NEW DICTIONARY
CHICAGO CITY

Elsa D. Plata.

NEW DICTIONARY
CHICAGO CITY

SPANISH-ENGLISH
ENGLISH-SPANISH
DICTIONARY

DICCIONARIO
INGLES-ESPAÑOL
ESPAÑOL-INGLES

Rapsa
REAL ANDINA
DE PUBLICACIONES

Compilación: Profesor Edgar Reinaldo Jalmes H
Licenciado en Idiomas
Director Editorial: Carlos Eduardo Puentes
Diseño Cubierta: Alexander Morales R.
Ilustraciones: Departamento de diseño RAPSA
Maquetacion y montaje: Mónica Aguiar C
Correcciones: Ingles-Español / Dra. Carolina Maria Camero B
Español-Ingles / Dra. Luz Ángela Bolaños B

© **Real Andina de Publicaciones**

ISBN: 958-33-4148-7

Impreso en Colombia / Printed in Colombia
Esta obra se termino de imprimir en los talleres litográficos de Real Andina de Publicaciones RAPSA en el mes de Noviembre del año 2002.

INDICE GENERAL

PREFACE

When beginning this work REAL ANDINA DE PUBLICACIONES proposed to offer the newest, updated and complete bilingual dictionary waited for so long in the Spanish and English speaking worlds. In addition to the precise translation of both lexicons, of a lot of encyclopedic files and the most detailed explanation of the protean terms, this is the vocabulary arisen from the technological and social progress of this time. There is also herein the variety of traditions and temperaments of those worlds reflected, and the literature up to the quotidian life of the man in the present time.

Never before as now, the Spanish and English speaking people have had a so easy and quick communication media. Those frequent and constant relationships, produce the necessity of a good dictionary in those languages, therefore the bilingual dictionary is the more natural vehicle for the understanding between persons of different speaking.

When a person looks to solve idiomatic doubts, he/she always chooses a dictionary that clearly provides to him/her what he/she whishes.

This is precisely what is looked for with the new CHICAGO city dictionary that you have at your hands in this precise moment, because that is the new advance to the ideal one.

The publisher with an interest in achieving the perfection of a dictionary fulfilling with all expectations of the persons consulting it, has included among others the following components in order to make the work as efficient as possible.

- Bicolor presentation of the text for the quick visualization of the words.
- Division of the words in syllables for the two languages.
- Pages for practices completely illustrated where the reader may find grammar forms of frequent usage such as the prepositions of place, movement; it teaches us as well to draft a letter, to make a telephone call, identifying the hour and English punctuation among others.
- A section where you can find appendixes that we referred the reader to, all dictionary along; numerical expressions, pronunciation, irregular and generic verbs, territory division of the U.S.A. and the most important cities of British islands.

The new CHICAGO city was elaborated with a complete didactic character. Nevertheless our labor will be compensated when the person consulting it for any doubt, finds the adequate, precise and better response so increasing his/her lexical knowledge. With this a purpose we hope to achieve the delivery of the best bilingual dictionary at present time.

REAL ANDINA DE PUBLICACIONES

PROLOGO

Al emprender esta obra REAL ANDINA DE PUBLICACIONES se propuso ofrecer el novísimo, actual y completo diccionario bilingüe que tanto se ha esperado en los mundos de habla hispana e inglesa. Además de la traducción exacta de ambos léxicos, de un caudal de archivos enciclopédicos y de la más detallada explicación de términos proteicos, he aquí el vocabulario surgido del progreso tecnológico y social de nuestros tiempos. Aquí también la variedad de tradiciones y temperamentos de esos dos mundos, reflejada y la literatura hasta la vida cotidiana del hombre del presente.

Nunca como en la actualidad han tenido los pueblos de lengua inglesa y los de la lengua española tan fáciles y frecuentes relaciones, aumentadas cada día por mejores y mas rápidos medios de comunicación. Estas frecuentes y constantes relaciones, hacen sentir la necesidad de un buen diccionario de esos idiomas, por esto el diccionario bilingüe es el vehículo mas natural para la comprensión entre pueblos de habla diferente.

Cuando una persona busca resolver dudas idiomáticas escoge siempre el diccionario que en una forma clara ha de brindarle la que desea.

Esto precisamente es lo que busca el nuevo diccionario CHICAGO city que ahora tiene el lector en las manos, pues es el nuevo avance hacia lo ideal.

La editorial en su afán por lograr la perfección de un diccionario que llene todas las expectativas del consultante ha incluido entre otros los siguientes componentes para hacer mas eficiente la obra.

• Presentación bicolor del texto para la rápida visualización de las palabras.
• Silabación de las palabras en los dos idiomas.
• Hojas de practicas profusamente ilustradas donde el lector podrá encontrar formas gramaticales de uso frecuente como son las preposiciones de lugar, movimiento, así como también nos enseña a redactar una carta, llamar por teléfono, identificar la hora y la puntuación inglesa entre otros.
• Una sección donde se encuentran los apéndices a los que hacemos referencia a lo largo del diccionario; expresiones numéricas, pronunciación, verbos irregulares, genéticos, la división territorial de los E.E.U.U. y las ciudades mas importantes de las islas Británicas.

El nuevo CHICAGO city fue elaborado con un carácter eminentemente didáctico. No obstante nuestra labor se vera recompensada cuando quien consulte alguna duda encuentre la respuesta adecuada, acertada y mejor así sus conocimientos léxicos. Con este propósito esperamos haber logrado entregar a ustedes el mejor diccionario bilingüe de la actualidad.

REAL ANDINA DE PUBLICACIONES

Part One Spanish-English

List of Abbreviations

adj.	adjetive	*math.*	mathematics
adv.	adverb	*neut.*	neuter
arith.	arithmetic	*num.*	numeral
conj.	conjunction	*p.p.*	past participle
contr.	contraction	*pers.*	personal
def.	definite	*pers. pron.*	personal pronoun
def. art.	definite article	*pl.*	plural
dem.	demonstrative	*poss.*	possessive
dem. adj.	demonstrative adjective	*prep.*	preposition
dem. pron.	demonstrative pronoun	*pron.*	pronoun
etc.	etcetera	*refl.*	reflexive
f.	feminine noun	*refl. pron.*	reflexive pronoun
fam.	familiar	*rel.*	relative
indef.	indefinite	*rel. adv.*	relative adverb
indef. art.	indefinite article	*rel. pron.*	relative pronoun
inf.	infinite	*sing.*	singular
interj.	interjection	*subj.*	subjuntive
interr.	interrogative	*v.*	verb
irr.	irregular	*v. irr.*	irregular verb.
m.	masculine noun		

Special Words and Abbreviations Used to Indicate Regional Occurrence

Am.[1]	Spanish-American
Andalusia	
Andes	(Ecuador, Perú, Bolivia)
Arg.	Argentina
Bol.	Bolivia
Carib.	(Cuba, Puerto Rico, Dominican Republic)
C.A.	Central America (Guatemala, El Salvador, Honduras, Nicáragua, Costa Rica)
Ch.	Chile
Col.	Colombia
C.R.	Costa Rica
Cuba	
Ec.	Ecuador
Guat.	Guatemala
Hond.	Honduras
Mex.	México
Nic.	Nicaragua
N. Sp.	Northern Spain
Pan.	Panama
Par.	Paraguay
Perú	
P.R.	Puerto Rico
Ríopl.	Río de la Plata región (Eastern Argentina, Uruguay)
S.A.	South America
Sal.	El Salvador
Spain	
Ur.	Uruguay
Ven.	Venezuela

[1] This abbreviation is employed to indicate general Spanish-American usage, usually with the implication of obsolescence in Spain. It is also used to identify words that are currently little used but which may occur in literary works of bygone days.

ALFABETO alphabet			A a (ei)	B b (bi)
C c (ci)	D d (di)	E e (i)	F f (ef)	G g (yi)
H h (eich)	I i (ai)	J j (yei)	K k (kei)	L l (el)
M m (em)	N n (en)	O o (ou)	P p (pi)	Q q (kiu)
R r (ar)	S s (es)	T t (ti)	U u (iu)	V v (ví)
W w (dabliú)	X x (éx)	Y y (uáy)	Z z (zi)	

Spanish Irregular and Orthographic Changing Verbs

The superior number, or numbers, after a verb entry indicate that it is conjugated like the model verb in this section which has the corresponding number. Only the tenses which have irregular forms or spelling changes are given. The irregular forms and spelling changes are shown in bold-face type.

1. pensar (if stressed, the stem vowel e becomes ie)
    Pres. Indic.   **pienso, piensas, piensa,** pensamos, pensáis, **piensan**.
    Pres. Subj.   **piense, pienses, piense,** pensemos, penséis, **piensen**.
    Imper.   **piensa** tú, **piense** usted, pensad vosoros, **piensen** ustedes.

2. contar (if stressed, the stem vowel o becomes ue)
    Pres. Indic.   **cuento, cuentas, cuenta,** contamos, contáis, **cuentan**.
    Pres. Subj.   **cuente, cuentes, cuente,** contemos, contéis, **cuenten**.
    Imper.   **cuenta** tú, **cuente** usted, contad vosotros, **cuenten** ustedes.

3.*a.* sentir (if stressed, the stem vowel e becomes ie; if unstressed, the stem vowel e becomes i when the following syllable contains stressed a, ie, or io)
    Pres. Indic.   **siento, sientes, siente,** sentimos, sentís, **sienten**.
    Pres. Subj.   **sienta, sientas, sienta, sintamos, sintáis, sientan**.
    Pret. Indic.   sentí, sentiste, **sintió,** sentimos, sentisteis, **sintieron**.
    Imp. Subj.   **sintiera** or **sintiese, sintieras** or **sintieses, sintiera** or **sintiese, sintiéra-mos** or **sintiésemos, sintierais** or **sintieseis, sintieran** or **sintiesen**.
    Imper.   **siente** tú, **sienta** usted, sentid vosotros, **sientan** ustedes.
    Pres. Part.   **sintiendo**.

b. erguir (this verb has same vowel changes as *sentir*, but the initial i of the diphthong ie is changed to y. For regular spelling changes see No. 12,*a*)
    Pres. Indic.   **yergo, yergues, yergue,** erguimos, erguís, **yerguen**.
    Pres. Subj.   **yerga, yergas, yerga, irgamos, irgáis, yergan**.
    Pret. Indic.   erguí, erguiste, **irguió,** erguimos, erguisteis, **irguieron**.
    Imp. Subj.   **irguiera** or **irguise, irguieras** or **irguieses, irguiera** or **irguieses, ir guiéramos** or **irguiésemos, irguierais** or **irguieseis, irguieran** or **ir guiesen**.
    Imper.   **yergue** tú, **yerga** usted, erguid vosotros, **yergan** ustedes.
    Pres. Part.   **irguiendo**.

4. dormir (if stressed, the stem vowel o becomes ue; if unstressed, the stem vowel o becomes u when the following syllable contains stressed a, ie, or ió).
    Pres. Indic.   **duermo, duermes, duerme,** dormimos, dormís, **duermen**.
    Pres. Subj.   **duerma, duermas, duerma, durmamos, durmáis, duerman**.
    Pret. Indic.   dormí, dormiste, **durmió,** dormimos, dormiteis, **duermieron**.
    Imp. Subj.   **durmiera** or **durmiese, durmieras** or **durmieses, durmiera** or **durmiese,durmiéramos** or **duermiésemos, durmierais** or **durmieseis, durmieran** or **durmiesen**.
    Imper.   **duerme** tú, **duerma** usted, dormid vosotros, **duerman** ustedes.
    Pres. Part.   **durmiendo**.

5. pedir (if stressed, the stem vowel e becomes i; if unstressed, the stem vowel e becomes i when the followings syllable contains stressed a, ie, or ió).
    Pres. Indic.   **pido, pides, pide,** pedimos, pedís, **piden**.
    Pres. Subj.   **pida, pidas, pida, pidamos, pidáis, pidan**.
    Pret. Indic.   pedí, pediste, **pidió,** pedimos, pedisteis, **pidieron**.

Imp. Subj.   pidiera or pidiese, pidieras or pidieses, pidiera or pidiese, pidiéramos or pidiésemos, pidierais or pidieseis, pidieran or pidiesen.

Imper.   pide tú, pida usted, pedid vosotros, pidan ustedes.

Pres. Part.   pidiendo.

6.   buscar (verbs ending in car change c to qu before e)

Pres. Subj.   busque, busques, busque, busquemos, busquéis, busquen.

Pret. Indic.   busqué, buscaste, buscó, buscamos, buscasteis, buscaron.

Imper.   busca tú, busque usted, buscad vosotros, busquen ustedes.

7.   llegar (verbs ending in gar change the g to gu before e)

Pres. Subj.   llegue, llegues, llegue, lleguemos, lleguéis, lleguen.

Pret. Indic.   llegué, llegaste, llegó, llegamos, llegasteis, llegaron.

Imper.   llega tú, llegue usted, llegad vosotros, lleguen ustedes.

8.   averiguar (verbs ending in guar change the gu to gü before e)

Pres. Subj.   averigüe, averigües, averigüe, averigüemos, averigüéis, averigüen.

Pret. Indic.   averigüé, averiguaste, averiguó, averiguamos, averiguasteis, averiguaron.

Imper.   averigua tú, averigüe usted, averiguad vosotros, averigüen ustedes.

9.   abrazar (verbs ending in zar change z to c before e)

Pres. Subj.   abrace, abraces, abrace, abracemos, abracéis, abracen.

Pret. Indic.   abracé, abrazaste, abrazó, abrazamos, abrazasteis, abrazaron.

Imper.   abraza tú, abrace usted, abrazad vosotros, abracen ustedes.

10.*a.*   convencer (verbs ending in cer preceded by a consonant change c to z before a and o)

Pres. Indic.   convenzo, convences, convence, convencemos, convencéis, convencen.

Pres. Subj.   convenza, convenzas, convenza, convenzamos, convenzáis, convenzan.

Imper.   convence tú, convenza usted, convenced vosotros, convenzan ustedes.

b.   esparcir (verbs ending in cir preceded by a consonant change c to z before a and o).

Pres. Indic.   esparzo, esparces, esparce, esparcimos, esparcís, esparcen.

Pres. Subj.   esparza, esparzas, esparza, esparzamos, esparzáis, esparzan.

Imper.   esparce tú, esparza usted, esparcid vosotros, esparzan ustedes.

c.   mecer (two verbs ending in cer preceded by a vowel change c to z before a and o; see No. 13.*a*): mecer and cocer.

Pres. Indic.   mezo, meces, mece, mecemos, mecéis, mecen.

Pres. Subj.   meza, mezas, meza, mezamos, mezáis, mezan.

Imper.   mece tú, meza usted, meced vosotros, mezan ustedes.

11.*a.*   dirigir (verbs ending in gir change g to j before a and o)

Pres. Indic.   dirijo, diriges, dirige, dirigimos, dirigís, dirigen.

Pres. Subj.   dirija, dirijas, dirija, dirijamos, dirijáis, dirijan.

Imper.   dirige tu, dirija usted, dirigid vosotros, dirijan ustedes.

b.   coger (verbs ending in ger change g to j before o and a)

Pres. Indic.   cojo, coges, coge, cogemos, cogéis, cogen.

Pres. Subj.   coja, cojas, coja, cojamos, cojáis, cojan.

Imper.   coge tú, coja usted, coged vosotros, cojan ustedes.

12.*a.* distinguir (verbs ending in **guir** drop the **u** before **o** and **a**)

    Pres. Indic.   **distingo**, distingues, distingue, distinguimos, distinguís, distinguen.
    Pres. Subj.   **distinga, distingas, distinga, distingamos, distingáis, distingan.**
    Imper.   distingue tú, **distinga** usted, distinguid vosotros, **distingan** ustedes.

b. delinquir (verbs ending in **quir** change **qu** to **c** before **o** and **a**)
    Pres. Indic.   **delinco**, delinques, delinque, delinquimos, delinguís, delinquen.
    Pres. Subj.   **delinca, delincas, delinca, delincamos, delincáis, delincan.**

13.*a.* conocer (verbs ending in **cer** when preceded by a vowel insert **z** before **c** when **c** is followed by **o** or **a**; see No. 10.*c.*)
    Pres. Indic.   **conozco**, conoces, conoce, conocemos, conocéis, conocen.
    Pres. Subj.   **conozca, conozcas, conozca, conozcamos, conozcáis, conozcan.**
    Imper.   conoce tu, **conozca** usted, conoced vosotros, **conozcan** ustedes.

b. lucir (verb ending in **cir** when preceded by a vowel insert **z** before **c** when **c** is followed by **o** or **a**; see No. 25)
    Pres. Indic.   **luzco**, luces, luce, lucimos, lucís, lucen.
    Pres. Subj.   **luzca, luzcas, luzcamos, luzcáis, luzcan.**
    Imper.   luce tú, **luzca** usted, lucid vosotros, **luzcan** ustedes.

14. creer (unstressed **i** between vowels is changed to **y**)
    Pret. Indic.   creí, creíste, **creyó**, creímos, creísteis, **creyeron.**
    Imp. Subj.   **creyera** or **creyese, creyeras** or **creyeses, creyera** or **creyese, creyéramos**
                    or **creyésemos, creyerais** or **creyeseis, creyeran** or **creyesen.**
    Pret. Part.   **creyendo**

15. reir (like No. 5, except that when the **i** of the stem would be followed by **ie** or **ió** the two **i**'s are reduced to one)
    Pres. Indic.   **rió, ríes, ríe**, reimos, reís, **ríen.**
    Pres. Subj.   **ría, rías, ría, riamos, riáis, rían.**
    Pret. Indic.   rei, reíste, **rió**, reímos, reísteis, **rieron.**
    Imp. Subj.   **riera** or **riese, rieras** or **rieses, riera** or **riese, riéramos** or **riésemos,**
                    rierais or **rieseis, rieran** or **riesen.**
    Imper.   **ríe** tu, **ría** usted, reíd vosotros, **rían** ustedes.
    Pres. Part.   **riendo.**

16. podrir or pudrir
    Prest. Indic.   **pudro, pudres, pudre**, podrimos or pudrimos, podris or pudrís, **pudren.**
    Pres. Subj.   **pudra, pudras, pudra, pudramos, pudráis, pudran.**
    Imp. Indic.   pudría or podría, etc. (Seldom *podría* because of confusion with *poder*)
    Prest. Indic.   podrí or pudrí, podriste or pudriste, **pudrió**, podrimos or pudrimos,
                    podristeis or pudristeis, **pudrieron.**
    Imp. Subj.   **pudriera** or **pudriese, pudrieras** or **pudrieses, pudriera** or **pudriese,**
                    pudriéramos or **pudriésemos, pudrierais** or **pudrieseis, pudrieran** or
                    pudriesen.
    Fut Indic.   pudriré or podriré, etc.
    Cond.   pudriría or podriría, etc.
    Pres. Part.   **pudriendo.**
    Past Part.   podrido or pudrido.

17. enviar
    Pres. Indic.   envío, envías, envía, enviamos, enviáis, envían.
    Pres Subj.   envíe, envíes, enviemos, enviéis, envíen.
    Imper.   envía tu, envíe usted, enviad vosotros, envíen ustedes.

18. continuar
    Pres. Indic.   continuo, continúas, continúa, continuamos, continuáis, continúan.
    Pres. Subj.   continúe, continúes, continúe, continuémos, continuéis, continúen.
    Imper.   cotinúa tu, continúe usted, continuad vosotros, continúen ustedes

19. gruñir (i of the diphthong **ie** or **ió** is lost after **ñ**)
    Pres. Indic.   gruñí, gruñiste, gruñó, gruñisteis, gruñeron.
    Pres. Subj.   gruñera or gruñese, gruñeras or gruñeses, gruñera or gruñese,
                     gruñéramos or gruñésemos, gruñerais or gruñeseis, gruñeran or gru
                     ñesen.
    Pres. Part.   gruñendo.

20. bullir (i of the diphthong **ie** or **ió** is lost after **ll**)
    Pret. Indic.   bullí, bulliste, bulló, bullimos, bullisteis, bulleron.
    Imp. Subj.   bullera or bullese, bulleras or bulleses, bullera or bullese, bullésemos,
                     bullerais or bulleseis, bulleran or bullesen.
    Pres. Part.   bullendo.

21. andar
    Pret. Indic.   anduve, anduviste, anduvo, anduvimos, anduvisteis, anduvieron.
    Imp. Subj.   anduviera or anduviese, anduvieras or anduvieses, anduviera or andu
                     viese, anduviéramos or anduviéses, anduvierais or anduvieseis, andu
                     vieran or anduviesen.

22. asir
    Pres. Indic.   asgo, ases, ase, asimos, asis, asen.
    Imp. Subj.   asga, asgas, asga, asgamos, asgáis, asgan.
    Imper.   ase tú, asga usted, asid vosotros, asgan ustedes.

23. caber
    Pres. Indic.   quepo, cabes, cabe, cabemos, cabéis, caben
    Imp. Subj.   quepa, quepas, quepa, quepamos, quepáis, quepan.
    Pret. Indic.   cupe, cupiste, cupo, cupimos, cupisteis, cupieron.
    Imp. Subj.   cupiera or cupiese, cupieras or cupieses, cupiera or cupiese, cupiéra
                     mos or cupiésemos, cupierais or cupieseis, cupieran or cupiesen.
    Fut. Indic.   cabré, cabrás, cabrá, cabremos, cabréis, cabrán.
    Cond.   cabría, cabrías, cabríamos, cabríais, cabrían.
    Imper.   cabe tu, quepa usted, cabed vosotros, quepan ustedes.

24. caer
    Pres. Indic.   caigo, caes, cae, caemos, caéis, caen.
    Pres. Subj.   caiga, caigas, caiga, caigamos, caigáis, caigan.
    Pret. Indic.   caí, caiste, cayó, caímos, caísteis, cayeron.
    Imp. Subj.   cayera or cayese, cayeras or cayases, cayera or cayese, cayéramos or

	cayésemos, cayerais or cayeseis, cayeran or cayesen.
Imper.	cae tú, caiga usted, caed vosotros, caigan ustedes.
Pres. Part.	cayendo

25. conducir (all verbs ending in ducir have the irregularities of conducir)

Pres. Indic.	conduzco, conduces, conduce, conducimos, conducís, conducen.
Imp. Subj.	conduzca, conduzcas, conduzca, conduzcamos, conduzcáis, conduzcan.
Pret. Indic.	conduje, condujiste, condujo, condujimos, condujisteis, condujeron
Imp. Subj.	condujera or condujese, condujeras or condujeses, condujera or condujese, condujéramos or condujeseis, condujeran or condujesen.
Imp.	conduce tú, conduzca usted, conducid vosotros, conduzcan ustedes.

26. dar

Pres. Indic.	doy, das, da, damos, dais, dan.
Pres. Subj.	dé, des, dé, demos, deis, den.
Pret. Indic.	di, diste, dio, dimos, disteis, dieron.
Imp. Subj.	diera or diese, dieras or dieses, diera or diese, diéramos or diésemos, dierais or dieseis, dieran or diesen.

27. decir[5]

Pres. Indic.	digo, dices, dice, decimos, decís, dicen.
Pres. Subj.	diga, digas, diga, digamos, digáis, digan.
Pret. Indic.	dije, dijiste, dijo, dijimos, dijisteis, dijeron.
Imp. Subj.	dijera or dijese, dijeras or dijeses, dijera or dijese, dijéramos or dijésemos, dijerais or dijeseis, dijeran or dijesen.
Fut. Indic.	diré, dirás, dirá, diremos, diréis, dirán.
Cond.	diría, dirías, diría, diríamos, diríais, dirían.
Imper.	di tú, diga usted, decid vosotros, digan ustedes.
Pres. Part.	diciendo.
Past Part.	dicho.

28. errar (like No. 1, except that the initial ie is spelled ye)

Pres. Indic.	yerro, yerras, yerra, erramos, erráis, yerran.
Pres. Subj.	yerre, yerres, yerre, erremos, erréis, yerren.
Imper.	yerra tú, yerre usted, errad vosotros, yerren ustedes.

29. estar

Pres. Indic.	estoy, estás, está, estamos, estáis, están.
Pres. Subj.	esté, estés, esté, estemos, estéis, estén.
Pret. Indic.	estuve, estuviste, estuvo, estuvimos, estuvisteis, estuvieron.
Imp. Subj.	estuviera or estuviese, estuvieras or estuvieses, estuviera or estuviese, estuviéramos or estuviésemos, estuvierais or estuvieseis, estuvieran or estuviesen.
Imper.	está tú, esté usted, estad vosotros, estén ustedes.

5. The compound verbs of *decir* have the same irregularities with the exception of the followin.

a. The future and conditional of the compound verbs bendecir and maldecir are regular: *bendeciré, maldeciré,* etc.; *bendeciría, maldeciría,* etc.

b. The familiar imperative is regular: *bendice* tu, *maldice* tu, *contradice* tu, etc.

c. The past participles of *bendecir* and maldecir are regular when used with haber or in the passive with ser: *bendecido, maldecido;* when used as an adjective with *estar* or with *ser* as a noun, the forms are: *bendito, maldito.*

30. haber
    Pres. Indic.   he, has, ha, hemos, habéis, han.
    Pres. Subj.   haya, hayas, hayamos, hayáis, hayan.
    Pret. Indic.   hube, hubiste, hubo, hubimos, hubisteis, hubieron.
    Imp. Subj.   hubiera or hubiese, hubieras or hubieses, hubiera or hubiese, hubiéra
                   mos or hubiésemos, hubierais or hubieseis, hubieran or hubiesen.
    Fut. Indic.   habré, habrás, habrá, habremos, habréis, habrán.
    Cond.   habría, habrías, habría, habríamos, habrían.

31. hacer
    Pres. Indic.   hago, haces, hace, hacemos, hacéis, hacen.
    Pres. Subj.   haga, hagas, haga, hagamos, hagáis, hagan.
    Pret. Indic.   hice, hiciste, hizo, hicimos, hicisteis, hicieron.
    Imp. Subj.   hiciera or hiciese, hicieras or hicieses, hiciera or hiciese, hiciéramos or
                   hiciésemos, hicierais or hicieseis, hicieran or hiciesen.
    Fut. Indic.   haré, harás, hará, haremos, haréis, harán.
    Cond.   haría, harías, haría, haríamos, haríais, harían.
    Imper.   haz tú, haga usted, haced vosotros, hagan ustedes.
    Past Part.   hecho.

32.a. huir
    Pres. Indic.   huyo, huyes, huye, huimos, huís, huyen.
    Pres. Subj.   huya, huyas, huya, huyamos, huyáis, huyan
    Pret. Indic.   huí, huiste, huyó, huimos, huisteis, huyeron
    Imp. Subj.   huyera or huyese, huyeras or huyeses,
                   huyéramos or huyésemos, huyerais or huyeseis, huyeran or huyesen.
    Imper.   huye tú, huya usted, huid vosotros, huyan ustedes.
    Pres. Part.   huyendo.

b.   argüir
    Pres. Indic.   arguyo, arguyes, arguye, argüís, arguyen.
    Pres. Subj.   arguya, arguyas, arguya, arguyamos, arguyáis, arguyan.
    Pret. Indic.   argüí, argüiste, arguyó, argüimos, argüisteis, arguyeron.
    Imp. Subj.   arguyera or arguyese, arguyeras or arguyeses, arguyera or arguyese,
                   arguyéramos or arguyésemos, arguyerais or arguyeseis, arguyeran or
                   arguyesen.
    Imper.   arguye tú, arguya usted, argüid vosotros, arguyan ustedes.
    Pres. Part.   arguyendo.

33. ir
    Pres. Indic.   voy, vas, va, vamos, vais, van.
    Pres. Subj.   vaya, vayas, vaya, vayamos, vayáis, vayan.
    Imp. Indic.   iba, ibas, iba, íbamos, ibais, iban.
    Pret. Indic.   fui, fuiste, fue, fuimos, fuisteis, fueron.
    Imp. Subj.   fuera or fuese, fueras or fueses, fuera or fuese, fuéramos or fuésemos,
                   fuerais or fueseis, fueran or fuesen.
    Imper.   ve tú, vaya usted, id vosotros, vayan ustedes.
    Pres. Part.   yendo.

34. jugar (cf. Nos. 2 and 7)
    Pres. Indic.   juego, juegas, juega, jugamos, jugáis, juegan.
    Pres. Subj.   juegue, juegues, juegue, juguemos, juguéis, jueguen.

Pret. Indic.	jugué, jugaste, jugó, jugamos, jugasteis, jugaron.
Imper.	juega tú, juegue usted, jugad vosotros, jueguen ustedes.

35. adquirir

Pres. Indic.	adquiero, adquieres, adquiere, adquirimos, adquirís, adquieren
Pres. Subj.	adquiera, adquieras, adquiera, adquiramos, adquiráis, adquieran.
Imper.	adquiere tú, adquiera usted, adquirid vosotros, adquieran ustedes.

36. oír

Pres. Indic.	oigo, oyes, oye, oímos, oís, oyen.
Pres. Subj.	oiga, oigas, oiga, oigamos, oigáis, oigan.
Pret. Indic.	oí, oíste, oyó, oímos, oísteis, oyeron.
Imp. Subj.	oyera or oyese, oyeras or oyeses, oyera or oyese, oyéramos or oyésemos, oyerais or oyeseis, oyeran or oyesen.
Imper.	oye tú, oiga usted, oíd vosotros, oigan ustedes.
Pres. Part.	oyendo.

37. oler (like No. 2, except that initial ue is spelled hue)

Pres. Indic.	huelo, hueles, huele, olemos, oléis, huelen.
Pres. Subj.	huela, huelas, huela, olamos, oláis, huelan.
Imper.	huele tú, huela usted, oled vosotros, huelan ustedes.

38. placer

Pres. Indic.	plazco, places, place, placemos, placéis, placen.
Pres. Subj.	plazca, plazcas, plazca, plazcamos, plazcáis, plazcan (There also the antiquated forms, plegue and plega, used now only in the third person in poetic language).
Pret. Indic.	In addition to the regular forms, there is the antiquated form plugo, used now only in poetic language.
Imp. Subj.	In addition to the regular forms, there are the antiquated forms, pluguiera and pluguiese, used now only in poetic language.

39. poder

Pres. Indic.	puedo, puedes, puede, podemos, podéis, pueden.
Pres. Subj.	pueda, puedas, pueda, podamos, podáis, puedan.
Pret. Indic.	pude, pudiste, pudo, pudimos, pudisteis, pudieron.
Imp. Subj.	pudiera or pudiese, pudieras or pudieses, pudiera or pudiesen.
Fut. Indic.	podré, podrás, podrá, podremos, podréis, podrán.
Cond.	podría, podrías, podría, podríamos, podríais, podrían.
Pres. Part.	pudiendo.

40. *poner*

Pres. Indic.	pongo, pones, pone, ponéis, ponen.
Pres. Subj.	ponga, pongas, ponga, pongamos, pongáis, pongan.
Pret. Indic.	puse, pusiste, puso, pusimos, pusisteis, pusieron.
Imp. Subj.	pusiera or pusiese, pusieras or pusieses, pusiera or pusiese, pusiéramos or pusiésemos, pusierais or pusieseis, pusieran or pusiesen.
Fut. Indic.	pondré, pondrás, pondrá, pondremos, pondréis, pondrán.
Cond.	pondría, pondrías, pondría, pondríamos, pondríais, pondrían.
Imper.	pon tú, ponga usted, poned vosotros, pongan ustedes.
Past. Part.	puesto.

41. querer

Pres. Indic.	quiero, quieres, quiere, queremos, queréis, quieren.
Pres. Subj.	quiera, quieras, quiera, queramos, queráis, quieran.
Pret. Indic.	quise, quisiste, quiso, quisimos, quisisteis, quisieron.
Imp. Subj.	quisiera or quisiese, quisieras or quisieses, quisiera or quisiese, qui siéramos or quisiésemos, quisierais or quisieseis, quisieran or quisie sen.
Fut. Indic.	querré, querrás, querrá, querremos, querréis, querrán.
Cond.	querría, querrías, querría, querríamos, querríais, querrían.
Imper.	quiere tú, quiera usted , quered vosotros, quieran ustedes.

42. saber

Pres. Indic.	sé, sabes, sabe, sabemos, sabéis, saben.
Pres. Subj.	sepa, sepas, sepa, sepamos, sepáis, sepan.
Pret. Indic.	supe, supiste, supo, supimos, supisteis, supieron.
Imp. Subj.	supiera or supiese, supieras or supieses, supiera or supiese, supiéra mos or supiésemos, supierais or supieseis, supieran or supiesen.
Fut. Indic.	sabré, sabrás, sabrá, sabremos, sabréis, sabrán.
Cond.	sabría, sabrías, sabría,sabríamos, sabríais, sabrían.
Imper.	sabe tú, sepa usted, sabed vosotros, sepan ustedes.

43. salir

Pres. Indic.	salgo, sales, sale, salimos, salís, salen.
Pres. Subj.	salga, salgas, salga, salgamos, salgáis, salgan.
Fut. Indic.	saldré, saldrás, saldrá, saldremos, saldréis, saldrán.
Cond.	saldría, saldrías, saldría, saldríamos, saldríais, saldrían.
Imper.[6]	sal tú, salga usted, salid vosotros, salgan ustedes.

44. ser

Pres. Indic.	soy, eres, es, somos, sois, son.
Pres. Subj.	sea, seas, sea, seamos, seáis, sean.
Imp. Indic.	era, eras, era, éramos, erais, eran.
Pret. Indic.	fui, fuiste, fue, fuimos, fuisteis, fueron.
Imp. Subj.	fuera or fuese, fueras or fueses, fuera or fuese, fuéramos or fuésemos, fuerais or fueseis, fueran or fuesen.
Imper.	sé tú, sea usted, sed vosotros, sean ustedes.

45. tener

Pres. Indic.	tengo, tienes, tiene, tenemos, tenéis, tienen.
Pres. Subj.	tenga, tengas, tenga, tengamos, tengáis, tengan.
Pret. Indic.	tuve, tuviste, tuvo, tuvimos, tuvisteis, tuvieron.
Imp. Subj.	tuviera or tuviese, tuviera or tuvieses, tuviera or tuviese, tuviéramos or tuviésemos, tuvierais or tuvieseis, tuvieran or tuviesen.
Fut. Indic.	tendré, tendrás, tendrá, tendremos, tendréis, tendrán.
Cond.	tendría, tendrías, tendría, tendríamos, tendríais, tendrían.
Imper.	ten tú, tenga usted, tened vosotros, tengan ustedes.

46. traer

Pres. Indic.	traigo, traes, trae, traemos, traéis, traen.
Pres. Subj.	traiga, traigas, traiga, traigamos, traigáis, traigan.
Pret. Indic.	traje, trajiste, trajo, trajimos, trajisteis, trajeron.
Imp. Subj.	trajera or trajese, trajeras or trajeses, trajera or trajese, trajéramos or

---

[6] The compound *sobresalir* is rgular in the familiar imperative: sobresale tú.

	trajésemos, trajerais or trajeseis, trajeran or trajesen.
Imper.	trae tú, traiga usted, traed vosotros, traigan ustedes.
Pres. Part.	trayendo.

47. **valer**

Pres. Indic.	valgo, vales, vale, valemos, valéis, valen.
Pres. Subj.	valga, valgas, valga, valgamos, valgáis, valgan.
Fut. Indic.	valdré, valdrás, valdrá, valdremos, valdréis, valdrían
Imper.	val or vale tú, valga usted, valed vosotros, valgan ustedes.

48. **venir**

Pres. Indic.	vengo, vienes, viene, venimos, venís, vienen.
Pres. Subj.	venga, vengas, venga, vengamos, vengáis, vengan.
Pret. Indic.	vine, viniste, vino, vinimos, vinisteis, vinieron.
Imp. Subj.	viniera or viniese, vinieras or vinieses, viniera or viniese, viniéramos or viniésemos, vinierais or vinieseis, vinieran or viniesen.
Fut. Indic.	vendré, vendrás, vendrá, vendremos, vendréis, vendrán.
Cond.	vendría, vendrías, vendría, vendríamos, vendríais, vendrían.
Imper.	ven tú, venga usted, venid vosotros, vengan ustedes.
Pres. Part.	viniendo.

49. **ver**

Pres. Indic.	veo, ves, ve, vemos, veis, ven.
Pres. Subj.	vea, veas, vea, veamos, veáis, vean
Imp. Indic.	veía, veías, veía, veíamos, veíais, veían.
Imper.	ve tú, vea usted, ved vosotros, vean ustedes.
Past. Part.	visto.

50. **yacer**

Pres. Indic.	yazco or yazgo, yaces, yace, yacemos, yacéis, yacen.
Pres. Subj.	yazca or yazga, yazcas or yazgas, yazca or yazga, yazcamos or yazgamos, yazcáis or yazgáis, yazcan or yazgan.
Imper.	yace tú, yazca or yazga usted, yaced vosotros, yazcan or yazgan ustedes.

51. Defective Verbs

    a. The following verbs are usted only in the forms that have an i in the ending: abolir, agredir, aterirse, empedernir, transgredir.

    b. atañer

    This verb is used only in the third person. It is most frequently used in the present indicative: atañe, atañen.

    c. concernir

    This verb is used only in the third person of the following tenses:

Pres. Indic.	concierne, conciernen.
Pres. Subj.	concierna, conciernan.
Imp. Indic.	concernía, concernían.
Imp. Subj.	concerniera or concerniese, concernieran or concerniesen.
Pres. Part.	concerniendo.

    d. soler

    This verb is used most frequently in the present and imperfect indicative. It is less frequently used in the present subjuntive.

Pres. Indic.	suelo, sueles, suele, solemos, soléis, suelen.
Pres. Subj.	suela, suelas, suela, solamos, soláis, suelan.
Imp. Indic.	solía, solías, solíamos, solíais, solían.

The preterit is seldom used. Of the compound tenses, only the present perfect is commonly used: he solido, etc. The other tenses are very rare.

e. roer

This verb has three forms in the first person of the present indicative: roo, royo, roigo, all of which are infrequently used. In the present subjunctive the preferable form is roa, roas, roa, etc., although the forms roya and roiga are found.

52. Irregular Past Participles

abrir–abierto
absorber–absorbido, absorto
bendecir–bendecido, bendito
componer–compuesto
cubrir–cubierto
decir–dicho
deponer–depuesto
descomponer–descompuesto
describir–descrito
descubrir–descubierto
desenvolver–desenvuelto
deshacer–deshecho
devolver–devuelto
disolver–disuelto
encubrir–encubierto
entreabrir–entreabierto
entrever–entrevisto
envolver–envuelto
escribir–escrito
freir–frito, freído
hacer–hecho
imprimir–impreso
inscribir–inscrito
maldecir–maldecido, maldito
morir–muerto
poner–puesto
prescribir–prescrito
proscribir–proscrito
proveer–proveído, provisto
resolver–resuelto
revolver–revuelto
romper–rompido, roto
satisfacer–satisfecho
subscribir–subscrito
ver–visto
volver–vuelto

Spanish/English

A

a. *prep.* to; in, into; on; by.

a·ba·ce·rí·a *f.* grocery; grocery store; **abacero** *m.* grocer.

a·bad *m.* abbot; **abadía** *f.* abbey.

a·ba·de·jo *m. N.Sp.* codfish.

a·ba·de·sa *f.* abbess.

a·ba·jar·se *v.* to lower oneself, humiliate oneself.

a·ba·je·ño *adj. Mex., C.A.* lowland; *n.* lowlander.

a·ba·jo *adv.* down, below; downstairs.

a·ba·lan·zar[9] *v.* to balance; to hurl, impel; **-se** to hurl oneself; to rush (upon), swoop down (upon); *Am.* to rear, balk.

a·ba·lear *v.* to "shoot up"

a·ban·de·ra·do *adj.* standard-bearing; *n.* standard-bearer.

a·ban·do·na·mien·to = **abandono**

a·ban·do·nar *v.* to abandon, desert; to give up.

a·ban·do·no *m.* abandon; desertion; neglect.

a·ba·ni·car[6] *v.* to fan.

a·ba·ni·co *m.* fan.

a·ba·ra·tar *v.* to cheapen, lower the price of.

a·bar·car[6] *v.* to embrace, contain, include; *Carib., Riopl.* to buy up, monopolize.

a·ba·rran·car·se[6] *v.* to fall into an opening; to get into a difficult situation.

a·ba·rro·te·rí·a *f. Mex., C.A., Andes* grocery, grocery store; **abarrotero** *m. Mex., C.A., Andes* grocer.

a·ba·rro·tes *m. pl.* small packages (*in hold of a ship*); *Mex., C.A., Andes* groceries; **tienda de** — *Mex., C.A., Andes* grocery store.

a·bas·te·cer[13] *v. irr.* to supply.

a·bas·te·ci·mien·to *m.* supply; pro-visions.

a·bas·to *m.* supply; **no dar** — **a** to be unable to cope with.

a·ba·ti·do *adj.* dejected, depressed, crestfallen, humbled; fallen; lowered.

aba·ti·mien·to *m.* discouragement, dejection, depression; descent, swoop, drop.

a·ba·tir *v.* to lower; to knock down; to depress; to humble; **-se** to become discouraged; to swoop down.

ab·di·car[6] *v.* to abdicate.

ab·do·men *m.* abdomen.

a·be·ce·da·rio *m.* alphabet; primer.

a·be·dul *m.* birch.

a·be·ja *f.* bee; **abejera** *f.* beehive; **abejón** *m.* drone; bumblebee; **abejorro** *m.* bumblebee.

a·be·rra·ción *f.* aberration, mental or moral deviation.

a·ber·tu·ra *f.* aperture, opening, hole, slit.

a·be·to *m.* fir (*tree and wood*).

a·bier·to *p.p. of* **abrir** opened; *adj.* open; frank; *Am.* proud, self-satisfied; *Am.* generous.

a·bi·ga·rra·do *adj.* motley; multicolored; variegated.

a·bi·gea·to *m.* cattle stealing.

a·bis·ma·do *p.p.* absorbed, buried in thought; overwhelmed.

a·bis·mal *adj.* abysmal.

a·bis·mar *v.* to overwhelm; to depress; **-se** to be plunged (into); to bury oneself (*in thought, grief, etc.*).

a·bis·mo *m.* abyss, precipice, chasm.

ab·ju·rar *v.* to abjure; to renounce solemnly.

a·blan·dar *v.* to soften.

ab·ne·ga·ción *f.* abnegation, self-denial, self-sacrifice.

ab·ne·ga·do *adj.* self-sacrificing.

ab·ne·gar·se[7] *v.* to deny oneself, sacrifice oneself.

a·bo·ba·do *adj.* stupid, silly.

a·bo·car[6] *v.* to bite; to bring near; to flow into.

a·bo·ci·nar *v.* to flare; to fall on one's face.

a·bo·chor·nar *v.* to overheat; to embar-rass; -se to get overheated; to blush; to be embarrassed.

a·bo·fe·tear *v.* to slap.

a·bo·ga·cí·a *f.* the legal profession; a law career.

a·bo·ga·do *m.* lawyer.

a·bo·gar[7] *v.* to advocate, plead in favor of; to inter-cede.

a·bo·len·go *m.* lineage, ancestry; inheritance, patrimony.

a·bo·li·ción *f.* abolition.

a·bo·lir[51] *v.* to abolish; to repeal.

a·bol·sar·se *v.* to bag (*said of trousers, skirts, etc.*).

a·bo·lla·do *p.p. & adj.* dented; bumped; bruised.

a·bo·lla·du·ra *f.* dent, bump.

a·bo·llar *v.* to dent; to bump; to crush, crumple; to bruise.

a·bom·bar *v.* to make bulge; **-se** *Riopl.* to get drunk.

a·bo·mi·na·ble *adj.* abominable, detestable.

a·bo·mi·nar *v.* to abominate, abhor, detest.

a·bo·na·do *m.* subscriber; *p.p. of* **abonar.**

a·bo·nar *v.* to credit with; to make a payment; to endorse, back (*a person*); to fertilize (*soil*); **-se** to subscribe.

a·bo·na·ré *m.* promissory note; I.O.U.

a·bo·no *m.* (*monetario*) payment; installment; endorsement; guarantee; (*del suelo*) fertilizer; (*suscripción*) subscription.

a·bor·dar v. to board (a ship); to dock, put into port; to approach; to undertake, take up (a matter, problem, etc.).

a·bo·ri·gen adj. aboriginal, indigenous, native; **aborígenes** m. pl. aborígenes, primitive inhabitants.

a·bo·rras·car·se[6] v. to become stormy.

a·bo·rre·cer[13] v. irr. to abhor, hate, detest.

a·bo·rre·ci·ble adj. abominable, hateful.

a·bo·rre·ci·mien·to m. abhorrence; hatred.

a·bor·tar v. to miscarry, have a miscarriage; to give birth prematurely; to fail.

a·bor·to m. abortion, miscarriage; monster.

a·bo·ta·gar·se[7] v. to bloat; to swell.

a·bo·to·na·dor m. buttonhook.

a·bo·to·nar v. to button, button up; to bud; **-se** to button up.

a·bo·ve·dar v. to vault, cover with a vault; to arch.

a·bo·za·lar v. to muzzle.

a·bra f. cove; mountain gap or pass; dale; Am. breach (in the jungle); Am. leaf (of a door).

a·bra·sa·dor adj. burning, very hot.

a·bra·sar v. to burn; to parch; **-se** to burn up, be consumed.

a·bra·zar[9] v. to hug, embrace; to include.

a·bra·zo m. hug, embrace.

a·bre·bo·te·llas m. bottle opener.

a·bre·la·tas m. can opener.

a·bre·va·de·ro m. drinking trough; watering place for cattle.

a·bre·var v. to water (livestock).

a·bre·via·ción f. abbreviation.

a·bre·viar v. to abbreviate, shorten, condense.

a·bre·via·tu·ra f. abbreviation.

a·bri·gar[7] v. to shelter, cover, protect; to wrap up; to harbor (fear), cherish (hope); **-se** to find shelter; to wrap oneself up.

a·bri·go m. shelter, cover, protection; wrap; overcoat.

a·bril m. April.

a·bri·llan·tar v. to polish, shine; to glaze.

a·brir[52] v. to open; to unlock.

a·bro·char v. to button; to clasp; to fasten.

a·bro·ga·ción f. repeal.

a·bro·gar[7] v. to abrogate, repeal, annul.

a·bro·jo m. thistle, thorn; **-s** reef.

a·bru·ma·dor adj. crushing, overwhelm·ing; oppressive; fatiguing.

a·bru·mar v. to crush, overwhelm; to trouble, annoy; **-se** to become foggy.

a·brup·to adj. abrupt, steep.

abs·ce·so m. abscess.

ab·so·lu·ción f. absolution; acquittal.

ab·so·lu·to adj. absolute; unconditional.

ab·sol·ver[2,52] v. irr. to absolve, free from guilt; to pardon, acquit.

ab·sor·ben·te adj. & m. absorbent.

ab·sor·ber[52] v. to absorb.

ab·sor·ción f. absorption.

ab·sor·to p.p. irr. of **absorber** & adj. absorbed, engrossed; amazed.

abs·te·ner·se[45] v. irr. to abstain, refrain.

abs·ti·nen·cia f. abstinence; fasting.

abs·trac·ción f. abstraction, reverie.

abs·trac·to adj. abstract.

abs·tra·er[46] v. irr. to abstract; to withdraw, remove; **-se** to be lost in thought.

abs·tra·í·do adj. lost in thought, absentminded; aloof.

ab·suel·to p.p. of **absolver** absolved, acquitted.

ab·sur·do adj. absurd, ridiculous, senseless; m. absurdity.

a·bue·la f. grandmother.

a·bue·lo m. grandfather; **-s** grandparents; ancestors.

a·bu·lia f. abulia, loss of will power.

a·bul·ta·do adj. bulky, bulgy.

a·bul·tar v. to bulge; to be bulky; to enlarge.

a·bun·dan·cia f. abundance, plenty.

a·bun·dan·te adj. abundant, plentiful.

a·bun·dar v. to abound, be plentiful.

a·bu·rri·do p.p. & adj. bored; boring, tiresome; weary.

a·bu·rri·mien·to m. weariness, dullness, boredom.

a·bu·rrir v. to bore, vex; **-se** to become bored or vexed.

a·bu·sar v. to abuse, mistreat; to misuse; **– de** to take unfair advantage of; to impose upon.

a·bu·so m. abuse; misuse.

a·cá adv. here, over here; this way, hither.

a·ca·ba·do m. a finishing material: paint, varnish.

a·ca·ba·mien·to m. finish, completion, end; death; Am. exhaustion, physical decline.

a·ca·bar v. to end, finish, complete; **– de** (+ inf.) to have just; **– por** (+ inf.) to end by; **– con** to put an end to, make short work of; to destroy; **-se** to be over, finished; to be consumed; Am. to wear oneself out; Riopl., Mex., C.A. to age or decline in health.

a·ca·de·mia f. academy; a special school; a scientific, literary, or artistic society.

a·ca·dé·mi·co adj. academic; m. acade·mician, member of an academy.

a·ca·e·cer[13] v. irr. to happen, occur.

a·ca·e·ci·mien·to m. event, happening.

a·ca·lo·ra·do adj. heated, excited, angry.

a·ca·lo·ra·mien·to m. heat, ardor, excitement.

a·ca·lo·rar v. (calentar) to heat, warm; (emocionar) to excite.

a·ca·llar v. to silence; to calm, quiet.

a·cam·par v. to encamp; to camp.

a·ca·na·lar v. to groove; to flute (as a column); to form a channel in.

a·can·ti·la·do adj. sheer, steep (cliff); m. bluff, cliff.

a·can·to·nar v. to quarter (troops).

a·ca·pa·rar *v.* to corner (*the market*); to monopolize; to gather in (*for one's gain or profit*).

a·ca·re·ar *v.* to bring face to face; to confront.

a·ca·ri·ciar *v.* to caress, pet; to cherish (*a hope or illusion*).

a·ca·rre·a·dor *m.* carter; carrier.

a·ca·rre·ar *v.* to cart, transport; to bring about (harm, disaster).

a·ca·rre·o *m.* cartage, carriage, transport, haul.

a·ca·so *adv.* perhaps; by chance; **por si** – just in case; *m.* chance, accident.

a·ca·ta·mien·to *m.* homage, reverence, respect.

a·ca·tar *v.* to revere, respect; to pay homage to; *Mex., C.A. Ven.* to realize; *Mex., C.A., Ven.* to notice, pay attention.

a·ca·te·rrar *v.* to chill; *Mex., Ven.* to bother, annoy; **-se** to get chilled, catch cold; *Riopl.* to get tipsy.

a·cau·di·llar *v.* to lead, command.

ac·ce·so *m.* access; entrance, admittance; attack; fit (*of madness, anger, etc.*).

ac·ce·so·rio *adj.* & *m.* accessory.

ac·ci·den·ta·do *adj.* seized with a fit; in a swoon; rough, uneven (*ground*).

ac·ci·den·tal *adj.* accidental, casual.

ac·ci·den·tar·se *v.* to have a seizure or fit; to swoon, faint.

ac·ci·den·te *m.* accident, mishap; chance; sudden fit, swoon.

ac·ción *f. (física)* action: act; gesture; *(militar)* battle; *(de bolsa)* share of stock; **– de gracias** thanksgiving.

ac·cio·nar *v.* to gesticulate, make gestures; *Am.* to act, be active.

ac·cio·nis·ta *m.* & *f.* shareholder, stockholder.

a·ce·ci·nar *v.* to dry-cure; to salt down.

a·ce·chan·za *f.* snare; ambush.

a·ce·char *v.* to lurk; to spy.

a·ce·cho *m.* ambush; spying; **al** (*or* **en**) – waiting in ambush, lying in wait.

a·ce·do *adj.* rancid; acid; sour; harsh, disagreeable.

a·cei·tar *v.* to oil, grease.

a·cei·te *m.* oil; **– alcanforado** camphorated oil; **– de hígado de bacalao** cod-liver oil; **– de oliva** olive oil; **– de ricino** castor oil.

a·cei·te·ra *f.* oil can; oil cruet (*bottle for the table*).

a·cei·to·so *adj.* oily.

a·cei·tu·na *f.* olive; **aceitunado** *adj.* olive green.

a·cei·tu·no *m.* olive tree.

a·ce·le·ra·ción *f.* acceleration.

a·ce·le·ra·dor *m.* accelerator.

a·ce·le·rar *v.* to accelerate, speed up; to quicken; to hurry, hasten.

a·cé·mi·la *f.* pack mule.

a·cen·dra·do *adj.* pure, without blemish; purified.

a·cen·drar *v.* to refine (*metals*); to purify, cleanse.

a·cen·to *m.* accent; emphasis.

a·cen·tuar[18] *v.* to accentuate; emphasize; to accent;

-se to become worse (*as an illness*).

a·cep·ción *f.* acceptation, usual meaning.

a·ce·pi·llar *v.* to brush; to plane.

a·cep·ta·ción *f.* acceptance; approval.

a·cep·tar *v.* to accept; to approve; to admit.

a·ce·quia *f.* irrigation canal or ditch; *Perú, Ch.* small stream; *Ven., Mex., Andes* sewer.

a·ce·ra *f.* sidewalk.

a·ce·ra·do *adj.* steely, made of steel; steel-like; sharp.

a·ce·rar *v.* to steel.

a·cer·bo *adj.* bitter; harsh, cruel.

a·cer·ca de *prep.* about, concerning.

a·cer·ca·mien·to *m.* approach; approac-hing; rapprochement (*coming together*).

a·cer·car[6] *v.* to bring near, draw up; **-se** to get near, approach.

a·ce·ro *m.* steel.

a·cé·rri·mo *adj.* very sour, very tart; very harsh; very strong, stanch, stalwart, steadfast.

a·cer·ta·do *adj.* accurate; right; sure.

a·cer·tar[1] *v. irr.* to hit (*the mark*), to hit upon; find by chance; to guess right; **– a** (+ *inf.*) to happen to.

a·cer·ti·jo *m.* riddle.

a·cia·go *adj.* ill-fated, unlucky.

a·ci·ca·la·do *p.p.* & *adj.* polished; dressed up; adorned; trim. neat.

a·ci·ca·lar *v.* to polish; to adorn; **-se** to dress up, doll up.

a·ci·ca·te *m.* spur; incentive.

a·ci·dez *f.* acidity, sourness.

á·ci·do *m.* acid; *adj.* acid, sour.

a·cier·to *m.* right guess; lucky hit; good aim; good judgment; **con** – effectively, su-ccessfully.

a·cla·ma·ción *f.* acclamation, applause.

a·cla·mar *v.* to acclaim, cheer, hail, applaud.

a·cla·ra·ción *f.* explanation.

a·cla·rar *v.* to clarify, explain; to clear up; to rinse; to dawn.

a·cli·ma·tar *v.* to acclimatize, accustom to a climate or new environment.

a·co·bar·dar *v.* to frighten, intimidate.

a·co·ge·dor *adj.* friendly; hospitable.

a·co·ger[11] *v.* to receive; to give shelter; **-se** to take refuge.

a·co·gi·da *f.* reception, welcome; refuge.

a·co·gi·mien·to *m.* reception, welcome.

a·co·ji·nar *v.* to cushion; to quilt.

a·col·char *v.* to quilt.

a·có·li·to *m.* acolyte, altar boy.

a·co·me·ter *v.* to attack; to undertake.

a·co·me·ti·da *f.* **acometimiento** *m.* attack, assault.

a·co·mo·da·di·zo *adj.* obliging; accom-modating.

a·co·mo·da·do *adj.* well-off, wealthy; suitable, convenient; *pp. of* **acomodar.**

a·co·mo·da·dor *m.* usher (*in a theater*).

a•co•mo•dar v. (cosa) to arrange, adjust; (a una persona) to lodge; to give employment to; **-se** to make oneself comfortable; to adapt oneself.

a•co•mo•do m. occupation, employment; arrangement.

a•com•pa•ña•dor m. companion; accom-panist.

a•com•pa•ña•mien•to m. accompaniment; retinue, company.

a•com•pa•ñan•te m. companion; escort; attendant; accompanist.

a•com•pa•ñar v. to accompany; to escort; to be with; to enclose (in a letter).

a•com•pa•sa•do adj. rhythmical; measured; slow, deliberate.

a•con•di•cio•na•do adj. conditioned; comfortable; air-conditioned; Am. adequate, suitable.

a•con•di•cio•nar v. to condition; to prepare; to arrange; **-se** to become conditioned or prepared.

a•con•go•jar v. to grieve; **-se** to grieve; to be distressed.

a•con•se•jar v. to advise, counsel.

a•con•te•cer[15] v. irr. to happen, occur.

a•con•te•ci•mien•to m. event, happening.

a•co•piar v. to gather, accumulate, store up.

a•co•pio m. storing; accumulation; stock, store, supply.

a•co•pla•mien•to m. coupling; joint, connection.

a•co•plar v. to couple, connect, to fit or join together; to yoke; to pair, fnate.

a•co•ra•za•do m. armored ship, battleship.

a•co•ra•zar[9] v. to armor.

a•cor•dar v. irr. (estar conforme) to arrange, to deci-de; (instrumento) to tune, put in harmony (stringed instrument); Perú, Ch., Riopl., Mex., Cuba to grant, **-se** to remember.

a•cor•de adj. in harmony; in tune; m. chord.

a•cor•de•lar v. to measure with a cord; to rope off, put a cord around.

a•cor•de•ón m. accordion.

a•cor•do•nar v. to tie with a cord, string, or rope; to rope off, tie a rope around (a place); to mill (a coin).

a•cor•ne•ar v. to gore, wound with a horn; to butt.

a•co•rra•lar v. to corral; to surround.

a•cor•ta•mien•to m. shortening.

a•cor•tar v. to shorten, diminish; **-se** to shrink; to be shy, bashful.

a•co•sar v. to pursue, harass.

a•cos•ta•do adj. reclining, lying down, in bed; tilted.

a•cos•tar[2] v. irr. to put to bed; to lay down; **-se** to lie down, go to bed; to tilt.

a•cos•tum•bra•do adj. accustomed, used, usual, habitual.

a•cos•tum•brar v. to accustom, train; to be used to, be accustomed to; **-se** to get accustomed.

a•co•ta•ción f. marginal note; stage directions (for a play); boundary mark; mark on a map showing altitude.

a•co•tar v. to mark off (with boundary marks); to make marginal notes or citations; to put the elevation marks on (maps).

a•cre adj. sour, tart, sharp; rude, harsh; m. acre.

a•cre•cen•ta•mien•to m. growth, increase.

a•cre•cen•tar[1] v. irr. to increase; to advance, promote.

a•cre•di•tar v. to credit; to bring fame or credit to; to accredit, authorize; **-se** to win credit or fame.

a•cre•e•dor adj. worthy, deserving; m. creditor.

a•cri•bi•llar v. to riddle; to perforate; to pierce.

a•crio•llar v. to make Spanish American; **-se** to become Spanish American like; to take on Spaish-American customs.

a•cró•ba•ta m. & f. acrobat.

ac•ta f. minutes (of a meeting); document; **levantar — to** write the minutes.

ac•ti•tud f. attitude; posture, pose.

ac•ti•var v. to activate, make active; to speed up, hasten.

ac•ti•vi•dad f. activity; energy.

ac•ti•vis•ta m. & f. activist.

ac•ti•vo adj. active, lively; m. assets.

ac•to m. act; action, deed; ceremony; **— continuo** (or **seguido**) immediately after; **en el —** immediately.

ac•tor m. actor; **actriz** f. actress.

ac•tua•ción f. action; intervention, parti-cipation, performance; **-es** legal proceedings.

ac•tual adj. present (time); of the present month; **-mente** adv. at present, nowadays.

ac•tua•li•dad f. present time; **-es** latest news, fashions, or events; **de —** current, up-to-date.

ac•tuar[18] v. to act, perform a function or act; to set in motion, cause to act.

a•cua•re•la f. water color.

a•cua•rio m. aquarium.

a•cuar•te•lar v. to quarter (troops).

a•cuá•ti•co adj. aquatic; **deportes -s** water sports.

a•cu•chi•llar v. to knife; to stab; to slash.

a•cu•dir v. to go or come (to aid, or in response to a call); to attend, be present; to resort or turn to for help.

a•cue•duc•to m. aqueduct, water channel or pipe.

a•cuer•do m. agreement; decision, resolu-tion; opinion; remembrance; **estar de —** to be in agreement; **ponerse de —** to come to an agrement; **tomar un —** to take a decision.

a•cu•llá adv. yonder, over there.

a•cu•mu•la•ción f. accumulation.

a•cu•mu•la•dor m. storage battery.

a•cu•mu•lar v. to accumulate, gather, pile up.

a•cu•ña•ción f. coinage, minting; wedging.

a•cu•ñar v. to mint, coin; to wedge.

a•cuo•so adj. watery.

a•cu•rru•car•se[6] v. to cuddle, nestle; to huddle.

a·cu·sa·ción *f.* accusation, charge.

a·cu·sa·do *p.p.* & *adj.* accused; *m.* defendant.

a·cu·sar *v.* to accuse, denounce; to acknowledge (*receipt*).

a·cu·se *m.* acknowledgment (*of receipt*).

a·cús·ti·ca *f.* acoustics (*science of sound*).

a·cha·car[6] *v.* to impute, attribute.

a·cha·co·so *adj.* sickly.

a·cha·pa·rra·do *adj.* shrub, of shrub size; squat, squatty.

a·cha·que *m.* slight chronic illness; excuse; pretext; infirmity.

a·chi·car[6] *v.* to shorten; to make small; to bail (*water*); to humiliate; *Col.* to kill; *Ríopl.* to tie, fasten; **-se** to get smaller; to shrink.

a·da·gio *m.* adage, proverb, wise saying; adagio (*musical Spanish America*).

a·dap·tar *v.* to adapt, fit, adjust.

a·de·cua·do *adj.* adequate, fit, suitable.

a·de·cuar *v.* to fit, adapt.

ade·fe·sio *m.* absurdity, nonsense; ridiculous sight, dress, or person.

a·de·lan·ta·do *p.p.* & *adj.* anticipated; advanced; ahead; forward, bold; **por –** in advance; *m.* governor of a province (*in colonial Spanish America*).

a·de·lan·ta·mien·to *m.* advancement, progress, betterment.

a·de·lan·tar *v.* to advance; to move forward; to progress; to better; **-se** to get ahead.

a·de·lan·te *adv.* forward, **ahead; en –** from now on.

a·de·lan·to *m.* advance; advancement, progress; betterment.

a·del·ga·zar[9] *v.* to thin out, taper; **-se** to get thin, slender.

a·de·mán *m.* gesture, gesticulation; attitude.

a·de·más *adv.* moreover, besides; **– de** *prep.* in addition to, besides.

a·den·tro *adv.* within, inside; **tierra –** inland; **mar –** out to sea; **hablar para sus -s** to talk to oneself.

a·de·re·za·mien·to *m.* dressing; adornment, decoration.

a·de·re·zar *v.* (*embellecer*) to fix up, adorn, beautify, garnish; (*condimentar*) to season, prepare; (*almidonar*) to starch, stiffen.

a·de·re·zo *m.* (*adorno*) adornment, garnish, trappings, finery, set of jewels; (*alimento*) seasoning; (*almidón*) starch, stiffener, filler (*used in cloth*).

a·des·tra·do *adj.* trained, skilled.

a·des·trar[1] *v.* to train; to guide.

a·deu·da·do *adj.* indebted; in debt; *p.p.* of **adeudar.**

a·deu·dar *v.* to owe; to debit, charge; **-se** to run into debt.

a·deu·do *m.* debt, indebtedness; duty (*on imports*); debit, charge.

ad·he·ren·cia *f.* adherence; attachment.

ad·he·rir[3] *v. irr.* to adhere, stick.

ad·he·sión *f.* adhesion; attachment.

a·dic·to *adj.* addicted; devoted; *m.* addict; follower.

a·dies·tra·do = adestrado.

a·dies·tra·mien·to *m.* training; drill.

a·dies·trar = adestrar.

a·di·ne·ra·do *adj.* wealthy.

¡a·diós! *interj.* good-bye!; farewell!; hello!; *Am.* you don't say!

a·di·ta·men·to *m.* addition; annex.

a·di·vi·na·ción *f.* divination, prediction; guess

a·di·vi·nan·za *f.* conundrum, riddle.

a·di·vi·nar *v.* to guess.

a·di·vi·no *m.* fortuneteller; soothsayer.

ad·je·ti·vo *m.* & *adj.* adjective.

ad·ju·di·car[6] *v.* to adjudge, award, assign; **-se** to appropriate.

ad·jun·tar *v.* to put with; to bring together; to enclose (*in a letter*).

ad·jun·to *adj.* adjoining; attached, enclosed.

ad·mi·ní·cu·lo *m.* accessory; gadget.

ad·mi·nis·tra·ción *f.* administration, management; headquarters; *Ven., Mex., Cuba* extreme unction, last sacrament.

ad·mi·nis·tra·dor *m.* administrator, manager.

ad·mi·nis·trar *v.* to administer; to manage; **-se** *Ven, Mex., Cuba* to receive the extreme unction or last sacrament.

ad·mi·nis·tra·ti·vo *adj.* administrative.

ad·mi·ra·ble *adj.* admirable, wonderful.

ad·mi·ra·ción *f.* admiration, wonder; **punto de –** exclamation point.

ad·mi·ra·dor *m.* admirer.

ad·mi·rar *v.* to admire; **-se** to be astonished or amazed; to wonder.

ad·mi·si·ble *adj.* admissible, allowable.

ad·mi·sión *f.* admission; acceptance; acknowledgment.

ad·mi·tir *v.* to admit; to let in; to accept; to allow, permit.

a·do·bar *v.* to fix, cook, prepare (*food*); to tan (*hides*); to pickle (*meats, fish*).

a·do·be *m.* adobe, sun-dried mud brick.

a·do·bo *m.* mending; sauce for seasoning or pickling; mixture for dressing skin   s or cloth; rouge.

a·doc·tri·na·mien·to *m.* indoctrination, teaching, instruction.

a·doc·tri·nar *v.* to indoctrinate, teach, instruct.

a·do·le·cer[13] *v. irr.* to suffer (*from an illness, defect, etc.*).

a·do·les·cen·cia *f.* adolescence.

a·do·les·cen·te *adj.* adolescent.

a·don·de *rel. adv.* where; **¿a dónde?** *interr. adv.* where to?; where?

a·dop·tar *v.* to adopt; to accept (*an opinion*):

a·dop·ti·vo *adj.* adoptive, related by adoption; adopted.

a·do·ra·ción *f.* adoration, worship.

a·do·rar *v.* to adore, worship.

a·dor·me·cer[13] *v. irr.* to make sleepy or drowsy; to lull; **-se** to get sleepy; to get numb; to asleep.

a·dor·mi·la·do *adj.* drowsy.

a·dor·nar *v.* to adorn, decorate, ornament.

a·dor·no *m.* adornment, ornament, decoration.

ad·qui·rir[35] *v. irr.* to acquire, gain, win, obtain.

ad·qui·si·ción *f.* acquisition; attainment.

a·dre·de *adv.* on purpose, intentionally.

a·dua·na *f.* customhouse.

a·dua·ne·ro *m.* customhouse officer; *adj.* customhouse.

a·duar *m.* gypsy camp; *Ríopl.* Indian camp or ranch.

a·du·cir[25] *v. irr.* to cite, allege, offer as proof.

a·due·ñar·se *v.* to take possession.

a·du·la·ción *f.* flattery.

a·du·la·dor *m.* flatterer.

a·du·lar *v.* to flatter.

a·dul·te·rar *v.* to adulterate, corrupt, make impure.

a·dul·te·rio *m.* adultery.

a·dúl·te·ro *m.* adulterer.

a·dul·to *m. & adj.* adult.

a·dus·to *adj.* stern, severe, austere.

ad·ve·ne·di·zo *m.* newcomer, stranger; upstart; *Mex., Carib., Andes* novice, beginner; *adj.* newly arrived; upstart; *Mex., Carib., Andes* inexpericend.

ad·ve·ni·mien·to *m.* advent, arrival, coming.

ad·ver·bio *m.* adverb.

ad·ver·sa·rio *m.* adversary, opponent; foe.

ad·ver·si·dad *f.* adversity; calamity.

ad·ver·so *adj.* adverse; contrary; unfa-vorable.

ad·ver·ten·cia *f.* notice; warning; advice.

ad·ver·tir[3] *v. irr.* to notice; to warn; to advise.

ad·ya·cen·te *adj.* adjacent.

a·é·re·o *adj.* aerial; airy; **correo** – air mail.

a·e·ro·di·ná·mi·co *adj.* aerodynamic; *f.* aerodynamics.

a·e·ró·dro·mo *m.* airport.

a·e·ro·flu·yen·te *adj.* streamlined.

a·e·ro·na·ve *f.* airship.

a·e·ro·lí·ne·a *f.* airline.

a·e·ro·pis·ta *f.* landing strip; runway.

a·e·ro·pla·no *m.* airplane.

a·e·ro·puer·to *m.* airport.

a·fa·bi·li·dad *f.* friendliness, pleasantness, courtesy; **afable** *adj.* affable, pleasant, courteous.

a·fa·ma·do *adj.* famous.

a·fán *m.* eagerness, anxiety, ardor.

a·fa·nar *v.* to urge, press; **-se** to hurry; to worry; to work eagerly; to toil.

a·fa·no·so *adj.* laborious; hardworking.

a·fa·sia *f.* aphasia.

a·fe·ar *v.* to make ugly; to disfigure; to blame, censure, condemn.

a·fec·ción *f.* affection, fondness; disease.

a·fec·ta·do *p.p. & adj.* affected; *Am.* hurt, harmed; *Am.* **estar – del corazón** to have heart trouble.

a·fec·tar *v. (promover)* to affect, move; *(fingir)* to pretend to have or feel; *Am.* to hurt, to harm, to injure.

a·fec·to *m.* affection; *adj.* fond; **– a** fond of; given to; prone to.

a·fec·tuo·so *adj.* affectionate, tender.

a·fei·ta·da *f. Am.* shave, shaving.

a·fei·tar *v.* to shave; **-se** to shave oneself; to put on make-up.

a·fei·te *m.* make-up, cosmetics.

a·fe·mi·na·do *adj.* effeminate.

a·fe·rra·do *adj.* stubborn, obstinate; *p.p. of* **aferrar.**

a·fe·rra·mien·to *m.* grasping, seizing; attachment; stubbornness; tenacity.

a·fe·rrar *v.* to seize, grasp, grapple; **-se** to take or seize hold of; to cling; **-se a una opinión** to cling to an opinion.

a·fian·zar[9] *v.* to fasten, secure; to steady; to give bail or bond.

a·fi·ción *f.* taste, inclination; fondness, affection.

a·fi·cio·na·do *adj.* fond; *m.* amateur, fan.

a·fi·cio·nar *v.* to inspire a liking or fondness; **-se a** to become fond of.

a·fi·che *m. Ríopl.* poster.

a·fi·la·dor *m.* grinder, sharpener.

a·fi·lar *v.* to sharpen; to grind; *Am.* to make love to, woo; *Am.* to flatter; *Am.* **– con** to flirt with.

a·fín *adj.* kindred, related; **ideas afines** related ideas.

a·fi·na·dor *m.* piano tuner.

a·fi·nar *v.* to refine, polish; to tune.

a·fi·ni·dad *f.* affinity; similarity; relationship.

a·fir·ma·ción *f.* affirmation, assertion.

a·fir·mar *v.* to affirm, assert; to make firm; *Am.* **– un golpe** to deal a blow.

a·fir·ma·ti·va *f.* affirmative.

a·fir·ma·ti·vo *adj.* affirmative.

a·flic·ción *f.* affliction, trouble, pain, grief.

a·fli·gir[11] *v.* to afflict, trouble, grieve; *Ríopl., Ven.* to mistreat, harm, beat, strike; **-se** to worry, grieve.

a·flo·jar *v.* to slacken; to loosen, unfasten; to let go; *Mex., Ríopl., Carib.* to let go of money, spend easily; *Mex., Ríopl., Carib.* **– un golpe** to give a blow.

a·fluen·te *m.* tributary; *adj.* abundant.

a·fluir[32] *v. irr.* to flow (into).

a·for·tu·na·do *adj.* fortunate; lucky.

a·fren·ta *f.* affront, offense, insult.

a·fren·tar *v.* to insult, offend, dishonor.

a·fren·to·so *adj.* outrageous, shameful, disgraceful.

a·fri·ca·no *adj. & m.* African.

a·fron·tar *v.* to face; to confront.

a·fue·ra *adv.* out, outside; **-s** *f. pl.* outskirts.

a•ga•char v. to lower; to bend down; **-se** to stoop, bend down, duck; to crouch; *Am.* to give in, yield; *Col.* **-se con algo** to make away with or steal something.

a•ga•lla f. gill; tonsil; *Col., Ven.* greed; tener **-s** to have guts, have courage; *Riopl., Ch., Carib.* to be unscrupulous and bold in business deals; *Riopl., Ch., Carib.* to be greedy or stingy; *C.A.* to be smart, astute, cunning.

a•ga•rrar v. to seize, grasp, grab; **-se** to cling, hold on.

a•ga•rro m. clench, clutch, grasp, grip, grab; **agarrón** m. tight clench, sudden grasp, grab; *Mex., Col., Ven., C.A.* pull, tug.

a•ga•sa•jar v. to entertain; to flatter.

a•ga•sajo m. entertainment, kind reception; friendliness; flattery.

a•ga•za•par v. to nab, seize (*a person*), **-se** to crouch; to squat.

a•gen•cia f. agency; *Ch.* pawnshop.

a•gen•ciar v. to negotiate; to procure by negotiation; to promote.

a•gen•te m. agent; *Am.* officer, official.

á•gil adj. agile, nimble, limber.

a•gi•li•dad f. agility, nimbleness.

a•gi•ta•ción f. agitation; excitement.

a•gi•ta•dor m. agitator; adj. agitating; stirring.

a•gi•tar v. to agitate, excite; to stir; to wave; to shake.

a•glo•me•ra•ción f. conglomeration, heap, pile, mass.

a•glo•me•rar v. to mass together; to cluster; **-se** to crowd together, pile up.

a•go•biar v. to oppress, weigh down; to overwhelm.

a•gol•par•se v. to crowd together, jam.

a•go•nía f. agony.

a•go•ni•zan•te adj. dying; m. dying person.

a•go•ni•zar⁹ v. to be dying.

a•go•re•ro adj. ominous, of bad omen; prophetic; m. augur, prophet, fortune-teller.

a•gos•tar v. to parch, dry up; pasture; to plow (*in August*).

a•gos•to m. August; harvest; **hacer su —** to make hay while the sun shines.

a•go•ta•do adj. & p.p. exhausted; out-of-print.

a•go•ta•mien•to m. exhaustion; draining.

a•go•tar v. to exhaust, use up; to drain off; **-se** (*acabarse*) to be exhausted, used up; (*terminarse la edición*) to go out of print.

a•gra•cia•do adj. graceful; m. winner (*of a favor, prize, etc.*).

a•gra•ciar v. to grace; to adorn.

a•gra•da•ble adj. agreeable, pleasant.

a•gra•dar v. to please, be agreable (to).

a•gra•de•cer¹³ v. irr. to thank for; to be grateful for.

a•gra•de•ci•do adj. thankful, grateful.

a•gra•de•ci•mien•to m. gratitude, thankfulness.

a•gra•do m. agreeableness; liking, pleasure; **de su —** to his liking.

a•gran•dar v. to enlarge; to aggrandize, make greater.

a•gra•var v. to aggravate, make worse; to make heavier; to oppress; **-se** to get worse.

a•gra•viar v. to offend, insult, affront.

a•gra•vio m. offense, insult, affront.

a•gre•dir⁵¹ v. to assail, assault, attack.

a•gre•gado m. attaché, person attached to a staff; aggregate, collection.

a•gre•gar⁷ v. to add; to join; to attach.

a•gre•si•vo adj. aggressive, offensive.

a•gre•sor m. agressor; assailant.

a•gres•te adj. rustic; wild (*fruit, flower, etc.*).

a•griar¹⁷ v. to sour, make sour; **-se** to sour, turn sour, become sour.

a•grí•co•la adj. agricultural.

a•gri•cul•tor m. agriculturist, farmer.

a•gri•cul•tu•ra f. agriculture.

a•gri•dul•ce adj. bittersweet, tart.

a•grie•tar•se v. to crack; to chap (*said of the skin*).

a•gri•men•su•ra f. survey, surveying (*of land*).

a•grio adj. sour; disagreeable.

a•gro•pe•cua•rio adj. farming (*crops and cattle*).

a•gru•pa•ción f. group; bunch; grouping; gathering.

a•gru•par v. to group, bunch up.

a•gru•ra f. sourness.

a•gua f. water; rain; **— abajo** downstream; **— arriba** upstream; **aguas inmundas** f. sewage.

a•gua•ca•te m. *Am.* avocado, alligator pear; *Am.* avocado tree; *Am.* phlegmatic person.

a•gua•ce•ro m. shower.

a•gua•da f. watering place; supply of drinking water; flood in a mine; wall wash; water color.

a•gua•de•ro m. watering place.

a•gua•do adj. watery; watered; *Am.* soft, unstarched; *Am.* weak, limp; *Andes* insipid, uninteresting, dull; **sopa aguada** thin soup; p.p. of **aguar**.

a•gua•i•tar v. *Col., Ven., Andes, Ch.* to spy; to watch; to wait for.

a•guan•tar v. to endure, bear; to resist, **-se** to be silent, restrain oneself.

a•guan•te m. endurance, fortitude, resistance.

a•guar⁹ v. to water, dilute with water; to spoil (*pleasure*); *Riopl., Ven., C.A.* to water (*livestock*); **-se** to become diluted; to get watery; to fill up with water; **se aguó la fiesta** the party was spoiled.

a•guar•dar v. to wait; to wait for.

a•guar•den•to•so adj. alcoholic; hoarse, raucous.

a•guar•dien•te m. brandy, hard liquor; **— de caña** rum.

a•gua•rrás m. turpentine, oil of turpentine.

a•gua•zal m. marsh, swamp.

a•gu•de•za f. sharpness; keenness; wit; witty remark or saying.

a·gu·do *adj.* sharp; sharp-pointed; keen, witty; acute; shrill.

a·güe·ro *m.* augury, prediction; sign, omen; *Ríop., Mex., Carib.* fortuneteller.

a·gui·jar *v. (picar)* to prick, goad, spur; *(animar)* to encourage, excite.

a·gui·jón *m.* prick; sting; spur, goad.

a·gui·jo·ne·ar *v.* to goad; to prick.

á·gui·la *f.* eagle; **es un –** he is a shark.

a·gui·le·ño *adj.* aquiline; eaglelike.

a·gui·nal·do *m.* Christmas or New Year's gift; bonus.

a·gu·ja *f.* needle; crochet hook; watch hand; church spire; railroad switch.

a·gu·je·re·ar *v.* to pierce, perforate; to riddle.

a·gu·je·ro *m.* hole; needle peddler; needle box; pincushion.

a·gu·zar[9] *v.* to sharpen; to goad, stimulate; **– las ore·jas** to prick up one's ears.

a·hí *adv.* there; **por –** over there.

a·hi·ja·do *m.* godchild.

a·hin·co *m.* effort, eagerness, zeal.

a·ho·gar[7] *v.* to drown; ; to choke, strangle; to smother; to quench, extinguish.

a·ho·go *m.* suffocation; breathlessness; anguish, grief.

a·hon·dar *v.* to deepen; to dig; to penetrate, go deep into.

a·ho·ra *adv.* now; **– mismo** right now; **por –** for the present; **– que** *Am.* as soon as; **ahorita** instantly, this very minute; **ahoritica, ahoritita** *Am.* this very second, in a jiffy.

a·hor·car[6] *v.* to hang, kill by hanging.

a·horrar *v.* to save; to spare; to avoid.

a·ho·rro *m.* saving, economy; **caja de -s** savings bank.

a·hue·car[6] *v.* to make hollow; to hollow out; **– la voz** to speak in a hollow voice; *Am.* **¡ahueca!** get out of here!; **-se** to become puffed up, get conceited.

a·hue·hue·te *m. Am.* a Mexican cypress.

a·hu·ma·do *adj.* smoked; smoky.

a·hu·mar *v.* to smoke; to fume.

a·hu·yen·tar *v.* to drive away; to scare away; **-se** to go away, flee; *Ven., Carib., Mex.* to stop frequenting a place.

ain·dia·do *adj.* Indian-like.

ai·rar *v.* to annoy, irritate; **-se** to get angry.

ai·re *m.* air; wind; tune; appearance; conceit; **-cito** *m.* breeze; a little tune; a certain air or appearance.

ai·re·ar *v.* to air, ventilate.

ai·ro·so *adj.* windy; airy; graceful, elegant; lively, spirited.

ais·la·dor *m.* insulator; isolator; *adj.* insulating; isolating.

ais·la·mien·to *m.* isolation; insulation.

ais·lar *v.* to isolate, place apart; to insulate.

a·jar *v.* to crumple, wither.

a·je·drez *m.* chess.

a·je·no *adj. (de otro)* another's; *(inconciente)* unaware; *(extranjero)* alien; **– a mi voluntad** beyond muy control; **– de cuidados** free from cares.

a·je·tre·ar·se *v.* to hustle and bustle; to get tired out.

a·je·tre·o *m.* bustle, hustle; hubbub; fuss; fatigue.

a·jí *m. S.A., Carib.* chili pepper, chili sauce.

a·jo *m.* garlic; garlic clove; garlic sauce; swear word.

a·juar *m.* furniture set; trousseau, bride's outfit; portion or dowry.

a·jus·ta·do *adj.* tight, fitting tight; agreed upon *(as a price)*; **– a la ley** in accordance with the law; *p.p. of* **ajustar.**

a·jus·ta·mien·to *m.* adjustment.

a·jus·tar *v.* to adjust; to fit tight; to regulate; to tighten; to settle *(accounts)*; to hire *(a person)*; *Col.* to stint, scrimp, save; *C.A.* **– una bofetada** to give a good slap; *C.A., Mex.* **hoy ajusta quince años** he is just fifteen years old today; **-se** to come to an agreement.

a·jus·te *m.* adjustment, fit; agreement; settlement *(of accounts)*.

a·jus·ti·ciar *v.* to execute, put to death.

al = a + el to the.

a·la *f.* wing; hat brim.

a·la·ban·za *f.* praise.

a·la·bar *v.* to praise.

a·la·ce·na *f.* cupboard; closet; *Am.* booth, stall, market stand.

a·la·crán *m.* scorpion.

a·la·do *adj.* winged.

a·lam·bi·ca·do *p.p. & adj.* distilled; overrefined, over-subtle *(applied to style)*.

a·lam·bi·que *m.* still.

a·lam·bra·da *f.* wire entanglement.

a·lam·bra·do *m.* wire fence; wire screening; wiring.

a·lam·bre *m.* wire.

a·la·me·da *f.* poplar grove; park.

á·la·mo *m.* poplar.

a·lan·ce·ar *v.* to lance, spear.

a·la·no *m.* mastiff.

a·lar·de *m.* boast, bluff, brag.

a·lar·de·ar *v.* to boast, brag.

a·lar·gar[7] *v.* to lengthen; to prolong; to strech out, extend.

a·la·ri·do *m.* shout, scream, howl.

a·lar·ma *f.* alarm.

a·lar·mar *v.* to alarm.

a·la·zán *adj.* chestnut-colored; sorrel.

al·ba *f.* dawn; alb *(white robe worn by priest)*.

al·ba·ce·a *m.* executor.

al·ba·ñal *m.* sewer.

al·ba·ñil *m.* mason, brickmason; **albañilería** *f.* masonry.

al·ba·ri·co·que *m.* apricot; **albaricoquero** *m.*

apricot tree.

al·ba·yal·de *m.* white lead.

al·ba·zo *m. Mex.* early morning serenade; *Mex.* bad surprise, surprise attack at dawn.

al·be·ar *v.* to show white (*in the distance*); *Am.* to rise at dawn.

al·be·drí·o *m.* free will.

al·béi·tar *m.* veterinary.

al·ber·ca *f.* water reservoir, tank; pool.

al·ber·gar[7] *v.* to house, shelter, lodge; **-se** to take shelter; to lodge.

al·bo *adj.* white; *Am.* white-footed (*horse*).

al·bón·di·ga *f.* meat ball; fish ball.

al·bor *f.* dawn; whiteness.

al·bo·ra·da *f.* dawn; reveille (*morning bugle call*).

al·bo·re·ar *v.* to dawn.

al·bo·ro·ta·dor *m.* agitator, troublemaker.

al·bo·ro·tar *v.* to disturb, upset; *Am.* to excite, arouse enthusiasm; **-se** to get upset; to mutiny; to riot; *Am.* to get excited; *Am.* to rear, balk (*said of a horse*).

al·bo·ro·to *m.* uproar, disturbance; riot; *Am.* excitement, enthusiasm; *Col., C.A.* popcorn, candied popcorn ball.

al·bo·ro·za·do *adj.* elated, excited.

al·bo·ro·zar[9] *v.* to gladden, **-se** to rejoice.

al·bo·ro·zo *m.* joy, delight.

al·bri·cias *f. pl.* good news; reward (*for good news*).

al·ca·cho·fa *f.* artichoke; *Ch.* sock, blow.

al·ca·hue·te *m.* procurer, pander; gobetween; **al·ca·hue·ta** *f.* baws, pro-curess, go-between.

al·cai·de *m.* warden (*of a fortress, prison, etc.*).

al·cal·de *m.* mayor; justice of the peace; **– mayor** mayor.

al·can·ce *m.* (*extensión*) reach, scope; (*capacidad*) talent, capacity; (*noticias*) last minute news, newspapter extra; **cortos -s** meagre intellect; **dar – a** to catch up with.

al·can·cí·a *f.* money box (*with slit for coin*); savings bank.

al·can·for *m.* camphor.

al·can·ta·ri·lla·do *m.* sewage system.

al·can·za·do *adj.* needy; broke, short of funds.

al·can·zar[9] *v.* to reach; to overtake; to obtain; to befall; to be enough; *Am.* to hand, pass, put within reach.

al·ca·ya·ta *f.* wall hook; meat hook.

al·cá·zar *m.* castle, fortress.

al·co·ba *f.* alcove, bedroom.

al·co·hol *m.* alcohol; **alcohólico** *adj.* alcoholic.

al·cor *m.* hill.

al·cor·no·que *m.* cork tree; cork wood; blockhead, dunce.

al·cu·za *f.* oil can; cruet, oil bottle.

al·da·ba *f.* knocker (*of a door*); crossbar, bolt, latch; handle (*of a door, chest, etc.*); **tener buenas -s** to have "pull", influential connections.

al·da·bón *m.* large iron knocker; large handle; **alda-**

bonazo *m.* knock, knocking.

al·de·a *f.* village; **aldehuela** *f.* little village, hamlet.

al·de·a·no *adj.* rustic, countrified; *m.* villager; peasant.

a·le·a·ción *f.* alloy; alloying.

ale·ar *v.* to alloy, mix (*metals*); to flutter; to flap (*wings, arms, etc.*).

a·lec·cio·nar *v.* to coach; to teach, instruct; to train; to drill.

a·le·da·ños *m. pl.* borders, frontiers.

a·le·gar[7] *v.* to allege, assert; *Am.* to argue, dispute.

a·le·ga·to *m.* allegation; assertion.

a·le·grar *v.* to cheer up, gladden; to brighten; **-se** to be glad, rejoice; to get tipsy.

a·le·gre *adj.* merry, gay, joyful, cheerful bright; tipsy

a·le·grí·a *f.* joy, mirth, gaiety, merriment.

a·le·ja·mien·to *m.* withdrawal; retirement, aloofness.

a·le·jar *v.* to remove, move away from; **-se** to move away; to withdraw, be aloof.

a·le·la·do *adj.* stupefied, open-mouthed; silly.

a·le·mán *adj. & m.* German.

a·len·tar[1] *v. irr.* to breathe; to encourage, cheer, cheer up; **-se** to take heart; *Am.* to recover (*from illness*).

a·ler·gia *f.* allergy.

a·le·ro *m.* eaves; projecting edge.

a·le·rón *m.* aileron, flap.

a·ler·to *adj.* alert, watchful; **¡alerta!** attention! look out!; **estar alerta** to be on the alert.

a·le·ta *f.* small wing; flap; fin (*of a fish*).

a·le·tar·ga·do *adj.* drowsy, sluggish.

a·le·tar·gar·se[7] *v.* to fall into a state of lethargy; to become drowsy.

a·le·ta·zo *m.* flap, blow with a wing.

a·le·te·ar *v.* to flap, flutter.

a·le·te·o *m.* flapping, flutter (*of wings*).

a·le·ve *adj.* treacherous.

a·le·vo·sí·a *f.* treachery.

a·le·vo·so *adj.* treacherous.

al·fa·be·to *m.* alphabet.

al·fal·fa *f.* alfalfa, **alfalfar** *m.* alfalfa field.

al·fa·re·rí·a *f.* pottery; alfarero *m.* potter.

al·fe·ñi·car[6] *v.* to frost with sugar (*a cake, cookie, etc.*); **-se** to get frail, delicate; to act affectedly.

al·fe·ñi·que *m.* sugar paste; delicate person.

al·fé·rez *m.* ensign; second lieutenant.

al·fil *m.* bishop (*in chess*).

al·fi·ler *m.* pin; brooch; **-es** pin money; **ponerse de veinticinco -es** to doll up, dress up.

al·fom·bra *f.* carpet; **alfombrilla** *f.* (*para el suelo*) carpet, rug; (*enfermedad*) measles; *Mex.* plant of the vervain family; *Carib.* black smallpox; *Carib.* skin eruption.

al·for·ja *f.* saddlebag; knapsack; food provisions for a trip; *Am.* **pasarse a la otra –** to take undue liberties.

al·for·za *f.* tuck, fold, pleat; scar.

al•ga•ra•bí•a *f.* jargon; chatter; uproar.

al•ga•rro•bo *m.* locust tree; carob tree.

al•ga•za•ra *f.* clamor; shouting; uproar.

ál•ge•bra *f.* algebra.

al•go *pron.* something; *adv.* somewhat.

al•go•dón *m.* cotton; **algodonal** *m.* cotton plantation.

al•gua•cil *m.* policeman, constable.

al•guien *pron.* somebody, someone.

al•gún(o) *adj.* some; any; *pron.* someone.

al•ha•ja *f.* jewel.

al•ha•ra•ca *f.* rumpus, clamor, racket.

a•lia•do *adj.* allied; *m.* ally.

a•lian•za *f.* alliance, union; *Andes* wedding ring; *Am.* mixture of liquors.

a•liar[17] *v.* to ally; to unite; **-se** to form an alliance; to unite.

a•li•ca•í•do *adj.* crestfallen, downcast, discouraged; drooping.

a•li•ca•tes *m. pl.* pliers, small pincers.

a•li•cien•te *m.* inducement, incentive, attraction.

a•lie•nis•ta *m.* alienist (*doctor who treats mental diseases*).

a•lien•to *m.* (*de los pulmones*) breath; (*ánimo*) encouragement.

a•li•ge•rar *v.* to lighten; to hasten.

a•li•men•ta•ción *f.* nourishment, food, nutrition; feeding.

a•li•men•tar *v.* to feed, nourish.

a•li•men•ti•cio *adj.* nutritious, nourishing.

a•li•men•to *m.* food.

a•li•ne•ar **v.** to line up, put into line; to range; **-se** to fall in line, form into a line.

a•li•ño *m.* ornament, decoration; neatness; condiment, dressing, seasoning.

a•li•sar *v.* to smooth; to polish; to plane.

a•lis•ta•mien•to *m.* enlistment; enrollment.

a•lis•tar *v.* to enlist; to enroll; to make ready; **-se** to enlist; to get ready; *Am.* to dress up.

a•li•viar *v.* to lighten; to alleviate, relieve, remedy, soothe; **-se** to get better, recover.

a•li•vio *m.* relief, remedy; aid, help; improvement.

al•ji•be *m.* cistern, reservoir, tank; water tanker; *Riopl.* well, artesian well, spring.

al•ma *f.* soul, spirit; inhabitant.

al•ma•cén *m.* warehouse; department store; store.

al•ma•ce•na•je *m.* storage.

al•ma•ce•nar *v.* to store, store up; to put in storage.

al•ma•ce•nis•ta *m. & f.* department store owner; warehouse owner or manager; wholesale merchant.

al•ma•na•que *m.* almanac, calendar.

al•me•ja *f.* clam.

al•men•dra *f.* almond; **almendrado** *m.* almond paste; **almendro** *m.* almond tree.

al•mí•bar *m.* syrup.

al•mi•dón *m.* starch; *Col., Ven.* paste (*for gluing*).

al•mi•do•nar *v.* to starch.

al•mi•nar *m.* turret.

al•mi•ran•te *m.* admiral.

al•mi•rez *m.* metal mortar.

al•mo•ha•da *f.* pillow; **almohadón** *m.* large cushion or pillow.

al•mo•ha•za *f.* currycomb (*for grooming horses*).

al•mo•ne•da *f.* auction.

al•mor•zar[2,9] *v. irr.* to lunch, eat lunch.

al•muer•zo *m.* lunch.

a•lo•ja•mien•to *m.* lodgind.

a•lo•jar *v.* to lodge; to house; to quarter (*troops*); **-se** to lodge, room.

a•lon•dra *f.* lark.

al•pa•ca *f.* alpaca (*sheeplike animal of South America*); alpaca wool; alpaca cloth.

al•par•ga•ta *f.* sandal (*usually of canvas and with hemp sole*).

al•que•ría *f.* farmhouse.

al•qui•lar *v.* to rent; to hire; **-se** to hire out.

al•qui•ler *m.* rent, rental; **de –** for rent, for hire.

al•qui•trán *m.* tar.

al•re•de•dor *adv.* about, around; **– de** *prep.* around; **-es** *m. pl.* environs, outskirts.

al•ta•ne•ría *f.* haughtiness.

al•ta•ne•ro *adj.* haughty, proud.

al•tar *m.* altar; **– mayor** high altar.

al•ta•voz *m.* loud-peaker.

al•te•ra•ción *f.* alteration, change; disturbance.

al•te•rar *v.* to alter, change; to disturb.

al•ter•car[6] *v.* to argue, dispute; to quarrel.

al•ter•nar *v.* to alternate; to take turns; **– con** to rub elbows with, be friendly with.

al•ter•na•ti•va *f.* alternative, choice, option.

al•ter•na•ti•vo *adj.* alternating, alternative.

al•ter•no *adj.* alternate.

al•te•za *f.* highness (*title*); lofty height.

al•ti•ba•jo *m.* downward thrust (*in fencing*); **-s** ups and downs; uneven ground.

al•ti•pla•ni•cie *f.* upland; high plateau.

al•ti•pla•no *m. Am.* high plateau.

al•ti•so•nan•te *adj.* high-sounding.

al•ti•tud *f.* altitude.

al•ti•vez *f.* haughtiness, arrogance.

al•ti•vo *adj.* haughty, proud, arrogant.

al•to *adj.* (*tamaño*) high; *m.* height; upper story (*of a building*); *Am.* heap, pile; **-s** *Am.* upper floors; *v.* **hacer –** to halt, stop; **pasar por –** to omit, overlook; **– ¡**halt!

al•to•par•lan•te *m.* loud-speaker.

al•tu•ra *f.* height, altitude.

a•lud *m.* avalanche.

a•lu•dir *v.* to allude, refer indirectly.

a•lum•bra•do *m.* lighting; *adj.* lit, lighted; tipsy.

a•lum•bra•mien•to *m.* childbirth; lighting.

a•lum•brar *v.* to light, give light; to enlighten; to give birth; **-se** to get tipsy.

a•lu•mi•nio *m.* aluminum.

a•lum•na•do *m.* student body.

a•lum•no *m.* student.

a•lu•sión *f.* allusion.

al•za *f.* rise; lift (*for shoes*).

al•za•da *f.* height (*of a horse*).

al•za•mien•to *m.* raising, lifting; uprising, insurrection.

al•zar[9] *v.* to lift, raise; to cut (*cards*); **-se** to rebel, rise up in arms; *Col., Ven., C.A., Mex., Andes* to puff up with pride; **-se con algo** to run off with something, steal something.

allá *adv.* there, over there; **más** – farther.

a•lla•nar *v.* to level, even off; to invade, break into (*a house*); to raid; – **una dificultad** to smooth out a difficulty.

a•lle•ga•do *adj.* near; related; allied; *m.* relative; partisan, follower.

a•lle•gar[7] *v.* to accumulate, heap up, gather.

a•llen•de *adv.* on the other side; beyond; – **el mar** across the sea, overseas.

a•llí *adv.* there; **por** – through that place, around there.

a•ma *f.* mistress, owner; – **de leche** wet nurse; – **de llaves** housekeeper.

a•ma•bi•li•dad *f.* kindness, courtesy.

a•ma•ble *adj.* kind, amiable.

a•ma•dor *m.* lover.

a•maes•trar *v.* to teach, coach, train.

a•ma•gar[7] *v.* to threaten; to feint, make a threatening motion; to strike at.

a•ma•go *m.* threat; indication.

a•mal•ga•mar *v.* to amalgamate, combine, mix, blend.

a•ma•man•tar *v.* to nurse, suckle.

a•ma•ne•cer[13] *v. irr.* to dawn; – **malo** to wake up ill; *m.* dawn, sunrise.

a•ma•ne•ci•da *f.* dawn, sunrise.

a•man•sar *v.* to tame; to subdue; to pacify.

a•man•te *m.* lover; – **de** fond of.

a•ma•ñar•se *v. Ec., Col., Ven* to be accustomed; to acclimate oneself.

a•ma•po•la *f.* poppy.

a•mar *v.* to love.

a•mar•gar[7] *v.* to embitter, make bitter.

a•mar•go *adj.* bitter; *m.* bitters; *Am.* mate (*Paraguayan tea*) without sugar.

a•mar•gor *m.* bitterness.

a•mar•gu•ra *f.* bitterness; grief.

a•ma•ri•lle•ar *v.* to show or have a yellow-ish tinge; to turn yellow.

a•ma•ri•llen•to *adj.* yellowish.

a•ma•ri•llo *adj.* yellow.

a•ma•rra *f.* cable; rope; strap.

a•ma•rrar *v.* to tie, fasten, rope; to moor (*a ship*); *Am.* **amarrárselas** to get "tight", drunk.

a•ma•sar *v.* to knead, mix; to mash; *Am.* to amass, accumulate (*a fortune*).

a•ma•tis•ta *f.* amethyst.

am•ba•gues *m. pl.* circumlocutions; **hablar sin** – to go straight to the point, speak plainly, not to beat about the bush.

ám•bar *m.* amber; **ambarino** *adj.* amber; like amber.

am•bi•ción *f.* ambition; aspiration.

am•bi•cio•nar *v.* to seek, aspire after; to covet.

am•bi•cio•so *adj.* ambitious, eager; greedy, grasping.

am•bien•te *m.* atmosphere, environment.

am•bi•güe•dad *f.* ambiguity.

am•bi•guo *adj.* ambiguous; uncertain, doubtful.

ám•bi•to *m.* precinct, enclosure.

am•bos *adj. & pron.* both.

am•bu•lan•cia *f.* ambulance; field hospital.

am•bu•lan•te *adj.* walking; itinerant; moving; wandering.

a•me•dren•tar *v.* to scare, frighten.

a•me•na•za *f.* menace, threat.

a•me•na•za•dor, amenazante *adj.* threatening.

a•me•na•zar[9] *v.* to menace, threaten.

a•men•guar[8] *v.* to lessen, diminish; to defame, dishonor.

a•me•ni•dad *f.* pleasantness.

a•me•ni•zar[9] *v.* to make pleasant, cheer, brighten.

a•me•no *adj.* pleasant, agreeable.

a•me•ri•ca•na *f.* suit coat.

a•me•ri•ca•no *adj. & m.* American.

a•me•tra•lla•dor *m.* gunner; **ametralladora** *f.* machine gun.

a•mi•ga•ble *adj.* friendly; affable, pleasant.

a•míg•da•la *f.* tonsil; **amigdalitis** *f.* tonsilitis.

a•mi•go *m.* friend; – **de** fond of.

a•mi•no•rar *v.* to lessen.

a•mis•tad *f.* friendship; friendliness.

a•mis•to•so *adj.* friendly.

a•mo *m.* master, owner, boss.

a•mo•do•rra•do *adj.* drowsy.

a•mo•do•rrar *v.* to make drowsy; **-se** to become drowsy.

a•mo•la•dor *m.* grinder, sharpener; *adj.* grinding, sharpening.

a•mo•lar *v. irr.* to grind, hone, sharpen; to annoy; *Col., Mex., C.A.* to ruin, harm; **-se** *Mex., C.A., Col.* to go to rack and ruin.

a•mol•dar *v.* to mold; to shape; to adjust; to adapt.

a•mo•nes•ta•ción *f.* admonition, advice, warning; **-es** marriage bans (*or* banns).

a•mo•nes•tar *v.* to admonish, advise, warn.

a•mo•ní•a•co *m.* ammonia.

a•mon•to•na•mien•to *m.* accumulation, pile, heap.

a•mon•to•nar *v.* to heap up, pile up, crowd up.

a•mor *m.* love; – **propio** self-esteem.

a•mor•ta•do *adj.* livid, bluish, purplish.

a·mor·da·zar[9] *v.* to gag; to muzzle.

a·mo·rí·o *m.* love affair; love-making.

a·mo·ro·so *adj.* loving, tender, affectionate.

a·mor·ta·jar *v.* to shroud.

a·mor·ti·gua·dor *m.* shock absorber; silencer, muffler.

a·mor·ti·guar[8] *v.* to muffle; to deafen (*a sound*); to deaden (*a blow or sound*); to soften, tone down (*a color or sound*).

a·mor·ti·zar[9] *v.* to pay on account; to liquidate, pay (*a debt*); to provide a sinking fund.

a·mos·car·se[6] *v.* to get peeved, annoyed; *Am.* to blush, be inhibited or embarrassed.

a·mos·ta·zar[6] *v.* to anger, irritate; -se to get angry or irritated.

a·mo·ti·nar *v.* to incite to rebellion; -se to mutiny; to riot.

am·pa·rar *v.* to protect; to defend; *Am.* to grant mining rights; -se to seek protection or refuge; to protect oneself.

am·pa·ro *m.* protection; habeas corpus (*protection against imprisonment*); *Am.* mining rights.

am·plia·ción *f.* enlargement, widening.

am·pliar[17] *v.* to enlarge, widen.

am·pli·fi·ca·dor *m.* amplifier.

am·pli·fi·car[6] *v.* to amplify, expand, extend, enlarge; to magnify.

am·plio *adj.* ample; wide, large, roomy.

am·pli·tud *f.* f. breadth, extent, width.

am·po·lla *f.* (*condición*) blister, water buble; (*vasija*) narrow-necked bottle or vase, cruet.

am·po·llar *v.* to blister; -se to blister.

am·pu·lo·so *adj.* inflated, wordy, bom-bastic, pompous.

am·pu·tar *v.* to amputate, cut off.

a·mue·blar *v.* to furnish (*with furniture*).

á·na·de *m.* & *f.* duck; anadeja *f.* duckling.

a·na·de·ar *v.* to waddle.

a·na·les *m. pl.* annals, historical records.

a·nal·fa·be·to *adj.* & *m.* illiterate; analfabetismo *m.* illiteracy.

a·ná·li·sis *m.* analysis.

a·na·li·zar[9] *v.* to analyze, examine.

a·na·lo·gí·a *f.* analogy, similarity.

a·ná·lo·go *adj.* analogous, similar, comparable.

a·na·ná, a·na·nás *f.* pineapple. *See* piña.

a·na·quel *m.* shelf; bookshelf; anaquelería *f.* shelves, bookshelves, library stacks.

a·na·ran·ja·do *adj.* orange-colored; *m.* orange color.

a·nar·quí·a *f.* anarchy.

a·na·to·mí·a *f.* anatomy.

an·ca *f.* haunch, hind quarter, rump; *Andes* popcorn.

an·cia·ni·dad *f.* old age.

an·cia·no *adj.* old, aged; *m.* old man.

an·cla *f.* anchor.

an·clar *v.* to anchor.

an·cho *adj.* wide, broad; loose; roomy; *Col., Ven.* self-satisfied, conceited; a sus anchas at one's ease; comfortable; leisurely; *m.* width.

an·cho·a, an·cho·va *f.* anchovy.

an·chu·ra *f.* width, breadth; comfort, ease.

an·chu·ro·so *adj.* vast, extensive; spacious.

an·da·da *f. Mex., Ven.* walk, stroll; -s track, footprints; volver a las -s to fall back into one's old ways or habits.

an·da·du·ra *f.* gait, pace.

an·da·luz *adj.* Andalusian, of or pertaining to Andalusia, Spain; *m.* Andalusian, native of Andalusia.

an·da·mia·da *f.* andamiaje *m.* scaffolding; framework.

an·da·mio *m.* scaffold, scaffolding.

an·da·na·da *f.* (*localidad*) grandstand; (*descarga*) broadside; soltar una – to discharge a broadside; to reprimand.

an·dan·te *adj.* walking; errant, wandering; moderately slow (*music*); caballero – knight-errant.

an·dan·zas *f. pl.* rambles, wanderings.

an·dar[21] *v. irr.* to walk; to go, go about; to run (*as a watch or machinery*); – con cuidado to be careful; anda en quince años he is about fifteen; a todo – at full (walking) speed; a más – walking briskly; ¡anda! move on! ¿qué andas haciendo? what are you doing?; *Am.* – andando to be walking around; *Am.* ¡ándale! hurry!

an·da·rie·go *adj.* fond of walking; roving; *m.* walker.

an·das *f. pl.* portable platform; litter.

an·dén *m.* railway station platform; *C.A., Col., Ven.*, sidewalk.

an·di·no *adj.* Andean, of or from the Andes.

an·dra·jo *m.* rag.

an·dra·jo·so *adj.* ragged, in rags.

a·néc·do·ta *f.* anecdote, story.

a·ne·gar[7] *v.* to drown; to flood.

a·ne·jo *adj.* annexed, attached.

a·nes·té·si·co *m.* & *adj.* anesthetic.

a·ne·xar *v.* to annex.

a·ne·xo *m.* annex; *adj.* annexed, joined.

an·fi·te·a·tro *m.* amphitheater.

an·fi·trión *m.* generous host.

án·gel *m.* angel.

an·gé·li·co *adj.* angelic.

an·gi·na *f.* angina, inflammation of the throat; *Mex., Ven.* tonsil; – del pecho angina pectoris.

an·glo·sa·jón *adj.* & *m.* Anglo-Saxon.

an·gos·tar *v.* to narrow; -se to narrow, become narrow; to contract.

an·gos·to *adj.* narrow.

an·gos·tu·ra *f.* narrowness; narrows (narrow part of a river, valley, strait, etc).

an·gui·la *f.* eel.

an·gu·lar *adj.* angular; **piedra** – corner-stone.

án·gu·lo *m.* angle, corner.

an·gu·lo·so *adj.* angular, sharp-cornered.

an·gus·tia *f.* anguish, sorrow, grief, worry.

an·gus·tiar *v.* to distress, grieve, worry.

an·gus·tio·so *adj.* anguished, worried, grievous; distressing.

an·he·lan·te *adj.* anxious, desirous, long-ing; panting.

an·he·lar *v.* to long for; to breathe hard; to pant.

an·he·lo *m.* longing.

an·he·lo·so *adj.* anxious; eager.

a·ni·dar *v.* to nest; to nestle; to dwell; to shelter.

a·ni·llo *m.* ring.

á·ni·ma *f.* soul, spirit.

a·ni·ma·ción *f.* animation, liveliness, life.

a·ni·mal *m.* animal; *adj.* animal; stupid; beastly; **animalejo** *m.* little animal; **animalucho** *m.* insignificant animal; hideous little beast.

a·ni·mar *v.* to animate, give life to; to inspire, encourage.

á·ni·mo *f.* spirit, mind; courage, valor; intention.

a·ni·mo·si·dad *f.* animosity, ill will; courage, energy.

a·ni·mo·so *adj.* spirited; courageous.

a·ni·ña·do *adj.* boyish; childish; **aniñada** girlish.

a·ni·qui·lar *v.* to annihilate, wipe out, destroy completely.

a·ni·ver·sa·rio *m.* anniversary.

a·no·che *adv.* last night.

a·no·che·cer[13] *v. irr.* to grow dark; to be or arrive at nightfall; *m.* nightfall.

a·no·che·ci·da *f.* nightfall.

a·no·na·dar *v.* to annihilate; to humiliate.

a·nó·ni·mo *adj.* anonymous; nameless; *m.* anonymous letter or note.

a·nor·mal *adj.* abnormal.

a·no·ta·ción *f.* annotation; note.

a·no·tar *v.* to annotate, provide with notes; to write down

an·qui·lo·sa·do *adj.* stiff-jointed; gnarled.

an·qui·lo·sar·se *v.* to become stiff in the joints; to become mentally stagnant.

an·sia *f.* anxiety, anguish; longing, eagerness; **-s** anguish; *Col., Ven., P.R.* nausea.

an·siar[17] *v.* to long for, desire eagerly.

an·sie·dad *f.* anxiety; worry.

an·sio·so *adj.* anxious, troubled; eager.

an·ta·go·nis·mo *m.* antagonism.

an·ta·go·nis·ta *m. & f.* antagonist, adversary, opponent.

an·ta·ño *adv.* yesteryear, formerly; **días de** – days of old.

an·te *prep.* before, in the presence of; **todo** above all; *m.* elk; buckskin.

an·te·a·no·che *adv.* night before last.

an·te·a·yer *adv.* day before yesterday.

an·te·bra·zo *m.* forearm.

an·te·cá·ma·ra *f.* antechamber, waiting room.

an·te·ce·den·te *m.* antecedent; *adj.* antecedent, preceding.

an·te·ce·sor *m.* ancestor; predecessor.

an·te·di·cho *adj.* aforesaid.

an·te·la·ción *f.* precedence, priority (*in time*).

an·te·ma·no: de – beforehand.

an·te·na *f.* antenna (*of a radio or wireless*); lateen yard (*of a ship*); **-s** antennae, feelers; **– emisora** *f.* broadcasting antenna; **– receptora** *f.* receiving antenna; **– parabólica** *f.* parabolic (*TV*) antenna.

an·te·no·che = **anteanoche**

an·te·o·je·ra *f.* blinder.

an·te·o·jo *m.* spyglass; small telescope; eyeglass; **-s** spectacles; **-s de larga vista** field glasses.

an·te·pa·sa·do *adj.* passed; **año** – year before last; *m.* ancestor.

an·te·pe·cho *m.* sill, railing.

an·te·po·ner[40] *v. irr.* to place before; to prefer.

an·te·pues·to *p.p. of* **anteponer**

an·te·rior *adj.* front, toward the front; earlier, previous; **el día** – the day before.

an·tes *adv.* before, formerly; **– de** *prep.* before; **– (de) que** *conj.* before.

an·te·sa·la *f.* anteroom, waiting room.

an·ti·a·é·re·o *adj.* antiaircraft.

an·ti·ci·pa·ción *f.* anticipation, advance consideration; **con** – in advance.

an·ti·ci·pa·do *adj.* early, ahead of time; advanced (*payment*); **por** – in advance; *p.p. of* **anticipar** anticipated.

an·ti·ci·par *v.* to anticipate; to advance, pay in advance; **-se** to get ahead (of).

an·ti·ci·po *m.* advance, advance payment.

an·ti·cle·ri·ca·lis·mo *m.* anticlericalism (*opposition or antagonism to the clergy*).

an·ti·cua·do *adj.* antiquated, out-of-date.

an·tí·do·to *m.* antidote.

an·ti·gua·lla *f.* antique; anything old.

an·ti·güe·dad *f.* antiquity, ancient times; **-es** antique objects, antiques.

an·ti·guo *adj.* ancient, old; antique.

an·tí·lo·pe *m.* antelope.

an·ti·pa·rras *f. pl.* goggles; spectacles.

an·ti·pa·tí·a *f.* antipathy, dislike; mutual antagonism.

an·ti·pá·ti·co *adj.* disagreeable; unlike-able, unpleasant.

an·ti·po·lio·mie·lí·ti·co *adj.* antipolio.

an·ti·sép·ti·co *adj. & m.* antiseptic.

an·to·ja·di·zo *adj.* fanciful, whimsical.

an·to·jar·se *v.:* **antojársele a uno** to take a notion or fancy to; to strike one's fancy; to want, desire.

an•to•jo *m.* whim, notion, fancy.

an•tor•cha *f.* torch.

an•tra•ci•ta *f.* anthracite, hard coal.

a•nual *adj.* annual, yearly.

a•nua•rio *m.* annual, yearbook.

a•nu•blar *v.* to cloud; to dim, obscure; **-se** to become cloudy.

a•nu•dar *v.* to knot; **anudársele a uno la garganta** to choke up with emotion.

a•nu•la•ción *f.* voiding, cancellation.

a•nu•lar *v.* to annul, void, cancel, abolish.

a•nun•cia•dor *m.* announcer; advertiser; *adj.* announcing; advertising.

a•nun•cian•te *m. & f.* announcer, advertiser.

a•nun•ciar *v.* to announce; to advertise.

a•nun•cio *m.* announcement; advertisement.

an•zue•lo *m.* fishhook; lure, attraction.

a•ña•di•du•ra *f.* addition.

a•ña•dir *v.* to add.

a•ñe•ja•do *adj.* aged (*wine, cheese, etc.*).

a•ñe•jo *adj.* old; of old vintage; stale.

a•ñi•cos *m. pl.* bits, shatters, fragments; **hacer(se)** – to shatters, break into a thousand pieces.

a•ñil *m.* indigo (*plant*); indigo blue.

a•ño *m.* year; **– bisiesto** leap year; **¿cuántos -s tiene usted?** how old are you?

a•ño•ran•za *f.* nostalgia, longing.

a•ño•rar *v.* to long for, yearn for, be homesick for; to make reminiscences.

a•ño•so *adj.* old, aged.

a•o•jar *v.* to bewitch, to cast the evil eye.

a•pa•bu•llar *v.* to crush, crumple.

a•pa•cen•tar[1] *v. irr.* to graze, pasture; to feed (*the spirit, desires, passions, etc.*); **-se** to graze, pasture.

a•pa•ci•bi•li•dad *f.* gentleness, mildness, pleasantness; **apacible** *adj.* pleasant, quiet, gentle.

a•pa•ci•gua•mien•to *m.* appeasement.

a•pa•ci•guar[8] *v.* to pacify, calm, appease; **-se** to calm down.

a•pa•chu•rrar *v. Mex., C.A., Carib., Andes* to crush. See **despachurrar.**

a•pa•dri•nar *v.* to sponsor; to act as a godfather; to act as a second in a duel.

a•pa•gar[7] *v.* to put out, extinguish; to deafen (*a sound*).

a•pa•gón *m.* blackout.

a•pa•la•brar *v.* to speak for, engage, reserve; **-se con** to make a verbal agreement with.

a•pa•le•ar *v.* to beat up, thrash; to thresh.

a•pa•ra•dor *m.* sideboard; cupboard; showcase; show window; workshop.

a•pa•ra•to *m.* apparatus; pomp.

a•pa•ra•to•so *adj.* pompous, ostentatious.

a•par•ce•ro *m.* co-owner of land; *Am.* pal, comrade.

a•pa•re•ar *v.* to mate; to match; to pair; **-se** to mate; to match; to pair.

a•pa•re•cer[13] *v. irr.* to appear, show up.

a•pa•re•ci•do *m.* ghost, specter, phantom.

a•pa•re•jar *v.* to prepare; to harness; to rig; to equip.

a•pa•re•jo *m.* harness; packsaddle; rigging (*of a boat*); preparation; fishing tackle; **-s** equipment, tools.

a•pa•ren•tar *v.* to appear, seem; to pretend, feign, affect.

a•pa•ren•te *adj.* apparent.

a•pa•ri•ción *f.* apparition, ghost; appear-ance.

apa•rien•cia *f.* appearance.

a•par•ta•do *m.* compartment; **– postal** post office letter box; *p.p. of* **apartar.**

a•par•ta•men•to *m.* apartment.

a•par•ta•mien•to *m.* separation; retirement; aloofness; retreat, refuge; *Am.* apartment, flat.

a•par•tar *v.* to set apart, separate; to remove; *Am.* **– las reses** to sort out cattle; **-se** to withdraw; to step aside; to go away.

a•par•te *adv.* apart; aside; *m.* aside (*in a play*); new paragraph; *Am.* sorting out of cattle.

a•pa•sio•na•do *adj.* passionate; very fond (of); impassioned, emotional.

a•pa•sio•nar *v.* to arouse passion; to fill with passion; **-se** to become impassioned; to fall ardently, in love.

a•pá•ti•a *f.* apathy, indolence, indifference.

a•pá•ti•co *adj.* apathetic, indifferent, indolent.

a•pe•ar *v.* (*de caballo*) dismount; (*bajar*) to lower, take down; to shackle (*a horse*); to fell (*a tree*); *Riopl.* to fire, dismiss from a position; **– el tratamiento** to omit the title (*in addressing a person*); **-se** to get off, alight; *Am.* **-se por la cola** (*or* **por las orejas**) to go off at a tangent, make an irrelevant remark.

a•pe•chu•gar *v.* to push with the chest; to push ahead; **– con** to accept reluctantly; to go through with (*something*) courageósly; *P.R.* to snatch, take possession of.

a•pe•dre•ar *v.* to stone, hit with stones.

a•pe•ga•do *adj.* devoted, attached; *p.p. of* **apegar-se.**

a•pe•gar•se[7] *v.* to become attached (to); to become fond (of).

a•pe•go *m.* attachment, fondness.

a•pe•la•ción *f.* appeal.

a•pe•lar *v.* to appeal.

a•pe•lo•to•nar *v.* to form or roll into a ball; to pile up, bunch together.

a•pe•lli•dar *v.* to call, name; **-se** to be named; to have the surname of.

a•pe•lli•do *m.* surname.

a•pe•nar *v.* to grieve, afflict; **-se** to be grieved; *Col., Ven., C.A., Carib.* to feel embarrassed, feel ashamed.

a•pe•nas *adv.* hardly, scarcely; *conj.* as soon as.

a•pén•di•ce *m.* appendix.

a•per•ci•bir *v.* to prepare beforehand; to supply; to warn, advise; to perceive; **-se a la pelea** to get ready to fight; *Am.* **-se de** to notice.

a•per•ga•mi•na•do *adj.* parchment-like; dried up.

a•pe•ri•ti•vo *m.* aperitif, appetizer; cocktail.

a•per•la•do *adj.* pearly, pearl-colored.

a•pe•ro *m.* farm equipment; **-s** tools, implements; *Riopl., Ch., Mex., Ven., Andes* saddle and trappings.

a•per•tu•ra *f.* opening (*act of opening or beginning*).

a•pes•tar *v.* to infect; to corrupt; to sicken; to stink; **-se** to turn putrid, become corrupted; *Am.* to catch cold.

a•pes•to•so *adj.* putrid, foul-smelling.

a•pe•te•cer[13] *v. irr.* to desire, crave.

a•pe•te•ci•ble *adj.* desirable; appetizing.

a•pe•ten•cia *f.* hunger, appetite; desire.

a•pe•ti•to *m.* appetite; hunger.

a•pe•ti•to•so *adj.* appetizing; gluttonous.

a•pia•dar•se *v.* to pity; **– de** to pity, take pity on.

á•pi•ce *m.* apex. top, summit.

a•pi•lar *v.* to pile up, stack, heap.

a•pi•ña•do *p.p. of* **apiñar** & *adj.* crowded, jammed; cone-shaped, shaped like a pine cone.

a•pi•ña•mien•to *m.* crowd, jam (*of people or animals*); crowding together.

a•pi•ñar *v.* to cram together; to crowd; **-se** to pile up, crowd together.

a•pio *m.* celery.

a•pi•so•nar *v.* to pack down, flatten by pounding.

a•pla•car[6] *v.* to appease, pacify, soothe.

a•pla•na•mien•to *m.* flattening, leveling; dejection, depression.

a•pla•nar *v.* to level; to flatten; to astonish; *Am.* **– las calles** to tramp the streets; **-se** to be flattened out; to be leveled to the ground; to lose one's strength; *Col.* to give in, yield.

a•plas•tar *v.* to squash, crush, flatten; *Am.* to tire out, break (*a horse*); **-se** *Am.* to plump oneself down; *Col., Andes* to overstay a call (*remaining seated*).

a•plau•dir *v.* to applaud, clap; to approve, praise.

a•plau•so *m.* applause; praise, approval.

a•pla•za•mien•to *m.* postponement; ad-journment.

a•pla•zar[9] *v.* to postpone; to adjourn.

a•pli•ca•ble *adj.* applicable, suitable, fitting.

a•pli•ca•ción *f.* application; effort, dili-gence; **-es** appliqué (*trimming laid on a dress*).

a•pli•ca•do *adj.* industrious, diligent.

a•pli•car[6] *v.* to apply; toput on, lay on; **-se** to apply oneself, work hard.

a•plo•ma•do *adj.* gray, lead-colored; *p.p.* of **aplomar.**

a•plo•mar *v.* to plumb (*a wall*); to make vertical; to make heavier; **-se** *Am.* to become ashamed or embarrassed; *Am.* to be slow.

a•plo•mo *m.* assurance, confidence, self-possession, serenity; **estar –** to be plumb, vertical.

a•po•ca•do *adj.* cowardly; timid; *p.p.* of **apocar.**

a•po•ca•mien•to *m.* timidity; bashfulness; belittling.

a•po•car[6] *v.* to lessen; to belittle, give little importance to; **-se** to humble oneself.

a•po•dar *v.* to nickname.

a•po•de•ra•do *m.* attorney; proxy, substi-tute.

a•po•de•rar *v.* to empower, give power of attorney; **-se de** to take possession of, seize.

a•po•do *m.* nickname.

a•po•ge•o *m.* apogee (*point at which a planet, satellite, or rocket is at the greatest distance from the earth*); highest point, height (*of glory, fame, etc.*).

a•po•li•lla•do *adj.* moth-eaten; wormeaten.

a•po•lo•gía *f.* apology.

a•po•ple•jía *f.* apoplexy; stroke.

a•po•rre•ar *v.* to beat; to maul; *Am.* to beat (*in a game*), dcfeat.

a•por•ta•ción *f.* contribution.

a•por•tar *v.* to bring; to contribute; to arrive in port; to reach an unexpected place (*after having gone astray*); **-se** *Am.* to appear, approach.

a•por•te *m.* contribution.

a•po•sen•to *m.* room; lodging.

a•pos•tar[2] *v. irr.* to bet; to post, station.

a•pós•tol *m.* apostle; religious leader.

a•pos•tó•li•co *adj.* apostolic (*pertaining to the apostles, or to the Pope and his authority*).

a•pos•tu•ra *f.* elegant bearing, graceful carriage.

a•po•yar *v.* to lean, rest; to back, support; to aid, favor; to confirm; **-se** to lean (on).

a•po•yo *m.* support; favor, protection.

a•pre•cia•ble *adj.* estimable, esteemed; valuable; appraisable; noticeable.

a•pre•cia•cion *f.* appreciation; valuation; estimation.

a•pre•ciar *v.* to appreciate, value, esteem; to price, fix the price of; to appraise.

a•pre•cio *m.* esteem, high regard; appraisal, valuation, estimate; *Mex., Ven., Cuba* **hacer –** to notice, pay attention.

a•pre•hen•der *v.* to apprehend, seize, arrest.

a•pre•hen•sión, aprensión *f.* apprehen-sion; fear, dread; seizure, arrest; *Am.* prejudice.

a•pre•hen•sor, aprensor *m.* captor.

a•pre•mian•te *adj.* pressing, urgent.

a•pre•miar *v.* to press, urge onward, hurry.

a•pre•mio *m.* pressure; urgency.

a•pren•der *v.* to learn.

a•pren•diz *m.*, apprentice.

a•pren•di•za•je *m.* apprenticeship; learning (*act of learning*).

a•pre•sar *v.* to seize, grab; to capture; to imprison.

a•pres•tar *v.* to prepare, make ready; **-se** to get ready.

a•pres•to *m.* preparation; readiness.

a•pre•su•ra•do *adj.* hasty.

a•pre•su•rar *v.* to hurry, hasten; **-se** to hurry, hasten.

a•pre•ta•do *adj.* tight; compact; stingy, miserly; difficult, dangerous; *p.p.* of apretar.

a•pre•tar[1] *v. irr.* to press, squeeze, tighten; to urge on; *Am.* to increase in strength or intensity (*as rain, wind, etc.*); *Am.* to redouble one's effort; **– a correr** to start to run; **-se** *Col.* to gorge, overeat.

a•pre•tón *m.* sudden pressure; squeeze; dash, short run; **– de manos** handshake.

a•pre•tu•ra *f.* jam, crush; tight squeeze, narrow place; difficulty, predicament; dire poverty.

a•prie•to *m.* tight spot, difficulty.

a•pri•sa *adv.* quickly, fast, speedily.

a•pris•co *m.* sheepfold.

a•pri•sio•nar *v.* to imprison; to tie, fasten.

a•pro•ba•ción *f.* approbation, approval; consent; pass, passing grade.

a•pro•bar² *v. irr.* to approve; to pass (*in an examination*).

a•pron•tar *v.* to make ready; to expedite; to hand over without delay; *Am.* to pay in advance.

a•pro•pia•ción *f.* appropriation; confis-cation.

a•pro•pia•do *adj.* appropriate, proper, fitting, suitable; *p.p. of* **apropiar.**

a•pro•piar *v.* to fit; to adapt; **-se** to take possession (of); to confiscate.

a•pro•ve•cha•ble *adj.* available; usable, fit to use.

a•pro•ve•cha•do *adj.* diligent, indus-trious; *p.p. of* **aprovechar.**

a•pro•ve•cha•mien•to *m.* use, utilization; exploitation; profit, benefit; progress.

a•pro•ve•char *v.* to profit, be profitable; to progress, get ahead; to utilize; **-se de** to take advantage of; **¡que aproveche!** may you enjoy it!

a•pro•xi•ma•do *adj.* approximate; near; nearly correct.

a•pro•xi•mar *v.* to place or bring near; to approximate; **-se** to get near, approach.

a•pro•xi•ma•ti•vo *adj.* approximate.

ap•ti•tud *f.* aptitude, capacity, ability.

ap•to *adj.* apt; competent.

a•pues•ta *f.* bet, wager.

a•pues•to *adj.* smart, stylish; good-look-ing.

a•pun•ta•ción *f.* note; memorandum; musical notation, set of musical symbols or signs.

a•pun•ta•lar *v.* to prop; to shore up.

a•pun•tar *v. (señalar)* no point; *(arma)* to aim; *(escribir)* to write down; *(a un actor)* to prompt; *(remendar)* to mend, to stitch; to sharpen; *(brotar)* to begin to show; **– el día** to begin to dawn; **-se** to sprout.

a•pun•te *m.* note, memorandum

a•pu•ña•lar *v.* to stab.

a•pu•ra•ción *f.* worry; trouble.

a•pu•ra•do *adj.* worried; needy; difficult; dangerous; in a hurry.

a•pu•rar *v. (acabar)* to exhaust, to drain to the last drop; *(preocupar)* to worry, annoy; *(acelerar)* to hurry, press; **-se** to be or get worried; to hurry up.

a•pu•ro *m.* need; worry; predicament; *Am.* rush, hurry.

a•que•jar *v.* to grieve, afflict.

a•quel, a•que•lla *dem. adj.* that (*at a distance*); **aquellos, aquellas** those; **aquél, aquélla** *m., f. dem, pron.* that one; the former; aquello that, that thing; **aquéllos, aquéllas** *m., f. pl.* those; the former.

a•quí *adv.* here; **por –** this way; through here; around here.

a•quie•tar *v.* to quiet, calm; to hush; **-se** to calm down, become calm.

a•qui•lón *m.* north wind.

a•ra *f.* altar.

á•ra•be *adj. & m.* Arab; Arabic.

a•ra•do *m.* plow; *Am.* plowed land, piece of cultivated land.

a•ra•go•nés *adj.* Aragonese, of or from Aragón, Spain; *m.* Aragonese.

a•ran•cel *m.* tariff; **– de aduanas** customs, duties; **arancelario** *adj.* pertaining to tariff.

a•ra•ña *f.* spider; chandelier.

a•ra•ñar *v.* to scratch; to claw.

a•ra•ño *m.* scratch; **arañazo** *m.* big scratch.

a•rar *v.* to plow.

ar•bi•tra•ción *f.* arbitration.

ar•bi•tra•dor *m.* arbitrator; referee, umpire.

ar•bi•tra•je *m.* arbitration.

ar•bi•trar *v.* to arbitrate; to umpire.

ar•bi•tra•rio *adj.* arbitrary.

ar•bi•trio *m.* free will, scheme, means; compromise, arbitration; sentence (*of a judge*); judgment.

ár•bi•tro *m.* arbitrator, sole judge, umpire.

ár•bol *m.* tree; mast; **arbolado** *adj.* wooded; *m.* grove of trees.

ar•bo•le•da *f.* grove.

ar•bus•to *m.* shrub.

ar•ca *f.* ark; chest, coffer; **arcón** *m.* large coffer or chest; bin.

ar•ca•da *f.* arcade; archway.

ar•cai•co *adj.* archaic.

ar•ca•no *adj.* hidden, secret; *m.* secret, mystery.

ar•ce *m.* maple, maple tree.

ar•ci•lla *f.* clay.

ar•co *m.* arc; arch; bow; violin bow; **– iris** rainbow.

ar•chi•pié•la•go *m.* archipelago (*group of many islands*)

ar•chi•sa•bi•do *adj.* very well-known.

ar•chi•vo *m.* archives; file; public records; *Am.* office, bussiness office; **archivero** *m.* keeper or archives; city clerk.

ar•der *v.* to burn; to be consumed (*with fever or passion*); *Col., Carib.* to smart, sting.

ar•did *m.* trick, scheme.

ar•dien•te *adj.* arden, burning, fervent; passionate; fiery.

ar•di•lla *f.* squirrel.

ar•di•te *m.* ancient coin of small value; bit, trifle; **no valer un –** not to be worth a penny.

ar•dor *m.* ardor; heat; fervor, eagerness.

ar·do·ro·so *adj.* ardent, fiery.

ar·duo *adj.* arduous, hard, difficult.

á·re·a *f.* area.

a·re·na *f.* sand; arena; **-s** kidney stones; **arenal** *m.* sand pit.

a·ren·ga *f.* address, speech.

a·re·nis·co *adj.* sandy; gritty; **piedra arenisca** sandstone.

a·re·no·so *adj.* sandy; gritty.

a·ren·que *m.* herring.

a·re·pa *f.* Col., Ven., Carib. a fried (griddle) cake made of corn meal that corresponds to the Mexican tortilla.

a·re·te *m.* earring.

ar·ga·ma·sa *f.* mortar.

ar·gen·tar *v.* to plate (with silver); to polish.

ar·gen·tino *adj.* silvery; Argentine; *m.* Argentine; Argentine gold coin worth 5 pesos.

ar·go·lla *f.* large iron ring; *Am.* plain finger ring, engagement ring; *Am.* **tener –** to be lucky.

ar·gu·cia *f.* cunning, astuteness; scheme; subtlety.

ar·güir[32] *v. irr.* to argue; to deduce, infer.

ar·gu·men·ta·ción *f.* argumentation, argument, reasoning.

ar·gu·men·to *m.* reasoning; substance, subjetc matter, resumé (of a play or story).

a·ri·dez *f.* barrenness; dryness; drought.

á·ri·do *adj.* arid, dry, barren; **-s** *m. pl.* grains and dry vegetables; **medida para -s** dry measure.

a·rie·te *m.* ram, battering ram; **– hidráulico** hydraulic ram.

a·ris·co *adj.* gruff, harsh, unsociable; *Am.* shy, distrustful.

a·ris·ta *f.* sharp edge; ridge; beard (of wheat or corn).

a·ris·to·cra·cia *f.* aristocracy.

a·ris·tó·cra·ta *m. & f.* aristocrat.

a·ris·to·crá·ti·co *adj.* aristocratic.

a·rit·mé·ti·ca *f.* arithmetic.

ar·ma *f.* arm, weapon; branch (of the army); **-s** armed forces; **– arrojadiza** missile weapon; **– blanca** sword or knife; **de -s tomar** ready for any emergency; ready to fight.

ar·ma·da *f.* armada, fleet.

ar·ma·dor *m.* shipbuilder; assembler.

ar·ma·du·ra *f.* armor; armature (of a generator or dynamo); framework; mounting.

ar·ma·men·to *m.* armament; equipment.

ar·mar *v.* to arm; to set up, assemble, rig up; **– una pendencia** to start a quarrel; *Col.* **– un trique** to lay a snare, set a trap; *Am.* **-se** to balk, to be stubborn; *Ven., Méx.* **-se con alguna cosa** to refuse to return something.

ar·ma·rio *m.* wardrobe, clothes closet; cabiner.

ar·ma·tos·te *m.* unwieldy object or machine; clumsy thing; heavy, clumsy fellow.

ar·ma·zón *f.* framework, skeleton; *m.* skeleton (of an animal); *Am.* shelf, set of shelves.

ar·me·lla *f.* staple; screw eye.

ar·mi·ño *m.* ermine.

ar·mis·ti·cio *m.* armistice.

ar·mo·nía *f.* harmony.

ar·mó·ni·co *adj.* harmonic; harmonious.

ar·mo·nio·so *adj.* harmonious, musical.

ar·mo·ni·zar[9] *v.* to harmonize.

ar·nés *m.* harness; coat of mail; **-es** harness and trappings; equipment, outfit.

a·ro *m.* hoop; rim (of a wheel); *Am.* finger ring; *Ch., Riopl.* earring.

a·ro·ma *f.* aroma, scent, perfume.

a·ro·má·ti·co *adj.* aromatic, fragrant, spicy; **sales aromáticas** smelling salts.

ar·pa *f.* harp.

ar·pí·a *f.* shrew.

ar·pón *m.* harpoon, spear.

ar·que·a·do *adj.* arched.

ar·que·ar *v.* to arch.

ar·qui·tec·to *m.* architect.

ar·qui·tec·tó·ni·co *adj.* architectural.

ar·qui·tec·tu·ra *f.* architecture.

a·rra·bal *m.* outlying district; **-es** outskirts, suburbs.

a·rra·ca·da *f.* earring.

a·rrai·gar[7] *v.* to root, take root; **-se** to become rooted, attached.

a·rran·ca·do *adj. Mex., Carib., C.A., Andes* without money, broke.

a·rran·car[6] *v.* to uproot; to pull out; to start, start out, *Ch., Mex.* to flee, run away.

a·rran·que *m.* start; pull; uprooting; automobile starter; **– de ira** fit or outburst of anger; **punto de –** starting point.

a·rra·sar *v.* to level; to tear down, raze; to fill to the brim; **-se** to clear up (said of the sky); **-se da lágrimas** to fill up with tears.

a·rras·tra·do *adj.* poor, destitute; mean, vile; wretched; rascally; **llevar una vida arrastrada** to lead a dog's life.

a·rras·trar *v.* to drag, haul; *Ven.* to harrow (land); **-se** to drag along, crawl.

a·rra·yán *m.* myrtle.

¡a·rre! *interj.* gee! get up there!

a·rre·ar *v.* to drive (mules, cattle), *Guat.* to rustle, steal cattle; *Am.* **-le a uno una bofetada** to give a person a slap.

a·rre·ba·ta·mien·to *m.* snatch; ecstasy; rage.

a·rre·ba·tar *v.* to snatch away; **-se de cólera** to have a fit of anger.

a·rre·ba·ti·ña *f.* grab, snatch; scramble; **arrebatón** *m.* quick or violent grab.

a·rre·ba·to *m.* rage; rapture, ecstasy; fit.

a·rre·bol *m.* red color of the sky; rouge; **-es** red clouds.

a·rre·ciar *v.* to increase in intensity, get stronger.

a·rre·ci·fe *m.* reef.

a·rre·drar *v.* to frighten, intimidate; **-se** to be or get scared.

a·rre·glar *v.* to arrange, put in order; to regulate; to fix; to adjust, settle; *Am.* to pay (*a debt*); *Am.* to correct, punish; **-se** to doll up, fix oneself up; to settle differences, come to an agreement.

a·rre·glo *m.* arrangement; adjustment; settlement; conformity, agreement; **con — a** according to.

a·rre·lla·nar·se *v.* to sprawl, lounge; to be self, satisfied.

a·rre·man·ga·do *adj. & p.p.* turned up; **nariz arre-mangada** turned up nose.

a·rre·man·gar[7] *v.* to stuck up, turn up, roll up (*the sleeves, trouser, etc.*); **-se** to roll up one's sleeves; **-se los pantalones** to roll up one's trouser.

a·rre·me·ter *v.* to attack, assail, assault.

a·rre·me·ti·da *f.* thrust, push, attack.

a·rre·mo·li·nar·se *v.* to whirl, swirl; to eddy; to mill around.

a·rren·da·mien·to *m.* renting; lease; rental, rent.

a·rren·dar[1] *v. irr.* to rent, lease, let; to hire; to tie (*a horse*); to bridle; *Am.* to head for.

a·rren·da·ta·rio *m.* renter, tenant.

a·rre·o *m.* raiment; ornament; *Am.* driving of horses or mules; *Ríopl. Ch., Méx., Ven.* drove of horses or mules; **-s** trappings; equipment; finery; *adv.* uninterruptedly, without interruption.

a·rre·pen·ti·do *adj.* repentant; *p.p. of* **arrepen-tirse.**

a·rre·pen·ti·mien·to *m.* repentance, regret.

a·rre·pen·tir·se[3] *v. irr.* to repent, regret.

a·rres·ta·do *adj.* daring, rash; *p.p. of* **arrestar.**

a·rres·tar *v.* to arrest; *Am.* to return, strike back (*a ball*); *Perú* to reprimand; **-se** to dare, venture.

a·rres·to *m.* arrest, imprisonment; detention; daring, rashness; rash act.

a·rriar[17] *v.* to haul down, lower (*the flag*); to lower (*the sails*); to slacken (*a rope*).

a·rri·ba *adv.* above; upstairs; **de — abajo** from top to bottom; up and down; **río —** upstream; **¡—! hurrah!**

a·rri·ba·da *f.* arrival; *Am.* back talk, impudent answer.

a·rri·bar *v.* to arrive; to put into port; *Am.* to prosper, better one's lot.

a·rri·bo *m.* arrival.

a·rrien·do = **a·rren·da·mien·to.**

a·rrie·ro *m.* muleteer.

a·rries·ga·do *adj.* risky, daring.

a·rries·gar[7] *v.* to risk; **-se** to dare, run a risk.

a·rri·mar *v.* to bring or place near; to lay aside; to strike (*a blow*); **-se** to lean (on); to get near; to seek shelter.

a·rrin·co·nar *v.* to corner; to put in a corner; to lay aside; to slight, neglect; **-se** to retire; to live a secluded life.

a·rris·ca·do *adj.* bold; daring; brisk; spirited (*horse*); craggy, rugged.

a·rris·car[6] *v.* to risk, venture; *Méx.* to roll up, curl up, tuck up, fold back; *Col.* to have vim and vigor; *Am.* **— a** to reach, amount to; **-se** to get angry; *Perú., C.A.* to dress up, doll up.

a·rro·ba *f.* weight of 25 pounds.

a·rro·ba·mien·to *m.* trance, rapture.

a·rro·bar·se *v.* to be entranced; to be in a trance; to be enraptured.

a·rro·di·llar·se *v* to kneel.

a·rro·gan·cia *f.* arrogance, pride.

a·rro·gan·te *adj.* arrogant, haughty, proud.

a·rro·gar·se[7] *v.* to appropriate, usurp, assume (*power or right*).

a·rro·ja·di·zo *adj.* missile; **arma arrojadiza** missile weapon.

a·rro·ja·do *adj.* daring, rash, fearless, *p.p. of* **arro-jar.**

a·rro·jar *v.* to throw, hurl, cast; to expel; *Am.* to throw up, vomit; **— un saldo** de to show a balance of; **-se a** to hurl oneself upon or at; to dare to.

a·rro·jo *m.* boldness, daring.

a·rro·lla·dor *adj.* sweeping, overwhelming, violent; winding (*that serves to wind or roll up*).

a·rro·llar *v.* to roll up, to sweep away; to trample upon; to destroy.

a·rro·par *v.* to wrap, cover; *Col.* to snap up, accept on the spot (*a deal*); **-se** to wrap up, cover up.

a·rros·trar *v.* to face, defy; **-se** to dare, dare to fight face to face.

a·rro·ya·da *f.* gully, valley of a stream; bed (*formed by a stream*); river flood.

a·rro·yo *m.* brook, small stream, rivulet; gutter; **arroyuelo** *m.* rivulet.

a·rroz *m.* rice; **arrozal** *m.* rice field.

a·rru·ga *f.* wrinkle.

a·rru·gar[7] *v.* to wrinkle; *Carib.* to bother, annoy; **-se** to get wrinkled; *Méx., Col.* to crouch with fear, be afraid.

a·rrui·nar *v.* to ruin, destroy; **-se** to become ruined; *Am.* to go "broke", lose all one's fortune.

a·rru·llar *v.* to lull; to coo.

a·rru·llo *m.* lullaby; cooing.

a·rrum·bar *v.* to lay aside (*as useless*), put away in a corner, discard; to dismiss, remove (*from office or a position of trust*); to take bearings; **— a su adversa-rio** to corner one's opponent, overpower him.

ar·se·nal *m.* arsenal; navy yard.

ar·sé·ni·co *m.* arsenic.

ar·te *m. & f.* art; skill, ability; cunning; craft; **por – de** by way or means of; **bellas -s** fine arts.

ar·te·fac·to *m.* piece of workmanship, manufactured object; handiwork; contrivance.

ar·te·ria *f.* artery.

ar·te·ro *adj.* crafty, astute.

ar•te•sa *f.* trough.

ar•te•sa•no *m.* artisan, craftsman; **artesanía** *f.* arts and crafts; workmanship, craftsmanship.

ar•te•so•na•do *m.* ceiling decorated with carved panels.

ár•ti•co *adj.* arctic.

ar•ti•cu•la•ción *f.* articulation; pronunci-ation; joint.

ar•ti•cu•lar *v.* to articulate; to join, unite.

ar•tí•cu•lo *m.* article; **– de fondo** editorial.

ar•tí•fi•ce *m.* artisan, craftsman.

ar•ti•fi•cial *adj.* artificial.

ar•ti•fi•cio *m.* artifice, clever device; craft, skill; cunning, deceit.

ar•ti•fi•cio•so *adj.* cunning, astute, deceitful; skillful.

ar•ti•lle•ría *f.* artillery, gunnery; **– de plaza** (or **de sitio**) heavy artillery; **– de montaña** light mountain artillery.

ar•ti•lle•ro *m.* artilleryman, gunner.

ar•ti•ma•ña *f.* trick.

ar•tis•ta *m. & f.* artist.

ar•tís•ti•co *adj.* artistic.

ar•ve•ja *f. C.A., Col., Ven.* pea, *Also referred to as* **alverja.**

ar•zo•bis•po *m.* archbishop.

ar•zón *m.* saddletree.

as *m.* ace.

a•sa *f.* handle.

a•sa•do *m.* roast; *p.p. & adj.* roasted.

a•sa•dor *m.* spit *(for roasting).*

a•sal•ta•dor *m.* assailant; highway robber.

a•sal•tar *v.* to assault, attack; **-le a uno una idea** to be struck by an idea; *Ríopl., Carib.* **- la casa de un amigo** to give a surprise party.

a•sal•to *m.* assault, attack; *Am.* surprise party.

a•sam•ble•a *f.* assembly, legislature; meeting.

a•sar *v.* to roast; **-se** to roast; to feel hot.

a•saz *adv.* enough, very.

as•cen•den•cia *f.* ancestry; origin.

as•cen•den•te *adj.* ascendant, ascending, upward, rising.

as•cen•der *v. irr.* to ascend, climb; to promote; to amount (to).

as•cen•dien•te *m.* ancestor; influence.

as•cen•sión *f.* ascension; ascent.

as•cen•so *m.* ascent, rise; promotion.

as•cen•sor *m.* elevator.

as•co *m.* disgust, loathing; nausea; **me da** – it makes me sick; it disgusts me; *Mex., Ven.* **poner a uno del** – to call a person all kinds of bad names; to soil.

as•cua *f.* ember.

a•se•a•do *adj.* clean, neat; *p.p. of* **asear.**

a•se•ar *v.* to adorn; to make neat and clean; **-se** to clean oneself up.

a•se•chan•za *f.* = **ace•cha•nza.**

a•se•diar *v.* to besiege, attack.

a•se•dio *m.* siege.

a•se•gu•rar *v.* to assure; to secure; to affirm; to insure; **-se** to make sure; to hold on; to get insured.

a•se•me•jar *v.* to liken, compre; **-se a** to resemble.

a•sen•ta•de•ras *f. pl.* buttocks.

a•sen•ta•dor *m.* razor strop.

a•sen•tar *v. (poner)* to set; to put down in writing; *(afirmar)* to assert; to iron out; to establish; *(afilar)* to hone, strop; **-se** to settle.

a•sen•ti•mien•to *m.* assent, acquiescence, agreement.

a•sen•tir *v. irr.* to assent, agree.

a•se•o *m.* neatness, cleanliness.

a•se•qui•ble *adj.* obtainable, available.

a•ser•ción *f.* assertion, affirmation.

a•se•rra•de•ro *m.* sawmill.

a•se•rrar *v. irr.* to saw.

a•se•rrín *m.* sawdust.

a•ser•to *m.* assertion.

a•se•si•nar *v.* to assassinate, murder.

a•se•si•na•to *m.* assassination, murder.

a•se•si•no *m.* assassin, murderer; *adj.* murderous.

a•ses•tar *v.* to point, aim, direct; **- un golpe** to deal a blow; **– un tiro** to fire a shot.

a•se•ve•ra•ción *f.* assertion, affirmation, contention.

a•se•ve•rar *v.* to assert, affirm.

as•fal•to *m.* asphalt.

as•fi•xia *f.* suffocation.

as•fi•xiar *v.* to suffocate, smother,

a•sí *adv.* so, thus, like this; therefore; **– –** so-so; **– que** so that; **– que** (or **como**) *conj.* as soon as; *Ríopl. Ch., Ven., Mex., Andes* **– no más** so-so; just so.

a•siá•ti•co *adj. & m.* Asiatic.

a•si•de•ro *m.* handle; hold.

a•si•duo *adj.* assiduous, diligent, persevering.

a•sien•to *m.* seat; site, location; bottom; entry *(in bookkeeping)*; **-s** dregs, sediment.

a•sig•na•ción *f.* assignment; allowance.

a•sig•nar *v.* to assign; to allot; to attribute; to appoint.

a•si•la•do *m.* inmate *(of an asylum).*

a•si•lar *v.* to house, shelter, to put in an asylum.

a•si•lo *m.* asylum, refuge, shelter.

a•si•mi•lar *v.* to assimilate, digest, absorb; to liken, compare.

a•si•mis•mo *adv.* likewise, also.

a•sir *v. irr.* to seize, take hold of.

a•sis•ten•cia *f.* presence; attendance; assistance, help; *Mex.* sitting room; **-s** allowance; *Col., Ven., Mex.* **casa de** – boarding house.

a•sis•ten•te *m.* assistant; helper; military orderly; *Col., Ven., P.R.* servant; **los -s** those present.

a•sis•tir *v.* to attend, be present; to help; *Am.* to board, serve meals.

as•no *m.* ass, donkey.

a·so·cia·ción *f.* association.

a·so·cia·do *m.* associate.

aso·ciar *v.* to associate; -se to join; to associate.

a·so·la·mien·to *m.* devastation, ravage, havoc, destruction.

a·so·lar² *v. irr.* to raze; to lay waste; to parch; -se to dry up, become parched; to settle (*as liquids*).

a·so·le·a·do *adj.* sunny; *p.p. of* asolear.

a·so·le·ar *v.* to sun; -se to bask in the sun; to get sunburnt.

a·so·mar *v.* to show, appear; — la cabeza to stick one's head out; -se to look out (*of window*); to peep out (*or* into); *Peru* to draw near, approach.

a·som·brar *v.* (*hacer sombra*) to cast a shadow, darken; (*asustar*) to astonish, amaze, frighten; -se to be astonished, amazed.

a·som·bro *m.* astonishment, amazement; fright.

a·som·bro·so *adj.* astonishing, amazing.

a·so·mo *m.* sign, indication; conjecture, suspicion; ni por — by no means.

as·pa *f.* wing of a windmill; blade (*of a propeller*); reel (*for winding yarn*).

as·pec·to *m.* aspect, look, appearance.

as·pe·re·za *f.* roughness, ruggedness; harshness; severity.

ás·pe·ro *adj.* rough, uneven, harsh; gruff.

as·pi·ra·ción *f.* aspiration, ambition, longing; inhalation, breathing in.

as·pi·ra·do·ra *f.* vacuum cleaner.

as·pi·ran·te *m. & f.* applicant; candidate.

as·pi·rar *v.* (*anhelar*) to aspire, long for, seek; (*inspirar*) to breathe in, to inhale; to aspirate (*a sound*).

as·que·ar *v.* to disgust, nauseate, sicken.

as·que·ro·so *adj.* loathsome, disgusting, sickening, filthy.

as·ta *f.* horn; antler; mast, pole, staff, flagstaff; lance; a media — at half mast.

as·te·ris·co *m.* asterisk, star (*used in printing*).

as·ti·lla *f.* splinter; splint.

as·ti·llar *v.* to chip; to splinter; -se to splinter, break into splinters.

as·ti·lle·ro *m.* dry dock; shipyard; lumber yard; rack (*for lances or spears*).

as·tro *m.* star; planet.

as·tro·nau·ta *m. & f.* astronaut.

as·tro·no·mí·a *f.* astronomy; astrónomo *m.* astronomer.

as·tu·cia *f.* shrewdness, cunning; trick.

as·tu·ria·no *adj.* Asturian, of or from Asturias, Spain; *m.* Asturian.

as·tu·to *adj.* astute, shrewd, wily, crafty.

a·sue·to *m.* recess, vacation; día de — holiday.

a·su·mir *v.* to assume.

a·sun·to *m.* topic, subject matter; business; affair.

a·sus·ta·di·zo *adj.* shy, scary, easily frightened, jumpy.

a·sus·tar *v.* to frighten, scare.

a·ta·can·te *m.* attacker; *adj.* attacking.

a·ta·car⁶ *v.* to attack; to tighten, fasten; to ram; to plug, wad (*a gun*).

a·ta·du·ra *f.* tie, knot; fastening.

a·ta·jar *v.* to intercept; to interrupt, cut off; to take a short cut; to cross aout.

a·ta·jo *m.* short cut; interception; *Am.* drove. See hatajo.

a·ta·la·ya *f.* lookout, watchtower; *m.* lookout, watchman, guard.

a·ta·ñer¹⁹·⁵¹ *v.* to concern.

a·ta·que *m.* attack; fit.

a·tar *v.* to tie, fasten; -se to get tied up; to be puzzled or perplexed.

a·ta·rea·do *adj.* busy, over-worked.

a·ta·re·ar *v.* to overwork, load with work; -se to toil, work hard; to be very busy.

a·tas·ca·de·ro *m.* muddy place; obstruction.

a·tas·car⁶ *v.* to stop up; to jam, obstruct; -se to get stuck; to stick; to jam, get, obstructed; to stall.

a·ta·úd *m.* coffin.

a·ta·viar¹⁷ *v.* to attire, deck, adorn; -se to dress up, doll up.

a·ta·vío *m.* attire, costume; ornaments, finery.

a·te·mo·ri·zar⁹ *v.* to frighten, scare.

a·ten·ción *f.* attention, care, thought; courtesy; -es business, affairs; en — a having in mind, considering.

a·ten·der¹ *v. irr.* to heed, pay attention; to attend to, take care of; to take into account or consideration.

a·ten·di·do *adj. Am.* attentive, courteous.

a·te·ner·se⁴⁵ *v. irr.* to rely (on); to accept, abide (*by*).

a·te·ni·do *adj. Mex., Carib., C.A., Andes* habitually dependent on another; *p.p. of* atenerse.

a·ten·ta·do *m.* offense, violation; crime, violence.

a·ten·tar¹ *v. irr.* to attempt, try; — contra la vida de alguien to attempt the life of someone.

a·ten·to *adj.* attentive; courteous, polite.

a·te·nuar¹⁸ *v.* to attenuate, lessen; to tone down; to dim; to make thin or slender.

a·te·o *m.* atheist; *adj.* atheistic.

a·ter·cio·pe·la·do *adj.* velvety.

a·te·ri·do *adj.* stiff, numb from cold.

a·te·rir·se³·⁵¹ *v. irr.* to become numb with cold.

a·te·rra·dor *adj.* terrifying, appalling.

a·te·rrar *v.* to terrify, frighten.

a·te·rri·za·je *m.* landing (*of a plane*); pista de — landing strip.

a·te·rri·zar⁹ *v.* to land (*said of a plane*).

a·te·rro·nar *v.* to make lumpy, form into lumps; -se to lump, form into lumps, become lumpy.

a·te·rro·ri·zar⁹ *v.* to terrify, frighten, appal.

a·te·so·rar *v.* to treasure; to hoard, lay up, accumulate.

a·tes·ta·do *adj.* crowded, jammed, stuffed;

witnessed; *p.p. of* **atestar**.

a·tes·tar *v.* (*legal*) to attest, testify, witness; (*llenar*) to fill up, cram, stuff, crowd; **-se** to stuff oneself with, to get stuffed with.

a·tes·ti·guar[8] *v.* to testify, witness; to attest.

a·ti·bo·rrar *v.* to stuff; **-se** to stuff oneself.

a·tie·sar *v.* to stiffen.

a·til·da·do *adj.* spruce, trim; painstaking in dress or style.

a·ti·nar *v.* to hit the mark; to guess right.

a·tis·bar *v.* to spy, look cautiously; to watch, pry; to catch a glimpse of; to peek.

a·tis·bo *m.* glimpse; insight; peek; spying.

a·ti·zar[9] *v.* to poke, stir (*the fire*); to kindle, rouse; to trim (*a wick*); **– un bofetón** to give a wallop.

a·tlán·ti·co *adj.* Atlantic; **el Atlántico** the Atlantic.

a·tlas *m.* atlas.

a·tle·ta *m. & f.* athlete.

a·tlé·ti·co *adj.* athletic.

a·tle·tis·mo *m.* athletics.

at·mós·fe·ra *f.* atmosphere, air.

at·mos·fé·ri·co *adj.* atmospheric.

a·to·le *m. Am.* Mexican drink made of corn meal.

a·to·lon·dra·do *p.p. & adj.* confused, muddled; stunned; heedless, harebrained, thoughtless.

a·to·lon·dra·mien·to *m.* thoughtlessness, recklessness; confusion, perplexity.

a·to·lon·drar *v.* to confuse, muddle, perplex; to stun; **-se** to get muddled, confused; to get stunned.

á·to·mo *m.* atom; small particle, tiny bit.

a·tó·ni·to *adj.* astonished, amazed.

a·ton·ta·do *adj.* stupefied, stupid, stunned.

a·ton·tar *v.* to stupefy, stun; to confuse.

a·to·rar *v.* to jam; to stop up, clog; *Am.* to hold up, stop; **-se** to get stuck (*in the mud*); to get clogged; to get jammed; to choke (*with food*).

a·tor·men·tar *v.* to torment; to worry, afflict; to tease, bother, vex.

a·tor·na·so·la·do = **tor·na·so·la·do**.

a·tor·ni·llar *v.* to screw; *Am.* to bother, torment.

a·to·rran·te *m. & f. Col. Ch., Riopl., Bol.* vagabond, tramp.

a·tra·ban·car[6] *v.* to rush awkwardly; to run over; **-se** *Riopl.* to get involved in difficulties; *Riopl.* to rush into things.

a·tra·bi·lia·rio *adj.* melancholy; bad-tempered.

a·tra·car *v.* (*llenar*) to cram, stuff; (*amarrar*) to moor, to approach land; (*atacar*) to hold up, assault; *Am.* to seize; *Col.* to pursue, harass; *Am.* to treat severely; *Mex., C.A.* to thrash, beat; **– al muelle** to dock, moor to the wharf; **-se** to stuff oneself, overeat; *Ch.* to have a fist fight; *Riopl.* to falter, stutter; **-se a** to come alongside of (*a ship*).

a·trac·ción *f.* attraction.

a·tra·co *m.* holdup, assault; *Am.* **darse un – de co·mida** to stuff oneself, gorge.

a·tra·cón *m.* stuffing, gorging; *C.A.* violen quarrel; **darse un – de comida** to sutff oneself, gorge.

a·trac·ti·vo *adj.* attractive; *m.* attractiveness, charm.

a·tra·er[46] *v. irr.* to attract.

a·tra·gan·tar·se *v.* to gobble up; to choke (*with food*).

a·tran·car[6] *v.* to bolt, fasten with a bolt; *Am.* **– le a una cosa** to face somethin, stand up against something; **-se** to get crammed, obstructed; *Am.* to be stubborn, stick to one's opinion; *Col.* to stuff oneself, choke (*with food*).

a·tra·par *v.* to trap, ensnare; to seize, grab; to overtake.

a·trás *adv.* back; behind; backward; *Am.* **echarse –** (*or* **para –**) to back out, go back on one's word.

a·tra·sa·do *adj.* late; behind time; backward; behind (*in one's work, payments, etc.*); slow (*said of a clock*); *p.p. of* atrasar.

a·tra·sar *v.* to delay; to be slow or behind time: **-se** to get behind, lose time; *Am.* to suffer a setback (*in one's health or fortune*).

a·tra·so *m.* backwardness; delay; setback; **-s** arrears.

a·tra·ve·sar[1] *v. irr.* to cross; to walk across; to through; to pierce; *Am.* to buy wholesale.

a·tre·ver·se *v.* to dare, risk, to be insolent, saucy.

a·tre·vi·do *adj.*, bold, daring; insolent.

a·tre·vi·mien·to *m.* boldness, daring; insolence.

a·tri·buir[32] *v. irr.* to attribute, ascribe, impute.

a·tri·bu·lar *v.* to grieve, distress; **-se** to grieve; to be distressed.

a·tri·bu·to *m.* attribute, quality.

a·tril *m.* lectern, reading desk; book stand; music stand.

a·trin·che·rar *v.* to entrench, fortify with trenches; **-se** to entrench oneself.

a·trio *m.* court, patio in front of a church; entrance hall.

a·tro·ci·dad *f.* atrocity.

a·tro·na·dor *adj.* thunderous, deafening.

a·tro·nar[2] *v. irr.* to deafen; to stun.

a·tro·pe·llar *v.* to run over, run down, knock down; to trample upon; to insult; **– por** to knock down, overcome with violence; **-se** to rush.

a·tro·pello *m.* violent atc; insult; outrage; trampling.

a·troz *adj.* atrocious, awful; inhuman.

a·tún *m.* tunny fish, tuna fish.

a·tur·di·do *adj. & p.p.* stupid, awkard; stunned, bewildered.

a·tur·di·mien·to *m.* daze, bewilderment, confusion.

a·tur·dir *v.* to stun; to deafen; to bewilder.

au·da·cia *f.* daring, boldness.

au·daz *adj.* daring, bold.

au·dien·cia *f.* audience, hearing; court of justice.

au·di·tor *m.* judge advocate.

au·di·to·rio *m.* audience.

au·ge f. boom (in the market); boost (in prices); topmost height (of fortune, fame, dignity, etc.); **estar** (or **ir**) **en —** to be on the increase.

au·gu·rar v. to foretell, predict.

au·gus·to adj. venerable; majestic.

au·la f. schoolroom, classroom; lecture hall.

au·llar v. to howl; to shriek; to bawl.

au·lli·do m. howl.

au·men·tar v. to augment, increase.

au·men·to m. increase, advance, rise.

aun (aún) adv. even, still, yet.

aun·que conj. though, although.

au·ra f. breeze; favor, applause; Am. bird of prey, buzzard, vulture.

áu·re·o adj. golden.

au·re·o·la f. aureole, halo.

au·re·o·mi·ci·na f. Aureomycin (trademark for chlortetracycline).

au·ro·ra f. dawn; beginning; **— boreal** aurora borealis, northern lights.

aus·cul·tar v. to sound, examine by listening to (the chest, lungs, heart, etc.).

au·sen·cia f. absence.

au·sen·tar·se v. to absent oneself; to be absent; to leave.

au·sen·te adj. absent.

aus·pi·cios m. pl. auspices, patronage; omens.

aus·te·ri·dad f. austerity, severity, sternness, harshness.

aus·te·ro adj. austere, stern, strict; harsh.

aus·tral adj. southern.

aus·tría·co adj. & m. Austrian.

aus·tro m. south wind.

au·tén·ti·co adj. authentic, true, genuine.

au·to m. auto, automobile; one-act play; writ, order; **— sacramental** one-act religious play; **-s** proceedings.

au·to·bús m. bus, autobus.

au·tóc·to·no adj. indigenous, native.

au·to·má·ti·co adj. automatic.

au·to·mo·triz adj. automotive, self-moving.

au·to·mó·vil m. automobile, auto.

au·to·mo·vi·lis·ta m. & f. motorist.

au·to·pis·ta f. expressway, superhighway, freeway, throughway, turnpike.

au·tor m. author.

au·to·ri·dad f. authority.

au·to·ri·ta·rio adj. authoritative; authoritarian, domineering; bossy.

au·to·ri·za·ción f. authorization; sanction.

au·to·ri·zar v. to authorize, give power (to).

au·xi·liar v. to aid, help; adj. auxiliary, helping, assisting; m. assistant.

au·xi·lio m. aid, help.

a·va·lua·ción f. valuation, appraisal, assessment.

ava·luar v. to value, appraise.

ava·lú·o m. valuation, appraisal.

a·van·ce m. advance, progress, headway; advanced payment; attack.

a·van·za·da f. advance guard; outpost; advanced unit, spearhead.

a·van·zar v. to advance.

a·va·ri·cia f. avarice, greed.

ava·rien·to adj. avaricious, miserly; m. miser.

a·va·ro adj. miserly, greedy; m. miser.

a·va·sa·llar v. to subject, dominate, subdue.

a·ve f. bird; fowl; **— de corral** domestic fowl; **— de rapiña** bird of prey.

a·ve·cin·dar·se v. to settle, locate, establish oneself, take up residence (in a community).

a·ve·lla·na f. hazelnut; **avellano** m. hazel; hazelnut tree; **avellanado** adj. hazel, light brown.

a·ve·na f. oats.

a·ve·nen·cia f. harmony, agreement; conformity.

a·ve·ni·da f. avenue; flood.

a·ve·nir v. irr. to adjust; to reconcile; **-se a** to adapt oneself to; **-se con alguien** to get along with someone.

a·ven·ta·dor m. fan (for fanning a fire); ventilator; winnower (machine for separating wheat from chaff).

a·ven·ta·jar v. to excel; to be ahead (of); **-se a** to get ahead of.

a·ven·tar v. irr. to fan; to winnow, blow chaff from grain; to throw out, expel; Am. to pitch, throw; Am. to dry sugar (in the open); Am. to rouse (game); **-se** to be full of wind; to flee, run away; Am. to attack, hurl oneself (on someone).

a·ven·tu·ra f. adventure; risk, danger; chance.

a·ven·tu·ra·do adj. adventurous, risk; bold, daring.

a·ven·tu·rar v. to venture, risk; **-se a** to risk, run the risk of; to dare.

a·ven·tu·re·ro adj. adventurous; m. adventurer.

a·ver·gon·zar v. irr. to shame; **-se** to feel ashamed.

a·ve·ría f. damage; aviary, birdhouse; Am. misfortune; Mex., Cuba mischief.

a·ve·riar v. to damage, spoil, hurt; **-se** to become damaged; to spoil.

a·ve·ri·guar v. to find out; to investigate.

a·ver·sión f. aversion, dislike; reluctance.

a·ves·truz m. ostrich.

a·ve·za·do p.p. & adj. accustomed; trained, practiced.

a·via·ción f. aviation.

a·via·dor m. aviator, flyer; purveyor, provider; Am. moneylener (to miners or laborers), promoter.

a·viar v. to equip; to supply; to prepare, make ready; Am. to lend money or equipment; **estar aviado** to be surrounded by difficulties; to be in a fix.

á·vi·do adj. eager; greedy.

a·vi·na·gra·do adj. sour; acid; cross.

a·vi·na·grar *v.* to sour, make sour or acid; **-se** to sour, become sour.

a·vío *m.* provision, supply; preparation; *Cuba, Mex.* loan of money or equipment; **-s** equipment; **-s de pescar** fishing tackle.

a·vión*m.* airplane; martin *(a bird similar to a swallow).*

a·vi·sar*v.* to inform, give notice, advise; to announce; to warn.

a·vi·so *m.* notice, advice, announcement; warning.

a·vis·pa*f.* wasp; **avispero** *m.* wasp's nes; **avispón** *m.* hornet.

a·vis·pa·do *adj.* lively, keen, clever, wideawake; *Am.* frightened, scared.

a·vis·par*v.* to spur, incite; **-se** to be on the alert; to be uneasy; *Am.* to be come frightened, scared.

a·vis·tar*v.* to glimpse, catch sight of; **-se** to see each other, meet.

a·vi·var*v.* to enliven, give life to; to revive; to brighten; to quicken.

a·vi·zor *adj.* alert, watchful.

a·vi·zo·rar*v.* to spy, watch closely.

a·vi·zo·rar *v.* to spy, watch closely.

a·ya*f.* child's nurse, governess; **ayo** *m.* tutor, guardian.

a·yer *adv.* yesterday.

a·yu·da *f.* aid, help.

a·yu·dan·te *m.* assistant.

a·yu·dar *v.* to aid, help.

a·yu·nar *v.* to fast.

a·yu·nas;en — fasting; **en** – **de** totally ignorant of.

a·yu·no *m.* fast; – **de** wholly ignorant of.

a·yun·ta·mien·to*m.* municipal govern-ment; town hall.

a·za·ba·che*m.* jet; **-s** jet ornaments.

a·za·da *f.* spade; hoe; **azadón** *m.* hoe.

a·za·frán *m.* saffron.

a·za·har *m.* orange or lemon blossom.

a·zar *m.* hazard; chance; accident; disaster.

a·zo·gue *m.* quicksilver.

a·zol·var*v.* to clog, obstruct; **ce** to clog, get clogged.

a·zo·rar *v.* to disturb, startle; to bewilder; **-se** to be startled, astonished; to be bewildered, perplexed; to be uneasy.

a·zo·tai·na *f.* flogging, lashing, beating.

a·zo·tar*v.* to whip, lash, beat; *Am.* to thresh *(rice);* – **las calles** to "beat the pavement", walk the streets.

a·zo·te*m.* whip; lash with a whip; scourge; affliction, calamity.

a·zo·te·a *f.* flat roof.

az·te·ca *adj., m. & f.* Aztec.

a·zú·car*m.* sugar.

a·zu·ca·rar*v.* to sugar; to sweeten; **-se** to become sweet; *Am.* to crystallize, turn to sugar.

a·zu·ca·re·ra *f.* sugar bowl; sugar mill.

a·zu·ca·re·ro *adj.* sugar *(used as adj.);* m. sugar manufacturer, producer or dealer; sugar bowl.

a·zu·ce·na *f.* white lily.

a·zu·fre *m.* sulphur.

a·zul *adj.* blue; – **celeste** sky-blue; – **marino** navy blue; – **turquí** indigo; *Am.* **tiempos -es** hard times.

a·zu·la·do *adj.* bluish.

a·zu·lar *v.* to dye or color blue.

a·zu·le·jo *m.* glazed tile; *Am.* bluebird; *adj.* bluish.

a·zu·zar⁹ *v.* to urge, egg on; to incite.

B

ba·ba *f.* drivel, slaver, saliva; slime, slimy secretion; A*m.* small alligator.

ba·be·ar *v.* to drivel; to slobber.

ba·be·ro *m.* baby's bib.

ba·bor *m.* port, port side *(of a ship).*

ba·bo·se·ar *v.* to slaver, drivel; to keep one's mouth open; to act like a fool.

ba·bo·so*adj.* driveling, slobbering; slimy; foolishly sentimental; *Am.* silly, idiotic, foolish; **babosa** *f.* slug *(creature like a snail, but without a shell).*

ba·bu·cha *f.* slipper; *Riopl.* **a** – pickaback, on the back or shoulders.

ba·ca·la·o, ba·ca·lla·o*m. Andulasia, Am.* codfish.

ba·ci·lo *m.* bacillus.

ba·cín *m.* pot. chamber pot; **bacinica** *f.* chamber pot.

bac·te·ria *f.* bacterium; **-s** bacteria.

bac·te·rio·lo·gí·a *f.* bacteriology.

bac·te·rio·ló·gi·co *adj.* bacteriological, pertaining to bacteriology.

bá·cu·lo *m.* staff, cane; aid, support.

ba·che *m.* rut, hole in the road.

ba·chi·ller *m.* bachelor *(one who holds degree);* talkative person; **bachillerato** *m.* bachelor's degree; studies for the bachelor's degree.

ba·da·jo *m.* clapper of a bell; foolish talker.

ba·da·na *f.* sheepskin.

ba·ga·je *m.* baggage; army pack mule.

ba·ga·te·la *f.* trifle.

ba·ga·zo *m.* waste pulp *(of sugarcane, olives, grapes, etc.).*

ba·gual*adj. Riopl.* wild, untamed, unruly; *Riopl.* rude, discourteous; *Riopl.* lanky, awkward; *m. Riopl.* wild horse.

ba·hí·a *f.* bay, harbor.

bai·la·dor *m.* dancer; *adj.* dancing.

bai·lar *v.* to dance; to spin around.

bai·la·rín *m.* dancer; **bailarina** *f.* dancer.

bai·le *m.* dance; ball; ballet.

bai·lo·te·ar*v.* to jig, jiggle; to dance poorly; to dan-ce around.

ba·ja *f.* fall *(of prices);* war casualty; **dar de** – to discharge, muster out.

ba·ja·da*f.* descent; slope, dip *(on a road);* **de** – on the way down; **subidas y -s** ups and downs.

ba•jar v. to go down; to drop (*as price or value*); to lower; to take or carry down; to humble; **-se** to get down or off; to alight; *Am.* to stop at a hotel.

ba•jel m. boat, ship.

ba•je•za f. vile act or remark; meanness; baseness; degradation.

ba•jí•o m. shoal, sand bank; *Am.* lowland.

ba•jo adj. low; short; soft, bass (*tone or voice*); shallow (*water*); subdued (*color*); humble; base; **piso** – first floor, ground floor; *prep.* under, underneath; m. bass.

ba•la f. bullet, shot, ball; bale (*of cotton*).

ba•la•da f. ballad.

ba•la•dí adj. trivial; flimsy.

ba•lan•ce m. balance; equilibrium; balance sheet; rocking, rolling.

ba•lan•ce•ar v. to balance; to rock, roll; to swing, sway; to waver.

ba•lan•ce•o m. rocking, rolling; swinging; balancing; wavering; wobbling.

ba•lan•za f. balance, scale.

ba•lar v. to bleat.

ba•laus•tra•da f. balustrade, banister, railing.

ba•laus•tre m. banister.

ba•la•zo m. shot; bullet wound; adj. *Ch.* clever, cunning.

bal•bu•ce•ar v. to stammer, stutter; to babble.

bal•bu•ce•o m. babble.

bal•cón m. balcony.

bal•da•do m. cripple; adj. & p.p. crippled.

bal•dar v. to cripple; to trump (*a card*).

bal•de m. pail; bucket; **de** – free of charge; **en** – in vain.

bal•dí•o adj. barren; fallow, uncultivated; m. fallow land; wasteland.

bal•dón m. infamy, insult.

bal•do•sa f. floor tile; paving stone.

ba•li•do m. bleat, bleating.

bal•ne•a•rio m. bathing resort; adj. pertaining to bathing resorts or medicinal springs.

ba•lom•pié m. football.

ba•lo•ta f. ballot.

ba•lo•tar v. to ballot, vote.

ba•lsa f. (*de agua*) pond, pool; (*embarcación*) raft; *Am.* marsh; *Am.* a species of ceiba (*a tropical tree*).

bál•sa•mo m. balsam, balm.

ba•luar•te m. bulwark.

ba•lle•na f. whale; whalebone.

bam•bo•le•ar v. to sway, swing, rock; **-se** to stagger; to sway.

bam•bú m. bamboo.

ba•na•na f. banana; **banano** m. banana tree.

ba•nas•ta f. large basket.

ban•ca f. bench; card game; banking; banking house.

ban•ca•rio adj. bank, pertaining to a bank.

ban•ca•rro•ta f. bankruptcy; failure, colapse.

ban•co m. bank; bench, stool; school (*of fish*); *Mex.* pile of grain; *Am.* small hill on a plain.

ban•da f. (*musical*) band; (*cinta*) ribbon, sash; (*grupo*) gang, group, party; flock (*lindero*) side, edge, border.

ban•da•da f. flock of birds; *Am.* gang.

ban•de•ja f. tray; *Mex., Ven., Col.* bowl.

ban•de•ra f. banner, flag; *Riopl., Cuba, Mex.* **parar uno** – to take the lead, be a gangleader.

ban•de•ri•lla f. dart with a small flag or streamers (*used in bullfights*); **clavar a uno una** – tog oad or taunt someone; **tercio de** – the banderilla phase of the bullfight; *Am.* **pegar una** – to touch for a loan.

ban•de•ri•lle•ro m. bullfighter who sticks the **banderillas** into the bull.

ban•de•rín m. small flag; signal flag; signal flag; pennant; recruiting office.

ban•de•ro•la f. streamer, small banner or flag; pennant

ban•di•da•je m. banditry, highway robbery; bandits.

ban•di•do m. bandit, gangster.

ban•do m. (*decreto*) decree, proclamation; (*partido*) party, faction.

ban•do•le•ro m. bandit.

ban•du•rria f. bandore (*stringed instrument*), *Am.* a species of wading bird.

ban•que•ro m. banker.

ban•que•ta f. bench (*without a back*); stool; footstool; *Mex.* sidewalk.

ban•que•te m. banquet.

ban•que•te•ar v. to banquet, feast.

ban•qui•llo m. bench, stool.

ba•ña•da f. shower, spray; dip, bath.

ba•ñar v. to bathe, wash; to dip; **-se** to take a bath.

ba•ñe•ra f. bathtub.

ba•ñis•ta m. & f. bather.

ba•ño m. (*aseo*) bath; bathtub; (*acabado*) cover, coating; – **de María** double bolier; *Am.* – **ruso** steam bath.

ba•que•ta f. rod; whip; **-s** drumsticks; **tratar a la** – to treat scornfully, despotically.

ba•quia•no, ba•quea•no m. *Riopl., Ven., Andes* native guide (*through the wilderness, pampas, etc.*); adj. *Riopl., Andes* having an instinctive sense of direction.

bar m. bar, taproom, tavern.

ba•ra•ja f. pack of cards.

ba•ra•jar v. to shuffle; to mix, jumble together; to scuffle, wrangle; *Am.* to hinder, obstruct.

ba•ran•da f. railing; **barandal** m. banister, railing.

ba•ran•di•lla f. balustrade, rail, railing.

ba•ra•ta f. barter, exchange; *Am.* bargain sale; *Peru, Ch.* cockroach.

ba•ra•te•ar v. to sell cheap; to cheapen; to cut the price of.

ba•ra•ti•ja f. trinket, trifle.

ba·ra·to *adj.* cheap; *m.* bargain sale; money given by the winning gambler.

ba·ra·tu·ra *f.* cheapness.

ba·ra·ún·da *f.* clamor, uproar, clatter.

bar·ba *f.* chin; beard; **-s** whiskers.

bar·ba·co·a *f. Am.* barbecue; barbecued meat.

bar·ba·do *adj.* bearded.

bar·ba·ri·dad *f.* cruelty, brutality; rudeness; **una —
de** a lot of; **¡que — !** what nonsense!; what an atrocity!

bar·ba·rie *f.* barbarousness; savagery; lack of culture, ignorance; cruelty, brutality.

bár·ba·ro *adj.* barbarous, cruel, savage; crude, coarse; *m.* barbarian.

bar·be·char *v.* to plow; to fallow.

bar·be·cho *m.* first plowing; plowed land; fallow, fallow land.

bar·be·ría *f.* barbershop.

bar·be·ro *m.* barber; *Am.* flatterer.

bar·bi·lla *f.* point of the chin.

bar·bón, bar·bu·do *adj.* bearded.

bar·ca *f.* boad, launch, barge.

bar·co *m.* boat, ship.

bar·do *m.* hard, minstrel, poet.

ba·rí·to·no *m.* baritone.

bar·niz *m.* varnish; glaze; printer's ink.

bar·ni·zar *v.* to varnish; to glaze.

ba·ró·me·tro *m.* barometer.

bar·que·ro *m.* boatman; bargeman.

bar·qui·llo *m.* rolled wafer; ice-cream cone.

bar·qui·na·zo *m.* tumble, bad fall, hard bump, somersault; *Am.* lurch (*of a vehicle or boat*).

ba·rra *f.* bar, rod; railing; sand bar; claque, audience; **— de jabón** bar of soap.

ba·rra·ba·sa·da *f.* mischief, mean prank; rash, hasty act.

ba·rra·ca *f.* hut, cabin; *Andes* large shed, warehouse.

ba·rran·ca *f.*, **barranco** *m.* ravine, gorge; *Am.* cliff.

ba·rre·mi·nas *m.* mine-sweeper.

ba·rre·na *f.* auger, drill; gimlet (*small tool for boring holes*); spinning dive of a plane).

ba·rre·nar *v.* to drill, bore; to scuttle (*a ship*); to blast (*a rock*).

ba·rren·de·ro *m.* sweeper.

ba·rrer *v.* to sweep; to sweep away; *Am.* to defeat; *Am.* **al —** altogether, as a whole.

ba·rre·ra *f.* barrier; obstacle.

ba·rre·ta *f.* small iron bar; *Mex., Cuba, Col.* pick, pickaxe.

ba·rri·ca *f.* cask, keg.

ba·rri·da *f. Am.* sweep, sweeping.

ba·rri·do *m.* sweep, sweeping; sweepings; *p.p. of* **barrer**.

ba·rri·ga *f.* belly; bulge.

ba·rri·gón, ba·rri·gu·do *adj.* big-bellied.

ba·rril *m.* barrel, keg.

ba·rrio *m.* district, neighborhood, quarter; **-s bajos** slums.

ba·rro *m.* (*tierra*) mud, clay; (*granillo*) pimple; *Am.* **hacer** (*or* **cometer) un —** to commit a blunder.

ba·rro·so *adj.* muddy; pimply; reddish.

ba·rro·te *m.* short, thick bar; brace, rung (*of a ladder or chair*).

ba·rrun·tar *v.* to foresee; to have a pre-sentiment; to conjecture.

ba·rrun·to *m.* foreboding, presentiment; guess; hint, indication, sign.

bár·tu·los *m.* household goods; implements, tools.

ba·ru·llo *m.* hubbub, racket, disorder.

ba·sa *f.* base, pedestal; basis, foundation.

ba·sar *v.* to base; to put on a base.

bas·ca *f.* nausea, sickness to one's stomach; **tener -
s** to be nauseated, sick to one's stomach.

bás·cu·la *f.* scale (*for weighing*), platform scale.

ba·se *f.* base, basis, foundation.

bá·si·co *adj.* basic.

bas·que·ar *v.* to heave, try to vomit; to be nauseated, sick to one's stomach.

bas·quet·bol *m.* basketball.

bas·tan·te *adj.* enough, sufficient; *adv.* enough.

bas·tar *v.* to be enough; to suffice.

bas·tar·di·lla *f.* italic type, italics.

bas·tar·do *adj.* bastard.

bas·ti·dor *m.* wing (*of a stage*); frame; embroidery frame; window sash; easel (*suppor for a picture, blackboard, etc.*); **entre -es** behind the scenes, off stage.

bas·ti·lla *f.* hem.

bas·ti·men·to *m.* supply, provisions; vessel, ship.

bas·to *adj.* coarse; *m.* club (*in cards*); *Am.* saddle pad.

bas·tón *m.* cane, walking stick.

ba·su·ra *f.* rubbish, scraps; garbage; refuse.

ba·su·re·ro *m.* garbage or rubbish dump; manure pile; garbage man, rubbish man; street cleaner.

ba·ta *f.* lounging robe; housecoat, wrapper, dressing gown; smock; **batín** *m.* smock.

ba·ta·ho·la *f.* hubbub, racket, uproar.

ba·ta·lla *f.* battle; struggle.

ba·ta·llar *v.* to battle, fight, struggle.

ba·ta·llón *m.* battalion.

ba·ta·ta *f.* sweet potato.

ba·te *m. Am.* baseball bat.

ba·te·a *f.* tray; trough; bowl; barge; *Am.* washtub.

ba·te·a·dor *m. Am.* batter (*in baseball*).

ba·te·ar *v. Am.* to bat.

ba·te·rí·a *f.* battery (*military, naval, or electric*); **—
de cocina** set of kitchen utensils; **— de jazz** a jazz combo; *Mex.* **dar —** to raise a rumpus; to plod, work hard.

ba·ti·dor *m.* beater; scout.

ba·tin·tín *m.* gong.

ba·tir *v.* (*combatir*) to beat, whip, defeat; (*recono-*

cer) reconnoiter, explore; (*mover*) to flap; *Ch.* to rinse (*clothes*); *Riopl.* to denounce; **-se** to fight; — **palmas** to clap, applaud.

ba·tis·fe·ra *f.* bathysphere.

ba·tu·rri·llo *m.* medley, mixture; hodgepodge.

ba·tu·ta *f.* orchestra conductor's baton or wand; **llevar la** – to lead; to be the leader.

ba·úl *m.* trunk, chest; **– mundo** large trunk.

bau·tis·mo *m.* baptism. christening; **nombre de** – Christian name.

bau·tis·ta *m.* & *f.* Baptist; baptizer.

bau·ti·zar⁹ *v.* to baptize, christen.

bau·ti·zo *m.* christening, baptism.

ba·ya *f.* berry.

ba·ye·ta *f.* flannel; flannelette; **bayetón** *m.* thick wool cloth; *Col.* long poncho lined with flannel.

ba·yo *adj.* bay, reddish-brown.

ba·za *f.* trick (*cardsplayed in one round*); **meter** – to meddle; to butt into a conver-sation; **no dejar meter** – not to let a person put a word in edgewise.

ba·zar *m.* bazaar; department store.

ba·zo *m.* spleen.

ba·zo·fia *f.* scraps, refuse, garbage; dregs.

be·a·ti·tud *f.* bliss, blessedness.

be·a·to *adj.* blessed; beatified; devout; overpious; hypocritical.

be·bé *m.* baby.

be·be·de·ro *m.* drinking trough; watering place; spout.

be·be·dor *m.* drinker; drunkard.

be·ber *v.* to drink; to drink in, absorb.

be·bi·da *f.* drink, beverage; **dado a la** – given to drink.

be·ca *f.* scholarship, fellowship; sash worn over the academic gown.

be·ca·rio *m.* scholar, fellow, holder of a scholarship.

be·ce·rro *m.* young bull (*less than a year old*); calf; calfskin.

be·cua·dro *m.* natural sign (*in music*).

be·del *m.* beadle.

be·fa *f.* scoff, jeer.

be·far *v.* to scoff, jeer at, mock.

be·ju·co *m.* cane; **silla de** – cane chair.

bel·dad *f.* beauty

bel·ga *adj.*, *m,* & *f.* Belgian.

bé·li·co *adj.* warlike.

be·li·ge·ran·te *adj.,m.*& *f.* belligerent.

be·lla·co *adj.* sly, deceitful; *m.* villain; rascal.

be·lla·que·ar *v.* to cheat; to play tricks; *Am.* to rear, stand up on the hind legs; *Am.* to balk; *Am.* to be touchy, oversensitive.

be·lla·que·rí·a *f.* cunning, trickery; sly act or remark.

be·lle·za *f.* beauty.

be·llo *adj.* beautiful.

be·llo·ta *f.* acorn.

be·mol *adj.* flat (*in music*); **tener** – to have difficulties.

ben·de·cir²⁷,⁵² *v.* irr. to bless.

ben·di·ción *f.* benediction, blessing; *Mex., C.A., Col., Ven.* echarle la – a una cosa to give something up for lost.

ben·di·to *adj.* blessed; saintly; **es un** – he is a saint, he is a simple soul; *p.p. of* **bendecir**.

be·ne·fac·tor *m.* benefactor; patron.

be·ne·fi·cen·cia *f.* beneficence, kindness, charity.

be·ne·fi·ciar *v.* to benefit, do good; to cultivate (*land*); to exploit (*a mine*); to treat (*metals*); *Col., Ven.* to slaughter (*cattle*) for marketing.

be·ne·fi·cio *m.* (*provecho*) benefit, profit; exploitation of a mine; (*cultivo*) cultivation of land; *Am.* fertilizer; *Am.* slaughtering (*of cattle*).

be·né·fi·co *adj.* beneficent, good, kind.

be·ne·mé·ri·to *m.* worthy, notable; *adj.* worthy.

be·ne·vo·len·cia *f.* benevolence, kindness.

be·né·vo·lo *adj.* benevolent good, kindly.

be·nig·no *adj.* benign, gentle, mild, kind.

be·o·do *adj.* drunk; *m.* drunkard.

be·ren·je·na *f.* eggplant; *Mex., C.A.* kind of squash; **berenjenal** *m.* eggplant patch; **meterse uno en un** – to get into a mess.

ber·gan·tín *m.* brigantine, brig (*squarerigged ship with two masts*).

ber·me·jo *adj.* crimson, bright red.

ber·me·llón *adj.* vermilion (*bright red*).

be·rrear *v.* to bellow; to scream; to sing off key.

be·rri·do *m.* bellow, bellowing; scream.

be·rrin·che *m.* fit of anger; tantrum.

ber·za *f.* cabbage.

be·sar *v.* to kiss.

be·so *m.* kiss.

bes·tia *f.* beast.

bes·tia·li·dad *f.* bestiality, brutality.

be·su·go *m.* sea bream (*a fish*).

be·su·que·ar *v.* to kiss repeatedly.

be·ta·bel *f. Mex.* beet.

be·tún *m.* bitumen (*combustible mineral*); black pitch; shoeblacking.

Bi·blia *f.* Bible.

bí·bli·co *adj.* Biblical.

bi·blio·te·ca *f.* library; set of volumes; bookcase.

bi·blio·te·car·io *m.* librarian.

bi·ci·cle·ta *f.* bicycle; **biciclista, bicicletista** *m.* & *f.* bicyclist, bicycle rider.

bi·cho *m.* insect, bug; any small animal; an insignificant person.

bie·la *f.* connecting rod (*of an engine*).

bien *adv.* well; **– que** although; **ahora** – now then; **más** – rather; **si** – although; *m.* good, benefit; **-es** property; **-es inmuebles** real estate, **-es raíces** real estate.

bie·na·ven·tu·ra·do *adj.* blessed, happy.

bie·na·ven·tu·ran·za *f.* blessedness; beatitude;

bliss.

bie•nes•tar *m.* well-being, comfort, welfare.

bien•he•chor *m.* benefactor.

bien•ve•ni•da *f.* welcome.

bien•ve•ni•do *adj.* welcome.

bif•tec, bis•tec, bis•té *m.* beefsteak.

bi•fur•ca•ción *f.* fork, forking, branching out; railway junction; branch railroad.

bi•fur•car•se[6] *v.* to fork, branch off, divide into two branches.

bi•ga•mí•a *f.* bigamy.

bi•go•te *m.* mustache.

bi•ki•ni *m.* bikini bathing suit.

bi•lis *f.* bile.

bi•llar *m.* billiards; billiard room.

bi•lle•te *m.* ticket; note; bill, banknote.

bi•llón *m.* billion.

bi•mes•tre *m.* two-month period; bimonthly salary, rent, etc.; *adj.* bimonthly; **bimestral** *adj.* bimonthly.

bio•gra•fí•a *f.* biography.

bio•lo•gí•a *f.* biology.

biom•bo *m.* folding screen.

bir•lar *v.* to snatch away; to steal; to kill or knock down with one blow.

bi•sa•bue•lo *m.* great-grandfather; **bisabuela** *f.* great-grandmother.

bi•sa•gra *f.* hinge.

bi•sies•to *adj.* leap (*year*).

bi•so•jo *adj.* squint-eyed.

bi•son•te *m.* bison; the American buffalo.

bis•tu•rí *m.* bistoury, surgical knife.

bi•to•que *m.* barrel plug, stopper; *Am.* faucet; *Col., Cuba, Mex.* injection point (*of a syringe*).

bi•za•rrí•a *f.* gallantry, bravery; generosity.

bi•za•rro *adj.* gallant, brave; generous.

biz•co *adj.* cross-eyed.

biz•co•cho *m.* hardtack, hard biscuit; cake; cookie; **– borracho** cake dipped in wine.

biz•nie•to *m.* great-grandson; **biznieta** *f.* great-granddaughter.

blan•co *adj.* (*color*) white; *m.* white man; (*nada escrito*) blank, blank sheet; (*objeto de tiro*) target, goal.

blan•cu•ra *f.* whiteness.

blan•cuz•co, blanquecino, blanquizco *adj.* whitish.

blan•dir *v.* to brandish, flourish, swing.

blan•do *adj.* bland, smooth; soft; **blanducho** *adj.* flabby; soft.

blan•du•ra *f.* softness; mildness, gentleness.

blan•que•ar *v.* to whiten, bleach; to whitewash; to show white; to begin to turn white.

blan•que•o *m.* whitening, bleach, bleaching.

blan•qui•llo *adj.* whitish; white (*flour*); *m. Mex., C.A.* egg; *Peru, Ch., Andes* white peach.

blas•fe•mar *v.* to blaspheme, curse, swear.

blas•fe•mia *f.* blasphemy.

bla•són *m.* coat of arms; honor, glory.

bla•so•nar *v.* to boast.

blin•da•je *m.* armor, armor plating.

blin•dar *v.* to armor.

bloc *m. Am.* tablet, pad of paper.

blo•ca•je *m.* action of blocking.

blon•do *adj.* blond.

blo•que *m.* block (*of stone, wood, etc.*); *Am.* tablet, pad of paper; *Cuba, Mex., Ríopl.* political bloc.

blo•que•ar *v.* to blockade.

blo•que•o *m.* blockade.

blu•sa *f.* blouse.

bo•a•to *m.* pomp, ostentation.

bo•ba•da *f.* foolishness, folly.

bo•ba•li•cón *adj.* foolish, silly; *m.* simple-ton, blockhead, dunce.

bo•be•ar *v.* to act like a fool; to fool around; to gawk, stare foolishly.

bo•be•rí•a *f.* foolishness, folly; nonsense; foolish remark.

bo•bi•na *f.* bobbin, reel; electric coil; **– distribuidora** feeding reel; **– receptora** rewind reel (*on a tape recorder*).

bo•bo *adj.* simple, foolish, stupid; *m.* booby, fool; dunce.

bo•ca *f.* mouth; opening; **– abajo** face downward; **– arriba** face upward; **a – de jarro** at close range; **bocaza** *f.* large mouth.

bo•ca•ca•lle *f.* street intersection.

bo•ca•do *m.* mouthful, morsel, bite; bit (*of a bridle*); **bocadillo, bocadito** *m.* snack; sandwich; tidbit; *Am.* piece of candy.

bo•ca•na•da *f.* mouthful; puff (*of smoke*).

bo•ce•to *m.* sketch; outline; skit.

bo•ci•na *f.* horn; trumpet; automobile horn; speaking tube; megaphone.

bo•chor•no *m.* sultry weather; suffocating heat; blush, flush; embarrassment.

bo•chor•no•so *adj.* sultry; embarrassing.

bo•da *f.* marriage, wedding; **– de negros** a noisy party; **-s de Camacho** lavish feast, banquet.

bo•de•ga *f.* cellar; wine cellar; storeroom; warehouse; *Cuba, Ven., Col.* grocery store; **bodeguero** *m.* keeper of a wine cellar; liquor dealer; *Cuba, Ven., Col.* grocer.

bo•do•que *m.* wad; lump; dunce; *Am.* bump, swelling.

bo•fe *m.* lung; *P.R.* snap easy job; **echar uno los -s** to throw oneself into a job; to work hard; *Am.* **ser un —** to be a bore; to be repulsive.

bo•fe•ta•da *f.* slap; **bofetón** *m.* big slap, blow, hard sock, wallop.

bo•ga *f.* vogue, fashion; rowin; *m.* rower.

bo•gar[7] *v.* to row.

bo•he•mio *adj. & m.* Bohemian.

bo•hí•o *m. Carib., Ven.* cabin, shack, hut.

bo·í·na *f.* cap.

bo·la *f.* (*esfera*) ball, bowling; (*mentira*) fib, lie; (*betún*) shoe polish; *Am.* disturbance, riot, false rumor; **no dar pie con** – not to do things right; not to hit the mark; to make mistakes; *Am.* **darle a la** – to hit the mark.

bo·le·a·da *f. Ríopl.* lassoing with **boleadoras**; *Ríopl.* hunting expedition (*with* **boleadoras**); *Mex.* shoeshine; *Col.* affront, insult.

bo·le·a·do·ras *f. pl. Am.* lasso with balls at the ends.

bo·le·ar *v.* to play billiards; to bowl; to lie fib; *Am.* to lasso with **boleadoras**; *Am.* to entangle; *Am.* to polish (shoes); *Am.* to dismiss; *Am.* to blackball, vote against; *Am.* to flunk; **-se** *Am.* to rear, balk (*said of a horse*); *Am.* to blush, be ashamed.

bo·le·ta *f.* certificate; pass; pay order; *Mex., C.A.* ballot; *Ch.* first draft of a deed.

bo·le·tín *m.* bulletin.

bo·le·to *m. Am.* ticket; **boletería** *f. Am.* ticket office.

bo·li·che *m.* bowl (*wooden ball for bowling*); bowling alley; *Ríopl.* cheap tavern; *Ch.* gambling joint; *Ríopl.* cheap store or shop, notions store, variety store.

bo·li·ta *f.* small ball; *Am.* ballot (*small ball used in voting*); *Col., Ven.* marble; *Am.* armadillo.

bo·lo *m.* one of the ninepins (*used in bowling*); dunce, stupid fellow; **-s** bowls, bowling; **jugar a los -s** to bowl.

bol·sa *f.* bag, purse; stock exchange; *Ríopl.* pocket.

bol·si·llo *m.* pocket; pocketbook.

bol·sis·ta *m.* stockbroker, market operator.

bo·llo *m.* bun, muffin; bump, lump; puff (*in a dress*); tuft (*on upholstery*); *Andes* loaf of bread; *Am.* a kind of tamale; **-s** *Am.* difficulties, troubles.

bom·ba *f.* pump; lamp globe; bomb; – **atómica** atomic bomb; – **de hidrógeno** hydrogen bomb; *Carib.* false news; *Am.* stanza improvised by a dancer; *Ríopl.* firecracker, skyrocket; *Mex., Col.* satirical remark; *Am.* large drum; – **para incendios** fire engine; *Am.* **estar con una** – to be drunk; **bombita** *f.* soap bubble; *Col.* shame, embarrassment.

bom·ba·chas *f. pl. Am.* loose-fitting breeches).

bom·ba·cho *adj.* loose-fitting (*trousers or breeches*).

bom·bar·de·ar *v.* to bomb.

bom·bar·de·o *m.* bombardment, bombing; **avión de** – bomber, bombing plane.

bom·bar·de·ro *m.* bombardier; bomber.

bom·be·a·r *v.* (*echar bombas*) to bomb; (*alabar*) to praise, extol; *Am.* to pump; *Col.* to fire, dismiss; *Am.* to puff hard on a cigar or cigarette.

bom·be·ro *m.* fireman; pumper.

bom·bi·lla *f.* electric-light bulb; *Am:* kerosene lamp tube; *Am.* small tube for drinking **mate**.

bom·bo *m.* large drum; bass drum; player on a bass drum; *Mex., Col., Ch.* pomp, ostentation; *Ríopl.*

buttocks, rump; **dar** – to praise, extol (*in the press or newspapers*); *Col., Ríopl.* **darse** – to put on airs; *Am.* **irse uno al** – to fail; *adj.* stunned; *Am.* lukewarm; *Am.* slightly rotten; *Am.* stupid, silly, simple; *Cuba* **fruta bomba** papaya (*tropical fruit*).

bom·bón *m.* bonbon, candy; – **de altea** marshmallow.

bo·na·chón *adj.* good-natured; naive, simple.

bo·nan·za *f.* faire weather; prosperity; rich vein of ore.

bon·dad *f.* goodness.

bon·da·do·so *adj.* good, kind.

bo·nia·to *m. Am.* sweet potato.

bo·ni·to *adj.* pretty; *m.* striped tunny (*a fish*).

bo·no *m.* certificate; bond.

bo·ñi·ga *f.* dung, manure.

bo·que·a·da *f.* gape, gasp.

bo·que·ar *v.* to open one's mouth; to gape, gasp; to be dying.

bo·que·te *m.* breach, gap, hole, opening.

bo·quia·bier·to *adj.* openmouthed.

bo·qui·lla *f.* (*abertura*) little mouth; small opening; (*de cigarro*) holder; (*de instrumento*) mouthpiece.

bor·bo·llón, bor·bo·tón *m.* spurt; spurt-ing; big buble; bubbling up; **a -es** in spurts.

bor·bo·tar *v.* to buble up; to spurt, gush forth; to boil over.

bor·da·do *m.* embroidery.

bor·da·du·ra *f.* embroidery.

bor·dar *v.* to embroider.

bor·de *m.* border, edge.

bor·de·ar *v.* to skirt, go along the edge of; *Am.* to trim with a border; *Am.* to make a **bordo** (*small, temporary dam*); **-se** *Ch., Mex., Ven.* to approach, get near.

bor·do *m.* board, side of a ship; tack (*of a ship*); *Mex., Ven.* ridge (*of a furrow*); *Mex.* small dam; **a** - on board.

bor·la *f.* (*indumentaria*) tassel; doctor's cap; (*título*) doctor's degree; (*cosmético*) powder puff; tuft; **tomar uno la** – to get a doctor's degree.

bor·lar·se *v. Am.* to get a doctor's degree.

bo·rra·che·ra *f.* drunkenness; drunken spree.

bo·rra·chín *m.* toper.

bo·rra·cho *adj.* drunk; *m.* drunkard; **borrachón** *m.* drunkard, heavy drinker.

bo·rra·dor *m.* rough draft; *Am.* rubbet eraser.

bo·rrar *v.* to blot out; to erase.

bo·rras·ca *f.* storm, tempest.

bo·rras·co·so *adj.* stormy.

bo·rre·go *m.* lamb; fool, simpleton; *Mex., C.A.* false news.

bo·rri·co *m.* donkey, ass; fool; sawhorse.

bo·rrón *m.* blotch (*of ink*), blot.

bo·rro·ne·ar *v.* to blot, blotch; to scribble; to blur; to make a rough skech.

bo·ru·ca *f.* racket, noise.

bos·ca·je *m.* grove, thicket, woods; landscape (*picture of natural scenery*).

bos·que m forest, woods; **bosquecillo** *m.* small forest, grove.

bos·que·jar *v.* to sketch; to outline.

bos·que·jo *m.* sketch, plan, outline, rough draft.

bos·te·zar⁹ *v.* to yawn.

bos·te·zo *m.* yawn.

bo·ta *f.* (*calzado*) boot; (*bolsa*) leather wine bag; *adj. Am.* stupid, clumsy; *Mex.* drunk.

bo·tar *v.* (*echar*) to launch; to fling; to throw away; (*rebotar*) to bounce; *Ven.* to waste, squander; *Am* to fire, dismiss; **-se** *Am.* to lie down.

bo·ta·ra·te *m.* fool; braggart; *Mex. Carib.* spendthrift.

bo·te *m.* (*jarro*) small jar; (*embarcación*) boat; (*rebote*) bounce; (*golpe*) blow; jump; *Riopl.* liquor bottle; *Mex., C.A.* jail; **estar de – en –** to be crowded, completely filled up.

bo·te·lla *f.* bottle.

bo·ti·ca *f.* drugstore.

bo·ti·ca·rio *m.* druggist.

bo·ti·ja *f.* earthen jug; fat person; *Am.* buried treasure; *Am.* belly; *Col.* **poner a uno como – verde** to dress down, scold, insult a person.

bo·tín *m.* booty, plunder; high shoe; *Am.* sock.

bo·ti·quín *m.* medicine cabinet; medicine kit; *Am.* liquor store, wine shop.

bo·tón *m.* bud; button; knob; handle; **-es** bellboy.

bó·ve·da *f.* arched roof; vault, underground cellar; burial place.

bo·xe·a·dor *m.* boxer.

bo·xe·ar *v.* to box, fight with the fists.

bo·xe·o *m.* boxing.

bo·ya *f.* buoy; float net; *Am.* crease, dent; *Am.* rich mineral vein; *Am.* **estar en la buena –** to be in good humor.

bo·zal *m.* (*de animal*) nuzzle; (*cascabel*) bells on a harness; (*novicio*) novice; (*negro*) Negro native of Africa; *Am.* headstall (*of a halter*); Spain person (*especially a Negro*) who speaks broken Spanish; *Am.* coarse, crude individual; *adj.* green, inexperienced; wild, untamed, stupid.

bo·zo *m.* down (*on the upper lip*); mustache; outside part of the mouth; headstall (*of a halter*).

bra·ce·ar *v.* to swing one's arms; to struggle; to crawl, swim with a crawl.

bra·ce·ro *m.* laborer; **de –** arm in arm; **servir – a una señora** to serve as an escort, give a lady one's arm.

bra·ce·te: **de –** arm in arm.

bra·man·te *m.* hemp cord, hemp string; Brabant linen; *adj.* roaring, bellowing.

bra·mar *v.* to bellow, roar, howl; to rage.

bra·mi·do *m.* roar; howl; bellow.

bra·sa *f.* red-hot coal.

bra·se·ro *m.* brazier (*pan for burning coal*), grate; hearth; *Riopl.* brick cooking stove.

bra·va·ta *f.* bravado, boastfulness, defiance.

bra·ve·ar *v.* to bluster; to bully.

bra·ví·o *adj.* savage, wild; rustic.

bra·vo *adj.* (*agresivo*) wild, ferocious, harsh; ill-tempered; (*valiente*) brave; *Carib., C.A., Andes* angry; *Am.* hot, highly seasoned.

bra·vu·ra *f.* fierceness; courage; bravado, show of boldness.

bra·za *f.* fathom; stroke.

bra·za·da *f.* armful; movement of the arms (*swimming stroke*); **a una –** at arm's length.

bra·za·le·te *m.* bracelet.

bra·zo *m.* arm; branch; **-s** day laborers; *Riopl., Cuba* **de –** arm in arm; **luchar a – partido** to wrestle; to fight hand to hand.

bre·a *f.* pitch; tar; canvas.

bre·cha *f.* breach, gap.

bre·gar⁷ *v.* to struggle; to fight.

bre·ña *f.* rough, craggy ground covered with brambles; bramble; **breñal** *m.* brambles; bush country

bre·ve *adj.* brief, short; **en –** shortly.

bre·ve·dad *f.* brevity, shortness.

bri·bón *adj.* idle, indolent; *m.* rascal, rogue; **bribonazo** *m.* scoundrel, cheat.

bri·da *f.* bridle; rein.

bri·ga·da *f.* brigade.

bri·llan·te *adj.* brilliant, bright; *m.* diamond.

bri·llan·tez *f.* brilliance, dazzle.

bri·llar *v.* to shine.

bri·llo *m.* luster, sparkle, shine.

brin·car⁶ *v.* to hop, skip. jump, bounce.

brin·co *m.* hop, skip, bounce, leap.

brin·dar *v.* to toast, drink to the health of; to offer.

brin·dis *m.* toast (*to a person's health*).

brí·o *m.* vigor, liveliness; valor, courage.

brio·so *adj.* lively; brave.

bri·sa *f.* breeze.

bri·tá·ni·co *adj.* British.

briz·na *f.* particle, chip, fragment; blade of grass.

bro·cal *m.* curb, curbstone (*of a well*).

bro·cha *f.* painter's brush; loaded, dice; **cuadro de – gorda** dadly done painting; **pintor de – gorda** house painter; **brochada** *f.* stroke of the brush, brush stroke; **brochazo** *m.* blow with a brush; brush stroke.

bro·che *m.* brooch; clasp, clip, fastener; hook and eye.

bro·ma *f.* jest, joke; fun, merriment; *Am.* disappointment, irritation; **de –** in jest; **fuera de –** all joking aside.

bro·me·ar *v.* to joke, jest.

bron·ca *f.* quarrel, dispute, wrangle; **armar una –** to cause a disturbance, raise a rumpus.

bron•ce *m.* bronze.

bron•ce•a•do *adj.* bronzed; bronze-col-ored; *m.* bronze finish.

bron•co *adj.* hoarse; raspy, harsh; coarse, rough; uncouth; wild, untamed (*horse*).

bron•quio *m.* bronchus, bronchial tube.

bro•quel *m.* buckler, shield (*worn on the arm*).

bro•tar *v.* to shoot forth; to bud; to break aut (*on the skin*); to gush, flow; to spring forth.

bro•za *f.* brushwood, underbrush; rubbish, refuse, trash; coarse, hard brush.

bru•ces: de – face downward.

bru•ja *f.* witch; hag owl; *adj. Mex.* broke, poor; **bru•jo** *m.* sorcerer, magician, wizard.

brú•ju•la *f.* (*compás*) compass; magnetic needle; (*mira*) peephole; gunsight.

bru•ma *f.* mist, fog; **brumoso** *adj.* foggy, misty, hazy.

bru•ñir[19] *v. irr.* to burnish, polish; to put on make-up.

brus•co *adj.* blunt, rude, abrupt.

bru•tal *adj.* brutal, beastly, savage.

bru•ta•li•dad *f.* brutality.

bru•to *adj.* (*tonto*) stupid, brutal; (*burdo*) coarse, rough; **peso –** gross weight; **diamante en –** diamond in the rough, unpolished diamond; *m.* brute, beast.

bu•cal *adj.* oral, pertaining to the mouth.

bu•ce•ar *v.* to dive; to dive into, plunge into; to explo-re thoroughly a subject.

bu•cle *m.* curl, ringlet.

bu•che *m.* crop (*of a bird*); mouthful (*of water*); wrinkle, bag (*in clothes*); *Riopl.. Mex., Ven.* goiter.

bu•dín *m.* pudding.

bue•n(o) *adj.* good; kind; useful; well, in good health; **de buenas a primeras** all of a sudden, unexpectedly, on the spur of the moment; **por la(s) buena(s) o por la(s) mala(s)** willingly or unwillingly, by hook or crook.

buey *m.* ox.

bú•fa•lo *m.* buffalo.

bu•fan•da *f.* muffler, scarf.

bu•far *v.* to snort; to puff with anger; **-se** *Mex.* to swell, bulge (as a wall).

bu•fe•te *m.* desk, writing table; lawyer's office.

bu•fi•do *m.* snort.

bu•fón *m.* buffoon, jester, clown; *adj.* comical, funny; **bufonada** *f.* wisecrack; jest.

bu•fo•ne•ar *v.* to clown; to jest.

bu•har•di•lla *f.* garret, attic; skylight.

bu•ho *m.* owl.

bu•ho•ne•ro *m.* peddler.

bui•tre *m.* vulture.

bu•je *m.* bushing; axle box.

bu•jí•a *f.* candle; candle power; candlestick; spark plug.

bu•la *f.* bull (*papal document*); papal seal.

bul•do•zer *m.* bulldozer.

bu•le•var *m.* boulevard.

bul•to *m.* (*cuerpo*) body, bundle, shadow, lump, swelling; (*tamaño*) bulk, volume; **a –** haphazardly, by guess; **escurrir el –** to dodge; **imagen de –** statue, sculpture; **una verdad de –** an evident truth.

bu•lla *f.* shouting, uproar; noisy crowd.

bu•lli•cio *m.* noise, uproar.

bu•lli•cio•so *adj.* boisterous, noisy; gay, lively; turbulent, stormy.

bu•llir[20] *v. irr.* to boil; to buzz about; to bustle; to stir, move; *Am.* to deride.

bu•ñue•lo *m.* fritter; botch, poor piece of work.

bu•que *m.* ship, boat.

bur•bu•ja *f.* bubble.

bur•do *adj.* coarse.

bur•gués *adj.* bourgeois, middle-class.

bur•la *f.* jest, mockery; **de –** in jest.

bur•la•dor *m.* practical joker; jester; scoffer; seducer.

bur•lar *v.* to mock, ridicule, deceive; **-se** de to scoff at; to make fun of.

bur•lón *m.* jester, teaser.

bu•rro *m.* ass, donkey; *Mex., Cuba, Riopl.* stepladder; *adj.* stupid; **burrito** *m.* small donkey; *Am.* saddle rack.

bus•ca *f.* search; hunting party; *Am.* **-s** profit on the side; graft.

bus•car[6] *v.* to seek, search, look for; *Andes* to provoke.

bús•que•da *f.* search.

bus•to *m.* bust (*upper part of body*).

bu•ta•ca *f.* armchair; orchestra seat; **butacón** *m.* large armchair.

bu•zo *m.* diver.

bu•zón *m.* mailbox; letter drop.

C

ca•bal *adj.* complete, entire; exact; **estar uno en sus -es** to be in one's right mind.

ca•bal•gar[7] *v.* to ride, mount (*a horse*); to ride horseback.

ca•ba•lla *f.* horse mackerel.

ca•ba•lla•da *f.* herd of horses; *Am.* non-sense, stupidity, blunder.

ca•ba•lle•jo *m.* nag; poor horse.

ca•ba•lle•res•co *adj.* gentlemanly; knightly; chivalrous, gallant.

ca•ba•lle•rí•a *f.* cavalry; horsemanship; mount, horse; knighthood; chivalry.

ca•ba•lle•ri•za *f.* stable; horses of a stable.

ca•ba•lle•ri•zo *m.* groom stableman.

ca•ba•lle•ro *m.* gentleman; knight, horse-man; *adj.*

gentlemanly.

ca·ba·lle·ro·si·dad *f.* chivalry, gentlemanly conduct.

ca·ba·lle·ro·so *adj.* chivalrous, gentle-manly.

ca·ba·lle·te *m.* (*de casa*) ridge of a roof; (*madero*) sawhorse; (*de la cara*) bridge of the nose.

ca·ba·llo *m.* horse; knight (*in chess*); *Am.* stupid or brutal person; **a** – on horseback; **caballuco** *m.* nag.

ca·ba·ña *f.* hut, cabin; *Am.* cattle rach.

ca·be·ce·ar *v.* to nod; to shake the head; to pitch (*as a boat*); *Am.* to begin to rise or fall (*said of a river*).

ca·be·ce·o *m.* nodding; pitching (*of a boat*).

ca·be·ce·ra *f.* head (*of bed or table*); seat, chief city (*of a district*).

ca·be·ci·lla *f.* small head; *m.* ringleader.

ca·be·lle·ra *f.* head of hair, long hair:; wig; tail of a comet.

ca·be·llo *m.* hair; **traer algo por los -s** to bring in a far-fetched fact or quotation; **-s de ángel** cotton candy.

ca·be·llu·do *adj.* hairy; **cuero** – scalp.

ca·ber²³ *v. irr.* to fit into, go into; to have enough room for; to befall; **no cabe duda** there is no doubt; **no cabe más** there is no room for more; **no – uno en sí** to be puffed up with pride; **no cabe en lo posible** it is absolutely impossible.

ca·bes·tro *m.* halter; leading ox; *Carib., Mex.* rope, cord; *Am.* advance payment; **cabestrillo** *m.* sling (*for an arm*).

ca·be·za *f.* (*parte superior*) head; upper part; (*director*) chief, leader; capital (*of a district*); *Carib.* source (*of a river*); **– de playa** beachhead; **– de puente** bridgehead; **– sonora** recording head.

ca·be·za·da *f.* butt (*with the head*); bump on the head; nod; shake of the head; pitching (*of a ship*); headgear (*of a harness*).

ca·be·za·zo *m.* butt (*with the head*); bump on the head.

ca·be·zu·do *adj.* big-headed; hard-headed, pig-headed, stubborn, headstrong

ca·be·zón *adj.* big-headed; pig-headed, stubborn; *Ch.* strong (*liquor*); *m.* large head; cavesson (*iron noseband used in breaking a horse*); *Col.* rapids or whirlpool in a river.

ca·bi·da *f.* space, room, capacity; **tener – con alguien** to have influence with someone.

ca·bil·do *m.* cathedral chapter; municipal council; council room; town hall.

ca·bi·na *f.* cabin (*of an airplane*).

ca·biz·ba·jo *adj.* crestfallen, downcast; pensive.

ca·ble *m.* cable.

ca·ble·gra·fiar¹⁷ *v.* to cable.

ca·ble·gra·ma *m.* cablegram.

ca·bo *m.* (*cosa*) end, tip, handle; piece of rope; (*geográfico*) cape, headland; (*persona*) foreman, corporal; **al –** finally; **al fin y al –** anyway, in the long run; **de – a rabo** from beginning to end; **estar al –**

de to be well informed about; **llevar a –** to carry out, finish.

ca·bra *f.* goat; *Col.* fraud, trick; *Am.* loaded dice; *Am.* light two-wheeled carriage; **cabrillas** *f. pl.* whitecaps (*small waves with white crests*); Pleiades (*constellation*); game of skipping stones on the water.

ca·brío *adj.* goatish; **macho –** he-goat; *m.* herd of goats.

ca·brio·la *f.* caper, leap, hop, skip; som-ersault; **hacer -s** to cut capers; to prance.

ca·brio·lar *v.* to prance; to caper; to romp. frolic, frisk.

ca·bri·to *m.* kid; **cabritilla** *f.* kid, kidskin.

ca·brón *m.* he-goat; cuckold (*man whose wife is unfaithful*).

ca·ca·hua·te *m.* Mex., C.A. peanut; Spain **cacahuete, cacahuey.**

ca·ca·o *m.* cocoa.

ca·ca·re·ar *v.* to cackle; to boast; *Am.* to run away from a fight.

ca·ca·re·o *m.* cackle.

ca·ce·rí·a *f.* hunt, hunting.

ca·ce·ro·la *f.* saucepan.

ca·cha *f.* handle (*of a knife or pistol*); *Am.* the horns of a bull; *C.A.* **hacer la –** to complete a task, to get.

ca·cha·rro *m.* earthen pot or vase, broken piece of a pot; crude utensil; *Am.* cheap trinket.

ca·cha·za *f.* slowness; calm; rum.

ca·cha·zu·do *adj.* slow, easy going.

ca·che·ta·da *f. Am.* slap on the face.

ca·che·te *m.* cheek; slap on the cheek.

ca·chim·bo *m. Am.* pipe (*for smoking*); *Cuba* small sugar mill; also **cachimba.**

ca·chi·va·che *m.* piece of junk; worthless fellow; *Mex., Carib., Ven.* trinket.

ca·cho·rro *m.* cub; small pistol; *Am.* rude, ill-bred person.

ca·chu·cha *f.* cap; rowboat; popular Andalusian dance, song and music; *Am.* slap.

ca·ci·que *m.* chief; political boss; *Mex.* tyrant; *Ch., Ven.* one who leads an easy life.

ca·ci·quis·mo *m.* political bossism (*rule by political bosses*).

cac·to *m.* cactus.

ca·cu·men *m.* acumen, keen insight.

ca·da *adj.* each, every; **– uno** each one; **– y cuando que** whenever; *Am.* **a – nada** every second.

ca·dal·so *m.* gallows; scaffold, platform.

ca·dá·ver *m.* corpse; **cadavérico** *adj.* deadly, ghastly, pale, like a corpse.

ca·de·na *f.* chain.

ca·den·cia *f.* cadence.

ca·den·cio·so *adj.* rhythmical.

ca·de·ra *f.* hip.

ca·de·te *m.* cadet.

ca·du·car⁶ *v.* to dote, be in one's dotage; to lapse,

expire; to become extinct, fall into disuse.

ca•du•co *adj.* decrepit, very old, feeble; perishable.

ca•er[24] *v. irr.* to fall; to fall down; to fall off; **-se** to fall down, tumble; **– a** to face, overlook; **– bien** to fit, be becoming; **– en cama** to fall ill; **– en la cuenta** to catch on, get the point; **– en gracia** to please; **al – de** la noche at nightfall; **dejar –** to drop.

ca•fé *m.* coffee; café; *Am.* annoyance, bad time.

ca•fe•í•na *f.* caffein.

ca•fe•tal *m.* coffee plantation.

ca•fe•te•ra *f.* coffeepot; woman café owner, coffe vendor or merchant; cofflee-bean picker.

ca•fe•te•rí•a *f.* café, bar, lunchroom.

ca•fe•te•ro *adj.* pertaining to coffe; *m.* coffee grower; coffe merchant; owner of a café or coffee-house; *Am.* coffe drinker.

ca•fe•to *m.* coffe bush.

ca•í•da *f.* fall, drop; descent; **a la – del sol** (*or* **de la tarde**) at sunset.

cai•mán *m.* cayman, alligator.

ca•ja *f.* case, box; **– de ahorros** savings bank; **– de cambios** transmission (*automobile*); **– de píldora** pillbox; **– fuerte** safe; **echar a uno con -s destempladas** to five someone the gate.

ca•je•ro *m.* cashier; box maker.

ca•je•ti•lla *f.* small box; package of ciga-rettes.

ca•jón *m.* large box, chest; drawer; vendor's booth or stand; *Ch., Mex.* narrow canyon; **– de muerto** coffin; *Mex.* **– de ropa** dry-goods and clothing store.

cal *f.* lime (*mineral*).

ca•la•ba•za *f.* pumpkin, squash; gourd; an ignorant person; **dar -s** to jilt, turn down (*a suitor*); to flunk, fail.

ca•la•bo•zo *m.* dungeon; prison cell.

ca•la•do *m.* drawn work; openwork (*in wood, metal, linen, etc.*), fretwork; draft (*of a ship*).

ca•la•mar *m.* squid, cuttlefish.

ca•lam•bre *m.* cramp.

ca•la•mi•dad *f.* calamity, misfortune.

ca•lan•dria *f.* lark, skylark.

ca•lar *v.* (*penetrar*) to pierce, penetrate; to soak through; to make openwork (*in cloth, metal*); (*probar*) to probe, search into; **-se el sombrero** to put on one's hat; to pull down one's hat.

ca•la•ve•ra *f.* skull; *m.* madcap, rounder, reckless fellow; *Mex.* taillight.

cal•car[6] *v.* to trace; to copy, imitate.

cal•ce•ta *f.* hose, stocking; **hacer –** to knit; **calcetería** *f.* hosiery shop; hosiery (*business of making hose*).

cal•ce•tín *m.* sock.

cal•ci•nar *v.* to burn, char, heat.

cal•cio *m.* calcium.

cal•co *m.* tracing, traced copy; exact copy; imitation.

cal•cu•la•do•ra *f.* calculator (*machine for performing mathematical operations*); **– electrónica** computer.

cal•cu•lar *v.* to calculate, figure, estimate.

cál•cu•lo *m.* to calculation, estimate; calcu-lus; gravel (*in the gall bladder, kidney, etc.*).

cal•de•ar *v.* to heat; to weld; **-se** *Am.* to become overheated, excited; *Am.* to get "lit up", get drunk.

cal•de•ra *f.* boiler; caldron, kettle; **calderilla** *f.* copper coin.

cal•do *m.* broth; gravy.

ca•le•fac•ción *f.* heat, heating.

ca•len•da•rio *m.* calendar; almanac.

ca•lén•du•la *f.* marigold.

ca•len•ta•dor *m.* heater.

ca•len•tar[1] *v. irr.* to warm, heat; to spank; *Am.* to annoy, bother; **-se** to warm oneself; to become heated, excited; to be in heat; *Am.* to become angry.

ca•len•tu•ra *f.* fever; *Col.* fit of temper; **– de pollo** feigned illness; **calenturón** *m.* high fever.

ca•len•tu•rien•to *adj.* feverish; *Ch.* tu-bercular.

ca•le•tre *m.* judgment, acumen, keen insight.

ca•li•brar *v.* to gauge, measure; to measure the caliber of.

ca•li•bre *m.* caliber; bore, gauge (*of a gun*); diameter (*of a pipe tube, wire*).

ca•li•can•to *m.* stone masonry.

ca•li•có *m.* calico, cotton cloth.

ca•li•dad *f.* quality.

cá•li•do *adj.* warm, hot.

ca•lien•te *adj.* warm, hot; heated; fiery; *Am.* angry; *Col.* bold, brave; *m. Am.* brandy in hot water; **calientito** *adj.* nice and warm.

ca•li•fi•ca•ción *f.* qualification; grade, mark (*in a course or examination*); judgment.

ca•li•fi•car[6] *v.* to qualify; to rate, consider, judge; to grade; *Am.* to compute (*election returns*); **-se** *Ch.* to qualify or register (*as a voter*).

ca•li•gra•fí•a *f.* penmanship.

ca•li•na *f.* haze, mist.

cá•liz *m.* chalice, communion cup; cup, goblet; calyx (*of a flower*).

cal•ma *f.* calm, quiet.

cal•man•te *adj.* soothing; *m.* sedative.

cal•mar *v.* to calm, quiet, soothe.

cal•mo *adj.* calm, quiet.

cal•mo•so *adj.* calm; soothing; phlegmatic, slow.

ca•lor *m.* heat, warmth; ardor.

ca•lo•rí•fe•ro *m.* heater, radiator; furnace.

ca•los•frí•o, calofrío *m.* chill.

ca•lum•nia *f.* slander.

ca•lum•niar *v.* to slander.

ca•lu•ro•so *adj.* (*literal*) hot, warm; (*figurado*) heated, excited; cordial, enthusiastic.

cal•va *f.* bald head; bald spot; barren spot.

cal•va•rio *m.* Calvary, place of the Cross; suffering, tribulation.

cal•vo *adj.* bald; barren.

cal•za *f.* wedge; shoehorn; *Col., Ven.* gold inlay, tooth fillin; **-s** breeches.

cal·za·da *f.* paved road; highway; *Mex., Carib.* wide avenue.

cal·za·do *m.* footwear.

cal·za·dor *m.* shoehorn.

cal·zar⁹ *v.* to put on (*shoes, gloves, spurs*); to put a wedge under a wheel; *Am.* to fill (*a tooth*).

cal·zón *m.* (*or* **calzones**) breeches, short trousers; *Mex., Ven.* drawers; *Mex.* white cotton trousers; **calzoncillos** *m. pl.* drawers, men's shorts; **calzoneras** *f. pl. Mex.* trousers open down the sides.

ca·lla·do *adj.* silent, quiet.

ca·llar *v.* to be silent; to hush; **-se** to be or keep silent.

ca·lle *f.* street.

ca·lle·ja *f.* small street, alley, lane; **callejuela** *f.* small, narrow street; lane.

ca·lle·je·ar *v.* to walk the streets, ramble.

ca·lle·je·ro *m.* street-rambler, street-stroller; street-loiterer; *adj.* fond of walkin the streets; rambling.

ca·lle·jón *m.* alley; lane; narrow pass; **sin salida** blind alley.

ca·llo *m.* callus, corn; **-s** tripe (*food*).

ca·llo·so *adj.* callous, hard.

ca·ma *f.* bed, couch, cot; litter; **caer en** – to fall ill, **guardar** – to be confined to bed; *Am.* **tenderle uno la** – **a otro** to help one in his love affairs; to set a trap for someone; **camastro** *m.* poor uncomfortable bed.

ca·ma·da *f.* litter; brood.

cá·ma·ra *f.* chamber, hall, parlor; house (*of a legislative body*); cabin, stateroom; chamber (*of a gun*); – **de aire** inner tube; – **fotográfica** camera.

ca·ma·ra·da *m.* comrade; **camaradería** *f.* comradeship, companionship.

ca·ma·re·ra *f.* waitress; chambermaid; stewardess.

ca·ma·re·ro *m.* waiter; chamberlain; steward; valet.

ca·ma·ri·lla *f.* political lobby; small group of politicians; "kitchen cabinet", group of unofficial advisers; small room.

ca·ma·rón *m.* shrimp.

ca·ma·ro·te *m.* cabin, stateroom.

cam·ba·la·che *m.* swap, barter, exchange.

cam·ba·la·che·ar *v.* to swap, barter, exchange.

cam·bia·dor *m.* barterer; money changer; *Am.* switchman.

cam·bian·te *adj.* changing; exchanging; **-s** *m. pl.* iridescent colors.

cam·biar *v.* to change; to exchange; to shift; – **de marcha** to shift gears.

cam·bia·ví·a *m. Carib., Mex., Andes* railway switchman. See **guardagujas** and **cambiador**.

cam·bio *m.* change; exchange; railway switch; **libre** – free trade; **en** – on the other hand; in exchange.

cam·bis·ta *m.* exchange broker; banker; *Am.* railway switchman.

ca·me·llo *m.* camel.

ca·mi·lla *f.* stretcher; cot; **camillero** *m.* stretcher bearer.

ca·mi·nan·te *m. & f.* walker, traveler.

ca·mi·nar *v.* to travel; to walk; *Am.* to progress, prosper.

ca·mi·na·ta *f.* long walk; hike; jaunt.

ca·mi·no *m.* road; course; *Riopl.* table runner; *Am.* hall runner; – **de hierro** railroad; – **real** highway; **de** – on the way.

ca·mión *m.* truck; wagon; *Mex.* bus; **camionero** *m.* truck driver; **camioneta** *f.* small truck; *C.A.* bus.

ca·mi·sa *f.* shirt; – **de fuerza** straitjacket; **meterse en** – **de once varas** to attempt more than one can manage, bite off more than one can chew; **camiseta** *f.* undershirt.

ca·mi·són *m.* long shirt; *Am.* nightgown; *Am.* gown; dress.

ca·mo·te *m. Am.* kind of sweet potato.

cam·pa·men·to *m.* encampment; camp.

cam·pa·na *f.* bell; *Riopl., Andes* spy, lookout (*for thieves*); **campanada** *f.* stroke of a bell; *Am.* **por – de vacante** once in a blue moon, very seldom.

cam·pa·na·rio *m.* bell tower.

cam·pa·ni·lla *f.* small bell; bubble; uvula; tassel; bell-flower.

cam·pa·ni·lla·zo *m.* loud ring of a bell.

cam·pa·ni·lle·o *m.* ringing; tinkling.

cam·pa·ña *f.* level, open country; campaing; period of active service.

cam·pear *v.* to pasture; to grow green (*said of the fields*); to excel; to be prominent, stand out; to be in the field; *Riopl.* to search the plains for lost cattle; *Col., Ven.* to act the bully.

cam·pe·cha·no *adj.* frank, open.

cam·pe·ón *m.* champion; defender.

cam·pe·o·na·to *m.* championship.

cam·pe·si·no *adj.* rural, rustic; *m.* peasant, countryman; farmer.

cam·pes·tre *adj.* rural, rustic.

cam·pi·ña *f.* largefield; open country.

cam·po *m.* country; field camp, **a – raso** in the open; **a – traviesa** (*or* **travieso**) cross-country.

cam·po·san·to *m.* churchyard, cemetery.

ca·mue·sa *f.* pippin (*a variety of apple*).

ca·mu·fla·je *m.* camouflage.

can *m.* dog; trigger (*of a gun*).

ca·na *f.* white hair, grey hair; *Carib.* a kind of palm; **echar una – al aire** to go out for a good time; to go out on a fling.

ca·na·dien·se *adj., m. & f.* Canadian.

ca·nal *m.* canal, channel; *f.* eaves trough.

ca·na·lla *f.* rabble, mob; *m.* mean fellow.

ca·na·na *f.* cartridge belt; **-s** *Col., Ven.* handcuffs.

ca·na·pé *m.* couch, lounge, sofa; settee.

ca·na·rio *m.* canary; native of the Canary Islands; *interj.* great Scott!!

ca·nas·ta *f.* basket; crate.

can•ce•la•ción *f.* cancellation.

can•ce•lar *v.* to cancel.

can•ci•ller *m.* chancellor.

can•ción *f.* song; a kind of lyric poem; **volver a la misma** – to repeat, harp on the same thing.

can•cha *f.* court (*for tennis, etc.*); sports ground or field; cockpit, enclosure for cockfights; *Peru* roasted corn or beans; *Am.* ¡abran –! gangway!; make room!

can•da•do *m.* padlock; *Col.* goatee.

can•de•la *f.* candle; fire, forest fire; light.

can•de•le•ro *m.* candlestick.

can•den•te *adj.* incandescent, white-hot, red-hot.

can•di•da•to *m.* candidate.

can•di•da•tu•ra *f.* candidacy.

can•di•dez *f.* candor, simplicity.

cán•di•do *adj.* candid, siple, innocent; white.

can•dil *m.* lamp; *Riopl.*, *Mex.* chandelier; **candileja** *f.* small oil lamp; oil receptacle (*of a lamp*); **-s** footlights (*of a stage*).

can•dor *m.* candor, simplicity, innocence; frankness, sincerity.

ca•ne•la *f.* cinnamon; an exquisite thing.

can•gre•jo *m.* crab.

can•gu•ro *m.* kangaroo.

ca•ní•bal *m.* cannibal.

ca•ni•ca *f.* marble (*small glass or marble ball*).

ca•ni•lla *f.* long bone (*of the arm or leg*); cock (*of a barrel*), faucet; spool (*for a sewing machine*); *C.A.* slender leg; *Ch.*, *Col.*, *Riopl.* calf (*of the leg*); *Mex.*, *Ven.* **tener** – to have physical strength; **canillita** *m.* *Riopl.*, *Ch.*, *C.A.*, *Andes* newspaper boy.

ca•ni•no *adj.* canine; **tener un hambre canina** to be ravenous; to be hungry as a dog.

can•je *m.* interchange, exchange.

can•je•ar *v.* to exchange, interchange.

ca•no *adj.* grey-headed, grey-haired.

ca•no•a *f.* canoe.

ca•non *m.* canon; precept, rule, principle.

ca•nó•ni•go *m.* canon (*churchman*).

ca•no•ni•zar⁹ *v.* to canonize,saint.

ca•no•so *adj.* grey, grey-haired.

can•sa•do *adj.* tired; tiresome, boring.

can•san•cio *m.* fatigue, weariness.

can•sar *v.* to tire, fatigue; **-se** to get tired.

can•tar *v.* to sing; to squeal, confess; *Am.* – **alto** to ask a high price; – **claro** (*or* **-las claras**) to speak with brutal frakness; *m.* song, epic poem.

cán•ta•ro *m.* pitcher, jug.

can•ta•triz *f.* singer.

can•te•ra *f.* quarry; *Riopl.*, *Mex.*, *Carib.* stone block.

cán•ti•co *m.* canticle, religious song.

can•ti•dad *f.* quantity.

can•ti•le•na *f.* song, ballad; monotonous repetition.

can•tim•plo•ra *f.* canteen; metal vessel for cooling water; *Col.* flask for carrying gunpowder.

can•ti•na *f.* mess hall; wine cellar; wine shop;

canteen; *Carib.*, *Mex.*, *Riopl.* barroom, tavern; *Col.* saddlebag.

can•ti•ne•la = **cantilena**.

can•ti•ne•ro *m.* bartender; tavern keeper.

can•to *m.* song; singing; canto (*division of a long poem*); stone; edge; *Col.* lap; *Am.* piece.

can•tón *m.* canton, region; corner; *Am.* cotton cloth.

can•tor *m.* singer; song bird.

can•tu•rre•ar, canturriar *v.* to hum, sing softly.

can•tu•rre•o *m.* hum, humming.

ca•ña *f.* cane, reed; tall, thin glass; stem; *Riopl.*, *Col.*, *Ven.* sugar-cane brandy; *Am.* a kind of dance; *Am.* blutt, boast.

ca•ña•da *f.* narrow canyon, dale, dell, gully, ravine; *Am.* brook.

cá•ña•mo *m.* hemp; hemp cloth; *Am.* hemp cord, rope; **cañamazo** *m.* canvas.

ca•ña•ve•ral *m.* cane field; reed patch; sugar-cane plantation.

ca•ñe•rí•a *f.* conduit, pipe line; tubing, piping; gas or water main.

ca•ño *m.* pipe, tube; spout; sewer; narrow channel; *Ven.* branch of a river, stream.

ca•ñón *m.* (*arma*) cannon, gun; barrel (*of a gun*); (*topográfico*) ravine, gorge, canyon; (*tubo*) pipe, tube; (*figurado*) beard stubble; pinfeather; quill (*of a feather*); chimney shaft; **cañonazo** *m.* cannon shot.

ca•ño•ne•ar *v.* to cannonade, bombard.

ca•ño•ne•o *m.* cannonade; bombardment.

ca•ño•ne•ro *m.* gunboat; gunner; **lancha cañone-ra** gumboat.

ca•o•ba *f.* mahogany.

ca•os *m.* chaos, confusion.

ca•pa *f.* (*ropa*) cape, cloak; (*cubierta*) covering, coatin; layer; scum; **so – de** under the guise of, under pretense of.

ca•pa•ci•dad *f.* capacity; ability.

ca•pa•ci•tar *v.* to enable, prepare, fit, qualify; *Col.* to empower, authorize.

ca•pa•taz *m.* boss, foreman, overseer.

ca•paz *adj.* capable, able, competent; spacious, roomy.

ca•pe•llán *m.* chaplain, priest, clergyman.

ca•pe•ru•za *f.* pointed hood.

ca•pi•lla *f.* chapel; hood.

ca•pi•ro•te *m.* hood; **tonto de** – dunce, plain fool.

ca•pi•tal *m.* capital, funds; *f.* capital, capital city; *adj.* capital; **capitalismo** *m.* capitalism; **capitalista** *m.* & *f.* capitalist; *adj.* capitalistic.

ca•pi•ta•li•zar⁹ *v.* to capitalize.

ca•pi•tán *m.* captain.

ca•pi•ta•ne•ar *v.* to command, lead.

ca•pi•to•lio *m.* capitol.

ca•pi•tu•lar *v.* to surrender; to come to an agreement.

ca•pí•tu•lo *m.* chapter.

ca•po•ral *m.* boss, leader; *Am.* foreman in a cattle

ranch.

ca·po·te m. cloak (with sleeves); bullfighter's cloak; Ch. thrashing, beating; **decir para su** — to say to oneself; Am. **de** — in an underhanded way; Ven., Carib. **dar** — to get ahead; to deceive.

ca·pri·cho m. caprice, whim, notion.

ca·pri·cho·so adj. capricious, whimsical; changeable, fickle.

ca·pri·chu·do adj. whimsical; stubborn, willful.

cáp·su·la f. capsule; percussion cap, cartridge shell; metal cap (on bottles).

cap·tar v. to win, attract; to capitivate; Am. to get, tune in on (a radio station).

cap·tu·ra f. capture.

cap·tu·rar v. to capture, arest.

ca·pu·cha f. hood.

ca·pu·llo m. cocoon; bud; acorn cup.

ca·ra f. face; expression, countenance; front; **de** — opposite; **echar** (or **dar**) **en** — to reproach, blame; **sacar la** — **por alguien** to take someone's part, defend him.

ca·ra·bi·na f. carbine, rifle.

ca·ra·col m. snail; winding stairs; Am. embroidered blouse; Am. curl.

ca·ra·co·le·ar v. to caper, prance around (said of horses); Col., Ven. to muddle, entangle; Am. to sidestep an obligation.

ca·ra·co·le·o m. prancing around; winding turn.

ca·rác·ter m. character; temper.

ca·rac·te·rís·ti·co adj. characteristic; **característica** f. characteristic, trait.

ca·rac·te·ri·zar v. to characterize.

¡ca·ram·ba! interj. great guns! great Scott!

ca·rám·ba·no m. icicle.

ca·ra·me·lo m. caramel.

ca·ra·mi·llo m. reed pipe, small flute; **armar un** — to raise a rumpus, create a disturbance.

ca·ran·cho m. Riopl. hawk, buzzard.

ca·rá·tu·la f. mask; Col., Ven., Riopl., Carib., Andes title page of a book; C.A., Mex., Andes dial, face of watch.

ca·ra·va·na f. caravan.

car·bó·li·co adj. carbolic.

car·bón m. carbon; coal; — **de leña** charcoal; **carbono** m. carbon.

car·bo·ne·ra f. coal bin; coal cellar; woman coal or charcoal vendor; Am. coal mine; **carbonero** m. coal dealer; charcoal vendor; adj. coal, relating to coal or charcoal.

car·bu·ra·dor m. carburetor.

car·ca·ja·da f. loud laughter, peal of laughter.

cár·cel f. jail, prison.

car·ce·le·ro m. jailer; adj. relating to a jail.

car·co·mi·do adj. worm-eaten; decayed.

car·dar v. to card, comb (wool).

car·de·nal m. cardinal; cardinal bird; bruise.

cár·de·no adj. dark-purple.

car·do m. thistle; a kind of cactus.

ca·re·ar v. to confront, bring face to face; to compare; **-se** to meet face to face.

ca·re·cer v. irr. to lack, be in need of.

ca·ren·cia f. lack, want.

ca·ren·te adj. lacking.

ca·re·ro adj. overcharging; profiteering; m. profiteer.

ca·res·tí·a f. dearth, scarcity; high price.

ca·re·ta f. mask.

car·ga f. load, burden; freight; cargo; charge of gunpowder; **volver a la** — to insist again and again.

car·ga·do p.p. & adj. loaded; strong (as tea or coffe); cloudy, sultry; — **de espaldas** round-shouldered, stoopshouldered.

car·ga·dor m. loader; stevedore; Am. carrier, errand boy, mover.

car·ga·men·to m. cargo.

car·gar v. (poner carga) to load; to charge; (atacar) to charge; (molestar) to bother, annoy; Am. to carry, lug; Am. to punish; — **con** to carry away; to assume (responsibility); — **con el muerto** to get the blame (unjustly).

car·go m. charge, position, duty, burden; loading; accusation; **hacerse** — **de** to take charge of; to realize.

car·gue·ro adj. load-carrying; freight-carrying; m. Am. beast of burden; Am. skilled loader of pack animals; Am. patient, long-suffering person.

ca·ri·be adj. Caribbean; m. Carib, Caribbean Indian; cannibal; savage.

ca·ri·ca·tu·ra f. caricature; cartoon.

ca·ri·cia f. caress.

ca·ri·dad f. charity; alms.

ca·ries f. decay (of a bone); tooth cavity.

ca·ri·ño m. affection, love; Am. gift.

ca·ri·ño·so adj. affectionate, loving.

ca·ri·ta·ti·vo adj. charitable.

car·me·sí adj. & m. crimson.

car·mín m. crimson.

car·nal adj. carnal, sensual.

car·na·val m. carnival.

car·ne f. meat, flesh; — **de gallina** "goose flesh", "goose pimples"; **echar -s** to put on weight, get fat; Am. — **de res** beef.

car·ne·a·da f. Riopl. butchering, slaugh-tering.

car·ne·ar v. Riopl. to butcher; Riopl. to kill.

car·ne·ro m. (animal) ram, male sheep; (carne) mutton; Am. a weak-willed person; Am. waste basket; Am. — **de la tierra** llama (or any fleecebearing animal); Am. **cantar uno el** — to die.

car·ni·ce·rí·a f. (tienda) meat market; (matanza) butchery, slaughter; C.A., Ec. slaughterhouse.

car·ni·ce·ro m. butcher; adj. carnivorous, flesh-eating; cruel.

car·ní·vo·ro adj. carnivorous.

car·no·si·dad *f.* fleshiness, fatness; abnormal growth (*on animal or plant tissues*).

car·no·so *adj.* fleshy; meaty; pulpy.

ca·ro *adj.* expensive; dear; *adv.* at a high price.

ca·ro·na *f.* saddle pad.

ca·ro·zo *m.* cob, cornboc.

car·pa *f.* carp (*fresh-water fish*); *Am.* canvas tent, circus tent; **– dorada** goldfish.

car·pe·ta *f.* (*cubierta*) table cover; desk pad; (*cartera*) portfolio, letter case or file; *Andes* office desk; *Am.* bookkeeping department; **carpetazo; dar –** to table (*a motion*); to set aside, pigeonhole or dismiss.

car·pin·te·rí·a *f.* carpentry; carpenter's workshop.

car·pin·te·ro *m.* carpenter; **pájaro –** woodpecker.

ca·rras·pe·ar *v.* to cough up; to clear one's throat; to be hoarse.

ca·rras·pe·ra *f.* hoarseness.

ca·rre·ra *f.* career; race, run; course; stocking run.

ca·rre·ta *f.* long, narrow wagon; cart; *Col., Ven.* wheelbarrow.

ca·rre·ta·je *m.* cartage (*transporting by cart, truck, etc.*); price paid for cartage.

ca·rre·te *m.* spool; reel; **– distribuidor** feeding reel; **– receptor** take-up reel (*tape recorder*).

ca·rre·tel *m.* reel, spool, bobbin; fishing reel; log reel (*of a boat*).

ca·rre·te·ra *f.* highway.

ca·rre·te·ro *m.* carter, teamster; cart maker; camino – highway.

ca·rre·ti·lla *f.* wheelbarrow; small cart; baggage truck; *Ríopl.* wagon; *Am.* jaw; *Col.* string, series (*of lies, blunders, etc.*); *Am.* firecracker; **repetir de –** to rattle off, repeat mechanically.

ca·rre·tón *m.* truck; wagon, cart.

ca·rril *m.* rail; rut; furrow.

ca·rri·llo *m.* (*de la cara*) cheek; (*mecánico*) pulley; cart.

ca·rri·zo *m.* reed; reed grass.

ca·rro *m.* cart; cartload; *Am.* car, auto, streetcar, coach; *Am.* **pararle a uno el –** to restrain someone; *Am.* **pasarle a uno el –** to suffer an injury or misfortune; **carroza** *f.* large and luxurious carriage; chariot; *Am.* hearse.

ca·rro·ce·ría *f.* chassis; frame for a parade float.

ca·rro·ña *f.* dead and decaying flesh; putrid, decaying carcass.

ca·rrua·je *m.* carriage, vehicle.

car·ta *f.* (*misiva*) letter; (*naipe*) card; (*documento*) charter; map; **– blanca** full authority, freedom to act; **– de naturaleza** naturalization papers; **– de venta** bill of sale; *Ch.* **retirar –** to repent, back down; *Am.* **ser la última – de la baraja** to be the worst or most insignificant person or thing.

car·te·ar·se *v.* to correspond, write to each other.

car·tel *m.* poster, handbill; cartel, written agreement; **cartela** *f.* tag, slip of paper, small card, piece of cardboard; **cartelera** *f.* billboard; **cartelón** *m.* large poster.

car·te·ra *f.* (*objeto*) wallet; briefcase; desk pad; (*puesto*) portfolio, cabinet post; **carterista** *m. & f.* pickpocket.

car·te·ro *m.* mailman, letter carrier, postman.

car·ti·lla *f.* primer; note, short letter; **leerle a uno la –** to scold, lecture someone concerning his duties.

car·to·gra·fíar [17] *v.* to chart; to make charts.

car·tón *m.* cardboard; pasteboard; **cartulina** *f.* fine cardboard.

car·tu·che·ra *f.* cartridge belt.

car·tu·cho *m.* cartridge; roll of coins; paper cone or bag.

ca·sa *f.* (*doméstica*) house, home; household; (*negocio*) business firm; square (*of a chessboard*); *Am.* bet, wager; **– de empeños** pawnshop; **– de huéspedes** boardinghouse; **echar la – por la ventana** to spend recklessly, squander everything; **poner –** to set up housekeeping.

ca·sa·be, ca·za·be *m. Am.* cassava; *Am.* cassava bread.

ca·sa·ca *f.* long military coat; **volver –** to be a turncoat, change sides or parties.

ca·sa·mien·to *m.* wedding; marriage.

ca·sar *v.* to marry; to match; *Am.* to graft (*trees*); **-se** to get married.

cas·ca·bel *m.* jingle bell, tinkle bell; snake's rattle; *Am.* rattlesnake; **cascabela** *f.* C.R. rattlesnake.

cas·ca·da *f.* cascade, waterfall.

cas·ca·jo *m.* coarse gravel; grushed stone; pebble; fragment; rubbish.

cas·ca·nue·ces *m.* nutracracker.

cas·car [6] *v.* to crack, break; **-se** to crack or break open.

cás·ca·ra *f.* shell, husk, hull, rind; bark of a tree; *Ríopl.* **dar a uno – de novillo** to give someone a whipping; **cascarudo** *adj.* having a thick husk; having a thick rind.

cas·ca·rra·bias *m. & f.* crab, grouch, illtempered person; *adj.* grouchy, cranky, irritable.

cas·co *m.* helmet; hoof; skull; broken piece of earthenware; cask; empty bottle; hull of a ship; *Mex., Ríopl.* compound, main buildings of a farm; **caliente de -s** hot-headed; **ligero -s** light-headed, frivolous; **romperse los -s** to rack one's brain.

ca·se·río *m.* hamlet, small settlement.

ca·se·ro *adj.* dometic; homemade; *m.* landlord; janitor, caretaker; *Ch.* customer; *Col., Peru, Ven.* delivery boy; **casera** *f.* landlady; housekeeper.

ca·se·ta *f.* small house, cottage; booth, stall.

ca·si *adv.* almost.

ca·si·lla *f.* (*puesto*) stall, booth; (*apartado*) post office box; pigeonhole; **sacarle a uno de sus -s** to change someone's way of life or habits; to irritate, annoy, try someone's patience; **salirse de sus -s** to lose one's temper; to do something out of the way.

ca•si•no *m.* club, society; clubhouse; recreation hall.

ca•so *m.* case; point; matter; event; **– que** (*or* **en – que**) in case that; **dado –** supposing; **hacer –** de to pay attention to; **hacer – omiso** de to omit; **no vie-ne al –** that is not to the point.

ca•so•rio *m.* wedding, marraige.

cas•pa *f.* dandruff.

cas•ta *f.* race, breed; caste, distintct class; quality, kind.

cas•ta•ña *f.* chestnut; jug; knot or roll of hair; *Am.* small barrel; *Mex.* trunk, large suitcase.

cas•ta•ñe•te•ar *v.* to rattle the castanets; to chatter (*said of the teeth*); to crackle (*said of the knees or joints*); **– con los dedos** to snap one's fingers.

cas•ta•ñe•te•o *m.* rattle or sound of cas-tanets; chatter, chattering (*of the teeth*).

cas•ta•ño *m.* chestnut (*tree and wood*); *adj.* chestnut-colored.

cas•ta•ñue•la *f.* castanet.

cas•te•lla•no *adj. & m.* Castilian.

cas•ti•dad *f.* chastity.

cas•ti•gar[7] *v.* to chastise, punish.

cas•ti•go *m.* punishment; correction.

cas•ti•llo *m.* castle.

cas•ti•zo *adj.* pure, correct (*language*); pure-blooded.

cas•to *adj.* chaste, pure.

cas•tor *m.* beaver; beaver cloth.

ca•sual *adj.* casual, accidental.

ca•sua•li•dad *f.* chance, accident.

ca•su•ca *f.* little house; hut, shanty.

ca•su•cha *f.* hut, hovel, shack.

ca•ta•du•ra *f.* aspect, apearance.

ca•ta•lán *adj.* Catalan, Catalonian, of or from Catalonia, Spain; *m.* Catalan.

ca•ta•le•jo *m.* telescope.

ca•ta•lo•gar[7] *v.* to catalogue.

ca•tá•lo•go *m.* catalogue.

ca•tar *v.* to look at, examine; to taste, sample.

ca•ta•ra•ta *f.* cataract; waterfall.

ca•ta•rro *m.* catarrh, cold.

ca•tás•tro•fe *f.* catastrophe, mishap.

ca•tear *v.* to explore, look around; *Ch., C.A., Mex.* to search or raid (*a home*); *Am.* to explore for ore; *Col., Riopl.* to test, try.

ca•te•cis•mo *m.* catechism.

cá•te•dra *f.* class; subjetct; chair, profes-sorship.

ca•te•dral *f.* cathedral.

ca•te•drá•ti•co *m.* professor.

ca•te•go•ría *f.* category, rank; kind, class.

ca•te•gó•ri•co *adj.* categorical, positive.

ca•te•qui•zar[9] *v.* to catechize, give religious instruction (to); to induce, persuade.

ca•tó•li•co *adj.* Catholic; universal; *m.* Catholic; **catolicismo** *m.* Catholicism.

ca•tre *m.* cot, small bed; *Am.* raft, float; *C.A.*, camp stool, folding stool; **– de tijera** folding cot.

ca•trín *m. Am.* dandy; *adj. Mex., C.A.* over-elegant, dressy.

cau•ce *m.* river bed.

cau•ción *f.* precaution; security, guarantee; bail.

cau•che•ro *m. Am.* rubber gatherer; *Am.* rubber producer; *adj. Am.* rubber, pertaining to rubber.

cau•cho *m.* rubber; **– sintético** synthetic rubber; *Am.* rubber tree; *Col.* rubber raincoat or cloak; **cauchal** *m.* rubber grove or plantation.

cau•dal *m.* (*monetario*) wealth; (*torrente*) river current; volume of water.

cau•da•lo•so *adj.* wealthy; abundant.

cau•di•lla•je *m.* military leadership; *Am.* political bossism; *Am.* tyranny.

cau•di•llo *m.* leader, chief; *Am.* political boss.

cau•sa *f.* cause; case, lawsuit; *Am.* light lunch, snak.

cau•sar *v.* to cause.

cau•te•la *f.* caution; cunning, craftiness; trick, deception.

cau•te•lo•so *adj.* cautious; crafty.

cau•ti•var *v.* to capture; to charm, fascinate.

cau•ti•ve•rio *m.* captivity.

cau•ti•vo *m.* captive, war prisoner.

cau•to *adj.* cautious.

ca•var *v.* to dig, spade; to excavate.

ca•ver•na *f.* cavern, cave.

ca•ver•no•so *adj.* cavernous, like a cavern; hollow; **voz cavernosa** deep, hollow voice.

ca•vi•dad *f.* cavity.

ca•ya•do *m.* shepherd's crook, staff.

ca•yo *m.* key, island reef.

ca•za *f.* hunt, hunting; wild game; *m.* attack plane; **dar –** to pursue, track down.

ca•za•dor *adj.* hunting; *m.* hunter.

ca•zar[9] *v.* to chase, hunt; to track down.

ca•za•tor•pe•de•ro *m.* destroyer, torpedo-boat.

ca•zo *m.* dipper; pot, pan.

ca•zue•la *f.* stewing pan; earthenware cooking pan; topmost theatre gallery; *Ven.* stewed hen; *P.R.* candied sweet potatoes with spices.

ce•ba•da *f.* barley; *Am.* brewing of **mate; cebadal** *m.* barley field.

ce•bar *v.* to feed, fatten (*animals*); to encourage, nourish (*a passion*); to prime (*a gun, pump, etc.*); to bait (*a fishhook*); *Riopl.* to brew and serve **mate** or tea; **-se** to vent one's fury.

ce•bo *m.* feed (*for animals*); bait; incentive.

ce•bo•lla *f.* onion.

ce•ce•ar *v.* to lisp.

ce•ce•o *m.* lisp, lisping.

ce•ci•na *f.* dried beef, jerked beef.

ce•da•zo *m.* sieve.

ce•der *v.* to cede, transfer; to yield, surrender, submit; to diminish, abate.

ce•dro *m.* cedar.

cé·du·la *f.* slip of paper; certificate; **– de vecindad** (*or* **– personal**) official identification card.

cé·fi·ro *m.* zephyr, soft breeze; *Am.* fine muslin.

ce·gar[1,7] *v. irr.* to blind; to become blind; to confuse; to fill up, stop up (*a hole*).

ce·gue·dad, ce·gue·ra *f.* blindness.

cei·ba *f. Am.* ceiba, silk-cotton tree.

ce·ja *f.* eyebrow; brow of a hill.

ce·jar *v.* to go backward; to back; to back down, give in, yield; to slacken.

ce·ji·jun·to *adj.* frowning; with knitted eyebrows.

ce·la·da *f.* ambush, snare, trap.

ce·la·jem. colored clouds; skylight; presage, portent; *P.R.* shadow, ghost; *Am.* **como un** – like lightning.

ce·lar *v.* to guard, watch; to watch over jealously; to conceal.

cel·da *f.* cell.

ce·le·bra·ción *f.* celebration.

ce·le·brar *v.* to celebrate; to praise, honor; to be glad.

cé·le·bre *adj.* famous; funny, witty; *Col.* graceful, pretty (*woman*).

ce·le·bri·dad *f.* fame, renown; celebrity, famous person; celebration.

ce·le·ri·dad *f.* swiftness, speed.

ce·les·te *adj.* celestial, heavenly.

ce·les·tial *adj.* celestial, heavenly, divine.

cé·li·be *adj.* unmarried; *m. & f.* unmarried person.

ce·lo *m.* (*humano*) zeal, ardor; envy; (*animal*) heat (*sexual excitement in animals*); **-s** jealousy, suspicion; **tener -s** to be jealous.

ce·lo·sí·a *f.* window lattice; Venetian blind.

ce·lo·so *adj.* jealous; zealous, eager; sus-picious.

cé·lu·la *f.* cell.

ce·lu·loi·de *m.* celluloid.

ce·llis·ca *f.* sleet; rain and snow.

ce·men·tar *v.* to cement.

ce·men·te·rio *m.* cementery.

ce·men·to *m.* cement; **– armado** reinforced con-crete.

ce·na *f.* supper.

ce·na·gal *m.* quagmire, muddy ground, swamp.

ce·na·go·so *adj.* muddy, miry.

ce·nar *v.* to eat supper.

cen·ce·rra·da *f.* racket. noise (*with cow-bells, tin cans, etc.*); tin pan serenade.

cen·ce·rre·ar *v.* to make a racket (*with combells, tin cans, etc.*).

cen·ce·rro *m.* cowbell.

cen·dalm. gauze; thin veil.

ce·ni·ce·rom. ash tray; ash pit; ash pan.

ce·ni·cien·ta *f.* a Cinderella.

ce·ni·cien·to *adj.* ashen, ash-colored.

ce·nit*m.* zenith.

ce·ni·za *f.* ashes, cinders.

ce·ni·zo *adj.* ash-colored.

cen·som. census.

cen·sor *m.* censor.

cen·su·ra *f.* censure, criticism, disapproval; censorship.

cen·su·ra·dor*m.* censor, critic; critical person; *adj.* critical.

cen·su·rar *v.* to censure, criticize, reprove; to cen-sor.

cen·ta·vo *v.* cent.

cen·te·lla *f.* lightning, flash; spark.

cen·te·lle·an·te *adj.* sparkling, flashing.

cen·te·lle·ar*v.* to twinkle; to sparkle, gillter; to flash.

cen·te·lle·o *m.* glitter, sparkle.

cen·te·nar *m.* one hundred; field or rye.

cen·te·na·rio *m.* centennial, one hundredth anniversary; *adj.* centennial; old, ancient.

cen·te·no *m.* rye.

cen·té·si·mo *adj. & m.* hundredth.

cen·tí·me·tro*m.* centimeter (*one hundredth part of a meter*).

cén·ti·mo *m.* one hundredth part of a **peseta**.

cen·ti·ne·la *m.* sentry, sentinel.

cen·tral *adj.* central; *f.* main office; head-quarters; *Am.* main sugar mill or refinery.

cen·trar *v.* to center.

cén·tri·co *adj.* central.

cen·tro *m.* center, middle.

ce·ñi·dor*m.* girdle, belt, sash.

ce·ñir[5,19] *v. irr.* (*rodear*) to gird, girdle; to tighten; to encircle; (*abreviar*) to diminish; to limit; **-se a** to limit oneself to.

ce·ñom. frown, scowl; **fruncir el** – to frown; to scowl.

ce·pa *f.* stump, stub (*of a tree or plant*); vinestock; origin, stock (*of a family*); *Am.* mass of plants growing from a common root; *Am.* excavation (*for a build-ding*), hole, pit (for planting trees); **de buena** – of good stock.

ce·pi·llom. brush; alms box; carpenter's plane, *Am.* flatterer; **– de dientes** tooth-brush.

ce·pom. branch, stock.

ce·ra *f.* wax.

ce·rá·mi·ca *f.* ceramics, pottery.

cer·ca*adv.* near, near by; **– de** *prep.* near, nearly; *f.* fence, low wall.

cer·ca·do *m.* enclosure; fenced-in garden; fence; *Am.* Peruvian political division; *p.p.* of **cercar**.

cer·ca·ní·a *f.* proximity; **-s** surroundings, vicinity.

cer·ca·no *adj.* near; neighboring.

cer·car[6] *v.* to fence, enclose; to surround; to besiege.

cer·ce·nar*v.* to clip off; to curtail, diminish, reduce.

cer·cio·rar*v.* to assure, affirm; **-se** to ascertain, find out.

cer·com. fence, enclosure; siege; circle; *Ch.* small farm or orchard.

cer·daf. bristle; *Am.* **ir en -s** to go halves or share in a deal.

cer·dom. hog, pig; pork.

cer•do•so *adj.* bristly.

ce•re•al *m.* cereal, grain.

ce•re•bro *m.* brain.

ce•re•mo•nia *f.* ceremony.

ce•re•mo•nial *adj. & m.* ceremonial.

ce•re•mo•nio•so *adj.* ceremonious.

ce•re•za *f.* cherry; **cerezo** *m.* cherry tree; cherry wood.

ce•ri•lla *f.* wax taper, wax match; earwax.

ce•ri•llo *m. Mex., C.A., Ven., Andes* match.

cer•ner¹ *v. irr.* to sift; to drizzle; *Am.* to strain through a sieve; **-se** to hover (*as a bird or plane*).

ce•ro *m.* zero; nothing.

cer•qui•ta *adv.* quite near, nice and near.

ce•rra•do *adj.* closed; cloudy; thick (*beard*); reserved (*person*); dull; *Am.* stubborn.

ce•rra•du•ra *f.* locking, closing; lock; **– de golpe** spring lock

ce•rra•je•rí•a *f.* locksmith's shop; lock-smith's trade.

ce•rra•je•ro *m.* locksmith.

ce•rrar¹ *v. irr.* to close, shut, lock; **-se** to close; **-se el cielo** to become overcast or cloudy.

ce•rra•zón *f.* cloudiness, darkness.

ce•rro *m.* hill.

ce•rro•jo *m.* latch, bolt.

cer•ta•men *m.* contest, literary contest; debate; competition.

cer•te•ro *adj.* acurate, exact; well-aimed; **tirador –** good shot.

cer•te•za *f.* certainty.

cer•ti•dum•bre *f.* certainty.

cer•ti•fi•ca•do *adj.* certified, registered; *m.* certificate.

cer•ti•fi•car⁶ *v.* to certify; to register (*a letter*).

cer•va•to *m.* fawn, young deer.

cer•ve•za *f.* beer; **cervecería** *f.* beer tavern; brewery.

ce•san•te *adj.* unemployed.

ce•sar *v.* to cease, stop; to quit.

ces•ta *f.* basket; a kind of racket for playing jai alai (*Basque ball game*).

ces•to *m.* large basket, hamper.

ce•tri•no *adj.* greenish-yellow, lemon-colored, citronlike; melancholy, gloomy.

ce•tro *m.* scepter, staff.

ci•ber•né•ti•ca *f.* cybernetics, computer science.

ci•ca•te•ro *adj.* miserly, stingy.

ci•ca•triz *f.* scar.

ci•ca•tri•zar⁹ *v.* to heal, close (*a wound*).

ci•clo *m.* cycle; period of time; school term.

ci•clón *m.* cyclone.

ci•clo•trón *m.* cyclotron.

cie•go *adj.* blind; **a ciegas** blindly; *m.* blindman.

cie•lo *m.* sky; heaven; **– de la boca** palate; **poner en el –** to praise, extol; **poner el grito en el –** to "hit the ceiling"; **cielito** *m. Am.* gaucho group dance and tune.

ciem•piés, ci•en•to•piés *m.* centipede.

cié•na•ga *f.* swamp, bog, quagmire, marsh.

cien•cia *f.* science; learning; skill; **a** (*or* **de**) **– cierta** with certainty.

cie•no *m.* mud, mire.

cien•tí•fi•co *adj.* scientific; *m.* scientist.

cie•rre *m.* clasp, fastener; zipper; closing, fastening, locking; method of closing.

cier•to *adj.* certain, true, sure; **por –** certainly; *Col., C.A.* **ciertas hierbas** so-and-so (*person not named*).

cier•vo *m.* deer; **cierva** *f.* doe, hind, female deer.

cier•zo *m.* north wind.

ci•fra *f.* cipher, number; figure; abridgment, summary; code; monogram; emblem.

ci•frar *v.* to write in code; to summarize; **– la esperanza en** to place one's hope in.

ci•ga•rra *f.* cicada, locust.

ci•ga•rre•ra *f.* cigar or cigarrette case; woman cigar maker or vendor.

ci•ga•rri•llo *m.* cigarrette.

ci•ga•rro *m.* cigar; cigarette.

ci•güe•ña *f.* stork; crank, handle (*for turning*).

ci•güe•ñal *m.* crankshaft.

ci•lín•dri•co *adj.* cylindrical.

ci•lin•dro *m.* cylinder; *Mex.* hand organ.

ci•ma *f.* peak, summit, top; **dar –** to complete, carry out.

ci•ma•rrón *adj. Riopl., Mex., Carib., Ven., Andes* wild, untamed; *Am.* **mate –** black, bitter **mate**.

ci•ma•rro•ne•ar *v. Riopl.* to drink **mate** without sugar.

cim•brar, cim•bre•ar *v.* to brandish, flourish, swing; to shake; to bend; *Am.* to swing around, change suddenly one's direction; **– a uno de un golpe** to knock a person down with a blow; **-se** to swing, sway; to vibrate, shake.

ci•mien•to *m.* foundation, base; source, root; **abrir los -s** to break ground for a building.

cinc *m.* zinc.

cin•cel *m.* chisel.

cin•ce•lar *v.* to chisel; to engrave.

cin•cha *f.* cinch, girth; *Am.* blows with the flat of a sword; *Col., Riopl.* **a revienta -s** unwillingly; hurriedly; at breakneck speed.

cin•char *v.* to cinch, tighten the saddle girth; *Am.* to hit with the flat of a sword.

ci•ne, ci•ne•ma *m.* cinema, motion picture; movie; **cinematógrafo** *m.* motion picture.

ci•ne•ma•to•gra•fí•a *f.* cinematography, the science of motion picture photography.

cín•gu•lo *m.* girdle, cord, belt.

cí•ni•co *adj.* cynical sarcastic, sneering; *m.* cynic.

cin•ta *f.* ribbon, band; tape; strip; movie film; coarse fishing net; *Am.* tin can.

cin•ta•ra•da *f.* beating, flogging; **cintarazo** *m.* blow with the flat of a sword.

cin·ti·lar v. to sparkle, twinkle; to glimmer.

cin·to m. belt; girdle.

cin·tu·ra f. waist; **meter en** – to subdue, subject.

cin·tu·rón m. belt; – **de seguridad** safety belt.

ci·prés m. cypress.

cir·co m. circus.

cir·cui·to m. circuit.

cir·cu·la·ción f. circulation; traffic.

cir·cu·lar v. to circulate; to circle; adj. circular; f. circular letter, notice.

cír·cu·lo m. circle; group; club; clubhouse.

cir·cun·dan·te adj. surrounding.

cir·cun·dar v. to surround.

cir·cun·fe·ren·cia f. circumference.

cir·cun·lo·cu·ción f. circumlocution, roundabout expression.

cir·cuns·pec·ción f. circumspection, decorum, prudence, restraint.

cir·cuns·pec·to adj. circumspect, prudent.

cir·cuns·tan·cia f. circumstance.

cir·cuns·tan·te adj. surrounding; present; **-s** m. pl. bystanders, onlookers. audience.

cir·cun·ve·ci·no adj. neighboring, surrounding.

ci·rio m. wax candle; saguaro cactus.

ci·rue·la f. plum; prune; – **pasa** prune, dried prune; **ciruelo** m. plum tree.

ci·ru·gí·a f. surgery.

ci·ru·ja·no m. surgeon.

cis·ne m. swan; Riopl. powder puff.

cis·ter·na f. cistern.

ci·ta f. date, appointment; citation, summons; quotation.

ci·ta·ción f. citation, quotation; summons.

ci·tar v. (convocar) to make a date or appointment with; (referir) to cite, quot; (incitar) incite, provoke; to summon.

ciu·dad f. city.

ciu·da·da·no m. citizen; resident of a city; adj. of or pertaining to a city; **ciudadanía** f. citizenship.

ciu·da·de·la f. citadel.

cí·vi·co adj. civic.

ci·vil adj. civil; polite, courteous.

ci·vi·li·dad f. civility, courtesy.

ci·vi·li·za·ción f. civilization.

ci·vi·li·za·dor adj. civilizing; m. civilizer.

ci·vi·li·zar⁹ v. to civilize.

ci·za·ña f. weed; vice; discord; **sembrar** – to sow discord.

cla·mar v. to clamor, shout; to whine.

cla·mor m. clamor, shout; whine; knell.

cla·mo·re·o m. clamoring; shouting.

cla·mo·re·ar v. to clamor, shout; to toll, knell.

clan·des·ti·no adj. clandestine, under-handed, secret.

cla·ra f. white of egg; bald spot; thin spot (in a fabric); **a las -s** clearly, opnly, frankly.

cla·ra·bo·ya f. skylight.

cla·re·ar v. (poner claro), to clarify, make clear; (haber más luz) to grow light, begin to dawn; to clear up; Am. to pierce through and through; **-se** to become transparent; to reveal oneself.

cla·ri·dad f. clarity, clearness; blunt remark, slam; fame.

cla·ri·do·so adj. Mex., Ven., C.A. blunt, outspoken, plainspoken.

cla·ri·fi·car⁶ v. to clarify, make clear.

cla·rín m. bugle; bugler; organ stop; Am. song bird.

cla·ri·ne·te m. clarinet; clarinet player.

cla·ri·to adj. & adv. quite clear, nice and clear.

cla·ri·vi·den·cia f. clairvoyance; keen insight.

cla·ro adj. clear; light (color); illustrious; adv. clearly; m. skylight; space, gap; clearing (in a forest); **pasar la noche de** – **en** – not to sleep a wink; Mex., Carib. **en** – without eating or sleeping; Am. **poner en** – to copy (a rough draft).

cla·se f. class; classroom; kind, sort.

clá·si·co adj. classic, classical.

cla·si·fi·ca·ción f. classification.

cla·si·fi·car⁶ v. to classify.

claus·tro m. cloister; meeting of a university faculty; – **de profesores** university faculty.

cláu·su·la f. clause.

clau·su·ra f. closing; seclusion, monastic life.

cla·va·do m. Mex. a dive.

cla·var v. to nail; to fix; to deceive, cheat; **-se** to be deceived; Mex., to fall into a trap; Mex. to dive.

cla·ve f. key, code; keystone; clef.

cla·vel m. carnation, pink.

cla·ve·te·ar v. to nail; to stud with nails.

cla·ví·cu·la f. collarbone.

cla·vi·ja f. peg; electric plug; peg (of a stringed instrument).

cla·vi·je·ro m. hat or clothes rack.

cla·vo m. nail; clove (spice); sharp pain or grief; sick headache; Mex. rich mineral vein; Am. bother, worry; Col. surprise, disappointment; Riopl. drug on the market (unsaleable article); **dar en el** – to hit the nail on the head; Am. **meter a uno en un** – to put a person in a predicament; Am. **ser un** – to be punctual, exact.

cle·men·cia f. mercy; **clemente** adj. merciful.

cle·ri·cal adj. clerical, of a clergyman or the clergy.

clé·ri·go m. clergyman.

cle·ro m. clergy.

cli·ché m. photographic plate; also **clisé**.

clien·te m. & f. client; customer; **clientela** f. cleintele, clients; customers.

cli·ma m. climate.

clí·max m. climax.

clí·ni·ca f. clinic.

clí·per m. clipper.

clo·a·ca f. sewer

clo·que·ar v. to cluck.

clo·que·o m. cluck, clucking.

clo·ro m. chlorine.

club m. club, society.

clue·ca f. brooding hen.

co·ac·ción f. compulsion, force; enforcement.

co·a·gu·lar v. to coagulate, thicken, clot; to curd, curdle; **-se** to coagulate, clot; to curd, curdle.

co·á·gu·lo m. coagulation, clot.

co·ar·tar v. to restrain, limit.

co·ba f. flattery; fib; **dar** − to flatter; to tease.

co·bar·de adj. cowardly; timid; weak; m. coward.

co·bar·dí·a f. cowardice.

co·ber·ti·zo m. shed, shanty.

co·ber·tor m. bedcover, quilt.

co·ber·tu·ra f. cover, covering.

co·bi·ja f. cover; shelter; roof; Am. blanket; Am. shawl, serape, poncho; **-s** Am. bedclothes.

co·bi·jar v. to cover; to shelter.

co·bra·dor m. collector; ticket collector.

co·bran·za f. collection (of a sum of money); cashing.

co·brar v. to collect (bills, debts); to charge; to cash (a draft, check, etc.); to recover, regain; to gain, acquire; Am. to demand payment; − **cariño a** to take a liking to.

co·bre m. copper; copper kitchen utensils; Am. copper coin; **-s** brass musical instruments; **batir el** − to hustle, work with energy; Am. **mostrar el** − to show one's worse side.

co·bri·zo adj. coppery, copper-colored.

co·bro m. collection (of bills); **poner en** − to put in a safe place; **ponerse en** − to take refuge, get to a safe place.

co·ca f. Am. (South American shrub and its leaves); Am. cocaine; Am. coca tea; Am. eggshell; Am. fruit skin or rind; Am. **de** − free of charge; in vain.

co·ca·í·na f. cocaine.

co·ce·ar v. to kick.

co·cer[2,10] v. irr. to cook; to boil; to bake.

co·ci·do m. Spanish stew; p.p. of **cocer**.

co·cien·te m. quotient.

co·ci·mien·to m. cooking; baking, liquid concoction (generally made of medicinal herbs).

co·ci·na f. kitchen; cuisine, cooking; − **económica** stove, range.

co·ci·nar v. to cook.

co·ci·ne·ro m. cook.

co·co m. coconut; coconut palm; bogeyman, globin; Am. derby hat; Mex., Caribe, Riopl. head; Am. blow on the head; **hacer -s a** to make eyes at, flirt with; Col., Ven., Andes **pelar a** − to crop the hair; **cocotal** m. grove of coconut palms; coconut plantation; **cocotero** m. coconut palm.

co·co·dri·lo m. crocodile.

co·che m. coach; car; taxi.

co·che·ro m. coachman; cabman; taxi driver.

co·chi·na·da f. filth, filthiness; filthy act or remark; dirty trick; herd of swine.

co·chi·ni·lla f. cochineal (insect).

co·chi·no m. hog, pig; dirty person; Ch. stingy person; Am. − **de monte** wild boar; adj. filthym dirty; Ch. miserly, stingy.

co·da·zo m. nudge; poke (with the elbow).

co·de·ar v. to elbow; to nudge; **-se con alguien** to rub elbows with someone.

co·di·cia f. greed; grediness.

co·di·ciar v. to covet.

co·di·cio·so adj. covetous, greedy.

có·di·go m. code of laws.

co·do m. elbow; bend; **alzar** (or **empinar**) **el** − to drink too much; **hablar por los -s** to talk too much; **meterse** (or **estar metido**) **hasta los -s** to be up to the elbows, be very busy.

co·dor·niz f. partridge.

co·e·tá·ne·o adj. contemporary.

co·fra·de m. & f. fellow member (of a brotherhood, club, society, etc.).

co·fra·dí·a f. brotherhood; sisterhood; guild; trade union.

co·fre m. coffer, jewel box; chest, trunk.

co·ger[11] v. to seize; to catch; to grasp; to gather; Am. **-se una cosa** to steal something.

co·go·te m. nape, boack of the neck.

co·he·char v. to bribe.

co·he·re·de·ro m. joint heir.

co·he·ren·te adj. coherent; connected.

co·he·te m. skyrocket; rocket; Riopl. **al** − in vain, uselessly.

co·he·te·rí·a f. rocketry; rocket weaponry; shop for making fireworks.

co·hi·bi·ción f. repression, inhibition, restraint.

co·hi·bi·do p.p. & adj. inhibited; embarrassed, uneasy.

co·hi·bir v. to restrain, repress; to inhibit.

coin·ci·den·cia f. coincidence.

coin·ci·dir v. to coincide.

co·je·ar v. to limp; **cojeamos del mismo pie** we both have the same weakness.

co·je·ra f. limp. lameness.

co·jín m. cushion; pad; **cojincillo** m. pad.

co·ji·ne·te m. small pillow or cushion, pad; bearing, ball bearing.

co·jo adj. lame, crippled; one-legged.

col f. cabbage; − **de Bruselas** Brussels sprouts.

co·la f. (rabo) tail; train of a dress; (hilera de gente) line of people; **piano de** − grand piano; **piano de media** − baby grand; **hacer** − to stand in line; Am. **comer** − to be the last one in a contest.

co·la·bo·ra·ción f. collaboration, mutual help.

co·la·bo·rar v. to collaborate, work together.

co·la·de·ra f. colander, strainer, sieve; Mex., Ven. drain.

co·lar[2] *v. irr.* to strain, filter; to bleach with lye; **-se** to slip in or out, sneak in.

col·cha *f.* quilt; bedspread; **-s** *Riopl.* saddle and trappings; *Riopl.* gaucho clothing.

col·chón *m.* mattress.

co·le·ar *v.* to wag the tail; to grab a bull by the tail and throw him over; *Am.* to flunk (*a student*); *Am.* to trail, tag behind (*a person*); *Col.* to bother, nag, harass; *Am.* to smoke one cigarette after another.

co·lec·ción *f.* collection; set; gathering.

co·lec·cio·nar *v.* to collect, make a collection.

co·lec·cio·nis·ta *m. & f.* collector (*of stamps, curios, etc.*).

co·lec·ta *f.* collection of voluntary gifts; assessment; collect (*a short prayer of the mass*).

co·lec·ti·vo *adj.* collective; *m. Am.* small bus.

co·lec·tor *m.* collector; water pipe, drain.

co·le·ga *m. & f.* colleague, fellow worker.

co·le·gia·tu·ra *f.* college fellowship or scholarship; *C.A.* tuition in a college.

co·le·gio *m.* boarding school; school, academy; college, body of professional men.

co·le·gir[5,11] *v.* to gather; to conclude, infer.

có·le·ra *f.* anger, rage; *m.* cholera (*disease*).

co·lé·ri·co *adj.* irritable; angry.

co·le·to *m.* leather jacket; one's inner self; *Am.* impudence, shamelessness; **decir para su –** to say to oneself; **echarse al –** to drink down; to devour.

col·ga·de·ro *m.* hanger; hook, peg; hat or clothes rack.

col·ga·du·ra *f.* drape, hanging; drapery; tapestry.

col·gan·te *adj.* hanging; dangling; **puente –** suspension bridge.

col·gar[2,7] *v. irr.* (*suspender*) to hang, suspend; to dangle; to drape (*walls*); (*achacar*) to impute, attribute; *Cuba* to flunk, fail (*a student*); *Col.* **-se** to fall behind.

co·li·brí *m.* hummingbird.

co·li·flor *f.* cauliflower.

co·li·gar·se[7] *v.* league together; band together.

co·li·lla *f.* small tail; butt (*of a cigarette*), stub (*of a cigar*).

co·li·na *f.* hill.

co·lin·dan·te *adj.* contiguous, neighbor-ing, adjacent.

co·lin·dar *v.* to border (on); to adjoining.

co·li·sión *f.* collision, clash.

col·mar *v.* to fill to the brim; **– de** to fill with; to shower with (*gifts, favors, etc.*); **-le a uno el plato** to exhaust. one's patience.

col·me·na *f.* beehive; *Mex.* bee.

col·mi·llo *m.* eyetooth, canine tooth; tusk; fang.

col·mo *m.* overfullness; limit; **– de la locura** height of folly; **¡eso es el –!** that's the limit! *adj.* overfull, filled to the brim.

co·lo·ca·ción *f.* placing, arrangement; position,

job.

co·lo·car[6] *v.* to place; to put in place, arrange; to give employment to.

co·lo·cho *m. C.A.* curly hair; wood shavings.

co·lom·bia·no *adj.* Colombian, of or pertaining to Colombia, South América.

co·lon *m.* colon (*of the large intestine*).

co·lo·nia *f.* colony; silk ribbon; *Mex.*, *Carib.* city district; *Am.* sugar plantation.

co·lo·nia·je *m. Am.* colonial period.

co·lo·nial *adj.* colonial.

co·lo·ni·za·ción *f.* colonization.

co·lo·ni·za·dor *m.* colonizer, colonist; *adj.* colonizing.

co·lo·ni·zar[9] *v.* to colonize.

co·lo·no *m.* colonist, settler; tenant farmer; *Carib.* owner of a sugar plantation; *Am.* bootlicker, flatterer.

co·lo·quio *m.* conversation, talk; literary dialogue; *Col.* street comedy, farce.

co·lor *m.* color; coloring; paint; rouge; **so – de** under the pretext of.

co·lo·ra·ción *f.* coloring.

co·lo·ra·do *adj.* red, reddish; colored: **ponerse –** to blush.

co·lo·ran·te *adj. & m.* coloring.

co·lo·rar *v.* to color; to stain; to dye.

co·lo·re·ar *v.* to color; to redden; to give color to.

co·lo·re·te *m.* rouge.

co·lo·ri·do *m.* coloring; color; *adj.* colored: colorful.

co·lo·sal *adj.* colossal, huge.

co·lum·brar *v.* to see faintly; to glimpse.

co·lum·na *f.* column.

co·lum·piar *v.* to swing; **-se** to swing; to sway.

co·lum·pio *m.* swing.

co·lla·do *m.* hillock, knoll.

co·llar *m.* necklace; dog collar; *Am.* collar (*of a draft horse*); **collera** *f.* collar (*for draft animals*).

co·ma *f.* comma; *m.* coma, stupor, prolonged unconsciousness.

co·ma·dre *f.* (*amiga*) woman friend; (*chismosa*) gossip; (*partera*) midwife; (*alcahueta*) go-between; *name used to express kinship between mother and godmother*; **comadrona** *f.* midwife.

co·ma·dre·ja *f.* weasel.

co·man·dan·cia *f.* command; position and headquarters of a commander.

co·man·dan·te *m.* major; commander.

co·man·dar *v.* to command (*troops*).

co·man·di·ta *f.* silent partnership; **sociedad en –** limited company.

co·man·do *m.* military command.

co·mar·ca *f.* district, region.

com·ba *f.* bulge, warp.

com·bar *v.* to warp, bend, twist; **-se** to warp; to sag; to bulge.

com·ba·te *m.* combat, battle, fight.

com•ba•tien•te *m.* combatant, fighter.

com•ba•tir *v.* to combat; to fight.

com•bi•na•ción *f.* combination.

com•bi•nar *v.* to combine, unite.

com•bu•ren•te *m.* the chemical agent that causes combustion, e.g., oxygen; *adj.* causing combustion.

com•bus•ti•ble *adj.* combustible; *m.* fuel.

com•bus•tión *f.* combustion.

co•me•de•ro *m.* trough (*for feeding animals*); *adj.* edible, eatable.

co•me•dia *f.* comedy; farce.

co•me•dian•te *m.* actor, comedian.

co•me•di•do *adj.* courteous, polite, obliging; *p.p. of* **comedirse**.

co•me•dir•se[5] *v. irr.* to be civil, polite, obliging; *Ec.* to meddler; *Am.* – **a hacer algo** to volunteer to do something.

co•me•dor *m.* dining room; great eater.

co•me•jén *m.* termite.

co•me•lón *m. Am.* big eater. *See* **comilón**.

co•men•da•dor *m.* commander (*of certain military orders*).

co•men•sal *m. & f.* table companion; dinner guest.

co•men•ta•dor *m.* commentator.

co•men•tar *v.* to comment.

co•men•ta•rio *m.* commentary; explanation.

co•men•ta•ris•ta *m. & f.* commentator.

co•men•zar[1,9] *v. irr.* to begin.

co•mer *v.* to eat; to dine; to take (*in chess or checkers*), **dar de** – to feed; **ganar de** – to earn a living; **-se** to eat; to eat up; to skip (*a letter, syllable, word, etc.*); *Ríopl., Col.* **-se uno a otro** to deceive each other.

co•mer•cial *adj.* commercial.

co•mer•cian•te *m.* merchant; storekeeper.

co•mer•ciar *v.* to trade; to have dealings (with).

co•mer•cio *m.* commerce, trade.

co•mes•ti•ble *adj.* edible, eatable; **-s** *m. pl.* food, groceries.

co•me•ta *m.* comet; *C.A.* person seldom seen; *f.* kite.

co•me•ter *v.* to commit; to entrust; to use (*a figure of speech*).

co•me•ti•do *m.* commission, assignment, charge; task, duty.

co•me•zón *f.* itch.

co•mi•cios *m. pl.* primaries, elections.

có•mi•co *adj.* comic, of comedy; comical, funny, amusing; *m.* comedian, actor.

co•mi•da *f.* meal; dinner; good; **comidilla** *f.* small meal; gossip; **la comidilla de la vecindad** the talk of the town.

co•mien•zo *m.* beginning, origin.

co•mi•li•to•na *f.* spread, big feast.

co•mi•lón *m.* big eater.

co•mi•llas *f. pl.* quotation marks.

co•mi•sa•rio *m.* commissary, deputy, delegate;

manager; *Am.* police inspector.

co•mi•sión *f.* commission; committee.

co•mi•sio•na•do *adj.* commissioned, charged, delegated; *m.* commissioner; *Am.* constable.

co•mi•sio•nar *v.* to commission.

co•mis•tra•jo *m.* mess, strange food concoction, mixture.

co•mi•té *m.* committee, commission.

co•mi•ti•va *f.* retinue, group of attendants or followers.

co•mo *adv. & conj.* as, like, such as; if, provided that, since, when; *Mex., Ven.* about, approximately; **¿cómo?** *interr. adv.* how?, what (did you say)?; *Am.* **¡cómo no!** yes, of course!

có•mo•da *f.* bureau, chest of drawers.

co•mo•di•dad *f.* comfort, convenience.

có•mo•do *adj.* comfortable; convenient; *m. Am.* bedpan.

com•pac•to *adj.* compact.

com•pa•de•cer[13] *v. irr.* to pity, sympathize with; **-se con** to be in harmony with; **-se de** to take pity on.

com•pa•draz•go *m.* compaternity (*spiritual affinity between the godfather and the parents of a child*); friendship; relationship; clique, group of friends.

com•pa•dre *m.* (*amigo*) pal, crony, comrade; (*padrino*) cosponsor; *name sted to express kinship between father and godfather*.

com•pa•ñe•ro *m.* companion; partner; mate; **compañerismo** *m.* companionship.

com•pa•ñí•a *f.* company; *Am.* – **del ahorcado** silent companarion, poor company.

com•pa•ra•ción *f.* comparison.

com•pa•rar *v.* to compare.

com•pa•ra•ti•vo *adj.* comparative.

com•pa•re•cer[13] *v. irr.* to appear (*before a judge or tribunal*).

com•par•ti•mien•to *m.* compartment.

com•par•tir *v.* to share; to divide into shares.

com•pás *m.* compass; measure; beat; **llevar el** – to beat time.

com•pa•sión *f.* compassion, pity.

com•pa•si•vo *adj.* compassionate, sympathetic.

com•pa•ti•ble *adj.* compatible, in harmony.

com•pa•trio•ta *m. & f.* compatriot, fellow countryman.

com•pe•ler *v.* to compel, force.

com•pen•diar *v.* to abstract, summarize, condense.

com•pen•dio *m.* summary condensation.

com•pen•sa•ción *f.* compensation; recompense.

com•pen•sar *v.* to balance; to make aqual; to compensate, recompense.

com•pe•ten•cia *f.* competition, rivalry; competente, ability.

com•pe•ten•te *adj.* competent; capable; adequate.

com•pe•ti•dor *m.* competitor; rival; *adj.* competing.

com•pe•tir[5] *v. irr.* to compete, vie.

com•pi•lar *v.* to compile.

com•pin•che *m.* chum, pal, comrade,

com•pla•cen•cia *f.* complacency, satisfaction, contentment.

com•pla•cer[38] *v. irr.* to please, humor; to comply; **-se** to take pleasure or satisfaction (in).

com•pla•cien•te *adj.* obliging, agreeable, willing to please.

com•ple•ji•dad *f.* complexity.

com•ple•jo *adj.* & *m.* complex.

com•ple•men•to *m.* complement; object (*of a verb*).

com•ple•ta•mien•to *m.* completion.

com•ple•tar *v.* to complete; to finish.

com•ple•to *adj.* complete, full, perfect.

com•pli•car[6] *v.* to complicate.

cóm•pli•ce *m.* & *f.* accomplice, companion in crime.

com•plot *m.* plot, conspiracy; intrigue.

com•po•nen•da *f.* adjustment; compro-mise.

com•po•nen•te *adj.* component, constit-uent; *m.* component, essential part.

com•po•ner[40] *v. irr.* to fix, repair; to fix up; to adorn, trim; to compose; to set up (*type*); to settle (*a dispu-te*); *Col.* to set (*bones*).

com•por•ta•mien•to *m.* conduct, behavior.

com•po•si•ción *f.* composition; settlement.

com•po•si•tor *m.* composer.

com•pos•tu•ra *f.* (*arreglo*) repair; settlement, adjustment; (*aseo*) neatness, composition; (*dignidad*) composure, dignity.

com•po•ta *f.* fruit preserves; **– de manzana** appleasauce.

com•pra *f.* purchase; buying; **ir de -s** to go shopping.

com•pra•dor *m.* buyer, purchaser.

com•prar *v.* to buy, purchaser.

com•pra•dor *m.* buyer, purchaser.

com•prar *v.* to buy, purchase.

com•pren•der *v.* to understand, grasp, comprehend; to comprise, embrace.

com•pren•si•ble *adj.* comprehensible, understandable.

com•pren•sión *f.* understanding; comprehension; keenness.

com•pren•si•vo *adj.* comprehensive; undeastanding.

com•pre•sión *f.* compression.

com•pre•sor *m.* compressor.

com•pri•mir *v.* to compress; to repress.

com•pro•ba•ción *f.* confirmation, check proof, test.

com•pro•ban•te *adj.* proving, verifying; *m.* proof; evidence; certificate; voucher; warrant.

com•pro•bar[2] *v. irr.* to verify; to check; to prove.

com•pro•me•ter *v.* (*exponer*) to compro-mise; to endanger; to bind; to force; (*concordar*) to come to an agreement; **-se** to promise, bind oneself; to become engaged; to compromise oneself.

com•pro•mi•so *m.* (*convenio*) compromise; (*obligación*) engagement; appointment; (*dificultad*) predicament, trouble.

com•puer•ta *f.* sluice (*gate to control the flow of water*), floodgate.

com•pues•to *p.p. of* **componer** & *adj.* repaired; fixed, adorned; composed; composite; compound; *m.* composite; compound.

com•pun•gir•se[11] *v.* to feel regret or remorse.

com•pu•ta•do•ra e•lec•tró•ni•ca *f.* electronic computer.

com•pu•tar *v.* to compute, calculate.

cóm•pu•to *m.* computation, calculation.

co•mul•gar[7] *v.* to commune, take communion.

co•mún *adj.* common; **por lo –** generally; *m.* toilet; **el – de las gentes** the majority of the people; the average person.

co•mu•ne•ro *adj.* common, popular; *Am.* pertaining to a community; *m.* commoner (*one of the common people*); *Col., Ven. Andes* member of an Indian community.

co•mu•ni•ca•ción *f.* communication.

co•mu•ni•car[6] *v.* to communicate; to notify; **-se** to communicate; to correspond; to be in touch (with); to connect.

co•mu•ni•ca•ti•vo *adj.* communicative, talkative.

co•mu•ni•dad *f.* community; common-wealth; the common people; commonness; guild.

co•mu•nión *f.* communion; political party.

co•mu•nis•mo *m.* communism; **comunista** *m.* & *f.* communist; *adj.* communistic, communist.

con *prep.* with; **– ser** in spite of being; **– tal que** provided that; **– todo** however.

con•ca•vi•dad *f.* hollow, cavity; hollowness.

cón•ca•vo *adj.* concave, hollow.

con•ce•bi•ble *adj.* conceivable.

con•ce•bir[5] *v. irr.* to conceive; to imagine; to understand, grasp.

con•ce•der *v.* to concede, grant; to admit.

con•ce•jal *m.* councilman, alderman.

con•cen•tra•ción *f.* concentration.

con•cen•trar *v.* to concentrate.

con•cep•ción *f.* conception.

con•cep•to *m.* concept, idea, thought.

con•cer•nir[51] *v. irr.* to concern.

con•cer•tar[1] *v. irr.* (*arreglar*) to arrange, plan, settle; to conclude (*a treaty or business deal*); (*concordar*) to harmonize; to agree.

con•ce•sión *f.* concession, grant; granting; acknowledgment.

con•cien•cia *f.* conscience.

con•cien•zu•do *adj.* conscientious.

con•cier•to *m.* concert; harmony; agreement; **de –** by common agreement.

con•ci•liar *v.* to conciliate, win over; to reconcile, bring into harmony; **– el sueño** to get to sleep.

con•ci•lio *m.* council.

con•ci•sion *f.* conciseness, brevity.

con•ci•so *adj.* concise, brief.

con•ciu•da•da•no *m.* fellow citizen, fellow countryman.

oon•cluir³² *v. irr* to conclude, finish; to infer.

con•clu•sión *f.* conclusion.

con•cor•dan•cia *f.* concord, agreement, harmony.

con•cor•dar² *v. irr.* to agree; to be in harmony; to put in harmony.

con•cor•dia *f.* concord, harmony, agreement.

con•cre•tar *v.* to summarize, condense; to limit; **-se a** to limit oneself to.

con•cre•to *adj.* concrete, real, specific; **en –** concretely; to sum up; *m. Am.* concrete.

con•cu•pis•cen•te *adj.* sensual.

con•cu•rren•cia *f.* gathering, audience; concurrence, simultaneous meeting or happening; competition.

con•cu•rri•do *adj.* well-patronized, wellattended, much frequented.

con•cu•rrir *v.* to concur, meet together; to happen at the same time or place; to attend; to agree.

con•cur•so *m.* gathering; contest; competitive examination; assistance.

con•cha *f.* shell; shellfish; prompter's box; *Mex.* **te-ner –** to be indifferent unruffled, tough.

con•cha•bar *v.* to unite, join; *Mex., S.A.* to hire (*labor*); **-se** to join, gang together; to conspire; *Riopl.* to hire oneself out, get a job.

con•cha•bo *m. Am.* hiring of a laborer or servant; *Riopl.* job, menial job.

con•de *m.* count; **condesa** *f.* countess.

con•de•co•ra•ción *f.* decoration; badge, medal.

con•de•co•rar *v.* to decorate (*with a badge or medal*).

con•de•na *f.* term in prison, sentence, penalty.

con•de•na•ción *f.* condemnation; conviction (*of a prisoner or criminal*); damnation.

con•de•nar *v.* to condemn; to sentence; *Am.* to annoy, irritate; **-se** to be damned, go to hell.

con•den•sar *v.* to condense.

con•des•cen•den•cia *f.* condescension, patronizing attitude.

con•des•cen•der¹ *v. irr.* to condescend; to condescenden; to comply, yield.

con•di•ción *f.* condition.

con•di•men•tar *v.* to season.

con•di•men•to *m.* condiment, seasoning.

con•dis•cí•pu•lo *m.* schoolmate, classmate.

con•do•ler•se² *v. irr.* to condole (with), sympathize (with), be sorry (for).

cón•dor *m. Am.* condor, vulture; *Am.* gold coin of Ecuador, Chile and Colombia.

con•du•cir²⁵ *v. irr.* to conduct, lead; to drive (*an auto*); **-se** to behave, act.

con•duc•ta *f.* conduct; behavior; convoy, escort; management.

con•duc•to *m.* conduit, pipe, channel; **por – de** through.

con•duc•tor *adj.* conducting; *m.* leader; chauffeur; guide; conductor (*electrical*); *Am.* conductor, ticket collector (*on trains, buses, streetcars*); *Am.* teamster, driver.

co•nec•tar *v.* to connect.

co•ne•je•ra *f.* burrow; rabbit warren (*piece of land for breeding rabbits*); den, joint, dive (*of ill repute*).

co•ne•jo *m.* rabbit; *Am.* guinea pig; **conejillo de Indias** guinea pig.

co•ne•xión *f.* connection.   •

co•ne•xo *adj.* connected; coherent.

con•fec•ción *f.* making; confection; manufactured article; workmanship; concoction, compound.

con•fec•cio•nar *v.* to make; to manufacture; to mix, put up (*a prescription*).

con•fe•de•ra•ción *f.* confederation, alliance, league.

con•fe•de•rar *v.* to confederate; **-se** to confederate, form into a confederacy

con•fe•ren•cia *f.* lecture; conference, meeting.

con•fe•ren•cian•te *m. & f.* lecturer.

con•fe•ren•cis•ta *m. & f.* lecturer.

con•fe•rir³ *v. irr.* to confer; to give, bestow.

con•fe•sar¹ *v. irr.* to confess.

con•fe•sión *f.* confession.

con•fe•sio•na•rio *m.* confessional, confessional box.

con•fe•sor *m.* confessor.

con•fia•do *adj.* confident, trusting, cre-dulous; presumptuous, sef-confident.

con•fian•za *f.* confidence, trust; familiarrity; informality, **reunión de –** informal gathering or party.

con•fian•zu•do *adj.* over-friendly, over-familiar; *Am.* meddlesome.

con•fiar¹⁷ *v.* to confide, entrust; to trust, hope firmly.

con•fi•den•cia *f.* confidence, trust; secret, confidential remark; **confidencial** *adj.* confidential.

con•fi•den•te *m.* confidant; spy, secret agent; settee or sofa for two people, love seat; *adj.* faithful, trustworthy.

con•fín *m.* limit, border, boundary; *adj.* bordering, limiting.

con•fi•nar *v.* to border (upon); to confine, exile to a specific place.

con•fir•ma•ción *f.* confirmation.

con•fir•mar *v.* to confirm.

con•fis•car[6] v. to confiscate.

con•fi•tar v. to candy (*with sugar syrup*); to make into candy or preserves; to sweeten.

con•fi•te m. candy, bonbon; **confitería** f. confectionery; candy shop; **confitura** f. confection.

con•flic•to m. conflict.

con•fluen•cia f. junction (*of two rivers*).

con•for•mar v. to adapt, adjust; **-se** to conform, comply, to agree; to be resigned (to); to be satisfied.

con•for•me adj. in agreement; resigned, satisfied; alike, similar; **– a** in accordance with.

con•for•mi•dad f. conformity; agreement, harmony; compliance; **– con la voluntad de Dios** resignation to the will of God; **en – con** in compliance with; **estar de – con** to be in accordance or agreement with.

con•for•tar v. to comfort, console.

con•fra•ter•ni•dad f. brotherhood.

con•fron•tar v. to confront; to face; to compare, check.

con•fun•dir v. to confound, confuse, mix up; to bewilder; to shame.

con•fu•sión f. confusion.

con•fu•so adj. confused, bewildered; blurred; vague.

con•ge•la•do p.p. & adj. frozen; icy.

con•ge•lar v. to congeal, freeze.

con•ge•nial adj. congenial.

con•ge•niar v. to be congenial (with); to harmonize, be in harmony (with).

con•go•ja f. anguish, grief, anxiety.

con•gra•tu•lar v. to congratulate.

con•gre•ga•ción f. congregation, assembly; religious fraternity.

con•gre•gar[7] v. to congregate, call together; to assemble; **-se** to congregate, assemble.

con•gre•sis•ta m. congressman; f. congresswoman.

con•gre•so m. congress, assembly; **– de los Diputados** House of Representatives.

con•je•tu•ra f. conjecture, guess, surmise.

con•je•tu•rar v. to conjecture, guess, surmise.

con•ju•ga•ción f. conjugation; coupling, joining together.

con•ju•gar[7] v. to conjugate.

con•jun•ción f. conjunction: union, com-bination.

con•jun•to m. total, whole, entirety; **en –** jas a whole; adj. joined; related, allied.

con•ju•ra•ción f. conspiracy; plot.

con•ju•ra•do m. conspirator.

con•ju•rar v. to conspire, plot; to join a conspiracy; to entreat; to conjure, to ward off.

con•me•mo•rar v. to commemorate.

con•me•mo•ra•ti•vo adj. memorial, serving to commemorate.

con•mi•go with me.

con•mi•na•ción f. threat.

con•mi•na•to•rio adj. threatening.

con•mo•ción f. commotion.

con•mo•ve•dor adj. moving, touching; stirring.

con•mo•ver[2] v. irr. to move, touch, affect (*with emotion*); to stir (*emotions*).

con•mu•ta•dor m. electric switch; **cuadro –** switchboard.

con•na•tu•ral adj. inborn.

co•no m. cone; pine cone.

co•no•ce•dor adj. knowing, aware, expert; m. connoisseur, judge, expert; **ser – de** to be judge of.

co•no•cer[13] v. irr. (*tener idea de*) to know, be acquainted with; to recognize; (*llegar a conocer*) to meet; **se conoce que** it is clear or evident that.

co•no•ci•do p.p. & adj. known; wellknown; m. acquaintance.

co•no•ci•mien•to m. (*inteligencia*) knowledge, understanding; acquaintance; (*documento*) bill of lading; **-s** knowledge, learning; **poner en –** to inform.

con•que conj. so then, well then, and so.

con•quis•ta f. conquest.

con•quis•ta•dor m. conqueror; adj. conquering, victorious.

con•quis•tar v. to conquer, defeat; to win.

con•sa•bi•do adj. aforementioned, aforesaid.

con•sa•gra•ción f. consecration.

con•sa•grar v. to consecrate.

cons•cien•cia f. consciousness.

cons•cien•te adj. conscious.

con•se•cu•ción f. attainment.

con•se•cuen•cia f. consequence; result; **a – de** as a result of; **por** (*or* **en**) **–** therefore; consequently.

con•se•cuen•te adj. consequent, logical; consistent; m. consequence, result.

con•se•cu•ti•vo adj. consecutive, successive.

con•se•guir[5,12] v. irr. to get, obtain; to reach, attain.

con•se•ja f. old wives' tale, fable.

con•se•je•ro m. adviser, counselor.

con•se•jo m. counsel, advice; council; council hall.

con•sen•ti•mien•to m. consent.

con•sen•tir[3] v. to consent, permit; to pamper, spoil.

con•ser•je m. janitor, caretaker.

con•ser•va f. preserve; pickled fruit or vegetables; *Ch.* filling (*for tarts or candy*).

con•ser•va•ción f. conservation.

con•ser•va•dor m. conservative; preserver; guardian: adj. conservative.

con•ser•var v. to conserve, keep; to preserve.

con•si•de•ra•ble adj. considerable.

con•si•de•ra•ción f. consideration.

con•si•de•ra•do adj. considerate, thought-ful; respected; prudent.

con•si•de•rar v. to considerar; to treat with consideration.

con•sig•na f. watchword, password; *Am.* checkroom.

con•sig•nar v. to consign; to deliver; to deposit; to assign; to check (*baggage*).

con•si•go with oneself; with himself (herself, themselves).

con•si•guien•te adj. consequent; m. consequence; **por** – consequently.

con•sis•ten•te adj. firm, substantial.

con•sis•tir v. to consist; to be based on; **¿en qué consiste?** why? what is the explanation for it?

con•so•cio m. associate, partner.

con•so•la•ción f. consolation.

con•so•lar² v. irr. to console, cheer.

con•so•li•dar v. to consolidate, make solid; to unite, combine.

con•so•nan•te m. perfect rhyme; f. consonant; adj. in harmony.

con•sor•te m. & f. consort; mate; companion.

cons•pi•cuo adj. conspicuous.

cons•pi•ra•ción f. conspiracy; plot.

cons•pi•ra•dor m. conspirator, plotter.

cons•pi•rar v. to conspire, plot.

cons•tan•cia f. (*firmeza*) constancy; perseverance; (*certeza*) evidence, certainty; *Am.* documentary proof, record.

cons•tan•te adj. constant; continual; firm, faithful.

cons•tar v. to be evident, clear; to consist (of), be composed (of); to be on record.

cons•ta•ta•ción f. *Am.* proof, check, evidence.

cons•te•la•ción f. constellation.

cons•ti•pa•do adj. suffering from a cold; m. cold in the head.

cons•ti•par v. to stop up (*the nasal passages*); to cause a cold; **-se** to catch cold.

cons•ti•tu•ción f. constitution.

cons•ti•tu•cio•nal adj. constitutional.

cons•ti•tuir³² v. irr. to constitute, form; to set up, establish; **-se en** to set oneself up as.

cons•ti•tu•ti•vo = **constituyente.**

cons•ti•tu•yen•te adj. constituent.

cons•tre•ñir[5,19] v. irr. to constrain; to compel, oblige.

cons•truc•ción f. construction; structure; building.

cons•truir³² v. irr. to construct, build.

con•sue•lo m. consolation, comfort; relief; cheer.

con•sue•tu•di•na•rio adj. habitual, cus-tomary; **derecho** – common law.

cón•sul m. consul.

con•su•la•do m. consulate.

con•sul•ta f. consultation, opinion.

con•sul•tar v. to consult.

con•sul•to•rio m. office for consultation; doctor's office or clinic.

con•su•ma•do p.p. of **consumar**; adj. con-summate, perfecto, complet; accomplished.

con•su•mar v. to consummate, complete.

con•su•mi•dor m. consumer; adj. consuming.

con•su•mir v. to consume; to waste; **-se** to be consumed; to burn out; to be exhausted; to waste away.

con•su•mo m. consumption (*of food, provisions, etc.*)

con•sun•ción f. consumptiom (*illness*).

con•ta•bi•li•dad f. accounting; book-keeping.

con•tac•to m. contact.

con•ta•do: **al** – in cash; **de** – immediately; **por de** – of course; **contados** adj. few, scarce, rare.

con•ta•dor m. accountant; purser, cashier; counter; meter (*for water, gas, or electricity*); – **geiger** Geiger counter; Geiger-Müller counter.

con•ta•du•rí•a f. accountant's or auditor's office; box office; cashier's office; accounting.

con•ta•giar v. to infect; to corrupt; to con-taminate.

con•ta•gio m. contagion; infection.

con•ta•gio•so adj. contagious; infectious.

con•ta•mi•nar v. to contaminate, defile; to corrupt.

con•tar² v. irr. to count; to tell, relate; – **con** to count on, rely on; **a** – **desde** starting from, beginning with.

con•tem•pla•ción f. contemplation; gazing; meditation.

con•tem•plar v. to contemplate, gaze at; to examine; to meditate.

con•tem•po•rá•ne•o adj. contemporary.

con•ten•der¹ v. irr. to contend, fight, to compete.

con•te•ner[45] v. irr. to contain; to restrain, check; **-se** to refrain; to restrain oneself.

con•te•ni•do m. contents; adj. restrained, moderate.

con•ten•ta•mien•to m. contentment, joy.

con•ten•tar v. to give pleasure, make happy; **-se** to be satisfied, pleased; *Am.* to make up, renew friendship.

con•ten•to adj. content, contented, satisfied, glad; m. gladness, contentment.

con•te•ra f. metal tip (*of a cane, umbrella, etc.*); tip, end; refrain of a song; **por** – as a finishing touch.

con•ter•tu•lio m. fellow-member.

con•tes•ta•ción f. answer, reply; argument.

con•tes•tar v. to answer, reply.

con•tex•tu•ra f. texture, composition; structure (*of animal or vegetable tissues*).

con•tien•da f. fight; dispute; contest.

con•ti•go with you (with thee).

con•ti•guo adj. contiguous, next, neighboring.

con•ti•nen•tal adj. continental.

con•ti•nen•te m. continent; countenance; adj. continent, moderate, sober.

con•tin•gen•cia f. contingency, possibility; risk.

con•tin•gen•te adj. continget, accidental; m. quota; military contingent.

con•ti•nua•ción f. continuation; continance; **a** – below, as follows.

con•ti•nuar[18] v. to continue; to last.

con•ti•nui•dad f. continuity.

con•ti•nuo adj. continuous, connected; continual;

steady, constant.

con•to•ne•ar•se *v.* to strut, swagger; to waddle.

con•to•ne•o *m.* strut; waddle.

con•tor•no *m.* (*circuito*) environs, surrounding country (*usually used in plural*); (*línea*) contour, outline.

con•tra *prep.* against; **el pro y el** – the pro and con; *f.* opposition; *Am.* antidore, remedy; **-s** *Am.* play-off, final game (*to determine the winner*); **llevar a uno la** – to contradict a person, take the opposite view.

con•tra•al•mi•ran•te *m.* rear admiral.

con•tra•ba•jo *m.* bass fiddle, string bass.

con•tra•ban•de•ar *v.* to smuggle.

con•tra•ban•dis•ta *m.* smuggler.

con•tra•ban•do *m.* contraband; smuggled goods; smuggling.

con•trac•ción *f.* contraction; *Ch. Peru* diligence, application, devotion.

con•tra•de•cir[27] *v. irr.* to contradict.

con•tra•dic•ción *f.* contradiction.

con•tra•dic•to•rio *adj* contradictory, contrary, opposing.

con•tra•di•cho *p.p. of* **contradecir**.

con•tra•er[46] *v. irr.* to contract; – **matrimonio** to get married; **-se** to shrink; to contract.

con•tra•fuer•te *m.* buttress; spur (*of a mountain*); **-s** secondary chain of mountains.

con•tra•ha•cer[31] *v. irr.* to counterfeit; to forge; to copy, imitate; to mimic.

con•tra•he•cho *p.p. of* **contrahacer** & *adj.* counterfeit; forged; deformed.

con•tra•lor *m. Am.* controller or comptroller (*of accounts or expenditures*). *See* **controlador.**

con•tra•or•den *f.* countermand; cancellation of an order.

con•tra•pe•lo; a – against the grain.

con•tra•pe•sar *v.* to counterbalance, balance; to off-set.

con•tra•pe•so *m.* counterpoise, counter-weight, counterbalance; *Am.* fear, uneasiness.

con•tra•riar[17] *v.* to oppose; to contradict; to irritate, vex.

con•tra•rie•dad *f.* opposition; contra-diction; bother, irritation; disappointment.

con•tra•rio *adj.* contrary; opposite; *m.* opponent.

con•tra•rres•tar *v.* to counteract; to resist, oppose; to strike back (*a ball*).

con•tra•se•ña *f.* password, watchword; mark; check (*for baggage*); – **de salida** theatre check (*to re-enter during the performance*).

con•tras•tar *v.* (*contrapesar*) to contrast; to test (*scales, weights, measures, etc.*); to assay (*metals*); (*resistir*) to resist, oppose.

con•tras•te *m.* contrast; assay, test; assayer, tester; assayer's office.

con•tra•ta *f.* contract, bargain, agreement.

con•tra•tar *v.* to contract for; to trade; to engage, hire (*men*); **-se** to come to, or make, an agreement.

con•tra•tiem•po *m.* accident, mishap.

con•tra•tis•ta *m. & f.* contractor.

con•tra•to *m.* contract.

con•tra•ven•ta•na *f.* shutter.

con•tri•bu•ción *f.* contribution; tax.

con•tri•buir[32] *v. irr.* to contribute.

con•tri•bu•yen•te *m.* contributor; taxpayer; *adj.* contributing.

con•trol *m. Am.* control.

con•tro•la•dor *m. Am.* controller.

con•tro•lar *v. Am.* to control.

con•tro•ver•sia *f.* controversy.

con•tu•ma•cia *f.* stubbornness, obstinacy; contempt of court, failure to appear in court; rebelliousness.

con•tu•maz *adj.* stubborn; rebellious.

con•tu•sión *f.* bruise.

con•va•le•cer[13] *v. irr.* to convalesce, recover from an illness.

con•ve•ci•no *adj.* near, neighboring; *m.* neighbor.

con•ven•ce•dor *adj.* convincing.

con•ven•cer[10] *v.* to convince.

con•ven•ci•mien•to *m.* conviction, belief; convincing.

con•ven•ción *f.* convention, assembly; pact, agreement; *Ríopl., Col., Ven., Mex., Carib.* political convention; **convencional** *adj.* conventional.

con•ve•ni•do *adj.* agreed; O.K., all right; *p.p. of* **convenir**.

con•ve•nien•cia *f.* convenience; comfort; utility, profit.

con•ve•nien•te *adj.* convenient, useful, profitable; fit, proper, suitable; opportune.

con•ve•nio *m.* pact, agreement.

con•ve•nir[48] *v. irr.* to agree; to convene, assemble; to be suitable, proper, advisable; to suit, fit; **-se** to agree.

con•ven•ti•llo *m. Ríopl., Ch.* tenement house.

con•ven•to *m.* convent.

con•ver•gen•te *adj.* convergent, coming together.

con•ver•ger[11], con•ver•gir[11] *v.* to converge.

con•ver•sa•ción *f.* conversation.

con•ver•sar *v.* to converse.

con•ver•sión *f.* conversion.

con•ver•tir[3] *v. irr.* to convert.

con•vic•ción *f.* conviction.

con•vic•to *p.p. irr. of* **convencer**; con-victed, guilty.

con•vi•da•do *m.* guest; *Am.* – **y con ollita** guest who abuses hospitality.

con•vi•dar *v.* to invite; **-se** to volunteer one's services; to invite oneself.

con•vin•cen•te *adj.* convincing.

con•vi•te *m.* invitation; banquet.

con•vo•ca•ción *f.* convocation.

con•vo•car[6] *v.* to convoke, call together.

con•vo•yar v. to convoy, escort.

con•vul•sión f. convulsion.

con•vul•si•vo adj. convulsive; **tos convulsiva** whooping cough.

con•yu•gal adj. conjugal, pertaining to marriage or a married couple; **vida** – married life.

cón•yu•ge m. husband; f. wife.

co•o•pe•ra•ción f. cooperation.

co•o•pe•ra•dor adj. cooperating, coopera-tive; m. cooperate, co-worker.

co•o•pe•rar v. to cooperate.

co•o•pe•ra•ti•vo adj. cooperative; **cooperativa** f. cooperative, cooperative society.

co•or•di•na•ción f. coordination.

co•or•di•nar v. to coordinate.

co•pa f. (vaso) goblet; (de árbol) treetop; (de sombrero) crown; (palo de la baraja) card in the suit of copas (Spanish deck of cards); Am. **empinar la** – to drink, get drunk.

co•par•tí•ci•pe adj. participant; m. & f. joint partner.

co•pe•te m. tuft; crest; top, summit; ornamental top on furniture; **de** – of high rank, important; proud; **estar uno hasta el** – to be stuffed; to be fed up; **tener mucho** – to be arrogant, haughty.

co•pia f. copy; imitation; abundance.

co•piar v. to copy.

co•pio•so adj. copious, abundant.

co•pi•ta f. little glass; little drink.

co•pla f. couplet; stanza (of variable length and meter); popular song.

co•po m. (de nieve) snowflake; (mechón) wad, tuft (of wool or cotton).

co•que•ta f. coquette, flirt.

co•que•te•ar v. to flirt.

co•que•te•rí•a f. coquetry, flirting.

co•ra•je m. courage, valor; anger.

co•ral m. coral; Am. red poisonous snake; **-es** coral beads; adj. choral, pertaining to a choir; **coralino** adj. coral, like coral.

co•ra•za f. cuirass, armor; armor plate or plating; shell (of a turtle).

co•ra•zón m. heart; core, center.

co•ra•zo•na•da f. presentiment, foreboding; hunch.

cor•ba•ta f. necktie; cravat; Am. colorful kerchief, scarf.

cor•cel m. charger, steed.

cor•co•va f. hump, hunch; **corcovado** adj. hunchbacked; m. hunchback.

cor•co•ve•ar v. to prance about, leap; Am. to kick, protest against.

cor•che•te m. hook and eye.

cor•cho m. cork; beehive; adj. Am. corklike, spongy.

cor•del m. cord, rope.

cor•de•ro m. lamb; lambskin.

cor•dial adj. codial, friendly; **dedo** – middle finger.

cor•dia•li•dad f. cordiality, friendliness, warmth.

cor•di•lle•ra f. mountain range.

cor•do•bés adj. Cordovan, of or pertaining to Cordova; m. native of Cordova.

cor•dón m. cord; braid; cordon, line of soldiers; Ríopl. – **de la acera** curb, curbstone of the sidewalk; **cordonería** f. lace or cord maker's shop; collection of cords and laces; cordmaker's work; braiding.

cor•don•ci•llo m. small cord, drawstring, lace, lacing; braid; mill (ridged edge of a coin); ridge, rib (of certain fabrics).

cor•du•ra f. good judgment, wisdom; sanity.

cor•na•da f. goring; butt with the horns; **dar -s** to gore, horn, butt with the horns.

cor•ne•ta f. cornet; bugle; horn; m. bubler.

cor•ni•sa f. cornice.

co•ro m. choir; chorus.

co•ro•na f. crown; wreath.

co•ro•nar v. to crown; to top.

co•ro•nel m. colonel.

co•ro•ni•lla f. small crown; crown of the head; **estar uno hasta la** – to be fed up, be satiated.

cor•pan•chón m. large body; carcass.

cor•pi•ño m. bodice.

cor•po•ra•ción f. corporation.

cor•po•ral adj. corporal, of the body; m. corporal (small piece of linen used at Mass).

cor•pó•re•o adj. corporeal, bodily; tangible, material.

cor•pu•len•to adj. corpulent, fat, stout.

co•rral m. yard; corral, cattle yard; **corralón** m. large corral; Am. lumber warehouse.

co•rre•a f. leather strap; resistance; Ch. **-s** leather blanket carrier; Am. **tener muchas -s** to be phlegmatic, calm.

co•rrec•ción f. correction; correctness.

co•rrec•to adj. correct, proper.

co•rre•di•zo adj. sliding, slipping; **nudo** – slip knot.

co•rre•dor m. (que corre) runner, racer; (pasillo) corridor; gallery around a patio; (revendedor) broker; Carib., Andes covered porch; Am. beater of wild game; adj. running; speedy.

co•rre•gi•dor m. corrector; Spanish magistrate.

co•rre•gir[5,11] v. irr. to correct; to reprove; to punish; **-se** to mend one's ways.

co•rren•ta•da f. Ch., Ríopl., C.A., Carib. strong river current.

co•rre•o m. mail; mail service; postman; post office; – **aéreo** air mail.

co•rre•ón m. large strap.

co•rre•o•so adj. flexible; leathery, tough; **correosidad** f. toughness; flexibility.

co•rrer v. (caminar) to run; to blow (said of the wind); (encarrera) to race; to chase; (pasar) to pass, elapse (time); to draw (a curtain); Am. to dismiss, throw out, **-se** to slip through; to slide; to be embarrassed.

co•rre•rí•a *f.* foray, raid for plunder; excursión, short trip; **-s** wanderings, travels; raids.

co•rres•pon•den•cia *f.* correspondence; letters, mail; agreement; interchage.

co•rres•pon•der *v.* to reciprocate, return (*love, favors*);to belong; to concern; to correspond (*one thing with another*).

co•rres•pon•dien•te *adj.* corresponding, agreeing; respective; *m.* correspondent.

co•rres•pon•sal *m.* correspondent; agent; newspaper reporter.

co•rre•te•ar *v.* to run around; to roam, rove; *Am.* to pursue, chase.

co•rri•da *f.* race; *Ch.* row, file; *P.R.*, night spree; *Am.* beating up of game; **– del tiempo** swiftness of time; **– de toros** bullfight; **de** – without stopping.

co•rri•do *adj.* embarrassed, ashamed; worldly-wise; flowing, fluent; **de** – without stopping; *Mex.*, *Col.*, *Ven.*, *Riopl.*, *Andes* popular ballad.

co•rrien•te *adj.* (*que corre*) running; flowing, fluent; (*común*) usual, common, ordinary; *Am.* frank, open, ¡–! all right! O.K.!; **el ocho del** – the eighth of the current month; **estar al** – to be up-to-date; to be well-informed (*about current news*); **poner a uno al** – to keep someone posted or well informed; *f.* current; flow; course; *Am.* **hay que llevarle la** –one must humor him.

co•rri•llo *m.* circle or group of gossipers.

co•rro *m.* group of takers or spectators.

co•rro•er[81] *v. irr.* to corrode.

co•rrom•per *v.* to corrupt; to seduce; to bribe; **-se** to rot; to become corrupted.

co•rrom•pi•do *adj.* corrupt; rotten, spoiled; degenerate; *p.p.* of **corromper**.

co•rrup•ción *f.* corruption.

co•rrup•to *adj.* corrupt, rotten.

cor•sé *m.* corset.

cor•ta•da *f. Col.*, *Ven.*, *Carib.* cut, slash.

cor•ta•dor *m.* cutter.

cor•ta•du•ra *m.* cut; gash; slash.

cor•tan•te *adj.* cutting; sharp.

cor•ta•plu•mas *m.* penknife.

cor•tar *v.* to cut; to cut off; to cut out; to cut our; to cut down; to interrupt; *Ven.* to harvest, pick (*fruit*); to gossip, speak ill of someone; **-se** to be embarrassed, ashamed; to sour, curdle (*said of milk*); *Am.* to become separated; cut off; *Mex.*, Cuba to leave in a hurry; *Am.* to die.

cor•te *m.* cut; cutting edge; fit, style; *Carib.*, *Mex.*, *Riopl.* cut (*in cards*); *Am.* harvest; *Am.* weeding; *Am.* gracefulness in dancing; *f.* royal court; retinue; *P.R.*, *Ven.* court of justice; **-s** Spanish parliament; **hacer la** – to court , woo; *Am.* **darse un** – to put on airs.

cor•te•dad *f.* smallness; timidity; bashfulness, shyness.

cor•te•jar *v.* to court, woo.

cor•te•jo *m.* cortege, procession; retinue; courtship; suitor.

cor•tés *adj.* courteous, polite.

cor•te•sa•na *f.* courtesan, prostitute.

cor•te•sa•no *m.* courtier; *adj.* courtlike; courteous.

cor•te•sí•a *f.* courtesy, politeness.

cor•te•za *f.* bark; crust; peel.

cor•ti•jo *m.* farmhouse.

cor•ti•na *m.* curtain.

cor•to *adj.* short; scanty; bashful.

cor•ve•ta *f.* buck, leap, bound (*of a horse*); **hacer -s** to prance.

cor•vo *adj. see* **curvo**.

co•sa *f.* thing; **– de** approximately, aboud; **no es** – it is not worth anything; **otra** – something else; **como si tal** – serene, as if nothing had happened; *Am.* **ni por una de estas nueve -s** absolutely not, not for anything in the world.

co•se•cha *f.* crop; harvest.

co•se•char *v.* to reap; to harvest.

co•ser *v.* to sew; to stitch.

cos•mé•ti•co *m. & adj.* cosmetic.

cos•qui•llas *f. pl.* ticklishness; tickling; **hacer–** to tickle; to excite (*one's desire or curiosity*); **tener –** to be ticklish.

cos•qui•lle•ar *v.* to tickle; to excite (*one's curiosity or desire*).

cos•qui•lle•o *m.* tickle, tickling sensation.

cos•qui•llo•so *adj.* ticklish; touchy.

cos•ta *f.* coast; cost, expense, price; **a toda** – at all costs, by all means.

cos•ta•do *m.* side; flank.

cos•tal *m.* sack; **estar hecho un – de huesos** to be nothing but skin and bones; to be very thin.

cos•ta•ne•ro *adj.* coastal, relating to a coast; sloping.

cos•tar[2] *v. irr.* to cost; **– trabajo** to be difficult.

cos•ta•rri•cen•se *adj.*, *m. & f.* Costa Rican.

cos•te, cos•to *m.* cost; expense.

cos•te•ar *v.* (*pagar*) to defray or pay costs; to pay, be profitable; (*pasar junto a*) to navigate along the coast; to go along the edge of; **no costea** it does not pay.

cos•te•ro *adj.* coastal; **navegación costera** coastal navigation.

cos•ti•lla *f.* rib; chop, cutlet.

cos•to•so *adj.* costly, expensive.

cos•tra *f.* crust; scab.

cos•tro•so *adj.* crusty; scabby.

cos•tum•bre *f.* custom, habit.

cos•tu•ra *f.* sewing; stitching; seam.

cos•tu•re•ra *f.* seamstress.

cos•tu•re•ro *m.* sewing table or cabinet; sewing box; sewing room.

cos•tu•rón *m.* coarse stitching; large seam; patch, mend; big scar.

co•te•jar *v.* to confront, compare.

co•te•jo *m.* comparison.

co•ten•se *m. Ch., Mex.* burlap.

co•ti•dia•no *adj.* daily.

co•ti•za•ble *adj.* quotable (*price*).

co•ti•za•ción *f.* quottion of prices; current price.

co•ti•zar[9] *v.* to quote (*prices*); *Ch.* to con-tribute one's share or quota; *Am.* to prorate, distribute proportionally.

co•to *m.* enclosure; landmark; limitation; limit, boundary; **poner – a** to set a limit to; to put an end to.

co•to•rra *f.* small parrot; magpie; talkative person, chatterbox.

co•to•rre•ar *v.* to chatter; to gossip.

co•va•cha *f.* small cave; grotto; *Mex., Cuba, Andes* hut, shanty; *Col.* cubbyhole, small dark room.

co•yo•te *m. Am.* coyote, prairie wolf; *Mex.* shyster, tricky; lawyer; *C.A.* agent, broker (*often illegal*).

co•yun•tu•ra *f.* joint; articulation; occasion; precise moment.

coz *f.* kick; recoil of a gun; gutt of a firearm; **dar (or tirar) coces** to kick.

crá•ne•o *m.* cranium, skull.

cra•so *adj.* fat; thick, coarse, gross; **ignorancia cra-sa** gross ignorance.

crá•ter *m.* crater of a volcano.

cre•a•ción *f.* creation.

cre•a•dor *m.* creator; *adj.* creating, creative.

cre•ar *v.* to create.

cre•cer[13] *v. irr.* to grow; to increase; **-se** to swell (*as a river*); to become or feel important.

cre•ci•da *f.* river flood.

cre•ci•do *adj.* grown, increased; large; swollen.

cre•cien•te *adj.* growing, increasing; crescent (*moon*); *f.* river flood; *m.* crescent.

cre•ci•mien•to *m.* growth, increase.

cre•den•cia•les *f. pl.* credentials.

cré•di•to *m.* credit; credence, belief; fame, reputation; letter of redit; **dar a –** to loan on credit.

cre•do *m.* creed; **en un –** in a jiffy, in a minute.

cré•du•lo *adj.* credulous, too ready to believe.

cre•en•cia *f.* belief, faith.

cre•er[14] *v.* to believe; to think, suppose; **¡ya lo creo!** I should say so!; yes, of course!

cre•í•ble *adj.* credible, believable.

cre•ma *f.* cream; custard; cold cream.

cre•pi•tar *v.* to crackle, snap; to creak; to rattle.

cre•pus•cu•lar *adj.* twilight.

cre•pús•cu•lo *m.* twilight.

cres•po *adj.* curly; artifical (*style*); angry; crisp.

cres•pón *m.* crepe.

cres•ta *f.* crest; top, summit; tuft, comb (*of a bird*).

cre•to•na *f.* cretonne.

cre•yen•te *m. & f.* believer; *adj.* believing.

cre•yón *m. Am.* crayon.

crí•a *f.* brood; suckling; breeding.

cri•a•de•ro *m.* tree nursery; breeding place; hotbed; rich mine.

cria•do *m.* servant; *adj.* bred; **mal –** ill-bred; **criada** *f.* maid, servant.

cria•dor *m.* breeder, raiser, rearer; creator; *adj.* creating, creative, breeding; nourishing.

crian•za *f.* breeding; nursing; manners.

criar[17] *v.* to breed; to bring up, rear, educate; to nurse.

cria•tu•ra *f.* creature; baby child.

cri•ba *f.* sieve.

cri•bar *v.* to sift.

cri•men *m.* crime.

cri•mi•nal *adj., m. & f.* criminal.

crin *f.* mane.

cri•nu•do *adj. Am.* with a long or thick mane.

crio•llo *m. Am.* Creole; native of America (*especially Spanish America*); *adj. Am.* national, domestic (*not foreign to Spanish America*).

cri•san•te•ma *f.,* **crisantemo** *m.* chry-santhemum.

cri•sis *f.* crisis.

cri•sol *m.* crucible, melting pot; hearth of a blast furnace.

cris•par *v.* to contract (*muscles*); to clench (*fists*); to put (*nerves*) on edge.

cris•tal *m.* crystal; glass; mirror; lens.

cris•ta•le•rí•a *f.* glassware shop or factory; glassware.

cris•ta•li•no *adj.* crystalline, transparent, clear; *m.* lens of the eye.

cris•ta•li•zar[9] *v.* to crystallize.

cris•tian•dad *f.* Christianity; Christendom.

cris•tia•nis•mo *m.* Christianity.

cris•tia•no *m.* Christian; person; **hablar en –** to speak clearly; *adj.* Christian.

cri•te•rio *m.* criterion, rule, standard; judgment.

crí•ti•ca *f.* criticism; censure; gossip.

cri•ti•ca•dor *adj.* critical; *m.* critic, faultfinder.

cri•ti•car[6] *v.* to criticize; to censure; to find fault with.

crí•ti•co *adj.* critica; *m.* critic, judge, *Am.* faultfinder, slanderer; **criticón** *m.* critic, knocker, faultfinder; *adj.* critical, over-critical, faultfinding.

cro•ar *v.* to croak.

cro•mo *m.* chromium.

cro•mo•so•ma *m.* chromosome.

cró•ni•ca *f.* chronicle, history; **cronista** *m. & f.* chronicler.

cró•ni•co *adj.* chronic.

cro•nó•me•tro *m.* chronometer, time piece.

cro•quis *m.* rough sketch.

cru•ce *m.* crossing; crossroads; cross-breeding.

cru•ce•ro *m.* (*cruciforme*) crossing; cross-bearer; crossroads; transept (*of a church*); crossbeam; cross (*a constellation*); (*buque*) cruiser.

cru•ce•ta *f.* crosspiece; crosstree; universal joint (*automobile*).

cru•ci•fi•car *v.* to crucify.

cru•ci•fi•jo *m.* crucifix.

cru•ci•gra•ma *m.* crossword puzzle.

cru•do *adj.* raw; uncooked; unripe; harsh; **agua cruda** hard water; **petróleo** – crude oil; *Mex.* **estar** – to have a hang-over; **cruda** *f. Mex.* hang-over.

cru•el *adj.* cruel.

cru•el•dad *f.* cruelty.

cru•ji•do *m.* creak, crack, craking; rustple.

cru•jir *v.* to creak, crackle; to grate (*one's teeth*); to rustle; to crunch.

cruz *f.* cross.

cru•za•da *f.* crusade; holy war; campaign.

cru•za•do *m.* crusader; *adj.* crossed; cross, crosswise, transverse.

cru•za•mien•to *m.* crossing; crossroads.

cru•zar⁹ *v.* to cross; *Am.* to fight, dispute; **-se con** to meet.

cua•co *m. Mex.* horse; *Am.* cassava flour.

cua•der•no *m.* notebook; memorandum book; booklet; *Mex., Ven.* pamphlet.

cua•dra *f.* hall, large room; stable; hospital or prison ward; *Am.* city block; *Am.* reception room.

cua•dra•do *adj.* square; *m.* square; square ruler; die, metal block or plate.

cua•dran•te *m.* dial, face of a clock or watch; sundial; quadrant (*fourth part of circle; instrument used in astronomy*).

cua•drar *v.* (*cuadriforme*) to square to form into a square; to form into a square; (*agradar*) to please; to conform; to harmonize; to well; *Am.* to be becoming (*said of clothes*); *Am.* to be ready; *Am.* to contribute a large sum; *Am.* to come out well, succeed; **-se** to stand at attention.

cua•dri•cu•lar *v.* to square off, divide into squares.

cua•dri•lla *f.* group, troupe, gang; armed band; quadrille, square dance.

cua•dro *m.* square; picture; scene; frame; flower bed; *Am.* blackboard; *Ch.* slaughterhouse.

cua•ja•da *f.* curd.

cua•ja•do *p.p.* & *adj.* coagulated, curdled; filled, covered; – **de** with (*flowers, dew, etc.*).

cua•jar *v.* to coagulate, thicken, curd, curdle; to turn out well; to jell; to please; *Am.* to chatter, prattle; **-se** to coagulate, curd; to become crowded, be filled; **la cosa no cuajó** the thing did not work, did not jell.

cua•ja•rón *m.* clot.

cual *rel. pron.* which; **cada** – each one; – **más**, – **menos** some people more, others less; **el** –, **la** –, **los -es**, **las -es** which; who; **lo** – which; adv. as, like; **¿cuál?** *interr. pron.* which one? what?

cua•li•dad *f.* quality; trait.

cual•quier(a) *indef. adj.* & *pron.* any, anyone; whichever; **un hombre cualquiera** any man whatever.

cuan•do *rel. adv.* & *conj.* when; **aun** – even though; **¿cuándo?** *interr. adv.* when?

cuan•tí•a *f.* quantity; rank, importance.

cuan•tio•so *adj.* plentiful, abundant; numerous.

cuan•to *rel. adj.* & *pron.* as much as, as many as; all that; – **antes** as soon as possible, immeditely; **en** – *conj.* as soon as; **en** – **a** to, for, with regard to; **unos -s** a few; **¿cuánto?** interr. adj. & pron. how much?; **¿cuántos?** how many?

cua•que•ris•mo *m.* the Quaker sect, or doctrine.

cuá•que•ro *m.* Quaker.

cua•ren•te•na *f.* quarantine; forty units of anything; period of forty days, months, or years.

cua•ren•tón *m.* man in his forties; **cuarentona** *f.* woman in her forties.

cua•res•ma *f.* Lent.

cuar•ta *f.* foruth, fourth part; span of a hand; *Am.* horse whip; *P.R.* **echar** – to beat, flog.

cuar•te•ar *v.* to quarter, divide into quarters; *P.R.* to whip; **-se** to crack, split (*said of walls or ceilings*); *Mex.* to back down, go back on one's word.

cuar•tel *m.* quarter, one fourth; quarters, barracks; district; quarter, mercy; **no dar** – to give no quarter.

cuar•te•la•da *f.* military coup d'état, uprising, insurrection.

cuar•te•la•zo *m. Am.* military coup d'état, insurrection.

cuar•te•rón *m.* quarter, fourth part; fourth of a pound; panel (*of a door or window*); *adj.* & *m.* quarter-breed (*one fourth Indian and three fourths Spanish*); quadroon (*person of quarter negro blood*).

cuar•te•to *m.* quartet; quatrain (*stanza of four lines*).

cuar•ti•lla *f.* (*hoja*) sheet of paper; (*medida*) about 4 quarts; about 1 1/2 pecks; fourth of an **arroba** (*about 6 pounds*); *Am.* three cents' worth; *Am.* **no valer uno** – not to be worth a penny.

cuar•ti•llo *m.* fourth of a peck; about a pint; fourth of a **real**.

cuar•to *m.* room; quarter, one fourth; **tener -s** to have money; *adj.* fourth.

cuar•zo *m.* quartz.

cua•te *adj., m.* & *f. Mex.* twin; pal, buddy.

cua•tre•ro *f m.* horse thief, cattle thief; *Am.* Indian who speaks "broken" Spanish.

cu•ba *f.* cask, barrel; tub, vat; bigbellied person; drunkard.

cu•ba•no *adj.* & *m.* Cuban.

cu•be•ta *f.* small barrel or keg; bucket; pail.

cú•bi•co *adj.* cubic.

cu•bier•ta *f.* cover; covering; envelope; deck (*of a ship*); *Am.* sheath.

cu•bier•to *p.p. of* cubrir; *m.* cover; place setting or one person at a table.

cu•bo *m.* cube; bucket, pail; hub of a wheel; mill pond; *Am.* finger bowl.

cu•bre•me•sa *f.* table cover.

cu•brir[52] *v.* to cover; to hide; to coat; to settle, pay (*a bill*); **-se** to cover oneself; to put on one's hat.

cu•ca•ra•cha *f.* cockroach.

cu•cli•llas: en – inasquatting position; **sentarse en –** to squat.

cu•cli•llo *m.* cuckoo.

cu•co *adj.* dainty, cute; sly, shrewd; *m.* cuckoo; a kind of caterpillar; card game; *Riopl.* peach, peach tree; *Am.* **hacer – a** to make fun of; to fool.

cu•cu•ru•cho *m.* paper cone; *Am.* peak, summit; *Peru, C.A., Mex.* cowl, cloak with a hood (*worn by penitents in Holy Week processions*)

cu•cha•ra *f.* spoon; scoop; *Am.* mason's trowel; **media – mediocre** person; *Am.* mason's helper; *Am.* **hacer – to** pout; *Am.* **meter uno su – to** butt into a conversation; to meddle; **cucharada** *f.* spoonful; scoop; **cucharón** *m.* large spoon; ladle; dipper; scoop.

cu•chi•che•ar *v.* to whisper.

cu•chi•che•o *m.* whispering, whisper.

cu•chi•lla *f.* large knife, cleaver; blade (*of any cutting instrument*); *Peru* penknife; *Riopl., Mex., P.R.* mountain ridge; *Am.* gore (*in a garment*); *Am.* narrow tract of land.

cu•chi•lla•da *f.* thrust with a knife, stab, slash; cut, gash.

cu•chi•llo *m.* knife; gore (*in a garment*); **– de monte** hunting knife; **cuchillería** *f.* cutlery; cutlery shop.

cue•ca *f. Am.* a Chilean dance.

cue•llo *m.* neck; collar.

cuen•ca *f.* river basin; narrow valley; wooden bowl; socket of the eye.

cuen•co *m.* earthen bowl.

cuen•ta *f.* (*cálculo*) count, calculation; bill; account; (*bolita*) bead (*of a rosary or necklace*); **a fin de -s** in the final analysis; **caer en la – to** see, get the point; **darse – to** realize; *Col.* **de toda – anyway; eso corre de mí – that** is my responsibility; I'll take charge of that; **eso no me tiene – that** does not pay me; it is of no profit to me; **en resumidas -s** in short; *P.R.* **hacerle – una cosa a uno** to be useful or profitable for one; **tomar en – to** take into account; **tomar una cosa por su – to** take charge of something, take the responsibility for it; **vamos a -s** let's understand or settle this.

cuen•ta•go•tas *m.* dropper (*for counting drops*).

cuen•to *m.* story, tale; **– de nunca acabar** never-ending tale; **déjese de -s** come to the point; **no viene a – it** is not opportune or to the point.

cuer•da *f.* cord, string, rope; chord; watch spring; **dar – a** to wind (*a watch*).

cuer•do *adj.* sane; wise.

cue•re•a•da *f. Mex., C.A., Col., Ven.* flogging, whipping; *Am.* skining of an animal.

cue•re•ar *v. Am.* to flog, whip; *Am.* to harm, dishonor;

Am. to beat (*in a game*); *Am.* to skin (*an animal*).

cuer•no *m.* horn; antenna, feeler; **poner -s a** to be unfaithful to, deceive (*a husband*); *Am.* **mandar al – to** send to the devil.

cue•ro *m.* hide, skin; leather; wineskin; *Col., Ven.* whip; **en -s** naked.

cuer•pe•a•da *f. Riopl.* dodge; evasion.

cuer•po *m.* body; bulk; corps; **en – without** hat or coat; **luchar – a – to** fight in single combat; *Am.* **sacar el – to** dodge; to escape, avoid doing somethin.

cuer•vo *m.* crow; raven; *Ven.* buzzard; *Am.* dishonest priest; *Riopl., Ch.* **hacer uno la del – to** leave abruptly and not return.

cues•ta *f.* hill, slope; **a -s** on one's shoulders or back; in one's care; **– abajo** downhill; **– arriba** uphill.

cues•tión *f.* question; controversy, dispute; problem, matter.

cues•tio•na•rio *m.* questionnaire, list of questions.

cue•va *f.* cave, cavern; cellar.

cui•co *m. Mex.* cop, policeman; *Am.* gossiper, tattletale, "squealer"; *Ch., Bol., Peru* half-breed; *Riopl.* short, chubby person.

cui•da•do *m.* care, attention; worry, misgiving; **al – de** in care of; **tener – to** be careful; **¡–!** look out!; be careful! **¡cuidadito!** be very careful!

cui•da•do•so *adj.* careful; attentive, anxious.

cui•dar *v.* to take care of, look after, keep; to make or do carefully.

cui•ta *f.* grief, care, anxiety; misfortune; *C.A.* bird dung.

cui•ta•do *adj.* unfortunate; timid, shy.

cu•la•ta *f.* haunch, buttock; rear; butt (*of a firearm*).

cu•la•ta•zo *f.* blow with the butt of a rifle; recoil, kick of a firearm.

cu•le•bra *f.* snake; coil; *Mex.* money belt.

cu•le•bre•ar *v.* to zigzag; to twist, wriggle.

cul•mi•na•ción *f.* culmination, climax.

cul•mi•nar *v.* to culminate; to come to a climax.

cul•pa *f.* fault; guilt; blame; **echar la – a** to blame; **tener la – to** be to blame.

cul•pa•bi•li•dad *f.* guilt; **culpable** *adj.* guilty.

cul•par *v.* to blame; to declare guilty.

cul•ti•va•ción *f.* cultivation.

cul•ti•va•dor *m.* cultivator; **máquina cultivadora** cultivator.

cul•ti•var *v.* to cultivate.

cul•ti•vo *m.* cultivation, culture.

cul•to *adj.* cultured; *m.* cult worship; religious sect; **rendir – a** to pay homage to; to worship.

cul•tu•ra *f.* culture; cultivation.

cum•bre *f.* summit; top.

cum•ple•a•ños *m.* birthday.

cum•pli•do *adj.* (*completo*) complete, full; perfecto; (*cortés*) courteous; *p.p.* fulfilled; due, fallen due; **tiene tres años -s** he is just over threee years old; *m.* courtesy, attention; compliment.

cum•pli•men•tar *v.* to compliment; to congratulate; to pay a courtesy visit.

cum•pli•mien•to *m.* fulfilment; courtesy; completion; compliment; **de** — formal, ceremonious.

cum•plir *v.* to fulfill; to comply; to carry out; to fall due; **– años** to have a birthday; to be (*so many*) years old.

cú•mu•lo *m.* pile, heap; accumulation; cumulus (*mass of clouds*).

cu•na *f.* cradle; origin; *Am.* coffin for the poor; *Am.* dive, den (*for gambling and dancing*).

cun•dir *v.* to spread (*as news, disease, liquids*); to propagate, extend, multiply.

cu•ña *f.* wedge; splinter; *Ch.*, *Riopl.* influential person.

cu•ña•do *m.* brother-in-law; **cuñada** *f.* sister-in-law.

cuo•ta *f.* quota; dues, fee; **– de entrada** admission fee.

cuo•ti•dia•no *adj.* everyday, daily.

cu•pé *m.* coupé.

cu•pón *m.* coupon.

cú•pu•la *f.* dome.

cu•ra *f.* cure; *m.* curate, priest.

cu•ra•ción *f.* cure.

cu•ran•de•ro *m.* healer (*not a doctor*); quack; medicine man (*among Indians*).

cu•rar *v.* to cure, heal; to treat; to cure (*meats, tobacco*); to tan (*skins*); *Am.* to load (*dice*), fix (*cards*); **– de** to take care of; **-se** to cure oneself; to get well; *Riopl.* to get drunk.

cu•rio•se•ar *v.* to snoop, peek, peer, pry; to observe with curiosity.

cu•rio•si•dad *f.* curiosity; neatness, daintiness.

cu•rio•so *adj.* curious; neat, dainty; **libros raros y -s** rare books.

cu•rro *adj.* showy, gaudy, flashy; *m.* dandy.

cu•rru•ta•co *m.* fop, dandy; *adj.* affected (*in one's dress*).

cur•si *adj.* common, in bad taste; cheap, ridiculous; **cursilería** *f.* bad taste, cheapness, false elegance; group of cheap, ridiculous people.

cur•so *m.* course, direction; scholastic year; course of study.

cur•ti•dor *m.* tanner.

cur•ti•du•rí•a *f.* tannery.

cur•tir *v.* to tan; to harden, accustom to hardships; *Col.*, *Ven.* to dirty, soil; **-se** to get tanned or sunburned; to become accustomed to hardships.

cur•va *f.* curve.

cur•vo *adj.* curved; bent, cooked; arched.

cús•pi•de *f.* summit, peak, top; spire, steeple.

cus•to•dia *f.* custody; guard, guardian; monstrance (*vessel in which the consecrated Host is exposed*).

cus•to•diar *v.* to guard, watch; to keep in custody.

cus•to•dio *m.* guardian, keeper.

cu•tí•cu•la *f.* cuticle.

cu•tis *m.* skin; complexion.

cu•yo *rel. poss. adj.* whose, of whom, of which.

CH

cha•ba•ca•no *adj.* crude, unpolished; inartistic; cheap, in bad taste; *m. Mex.* a variety of apricot.

cha•co•ta *f.* fun; jest; **echar a –** to take as a joke; **hacer – de** to make fun of.

cha•co•te•ar *v.* to frolic, joke, make merry; to be boisterous; to show off.

cha•cra *f. Ec.*, *Peru*, *Ch.* small farm; *Col.*, *Ec.* cultivated field.

cha•gra *f. Col.*, *Ec.* farm, piece of farm land; *m. & f. Ec.* peasant; *adj.* uncivilized, unrefined.

chal *m.* shawl.

cha•lán *m.* horse trader; *Am.* broncobuster, horse breaker.

cha•le•co *m.* waistcoat, vest.

cha•lu•pa *f.* sloop, sailboat; launch; *Mex.*, *Col.*, *Ven.*, *Riopl.* canoe; *P.R.* raft; *Mex.* Mexican tortilla with sauce.

cha•ma•co *m. Mex.*, *C.A.* boy; **chamaquito** *m. Mex.*, *C.A.* little boy.

cha•ma•rra *f.* coarse wool jacket or swater; *Mex.* sheepskin jacket, leather jacket; *Am.* heavy wool blanket.

cha•ma•rre•ta *f.* short loose jacket; *Am.* square poncho.

cham•ber•go *m.* gaucho sombrero.

cham•bón *adj.* clumsy, awkward, unskillful; *m.* bungler, clumsy performer, awkard workman; clumsy player.

cham•pa•ña *f.* champagne.

cham•pú *m.* shampoo.

cham•pu•rra•do *m. Mex.* a mixed drink of chocolate and **atole**; *Col.* a mixed alcoholic beverage.

cham•pu•rrar, *Am.* **champurrear** *v.* to mix (*drinks*).

cha•mus•ca•da, cha•mus•ca•du•ra *f. Am.* singe, scorch.

cha•mus•car[6] *v.* to scorch; to singe; to sear; *Am.* to sell at a low cost; **-se** to get scorched, singed, or seared; *Am.* to get peeved, offended.

cha•mus•qui•na *f.* singe, scorch.

chan•ce•ar *v.* to fool, joke; *adj.* jolly.

chan•ce•ro *m.* jester, joker; adj. jolly.

chan•cla *f.* slipper, old shoe; **chancleta** *f.* slipper; *m.*
Am. good-for-nothing.

chan•clo *m.* galosh, overshoe; clog; rubber overshoe;
-s rubbers.

chan•cho *m. S.A.* pig, pork.

chan•ga•dor *m. Riopl.* carrier, porter; *Am.* handy
man, person who does odd jobs.

chan•go *m. Mex.* monkey; **ponerse** – to be alert,
wary.

chan•ta•je *m.* blackmail, blackmailing.

chan•za *f.* joke, jest.

cha•pa *f.* metal plate; veneer (*thin leaf of wood*); rosy
spot on the cheeks; *Mex., C.A., Andes* lock; *Am.* Indian
spy; **-s** game of tossing coins; **hombre de** – serious,
reliable man.

cha•pa•do *adj.* veneered (*covered with a thin layer
of wood or other material*); **– a la antigua** oldfashioned.

cha•pa•le•ar = chapotear.

cha•pa•rro *m.* scrub oak; short, chubby person; *Am.*
a kind of tropical shrub with rough leaves; *Am.* short
whip; *adj. Mex. C.A.* short, squatty.

cha•pa•rrón *m.* downpour, heavy shower.

cha•pi•tel *m.* spire, steeple; capital (*of a column*).

cha•po•te•ar *v.* to splash, paddle in the water.

cha•po•te•o *m.* splash.

cha•pu•ce•ar *v.* to fumble; to botch, bungle, do or
make clumsily; *Am.* to deceive, trick.

cha•pu•lín *m. Mex., C.A.* grasshopper.

cha•pu•rrar *v.* to speak (*a language*) brokenly; to mix
(*drinks*).

cha•puz *m.* dive, duck, ducking.

cha•pu•za *f.* botch, clumsy piece of work; *Am.* foul
trick, fraud.

cha•pu•zar[2] *v.* to duck; to dive.

cha•que•ta *f.* jacket; **chaquetón** *m.* long jacket, coat.

cha•ra•mus•ca *f. Mex.* twisted candy stick or cane;
Col., Ven. brushwood, firewood; *C.A.* hubbub,
uproar.

cha•ra•mus•que•ro *m. Am.* candy-stick maker or
vendor.

char•ca *f.* pond.

char•co *m.* puddle, pool; **pasar el** – to cross the pond,
cross the ocean.

char•la *f.* chat, chatter, prattle.

char•la•du•rí•a *f.* chater, gossip.

char•lar *v.* to chat, chatter, prate.

char•la•tán *m.* chatterer, prater; gossiper; charlatán,
quack.

cha•rol *m.* varnish; patent leather; *Col.* tray; **charola**
f. Mex. tray.

cha•ro•lar *v.* to varnish, polish.

char•qui *m.* jerky, jerked beef.

cha•rro *m. Spain* a villager of Salamanca province;
Mex. Mexican horseman of special costume and
cultural status.

cha•rrú•a *m. & f. Am.* Charruan Indian (*Indian of
Uruguay*).

chas•ca•rri•llo *m.* joke, funny story.

chas•co *m.* joke, prank; surprise; disillusionment,
disappointment; **llevarse** – to be disappointed,
surprised or fooled; *adj. Am.* thick, curly (*hair*); *Am.*
ruffed (*plumage*).

chas•que•ar *v.* to play a trick on; to disappoint; to
crack (*a whip*); to smack (*the lips*); to click (*the tongue*);
Col., Ven. to chatter (*said of the teeth*);
Am. to munch (*food*); **-se** to be disappointed or
disillusioned; to be tricked or fooled.

chas•qui *m. Andes, Riopl.* courier, messenger.

chas•qui•do *m.* crack of a whip; crackle; smack (*op
the lips*); click (*of the tongue*).

cha•ta *f.* bedpan; scow, barge, flatbottomed boat; *Am.*
platform wagon, platform car, flatcar; **chatita** *f.*
Mex. "honey", "cutie", "funny face".

cha•to *adj.* snub-nosed, flat-nosed; flat; flattened;
squatty; *Mex.* **quedarse uno** – to be left flat or in
the lurch; to be dissappointed.

cha•val *m.* lad; young man.

cha•yo•te *m. Am.* vegetable pear (*a tropical fruit
growing on a vine*); *Am.* dunce, silly fool.

che *interj. Riopl.* word used to attract attention among
intimates; say ¡listen! hey!; nickname for citizens
of Argentina.

che•que *m.* check, bank check.

chi•ca *f.* little girl; girl; maid, servant.

chi•cle *m. Am.* chicle; *Am.* chewing gum.

chi•co *adj.* small, little; *m.* child, boy; *Col.* each game
of billiards; *Am.* **= chicozapote** (*tropical fruit and
tree from which chicle is extracted*).

chi•co•te *m.* cigar; piece of rope; *Am.* whip; *Col.,
Ven.* cigar butt.

chi•co•te•ar *v. Riopl., Col., Peru* to lash, whip, flog;
Am. to fight, quarrel; *Am.* to kill.

chi•co•te•o *m. Riopl.* whipping; *Am.* shooting, killing;
Am. crackling, rattling (*as of machine guns*); *Am.*
quarreling.

chi•cha *f. Peru, Col., Riopl., C.A.* chicha (*a popular
alcoholic beverage*); *Peru* thick-soled shoe; **no ser
ni – ni limonada** to be worth nothing, be neither fish
nor fowl.

chí•cha•ro *m.* pea; *Col.* bad cigar; *Am.* apprentice.

chi•cha•rra *f.* cicada, locust; talkative person; *Mex.*
person with a shrill voice; *Am.* rickety, squeaky car;

Ch. harsh-sounding musical instrument or bell; *C.A.*, *Mex.*, *Cuba* piece of gried pork skin.

chi•cha•rrón *m.* crackling, crisp piece of fried pork skin; burned piece of meat; sunburnt person; *Am.*dried-up, wrinkled person; *Am.* bootlicker, flatterer.

chi•che *m. Mex., C.A.* breast, teat; wet nurse.

chi•chón *m.* bump, lump; *Am.* joker, jester; **chichona** *adj. Mex., C.A.* large-breasted.

chi•fla•do *adj.* "cracked", "touched", crazy; *p.p. of* **chiflar**.

chi•fla•du•ra *f.* craziness, mania; mockery, jest.

chi•flar *v.* to whistle; to hiss; *Am.* to sing (*said of birds*); **-se** to lose one's head; to become unbalanced, crazy.

chi•fli•do *m.* whistle; hiss; *Am.* **en un –** in a jiffy, in a second.

chi•le *m.* chili, red pepper.

chi•le•no *adj. & m.* Chilean.

chi•llan•te *adj.* flashy, bright, showy, loud; shrieking.

chi•llar *v.* to shriek, scream; to hiss; *Am.* to shout, protest, moan; *Am.* to "squeal", turn informer; *Riopl.*, *Ven., C.A., P.R.* **no –** not to say a word; *Mex.* **-se** to be piqued, offended.

chi•lli•do *m.* shriek, scream.

chi•llón *adj.* shrieking, screaming; shrill; loud, gaudy; *Col.*, *Andes* whining, discontented; *Riopl.* touchy.

chi•me•ne•a *f.* chimney; fireplace, hearth.

chi•na *f.* (*de la China*) Chinese woman; China silk or cotton; porcelain; (*piedra*) pebble; marble; *Andes*, *Ch., Riopl., Col.* girl, young woman (*usually half-breed or Indian*); *Am.* servant girl; *P.R.* sweet orange; *Col.* spinning top; **chinita** *f. Am.* little Indian girl; darling.

chin•che *f.* bedbug; thumbtack; tiresome person, bore; *Col., Ven., Riopl.* touchy or irritable person; *Am.* plump, squatty person.

chin•cho•rro *m. Ven., Col.* hammock.

chi•no *adj.* Chinese; *Mex.* curly; *m. Riopl.* Chinese; Chinaman; *Am.* pig; *Am.* half-breed (*Negro and Indian, white and Indian*); *Am.* Indian; *Col.* house servant; *Am.* coarse, rough, ugly person; *Col.* straight, coarse hair.

chi•que•ro *m.* pigsty, pigpen; pen for bulls; goat shelter.

chi•qui•lín *m. Am.* tot, little boy; **chiquilina** *f. Am.* little girl.

chi•qui•to *adj.* tiny, very small; *m.* tiny tot, tiny child; **chiquitico** *adj.* tiny.

chi•ri•pa *f.* stroque of good luck.

chi•ri•pá *m. Riopl.* loose riding trousers (*square of cloth draped from the waist and between the legs*).

chi•ro•la *f. Mex., Ven., Ríopl.* "jug"; jail; *Am.* coin of low value.

chi•ro•na *f.* "jug"; jail.

chi•rria•do *adj. Col.* attractive; lively.

chi•rriar[17] *v.* to squeak, creak; to sizzle; to chirp; to sing out of tune; *Col.* to go on a spree.

chi•rri•do *m.* creak, squeak; chirp; squeaking, creaking; chirping.

chis•gue•te *m.* squirt.

chis•me *m.* gossip, piece of gossip; trifle, trinket, knickknack, gadget.

chis•me•ar *v.* to gossip; to tattle.

chis•me•rí•a *adj.* gossiping, talebearing.

chis•me•ro *adj.* gossiping; *m.* gossip.

chis•mo•so *adj.* gossiping; *m.* gossip, talebearer, tattletale.

chis•pa *f.* spark; small diamond; wit; *Col.* false rumor lie; *Am.* two-wheeled cart; *Mex.* brazen, shameless woman; *Am.* **da –** it clicks, works, functions; *Am.* **ponerse –** to get drunk.

chis•pe•an•te *adj.* sparkling

chis•pe•ar *v.* to spark; to sparkle; to twinkle; to drizzle.

chis•po•rro•te•ar *v.* to sputter, throw off sparks.

chis•te *m.* joke, jest; **dar en el –** to guess right, hit the nail on the head.

chis•te•ra *f.* top hat; fish basket.

chis•to•so *adj.* funny, amusing, humorous.

¡chi•to! **¡chi•tón!** *interj.* hush!

chi•va *f.* female goat; *Am.* goatee; *Pan., Col.* flivver, small bus; **chivo** *m.* he-goat; *Am.* fit of anger; *Am.* insulting remark; *Am.* **estar hecho un –** to be very angry; *adj. Am.* angry; **chivato** *m. Cuba* informer, squealer.

cho•can•te *adj.* striking, surprising; shocking; disgusting; *Col., Andes* tiresome, annoying, impertinent.

cho•car[6] *v.* to bump, collide, clash; to fight; to shock, surprise, disgust; **me choca ese hombre** I loathe that man.

cho•ca•rre•ar *v.* to tell coarse jokes; to clown.

cho•ca•rre•rí•a *f.* coarse joke; **chocarrero** *adj.* coarse, vulgar; clownish.

cho•clo *m.* overshoe; clog; *Mex.* low shoe or slipper; *Andes, Col., Ch., Ríopl.* ear of corn; *Am.* corn stew; *Am.* spike, ear of wheat.

cho•co•la•te *m.* chocolate.

cho•che•ar *v.* to be in one's dotage, act senile.

cho•che•ra, cho•chez *f.* senility, dotage: **choche-ras, chocheces** senile actions or habits.

cho•cho *adj.* doting; *m.* childish old man.

chó•fer *m.* chauffeur.

cho•lo *m. Andes, Ríopl., Ch.* half-breed; *Am.* half-civilized Indian; *Am.* coarse, rude; *C.R.* dark-skinned; *Ch.* black (*dog*).

cho•po *m.* black poplar; *adj. Am.* stupid.

cho•que *m.* collision, bump; shock; clash, conflict; dispute.

cho•ri•zo *m.* sausage; *Am.* string of things; *Am.*fool.

cho•rra•zo *m.* spurt, large stream or jet.

cho•rre•ar *v.* to drip; to spout.

cho•rro m. spurt, jet; stream, flow; Am. strand of a whip; Am. river rapids.

cho•te•a•dor m. Am. joker, jester.

cho•te•ar v. Cuba to make fun of, jeer, jest, mock, kid; Mex., C.A. to idle, fool around; Am. to pamper.

cho•te•o m. Cuba joking, jeering, kidding.

cho•za f. hut, cabin.

chu•bas•co m. squall, sudden shower; **aguantar el −** to weather the storm.

chu•che•rí•a f. trifle, trinket; knickknack; tidbit.

chue•co adj. Am. crooked, bent; Col. crook-legged, bow-legged, knock-kneed; Am. worn-out, dejected; Mex. disgusted, annoyed; Am. **comerciar en −** to trade in stolen goods.

chu•le•ta f. cutlet, chop; blow, slap.

chu•lo m. dandy; effeminate man; clownish fellow; bullfighter's assistant; Col. buzzard; Am. coarse, thick brush; adj. C.A., Col., Mex. goodlooking, pretty.

chum•pi•pe m. C.A. turkey; also **chompipe**.

chu•pa•da f. sucking; suction; suck, sip, Mex., C.A., Ven., Andes puff from a cigarette; Riopl. big swallow of liquor.

chu•pa•dor m. sucker; teethin ring; Am. toper, heavy drinker; Am. smoker.

chu•pa•flor, chu•pa•rro•sa m. Am. hummingbird.

chu•par v. to suck; to sip; to absorb, take in; Am. to smoke; C.A., Riopl., Andes to drink, get drunk; **-se** to shrivel up.

chu•rras•co m. Riopl., Andes roasted meat; Riopl., Andes barbecued meat; Riopl., Andes large piece of meat for barbecuing.

chu•rras•quear v. Riopl., Andes to barbecue, roast over coals; Riopl., Andes to prepare (meat) for barbecuing; Riopl., Andes to eat barbecued meat.

chu•rras•qui•to m. small piece of roast.

chu•rri•gue•res•co adj. baroque, ornate (architecture).

chus•ca•da f. jest, joke.

chus•co adj. funny, witty; ridiculous; Peru **perro −** mongrel dog.

chus•ma f. rabble, mob.

D

da•ble adj. feasible, possible.

da•ca = da acá.

dá•di•va f. gift.

da•di•vo•so adj. liberal, generous.

da•do m. die; **-s** dice.

da•dor m. giver.

da•ga f. dagger.

da•ma f. lady; **jugar a las -s** to play checkers.

da•mi•se•la f. damsel, girl.

dan•za f. dance.

dan•zan•te m. & f. dancer.

dan•zar[9] v. to dance.

dan•za•ri•na f. dancer.

da•ñar v. to harm, hurt, damage; **-se** to spoil, rot; to get hurt; to get damaged.

da•ñi•no adj. harmful; destructive.

da•ño m. damage, harm, loss.

da•ño•so adj. harmful.

dar[25] v. irr. (hacer don) to give, confer; (golpear) to strike, hit; (emitir) give off, emit; **− a luz** to give birth to; to publish; **− con** to encounter, find; **− de comer** to feed; **− de sí** to give, stretch; **− en** to hit upon; to persist in; **− largas a un asunto** to prolong or postpone a mater; C.A., Ven., Col. **− cuero (guasca, puños)** to beat, thrash, lash; **lo mismo da** it makes no difference; **-se** to give up; **dárselas de** to boast of.

dar•do m. dart, arrow.

da•res y to•ma•res m. pl. give-and-take, dispute; dealings.

dár•se•na f. dock, wharf.

da•tar v. to date; **− de** to date from.

dá•til m. date (fruit of the date palm).

da•to m. datum, fact; **-s** data.

de prep. of, from; about, concerning; in (after a superlative); if (before inf.); **− no llegar** if he does not arrive; el **− la gorra azul** the one with the blue cap; **el mejor − América** the best in America; **más − lo que dice** more than he says.

de•ba•jo adv. under, underneath; **− de** prep. under.

de•ba•te m. debate; dispute, quarrel.

de•ba•tir v. to debate, argue, discuss; to figth; **-se** to struggle.

de•be m. debit.

de•be•lar v. to subdue, defeat.

de•ber v. to owe; to have to (must, should, ought); **debe de ser** it must be, probably is; **¡me la debes!** I have an account to settle with you!

de•ber m. duty, obligation; debt; debit, debit side (in bookkeeping).

de•bi•do adj. due, owing; just, appropriate.

dé•bil adj. weak, feeble.

de•bi•li•dad f. debility, weakness.

de•bi•li•ta•ción f., **debilitamiento** m. weakening; weakness.

de•bi•li•tar v. to weaken.

dé•bi•to m. debt; debit.

de•bu•tar v. to make a debut, make a first public appearance.

dé•ca•da f. decade, ten years; series of ten.

de•ca•den•cia f. decadence, decline, falling off.

de•ca•er[24] v. irr. to decay, decline, wither, fade; to fall to leeward.

de•cai•mien•to m. decline, decay; dejection;

weakness.

de•ca•no *m.* dean; senior member of a group.

de•can•ta•do *p.p. & adj.* much talked about; overrated.

de•ca•pi•tar *v.* to behead.

de•cen•cia *f.* decency; **decente** *adj.* decent; respectable; fair.

de•ce•nio *m.* decade.

de•cep•ción *f.* disillusion, disappointment.

de•cep•cio•nan•te *adj.* disappointing.

de•cep•cio•nar *v.* to disillusion, disappoint.

de•ci•bel *m.* decibel (*unit for the measure-ment of the intensity of sound*).

de•ci•dir *v.* to decide, resolve; **-se a** to make up one's mind to; to decide to.

dé•ci•ma *f.* tenth; tithe; stanza of ten octosyllabic lines.

dé•ci•mo *adj.* tenth.

de•cir[27] *v. irr.* to say; to tell; to speak; **es** − that is; **querer** − to mean, signify.

de•ci•sión *f.* decision.

de•ci•si•vo *adj.* decisive, final.

de•cla•mar *v.* to declaim, recite.

de•cla•ra•ción *f.* declaration; statement, deposition, testimony.

de•cla•rar *v.* to declare, state, affirm; to testify; **-se** to propose, declare one's love; to give one's views or opinion.

de•cli•nar *v.* to decline; to go down; to lose vigor, decay; to bend down.

de•cli•ve *m.* declivity, slope.

de•co•ra•ción *f.* decoration, ornament; stage setting.

de•co•rar *v.* to decorate, adorn.

de•co•ra•ti•vo *adj.* decorative, ornamental.

de•co•ro *m.* decorum, propriety; dignity; honor.

de•co•ro•so *adj.* decorous, becoming, proper, decent.

de•cré•pi•to *adj.* decrepit, old, feeble.

de•cre•tar *v.* to decree.

de•cre•to *m.* decree; decision, order.

de•cha•do *m.* model, pattern, example.

de•dal *m.* thimble.

de•di•car[6] *v.* to dedicate; to devote; **-se** to apply oneself.

de•di•ca•to•ria *f.* dedication, inscription.

de•do *m.* (*de la mano*) finger; (*del pie*) toe; − **del corazón** middle finger; − **meñique** little finger; − **pulgar** thumb; **no mamarse el** − not to be easily fooled; **dedillo** *m.* small finger; **saber al dedillo** to know perfectly, know by heart.

de•duc•ción *f.* deduction; inference.

de•du•cir[25] *v. irr.* to deduce, conclude; to deduct.

de•fec•to *m.* defect, fault.

de•fec•tuo•so *adj.* defective, faulty.

de•fen•der[1] *v. irr.* to defend.

de•fen•sa *f.* defense; *Am.* automobile bumper.

de•fen•si•vo *adj.* defensive; *m.* defense, safeguard;

defensiva *f.* defensive.

de•fen•sor *m.* defender.

de•fi•cien•cia *f.* deficiency; **deficiente** *adj.* deficient.

dé•fi•cit *m.* deficit, shortage.

de•fi•ni•ción *f.* definition.

de•fi•ni•do *adj.* definite; *p.p. of* **definir**.

de•fi•nir *v.* to define, explain; to determine.

de•fi•ni•ti•vo *adj.* definitive, conclusive, final; **en definitiva** in short, in conclusion; definitely.

de•for•ma•ción *f.* deformation, deformity.

de•for•mar *v.* to deform; **-se** to become deformed; to lose its shape or form.

de•for•me *adj.* deformed; ugly.

de•for•mi•dad *f.* deformity.

de•frau•dar *v.* to defraud, cheat, rob of.

de•fun•ción *f.* death, decease.

de•ge•ne•ra•do *adj. & m.* degenerate.

de•ge•ne•rar *v.* to degenerate.

de•glu•ción *f.* swallowing.

de•glu•tir *v.* to swallow.

de•go•llar[2] *v. irr.* to behead; to slash the throat; to cut (*a dress*) low in the neck.

de•gra•dar *v.* to degrade; to debase.

de•güe•llo *m.* beheading; throat-slashing.

de•he•sa *f.* pasture, grazing ground.

dei•dad *f.* deity.

de•ja•dez *f.* lassitude, languor, listlessness; self-neglect, slovenliness.

de•ja•do *adj.* indolent, listless; slovenly.

de•jar *v.* (*abandonar*) to leave; to quit; to abandon; to omit; (*permitir*) to permit, let; (*soltar*) to let go; − **de** to stoop, cease; − **caer** to drip; *Am.* **no -se** not to be an easy mark, not to let others pick on one.

de•jo *m.* (*sabor*) aftertaste; slight taste; (*acento*) slight accent, peculiar inflection.

del = de + el of the.

de•lan•tal *m.* apron.

de•lan•te *adv.* before, in front; − **de** *prep.* in front of.

de•lan•te•ra *f.* lead, forepart, front.

de•lan•te•ro *adj.* front, foremost, first.

de•la•tar *v.* to denounce, acuse, inform against.

de•la•tor *m.* accuser, informer.

de•le•ga•ción *f.* delegation.

de•le•ga•do *m.* delegate.

de•le•gar[7] *v.* to delegate.

de•lei•ta•ble *adj.* delightful, enjoyable.

de•lei•tar *v.* to delight, please.

de•lei•te *m.* delight, joy, pleasure.

de•lei•to•so *adj.* delightful.

de•le•tre•ar *v.* to spell.

de•lez•na•ble *adj.* perishable,brittle.

del•fín *m.* dolphin; dauphin.

del•ga•dez *f.* thiness; slimness; fineness.

del•ga•do *adj.* thin, slender, slim.

de•li•be•ra•do *adj.* deliberate; *p.p. of* deliberar

de•li•be•rar *v.* to deliberate, consider, ponder.

de•li•ca•de•za *f.* fineness; delicacy, softness, exquisiteness.

de•li•ca•do *adj.* delicate; weak, frail; exquisite, dainty; tender.

de•li•cia *f.* delight.

de•li•cio•so *adj.* delicious, delightful.

de•lin•cuen•te *adj., m. & f.* delinquent.

de•li•ne•a•ción *f.* **delineamiento** *m.* delineation, design, outline, drawing; portrayal.

de•li•ne•ar *v.* to delineate, sketch, outline.

de•li•ran•te *adj.* delirious, raving.

de•li•rar *v.* to be delirious; to rave, talk wildly or foolishly.

de•li•rio *m.* delirium. temporary madness; wild excitement; foolishness.

de•li•to *m.* crime; misdemeanor.

de•ma•cra•do *adj.* scrawny, emaciated, thin.

de•man•da *f.* demand; petition; question; claim; complaint; lawsuit.

de•man•da•do *m.* defendant; *p.p. of* **demandar**.

de•man•dan•te *m. & f.* plaintiff.

de•man•dar *v.* to demand; to petition; to sue, file a suit; to indict.

de•más *indef. adj. & pron.:* **los** – the rest; the others; **las** – **personas** the other people; **lo** – the rest; **por** – useless; uselessly; **por lo** – as to the rest; moreover.

de•ma•sí•a *f.* excess; boldness, insolence; offense, outrage; **en** – excessively.

de•ma•sia•do *adv.* too much, excessively; too; *adj.* too much, excessive.

de•men•te *adj.* demented, insane, crazy.

de•mo•cra•cia *f.* democracy; **demócrata** *m & f.* democrat; **democrático** *adj.* democratic.

de•mo•ler² *v. irr.* to demolish, tear down.

de•mo•nio *m.* demon, devil; evil spirit.

de•mon•tre *m.* devil; ¡ – ! the deuce!

de•mo•ra *f.* delay.

de•mo•rar *v.* to delay; to retard; **-se** to linger; to be delayed.

de•mos•tra•ción *f.* demonstration; proof, explanation.

de•mos•trar² *v. irr.* to demonstrate, show, prove, explain.

de•mos•tra•ti•vo *adj.* demonstrative.

de•mo•vi•li•zar⁹ *v.* to demobilize.

de•mu•dar *v.* to change, alter; to disguise; **-se** to change color or one's facial expression; to turn pale.

den•go•so, den•gue•ro *adj.* affected; finicky.

den•gue *m.* primness; coyness, affectation; dengue, breakbone fever; *Am.* marigold; *Col.* zigzag; *Am.* swagger; **hacer -s** to act coy, make grimaces.

de•ni•grar *v.* to blacken, defame, revile, insult.

de•no•da•do *adj.* dauntless, daring.

de•no•mi•na•ción *f.* denomination; name, title, designation.

de•no•mi•nar *v.* to name, call, entitle.

de•nos•tar² *v. irr.* to insult, outrage, revile.

de•no•tar *v.* to denote, indicate, mean.

den•si•dad *f.* density.

den•so *adj.* dense, compact; thick.

den•ta•do *adj.* toothed, notched.

den•ta•du•ra *f.* set of teeth.

den•tar¹ *v. irr.* to tooth, furnish (*a saw*) with teeth; to indent: to cut teeth, grow teeth (*referring to a child*).

den•te•lla•da *f.* bite; tooth mark; **a -s** with big bites.

den•ti•ción *f.* teething.

den•tí•fri•co *m.* dentrifice, tooth cleanser; **pasta dentífrica** toothpaste; **polvos dentríficos** toothpowder.

den•tis•ta *m* dentist.

den•tro *adv.* inside, within; – **de** *prep.* inside of; **por** – on the inside.

de•nue•do *m.* spirit, courage, daring.

de•nues•to *m.* affront, insult.

de•nun•cia *f.* denunciation, condemnation, accusation; miner's claim.

de•nun•ciar *v.* to denounce, accuse; to proclaim, advise, give notice; to claim (*a mine*).

de•pa•rar *v.* to furnish, offer, supply.

de•par•ta•men•to *m.* department; com-partment; apartment.

de•par•tir *v.* to talk, converse.

de•pen•den•cia *f.* dependence: dependency; branch office.

de•pen•der *v.* to depend, rely (on).

de•pen•dien•te *m.* clerk; dependent, subordinate; *adj.* dependent.

de•plo•rar *v.* to deplore, lament, regret.

de•po•ner⁴⁰ *v. irr.* to set aside; to depose, remove (*an official*); to testify, declare; to have a bowel movement; *Am.* to vomit.

de•por•tar *v.* to deport, banish.

de•por•te *m.* sport; pastime, recreation.

de•por•tis•ta *m.* sportsman; *f.* sportswoman.

de•por•ti•vo *adj.* sport, sports (*used as an adj.*); **copa deportiva** loving cup.

de•po•si•ción *f.* declaration, assertion; testimony; dismissal, removal (*from office or power*); bowel movement.

de•po•si•tar *v.* to deposit; to deliver, intrust.

de•po•si•ta•rio *m.* receiver, trustee.

de•pó•si•to *m.* deposit; storage; warehouse; **- de**

agua reservoir.

de•pra•va•do *adj.* depraved, corrupt, degenerate.

de•pra•var *v.* to corrupt, pervert, contaminate.

de•pre•ciar *v.* to depreciate, lesseen the value of.

de•pre•sión *f.* depression; dip, sag.

de•pri•men•te *adj.* depressing.

de•pri•mir *v.* to depress; to press down; to humiliate, belittle.

de•pues•to *p.p. of* **deponer**.

de•pu•rar *v.* to purify.

de•re•cha *f.* right hand; right side; right wing (*in politics*): **a la –** to the right; **derechazo** *m.* a blow with the right hand, a right (*boxing*).

de•re•cho *adj.* right; straight; *m.* law; duty, tax; fee.

de•re•chu•ra *f.* straightness.

de•ri•va *f.* drift (*of a boat or plane*); irse (*or* **andar**) **a la –** to drift, be drifting.

de•ri•var *v.* to derive; to come (from).

de•ro•gar[7] *v.* to revoke, repeal, abolish.

de•rra•ma•mien•to *m.* spill, spilling, shedding; overflow; scattering; **– de sangre** bloodshed.

de•rra•mar *v.* to spill; to spread, scatter; to shed.

de•rra•me *m.* spill, spilling, shedding; overflow; discharge (*of secretion, blood, etc.*); slope.

de•rre•dor *m.* circuit; contour; **al –** around: **en -** around.

de•rren•ga•do *p.p. & adj.* lame, crippled; dislocated (*said of hip or spine*).

de•rren•gar[1,7] *v. irr.* to dislocate or sprain (*hip or spine*); to cripple; to bend.

de•rre•ti•mien•to *m.* thaw, thawing, melting.

de•rre•tir[5] *v. irr.* to melt, dissolve; **-se** to be consumed; to melt.

de•rri•bar *v.* to demolish, knock down, fell; to overthrow; **-se** to lie down, throw oneself down.

de•rro•ca•mien•to *m.* overthrow.

de•rro•car[4] *v.* to fling down; to fell; to overthrow.

de•rro•cha•dor *m.* squanderer, spendthrift; *adj.* wasteful, extravagant.

de•rro•char *v.* to waste; to squander.

de•rro•che *m.* waste; dissipation; lavish spending.

de•rro•ta *f.* rout, defeat; ship's route or course.

de•rro•tar *v.* to defeat; to squander; to destroy, ruin; to lose or shift its course (*said of a ship*).

de•rro•te•ro *m.* course, direction; ship's course; book of marine charts.

de•rrum•ba•de•ro *m.* precipice.

de•rrum•ba•mien•to *m.* landslide; collapse.

de•rrum•bar *v.* to fling down: *Am.* to knock down; *Am.* to go down in a hurry; **-se** to crumble away; to topple over; *Col., Ven.* to dwindle (*as a business*).

de•rrum•be *m.* landslide; collapse.

de•sa•bo•to•nar *v.* to unbutton.

de•sa•bri•do *adj.* tasteless, insipid; harsh; sour.

de•sa•bri•gar[7] *v.* to uncover; **-se** to uncover oneself.

de•sa•bri•mien•to *m.* tastelessness; harsh-ness; sourness.

de•sa•bro•char *v.* to unfasten, unbutton, unclasp; **-se** to unbutton oneself, unfasten one's clothes.

de•sa•ca•to *m.* irreverence, disrespect; profanation.

de•sa•cier•to *m.* mistake, error.

de•sa•cos•tum•bra•do *adj.* unaccustomed; unusual; *p.p. of* **desacostumbrar**.

de•sa•cos•tum•brar *v.* to disaccustom, rid of a habit; **-se** to become unaccustomed; to lose a custom.

de•sa•cre•di•tar *v.* to discredit; to disgrace.

de•sa•cuer•do *m.* disagreement; discord; blunder; forgetfulness.

de•sa•fiar[17] *v.* to challenge; to compete: to defy.

de•sa•fi•na•do *adj.* out of tune.

de•sa•fi•nar *v.* to be discordant; to be out of tune; **-se** to get out of tune.

de•sa•fí•o *m.* challenge, defiance; duel; contest.

de•sa•for•tu•na•do *adj.* unfortunate, unlucky.

de•sa•fue•ro *m.* violation; outrage, abuse.

de•sa•gra•da•ble *adj.* disagreeable, unpleasant.

de•sa•gra•dar *v.* to displease.

de•sa•gra•de•ci•do *adj.* ungrateful.

de•sa•gra•do *m.* displeasure; discontent.

de•sa•gra•viar *v.* to make amends; to compensate for a damage or injury; to right a wrong; to apologize; to vindicate.

de•sa•gra•vio *m.* reparation; compensation for a wrong or injury; vindication; apology.

de•sa•gua•de•ro *m.* drain, drain pipe, water outlet.

de•sa•guar[8] *v.* to drain, draw off; to flow (into); *Ch.* to wash (*something*) two or more times; *Am.* to extract the juice from; *Col., Ven., Mex.* to urinate; **-se** to drain.

de•sa•güe *m.* drainage; drain.

de•sa•gui•sa•do *m.* outrage, violence, wrong.

de•sa•ho•ga•do *p.p. & adj. (aliviado)* relieved; (*espacioso*) roomy, spacious; **estar –** to be in easy or comfortable circumstances; to be well-off.

de•sa•ho•gar[7] *v.* to relieve from pain or trouble; **-se** to find relief or release; to unbosom oneself, disclose one's feelings.

de•sa•ho•go *m.* relief from pain or trouble; release; ease, comfort, relaxation; freedom, unrestraint.

de•sai•rar *v.* to slight, snub, disdain; to rebuff; to disappoint; to neglect.

de•sai•re *m.* rebuff, snub, slight, disdain.

de•sa•len•tar[1] *v. irr.* to put out of breath; to discourage; **-se** to get discouraged.

de•sa•lien•to *m.* discouragement, dejection.

de•sa•li•ña•do *adj.* disheveled, slovenly, unkempt, untidy; disorderly.

de•sa•li•ño *m.* slovenliness, untidiness; neglect, carelessness; disorder.

de•sal•ma•do *adj.* soulless, cruel, inhuman.

de•sa•lo•jar *v.* to dislodge; to evict, expel from a lodging; to vacate.

de•sa•ma•rrar v. to untie, unfasten; to unmoor (*a ship*).

de•sam•pa•rar v. to abandon, forsake.

de•sam•pa•ro m. desertion, abandonment.

de•sa•mue•bla•do adj. unfurnished.

de•san•grar v. to bleed, draw blood from; to drain; -se to bleed, lose blood.

de•sa•ni•ma•do adj. discouraged; lifeless; dull (*said of a party, meeting, etc.*).

de•sa•ni•mar v. to dishearten, discourage.

de•sa•pa•re•cer[13] v. irr. to disappear; to hide: -se to disappear, vanish.

de•sa•pa•ri•ción f. disappearance.

de•sa•pa•sio•na•do adj. dispassionate; free from passion; calm; impartial.

de•sa•pe•go m. aloofness, indifference, detachment.

de•sa•per•ci•bi•do adj. unprepared; unprovided; unnoticed.

de•sa•pro•ba•ción f. disapproval.

de•sa•pro•bar[2] v. irr. to disapprove.

de•sar•mar v. to disarm; to dismount, take apart.

de•sar•me m. disarmament.

de•sa•rrai•gar[7] v to root out, uproot.

de•sa•rre•gla•do p.p & adj. disordered; disorderly; slovenly.

de•sa•rre•glar v. to disarrange, disorder, disturb, upset.

de•sa•rre•glo m. disorder, confusión.

de•sa•rro•llar v. to unroll, unfold; to develop, explain; -se to develop; to unfold.

de•sa•rro•llo m. development.

de•sa•se•a•do adj. unkempt, untidy

de•sa•se•o m. slovenliness, untidiness.

de•sa•sir[22] v. irr. to loosen, unfasten; -se to get loose (from); to let go (of).

de•sa•so•sie•go m. unrest, uneasiness, restlessness.

de•sas•tra•do adj. unfortunate, unhappy; ragged, dirty, untidy.

de•sas•tre m. disaster.

de•sas•tro•so adj. disastrous, unfortunate.

de•sa•tar v. to untie, loosen; to dissolve; to unravel, clear up: -se to let loose, let go; to break loose; -se en improperios to let out a string of insults.

de•sa•ten•ción f. inattention, lack of attention; discourtesy.

de•sa•ten•der[1] v. irr. to disregard, pay no attention (to); to slight, neglect.

de•sa•ten•to adj. inattentive; discourteous.

de•sa•ti•na•do adj. senseless; reckless.

de•sa•ti•nar v. to act foolishly; to talk nonsense; to blunder; to rave; to lose one's bearings.

de•sa•ti•no m. blunder error; folly, nonsense.

de•sa•tra•car[6] v. to push off (*from shore or from another ship*); to cast off, unmoor.

de•sa•ve•nen•cia f. disagreement, discord; dispute; misunderstanding.

de•sa•yu•nar•se v. to eat breakfast; – con la noticia to hear a piece of news for the first time.

de•sa•yu•no m. breakfast.

de•sa•zón f. uneasiness, anxiety; insipidity, flatness, tastelessness; displeasure.

des•ban•dar•se v. to disband, scatter, disperse; to desert the army or a party.

des•ba•ra•tar v. to destroy, ruin; to upset, disturb; to disperse, put to flight; to talk nonsense; -se to be upset, be in disorder; to fall to pieces.

des•bo•ca•do adj. runaway (*horse*), dashing headlong; foul-mouthed, abusive; broken-mouthed (*jar, pitcher, etc.*).

des•bor•da•mien•to m. overflow, flood.

des•bor•dan•te adj. overflowing; Am. frantic.

des•bor•dar v. to overflow, flood; -se to spill over; to get overexcited.

des•ca•ba•lar v. to bleak (*a given amount, making it thereby incomplete*).

des•ca•be•llo m. the act of killing the bull by piercing the brain with the sword.

des•ca•be•za•do p.p. beheaded; adj. headless; harebrained, thoughtless.

des•ca•be•zar[9] v. to behead; to chop off the head or tip of; – el sueño to take a nap; -se to break one's head; to rack one's brain.

des•ca•e•ci•do adj. feeble weak; – de ánimo depressed, dejected, despondent.

des•ca•e•ci•mien•to m. languor, weakness; depression, dejection.

des•ca•la•bra•du•ra f. blow or wound on the head; scar on the head.

des•ca•la•brar v. to wound on the head; to hurt, injure; to damage; -se to suffer a head wound or skull fracture.

des•ca•la•bro m. loss, misfortune.

des•cal•zar[9] v. to take off (*someone's*) shoes or (and) stockings; -se to lose a shoe (*said of horses*).

des•cal•zo adj. barefoot; shoeless.

des•ca•mi•nar v. to mislead, lead astray; -se to go astray.

des•ca•mi•sa•do adj. shirtless; in rags; m. ragamuffin, ragged fellow.

des•can•sar v. to rest.

des•can•so m. rest; staircase landing.

des•ca•ra•do adj. shameless, impudent, brazen.

des•car•ga f. discharge; unloading.

des•car•gar[7] v. to discharge; to unload.

des•car•go m. discharge (*of a duty or obligation*); unloading; relief.

des•car•gue m. unloading; discharge.

des•car•na•do adj. fleshless, scrawny.

des•car•nar v. to pull the flesh from the bone; to corrode, eat away; -se to become thin, emaciated.

des•ca•ro m. effrontery, shamelessness, impudence, audacity.

des•ca•rriar[17] v. to mislead, lead astray; to separate (*cattle*) from the herd; -se to stray; to go astray.

des•ca•rri•lar v. to derail (cause a train to run off the track); to wreck (a train); **-se** to get or run off the track; to go astray.

des•car•tar v. to discard; to put aside.

des•cas•ca•ra•do p.p. & adj. peeled off; chipped off.

des•cas•ca•rar v. to shell, hull, husk; to peel; to chip off (plaster); Am. to defame, discredit; Col. to flay; **-se** to chip off, peel off.

des•cen•den•cia f. descent, lineage; descendants, offspring.

des•cen•den•te adj. descending, downward.

des•cen•der¹ v. irr. to descend, go down; to get down; to come (from), originate.

des•cen•dien•te m. & f. descendant; adj. descending.

des•cen•di•mien•to m. descent.

des•cen•so m. descent; fall

des•ci•frar v. to decipher, puzzle out, figure out.

des•col•gar²·⁷ v. irr. to unhang, take down; to let down; **-se** to climb down (a rope, tree, etc.); to drop in, appear unexpectedly.

des•co•lo•rar v. to discolor; to fade; **-se** to fade, lose its color; to discolor.

des•co•lo•ri•do adj. pale.

des•co•llar² v. irr. to excel; to stand out, tower (above).

des•co•me•di•do adj. rude, discourteous, impolite; unobliging.

des•com•ple•tar v. to make incomplete, break (a unit, sum, set, etc.).

des•com•po•ner⁴⁰ v. irr. (estorbar) to upset, disturb; (echar a perder) to put out of order; to decompose; **-se** to decompose, rot; to become upset, ill; to get out of order; Col., Ven., C.A., Carib., Mex. **se me descompuso el brazo** I dislocated my arm, my arm got out of joint.

des•com•po•si•ción f. decomposition; decay, corruption; disorder, confusion.

des•com•pues•to p.p. of **descomponer**; adj. out of order; insolent; brazen; immodest.

des•co•mu•nal adj. colossal, enormous, monstrous.

des•con•cer•tan•te adj. disconcerting, disturbing, confusing, baffing, embarrassing.

des•con•cer•tar¹ v. irr. to disconcert, bewilder, confuse; to disturb; **-se** to be confused, perplexed.

des•con•cier•to m. disorder; confusion; disagreement; feeling of discomfort.

des•con•cha•du•ra f. chip (chipped off place); chipping off, peeling off (of plaster, varnish, etc.).

des•con•char v. to scrape off (plaster or stucco); **-se** to peel off, chip off (as plaster).

des•co•nec•tar v. to disconnect.

des•con•fia•do adj. distrustful, suspicious.

des•con•fian•za f. mistrust, distrust.

des•con•fiar¹⁷ v. to distrust; to lose confidence.

des•co•no•cer¹⁸ v. irr. to fail to recognize or remember; to disown; to disregard, slight; not to know.

des•co•no•ci•do adj. unknown; unrecog-nizable; m. stranger.

des•co•no•ci•mien•to m. disregard; ignorance.

des•con•so•la•do p.p. & adj. disconsolate, forlorn; disheartened, grieved.

des•con•so•la•dor adj. disheartening, saddening.

des•con•so•lar² v. irr. to sadden, grieve; to discourage; **-se** to become disheartened, grieved.

des•con•sue•lo m. dejection, sadness, distress.

des•con•tar² v. irr. to discount, deduct; to allow for.

des•con•ten•ta•di•zo adj. discontented, fretful, hard to please.

des•con•ten•tar v. to displease.

des•con•ten•to adj. discontent, displeased; m. discontent, displeasure.

des•co•ra•zo•na•do adj. disheartened, discouraged, depressed.

des•cor•char v. to uncork; to remove the bark from (a cork tree); to force or break open.

des•cor•tés adj. discourteous, rude, impolite.

des•cor•te•sí•a f. discourtesy, rudeness, impoliteness.

des•cor•te•zar⁹ v. to bark, strip the bark from (trees); to remove the crust or shell from; to peel; to civilize, remove the rough manners from.

des•co•ser v. to rip, unsew, unstitch; **-se** to rip, come unstitched; to talk too much or indiscreetly.

des•co•si•do m. rip; adj. too talkative, indiscreet; disorderly; p.p. of **descoser**.

des•cos•trar v. to flake; to scale off; to remove the crust from; **-se** to flake, scale off.

des•co•yun•ta•do p.p. & adj. dislocated, out of joint.

des•co•yun•tar v. to dislocate, put out of joint; **-se** to get out of joint.

des•cré•di•to m. discredit.

des•cre•í•do adj. incredulous, unbelieving; m. unbeliever.

des•crei•mien•to m. unbelief, lack of faith.

des•cri•bir⁵² v. to describe.

des•crip•ción f. description.

des•crip•ti•vo adj. descriptive.

des•cri•to p.p. irr. of **describir**.

des•cuar•ti•zar⁹ v. to quarter (an animal); to tear or cut into parts.

des•cu•bier•to p.p. of **descubrir** & adj. (sin cubierta) uncovered; hatless, bareheaded; (hallado) discovered; m. deficit, shortage; **al –** openly, in the open; **en –** uncovered; unpaid.

des•cu•bri•dor m. discoverer.

des•cu•bri•mien•to m. discovery; find; invention.

des•cu•brir⁵² v. to discover; to uncover; **-se** to uncover; to take off one's hat.

des•cuen•to m. discount; deduction.

des•cui•da•do *adj.* careless, negligent; untidy, slovenly; unaware; thoughtless.

des•cui•dar *v.* to neglect; to overlook; to be careless or negligent; **-se** to be careless or negligent.

des•cui•do *m.* carelessness; neglect; oversight; disregard; inattention; slip, error.

des•de *prep.* from; since; **– luego** of course; **– que** *conj.* since, ever since.

des•de•cir²⁷ *v. irr.* to be out of harmony (*with*); to detract (*from*), **-se** to retract; to contradict oneself.

des•dén *m.* disdain, scorn.

des•den•ta•do *adj.* toothless.

des•de•ñar *v.* to disdain, scorn.

des•de•ño•so *adj.* disdainful, scornful.

des•di•cha *f.* misfortune; misery; poverty.

des•di•cha•do *adj.* unfortunate; unhappy, wretched; miserable; *m.* wretch.

des•do•bla•mien•to *m.* unfolding

des•do•blar *v.* to unfold; to spread out.

des•do•rar *v.* to remove the gilt from: to tarnish; to dishonor.

des•do•ro *m.* tarnish, blemish; dishonor.

de•se•a•ble *adj.* desirable.

de•se•ar *v.* to desire, want.

de•se•ca•ción *f.*, **desecamiento** *m.* drying; drainage.

de•se•car⁶ *v.* to dry; to dry up; to drain (*land*).

de•se•char *v.* to discard; to reject; to refuse, decline; *Col.* to cut across, take a short cut.

de•se•cho *m.* remainder, residue; waste material; piece of junk; discard; **-s** refuse, scraps, junk; **hierro de** – scrap iron; **papel de** – wastepaper, scraps of paper.

de•sem•ba•lar *v.* to unpack.

de•sem•ba•ra•zar⁹ *v.* to rid, free, clear; *Ch.* to give birth; **–se** to get rid of

de•sem•ba•ra•zo *m.* freedom, ease, naturalness; *Ch.* childbirth.

de•sem•bar•ca•de•ro *m.* dock, wharf, pier.

de•sem•bar•car⁶ *v.* to disembark, land; to unload; to go ashore.

de•sem•bar•co, de•sem•bar•que *m.* landing; unloading.

de•sem•bo•ca•du•ra *f.* mouth (*of a river, canal, etc.*); outlet.

de•sem•bo•car⁶ *v.* to flow (into); to lead (to).

de•sem•bol•sar *v.* to disburse, pay out.

de•sem•bol•so *m.* disbursement, outlay, expenditure.

de•sem•bra•gar⁷ *v.* to throw out the clutch; to disconnect.

de•se•me•jan•te *adj.* unlike.

de•sem•pa•car⁶ *v.* to unpack.

de•sem•pe•ñar *v.* to recover, redeem, take out of pawn; **– un cargo** to perform the duties of a position; **– un papel** to play a part; **–se** to get out of debt.

de•sem•pe•ño *m.* fulfillment, carrying out, discharge; performance (*of a duty*); acting (*of a role*); redeeming (*of a thing pawned*).

de•sem•ple•a•do *adj.* unemployed.

de•sem•ple•o *m.* unemployment.

de•sem•pol•var *v.* to dust, remove the dust from.

de•sen•ca•de•nar *v.* to unchain, free from chains; to loosen, set free; **-se** to free oneself; to break loose.

de•sen•ca•ja•do *p.p. & adj.* disjointed; disfigured; sunken (*eyes*); emaciated.

de•sen•can•tar *v.* to disillusion, disappoint-ment.

de•sen•can•to *m.* disilluion, disappoint-ment.

de•sen•fa•do *m.* ease, freedom; calmness.

de•sen•fre•na•do *p.p. & adj.* unbridled; wanton, reckless; loose, immoral.

de•sen•gan•char *v.* to unhitch; to unhook: to unfasten

de•sen•ga•ña•dor *adj.* disappointing, disillusioning.

de•sen•ga•ñar *v.* to undeceive, disillusion, disappoint.

de•sen•ga•ño *m.* disillusion, disappoint-ment, blighted hope.

de•sen•gra•nar *v.* to throw out of gear.

de•sen•ma•ra•ñar *v.* to untangle; to unravel.

de•sen•mas•ca•rar *v.* to unmask.

de•sen•re•dar *v.* to disentangle, unravel.

de•sen•ro•llar *v.* to unroll.

de•sen•sar•tar *v.* to unstring; to unthread; to unfasten from a ring.

de•sen•si•llar *v.* to unsaddle

de•sen•ten•der•se¹ *v. irr.* to neglect, ignore, pay no attention to; to pretend not to see, hear or understand.

de•sen•ten•di•do *adj.* unmindful, heedless; *p.p. of* **desentenderse; hacerse el** – to pretend not to notice.

de•sen•te•rrar¹ *v. irr.* to unearth, dig up.

de•sen•to•na•do *adj.* inharmonious, out of tune.

de•sen•to•nar *v* to be out of tune; to he out of harmony; to sing off key, play out of tune.

de•sen•vol•tu•ra *f.* freedom, ease, abandon; boldness, impudence.

de•sen•vol•ver²·⁵² *v. irr.* to unroll, unfold; to unwrap: to develop.

de•sen•vol•vi•mien•to *m.* development, unfolding.

de•sen•vuel•to *adj.* free, easy; forward, bold; shameless, brazen; *p.p. of* **desenvolver**.

de•se•o *m.* desire, wish.

de•se•o•so *adj.* desirous, eager.

de•se•qui•li•bra•do *adj.* unbalanced; *p.p. of* **desequilibrar**.

de•se•qui•li•brar *v.* to unbalance; to derange.

de•se•qui•li•brio *m.* lack of balance; derangement,

mental disorder.

de•ser•ción *f.* desertion.

de•ser•tar *v.* to desert; to abandon; **-se de** to desert.

de•ser•tor *m.* deserter; quitter.

de•ses•pe•ra•ción *f.* despair; desperation; fury.

de•ses•pe•ra•do *adj.* desperate; despairing; hopeless; *p.p. of* **desesperar**.

de•ses•pe•ran•za•do *p.p.* & *adj.* discouraged; hopeless; desperate, in despair.

de•ses•pe•ran•zar[9] *v.* to discourage, deprive of hope; **-se** to be discouraged; to despair, lose one's hope.

de•ses•pe•rar *v.* to despair, lose hope; to make (*someone*) despair; **-se** to despair, be desperate; to be furious.

des•fa•cha•tez *f.* shamelessness, effrontery, impudence.

des•fal•car[6] *v.* to embezzle; to remove a part of.

des•fal•co *m.* embezzlement; diminution, decrease.

des•fa•lle•cer[13] *v. irr.* to grow weak; to faint.

des•fa•lle•ci•mien•to *m.* faintness; weakness; languor; swoon, faint.

des•fa•vo•ra•ble *adj.* unfavorable.

des•fi•gu•rar *v.* to disfigure; to deface; to distort.

des•fi•la•de•ro *m.* narrow passage, narrow gorge; road on the edge of a precipice.

des•fi•lar *v.* to march, parade, pass by.

des•fi•le *m.* parade.

des•ga•na *f.* lack of appetite; reluctance.

des•ga•rra•do *p.p. torn; adj.* shameless; impudent.

des•ga•rra•du•ra *f.* tear.

des•ga•rrar *v.* to tear, rend; to expectorate, cough up; **-se** to tear; to separate oneself (from).

des•gas•tar *v.* to waste, consume, wear away; **-se** to waste away, lose one's strength or vigor; to war off.

des•gas•te *m.* waste, war and tear.

des•gra•cia *f.* misfortune, mishap; disgrace.

des•gra•cia•do *adj.* unfortunate, wretched.

des•gra•nar *v.* to thrash, thresh (*grain*); to remove the grain from; to shell (*peas, beans, etc.*).

des•gre•ña•do *adj.* disheveled.

des•ha•bi•ta•do *adj.* uninhabited, deserted; empty, vacant.

des•ha•cer[31] *v. irr.* to undo; to dissolve; to destroy; to untie; **-se** to dissolve; to melt; to waste away; **-se de** to get rid of.

des•ha•rra•pa•do, de•sa•rra•pa•do *adj.* ragged, shabby, tattered.

des•he•cha *f.* simulation, pretense; **hacer la –** to feign,

pretend.

des•he•cho *p.p. of* **deshacer** & *adj.* undone; ruinted; destroyed, in pieces; violent (*said of rainstorms*); worn-out, fatigued; *Am.* disorderly, untidy.

des•he•lar[1] *v. irr.* to melt; to thaw; **-se** to melt; to thaw.

des•her•bar[1] *v. irr.* to weed.

des•hie•lo *m.* thaw.

des•hier•be *m.* weeding.

des•hi•la•char *v.* to ravel, fray.

des•hi•lar *v.* to unravel; **-se** to unravel; to fray.

des•ho•jar *v.* to strip off the leaves, petals, or pages; **–se** to lose its leaves (*said of a plant or book*); to lose petals.

des•ho•lle•jar *v.* to husk, hull; to peel, pare, skin; to shell (*beans*).

des•ho•nes•to *adj.* immodest; unchaste, lewd.

des•hon•ra *f.* dishonor; disgrace.

des•hon•rar *v.* to dishonor, disgrace; to insult, offend; to seduce.

des•hon•ro•so *adj.* dishonorable; shame-dul.

des•ho•ra *f.* inopportune time; **a –** (*or* **a –s**) unexpectedly; **comer a –** to piece, eat between meals.

des•hue•sar *v.* to stone, remove the pits or stones from (*fruits*); to bone, remove the bones from (*an animal*).

de•si•dia *f.* indolence, laziness.

de•si•dio•so *adj.* indolent, negligent, lazy; listless.

de•sier•to *adj.* deserted, uninhabited; alone, lonely; *m.* desert, wilderness.

de•sig•na•ción *f.* designation; appointment.

de•sig•nar *v.* to designate, appoint, select; to design, plan, intend.

de•sig•nio *m.* design, plan, purpose,

de•si•gual *adj.* unequal, uneven; variable, changeable.

de•si•gual•dad *f.* inequality; unevenness; roughness (*of the ground*).

de•si•lu•sión *f.* disillusion, disappointment.

de•si•lu•sio•nar *v.* to disillusion, disappoint; **-se** to become disillusioned; to lose one's illusions.

de•si•nen•cia *f.* termination, ending (*of a word*).

de•sin•fec•tan•te *adj.* disinfecting; *m.* disinfectant.

de•sin•fec•tar *v.* to disinfect.

de•sin•fla•do *adj.* deflated, not inflated, flat.

de•sin•te•rés *m.* disinterestedness, unselfishness, impartiality.

de•sin•te•re•sa•do *adj.* disinterested, un-selfish, fair, impartial.

de•sis•tir *v.* to desist, stop, cease.

des•la•va•do *p.p.* & *adj.* half-washed; weakened; faded; pale; saucy.

des•la•var *v,* to wash away; to fade; to wash superficially.

des•le•al *adj.* disloyal, faithless.

des•le•ír[15] *v, irr.* to dissolve; to dilute, make thin or weak; **-se** to ecome diluted.

des·lin·dar v. to mark off, mark the boundaries of.

des·liz m. slip, slide; error.

des·li·za·dor m. glider.

des·li·za·mien·to m. slip, slipping; glide; sliding, skidding.

des·li·zar[9] v. to slip, slide; **-se** to slip; to skid: to glide; to slip out.

des·lu·ci·do p.p. & adj. tarnished; dull; discredited; dingy, shabby; awkward, ungraceful; inelegant.

des·lu·cir[13] v. irr. to tarnish, dull the luster of; to discredit.

des·lum·bra·dor adj. dazzling, glaring.

des·lum·bra·mien·to m. dazzle, glare; daze, confusion.

des·lum·brar v. to dazzle.

des·lus·tra·do adj. & p.p. tarnished; dim, dull; opaque.

des·lus·trar v. to tarnish; to soil, stain (one's honor or reputation).

des·lus·tre m. tarnish; disgrace.

des·ma·de·ja·do p.p. & adj. enervated, exhausted; depressed.

des·ma·de·jar v. to enervate, weaken.

des·mán m. misconduct, abuse, insult; calamity, disaster.

des·man·te·lar v. to dismantle, strip of furniture, equipment, etc.

des·ma·ña·do adj. unskillful, awkward, clumsy.

des·ma·yar v. to dismay; to lose strength, courage; **-se** to faint.

des·ma·yo m. faint, swoon; dismay, discouragement.

des·ma·za·la·do adj. dejected, depressed.

des·me·jo·rar v. to impair; to make worse; **-se** to grow worse; to waste away, lose one's health.

des·men·tir[3] v. irr. to contradict; to give the lie; **-se** to contradict oneself; to retract, take back one's word.

des·me·nu·zar[9] v. to crumble, break into bits; to mince; to shred; **-se** to crumble, fall to pieces.

des·me·re·cer[13] v. irr. to become unworthy of; to deteriorate, lose merit or value; to be inferior to.

des·mi·ga·jar v. to crumb (bread); to crumble; **-se** to crumble.

des·mo·char v. to cut off, chop off (the top or tip).

des·mo·la·do adj. toothless, without molars.

des·mon·tar v. to dismount; to cut down (a forest); to clear or level off (ground); to dismantle, take apart; to tear down; **-se** to dismount, alight, get off.

des·mo·ro·nar v. to crumble; **-se** to crumble down, fall gradually to pieces.

des·na·tar v. to skim, take the cream from (milk).

des·na·tu·ra·li·za·do adj. unnatural, cruel; **alcohol** – denatured alcohol (made unfit for drinking); **madre desnaturalizada** unnatural mother (one without motherly instincts).

des·nu·dar v. to undress, uncover; **-se** to undress.

des·nu·dez f. nudity, nakedness.

des·nu·do adj. nude, naked, bare.

de·so·be·de·cer[13] v. irr. to disobey.

de·so·be·dien·cia f. disobedience; **desobediente** adj. disobedient.

de·so·cu·pa·ción f. unemployment; idleness; vacationing.

de·so·cu·pa·do adj. unoccupied; unemployed, idle; empty, vacant.

de·so·cu·par v. to empty, vacate; **-se de un negocio** to get rid of, or not pay attention to, a business

de·so·ír[36] v. irr. to turn a deaf ear to, not to heed; to refuse (a petition)

de·so·la·ción f. desolation; ruin; loneli-ness; anguish, affliction, grief.

de·so·la·do adj. desolate; p.p. of **desolar**.

de·so·lar[2] v. irr. to lay waste, ruin; **-se** to be in anguish; to grieve.

de·so·llar[2] v. irr. to skin, flay; to fleece, extort money from.

de·sor·bi·ta·do adj. out of its orbit; out of place or proportion; decentered; Ch., Andes popeyed, with bulging eyes; Am. crazy, eccentric.

de·sor·den m. disorder, confusion.

de·sor·de·na·do adj. disorderly; lawless, unsettled; p.p. of **desordenar**.

de·sor·de·nar v. to disturb, confuse, upset.

de·so·rien·tar v. to throw off one's bearings; to lead astray; to misdirect, mislead; to confuse; **-se** to lose one's bearings; to go astray, get lost.

des·pa·bi·la·do adj. wakeful; wide-awake; bright, lively.

des·pa·bi·lar v. to snuff, trim the wick of (a candle); to enliven, awaken (the mind), sharpen (the wits); **-se** to wake up, rouse oneself, shake off drowsiness.

des·pa·cio adj. slowly.

des·pa·cio·so adj. slow.

des·pa·char v. to dispatch; to send; to facilitate; to ship.

des·pa·cho m. (oficina) office, bureau; salesroom; (comunicación) dispatch; (envío) sending; shipment; (sin demora) promptness; Ch. country store, farm store.

des·pa·chu·rrar v. to crush, squash.

des·pa·re·jo adj. unequal, uneven.

des·par·pa·jar v. to upset, disarrange; to rant, talk too much; Mex. to disperse, scatter.

des·par·pa·jo m. ease, freedom of manner; freshness, pertness; Col. dispersion, scattering; Am. disorder, jumble.

des·pa·rra·mar v. to scatter, spread; to spill; to squander, **-se** to "spread" oneself, spend lavishly; to scatter; to spill.

des·pa·rra·mo m. Ch., C.A. scattering, spreading, spilling; Riopl., Carib. disorder, commotion.

des·pa·ta·rrar·se *v.* to sprawl; to fall sprawling to the ground.

des·pe·cho *m.* spite; grudge; despair; weaning; **a — de** in spite of.

des·pe·da·zar[9] *v.* to break, cut, tear into pieces.

des·pe·di·da *f.* farewell; departure; dismissal.

des·pe·dir[5] *v. irr.* (*cesar*) to discharge, dismiss; (*emitir*) emit, throw off, give off; to see (*a person*) off (*at a station, airport, etc.*); **-se** to take leave, say good-bye.

des·pe·gar[7] *v.* to detach; to unfasten; to take off (*said of a plane*); *Am.* to unhitch; **no — los labios** not to say a word, not to open one's mouth; **-se** to grow apart; to come loose or become detached.

des·pe·go = desapego.

des·pe·gue *m.* takeoff (*of an airplane*).

des·pe·ja·do *adj.* clear, cloudless; smart, bright; *p.p. of* despejar.

des·pe·jar *v.* to clear; to remove obstacles from; **-se** to clear up (*as the sky*); to clear one's mind.

des·pe·lle·jar *v.* to skin, flay.

des·pen·sa *f.* pantry; storeroom (*for food*); food provisions.

des·pen·se·ro *m.* butler; steward.

des·pe·ña·de·ro *m.* steep cliff, precipice.

des·pe·ñar *v.* to fling down a precipice; **-se** to fall down a precipice; to throw oneself down a cliff.

des·pe·pi·tar *v.* to seed, remove the seeds from; **-se** to talk or shout vehemently; to rave, talk wildly; **-se por una cosa** to long for something; to be crazy about something.

des·per·di·cia·do *adj.* wasteful; *p.p. of* **desperdiciar.**

des·per·di·ciar *v.* to squander; to waste.

des·per·di·cio *m.* waste; extravagance; **-s** leftovers, garbage; residue.

des·per·di·gar[7] *v.* to disperse; to scatter; to strew.

des·pe·re·zar·se[9] *v.* to stretch oneself.

des·per·fec·to *m.* damage; flaw, defect.

des·per·ta·dor *m.* alarm clock.

des·per·tar[1] *v. irr.* to awaken; to wake up; **-se** to wake up.

des·pia·da·do *adj.* pitiless, heartless, cruel.

des·pier·to *adj.* awake; wide-awake.

des·pil·fa·rra·do *adj.* wasteful, extravagant; ragged; *p.p. of* **despilfarrar.**

des·pil·fa·rrar *v.* to squander; to waste.

des·pil·fa·rro *m.* extravagance, squan-dering; waste.

des·pis·tar *v.* to throw off the track.

des·plan·te *m.* arrogance; impudent remark or act.

des·pla·zar[9] *v.* to displace.

des·ple·gar[1,7] *v. irr.* to unfold; to unfurl; to show, manifest.

des·plo·mar *v.* to cause (*a wall*) to lean; **-se** to slump; to topple over, tumble down, collapse.

des·plo·me *m.* collapse; toppling over; landslide.

des·plu·mar *v.* to pick, pluck (*a fowl*); to fleece, skin, rob, strip; **-se** to molt, shed the feathers.

des·po·bla·do *adj.* uninhabited, desolate; **—de ár-boles** treeless; *m.* open country; uninhabited place; wilderness.

des·po·jar *v.* to despoil, rob; to strip (of), deprive (of); **-se** to undress; to deprive oneself.

des·po·jo *m.* plundering, robbery; spoil, booty; leftover, scrap; **-s** remains.

des·por·ti·lla·du·ra *f.* chip; nick.

des·por·ti·llar *v.* to chip; to nick.

des·po·sar *v.* to marry; **-se** to become formally engaged; to get married.

dés·po·ta *m. & f.* despot, tyrant.

des·pó·ti·co *adj.* despotic, tyrannical.

des·po·tis·mo *m.* despotism, tyranny.

des·pre·cia·ble *adj.* contemptible; worthless; insignificant, negligible.

des·pre·ciar *v.* to despise, scorn.

des·pre·cio *m.* scorn, contempt.

des·pren·der *v.* to unfasten, loosen; to detach; **-se** to get loose, come unfastened; to climb down; to get rid (of); to be inferred, be deduced.

des·pren·di·mien·to *m.* detachment; generosity; unfastening; landslide.

des·preo·cu·pa·do *p.p. & adj.* unbiased; liberal, broadminded; unconventional, carefree; *Am.* careless, slovenly; *Am.* indifferent to criticism.

des·pres·ti·giar *v.* to discredit, harm the reputation of; **-se** to lose one's prestige.

des·pres·ti·gio *m.* discredit, loss of prestige.

des·pre·ve·ni·do *adj.* unprepared; unaware.

des·pro·pó·si·to *m.* absurdity, nonsense.

des·pro·vis·to *adj.* destitute; lacking; devoid.

des·pués *adv.* after, afterward; then, later; **— de** *prep.* after; **— (de) que** *conj.* after.

des·pun·ta·do *adj.* blunt, dull; *p.p. of* **despuntar.**

des·pun·tar *v.* (*quitar la punta*) to blunt; to cut off (*a point*); nip; (*brotar*) to bud or sprout; (*sobresalir*) to excel; to be clever, witty; **— el alba** to begin to dawn.

des·qui·tar *v.* to retrieve, restore (*a loss*) **-se** to get even, take revenge; to win back one's money; to make up (for).

des·qui·te *m.* retaliation, revenge; getting even; recovery of a loss; return game or match.

des·ra·zo·na·ble *adj.* unreasonable.

des·ta·ca·do *adj.* outstanding; *p.p. of* **destacar.**

des·ta·ca·men·to *m.* military detachment.

des·ta·car[6] *v.* to detach (*troops*) to make stand out; to stand out; **hacer —** to emphasize; to make stand out; **-se** to stand out.

des·ta·par *v.* to uncover; to uncork; *Am.* to start running; **-se** to uncover, get uncovered; to get uncorked; *Am.* to burst out talking.

des·tar·ta·la·do *adj.* in disorder; in rack and ruin;

dismantled, stripped of furniture.

des·te·cha·do *adj.* roofless.

des·te·llar *v.* to flash; to sparkle, twinkle; to gleam.

des·te·llo *m.* flash, sparkle, gleam.

des·tem·pla·do *adj.* out of tune, out of harmony; immoderate; **sentirse** − not to feel well; to feel feverish.

des·te·ñir[5,19] *v. irr.* to discolor; to fade; to bleach; **-se** to become discolored; to fade.

des·ter·ni·llar·se *v.* − **de risa** to split one's sides with laughter.

des·te·rra·do *m.* exile; outcast; *p.p. & adj.* exiled, banished.

des·te·rrar[1] *v. irr.* to exile, banish; to remove earth (from).

des·te·tar *v.* to wean

des·tie·rro *m.* exile.

des·ti·la·ción *f.* distillation.

des·ti·la·de·ra *f.* still; *Am.* filter.

des·ti·lar *v.* to distill; to drip, trickle; to filter.

des·ti·le·rí·a *f.* distillery

des·ti·na·ción *f.* destination.

des·ti·nar *v.* to destine; to employ.

des·ti·na·ta·rio *m.* addressee.

des·ti·no *m.* destiny, fate; destination; employment, job.

des·ti·tu·í·do *adj.* destitute; *p.p. of* **destituir**.

des·ti·tu·ír[32] *v. irr.* to deprive.

des·tor·ni·lla·dor *m.* screwdriver.

des·tor·ni·llar *v.* to unscrew.

des·tra·bar *v.* to unlock, unfasten; to untie, to separate; to unfetter.

des·tre·za *f.* dexterity, skill, ability.

des·tro·nar *v.* to dethrone, depose, overthrow.

des·tro·zar[9] *v.* to shatter, cut to pieces; to destroy; to squander.

des·tro·zo *m.* destruction; ruin.

des·truc·ción *f.* destruction.

des·truc·ti·vo *adj.* destructive.

des·truc·tor *adj.* destructive; *m.* destroyer

des·tru·ír[32] *v. irr.* to destroy; to ruin.

de·su·nir *v.* to divide, separate.

de·su·sa·do *adj.* unusual, unaccustomed; obsolete, out of use.

de·su·so *m.* disuse; obsoleteness.

des·va·í·do *adj.* lanky, tall and awkward; gaunt; dull, faded.

des·va·i·nar *v.* to shell (*peas, beans, etc.*).

des·va·li·do *adj.* abandoned; destitute; helpless.

des·va·li·jar *v.* to ransack the contents of a valise; to rob.

des·ván *m.* garret, attic.

des·va·ne·cer[13] *v. irr.* to fade, dissolve; to make vain; to make dizzy; **-se** to evaporate; to vanish; to fade out, disappear; to get dizzy.

des·va·ne·ci·do *adj.* (*desmayado*) dizzy, faint; (*or-*

gulloso) proud, haughty; *p.p. of* **desvanecer**.

des·va·ne·ci·mien·to *m.* dizziness, faintness; vanity.

des·va·ri·ar[17] *v.* to rave, be delirious; to rant, talk excitedly; to talk nonsense.

des·va·rí·o *m.* raving; delirium; madness; inconstancy.

des·ve·la·do *adj.* sleepless, awake; watchful; *p.p. of* **desvelar**.

des·ve·lar *v.* to keep (*another*) awake; **-se** to keep awake; to have insomnia, lose sleep; to be worried, anxious.

des·ve·lo *m.* lack of sleep: restlessness; vigilance, watchfulness; worry, anxiety.

des·ven·ci·ja·do *adj.* tottering, rickety, shaky, falling apart.

des·ven·ta·ja *f.* disadvantage.

des·ven·tu·ra *f.* misfortune, unhappiness.

des·ven·tu·ra·do *adj.* unfortunate, unhappy, miserable, wretched.

des·ver·gon·za·do *adj.* shameless, brazen.

des·ver·güen·za *f.* shamelessness; disgrace; shame; insolence; impudent word.

des·ves·tir[5] *v. irr.* to undress; **-se** to undress.

des·via·ción *f.* deviation, turning aside, shift; detour.

des·viar[17] *v.* to deviate, turn aside; to swerve; **-se** to shift direction; to branch off, turn off the main road; to swerve.

des·ví·o *m.* deviation, turning aside; indifference; coldness; side track, railroad siding; detour.

des·vir·tuar[18] *v.* to impair, diminish the value or quality of.

des·vi·vir·se *v.* − **por** to long for; to be excessively fond of, be crazy about, make a fuss over; to do one's best for; **ella se desvive por complacerme** she does her utmost to please me.

des·yer·bar = **desherbar**.

de·ta·llar *v.* to detail, report in detail; to retail.

de·ta·lle *m.* detail; retail; **¡ahí está el** − **!** that's the point.

de·ta·llis·ta *m. & f.* retailer; detailer; person fond of detail.

de·tec·ti·ve, de·tec·ti·vo *m.* detective.

de·ten·ción *f.* detention, arrest; stop, halt; delay.

de·te·ner[45] *v. irr.* to detain, stop; to arrest; **-se** to halt; to delay oneself, stay.

de·te·ni·mien·to *m.* detention; delay; care, deliberation.

de·te·rio·rar *v.* to deteriorate, damage; **-se** to deteriorate, become impaired or damaged; to wear out.

de·te·rio·ro *m.* deterioration, impairment.

de·ter·mi·na·ción *f.* determination; firmness.

de·ter·mi·nar *v.* to determine; to decide; **-se** to

resolve, decide.

de•tes•ta•ble *adj.* detestable; hateful.

de•tes•tar *v.* to detest.

de•to•na•ción *f.* detonation, report (*of a gun*), loud explosion; pop.

de•to•nar *v.* to detonate, explode with a loud noise; to pop.

de•trás *adv.* behind; **– de** *prep.* behind; **por –** from the rear, by the rear, from behind.

deu•da *f.* debt; indebtedness.

deu•do *m.* relative, kinsman.

deu•dor *m.* debtor; *adj.* indebted, obligated.

de•va•nar *v.* to spool, wind on a spool; **-se los sesos** to rack one's brain.

de•va•ne•o *m.* frenzy; dissipation; wandering; idle pursuit; giddiness.

de•vas•tar *v.* to devastate, lay waste, destroy.

de•ve•nir[48] *v. irr.* to befall; *to* become, be transformed into.

de•vo•ción *f.* devotion; piety; attachment.

de•vo•cio•na•rio *m.* prayer book.

de•vo•lu•ción *f.* return, giving back; replacement.

de•vol•ver[2,52] *v. irr.* to return, give back, pay back.

de•vo•ra•dor *adj.* devouring; absorbing; ravenous; *m.* devourer.

de•vo•rar *v.* to devour, gobble up.

de•vo•to *adj.* devout, religious, pious; very fond (of.)

de•vuel•to *p.p. of* **devolver**.

dí•a *m.* day; **al otro –** on the next day; **hoy –** nowadays; **un – sí y otro no** every other day.

dia•blo *m.* devil, demon.

dia•blu•ra *f.* deviltry, mischief, devilish prank.

dia•bó•li•co *adj.* diabolic, devilish, fiendish.

diá•co•no *m.* deacon.

dia•de•ma *f.* diadem, crown.

diá•fa•no *adj.* transparent, clear; sheer.

diag•nos•ti•car[4] *v.* to diagnose.

dia•gra•ma *m.* diagram; graph.

dia•lec•to *m.* dialect.

dia•lo•gar[7] *v.* to dialogue.

diá•lo•go *m.* dialogue.

dia•man•te *m.* diamond.

diá•me•tro *m.* diameter.

dian•tre *m.* devil.

dia•pa•són *m.* pitch (*of a sound*); tuning fork.

dia•po•si•ti•va *f. Spain* slide, lantern slide.

dia•rio *adj.* dialy; *m.* newspaper; daily expense; journal, diary.

dia•rre•a *f.* diarrhea.

di•bu•jan•te *m. & f.* draftsman; designer.

di•bu•jar *v.* (*diseñar*) to draw, make a drawing of; (*describir*) depict, portray; describe; **-se** to appear,

show.

di•bu•jo *m.* drawing; delineation, portrayal, picture; **– natural** drawing of the human figure, drawing from life.

dic•ción *f.* diction; word; choice of words, style.

di•ciem•bre *m.* December.

dic•ta•do *m.* dictation; title; dictate; **escribir al –** to take dictation.

dic•ta•dor *m.* dictator.

dic•ta•du•ra *f.* dictatorship.

dic•ta•men *m.* opinion, judgment.

dic•ta•mi•nar *v.* to give an opinion or judgment.

dic•tar *v.* to dictate.

di•cha *f.* happiness; good luck.

di•cha•ra•che•ro *adj.* fond of making wisecracks; witty.

di•cha•ra•cho *m.* wisecrack, smart remark; malicious remark.

di•cho *p.p. of* **decir** said; **– y hecho** no sooner said than done; *m.* saying, popular proverb.

di•cho•so *adj.* happy, lucky.

dien•te *m.* tooth; tusk; **– de león** dandelion; **de -s afuera** insincerely; *Am.* **pelar el –** to smile affectedly.

di•é•re•sis *f.* diaeresis (*as in* **vergüenza**).

die•sel *m.* diesel; diesel motor.

dies•tra *f.* ritht hand.

dies•tro *adj.* skillful; right; *m.* matador; skillful swordsman; halter.

die•ta *f.* diet; assembly; salary, fee.

diez•mo *m.* tithe.

di•fa•ma•ción *f.* libel, slander.

di•fa•ma•dor *m.* slanderer.

di•fa•mar *v.* to defame, libel, malign, slander.

di•fa•ma•to•rio *adj.* scandalous, slandering.

di•fe•ren•cia *f.* difference.

di•fe•ren•ciar *v.* to differentiate, distinguish; to differ, disagree; **-se** to distinguish oneself; to become different.

di•fe•ren•te *adj.* different.

di•fe•rir[3] *v. irr.* to defer, put off, delay; to differ, disagree; to be different.

di•fí•cil *adj.* difficult.

di•fi•cul•tad *f.* difficulty.

di•fi•cul•tar *v.* to make difficult; **– el paso** to impede or obstruct the passage; **-se** to become difficult.

di•fi•cul•to•so *adj.* difficult, hard.

dif•te•ria *f.* diphtheria.

di·fun·dir *v.* to diffuse, spread out, scatter; to broadcast by radio.

di·fun·to *adj.* deceased, dead; *m.* corpse.

di·fu·sión *f.* diffusion, spreading, scattering; wordiness; broadcasting.

di·fu·so *adj.* diffuse; diffused, widespread.

di·ge·ri·ble *adj.* digestible.

di·ge·rir[3] *v. irr.* to digest.

dig·nar·se *v.* to deign, condescend.

dig·na·ta·rio *m.* dignitary (*person in a high office*).

dig·ni·dad *f.* dignity.

dig·no *adj.* worthy; dignified.

di·gre·sión *f.* digression.

di·je *m.* trinket, small piece of jewelry; locket; woman of fine qualities, a "jewel"; *Am.* locket or charm.

di·la·ción *f.* delay.

di·la·ta·do *adj.* vast, spacious; extensive; *p.p. of* **dilatar**

di·la·tar *v.* to dilate, widen, enlarge; to expand; to lengthen, extend; to spread out; to defer, put off, retard; **-se** to expand; to be diffuse, wordy; *Am.* to delay oneself, take long.

di·li·gen·cia *f.* diligence, care, industry; speed; stagecoach; business, errand.

di·li·gen·te *adj.* diligent; quick; speedy

di·luir[32] *v. irr.* to dilute.

di·lu·vio *m.* flood.

di·men·sión *f.* dimension.

di·mes: — y diretes quibbling, arguing; **andar en — y diretes** to quibble, argue.

di·mi·nu·ción *f.* diminution, decrease.

di·mi·nu·ti·vo *adj.* diminutive, tiny; diminishing; *m.* diminutive.

di·mi·nu·to *adj.* tiny, little.

di·mi·sión *f.* resignation (*from an office*).

di·mi·tir *v.* to resign give up (*a position, office, etc.*).

di·ná·mi·ca *f.* dynamics; **dinámico** *adj.* dynamic.

di·na·mis·mo *m.* vigor, forcefulness; dynamic force or energy.

di·na·mi·ta *f.* dynamite.

dí·na·mo *m.* dynamo.

di·nas·tí·a *f.* dynasty.

di·ne·ral *m.* a lot of money.

di·ne·ro *m.* money; currency; *Peru* Peruvian silver coin equivalent to about ten cents; **— contante y sonante** ready cash, hard cash.

dios *m.* god; **Dios** God; **a la buena de —** without malice; without plan, haphazard, at random.

dio·sa *f.* goddess.

di·plo·ma·cia *f.* diplomacy; tact.

di·plo·má·ti·co *adj.* diplomatic; tactful; *m.* diplomat.

di·pu·ta·ción *f.* deputation; committee.

di·pu·ta·do *m.* deputy; representative.

di·pu·tar *v.* to depute, delegate, commission.

di·que *m.* dike; barrier; **— de carena** dry dock.

di·rec·ción *f.* direction, course; advice, guidance; management; board of directors; office of the board of directors; address.

di·rec·ti·vo *adj.* directive, directing, guiding; **mesa directiva** board of directors.

di·rec·to *adj.* direct, straight.

di·rec·tor *m.* director, manager; *adj.* directing

di·rec·to·rio *adj.* directory, directive, directing; *m.* directory, book of instructions; directorate, board of directors.

di·ri·gen·te *adj.* directing, leading; *m.* leader, director.

di·ri·gir[11] *v.* to direct, manage, govern; to guide; to address (*letters, packages*); to dedicate; **-se a** to address (*a person*); to go to or toward.

dis·cer·ni·mien·to *m.* discernment, keen judgment, insight, discrimination.

dis·cer·nir[3] *v. irr.* to discern; to distinguish; to discriminate.

dis·ci·pli·na *f.* discipline, training; rule of conduct; order; any art or science; scourge, whip.

dis·ci·pli·nar *v.* to discipline, train; to drill; **-se** to discipline oneself; to scourge oneself.

dis·cí·pu·lo *m.* pupil; disciple.

dis·co *m.* disk; discus; phonograph record.

dís·co·lo *adj.* unruly, disobedient; unfriendly.

dis·cor·dan·cia *f.* discord, disagreement

dis·cor·dia *f.* discord.

dis·cre·ción *f.* discretion; keenness; wit; **darse** (*or* **rendirse**) **a —** to surrender unconditionally; **discrecional** *adj.* optional.

dis·cre·pan·cia *f.* discrepancy.

dis·cre·to *adj.* discreet, prudent; clever.

dis·cul·pa *f.* excuse; apology.

dis·cul·pa·ble *adj.* excusable.

dis·cul·par *v.* to excuse, free from blame; **-se** to excuse oneself, apologize.

dis·cu·rrir *v.* (*charlar*) to discuss; (*recorrer*) to ramble about; (*imaginar*) to invent, think out.

dis·cur·se·ar *v.* to make speeches.

dis·cur·so *m.* discourse; speech; reasoning; lapse of time.

dis·cu·sión *f.* discussion.

dis·cu·ti·ble *adj.* debatable, questionable.

dis·cu·tir *v.* to discuss.

di·se·car[6] *v.* to dissect; to stuff and mount (*the skins of animals*).

di·se·mi·na·ción *f.* dissemination, spread, scattering.

di·se·mi·nar *v.* to disseminate, scatter, spread.

di·sen·sión *f.* dissension, dissent, disagreement.

di·sen·te·rí·a *f.* dysentery.

di·sen·tir[3] *v. irr.* to dissent, differ, disagree.

di·se·ña·dor *m.* designer.

di·se·ñar *v.* to design; to sketch, outline.

di·se·ño *m.* design; sketch, outline.

di·ser·tar *v.* to discourse, discuss.

dis·for·me *adj.* deformed; ugly, hideous; out of proportion.

dis·fraz *m.* disguise, mask; masquerade costume.

dis·fra·zar[9] *v.* to disguise, conceal; **-se** to disguise oneself; to masquerade.

dis·fru·tar *v.* to enjoy; to reap benefit or advantage; to make use of.

dis·fru·te *m.* enjoyment, benefit, use.

dis·gus·tar *v.* to disgust, displease; **-se** to get angry; to get bored.

dis·gus·to *m.* displeasure; unpleassant-ness; annoyance; quarrel; grief; disgust.

di·si·den·te *m. & f.* dissident; protester.

di·si·mu·la·do *adj.* underhanded, sly, cunning; *p.p. of* **disimular**.

di·si·mu·lar *v.* to feign, hide, mask; to overlook, excuse.

di·si·mu·lo *m.* dissimulation, feigning, pretense; slyness; reserve.

di·si·pa·ción *f.* dissipation; waste, extravagance.

di·si·par *v.* to dissipate, scatter; to squander; **-se** to vanish.

dis·lo·car[6] *v.* to dislocate, put out of joint; **-se** to become dislocated, get out of joint.

dis·mi·nu·ción = **diminución.**

dis·mi·nu·ír[32] *v. irr.* to diminish, decrease, lessen.

di·so·cia·ción *f.* dissociation, separation.

di·so·ciar *v.* to dissociate, separate.

di·so·lu·ción *f.* dissolution, breaking up; dissoluteness, lewdness.

di·so·lu·to *adj.* dissolute, loose, immoral, dissipated.

di·sol·ver[2,52] *v. irr.* to dissolve; to melt.

di·so·nan·cia *f.* discord.

dis·pa·ra·da *f. C.A., Mex., Carib., Riopl.* rush, run.

dis·pa·rar *v.* to shoot, fire, discharge; to throw; **-se** to run away, dart out.

dis·pa·ra·ta·do *adj.* absurd, foolish, senseless.

dis·pa·ra·tar *v.* to talk nonsense; to blunder; to act foolishly.

dis·pa·ra·te *m.* nonsense, blunder.

dis·pa·ri·dad *f.* inequality.

dis·pa·ro *m.* shooting, discharge, explosion; shot; sudden dash, run.

dis·pen·sa *f.* dispensation; exemption.

dis·pen·sar *v.* to excuse, absolve, pardon; to grant, give.

dis·pen·sa·rio *m.* dispensary; pharma-ceutical laboratory; pharmacopoeia (*book containing list and description of drugs*).

dis·per·sar *v.* to disperse, scatter.

dis·per·sión *f.* dispersion, dispersal.

dis·pli·cen·cia *f.* displeasure, discontent, dislike.

dis·pli·cen·te *adj.* unpleasant, disagree-able, cross.

dis·po·ner[40] *v. irr.* (*arreglar*) to dispose; to arrange, put in order; to prepare; (*mandar*) to order, command; **-se** to get ready; to make one's will and testament.

dis·po·ni·ble *adj.* spare, available; on hand.

dis·po·si·ción *f.* disposition; arrangement; order, command; aptitude; disposal.

dis·pues·to *p.p. of* **disponer** & *adj.* disposed; ready; fit; smart, clever.

dis·pu·ta *f.* dispute.

dis·pu·tar *v.* to dispute.

dis·tan·cia *f.* distance.

dis·tan·te *adj.* distant.

dis·tar *v.* to be distant, far (from).

dis·ten·der[1] *v. irr.* to distend, stretch; to inflate; **-se** to distend, expand.

dis·tin·ción *f.* distinction.

dis·tin·gui·do *adj. & p.p.* distinguished.

dis·tin·guir[12] *v.* to distinguish; **-se** to distinguish oneself, excel; to differ, be different.

dis·tin·ti·vo *adj.* distinctive, distinguish-ing; *m.* distinguishing characteristic; mark, sign; badge.

dis·tin·to *adj.* distinct, plain, clear; different.

dis·trac·ción *f.* distraction; diversion, amusement; lack of attention.

dis·tra·er[46] *v. irr.* to distract; to divert, amuse; to lead astray; to divert (*funds*); **-se** to have a good time; to be absentminded; to be inattentive.

dis·tra·í·do *adj.* distracted; inattentive; absentminded; *Am.* slovenly, untidy.

dis·tri·bu·ción *f.* distribution, apportion-ment.

dis·tri·bui·dor *m.* distributor; *adj.* distributing.

dis·tri·bu·ír[32] *v. irr.* to distribute; to sort, classify.

dis·tri·to *m.* district; region.

dis·tur·bio *m.* disturbance.

di·suel·to *p.p. of* **disolver.**

di·va·ga·ción *f.* rambling, digression.

di·va·gar[7] *v.* to ramble; to digress.

di·ván *m.* divan, sofa.

di·ver·gen·cia *f.* divergence; difference (*of opinion*).

di·ver·gir[11] *v.* to diverge; to differ.

di·ver·si·dad *f.* diversity; variety.

di·ver·sión *f.* amusement.

di·ver·so *adj.* diverse, different; **-s** several, various.

di·ver·ti·do *adj.* amusing, funny.

di·ver·tir[3] *v. irr.* to amuse, entertain; to divert, turn aside; **-se** to have a good time, amuse oneself.

di·vi·den·do *m.* dividend.

di·vi·dir *v.* to divide, split.

di·vi·ni·dad *f.* divinity, deity; **¡qué –!** what a beauty!

di·vi·no *adj.* divine.

di·vi·sa *f.* device, emblem.

di·vi·sar *v.* to sight; to make out, distinguish.

di·vi·sión *f.* division.

di·vor·ciar *v.* to divorce; to separate.

di·vor·cio *m.* divorce.

di·vul·gar[7] *v.* to divulge, spread, make public, give out.

diz = dice; dizque they say that. . .

do·bla·di·llar *v.* to hem.

do·bla·di·llo *m.* hem; **– de ojo** hemstitch.

do·blar *v.* to bend, fold; to double; to toll, knell; *Ríopl.* to knock down; **– la esquina** to turn the corner; **-se** to stoop; to bend down; to give in.

do·ble *adj.* double, twofold; doublefaced, hypocritical; *Am.* broke, poor; *m.* fold; toll, tolling of bells, knell.

do·ble·gar[7] *v.* to bend; to fold; **-se** to bend over; to stoop; to submit, yield.

do·blez *m.* fold, crease; duplicity, hypocrisy.

do·ce·na *f.* dozen.

do·cen·te *adj.* teaching; educational; **cuerpo –** faculty (*of a school*).

dó·cil *adj.* docile, obedient, manageable, meek; flexible; **docilidad** *f.* obedience, meekness, gentleness; flexibility.

doc·to *adj.* learned; expert.

doc·tor *m.* doctor.

doc·to·rar *v.* to grant a doctor's degree to; **-se** to get a doctor's degree.

doc·tri·na *f.* doctrine.

do·cu·men·tar *v.* to document.

do·cu·men·to *m.* document.

do·gal *m.* halter; noose.

dog·ma *m.* dogma; **dogmático** *adj.* dogmatic, pertaining to dogma; positive.

do·len·cia *f.* ailment; ache, aching.

do·ler[2] *v. irr.* to ache, hurt, cause pain; to cause grief; **-se de** to feel pity for, feel sorry for; to repent from.

do·lien·te *adj.* sorrowful; suffering; aching; *m.* sick person, patient; mourner.

do·lor *m.* pain, ache; sorrow, grief.

do·lo·ri·do *adj.* aching, sore; afficted; repentant; doleful.

do·lo·ro·so *adj.* painful; sorrowful.

do·ma *f.* breaking of horses.

do·ma·dor *m.* horsebreaker, broncobuster.

do·mar *v.* to tame, subdue.

do·me·ñar *v.* to tame; to subdue; to dominate.

do·mes·ti·car[6] *v.* to domesticate, tame.

do·més·ti·co *adj.* domestic; *m.* house servant.

do·mi·ci·liar *v.* to house, lodge; *Ríopl.* to address (*a letter*); **-se** to take up residence; to settle down; to dwell, reside.

do·mi·ci·lio *m.* home, dwelling.

do·mi·na·ción *f.* domination, rule, authority.

do·mi·na·dor *adj.* dominant, dominating; domineering, bossy; *m.* ruler, boss.

do·mi·nan·te *adj.* dominant; domineering; tyrannical; prevailing, predominant.

do·mi·nar *v.* to dominate, rule, lead; to stand out, tower above; to master.

dó·mi·ne *m.* teacher; pedagogue; pedant.

do·min·go *m.* Sunday; **– de ramos** Palm Sunday.

do·mi·nio *m.* domain; dominion; authority; mastery (*of a science, art, language, etc.*).

do·mi·nó *m.* domino.

don *m.* gift; ability, knack; Don (*title used only before Christian names of men*).

do·na·ción *f.* donation; grant.

do·na·dor *m.* donor, giver.

do·nai·re *m.* grace, elegance; wit; humor; witty remark.

do·nai·ro·so *adj.* elegant, graceful; witty.

do·nar *v.* to donate.

don·ce·lla *f.* virgin, maiden; maidservant; *Col.* felon (*sore or inflammation near a finger or toenail*).

don·de *rel. adv.* where, in which; **a – (adonde)** where, to which; *C.A., Ríopl.* to the house of; **de –** from where, from which; **en –** where, in which; **por –** where, through which; wherefore; **– no** otherwise; if not; **¿dónde?** *interr. adv.* where?; **¿por –?** which way?

don·de·quie·ra *adv.* wherever; anywhere.

don·jua·nis·mo *m.* Don Juanism, conduct reminiscent of Don Juan Tenorio.

do·no·so *adj.* witty, gay; graceful.

do·ña *f.* Doña (*title used only before Christian names of women*).

do·ra·do *p.p. & adj.* gilded, gilt; golden; *m.* gilding; *Am.* a kind of hummingbird; **doradillo** *adj. Am.* honeycolored, golden (*applied to horses*).

do·rar *v.* to gild.

dor·mir[4] *v. irr.* to sleep; **-se** to go to sleep, fall asleep; to become numb.

dor·mi·tar *v.* to doze.

dor·mi·to·rio *m.* dormitory; bedroom.

dor·so *m.* back, reverse.

do·sel *m.* canopy.

do·sis *f.* dose.

do·ta·ción *f.* endowment, endowing; donation,

foundation; dowry; complement (*personnel of a warship*); office force.

do•tar *v.* to endow; to provide with a dowry.

do•te *m. & f.* dowry; *f.* natural gift, talent, or quality.

dra•ga *f.* dredge, dredging machine.

dra•ga•do *m.* dredging.

dra•ga•mi•nas *m.* mine sweeper.

dra•gar[7] *v.* to dredge.

dra•gón *m.* dragon.

dra•ma *m.* drama.

dra•má•ti•co *adj.* dramatic; *m.* dramatic actor; playwright, dramatist.

dra•ma•ti•zar[9] *v.* to dramatize.

dra•ma•tur•go *m.* playwright, dramatist.

dre•na•je *m. Am.* drainage.

dre•nar *v. Am.* to drain.

dril *m.* drill (*strong cotton or linen cloth*).

dro•ga *f.* (*medicina*) drug, medicine; (*mentira*) lie, fib; trick; (*molestia*) bother, nuisance; *Peru, Carib.* bad debt; *Riopl.* drug on the market, unsalable article.

dro•gue•rí•a *f.* drugstore; drug business.

dro•gue•ro *m.* druggist; *Am.* cheat, debt evader.

dro•guis•ta *m. & f.* druggist; cheat, crook.

du•cha *f.* shower bath; douche.

du•cho *adj.* expert, skillful.

du•da *f.* doubt.

du•da•ble *adj.* doubtful.

du•dar *v.* to doubt; to hesitate.

du•do•so *adj.* doubtful; uncertain.

due•la *f.* stave (*of a barrel*); *Mex., Andes* long, narrow floor board.

due•lo *m.* (*luto*) grief, sorrow; mourning; mourners; (*pleito*) duel; **estar de –** to be in mourning; to mourn.

duen•de *m.* goblin.

due•ña *f.* owner, landlady; duenna, chaperon or governess.

due•ño *m.* owner; master.

due•to, duo *m.* duet.

dul•ce *adj.* sweet; pleasant, agreeable; fresh (*water*); soft (*metal*); *m.* sweetmeat; candy; preserves; *Am.* sugar, honey; **dulcería** *f.* candy shop.

dul•ci•fi•car[6] *v.* to sweeten; to soften.

dul•zón *adj.* over-sweet, sickeningly sweet.

dul•zu•ra *f.* sweetness; meekness.

du•na *f.* dune, sand dune.

du•pli•ca•do *adj. & m.* duplicate; **por –** in duplicate; *p.p. of* **duplicar.**

du•pli•car[6] *v.* to duplicate, double; to repeat.

du•pli•ci•dad *f.* duplicity, deceit, deceitfulness, treachery.

du•que *m.* duke.

du•ra•bi•li•dad *f.* durability, durable quality, wear.

du•ra•ble *adj.* durable.

du•ra•ción *f.* duration.

du•ra•de•ro *adj.* durable, lasting.

du•ran•te *prep.* during, for.

du•rar *v.* to last, endure; to wear well.

du•raz•no *m.* peach; peach tree; **duraznero** *m.* peach tree.

du•re•za *f.* hardness; harshness.

dur•mien•te *adj.* sleeping; *m.* sleeper; crossbeam; *Col., Ven., Mex., Ch.,* railroad tie.

du•ro *adj.* (*sólido*) hard; firm, solid; untiring; (*cruel*) cruel; harsh; rigid; (*tacaño*) stubborn; stingy; **a duras penas** with difficulty; *Am.* **– y parejo** eagerly, tenaciously; *Am.* **hacer –** to resist stubbornly; *m.* **duro** (*Spanish dollar*).

E

e *conj.* and (*before words beginning with* **i** *or* **hi**).

é•ba•no *m.* ebony.

e•brio *adj.* drunk.

e•bu•lli•ción *f.* boiling, bubbling up.

e•cle•siás•ti•co *adj.* ecclesiastic, belonging to the church; *m.* clergyman.

e•clip•sar *v.* to eclipse; to outshine, surpass.

é•clo•ga *f.* eclogue, pastoral poem, idyll.

e•co *m.* echo.

e•co•no•mí•a *f.* economy; **– política** economics, political economy.

e•co•nó•mi•co *adj.* economic; economical, saving; **economista** *m.* economist.

e•co•no•mi•zar[9] *v.* to economize; save.

e•cua•ción *f.* equation.

e•cua•dor *m.* equator.

e•char *v.* (*tirar*) to throw, cast; to expel; to throw out; (*emitir*) to give off; to sprout; **– a correr** to run away; **-(se) a perder** to spoil; **– a pique** to sink; **-(se) a reír** to burst out laughing; **– carnes** to get fat; **– de menos** to miss; **– de ver** to notice; to make out; **– mano** to seize; **– papas** to fib; **– raíces** to take root; **– suertes** to draw lots; **-se** to lie down; *Am.* **echársela** to boast.

e•dad *f.* age.

e•dén *m.* Eden; paradise.

e•di•ción *f.* edition, publication.

e•di•fi•ca•ción *f.* edification (*moral or spiritual uplift*);

construction.

e·di·fi·car⁶ v. to construct, build; to edify, uplift.

e·di·fi·cio m. edifice, building.

e·di·tar v. to publish.

e·di·tor m. publisher; adj. publishing.

e·di·to·rial adj. publishing, editorial; m. editorial; f. publishing house.

e·dre·dón m. down quilt, comforter, quilted blanket.

e·du·ca·ción f. education, training; breeding, manners.

e·du·ca·dor m. educator; adj. educating.

e·du·can·do m. pupil; inmate (of an orphanage, boarding school, etc.).

e·du·car⁶ v. to educate, teach, train, raise, bring up.

e·du·ca·ti·vo adj. educational.

e·fec·ti·vo adj. effective; real; in operation, active; m. cash.

e·fec·to m. (resultado) effect, result; (fin) end, purpose; -s goods, personal property; en – in fact, actually; llevar a – to carry out; surtir – to come out as expected; to give good results.

e·fec·tuar¹⁸ v. to effect, bring about.

e·fi·ca·cia f. efficacy; efficiency; effectiveness.

e·fi·caz adj. effective; active; efficient.

e·fi·cien·cia f. efficiency; eficiente adj. efficient.

e·fí·me·ro adj. ephemeral, short-lived, brief.

e·flu·vio m. emanation, exhalation, vapors.

e·fu·sión f. effusion, unrestrained expression of feeling, gushy manner; – de sangre bloodshed.

e·fu·si·vo adj. effusive, too demonstrative, over-emotional.

e·gip·cio adj. & m. Egyptian.

e·go·cén·tri·co adj. egocentric, selfcentered.

e·go·ís·mo m. selfishness.

e·go·ís·ta adj. selfish; m. & f. selfish person.

e·go·la·trí·a f. self-worship.

e·je m. axis; axle.

e·je·cu·ción f. execution; carryng out.

e·je·cu·tar v. to execute; to carry out; to perform, do.

e·je·cu·ti·vo adj. executive; active; m. executive.

e·je·cu·tor m. executor; – de la justicia executioner.

e·jem·plar adj. exemplary, model; m. copy; specimen.

e·jem·plo m. example; model, pattern.

e·jer·cer¹⁰ v. to practice (a profession); to exert.

e·jer·ci·cio m. exercise; practice; military drill; exercise (of authority); hacer – to take exercise.

e·jer·ci·tar v. to practice, exercise; to drill, train; -se to train oneself; to practice.

e·jér·ci·to m. army.

e·ji·do m. public land, common.

e·jo·te m. Mex., Guat., string bean.

el def. art. m. the; – de the one with, that one with; – que rel. pron. he who, the one that; él pers. pron. he; him, it (after a prep.).

e·la·bo·ra·ción f. manufacture, making; development.

e·la·bo·rar v. to elaborate.

e·las·ti·ci·dad f. elasticity.

e·lás·ti·co adj. elastic; flexible; m. elastic; elastic tape; wire spring; -s Am. suspenders.

e·lec·ción f. election; choice.

e·lec·to adj. elect, chosen; m. elect, person chosen.

e·lec·tor m. elector, voter; adj. electoral, electing.

e·lec·to·ral adj. electoral.

e·lec·tri·ci·dad f. electricity.

e·lec·tri·cis·ta m. electrician; electrical engineer.

e·léc·tri·co adj. electric, electrical.

e·lec·tri·zar⁹ v. to electrify; to thrill, excite; Am. to anger, irritate.

e·lec·tro·car·dió·gra·fo m. electrocar-diograph.

e·lec·troi·mán m. electromagnet.

e·lec·tró·ni·co adj. electronic; electrónica f. electronics.

e·le·fan·te m. elephant.

e·le·gan·cia f. elegance, grace, distinguished manner.

e·le·gan·te adj. elegant, graceful, polished; stylish.

e·le·gir⁵·¹¹ v. irr. to elect, choose.

e·le·men·tal adj. elementary; elemental, fundamental.

e·le·men·to m. element; -s elements, fundamentals; personnel; – químicos chemical elements, simple substances; Am. ser (or estar) hecho un – to be an idiot, a fool.

e·le·va·ción f. elevation; height; rise; rapture.

e·le·va·dor m. Am. elevator, hoist.

e·le·var v. to elevate, raise, lift; -se to go up; to soar.

e·li·mi·na·ción f. elimination, removal.

e·li·mi·nar v. to eliminate.

e·lo·cuen·cia f. eloquence.

e·lo·cuen·te adj. eloquent.

e·lo·giar v. to praise.

e·lo·gio m. praise.

e·lo·te m. Mex., C.A. ear of corn, corn on the cob.

e·lu·ci·da·ción f. elucidation, explanation.

e·lu·ci·dar v. to elucidate, illustrate, explain.

e·lu·dir v. to elude, avoid, dodge.

e·lla pers. pron. she; her, it (after a prep.).

e·llo pron. it; – es que the fact is that.

e·ma·na·ción f. emanation, flow; fumes, vapor, odor, manifestation.

e·ma·nar v. to emanate, spring, issue.

e·man·ci·pa·ción f. emancipation.

e·man·ci·par v. to emancipate, set free; -se to become free.

em·ba·ja·da f. embassy; errand, mission.

em·ba·ja·dor m. ambassador.

em·ba·la·dor m. packer.

em·ba·la·je m. packing.

em·ba·lar v. to pack; to bale, crate.

em·bal·do·sar v. to pave with flagstones or tiles.

em·bal·sa·mar v. to embalm; to scent, perfume.

em·ba·ra·zar⁹ v. (impedir) to hinder, to obstruct; (preñar) to make pregnant; **-se** to become pregnant; to become embarrassed.

em·ba·ra·zo *m.* (*obstáculo*) impediment, obstacle; (*preñez*) pregnancy; (*timidez*) bashfulness, awkwardness.

em·ba·ra·zo·so *adj.* embarrassing; cumbersome, unwieldly.

em·bar·ca·ción *f.* ship, boat; embarkation.

em·bar·ca·de·ro *m.* wharf, pier.

em·bar·ca·dor *m.* shipper.

em·bar·car[6] *v.* to embark; to ship: *Am.* to ship by train or any vehicle; **-se** to embark, sail; to engage (in); *Am.* to board, get on a train.

em·bar·co *m.* embarkation.

em·bar·gar *v.* to impede; to restrain; to attach, confiscate; to lay an embargo on; **estar embargado de emoción** to be overcome with emotion.

em·bar·go *m.* embargo, restriction on commerce; attachment, confiscation; **sin —** nevertheless.

em·bar·que *m.* shipment.

em·ba·rra·do *p.p.* & *adj.* smeared; plastered; muddy.

em·ba·rrar *v.* to smear, daub.

em·bau·ca·dor *m.* cheat, impostor.

em·bau·car[6] *v.* to fool, trick, swindle, deceive.

em·be·be·ci·do *p.p.* & *adj.* absorbed; amazed.

em·be·be·ci·mien·to *m.* absorption; rapture.

em·be·ber *v.* to imbibe, absorb; to soak; to shrink; **-se** to be fascinated; to be absorbed.

em·be·le·sar *v.* to enrapture, delight, charm.

em·be·le·so *m.* delight, ecstasy.

em·be·lle·cer[13] *v. irr.* to embellish, beautify, adorn.

em·bes·ti·da *f.* sudden attack, onset, assault.

em·bes·tir[5] *v. irr.* to attack, assail.

em·be·tu·nar *v.* to cover with pitch; to black.

em·blan·que·cer[13] *v. irr.* to whiten; to bleach; to become white; **-se** to whiten, become white.

em·ble·ma *m.* emblem.

em·bo·bar *v.* to fool; to amuse; to fascinate; to amaze; **-se** to be amazed; to be fascinated.

em·bo·bi·na·do *m.* reel assembly (*of a tape recorder or computer*).

em·bo·ca·du·ra *f.* mouth (*of a river*); entrance (*through a narrow passage*); mouthpiece (*of a wind instrument*); bit (*of a bridle*); taste flavor (said of *wines*).

em·bo·la·do *m.* bull whose horns have been tipped with falls; impotent, ineffectual person; *p.p. of* **embolar**.

em·bo·lar *v.* (*al toro*) to tip a bull's horns with balls; (*dar lustre*) to polish, to black; **-se** *C.A.* to get drunk.

ém·bo·lo *m.* piston; plunger (*of a pump*); embolus (*clot in a blood vessel*).

em·bol·sar *v.* to put into a pocket or purse; **-se** to pocket, put into one's pocket.

em·bo·rra·char *v.* to intoxicate; **-se** to get drunk.

em·bo·rro·nar *v.* to blot; to scribble.

em·bos·ca·da *f.* ambush.

em·bos·car[6] *v.* to ambush; **-se** to lie in ambush; to go into a forest.

em·bo·ta·do *adj.* dull, blunt; *p.p. of* **embotar**.

em·bo·ta·mien·to *m.* dullness, bluntness; dulling, blunting.

em·bo·tar *v.* to dull, blunt; to enervate, waken.

em·bo·te·lla·dor *m.* bottling machine; **embotelladora** bottling works.

em·bo·te·llar *v.* to bottle; to bottle up; *Am.* to jail.

em·bo·za·do *adj.* cloaked; muffled, covered up to the face.

em·bo·zar[7] *v.* to muffle; to cloak, conceal, disguise; to muzzle; **-se** to muffle oneself, wrap oneself.

em·bra·gar *v.* to engage or throw in the clutch.

em·bra·gue *m.* clutch (*of a machine*); coupling.

em·bria·gar[7] *v.* to intoxicate; **-se** to get drunk, intoxicated.

em·bria·guez *f.* to intoxication; drunkeness.

em·bro·llar *v.* to involve, ensnare, entangle; tu confuse.

em·bro·llo *m.* confusion, tangle; trickery, lie, deception.

em·bro·mar *v.* to chaff, make fun of, "kid"; *Am.* to bother, molest; *Am.* to delay unnecessarily; *Col., Ven.* to ruin, harm; **-se** *Am.* to be bothered, disgusted; *Mex.* to get delayed.

em·bru·jar *v.* to bewitch, enchant.

em·bru·jo *m.* charm, enchantment; glamour.

em·bru·te·cer[13] *v. irr.* to stupefy, render brutish; to dull the mind, make insensible.

em·bu·do *m.* funnel; trick.

em·bus·te *m.* lie, fraud; trinket.

em·bus·te·ro *m.* liar; *adj.* deceitful, tricky.

em·bu·ti·do *m.* sausage; inlaid work; *Am.* insertion of embroidery or lace; *p.p. of* **embutir**.

em·bu·tir *v.* to insert, inlay; to stuff.

e·mer·ger[11] *v.* to emerge, come out.

e·mi·gra·ción *f.* emigration.

e·mi·gran·te *m.* & *f.* emigrant.

e·mi·grar *v.* to emigrate; to migrate.

e·mi·nen·cia *f.* eminence; height.

e·mi·nen·te *adj.* eminent, high, lofty.

e·mi·sión *f.* issue (*of bonds, money, etc.*); radio broadcast.

e·mi·sor *adj.* emitting; broadcasting; *m.* radio transmitter; **emisora** *f.* broadcasting station.

e·mi·tir *v.* to emit, give off; to utter; to send forth; to issue; to broadcast.

e·mo·ción *f.* emotion.

e·mo·cio·nal *adj.* emotional.

e·mo·cio·nan·te *adj.* moving, touching, thrilling.

e·mo·cio·nar *v.* to cause emotion, touch, move; **-se** to be touched, moved, stirred.

e·mo·ti·vo *adj.* emotional.

em·pa·ca·dor *m.* packer.

em·pa·car[6] *v.* to pack up, wrap up, bale, crate; *Riopl.* to goad, irritate (*an animal*); **-se** to be stubborn; to get angry; *Riopl.* to balk; *Riopl.* to put on airs.

em·pa·cha·do *p.p. & adj.* (*relleno*) clogged; stuffed; upset from indigestion; (*tímido*) embarrassed; bashful.

em·pa·char *v.* to stuff, cram; to cause indigestion; **-se** to get upset; to get clogged; to be stuffed; to suffer indigestion; to get embarrassed.

em·pa·cho *m.* indigestion; bashfulness; **no tener -en** lo have no objection to; to feel free to.

em·pa·la·gar[7] *v.* to cloy; to pall on, become distasteful; to disgust.

em·pa·la·ga·so *adj.* cloying; sickeningly sweet; boring, wearisome.

em·pa·li·za·da *f.* stockade, palisade.

em·pal·mar *v.* to splice; to join; **– con** to join (*as railroads or highways*).

em·pal·me *m.* junction; joint, connection; splice.

em·pa·na·da *f.* pie, meat pie; swindle, fraud.

em·pa·ni·zar[9] *v.* Carib., *C.A.*, *Mex.* to bread.

em·pa·ña·do *adj. & p.p.* tarnished; dim, blurred.

em·pa·ñar *v.* to blur, dim, tarnish.

em·pa·pa·da *f. Am.* drenching, soaking.

em·pa·par *v.* to soak, drench, saturate.

em·pa·pe·la·dor *m.* paper hanger.

em·pa·pe·lar *v.* to paper; to wrap in paper.

em·pa·que *m.* (*bulto*) packing; (*parecer*) looks, appearance, air; airs, importance; *Am.*, *Peru* impudence.

em·pa·que·tar *v.* to pack; to pack in; to make a package; **-se** to dress up, doll up.

em·pa·re·da·do *adj.* shut up, confined between walls; *m.* sandwich; prisoner confined in a narrow cell.

em·pa·re·jar *v.* to even up, level off; to match; to pair off; to overtake, catch up with.

em·pa·ren·ta·do *adj. & p.p.* related by marriage.

em·pa·ren·tar *v.* to become related by marriage.

em·pa·rra·do *m.* vine arbor.

em·pas·tar *v.* to paste; to fill (*a tooth*); to bind (*books*); **-se** to get lost in the pasture; *Mex.* to become overgrown with grass.

em·pas·te *m.* tooth filling; binding (*of a book*).

em·pa·tar *v.* (*igualar*) to tie (*in a game*), have an equal score; to have an equal number of votes; (*impedir*) to hinder, obstruct; *Col.*, *Ven.*,*Carib.* to tie, join.

em·pa·te *m.* tie, draw, equal score, equal number of votes; hindrance, obstruction ; *Am.* joint, junction.

em·pe·ci·na·do *adj. Am.* stubborn.

em·pe·der·ni·do *adj.* hardened, hardhearted.

em·pe·der·nir[51] *v.* to harden, toughen; **-se** to become hardened.

em·pe·dra·do *m.* cobblestone pavement; *p.p. & adj.* paved with stones.

em·pe·drar[1] *v. irr.* to pave with stones.

em·pei·ne *m.* instep; groin (*hollow between lower part of abdomen and thigh*).

em·pe·llón *m.* push, shove; **a -es** by pushing.

em·pe·ñar *v.* (*dar en prenda*) to pawn; (*obligar*) to obligue, compel; **-se** to persist, insist; to apply oneself; to go into debt; **-se por** to plead for, intercede for; **se empeñaron en una lucha** they engaged in a fight.

em·pe·ño *m.* (*fianza*) pledge, pawn; (*deseo*) persistence, insistence; eagerness; perseverance; *Am.* pawnshop; **tener – en** to be eager to.

em·pe·o·rar *v.* to impair, to make worse; to grow worse, **-se** to grow worse.

em·pe·que·ñe·cer[13] *v. irr.* to diminish, make smaller; belittler.

em·pe·ra·dor *m.* emperor; **emperatriz** *f.* empress.

em·pe·ri·fo·llar *v.* to decorate, adorn; **-se** to dress up, deck out, doll up.

em·pe·ro *conj.* however, nevertheless.

em·pe·zar[1,9] *v. irr.* to begin.

em·pie·zo *m.* Carib., *Mex.*, *C.A.* beginning

em·pi·na·do *adj.* steep; lofty.

em·pi·nar *v.* to raise, lift; to incline, bend; **– el codo** to drink; **-se** to stand on tiptoes, to rear (*said of horses*); to rise high; *Am.* to overeat.

em·pio·ja·do *adj.* lousy, full of lice.

em·plas·to *m.* plaster, poultice.

em·ple·a·do *m.* employee; *p.p. of* **emplear**.

em·ple·ar *v.* to employ; to invest, spend; **-se en** to be employed in.

em·ple·o *m.* employment, position, job; employ; occupation; aim; investment.

em·plu·mar *v.* to feather; to adorn with feathers; to tar and feather; *C.A.* to deceive; *Ec.* to send away to a house of correction or prison; *Am.* **– con algo** to run away with something, steal it; *Ch.*, *Col.*, *Ven.* **-las** (*or* **emplumárselas**) to take to one's heels, flee, escape.

em·po·bre·cer[13] *v. irr.* to impoverish; **-se** to become poor.

em·po·bre·ci·mien·to *m.* impoverishment.

em·pol·va·do *adj.* dusty, covered with dust or powder.

em·pol·var *v.* to sprinkle powder; to cover with dust; **-se** to get dusty; to powder one's face.

em·po·llar *v.* to hatch, brood.

em·pon·zo·ñar *v.* to poison.

em·pren·de·dor *adj.* enterprising.

em·pren·der *v.* to undertake.

em·pre·ñar *v.* to impregnate, make pregnant.

em·pre·sa *f.* enterprise, undertaking; sym-bol; company, management.

em·pre·sa·rio *m.* manager; impresario, promoter.

em·prés·ti·to *m.* loan.

em·pu·jar *v.* to push, shove.

em·pu·je *m.* push; shove; impulse; energy.

em·pu·jón *m.* shove, push.

em·pu·ñar *v.* to grasp, grab, clutch, seize.

é·mu·lo *m.* rival, competitor.

en *prep.* in, on, upon.

e·na·guas *f. pl.* underskirt, petticoat; short skirt.

e·na·je·na·mien·to *m.* trance; abstraction, absence of mind; transfer (*of property*); **—mental**, mental disorder; **– de los sentidos**, loss of consciousness.

e·na·je·nar *v.* (*distraer*) to enrapture, charm; to deprive (*of one's sense*); (*trasladar*) to trasfer property; to dispossess; **– el afecto de**, to alienate the affection of; **-se** to be enraptured, be in a trance.

e·nal·te·cer[13] *v.* to extol, exalt.

e·na·mo·ra·do *adj.* in love; *m.* lover.

e·na·mo·rar *v.* to make love, woo, court; to enamor; **—se** to fall in love.

e·na·no *m.* dwarf.; *adj.* dwarfish, tiny, little.

e·nar·bo·lar *v.* to hoist, lift raise on high; to brandish (*a sword, cane, etc.*); **-se** to rear, balk.

e·nar·ca·do *p.p.* arched.

e·nar·car[6] *v.* to arch; to hoop (*barrels, kegs, etc*); **– las cejas**, to arch one's eyebrows.

e·nar·de·cer[13] *v. irr.* to excite, kindle, fire with passion; **se** to become excited; to become passionate; to get angry.

e·nar·de·ci·mien·to *m.* ardor, passion, unbridled, enthusiasm; inflaming.

en·ca·be·za·do *m.* headline; heading.

en·ca·be·za·mien·to *m.* heading; headline; list or roll of taxpayers; registration of taxpayers.

en·ca·be·zar[6] *v.* to give a heading or title to; to head; to lead; to make up (*a list or tax roll*); to strengthen (*wine*).

en·ca·bri·tar·se *v.* to rear, rise up on the hind legs.

en·ca·de·nar *v.* to chain; to link togheter.

en·ca·jar *v.* to thrust in, fit into, insert; **-se** to squeeze into; to intrude, meddle.

en·ca·je *m.* lace; adjustment; fitting together; socket, groove, hole; inlaid work.

en·ca·jo·nar *v.* to box (*put or pack in a box*).

en·ca·llar *v.* to strand, run aground; to get stuck.

en·ca·ma·do *p.p.* confined in bed.

en·ca·mi·nar *v.* to direct, guide; **-se** to betake oneself, go (toward); to start out on a road.

en·ca·ne·cer[13] *v.* to get grey, get grey – haired.

en·ca·ni·ja·do *adj.* emaciated, thin, sickly.

en·ca·ni·jar·se *v.* to get thin, emaciated.

en·can·ta·do *p.p. & adj.* delighted, charmed; enchanted.

en·can·ta·dor *adj.* charming; *m.* charmer, enchanter.

en·can·ta·mien·to *m.* enchantment.

en·can·tar *v.* to charm, enchant.

en·can·to *m.* charm, enchantment, delight.

en·ca·pi·llar *v. P.R.* to confine in the death cell.

en·ca·po·ta·do *p.p. & adj.* cloaked; overcast, cloudy; in a bad humor.

en·ca·po·tar·se *v.* to become overcast, cloudy; to cover up, put on a cloak or raincoat; to frown.

en·ca·pri·char·se *v.* to persist in one's whims; to get stubborn.

en·ca·ra·mar *v.* to raise; to elevate; to extol; **-se** to climb; to climb upon, get upon, perch upon; *Ch.* to be ashamed; *Carib.* to go to one's head (*said of liquor*).

en·ca·rar *v.* to face; to aim; **-se con** to face; to confront.

en·car·ce·la·ción *f.* imprisonment.

en·car·ce·la·mien·to = encarcelación.

en·car·ce·lar *v.* to imprison, jail.

en·ca·re·cer[13] *v. irr.* (*alzar precio*) to go up in value; to make dear, raise the price of; (*ponderar*) to exaggerate; to extol; to recommend highly, to enhance.

en·ca·re·ci·da·men·te *adv.* earnestly.

en·car·gar[7] *v.* (*dar cargo*) to put in charge; to entrust; to commission; (*aconsejar*) to recommend, advise; (*pedir*) to order; to beg; **-se de** to take charge of.

en·car·go *m.* recommendation, advise; charge; order; commission; errand.

en·ca·ri·ña·do *adj. & p.p.* attached, fond, enamored.

en·ca·ri·ña·mien·to *m.* affection, fondness, attachment.

en·ca·ri·ñar *v.* to awaken love or affection; **-se** to become fond (of), attached (to).

en·car·na·do *adj.* flesh-colored; red; *p.p. of* **encarnar**.

en·car·nar *v.* to incarnate, embody; to bait (*a fishhook*).

en·car·ni·za·do *adj.* bloody; hard–fought, fierce.

en·car·ni·zar[9] *v.* to infuriate, enrage; **-se** to get furious, enraged; to fight with fury.

en·ca·si·llar *v.* to pigeonhole, put in a piogenhole or compartment; to put in a stall; to classify, sort out.

en·cen·der[1] *v. irr.* to light, kindle; to set on fire; **-se** to take fire, be on fire; to get red.

en·cen·di·do *adj.* red; *p.p. of* **encender**; *m.* ignition (*of a motor*).

en·ce·ra·do *m.* blackboard; oilcloth; wax coating; *p.p. & adj.* waxed; waxcolored; **papel** – wax paper.

en·ce·rar *v.* to wax; to thicken (*lime*).

en·ce·rra·mien·to *m.* enclosure, confi-nement; locking up; retreat; prison.

en·ce·rrar[1] *v. irr.* to enclose; to lock up; to contain; **– se** to lock oneself up, go into seclusion.

en·cí·a *f.* gum (*of the teeth*).

en·ci·clo·pe·dia *f.* encyclopedia.

en·cie·rro *m.* confinement; retreat; prison.

en·ci·ma *adv.* above, overhead, over, on top, besides, in addition; **– de** on top of; **por – de** over; *Am.* **de –** besides, in addition; *Col., C.A., Riopl., Carib.* **echár-selo todo –** to spend everything on clothes.

en·ci·na *f.* live oak.

en·cin·ta *adj.* pregnant.

en·cin·ta·do *m.* curb (*of a sidewalk*).

en·claus·trar *v.* to cloister.

en·cla·var *v.* to nail, fix, fasten.

en·clen·que *adj.* sickly, wan: weak, feeble.

en·co·ger[11] *v.* to shrink, shrivel, shorten, contract; **-se** to shrink; to shrivel; **-se de hombros** to shrug one's shoulders.

en·co·gi·do *p.p.* & *adj.* shrunk, shrivelled; timid, shy.

en·co·gi·mien·to *m.* shrinking; timidity; **— de hombros** shrug.

en·co·le·ri·zar[9] *v.* to anger; **-se** to get angry.

en·co·men·dar[1] *v. irr.* (*encargar*) to charge, advise; to entrust; (*recomendar*) to recommend, commend; **-se** to put oneself in the hands (of); to send regards; to pray (to).

en·co·miar *v.* to extol, praise.

en·co·mien·da *f.* charge, commission; recommendation; royal land grant (*including Indian inhabitants*); *Am.* warehouse (*for agricultural products*); *Am.* parcel-post package.

en·co·mio *m.* encomium, high praise.

en·co·na·do *p.p.* & *adj.* inflamed; infected; sore; angry.

en·co·nar *v.* to inflame; to infect; to irritate; **-se** to become inflamed, infected; to get irritated.

en·co·no *m.* rancor, animosity, ill will; *Cuba, Mex.* inflammation, swelling.

en·con·tra·do *adj.* opposite; opposing; contrary; *p.p. of* **encontrar**.

en·con·trar[2] *v. irr.* to encounter, meet; to find; **-se** to meet; to coincide; to be; to be found, be situated; to collide; to conflict; **-se con** to come across, meet up with.

en·con·trón, en·con·tro·na·zo *m.* bump, collision; **darse un —** to collide (with) bump (into); to bump into each other.

en·cor·de·lar *v.* to string; to tie with strings.

en·cor·var *v.* to curve, bend; **-se** to bend down; to stoop.

en·cres·par *v.* (*rizar*) to curl; to ruffle; (*agitar*) to irritate; **-se** to curl; to get ruffled; to become involved or entangled (*a matter or affair*); to become rough (*said of the sea*).

en·cru·ci·ja·da *f.* crossroads, street intersection; ambush.

en·cua·der·na·ción *f.* binding (*of books*).

en·cua·der·nar *v.* to bind (*books*).

en·cua·drar *v.* to enclose in a frame; to encompass; to fit (into); *Am.* to suit; *Ven.* to summarize briefly, give a synthesis of.

en·cu·bier·to *p.p. of* **encubrir**.

en·cu·brir[52] *v.* to cover, hide.

en·cuen·tro *m.* (*hallazgo*) encounter, meeting; find, finding; (*conflicto*) conflict, clash; collision; **salir al — de** to go out to meet; to make a stand against,

oppose; *Am.* **llevarse de —** to run over, knock down; to drag along.

en·cue·ra·do *adj. Am.* naked.

en·cue·rar *v. Am.* to strip of clothes; *Am.* to skin, fleece, strip of money; **-se** *Am.* to strip, get undressed.

en·cues·ta *f.* search, inquiry, investigation; survey.

en·cum·bra·do *p.p.* & *adj.* elevated; exalted; high, lofty.

en·cum·bra·mien·to *m.* elevation; exaltation; height; eminence.

en·cum·brar *v.* to elevate; to exalt, extol; **-se** to climb to the top; to rise up; to hold oneself high; to soar.

en·cur·ti·do *m.* pickle; *p.p. of* **encurtir**.

en·cur·tir *v.* to pickle.

en·chi·la·da *f. Mex., C.A.* rolled **tortilla** seved with chili.

en·chue·car[6] *v.* to bend, twist; **-se** *Col., Ven., Mex., Riopl.* to get bent or twisted.

en·chu·far *v.* to plug in; to telescope; to fit (*a tube or pipe*) into another.

en·chu·fe *m.* socket; plug; electric outlet; *Spain* influence; position obtained through influence.

en·de : por — hence, therefore.

en·de·ble *adj.* weak, feeble; flimsy.

en·de·mo·nia·do *adj.* possessed by the devil; devillish, fiendish; mischievous.

en·den·tar[1] *v. irr.* to indent, form notches in; to furnish (*a saw, wheel, etc.*) with teeth; to mesh.

en·de·re·zar[9] *v.* to straighten; to set upright; to right, correct; to direct; to address; **-se** to go straight (to); to straighten up.

en·deu·da·do *p.p.* & *adj.* indebted; in debt.

en·deu·dar·se *v.* to get into debt, become indebted.

en·dia·bla·do *adj.* devilish; possessed by the devil; ugly; mean, wicked; *Col., Ven., Mex., Riopl.* dangerous, risky.

en·do·min·ga·do *p.p.* & *adj.* dressed up in one's Sunday, or best, clothes.

en·do·san·te *m.* endorser.

en·do·sar *v.* to endorse (*a check, draft, etc.*).

en·do·se, en·do·so *m.* endorsement.

en·dul·zar[9] *v.* to sweeten; to soften.

en·du·re·cer[13] *v. irr.* to harden; **-se** to get hardened; to get cruel.

e·ne·mi·go *m.* enemy; devil; *adj.* hostile; unfriendly; **ser — de una cosa** to dislike a thing.

e·ne·mis·tad *f.* enmity, hatred.

e·ne·mis·tar *v.* to cause enmity between; **-se con** to become an enemy of.

e·ner·gí·a *f.* energy; **— nuclear** nuclear energy.

e·nér·gi·co *adj.* energetic.

e·ne·ro *m.* January.

e·ner·var *v.* to enervate, weaken.

en·fa·dar *v.* to anger; **-se** to get angry.

en·fa·do *m.* anger, disgust.

en·fa·do·so *adj.* annoying.

en•far•dar *v.* to bale, pack.

én•fa•sis *m.* emphasis; **enfático** *adj.* emphatic.

en•fer•mar *v.* to become ill; to make ill; to weaken; — **se** to become ill.

en•fer•me•dad *f.* sickness, illness.

en•fer•me•rí•a *f.* infirmary.

en•fer•me•ro *m.* male nurse; **enfermera** *f.* nurse (*for the sick*).

en•fer•mi•zo *adj.* sickly; unhealthy.

en•fer•mo *adj.* sick, ill; feeble; *m.* patient.

en•fla•que•cer[13] *v. irr.* to become thin; to make thin; to weaken.

en•fo•car[6] *v.* to focus.

en•fre•nar *v.* to bridle; to brake, put the brake on; to cleck, curb.

en•fren•tar *v.* to put face to face; **-se con** to confront, face, meet face to face.

en•fren•te *adv.* in front, opposite; — **de** in front of, opposite.

en•fria•mien•to *m.* cooling; chill; refrig-eration.

en•friar[17] *v.* to cool, chill; *Carib.* to kill; **-se** to cool, cool off, to get chilled.

en•fu•re•cer[13] *v. irr.* to infuriate, enrage; **-se** to rage, to get furious; to get rough, stormy (*said of the sea*).

en•fu•rru•ñar•se *v.* to get angry; to grumble.

en•ga•la•nar *v.* to adorn, decorate; **-se** to dress up, primp.

en•gan•cha•mien•to = **enganche**

en•gan•char *v.* to hitch; to hook; to ensnare; to draft; to attract into the army; *Col., Ven., Mex., Riopl.* to hire (*labor with false promises*); **-se** to engage, inter-lock; to get hooked; to enlist in the army.

en•gan•che *m.* hooking; coupling; draft (*into the army*); *Col., Ven., Mex., Riopl.* enrolling of laborers (*for a rubber plantation or other risky business under false promises*); *Mex.* down payment.

en•ga•ña•dor *adj.* deceitful, deceiving; *m.* deceiver.

en•ga•ñar *v.* to deceive; to while away (*time*); to ward off (*hunger or sleep*); **-se** to deceive oneself; to be mistaken.

en•ga•ño *m.* deceit, trick, fraud; mistake, misunderstanding: *Ch., C.A.* bribe.

en•ga•ño•so *adj.* deceitful; tricky; misleading.

en•gas•tar *v.* to mount, set (*jewels*).

en•gas•te *m.* setting (*for a gem or stone*).

en•ga•tu•sar *v.* to coax, entice; to fool.

en•gen•drar *v.* to engender, beget, produce; to cau-se.

en•gol•far•se *v.* to get deep (into); to go deeply (into); to become absorbed, lost in thought.

en•go•mar *v.* to gum: to glue.

en•gor•dar *v.* to fatten; to get fat; to get rich.

en•go•rro•so *adj.* cumbersome; bother-some.

en•gra•na•je *m.* gear, gears, gearing.

en•gra•nar *v.* to gear, throw in gear; to mesh gears.

en•gran•de•cer[13] *v. irr.* to aggrandize, make greater; to magnify; to exalt.

en•gra•ne *m.* engagement (*of gears*); gear.

en•gra•sar *v.* to lubricate, grease; to stain with grease; to fertilize, manure; to dress (*cloth*).

en•gre•í•do *adj. & p.p.* conceited, vain; *Col.* attached, fond.

en•gre•ír[15] *v. irr.* to make vain, conceited; **-se** to puff up, get conceited; *Col.* to become fond (of), become attached (to).

en•gro•sar[2] *v. irr.* to enlarge; to thicken; to fatten; to get fat.

en•gru•do *m.* paste (*for gluing*).

en•gu•llir[20] *v.* to gobble, devour; to gorge.

en•he•brar *v.* to thread (*a needle*); to string (*beads*).

en•hies•to *adj.* straight, upright, erect.

en•ho•ra•bue•na *f.* congratulation; *adv.* safely; well and good; all right; with much pleasure.

e•nig•ma *m.* enigma, riddle, puzzle.

en•ja•bo•nar *v.* to soap; to soft-soap, flatter.

en•ja•e•zar[9] *v.* to harness.

en•jal•be•gar[7] *v.* to whitewash; **-se** to paint (*one's face*).

en•jam•bre *m.* swarm of bees; crowd.

en•jau•lar *v.* to cage; to confine; to jail.

en•jua•gar[7] *v.* to rinse, rinse out.

en•jua•gue *m.* mouth wash; rinse; rinsing; scheme, plot.

en•ju•gar[7] *v.* to dry; to wipe; **-se** to dry oneself.

en•jui•ciar *v.* to indict; to prosecute, bring suit against; to try (*a case*); to judge.

en•jun•dia *f.* substance, essence; fat; force, strength.

en•ju•to *adj.* dried; thin, skinny; **-s** *m. pl.* dry kindling.

en•la•ce *m.* link; tie, bond; marriage.

en•la•dri•lla•do *m.* brick pavement or floor.

en•la•dri•llar *v.* to pave with bricks.

en•la•tar *v.* to can; *Col.* to roof with tin.

en•la•zar[9] *v.* to join, bind, tie; to rope; *Ven., Mex.* to lasso; **-se** to join; to marry; to become related through marriage.

en•lo•dar *v.* to cover with mud; to smear, sully, soil, dirty; **-se** to get in the mud; to get muddy.

en•lo•que•cer[13] *v. irr.* to make crazy; to drive mad; to lose one's mind; **-se** to go crazy.

en•lo•sa•do *m.* flagstone pavement; *p.p. of* **enlosar.**

en•lo•sar *v.* to pave with flagstones.

en•man•te•ca•do *m. Am.* ice cream. *See* **manteca-do.**

en•man•te•car[6] *v.* to butter; to grease (*with lard or butter*)

en•ma•ra•ñar *v.* to entangle; to snarl; to confuse; mix up.

en•mas•ca•rar *v.* to mask; **-se** to put on a mask; to masquerade.

en•men•dar[1] *v. irr.* to amend, correct; to indemnify, compensate; **-se** to reform, mend one's ways.

en•mien•da *f.* correction; amendment; reform;

indemnity, compensation.

en·mo·he·cer[13] *v.* to rust; to mold; **-se** to rust, become rusty; to mold.

en·mu·de·cer[13] *v. irr.* to silence; to remain silent; to lose one's voice; to become dumb.

en·ne·gre·cer[13] *v. irr.* to blacken; to darken; **-se** to become dark; to get cloudy.

en·no·ble·cer[13] *v. irr.* to ennoble, dignify.

e·no·ja·di·zo *adj.* irritable, ill-tempered.

e·no·ja·do *adj.* angry.

e·no·jar *v.* to make angry, vex, annoy; **-se** to get angry.

e·no·jo *m.* anger; annoyance.

e·no·jo·so *adj.* annoying, bothersome.

e·nor·gu·lle·cer[13] *v. irr.* to fill with pride; **-se** to swell up with pride; to be proud.

e·nor·me *adj.* enormous.

en·ra·ma·da *f.* arbor, bower; shady grove.

en·ra·re·cer[13] *v. irr.* to rarefy, thin, make less dense (*as air*); **-se** to become rarefied; to become scarce.

en·ra·re·ci·mien·to *m.* rarity, thinness (*of the air*); rarefaction (*act of making thin, rare or less dense*).

en·re·da·de·ra *f.* climbing vine.

en·re·dar *v.* (*enmarañar*) to entangle, snare; to snarl; to mix up; to wind (*on a spool*); (*enemistar*) to raise a rumpus; **-se** to get tangled up, mixed up; to get trapped; **-se con** to have an affair with.

en·re·dis·ta *m. Am.* liar; *Am.* talebearer.

en·re·do *m.* tangle; confusion; lie; plot.

en·re·do·so *adj.* tangled up; *Am.* tattler.

en·re·ja·do *m.* trellis; grating.

en·re·ve·sa·do *adj.* turned around; intricate, complicated; unruly

en·ri·que·cer[13] *v. irr.* to enrich; to become rich; **-se** to become rich.

en·ro·je·cer[13] *v. irr.* to redden; **-se** to get red, blush.

en·ro·llar *v.* to roll, roll up; to coil.

en·ron·que·cer[13] *v. irr.* to make hoarse; to become hoarse; **-se** to become hoarse.

en·ros·car[6] *v.* to coil; to twist, twine; **-se** to coil; to curl up.

en·sa·car[6] *v.* to sack, bag, put in a bag or sack.

en·sa·la·da *f.* salad; hodgepodge, mixture.

en·sal·zar[9] *v.* to exalt, praise.

en·san·char *v.* to widen, enlarge; **-se** to expand; to puff up.

en·san·che *m.* widening, expansion, extension.

en·san·gren·ta·do *adj.* gory, bloody; *p.p. of* **ensangrentar**.

en·san·gren·tar *v.* to stain with blood; **-se** to be covered with blood; to get red with anger.

en·sar·tar *v.* to string; to thread; to link; to rattle off (*tales, stories, etc.*); *Ch.* to tie to a ring; *Am.* to swindle, trick; **-se** *Andes* to fall into a trap.

en·sa·yar *v.* to try; to attempt; to test; to rehearse; **-se** to practice, train oneself.

en·sa·yo *m.* trial, attempt; rehearsal: test; experiment; essay.

en·se·na·da *f.* small bay, cove.

en·se·ñan·za *f.* teaching; education, training.

en·se·ñar *v.* to show; to teach; to train; to point out.

en·se·res *m. pl.* household goods; utensils; implements; equipment.

en·si·llar *v.* to saddle; *Ch.* to abuse, mistreat, domineer; *Ríopl.* — **el picazo** to get angry.

en·si·mis·mar·se *v.* to become absorbed in thought; *Col., Ven., Ch.* to become conceited or vain.

en·so·ber·be·cer[13] *v. irr.* to make proud or haughty; **-se** to puff up with pride; to become haughty; to get rough, choppy (*said of the sea*).

en·sor·de·cer[13] *v. irr.* to deafen; to become deaf.

en·sor·ti·jar *v.* to curl; to ring the nose of (*an animal*); **-se** to curl.

en·su·ciar *v.* to dirty, soil; to stain; **-se** to get dirty; to soil oneself.

en·sue·ño *m.* illusion, dream.

en·ta·blar *v.* to board up: to plank; to splint; **– una conversación** to start a conversation; **– un pleito** to bring a lawsuit.

en·ta·bli·llar *v.* to splint; *Mex.* to cut (*chocolate*) into tablets or squares.

en·ta·llar *v.* to fit closely (*a dress*); to carve.

en·ta·pi·zar[9] *v.* to cover with tapestry; to drape with tapestries; to upholster.

en·ta·ri·mar *v.* to floor (*with boards*).

en·te *m.* entity, being; queer fellow.

en·te·co *adj.* sickly, skinny.

en·ten·der[1] *v. irr.* to understand; **– de** to know, be an expert in; **– en** to take care of; to deal with; **-se con** to have dealings or relations with; to have an understanding with.

en·ten·di·do *p.p.* understood; *adj.* wise, prudent; well-informed; able, skilful; **no darse por –** to pretend not to hear or understand; not to take the hint.

en·ten·di·mien·to *m.* understanding; intellect; mind.

en·te·ra·do *p.p. & adj.* informed; aware.

en·te·rar *v.* to inform, acquaint; **-se** to know, learn, find out; to understand, get the idea

en·te·re·za *f.* entirety; integrity; fortitude; serenity; firmness; perfection.

en·ter·ne·ce·dor *adj.* touching, moving, pitiful.

en·ter·ne·cer[13] *v. irr.* to soften, touch, stir, move; **-se** to become tender; to be touched, stirred.

en·te·ro *adj.* (*completo*) entire, whole; (*justo*) just, right; firm; *m.* integer, whole number; *Col.* payment, reimbursement; *Ch.* balance of an account; **caballo –** stallion.

en·te·rra·mien·to *m.* burial.

en·te·rrar[1] *v. irr.* to bury; *Am.* to sink, stick into.

en·ti·biar *v.* to make lukewarm; **-se** to become lukewarm.

en·ti·dad *f.* entity; unit, group, organization; **de –** of value or importance.

en•tie•rro *m.* burial; funeral; grave; *Am.* hidden treasure.

en•tin•tar *v.* to ink; to stain with ink; to dye.

en•tol•dar *v.* to cover with an awning; **-se** to puff up with pride; to become overcast, cloudy.

en•to•na•ción *f.* intonation.

en•to•nar *v.* to sing in tune; to start a song (*for others to follow*); to be in tune; to harmonize; **–se** to put on airs.

en•ton•ces *adv.* then, at that time; **pues** – well then.

en•tor•na•do *adj.* half-open; half-closed, ajar.

en•tor•nar *v.* to half-open.

en•tor•pe•cer[13] *v. irr.* to stupefy; to benumb, make numb; to delay, obstruct; to thwart, frustrate.

en•tor•pe•ci•mien•to *m.* numbness; dullness; delay, obstruction.

en•tra•da *f.* (*apertura*) entrance; entry; gate; opening; (*acción o privilegio*) entering, admission; entrée (*dish or dinner course*); *Am.* attack, assault, goring; *Mex.* beating; **-s** cash receipts.

en•tram•bos *adj. & pron.* both.

en•tram•par *v.* to trap, ensnare; to trick; to burden with debts; **-se** to get trapped or entangled; to run into debt.

en•tran•te *adj.* entering; incoming; **el año** – next year.

en•tra•ña *f.* entrail; innermost recess; heart; disposition, temper; **-s** entrails, "innards", insides; **hijo de mis -s** child of my heart; **no tener -s** to be cruel.

en•trar *v.* to enter, go in, come in; to attack; **me entró miedo** I became afraid; **-se** to slip in, gest in, sneak in; to enter.

en•tre *prep.* between; among; **dijo – sí** he said to himself; – **tanto** meanwhile; *Am.* – **más habla menos dice** the more he talks the less he says.

en•tre•a•bier•to *p.p. of* **entreabrir**; *adj.* ajar, half-open, partly open.

en•tre•a•brir[52] *v.* to half–open.

en•tre•ac•to *m.* intermission; intermezzo (*entertainment between the acts*); small cigar.

en•tre•ca•no *adj.* greyish.

en•tre•ce•jo *m.* space between the eyebrows; **fruncir el** – to wrinkle one's brow.

en•tre•cor•ta•do *adj.* hesitating, faltering (*speech*); breathless, choking; *p.p.* interrupted.

en•tre•cor•tar *v.* to cut halfway through or in between; to interrupt at intervals.

en•tre•cru•zar[9] *v.* to intercross, cross; to interlace; **-se** to cross.

en•tre•di•cho *m.* prohibition, injunction.

en•tre•ga *f.* (*acto de ceder*) delivery; surrender; (*parte suelta*) installment (*of a book*); **novela por -s** serial novel.

en•tre•gar[7] *v.* to deliver, hand over; **-se** to surrender, submit, give up; to devote oneself (to); to abandon oneself (to).

en•tre•la•zar[9] *v.* to interlace; to weave together.

en•tre•més *m.* relish, side disch (*of olives, pickles, etc.*); one-act farce (*formerly presented between the acts of a play*).

en•tre•me•ter *v.* to insert; to place between; **-se** to meddle; to intrude.

en•tre•me•ti•do *adj.* meddlesome; *m.* meddler; intruder.

en•tre•me•ti•mien•to *m.* intrusion, meddling.

en•tre•mez•clar *v.* to intermix, intermingle.

en•tre•na•dor *m. Am.* trainer.

en•tre•na•mien•to *m. Am.* training, drill.

en•tre•nar *v. Am.* to train, drill; **-se** *Am.* to train.

en•tre•sa•car[6] *v.* to pick out, select.

en•tre•sue•lo *m.* mezzanine; second floor.

en•tre•tan•to *adv.* meanwhile.

en•tre•te•jer *v.* to weave together; to intertwine.

en•tre•te•ner[45] *v. irr.* to delay, detain; to amuse, entertain; **-se** to amuse oneself: to delay oneself; – **el tiempo** to while away the time.

en•tre•te•ni•do *adj.* entertaining, amusing; *p.p. of* **entretener**.

en•tre•te•ni•mien•to *m.* entertainment; pastime; delay.

en•tre•ver[49] *v.* to glimpse, catch a glimpse of; to half-see, see vaguely.

en•tre•ve•rar *v.* to intermingle, intermix.

en•tre•vis•ta *f.* interview; date, appointment.

en•tre•vis•tar *v.* to interview; **-se con** to have an interview with.

en•tre•vis•to *p.p. of* **entrever**

en•tris•te•cer[13] *v. irr.* to sadden, make sad; **–se** to become sad.

en•tro•me•ter = **entremeter.**

en•tro•me•ti•do = **entremetido.**

en•tu•me•cer[13] *v. irr.* to make numb; **-se** to get numb; to surge; to swell.

en•tu•mi•do *adj.* numb, stiff; *Am.* timid, shy, awkward.

en•tu•mir•se *v.* to get numb.

en•tur•biar *v.* to make muddy; to muddle; to disturb; to obscure; **-se** to get muddy; to get muddled.

en•tu•sias•mar *v.* to excite, fill with enthusiasm; **-se** to get enthusiastic, excited.

en•tu•sias•mo *m.* enthusiasm.

en•tu•sias•ta *m. & f.* enthusiast; **entusiástico** *adj.* enthusiastic.

e•nu•me•ra•ción *f.* enumeration, counting.

e•nu•me•rar *v.* to enumerate.

e•nun•ciar *v.* to express, state, declare.

en•vai•nar *v.* to sheathe.

en•va•len•to•nar *v.* to make bold or haugh-ty; **-se** to get bold; to brag, swagger.

en•va•ne•cer[13] *v. irr.* to make vain; **-se** to become vain.

en•va•sar v. to pack, put up in any container; to bottle; to can.

en•va•se m. packing; container, jar, bottle, can (*for packing*).

en•ve•je•cer[13] v. irr. to make old; to grow old, get old; -se to grow old, get old.

en•ve•ne•na•mien•to m. poisoning.

en•ve•ne•nar v. to poison; to infect.

en•ver•ga•du•ra f. span (*of an airplane*); spread (*of a bird's wings*); breadth (*of sails*).

en•vés m. back or wrong side.

en•via•do m. envoy.

en•viar[17] v. to send; – a uno a paseo to give someone his walking papers.

en•vi•ciar v. to vitiate, corrupt; -se to become addicted (to), overly fond (of).

en•vi•dar v. to bid (*in cards*); to bet.

en•vi•dia f. envy.

en•vi•dia•ble adj. enviable, desirable.

en•vi•diar v. to envy.

en•vi•dio•so adj. envious.

en•vi•le•cer[13] v. irr. to revile, malign, degrade; -se to degrade or lower oneself.

en•ví•o m. remittance, sending; shipment.

en•vi•te m. bid; stake (*in cards*); offer; push.

en•vol•to•rio m. bundle, package.

en•vol•tu•ra f. wrapping, cover; wrapper.

en•vol•ver[2,52] v. irr. to involve, entangle; to wrap; to wind (*a thread, rope, etc.*); to surround; -se to become involved, entangled; to cover up, wrap up.

en•vuel•to p.p. of envolver.

en•ye•sar v. to plaster; to chalk.

en•zol•var v. Am. to clog, obstruct; Am. -se to clog, get clogged. See azolvar.

¡e•pa! interj. Riopl.,Ven., Col., Mex. hey! listen! stop! look out!

é•pi•co adj. epic.

e•pi•de•mia f. epidemic.

e•pi•so•dio m. episode.

e•pís•to•la f. epistle; letter.

e•pi•ta•fio m. epitaph.

é•po•ca f. epoch.

e•po•pe•ya f. epic. poem.

e•qui•dad f. equity, justice, fairness.

e•qui•dis•tan•te adj. equidistant, equally distant, halfway, midway.

e•qui•li•brar v. to balance, poise.

e•qui•li•brio m. equilibrium, balance; poise.

e•qui•pa•je m. baggage, luggage; equipment, outfit; crew.

e•qui•par v. to equip, fit out; to man, equip and provision (*a ship*).

e•qui•po m. (*materiales*) equipment, equipping; outfit, (*grupo*) work crew; sport team; – de novia trousseau.

e•qui•ta•ción f. horsemanship; horseback riding.

e•qui•ta•ti•vo adj. fair, just.

e•qui•va•len•te adj. equivalent.

e•qui•va•ler[47] v. irr. to be equivalent.

e•qui•vo•ca•ción f. error, mistake.

e•qui•vo•ca•do p.p. & adj. mistaken.

e•qui•vo•car[6] v. to mistake; -se to be mistaken; to make a mistake.

e•quí•vo•co adj. equivocal, ambiguous, vague; Am. mistaken; m. pun, play on words; Am. mistake, error.

e•ra f. era, age; threshing floor.

e•ra•rio m. public treasury.

er•gui•do adj. erect; p.p. of erguir.

er•guir[3] v. irr. to erect, set upright; to lift (*the head*); -se to sit up or stand erect; to become proud and haughty.

e•rial m. uncultivated land; adj. unplowed, untilled.

e•ri•gir[11] v. to erect, build; to found.

e•ri•za•do adj. bristly, prickly; – de bristling with.

e•ri•zar[9] v. to set on end, make bristle; -se to bristle; to stand on end (*hair*).

e•ri•zo m. hedgehog, porcupine; thistle; – de mar sea urchin; ser un – to be irritable, harsh.

er•mi•ta•ño m. hermit.

e•ro•sión f. erosion.

e•rra•bun•do adj. wandering.

e•rra•do adj. mistaken, wrong, in error; p.p. of errar.

e•rran•te adj. errant, roving, wandering.

e•rrar[28] v. irr. to err, make mistakes; to miss (*target, road*); to rove, wander.

e•rra•ta f. misprint, printer's error.

e•rró•ne•o adj. erroneous, mistaken, wrong, incorrect.

e•rror m. error, fault, mistake.

e•ruc•tar v. to belch.

e•ruc•to m. belch.

e•ru•di•ción f. erudition, learning.

e•ru•di•to adj. erudite, scholarly, learned; m. scholar.

e•rup•ción f. eruption; outburst; rash.

es•bel•to adj. slender.

es•bo•zar[9] v. to sketch, outline.

es•bo•zo m. sketch, outline.

es•ca•be•char v. to pickle.

es•ca•be•che m. pickled fish; pickle (*solution for pickling*).

es•ca•bel m. stool; footstool.

es•ca•bro•si•dad f. roughness, unevenness; harshness; improper word or phrase.

es•ca•bro•so adj. rough; rugged; scabrous, rather indecent.

es•ca•bu•llir•se[20] v. irr. to slip away; to slip through; to scoot, scamper, scurry.

es•ca•la f. ladder; scale; port of call; stopover; hacer – en to stop over at; escalafón m. army register.

es•ca•lar v. to scale; to climb.

es·cal·dar v. to scald; to make red-hot; **-se** to get scalded.

es·ca·le·ra f. stairs, staircase; ladder; **– mecánica** escalator.

es·cal·far v. to poach (eggs).

es·ca·li·na·ta f. flight of stairs (usually on the outside).

es·ca·lo·friar·se[17] v. to become chilled.

es·ca·lo·frí·o m. chill; **-s** chills and fever.

es·ca·lón m. step (of a ladder or staircase); stepping stone; Am. **– es** tribe of **quichua** Indians.

es·ca·lo·nar v. to echelon (arrange in step–like formation); to terrace; **-se** to rise in terraces.

es·ca·ma f. scale, fish scale; flake.

es·ca·mo·so adj. scaly.

es·ca·mo·te·ar v. to whisk out of sight; to steal or snatch away with cunning; to conceal by a trick or sleight of hand.

es·can·da·li·zar[9] v. to scandalize, shock; **-se** to be shocked.

es·cán·da·lo m. scandal; bad example.

es·can·da·lo·so adj. scandalous, shocking; Mex., C.A., Col., Andes showy, loud (color).

es·ca·pa·da f. escape, flight.

es·ca·par v. to escape, flee, avoid; **-se** to run away, escape.

es·ca·pa·ra·te m. show window; glass case, glass cabinet or cupboard.

es·ca·pa·to·ria f. escape, loophole, excuse.

es·ca·pe m. escape; vent; outlet; exhaust; **a –** rapidly, at full speed.

es·ca·ra·ba·jo m. black beetle.

es·ca·ra·mu·za f. skirmish; quarrel.

es·car·bar v. to scrape, scratch; to dig out; to pry into, investigate.

es·car·ce·ar v. Ch., Riopl. to prance.

es·car·cha f. frost; frosting.

es·car·char v. to frost; to freeze.

es·car·dar v. to weed; to weed out.

es·car·la·ta f. scarlet; scarlet fever: scarlet cloth; **escarlatina** f. scarlet fever.

es·car·men·tar[1] v. irr. to punish (as an example or warning); to profit by one's misfortunes, punishment, etc.; **– en cabeza ajena** to profit by another's mistake or misfortune.

es·car·mien·to m. lesson, example, warning; punishment.

es·car·ne·cer[13] v. irr. to jeer, insult, mock.

es·car·nio m. scoff, jeer.

es·car·pa f. steep slope, bluff, cliff; scarp (of a fortification).

es·car·pa·do adj. steep; rugged.

es·car·pia f. hook (for hanging something).

es·ca·se·ar v. to be scarce; to grow less, become scarce, to stint.

es·ca·sez f. scarcity, lack, scantiness.

es·ca·so adj. scarce, limited; scant; scanty; stingy.

es·ca·ti·mar v. to stint, skimp: to curtail.

es·ce·na f. scene; scenery; theatre, stage.

es·ce·na·rio m. stage.

es·ce·ni·fi·ca·ción f. dramatization, stage adaptation.

es·cep·ti·cis·mo m. scepticism, doubt, unbelief.

es·cép·ti·co m. & adj. sceptic.

es·cla·re·cer[13] v. irr. to lighten, illuminate; to elucidate, make clear, explain.

es·cla·re·ci·mien·to m. clarification, illumination, illustration; worth, nobility.

es·cla·vi·tud f. slavery.

es·cla·vi·zar[9] v. to enslave.

es·cla·vo m. slave.

es·clu·sa f. lock (of a canal); sluice, floodgate.

es·co·ba f. broom.

es·co·ba·zo m. blow with a broom.

es·co·bi·lla f. whisk broom; small broom.

es·co·cer[2,10] v. irr. to sting, smart.

es·co·cés adj. Scotch; m. Scotch; Scotchman.

es·co·ger[11] v. to choose, select, pick out.

es·co·lar adj. scholastic, academic; m. scholar, student.

es·co·lás·ti·co adj. & m. scholastic.

es·col·ta f. escort; convoy.

es·col·tar v. to escort; to convoy.

es·co·llo m. reef; danger; obstacle.

es·com·bro m. debris, rubbish; mackerel.

es·con·der v. to hide, conceal; **-se** to hide, go into hiding.

es·con·di·das: a – on the sly, under cover; Am. **jugar a las –** to play hide-and-seek.

es·con·di·te m. hiding place; Spain **jugar al –** to play hide-and-seek.

es·con·dri·jo m. hiding place.

es·co·pe·ta f. shotgun.

es·co·pe·ta·zo m. gunshot; gunshot wound; sudden bad news; Am. offensive or ironic remark.

es·co·plo m. chisel.

es·co·ria f. slag; scum; **escorial** m. dump, dumping place; pile of salg.

es·cor·pión m. scorpion.

es·co·te m. low neck; **convite a –** Dutch treat (where everyone pays his share).

es·co·ti·lla f. hatchway; **escotillón** m. hatch, hatchway; trap door.

es·co·zor m. smarting sensation, sting.

es·cri·ba·no m. court clerk; lawyer's clerk; notary.

es·cri·bien·te m. clerk, office clerk.

es·cri·bir[52] v. to write.

es·cri·to p.p. of **escribir** written; m. writing, manuscript.

es·cri·tor m. writer.

es·cri·to·rio m. desk; office.

es·cri·tu·ra f. writing, handwriting; deed, document; **Sagrada Escritura** Holy Scripture.

es·crú·pu·lo *m.* scruple, doubt.

es·cru·pu·lo·so *adj.* scrupulous; particular, exact.

es·cru·ta·dor *adj.* scrutinizing, examining; peering; penetrating; *m.* scrutinizer, examiner; inspector of election returns.

es·cru·tar *v.* to scrutinize.

es·cru·ti·nio *m.* scrutiny, careful inspection.

es·cua·dra *f.* squadron; fleet; square (*instrument of drawing or testing right angles*).

es·cua·drón *m.* squadron.

es·cua·li·dez *f.* squalor.

es·cuá·li·do *adj.* squalid, filthy; thin, emaciated.

es·cu·char *v.* to listen; to heed.

es·cu·dar *v.* to shield.

es·cu·de·ro *m.* squire.

es·cu·do *m.* shield; escutcheon, coat of arms; gold crown (*ancient coin*); *Am.* Chilean gold coin.

es·cu·dri·ñar *v.* to scrutinize, search, pry into.

es·cue·la *f.* school.

es·cue·lan·te *m. & f. Col.* schoolboy; schoolgirl.

es·cue·to *adj.* plain, unadorned, bare.

es·cul·car[6] *v. Am.* to search; *Carib., Col., Ven.,* to frisk (*a person's pockets*).

es·cul·pir *v.* to sculpture; to engrave.

es·cul·tor *m.* sculptor.

es·cul·tu·ra *f.* sculpture.

es·cu·pi·de·ra *f.* cuspidor.

es·cu·pir *v.* to spit.

es·cu·rrir *v.* to drip; to drain; to trickle; -se to ooze out, trickle; to slip out, sneak out.

e·se, e·sa *dem. adj.* that; esos, esas those; ése, ésa *m., f. dem. pron.* that one; ésos, ésas *m., f. pl.* those.

e·sen·cia *f.* essence.

e·sen·cial *adj.* essential.

es·fe·ra *f.* sphere; clock dial.

es·fé·ri·co *adj.* spherical.

es·for·za·do *adj.* strong; valiant; courageous.

es·for·zar[2,9] *v. irr.* to give or inspire strength; to encourage; -se to make an effort, to strive, try hard.

es·fuer·zó *m.* effort; spirit, courage, vigor; stress.

es·fu·mar *v.* to shade, tone down; -se to vanish, disappear.

es·gri·ma *f.* fencing.

es·gri·mir *v.* to fence; to brandish; to wield (*the sword or pen*).

es·la·bón *m.* link of a chain; steel knife sharpener; black scorpion.

es·la·bo·nar *v.* to link; to join; to connect.

es·mal·tar *v.* to enamel; to beautify, adorn.

es·mal·te *m.* enamel; enamel work; smalt (*a blue pigment*).

es·me·ra·do *adj.* painstaking, careful, conscientious; *p.p. of* esmerar.

es·me·ral·da *f.* emerald; *Am.* an eel-like fish; *Col.* hummingbird; *Mex.* variety of pineapple.

es·me·rar *v.* to polish, clean; -se to strive, take special pains; use great care.

es·me·ro *m.* care, precision.

es·mo·quin *m.* tuxedo, dinner coat.

e·so *dem. pron.* that, that thing, that fact; — es that is it; a — de at about (*referring to time*); *Am.* ¡eso! that's right!

es·pa·ciar[17] *v.* to space; to spread; to expand; -se to enlarge (*upon a subject*); to relax, amuse oneself.

es·pa·cio *m.* space; interval; slowness, delay; *adv. Mex.* slowly.

es·pa·cio·so *adj.* spacious; slow.

es·pa·da *f.* sword; skilled swordsman; matador (*bullfighter who kills the bull*); -s swords (*Spanish card suit*).

es·pal·da *f.* back, shoulders; -s back, back part; a -s behind one's back; de -s on one's back; dar la — a to turn one's back on; espaldilla *f.* shoulder blade.

es·pal·dar *m.* back (*of a chair*); trellis (*for plants*); backplate of a cuirass (*armor*).

es·pan·ta·di·zo *adj.* scary, shy, timid.

es·pan·ta·jo *m.* scarecrow.

es·pan·ta·pá·ja·ros *m.* scarecrow.

es·pan·tar *v.* to frighten, scare; to scare away; *Col.* to haunt; -se to be scared; to be astonished; *Mex.* espantárselas to be wide-awake, catch on quickly.

es·pan·to *m.* fright, terror; astonishment, *Col., Ven., Mex.* ghost.

es·pan·to·so *adj.* frightful, terrifying; wonderful.

es·pa·ñol *adj.* Spanish; *m.* Spaniard; Spanish language.

es·pa·ra·dra·po *m.* court plaster, adhesive tape. See tela adhesiva.

es·par·cir[10] *v.* to scatter, spread; -se to relax, amuse oneself.

es·pá·rra·go *m.* asparagus.

es·par·to *m.* esparto grass (*used for making ropes, mats, etc.*).

es·pas·mo *m.* spasm; horror.

es·pá·tu·la *f.* spatula.

es·pe·cia *f.* spice.

es·pe·cial *adj.* special; en — in particular, specially.

es·pe·cia·li·dad *f.* specialty.

es·pe·cia·lis·ta *m. & f.* specialist.

es·pe·cia·li·zar[9] *v.* to specialize; -se en to specialize in.

es·pe·cie *f.* species; kind, sort; pretext; idea.

es·pe·ci·fi·car[6] *v.* to specify; to name.

es·pe·cí·fi·co *adj.* specific; *m.* specific (*medicine*).

es·pé·ci·men *m.* specimen, sample.

es·pec·ta·cu·lar *adj.* spectacular.

es·pec·tá·cu·lo *m.* spectacle.

es·pec·ta·dor *m.* spectator.

es·pec·tro *m.* spectre, ghost; spectrum.

es·pe·cu·la·ción *f.* speculation.

es·pe·cu·la·dor *m.* speculator.

es·pe·cu·lar *v.* to speculate.

es·pe·cu·la·ti·vo *adj.* speculative.

es·pe·jis·mo *m.* mirage; illusion.

es·pe·jo *m.* mirror; model; **– de cuerpo entero** full-length mirror.

es·pe·luz·nan·te *adj.* hair-raising, terrifying.

es·pe·luz·nar·se *v.* to be terrified; to bristle with fear.

es·pé·ra *f.* wait; stay (*granted by judge*), delay; extension of time (*for payment*); **sala de –** waiting room; **estar en – de** to be waiting for; to be expecting.

es·pe·ran·za *f.* hope; expectation.

es·pe·ran·za·do *adj.* hopeful.

es·pe·ran·zar[9] to give hope to.

es·pe·rar *v.* (*tener esperanza*) to hope; to expect; to trust; (*permanecer*) to wait, wait for; **– en alguien** to place hope or confidence in someone.

es·pe·re·zar·se = **desperezarse**.

es·per·pen·to *m.* ugly thing; nonsense.

es·pe·sar *v.* to thicken; to make dense; **-se** to thicken; to become thick or dense.

es·pe·so *adj.* thick, dense; compact; slovenly; *Riopl.* bothersome, boring.

es·pe·sor *m.* thickness.

es·pe·su·ra *f.* density, thickness; thicket; thickest part (*of a forest*).

es·pe·tar *v.* to spring (*a joke, story, etc.*) on (*a person*), surprise with (*a joke, speech, story, etc.*); to pop (*a question*); to run a spit thorugh (*meat, fish, etc. for roasting*); to pierce; **-se** to be stiff, pompous.

es·pí·a *m. & f.* spy.

es·piar[17] *v.* to spy; *Col., Mex.* **-se** to bruise the hoofs, get lame (*said of horses*).

es·pi·ga *f.* ear of wheat; peg; spike.

es·pi·gar[7] *v.* to glean; to grow spikes (*said of corn or grain*); **-se** to grow tall and slender.

es·pi·na *f.* thorn; sharp splinter; fish bone; spine; fear, suspicion; **darle a uno mala –** to arouse one's suspicion.

es·pi·na·ca *f.* spinach.

es·pi·na·zo *m.* spine, backbone.

es·pi·ni·lla *f.* shin (*front part of leg*); blackhead (*on the skin*).

es·pi·no *m.* hawthorn; thorny shrub; thorny branch.

es·pi·no·so *adj.* thorny; difficult, dangerous.

es·pio·na·je *m.* espionage, spying.

es·pi·ral *adj. & f.* spiral.

es·pi·rar *v.* to exhale; to emit, give off; to die. *See* **expirar**.

es·pí·ri·tu *m.* spirit; soul; courage; vigor; essence; ghost.

es·pi·ri·tual *adj.* spiritual.

es·pi·ta *f.* spigot, faucet, tap; toper, drunkard.

es·plen·di·dez *f.* splendor.

es·plén·di·do *adj.* splendid.

es·plen·dor *m.* splendor.

es·plen·do·ro·so *adj.* resplendent, shining.

es·plie·go *m.* lavender (*plant*).

es·po·le·ar *v.* to spur; to incite.

es·po·le·ta *f.* bomb fuse.

es·po·lón *m.* spur (*on a cock's leg*); ram (*of a boat*); spur; buttress.

es·pol·vo·re·ar *v.* to powder, sprinkle with powder.

es·pon·ja *f.* sponge; sponger, parasite; *Col., Peru., Ch., Riopl.* souse, habitual drunkard.

es·pon·ja·do *adj.* fluffy, spongy; puffed up; *p.p. of* **esponjar**.

es·pon·jar *v.* to fluff; to make spongy or porous; **-se** to fluff up: to become spongy or porous; to swell, puff up; to puff up with pride.

es·pon·jo·so *adj.* spongy.

es·pon·sa·les *m. pl.* betrothal.

es·pon·ta·nei·dad *f.* spontaneity, ease, naturalness.

es·pon·tá·ne·o *adj.* spontaneous.

es·po·sa *f.* wife; **-s** handcuffs.

es·po·so *m.* husband.

es·pue·la *f.* spur.

es·pul·gar[7] *v.* to delouse, remove lice or fleas from: to scrutinize.

es·pu·ma *f.* foam, froth; scum; **– de jabón** suds.

es·pu·mar *v.* to skim, to froth, foam.

es·pu·ma·ra·jo *m.* froth, foam (*from the mouth*); **echar -s** to froth at the mouth; to be very angry.

es·pu·mo·so *adj.* foamy.

es·pu·to *m.* sputum, spit, saliva.

es·que·la *f.* note, letter; announcement.

es·que·le·to *m.* skeleton; carcass; frame-work; *Mex., C.A., Col., Ven.* blank (to fill out); *Am.* outline.

es·que·ma *f.* scheme, outline.

es·quí *m.* ski, skiing; **– náutico, – acuatico** water ski.

es·quiar[17] *v.* to ski.

es·qui·la *f.* small bell, cow bell; sheep-shearing.

es·qui·lar *v.* to shear; to clip; to crop.

es·qui·na *f.* corner, angle; **esquinazo** *m.* corner; *Am.* serenade; **dar esquinazo** to avoid meeting someone; to "ditch" someone.

es·qui·var *v.* to avoid, dodge; to shun; **-se** to withdraw, shy away.

es·qui·vez *f.* shyness; aloofness; disdain.

es·qui·vo *adv.* reserved, unsociable; shy; disdainful, aloof.

es·ta·bi·li·dad *f.* stability.

es·ta·ble *adj.* stable, firm, steady.

es·ta·ble·cer[13] *v. irr.* to establish; to found; to decree; ordain.

es·ta·ble·ci·mien·to *m.* establishment; foundation;

statute, law.

es·ta·blo *m.* stable; **establero** *m.* groom.

es·ta·ca *f.* stake, club; stick; picket.

es·ta·ca·da *f.* stockade; picket fence; *Am.* predicament.

es·ta·car⁶ *v.* to stake; to tie to a stake; to stake off, mark with stakes; *Am.* to fasten down with stakes; -**se** to remain stiff or rigid.

es·ta·ción *f.* station; season; railway station.

es·ta·cio·nar *v.* to station; to place; to park (*u car*); **se** to remain stationary; to park.

es·ta·cio·na·rio *adj.* stationary; motion-less.

es·ta·da *f.* sojourn, stay.

es·ta·dí·a *f.* detention, stay; stay in port (*beyond time allowed for loading and unloading*); *C.A., Carib.* sojourn, stay (*in any sense*).

es·ta·dio *m.* stadium.

es·ta·dis·ta *m.* statesman.

es·ta·dís·ti·ca *f.* statistics.

es·ta·do *m.* state, condition; station, rank; estate; — **mayor** army staff; **hombre de** — statesman; *Am.* **en** – **interesante** pregnant.

es·ta·dou·ni·den·se *adj.* from the United States, American.

es·ta·fa *f.* swindle, fraud, trick.

es·ta·fa·dor *m.* swindler, crook.

es·ta·far *v.* to swindle, defraud, cheat.

es·ta·llar *v.* to explode, burst; to creak, crackle.

es·ta·lli·do *m.* explosion, outburst; crash; creaking; crack (*of a gun*), report (*of a gun or cannon*).

es·tam·bre *m.* woolen yarn; stamen (*of a flower*).

es·tam·pa *f.* image; print; stamp: cut, picture; footprint; figure, appearance.

es·tam·pa·do *m.* print, printed fabric; printing.

es·tam·par *v.* to stamp, print.

es·tam·pi·da *f.* crack, sharp sound; *Col., Ven., C.A.* stampede (*sudden scattering of a herd of cattle or horses*).

es·tam·pi·do *m.* crack, sharp sound; report *of* a gun.

es·tam·pi·lla *f.* stamp, seal; *Mex., C.A., Andes* postage stamp.

es·tan·car⁶ *v.* to stem; to stanch; to stop the flow *of*, to corner (*a market*); -**se** to stagnate, become stagnant.

es·tan·cia *f.* (*permanencia*) stay; (*lugar*) hall, room; mansion; *Riopl.* farm, cattle ranch; *Carib.* main building of a farm or ranch.

es·tan·cie·ro *m. Riopl.* rancher, ranchowner, cattle raiser; *adj.* pertaining to an **estancia**.

es·tan·co *m.* monopoly; government store (*for sale of monopolized goods such as tobacco, stamps and matches*); tank, reservoir ; *Ec., C.A.* liquor store.

es·tán·dar *m. Am.* standard, norm.

es·tan·dar·di·zar, es·tan·da·ri·zar⁹ *v. Am.* to standardize.

es·tan·dar·te *m.* st andard, flag, banner.

es·tan·que *m.* pond, pool, reservoir.

es·tan·qui·llo *m.* tobacco store; *Am.* small store; *C.A., Mex.* small liquor store, tavern.

es·tan·te *m.* shelf; bookshelf; *Am.* prop, support; **estantería** *f.* shelves; bookcases.

es·ta·ño *m.* tin.

es·ta·qui·lla *f.* peg; spike.

es·tar²⁹ *v. irr.* to be; -**le bien a uno** to be becoming to one; – **de prisa** to be in a hurry; **¿a cuántos estamos?** what day *of* the month is it today?; -**se** to keep, remain.

es·tá·ti·co *adj.* static; **estática** *f.* statics; radio static.

es·ta·tua *f.* statue.

es·ta·tu·ra *f.* stature, height .

es·ta·tu·to *m.* statute.

es·te, es·ta *dem. adj.* this; **estos, estas** these; **éste, ésta** *m., f., dem. pron.* this one, this thing; the latter; **esto** this, this thing; **éstos, éstas** *m., f. pl.* these; the latter.

es·te *m.* east; east wind.

es·te·la *f.* wake *of* a ship.

es·te·nó·gra·fo *m.* stenographer.

es·ten·tó·re·o *adj.* loud, thundering (*voice*).

es·te·pa *f.* steppe, treeless plain.

es·te·ra *f.* matting; mat.

es·ter·co·lar *v.* to manure, fertilize with manure.

es·ter·co·le·ro *m.* manure pile, manure dump, manure collector.

es·te·re·os·co·pio *m.* stereoscope.

es·te·re·o·ti·po *m.* stereotype.

es·té·ril *adj.* sterile, barren.

es·te·ri·li·dad *f.* sterility, barrenness.

es·te·ri·li·zar⁹ *v.* to sterilize.

es·ter·ii·na *adj.* sterling; **libra** – pound sterling.

es·te·ro *m.* estuary.

es·ter·tor *m.* death-rattle; snort.

es·té·ti·co *adj.* aesthetic; **estética** *f.* aesthetics.

es·te·tos·co·pio *m.* stethoscope.

es·ti·ba·dor *m.* stevedore, longshoreman.

es·ti·bar *v.* to stow (*in a boat*); to pack down, compress.

es·tiér·col *m.* manure; fertilizer.

es·tig·ma *m.* stigma; brand, mark *of* disgrace; birthmark.

es·ti·lar *v.* to use, be accustomed to using; -**se** to be in style (*said of clothes*).

es·ti·le·te *m.* stiletto, narrow-bladed dagger; stylet (*instrument for probing wounds*); long, narrow sword.

es·ti·lo *m.* style; fashion.

es·ti·ma *f.* esteem.

es·ti·ma·ción *f.* esteem, regard; valuation.

es·ti·mar *v.* to esteem, regard highly; to estimate, appraise; to judge, think.

es·ti·mu·lan·te *adj.* stimulant, stimulating; *m.* stimulant.

es·ti·mu·lar *v.* to stimulate, excite, goad.

es·tí·mu·lo *m.* stimulation, incitement; stimulus.

es·tí·o *m.* summer.

es·ti·pu·la·ción *f.* stipulation, specification, provision, proviso.

es·ti·pu·lar *v.* to stipulate, specify.

es·ti·ra·do *p.p.* & *adj.* stretched; extented, draw out; stuck-up, conceited.

es·ti·rar *v.* to stretch, extend; **– la pata,** to die; **-se** to stretch out; *Am.* to die.

es·ti·rón *m.* hard pull, tug; stretch; **dar un –** to grow suddenly (*said of a child*).

es·tir·pe *f.* lineage, family, race.

es·ti·val *adj.* summer, relating to the summer.

es·to·ca·da *f.* thrust, stab; stab wound.

es·to·fa *f.* stuff, cloth; class, quality; **gente de baja – low** class people, rabble.

es·to·fa·do *m.* stew, stewed meat; *p.p.* of **esto-far.**

es·to·far *v.* to quilt; to stew.

es·toi·co *adj.* & *m.* stoic.

es·to·la *f.* stole; **– de visón** mink wrap.

es·tó·ma·go *m.* stomach.

es·to·pa *f.* burlap; oakum (*loose fiber of old ropes*).

es·to·que *m.* long, narrow sword.

es·tor·bar *v.* to hinder; to obstruct.

es·tor·bo *m.* hindrance; nuisance, bother.

es·tor·nu·dar *v.* to sneeze.

es·tor·nu·do *m.* sneeze.

es·tra·do *m.* dais (*platform for a throne, seats of honor, etc.*) main part of a parlor or drawing room.

es·tra·ga·do *p.p.* & *adj.* corrupted; spoiled; ruined; tired, worn out.

es·tra·gar *v.* corrupt, contaminate; to spoil; to ruin.

es·tra·go *m.* havoc, ruin; massacre.

es·tran·gu·la·dor *m.* strangler, choke (*of an automobile*); *adj.* strangling.

es·tran·gu·lar *v.* to strangle; to choke, throttle.

es·tra·ta·ge·ma *f.* stratagem, scheme.

es·tra·te·gia *f.* strategy.

es·tra·té·gi·co *adj.* strategic; *m.* strategist, person trained or skilled in strategy.

es·tra·to *m.* stratum, layer (*of mineral*).

es·tra·to·rre·ac·tor *m.* supersonic jet plane.

es·tra·tos·fe·ra *f.* stratosphere.

es·tre·char *v.* to tighten; to narrow down; to embrace, hug; **– la mano,** to squeeze, grasp another's hand; to shake hands.

es·tre·chez, es·tre·chu·ra *f.* narrowness; tightness; austerity; dire straits; poverty; closeness.

es·tre·cho *adj.* narrow; tight; *m.* strait, narrow passage.

es·tre·lla *f.* star; **– de mar,** starfish.

es·tre·lla·do *adj.* starry; spangle with stars, **huevos -s,** fried eggs.

es·tre·llar *v.* to shatter; to dash to pieces; to star, spangle with stars; **-se** to shatter, break into pieces; to fail.

es·tre·me·cer[13] *v. irr.* to shake; **-se** to shiver, shudder; to vibrate.

es·tre·me·ci·mien·to *m.* shiver, shudder; vibration; shaking.

es·tre·nar *v.* to wear for the first time; to perform (*a play*) for the first time; to inaugurate; to begin.

es·tre·no *m.* debut, first appearance or performance.

es·tre·ñi·mien·to *m.* constipation.

es·tre·ñir[5,19] *v. irr.* to constipate; **-se** to become constipated.

es·tré·pi·to *m.* racket, noise, crash.

es·tre·pi·to·so *adj.* noisy; boisterous.

es·tria·do *p.p.* & *adj.* fluted, grooved; streaked.

es·triar[17] *v.* to groove, to flute (*as a column*).

es·tri·ba·ción *f.* spur (*of mountain or mountain range*).

es·tri·bar *v.* to rest (upon); **eso estriba en que...** the basis or reason for it is that...

es·tri·bi·llo *m.* refrain.

es·tri·bo *m.* (*de caballo o vehículo*) stirrup; footboard, running board; (*apoyo*) support; brace; spur (*of a mountain*); **perder los -s** to lose one's balance; to lose control of oneself.

es·tri·bor *m.* starboard.

es·tric·to *adj.* strict.

es·tro·fa *f.* strophe, stanza.

es·tro·pa·jo *m.* fibrous mass (*for scrub-bing*); **tratar a uno como un –** to treat someone scornfully.

es·tro·pe·ar *v.* to spoil, ruin, damage; to cripple.

es·truc·tu·ra *f.* structure.

es·truc·tu·ral *adj.* structural.

es·truen·do *m.* clatter; clamor, din, racket.

es·truen·do·so *adj.* thunderous, uproarious, deafening.

es·tru·ja·mien·to *m.* crushing, squeezing.

es·tru·jar *v.* to squeeze, press, crush.

es·tru·jón *m.* squeeze, crush; smashing.

es·tua·rio *m.* estuary.

es·tu·co *m.* stucco.

es·tu·che *m.* jewel box; instrument case, kit; small casket; sheath.

es·tu·dian·ta·do *m.* the student body (*of a school or college*).

es·tu·dian·te *m.* & *f.* student.

es·tu·diar *v.* to study.

es·tu·dio *m.* study; studio.

es·tu·dio·so *adj.* studious; *m.* learner.

es·tu·fa *f.* heater; stove; hothouse; steam room; steam cabinet.

es·tu·pe·fac·to *adj.* stunned; speechless.

es·tu·pen·do *adj.* stupendous, marvelous.

es·tu·pi·dez *f.* stupidity.

es·tú·pi·do *adj.* stupid.

e·ta·pa *f.* stage, lap (*of a journey or race*); army food rations; epoch, period.

é·ter *m.* ether.

e·té·re·o *adj.* ethereal; heavenly.

e·ter·ni·dad *f.* eternity.

e·ter·ni·zar[9] *v.* to prolong excessively; to perpetuate, make eternal.

e·ter·no *adj.* eternal, everlasting.

é·ti·ca *f.* ethics; ético *adj.* ethical, moral.

e·ti·que·ta *f.* etiquette; formality; tag; **de** – formal (*dress, function, etc*).

eu·ca·lip·to *m.* eucalyptus.

eu·ro·pe·o *adj.* & *m.* European.

e·va·cua·ción *f.* evacuation; bowel movement.

e·va·cuar[18] *v.* to evacuate, empty; to vacate.

e·va·dir *v.* to evade, elude; -**se** to slip away, escape.

e·va·luar[18] *v.* to evaluate, appraise.

e·van·ge·lio *m.* gospel.

e·va·po·rar *v.* to evaporate; -**se** to evap-orate; to vanish, disappear.

e·va·sión *f.* evasion, dodge, escape.

e·va·si·va *f.* evasion, dodge, escape.

e·va·si·vo *adj.* evasive.

e·va·sor *m.* evader, dodger.

e·ven·to *m.* event.

e·vi·den·cia *f.* evidence. ·

e·vi·den·ciar *v.* to prove, show, make evident.

e·vi·den·te *adj.* evident

e·vi·ta·ble *adj.* avoidable.

e·vi·tar *v.* to avoid, shun.

e·vo·car[6] *v.* to evoke, call forth.

e·vo·lu·ción *f.* evolution.

e·vo·lu·cio·nar *v.* to evolve; to perform maneuvers; to go throught changes.

e·xa·cer·bar *v.* to exasperate, irritate; to aggravate, make worse.

e·xac·ti·tud *f.* exactness, presicion; punc-tuality.

e·xac·to *adj.* exact, precise; punctual.

e·xa·ge·rar *v.* to exaggerate.

e·xal·ta·ción *f.* exaltation; excitement.

e·xal·ta·do *adj.* elated; excited; hotheaded.

e·xal·tar *v.* to exalt, elevate, glorify; to praise; -**se** to get excited; to become upset emotionally.

e·xa·men *m.* examination; inspection.

e·xa·mi·nar *v.* to examine; to inspect.

e·xan·güe *adj.* lacking blood; anemic; exahusted.

e·xá·ni·me *adj.* lifeless, motionless; weak, faint.

e·xas·pe·rar *v.* to exasperate, irritate, annoy.

ex·ca·var *v.* to excavate, dig, dig out.

ex·ce·den·te *m.* surplus; *adj.* exceeding, extra.

ex·ce·der *v.* to exceed, surpass; to overdo; -**se** to go beyond the proper limit; to misbehave.

ex·ce·len·cia *f.* excellence, superiority; excellency (*title*).

ex·ce·len·te *adj.* excellent.

ex·cel·so *adj.* lofty, elevated; sublime; **El Excelso** the Most High.

ex·cén·tri·co *adj.* eccentric; queer, odd.

ex·cep·ción *f.* exception.

ex·cep·cio·nal *adj.* exceptional, unusual.

ex·cep·to *adj.* except, with the exception of.

ex·cep·tuar[18] *v.* to except.

ex·ce·si·vo *adj.* excessive.

ex·ce·so *m.* excess; crime; – **de equipaje** excess baggage; **en** – in excess, excessively.

ex·ci·ta·ción *f.* excitement.

ex·ci·tan·te *adj.* exciting; stimulating.

ex·ci·tar *v.* to excite, stir; -**se** to get excited.

ex·cla·ma·ción *f.* exclamation.

ex·cla·mar *v.* to exclaim.

ex·cluir[32] *v. irr.* to exclude.

ex·clu·si·vo *adj.* exclusive.

ex·co·mu·ni·car[6] *v.* to excommunicate.

ex·co·mu·nión *f.* excommunication.

ex·cre·cen·cia, ex·cres·cen·cia *f.* excrescence (*abnormal growth or tumor*).

ex·cre·men·to *m.* excrement.

ex·cur·sión *f.* excursion, tour, outing.

ex·cu·sa *f.* excuse.

ex·cu·sa·do *p.p.* & *adj.* excused; exempt; superfluous; unnecessary; reserved, private; *m.* toilet.

ex·cu·sar *v.* (*disculpar*) to excuse; to exempt: (*evitar*) to avoid, shun; -**se** to excuse oneself, apologize; to decline.

e·xen·ción *f.* exemption.

e·xen·tar *v.* to exempt. *See* eximir.

e·xen·to *adj.* exempt, freed; free, unob-structed.

e·xe·quias *f.* pl. obsequies, funeral rites.

ex·ha·lar *v.* to exhale; to emit, give off; to breathe forth; -**se** to evaporate; to run away.

ex·hi·bi·ción *f.* exhibition; exposition; *Mex.* payment *of* an installment.

ex·hi·bir *v.* to exhibit; *Mex.*, to pay for in installments (*stocks, policies, etc.*); -**se** to exhibit oneself, show off.

ex·hor·tar *v.* to exhort, admonish.

e·xi·gen·cia *f.* demand; urgent want; emergency.

e·xi·gen·te *adj.* demanding; exacting; urgent.

e·xi·gir[11] *v.* to require; to demand; to exact.

e·xi·guo *adj.* scanty, meager.

e·xi·mio *adj.* very distinguished.

e·xi·mir *v.* to exempt, except, excuse; -**se de** to avoid, shun.

e·xis·ten·cia *f.* existence; -**s** stock on hand, goods; **en** – in stock, on hand.

e·xis·ten·te *adj.* existent, existing; in stock.

e·xis·tir *v.* to exist.

é·xi·to *m.* outcome, result; success; **tener buen (mal)** – to be successfull (unsuccessfull).

é·xo·do *m.* exodus, emigration.

e·xo·ne·rar *v.* to exonerate, free from blame; to re-lieve *of* a burden or position; to dismiss.

e·xor·bi·tan·te *adj.* exorbitant, excessive, extravagant.

e·xó·ti·co *adj.* exotic, foreing, strange; quaint.

ex·pan·sión *f.* expansion; relaxation; recreation.

ex·pan·si·vo *adj.* expansive; demons-trative; effusive.

ex·pa·triar *v.* to expatriate, exile; -se to expatriate oneself, renounce one´s citizenship, to emigrate.

ex·pec·ta·ción *f.* expectation.

ex·pec·ta·ti·va *f.* expectation; hope, pros-pect; **estar en – de algo,** to be expecting, or on the lookout for, something.

ex·pec·to·rar *v.* to expectorate, cough up.

ex·pe·di·ción *f.* expedition; dispatch, promptness; papal dispatch or bull.

ex·pe·di·cio·na·rio *adj.* expeditionary; *m.* member *of* an expedition; explorer.

ex·pe·dien·te *m.* certificate, papers pertaining to a business matter; expedient, means; dispatch, promptness.

ex·pe·dir[5] *v. irr.* to dispatch; to issue *o*fficially; to remit, send.

ex·pe·ler *v.* to expel, eject.

ex·pe·rien·cia *f.* experience; experiment.

ex·pe·ri·men·ta·do *adj. & p.p.* expe-rienced.

ex·pe·ri·men·tal *adj.* experimental.

ex·pe·ri·men·tar *v.* to experiment, try, test; to experience, feel.

ex·pe·ri·men·to *m.* experiment, trial.

ex·per·to *adj.* expert, skillful; *m.* expert.

ex·pia·ción *f.* expiation, atonement.

ex·piar[17] *v.* to atone for; t*o* make amends for; to purify.

ex·pi·rar *v.* to die, to expire, come to an end.

ex·pla·yar *v.* to become extended; to relax in the open air; to enlarge upon a subject; -se **con un amigo,** to unbosom oneself, speak with utmost frankness with a friend.

ex·pli·ca·ble *adj.* explainable.

ex·pli·ca·ción *f.* explanation.

ex·pli·car[6] *v.* to explain, **– una cátedra,** to teach a course; -se to explain – oneself; to account for one´s conduct.

ex·pli·ca·ti·vo *adj.* explanatory, explaining.

ex·plí·ci·to *adj.* explicit; express, clear, definite.

ex·plo·ra·ción *f.* exploration.

ex·plo·ra·dor *m.* explorer, scout, *adj.* exploring.

ex·plo·rar *v.* to explore.

ex·plo·sión *f.* explosion.

ex·plo·si·vo *adj. & m.* explosive.

ex·plo·ta·ción *f.* exploitation; operation *of* a mine; development *of* a business; plant.

ex·plo·tar *v.* to exploit, operate, develop; to utilize, profit by, to make unfair use *of; Am.* to explode.

ex·po·ner[40] *v. irr. (dejar ver)* to expose, reveal; to show, exhibit; to display; *(sin protección)* to leave unprotected, to expose *(film); (explicar)* to expound; to explain; -se **a,** to expose oneself to; to run the risk of.

ex·por·ta·ción *f.* exportation; export.

ex·por·tar *v.* to export.

ex·po·si·ción *f.* exposition; exhibition; explanation; exposure.

ex·prés *m. Am.* express; *Am.* express company.

ex·pre·sar *v.* to express; -se to express oneself, speak.

ex·pre·sión *f.* expression; utterance; -es, regards.

ex·pre·si·vo *adj.* expressive, affectionate.

ex·pre·so *adj.* expressed, express, clear, exact; fast; *m.* express train.

ex·pri·mir *v.* to squeeze, extract *(juice);* to wring out; to express, utter.

ex·pues·to *p.p* of **exponer** & *adj.* exposed; expressed; displayed; risky, dangerous; **lo –** what has been said.

ex·pul·sar *v.* to expel, eject.

ex·pul·sión *f.* expulsion, expelling.

ex·qui·si·tez *f.* exquisiteness.

ex·qui·si·to *adj.* exquisite.

ex·ta·sia·do *adj.* rapt, in ecstasy; *p.p of* **extasiar.**

ex·ta·siar[17] *v.* to delight; -se to be in ecstasy, to be entranced.

éx·ta·sis *m.* ecstasy.

ex·ten·der[1] *v. irr.* to extend; to spread; to unfold, to draw up *(a document);* -se to extend, spread; to expatiate, be too wordy.

ex·ten·sión *f.* extension; extent; expanse; expansion.

ex·ten·si·vo *adj.* extensive.

ex·ten·so *p.p. of* **extender** extended; *adj.* extensive, vast, spacious; **por –** extensively, in detail.

ex·te·nua·do *adj.* wasted, weak, emaciated.

ex·te·rior *adj.* exterior, outer; *m.* exterior; outside; outward appearance.

ex·ter·mi·nar *v.* to exterminate.

ex·ter·mi·nio *m.* extermination, destruction.

ex·ter·no *adj.* external, outward.

ex·tin·guir[12] *v.* to extinguish, put out; to destroy.

ex·tin·to *adj.* extinct.

ex·tin·tor *m.* extinguisher; **– de espuma** fire extinguisher.

ex·tir·par *v.* to eradicate, pull out by the roots, root out, remove completely; to destroy completely.

ex·tor·sión *f.* extortion.

ex·tor·sio·nar *v. Am.* to extort, extract money, blackmail.

ex·tor·sio·nis·ta *m. Am.* extortioner, profiteer, racketeer.

ex·trac·to *m.* extract; abstract, summary.

ex·tra·er[46] *v. irr.* to extract.

ex·tran·je·ro *adj.* foreign; *m.* foreigner.

ex·tra·ña·mien·to *m.* wonder, surprise, amazement.

ex·tra·ñar *v.* to wonder at; to banish; *Am.* to miss *(a person or thing);* -se to marvel, be astonished.

ex·tra·ñe·za *f.* strangeness; surprise, astonishment; oddity, odd thing.

ex·tra·ño *adj.* strange; rare; odd; *m.* stranger.

ex·tra·or·di·na·rio *adj.* extraordinary.

ex·tra·va·gan·cia *f.* extravagance; folly.

ex·tra·va·gan·te *adj.* extravagant, fan-tastic; queer, odd.

ex·tra·viar[17] *v.* to lead astray; to strand; to misplace; **-se** to lose one's way; to get stranded; to get lost; to miss the road.

ex·tra·ví·o *m.* deviation, straying; error; misconduct; damage.

ex·tre·ma·do *adj.* extreme; extremely good or extremely bad; *p.p.* of **extremar**.

ex·tre·mar *v.* to carry to an extreme; **-se** to take great pains, exert great effort.

ex·tre·mi·dad *f.* extremity; extreme degree; remotest part; **-es** extremities, hands and feet.

ex·tre·mo *adj.* extreme, last; farthest; excessive; utmost; *m.* extreme, highest degree or point; end, extremity; extreme care; **con (en** *or* **por) –** very much, extremely.

e·xu·be·ran·te *adj.* exuberant; luxuriant.

F

fa *m.* fourth note *of* the musical scale (*solfa* syllables).

fá·bri·ca *f.* manufacture; factory, mill; structure.

fa·bri·ca·ción *f.* manufacture.

fa·bri·can·te *m.* manufacturer, maker.

fa·bri·car[6] *v.* to manufacture, make; to construct, build; to fabricate, make up, invent.

fa·bril *adj.* manufacturing

fá·bu·la *f.* fable, tale; falsehood.

fa·bu·lo·so *adj.* fabulous; false, imaginary.

fac·ción *f.* faction, band, party; battle; **-es** features; **estar de –** to be on duty.

fa·ce·to *adj. Am.* cute, funny; *Am.* affected.

fá·cil *adj.* easy; docile, yielding, manageable; likely; probable.

fa·ci·li·dad *f.* facility, ease; opportunity.

fa·ci·li·tar *v.* to facilitate, make easy; to furnish, give; **– todos los datos** to furnish all the data.

fa·cón *m. Riopl., Bol.* dagger, large knife; **faconazo** *m. Riopl., Bol.,* stab.

fac·ti·ble *adj.* feasible.

fac·tor *m.* factor; element, joint cause; commercial agent; baggage man.

fac·to·rí·a *f.* trading post; *Am.* factory.

fac·tu·ra *f.* (*cuenta*) invoice, itemized bill; (*hechura*) make; workmanship, form; *Am.* roll, biscuit, muffin; **– simulada** temporary invoice, memorandum.

fac·tu·rar *v.* to invoice, bill; to check (*baggage*).

fa·cul·tad *f.* faculty; ability, aptitude; power, right; permission; branch *of* learning; school or college *of* a university.

fa·cul·ta·ti·vo *m.* doctor, physician.

fe·cun·dia *f.* eloquence, fluency, facility in speaking, gift of expression.

fa·cha *f.* appearance, figure, aspect, looks.

fa·cha·da *f.* facade, front (*of a building*); title page.

fa·chen·da *f.* ostentation, vanity.

fa·chen·do·so *adj.* vain, boastful, ostentatious.

fa·e·na *f.* task, job, duty; *Carib., Mex., C.A.* extra job; *Ch.* work crew, labor gang.

fa·ja *f.* sash; girdle; band, *Am.* belt, waist band.

fa·jar *v.* to girdle; to bind, wrap, or bandage with a strip of cloth; *Am.* to beat, strike, thrash; *Am.* **– un latiga-zo a uno** to whip, thrash someone; **-se** to put on a sash or belt; *Am.* **-se con** to have a fight with, come to blows with.

fa·jo *m.* bundle; sheaf.

fa·laz *adj.* illusive, illusory; deceitful, deceiving.

fal·da *f.* skirt; lap; hat brim; foothill,, slope; **faldón** *m.* coattail; shirttail.

fal·de·ar *v.* to skirt (*a hill*).

fal·sa·rio *m.* crook, forger; liar.

fal·se·ar *v.* to falsity, misrepresent; to counterfeit; to forge; to pick (*a lock*); to flag, grow weak; to hit a wrong note.

fal·se·dad *f.* falsehood, lie; deceit.

fal·si·fi·ca·ción *f.* falsification, forgery; counterfeit.

fal·si·fi·car[6] *v.* to falsity, make false; to counterfeit; to forge.

fal·so *adj.* false; untrue, unreal; deceitful; counterfeit; sham; *C.A.* cowardly; *m.* inside facing of a dress; lining; *Mex.* false testimony, slander; en – upon a false foundation; without proper security; *Am.* **co·ger a uno en –** to catch one lying.

fal·tar *v.* to be lacking, wanting; to be absent or missing; to fail, be of no use or help; to fail to fulfill (*a promise or duty*); to die; *Mex., C.A* to insult; **– poco para las cinco** to be almost five o'clock; **¡no faltaba más!** that's the last straw!; why, the very idea!

fal·ta *f.* (*defect*o) lack, want; fault, mistake; defect; absence; (*infracción*) misdemeanor, offense; **a – de** for want of; **hacer –** to be necessary; to be missing; **me hace –** I need it; **sin –** without fail.

fal·to *adj.* lacking; deficient, short; *Am.* foolish, stupid.

fal·tri·que·ra *f.* pocket.

fa·lla *f.* fault, defect; failure; fault (*fracture in the earth's crust*); *Riopl.* baby's bonnet.

fa·llar *v.* (*juzgar*) to render a verdict; (*fracasar*) to fail, be deficient; to default; to miss; to fail to hit; to give way, break; to trump.

fa·lle·cer[13] *v. irr.* to die.

fa·lle·ci·mien·to *m.* decease, death.

fa·lli·do *adj.* frustrated; bankrupt.

fa·llo *m.* verdict, judgment; decision; *adj.* lacking (*a card, or swit, in card games*); *Ch.* silly, foolish.

fa·ma *f.* fame, reputation; rumor, report; *Ch.* bull's-eye, center of a target.

fa·mé·li·co *adj.* ravenous, hungry, starved.

fa·mi·lia *f.* family

fa·mi·liar *adj.* domestic, homelike; familiar, well-known; friendly, informal; colloquial (*phrase or expression*); *m.* intimate friend; member of a household; domestic servant; familiar spirit, demon; *Am.* relative.

fa·mi·lia·ri·dad *f.* familiarity, informality.

fa·mi·lia·ri·zar[9] *v.* to familiarize, acquaint; **-se** to acquaint oneself, become familiar (with).

fa·mo·so *adj.* famous; excellent.

fa·nal *m.* beacon, lighthouse; lantern; headlight; bell jar, glass cover.

fa·ná·ti·co *adj. & m.* fanatic.

fa·na·tis·mo *m.* fanaticism.

fa·ne·ga *f.* Spanish bushel; **– de tierra** land measure (*variable according to region*).

fan·fa·rrón *m.* braggart, boaster; bluffer.

fan·fa·rro·na·da *f.* boast, brag, swagger, bluff.

fan·fa·rro·ne·ar *v.* to bluff, brag; to swagger.

fan·go *m.* mud, mire.

fan·go·so *adj.* muddy, miry.

fan·ta·se·ar *v.* to fancy; to imagine.

fan·ta·sí·a *f.* fantasy, imagination, fancy, whim; **-s** string of pearls; *Ven.* **tocar por –** to play by ear.

fan·tas·ma *m.* phantom, image; vision, ghost; *f.* scarecrow.

fan·tas·ma·gó·ri·co *adj.* fantastic, unreal, illusory.

fan·tás·ti·co *adj.* fantastic.

far·del *m.* knapsack, bag; bundle.

far·do *m.* bundle; bale; *Ríopl., Andes* **pasar el –** to "pass the buck", shift the responsibility to someone else.

fa·rin·ge *f.* pharynx.

fa·rín·ge·o *adj.* pharyngeal.

far·ma·céu·ti·co *m.* pharmacist, druggist; *adj.* pharmaceutical (*pertaining to a pharmacy or pharmacists*).

far·ma·cia *f.* pharmacy; drugstore.

fa·ro *m.* lighthouse; beacon; *Am.* headlight.

fa·rol *m.* (*linterna*) lantern; street lamp; (*fachendoso*) conceit, self-importance; *Ríopl.* balcony; *Am.* presumptuous man; *Am.* bluff; **darse –** to show off; to put on airs.

fa·ro·la *f.* street light; lamppost.

fa·ro·le·ro *adj.* vain, ostentatious; *m.* lamp maker or vendor; lamplighter (*person*).

fa·rra *f. Ríopl., Ch., Col., Ven., Andes* spree, revelry, wild party, noisy merrymaking; *Ríopl., Ch., Col., Ven., Andes* **ir de –** to go on a spree.

far·sa *f.* farce; company of actors; sham, fraud.

far·san·te *m.* charlatan, bluffer; quack; comedian; wag.

fas·ci·na·ción *f.* fascination; glamour.

fas·ci·na·dor *adj.* fascinating, glamorous; charming.

fas·ci·nar *v.* to fascinate, bewitch, charm; to allure.

fa·se *f.* phase, aspect.

fas·ti·diar *v.* to annoy, bother; to bore; *Col., P.R.* to hurt, harm, ruin.

fas·ti·dio *m.* boredom; disgust; nuisance, annoyance.

fas·ti·dio·so *adj.* annoying, bothersome; boring, tiresome.

fa·tal *adj.* fatal; mortal, deadly; unfortunate.

fa·ta·li·dad *f.* fatality, destiny; calamity, misfortune.

fa·ti·ga *f.* fatigue, weariness; toil; **-s** hardships.

fa·ti·gar[7] *v.* to fatigue, weary; to bother.

fa·ti·go·so *adj.* fatiguing, tiring.

fa·tuo *adj.* foolish, stupid; vain; **fuego –** will-o'-the-wisp.

fa·vor *m.* favor; kindness; help, aid; protection; *Am.* ribbon bow; **a – de** in favor of; **hágame el –** please.

fa·vo·ra·ble *adj.* favorable.

fa·vo·re·cer[13] *v. irr.* to favor, help, protect.

fa·vo·ri·tis·mo *m.* favoritism.

fa·vo·ri·to *adj. & m.* favorite.

faz *f.* face.

fe *f.* faith; **– de bautismo** baptismal certificate.

fe·al·dad *f.* ugliness, homeliness; foulness, foul or immoral action.

fe·bre·ro *m.* February.

fe·bril *adj.* feverish.

fé·cu·la *f.* starch.

fe·cun·dar *v.* to fertilize

fe·cun·do *adj.* fruitful, fertile, productive.

fe·cha *f.* date.

fe·char *v.* to date.

fe·cho·rí·a *f.* misdeed, misdemeanor.

fe·de·ra·ción *f.* federation, union.

fe·de·ral *adj.* federal.

fe·li·ci·dad *f.* happiness; **¡-es!** congratu-lations!

fe·li·ci·ta·ción *f.* congratulation.

fe·li·ci·tar *v.* to congratulate.

fe·li·grés *m.* parishioner.

fe·liz *adj.* happy; lucky.

fel·pu·do *adj.* plushy, like plush; *m.* small plushlike mat; door mat.

fe·me·nil *adj.* womanly, feminine.

fe·me·ni·no *adj.* feminine.

fe·men·ti·do *adj.* false; treacherous.

fe·ne·cer[13] *v. irr.* to die; to finish, end.

fé·ni·co *adj.* carbolic; **ácido –** carbolic acid.

fé·nix *m.* phoenix (*mythical bird*).

fe·nó·me·no *m.* phenomenon.

fe·o *adj.* ugly, homely: *Am.* bad (*referring to taste or odor*); **feote** *adj.* hideous, very ugly.

fé·re·tro *m.* bier; coffin.

fe·ria *f.* fair; market; *Mex.* change (*money*); *Am.* tip: **-s** *Am.* present given to servants or the poor during holidays.

fe·rian·te *m. & f.* trader at fairs; trader; peddler.

fer·men·tar *v.* to ferment.

fer•men•to m. ferment; yeast, leaven.

fe•ro•ci•dad f. ferocity, fierceness

fe•roz adj. ferocious, wild, fierce.

fé•rre•o adj. ferrous (pertaining to or derived from iron); ironlike; harsh; **vía férrea** railroad.

fe•rre•te•rí•a f. hardware shop; hardware.

fe•rro•ca•rril m. railroad.

fe•rro•via•rio adj. railway, railroad (used as adj.); m. railroad man; railroad employee.

fér•til adj. fertile, productive; **fertilidad** f. fertility.

fer•ti•li•zar⁹ v. to fertilize.

fer•vien•te adj. fervent, ardent.

fer•vor m. fervor, zeal, devotion.

fer•vo•ro•so adj. fervent, ardent; pious, devout; zealous.

fes•te•jar v. to feast, entertain; to celebrate; to woo; Mex. to thrash, beat.

fes•te•jo m. entertainment, festival, celebration; courtship; Am. revelry.

fes•tín m. feast; banquet.

fes•ti•vi•dad f. festival; holiday; holy day; festivity, gaiety, rejoicing.

fes•ti•vo adj. festive, gay; **día** – holiday.

fé•ti•do adj. foul; foul-smelling.

fia•do p.p. of **fiar; al** – on credit.

fia•dor m. guarantor, backer, bondsman; Ec., Ch. chin strap, hat guard.

fiam•bre m. cold meat; cold or late news; Riopl., Mex., Col., Ven. cold meat salad; Am. flop, failure (referring to a party).

fian•za f. bond, security, surety, guarantee; bail.

fiar¹⁷ to trust; to guarantee, back; Am. to borrow on credit; **-se de** to place confidence in.

fi•bra f. fiber; **fibroso** adj. fibrous.

fic•ción f. fiction.

fic•ti•cio adj. fictitious.

fi•cha f. (pieza) chip; token; domino; (tarjeta) file card; Am. check (used in barbershops and stores); Am. rascal scamp; **fichero** m. file, card index, fling cabinet.

fi•de•dig•no adj. trustworthy, reliable.

fi•de•li•dad f. fidelity, faithfulness.

fi•de•o m. vermicelli, thin noodle; thin person.

fie•bre f. fever; excitement, agitation; Ch. astute person.

fiel adj. faithful; true, accurate; m. public inspector; pointer of a balance or scale; pin of the scissors; **los -es** the worshipers, the congregation.

fiel•tro m. felt; felt hat; felt rug.

fie•ra f. wild beast; Am. go-getter, hustler; **ser una – para el trabajo** to be a demon for work.

fie•re•za f. ferocity, fierceness; cruelty ugliness.

fie•ro adj. fierce, ferocious, wild; cruel; ugly, horrible; huge; m. threat; **echar** (or **hacer**) **-s** to threaten; to boast.

fie•rro m. Am. iron; Am. iron bar; Am. cattle brand; -

s Am. tools, implements. See **hierro**.

fies•ta f. festivity, celebration, entertainment; holiday; **estar de** – to be in a holiday mood; **hacer -s a uno** to fawn on a person.

fies•te•ro adj. fond of parties, fond of entertaining; gay, festive; playful; m. merry-maker.

fi•gón m. cheap eating house, "joint."

fi•gu•ra f. figure; shape, form; countenance; face card.

fi•gu•ra•do adj. figurative.

fi•gu•rar v. to figure; to form; to represent, symbolize; **-se** to imagine; **se me figura** I think, guess, or imagine.

fi•gu•rín m. fashion plate; dandy.

fi•jar v. to fix, fasten; to establish; **-se** to settle; **-se en** to notice, pay attention to.

fi•je•za f. firmness, solidity, steadiness.

fi•jo adj. fixed; firm; secure.

fi•la f. row, tier; rank.

fi•la•men•to m. filament.

fi•le•te m. (moldura) edge, rim: (carne) fillet, tenderloin; (freno) snaffle bit (for horses); hem; screw thread.

fi•lial adj. filial.

fil•mar v. to film, screen (a play or novel).

fi•lo m. cutting edge; Andes hunger; **por** – exactly; Am. **de** – resolutely.

fi•lón m. seam, leyer (of metallic ore).

fi•lo•so adj. Am. sharp, sharp-edged.

fi•lo•so•fí•a f. philosophy.

fi•lo•só•fi•co adj. philosophic, philo-sophical.

fi•ló•so•fo m. philosopher.

fil•trar v. to filter; **-se** to leak through, leak out; to filter.

fil•tro m. filter.

fi•lu•do adj. Am. sharp, sharp-edged.

fin m. end, ending; purpose; **al** – at last; **al** – **y al cabo** at last; anyway; in the end: **a – de que** so that; **a -es del mes** toward the end of the month; **en** – in conclusion; well; in short.

fi•na•do m. the deceased.

fi•nal adj. final.

fi•na•li•zar⁹ v. to finish; to end.

fi•nan•cia•mien•to m. Am. financing.

fi•nan•ciar v. Am. to finance.

fi•nan•cie•ro adj. financial; m. financier.

fi•nan•cis•ta m. Am. financier.

fi•nan•za f. Am. finance; **-s** Am. public treasury, government funds.

fin•ca f. real estate; property; country house; Am. ranch, farm.

fin•car v. to buy real estate; Am. to rest (on), be based (on); Am. to build a farmhouse or country house.

fi•ne•za f. fineness; nicety; courtesy; favor, kindness; present.

fin•gi•mien•to m. pretense, sham.

fin·gir[11] v. to feign, pretend, fake; to imagine.

fi·ni·qui·to m. settlement (of an account); quittance, final receipt; **dar** – to finish up.

fi·no adj. fine; nice; delicate; sharp; subtle; refined.

fi·nu·ra f. fineness; nicety; subtlety; courtesy, good manners.

fior·do m. fjord.

fir·ma f. signature; firm, firm name.

fir·ma·men·to m. firmament, sky.

fir·man·te m. & f. signer.

fir·mar v. to sign.

fir·me adj. firm; solid, hard; **de** – with-out stopping, hard, steadily.

fir·me·za f. firmness.

fis·cal m. public prosecutor, district attorney; adj. fiscal.

fis·gar[7] v. to pry; to snoop; to spy on.

fis·gón m. snoop, snooper; adj. snooping; curious.

fis·go·ne·ar v. to pry about; to snoop.

fí·si·ca f. physics.

fí·si·co adj. physical; Am. vain, prudish, affected; Am. real; m. physicist.

fi·sio·lo·gí·a f. physiology.

fi·sio·ló·gi·co adj. physiological.

fi·sio·no·mí·a f. face, features.

fla·co adj. lean, skinny; frail, weak; **su lado** – his weak side, his weakness.

fla·cu·ra f. thinness.

fla·ma f. flame.

fla·man·te adj. bright, shiny; brandnew.

fla·me·an·te adj. flaming, flashing.

fla·me·ar v. to flame; to flap, flutter (in the wind).

fla·men·co adj. Flemish; C.A., P.R. skinny; m. Flemish, Flemish language; flamingo; Andalusian dance.

flan m. custard.

flan·co m. flank, side.

flan·que·ar v. to flank.

flaps m. pl. flaps (of an airplane).

fla·que·ar v. to weaken, flag.

fla·que·za f. thinness, leanness; weakness, frailty.

flau·ta f. flute; **flautista** m. & f. flute player.

fle·co m. fringe; bangs, fringe of hair.

fle·cha f. arrow, dart.

fle·char v. to dart, shoot (an arrow); to strike, wound or kill with an arrow; to cast an amorous or ardent glance; Ven. to prick, sting; Am. to burn (said of the sun).

fle·ta·men·to m. charter, charter party (of a ship).

fle·tar v. to charter (a ship); to freight; Ch. to hire (pack animals); Peru to let loose (strong words); Am. to scatter (false rumors); **-se** Col., Mex., Carib., Ch. to run away, slip away; Am. to slip in uninvited; Am. **salir fletado** to leave on the run.

fle·te m. freight, freightage; cargo: load: Am. fine horse, race horse; Am. bother, nuisance; Col., Ven. **salir sin -s** to leave in a hurry.

fle·xi·bi·li·dad f. flexibility; **flexible** adj. flexible.

fle·xión f. bending, bend; sag.

flo·je·ar v. to slacken; to waken; to idle, to be lazy.

flo·je·dad f. laxity, looseness; slackness; laziness; slack.

flo·je·ra = flojedad.

flo·jo adj. (mal atado) lax; loose, slack; (sin fuerza) lazy; weak.

flor f. flower, blossom; compliment; – **de la edad** prime; – **de lis** iris (flower); – **y nata** the best, the cream, the chosen few; **a – de** flush with; **echar -es** to throw a bouquet; to compliment, flatter.

flo·re·ado p.p. & adj. flowered; made of the finest wheat.

flo·re·ar v. to decorate with flowers; to brandish, flourish; to make a flourish on the guitar; to flatter, compliment; to bolt, sift out (the finest flour); Am. to flower, bloom; Am. to choose the best; **-se** C.A. to shine, excel; Am. to burst open like a flower.

flo·re·cer[13] v. irr. to flower, bloom; to flourish, thrive.

flo·re·cien·te adj. flourishing, thriving; prosperous.

flo·re·ci·mien·to m. flourishing, flowering, bloom.

flo·re·o m. flourish; idle talk; flattery, compliment.

flo·re·rí·a f. florist's shop.

flo·re·ro m. florist; flower vase; flatterer; adj. flattering.

flo·res·ta f. wooded place, grove; arbor.

flo·re·te m. fencing foil.

flo·ri·do adj. flowery.

flo·ta f. fleet; Col., **echar -s** to brag, boast.

flo·ta·dor m. floater; float; pontoon (of a hydroplane); adj. floating.

flo·tan·te adj. floating; m. Col., Ven. bluffer, braggart.

flo·tar v. to float.

flo·te: **a** – afloat.

fluc·tua·ción f. fluctuation; wavering, hesitation.

fluc·tuar[18] v. to fluctuate; to waver; to hesitate.

fluen·te adj. fluent, flowing.

flui·dez f. fluidity, easy flow, fluency.

fluí·do adj. fluid, flowing, fluent; m. fluid.

fluir[32] v. irr. to flow.

flu·jo m. flux; flow; flood tide.

fluo·res·cen·te adj. fluorescent.

flux f. flush (in cards); P.R., Col., Ven. suit of clothes; **hacer** – to use up one´s funds, lose everything; Am. **tener uno** – to be lucky.

fo·ca f. seal, sea lion.

fo·co m. focus, center; Am. electric-light bulb.

fo·fo adj. spongy, porous; light (in weight), soft.

fo·ga·ta f. fire, blaze, bonfire.

fo·gón m. hearth, fireplace; grill (for cooking); vent of a gun; C.A., Mex. fire, bonfire; **fogonazo** m. flash (of gunpowder).

fo·go·so adj. fiery, ardent; lively, spirited.

fo·lla·je m. foliage.

fo·lle·tín m. small pamphlet; serial story.

fo•lle•to *m.* pamphlet.

fo•men•tar *v.* to foment, encourage, promote, foster.

fo•men•to *m.* promotion, encouragement; development; aid.

fon•da *f.* inn; restaurant.

fon•de•ar *v.* to cast anchor; to sound, make sounding; to search (*a ship*); a sound out; -**se** *Cuba*, to save up for the future.

fon•de•ro *m. Am.* innkeeper.

fon•di•llos *m. pl.* seat of trousers.

fon•dis•ta *m. & f.* innkeeper.

fon•do *m.* (*hondura*) bottom; depth; background; back, rear end; (*esencia*) mature, heart, inner self; fund; *Cuba, Ven.* underskirt; -**s** funds; **a** – thoroughly; **echar a** – to sink.

fon•du•cho *m.* cheap eating place.

fo•ne•ma *m.* phoneme.

fo•né•ti•ca *f.* phonetics, study *of* pronun-ciation.

fo•nó•gra•fo *m.* phonograph.

fo•no•lo•gí•a *f.* phonology.

fo•ra•ji•do *m.* outlaw, fugitive; highway-man, bandit.

fo•rá•ne•o *adj.* foreign; *m.* outsider, stranger.

fo•ras•te•ro *m.* strandger; foreigner; outsider; *adj.* foreign.

for•ce•je•ar, for•ce•jar *v.* to struggle; to strive; to oppose, resist.

for•ja *f.* forge; forging; blacksmith's shop.

for•ja•dor *m.* forger (*of metals*); smith, blacksmith; inventor (*of lies, stories, trichs, etc.*).

for•jar *v.* to forge; to form, shape; to invent, feign, fake.

for•ma *f.* form, shape, figure; manner; format (*size and shape of a book*); host (*unleavened bread for communion*).

for•ma•ción *f.* formation.

for•mal *adj.* formal; seriuos, trustworthy, punctual; reliable.

for•ma•li•dad *f.* formality; seriousness, reliability; gravity, dignity; punctuality, red tape.

for•ma•lis•mo *m.* formality, red tape (*excess of formalities*); **formalista** *adj.* fond *of* excessive formalities, fond of red tape.

for•ma•li•zar⁹ *v.* to give proper form to; to legalize; tomake official; -**se** to settle down, become serious.

for•mar *v.* to form; to shape, mold; -**se** to get into line; to be molded, educated; to take form.

for•mi•da•ble *adj.* formidable; fearful.

for•món *m.* wide chisel.

fór•mu•la *f.* formula.

for•mu•lar *v.* to formulate, word.

for•ni•do *adj.* stout, strong, sturdy.

fo•ro *m.* stage; back, rear (*of a stage*); forum, court; bar (*profession of law*).

fo•rra•je *m.* forage, green grass, fodder, feed.

fo•rra•je•ar *v.* to forage, gather forage.

fo•rrar *v.* to line; to cover, put a sheath, case, or covering on; -**se** *Riopl., C.A.* to eat well ; *Am.* to supply oneself with provisions; *Riopl., Mex., Cuba,* to save money.

fo•rro *m.* lining; sheathing, casing; covering; book cover.

for•te•le•cer¹³ *v. irr.* to fortify; to strengthen.

for•ta•le•za *f.* fortress; fortitude; strength, vigor; *Ch.* stench, stink.

for•ti•fi•ca•ción *f.* fortification; fort.

for•ti•fi•car⁶ *v.* to fortify.

for•tui•to *adj.* fortuitous, accidental, unexpected.

for•tu•na *f.* fortune; fate, chance; wealth; **por** – fortunately.

for•zar⁹ *v. irr.* to force; to compel; to take (*a fort*); to rape; – **la entrada en** to break into.

for•zo•zo *adj.* compulsory; necessary.

fo•sa *f.* grave; cavity.

fos•co *adj.* dark; cross, irritable, frowning.

fos•fa•to *m.* phosphate.

fos•fo•re•cer¹³, fos•fo•res•cer *v.* to glow.

fós•fo•ro *m.* phosphorus; match.

fó•sil *adj. & m.* fossil.

fo•so *m.* hole, pit; stage pit; ditch.

fo•to•gra•ba•do *m.* photoengraving.

fo•to•gra•fí•a *f.* photograph; photography.

fo•to•gra•fiar¹⁷ *v.* to photograph.

fo•tó•gra•fo *m.* photographer.

fra•ca•sa•do *adj.* failed; *m.* failure.

fra•ca•sar *v.* to fail, to come to ruin; to crumble to pieces.

fra•ca•so *m.* failure, ruin; calamity; crash.

frac•ción *f.* fraction.

frac•tu•ra *f.* fracture; break, crack.

frac•tu•rar *f.* fracture, break.

fra•gan•cia *f.* fragance, scent, perfume.

fra•gan•te *adj.* fragrant; **en** – in the act.

fra•ga•ta *f.* frigate.

frá•gil *adj.* fragile, breakable, frail, weak.

frag•men•to *m.* fragment.

fra•gor *m.* clang, din; crash.

fra•go•ro•so *adj.* deafening, thunderous.

fra•go•so *adj.* rugged, craggy, rough, uneven; noisy.

fra•gua *f.* forge; blacksmith's shop.

fra•guar *v.* to forge; to sheme, hatch (*a plot*).

frai•le *m.* friar; priest; **frailuco** *m.* little old friar.

fram•bue•sa *f.* raspberry; **frambueso** *m.* raspberry bush.

fran•cés *adj.* French; *m.* Frenchman; French language.

fran•co *adj.* (*sincero*) frank, open, candid, sincere; (*exento*) free; *m.* franc; **francote** *adj.* very frank, blunt, outspoken.

fra•ne•la *f.* flannel.

fran•ja *f.* fringe, border; stripe, braid.

fran•que•ar *v.* to exempt; to free; to frank (*a letter*); to dispatch, send; to make grants; – **el paso**, to permit the passage (of); **-se** to unbosom oneself, disclose one´s innermost thoughts and feelings.

fran·que·o *m.* postage; franking (*of a letter*); freeing (*of slaves or prisoners*).

fran·que·za *f.* frankness; freedom.

fran·qui·cia *f.* franchise, grant, privilege; freedom or exemption (*from fees*).

fras·co *m.* flask, vial, small bottle.

fra·se *f.* phrase; sentence.

fra·ter·nal *adj.* fraternal, brotherly.

fra·ter·ni·dad *f.* fraternity; brotherhood.

frau·de *m.* fraud.

frau·du·len·to *adj.* fraudulent, tricky, deceitful, dishonest.

fray *m.* (*contr. of* **fraile**, *used before Christian name*) friar.

fra·za·da *f.* blanket.

fre·cuen·cia *f.* frequency; **con –** frequently.

fre·cuen·tar *v.* to frequent.

fre·cuen·te *adj.* frequent.

fre·ga·de·ro *m.* sink.

fre·ga·do *m.* scrub, scrubbing; *p.p. of* **fregar**; *adj.* *Ch.*, *Andes* bothersome, annoying; *Col.*, stubborn; *Mex.*, *C.A.* brazen.

fre·gar[7] *v. irr.* to scour; to scrub; to rub; to wash (*dishes*); *Am.* to molest, annoy.

fre·go·na *f.* scrub woman; dishwasher, kitchen maid.

fre·ír[15] *v. irr.* to fry; to tease, bother.

fre·ne·sí *m.* frenzy, madness.

fre·né·ti·co *adj.* frantic; furious; in a frenzy.

fre·no *m.* bridle; brake; control; bit (*for horses*).

fren·te *f.* forehead; countenance; *m.* front; **en – de**, in front of; **– a**, in front of, facing; **hacer –** to face.

fre·sa *f.* strawberry.

fres·ca *f.* fresh air; fresh remark.

fres·co *adj.* (*bastante frío*) fresh; cool, (*sereno*) calm, serene; (*descarado*) forward, bold; *m.* coolness; cool air; fresco (*painting*); *C.A.*, *Col.*, refreshment; **al –** in the open air; **pintura al –** painting in fresco.

fres·cor *m.* freshness, coolness.

fres·cu·ra *f.* (*temperatura baja*) freshness; coolness; (*serenidad*) calm; freeedom; ease; (*insolencia*) boldness, impudence; impudent remark.

fres·no *m.* ash, ash tree.

fres·que·ci·llo *adj.* nice and cool; *m.* cool air, fresh breeze; **fresquecito, fresquito,** *adj.* nice and cool.

frial·dad *f.* coldness; coolness, indeference.

fric·ción *f.* friction, rub, rubbing.

fric·cio·nar *v.* to rub; to massage.

frie·ga *f.* rub, rubbing; *Am.* bother, nuisance, irritation; *Am.* flogging, beating.

fri·go·rí·fi·co *adj.* freezing; *m.* Spain refrigerator, icebox; *Riopl.* meatpacking house.

fri·jol *m.* bean; kidney bean, navy bean.

frí·o *adj.* cold; frigid; cool, indifferent; *m.* cold; **-s** *Mex.*, chills and fever; *Col.*, *C.A.* *Ven.*, malaria.

frio·len·to *adj.* cold-blooded, sensitive to cold; chilly.

frio·le·ra *f.* trifle.

fri·ta·da *f.* dish or fried food.

fri·to *p.p. irr. of* **freír**, fried; *m.* fry, dish or fried food.

fri·tu·ra *f.* fry, dish or fried food; fritter.

fri·vo·li·dad *f.* frivolity; **frívolo** *adj.* frivolous.

fron·da *f.* leaf; fern leaf; foliage.

fron·do·so *adj.* leafy.

fron·te·ra *f.* frontier, border; **fronterizo** *adj.* **fron·tier** (*used as an adj.*); opposite, facing.

fron·te·ro *adj.* facing, opposite.

fron·tis *m.* façade, front (*of a building*).

fron·tis·pi·cio *m.* front, façade (*front of a building*); title page.

fron·tón *m.* main wall of handball court; handball court; jai alai court; game of *pelota*.

fro·ta·ción *f.* friction, rubbing.

fro·tar *v.* to rub; to scour.

fro·te *m.* rubbing; friction.

fruc·ti·fi·car[6] *v.* to fruit, bear of produce fruit; to yield profit.

fruc·tuo·so *adj.* fruitful.

fru·gal *adj.* frugal, economical, saving, thrifty; **fru·galidad** *f.* frugality, thrift.

frun·cir[10] *v.* to wrinkle; to gather in pleats; to contract, shrivel; **– las cejas**, to frown; to knit the eyebrows; **– los labios**, to purse or curl the lips.

frus·le·rí·a *f.* trifle, trinket.

frus·tra·ción *f.* frustration; failure.

frus·trar *v.* to frustrate, thwart, foil; **-se** to fail, be thwarted.

fru·ta *f.* fruit (*not a vegetable*); **frutería** *f.* fruit store.

fru·te·ro *m.* fruit vendor; fruit dish; *adj.* fruit (*used as adj.*); **buque –** fruit boat; **plato –** fruit dish.

fru·to *m.* fruit (*any organic product of the earth*); result; benefit, profit.

¡fu·che! *interj.* *Mex.* phew! ugh! pew! phooey!

fue·go *m.* (*incendio*) fire; (*pasión*) passion; (*erupción*) skin eruption; *Am.* cold sore; **-s artificiales**, fireworks; **hacer –** to fire, shoot; **estar hecho un –** to be very angry; **romper –** to begin to fire, start shooting.

fue·lle *m.* (*instrumento*) bellows; (*arruga*) pucker, wrinkle, fold; (*hablador*) tattletale, windbag, gossiper.

fuen·te *f.* fountain; source, origin; spring; platter, serving dish.

fue·ra *adv.* outside, out; **– de** *prep.* outside of; in addition to.

fue·re·ño *m.* *Mex.*, *Ven.*, *Andes* outsider, stranger.

fue·ro *m.* law, statute; power, jurisdiction; code of laws; exemption, privilege.

fuer·te *adj.* (*robusto*) strong; loud; secure, fortified; (*grave*) grave, serious; (*áspero*) excessive; *Ch.* stinking; *m.* fort; forte, strong point; forte (*music*);

Mex, alcohol, liquor; *adv*. strongly; excessively; loud; hard.

fuer•za *f*. force; power, strength; violence,compulsion; **a – de**, by dint of; **a la – (por –, por la –, de por –,** *Am.* **de –)** by force, forcibly; necessarily; **ser –** to be necessary.

fue•te *m. Col., Cuba. Ríopl., Mex., Ven., Andes* whip; **fuetazo** *m. Am.* lash.

fu•ga *f*. flight, escape; leak, leakage; fugue (*musical composition*).

fu•gar•se[7] *v*. to flee, escape.

fu•gaz *adj*. fleeing; fleeting, brief, passing.

fu•gi•ti•vo *adj*. fugitive; fleeting, passing; perishable; *m*. fugitive.

fu•la•no *m*. so-and-so (*referring to person*).

ful•gor *m*. radiance, brilliance.

ful•gu•rar *v*. to gleam, flash, shine.

ful•mi•nar *v*. to thunder, thunder forth; to utter (*threats*).

fu•lo *m. Pan.* blond.

fu•lle•ro *m*. cardsharp; cooked gambler; cheat.

fu•ma•da *f*. puff, whiff (*of smoke*).

fu•ma•de•ro *m*. smoking room.

fu•ma•dor *m*. smoker, habitual smoker.

fu•mar *v*. to smoke (*tabacco*); *Am*. **-se a uno** to swindle or cheat someone.

fu•mi•gar[7] *v*. to fumigate.

fun•ción *f*. (*actividad*) function; functioning; (*empleo*) office; occupation; (*espectáculo*) show, performance; religious festival.

fun•cio•na•mien•to *m*. functioning, action, working, operation.

fun•cio•nar *v*. to function; to work, run (*said of machines*).

fun•cio•na•rio *m*. public employee, officer or official.

fun•da *f*. cover, case; *Col*. skirt; **– de almohada,** pillowcase.

fun•da•ción *f*. foundation.

fun•da•dor *m*. founder.

fun•da•men•tal *adj*. fundamental.

fun•da•men•to *m*. foundation, groudwork; basis; *Col*. skirt.

fun•dar *v*. to found, establish; to erect; to base, ground.

fun•dir *v*. to smelt, fuse, melt; to cast, mold; *Am*: to ruin; **-se** to fuse, melt together; to unite; *Ríopl., Mex*. to be ruined.

fun•do *m*. farm, country estate; property, land.

fú•ne•bre *adj*. funeral; funereal, gloomy, dismal.

fu•ne•ral *adj. & m*. funeral.

fu•ne•ra•ria *f*. undertaking establishment, funeral parlor.

fu•nes•to *adj*. ill-fated, unlucky; sad, unfortunate.

fun•go•si•dad *f*. fungus, fungous growth.

fur•gón *m*. freight car, boxcar; **furgonada** *f*. carload.

fu•ria *f*. fury, rage; speed.

fu•ri•bun•do *adj*. furious.

fu•rio•so *adj*. furious.

fu•ror *m*. fury, rage, anger; frenzy.

fur•ti•vo *adj*. furtive, sly, secret.

fu•se•la•je *m*. fuselage (*of an airplane*).

fu•si•ble *adj*. fusible; *m*. electric fuse.

fu•sil *m*. gun, rifle.

fu•si•lar *v*. to shoot, execute.

fu•sión *f*. fusion; melting; **– nuclear** nuclear fusion.

fus•ti•gar[7] *v*. to lash, whip; to censure severely, scold sharply.

fú•til *adj*. futile, useless; trivial; **futilidad,** *f*. futility, uselessness.

fu•tu•ro *adj*. future; *m*. fiancé, future husband; future.

G

ga•ba•cho *adj*. from or of the Pyrenees; Frenchlike; *Am*. **me salió –** it turned out wrong; *m*. Frenchman (*used depreciatively*).

ga•bán *m*. overcoat.

ga•be•ta – gaveta.

ga•bi•ne•te *m*. cabinet (*of a goverment*); studio, study, library room; dressing room; sitting room; private room; dentist's office; laboratory; *Am*. glassed-in **mirador.**

ga•ce•ta *f*. gazette, official newspaper; professional periodical; *Am*. any newspapaer.

ga•ce•ti•lla *f*. short newspaper article; column of short news items; gossip column; *m. & f*. newsmonger, tattletale; **gacetillero** *m*. newspaper reporter; newsmonger.

ga•cha *f*. watery mass or mush; *Col*. china or earthenware bowl; **-s** porridge, mush; caresses; **-s de avena** oatmeal.

ga•cho *adj*. dropping; bent downward; turned down; stooping; slouching; with horns curved downward; **sombrero –** slouch hat; **a gachas** on all fours, **con las orejas gachas,** with drooping ears; crestfallen, discouraged.

ga•fas *f. pl*. spectacles; grappling hooks.

gai•ta *f*. flageolet, a kind of flute; *Am*. good-for-nothing, lazy bum; **– gallega** bagpipe; **sacar la –** to stick out one's neck; **gaitero** *m*. piper, bagpipe player.

ga•je *m*. fee; **-s** wages, salary; fees.

ga•la *f*. elegance; full dress or uniform; ostentation; *Am*. award, prize, tip; -s finery, regalia, best clothes; **-s de novia** trousseau; **hacer – de** to boast of.

ga•lán *m*. gallant, lover; leading man (*in a play*).

ga•lan•te *adj*. gallant, attentive to ladies; polite.

ga•lan•te•a•dor *m*. gallant, lady's man; flatterer.

ga•lan•te•ar *v*. to court, woo; to make love.

ga•lan•te•o *m*. wooing, courtship.

ga·lan·te·rí·a *f.* gallantry, compliment, attention to ladies; courtesy; gracefulness; generosity.

ga·lar·dón *m.* recompense, reward.

ga·le·o·te *m.* galley slave.

ga·le·ra *f.* galley; large wagon; women's jail; printer's galley; *Mex.* jail; *Ch.*, *Ríopl.* tall hat.

ga·le·ra·da *f.* galley, galley proof; wagon load, van load.

ga·le·rí·a *f.* gallery; corridor.

gal·go *m.* greyhound; *adj. Col.* gluttonous, always hungry.

ga·li·cis·mo *m.* gallicism.

ga·li·llo *m.* uvula.

ga·lón *m.* gallon, braid, trimming; gallon.

ga·lo·ne·a·do *adj.* gallooned, trimmed with braid.

ga·lo·pa·da *f.* gallop: **pegar una –** to break into a gallop.

ga·lo·par *v.* to gallop.

ga·lo·pe *m.* gallop; **a (al *or* de) –** at a gallop: speedily.

ga·lo·pe·ar **= galopar**.

gal·pón *m. Ríopl.*, *Andes* large open shed.

ga·llar·de·te *m.* streamer.

ga·llar·dí·a *f.* elegance; gracefullness; bravery.

ga·llar·do *adj.* elegant, graceful; brave.

ga·lle·go *adj.* Galician, from or of Galicia, Spain; *m.* Galician; *Carib.*, *Ríopl.* Spaniard (*used as a nickname*).

ga·lle·ta *f.* cracker; hardtrack, hard biscuit; hard cookie; blow, slap; small pot; *Ríopl.* bread of coarse meal or bran; *Ch.*, reproof; *Am.* **colgarle la – a uno**, to fire, dismiss someone; *Am.* **tener –** to have strength, muscle.

ga·lli·na *f.* hen; *m. & f.* chikenhearted person.

ga·lli·ne·ro *m.* chiken coop, house, or yard; flock of chikens; basket for carrying chikens; poultryman; noisy gathering; top gallery of a theater.

ga·llo *m.* cock, rooster; aggressive, bossy person; cork float; false note (*in singing*); frog (*in one's throat*); *Am.* secondhand clothing; *Am.* fire wagon; *Mex.*, *Ríopl.* serenade.

ga·mo *m.* buck, male deer.

ga·mu·za *f.* chamois, chamois skin (*soft leather made from the skin of sheep, goats, deer, etc.*).

ga·na *f.* desire, appetite; **de buena (mala) –** willingly (unwillingly); **tener –** (*or* **-s**) to feel like, want to; **no me da la –** I don't want to.

ga·na·de·ro *m.* cattleman; cattle dealer; *adj.* cattle, pertaining to cattle.

ga·na·do *m.* cattle; herd; livestock; **– mayor**, cattle; horses; mules; **– menor**, sheep; **– de cerda** swine.

ga·na·dor *m.* winner; *adj.* winning.

ga·nan·cia *f.* profit, gain; *Am.* something extra, something to boot, something extra.

ga·nan·cio·so *adj.* winning; profitable; *m.* winner.

ga·nar *v.* to win; to profit, gain; to earn; to get ahead of.

gan·cho *m.* hook; hooked staff; *Mex.*, *Cuba*, *Ríopl.*, *Col.*, *C.A.* hairpin; *Am.* bait, lure, trick; **aguja de –** crochet hook; **echara uno el –** to hook someone; **tener –** to be attractive, alluring.

gan·dul *m.* bum, loafer.

gan·ga *f.* bargain; snap, easy job; kind of prairie hen.

gan·go·so *adj.* twangy, nasal (*voice*).

gan·gre·na *f.* gangrene.

gan·gre·nar *v.* to gangrene, cause gangrene; **-se** to gangrene.

ga·no·so *adj.* desirous; *Am.* lively, spirited (*horse*).

gan·so *m.* goose, gander; lazy, slovenly person; dunce.

gan·zú·a *f.* hook; picklock (*tool for picking locks*); *m. & f.* burglar.

ga·ra·ba·to *m.* hook; scrawl, scribble; **hacer -s** to scribble, write poorly.

ga·ra·je *m.* garage.

ga·ran·tí·a *f.* to guaranty; security; bail, bond.

ga·ran·ti·zar² *v.* to guarantee, vouch for.

ga·ra·ñón *m.* jackass, male ass, male camel (*for breeding*); *Ríopl.*, *Mex.*, *C.A.* stallion.

ga·ra·pi·ñar *v.* to candy (*almonds, fruits, etc.*).

gar·ban·zo *m.* chickpea.

gar·bo *m.* elegance, graceful air, good carriage.

gar·bo·so *adj.* graceful; elegant; sprightly.

gar·du·ña *f.* marten.

gar·fio *m.* hook.

gar·gan·ta *f.* throat, neck; groge, ravine; **garganti-lla** *f.* necklace.

gár·ga·ra *f.* gargling; **-s** *Am.* gargle, gargling solution; **hacer -s** to gargle.

gar·ga·re·ar *v. Am.* to gargle.

gar·ga·ris·mo *m.* gargling; gargle, gargling solution.

gar·ga·ri·zar² *v.* to gargle.

ga·ri·ta *f.* sentry box; watchman's booth; *Col.* vendor's booth.

ga·ri·to *m.* gambling house, gambling joint; gambler's winnings.

ga·rra *f.* claw, paw; hook; *Am.* strength; *Col.* leather or cloth remnant; *Am.* skinny person or animal; *Am.* margin of profit in a business deal; **echar la –** to arrest; to grab; *Mex.*, *C. A.*, *Ven.*, *Andes* **hacer -s** to tear to pieces.

ga·rra·fa *f.* decanter; **garrafón** *m.* large decanter; demijohn.

ga·rra·pa·ta *f.* tick (*an insect*).

ga·rra·pa·te·ar *v.* to scribble, scrawl, write poorly.

ga·rro·cha *f.* pole; iron-pointed staff; *Am.* goad (*for goading oxen*).

ga·rro·te *m.* club, cudgel, heavy stick; *Mex.*, *Ur.* brake; **dar –** to strangle; *Am.* to brake, set the brakes; **garrotazo** *m.* blow with a club; huge stick.

ga·rro·te·ro *m. Mex.*, *Ven.* brakeman; *Am.* beater (*one who beats with a club*); *adj. Am.* stingy.

ga·rru·cha *f.* pulley.

ga·rú·a *f. C.A.*, *Ríopl.*, *Ven.*, *Andes* drizzle.

gar•za *f.* heron.

gar•zo *adj.* blue, bluish; blue-eyed.

gas *m.* gas, vapor; *Col.*, *Ríopl.*, *Ven.*, gasoline.

ga•sa *f.* gauze.

ga•se•o•sa *f.* soda water; soda pop.

ga•se•o•so *adj.* gaseous.

ga•so•li•na *f.* gasoline.

gas•ta•dor *adj.* lavish, extravagant, wasteful; *m.* spendthrift, lavish spender.

gas•tar *v.* to spend; to wear; to use; to waste; **-se** to wear out, to get old.

gas•to *m.* expense, expenditure; wear.

ga•tas; a – on all fours; **andar a** – to creep, crawl; **salir a** – to crawl out of a difficulty.

ga•te•a•do *adj.* catlike; veined, streaked; *m. Am.* light-colored horse with black streaks.

ga•te•ar *v.* to creep; to crawl; to walk on all fours; to claw, scratch; to steal.

ga•ti•llo *m.* kitten, trigger; forceps (*for extracting teeth*), petty thief.

ga•to *m.* cat; moneybag; jack (*for lifting weigths*); sneak thief; sly fellow; *Am.* trigger; *Am.* outdoor market; *Am.* hot- water bottle; *Am.* a gaucho song and tap dance (*by extension, the dancer*); *Am.* blunder.

ga•lu•pe•rio *m.* fraud, intrigue.

gau•cha•da *f. Ríopl.* gaucho deed or exploit.

gau•cha•je *m. Ríopl.* band of Gauchos, Gaucho folk.

gau•ches•co *adj. Am.* relating to Gauchos.

gau•cho *m. Am.* Gaucho, Argentine and Uruguayan cowboy; *Ríopl.*, *Ven.* good horseman; *adj. Am.* relating to Gauchos, Gaucho-like; *Am.* sly, crafty.

ga•ve•ta *f.* drawer.

ga•vi•lla *f.* sheaf; gang, band (*of rogues, thieves, etc.*).

ga•vio•ta *f.* sea gull.

ga•za *f.* loop; *Carib.* noose of a lasso.

gaz•mo•ñe•rí•a *f.* prudery, affected modesty; **gaz•moño** *adj.* prudish, affected, coy.

gaz•na•te *m.* windpipe: a kind of fritter; *Andes* a sweetmeat made of pineapple or coconut.

ge•la•ti•na *f.* gelatin; jelly

ge•ma *f.* gem, jewel; bud.

ge•me•lom twin; **-s** twins; binoculars, opera glasses, field glasses; cuff links.

ge•mi•do *m.* moan; wail, cry.

ge•mir⁵ *v. irr.* to moan; to wail, cry.

gen•dar•me *m. Mex.*, *Ven.*, *Ríopl.*, *C.A.* policeman.

ge•ne•ra•ción *f.* generation.

ge•ne•ra•dor *m.* generator; **– molecular** atom smasher.

ge•ne•ral *adj. & m.* general; **por lo –** generallly.

ge•ne•ra•li•dad *f.* generality; majority.

ge•ne•ra•li•zar⁹ *v.* to generalize; **-se** to spread, become general.

gé•ne•ro *m.* (*clase*) kind, sort, class; gender; (*tela*) goods, material, cloth; **– humano** human race.

ge•ne•ro•si•dad *f.* generosity.

ge•ne•ro•so *adj.* generous; best (*wine*).

ge•nial *adj.* genial, jovial, pleasant.

ge•nio *m.* genius; temperament, disposition; spirit.

gen•te *f.* (*personas*) people; crowd; (*pueblo*) race, nation; clan; *Am.* **– bien** upper-class or important person; *Am.* **ser –** to be a somebody; to be cultured; to be socially important.

gen•til *adj.* graceful; genteel; courteous; gentile; *m.* pagan; gentile.

gen•ti•le•za *f.* grace, courtesy; nobility; favor.

gen•tí•o *m.* crowd, throng.

gen•tu•za *f.* rabble.

ge•nui•no *adj.* genuine.

ge•o•fí•si•ca *f.* geophysics.

ge•o•gra•fí•a *f.* geography; **geográfico.** *adj* geographical.

ge•o•lo•gí•a *f.* geology; **geológico** *adj.* geological.

ge•o•me•trí•a *f.* geometry; **geométrico** *adj.* geometric.

ge•ra•nio *m.* geranium.

ge•ren•cia *f.* management, administration.

ge•ren•te *m.* manager.

ger•men *m.* germ; origin, source.

ger•mi•nar *v.* to germinate.

ge•run•dio *m.* gerund; present participle.

ges•ti•cu•lar *v.* to gesticulate.

ges•tión *f.* action, step, maneuver; intervention; **-es** negotiations.

ges•tio•nar *v.* to manage; to take steps; to negotiate or carry out (*a deal, transaction, etc*).

ges•to *m.* face, expression; grimace; gesture; **estar de buen** (*or* **mal**) – to be in a good (*or* bad) humor; **hacer -s a** to make faces at.

gi•ba *f.* hump, hunch.

gi•gan•te *adj.* gigantic; *m.* giant.

gi•gan•tes•co *adj.* gigantic.

gim•na•sia *f.* gymnastics; **gimnasio** *m.* gymnasium; German institute (*for secondary instruction*).

gi•mo•te•ar *v.* to whimper, whine.

gi•mo•te•o *m.* whimper, whining.

gi•ne•bra *f.* gin (*liquor*).

gi•ra *f.* excursion, tour; outing, picnic.

gi•ra•dor *m.* drawer (*of a check or draft*).

gi•rar *v.* to revolve, rotate, whirl; to send, issue, or draw (*checks, drafts, etc.*); to manage (*a business*).

gi•ra•sol *m.* sunflower.

gi•ra•to•rio *adj.* rotary, revolving.

gi•ro *m.* (*movimiento circular*) rotation; bend, turn; (*dirección*) direction, trend; (*estructura*) turn of phrase; (*monetario*) draft; **– postal** money order; *adj.* yellowish (*rooster*); *Am.* black and white (*rooster*); *Am.* cocky.

gi•ta•no *adj.* gypsy; gypsylike; sly, clever; *m.* gypsy.

gi•to•ma•te *Am.* = **jitomate**.

gla•cial *adj.* glacial, icy, very cold.

gla•ciar *m.* glacier.

glán·du·la f. gland.

gla·se·ar v. to glaze (paper, fruits, etc.), make glossy.

glo·bo m. globe, sphere; world; balloon.

glo·ria f. glory; gloria (song of praise to God).

glo·riar·se[17] v. to glory (in), delight (in), be proud (of); to boast (of).

glo·rie·ta f. arbor, bower; secluded nook in a park (with benches).

glo·ri·fi·car[6] v. to glorify; **-se** to glory (in), take great pride (in).

glo·rio·so adj. glorious.

glo·sar v. to gloss, comment upon, explain (a text).

glo·sa·rio m. glossary.

glo·tal adj. glottal.

glo·tis f. glottis.

glo·tón adj. gluttonous; m. glutton.

glo·to·ne·rí·a f. gluttony.

go·ber·na·dor adj. governing; m. governor, ruler.

go·ber·nan·te adj. governing, ruling; m. governor, ruler.

go·ber·nar[1] v. irr. to govern, rule; to lead, direct; to steer (a boat).

go·bier·no m. government; management; control; helm, rudder.

go·ce m. enjoyment; joy.

go·le·ta f. schooner, sailing vessel.

gol·fo m. gulf; open sea; faro (gambling game); vagabond, bum, ragamuffin.

go·lon·dri·na f. swallow; swallow fish.

go·lo·si·na f. sweet, dainty, tidbit; trifle; appetite, desire.

go·lo·so adj. sweet-toothed, fond of sweets; gluttonous.

gol·pa·zo m. bang, whack, heavy blow, hard knock.

gol·pe m. blow, hit, stroke; knock; beat; Col. facing (of a garment); Am. sledge hammer; **– de fortuna** stroke of good luck; **– de gente** crowd, throng; **– de gracia** death blow; finishing stroke; **de –** suddenly; **de un –** all at once; **pestillo de –** spring latch; Am. **al –** instantly, at once; Am. **al – de vista** at one glance.

gol·pe·ar v. to strike, hit; to knock, to beat; Am. to knock at a door.

gol·pe·te·ar v. to tap, knock or pound continuously; to flap; to rattle.

gol·pe·te·o m. tapping, pounding, knocking; flapping; rattling.

go·lle·rí·a f. dainty, delicacy; superfluous thing.

go·ma f. gum; rubber; elastic; eraser; tire; **– de repuesto** spare tire; Am. **estar de –** to have a hang–over (after excessive drinking).

go·me·ro adj. rubber, pertaining to rubber; m. Riopl. gum or rubber tree; Am. rubber producer; Am. rubberplantation worker; Ven. glue container or bottle.

go·mí·fe·ro adj. rubber-bearing, rubber-producing.

go·mo·so adj. gummy, sticky; m. dandy.

gor·di·flón adj. fat; chubby.

gor·do adj. fat; plump; m. suet, fat, **gorda** f. Mex. thick tortilla or cornmeal cake; **se armó la gorda** all hell broke loose; there was a big rumpus.

gor·du·ra f. fatness; stoutness; fat.

gor·go·jo m. weevil; puny person; Am. wood borer, wood louse; **gorgojoso** adj. infested with weevils.

go·ri·la m. gorilla.

gor·je·a·dor m. warbler; adj. warbling; **pájaro –** warbler.

gor·je·ar v. to warble; to chirp.

gor·je·o m. warble; warbling.

go·rra f. cap; bonnet; **de –** at another's expense; **vivir de –** to sponge, live at another's expense.

go·rrión m. sparrow.

go·rro m. cap; bonnet.

go·rrón m. sponge, parasite; bum; rake (dissolute fellow).

go·ta f. (líquido) drop; (enfermedad) gout; **sudar la – gorda** to sweat profusely, toil, work hard.

go·te·ar v. to drip; to leak; to dribble, trickle; to sprinkle, begin to rain; **-se** to leak.

go·te·o m. trickle, drip.

go·te·ra f. leak, hole (in the roof); eaves; trough; **-s** Mex. surroundings, outskirts.

go·te·ro m. Carib., Mex. dropper (for counting drops).

gó·ti·co adj. Gothic; m. Goth; Gothic language.

go·zar[9] v. to enjoy; to possess, have; **-se** to rejoice.

goz·ne m. hinge.

go·zo m. pleasure, joy.

go·zo·so adj. joyful, glad, merry.

goz·que, **goz·que·jo**, **goz·que·ci·llo** m. a small dog.

gra·ba·ción f. recording (tape).

gra·ba·do adj. engraved; recorded; m. engraving; woodcut, print; **– al agua fuerte** etching.

gra·ba·do·ra f. tape recorder.

gra·bar v. to engrave; to carve; to fix, impress, to record on tape; **– al agua fuerte** to etch.

gra·ce·ja·da f. C.A. clownish act or expression.

gra·ce·jo m. grace; cuteness; humor, wit.

gra·cia f. (humorismo) witty remark; joke; humor; (garbo) grace, gracious act; (favor) favor; pardon; **caer en –** to please; **hacer –** to amuse, make (someone) laugh; **¡-s!** thanks!; **dar -s** to thank.

gra·cio·so adj. (chistoso) amusing; funny; witty; (con garbo) graceful, attractive; m. comedian, clown.

gra·da f. step of staircase, harrow; **-s** steps; seats of an amphitheater; bleachers.

gra·da·ción f. gradation.

gra·de·rí·a f. series of steps; rows of seats (in an amphitheater or stadium); **– cubierta** grandstand; **-s** bleachers.

gra·do m. (medida) degree; step; (título) degree; **de (buen) –** willingly, with pleasure; **de mal –** unwillingly; **de – en –** by degrees, gradually.

gra·dua·ción f. graduation; military rank.

gra·dual *adj.* gradual; *m.* response sung at mass.

gra·duar[16] *v.* to graduate, give a diploma, rank or degree to; to gauge; to classify, grade; **-se** to graduate, take a degree.

grá·fi·co *adj.* graphic; vivid, lifelike; **gráfica** *f.* graph, diagram, chart.

gra·fi·to *m.* graphite.

gra·jo *m.* jay.

gra·ma *f.* grama grass.

gra·má·ti·ca *f.* grammar; **gramatical** *adj.* grammatical; **gramático** *adj.* grammatical; *m.* grammarian.

gra·mo *m.* gram.

gran *contr. of* **grande**.

gra·na *f.* cochineal, kermes (*insects used for producing a red dye*); scarlet color; scarlet cloth; any small seed.

gra·na·da *f.* pomegranate; grenade, shell, small bomb; **– de mano** hand grenade.

gra·na·do *m.* pomegranate tree; *adj.* notable; illustrious; select.

gran·de *adj.* large, big; great, grand; *Mex., C.A., Ven., Andes* **mamá (papá)** – grandmother (grandfather); *m.* grandee (*Spanish or Portuguese nobleman*); **en** – on a large scale.

gran·de·za *f.* greatness; grandeur, splendor; bigness; size; grandeeship; body of gran-dees.

gran·dio·si·dad *f.* grandeur, grandness; greatness; **grandioso** *adj.* grandiose; great, grand, magnificent.

gra·ne·ro *m.* granary; grain bin; country or region rich in grain.

gra·ni·to *m.* granite; small grain; small pimple.

gra·ni·za·da *f.* hailstorm; shower, volley.

gra·ni·zar[9] *v.* to hail.

gra·ni·zo *m.* hail; hailstorm; web or film in the eye; *adj. Mex.* spotted (*horse*).

gran·ja *f.* grange, farm; country house.

gran·je·ar *v.* to earn, gain; to acquire, obtain; *Ch., C.A.* to steal; **se** to win for oneself (*favor, goodwill, esteem, etc.*).

gran·je·rí·a *f.* farming; business profit.

gran·je·ro *m.* farmer.

gra·no *m.* (*cereal*) grain; seed; grain (*unit of measure*); **ir al** – to come to the point.

gra·nu·ja *m.* ragamuffin, urchin; scamp.

gra·nu·lar *v.* to granulate; **-se** to become granulated; to break out with pimples.

gra·pa *f.* champ; staple; (*carbunclo*) pimple.

gra·sa *f.* grease, fat; tallow; *Mex., Riopl., Ven.* shoe polish; *Am.* **dar** -- to polish (*shoes*).

gra·sien·to *adj.* greasy, oily.

gra·so·so *adj.* greasy, oily.

gra·ti·fi·ca·ción *f.* gratuity, bonus, tip; recompense, reward.

gra·tis *adv.* gratis, for nothing, free of charge.

gra·ti·tud *f.* gratitude.

gra·to *adj.* pleasing, pleasant; gratuitous; **su grata** your favor, your letter.

gra·tui·to *adj.* gratuitous, free, free of charge.

gra·va *f.* gravel.

gra·va·men *m.* burden; mortgage.

gra·ve *adj.* grave; serious; weighty, heavy; grievous; deep, low (*in pitch*).

gra·ve·dad *f.* (*fuerza*) gravity; (*seriedad*) seriousness; gravity; (*tono*) depth (*of a sound*).

gra·vo·so *adj.* burdensome; **serle a uno** – to be burdensome; to weigh on one's conscience.

graz·nar *v.* to caw, croak, squawk, cackle, quack

graz·ni·do *m.* caw, croak, squawk, cackle, quack.

gre·ca *f.* fret; ornamental design.

gre·da *f.* clay, chalk; chalk cleaner.

gre·mio *m.* guild, society, brotherhood; trade union; fold (*referring to the Church*).

gre·ña *f.* shock of hair, tangled mop of hair (*usually* **greñas**); **greñudo** *adj.* shaggy, with long, unkempt hair.

grey *f.* flock; congregation (*of a church*).

grie·go *adj.* Greek, Grecian; *m.* Greek.

grie·ta *f.* crevice; crack; fissure.

gri·fo *m.* faucet; *Am.* cheap tavern (*where* **chicha** *is sold*); *Peru* gas station; *Am.* colored person; *Col.* drug addict; *Am.* drunkard; *adj.* curly, kinky, woolly (*hair*); *Col.* vain, conceited; **letra grifa** script; **ponerse** – to bristle, stand on end (*said of hair*).

gri·llo *m.* cricket; sprout, shoot; **-s** fetters; obstacle, hindrance.

gri·ma *f.* uneasiness; displeasure, disgust; *Riopl., Carib.* sadness, compassion, pity; *Am.* bit, small particle; **dar** – to disgust; to make uneasy; *Am.* to make sad, inspire pity.

grin·go *adj. Ch., Riopl.* (*Italian*) foreign (*not Spanish*); *m. Ch., Riopl.* (*Italian*) foreigner (*not Spanish*); *Mex., C.A., Andes, Col., Ven.* Yankee or English speaking person.

gri·pe *f.* grippe, flu, influenza.

gris *adj.* grey; **grisáceo** *adj.* greyish.

gri·ta *f.* shouting, hooting; clamor, uproar.

gri·tar *v.* to shout, cry.

gri·te·rí·a *f.* shouting, clamor, uproar.

gri·to *m.* shout, cry; **poner el – en el cielo** to complain loudly, "hit the ceiling".

gro·se·lla *f.* currant; **– blanca** gooseberry; **grosellero** *m.* currant bush.

gro·se·rí·a *f.* rudeness; coarseness; crudeness; insult.

gro·se·ro *adj.* rough, coarse; rude, impolite.

gro·sor *m.* thickness.

gro·tes·co *adj.* grotesque, fantastic; absurd.

grú·a *f.* crane, derrick.

grue·sa *f.* gross, twelve dozen.

grue·so *adj.* (*voluminoso*) fat, stout; thick; bulky, big, heavy; (*burdo*) dense; coarse; *m.* thickness; bulk;

density; main part; **en –** in gross, in bulk, by wholesale.

gru•lla f. crane (bird).

gru•ñi•do m. growl, grumble; grunt.

gru•ñir[19] v. irr. to grunt; to growl; to snarl; to grumble.

gru•ñón adj. growling; grunting; grumbly; m. growler; grumbler.

gru•pa f. rump; **volver -s** to turn around (usually on horseback).

gru•po m. group; set.

gru•ta f. grotto, cavern.

gua•cal m. Col., Mex., C.A. crate (for transporting fruit, vegetables, etc.). Also **huacal**.

gua•ca•ma•yo m. Am. macaw (large parrot); Am. flashily dressed person.

gua•ca•mo•le m. Mex., C.A., Cuba avocado salad; also **guacamol**.

gua•cho m. birdling, chick; young animal; Andes, Ríopl. orphan; Andes, Ríopl. foundling, abandoned child; adj. Am. odd, not paired; Andes, Ríopl. forlorn, alone, abandoned.

gua•dal m. Am. small dune, sand hill; Ven. quagmire, bog, swamp; Am. growth of bamboo grass.

gua•da•ña f. scythe.

gua•gua f. Carib., Ven. bus; trifle, insignificant thing; m. & Andes, Ch., Ríopl. baby; **de –** for nothing, gratis, free.

gua•je m. Am. a species of gourd; Am. vessel or bowl made of a gourd; Am. simpleton, fool; Am. trifle, trinket, piece of junk; adj. Am. foolish; Am. **hacerse uno –** to play the fool; Am. **hacer a uno –** to fool, deceive semeone.

gua•ji•ro m. Indian of the Guajira peninsula (in Venezuela and Colombia); Cuba rustic, peasant.

gua•jo•lo•te m. Mex. turkey; Am. fool.

gua•na•co m. Andes, Ch., Ríopl. guanaco (a kind of llama); An. tall, lanky, gawky person; Am. fool, simpleton; nickname for Salvadoreans.

gua•na•jo m. Am. turkey; Am. fool, dunce.

gua•no m. Carib. palm tree; Carib. palm leaves (used for thatching); Am. guano, bird dung; fertilizer.

guan•ta•da f. wallop, blow, slap.

guan•te m. glove; Andes whip, scourge; **echar el – a uno** to seize or grab a person; **guantelete** m. gauntlet.

gua•po adj. handsome, good-looking; ostentatious, showy; daring, brave; Ch., Andes harsh, severe; Carib., Mex. angry; m. brawler, quarreler, bully.

gua•ra•che m. Mex. Mexican leather sandal, Mex. tire patch. Also **huarache**.

gua•ra•ní adj. pertaining to the Guarani Indans of Paraguay; m. & f. Guarani Indian.

gua•ra•po m. Col., C.A., Andes juice of the sugar cane; Col., C.A., Andes sugar-cane liquor; Col., C.A., Andes low-grade brandy.

guar•da m. & f. guard; keeper; Ríopl. ticket collector on a streetcar, f. custody, care, keeping; observance of a law; **-s** outside ribs of a fan; flyleaves.

guar•da•ba•rros, **guar•da•fan•go** m. fender.

guar•da•bos•ques m. forest ranger, forester, forest keeper.

guar•da•bri•sa f. windshield.

guar•da•fre•nos m. brakeman.

guar•da•gu•jas m. switchman.

guar•da•pa•pe•les m. file, filing cabinet or box.

guar•da•pe•lo m. locket.

guar•dar v. to guard, watch over; to keep; to store; to observe (laws, customs); **-se de** to guard against, keep from, avoid.

guar•da•rro•pa m. wardrobe; cloakroom; keeper of a cloakroom.

guar•dia f. guard, body of guards; defense, protection; m. guard, guardsman.

guar•dia•ma•ri•na f. midshipman.

guar•dián m. guardian, keeper; guardian, superior of a Franciscan·monastery.

gua•re•cer[13] v. irr. to protect, shelter; **-se** to take shelter.

gua•ri•da f. den, cave, lair.

gua•ris•mo m. number.

guar•ne•cer[13] v. irr. to garnish, decorate; to adorn; to trim; to harness; to garrison; to set (jewels).

guar•ni•ción f. adornment; trimming; setting of a jewel; guard of a sword; garrison, **-es** trappings, harness.

gua•ro m. C.A. rum.

guas•ca f. Andes, Ch., Ríopl. leather thong; Andes, Ch., Ríopl. rope, cord; Andes, Ch. whip: Andes, Ch., Ríopl. **dar –** to whip: beat, thrash.

gua•so m. Am. stang, male deer; Ch., Andes Ríopl. peasant; Cuba halfbreed; Am. lasso; adj. rustic, peasantlike.

gua•són adj. funny, comical; m. joker, jester.

gua•ta f. Am. padding; Ven. fib; Col. a species of potato; Ch., Andes paunch, belly; Am. **echar –** to get fat.

gua•te•mal•te•co m. & adj. Guatemalan.

gua•ya•ba f. guava (pear-shaped tropical fruit); **gua•yabo** m. guava tree; Am. lie, fraud, trick.

gu•ber•na•ti•vo *adj.* governmental, administrative.

gue•de•ja *f.* forelock; lock of hair; lion's mane.

güe•ro *adj. Mex.* blond; *m. Ven.* cassava liquor. *See* **huero**.

guer•rra *f.* war; **– a muerte** war to the finish; **dar –** to bother, trouble.

gue•rre•ar *v.* to war, *Am.* to do mischief or to bother (*said of children*).

gue•rre•ro *adj.* warlike, martial; *m.* warrior, soldier.

gue•rri•lla *f.* small war; skirmish; body of soldiers; band of fighters.

gue•rri•lle•ro *m.* guerrilla fighter.

guí•a *m. & f.* guide, leader; *f.* guidebook, directory; signpost; shoot, sprout; *Riopl.* garland of flowers.

guiar[17] *v.* to guide; to drive (*a car*).

gui•ja *f.* pebble; **guijarro** *m.* pebble.

gui•jo *m.* gravel.

guin•da *f.* a kind of cherry.

guin•di•lla *f. Spain* small hot pepper.

gui•ña•da *f.* wink.

gui•ña•po *m.* tag, tatter, rag; ragamuffin, ragged person.

gui•ñar *v.* to wink.

gui•ño *m.* wink.

guión *m.* hyphen; repeat sign (*in music*); cross (*carrried before a prelate in a procession*); guide, leader (*among birds and animals*); leader in a dance.

guir•nal•da *f.* garland, wreath.

gui•sa *f.* way, manner; **a – de** like, in the manner of.

gui•sa•do *m.* stew.

gui•san•te *m.* pea; **– de olor** sweet pea.

gui•sar *v.* to cook; to prepare, arrange.

gui•so *m.* dish, dish of food.

guis•quil *m. C.A.* chayote (*a pear-shape fruit*).

gui•ta•rra *f.* guitar.

gu•la *f.* gluttony.

gu•sa•no *m.* worm; caterpillar; **– de la conciencia** remorse; **– de luz** glowworm; *Col., Mex.* **matar el –** to satisfy a need or desire (*particularly hunger or thirst.*)

gus•tar *v.* (*agradar*) to please, be pleasing; (*saborear*) to taste; to experience; **– le a uno una cosa** to like something; **– de** to have a liking for, be fond of.

gus•to *m.* (*agrado*) pleasure; whim, fancy; (*sabor*) taste, flavor; **dar –** to please; **estar a –** to be comfortable, contented, **tener – en** to be glad to; **tomar el – a una cosa** to become fond of something.

gus•to•so *adj.* (*con agrado*) glad; pleasant; willing; merry; (*sabroso*) tasty; *adv.* willingly.

H

ha•ba *f.* large bean; Lima bean.

ha•ber[30] *v. irr.* to have (*auxiliary verb*); **habérselas con** to have it out with; **ha de llegar mañana** he is to arrive tomorrow; **ha de ser verdad** it must be true; **hay** (**había, hubo,** *etc.*) there is, there are (there was, there were, *etc.*); **hay que** (+ *inf.*) it is necessary; **no hay de qué** you are welcome; **¿qué hay?** what's the matter?

ha•ber *m.* credit, credit side (*in bookkeeping*), **-es** property, goods, cash, assets.

ha•bi•chue•la *f.* bean; **– verde** string bean.

há•bil *adj.* skilful, capable, able.

ha•bi•li•dad *f.* ability, skill.

ha•bi•li•tar *v.* to enable; to equip; to qualify.

ha•bi•ta•ción *f.* apartment; room; lodging.

ha•bi•tan•te *m.* inhabitant; resident.

ha•bi•tar *v.* to inhabit; to live, reside.

há•bi•to *m.* habit; custom.

ha•bi•tual *adj.* habitual, customary.

ha•bi•tuar[18] *v.* to accustom; **-se** to get used, accustomed.

ha•bla *f.* speech; language, dialect; **al –** with in speaking distance; in communication (with)

ha•bla•dor *m.* talker; gossip; *adj.* talkative.

ha•bla•du•rí•a *f.* gossip, rumor; empty talk; impertinent remark.

ha•blar *v.* to speak; to talk; **– alto** (*or* **en voz alta**) to speak loudly; **– bajo** (**quedo** *or* **en voz baja**) to speak softly; **– por los codos** to chatter constantly.

ha•bli•lla *f.* gossip, rumor, malicious tale.

ha•ce•de•ro *adj.* feasible.

ha•ce•dor *m.* maker; **el Supremo Hacedor** the Maker.

ha•cen•da•do *m.* landholder; *Riopl., Ch., Ven.* owner of a farm, plantation, or ranch.

ha•cen•do•so *adj.* industrious, diligent.

ha•cer[31] *v. irr.* (*crear*) to do; to make; (*formar*) to form; to accustom; (*causar*) to cause, order (*followed by inf.*); **– caso** to mind, pay attention; **– frío** (**calor**) to be cold (*warm*); **– la maleta** to pack one's suitcase; **– un papel** to play a part; *Am.* **– aprecio** to pay attention; *Riopl., Mex.* **– caras** (*or* **caritas**) to flirt; **no le hace** it makes no difference; **-se** to become, grow, get to be; **–se a** to get used to; **-se de rogar** to want to be coaxed.

ha•cia *prep.* toward; about; **– adelante** forward; **– atrás** backward.

ha•cien•da *f.* estate; property; finance; large farm; *Riopl.* cattle, livestock.

ha•ci•na *f.* shock (*of grain*), stack, pile.

ha•ci•nar *v.* to shock (*grain*); stack, pile up; to accumulate.

ha·cha *f.* ax; hatchet; torch.

ha·che·ro *m.* axman, woodcutter.

ha·da *f.* fairy.

ha·do *m.* fate, fortune, destiny.

ha·la·gar⁷ *v.* to coax, to flatter; to allure, attract.

ha·la·go *m.* flattery; caress; allurement.

ha·la·güe·ño *adj.* alluring, attractive; flattering; promising.

ha·lar = **jalar.**

hal·cón *m.* falcon.

há·li·to *m.* breath; vapor.

ha·llar *v.* to find; to discover, find out; **-se** to be; to fare, get along.

ha·llaz·go *m.* find; discovery; reward (*for finding something*).

ha·ma·ca *f.* hammock.

ham·bre *f.* hunger; famine; appetite; **tener** – to be hungry; **hambruna** *f. Am.* great hunger, starvation.

ham·bre·ar *v.* to starve, to be hungry.

ham·brien·to *adj.* hungry; greedy; *C.A., Mex., Andes* stingy.

ham·pa *f.* underworld.

han·gar *m.* hangar.

ha·ra·gán *adj.* lazy, indolent; *m.* loafer, idler.

ha·ra·ga·ne·ar *v.* to lounge, loaf, be lazy.

ha·ra·ga·ne·rí·a *f.* laziness.

ha·ra·pien·to *adj.* tattered, ragged.

ha·ra·po *m.* rag, tatter; **andar hecho un** – to be in tatters.

ha·ra·po·so *adj.* tattered, ragged.

ha·ri·na *f.* flour; **eso es – de otro costal** that is something entirely different; **harinoso** *adj.* floury; flourlike.

har·mo·ní·a *f.* harmony.

har·tar *v.* to fill up, gorge, to sate, satiate, **-se** to have one's fill; to overeat, eat too much.

har·to *adj.* full; sated, satiated; fed up; too much; *adv.* too much; *Mex., C.A., Col., Ven., Ríopl., Andes* much, very much.

has·ta *prep.* till, until; up to; – **luego** good-bye, see you later; *conj.* even: – **que** until.

has·tiar¹⁷ *v.* to surfeit; to cloy; to disgust.

has·tí·o *m.* surfeit, excess; boredom; loathing, disgust.

ha·to *m.* herd; flock; sheepfold; shepherd's hut; gang, crowd; pile; *Col., Ven.* cattle ranch.

ha·ya *f.* beech; **hayuco** *m.* beechnut.

haz *f.* face; surface; *m.* fagot, bundle, bunch.

ha·za·ña *f.* deed, exploit, feat.

he (*used with* **aquí** *or* **allí**) behold, here is, here you have; **heme aquí** here I am; **helo aquí** here it is.

he·bi·lla *f.* buckle.

he·bra *f.* thread; fiber; fine string; *Am.* **de una** – allat once, at one stroke, *Am.* **ni** – absolutely nothing; **hebroso** *adj.* fibrous, stringy.

he·ca·tom·be *m.* massacre, great slaughter; hecatomb (*sacrifice of 100 oxen*).

he·chi·ce·ra *f.* witch, enchantress; hag.

he·chi·ce·rí·a *f.* witchcraft; magic; charm; enchantment.

he·chi·ce·ro *adj.* bewitching, charming; *m.* magician; charmer; sorcerer.

he·chi·zar⁹ *v.* to bewitch; to charm.

he·chi·zo *m.* charm; enchantment.

he·cho *m.* fact; act, deed; **de** – in fact; *p.p. of* **hacer** done, made.

he·chu·ra *f.* make; shape, cut; workmanship.

he·der¹ *v. irr.* to stink; to reek.

he·dion·dez *f.* stink, stench.

he·dion·do *adj.* foul-smelling; stinking; filthy; *m. Ríopl.* skunk.

he·dor *m.* stink, stench.

he·la·da *f.* frost.

he·la·do *adj.* frozen; freezing; frosty; icy; *m.* ice cream; ice, sherbet; **heladería** *f. Am.* ice–cream parlor.

he·la·do·ra *f.* freezer.

he·lar¹ *v. irr.* to freeze.

he·le·cho *m.* fern.

hé·li·ce *f.* screw propeller; helix, spiral.

he·li·cóp·te·ro *m.* helicopter.

he·lio *m.* helium.

he·li·puer·to *m.* heliport.

hem·bra *f.* female; staple; nut (*of a screw*); **macho y** – hook and eye.

he·mis·fe·rio *m.* hemisphere.

hen·chir⁵ *v. irr.* to swell, stuff, fill.

hen·de·du·ra, hen·di·du·ra *f.* crack, crevice, fissure.

hen·der¹ *v. irr.* to split, creack, cleave.

he·ne·quén *m. Mex., Ven., C.A., Col.* sisal, sisal hemp.

he·no *m.* hay; **henil** *m.* hayloft.

he·ral·do *m.* herald.

her·ba·zal *m.* field of grass.

her·bo·so *adj.* grassy; weedy.

he·re·dad *f.* parcel of land; rural property, estate.

he·re·dar *v.* to inherit; to bequeath, leave in a will.

he·re·de·ro *m.* heir; successor; **heredera** *f.* heiress.

he·re·di·ta·rio *adj.* hereditary.

he·re·je *m.* heretic; **cara de** – hideous face.

he·re·jí·a *f.* heresy; offensive remark.

he·ren·cia *f.* inheritance; heritage; heredity.

he·ri·da *f.* wound; injury.

he·ri·do *adj.* wounded; *m.* wounded man; *Am.* small drainage channel.

he·rir³ *v. irr.* to wound; to hurt; to strike; to offend.

her·ma·na *f.* sister.

her·ma·nas·tro *m.* stepbrother, half brother; **hermanastra,** *f.* stepsister, half sister.

her·man·dad *f.* brotherhood, fraternity.

her·ma·no *m.* brother.

her·mé·ti·co *adj.* hermetic; airtight; tight–lipped;

close-mouthed; **hermetismo** *m.* complete silence.

her•mo•se•ar *v.* to beautify, adorn.

her•mo•so *adj.* beautiful, handsome.

her•mo•su•ra *f.* beauty.

hé•ro•e *m.* hero; **heroína** *f.* heroine.

he•roi•co *adj.* heroic.

he•ro•ís•mo *adj.* heroism.

he•rra•du•ra *f.* horseshoe.

he•rra•je *m.* ironwork; iron trimmings; horseshoes and nails; *Am.* silver saddle trimmings; horseshoe.

he•rra•mien•ta *f.* set of tools; iron tool.

he•rrar[1] *v. irr.* to shoe (*a horse*); to brand; to trim with iron.

he•rre•rí•a *f.* blacksmith's shop or trade; forge; ironworks.

he•rre•ro *m.* blacksmith.

he•rre•te *m.* metal tip (*for a shoelace, for instance*); *Am.* branding iron.

her•vi•de•ro *m.* bubbling sound (*of boiling water*); bubbling spring; swarm, crowd; **un – de gente** a swarm of people.

her•vir[3] *v. irr.* to boil; **– de gente**, to swarm with people.

her•vor *m.* boiling; boiling point; **soltar el – to come to a boil.

hez *f.* scum; **la – del pueblo**, the scum of society; **heces**, dregs, sediment.

hi•dal•go *m.* hidalgo (*Spanish nobleman*); *adj.* noble, courteous.

hi•dal•guí•a *f.* nobility, generosity; courtesy.

hi•dráu•li•co *adj.* hydraulic; **fuerza hidráulica**, water power; **ingeniero –** hydraulic engineer.

hi•dro•a•vión *m.* hydroplane, seaplane.

hi•dró•ge•no *m.* hydrogen.

hi•dro•pla•no *m.* hydroplane.

hie•dra *f.* ivy.

hiel *f.* gall, bile; bitterness.

hie•lo *m.* ice; frost.

hier•ba *f.* grass; herb; weed; *Riopl.*, *Andes* mate (*Paraguayan tea*); *Mex.*, *Ven.*, *Cuba* marihuana (*a narcotic*); *C.A.* **ciertas -s** so-and-so (*person not named*).

hier•ba•bue•na *f.* mint. *Also* **yerbabuena**.

hie•rro *m.* iron; brand; iron tool, instrument, or weapon; **-s** irons, chains, handcuffs.

hí•ga•do *m.* (*órgano*) liver; (*valentía*) courage; valor; **malos -s** ill will.

hi•gie•ne *f.* hygiene; **higiénico** *adj.* hygienic, sanitary.

hi•go *m.* fig; **higuera** *f.* fig tree; **higuerilla** *f. Am.* castor-oil plant.

hi•ja *f.* daughter; native daughter.

hi•jo *m.* son; native son; offspring, fruit, result.

hi•la•chas *f. pl.* lint; **mostrar una la hilacha** to show one's worst side or nature; **hilachos** *m. pl. Am.* rags, tatters.

hi•la•do *m.* yarn; *p.p. of* **hilar**.

hi•lan•de•ra *f.* spinner.

hi•lan•de•rí•a *f.* spinning mill; art of spinning; spinning.

hi•lan•de•ro *m.* spinner; spinning room.

hi•lar *v.* to spin, make into thread; **– muy delgado** to be very subtle.

hi•las *f. pl.* lint, fine ravelings (*for dessing wounds*).

hi•la•za *f.* coarse thread; yarn.

hi•le•ra *f.* file, row, line; **– de perlas** strand or strings of pearls.

hi•lo *m.* (*hebra*) thread; fine yarn; string; (*alambre*) filament; thin wire; (*tela*) linen; **a –** without interruptions; **al –** along the thread; *Am.* very well; all right; **de –** straight, without stopping; *Am* **de un –** constantly, without stopping; **tener el alma en un –** to be frightened to death, to be in great anxiety or suspense.

hil•ván *m.* basting stich; basting; *Am.* hem.

hil•va•nar *v.* to baste; to put together, connect; to do hastily; *Am.* to hem.

him•no *m.* hymn.

hin•ca•pié: **hacer –** to emphasize, stress; to insist (upon).

hin•car[6] *v.* to drive, thrust (into); **-se** (*or* **-se de rodillas**) to kneel down.

hin•cha•do *adj. & p.p.* swollen; inflated; presumptuous.

hin•char *v.* to swell; **-se** to swell; to swell up, puff up.

hin•cha•zón *f.* swelling; inflation; conceit; bombast, inflated style.

hi•no•jos: **de –** on one's knees.

hi•pér•bo•le *f.* hyperbole.

hi•per•bó•li•co *m.* hyperbolic.

hi•po *m.* hiccough; sob; longing; grudge, ill will.

hi•po•cre•sí•a *f.* hypocrisy.

hi•pó•cri•ta *adj.* hypocritical, insincere; *m. & f.* hypocrite.

hi•pó•dro•mo *m.* race track.

hi•po•te•ca *f.* mortgage.

hi•po•te•car[6] *v.* to mortgage.

hi•pó•te•sis *f.* hypothesis, theory.

hir•vien•te *adj.* boiling.

his•pa•nis•ta *m. & f.* Hispanist; one who is interested in Hispanic studies

his•pa•no *adj.* Hispanic, Spanish; *m.* Spaniard.

his•pa•no•a•me•ri•ca•no *adj.* Spanish-American.

his•té•ri•co *adj.* hysterical.

his•to•ria *f.* history; story; tale; fable; **dejarse de -s** to stop fooling and come to the point; **historieta** *f.* story, anecdote.

his•to•ria•dor *m.* historian.

his•to•rial *m.* record, data (*concerning a person or firm*); *adj.* historic.

his•tó•ri•co *adj.* historic, historical.

ho•ci•co *m.* snout; **caer de -s** to fall on one's face; **meter el – en todo**, to meddle, stick one's nose in everything.

ho·ga·ño *adv.* nowadays.

ho·gar *m.* hearth, fireplace; home.

ho·ga·re·ño *adj.* home-loving, domestic; homelike.

ho·gue·ra *f.* bonfire.

ho·ja *f.* leaf; petal; sheet of paper or metal; blade; **– de lata,** tin plate.

ho·ja·la·ta *f.* tin plate.

ho·jal·dre *m.* & *f.* puff pastry.

ho·ja·ras·ca *f.* fallen leaves; dry foliage; superfluous ornament; trash; useless words.

ho·je·ar *v.* to leaf, turn the pages of; to browse.

ho·jue·la *f.* leaflet, small leaf; thin leaf (*of metal*); flake; thin pancake; **– de estaño,** tin foil.

¡ho·la! *interj.* hello!; hi!; ah!

ho·lan·dés *adj.* Dutch; *m.* Dutchman; Dutch language.

hol·ga·do *adj.* (*libre*) free, at leisure; comfortable; (*ancho*) wide, loose; roomy, spacious; *p.p. of* **holgar.**

hol·gar *v. irr.* to rest; to loaf; **-se** to be glad; to relax, have a good time; **huelga decir** needless to say.

hol·ga·zán *m.* idler, loafer; *adj.* lazy, idle.

hol·ga·za·ne·ar *v.* to loiter, lounge, idle, bum around.

hol·ga·za·ne·ría *f.* idlness, laziness.

hol·go·rio *m.* spree.

hol·gu·ra *f.* (*descanso*) ease; rest, comfort; (*lugar*) roominess, plenty of room.

ho·lo·caus·to *m.* holocaust, burnt offering, sacrifice.

ho·llar *v.* to tread, trample upon.

ho·lle·jo *m.* skin, peel; husk.

ho·llín *m.* soot.

hom·bra·da *f.* manly act; show of bravery.

hom·bre *m.* man; **hombría** *f.* manliness, manly strength; **– de bien** honesty.

hom·bro *m.* shoulder; **arrimar** (*or* **meter) el –** to help.

hom·bru·no *adj.* mannish, masculine.

ho·me·na·je *m.* homage, honor.

ho·mi·ci·da *m.* murderer; *f.* murderess; *adj.* homicidal, murderous.

ho·mi·ci·dio *m.* homicide, murder.

ho·mo·gé·ne·o *adj.* homogeneous, of the same kind or nature.

hon·da *f.* sling, slingshot.

hon·do *adj.* deep; low; *m.* bottom, depth.

hon·do·na·da *f.* hollow, dip, gully, ravine.

hon·du·ra *f.* depth; **meterse en -s** to go beyond one's depth; to get into trouble.

ho·nes·ti·dad *f.* chastity, modesty, decency; decorum, propriety.

ho·nes·to *adj.* chaste, modest, decent; just, honest.

hon·go *m.* mushroom; fungus; derby hat.

ho·nor *m.* honor; glory; dignity.

ho·no·ra·rio *m.* fee (*for professional services*); *adj.* honorary.

ho·no·rí·fi·co *adj.* honorary; **mención honorífi-ca,** honorable mention.

hon·ra *f.* honor; reputation; **-s** obsequies, funeral rites.

hon·ra·dez *f.* honesty, honor, integrity.

hon·ra·do *adj.* honest, honorable; honored.

hon·rar *v.* to honor; **-se** to be honored; to consider it an honor.

hon·ro·so *adj.* honorable; honoring.

ho·ra *f.* hour; time; **-s** canonical hours, office (*required daily prayers for priests and nuns*); **es – de,** it is time to; **no ver la – de** (+ *inf.*) to be anxious to; **¿qué – es?** what time is it?.

ho·ra·dar *v.* to pierce, bore, perforate.

ho·ra·rio *m.* shedule, timetable; hour hand.

hor·ca *f.* (*cadalso*) gallows; (*horcón*) pitchfork; *P.R.* birthday present; **– de ajos,** string of garlic.

hor·ca·ja·das: a – astride (*with one leg on each side*); **ponerse a –** to straddle.

hor·cón *m.* forked pole, forked prop; *Mex., Cuba, Ven.* post, roof support; *Am.* roof.

hor·da *f.* horde.

ho·ri·zon·tal *adj.* horizontal.

ho·ri·zon·te *m.* horizon.

hor·ma *f.* form, mold; block (*for shaping a hat*); shoe last; shoe tree.

hor·mi·ga *f.* ant.

hor·mi·gón *m.* concrete.

hor·mi·gue·ar *v.* to swarm; to be crawling with ants; **me hormiguea el cuerpo** I itch all over.

hor·mi·gue·o *m.* itching, creeping sensa-tion; tingle, tingling sensation.

hor·mi·gue·ro *m.* ant hill; ant nest; swarm; **oso –** anteater.

hor·na·da *f.* batch of bread, baking.

hor·ne·ar *v.* to bake (*in a oven*).

hor·ni·lla *f.* burner; grate (*of a stove*).

hor·ni·llo *m.* kitchen stove; hot plate.

hor·no *m.* furnace; oven; kiln (*for baking bricks*).

hor·qui·lla *f.* hairpin; forked pole; small pitchfork.

ho·rren·do *adj.* horrible, hideous.

ho·rri·ble *adj.* horrible.

ho·rri·pi·lan·te *adj.* horrifying.

ho·rror *m.* horror; atrocity; **dar –** to cause fright; to horrify; **tenerle – a uno,** to feel a strong dislike for one.

ho·rro·ri·zar *v.* to horrify, shock, terrify.

ho·rro·ro·so *adj.* horrid; frighful, hideous.

hor·ta·li·za *f.* vegetables; vegetable garden.

hor·te·la·no *m.* gardener.

hos·co = fosco.

hos·pe·da·je *m.* board and lodging; lodging.

hos·pe·dar *v.* to lodge, give lodging; **-se** to take lodging; to room; to stop (*at a hotel*).

hos·pe·de·ro *m.* innkeeper.

hos·pi·cio *m.* asylum; orphanage, orphan asylum; poorhouse; **hospiciano** *m.* inmate of a poorhouse or asylum.

hos·pi·tal *m.* hospital; **– de primera sangre,** first-aid station.

hos·pi·ta·li·dad *f.* hospitality.

hos·tia *f.* host (*consecrated wafer*).

hos·ti·gar[7] *v.* to harass, vex; to beat, lash, *C.A., Col.* to cloy.

hos·til *adj.* hostile; **hostilidad** *f.* hostility.

ho·tel *m.* hotel; villa; **hotelero** *m.* hotel–keeper; *adj.* pertaining to hotels.

hoy *adv.* today; **– día** nowdays; **de – en adelante** from now on; **– por –** at present; **de – más** henceforth.

ho·ya *f.* pit; hole; grave; valley; *Am.* river basin.

ho·yo *m.* hole; pit; grave; *Ríopl. Carib.* dimple.

ho·yue·lo *m.* dimple; tiny hole.

hoz *f.* sickle; narrow ravine.

ho·zar[9] *v.* to root, turn up the earth with the snout (*as hogs*).

hua·cal = **guacal.**

hua·ra·che = **guarache.**

hua·so = **guaso.**

hue·co *adj.* (*vacío*) hollow, empty; (*vano*) vain, affected; puffed up; high-sounding; *m.* gap, space, hole.

huel·ga *f.* labor strike; rest; leisure; **declararse en –** to strike.

huel·guis·ta *m.* striker.

hue·lla *f.* trace; footprint.

huér·fa·no *adj.* & *m.* orphan.

hue·ro *adj.* empty; rotten, spoiled (*egg*). *See* **güero.**

huer·ta *f.* orchard and vegetable garden; irrigated land.

huer·to *m.* small orchard and vegetable garden; garden patch.

hue·so *m.* bone; stone, pit; big seed; **la sin –** the tongue; **soltar la sin –** to talk too much; **no dejarle un – sano** to pick him to pieces.

hués·ped *m.* (*convidado*) guest; (*anfitrión*) host; **ser – en su casa** to be seldom at home.

hues·te *f.* host, army, multitude.

hue·su·do *adj.* bony.

hue·vo *m.* egg; **– duro** hard-boiled egg; **– estrellado** fried egg; **– pasado por agua** soft–boiled egg; **–s revueltos** scrambled eggs; *Mex; C.A.;Col; Ven;***-s pericos** scrambled eggs; *Ven; Andes* **costar un –** to be very expensive.

hu·í·da *f.* flight; escape.

hu·ír[32] *v. irr.* to flee, escape; to avoid, shun.

hui·za·che *m. Mex., C.A.* huisache (*a species of acacia*).

hu·le *m.* rubber; oilcloth; *Col., Ven.* rubber tree.

hu·lla *f.* soft coal.

hu·ma·ni·dad *f.* humanity, mankind; humaneness; **– es** humanities, letters.

hu·ma·ni·ta·rio *adj.* humanitarian, huma-ne, kind, charitable.

hu·ma·no *adj.* human; humane; *m.* man, human being.

hu·ma·re·da *f.* cloud of smoke.

hu·me·an·te *adj.* smoking, smoky; steaming.

hu·me·ar *v.* to smoke, give off smoke; to steam, *Am.* to fumigate.

hu·me·dad *f.* humidity, moisture, dampness.

hu·me·de·cer[13] *v. irr.* to moisten, wet, dampen.

hú·me·do *adj.* humid, moist, wet, damp.

hu·mil·dad *f.* humility; humbleness; meekness.

hu·mil·de *adj.* humble, lowly, meek.

hu·mi·lla·ción *f.* humiliation; submission.

hu·mi·llar *v.* to humiliate, humble, lower, crush; **-se** to humiliate oneself; to bow humbly.

hu·mi·llos *m. pl.* airs, conceit, vanity.

hu·mo *m.* smoke, fume, vapor; **-s** conceit, vanity.

hu·mor *m.* humor; mood, disposition.

hu·mo·ra·da *f.* pleasantry, witty remark; caprice, notion.

hu·mo·ris·mo *m.* humor, humorous style.

hu·mo·rís·ti·co *adj.* humorous.

hu·mo·so *adj.* smoky.

hun·di·mien·to *m.* sinking, collapse, cave-in.

hun·dir *v.* (*sumir*) to sink, submerge; (*batir*) to crush, oppress; to destroy; **-se** to sink; to collapse, cave in.

hu·ra·cán *m.* hurricane.

hu·ra·ño *adj.* diffident, shy, bashful; unsociable.

¡hu·rra! *interj.* hurrah!

hur·ta·di·llas: a – on the sly, secretly, stealthily.

hur·tar *v.* to steal, rob; **-se** to withdraw, slipaway; to hide; **– el cuerpo** to dodge; to flee.

hur·to *m.* robbery, theft; stolen article; **a –** stealthily, on the sly.

hus·me·ar *v.* to scent, smell, follow the track of; to nose, pry (into).

hus·me·o *m.* sniff, sniffing, smelling; prying.

hu·so *m.* spindle.

I

ibé·ri·co, ibe·ro *adj.* Iberian; **iberoamericano** *adj.* Ibero-American (*Spanish or Portuguese American*).

i·da *f.* departure; sally; **billete de – y vuelta** round-trip ticket; **-s y venidas** goings and comings.

i·dea *f.* idea; notion.

i·deal *m.* & *adj.* ideal.

i·dea·lis·mo *m.* idealism.

i·dea·lis·ta *adj.* idealistic; *m.* & *f.* idealist; dreamer.

i·dear *v.* to form an idea of; to devise, think out, plan.

í·dem *idem* (*abbreviation:* id.), ditto, the same.

i·dén·ti·co *adj.* identical.

i·den·ti·dad *f.* identity.

i·den·ti·fi·car[6] *v.* to identify.

i•di•lio *m.* idyl.

i•dio•ma *m.* language, tongue.

i•dio•ta *m.* &. *f.* idiot; *adj.* idiotic, foolish.

i•dio•tis•mo *m.* idiom; idiocy.

ido•la•trar *v.* to idolize, worship.

í•do•lo *m.* idol.

i•dó•neo *adj.* fit, suitable; qualified.

i•gle•sia *f.* church.

ig•ni•ción *f.* ignition.

ig•no•mi•nia *f.* infamy, shame, disgrace.

ig•no•mi•nio•so *adj.* ignominious; infamous, shameful, disgraceful.

ig•no•ran•cia *f.* ignorance.

ig•no•ran•te *adj.* ignorant.

ig•no•rar *v.* to be ignorant of, not to know.

ig•no•to *adj.* unknown, undiscovered.

i•gual *adj.* (*semejante*) equal; (*liso*) even, smooth; uniform; (*siempre*) constant; **serle – a uno** to be all the same to one, make no difference to one; *m.* equal; **al –** equally.

i•gua•lar *v.* to equal; to equalize; to match; to level; smooth; to adjust; to be equal.

i•gual•dad *f.* equality.

i•gua•li•ta•rio *adj.* equalitarian (*promoting the doctrine of equality*).

i•gua•na *f.* iguana.

i•ja•da *f.* loin; flank (*of an animal*); pain in the side; **ijar** *m.* flank (*of an animal*).

i•le•gal *adj.* illegal, unlawful.

i•le•gí•ti•mo *adj.* illegitimate; illegal.

i•le•so *adj.* unharmed, uninjured, unhurt, safe and sound.

i•lí•ci•to *adj.* illicit, unlawful.

i•li•mi•ta•do *adj.* unlimited.

i•lu•mi•na•ción *f.* illumination.

i•lu•mi•nar *v.* to iluminate; to light; to enlighten.

i•lu•sión *f.* illusion.

i•lu•si•vo *adj.* illusive.

i•lu•so *adj.* deluded; *m.* visionary, dreamer.

i•lu•so•rio *adj.* illusive; deceptive; worthless.

i•lus•tra•ción *f.* illustration; elucidation, explanation.

i•lus•tra•dor *m.* illustrator.

i•lus•trar *v.* to illustrate.

i•lus•tre *adj.* illustrious, distinguished.

i•ma•gen *f.* image.

i•ma•gi•na•ble *adj.* imaginable, conceivable.

i•ma•gi•na•ción *f.* imagination.

i•ma•gi•nar *v.* to imagine.

i•ma•gi•na•rio *adj.* imaginary.

i•ma•gi•na•ti•vo *adj.* imaginative; **imaginativa** *f.* imagination.

i•mán *m.* magnet; attraction.

im•bé•cil *adj.* imbecile, stupid.

im•bo•rra•ble *adj.* indelible, not erasable; unforgettable.

im•buir³² *v. irr.* to imbue; to instill, infuse, inspire (with).

i•mi•ta•ción *f.* imitation.

i•mi•ta•dor *m.* imitator; follower; *adj.* imitative, imitating.

i•mi•tar *v.* to imitate.

im•pa•cien•cia *f.* impatience.

im•pa•cien•te *adj.* impatient.

im•par *adj.* odd; **número –** odd number.

im•par•cial *adj.* impartial; **imparcialidad** *f.* impartiality, fairness, justice.

im•pa•si•ble *adj.* impassive, insensitive, insensible, unfeeling, unmoved.

im•pá•vi•do *adj.* fearless; calm; *Am.* impudent, brazen.

im•pe•di•men•to *m.* impediment, hindrance, obstacle.

im•pe•dir⁵ *v. irr.* to impede, prevent, hinder.

im•pe•ler *v.* to impel, push; to incite, spur.

im•pe•ne•tra•ble *adj.* impenetrable; impervious; incomprehensible.

im•pen•sa•do *adj.* unforessen, unexpected; offhand, done without thinking; **impensadamente** *adj.* offhand, without thinking; unexpectedly.

im•pe•rar *v.* to rule, command, dominate.

im•pe•ra•ti•vo *adj.* imperative; urgent, compelling; *m.* imperative mood.

im•per•cep•ti•ble *adj.* imperceptible.

im•per•di•ble *m.* safety pin; *adj.* safe, that cannot be lost.

im•pe•re•ce•de•ro *adj.* imperishable, enduring, everlasting.

im•per•fec•to *adj.* imperfect; *m.* imperfect tense.

im•pe•rial *adj.* imperial; *f.* coach top; top seats on a coach or bus.

im•pe•ri•cia *f.* inexperience.

im•pe•rio *m.* empire; command, rule; sway, influence.

im•pe•rio•so *adj.* imperious, arrogant, domineering; urgent.

im•per•me•a•ble *adj.* waterproof, impervious, rainproof; *m.* raincoat.

im•per•so•nal *adj.* impersonal.

im•per•ti•nen•cia *f.* impertinence; impudence; insolent remark or act; **decir -s** to talk nonsense; to make insolent remarks.

im•per•ti•nen•te *adj.* impertinent, impudent; meddlesome; irrelevant, not to the point; **-s** *m. pl.* lorgnette (*eyeglasses mounted on a handle*).

ím•pe•tu *m.* impetus; violent force; impulse; *C.A.*, *Ríopl* vehement desire; **– de ira** fit of anger.

im•pe•tuo•so *adj.* impetuous, violent.

im•pí•o *adj.* impious, irreligious; profane.

im•pla•ca•ble *adj.* implacable; relentless.

im•plan•ta•ción *f.* implantation, establishment, introduction (*of a system*).

im•plan•tar *v.* to implant, establish, introduce.

im•pli•car *v.* to imply; to implicate, involve.

im•plo•rar *v.* to implore, entreat, beg.

im·po·nen·te *adj.* imposing.

im·po·ner[40] *v. irr.* to impose; to invest (*money*); — **miedo** to inspire fear; — **respeto** to inspire or command respect; **-se** to inspire fear or respect; to dominate; *Am.* **-se a** to get accustomed or used to.

im·por·tan·cia *f.* importance.

im·por·tan·te *adj.* important.

im·por·tar *v.* to be important; to matter; to amount to; to be necessary; to concern; to import.

im·por·te *m.* amount, price, value.

im·por·tu·nar *v.* to importune, nag, tease, pester.

im·por·tu·no *adj.* annoying, persistent.

im·po·si·bi·li·dad *f.* impossibility.

im·po·si·bi·li·ta·do *p.p.* & *adj.* disabled, unfit; helpless.

im·po·si·bi·li·tar *v.* to make impossible; to disable.

im·po·si·ble *adj.* impossible; intolerable, unbearable; *Col., Ven.* disabled, (*because of illness*); *Am.* slovenly, untidy.

im·po·si·ción *f.* imposition; burden; tax.

im·pos·tor *m.* impostor, cheat; **impostura** *f.* imposture, fraud, deceit.

im·po·ten·cia *f.* impotence.

im·po·ten·te *adj.* impotent, powerless.

im·pre·ci·so *adj.* vague, indefinite; inaccurate.

im·preg·nar *v.* to impregnate, saturate.

im·pren·ta *f.* press; printing shop; printing.

im·pres·cin·di·ble *adj.* essential, indispensable.

im·pre·sión *f.* impression; printing; mark; footprint.

im·pre·sio·nan·te *adj.* impressive.

im·pre·sio·nar *v.* to impress; to move, affect, stir; **-se** to be stirred, move.

im·pre·so *p.p. irr.* of **imprimir** printed; impressed, imprinted; *m.* printed matter.

im·pre·sor *m.* printer.

im·pre·vi·sión *f.* carelessness, lack of foresight.

im·pre·vis·to *adj.* unforeseen, unexpected.

im·pri·mir *v.* to print; to imprint, impress.

im·pro·ba·ble *adj.* improbable, unlikely.

im·pro·pe·rio *m.* affront, insult.

im·pro·pio *adj.* improper; unsuitable.

im·pro·vi·sar *v.* to improvise.

im·pro·vi·so *adj.* unforeseen, **de —** suddenly; *Col., Ven., Mex.* **en un —** in a moment, in the twinkling of an eye.

im·pru·den·cia *f.* imprudence, indiscretion, rash act.

im·pru·den·te *adj.* imprudent; unwise; indiscreet.

im·pues·to *p.p.* of **imponer** imposed; informed; *Am.* **estar - a** to be used or accustomed to; *m.* tax, duty.

im·pul·sar *v.* to impel, push, move, to force.

im·pul·so *m.* impulse; push.

im·pu·re·za *f.* impurity.

im·pu·ro *adj.* impure.

im·pu·tar *v.* to impute, attribute.

i·na·ca·ba·ble *adj.* unending, endless.

i·na·ca·ba·do *adj.* unfinished.

i·nac·ce·si·ble *adj.* inaccessible, unobtainable.

i·nac·ción *f.* inaction, inactivity, idleness.

i·na·cep·ta·ble *adj.* unacceptable, unsatisfactory.

i·nac·ti·vi·dad *f.* inactivity.

i·nac·ti·vo *adj.* inactive.

i·na·de·cua·do *adj.* inadequate.

i·nad·ver·ten·cia *f.* oversight; inattention, heedlessnes.

i·nad·ver·ti·do *adj.* careless, heedless; unnoticed.

i·na·fec·ta·do *adj.* unaffected.

i·na·go·ta·ble *adj.* inexhaustible

i·na·guan·ta·ble *adj.* insufferable, unbearable.

i·na·lám·bri·co *adj.* wireless.

i·nal·te·ra·ble *adj.* unalterable, unchangeable.

i·nal·te·ra·do *adj.* unchanged.

i·na·mo·vi·ble = **inmovible**.

i·na·ni·ción *f.* starvation.

i·na·ni·ma·do *adj.* inanimate, lifeless.

i·na·pe·ten·cia *f.* lack of appetite.

i·na·pli·ca·ble *adj.* inapplicable, unsuitable; **— al caso** irrelevant.

i·na·pre·cia·ble *adj.* invaluable; inappreciable, too small to be perceived, very slight.

i·na·se·qui·ble *adj.* inaccessible, not obtainable; hard to attain or obtain.

i·nau·di·to *adj.* unheard-of; unprecedented.

i·nau·gu·ra·ción *f.* inauguration.

i·nau·gu·rar *v.* to inaugurate, begin, open.

in·cai·co, in·cá·si·co *adj.* Incan (*of or pertaining to the Incas*).

in·cal·cu·la·ble *adj.* incalculable; innumerable, untold.

in·can·des·cen·te *adj.* incandescent.

in·can·sa·ble *adj.* untiring, tireless.

in·ca·pa·ci·dad *f.* incompetence, inability, unfitness.

in·ca·pa·ci·tar *v.* to cripple, disable, handicap, unfit, make unfit.

in·ca·paz *adj.* incapable, unable.

in·cau·to *adj.* unwary, heedless, reckless.

in·cen·diar *v.* to set fire to; **-se** to catch fire.

in·cen·dio *m.* conflagration, fire.

in·cen·ti·vo *m.* incentive, inducement.

in·cer·ti·dum·bre *f.* uncertainty, doubt.

in·ce·san·te *adj.* incessant.

in·ci·den·tal *adj.* incidental.

in·ci·den·te *adj.* incidental; *m.* incident.

in·cien·so *m.* incense.

in·cier·to *adj.* uncertain, doubtful; unstable; unknown; untrue.

in·ci·sión *f.* incision, cut, slit, gash.

in·ci·ta·mien·to *m.* incitement, inducement, incentive.

in·ci·tar *v.* to incite, rouse, stir up.

in·ci·vil *adj.* uncivil, rude, impolite.

in·cle·men·cia *f.* inclemency, severity, harshness; **inclemente** *adj.* unmerciful, merciless.

in•cli•na•ción *f.* inclination, affection; tendency, bent; bow; incline; slope.

in•cli•nar *v.* (*bajar*) to incline; (*persuadir*) to persuade; **-se** to bow; to stoop; to incline, slope, slant; to lean, bend.

in•cluir[32] *v. irr.* to include; to inclose.

in•clu•si•ve *adv.* inclusive, including; even; **inclusivo** *adj.* inclusive; comprehensive.

in•clu•so *adj.* inclosed; included; including; even.

in•cóg•ni•to *adj.* unknown; **de – incóg•nito** (*with one's name or rank unknown*); **incógnita** *f.* unknown quantity (*in mathematics.*).

in•co•he•ren•te *adj.* incoherent, disconnected, rambling.

in•co•lo•ro *adj.* colorless.

in•com•bus•ti•ble *adj.* incombustible; fireproof.

in•co•mo•dar *v.* to inconvenience, disturb; trouble, annoy.

in•co•mo•di•dad *f.* inconvenience, discomfort; bother, annoyance.

in•có•mo•do *adj.* inconvenient, bothersome: uncomfortable.

in•com•pa•ra•ble *adj.* incomparable.

in•com•pa•si•vo *adj.* merciless, pitiless.

in•com•pa•ti•ble *adj.* incompatible; unsuitable, uncongenial.

in•com•pe•ten•cia *f.* incompetence, inability, unfitness; **incompetente** *adj.* incompetent, unfit.

in•com•ple•to *adj.* incomplete.

in•com•pren•si•ble *adj.* incomprehen-sible.

in•con•di•cio•nal *adj.* unconditional.

in•co•ne•xo *adj.* unconnected; incoherent, disconnected.

in•con•fun•di•ble *adj.* unmistakable.

in•con•gruen•te *adj.* unsuitable, not appropriate; not harmonious.

in•con•quis•ta•ble *adj.* unconquerable.

in•cons•cien•cia *f.* unconsciousness; unawareness.

in•cons•cien•te *adj.* unconscious; unaware.

in•con•se•cuen•te *adj.* inconsistent; illogical.

in•con•si•de•ra•do *adj.* inconsiderate, thoughtless.

in•cons•tan•cia *f.* inconstancy, changeableness, fickleness.

in•cons•tan•te *adj.* inconstant, fickle, changeable, variable.

in•con•ta•ble *adj.* countless, innumerable.

in•con•ve•nien•cia *f.* inconvenience; trouble.

in•con•ve•nien•te *adj.* inconvenient; improper; *m.* obstacle; objection.

in•cor•po•rar *v.* to incorporate, unite; to embody; to include; **-se a** to join.

in•co•rrec•to *adj.* incorrect.

in•cre•du•li•dad *f.* incredulity, unbelief.

in•cré•du•lo *adj.* incredulous, unbelieving; *m.* unbeliever.

in•cre•í•ble *adj.* incredible, unbelievable.

in•cre•men•to *m.* increment, increase.

in•crus•tar *v.* to inlay; to encrust (*cover with a crust or hard coating*); **-se en** to penetrate, impress itself deeply into.

in•cu•ba•do•ra *f.* incubator.

in•cul•car[6] *v.* to inculcate, instill, impress.

in•cul•to *adj.* uncultured; uncultivated; unrefined.

in•cum•ben•cia *f.* concern, duty, obligation; **no es de mi** – it does not concern me, it is not within my province.

in•cu•ra•ble *adj.* incurable.

in•cu•rrir *v.* to incur, fall (into); **– en un error** to fall into or commit an error; **– en el odio de** to incur the hatred of.

in•cur•sión *f.* raid, invasion.

in•da•ga•ción *f.* investigation, inquiry.

in•da•ga•dor *m.* investigator; inquirer; *adj.* investigating; inquiring.

in•da•gar[7] *v.* to find out, investigate; to inquire.

in•de•bi•do *adj.* undue, improper; illegal;

in•de•bi•da•men•te *adv.* unduly, illegally.

in•de•cen•cia *f.* indecency, obscenity, indecent act or remark.

in•de•cen•te *adj.* indecent, improper.

in•de•ci•ble *adj.* inexpressible, untold.

in•de•ci•so *adj.* undecided; doubtful, uncertain.

in•de•fec•ti•ble *adj.* unfailing; **-mente** unfailingly.

in•de•fen•so *adj.* defenseless, unprotected.

in•de•fi•ni•ble *adj.* indefinable.

in•de•fi•ni•do *adj.* indefinite.

in•de•le•ble *adj.* indelible.

in•dem•ni•za•ción *f.* indemnity, compensation.

in•dem•ni•zar[9] *v.* to indemnify, compensate.

in•de•pen•den•cia *f.* indepedence.

in•de•pen•dien•te *adj.* independent.

in•des•crip•ti•ble *adj.* indescribable.

in•de•se•a•ble *adj.* undesirable, unwelcome.

in•dia•da *f. Riopl., C.A., Col.* community, group, or crowd of Indians; *Col., Ven., Carib., Andes* an Indianlike remark or act; *Am.* an uncontrollable fit of anger.

in•dia•nis•ta *m. & f.* student of Indian culture; *adj.* pertaining to Indian culture.

in•dia•no *adj.* of or pertaining to the West or East Indies; *m.* Spaniard who goes back to settle in his country after having lived for some time in Spanish America.

in•di•ca•ción *f.* indication.

in•di•car[6] *v.* to indicate, show, point out.

in•di•ca•ti•vo *adj.* indicative; *m.* indicative, indicative mood.

ín•di•ce *m.* index; catalogue; sign; pointer; forefinger.

in•di•cio *m.* indication, sign.

in•di•fe•ren•cia *f.* indifference.

in•di•fe•ren•te *adj.* indifferent.

in•dí•ge•na *adj.* indigenous; native; *m. & f.* native

inhabitant; *Am.* Indian.

in·dig·na·ción *f.* indignation.

in·dig·na·do *p.p.* & *adj.* indignant, irritated, angry.

in·dig·nar *v.* to irritate, anger; **-se** to become indignant, angry.

in·dig·ni·dad *f.* indignity, affront, insult; unworthy or disgraceful act.

in·dig·no *adj.* unworthy; low, contemptible.

in·dio *adj.* & *m.* Indian; Hindu.

in·di·rec·ta *f.* hint, indirect remark, innuendo, insinuation.

in·di·rec·to *adj.* indirect.

in·dis·ci·pli·na·do *adj.* undisciplined, untrained.

in·dis·cre·to *adj.* indiscreet, imprudent, unwise, rash.

in·dis·cu·ti·ble *adj.* indisputable, unquestionable.

in·dis·pen·sa·ble *adj.* indispensable.

in·dis·po·ner[40] *v. irr.* to indispose; to make ill; **– a uno con otro** to prejudice someone against another; **-se** to become ill; **-se con** to fall out with, quarrel with.

in·dis·po·si·ción *f.* indisposition, upset, slight illness; reluctance, unwillingness.

in·dis·pues·to *p.p.* of **indisponer** & *adj.* indisposed, unwilling; ill.

in·dis·pu·ta·ble *adj.* unquestionable.

in·dis·tin·to *adj.* indistinct, dim. vague, not clear.

in·di·vi·dual *adj.* individual.

in·di·vi·dua·li·dad *f.* individuality.

in·di·vi·duo *adj.* individual; indivisible; *m.* individual; person; member.

in·dó·cil *adj.* unruly, disobedient, headstrong.

in·doc·to *adj.* uneducated, ignorant.

ín·do·le *f.* disposition, temper; kind, class.

in·do·len·cia *f.* indolence, laziness; insensitiveness, indifference.

in·do·len·te *adj.* indolent, lazy; insensitive, indifferent.

in·do·ma·ble *adj.* indomitable, uncon-querable; unmanageable; untamable.

in·dó·mi·to *adj.* untamed; uncontrollable, unruly.

in·du·cir[25] *v. irr.* to induce; to persuade.

in·du·da·ble *adj.* unquestionable, certain.

in·dul·gen·cia *f.* indulgence, tolerance, forgiveness; remission of sins.

in·dul·gen·te *adj.* indulgent, lenient.

in·dul·tar *v.* to pardon, set free; to exempt.

in·dul·to m. pardon, forgiveness; exemption; privilege.

in·du·men·ta·ria *f.* costume, dress; manner of dressing.

in·dus·tria *f.* industry; cleverness, skill; **de –** intentionally, on purpose.

in·dus·trial *adj.* industrial; *m.* industrialist; manufacturer.

in·dus·trio·so *adj.* industrious.

i·né·di·to *adj.* unpublished.

i·ne·fa·ble *adj.* ineffable, inexpressible.

i·ne·fi·caz *adj.* ineffective; inefficient.

i·nep·to *adj.* incompetent; unsuitable.

i·ne·quí·vo·co *adj.* unmistakable.

i·ner·cia *f.* inertia, lifelessness; inactivity.

i·ner·me *adj.* unarmed, defenseless.

i·ner·te *adj.* inert; inactive, sluggish, slow.

i·nes·pe·ra·do *adj.* unexpected.

i·nes·ta·ble *adj.* unstable; unsettled; unsteady.

i·nes·ti·ma·ble *adj.* inestimable, invaluable.

i·ne·vi·ta·ble *adj.* inevitable, unavoidable.

i·ne·xac·to *adj.* inexact, inaccurate.

i·nex·pe·rien·cia *f.* inexperience.

i·nex·per·to *adj.* unskilful, unskilled, inexperienced.

i·nex·pli·ca·ble *adj.* inexplicable.

i·nex·tin·gui·ble *adj.* inextinguishable, unquenchable.

in·fa·li·ble *adj.* infallible.

in·fa·me *adj.* infamous; *m.* scoundrel.

in·fa·mia *f.* infamy, dishonor; wickedness.

in·fan·cia *f.* infancy.

in·fan·te *m.* infant; infante (*royal prince of Spain, except the heir to the thome*); infantryman.

in·fan·te·rí·a *f.* infantry.

in·fan·til *adj.* infantile, childlike, childish.

in·fa·ti·ga·ble *adj.* tireless, untiring.

in·faus·to *adj.* unfortunate; unhappy.

in·fec·ción *f.* infection; **infeccioso** *adj.* infectious.

in·fec·tar *v.* to infect; to corrupt: **-se** to become infected.

in·fe·liz *adj.* unhappy, unfortunate; *m.* poor wretch.

in·fe·rior *adj.* inferior; lower; *m.* inferior.

in·fe·rio·ri·dad *f.* inferiority.

in·fe·rir[3] *v. irr.* (*concluir*) to infer; to imply; (*causar*) to inflict.

in·fer·nal *adj.* infernal.

in·fes·tar *v.* to infest, invade, overrun, plague; to corrupt, infect.

in·fi·cio·nar *v.* to infect; to contaminate.

in·fiel *adj.* unfaithful, faithless; infidel; inaccurate.

in·fier·ni·llo *m.* chafing dish.

in·fier·no *m.* hell; **en el quinto –** very far away.

in·fil·trar *v.* to filter through; **-se** to leak (into), filter (through), infiltrate.

in·fi·ni·dad *f.* infinity; **una – de** a large number of.

in·fi·ni·to *adj.* infinite; adv. infinitely; *m.* infinity.

in·fla·ma·ción *f.* inflammation.

in·fla·ma·do *p.p.* & *adj.* inflamed; sore.

in·fla·mar *v.* to inflame, excite; to kindle, set on fire; **-se** to become inflamed.

in·flar *v.* to inflate; to exaggerate, **-se** to become inflated; to swell up with pride.

in·fle·xi·ble *adj.* inflexible, stiff, rigid; unbending.

in·fle·xión *f.* inflection.

in·fli·gir[11] *v.* to inflict.

in·flu·en·cia *f.* influence.

in·flu·en·za *f.* influenza, grippe, flu.

in·flu·ír³² *v. irr.* to influence.

in·flu·jo *m.* influence; influx, inward flow.

in·flu·yen·te *adj.* influential.

in·for·ma·ción *f.* information.

in·for·mal *adj.* informal; unconventional; unreliable, not dependable, not punctual.

in·for·mar *v.* to inform; to give form to; to give a report; to present a case; **-se** to find out.

in·for·me *m.* report, account; information; brief; *adj.* formless, shapeless.

in·for·tu·nio *m.* misfortune, mishap; misery.

in·frac·ción *f.* infraction, beach, violation (*of a law, treaty, etc.*).

in·frac·tor *m.* transgressor, lawbreaker, violator (*of a law*).

in·fras·cri·to *m.* undersigned, subscriber, signer (*of a letter, document, etc.*); **el — secretario** the secretary whose signature appears below.

in·frin·gir¹¹ *v.* to infringe, break, violate.

in·fruc·tuo·so *adj.* fruitless.

ín·fu·las *f.* pl. airs, false importance; **darse — to** put on airs.

in·fun·da·do *adj.* groundless, without foundation.

in·fun·dir *v.* to infuse, inspire; to instill.

in·fu·sión *f.* infusion (*liquid extract obtained by steeping*); infusion, inspiration; **poner en -** to steep (*as tea leaves*).

in·ge·nie·rí·a *f.* engineering.

in·ge·nie·ro *m.* engineer.

in·ge·nio *m.* genius; talent; ingenuity; mentality, mental power, mind; with; **— de azúcar** sugar refinery; sugar plantation.

in·ge·nio·si·dad *f.* ingenuity, cleverness.

in·ge·nio·so *adj.* ingenious, clever.

in·ge·nui·dad *f.* candor, frankness; unaffected simplicity.

in·ge·nuo *adj.* frank, sincere; simple, unaffected; naive.

in·ge·rir = **injerir**.

in·ges·tión *f.* ingestion.

in·gle *f.* groin.

in·glés *adj.* English; **a la inglesa** in the English fashion; *Am.* **ir a la inglesa** to go Dutch treat; *m.* Englishman; the English language.

in·go·ber·na·ble *adj.* ungovernable, unruly, uncontrollable.

in·gra·ti·tud *f.* ingratitude.

in·gra·to *adj.* ungrateful, trankless; harsh; cruel, disdainful.

in·gre·dien·te *m.* ingredient.

in·gre·sar *v.* to enter, **— en** to join (*a society, club, etc.*).

in·gre·so *m.* entrance; entry; **-s** receipts, profits; revenue.

in·há·bil *adj.* unskilled; unskilful; unfit.

in·ha·bi·li·dad *f.* inability; unfitness.

in·ha·bi·li·tar *v.* to disqualify; to unfit, disable.

in·he·ren·te *adj.* inherent.

in·hos·pi·ta·la·rio *adj.* inhospitable.

in·hu·ma·no *adj.* inhuman, cruel.

i·ni·cia·dor *m.* initiator; pioneer; *adj.* initiating.

i·ni·cial *adj. & f.* initial

i·ni·ciar *v.* to initiate; to begin.

i·ni·cia·ti·va *f.* initiative.

i·ni·cuo *adj.* wicked.

i·ni·qui·dad *f.* iniquity, wickedness; sin.

in·je·rír³ *v. irr.* to inject, insert; **-se** to interfere, meddle.

in·jer·tar *v.* to graft.

in·jer·to *m.* graft.

in·ju·ria *f.* affront, insult; harm, damage.

in·ju·riar *v.* to insult, offend; to harm, damage.

in·ju·rio·so *adj.* insulting, offensive; harmful.

in·jus·ti·cia *f.* injustice.

in·jus·ti·fi·ca·do *adj.* unjustified; unjustifiable.

in·jus·to *adj.* injust, unfair.

in·ma·cu·la·do *adj.* immaculate, clean; pure.

in·me·dia·ción *f.* vicinity; nearness; **-es** environs, outskirts.

in·me·dia·to *adj.* near, close; *Am.* **de —** immediately; suddenly; **inmediatamente** *adv.* immediately, at once.

in·men·si·dad *f.* immensity, vastness; vast number.

in·men·so *adj.* immense, vast, huge; boundless.

in·mer·sión *f.* immersion, dip.

in·mi·gra·ción *f.* immigration.

in·mi·gran·te *adj., f. & f.* inmigrant.

in·mi·grar *v.* to immigrate.

in·mien·te *adj.* imminent.

in·mis·cuir³² *v. irr.* to mix; **-se** to meddle, interfere.

in·mo·ble *adj.* motionless; unshaken.

in·mo·ral *adj.* immoral; **inmoralidad** *f.* immorality.

in·mor·tal *adj.* immortal; **inmortalidad** *f.* immortality.

in·mo·vi·ble *adj.* immovable, fixed; steadfast.

in·mó·vil *adj.* motionless, still; immovable.

in·mun·di·cia *f.* filth, dirt; nastiness.

in·mun·do *adj.* filthy, dirty; impure; nasty.

in·mu·ne *adj.* immune; exempt.

in·mu·ni·dad *f.* immunity.

in·mu·ta·ble *adj.* unchangeable, invariable.

in·mu·tar *v.* to alter, change; **-se** to show emotion (*either by turning pale or blushing*).

in·na·to *adj.* innate, natural, inborn.

in·ne·ce·sa·rio *adj.* unnecessary.

in·ne·ga·ble *adj.* undeniable, not to be denied.

in·no·cuo *adj.* innocuous, harmless; **innocuidad** *f.* harmlessness.

in·no·va·ción *f.* innovation; novelty.

in·nu·me·ra·ble *adj.* innumerable.

i·nob·ser·van·cia *f.* nonobservance, violation (*of a*

law), lack of observance (*of a law, rule or custom*).

i•no•cen•cia *f.* innocence.

i•no•cen•te *adj.* innocent; *m.* innocent person; **i•no•cen•tón** *adj.* quite foolish or simple; easily fooled; *m.* dupe, unsuspecting victim.

i•no•cu•lar *v.* to inoculate.

i•no•do•ro *adj.* adorless; *m. C.A., Ven., Col.* toilet, water closet.

i•no•fen•si•vo *adj.* inoffensive; harmless.

i•nol•vi•da•ble *adj.* unforgettable.

i•no•pi•na•do *adj.* unexpected.

i•no•por•tu•no *adj.* inopportune, untimely, unsuitable.

in•quie•tar *v.* to worry, disturb, make uneasy; **-se** to become disturbed, uneasy.

in•quie•to *adj.* restless; uneasy, anxious.

in•quie•tud *f.* restlessness; anxiety, uneasiness; fear.

in•qui•li•no *m.* tenant, renter; lodger.

in•qui•na *f.* aversion, grudge, dislike.

in•qui•rir[35] *v. irr.* to inquire, investigate; to find out.

in•qui•si•ción *f.* inquisition; inquiry, investigation.

in•sa•cia•ble *adj.* insatiable, never satisfied, greedy.

in•sa•lu•bre *adj.* unhealthy, unhealthful, unwholesome.

in•sa•no *adj.* insane, crazy; unhealthy.

ins•cri•bir[52] *v.* to inscribe; to register, enroll; to record; **-se** to register.

ins•crip•ción *f.* inscription; registration.

ins•crip•to, ins•cri•to *p.p.* of **inscribir.**

in•sec•to *m.* insect.

in•se•gu•ro *adj.* insecure; unsafe; doubtful, uncertain.

in•sen•sa•to *adj.* senseless; foolish.

in•sen•si•bi•li•dad *f.* insensibility, unconsciousness; lack of feeling.

in•sen•si•ble *adj.* insensible; unfeeling; imperceptible.

in•se•pa•ra•ble *adj.* inseparable.

in•ser•ción *f.* insertion; insect.

in•ser•tar *v.* to insert.

in•ser•to *adj.* inserted.

in•ser•vi•ble *adj.* useless.

in•si•dio•so *adj.* insidious; sly, crafty.

in•sig•ne *adj.* famous.

in•sig•nia *f.* badge, medal, decoration; flag, pennant; **-s** insignia.

in•sig•ni•fi•can•te *adj.* insignificant.

in•si•nua•ción *f.* insinuation; intimation, hint.

in•si•nuar[18] *v.* to insinuate, hint; **-se** to insinuate oneself (*into another's friendship*); to creep (into) gradually.

in•si•pi•dez *f.* flatness, tastelessness, dullness; **insípido** *adj.* insipid; tasteless.

in•sis•ten•cia *f.* insistence, persistence, obstinacy; **insistente** *adj.* insistent, persistent.

in•sis•tir *v.* to insist; to persist.

in•so•cia•ble *adj.* unsociable.

in•so•la•ción *f.* sunstroke.

in•so•len•cia *f.* insolence.

in•so•len•tar•se *v.* to sauce, become insolent, act with insolence.

in•so•len•te *adj.* insolent.

in•só•li•to *adj.* unusual; uncommon.

in•sol•ven•te *adj.* insolvent, bankrupt.

in•som•ne *adj.* sleepless.

in•son•da•ble *adj.* fathomless, deep; impenetrable.

in•so•por•ta•ble *adj.* unbearable.

in•sos•pe•cha•do *adj.* unsuspected.

ins•pec•ción *f.* inspection.

ins•pec•cio•nar *v.* to inspect.

ins•pec•tor *m.* inspector; overseer.

ins•pi•ra•ción *f.* inspiration; inhalation, breathing in.

ins•pi•rar *v.* to inspire; to inhale.

ins•ta•la•ción *f.* installation.

ins•ta•lar *v.* to install.

ins•tan•cia *f.* instance, urgent request; petitions; **a -s de** at the request of.

ins•tan•tá•ne•a *f.* snapshot.

ins•tan•tá•ne•o *adj.* instantaneous; subden.

ins•tan•te *m.* instant, moment; **al** — at once, immediately; **por -s** continually; from one moment to another; *adj.* instant, urgent.

ins•tar *v.* to urge, press; to be urgent.

ins•ti•gar[7] *v.* to instigate, urge on, incite.

ins•tin•ti•vo *adj.* instinctive.

ins•tin•to *m.* instinct.

ins•ti•tu•ción *f.* institution; establishment, foundation; **-es** institutes, collection of precepts and principles.

ins•ti•tuir[32] *v. irr.* to institute; — **por heredero** to appoint as heir.

ins•ti•tu•to *m.* institute; established principle, law, or custom; — **de segunda enseñanza** high school.

ins•ti•tu•triz *f.* governess.

ins•truc•ción *f.* instruction; education.

ins•truc•ti•vo *adj.* instructive.

ins•truir[32] *v. irr.* to instruct, teach; to inform

ins•tru•men•to *m.* instrument.

in•su•fi•cien•cia *f.* insufficiency, deficiency; incompetence; dearth, scarcity, lack.

in•su•fi•cien•te *adj.* insufficient.

in•su•fri•ble *adj.* insufferable, unbearable.

ín•su•la *f.* island.

in•sul•tan•te *adj.* insulting, abusive.

in•sul•tar *v.* to insult; **-se** to be seized. with a fit.

in•sul•to *m.* insult; sudden fit or attack.

in•su•pe•ra•ble *adj.* insuperable; insurmountable.

in•sur•gen•te *adj., m. & f.* insurgent.

in•su•rrec•ción *f.* insurrection, uprising, revolt.

in•su•rrec•to *m.* insurgent, rebel; *adj.* rebellious.

in•tac•to *adj.* intact.

in•ta•cha•ble *adj.* faultless, irreproach-able.

in·te·gral *adj.* integral; j. integral (*math*).

in·te·gran·te *adj.* integral; integrating.

in·te·gri·dad *f.* integrity; wholeness; honesty; purity.

ín·te·gro *adj.* whole, complete; honest, upright.

in·te·lec·to *m.* intellect.

in·te·lec·tual *adj.* intellectual.

in·te·li·gen·cia *f.* intelligence.

in·te·li·gen·te *adj.* intelligent.

in·tem·pe·ran·cia *f.* intemperance, excess.

in·tem·pe·rie *f.* open air; bad weather; **a la -** unsheltered, outdoors, in the open air; exposed to the wather.

in·ten·ción *f.* intention; **intencional** *adj.* intentional.

in·ten·den·te *m.* manager, superintendent, supervisor; *Ríopl.* governor of a province; *Am.* police commissioner.

in·ten·si·dad *f.* intensity; stress.

in·ten·so *adj.* intense; intensive; ardent, vehement.

in·ten·tar *v.* to attempt, try; to intend.

in·ten·to *m.* intent, purpose, intention; **de –** on purpose.

in·ter·ca·lar *v.* to insert, place between.

in·ter·cam·bio *m.* interchange; exchange.

in·ter·ce·der *v.* to intercede.

in·ter·cep·tar *v.* to intercept.

in·ter·ce·sión *f.* intercession, mediation.

in·ter·dic·ción *f.* interdiction; prevention.

in·te·rés *m.* interest.

in·te·re·san·te *adj.* interesting.

in·te·re·sar *v.* to interest; to give an interest or share; **-se** to be or become interested.

in·ter·fe·ren·cia *f.* interference.

ín·te·rin *m.* interim meantime; **en al –** in the meantime.

in·te·ri·no *adj.* acting, temporary.

in·te·rior *adj.* interior; inner; internal; *m.* interior, inside.

in·ter·jec·ción *f.* interjection, exclamation.

in·ter·lo·cu·tor *m.* participant in a dialogue.

in·ter·me·dio *adj.* intermediate; intervening; *m.* intermission; interval; **por – de** by means of, through the intervention of.

in·ter·mi·na·ble *adj.* interminable, unending, endless.

in·ter·mi·sión *f.* intermission, interruption, pause, interval.

in·ter·mi·ten·te *adj.* intermittent, occurring at intervals; **calentura** (*or* **fiebre**) **–** intermittent fever.

in·ter·na·cio·nal *adj.* international.

in·ter·na·do *m.* a boarding student.

in·ter·nar *v.* to intern, confine; **-se** to penetrate, go into the interior.

in·ter·no *adj.* internal; interior; *m.* boarding-school student.

in·ter·o·ce·á·ni·co *adj.* interoceanic; transcontinental.

in·ter·pe·lar *v.* to interrogate, question, demand explanations; to ask the aid of.

in·ter·po·ner[40] *v. irr.* to interpose, put between, insert; to place as a mediator; **-se** to intervene, mediate.

in·ter·pre·ta·ción *f.* interpretation.

in·ter·pre·tar *v.* to interpret.

in·tér·pre·te *m. & f.* interpreter.

in·ter·pues·to *p.p.* of **interponer**.

in·te·rro·ga·ción *f.* interrogation, question; **signo de –** question mark.

in·te·rro·ga·dor *m.* questioner; *adj.* questioning.

in·te·rro·gar[7] *v.* to interrogate, question.

in·te·rro·ga·ti·vo *adj.* interrogative.

in·te·rro·ga·to·rio *m.* interrogation, questioning.

in·te·rrum·pir *v.* to interrupt.

in·te·rrup·ción *f.* interruption.

in·te·rrup·tor *m.* interrupter; electric switch.

in·ter·sec·ción *f.* intersection.

in·ter·va·lo *m.* interval.

in·ter·ven·ción *f.* intervention; mediation; **participation**; auditing of accounts.

in·ter·ve·nir[48] *v. irr.* to intervene; to mediate: to audit (*accounts*).

in·ter·ven·tor *m.* inspector; controller, comptroller; auditor.

in·tes·ti·no *m.* intestine; *adj.* intestine, internal.

in·ti·ma·ción *f.* intimation; hint, insinuation, suggestion.

in·ti·mar *v.* to announce, notify; to intimate, hint; to become intimate, become friendly.

in·ti·mi·dad *f.* intimacy.

in·ti·mi·dar *v.* to intimidate.

ín·ti·mo *adj.* intimate.

in·ti·tu·lar *v.* to entitle; to give a title to (*a person or a thing*); **-se** to be entitled, be called; to call oneself (*by a certain name*).

in·to·le·ra·ble *adj.* intolerable.

in·to·le·ran·cia *f.* intolerance; **intolerante** *adj.* intolerant, narrow-minded.

in·to·xi·can·te *m.* poison.

in·to·xi·car[6] *v.* to poison.

in·tran·qui·lo *adj.* disturbed, uneasy.

in·tran·qui·li·dad *f.* uneasiness, restlessness.

in·tran·si·gen·cia *f.* uncompromising act or attitude; intolerance.

in·tran·si·gen·te *adj.* uncompromising, unwilling to compromise or yield; intolerant.

in·tra·ta·ble *adj.* unsociable; rude; unruly.

in·tra·ve·no·so *adj.* intravenous (*within a vein or the veins; into a vein*).

in·tre·pi·dez *f.* fearlessness, courage.

in·tré·pi·do *adj.* intrepid, fearless.

in·tri·ga *f.* intrigue; scheme; plot.

in·tri·gan·te *m. & f.* intriguer, plotter; *adj.* intriguing.

in·tri·gar[7] *v.* to intrigue.

in·trin·ca·do *adj.* intricate, complicated, entangled.

in·tro·duc·ción *f.* introduction.

in•tro•du•cir[25] v. irr. to introduce; **-se** to introduce oneself; to get in: to penetrate.

in•tro•mi•sión f. meddling; insertion.

in•tru•so adj. intrusive, intruding; m. intruder.

in•tui•ción f. intuition.

in•tuir[32] v. irr. to sense, feel by intuition.

i•nun•da•ción f. inundation, flood.

i•nun•dar v. to inundate, flood.

i•nu•si•ta•do adj. unusual, rare.

i•nú•til adj. useless.

i•nu•ti•li•dad f. uselessness.

inu•ti•li•li•zar[9] v. to make useless, put out of commission; to disable, to ruin, spoil.

in•va•dir v. to invade.

in•va•li•dar v. to render invalid; to void, annul.

in•vá•li•do adj. invalid; void, null, sickly, weak; m. invalid.

in•va•ria•ble adj. invariable.

in•va•sión f. invasion.

in•va•sor m. invader; adj. invading; **ejército –** invading army.

in•ven•ci•ble adj. invincible, uncon-querable.

in•ven•ción f. invention.

in•ven•di•ble adj. unsaleable.

in•ven•tar v. to invent.

in•ven•ta•riar[17] v. to inventory, take an inventory of.

in•ven•ta•rio m. inventory.

in•ven•ti•va f. inventiveness, power of inventing, ingenuity

in•ven•ti•vo adj. inventive.

in•ven•to m. invention.

in•ven•tor m. inventor; storyteller; fibber.

in•ver•ná•cu•lo m. greenhouse, hothouse.

in•ver•na•de•ro m. winter quarters; winter resort; winter pasture; greenhouse, hothouse.

in•ver•nal adj. wintry, winter.

in•ver•nar[1] v. irr. to winter, spend the winter.

in•ve•ro•sí•mil, in•ve•ri•sí•mil adj. unlikely, improbable.

in•ver•sión f. inversion; investment.

in•ver•so adj. inverse, inverted; reverse; **a (or por) la inversa** on the contrary.

in•ver•tir[3] v.irr. to invert; to reverse; to invest; to employ, spend (time).

in•ves•ti•ga•ción f. investigation.

in•ves•ti•ga•dor m. investigator; adj. investigating.

in•ves•ti•gar[7] v. to investigate.

in•vic•to adj. unconquered; always victorious.

in•vier•no m. winter; C.A., Col., Ven., Ec., Peru the rainy season.

in•vi•si•ble adj. invisible.

in•vi•ta•ción f. invitation.

in•vi•tar v. to invite.

in•vo•car[6] v. to invoke.

in•vo•lun•ta•rio adj. involuntary.

in•yec•ción f. injection.

in•yec•ta•do p.p. injected; adj. bloodshot, inflamed.

in•yec•tar v. to inject.

ir[33] v. irr. to go; to walk; **– corriendo** to be running, **– entendiendo** to understand gradually; to begin to understand; **– a caballo** to ride horseback; **– a pie** to walk; **– en automóvil** to drive, ride in an automobile; **no irle ni venirle a uno** to make no difference to one; **¿cómo le va?** how are you?; **no me va nada en eso** that doesn't concern me; **¡vamos!** let's go! come on!; **¡vaya!** well now!; **¡vaya un hombre!** what a man!; **-se** to go, go away; to escape; **-se abajo** to fall down, topple over; to collapse; **-se a pique** to founder, sink.

i•ra f. ire, anger.

i•ra•cun•do adj. irritable; angry

i•ris m. iris (of the eye); **arco –** rainbow.

i•ri•sa•do aj. iridescent, rainbow-hued.

i•ro•nía f. irony.

i•ró•ni•co adj. ironic, ironical.

i•rra•cio•nal adj. irrational, unreasonable.

i•rra•diar v. to radiate.

i•rre•al adj. unreal.

i•rre•fle•xión f. thoughtlessness.

i•rre•fle•xi•vo adj. thoughtless.

i•rre•fle•na•ble adj. uncontrollable.

i•rre•gu•lar adj. irregular.

i•rre•li•gio•so adj. irreligious.

i•rre•me•dia•ble adj. irremediable; hopeless, incurable.

i•rre•pro•cha•ble adj. irreproachable, fawless.

i•rre•sis•ti•ble adj. irresistible.

i•rre•so•lu•to adj. irresolute, undecided, hesitating.

i•rres•pe•tuo•so adj. disrespectful

i•rre•ve•ren•cia f. irreverence.

i•rre•ve•ren•te adj. irreverent.

i•rri•ga•ción f. irrigation.

i•rri•gar[7] v. to irrigate.

i•rri•sión f. mockery, ridicule, derision.

i•rri•ta•ción f. irritation.

i•rri•tan•te adj. irritating.

i•rri•tar v. to irritate.

i•rrum•pir v. to enter violently; to invade.

i•rrup•ción f. sudden attack, raid, invasión.

is•la f. island.

is•le•ño m. islander.

is•lo•te m. islet, small rocky island.

ist•mo m. isthmus.

i•ta•lia•no adj. & m. Italian.

i·ti·ne·ra·rio *m.* itinerary; timetable, schedule; railroad guide.

i·zar⁹ *v.* to hoist; to heave.

iz·quier·da *f.* letf hand; left side; left wing (*in politics*) **a la –** to the left; **izquierdista** *m. & f.* leftistk radical.

iz·quier·do *adj.* letf; left-handed.

J

ja·ba·lí *m.* wild boar.

ja·ba·li·na *f.* javelin; wild sow.

ja·bón *m.* soap; *Riopl.* fright, fear; **dar –** to soft-soap, flatter; **dar un –** to give a good scolding; to beat, thrash.

ja·bo·na·du·ra *f.* washing, soaping; **-s** suds, lather; **dar a uno una –** to reprimand or scold someone.

ja·bo·nar *v.* (*lavar*) to lather, soap; (*reprender*) to scold; reprimand.

ja·bo·ne·ra *f.* soap dish; woman soap vendor or maker.

ja·ca *f.* pony; small horse; **jacó** *m.* small nag; poor horse.

ja·cal *m. Mex.* shack, adobe hut; **jacalucho** *m. Am.* poor, ugly shack.

ja·cin·to *m.* hyacinth.

jac·tan·cia *f.* boast, brag; boasting.

jac·tan·cio·so *adj.* braggart, boastful.

jac·tar·se *v.* to brag, boast.

ja·cu·la·to·ria *f.* short, fervent prayer.

ja·de·an·te *adj.* brathless, panting, out of breath.

ja·de·ar *v.* to pant.

ja·deo *m.* pant, panting.

ja·ez *m.* harness; kind, sort; **jaeces** trappings.

ja·lar *v.* to pull; to haul; to jerk; *C.A.* to court, make love; *Ven., Andes* to flunk (*a student*); *Mex.* **¡jala!** (*or* **¡jálale!**) get going! get a move on there!; **-se** *Am.* to get drunk; *Mex.* to gó away, move awaý.

ja·le·a *f.* jelly.

ja·le·ar *v.* to shout (*to hunting dogs*); to rouse, beat up (*game*); to shout and clap (*to encourage dancers*).

ja·le·o *m.* shouting and clapping (*to encourage dancers*); an Añdalusian dance; revelry, merrymaking; jesting; gracefulness.

ja·le·ti·na *f.* gelatin.

ja·lón *m.* marker (*for boundaries*); *Am.* pull, jerk, tug; *Mex., C.A.* swallow of liquor; *Bol., C.A.* stretch., distance.

ja·lo·ne·ar *v. C.A., Mex.* to pull, jerk.

ja·más *adv.* never.

ja·món *m.* ham; *P.R.* fix, difficulty.

ja·po·nés *adj. & m.* Japanese.

ja·que *m.* check (*in chess*); braggart, bully; **– mate** checkmate (*in chess*); **tener a uno en –** to hold someone under a threat.

ja·que·ca *f.* headache; sick headache.

ja·ra *f.* rockrose (*shrub*); *Ven., Col,* reed; **jaral** *m.* bramble of rockroses; *Am.* reeds, chump of reeds.

ja·ra·be *m.* syrup; sweet beverage; *Mex., C.A.* a kind of tap dance; *Mex,* song and musical accompaniment of the **jarabe.**

ja·ra·na *f.* merrymaking, revelry; trick; fib; jest; *Col., Ec., Carib.* a dance; *Mex.* small guitar; **ir de –** to go on a spree.

jar·cia *f.* rigging (*ropes, chains, etc. for the masts, yards and sails of a ship*); fishing tackle; pile, heap; jumble of things.

jar·dín *m.* flower garden.

jar·di·ne·ro *m.* gardener.

ja·rra *f.* jar, vase, pitcher; **de** (*or* **en**) **-s** akimbo (with hands on the hips).

ja·rro *m.* jar, jug, pitcher.

ja·rrón *m.* large vase or jar.

jas·pe *m.* jasper: veined marble; **jaspeado** *adj.* veined, streaked, mottled.

jau·la *f.* cage; cagelike cell or prison; *Am.* roofless cattle car or freight car.

jau·ría *f.* pack of hounds.

jaz·mín *m.* jasmine.

je·fa·tu·ra *f.* position of chief; headquarters of a *chief.*

je·fe *m.* chief, leader, head.

jen·gi·bre *m.* ginger.

je·rez *m.* sherry wine.

jer·ga *f.* (*tela*) thick coarse cloth; straw mattress; (*dialecto*) jargon; slang: *Am.* saddle pad; *Col.* poncho made of coarse cloth.

jer·gón *f.* (*material*) straw mattress; ill-fitting suit or dress; (*persona*) big clumsy fellow; *Riopl., Mex., Ven.* cheap coarse rug.

je·ri·gon·za *f.* jargon; slàng.

je·rin·ga *f.* syringe; **jeringazo** *m.* injection; squirt.

je·rin·gar⁷ *v.* to inject; to squirt; to bother, molest, vex, annoy.

je·sui·ta *m.* Jesuit.

je·ta *f.* snout; thick lips.

ji·ba = **giba.**

jí·ba·ro *adj. P.R.* rustic, rural, rude, uncultured; *m. P.R.* bumpkin, peasant.

jí·ca·ra *f.* chocolate cup; *Am.* small bowl made out of a gourd; *Am.* any small bowl; *Am.* bald head.

jil·gue·ro *m.* linnet.

ji·ne·te *m.* horseman, rider.

ji·ne·tea·da *f. Riopl., C.A.* roughriding; horse-breaking.

ji·ne·te·ar *v.* to ride horseback; to perfor on horseback; *Am.* to break in (*a horse*); *Am.* to ride a bronco or bull.

ji·ra *f.* excursion, tour; outing, picnic: strip of cloth.

ji·ra·fa *f.* giraffe; boom mike (*broadcasting*).

ji·to·ma·te *m.* Mex tomato. Also **gitomate.**

jo·fai·na *f.* basin, washbowl.

jol·go·rio = holgorio.

jor·na·da f. day's journey; military expedition; working day; act (of a Spanish play).

jor·nal m. day's wages; bookkeeping journal; **a** – by the day.

jor·na·le·ro m. day laborer.

jo·ro·ba f. hump; nuisance, annoyance.

jo·ro·ba·do adj. hunchbacked; annoyed, bothered, in a bad fix; m. lunchback.

jo·ro·bar v. to bother, pester, annoy.

jo·ron·go m. Mex. Mexican poncho.

jo·ta f. name of the letter j: iota (anything insignificant); Aragonese and Valencian dance and music; Am. (= **ojota**) leather sandal; **no saber una** – not to know anything.

jo·ven adj. young m. & f. youth; young man; young woman.

jo·vial adj. jovial, jolly, merry; **jovialidad** f. gaiety, merriment, fun.

jo·ya f. jewel; piece of jewelry; **-s** jewels; trousseau.

jo·ye·rí·a f. jeweler's shop.

jo·ye·ro m. jeweler, jewel box.

jua·ne·te m. bunion.

ju·bi·la·ción f. retirement (from a position or office); pension.

ju·bi·lar v. to pension; to retire; **-se** to be pensioned or retired; to rejoice; Col. to decline, fall into decline; Ven., Guat. to play hooky or truant.

ju·bi·leo m. jubilee; time of rejoicing; concession by the Pope of plenary (complete) indulgence.

jú·bi·lo m. joy, glee.

ju·bi·lo·so adj. jubilant, joyful.

ju·bón m. jacket; bodice.

ju·dí·a f. bean; string bean; Jewess; **-s tiernas** (or **verdes)** string beans.

ju·di·cial adj. judicial; – **mente** adv. judicially.

ju·dí·o adj. Jewish; m. Jew.

ju·do m. judo.

jue·go m. game; play; sport; gambling; pack of cards; set; – **de palabras** pun, play on words; – **de te** tea set; **hacer** – to match; **poner en** – to coordinate; to set in motion.

juer·ga f. spree, revelry, wild festivity; **irse de** – to go out on a spree; **juerguista** m. & f. merrymaker.

jue·ves m. Thursday.

juez m. judge; juror, member of a jury; – **arbitrador** (or **árbitro)** arbitrator, umpire.

ju·ga·da f. play, move; stroke; trick

ju·ga·dor m. player; gambler; – **de manos** juggler.

ju·gar³⁴ v. irr. to play; to gamble; to toy; – **a la pelota** to play ball; Am. – **a dos cartas** to be double-face.

ju·ga·rre·ta f. bad play, wrong play; mean trick; tricky deal; Am. noisy game.

ju·go m. juice; sap.

ju·go·si·dad f. juiciness; **jugoso** adj. juicy.

ju·gue·te m. plaything, toy; jest, joke; – **cómico** skit;

por (or **de)** – jokingly.

ju·gue·te·ar v. to play around, romp, frolic; to toy; to tamper (with), fool (with).

ju·gue·tón adj. playful.

jui·cio m. judgment; sense, wisdom; opinion; trial; **perder el** – to lose one's mind, go crazy.

jui·cio·so adj. judicious, wise; sensible.

ju·lio m. July.

ju·men·to m. ass, donkey.

jun·co m. rush, reed; junk (Chinese sailboat).

jun·gla f. Am. jungle.

ju·nio m. June.

jun·qui·llo m. reed; jonquil (yellow flower similar to the daffodil), species of narcissus.

jun·ta f. (reunión) meeting, conference; (funcionarios) board, council.

jun·tar v. to join, unite; to connect; to assemble; to collect; **-se** to assemble, gather; to be closely united; to associate (with).

jun·to adj. joined, united; **-s** together; adv. near; – **a** near to, close to; **en** – all together, in all; **por** – all together, in a lump; wholesale.

jun·tu·ra f. juncture; junction; joint, seam.

ju·ra·do m. jury; juror, juryman; adj. & p.p.sworn.

ju·ra·men·tar v. to swear in; **-se** to take an oath, be sworn in.

ju·ra·men·to m. oath; vow; curse.

ju·rar v. to swear, vow; to take oath; to curse

ju·ris·con·sul·to m. jurist, expert in law; lawyer.

ju·ris·dic·ción f. jurisdiction.

ju·ris·pru·den·cia f. jurisprudence, law.

ju·ro; de – adv. certainly, of course.

jus·ta f. joust, tournament, combat (between horsemen with lances); contest.

jus·ti·cia f. justice; court of justice; judge; police.

jus·ti·cie·ro adj. stricly just, austere (in matters of justice).

jus·ti·fi·ca·ción f. justification.

jus·ti·fi·can·te adj. justifying; m. voucher; writter excuse; proof.

jus·ti·fi·car⁶ v. to justify, to vindicate, clear of blame.

jus·to adj. just; pious; exact, correct; tight; adv. duly; exactly; tightly; m. jusst man; **los -s** the just.

ju·ve·nil adj. juvenile, young, youthful.

ju·ven·tud f. youth; young people.

juz·ga·do m. court, tribunal.

juz·gar⁷ v. to judge.

K

ker·me·sse f. country fair; bazaar for charity.

ke·ro·se·na f. kerosene, coal oil.

ki·lo m. kilo, kilogram.

ki·lo·gra·mo m. kilogram.

ki·ló·me·tra·je *m.* number of kilometers.
ki·ló·me·tro *m.* kilometer.

L

la *def. art. f.* the; **– de** the one with; that one with; *obj. pron.* her; it; **– que** *rel. pron.* she who, the one that; which.
la *m.* sixth note on the musical scale.
la·be·rin·to *m.* labyrinth, maze; labyrinth, internal ear.
la·bia *f.* fluency, talkativeness, gift of gab; **tener mucha –** to be a good talker.
la·bial *adj.* labial.
la·bio *m.* lip.
la·bio·den·tal *adj.* labiodental.
la·bor *f.* (*trabajo*) labor, work; (*cosido*) embroidery; needlework; (*agrícola*) tillage; **– de punto** knitting; **laborable** *adj.* workable; tillable; **día laborable** work day; **laboral** *adj.* pertaining to labor.
la·bo·ra·to·rio *m.* laboratory.
la·bo·rio·si·dad *f.* laboriousness, industry.
la·bo·rio·so *adj.* laborious; industrious.
la·bra·do *p.p. & adj.* (*agrícola*) tilled, cultivated; (*hecho*) wrought; manufactured; carved; *m.* carving; **– en madera** woodwork, carving; **-s** cultivated lands.
la·bra·dor *m.* farmer; peasant.
la·bran·za *f.* farming, tillage, plowing; cultivated land, farm.
la·brar *v.* (*la tierra*) to till, cultivate, farm; to plow; (*crear*) to carve; to embroider, to work (*metals*); to build (*a monument*).
la·brie·go *m.* peasant.
la·ca *f.* lacquer; shellac.
la·ca·yo *m.* lackey, footman, flunky.
la·cio *adj.* withered; languid; limp; straight (*hair*).
la·cra *f.* trace of an illness; blemish, defect; *Am.* sore, ulcer, scab, scar.
la·cre *m.* red sealing wax; *adj. Am.* red.
lac·tar *v.* to nurse, suckle; to feed with milk.
lác·te·o *adj.* milky; **fiebre láctea** milk fever; **régimen –** milk diet; **Vía Láctea** Milky Way.
la·de·ar *v.* to tilt, tip; to go alongside the slope or side of; to turn aside (*from a way or course*); **-se** to tilt; to sway; to incline or lean (*towards*); to move to one side; *Am.* to fall in love.
la·de·o *m.* inclination; tilt.
la·de·ra *f.* slope.
la·di·no *adj.* crafty, sly, shrewd; conversant with two or three languages; *m.* Sephardic Jew (*spanish-speaking*); Romansch (*a Romance language of Switzerland*); *Guat.* Spanish-speaking person (*as opposed to one who speaks an Indian language*);

Am. mestizo, half-breed; *Mex.*, *Ven.* talker, talkative person.
la·do *m.* side; **al –** near, at hand, at one's side; **de –** tilted, obliquely; sideways; **– a –** side by side; **¡a un –!** gangway! **hacerse a un –** to move over, step aside, move to one side; *Mex.*, *Ven.* **echársela de –** to boast.
la·drar *v.* to bark.
la·dri·do *m.* bark, barking.
la·dri·llo *m.* brick.
la·drón *m.* thief, robber; **ladronzuelo** *m.* petty thief.
la·gar·ti·ja *f.* small lizard.
la·gar·to *m.* lizard; rascal, sly fellow.
la·go *m.* lake.
lá·gri·ma *f.* tear; **llorar a – viva** to weep abundantly.
la·gri·me·ar *v.* to weep, shed tears.
la·gu·na *f.* lagoon; gap, blank space.
lai·co *adj.* lay; *m.* layman.
la·ja *f.* slab; flat stone.
la·me·de·ro *m.* salt lick (*for cattle*).
la·men·ta·ble *adj.* lamentable, pitiful.
la·men·ta·ción *f.* lamentation.
la·men·tar *v.* to lament, deplore; **-se** to moan, complain, wail.
la·men·to *m.* lament, moan, cry.
la·mer *v.* to lick; to lap.
la·mi·da *f. Mex.*, *C.A.* lick; also **lambida**.
lá·mi·na *f.* metal plate; sheet of metal; engraving; book illustration.
lám·pa·ra *f.* lamp.
lam·pi·ño *adj.* hairless; beardless.
la·na *f.* wool; *Am.* tramp, vagabond.
la·nar *adj.* wool-bearing; of wool.
lan·ce *m.* occurrence, event; cast, throw, move, turn; accident; quarrel: predicament.
lan·ce·ar *v.* to lance, spear.
lan·cha *f.* launch; boat; slab; **lanchón** *m.* barge.
lan·gos·ta *f.* lobster; locust.
lan·gui·de·cer *v. irr.* to languish.
lan·gui·dez *f.* languor, faintness, weakness.
lán·gui·do *adj.* languid.
la·ni·lla *f.* nap (*of cloth*).
la·nu·do *adj.* woolly; *Ven.* coarse, crude, ill-bred; *Am.* dull, slow, weak-willed; *Ch.*, *C.A.*, *Col.* wealthy.
lan·za *f.* lance, spear; *Col.* swindler, cheat; *m.* **lanzabombas** bomb launcher; *m.* **lanzacohetes** rocket launcher; *m.* **lanzallamas** flame, thrower.
lan·za·da *f.* thrust (*with a spear*).
lan·za·de·ra *f.* shuttle.
lan·za·mien·to *m.* launching (*boat or rocket*).
lan·zar[9] *v.* to fling, throw; to eject; to launch; **-se** to rush, fling oneself; to dart out.
lan·za·zo *m.* thrust with a lance.
la·pi·ce·ro *m.* pencil (*a mechanical pencil, one with an adjustable lead*).
lá·pi·da *f.* slab, tombstone; stone tablet.

la•pi•dar *v.* to stone; *Col., Ch.* to cut precious stones.
lá•piz *f.* pencil; crayon; **– para los labios** lipstick.
lap•so *m.* lapse.
lar•do *m.* lard.
lar•gar[7] *v.* to loosen; to let go; to set free; to unfold (*a flag or sails*); *Am.* to hurl, throw; *Col.* to strike (*a blow*); *Riopl.* to give, hand over; **-se** to go away, slip away; to leave.
lar•go *adj.* long; generous; *m.* length; largo (*music*); **a la larga** in the long run; slowly; **a lo –** along; lengthwise; **¡ – de aquí!** get out of here!
lar•gor *m.* length.
lar•gu•cho *adj.* lanky.
lar•gue•za *f.* generosity, liberality; length.
lar•guí•si•mo *adj.* very long.
lar•gu•ra *f.* length.
la•rin•ge *f.* larynx.
la•rín•ge•o *adj.* laryngeal.
lar•va *f.* larva.
las *def. art. f. pl.* the; *obj. pron.* them: **– que** *rel. pron.* those which; which.
las•ci•via *f.* lewdness.
las•ci•vo *adj.* lascivious, lewd.
lás•ti•ma *f.* pity; compassion, grief.
las•ti•ma•du•ra *f.* sore, hurt.
las•ti•mar *v.* to hurt; to offend; **-se** to get hurt; **-se de** to feel pit for.
las•ti•me•ro *adj.* pitiful; mournful.
las•ti•mo•so *adj.* pitiful.
las•tre *m.* ballast, weight.
la•ta *f.* (*metal*) tin plate; tin can, can; (*madero*) small log; thin board; (*pesadez*) annoyance; embarrassment; boring speech; *Am.* gaucho saber; *Am.* prop.
la•ten•te *adj.* latent.
la•te•ral *adj.* lateral, side; [1] (*phonetically*).
la•ti•do *m.* palpitation, throb, beat; bark, howl.
la•ti•fun•dio *m.* large landed estate.
la•ti•ga•zo *m.* lash, stroke with a whip; crack of a whip; harsh reprimand; unexpected blow or offense.
lá•ti•go *m.* whip; *Am.* whipping, beating; *Ch.* end or goal of a horse race.
la•tín *m.* Latin language.
la•ti•no *adj.* Latin; *m.* Latinist, Latin scholar; Latin.
la•tir *v.* to throb, beat, palpitate; to bark.
la•ti•tud *f.* latitude, extent, breadth.
la•tón *m.* brass.
la•tro•ci•nio *m.* larceny, theft, robbery.
la•úd *m.* lute; catboat (*long, narrow boat with a lateen sail*).
lau•da•ble *adj.* laudable, praiseworthy.
lau•rel *m.* laurel; laurel wreath.
lau•ro *m.* laurel; glory, fame.
la•va *f.* lava; washing of minerals.
la•va•ble *adj.* washable.
la•va•bo *m.* lavatory, washroom; washstand; washbowl.
la•va•de•ro *m.* washing place.
la•va•do *m.* wash, washing; laundry, laundry work.
la•va•dor *m.* washer; cleaner; *adj.* washing; cleaning; **lavadora** *f.* washer, washing machine.
la•va•du•ra *f.* washing; slops, dirty water.
la•va•ma•nos *m.* lavatory, washbowl, washstand.
la•van•de•ra *f.* laundress, washerwoman.
la•van•de•rí•a *f.* laundry.
la•var *v.* to wash; to launder; to whitewash.
la•va•ti•va *f.* enema; syringe; bother, nuisance.
la•va•to•rio *m.* washing (*act of washing*); wash (*liquid or solution for washing*); lavatory (*ceremonial act of washing*); washbowl, washstand; *Am.* washroom.
la•va•zas *f. pl.* slops, dirty water.
la•za•da *f.* bow, bowknot; *Am.* throwing of the lasso, lassoing.
la•zar[9] *v.* to rope, lasso; to noose.
la•za•ri•llo *m.* blindman's guide.
la•zo *m.* (*nudo*) bow, knot; slipknot; lasso, lariat; (*vínculo*) tie, bond; (*trampa*) snare, trap; trick.
le *obj. pron.* him; you (*formal*); to him; to her; to you (*formal*).
le•al *adj.* loyal.
le•al•tad *f.* loyalty.
le•brel *m.* greyhound.
le•bri•llo *m.* earthenware basin or tub.
lec•ción *f.* lesson; reading; **dar la –** to recite the lesson; **dar –** to teach; **tomarle a uno la –** to have someone recite his lesson.
lec•tor *m.* reader; lecturer.
lec•tu•ra *f.* reading; **libro de –** reader.
le•cha•da *f.* whitewash; *Am.* milking.
le•che *f.* milk; *Col., Ven., C.A., Andes, Riopl.* luck (*in games*).
le•che•rí•a *f.* dairy, creamery; **lechero** *adj.* milk; milch; giving milk (*applied to animals*); *Am.* lucky (*in games of chance*); *m.* milkman; **lechera** *f.* milkmaid; milk can; milk pitcher.
le•cho *m.* bed; river bed.
le•chón *m.* suckling pig; pig.
le•cho•so *adj.* milky; *m.* papaya tree; **lechosa** *f.* papaya (*tropical fruit*).
le•chu•ga *f.* lettuce.
le•chu•za *f.* screech owl, barn owl.
le•er[14] *v.* to read.
le•ga•ción *f.* legation.
le•ga•do *m.* (*donación*) legacy; legato; (*representante*) representative, ambassador.
le•gal *adj.* legal, lawful; truthful; reliable; *Col., Ven., Andes* excellent, best; *Am.* just, honest.
le•ga•li•zar[9] *v.* to legalize.
le•gar[7] *v.* to will, bequeath; to send as a delegate.
le•gen•da•rio *adj.* legendary.
le•gión *f.* legion.
le•gis•la•ción *f.* legislation.

le·gis·la·dor *m.* legislator; *adj.* legislating, legislative.

le·gis·lar *v.* to legislate.

le·gis·la·ti·vo *adj.* legislative.

le·gis·la·tu·ra *f.* legislature, legisltive assembly.

le·gí·ti·mo *adj.* legitimate; real, genuine.

le·go *adj.* lay; ignorant; *m.* layman.

le·gua *f.* league (*about 3 miles*).

le·gu·le·yo *m.* shyster.

le·gum·bre *f.* vegetable.

le·í·da *f. Am.* reading. See **lectura**.

le·ís·ta *m. & f.* one who uses the pronoun le for masculine direct object (*le conozco*).

le·ja·ní·a *f.* distance; distant place.

le·ja·no *adj.* distant; remote.

le·jí·a *f.* lye; harsh reprimand.

le·jos *adv.* far, far away; **a lo –** in the distance; *Am.* **a un –** in the distance; **de** (*or* **desde**) **–** from afar; *m.* view, perspective; background.

le·lo *adj.* silly, stupid, foolish.

le·ma *m.* motto; theme; slogan.

len·ce·rí·a *f.* dry goods; dry-goods store; linen room or closet.

len·gua *f.* tongue; language, interpreter; **– de tierra** point, neck of land.

len·gua·do *m.* flounder, sole (*a fish*).

len·gua·je *m.* language (*manner of expression*).

len·gua·raz *adj.* talkative, loose-tongued.

len·güe·ta *f.* small tongue; lengüetada *f.* lick.

len·te *m. & f.* lens; **-s** *m.* pl. eyeglasses.

len·te·ja *f.* lentil; lentil seed; **lentejuela** *f.* spangle.

len·ti·tud *f.* slowness.

len·to *adj.* slow; dull.

le·ña *f.* firewood; kindling; beating;

le·ñe·ra *f.* woodshed; woodbox.

le·ña·dor *m.* woodcutter, woodman.

le·ño *m.* log; timber; piece of firewood.

le·ón *m.* lion; **leona** *f.* lioness; **leonera** *f.* lion´s den or cage; dive, gambling joint; disorderly room.

le·on·ti·na *f. Mex., Carib., Col.* watch chain.

le·o·par·do *m.* leopard.

le·o·pol·di·na *f. Mex., Ven.* watch chain.

ler·do *adj.* dull, heavy, stupid, slow.

les *adj. prom.* to them; to you (*formal*).

le·sión *f.* wound, injury.

le·sio·nar *v.* to injure; to wound; to hurt; to damage.

les·na - lezna.

le·tar·go *m.* lethargy, stupor, drowsiness.

le·tra *f.* letter (*of the alphabet*); printing type; hand, handwriting; letter (*exact wording or meaning*); words of a song; **– abierta** letter of credit; **– de cambio** draft, bill of exchange; **– mayúscula** capital letter; **– minúscula** small letter; **al pie de la –** literally; **-s** letters, learning.

le·tra·do *adj.* learned; *m.* lawyer.

le·tre·ro *m.* notice, poster, sign; legend (*under an illustration*).

le·va *f.* levy, draft; weighing anchor, setting sail; **echar –** to draft, conscript; *Col.* **echar -s** to boast.

le·va·du·ra *f.* leaven, yeast.

le·van·ta·mien·to *m.* (*revuelta*) uprising, revolt, insurrection; (*altura*) elevation; lifting, raising; adjournment (*of a meeting*); **– de un plano** surveying.

le·van·tar *v.* to raise, lift; to set up; to erect; to rouse, stir up; to recruit; *Ch.* to break land, plow; **– el campo** to break camp; **– la mesa** to clear the table; **– la sesión** to adjourn the meeting; **– un plano** to survey, map out; **– falso testimonio** to bear false witness; **-se** to stand up, get up, rise; to rebel.

le·van·te *m.* east; east wind.

le·van·tis·co *adj.* turbulent; rebellious.

le·var *v.* to weigh (*anchor*); **– el ancla** to weigh anchor; **-se** to weigh anchor, set sail.

le·ve *adj.* light; slight, unimportant.

le·vi·ta *f.* frock coat; *m.* Levite, member of the tribe of Levi.

lé·xi·co *m.* lexicon, dictionary; vocabulary; glossary.

ley *f.* law; rule; loyalty; standard quality; **de buena –** of good quality; **plata de –** sterling silver; **-es** jurisprudence, law; system of laws.

le·yen·da *f.* legend; reading; inscription.

lez·na *f.* awl.

liar [17] *v.* to tie, bind; to roll up; to deceive; **-se** to bind oneself; to get tangled up.

li·be·lo *m.* libel.

li·bé·lu·la *f.* dragon fly.

li·be·ra·ción *f.* liberation; deliverance.

li·be·ral *adj.* liberal; generous; **liberalidad** *f.* liberality; generosity.

li·ber·tad *f.* liberty.

li·ber·ta·dor *m.* liberator, deliverer.

li·ber·tar *v.* to liberate, free, set free; **-se** to get free; to escape.

li·ber·ti·na·je *m.* license, licentiousnes, lack of moral restraint.

li·ber·ti·no *m.* libertine (*person without moral restraint*).

li·bra *f.* pound; Libra (*sign of the Zodiac*).

li·bra·dor *m.* drawer (*of a bill, draft, etc.*); deliverer, liberator; measuring scoop.

li·bran·za *f.* bill of exchange, draft.

li·brar *v.* to free, set free; to issue; to draw (*a draft*); **– guerra** to wage war; **-se** to save oneself; to escape; **-se de** to get rid of, escape from.

li·bre *adj.* free; unmarried; loose; vacant.

li·bre·a *f.* livery (*uniform*).

li·bre·rí·a *f.* bookstore.

li·bre·ro *m.* bookseller; *Am.* bookcase, bookshelves.

li·bre·ta *f.* notebook, memorandum book.

li·bro *m.* book; **– de caja** cashbook; **– mayor** ledger.

li·cen·cia *f.* license; permission; furlough, leave;

looseness; license to practice.

li·cen·cia·do *m.* licenciate (*person having a degree aproximately equivalent to a master's degree*); *Riopl.*, *Mex.*, *C.A.* lawyer.

li·cen·ciar *v.* to license; to give a license or permit; to dismiss, discharge (*from the army*); to confer the degree of **licenciado**; **-se** to get the degree of **licenciado**.

li·cen·cia·tu·ra *f.* degree of **licenciado**.

li·cen·cio·so *adj.* licentious, lewd.

li·ce·o *m.* lyceum; high school; *Col.* primary school or high school.

lí·ci·to *adj.* lawful; permissible, allowable.

li·cor *m.* liquid; liquor.

lid *f.* fight; contest.

lí·der *m.* *Am.* leader.

li·diar *v.* to fight; to combat; to contend.

lie·bre *f.* hare; coward.

lien·zo *m.* cotton or linen cloth; canvas; painting.

li·ga *f.* (*alianza*) league; alliance; (*cinta*) garter; alloy; birdlime.

li·ga·du·ra *f.* binding; tie, bond.

li·gar[7] *v.* to bind, tie, unite; to alloy (*combine metals*); **-se** to unite, combine, form an alliance.

li·ge·re·za *f.* swiftness; flippancy; frivolity.

li·ge·ro *adj.* (*leve*) light; (*rápido*) swift; nimble; flippant; adv. *Am.* quickly; **a la ligera** quickly, superficially.

li·ja *f.* sandpaper.

li·jar *v.* to sandpaper.

li·la *f.* lilac; pinkish-purple.

li·ma *f.* file; lime (*fruit*); finishing, polishing.

li·mar *v.* to file; to file down; to smooth, polish.

li·me·ño *adj.* of or from Lima, *Peru*.

li·mi·ta·ción *f.* limitation; district.

li·mi·tar *v.* to limit; to restrict; to bound.

lí·mi·te *m.* limit; boundary.

li·mo *m.* slime.

li·món *m.* lemon; lemon tree; **limonada** *f.* lemonade; **limonero** *m.* lemon tree; lemon dealer or vendor.

li·mos·na *f.* alms, charity.

li·mos·ne·ro *m.* beggar.

lim·pia·bo·tas *m.* bootblack; *Ch.* bootlicker, flatterer.

lim·pia·dien·tes *m.* toothpick.

lim·piar *v.* to clean; to wipe; to cleanse, purify; *Am.* to beat up, whip, lash.

lím·pi·do *adj.* limpid, clear.

lim·pie·za *f.* cleanliness, neatness; purify; honesty.

lim·pio *adj.* clean; neat; pure; **poner en –** to make a clean copy; *Am.* **– y soplado** absolutely broke, wiped out.

li·na·je *m.* lineage, family, race.

li·na·za *f.* linseed.

lin·ce *m.* lynx; sharp-sighted person.

lin·char *v.* to lynch.

lin·dar *v.* to border, adjoin.

lin·de *m. & f.* limit, border, boundary; landmark.

lin·de·ro *adj.* bordering upon; *m.* *Carib.*, *C.A.* landmark, boundary.

lin·de·za *f.* prettiness; exquisiteness; neatness; witty act or remark.

lin·do *adj.* pretty; **de lo –** wonderfully; very much; to the utmost.

lí·ne·a *f.* line; limit.

li·ne·al *adj.* lineal, linear.

li·no *m.* linen; flax; **linón** *m.* lawn, thin linen or cotton.

li·no·ti·pia *f.* linotype.

lí·o *m.* (*bulto*) bundle; (*enredo*) fib; mess, confusion; **armar un –** to raise a rumpus; to cause confusion; **hacerse un –** to be confused, get tangled up; **meterse en un –** to get oneself into a mess.

li·qui·da·ción liquidation; settlement (*of an account*).

li·qui·dar *v.* to liquidate; to settle (*an account*).

lí·qui·do *m.* liquid.

li·ra *f.* lyre, small harp; a type of metrical composition; lira (*Italian coin*).

lí·ri·co *adj.* lyric, lyrical; *Am.* fantastic; *m.* *Riopl.* visionary, dreamer.

li·rio *m.* lily.

li·ris·mo *m.* lyricism (*lyric quality*); *Am.* idle dream, fantasy.

li·sia·do *adj.* lame, hurt, injured.

li·so *adj.* smooth, even; flat; evident, clear; *Am.* crafty, sly; *Col.*, *Ven.*, *C.A.*, *Andes* fresh, impudent.

li·son·ja *f.* flattery.

li·son·je·ar *v.* to flatter; to fawn on; to please.

li·son·je·ro *adj.* flattering, pleasing; *m.* flatterer.

lis·ta *f.* list; strip; stripe; **pasar –** to call the roll.

lis·ta·do *adj.* striped.

lis·tar *v.* to register, enter in a list; *Riopl.*, *Mex.*, *Ven.* to stripe, streak.

lis·to *adj.* ready, prompt; clever; *Riopl.*, *Ch.* mischievous.

lis·tón *m.* ribbon, tape; strip.

li·su·ra *f.* smoothness; sincerity, frankness; *Am.* freshness, impudence; *Andes* insulting or filthy remark.

li·te·ra *f.* berth (*on a boat or train*); litter (*for carrying a person*).

li·te·ra·rio *adj.* literary.

li·te·ra·to *adj.* literary, learned; *m.* literary man, writer.

li·te·ra·tu·ra *f.* literature.

li·ti·gio *m.* litigation, lawsuit.

li·to·ral *adj.* seaboard, coastal; *m.* coast, shore.

li·tro *m.* liter (about 1.05 quarts).

li·vian·dad *f.* lightness; frivolity; lewdness.

li·via·no *adj.* (*leve*) light; slight, unimportant; (*lascivo*) frivolous, fickle; lewd; unchaste.

lí•vi•do *adj.* livid, having a dull-bluish color; pale.

lo *obj. pron.* him; you *(formal)*; it; so; *dem. pron.* – **de** that of, that affair of, that matter of; – **bueno** the good, what is good; **se – bueno que Vd. es** I know how good you are; – **que** that which, what.

lo•a•ble *adj.* laudable, worthy of praise.

lo•ar *v.* to praise.

lo•ba•ni•llo *m.* growth, tumor.

lo•bo *m.* wolf.

ló•bre•go *adj.* dark, gloomy.

lo•bre•guez *f.* darkness, gloominess.

ló•bu•lo *m.* lobe.

lo•cal *adj.* local; *m.* place, quarters; site; premises.

lo•ca•li•dad *f.* location; locality, town; place; seat *(in a theater)*.

lo•ca•li•za•ción *f.* localization, localizing.

lo•ca•li•zar[9] *v.* to localize.

lo•co *adj.* insane, mad, crazy; – **de remate** stark mad; *m.* lunatic, insane person.

lo•co•mo•tor *adj.* locomotive.

lo•co•mo•to•ra *f.* locomotive; – **diesel**, diesel locomotive.

lo•cuaz *adj.* loquacious, talkative.

lo•cu•ción *f.* phrase; diction.

lo•cu•ra *f.* madness, insanity.

lo•cu•tor *m.* radio announcer.

lo•da•zal *m.* muddy place; mire.

lo•do *m.* mud; **lodoso** *adj.* muddy, miry.

lo•ga•rit•mo *m.* logarithm.

lo•gia *f.* lodge *(secret society)*.

ló•gi•ca *f.* logic; reasoning.

ló•gi•co *adj.* logical.

lo•grar *v.* to gain, obtain, accomplish; – (+ *inf.*) to succeed in; **-se** to succeed; to turn out well.

lo•gre•ro *m.* usurer; profiteer.

lo•gro *m.* profit, gain; usury; attainment; realization.

lo•ís•ta *m. & f.* one who uses the pronoun *lo* for the masculine direct object *(lo conozco)*.

lo•ma *f.* small hill; **lomerío** *m. Am.* group of hills.

lom•briz *f.* earthworm.

lo•mo *m.* back *(of an animal, book, knife, etc.)*; loin; ridge between two furrows; *Mex., Ven.* **hacer -** to bear with patience, resing oneself.

lo•na *f.* canvas.

lon•che *m. Col., Ven., Mex.* lunch; **lonchería** *f. Col., Ven., Mex.* lunchroom.

lon•ga•ni•za *f.* pork sausage.

lon•ge•vi•dad *f.* longevity, long life; span of life, length of life.

lon•gi•tud *f.* longitude; length.

lon•gi•tu•di•nal *adj.* longitudinal, lengthwise; **-men•te** adv. longitudinally, lengthwise.

lon•ja *f.* (*mercado*) exchange; market; (*carne*) slice of meat; (*correa*) leather strap; *Riopl.* raw hide.

lon•ta•nan•za *f.* background; **en-** in the distance, in the background.

lo•ro *m.* parrot.

los *def. art. m. pl.* the; *obj. pron.* them; – **que** *rel. pron.* those which; which.

lo•sa *f.* flagstone; slab; gravestone.

lo•te *m.* lot, share, part; *Am.* remnant lot; *Col.* swallow of liquor; *Am.* blockhead, dunce.

lo•te•ar *v. Am.* to subdivide into lots; *Am.* to divide into portions.

lo•te•rí•a *f.* lottery; raffle.

lo•za *f.* fine earthenware; crockery; – **fina** chinaware.

lo•za•ní•a *f.* luxuriance *(rich foliage or growth)*; vigor.

lo•za•no *adj.* luxuriant; exuberant, vigorous, lusty.

lu•bri•car[6] *v.* to lubricate, or grease.

lu•ce•ro *m.* morning star; any bright star; star on the forehead of certain animals; splendor, brightness.

lú•ci•do *adj.* lucid, clear; shining, bright.

lu•cien•te *adj.* shining, bright.

lu•ciér•na•ga *f.* firefly; glowworm.

lu•ci•mien•to *m.* splendor; brilliance; success.

lu•cir[13] *v. irr.* (*brillar*) to shine; to illuminate; to brighten; (*superar*) to excel; (*alardear*) to show off; **-se** to shine, be brilliant; to show off; to be successful.

lu•cra•ti•vo *adj.* lucrative, profitable.

lu•cro *m.* profit, gain.

luc•tuo•so *adj.* sad, mournful, dismal.

lu•cha *f.* fight; struggle; dispute; wrestling match.

lu•cha•dor *m.* fighter; wrestler.

lu•char *v.* to fight; to wrestle; to struggle; to dispute.

lue•go *adv.* soon, presently; afterwards, then, next; **desde –** immediately, at once; naturally; – **de** after; – **que** as soon as; **hasta –** good-bye, so long; – – right away.

luen•go *adj.* long; **-s años** many years.

lu•gar *m.* (*sitio*) place; site; town; space; (*empleo*) position, employment; (*ocasión*) time, occasion, opportunity; **dar – a** to give cause or occasion for; **hacer** (*or* **dar**) **–** to make room; **en – de** instead of.

lú•gu•bre *adj.* mournful, gloomy.

lu•jo *m.* luxury, extravagance.

lu•jo•so *adj.* luxurious; elegant; showy.

lu•ju•ria *f.* lust, lewdness, sensuality.

lu•ju•rio•so *adj.* lustful, lewd, sensual.

lum•bre *f.* fire; brightness.

lu•mi•no•so *adj.* luminous, bright, shining.

lu•na *f.* moon; mirror, glass for mirrors.

lu•nar *adj.* lunar; *m.* mole; blemish, spot.

lu•ná•ti•co *adj. & m.* lunatic.

lu•nes *m.* Monday; *Ch.* **hacer San Lunes** to lay off on Monday.

lun•far•do *m.* social dialect of the Buenos Aires underworld.

lus•tre *m.* luster, shine; glory.

lus•tro•so *adj.* lustrous, glossy, shining.

lu•to *m.* mourning; sorrow, grief.

luz *f.* light; clarity; hint, guidance; **dar a** – to give birth; to publish; **entre dos luces** at twilight.

LL

lla·ga *f.* wound; ulcer, sore.
lla·ma *f.* flame; llama (*a South American beast of burden*).
lla·ma·da *f.* call; beckon, sign; knock; reference mark (*as an asterisk*).
lla·ma·dor *m.* knocker (*of a door*); caller.
lla·ma·mien·to *m.* call, calling; calling together; appeal.
lla·mar *v.* to call; to summon; to name; to invoke; **- a la puerta** to knock at the door; **-se** to be called, named; *Am.* to break one's word or promise.
lla·ma·ra·da *f.* flash; sudden flame or blaze; sudden flush, blush.
lla·ma·ti·vo *adj.* showy, loud, gaudy, flashy; thirst-exciting.
lla·me·an·te *adj.* flaming.
lla·na *f.* mason's trowel.
lla·ne·ro *m. Ven., Col.* plainsman.
lla·ne·za *f.* simplicity; frankness; sincerity; plainness.
lla·no *adj.* plain, simple; even, smooth, level; frank; *m.* plain, flat ground.
llan·ta *f.* Spain rim of a wheel; *Am.* tire; tire casing; *Peru* large sunshade (*used in Peruvian markets*).
llan·to *m.* crying; weeping; tears.
lla·nu·ra *f.* extensive plain; prairie; evenness, flatness.
lla·pa *f. Andes, Ríopl.* a small gift from the vendor to the purchaser; also **yapa, ñapa**.
lla·ve *f.* key; faucet; clef; **- de tuercas** wrench; **- inglesa** monkey wrench; **- maestra** master key.
lla·ve·ra *f. Am.* housekeeper.
lla·ve·ro *m.* key ring; key maker; keeper of the keys.
lla·vín *m.* small key.
lle·ga·da *f.* arrival.
lle·gar *v.* to arrive; to reach; to amount; **- a ser**, to get or come to be; **- a las manos** to come to blows; **-se** to approach, get near.
lle·nar *v.* to fill; to stuff; **-se** to fill up; to overeat; **-se de** to get filled with; to get covered with, spattered with.
lle·no *adj.* full; *m.* fullness, completeness; **de** – totally, completely; **un – completo** a full house (*said of a theater*).
lle·nu·ra *f.* fullness; abundance.
lle·va·de·ro *adj.* bearable, tolerable.
lle·var *v.* (*transportar*) to carry; to bear; to transport; to wear; (*conducir*) to take; to lead; (*cobrar*) to charge; to ask a certain price; to keep (*accounts*); **- ventaja** to be ahead, have the advantage; **- un año**

a to be one year older than; **– un mes aquí**, to have been here one month; **– un castigo**, to suffer punishment; **-se** to carry away; **-se bien con** to get along with.
llo·rar *v.* to cry, weep.
llo·ri·que·ar *v.* to whimper, whine, weep.
llo·ri·que·o *m.* whimper, whining.
llo·ro *m.* weeping.
llo·rón *adj.* weeping; **sauce** – weeping willow; *m.* weeper, crybaby, whiner.
llo·ro·na *f.* weeping woman; **-s** *Am.* large spurs.
llo·ro·so *adj.* tearful; weeping.
llo·ve·di·zo *adj.* rain (*used as adj.*); **agua llovediza** rain water.
llo·ver [2] *v. irr.* to rain, shower.
llo·viz·na *f.* drizzle.
llo·viz·nar *v.* to drizzle, sprinkle.
llu·via *f.* rain; shower.
llu·vio·so *adj.* rainy.

M

ma·ca·na *f. Am.* club, cudgel, stick; *Am.* lie, absurdity, nonsense.
ma·ca·nu·do *adj. Ríopl.* tremendous! great!.
ma·ca·rrón *m.* macaroon; **-es** macaroni.
ma·ce·ta *f.* (*tiesto*) flowerpot; (*martillo*) small mallet; stonecutter's hammer; handle of tools; *Am.* head; *adj. Am.* slow.
ma·ci·len·to *adj.* thin, emaciated; pale.
ma·ci·zo *adj.* solid, firm; massive; *m.* massiveness; firmness; thicket; clump.
ma·cha·car [6] *v.* to pound, crush; to insist, harp on.
ma·cha·cón *adj.* persistent; tenacious.
ma·che·te *m.* machete, large heavy knife; **machetazo** *m.* large machete; blow with a machete.
ma·chis·mo *m.* the quality of being a male, proven daring.
ma·cho *m.* male; he-mule; hook (*of a hook and eye*); abutment; pillar; stupid fellow; sledgehammer; C.R. a blond; North American; *Am.* **pararle a uno el** – to halt or repress a person; *adj.* masculine, male; strong.
ma·chu·car [6] *v.* to pound, beat, bruise; *Am.* to crush; *Am.* to break (a horse).
ma·chu·cón *m.* smach; bruise.
ma·de·ja *f.* skein; mass of hair; limp, listless person.
ma·de·ra *f.* wood; timber; lumber; **maderero** *m.* lumberman, lumber dealer.
ma·de·ra·je *m.* timber, lumber; timber work; woodwork.
ma·de·ra·men *m.* timber; timber work; woodwork.
ma·de·ro *m.* beam; plank; timber, piece of lumber;

blockhead, dunce.

ma·dras·tra *f.* stepmother.

ma·dre *f.* mother; womb; root, origin; river bed; **salir-se de** – to overflow (*said a rivers*).

ma·dre·pe·ña *f. Am.* moss.

ma·dre·per·la *f.* mother-of-pearl.

ma·dre·sel·va *f.* honeysuckle.

ma·dri·gue·ra *f.* burrow; den, lair.

ma·dri·le·ño *adj.* Madrilenian, from or pertaining to Madrid; *m.* Madrilenian.

ma·dri·na *f.* (*patrocinadora*) godmother; bridesmaid; sponsor; (*correa*) strap for yoking two horses; (*ganado*) leading mare; prop: *Am.* small herd of tame cattle (*used for leading wil cattle*).

ma·dru·ga·da *f.* dawn; early morning; **de** – at daybreak.

ma·dru·ga·dor *m.* early riser.

ma·dru·gar[7] *v.* to rise early; to be ahead of others; to "get the jump" on someone.

ma·du·rar *v.* to mature; to ripen.

ma·du·rez *f.* maturity; ripeness.

ma·du·ro *adj.* ripe; mature; prudent, wise; *Am.* bruised, sore.

ma·es·trí·a *f.* mastery; great skill.

ma·es·tro *m.* master, teacher; chief craftsman; *adj.* master; masterly, skillful; **llave maestra** master key; **obra maestra** masterpiece.

ma·gia *f.* magic; charm.

má·gi·co *adj.* magic; *m.* magician.

ma·gín *m.* imagination, fancy.

ma·gis·te·rio *m.* teaching profession.

ma·gis·tra·do *m.* magistrate, judge.

ma·gis·tral *adj.* masterly; masterful; authoritative.

mag·ná·ni·mo *adj.* magnanimous, noble, generous.

mag·né·ti·co *adj.* magnetic; attractive.

mag·ne·to·fó·ni·co *adj.* recording (*tape or wire*).

mag·ne·tó·fo·no *m.* tape recorder.

mag·ni·fi·cen·cia *f.* magnificence, splendor.

mag·ní·fi·co *adj.* magnificent, splendid.

mag·ni·tud *f.* magnitude, greatness.

ma·go *m.* magician, wizard; **los tres Reyes Magos** the Three Wise Men.

ma·gra *f.* slice of ham.

ma·gro *adj.* lean.

ma·guey *m.* maguey, century plant.

ma·gu·llar *v.* to bruise; to maul; to mangle; *Riopl., Ch., Col., Andes, P.R.* to crumple.

ma·ho·me·ta·no *adj. & m.* Mohammedan.

ma·íz *m.* corn; **maizal** *m.* cornfield.

ma·ja·da *f.* sheepfold; dung, manure; *Riopl., Ch.* flock of sheep or goats.

ma·ja·de·rí·a *f.* foolishness, nonsense.

ma·ja·de·ro *adj.* foolish; bothersome.

ma·jar *v.* to pound; to crush; to bruise; to crumple; to mash; to annoy, bother.

ma·jes·tad *f.* majesty; dignity.

ma·jes·tuo·so *adj.* majestic, stately.

ma·jo *adj.* gaudy, showy; gaily attired; pretty; *m.* dandy; **maja** *f.* belle.

mal *m.* evil; illness; harm; wrong. *See* **malo.**

ma·la·ba·ris·ta *m. & f.* juggler; *Ch.* sly thief.

ma·la·ca·te *m.* hoist, hoisting machine; winch; *Am.* spindle (*for cotton*); *Am.* **parecer uno un** – to be constantly on the go, be in constant motion.

ma·la·gue·ña *adj.* song and dance of Málaga.

ma·lan·dan·za *f.* misfortune.

ma·la·ven·tu·ra *f.* misfortune, disaster.

ma·la·zo *adj.* perverse, evil, wicked; vicious.

mal·ba·ra·tar *v.* to undersell, sell at a loss; to squander.

mal·con·ten·to *adj.* discontented; *m.* malcontent, troublemaker.

mal·cria·do *adj.* ill-bred, rude.

mal·dad *f.* badness, evil, wickedness

mal·de·cir[27,52] *v. irr.* to curse; to damn.

mal·di·ción *f.* curse.

mal·dis·pues·to *adj.* unwilling, not inclined.

mal·di·to *p.p. of* **maldecir** & *adj.* cursed; wicked; dammed; *Am.* tricky; *Am.* bold, boastful.

ma·le·an·te *m.* crook, rogue, rascal, villain.

ma·le·cón *m.* mole; dike.

ma·le·di·cen·cia *f.* slander.

ma·le·fi·cio *m.* spell, charm, witchery.

ma·lé·fi·co *adj.* evil, harmful.

ma·les·tar *m.* indisposition; slight illness; discomfort.

ma·le·ta *f.* travelling bag; suitcase; *Col., Ven., C.A.* bundle of clothes; *Col.* hump (*on the back*); *Am.* saddlebag; *C.A.* rogue, rascal; *Am.* lazy fellow.

ma·le·tín *m.* small valise, satchel.

ma·le·vo *adj. Bol., Ríopl.* bad, wicked.

ma·lé·vo·lo *adj.* bad, evil, wicked.

ma·le·za *f.* underbrush; thicket; weeds.

mal·gas·tar *v.* to squander, waste.

mal·he·chor *m.* malefactor, evildoer, criminal.

mal·ho·ra *f. Ríopl., C.A., Ven.* trouble, misfortune.

mal·hu·mo·ra·do *adj.* ill-humored.

ma·li·cia *f.* malice; wickedness; shrewdness; suspicion; *Ch.* bit of brandy or cognac added to another drink.

ma·li·ciar *v.* to suspect.

ma·li·cio·so *adj.* malicious; wicked; shrewd; suspicious.

ma·lig·no *adj.* malign, malignant; pernicious, harmful.

mal·man·da·do *adj.* disobedient; stubborn.

mal(o) *adj.* bad, evil; wicked; ill; dtfficult; *Am.* **a la mala** treacherously; *Ríopl.* **de malas** by force; **estar de malas** to be out of luck; **por la mala** unwillingly, by force; **venir de malas** to come with evil intentions; **mal** *adv.* badly; poorly; wrongly.

ma·lo·grar *v.* to waste, lose; **-se** to turn out badly; to fail.

ma·lón *m.* mean trick; *Riopl.* surprise Indian raid; *Ven.* tin-pan serenade, boisterous surprise party.

mal·pa·gar[7] *v.* to underpay, pay poorly.

mal·par·to *m.* miscarriage, abortion.

mal·que·ren·cia *f.* aversion, dislike, ill will.

mal·sa·no *adj.* unhealthy; sickly.

mal·ta *f.* malt.

mal·tra·tar *v.* to treat badly; to misuse, abuse.

mal·tra·to *m.* mistreatment, abuse.

mal·tre·cho *adj.* battered, bruised, injured.

mal·va·do *adj.* wicked; malicious.

mal·ver·sa·ción *f.* graft, corruption, misuse of public funds.

mal·ver·sar *v.* to misuse (*funds in one's trust*); to embezzle.

ma·lla *f.* mesh; coat of mail; *Ch.* species of potato; **hacer -** to knit.

ma·má *f.* mamma.

ma·ma·da *f.* suck, sucking.

ma·mar *v.* to suckle; to suck; to gorge; **-se** *Riopl.*, *C.A.* to get drunk; *Col.* to go back on one's promise; *Am.* to fold up, crack up; **-se a uno** to get the best of someone, deceive someone; *Col.*, *C.A.* to kill someone.

ma·mí·fero *m.* mammal; *adj.* mammalian, of mammals.

ma·món *adj.* suckling; *m.* suckling (*very young animal or child*); shoot, sucker (*of a tree*); *Riopl.* cherimoya (*tree and fruit*); *Am.* papaya (*tree and fruit*); *Mex.* a kind of cake; *C.A.* public employee.

mam·pa·ra *f.* screen.

mam·pos·te·ría *f.* masonry, stone masonry.

ma·na·da *f.* herd; drove; pack; flock.

ma·nan·tial *m.* spring; source, origin.

ma·nar *v.* to spring, flow (*from*); to abound.

ma·na·za *f.* large hand.

ma·na·zo *m.* *Riopl.* slap. *See* **manotazo.**

man·ca·rrón *m.* one-armed or onehanded man; cripple; old nag; *Riopl.*, *Andes* crude, clumsy fellow; *Am.* disabled workman; *Am.* dike, small dam.

man·ce·bo *m.* youth, young man; bachelor.

man·ce·ra *f.* handle of a plough.

man·ci·lla *f.* stain, spot; dishonor.

man·co *adj.* one-armed; one-handed maimed; lame (*referring to an arm or the front leg of an animal*); faulty, detective; *m.* *Ch.* nag.

man·cuer·na *f.* pair of animals tied together; *Mex.*, *C.A. f. pl.* cuff links.

man·cha *f.* spot, stain, blemish; *Am.* cloud, swarm; *Ven.*, *Cuba*, *Col.* roving herd of cattle.

man·char *v.* to stain, soil, spot; to tarnish.

man·che·go *adj.* of or belonging to La Mancha (*region of Spain*); *m.* inhabitant of La Mancha.

man·chón *m.* large stain; large patch.

man·da·dero *m.* messenger, errand boy.

man·da·do *m.* (*orden*) command, order; (*recado*) errand; *p.p.* of **mandar; bien -** well-behaved; **mal -** illbehaved.

man·da·mien·to *m.* command, order; writ; commandment.

man·dar *v.* (*pedir*) to command, order; rule; (*enviar*) to send; to bequeath, will; *Col.*, *Ven.* to throw, hurl; **- hacer** to have made, order; *Col.*, *Ven.*, *Mex.*, *Carib.*, *Andes* **- una bofetada** to give a slap; *Col.*, *Ven.*, *Mex.*, *Carib.*, *Andes* **- una pedrada** to throw a stone; **-se** *Am.* to be impudent; **-se mudar** *Riopl.*,*Carib.* to go away.

man·da·ta·rio *m.* attorney, representative; *Am.* magistrate, chief.

man·da·to *m.* mandate; order, command; term of office.

man·dí·bu·la *f.* jaw, jawbone.

man·do *m.* command, authority, power.

man·dón *adj.* bossy, dormineering; *m.* bossy person; *Am.* boss or foreman of a mine; *Am.* race starter.

ma·nea·dor *m.* *Riopl.*, *Ven.*, *Col.* hobble, leather lasso (*for the legs of an animal*), *Am.* whip; *Ven.*, *Andes* halter.

ma·ne·ar *v.* to hobble, lasso, tie the legs of (*an animal*); **-se** *Col.*, *Ven.* to get tangled up.

ma·ne·ci·lla *f.* small hand; hand of a watch or clock.

ma·ne·ja·ble *adj.* manageable.

ma·ne·jar *v.* to manage, handle; to drive (*a car*); **-se** to move about, get around (*after an illness or accident*); *Carib.*, *Ven.* to behave oneself.

ma·ne·jo *m.* handling; management; trick, intrigue.

ma·ne·ra *f.* manner, way, mode; side opening in a skirt; front opening in breeches; **-s** customs; manners, behavior; **a – de** (or **a la – de**) like, in the style of; **de – que** so that; **sobre –** exceedingly; extremely.

man·ga *f.* sleeve; bag; hose (*for watering*); body of troops; *Am.* multitude, herd, swarm; *Am.* cattle chute (*narrow passageway*); *Am.* corral; **– de agua** waterspout, whirlwind over the ocean; *Am.* **– de hulo** raincape; **por anqas o por -s** by hook or crook, in one way or another.

man·ga·na *f.* lariat, lasso.

man·ga·ne·so *m.* manganese.

man·go *m.* handle; *Am.* mango (*tropical tree and its fruit*).

man·gue·ra *f.* hose (*for water*); waterspout; *Riopl.* large corral (*for livestock.*).

man·gui·to *m.* muff; knitted half-sleeve (*worn on the forearm*); oversleeve.

ma·ní *m.* *Carib.*, *C.A.*, *Ch.*, *Andes*, *Ven.*, *Col.* peanut; **manicero** *m.* *Carib.*, *C.A.*, *Ch.*, *Andes*, *Ven.*, *Col.* peanut vendor.

ma·ní·a *f.* mania, frenzy; craze, whim.

ma·nia·tar *v.* to tie the hands; to handcuff; to hobble (*an animal*).

ma·niá·ti·co *m.* crank, queer fellow; *adj.* cranky,

queer, odd.

ma·ni·co·mio *m.* insane asylum.

ma·ni·cu·ra *f.* manicure; manicurist.

ma·ni·cu·rar *v.* to manicure.

ma·ni·do *adj.* rotting; *Riopl., Carib., Col., Andes* trite, commonplace.

ma·ni·fes·ta·ción *f.* manifestation; demonstration.

ma·ni·fes·tar[1] *v. irr.* to manifest; to show.

ma·ni·fies·to *adj.* manifest, clear, plain; *m.* manifesto, public declaration; customhouse manifest.

ma·ni·gua *f. Col., Riopl., Cuba, P.R.* Cuban jungle or thicket; *Carib.* **coger** – to get feverish; *Riopl., Carib.* **irse a la** – to rise up in rebellion.

ma·ni·ja *f.* handle; crank; fetter.

ma·ni·lla *f.* small hand; bracelet; **-s de hierro**handcuffs.

ma·nio·bra *f.* maneuver; operation.

ma·nio·brar *v.* to maneuver.

ma·ni·pu·la·ción *f.* manipulation.

ma·ni·pu·lar *v.* to manipulate, handle.

ma·ni·quí *m.* manikin, model, dummy, figure of a person; puppet.

ma·ni·ve·la *f.* crank.

man·jar *m.* dish, food; choice bit of food.

ma·no *f.* (*del cuerpo*) hand; forefoot; (*reloj*) clock hand; (*acabado*) coat of paint or varnish; quire (25 *sheets*) of paper; *Am.* adventure, mishap; *Am.* handful; **– de obra** workmanship; labor; **a** – at hand; by hand; *Am.* **estamos a** – we are even, we are quits; *Am.* **doblar las -s** to give up; **ser** – to be first (*in a game*) to lead (*in a game*); **venir a las -s** to come to blows.

ma·no·jo *m.* handful; bunch.

ma·no·pla *f.* gauntlet; heavy glove; huge hand.

ma·no·se·ar *v.* to handle, touch, feel with the hand; *Am.* to fondle, pet, caress.

ma·no·ta·da *f.* slap, blow; sweep fo the hand; *Col.* handful, fistful; **manotazo** *m.* slap.

ma·no·te·ar *v.* to gesticulate; to strike with the hands; *Riopl.* to embezzle, steal; *Am.* to snatch away (*what is given*).

man·sal·va: a – without danger or rish; treacherously; **matar a** – to kill without warning or without giving a person a chance to defend himself.

man·se·dumbre *f.* meekness; gentleness.

man·sión *f.* sojourn, stay; abode, dwelling.

man·so *adj.* meek; mild, gentle; tame; *Riopl. Ch.* cultivated (*plant*), civilized (*Indian*); *m.* leading sheep, goat, or ox.

man·ta *f.* blanket; large shawl; tossing in a blanket; *Mex., C.A., Ven., Riopl.* coarse cotton cloth; *Am.* poncho; *Am.* – **mojada** dull person, dunce; **darle a uno una** – to toss someone in a blanket.

man·te·ar *v.* to toss (*someone*) in a blanket.

man·te·ca *f.* fat; lard; butter; *Am.* – **de cacao** cocoa butter; *Am.* – **de coco** coconut oil; **mantequera** *f.*

churn; butter dish; woman who makes or sells butter.

man·te·ca·do *m.* ice cream.

man·tel *m.* tablecloth; altar cloth; *C.A., Mex.* **estar de - es largos** to dine in style.

man·te·ner[45] *v. ir.* to maintain; to support; to sustain; to defend; **-se** to continue, remain; to support oneself; **-se firme** to remain firm; **-se quieto** to stay or keep quiet.

man·te·ni·mien·to *m.* maintenance, support; sustenance; livelihood.

man·te·qui·lla *f.* butter; **mantequillería** *f. Am.* creamery, dairy (for *making butter*).

man·ti·lla *f.* mantilla (*Spanish veil or scarf for the head*); saddlecloth.

man·to *m.* mantle, cloak; cape; large mantilla; mantel, mantelpiece.

man·tón *m.* large shawl; – **de Manila** embroidered silk shawl.

ma·nua·ble *adj.* handy, easy to handle.

ma·nual *adj.* manual; handy; *m.* manual, handbood.

ma·nu·brio *m.* crank; handle.

ma·nu·fac·tu·rar *v.* to manufacture.

ma·nu·fac·tu·re·ro *adj.* manufacturing; *m.* manufacturer.

ma·nus·cri·to *adj.* written by hand; *m.* manuscript.

ma·nu·ten·ción *f.* maintenance; support; conservation.

man·za·na *f.* apple; block of houses; *Riopl., Ch., Col., Ven., C.A.* Adam's apple; **manzano** *m.* apple tree.

ma·ña *f.* skill, knack; cunning; **malas -s** bad tricks or habits.

ma·ña·na *f.* morning; *Riopl.,* **media** – mid-morning snack; *adv.* tomorrow, in the near future; **pasado** – day after tomorrow; **muy de** – very early in the morning; *m.* morrow; **mañanitas** *f. pl. Mex., C.A.* popular song sung early in the morning to celebrate a birthday, saint's day, etc.

ma·ña·ne·ro *m.* early riser; *adj.* early rising; **mañanista** *m. & f. Am.* procrastinator, one who puts things off until tomorrow.

ma·ñe·ro *adj.* astute, artful, clever; *Am.* tricky; *Ch.* shy (*animal*); *Riopl.* indolent, lazy (*child*).

ma·ño·so *adj.* skillful; clever; sly; tricky; deceitful; *Am.* slow, lazy; *Am.* greedy, gluttonous (*child*).

ma·pa *m.* map, chart.

ma·pa·che *m. Ch.* raccoon.

ma·pu·ri·te, ma·pu·ri·to *m. Col., Ven.* **zorrino, zorrillo.**

má·qui·na *f.* machine; engine; – machine; – **de escribir** typ

ma·qui·na·ción *f.* machina plot, sheme.

ma·qui·na·dor *m.* sheme

ma·qui·nal *adj.* mechanica ·mechanically, automatic manner.

ma·qui·nar v. to plot, scheme.

ma·qui·na·ria f. machinery; mechanism; mechanics.

ma·qui·nis·ta m. engineer, locomotive engineer; machinist; mechanic.

mar m. & f. sea; **– alta** rough sea; **– llena** high tide (see **pleamar**); **– de fondo** swell; **a –es** abundantly; **baja – low tide**; **en alta –** on the high seas; **la – de cosas** a lot of things.

ma·ra·ca f. Carib., Col., Ven. maraca (rhythm instrument made of a dried gourd filled with seeds or pebbles).

ma·ra·ña f. tangle; snarl; thicket, maze; plot, intrigue.

ma·ra·ve·dí m. maravedi (an old Spanish coin).

ma·ra·vi·lla f. wonder, marvel; marigold; **a las mil – s** wonderfully, perfectly.

ma·ra·vi·llar v. to astonish, dazzle; **-se** to wonder, marvel.

ma·ra·vi·llo·so adj. marvellous, wonderful.

mar·be·te m. label, stamp; baggage tag or check.

mar·ca f. marck, stamp; sign; brand, make; gauge, rule; march, frontier province; **– de fábrica** trademark; **de –** of excellent quality.

mar·car[6] v. to mark, stamp, brand; to note, observe.

mar·cial adj. martial, warlike; frank, abrupt.

mar·co m. frame; marck (German coin); mark (unit of weight, equal to 8 ounces).

mar·cha f. march; course, progress; speed; gait; running, functioning; movement of a watch.

mar·cha·mo m. customhouse mark; Am. tax on each slaughtered animal.

mar·chan·te m. (vendedor) merchant, dealer; (cliente) customer, regular client.

mar·char v. to march, mark step; to walk; to parade; to run (said of machinery); **-se** to go away.

mar·chi·tar v. to wither; **-se** to wither; to fade; to shrivel up.

mar·chi·to adj. withered; faded; shriveled up.

ma·re·a f. tide; Ríopl., Ch. sea fog.

ma·re·a·do adj. seasick; dizzy.

ma·re·ar v. (navegar) to navigate, sail; (fastidiar) to annoy, upset (a person); to make dizzy, **-se** to get seasick, nauseated; dizzy.

ma·re·o m. seasickness; nausea; vexation, annoyance.

mar·fil m. ivory; Ven. fine-toothed comb.

mar·ga·ri·ta f. marguerite, daisy; pearl.

mar·gen m. & f. margin, border; river bank; **dar - a** to give an occasion to.

ma·ri·cón m. sissy, effeminate; m. sissy.

ma·ri·do m. husband.

ma·rim·ba f. marimba.

ma·ri·na f. (costa) seacoast, shore; (fuerza naval) fleet; navy; (arte u oficio) seascape; seamanship; **– de guerra** navy; **– mercante** merchant marine.

ma·ri·ne·ro m. mariner, seaman, sailor.

ma·ri·no adj. marine, m. mariner, seaman, sailor.

ma·ri·po·sa f. butterfly; moth; Am. blindman's buff (a game).

ma·ris·cal m. marshal; blacksmith; **– de campo** field marshal.

ma·ris·co m. shellfish.

ma·rí·ti·mo adj. maritime, marine.

mar·mi·ta f. kettle, boiler, teakettle.

már·mol m. marble.

mar·mó·re·o adj. marble, of marble, like marble.

ma·ro·ma f. rope; Am. somersault; Am. acrobatic performance; Col. sudden change of political views; **andar en la –** to walk the tightrope; **maromero** m Carib. acrobat.

mar·qués m. marquis.

mar·que·sa f. marquise; Ch. couch.

ma·rra·no m. pig, hog; filthy person.

ma·rra·zo m. Am. bayonet, dagger.

ma·rrón adj. maroon.

ma·rro·quí adj. from Morocco; pl. **marroquíes**.

ma·rru·lle·ro adj. sly, wily.

mar·tes m. Tuesday; **– de carnestolendas** Shrove Tuesday (Tuesday before Lent).

mar·ti·llar v. to hammer, pound.

mar·ti·llo m. hammer.

mar·ti·ne·te m. pile driver; drop hammer; hammer of a piano.

már·tir m. & f. martyr.

mar·ti·rio m. martyrdom; torture, torment.

mar·ti·ri·zar[9] v. to martyr; to torture, torment.

mar·zo m. March.

mas conj. but.

más adj. more; most; adv. more; most; plus; **- bien** rather; **– de** more than, over; **– que** more than; **no . . . – que** only; **a – de** in addition to; **a lo –** at the most; **está de –** it is superfluous, unnecessary; Am. **no – only**; Am. **no quiero – nada** (instead of **no quiero nada –**) I don't want anything more.

ma·sa f. (volumen) mass; volume; (pueblo) crowd, the masses; (pasta) dough, paste; mortar; **– coral** glee club, choral society; **agarrarle a uno con las manos en la –** to catch someone in the act; **masilla** f. putty.

ma·sa·je m. massage.

mas·ca·da f. chewing; Am. mouthful; Ríopl. chew or quid of tobacco; Am. reprimand, scolding; Mex. silk handkerchief, scarf.

mar·car[6] v. to chew.

más·ca·ra f. mask; **-s** masquerade; m. & f. masquerader; **mascarada** f. masquerade.

mas·cu·li·no adj. masculine.

mas·cu·llar v. to mumble; to munch.

ma·són m. mason, freemason; **masonería** f. masonry, freemasonry.

mas·ti·car[6] v. to chew.

más·til m. mast; post.

mas·tín m. mastiff.

mas•tuer•zo *m.* (*flor*) nasturtium; (*tonto*) simkpleton, fool.

ma•ta *f.* shrub, plant, bush; grove; clump of trees; *Ven.*, *Col.* thicket, jungle; **– de pelo** head of hair.

ma•ta•de•ro *m.* slaughterhouse; hard work.

ma•ta•dor *m.* killer, murderer; bullfighter who kills the bull.

ma•tan•za *f.* massacre, butchery; slaughter of livestock;*Mex.* slaughterhouse.

ma•tar *v.* to kill; to murder; **-se** to commit suicide, to overwork; **-se con alguien** to fight with somebody.

ma•ta•sa•nos *m.* quack, quack doctor.

ma•te *m.* checkmate (*winning move in chess*); *Ríopl.*, *Ch.* Paraguayan tea (*used also in Argentina and Uruguay*); *Andes, Col.* teapot (*for* **mate**), any small pot; *Am.* bald head; *adj.* unpolished, dull (*surface*).

ma•te•ar *v.* to plant seeds or shoots; to hunt among the bushes; *Ríopl., Ch.* to drink **mate**; *Am.* to checkmate (*make the winning move in chess*).

ma•te•má•ti•cas *f.* pl. mathematics.

ma•te•má•ti•co *adj.* mathematical; *m.* mathematician.

ma•te•ria *f.* matter; material; subject; pus: **– prima** (*or* **primera –**) raw material.

ma•te•rial *adj.* material; rude, coarse; *m.* ingredient; material; equipment; *Ven.* **de –** made of adobe.

ma•ter•nal *adj.* maternal.

ma•ter•ni•dad *f.* maternity, motherhood.

ma•ter•no *adj.* maternal.

ma•ti•nal *adj.* morning, of the morning.

ma•ti•né *m. Am.* matinée.

ma•tiz *m.* tint, shade, color, hue; shading.

ma•ti•zar⁹ *v.* to blend (*colors*); to tint; to shade, tone down.

ma•tón *m.* bully.

ma•to•rral *m.* thicket.

ma•to•so *adj.* bushy; weedy, full of weeds.

ma•tre•ro *adj.* astute, shrewd; cunning, sly; *m. Col.* trickster, swindler; *Ríop.* bandit, outlaw, cattle thief.

ma•trí•cu•la *f.* register, list; matriculation, registration; certificate of registration.

ma•tri•cu•lar *v.* to matriculate, enroll, register.

ma•tri•mo•nio *m.* matrimony, marriage; married couple.

ma•triz *f.* matrix, mold, form; womb; screw nut; *adj.* main, principal, first; **casa –** main office (*of a company*).

ma•tun•go *m. Ríopl.* nag, old worn-out horse.

ma•tu•ti•no *adj.* morning, of the morning.

mau•llar *v.* to mew.

mau•lli•do, ma•ú•llo *m.* mew.

má•xi•ma *f.* maxim, rule; proverb.

má•xi•me *adj.* principally, especially.

má•xi•mo *adj. & m.* maximûm.

ma•ya *f.* daisy; May queen; *m. & f.* Maya, Mayan Indian; *m.* Mayan language.

ma•yo *m.* May; Maypole; *Am.* Mayo Indian (*from Sonora, Mexico*); *Am.* language of the Mayo Indian.

ma•yo•ne•sa *f.* mayonnaise; dish served with mayonnaise.

ma•yor *adj.* greater; larger; older; greatest; largest; oldest; main; major; high (*altar, mass*); *m.* major; chief; **-es** elders; ancestors; **– de edad** of age; **por –** (*or* **al por –**) wholesale;*f.* major premise (*of a syllogism*).

ma•yo•ral *m.* head shepherd; stagecoach driver; foreman; overseer, boss.

ma•yo•raz•go *m.* primogeniture (*right of inheritance by the first-born*); firstborn son and heir; family estate left to the eldest son.

ma•yor•do•mo *m.* majordomo, steward, butler; manager of an estate.

ma•yo•re•ar *v. Am.* to wholesale, sell at wholesale.

ma•yo•re•o *m. Am.* wholesale.

ma•yo•rí•a *f.* majority.

ma•yo•ris•ta *m. Am.* wholesale dealer.

ma•za *f.* mace (*wapon, staff*); **– química** chemical mace.

maz•mo•rra *f.* dungeon.

ma•zo *m.* mallet; sledgehammer; bunch, handful.

ma•zor•ca *f.* ear of corn; *Ríopl.* tyrannical government; *Am.* cruel torture (*imposed by tyrants*).

me *obj. pron.* me; to me; for me; myself.

me•cá•ni•co *adj.* mechanical; *m.* mechanic, machinist, repairman; driver, chauffeur.

me•ca•nis•mo *m.* mechanism.

me•ca•no•gra•fí•a *f.* stenography, typewriting.

me•ca•nó•gra•fo *m.* stenographer, typist.

me•ca•te *m. Mex., C.A., Col., Ven.* rope, cord.

me•ce•dor *m.* swing; *adj.* swinging, rocking.

me•ce•do•ra *f.* rocking chair.

me•cer¹⁰ *v.* to swing, rock, sway; to shake.

me•cha *f.* wick; lock of hair; fuse; strip of salt pork or bacon (*for larding meat*); *Ven.* tip of a whip; *Am.* scare, fright; *Andes, Col.* fib; *Andes, Col.* jest, joke; *Col.* trifle, worthless thing.

me•char *v.* to lard (*meat or fowl*).

me•che•ro *m.* (*canutillo*) lamp burner; gas jet; candlestick socket; (*encendedor*) pocket lighter; large wick; *Col.* disheveled hair; *Am.* joker, jester.

me•chón *m.* large wick; large lock of hair.

me•da•lla *f.* medal.

mé•da•no *m.* dune, sand hill, sand bank; *Ríopl.*, Carib. sandy marshland.

me•dia *f.* stocking; *Col., Ríopl., Ven.* **– corta** (*or* **––**) sock.

me•dia•ción *f.*mediation.

me•dia•dor *m.* mediator.

me•dia•dos: a – de about the middle. of.

me•dia•ne•ro *m.* mediator; go-between; *adj.* mediating; intermediate; **pared medianera** partition wall.

me•dia•ní•a *f.* mediocrity; average; middle ground;

moderate circumstances; moderation; *Col.* partition wall.

me·dia·no *adj.* medium; moderate, middle-sized; average; mediocre.

me·dia·no·che *f.* midnight.

me·dian·te *adj.* intervening; **Dios** — God willing; *prep.* by means of, through, with the help of.

me·diar *v.* to mediate, intervene; to intercede; to arrive at, or be in, the middle.

me·di·ble *adj.* measurable.

me·di·ca·men·to *m.* medicament, medicine.

me·di·cas·tro *m.* quack, quack doctor.

me·di·ci·na *f.* medicine.

me·di·ci·nar *v.* to doctor, treat, prescribe medicine for; **-se** to take medicine.

me·di·ción *f.* measurement; measuring.

mé·di·co *m.* doctor, physician; *adj.* medical.

me·di·da *f.* measure; measurement; gauge, rule; — **para áridos** dry measure; **a — del deseo** according to one's desire; **a — que** as, in proportion as; at the same time as. *

me·dio *adj.* half, middle; intermediate; medium, average; **media noche** midnight; **hacer una cosa a medias** to do something halfway; **ir a medias** to go halves; *adv.* half, not completely; *m.* middle; means, way; medium; environment; **-s** means, resources; **meterse de por** — to intervene, meddle in a dispute.

me·dio·cre *adj.* mediocre; **mediocridad** *f.* mediocrity.

me·dio·dí·a *m.* midday, noon; south.

me·dio·e·val, me·die·val *adj.* medieval.

me·dir⁵ *v. irr.* to measure; to scan (*verses*); *Col.*, *Ven.*, *Mex.* — **las calles** to walk the streets, be out of a job; **-se** to measure one's words or actions; *Mex.*, *C.A.*, *Ven.*, *Col.*, *Riopl.* **-se con otro** to try one's strength or ability against another; to fight with another.

me·di·ta·ción *f.* meditation.

me·di·tar *v.* to meditate, to muse.

me·drar *v.* to flourish, thrive; to prosper.

me·dro·so *adj.* timid, faint-hearted; fearful, dreadful.

mé·du·la *f.* marrow; pith; — **oblongada** medulla oblongata (*the posterior part of the brain tapering off into the spinal cord.*).

me·gá·fo·no *m.* megaphone.

me·ji·ca·no *adj.* Mexican; *m.* Mexican; the Aztec language; inhabitant of Mexico City. *Also* **mexica·no**.

me·ji·lla *f.* cheek.

me·jor *adj.* better; **el** — the best; *adv.* better; **a lo** — suddenly, unexpectedly; **tanto** — so much the better.

me·jo·ra *f.* betterment; improvement.

me·jo·ra·mien·to *m.* improvement.

me·jo·rar *v.* to better, improve; to get better, recover; **-se** to get better, recover.

me·jo·rí·a *f.* betterment, improvement; superiority.

me·la·do *adj.* honey-colored; *m.* sugarcane syrup;

honey cake.

me·lan·co·lí·a *f.* melancholy, gloom.

me·lan·có·li·co *adj.* melancholy, gloomy.

me·la·za *f.* molasses.

me·le·na *f.* mane.

me·lin·dre *m.* (*acto*) affectation; affected act or gesture; whim; (*comestible*) fritter, marzipan (*sweetmeat made of almond paste*).

me·lin·dro·so *adj.* affected; too particular, finicky, fussy.

me·lo·co·tón *m.* peach; **melocotonero** *m.* peach tree.

me·lo·dí·a *f.* melody; **melodioso** *adj.* melodious.

me·lón *m.* melon; cantaloupe; muskmelon; melon vine.

me·lo·si·dad *f.* sweetness; softness, gentleness.

me·lo·so *adj.* honeyed; soft, sweet; *m. Am.* honey-voiced person; *Am.* overaffectionate person.

me·lla *f.* nick; dent; **hacer** — to make a dent or impression; to cause pain, worry, or suffering.

me·llar *v.* to notch; to nick; to dent; to impair, damage.

me·lli·zo *adj. & m.* twin.

mem·bre·te *m.* heading; letterhead; memorandum.

mem·bri·llo *m.* quince (*tree and its fruit*).

mem·bru·do *adj.* sinewy, robust, strong, muscular.

me·mo·ra·ble *adj.* memorable, notable.

me·mo·rán·dum *m.* memorandum, note; memorandum book, notebook.

me·mo·ria *f.* memory; remembrance; reminscence; memoir, note, account; memorandum; **de** — by heart; **hacer** — to remember, recollect; — **de gallo** poor memory; **-s** regards; memoirs.

me·mo·rial *f.* memorandum book; memorial, brief, petition.

men·ción *f.* mention.

men·cio·nar *v.* to mention.

men·di·gar⁷ *v.* to beg; to ask alms.

men·di·go *m.* beggar.

men·dru·go *m.* crumb of bread

me·ne·ar *v.* to move, shake, stir; to wiggle; to wag; **-se** to hustle about; to wag; to wiggle.

me·ne·o *m.* shaking; swaying; wagging; wiggle; wiggling.

me·nes·ter *m.* need; job, occupation; **-es** bodily needs; implements, tools; tasks, chores; **ser** — to be necessary.

me·nes·te·ro·so *adj.* needy, in want.

men·gua *f.* diminution, decrease; waning; poverty, want; discredit.

men·guan·te *adj.* waning, diminishing, declining.

men·guar⁸ *v.* to diminish, decrease; to wane.

men·jur·je *m.* stuff, mixture.

me·nor *adj.* smaller, lesser, younger; smallest, least, youngest; minor; *m. & f.* **- de edad** minor; *m.* minor (*music*); Minorite, Franciscan; *f.* minor premise (*of* *a syllogism*); **por – (al por –)** at retail; in small quantities.

me·no·rí·a = **minoría**.

me·nos *adv.* less; least; except: *adj. & pron.* less, least; *m.* minus; **– de (or – que)** less than; **a lo – (al –, or por lo –)** at least; **a – que** unless; **echar de –** to miss, feel or notice the absence of; **no puede – de hacerlo** he cannot help doing it; **venir a –** to decline; to become weak or poor.

me·nos·ca·bar *v.* to diminish, lessen; to impair, damage; **– la honra de** to undermine the reputation of.

me·nos·ca·bo *m.* impairment; damage; diminution, lessening.

me·nos·pre·ciar *v.* to despise, scorn; to underestimate.

me·nos·pre·cio *m.* scorn, contempt; underestimation.

men·sa·je *m.* message.

men·sa·je·ro *m.* messenger.

mens·truo *m.* menstruation.

men·sual *adj.* monthly.

men·sua·li·dad *f.* monthly allowance; monthly payment.

men·su·ra·ble *adj.* measurable.

men·ta *f.* mint; peppermint; *Riopl.* rumor, hearsay; *Riopl., Andes* **por -s** by hearsay; *Riopl.* **persona de –** famous person.

men·ta·do *adj.* famous; *p.p.* mentioned.

men·tal *adj.* mental.

men·ta·li·dad *f.* mentality.

men·tar[1] *v. irr.* to mention; to call, name.

men·te *f.* mind; intellect.

men·te·ca·to *adj.* foolish, simple; *m.* fool.

men·tir[3] *v. irr.* to lie, tell lies.

men·ti·ra *f.* lie, falsehood, fib; white spot on the fingernails.

men·ti·ro·so *adj.* lying; deceptive, false; *m.* liar, fibber; **mentirosillo** *m.* little fibber.

men·tís: **dar un –** to give the lie (to).

men·tón *m.* chin.

me·nú *m.* menu.

me·nu·de·ar *v.* to occur frequently; to repeat over and over; to fall incessantly *(as rain, stones projectiles, etc.)*; to tell in detail; *Am.* to retail, sell at retail; *Am.* to meet together often.

me·nu·de·o *m.* retail; **vender al –** to retail, sell at retail.

me·nu·do *adj.* minute, small; insignificant; exact, detailed; **dinero –** change; **a –** often; **por –** in detail; retail; *m.* entrails; «innards»; change, small coins.

me·ñi·que *adj.* tiny, wee; **dedo –** little finger.

me·o·llo *m.* marrow; pith; kernel; substance; brain; brains.

me·ple *m. Riopl.* maple.

mer·ca *f.* purchase.

mer·ca·chi·fle *m.* peddler, vendor; cheap merchant; cheap fellow.

mer·ca·der *m.* trader, merchant.

mer·ca·de·rí·a *f.* merchandise; trade.

mer·ca·do *m.* market; mart.

mer·can·cí·a *f.* merchandise; goods.

mer·can·til *adj.* mercantile, commercial.

mer·car[6] *v.* to purchase, buy.

mer·ced *f.* favor; present, gift; mercy; **Vuestra Merced** Your Honor; **a – de** at the mercy of; at the expence of.

mer·ce·rí·a *f.* notions *(pins, buttons, etc.)*; notions store; *Riopl., P.R.* drygoods store.

mer·cu·rio *m.* mercury; quicksilver.

me·re·ce·dor *adj.* worthy, deserving.

me·re·cer[13] *v. irr.* to deserve.

me·re·ci·do *adj. & p.p.* deserved; *m.* deserved punishment.

me·re·ci·mien·to *m.* merit.

me·ren·dar[1] *v. irr.* to have an afternoon snack or refreshment; *Carib., Ven.* **-se uno a alguien** to fleece or skin someone *(in a game or business deal)*; to kill someone.

me·ren·de·ro *m.* lunchroom.

me·ri·dia·no *adj. & m.* meridian.

me·ri·dio·nal *adj.* southern; *m.* southerner.

me·rien·da *f.* light afternoon meal; afternoon refreshments.

mé·ri·to *m.* merit; **de –** notable.

me·ri·to·rio *adj.* meritorious, worthy, deserving; *m.* employee without salary *(learning trade or profession)*.

mer·lu·za *f.* hake *(species of codfish)*; drunken state.

mer·ma *f.* reduction, decrease.

mer·mar *v.* to dwindle; to decrease, reduce.

mer·me·la·da *f.* marmalade.

me·ro *adj.* mere, pure; *Mex., C.A.* exact, real; **la mera verdad** the real truth; *adv. Mex., C.A.* very, very same, exactly; *Mex., C.A.* soon; *Col.* only; *Mex., C.A* **una mera de las tres** only one of the three; *Mex., C.A.* **ya –** (*or* **merito**) very soon; *Mex., C.A.* **allí –** (*or* **merito**) right there; *m.* species of perch; *Ch.* species of thrush.

me·ro·de·ar *v.* to rove in search of plunder.

mes *m.* month.

me·sa *f.* table; executive board; staircase landing; mesa, plateau; **levantar la –** to clear the table; **poner la –** to set the table; *Col., Carib., C.A., Mex.* **quitar la –** to clear the table.

me·sa·da *f.* monthly salary or allowance.

me·sar·se *v.* to tear *(one's hair or beard)*.

me·se·ro *m. Mex., C.A., Ven., Col.* waiter.

me·se·ta *f.* plateau; staircase landing.

me·són *m.* inn *(usually a large one-story shelter for men and pack animals)*.

me•so•ne•ro *m.* innkeeper.

mes•ti•zo *adj.* half-breed; hybrid; **perro –** mongrel dog; *m.* mestizo, half-breed.

me•su•ra *f.* moderation; composure; dignity; politeness.

me•su•ra•do *adj.* moderate, temperate; dignified.

me•ta *f.* goal; objective.

me•tá•fo•ra *f.* metaphor.

me•tal *m.* metal.

me•tá•li•co *adj.* metallic, metal; *m.* specie, coined money; cash in coin.

me•ta•lur•gia *f.* metallurgy.

me•ta•te *m. Mex.* flat stone (*used for grinding corn, etc.*).

me•tá•te•sis *f.* metathesis.

me•teo•ri•to *m.* meteorite.

me•teo•ro *m.*meteor.

me•teo•ro•lo•gí•a *f.* meteorology; **meteorológico** *adj.* meteorological; **oficina meteorológica** weather bureau.

me•ter *v.* to put (in); to get(in); to insert; to smuggle; to make (*noise, trouble, etc.*); to cause (*fear*); *Carib.* to strike (*a blow*); *Riopl., Carib.* -**le**, to hurry up; -**se** to meddle, interfere; to plunge (*into*); -**se monja** (*Am.* -**se de monja**) to become a nun; also -**se a monja**; -**se con** to pick a quarrel with.

me•tó•di•co *adj.* methodical.

mé•to•do *m.* method.

mé•tri•co *adj.* metric.

me•tro *m.* meter; subway.

me•tró•po•li *f.* metropolis.

me•tro•po•li•ta•no *adj.* metropolitan; *m.* archbishop.

me•xi•ca•no = mejicano (*pronounced identically*).

mez•cal *m. Mex.* mescal (*a species of* **maguey** *and an alcoholic beverage made from it*).

mez•cla *f.* mixture; mortar; mixed cloth; **mezclilla** *f.* mixed cloth (*generally black and white*); tweed.

mez•clar *v.* to mix, blend; -**se** to mix, mingle; to meddle.

mez•co•lan•za *f.* jumble, mess, mixture.

mez•quin•dad *f.* meanness; stinginess; dire poverty.

mez•qui•no *adj.* poor, needy; mean, stingy, meager; small, tiny; *m. Col., Mex.* wart (*usually on a finger*).

mi *adj.* my.

mí *pers. pron.* (*used after prep.*) me. myself.

mia•ja = migaja.

miau *m.* mew.

mi•co *m.* long-tailed monkey; *C.A.* jack (*for lifting heavy objects*).

mi•cro•bio *m.* microbe.

mi•cró•fo•no *m.* microphone.

mi•cros•co•pio *m.* microscope; – **electrónico** electron microscope; **microscópico** *adj.* microscopic.

mie•do *m.* fear; dread; **tener –** to be afraid.

mie•do•so *adj.* afraid, fearful, timid.

miel *m.* honey; molasses.

miem•bro *m.* member; limb.

mien•tes *f. pl.* thought, mind; **parar – en** to consider, reflect on; **traer a las –** to recall; **venírsele a uno a las –** to occur to one, come to one's mind.

mien•tras *conj.* while; – **que** while; – **tanto** in the meantime, meanwhile; – **más... – menos...** the more... the less...

miér•co•les *m.* Wednesday.

mies *f.* ripe grain; harvest; **-es** fields of grain.

mi•ga *f.* crumb; soft part of bread; substance; **-s** crumbs; fried crumbs of bread; **hacer buenas -s** (*or* **malas -s**) **con** to get along well (*or badly*) with.

mi•ga•ja *f.* crumb; bit, fragment, small particle.

mi•gra•ción *f.* migration.

mi•la•gro *m.* miracle; wonder.

mi•la•gro•so *adj.* miraculous.

mi•li•cia *f.* militia; military science; military profession.

mi•li•tar *adj.* military; *m.* soldier, military man; *v.* to serve in the army; to militate, fight (*against*).

mil•pa *f. Mex., C.A.* cornfield.

mi•lla *f.* mile.

mi•llar *m.* thousand; **-es** thousands, a great number.

mi•llón *m.* million; **millonario** *adj. & m.* millionaire; **millonésimo** *adj. & m.* millionth.

mi•mar *v.* to pamper, spoil, humor, to pet.

mim•bre *m.* wicker; **mimbrera** *f.* willow.

mí•mi•co *adj.* mimic.

mi•mo *m.* pampering; caress; coaxing.

mi•mo•so *adj.* tender, sensitive; delicate; finicky, fussy.

mi•na *f.* mine; source; fortune.

mi•nar *v.* to mine; to undermine; to sow with explosive mines.

mi•ne•ral *m.* mineral; mine; ore; wealth, fortune; *adj.* mineral.

mi•ne•rí•a *f.* mining; miners.

mi•ne•ro *m.* miner; wealth, fortune; source; *adj.* mining; **compañía minera,** mining company.

mi•nia•tu•ra *f.* miniature.

mí•ni•mo *adj.* least, smallest; *m.* minimum.

mi•ni•no *m.* kitten, kitty, pussy.

mi•nis•te•rio *m.* ministry; administration, ministering; portfolio (*office of a cabinet member*); minister's office.

mi•nis•trar *v.* to minister; to give (*money, aid, etc.*).

mi•nis•tro *m.* minister; cabinet member; office of justice.

mi•no•rí•a *f.* minority.

mi•no•ri•dad *f.* minority (*in age*).

mi•nu•cio•so *adj.* minute, detailed; scrupulous.

mi•nús•cu•lo *adj.* small; **letra minúscula** small letter.

mi•nu•ta *f.* minutes; memorandum; first draft (*of a contract, deed, etc.*); memorandum list; lawyer's bill; *Am.* **a la -** breaded and fried (*said of meat or fish*).

mi•nu•to *m.* minute; **minutero** *m.* minute hand.

mí•o *poss. adj.* my, of mine; *poss. pron.* mine; *Riopl.*, *Ch.* **detrás** – behind me.

mio•pe *adj.* shortsighted, nearsighted; *m. & f.* nearsighted person.

mi•ra *f.* (*de puntería*) gun sight; guiding point; (*intención*) intention, design; outlook; **estar a la – de** to be on the lookout for; to be on the alert for; **poner la – en** to fix one's eyes on; to aim at.

mi•ra•da *f.* glance, gaze, look.

mi•ra•dor *m.* mirador, enclosed balcony (*commanding an extensive view*); watchtower; lookout site; onlooker, spectator; *Riopl.* penthouse (*small house built on a roof for recreation*).

mi•ra•mien•to *m.* consideration, respect, regard; reverence; circumspection, prudence.

mi•rar *v.* to look; to glance; to behold; to see; **– por alguien**, to take care of someone; **¡mira (tú)!** look!.

mi•rí•a•da *f.* myriad, multitude, great number.

mir•lo *m.* blackbird.

mi•rón *m.* bystander, onlooker, spectator; *adj.* curious.

mir•to *m.* myrtle.

mi•sa *f.* mass; **– del gallo** midnight mass.

mis•ce•lá•ne•o *adj.* miscellaneous.

mi•se•ra•ble *adj.* miserable, unhappy; forlorn; miserly, stingy; mean.

mi•se•ria *f.* misery; poverty; stinginess; bit, trifle.

mi•se•ri•cor•dia *f.* mercy, compassion, pity.

mi•se•ri•cor•dio•so *adj.* merciful, compassionate.

mí•se•ro *adj.* miserable, unhappy; forlorn; stingy.

mi•sión *f.* mission.

mi•sio•ne•ro *m.* missionary.

mis•mo *adj.* same; self; very; **ahora –** right away.

mis•te•rio *m.* mystery; secret.

mis•te•rio•so *adj.* mysterious.

mís•ti•co *adj.* mystical, mystic; *m.* mystic.

mi•tad *f.* half; middle.

mi•ti•gar[7] *v.* to mitigate, soften, soothe.

mi•tin *m.* meeting.

mi•to *m.* myth; **mitología** *f.* mythology.

mi•tra *f.* bishop's miter.

mix•to *adj.* mixed; half-breed; *m.* composite; match; explosive compound.

mo•bi•lia•rio *m.* furniture.

mo•bla•je = mueblaje.

mo•ce•dad *f.* youth; youthfulness; youthful prank.

mo•ce•tón *m.* tall, robust lad.

mo•ción *f.* motion.

mo•co•so *adj.* sniffling; *m.* brat, scamp; sniffling boy.

mo•char *v. Am.* to cut off; chop off, cut, trim (*see* **desmochar**); *Am.* to snitch, pilfer; *Col.* to depose, dismiss, put out of a job.

mo•chi•la *f.* knapsack; soldier's kit.

mo•cho *adj.* cut off; cropped, shorn; *Am.* maimed, multilated; *Mex.* reactionary, conservative; *m.* butt of a firearm; *Col.*, *Ven.* nag: *Carib.* cigar butt.

mo•da *f.* mode, custom, style, fashion; **de –** fashionable.

mo•de•lar *v.* to model.

mo•de•lo *m.* model, copy, pattern; *m. & f.* life model.

mo•de•ra•ción *f.* moderation.

mo•de•ra•do *adj.* moderate; conservative.

mo•de•rar *v.* to moderate, temper; to regulate; to restrain.

mo•der•no *adj.* modern.

mo•des•tia *f.* modesty.

mo•des•to *adj.* modest.

mó•di•co *adj.* moderate, reasonable (*prise*).

mo•di•fi•ca•ción *f.* modification.

mo•di•fi•car[6] *v.* to modify.

mo•dis•mo *m.* idiom.

mo•dis•ta *f.* dressmaker; milliner.

mo•do *m.* mode, manner, way; mood (*grammar*); **a** (*or* **al**) **– de** like, in the manner of; **de - que** so that; and so; **de todos -s** at any rate, anyway.

mo•do•rra *f.* drowsiness; gid (*a disease of sheep*).

mo•du•lar *v.* to modulate, tone down.

mo•fa *f.* scoff, jeer, taunt; mockery.

mo•far *v.* to mock, scoff, jeer; **-se** de to make fun of, scoff at.

mo•fle•te•m *m.* fat cheek; **mofletudo** *adj.* fat-cheeked.

mo•hín *m.* grimace; wry face.

mo•hi•no *adj.* moody, discontented, sad, melancholy; black (*referring to a horse, cow or bull*).

mo•ho *m.* rust; mold.

mo•ho•so *adj.* musty, moldy; rusty.

mo•ja•da *f.* drench, drenching, wetting.

mo•ja•do *adj.* wet, damp, moist; *p.p. of* **mojar.**

mo•ja•du•ra *f.* wetting, dampening, drenching.

mo•jar *v.* to dampen, wet, moisten; *Riopl.*, *Ch.* to accompany (*a song*); *Am.* to bribe; *Riopl.*, *Carib.*, *Mex.* to celebrate by drinking; *Am.* **mojársele a uno los papeles** to get things mixed up.

mo•ji•cón *m.* punch, blow; muffin, bun.

mo•ji•ga•te•rí•a *f.* prudery; false humility; affected piety.

mo•ji•ga•to *adj.* prudish; affectedly pious, overzealous (*in matters of religion*); hypocritical; *m.* prude; hypocrite.

mo•jón *m.* landmark; milestone; heap, pile.

mol•de•m *m.* mold; cast; form; pattern, model; **venir de – to** come pat, be to the point; **letras de –** printed letters; print.

mol•de•ar *v.* to mold; to cast; to decorate with moldings.

mol·du·ra *f.* molding.

mo·le *f.* mass, bulk; *adj.* soft, mild; *m. Mex.* **– de guajolote** a Mexican dish of turkey served with a chili gravy.

mo·lé·cu·la *f.* molecule.

mo·ler[2] *v. irr.* to mill; to grind; to tire, fatigue; to wear out, destroy; to bother; **– a palos** to give a thorough beating.

mo·les·tar *v.* to molest, disturb; to bother, annoy.

mo·les·tia *f.* bother, annoyance; discomfort.

mo·les·to *adj.* bothersome, annoying; uncomfortable.

mo·li·cie *f* softness; fondness for luxury.

mo·lien·da *f.* grind, grinding, milling, portion to be, or that has been, ground; grinding season (*for sugar cane or olives*); fatigue, weariness; bother.

mo·li·ne·ro *m.* miller.

mo·li·ne·te *m.* small mill; ventilating fan; pin wheel; twirl, whirl, flourish.

mo·li·ni·llo *m.* small mill or grinder; chocolate beater; restless person.

mo·li·no *m.* mill; restless person; **– de viento** windmill.

mo·lle·ra *f.* crown of the head; judgment, good sense; **ser duro de –** to be stubborn; **no tener sal en la –** to be dull, stupid.

mo·men·tá·ne·o *adj.* momentary; sudden, quick.

mo·men·to *m.* moment; importance; momentum; **al –** immediately, without delay; **a cada –** continually; frequently.

mo·na *f.* female monkey; mimic; drunkenness; **dormir la –** to sleep it off; **pillar una –** to get drunk.

mo·na·da *f.* (*típico de mono*) monkeyshine; monkey face; (*cosa graciosa*) cute little thing; cute gesture; nonsense; flattery.

mo·nar·ca *m.* monarch.

mo·nar·quí·a *f.* monarchy.

mo·nas·te·rio *m.* monastery.

mon·da·dien·tes *m.* toothpick.

mon·dar *v.* to pare; to peel; to prune; to clean out; *Am.* to beat, thrash; *Am.* to beat, defeat; **-se los dientes** to pick one's teeth.

mo·ne·da *f.* coin; money; **– corriente,** currency; **– menuda** (*or* **suelta**) change, small coins; **casa de – mint.**

mo·ne·rí·a *f.* monkeyshine, antic; trifle, trinket, cute littlee thing.

mo·ne·ta·rio *adj.* monetary, pertaining to money; financial.

mo·ni·go·te *m.* puppet, ridiculous figure; dunce.

mo·ni·to·re·ar *v.* to monitor (*a radio or TV program*).

mon·ja *f.* nun.

mon·je *m.* monk.

mo·no *m.* monkey; silly fool; mimic; coveralls; *Ch.* pile of fruit or vegetables (*in a market*); **-s** *Ch.* worthless household·utensils and furniture; *Am.* **meterle a uno los -s en el cuerpo** to frighten,

terrify someone; *adj.* pretty, neat, cute; *Am.* sorrel, reddishbrown; *Col.* blond.

mo·no·lo·gar[7] *v.* to soliloquize, talk to oneself; to recite monologues; to monopolize the conversation.

mo·nó·lo·go *m.* monologue.

mo·no·po·lio *m.* monopoly.

mo·no·po·li·zar[9] *v.* to monopolize; to corner (*a market*).

mo·no·sí·la·bo *adj.* monosyllabic, of one syllable; *m.* monosyllable.

mo·no·to·ní·a *f.* monotony; **monótono** *adj.* monotonous.

mon·ser·ga *f.* gabble.

mons·truo *m.* monster.

mons·truo·si·dad *f.* monstrosity; monster, freak.

mons·truo·so *adj.* monstrous.

mon·ta *f.* amount, sum; value, importance; **de poca –** of little value or importance.

mon·ta·je *m.* assembly, assembling (*of machinery*); mount, support for a cannon.

mon·tan·te *m.* broadsword; transom; upright; post; *Carib., Ven.* sum, amount, cost; *f* high tide.

mon·ta·ña *f.* mountain; **– rusa** roller coaster.

mon·ta·ñés *adj.* mountain (*used as adj.*) of, from or pertaining to the mountains; *m.* mountaineer, native of the province of Santander, Spain.

mon·ta·ño·so *adj.* mountainous.

mon·tar *v.* to mount; to ride horseback; to amount (to); to set (*jewels*); to cock (*a gun*); to assemble, set up (*machinery*); *Carib., C.A.* to organize, establish.

mon·ta·raz *adj.* wild, primitive, uncivilized; *m.* forester.

mon·te *m.* mount, mountain; forest; thicket; monte (*a card game*); *C.A., Mex.* grass, pasture; *Am.* country, outskirts; **montecillo** *m.* mound, small hill; **montepío** *m.* pawnshop.

mon·te·ra *f.* cap; *Andes* Bolivian coneshaped hat (*worn by Indians*).

mon·tés *adj.* wild, mountain (*used as adj.*); **cabra –** mountain goat; **gato –** wildcat.

mon·tí·cu·lo *m.* mound.

mon·tón *m.* pile, heap; mass, great number; **a -es** in abundance, in heaps, by heaps.

mon·to·ne·ra *f. Col., Ven., Riopl.* band of mounted rebels or guerrilla fighters; *Col.* pile of wheat, hay, straw, etc.; *Am.* pile, heap (*of anything*).

mon·tuo·so *adj.* hilly; mountainous.

mon·tu·ra *f.* mount, horse; saddle and trappings.

mo·nu·men·to *m.* monument; **monumental** *adj.* monumental.

mo·ño *m.* knot or roll of hair; bow of ribbon; crest, tuft of feathers; *Mex.* forelock (*lock of hair on the fore part of the head*); *Am.* crest, peak (*of anything*); *Col.* whim; *Am.* a Colombian popular dance; **-s**

frippery, gaudy ornaments; *Col.* **estar con el - torcido** to be in an ugly humor.

mo•ra *f.* blackberry; mulberry; brambleberry; *Ch.* blood pudding, sausage.

mo•ra•da *f.* dwelling, residence; stay.

mo•ra•do *adj.* purple.

mo•ra•dor *m.* dweller, resident.

mo•ral *adj.* moral; *f.* ethics, moral philosophy; morale; *m.* mulberry tree; blackberry bush.

mo•ra•le•ja *f.* moral, lesson, maxim.

mo•ra•li•dad *f.* morality.

mo•ra•lis•ta *m.* & *f.* moralist.

mo•rar *v.* to live, dwell, reside.

mor•bi•dez *f.* softness; mellowness.

mór•bi•do *adj.* morbid, soft.

mor•bo•so *adj.* morbid, unhealthy, diseased.

mor•ci•lla *f.* blood pudding, blood sausage; gag (*an amusing remark by a comedian*).

mor•da•ci•dad *f.* sharpness (*of tongue*).

mor•daz *adj.* biting, cutting, sarcastic.

mor•da•za *f.* gag (*for the mouth*).

mor•de•dor *adj.* biting; snappy; *m.* biter; slanderer.

mor•de•du•ra *f.* bite; sting.

mor•de•lón *adj. Col.*, *Ven.* biting, snappy; *m. Am.* biter; *Mex.* public official who accepts a bribe.

mor•der² *v. irr.* to bite; to nip; to gnaw; to corrode; to backbite, slander; *Ven.* to swindle; *Mex.*, *C.A.* to "shake down", exact a bribe.

mor•di•da *f. Am.* bite; *Mex.*, *C.A.*, *Carib.*, *Ven.* graft, money obtained by graft.

mor•dis•car⁶, **mor•dis•que•ar** *v.* to nibble; to gnaw.

mor•dis•co *m.* bite; nibble.

mo•re•no *adj.* brown; dark, brunette; *m. Ríopl.*, *Carib.*, *Mex.*, *Ven.*, *Andes* colored person.

mo•re•tón *m.* bruise, black-and-blue mark.

mor•fe•ma *m.* morpheme.

mor•fi•na *f.* morphine; **morfinómano** *m.* morphine addict, drug fiend.

mo•ri•bun•do *adj.* dying.

mo•rir⁴·⁵² *v. irr.* to die; **-se** to die; to die out, be extinguished.

mo•ris•co *adj.* Moorish; Moresque, in the Moorish style; *m.* Morisco (*Christianized Moor*); language of the Moriscos.

mo•ro *adj.* Moorish; *Mex.*, *Ven.*, *Riopl.*, *Cuba* dappled, spotted (*horse*); *Col.*, *Ch.*, *Andes* unbaptized; *m.* Moor; *Am.* frosted cookie.

mo•ro•cho *adj. Am* robust, strong; *Ríopl.* of dark complexion; *Ch.* rough, tough; *Andes* of low social condition.

mo•rral *m.* nose bag; knapsack; hunter's bag.

mo•rri•ña *f.* melancholy blues, sadness.

mor•sa *f.* walrus.

mor•ta•ja *f.* shroud; *Am.* cigarette paper.

mor•tal *adj.* mortal; fatal; deadly; *m.* mortal; **mortalidad** *f.* mortality; death rate.

mor•tan•dad *f.* mortality, death rate; massacre, slaughter.

mor•te•ci•no *adj.* deathly pale; dying; **hacer la mortecina** to pretend to be dead.

mor•te•re•te *m.* small mortar, small canon.

mor•te•ro *m.* mortar (*for grinding*).

mor•tí•fe•ro *adj.* deadly, fatal.

mor•ti•fi•car⁶ *v.* to mortify; to torment; to vex, annoy; **-se** to do penance; to be grieved; *Mex.*, *C.A.*, *Ven.* to be embarrassed.

mor•tuo•rio *adj.* funeral; funereal; mournful; *m.* funeral, burial.

mo•sai•co *adj.* & *m.* mosaic.

mos•ca *f.* fly; bore; bother; *Am.* sponger, parasite; *Mex.*, *C.A.*, *Ven.* bull'seye, center of a target; **moscón** *m.* large fly; *Am.* **ir de moscón** to go along as a chaperone.

mos•que•ar *v.* to brush off or drive away flies; to whip, beat; *Ríopl.* to rage, be furious; **-se** to show pique or resentment; *Ch.* to go away.

mos•qui•to *m.* mosquito; gnat; *Am.* Mosquito Indian of Nicaragua; **mosquitero** *m.* mosquito net.

mos•ta•cho *m.* mustache.

mos•ta•za *f.* mustard; mustard seed; bird shot.

mos•tra•dor *m.* demonstrator; store counter; clock dial.

mos•trar² *v. irr.* to show; to demonstrate, to exhibit.

mos•tren•co *adj.* (*sin dueño*) ownerless; homeless; stray (*animal*); (*torpe*) slow, dull; fat, heavy; *m.* dunce; *C.A.* worthless animal.

mo•ta *f.* mote, speck; knot in cloth; slight defect; mound, knoll; *Col.*, *Ven.*, *Carib.* powder puff; *Am.* tulf.

mo•te *m.* motto; slogan; nickname; *Andes*, *Ch.*, *Col.* stewed corn; *Andes* grammatical error (*made by illiterate people and children*); *Am.* **– pelado** hominy.

mo•tear *v.* to speck, speckle; to spot; *Am.* to mispronounce, enunciate badly.

mo•te•jar *v.* to jeer at; to call bad names; to insult; to censure; **– de** to brand as.

mo•tín *m.* mutiny; riot.

mo•ti•var *v.* to cause; to give a cause for.

mo•ti•vo *m.* motive, reason; motif, theme; *m.* **con - de** because of; on the occasion of; *adj.* motive.

mo•to•ci•cle•ta *f.* motorcycle; **motociclista** *m.* & *f.* motorcyclist, motorcycle rider.

mo•tor *m.* motor; **– de reacción** jet engine; *adj.* motor, causing motion.

mo•to•ris•ta *m.* & *f.* motorist; motorman, motorwoman.

mo•triz *adj.* motive, impelling, driving; **fuerza –** power, driving force.

mo•ve•di•zo *adj.* movable; shaky; shifting; **arena**

movediza quicksand.

mo•ver[2] *v. irr.* (*fisicamente*) to move; (*persuadir*) to persuade; to stir, excite; to touch, affect; **-se** to move.

mo•vi•ble *adj.* movable; mobile; fickle.

mó•vil *m.* motive, inducement, incentive; *adj.* mobile, movable; unstable.

mo•vi•li•za•ción *f.* mobilization.

mo•vi•li•zar[9] *v.* to mobilize.

mo•vi•mien•to *m.* movement; motion; commotion; disturbance.

mo•za *f.* maid; girl; last hand of a game; *Ch.* last song or dance of a fiesta.

mo•zal•be•te *m.* youth, lad.

mo•zá•ra•be *adj.* Mozarabic (*Christian in Moslem Spain*).

mo•zo *adj.* young; unmarried; *m.* youth; manservant; waiter; porter; errand boy; **buen –** handsome man.

mo•zue•la *f.* lass, young girl.

mo•zue•lo *m.* lad, young boy.

mu•ca•ma *f. Andes, Ríopl.* servant girl; **mucamo** *m. Andes, Ríopl.* servant.

mu•co•so *adj.* mucous; slimy; **membrana mucosa** mucous membrane.

mu•cha•cha *f.* child; girl; servant, maid.

mu•cha•cho *m.* child; boy, lad.

mu•che•dum•bre *f.* multitude; crowd.

mu•cho *adj.* much, a lot of; long (*refering to time*); **-s** many; *adv.* much; a great deal; **ni con –** not by far, not by a long shot; **ni – menos** not by any means, nor anything like it; **por – que** no matter how much; **no es – que** it is no wonder that.

mu•da *f.* change; change of clothes; molt; (*act or time of shedding feathers*); *Ríopl.* relay of draft animals.

mu•da•ble *adj.* changeable; fickle.

mu•dan•za *f.* change; removal; inconstancy.

mu•dar *v.* to change; to remove; to molt; **– de casa** to move; **– de traje** to change one's clothes; to change one's habits; to move, change one's abode.

mu•dez *f.* muteness, dumbness.

mu•do *adj.* mute, dumb; silent; *m.* dumb person.

mue•bla•je *m.* furniture.

mue•ble *m.* piece of furniture; **-s** furniture, household goods; *adj.* movable; **bienes -s** chattels movable possessions.

mue•ca *f.* grimace; wry face.

mue•la *f.* (*diente*) molar tooth; (*piedra*) millstone; grindstone; **– cordal** (*or* **– del juicio**) wisdom tooth.

mue•lle *adj.* soft; voluptuous; *m.* spring; wharf; loading platform; **– real** main spring of a watch.

muer•te *f.* death.

muer•to *p.p. of* **morir** & *adj.* dead; withered; faded; **naturaleza muerta** still life; *m.* corpse.

mues•ca *f.* notch; groove.

mues•tra *f.* sample; pattern, model; shop ign; sign, indication; presence, bearing; face, dial (*of a clock or watch*); **muestrario** *m.* book or collection of samples.

mu•gi•do *m.* moo; mooing, lowing of cattle.

mu•gir[11] *v.* to moo, low.

mu•gre *f.* dirt, grime.

mu•grien•to *adj.* grimy, dirty.

mu•jer *f.* woman; wife.

mu•je•ril *adj.* womanly, feminine; womanish, like a woman.

mu•la *f.* mule; *Am.* cushion for carrying loads; *Am.* worthless merchandise; *Ríopl.* cruel, treacherous person; *Am.* **echar a uno la –** to give someone the dickens, scold someone.

mu•la•dar *m.* rubbish pile or dump; dunghill, pile of manure.

mu•la•to *adj.* & *m.* mulatto.

mu•le•ta *f.* crutch; red cloth draped over a rod (*used by bullfighters.*)

mu•le•ti•lla *f.* cane with a crutchlike handle; red cloth draped over a rod (*used by bullfighters*); cliché (*hackneyed or trite phrase*); refrain; repetitious word or phrase; braid frog (*fastener for a coat*).

mu•lo *m.* mule.

mul•ta *f.* fine.

mul•ti•co•lor *adj.* many-colored, motley.

múl•ti•ple *adj.* multiple.

mul•ti•pli•ca•ción *f.* multiplication.

mul•ti•pli•car[6] *v.* to multiply.

mul•ti•pli•ci•dad *f.* multiplicity, manifold variety.

múl•ti•plo *m.* multiple number.

mul•ti•tud *f.* multitude; crowd.

mu•lli•do *adj.* soft; fluffy; *m.* stuffing for mattreses or pillows; soft cushion or mattress.

mu•llir[20] *v.* to fluff; to soften.

mun•da•nal *adj.* worldly.

mun•da•no *adj.* mundane, worldly.

mun•dial *adj.* universal; **la guerra –** the World War.

mun•do *m.* world; trunk; **todo el –** everybody.

mu•ni•ción *f.* ammunition; buckshot; **-es de guerra** war supplies.

mu•ni•ci•pal *adj.* municipal; **municipalidad** *f.* municipality; town hall; city government.

mu•ni•ci•pio *m.* municipality.

mu•ñe•ca *f.* doll; wrist; manikin (*figure for displlaying clothes*); **muñeco** *m.* boy doll; dummy, puppet.

mu•ñon *m.* stump (*of an arm or leg*).

mu•ra•lla *f.* surrounding wall; rampart.

mur•cia•no *adj.* of or from Murcia, Spain; *m.* native of Murcia.

mur•cié•la•go *m.* bat.

mur•ga *f.* brass band.

mur•mu•llo *m.* murmur, rumor; whisper; muttering.

mur•mu•ra•ción *f.* slander, gosip; grumbling.

mur•mu•rar *v.* to murmur; to slander, gossip; to whisper; to grumble.

mu•ro *m.* wall.

mu•rria *f.* sulkiness, sullenness, melancholy, blue; **tener —** to be sulky; to have the blues.

mu•sa *f.* Muse; muse, poetic inspiration; poetry; **-s** fine arts.

mus•cu•lar *adj.* muscular.

mus•cu•la•tu•ra *f.* muscles; muscular systm.

mús•cu•lo *m.* mucle.

mus•cu•lo•so *adj.* muscular, sinewy.

mu•se•li•na *f.* muslin.

mu•se•o *m.* museum.

mus•go *m.* moss.

mus•go•so *adj.* mossy.

mú•si•ca *f.* music.

mu•si•cal *adj.* musical.

mú•si•co *adj.* musical; *m.* musician.

mu•si•tar *v.* to mutter, mumble; to whisper.

mus•lo *m.* thigh.

mus•tio *adj.* sad; withered; humble.

mu•ti•lar *v.* to mutilate; to butcher; to mar.

mu•tis•mo *m.* muteness, silence.

mu•tuo *adj.* mutual; reciprocal.

muy *adv.* very; greatly; most.

N

na•bo *m.* turnip.

ná•car *m.* mother-of-pearl; pearl color.

na•ca•ra•do *adj.* pearly.

na•cer[13] *v. irr.* (*salir del vientre*) to be born; (*brotar*) to spring, originate; to bud; to sprout, grow (*said of plants*); **— de pie** (*or* **— de pies**) to be born lucky.

na•cien•te *adj.* rising (*sun*); *m.* orient, east.

na•ci•mien•to *m.* birth; origin; beginning; descent; source; crèche (*representation of the Nativity*).

na•ción *f.* nation.

na•cio•nal *adj.* national; *m.* national, citizen.

na•cio•na•li•dad *f.* nationality.

na•da *f.* nothingness; *indef.* pron, nothing, not. . . anything; *adv.* not at all; **de —** you are welcome, don't mention it (*as a reply to* «**gracias**»); *Am.* **a cada —** constantly; **una nadita** a trifle, just a little.

na•da•da *f.* swim.

na•da•dor *m.* swimmer; *Ven.* fish-net float.

na•dar *v.* to swim; to float.

na•de•ría *f.* a mere nothing, trifle, worthless thing.

na•die *indef. pron.* nobody, no one, not ... anyone.

naf•ta *f.* naphtha.

na•guas **= enaguas.**

ná•huatl *adj.* the language of the Aztec Indians.

nai•pe *m.* playing card.

nal•gas *f. pl.* buttocks; rump; **nalgada** *f.* spank, **-s** spanking.

na•na *f.* grandma; lullaby; *Mex.*, *Ríopl.*, *Ven.* child's nurse; Spain nice old lady.

na•ran•ja *f.* orange; **— tangerina** tangerine; **naranja-da** *f.* orangeade, orange juice; orange marmalade; **naranjal** *m.* orange grove; **naranjo** *m.* orange tree.

nar•ci•so *m.* narcissus; daffodil; fop, dandy.

nar•có•ti•co *adj. & m.* narcotic.

nar•co•ti•zar⁹ *v.* to dope, drug with narcotics.

na•riz *f.* nose; nostril; **narices** nostril.

na•rra•ción *f.* narration, account, story.

na•rrar *v.* to narrate, tell, relate.

na•rra•ti•vo *adj.* narrative; **narrativa** *f.* narrative.

na•ta *f.* cream; best part; scum; **-s** whipped cr eam with sugar; custard; **natoso** *adj.* creamy.

na•ta•ción *f.* swimming.

na•tal *adj.* natal; native; **natalicio** *m.* birthday; **nata-lidad** *f.* birth rate.

na•ti•llas *f. pl.* custard.

na•ti•vo *adj.* native.

na•tu•ral *adj.* natural; native; simple, unaffected; *m.* & *f.* native; *m.* nature, disposition; **al —** without affectation; **del —** from nature, from life.

na•tu•ra•le•za *f.* nature; disposition; nationality; naturalization; **— muerta** still life.

na•tu•ra•li•dad *f.* naturalness; simplicity; birthright.

na•tu•ra•lis•ta *adj.* naturalistic; *m. & f.* naturalist.

na•tu•ra•li•za•ción *f.* naturalization.

na•tu•ra•li•zar⁹ *v.* to naturalize; to acclimatize, accustom to a new climate; **-se** to become naturalized.

nau•fra•gar⁷ *v.* to be shipwrecked; to fail.

nau•fra•gio *m.* shipwreck; failure, ruin.

náu•fra•go *m.* shipwrecked person.

náu•sea *f.* nausea; **dar -s** to nauseate, sicken; to disgust; **tener -s** to be nauseated, be sick to one's stomach.

nau•sea•bun•do *adj.* nauseating, sickening.

nau•sea•do *adj.* nauseated, sick to one's stomach.

náu•ti•ca *f.* navigation (*science of navigation*).

nar•va•ja *f.* jackknife, pocketknife; penknife; razor.

na•va•ja•zo *m.* stab with a jackknife or razor; stab wound.

na•val *adj.* naval.

na•va•rro *adj.* Navarrese, of or pertaining to Navarre, Spain; *m.* Navarrese.

na•ve *f.* ship, boat; nave; **— cósmica** spaceship; **— cósmica pilotada** manned space vehicle.

na•ve•ga•ble *adj.* navigable.

na•ve•ga•ción *f.* navigation; sea voyage; **— áerea** aviation.

na•ve•ga•dor na•ve•gan•te *m.* navigator; *adj.* navigating.

na•ve•gar⁷ *v.* to navigate; to sail.

na•vi•dad *f.* Nativity; Christmas; **-es** Christmas season.

na•ví•o *m.* vessel, ship; **— de guerra** warship.

ne•bli•na *f.* fog, mist.

ne·ce·dad *f.* foolishness, nonsense.

ne·ce·sa·rio *adj.* necessary.

ne·ce·ser *m.* toilet case; sewing kit.

ne·ce·si·dad *f.* necessity, need, want.

ne·ce·si·ta·do *adj.* needy; in need, destitute, poor; *p.p. of* **necesitar**; *m.* needy person.

ne·ce·si·tar *v.* to need; to necesitate.

ne·cio *adj.* stupid, ignorant; foolish; stubborn; *Col.* touchy.

ne·fan·do *adj.* abominable; wicked.

ne·ga·ción *f.* negation, denial; negative (*negative particle*).

ne·gar[1,7] *v. irr.* to deny; to refuse; to prohibit; to disown; **-se** to refuse, decline.

ne·ga·ti·va *f.* negative; denial, refusal.

ne·ga·ti·vo *adj.* negative.

ne·gli·gen·cia *f.* negligence, neglect, carelessness.

ne·gli·gen·te *adj.* negligent, neglectful, careless.

ne·go·cia·ción *f.* negotiation; business; business house; management; transaction, deal.

ne·go·cian·te *m.* merchant, trader, dealer; businessman; *adj.* negotiating.

ne·go·ciar *v.* to negotiate; to trade; to transact.

ne·go·cio *m.* business; business deal; negotiation, transaction; *Ríopl., Carib., C.A., Ven., Andes* store; **hombre de -s** businessman.

ne·gre·ar *v.* to become black; to appear black, look black (*in the distance*).

ne·gro *adj.* black; dark; sad, gloomy; unfortunate; *m.* black color; negro; *Ríopl. C.A., Ven., Col.* dear, darling; **negra** *f.* negress; *Ríopl., C.A., Ven., Col.* dear, darling.

ne·gru·ra *f.* blackness.

ne·gruz·co *adj.* blackish.

ne·na *f.* baby girl; **nene** *m.* baby boy.

ne·po·tis·mo *m.* nepotism.

ner·vio *m.* nerve.

ner·vio·so, nervoso *adj.* nervous; sinewy, strong.

ner·vio·si·dad, nervosidad *f.* nervousness; flexibility; vigor.

ner·vu·do *adj.* sinewy, tough, powerful.

ne·to *adj.* clear, pure; net (*profit, price, etc.*); **netamente** *adv.* clearly, distinctly.

neu·má·ti·co *m.* tire; *adj.* pneumatic.

neu·tra·li·dad *f.* neutrality.

neu·tra·li·zar[9] *v.* to neutralize, counteract.

neu·tro *adj.* neutral; neuter; sexless.

ne·va·da *f.* snowfall.

ne·va·do *adj.* snowy, white as snow; covered with snow.

ne·var[1] *v. irr.* to snow.

ne·vas·ca *f.* snowstorm.

ne·ve·ra *f.* icebox; refrigerator; ice storehouse; ice or ice-cream vendor (*woman*).

ni *conj. & adv.* nor; not even; neither; **– siquiera** not even.

ni·cho *m.* niche; recess, hollow in a wall.

ni·da·da *f.* nestful of eggs; brood of chicks; hatch, brood.

ni·do *m.* nest; abode; *Am.* **patearle el – a alguien** to "upset the applecart", upset someone's plans.

nie·bla *f.* fog, mist; confusion.

nie·to *m.* grandson, grandchild, **nieta** *f.* granddaughter.

nie·ve *f.* snow; *Mex., Ríopl., Ven.* sherbet, ice cream; **tiempo de -s** snowy season.

ni·mio *adj.* miserly, stingy; *Am.* very small, insignificant.

nin·fa *f.* nymph.

nin·gun(o) *indef. adj. & pron.* no one, none, not . . . any; nobody.

ni·ña *f.* girl; baby girl; *Andes, Ríopl., Mex., Carib.* lady, mistress (*title of respect and endearment given to adults*); **- del ojo** pupil of the eye.

ni·ña·da *f.* childishness, childish act or remark.

ni·ñe·ra *f.* child's nurse.

ni·ñe·rí·a *f.* childish act; child's play; trifle; foolishness.

ni·ñez *f.* infancy; childhood.

ni·ño *m.* child, boy; infant; *Am.* master (*title of respect given to a young man by his servants*); *adj.* childlike, childish; very young, immature.

ní·quel *m.* nickel.

ni·que·la·do *adj.* nickel-plated; *m.* nickel plating; nickel plate.

ni·ti·dez *f.* clarity, clearness.

ní·ti·do *adj.* clear.

ni·tra·to *m.* nitrate; saltpeter.

ni·tro *m.* niter, saltpeter.

ni·tró·ge·no *m.* nitrogen.

ni·vel *m.* level.

ni·ve·lar *v.* to level; to grade; to equalize.

no *adv.* no: not; nay; **– bien** as soon as; **un – sé qué** something indefinable; **por sí o por – just** in case, anyway.

no·ble *adj.* noble; *m.* nobleman.

no·ble·za *f.* nobility; nobleness.

no·ción *f.* notion, idea.

no·ci·vo *adj.* noxious, harmful, injurious.

noc·tur·no *adj.* nocturnal, night, nightly; *m.* nocturne (*musical or lyrical composition*).

no·che *f.* night; darkness; **a la** – tonight; **de –** by (at) night; **por (en) la –** at night, in the evening; **dejar a uno a buenas -s** to leave a person in the lurch.

No·che·bue·na *f.* Christmas Eve.

no·cher·nie·go *m.* night owl (*person*).

no·dri·za *f.* child's nurse; wet nurse.

no·gal *m.* walnut (*tree and wood*).

no·más *Am.* = **no más** just; only.

nom·bra·día *f.* renown, fame.

nom·bra·mien·to *m.* nomination; appointment; naming.

nom•brar v. to nominate; to name; to appoint.
nom•bre m. name; fame; noun; watchword; **- de pila** (*or* **– de bautismo**) Christian name.
no•me•ol•vi•des f. forget-me-not.
nó•mi•na f. list (*of names*); pay roll.
no•mi•na•ción f. nomination; appointment.
no•mi•nal adj. nominal; **valor –** small, insignificant value.
no•mi•nar v. to nominate.
non adj. odd, uneven; m. odd number, uneven number; **estar** (*or* **quedar**) **de –** to be left alone, be left without a partner or companion.
no•na•da f. trifle, mere nothing.
no•pal m. nopal, prickly pear tree (*species of cactus*).
nor•des•te adj. & m. northeast.
no•ria f. draw well; chain pump.
nor•ma f. norm, standard, model.
nor•mal adj. normal; standard; f. perpendicular line.
nor•ma•li•zar[9] v. to normalize, make normal; to standardize.
no•ro•es•te adj. & m. northwest.
nor•ta•da f. strong north wind.
nor•ta•zo m. Mex., Ven. sudden gust of wind, strong north wind.
nor•te m. north; north wind; guide; North Star; direction.
nor•tea•me•ri•ca•no adj. North American; American (*from or of the United States*).
nor•te•ño adj. northern; m. northerner.
no•rue•go adj. & m. Norwegian.
nos•tal•gia f. nostalgia, longing, homesickness.
nos•tál•gico adj. homesick; lonesome; longing.
no•ta f. note; mark; fame.
no•ta•ble adj. notable; noticeable.
no•tar v. to note, observe; to mark; to write down.
no•ta•rio m. notary.
no•ti•cia f. notice, information; news; **recibir -s** to receive word, hear (*from*).
no•ti•cia•rio m. news sheet, news column, news bulletin; **noticiero** m. **= noticiario**; adj. news (*used as adj.*); newsy, full of news.
no•ti•cio•so adj. newsy, full of news; wellinformed.
no•ti•fi•ca•ción f. notification, notifying; notice; summons.
no•ti•fi•car[6] v. to notify.
no•to•rio adj. well-known; obvious, evident.
no•va•to m. novice, beginner.
no•ve•dad f. novelty; latet news, event, or fashion; change; newness; **hacerle a uno –** to seem strange or new to one; to excite one's curiosity or interest; **sin –** as usual; well.
no•vel adj. new, inexperienced.
no•ve•la f. novel, fiction.
no•ve•les•co adj. novelistic, fictional; fantastic.
no•ve•lis•ta m. & f. novelist.

no•via f. fiancée; sweetheart; bride.
no•viaz•go m. betrothal, engagement; courtship.
no•vi•cio m. novice; beginner; apprentice; adj. inexperienced.
no•viem•bre m. November.
no•vi•lla f. heifer, young cow.
no•vi•lla•da f. herd of young bulls; bullfight (*using young bulls*).
no•vi•lle•ro m. a novice bullfighter; a fighter of 3-year-old bulls.
no•vi•llo m. young bull; steer; **-s** bullfight (*using young bulls*); **hacer -s** to play hooky, cut classes; to play truant.
no•vio m. fiancé; sweetheart; bridegroom.
nu•ba•rrón m. large storm cloud.
nu•be f. cloud; film on the eyeball; **poner por las -s** to praise to the skies.
nu•bla•do m. storm cloud; imminent danger; adj. cloudy.
nu•blar v. to cloud; to darken, obscure; **-se** to grow cloudy.
nu•blo•so adj. cloudy; gloomy.
nu•ca f. nape.
nu•cle•ar adj. nuclear.
nú•cle•o m. nucleus; kernel.
nu•di•llo m. small knot, knuckle; loop, knitted stitch.
nu•do m. (*vínculo*) knot; joint; union. bond, tie; (*crisis*) crisis, turning point (*of a play*); knot, nautical mile; **– ciego** hard knot.
nu•do•so adj. knotty, gnarled, knotted.
nue•ra f. daughter-in-law.
nue•va f. news.
nue•ve•ci•to adj. nice and new, brandnew.
nue•vo adj. new; newly arrived; **de –** again; **¿qué hay de –?** what's new? what's the news?.
nu•ez f. walnut; nut; **–** (*or* **– de Adán**) Adam's apple; **– moscada** (*or* **– de especia**) nutmeg.
nu•li•dad f. nullity (*state or quality of being mull*); incompetence; nonentity, a nobody.
nu•lo adj. null, void; useless.
nu•me•ral adj. & m. numeral.
nu•me•rar v. to number; to calculate; to enumerate.
nu•mé•ri•co adj. numerical.
nú•me•ro m. number; numeral.
nu•me•ro•so adj. numerous.
nun•ca adv. never; **no . . . –** not . . . ever; **mas que –** more than ever.
nun•cio m. herald, messenger; nuncio, Papal envoy.
nup•cial adj. nuptial, relating to marriage or weddings.
nup•cias f. pl. nuptials, wedding.
nu•tria f. otter.
nu•tri•ción f. nutrition; nourishment.
nu•tri•do adj. full, abundant; substantial; p.p. of **nutrir**.
nu•tri•men•to, nu•tri•mien•to m. nutrition;

nourishment, food.

nu•trir *v.* nourish, feed.

nu•tri•ti•vo *adj.* nutritious, nourishing.

ny•lon *m.* nylon.

Ñ

ñan•du *m.* nandu; American ostrich.

ña•pa *f. Andes, Ríopl., Cuba, Ven., Col.* additional amount, something extra; *Am.* **de — to** boot, in addition, besides.

ña•to *adj. C.A., Col., Ven., Andes* flatnosed, pug-nosed, snub-nosed; *Am.* ugly, deformed; *Am.* insignificant.

ño•ñe•ría *f.* silly remark or action; *Am.* dotage.

ño•ño *adj.* feeble-minded; silly; *Am.* old, decrepit, feeble; *Col., Ec.* oldfashioned, out of style.

O

o *conj.* or, either.

oa•sis *m.* oasis.

o•be•de•cer[13] *v. irr.* to obey; **— a cierta causa** to arise from, be due to, a certain cause; **esto obedece a que** . . . this is due to the fact that . . .

o•be•dien•cia *f.* obedience.

o•be•dien•te *adj.* obedient.

o•ber•tu•ra *f.* musical overture.

o•bis•po *m.* bishop; *Cuba, Andes* **a cada muerte de** (*or* **por la muerte de un**) — once in a blue moon.

ob•je•ción *f.* objection.

ob•je•tar *v.* to object.

ob•je•ti•vo *adj.* objective; *m.* objective (*lens of any optical instrument*); objective.

ob•je•to *m.* object, purpose, aim; thing.

o•blea *f.* wafer.

o•blí•cuo *adj.* oblique, slanting, bias.

o•bli•ga•ción *f.* obligation; duty; bond, security; engagement.

o•bli•gar[7] *v.* to oblige; to obligate, bind, compel, put under obligation; **-se** to bind oneself, obligate oneself.

o•bli•ga•to•rio *adj.* obligatory; compulsory; binding.

o•bo•e *m.* oboe.

ó•bo•lo *m.* mite, small contribution.

o•bra *f.* (*resultado de acción*) work; act; labor, toil; (*creación artística*) book; building (*under construction*); masterpiece of art; repair; **— de** approximately; **por — de** through, by virtue or power of; **hacer mala —** to interfere, hinder; **poner por —** to undertake, begin; to put into practice.

o•brar *v.* to work; to act; to operate; to function; to perform; to make; to do; **obra en nuestro poder** we are in receipt of; **la carta que obra en su**

---

poder the letter that is in his possession.

o•bre•ro *m.* workman, laborer.

obs•ce•ni•dad *f.* obscenity.

obs•ce•no *adj.* obscene.

obs•cu•re•cer[13] *v. irr.* to obscure, darken; to tarnish; to grow dark; **-se** to get dark or cloudy.

obs•cu•ri•dad *f.* obscurity, darkness; dimness.

obs•cu•ro *adj.* obscure; dark; dim; **a obscuras** (**= a oscuras**) in the dark; *m.* shade (*in painting*).

ob•se•quiar *v.* to regale, entertain; to court; *Am.* to give, make a present of.

ob•se•quio *m.* attention, courtesy; gift; **en — de** for the sake of, in honor of.

ob•se•qui•oso *adj.* attentive, courteous, obliging; obsequious, servile.

ob•ser•va•ción *f.* observation; remark.

ob•ser•va•dor *m.* observer; *adj.* observing.

ob•ser•van•cia *f.* observance (*of a law, rule, custom, etc.*).

ob•ser•van•te *adj.* observant (*of a law, custom, or rule*).

ob•ser•var *v.* to observe; to watch; to remark.

ob•ser•va•to•rio *m.* observatory.

ob•se•sión *f.* obsession.

ob•se•sio•nar *v.* to obsess.

obs•tá•cu•lo *m.* obstacle.

obs•tan•te: no — notwithstanding; newerthless.

obs•tar *v.* to hinder, impede, obstruct.

obs•ti•na•ción *f.* obstinacy, stubbornness.

obs•ti•na•do *adj.* obstinate, stubborn.

obs•ti•nar•se *v.* to persist (in); to be obstinate, stubborn (about).

obs•truc•ción *f.* obstruction.

obs•truir[32] *v. irr.* to obstruct, block.

ob•te•ner[45] *v. irr.* to obtain, get; to attain.

ob•te•ni•ble *adj.* obtainable, available.

ob•tu•ra•dor *m.* choke (*of an automobile*); throttle; plug, stopper; shutter (*of a camera*).

ob•viar *v.* to obviate, clear away, remove.

ob•vio *adj.* obvious.

o•ca•sión *f.* occasion, opportunity, cause; danger, rish; **de —** reduced, bargain; **avisos de —** want "ads" (*advertisements*); *Am.* **esta —** this time.

o•ca•sio•nal *adj.* occasional.

o•ca•sio•nar *v.* to occasion, cause.

o•ca•so *m.* sunset; setting (*of any star or planet*); west; decadence, decline, end.

oc•ci•den•tal *adj.* occidental, western.

oc•ci•den•te *m.* occident, west.

o•cé•a•no *m.* ocean.

o•ce•lo•te *m.* ocelot.

o•cio *m.* leisure, idleness; recreation, pastime.

o•cio•si•dad *f.* idleness, leisure.

o•cio•so *adj.* idle, useless.

oc•tu•bre *m.* October.

ocu•lar *adj.* ocular; **testigo** – eye witness; *m.* eyepiece, lens (*for the eye in a microscope or telescope*).

o•cu•lis•ta *m. & f.* oculist; *Am.* flatterer.

o•cul•tar *v.* to hide, conceal.

o•cul•to *adj.* hidden, concealed; *m. Am.* species of mole (*small animal*).

o•cu•pa•ción *f.* occupation; employment.

ocu•pan•te *m. & f.* occupant.

o•cu•par *v.* to occupy; to employ; **-se en** (*AM.* **-se de**) to be engaged in: to pay attention to, be interested in.

o•cu•rren•cia *f.* occurrence, event; witticism, joke, bright or funny idea.

o•cu•rren•te *adj.* witty, funny, humorous; occurring.

o•cu•rrir *v.* to occur.

o•cur•so *m. Ríopl.* petition, application.

o•da *f.* ode.

o•diar *v.* to hate.

o•dio *m.* hatred.

o•dio•so *adj.* odious, hateful.

o•dre *m.* wine bag; drunk.

o•es•te *m.* west; west wind.

o•fen•der *v.* to offend; to displease; **-se** to get offended; to become angry, take offense.

o•fen•sa *f.* offense.

o•fen•si•vo *adj.* offensive; obnoxious; attacking; **ofensiva** *f.* offensive.

o•fen•sor *m.* offender, *adj.* offending.

o•fer•ta *f.* offer; promise.

o•fi•cial *m.* official, officer; skilled workman; *adj.* official.

o•fi•ciar *v.* to officiate, serve, minister, perform the duties of a priest or minister; to communicate officially; **– de** to serve as, act as.

o•fi•ci•na *f.* office; shop; oficinesco *adj.* clerical, pertaining to an office.

o•fi•cio *m.* office, position; trade; function; official communication; religious office (*prayers*).

o•fi•cio•so *adj.* officious, meddlesome.

o•fre•cer[13] *v. irr.* to offer; to promise; **-se** to offer, occur, present itself; to offer oneself, volunteer; **¿qué se le ofrece a ud.?** What do you wish?

o•fre•ci•mien•to *m.* offer; offering.

o•fren•da *f.* offering, gift.

o•fus•ca•mien•to *m.* clouded vision, blindness; cloudiness of the mind, bewilderment, metal confusion.

o•fus•car[6] *v.* to darken, cast a shadow on; to blind; to could; to bewilder, confuse.

o•gro *m.* ogre.

o•í•do *m.* hearing; ear; **al –** confidentialy; **de** (*or* **al**) **–** by ear; de **-s** (*or* **de oídas**) by hearsay or rumor.

o•i•dor *m.* hearer, listener; judge.

o•ír[36] *v. irr.* to hear; to listen; to understand; **- misa** to attend mass; **– decir que**, to hear that; **– hablar de**

to hear about.

o•jal *m.* buttonhole; hole.

¡o•ja•lá! *interj.* God grant!; I hope so!; **– que**, would that. I hope that.

o•ja•zo *m.* large eye.

o•jea•da *f.* glimpse, quick glance.

o•jear *v.* to eye, stare; to bewich; to beat up, rouse (*wild game*).

o•je•ra *f.* dark circle under the eye; eyecup.

o•je•ri•za *f.* grudge, spite.

o•je•ro•so *adj.* with dark circles under the eye.

o•ji•va *f.* pointed arch; ojival *adj.* pointed (*arch*); **ventana ojival** window with a pointed arch.

o•jo *m.* (*órgano*) eye; (*agujero*) keyhole; hole; ¡-! careful! look out; **a –** by sight, by guess; **a -s vistas** visibly, clearly; **– de agua** spring (*of water*); **– de buey** porthole; **mal** (*or* **mal de**) **–** evil eye; *Am.* **hacer –** to cast the evil eye; *Am.* **pelar el –** to be alert, keep one's eye peeled; *Mex.*, *Ven.* **poner a uno los -s verdes** to deceive someone; **tener entre -s a** to have ill will toward, have a grudge against.

o•jo•ta *f. Andes.*, *Ch.*, *Ríopl.* leather sandal.

o•la *f.* wave.

o•le•a•da *f.* big wave; swell; surge; abundant yield of oil.

o•le•a•je, olaje *m.* swell, surge, succession of waves.

o•le•o *m.* oil, holy oil; **pintura al** – oil painting.

o•leo•so *adj.* oily.

o•ler[37] *v. irr.* to smell; to scent; **– a** to smack of; to smell like; *Am.* **olérselas** to suspect it; "smell a rat".

ol•fa•te•ar *v.* to scent, sniff, smell.

ol•fa•teo *m.* sniff, sniffing.

ol•fa•to *m.* sense of smell.

o•li•gar•quí•a *f.* oligarchy.

o•li•va *f.* olive; olive tree; olivar *m.* olive grove; **olivo** *m.* olive tree.

ol•mo *m.* elm.

o•lor *m.* (*en el olfato*) smell, odor, fragance; (*fama*) smack, trace, suspicion; *Am.* spice; **olorcillo** *m.* faint odor.

o•lo•ro•so *adj.* fragrant.

o•lo•te *m. Mex.*, *C.A.* cob, corncob.

ol•vi•da•di•zo *adj.* forgetful.

ol•vi•dar *v.* to forget; to neglect; **-se de** to forget; **olvidársele a uno algo** to forget something.

ol•vi•do *m.* forgetfulness; oblivion; neglect;: **echar al** – to cast into oblivion; to forget on purpose.

o•lla *f.* pot, kettle; olla (*vegetable and meat stew*); **- podrida** Spanish stew of mixed vegetables and meat.

om•bli•go *m.* navel; middle, center.

om•bú *m.* umbra tree.

o•mi•sión *f.* omision; oversight, neglect.

o•mi•so *adj.* careless, neglectful; *N. Arg.* guilty; **hacer caso** – to omit.

o•mi•tir *v,* to omit; to overlook.

óm•ni•bus *m.* omnibus, bus.

om•ni•po•ten•te *adj.* omnipotent, almighty.

on•da *f.* wave; ripple; sound wave; scallop.

on•de•ar *v.* to wave; to waver; to ripple; to sway, swing.

on•du•la•ción *f.* undulation, waving motion; wave; — **permanente**, permanent wave.

on•du•la•do *p.p. & adj.* wavy; scalloped (edge); — **permanente** permanent wave.

on•du•lan•te *adj.* wavy, waving.

on•du•lar *v.* to undulate, wave.

on•za *f.* ounce; ounce, wildcat; *Riopl.*, Bol. small tiger.

o•pa•ci•dad *f.* opacity; sadness.

o•pa•co *adj.* opaque, dim, dull.

ó•pa•lo *m.* opal.

ó•pe•ra *f.* opera.

o•pe•ra•ción *f.* operation; business transaction.

o•pe•ra•dor *m.* operator, surgeon.

o•pe•rar *v.* to operate; to take effect, work; to speculate *(in business)*; to manipulate, handle.

o•pe•re•ta *f.* operetta.

opi•nar *v.* to express an opinion; to think; to judge; to argue.

o•pi•nión *f.* opinion; reputation

o•pio *m.* opium.

o•po•ner⁹ *v. irr.* to oppose; **-se** to disapprove; **-se** a to oppose, be against.

o•por•to *m.* port wine.

o•por•tu•ni•dad *f.* opportunity.

o•por•tu•no *adj.* opportune; convenient, timely.

o•po•si•ción *f.* opposition; competition; **-es** competitive examinations.

o•po•si•tor *m.* opponent, competitor.

o•pre•sión *f.* oppression.

o•pre•si•vo *adj.* oppressive.

o•pre•sor *m.* oppressor.

o•pri•mir *v.* to oppress; to crush; to press down.

o•pro•bio *m.* infamy; insult; shame; dishonor.

op•tar *v.* to choose, select; — **por** to decide upon; to choose.

óp•ti•ca *f.* optics.

óp•ti•co *adj.* optical, optic; *m.* optician.

op•ti•mis•mo *m.* optimism; **optimista** *m. & f.* optimist; *adj.* optimistic.

óp•ti•mo *adj.* very good, very best.

o•pues•to *p.p. of* **oponer** opposed; *adj.* opposite; contrary.

o•pu•len•cia *f.* opulence, abundance, wealth.

o•pu•len•to *adj.* opulant, wealthy.

o•que•dad *f.* cavity, hollow; chasm.

o•ra *conj.* now, then; whether; either.

o•ra•ción *f.* oration; prayer; sentence.

o•ra•cu•lo *m.* oracle.

o•ra•dor *m.* orator, speaker.

o•ral *adj.* oral.

o•rar *v.* to pray.

o•ra•to•rio *f.* oratory, eloquence.

o•ra•to•rio *m.* oratory, private chapel; oratorio *(a religious musical composition)*; *adj.* oratorical, pertainig to oratory.

or•be *m.* orb, sphere, globe; the earth; world, universe.

ór•bi•ta *f.* orbit; eye socket.

or•den *m. (colocación)* order; succession; series; class, group; relation; proportion; *f. (mando)* order, command; *(sociedad)* honorary or religious order; *m. & f.* sacrament of ordination; **a sus órdenes** at your service.

or•de•na•do *p p. & adj.* ordered; ordained; orderly; neat.

or•de•nan•za *f.* ordinance, decree, law; command, order; *m.* orderly *(military)*.

or•de•nar *v.* to arrange, put in order; to order, command; to ordain; **-se** to become ordained.

or•de•ña *f.* milking.

or•de•ñar *v.* to milk.

or•di•na•riez *f.* commonness, lack of manners.

or•di•na•rio *adj.* ordinary; usual; common, coarse; *m.* ordinary *(a bishop or judge)*; ordinary mail; daily household expense; **de** — usually, ordinarily.

o•re•ar *v.* to air; **-se** to be exposed to the air, to dry in the air.

o•re•ja *f.* ear; hearing, loop; small flap; *Am.* handle *(shaped like an ear)*; **orejano** *adj.* unbranded *(cattle)*; *Ven., Col.* cautious; *m. Cuba* aloof, unsociable person; **orejera** *f.* ear muff; ear flap; **orejón** *m.* pull by the ear; *Col.* rancher or inhabitant of the **sabana**; *adj. Col.* long-eared, long-horned; *Col.* unbranded *(cattle)*; *Col.* coarse, crude, uncouth.

or•fan•dad *f.* orphanage *(state of being an orphan)*.

or•fa•na•to *m.* orphanage, orphan asylum.

or•fa•na•to•rio *Am.* = **orfanato**.

or•fe•bre *m.* goldsmith; silversmith.

or•feón *m.* glee club, choir.

or•gá•ni•co *adj.* organic.

or•ga•ni•llo *m.* hand organ, hurdy-gurdy.

or•ga•nis•mo *m.* organism.

or•ga•ni•za•ción *f.* organization.

or•ga•ni•za•dor *m.* organizer.

or•ga•ni•zar⁹ *v.* to organize; to arrange.

ór•ga•no *m.* organ; **organillo** *m.* hand organ.

or•gí•a *f.* orgy, wild revel.

or•gu•llo *m.* pride; haughtiness, arrogance.

or•gu•llo•so *adj.* proud; haughty, arrogant.

o•rien•tal *adj.* oriental, eastern.

o•rien•tar *v.* to orientate, orient; **-se** to orient oneself, find one's bearings.

o•rien•te *m.* orient, east; east wind; source, origin.

o•ri•fi•ca•ción *f.* gold filling.

o•ri•fi•cio *m.* orifice, small hole, aperture, outlet.

o•ri•gen *m.* origin; source.

o•ri•gi•nal *adj.* original; strange, quaint; *m.* original; manuscript, copy; queer person; **originalidad** *f.*

originality.

o•ri•gi•nar v. to originate, cause to be; **-se** originate, arise.

o•ri•lla f. shore, bank; beach; edge, border; **-s** Am. outskirts, environs.

o•ri•llar v. to border, trim the edge of; to skirt, go along the edge of; to reach the edge or shore.

o•rín m. rust; **orines** m. pl. urine.

o•ri•na f. urine.

o•ri•nar v. to urinate.

o•riol m. oriole.

o•riun•do adj. native; **ser – de** to hail from, come from.

or•la f. border; trimming, fringe.

or•lar v. to border, edge, trim with a border or fringe.

or•na•do adj. ornate; p.p. adorned, ornamented.

or•na•men•tar v. to ornament, adorn.

or•na•men•to m. ornament; decoration; **-s** sacred vestments.

or•nar v. to adorn.

o•ro m. gold; gold ornaments; **-s** "gold coins" (Spanish card suit).

o•ron•do adj. self-satisfied, puffed up, vain; Am. serene, calm.

o•ro•pel m. tinsel.

or•ques•ta f. orchestra.

or•quí•dea f. orchid.

or•ti•ga f. nettle.

or•to•gra•fí•a f. orthography, spelling.

or•to•grá•fi•co adj. orthographic (pertaining to orthography or spelling).

o•ru•ga f. caterpillar.

or•zue•lo m. sty (on the eyelid).

o•sa•dí•a f. boldness, daring.

o•sa•do adj. bold, daring.

o•sar v. to dare, venture.

os•ci•la•ción f. oscillation, sway; fluctuation, wavering.

os•ci•lar v. to oscillate, swing, sway; to waver.

os•cu•re•cer = obscurecer.

os•cu•ri•dad = obscuridad.

os•cu•ro = obscuro.

o•so m. bear; **– blanco** polar bear; **– hormiguero** anteater; **– marino** seal.

os•ten•ta•ción f. ostentation, show, display.

os•ten•tar v. to display, show; to show off; to boast.

os•ten•to•so adj. ostentatious, showy.

os•tión m. large oyster.

os•tra f. oyster.

o•ta•te m. Méx., C.A. species of bamboo; Méx., C.A. bamboo stock or cane.

o•te•ro m. hillock, small hill, knoll.

o•to•ñal adj. autumnal, of autumn.

o•to•ño m. autumn, fall.

o•tor•gar[7] v. to grant; to promise; to consent to.

o•tro adj. another; **otra vez** again; Am. **como dijo el**

– as someone said.

o•tro•ra adv. formerly, in other times.

o•va•ción f. ovation, enthusiastic applause.

o•val, ovalado adj. oval; **óvalo** m. oval.

o•va•ri•co adj. ovarian.

o•va•rio m. ovary.

o•ve•ja f. sheep.

o•ve•je•ro m. shepherd; sheep dog.

o•ve•ju•no adj. sheep, pertaining or relating to sheep.

o•ve•ro adj. peach-colored (applied to horses and cattle); Ríopl. mottled, spotted; Ríopl. multicolored; Ríopl. **ponerle a uno –** to insult someone.

o•ve•rol, overoles m. Ch., Col. overalls.

o•vi•llar v. to ball, wind or form into a ball; **-se** to curl up into a ball.

o•vi•llo m. ball of yarn or thread; tangle; **hacerse uno un –** to curl up into a ball; to become entangled, confused.

ovino, a adj. ovine, of sheep.

oviparo, a adj. oviparous II. m. f. oviparous animal.

ovni m. ufo, unidentified, flying object.

ovulación f. ovulation.

ovular I. adj. ovular. II. intr. to ovulat

ovulo m. ovule.

o•xi•da•do p.p. rusted; adj. rusty.

o•xi•dar v. to oxidize; to rust; **-se** to become oxidized; to rust.

o•xí•ge•no m. oxygen.

o•yen•te m. & f. listener, auditor, hearer; adj. listening.

P

pa•be•llón m. pavilion; canopy; banner, flag; shelter, covering; external ear.

pa•bi•lo m. wick; snuff (of a candle).

pa•cer[13] v. irr. to pasture; to graze.

pa•cien•cia f. patience.

pa•cien•te adj. patient; m. & f. patient.

pa•cien•zu•do adj. patient, long-suffering.

pa•ci•fi•car[6] v. to pacify; to appease.

pa•cí•fi•co adj. pacific, peaceful, calm.

pac•to m. pact, agreement.

pa•de•cer[13] v. irr. to suffer.

pa•de•ci•mien•to m. suffering.

pa•dras•tro m. stepfather; hangnail.

pa•dre m. father; **-s** parents; ancestors; adj. Am. very great, stupendous.

pa•dre•nues•tro m. paternoster, the Lord's Prayer.

pa•dri•no m. godfather; sponsor, patron; second in a due; best man (at a wedding).

pae•lla f. a popular rice dish with chiken, vegetables, etc.

pa•ga f. payment; pay, salary.

pa•ga•de•ro adj. payable.

pa•ga•do *p.p.* & *adj.* paid; elf-atified, conceited; **– de sí mismo** pleased with oneself.

pa•ga•dor *m.* payer; paymaster; paying teller (*in a bank*).

pa•ga•nis•mo *m.* paganism, heathenism.

pa•ga•no *adj.* pagan; *m.* pagan; payer; dupe, sucker.

pa•gar[7] *v.* to pay; to pay for; to requite, return (*love*); **-se de** to be proud of; to boast of; to be pleased with; *Riopl.* **-se de palabras** to let oneself be tricked; *Am.* **– a nueve** to pay in excess.

pa•ga•ré *m.* promissory note; L.O.U.

pá•gi•na *f.* page.

pá•gi•nar *v.* to page.

pa•go *m.* (*premio*) payment; prize, reward; (*distrito*) country district; *Riopl.* one´s native farm land or district; *adj.* paid; *Am.* **estar** – to be quits.

pai•la *f.* large pan; *C.A.* saucer.

pa•ís *m.* nation, country; region.

pai•sa•je *m.* landscape.

pai•sa•na•je *m.* peasantry, country people; civilians; *Andes* gang of farm laborers.

pai•sa•no *m.* countryman; peasant; fellow countryman; civilian.

pa•ja *f.* straw; chaff; rubbish; *Andes* grass for pasture; **echar-s** to draw lots; **por quítame allá esas -s** for an insignificant reason or pretext; **en un quítame allá esas -s** in a jiffy, in a second; **a humo de -s** thoughtlessly; **no lo hizo a humo de -s** he did not do it without a special reason or intention.

pa•jar *m.* straw loft, barn.

pá•ja•ro *m.* bird; shrewd, cautious person; *Ch.* absent-minded person; *Ch.*, *Riopl.* person of suspicious conduct; **– carpintero** woodpecker; **– mosca** humming bird.

pa•je *m.* page, valet, attendant.

pa•ji•zo *adj.* made of straw; covered with straw; straw colored.

pa•jo•nal *m.* plain or field of tall coarse grass.

pa•la *f.* shovel; trowel; scoop; paddle; blade of an oar; racket; upper (*of a shoe*), cunning, craftiness; **meter la** – to deceive with cunning; *Am.* **hacer la** – to deceive with cunning; to stall, pretend to work; to flatter; **palada** *f.* scoop, shovelful; stroke of an oar.

pa•la•bra *f.* word; promise; **de** – by word of mouth; **cuatro -s** a few words; **empeñar la** – to promise, pledge; **tener la** – to have the floor; *Am.* ¡ – ! I mean it, it is true!.

pa•la•bre•ro *adj.* wordy, talkative.

pa•la•bri•ta *f.* a little word, a few word; a word of advice.

pa•la•cio *m.* palace; **palaciego** *m.* courtier; *adj.* relating to a palace or court; court (*used as an adj.*).

pa•la•dar *m.* palate; taste, relish.

pa•la•de•ar *v.* to relish, taste with relish.

pa•la•dín *m.* knight; champion; defender.

pa•lan•ca *f.* lever; crowbar; bar used for carrying a load.

pa•lan•ga•na *f.* washbowl, basin; *S.A.* platter; *Ch.* large wooden bowl; *m.* Andes bluffer, charlatan.

pa•la•tal *adj.* palatal.

pal•co *m.* theater box; **– escénico** stage.

pa•len•que *m.* palisade, fence; enclosure; *Riopl.* hitching post or plank.

pa•le•ta *f.* small flat shovel; mason´s trowel; shoulder blade; blade (*of a rudder, of a ventilating fan*); paddle (*of a paddle wheel*); painter´s palette; *Am.* candy, sweetmeat or ice cream attached to a stick; *Am.* a wooden paddle to stir with, or for beating clothes; **en dos -s** in a jiffy, in a second; **paletilla** *f.* shoulder blade.

pa•li•de•cer[13] *v. irr.* to turn pale.

pa•li•dez *f.* pallor, paleness.

pá•li•do *adj.* pallid, pale.

pa•li•llo *m.* small stick; toothpick; **tocar todos lo -s** (*Ch.* **menear uno los -s**) to try every possible means.

pa•li•za *f.* beating (*with a stick*), thrashing.

pa•li•za•da *f.* palisade; stockade.

pal•ma *f.* palm tree; palm leaf; palm of tha hand; **batir -s** to clap, applaud; **llevarse la** – to triumph, win, carry off the honors; to be the best.

pal•ma•da *f.* slap, clap.

pal•ma•rio *adj.* clear, evident.

pal•ma•to•ria *f.* small candlestick with handle.

pal•me•ar *v.* to clap, applaud; *Am.* to pat, clap on the back; *Riopl.* to flatter.

pal•me•ra *f.* palm tree.

pal•mo *m.* span (*about 9 inches*); **– a** – slowly, foot by foot.

pal•mo•te•ar *v.* to clap, applaud.

pa•lo *m.* stick; pole; log; mast; wood; blow with a stick; suit (*in a deck of cards*); *Am.* tree; *Riopl.* reprimand, reproof; *P.R.*, *Ven.* large swallow of liquor; **– del Brasil,** Brasil wood; *Ven.* **– a pique** rail fence, barbed wire fence; *Mex.*, *C.A.* **a medio** – half-done; half-drunk; *Am.* **a – entero,** drunk.

pa•lo•ma *f.* dove; pigeon; pleasant, mild person; **-s** whitecaps.

pa•lo•mar *m.* dovecot (*shelter for doves or pigeons*).

pa•lo•mi•lla *f.* little dove; moth; small butterfly; **-s** whitecaps.

pa•lo•mi•ta *f.* little dove; **-s** *Am.* popcorn.

pal•pa•ble *adj.* palpable (*shat can be felt ot touched*); clear, obvious, evident.

pal•par *v.* to feel; to touch; to grope.

pal•pi•ta•ción *f.* palpitation; beat, throb.

pal•pi•tan•te *adj.* palpitating, throbbing, trembling; exciting; **la cuestión** – the burning question.

pal•pi•tar *v.* to palpitate; to throb, beat.

pal•ta *f.* *Col.*, *Ven.*, *Andes.*, *Riopl.*, *Ch.* avocado, alligator pear; **palto** *m.* *Col.*, *Ven.*, *Andes.*, *Riopl.*, *Ch.* avocado tree. See **aguacate**.

pa·lú·di·co *adj.* marshy; **fiebre palúdica** malarial, or marsh fever; malaria; **paludismo** *m.* malaria.

pam·pa *f. Am.* pampa (*vast treeless plain of South America*); *Am.* prairie; *Ch.* drill field (*military*); *m.* & *f.* pampa Indian of Argentina; *m. Am.* language of the pampa Indian; *adj. Am.* pertaining to the pampa Indian *Ríopl.* **caballo** – horse with head and body of different colors; *Ríopl.* **trato** – dubious or dishonest deal; *Am.* **estar a la** – to be in the open; *Ríopl.* **tener todo a la** – to be ragged or to be indecently exposed; *Ch.* **quedar en-** to be left without clothes; to be left in the lurch.

pam·pea·no *adj. Ríopl.* of, or pertaining to, the pampa.

pam·pe·ro *adj. Ríopl.* of, or pertaining to the pampa; *m. Ríopl.* inhabitant of the pampas; *Ríopl.* violent wind of the pampa.

pan *m.* bread; losf of bread; wheat; **-es** fields of grain; breadstuffs; *Am.* **echar -es** to brag, boast.

pa·na *f.* corduroy.

pa·na·de·ría *f.* bakery.

pa·na·de·ro *m.* baker; *Ch.* flatterer.

pa·nal *m.* honeycomb; sweetmeat (*made of sugar, egg white, and lemon*).

pa·na·me·ri·ca·no *adj.* Pan-American.

pan·de·ar·se *v.* to bulge, warp; to sag.

pan·deo *m.* sag; bulge.

pan·di·lla *f.* gang, band.

pa·ne·la *f. Col., C.A.* unrefined sugar.

pan·fle·to *m. Am.* pamphlet.

pá·ni·co *m.* panic; *adj.* panic, panicky.

pa·nne *f.* accident, car trouble.

pa·no·cha *f.* ear of corn; *Mex.* Mexican raw sugar; *Col., C.A.* a kind of tamale.

pan·qué *m. Col., C.A., Mex.* small cake, cup cake; *Am.* pancake.

pan·ta·lón *m.* trousers; pants; **un par de –es** a pair of trousers.

pan·ta·lla *f.* light shade; screen; fireplace scren; motion-picture screen; *C.R.* fan, palm leaf fan; *P.R.* earring.

pan·ta·no *m.* swamp; dam; difficulty.

pan·ta·no·so *adj.* swampy, marshy; muddy.

pan·te·ón *m.* cemetery.

pan·te·ra *f.* panther.

pan·to·rri·lla *f.* calf (*of the leg*).

pan·tu·fla *f.* bedroom slipper.

pan·za *f.* paunch, belly.

pan·zón, panzudo *adj.* big-bellied.

pa·ñal *m.* diaper; **estar en -es** to be in one's infancy; to have little or no knowledge of a thing.

pa·ño *m.* cloth (*any cloth, especially woolen*); blotch or spot on the skin; film on the eyeball; *Mex., Cuba* parcel of tillable land; *Mex.* kerchief, shawl; **– de mano** towel; **– de mesa** tablecloth; **al** – off-stage;

-s clothes, garments; **-s menores** underwear; pañero *m.* clothier.

pa·ño·lón *m.* scarf, large kerchief; shawl.

pa·ñue·lo *m.* hankerchief.

pa·pa *m.* Pope; *f.* potato; fib, lie; *Am.* snap, easy job; **-s** pap (*soft food for babies*); soup; *Ríopl., Ch.* **cosa** – someting good to eat; excellent thing; **echar -s** to fib, lie; *Am.* **importarle a uno una** – not to matter to one a bit; *Am.* **no saber ni** – not to a know a thing; to be completely ignorant.

pa·pá *m.* papa; *Mex., C.A., Andes* **– grande** grandfather.

pa·pa·ga·yo *m.* parrot; talker, chatterer.

pa·pal *adj.* papal.

pa·pa·lo·te, papelote *m. Carib., Mex.* kite.

pa·pa·mos·cos *m.* flycatcher (*a bird*); simpleton, half-wit, dunce.

pa·pa·na·tas *m.* simpleton, fool, dunce.

pa·pa·rru·cha *f.* fib, lie, **paparruchero** *m.* fibber.

pa·pa·ya *f.* papaya.

pa·pel *m.* (*hoja*) paper; sheet of paper; document; (*parte dramática*) role; **– de estraza** brown wrapping paper **– de lija** sandpaper; **– de seda** tissue paper; **– moneda** paper money; **– secante** blotting paper; **hacer el – de** to play the role of; **hacer buen (or mal)** – to cut a good (*or bad*) figure.

pa·pe·le·ra *f.* folder, file, case or device for keeping paper; *Am.* wastepaper basket; **papelero** *m.* paper manufacturer; *adj.* pertaining to paper; vain, ostentatious.

pa·pe·le·ría *f.* stationery store; stationery; lot of papers.

pa·pe·le·ta *f.* card, file card, slip of paper.

pa·pe·lu·cho *m.* worthless piece of paper.

pa·pe·ra *f.* goiter; **-s** mumps.

pa·que·te *m.* package; bundle; dandy; packet boat (*mail boat*); *adj. Am.* olled up, dressed up; *Ríopl., Col.* important, pompous; *Ríopl., Col.* insincere.

par *adj.* even; *n.* pair, couple; peer; **a la** – at par; jointly; at the same time; **al – de** on a par with; **bajo** – below par; **sin** – peerless, without an equal, having no equal; **sobre** – above par; **de – en** – wide-open.

pa·ra *prep.* for; to; towar; in order to; ¿– **qué**? what for; **– que** so that; **– siempre** forever; **– mis adentros** to myself; **sin qué ni – qué** without rhyme or reason; *m. Ríopl.* Paraguayan tobacco; *Ríopl.* Paraguayan (*used as nickname*).

pa·ra·bién *m.* congratulations; **dar el** – to congratulate.

pa·ra·bri·sa *m.* windshield.

pa·ra·caí·das *m.* parachute; **paracaidistas** *m.* & *f.* parachutist.

pa·ra·cho·ques *m.* bumper.

pa·ra·da *f.* stop; stopping place; bet, stake; military review; *P.R.* parade; *Ríopl.* boastfulness; *Ríopl.* **te-**

ner mucha – to dress very well.

pa•ra•de•ro *m.* stopping place; whereabouts; end.

pa•ra•do *p.p.* & *adj.* stopped; unoccupied, unemployed, fixed, motionless; *Ch., P.R.* standing, erect, straight up; *Ch., P.R.* stif, proud; *Riopl.* cold, unenthusiastic; *P.R., Ch., Andes* **caer uno –** to land on one's feet; to be lucky; *Am.* **estar bien –** to be well-fixed, well-established; to be lucky; *m. Am.* air, appearance.

pa•ra•do•ja *f.* paradox.

pa•ra•fi•na *f.* paraffin.

pa•ra•guas *m.* umbrella; **paragüero** *m* umbrella stand; umbrella maker or seller.

pa•ra•gua•yo *adj.* & *m.* Paraguayan.

pa•raí•so *m.* paradise, heaven; upper gallery (*in a theater*).

pa•ra•je *m.* place; spot; situation.

pa•ra•le•lo *adj.* parallel; similar; *m.* parallel; similarity; **paralela** *f.* parallel line; **paralelismo** *m.* parallelism.

pa•rá•li•sis *f.* paralysis.

pa•ra•li•zar[9] *v.* to paralyze; to stop.

pá•ra•mo *m.* high, bleak plain; cold region; *Andes* blizzard or a cold drizzle.

pa•ran•gón *m.* comparison.

pa•ran•go•nar *v.* to compare.

pa•ra•nin•fo *m.* assembly hall, lecture hall, auditorium.

pa•ra•pe•to *m.* parapet.

pa•rar *v.* to stop; to end, end up, come to an end; to parry (*in fencing*); to set up (*type*); *Am.* to stand, place in upright position; **– atención** to notice; **– mientes en** to observe, notice; *Riopl.* **– las orejas** to prick up one's ears; to pay close attention; **-se** to stop; *Am.* to stand up, get up.

pa•ra•rra•yos *m.* lightning rod.

pa•rá•si•to *m.* parasite; *adj.* parasitic.

pa•ra•sol *m.* parasol.

par•ce•la *f.* parcel of land; particle, small piece.

par•cial *adj.* partial; *m.* follower, partisan; **parciali-dad** *f.* partiality; faction, party.

par•che *m.* mending patch; sticking plaster; medicated plaster; drum.

par•dal *m.* sparrow; linnet; sly fellow.

par•de•ar *v.* to grow dusky; to appear brownish-grey.

par•do *adj.* dark-grey; brown; dark; cloudy; *m.* leopard; *Carib., Riopl.* mulatto; **pardusco** *adj.* greyish; brownish.

pa•re•ar *v.* to pair, couple, match, mate.

pa•re•cer[13] *v. irr.* to seem; to appear, show up; **-se** to resemble each other, look alike; *m.* opinion; appearance; looks; **al –** apparently, seemingly.

pa•re•ci•do *adj.* alike, similar; **bien –** good-looking; *p.p.* of **parecer**; *m.* similarity, likeness, resemblance.

pa•red *f.* wall; **– maestra** main wall; **– medianera** partition wall.

pa•re•ja *f.* pair; couple; match; partner; *Am.* team of two horses; *Riopl.* horse race.

pa•re•je•ro *m. Riopl.* race horse; *Riopl.* over-familiar person, backslapper, hail-fellow-well-met.

pa•re•jo *adj.* even; smooth; equal; *adv. Riopl.* hard.

pa•ren•te•la *f.* relatives, kin.

pa•ren•tes•co *m.* kinship, relationship.

pa•rén•te•sis *m.* parenthesis; digression; **entre –** by the way.

pa•ria *m.* & *f.* outcast.

pa•ri•dad *f.* par, equality.

pa•rlen•te *m.* & *f.* relative, relation.

pa•rir *v.* to give birth; to bear (*children*).

par•la•men•tar *v.* to converse; to parley, discuss terms with an enemy.

par•la•men•ta•rio *adj.* parliamentary; *m.* member of parliament; envoy to a parley.

par•la•men•to *m.* speech (*of a character in a play*); parley; parliament, legislative assembly.

par•lan•chín *adj.* talkative; *m.* talker, chatterer.

par•le•ro *adj.* talkative; gossipy; chattering, chirping.

par•lo•te•ar *v.* to prate, prattle, chatter, chat.

par•lo•te•o *m.* chatter, prattle, idle talk.

pa•ro *m.* work stoppage; lockout; *Am.* throw (*in the game of dice*); *Am.* **– y pinta** game of dice.

pa•ro•dia *f.* parody, take-off, humorous imitation.

pa•ro•diar *v.* to parody, take off, imitate.

pa•ró•ti•das *f. pl.* mumps.

par•pa•de•ar *v.* to wink; to blink; to flutter the eyelids; to twinkle.

par•pa•de•o *m.* winking; blinking; fluttering of the eyelids; twinkling.

pár•pa•do *m.* eyelid.

par•que *m.* park; *Am.* ammunition.

pa•rra *f.* grapevine; earthenware jug.

pa•rra•fa•da *f.* chat.

pá•rra•fo *m.* paragraph; **echar un – con** to have a chat with.

pa•rran•da *f.* revel, orgy, spree; *Col.* gang, band; **andar** (*or* **ir**) **de –** to go on a spree.

pa•rran•de•ar *v.* to revel, make merry, go on a spree.

pa•rri•lla *f.* grill, gridiron, broiler; grate.

pá•rro•co *m.* parish priest.

pa•rro•quia *f.* parish; parish church; clientele, customers.

pa•rro•quia•no *m.* client, customer; parishioner; *adj.* parochial, of a parish.

par•si•mo•nia *f.* thrift, economy; moderation; prudence.

par•si•mo•nio•so *adj.* thrifty; stingy; cautious; slow.

par•te *f.* part; share; place; party (*legal term*); **-s** qualities; **parte** *m.* notice, announcement; *Am.* unnecessary excuses or explanations; **de algún tiempo a esta –** for some time past; **de – de** on behalf of; in favor of; **de – a –** through, from one side to the other; **dar –** to inform; **echar a mala –** to take amiss; **en –** partly; **por todas -s** everywhere;

m. telegram; message.

par•te•ra *f.* midwife.

par•ti•ción *f.* partition, division.

par•ti•ci•pa•ción *f.* participation, share; notice.

par•ti•ci•pan•te *m. & f.* participant; *adj.* participating, sharing.

par•ti•ci•par *v.* to participate, share; to inform, notify.

par•ti•ci•pe *m. & f.* participant; *adj.* participating.

par•ti•ci•pio *m.* participle.

par•tí•cu•la *f.* particle.

par•ti•cu•lar *adj.* particular, special; peculiar; private, personal; odd, strange; **en –** specially; **lecciones -es** private lessons; *m.* private citizen; individual; point, detail; matter.

par•ti•da *f.* (*salida*) departue, leave; (*entidad*) item, entry; record; band, group; squad; shipment; game; set (*in tennis*); *Am.* part in the hair; **– de bautismo (de matrimonio** *or* **de defunción)** birth (marriage, or death) certificate; **– de campo** picnic; **– de caza** hunting party; **– doble** double-entry bookkeeping; *Mex., Riopl.* **confesar la –** to tell the truth, speak plainly; **jugar una mala -** to play a mean trick.

par•ti•da•rio *m.* partisan, follower, supporter.

par•ti•do *m.* party, faction, group; contest; game; profit; district; Bol. **a** (*or* **al) –** in equal shares; *Am.* **dar –** to give a handicap or advantage (*in certain games*); **darse a –** to yield, give up; **sacar – de** to derive advantage from, make the best of; **tomar un –** to decide, make a decision.

par•tir *v.* (*dividir*) to split, divide; to crack, break; (*salir*) to depart, leave; **a – de hoy** starting today; from this day on; *Am.* **a** (*or* **al) –** in equal parts; *Am.* **– a uno por el eje** to ruin someone.

par•ti•tu•ra *f.* musical score.

par•to *m.* childbirth, delivery; product, offspring; **estar de –** to be in labor.

par•va•da *f.* pile of unthreshed grain; brood; *Andes* flock (*of birds or children*).

par•ve•dad *f.* smallness; trifle; snack, bit of food.

pár•vu•lo *m.* child; *adj.* small; innocent.

pa•sa *f.* raisin; woolly hair of negros.

pa•sa•da *f.* passing, passage; *Am.* stay *Am.* embarrassment, shame; **una mala –** a mean trick; **de –** on the way; incidentally, by the way; **dar una – por** to pass by, walk by.

pa•sa•di•zo *m.* aisle; narrow hall; narrow pass ageway.

pa•sa•do *m.* pat; *p.p.* past, gone; *adj.* overripe, spoiled *Mex.* dried (*fruits*). *Col.* thin, bony (*animal*); **– mañana** day after tomorrow; **el año –** last year; **en días -s** in days gone by.

pa•sa•je *m.* passage; fare, ticket; total number of passengers; *Carib., Mex. Col.* private alley; *Col., Ven.* anecdote.

pa•sa•je•ro *adj.* passing, temporary, fleeting;

transitory; *m.* passenger; guest (*of a hotel*).

pa•sa•ma•no *m.* railing, hand rail; gangplank; gangway (*of a ship*).

pa•sa•por•te *m.* passport.

pa•sar *v.* to pass; to cross; to surpass, exceed; to pierce; to go forward; to go over (in, by, to); to enter; to carry over, take across; to happen; to get along; to swallow; to overlook; to tolerate; to suffer; **– las de Caín** to have a hard time; **– por alto** to omit, overlook; **– por las armas** to execute; **-se** to transfer, change over; to get overripe, spoiled; to exceed, go beyond; **se me pasó decirte** I forgot to tell you; *Ch.* **pasársela a uno** to deceive someone, break someone's confidence; **un buen –** enough to live on.

pa•sa•re•la *f.* gangplank.

pa•sa•tiem•po *m.* pastime; *Am.* cookie.

pas•cua *f.* Easter, Jewish Passover; **– florida** (*or* **de resurrección)** Easter Sunday; **- de Navidad** Christmas.

pa•se *m.* pass, permit; thrust (*in fencing*); pass (*with the cape in bullfighting*).

pa•se•ar *v.* to walk; to take a walk; to ride; **-se** to take a walk; to parade; **-se en automóvil** to take an automobile ride; **-se a caballo** to go horseback riding.

pa•se•o *m.* walk, ride; parade; public park; boulevard; **– en automóvil** automobile ride; **dar un –** to take a walk.

pa•si•llo *m.* aisle; hallway, corridor; short step; short skit; *Col.*, Ec. a type of dance music; *Mex.* runner, hall carpet.

pa•sión *f.* passion; suffering.

pa•si•vo *adj.* passive; inactive; *m.* liabilities, debts; debit, debit side (*in bookkeeping*).

pas•mar *v.* to astound, stun; **-se** to be amazed, stunned; to marvel; to get a sudden chill; to get frostbitten; *P.R.* to become dried up, shriveled up; *P.R., Mex.* to get bruised by the saddle or pack (*said of horses and mules*).

pas•mo *m.* amazement, astonishment; wonder, awe.

pas•mo•so *adj.* astonishing, astounding; marvellous.

pa•so *m.* pass; step; pace; gait; passage; passing; skit; incident; *P.R., Ch., Andes* ford; *Mex.* ferry, ferryboat wharf; *adv.* slowly; **de -** by the way, in passing; **al – que** while; **salir del –** to get out of a difficulty; *Am.* **marcar el –** to mark step, obey humbly; *adj.* dried (*figs, grapes, prunes, etc.*); **paso a nivel** grade crossing.

pas•ta *f.* paste; dough; moodles; book cover, binding; *Am.* cookie, cracker; **de buena –** of good temper or disposition.

pas•tal *m. Am.* range, grazing land, large pasture.

pas•tar *v.* to pasture, graze.

pas•te•ar *v. Mex., Riopl.* to graze, pasture.

pas•tel *m.* pie; pastry roll; filled pastry; trick, fraud; secret pact, plot; pastel crayon; **pintura al –** pastel painting.

pas•te•le•ría *f.* pastry shop, bakery; pastry.

pas•te•le•ro *m.* pastry cook; *Cuba* turncoat (*person who changes easily from one political party to another*); *Riopl.* political intriguer.

pas•te•ri•zar⁹, pasteurizar⁹ *v.* to pasteurize.

pas•ti•lla *f.* tablet (*of medicine, candy, etc.*); bar (*of chocolate*); cake (*of soap*).

pas•ti•zal *m.* pasture, grassland.

pas•to *m.* pasture; grassland; grazing; nourishment; *Am.* grass; **a todo** — without restraint.

pas•tor *m.* shepherd; pastor.

pas•to•ral *adj.* pastoral; *f.* pastoral play; idyll; pastoral letter; **pastorela** *f.* pastoral, pastoral play; **pastoril** *adj.* pastoral.

pas•to•so *adj.* pasty, soft; mellow (*said of the voice*); *Am.* grassy.

pas•tu•ra *f.* pasture; fodder, feed.

pa•ta *f.* foot, leg (*of an animal, table, chair, etc.*); female duck; **– de gallo** crow's-foot (*wrinkle at the corner of the eye*); *Ch., Andes* **– de perro** wanderer; *Riopl.* **hacer – ancha** to stand firm, face a danger; **meter la –** to put one's foot in it, make an embarrassing blunder; **-s arriba** upside down, head over heels.

pa•ta•cón *m. Riopl.* silver coin worth about one peso.

pa•ta•da *f.* kick; stamp (*with the foot*); footprint; "kick", intoxicating effect; **a -s** with kicks; in great abundance; *Andes* **en dos -s** in a jiffy, in a second.

pa•ta•le•ar *v.* to kick around; to stamp.

pa•ta•le•o *m.* kicking; stamping.

pa•ta•le•ta *f.* convulsion; fainting fit.

pa•tán *m.* boor, ill-mannered person; rustic; *adj.* rude, boorish, ill-mannered.

pa•ta•ta *f.* potato.

pa•te•ar *v.* to kick; to stamp the foot; to tramp about, to trample on; to humiliate; *Am.* to kick, spring back (*as a gun*); *Ch.* to have a kick or intoxicating effect.

pa•ten•tar *v.* to patent.

pa•ten•te *adj.* patent, evident, clear; *f.* patent; grant; privilege, *Carib.* **de –** excellent, of best quality.

pa•ten•ti•zar⁹ *v.* to evidence, reveal, show.

pa•ter•nal *adj.* paternal; fatherly.

pa•ter•ni•dad *adj.* paternity, fatherhood; authorship.

pa•ter•no *adj.* paternal, fatherly.

pa•té•ti•co *adj.* pathetic.

pa•ti•bu•la•rio *adj.* harrowing, frightful, hair-raising; criminal.

pa•tí•bu•lo *m.* scaffold, gallows.

pa•ti•lla *f.* small foot or paw; *Col., Ven.* watermelon; *Riopl.* stone or brick bench (*near a wall*); *Riopl.* railing of a balcony; *Ch.* slip from a plant; **-s** side whiskers; **Patillas** the Devil.

pa•tín *m.* skate; a small patio; goosander (*a kin of duck*); **– de ruedas** roller skate; **patinadero** *m.* skating rink.

pa•ti•nar *v.* to skate; to skid.

pa•tio *m.* patio, open court, courtyard; *Am.* railway switchyard; *Am.* **pasarse uno al –** to take undue liberties.

pa•ti•tuer•to *adj.* crook-legged; knockkneed; bowlegged.

pa•ti•zam•bo *adj.* knock-kneed.

pa•to *m.* duck; **pagar el –** to be the goat; to get the blame; *Riopl.* **andar –** to be flat broke, penniless; *Am.* **hacerse –** to play the fool; *Mex., Riopl.* **pasarse de – a ganso** to take undue liberties; *Am.* **ser el – de la boda** to be the life of the party; **patito** *m.* duckling.

pa•to•cha•da *f.* stupidity, blunder, nonsense.

pa•to•jo *adj.* crooked-legged; bowlegged; *m. & f. Guat.* child; young person.

pa•tra•ña *f.* fabulous tale; lie, falsehood.

pa•tria *f.* fatherland, native country.

pa•triar•ca *m.* patriarch, **patriarcal** *adj.* patriarchal.

pa•tri•mo•nio *m.* patrimony; inheritance.

pa•trio *adj.* native, of one's native country; paternal, belonging to the father.

pa•trio•ta *m. & f.* patriot.

pa•trió•ti•co *adj.* patriotic.

pa•trio•tis•mo *m.* patriotism.

pa•tro•ci•nar *v.* to patronize, favor, sponsor.

pa•tro•ci•nio *m.* patronage, protection.

pa•trón *m.* (*protector*) patron; patron saint; sponsor; (*amo*) master, boss; proprietor, landlord; host; skipper; (*dechado*) pattern, standard, model; **patrona** *f.* landlady; patroness; hostess.

pa•tro•na•to *m.* board of trustees; foundation (*for educational, cultural, or charitable purposes*).

pa•tro•no *m.* patron, protector; trustee; patron saint.

pa•tru•lla *f.* patrol; squad, gang.

pa•tru•llar *v.* to patrol.

pau•sa *f.* pause, stop, rest.

pau•sar *v.* to pause.

pau•ta *f.* norm, rule, standard; guide lines (*for writing*).

pa•va *f.* turkey hen; *Riopl.* kettle, teapot, teakettle; *Andes, Ch.* jest, coarse joke; **pelar la –** to talk by night at the window (*said of lovers*).

pa•ve•sa *f.* cinder; small firebrand; burnt wick or snuff of a candle; **-s** cinders.

pa•vi•men•tar *v.* to pave.

pa•vi•men•to *m.* pavement.

pa•vo *m.* turkey; *Ch.* sponger, parasite; **– real** peacock; **comer –** to be a wallflower at a dance; *adj.* silly, foolish; vain.

pa•vón *m.* peacock.

pa•vo•ne•ar•se *v.* to strut, swagger.

pa•vo•ne•o *m.* strut, swagger.

pa•vor *m.* awe, dread, terror.

pa•vo•ro•so *adj.* frightful, dreadful.

pa•ya•dor *m. Riopl.* one who sings an improvised song accompanied on the guitar.

pa•ya•sa•da *f.* clownish act or remark.

pa•ya•se•ar v. to clown, play the fool.

pa•ya•so m. clown.

paz f. peace.

paz•gua•to adj. simple, dumb, stupid; m. simpleton.

pe•a•je m. toll (for crossing a bridge or ferry).

peal = **pial.**

pe•a•lar = **pialar.**

pe•a•tón m. pedestrian.

pe•ca f. freckle.

pe•ca•do m. sin.

pe•ca•dor m. sinner; adj. sinful.

pe•ca•mi•no•so adj. sinful.

pe•car⁶ v. to sin; **– de bueno** to be too good; **– de oscuro** to be exceedingly unclear, too complicated.

pe•ce•ra f. fish bowl.

pe•co•so adj. freckly, freckled.

pe•cu•la•do m. embezzlement.

pe•cu•liar adj. peculiar; **peculiaridad** f. peculiarity.

pe•cha•da f. Ríopl. bump, push, shove with the chest; Am. bumping contest between two riders; Ríopl., Ch. overthrowing an animal (by bumping it with the chest of a horse).

pe•char v. Ríopl., Ch., Bol. to bump, push, shove with the chest; Ríopl., Ch., Bol. to drive ones' horse against; Ch., Ríopl. to borrow, strike (someone) for a loan.

pe•che•ra f. shirtfront; chest protector; bib (of an apron).

pe•cho m. chet; beast; bosom; heart; courage; **dar el – to** nurse; **tomar a -s** to take to heart; P.R., Col. **a todo** – shouting; Am. **en -s de camisa** in shirt sleeves.

pe•chu•ga f. breast, breast meat of a fowl; bosom; C.A., Col., Ch., Andes courage, nerve, audacity, impudence.

pe•da•go•gía f. pedagogy, science of education.

pe•da•gó•gi•ca adj. pedagogic, relating to education or teaching.

pe•da•go•go m. pedagogue, teacher, educator.

pe•dal m. pedal.

pe•da•le•ar v. to pedal.

pe•dan•te adj. pedantic, affected, vain, superficial; m. pedant; **pedantesco** adj. pedantic.

pe•da•zo m. piece, portion, bit; **hacer -s** to tear or break into pieces; **caerse a -s** fall into pieces.

pe•der•nal m. flint.

pe•des•tal m. pedestal, base.

pe•des•tre adj. pedestrian, walking, going on foot; commonplace, vulgar, low.

pe•di•do m. commercial order; request, petition; p.p.of **pedir.**

pe•di•güe•ño adj. begging, demanding.

pe•dir⁵ v. irr. to ask, beg, petition; to ask for; to demand; to require; to order (merchandise); **a – de boca** exactly as desired.

pe•do m. wind, flatulence; Mex. **andar** - to be drunk.

pe•dra•da f. hit or blow with a stone; throw with a stone; mark or bruise made by a stone (thrown); **a - s** by stoning; with stones; **dar una –** to hit with a stone; **echar a alguien a -s** to stone someone out; **matar a -s** to stone to death.

pe•dre•gal m. rocky ground, ground strewn with rocks.

pe•dre•go•so adj. rocky, stony, pebbly.

pe•dre•ría f. precious stones; precious stone ornament; jewelry.

pe•drus•co m. boulder.

pe•dún•cu•lo m. stem (of a leaf, flower or fruit), stalk.

pe•ga•jo•so adj. sticky; contagious.

pe•gar⁷ v. (golpear) to hit, strike, slap, beat; (adherir) to stick, paste, glue; to sew on (a button); to infect; tobe becoming; to be fitting, opportune, to the point; Am. to tie, fasten; Am. to yoke; **– fuego** to set on fire; **– un chasco** to play a trick; to surprise, disappoint; **– un susto** to give a sacre; **– un salto (una carre-ra)** to take a jump (a run); **-se** to stick, cling: **pegársela a uno** to fool somebody.

pe•go•te m. sticky thing; sticking plaster; clumsy patch; sponger; thick, sticky concoction; clumsy addition or insertion (in a literary or artistic work).

pei•na•do m. coiffure, hairdo; hairdressing; p.p. combed; groomed; adj. effeminate; **bien** – spruce, trim.

pei•na•dor m. hairdresser; short wrapper or dressing gown; **peinadora** f. woman hairdresser.

pei•nar v. to comb; Ríopl. to flatter.

pei•ne m. comb.

pei•ne•ta f. large ornamental comb.

pe•la•di•lla f. small pebble.

pe•la•do p.p. & adj. peeled; plucked; skinned; hairless; featherless; barren, treeless, bare; penniless; broke; m. Mex. ragged fellow (generally a peon); Mex. ill-bred person; Col. child.

pe•la•fus•tán m. tramp. vagabond.

pe•la•ga•tos m. ragged fellow, tramp.

pe•la•je m. animal's coat, fur; external appearance.

pe•lar v. to cut the hair of; to pluck the feathers or hair from; to peel, shell, skin, husk; to fleece, rob; Am. to beat, thrash; Am. to slander; C.R. **– los dientes** to show one's teeth; to smile affectedly; C.A., Mex., Carib., Col., Andes **– los ojos** to keep one's eyes peeled; to open one's eyes wide; **-se** to peel off; to lose one's hair; Col., Ven. to be confused; Col., Ven. to be careless, unaware; Col., Ven. to slip away; Col., Ven., to die; **pelárselas por algo** to be dying for something, want something very much.

pel•da•ño m. step (of a staircase).

pe•le•a f. fight, quarrel.

pe•le•ar v. to fight; to quarrel.

pe•le•te•ría *f.* fur store; fur trade; furs; *Am.* leather goods, leather shop; *Cuba* shoe store.

pe•lí•cu•la *f.* thin skin; membrane; film; motion-picture film.

pe•li•grar *v.* to be in danger.

pe•li•gro *m.* danger.

pe•li•gro•so *adj.* dangerous.

pe•li•llo *m.* short, fine hair; **-s** trouble, nuisance; **echar -s a la mar** to "bury the hatchet", become reconsiled; **no pararse en -s** not to stop at small details, not to bother about trifles; **no tener -s en la lengua** to speak frankly.

pe•li•rro•jo *adj.* redheaded, red-haired.

pe•lo *m.* (*cabello*) hair; (haz) nap (*of cloth*); (fibra) grain (*in wood*); **al —** perfectly; agreed; apropos, to the point; along the grain, **eso me viene al —** that suits me perfectly; **con todos sus -s y señales** with every possible detail; *Am.* **por** (*or* **en**) **un —** on the point of, almost, by a hair's breadth; **montar en —** to ride bareback; **tomar el — a** to kid, make fun of; *Ríopl.*, *Carib.*, *Mex.*, *Andes* **no aflojar un —** not to yield an inch.

pe•lo•ta *f.* ball; ball game; *Am.* boat made of cowhide; **en —** (*or* **en -s**) maked; *Am.* **darle a la —** to hit upon by chance; **pelotilla** *f.* pellet, little ball.

pe•lo•ta•ri *m.* pelota (*jai-alai*) player.

pe•lo•te•ra *f.* brawl, row, riot; *C.A.*, *Ven.* crowd.

pe•lo•tón *m.* large ball; crowd, gang; heap, pile; platoon of soldiers; firing squad.

pe•lu•ca *f.* wig.

pe•lu•do *adj.* hairy; shaggy; *m.* plush carpet with shaggy pile; *Am.* a species of armadillo; *Ríopl.* **agarrar un —** to get drunk.

pe•lu•que•ría *f.* barbershop, hairdreeser's shop.

pe•lu•que•ro *m.* hairdresser, barber.

pe•lu•sa *f.* down; fuzz; nap (*of cloth*).

pe•lle•jo *m.* hide; skin; peel; **salvar el —** to save one's skin, escape punishment; *Am.* **jugarse el —** to gamble one's life.

pe•lliz•car[6] *v* to pinch, nip.

pe•lliz•co *m.* pinching, nipping; pinch, nip.

pe•na *f.* penalty; grief, worry; hardship; toil; *Mex.*, *Carib.*, *C.A.*, *Col.*, *Ven.* embarrassment; **a duras -s** with great difficulty; harly; **me da —** it grieves me, *C.A.*, *Ven.*, *Col.*, *Carib.* it embarrasses me; **valer la —** to be worthwhile; **tener** (*or* **estar con**) **mucha —** to be terribly sorry; *Am.* to be greatly embarrassed.

pe•na•cho *m.* tuft, crest; plume.

pe•nal *adj.* penal; **código —** penal code.

pe•na•li•dad *f.* hardship; trouble; penalty.

pe•nar *v.* to suffer; to worry, fret; to impose a penalty; **— por** to long for; to suffer because of.

pen•ca *f.* leaf of a cactus plant; *Am.* sweetheart; *Ven.* **coger una —** to get drunk.

pen•co *m.* nag, horse; *Am.* boor.

pen•den•cia *f.* quarrel; scuffle, fight.

pen•den•cie•ro *adj.* quarrelsome.

pen•der *v.* to hang; to dangle; to depend.

pen•dien•te *f.* slope; *m.* earring; pendant; *Am.* watch chain; *adj.* hanging, dangling; pending.

pen•dón *m.* banner.

pén•du•lo *m.* pendulum.

pe•ne•tra•ción *f.* penetration; acuteness; keen judgment.

pe•ne•tran•te *adj.* penetrating; acute; keen.

pe•ne•trar *v.* to penetrate; to pierce; to fathom, comprehend.

pe•ni•ci•li•na *f.* penicillin.

pe•nín•su•la *f.* peninsula.

pe•nin•su•lar *adj.* peninsular.

pe•ni•ten•cia *f.* penance.

pe•ni•ten•cia•ria *f.* penitentiary.

pe•ni•ten•te *adj.* repentant, penitent; *m. & f.* penitent.

pe•no•so *adj.* painful; hard, difficult; embarrassing; fatiguing; *Mex.*, *Carib.*, *C.A.*, *Ven.*, *Col.* timid, shy.

pen•sa•dor *m.* thinker; *adj.* thinking.

pen•sa•mien•to *m.* thought; mind; pansy.

pen•sar[1] *v. irr.* to think; to think over, to intend.

pen•sa•ti•vo *adj.* pensive.

pen•sión *f.* pension; board; scholarship for study; boaringhouse; *Col.* apprehension, anxiety; **- completa** room and board.

pen•sio•na•do *m.* pensioner (*person receiving a pension*); *adj. & p.p.* pensioned.

pen•sio•nar *v.* to pension.

pen•sio•nis•ta *m. & f.* boarder; pensioner (*person receiving a pension*).

pen•ta•gra•ma *m.* musical staff.

pe•núl•ti•mo *adj.* next to the last.

pe•num•bra *f.* partial shadow, dimness.

pe•num•bro•so *adj.* dim.

pe•ña *f.* rock, large stone.

pe•ñas•co *m.* large rock; crag.

pe•ñas•co•so *adj.* rocky.

pe•ón *m.* unskilled laborer; foot soldier; spinning top; pawn (*in chess*); *Ch.*, *Ríopl.*, *C.A.*, *Carib.*, *Mex.* farm hand; *Am.* apprentice; *Mex.* **— de albañil** mason's helper.

pe•o•na•da *f.* gang of laborers or peons.

pe•or *adj. & Adv.* worse; worst; **— que** worse than, **— que —** that is even worse; **tanto —** so much the worse.

pe•pa *f.* *Andes*, *Col.*, *Ven.*, *C.A.*, *Mex.*, *Ríopl.* seed (*or an apple, melon, etc.*); *Am.* marble (*to play with*); **Pepa** *nickname for* **Josefa**.

pe•pe•nar *v. Mex.* to pick up; *Am.* to seize, grab.

pe•pi•no *m.* cucumber.

pe•pi•ta *f.* seed (*of an apple, melon, etc.*); pip (*a disease of birds*); nugget (*lump of gold or other minerals*); *Am.* fruit stone, pit; **Pepita = Josefita** *dim. of* **Josefa**.

pe•que•ñez *f.* smallness; childhood; trifle; meanness.

pe•que•ño *adj.* small, little; young; low, humble; *m.*

child.

pe•ra *f.* pear; goatee; sinecure, easy job; *Am.* Peruvian alligator pear (*see* **aguacate**); *Am.* **hacerle a uno la** – to play a trick on someone; **peral** *m.* pear tree; pear orchard.

per•cal *m.* percale (*fine cotton cloth*)

per•can•ce *m.* misfortune, accident; occurrence.

per•cep•ción *f.* perception; idea.

per•cep•ti•ble *adj.* perceptible, noticeable.

per•ci•bir *v.* to perceive; to collect, receive.

per•cu•di•do *adj.* dirty, grimy.

per•cu•dir *v.* to soil, make dirty or grimy; **-se** to get grimy.

per•cha *f.* clothes or hat rack; pole; perch, roost; perch (*a fish*); **perchero** *m.* clothes or hat rack.

per•der[1] *v.irr.* to lose; to squander; to ruin, harm; to miss (*a train*); **– de vista** to lose sight of; **-se** to lose one's way; to get lost; to go astray; to get spoiled; to become ruined.

per•di•ción *f.* perdition, damnation, hell, ruin.

pér•di•da *f.* loss; damage.

per•di•da•men•te *Adv.* excessively.

per•di•do *p.p.* & *adj.* lost; strayed; mislaid; ruined; **estar – por alguien** to be crazy about, or very fond of, someone; *m.* rake, dissolute fellow; bum, vagabond.

per•di•gón *m.* young partridge; bird shot, buckshot; losing gambler.

per•diz *f.* partridge.

per•dón *m.* pardon; forgiveness; remission.

per•do•nar *v.* to pardon; to forgive.

per•du•la•rio *m.* rake, dissolute person; reckless fellow; good-for-nothing; tramp.

per•du•ra•ble *adj.* lasting, everlasting.

per•du•rar *v.* to last, endure.

pe•re•ce•de•ro *adj.* perishable.

pe•re•cer[13] *v. irr.* to perish; to die; **-se** to long (for), pine (for).

pe•re•gri•na•ción *f.* pilgrimage; long journey.

pe•re•gri•no *m.* pilgrim; *adj.* foreing, strange; rare; beautiful, perfect; travelling, wandering; **ave peregrina** migratory bird, bird of passage.

pe•re•jil *m.* parsley; **-es** frippery, showy clothes or ornaments.

pe•ren•ne *adj.* perennial, enduring, perpetual.

pe•re•za *f.* laziness; idleness.

pe•re•zo•so *adj.* lazy; *m. Am.* sloth (*an animal*); *Am.* safety pin; *Am.* bed cushion.

per•fec•ción *f.* perfection; **a la** – to perfection, perfectly.

per•fec•cio•na•mien•to *m.* perfecting, perfection; completion.

per•fec•cio•nar *v.* to perfect, finish, complete.

per•fec•to *adj.* perfect.

per•fi•dia *f.* perfidy, treachery.

pér•fi•do *adj.* perfidious, treacherous, faithless.

per•fil *m.* profile; outline; *Am.* pen or pen point.

per•fi•lar *v.* to silhouette; to outline; **-se** to show one's profile; to be silhouetted.

per•fo•ra•ción *f.* perforation, hole; puncture; perforating, boring, drilling.

per•fo•rar *v.* to perforate, pierce; to drill, bore.

per•fu•mar *v.* to perfume, scent.

per•fu•me *m.* perfume; fragance.

per•fu•me•ría *f.* perfumery; perfume shop.

per•ga•mi•no *m.* parchment.

pe•ri•cia *f.* expertness, skill.

pe•ri•co *m.* parakeet, small parrot; *Col.* **huevos -s** scrambled eggs.

pe•ri•fo•llos *m.* pl. frippery, finery, showy ornaments.

pe•ri•fra•se•ar *v.* to paraphrase.

pe•ri•ge•o *m.* perigee.

pe•ri•lla *f.* small pear; pear-shaped ornament; knob; pommel of a saddle; goatee; **de** – apropos, to the point.

pe•rí•me•tro *m.* perimeter.

pe•rió•di•co *m.* newspaper; periodical; *adj.* periodic, periodical.

pe•rio•dis•mo *m.* journalism; **periodista** *m.* & *f.* journalist; newspaper editor or publisher; **periodístico** *adj.* journalistic.

pe•río•do *m.* period; cycle; sentence.

pe•ri•pe•cia *f.* vicissitude, change in fortune; unforeseen incident.

pe•ri•pues•to *adj.* dressed up, dolled up, decked out.

pe•ri•to *adj.* learned; experienced; skillful; skilled; *m.* expert.

per•ju•di•car[6] *v.* to damage, impair, harm.

per•ju•di•cial *adj.* harmful, injurious.

per•jui•cio *m.* damage, ruin, mischief; harm.

per•ju•rar *v.* to perjure oneself; to commit perjury; to curse, swear.

per•ju•rio *m.* perjury.

per•la *f.* pearl; **de -s** perfectly, just right, to the point.

per•li•no *adj.* pearly, pearl-colored.

per•ma•ne•cer[13] *v. irr.* to remain, stay.

per•ma•nen•cia *f.* permanence, duration; stability; stay, sojourn.

per•ma•nen•te *adj.* permanent.

per•mi•so *m.* permission; permit.

per•mi•tir *v.* to permit, let; to grant.

per•mu•ta *f.* exchange, barter.

per•mu•tar *v.* to exchange; to barter; to change around.

per•ne•tas: en – barelegged, with bare legs.

per•ni•cio•so *adj.* pernicious, harmful.

per•no *m.* bolt; spike; **-s** *Am.* tricks, frauds.

pe•ro *conj.* but, except, yet; *m.* objection, exception; defect; a variety of apple tree; a variety of apple; **perón** *m. Am.* a variety of apple.

pe•ro•gru•llada *f.* platitude, trite or commonplace remark.

pe·ro·ra·ción *f.* peroration, speech, harangue.

pe·ro·rar *v.* to make an impassioned speech; to declaim, harangue; to plea, make a plea.

pe·ro·ra·ta *f.* harangue, speech.

per·pen·di·cu·lar *adj., m. & f.* perpendicular.

per·pe·tuar[18] *v.* to perpetuate.

per·pe·tuo *adj.* perpetual; **perpetua** *f.* everlasting.

per·ple·ji·dad *f.* perplexity.

per·ple·jo *adj.* perplexed, bewildered.

pe·rra *f.* bitch, female dog; drunkenness; **– chica** five-centime copper coin; **– grande** (*or* **gorda**) ten-centime copper coin.

pe·rra·da *f.* pack of dogs; **hacer una –** to play a mean trick.

pe·rre·ra *f.* kennel; toil, hard work, hard job; tantrum; *Carib., Mex., Ven.* brawl, dispute.

pe·rri·lla *f. Am.* sty (*on the eyelid*). *See* **orzuelo**.

pe·rro *m.* dog; **– de busca** hunting dog; **– dogo** bulldog; **– de lanas** poodle; *adj.* dogged, tenacious; *Mex., C.A.* hard, selfish, mean, stingy; *Ven.*, vagabond.

pe·rru·no *adj.* canine, doglike.

per·se·cu·ción *f.* persecution; pursuit.

per·se·gui·dor *m.* pursuer; persecutor.

per·se·gui·mien·to *m.* pursuit; perse-cution.

per·se·guir[5,12] *v. irr.* to pursue; to persecute; to harass, annoy.

per·se·ve·ran·cia *f.* perseverance.

per·se·ve·rar *v.* to persevere.

per·sia·na *f.* Venetian blind; window shade.

per·sist·en·cia *f.* persistence; **persistente** *adj.* persistent.

per·sis·tir *v.* to persist.

per·so·na *f.* person; personage.

per·so·na·je *m.* personage; character (*in a book or play*).

per·so·nal *adj.* personal; *m.* personnel.

per·so·na·li·dad *f.* personality; indivi-duality; persón, personaje

pers·pec·ti·va *f.* perspective; view; appearance; outlook; prospect.

pers·pi·ca·cia *f.* keenness of mind, penetration, keen insight.

pers·pi·caz *adj.* keen, shrewd.

per·sua·dir *v.* to persuade.

per·sua·sión *f.* persuasion.

per·sua·si·vo *adj.* persuasive.

per·te·ne·cer[13] *v. irr.* to belong; to pertain; to concern.

per·te·ne·cien·te *adj.* pertaining, belonging, concerning.

pér·ti·ga *f.* pole, bar, rod; **salto con –** pole vault.

per·ti·nen·te *adj.* pertinent, to the point, apt, fitting.

per·tre·chos *m. pl.* military supplies; tools, implements.

per·tur·ba·ción *f.* uneasiness, agitation, disturbance.

per·tur·bar *v.* to perturb, disturb.

pe·rua·no *adj. m. & f.* Peruvian.

pe·ru·le·ro *adj. m. & f.* Peruvian (*slang expression*).

per·ver·si·dad *f.* perversity, wickedness.

per·ver·so *adj.* perverse, wicked; *m.* pervert.

per·ver·tir[3] *v. irr.* to pervert; to; corrupt to distort; **-se** to become perverted; to go wrong.

pe·sa *f.* weight (*for scales*); **– de reloj** clock weight; **-s y medidas** weights and measures.

pe·sa·dez *f.* heaviness; dullness, drowsiness; slowness; bother; stubbornness.

pe·sa·di·lla *f.* nightmare.

pe·sa·do *adj.* heavy; sound (*sleep*); tiresome, boring; annoying; slow; dull.

pe·sa·dum·bre *f.* grief, sorrow; weight, heaviness.

pé·sa·me *m.* condolence, expression of simpathy.

pe·san·tez *f.* gravity; heaviness.

pe·sar *v.* (*penar*) to cause grief, sorrow, or regret; (*tener gravedad*) to weigh; to consider, to have weight, value, or importance; *m.* grief, sorrow; **a – de** in spite of.

pe·sa·ro·so *adj.* grieved, sad; repentant.

pes·ca *f.* fishing; catch, fish caught.

pes·ca·de·ría *f.* fish market; **pescadero** *m.* fishmonger, dealer in fish.

pes·ca·do *m.* fish (*especially after being caught*); salted codfish.

pes·ca·dor *m.* fisherman.

pes·car[6] *v.* to fish; to catch; to catch unaware, cath in the act.

pes·co·zón *m.* blow on the back of the head or neck.

pes·cue·zo *m.* neck.

pe·se·bre *m.* manger.

pe·se·ta *f.* peseta (*monetary unit of Spain*).

pe·si·mis·mo *m.* pessimism; **pesimista** *m. & f.* pessimist; *adj.* pessimistic.

pé·si·mo *adj.* very bad.

pe·so *m.* weight; weighing; burden; importance; *Am.* peso (*monetary unit of several Spanich American countries*).

pes·que·ra *f.* fishery (*place for catching fish*); **pes·quería** *f.* fishery; fishing.

pes·que·ro *adj.* fishing; **buque –** fishing boat; **in·dustria pesquera** fishing industry.

pes·qui·sa *f.* investigation, inquiry; *m. Am.* police investigator.

pes·ta·ña *f.* eyelash; edging, fringe; **quemarse las -s** to burn the midnight oil, study hard at night.

pes·ta·ñe·ar *v.* to blink; to wink; to flicker.

pes·te *f.* pest, pestilence, plague; epidemic; stench, stink, foul odor; overabundance, excess; *Am.* smallpox; *Col.*, head cold; **echar -s** to utter insults.

pes·ti·llo *m.* bolt; latch; lock.

pe·ta·ca *f.* tobacco pouch; cigar case; leather covered hamper (*used as a pack*); *Mex., Ven.* leather covere trunk, suitcase; *adj. Andes* heavy, clumsy.

pé·ta·lo *m.* petal.

pe•ta•te *m.* bundle; impostor; *Mex., C.A., Ven., Col.* mat (*of straw or palm leaves*); *Am.* dunce; *Andes* coward; **liar el** – to pack up and go; *Mex.* to die; *Col., Ven.* **dejar a uno en un** – to ruin a person, leave him penniless.

pe•ti•ción *f.* petition, request.

pe•ti•rro•jo *m.* robin, robin redbreast.

pe•ti•so *adj. Riopl., Ch., Andes* small, short, dwarfish; *m. Am.* small horse, pony.

pé•tre•o *adj.* stone, stony.

pe•tró•le•o *m.* petroleum.

pe•tro•le•ro *m.* oil man; dearle in petroleum; **compañía petrolera** oil comopany.

pe•tu•lan•cia *f.* flippancy; insolence; **petulante** *adj.* pert, impertinent, flippant.

pez *m.* fish; *f.* pitch, tar.

pe•zón *m.* nipple; stem, stalk (*of a fruit, leaf or flower*); small point of land.

pe•zu•ña *f.* hoof.

pia•do•so *adj.* pious; kind, merciful.

pial *m. Mex.* lasso, lariat (*thrown in order to trip an animal*); *Riopl.* snare, trap.

pia•lar *v.* to lasso by tripping with a **pial**.

pia•no *m.* piano; – **de cola** grand piano; – **vertical** upright piano.

piar[17] *v.* to peep, chirp; to cry, whine.

pi•ca *f.* pike, spear; picador's goad or lance; stonecutter's hammer; *Ven.* tapping of rubber trees; *Col.* trail; *Col.* , *Ch.* pique, resentment; *Am.* cockfight.

pi•ca•da *f.* prick; bite (*as of an insect or fish*); puncture; sharp pain; dive (*of a plane*); *Cuba, Riopl.* path, trail (*cut through a foret*); *Am.* narrow ford; *Col., Ven., Mex.* peck.

pi•ca•di•llo *m.* meat an vegetable hash; minced meat, mincemeat.

pi•ca•dor *m.* picador (*mounted bullfighter armed with a goad*); horse-breaker; chopping block; *Ven.* tree tapper.

pi•ca•du•ra *f.* biting; pricking; bite; sting; puncture; cut tobacco.

pi•can•te *adj.* (*acerbo*) pricking, biting, stinging; (*con chile o ají*) spicy; highly seasoned; *m.* strong seasoning; *Am.* highly seasoned sauce (*usually containing chili pepper*).

pi•ca•plei•tos *m.* quarrelsome person (*one who likes to pick a fight*); shyster.

pi•ca•por•te *m.* latch; latchkey; door knocker.

pi•car[6] *v.* to prick; to pierce; to bite (*said of fish or insects*); to sting; to peck; to nibble; to mince, chop up; to goad; to stick, poke; to hew, chisel; to pique, vex to itch, smart, burn; *Am.* to chop (*wood*); *Am.* to open a trail; *Am.* to tap (*a tree*); *Am.* to slaughter (*cattle*); – **muy alto** to aim very high; – **en** to border on, be somewhat of; *Mex., Ven.* **¡picale!** hurry! **-se** to be piqued, angry; to be motheaten; to begin to sour; to begin to rot; *C.A., Ven.* to get tipsy; – **se de** to boast of.

pi•car•día *f.* roguishness; offensive act or remark; roguish trick; mischief.

pi•ca•res•co *adj.* picaresque, roguish.

pí•ca•ro *m.* rogue, rascal; *adj.* roguish; mischievous; crafty, sly; low, vile; **picarón** *m.* big rascal.

pi•ca•zón *f.* itch, itching.

pi•co *m.* beak, bill; sharp point; peak; pickaxe, pick, spout; mouth; additional amount, a little over; *C.A., Carib., Riopl., Ven.* a small balance; *Mex.* a goodly sum; **tener el – de oro** to be very eloquent; **tener mucho –** to be very talkative.

pi•co•ta•da *f.* **picotazo** *m.* peck.

pi•co•te•ar *v.* to peck; to chatter; *Am.* to mince, cut into small pieces.

pi•chel *m.* pitcher; mug.

pi•chón *m.* pigeon; *C.A.* any male bird (*except a rooster*); *Am.* dupe, easy mark; *Am.* novice, inexperienced person, apprentice; *adj. Am.* timid, shy.

pie *m.* foot; leg; stand; stem; base; *Am.* down payment; *Mex.* strophe, stanza; *Am.* – **de amigo** wedge; prop; – **de banco** silly remark; **a – juntillas** steadfastly, firmly; **al – de la letra** to the letter, literally, exactly; **de –** (*or* **en –**) standing; **a cuatro -s** on all fours; **dar –** to give an opportunity or occasion; *Am.* **estar a – en** to be ignorant of; **ir a –** to walk.

pie•ce•ci•to, pie•ci•to *m.* little foot.

pie•dad *f.* piety; pity; mercy; **monte de –** pawnshop.

pie•dra *f.* stone; gravel; hailstone; *Ven.* piece of a domino set; – **angular** (*or* **fundamental**) cornerstone; – **caliza** limestone; – **pómez** pumice, pumice stone; **a – y lodo** shut tight; **ser – de escándalo** to be an object; of scandal.

piel *f.* skin; hide; leather; fur.

pié•la•go *m.* high seas; sea; great abundance, great plenty.

pien•so *m.* feed; thought; **ni por –** not even in thought.

pier•na *f.* leg; **dormir a – suelta** to sleep like a log, sleep soundly; *Am.* **ser una buena –** to be a good fellow, be always in a good mood.

pie•za *f.* (*pedazo*) piece; part; (*cuarto*) room; (*comedia*) play; **de una –** solid, in one piece; *Am.* **ser de una –** to be an honest, upright man.

pig•men•to *m.* pigment.

pi•ja•ma *m.* pajamas.

pi•la *f.* (*pieza cóncava*) basin; baptismal font; trough; (*cúmulo*) pile; heap; electric battery; – **atómica** atomic pile; *Am.* fountain; *Andes* hairless dog; *Am.* bald head; **nombre de –** Christian name; *Andes* **andar –** to go naked; *Mex.* **tener las -s** (*or* **tener por -s**) to have a lot, have heaps.

pi•lar *m.* pillar, column; basin of a fountain.

pil•cha *f. Riopl.* any article of clothing; *Am.* mistress; **-s** *Riopl.* belongings.

píl·do·ra f. pill.

pil·ma·ma f. Mex. child's nurse, wet nurse.

pi·lón m. basin (of a fountain); watering trought; sugar loaf; large wooden or metal mortar (for grinding grain); counterpoise; Mex. an additional amount, premium (given to a buyer); Mex. **de −** to boot, in addition, besides; **piloncillo** m. Am. unrefined sugar loaf.

pi·lo·tar, pilotear v. to pilot.

pi·lo·te m. pile (for building).

pi·lo·to m. pilot; Mex. generous entertainer or host.

pi·lla·je m. pillage, plunder.

pi·llar v. to pillage, plunder; to pilfer; to seize, snatch, grasp; to catch; Am. to surprise, catch in the act.

pi·llo adj. roguish; sly, crafty; m. rogue, rascal; Am. a species of heron; Am. long-legged person; **pilluelo** m. little rascal, scamp.

pi·men·te·ro m. pepper plant; pepperbox pepper shaker.

pi·men·tón m. large pepper; cayenne, red pepper; paprika.

pi·mien·ta f. black pepper.

pi·mien·to m. green pepper; red pepper.

pim·po·llo m. rosebud; bud; shoot, sprout; attractive youth.

pi·ná·cu·lo m. pinnacle, top, summit.

pi·nar m. pine grove.

pin·cel m. artist's brush; **pincelada** f. stroke of the brush.

pin·char v. to prick; to puncture.

pin·cha·zo m. prick; puncture; stab.

pin·ga·jo m. tag, tatter, rag.

pin·go m. Ríopl., Andes saddle horse; Mex. devil.

pin·güe adj. abundant, copious; fat, greasy.

pi·no m. pine; Am. filling for a meat pie; **hacer -s** (or **hacer pinitos**) to begin to walk (said of baby); to begin to do things (said of a novice).

pin·ta f. spot, mark; outward sign, asspect; pint; Mex. **hacer −** to play hooky, cut class.

pin·tar v. to paint, to describe, depict; to feign; to begin to turn red, begin to ripen (said of fruit); to fancy, imagine; Mex. to play hooky, play truant; Am. to fawn, flatter; **no − nada** to be worth nothing, count for nothing; **las cosas no pintaban bien** things did not look well; Mex. **− venados** to play hooky; **-se** to put on make-up; Am. to excel (in); to praise oneself; Ven. to go a way.

pin·ta·rra·je·ar v. to daub; to smear with paint or rouge.

pin·to adj. Am. spotted, speckled.

pin·tor m. painter, artist; **− de brocha gorda** house painter; poor artist; adj. Am. boastful, conceited.

pin·to·res·co adj. picturesque.

pin·tu·ra f. painting; picture; paint, color; description.

pin·zas f. pl. pincers; tweezers; claws (of lobsters, crabs, etc.); Ríopl., Mex.,Carib. pliers, tongs.

pi·ña f. pineapple; pine cone; piña cloth; cluster; Cuba pool (a billiard game).

pi·ña·ta f. pot; hanging pot or other container (filled with candies, fruit, etc.).

pi·ñón m. pine nut; nut pine; pinion.

pío adj. pious, devout; kind; merciful; dappled, spotted (horse); **obras pías** pious works, charitable deeds.

pio·jo m. louse.

pio·jo·so adj. lousy; mean, stingy.

pi·pa f. tobacco pipe; keg, barrel; reed pipe (musical instrument); fruit seed (of a lemon, orange, melon); Col. green coconut; Am. potato; Ven. **estar −** to be drunk; m. Am. species of green frog.

pi·piar[17] v. to peep, chirp.

pi·pio·lo m. novice, beginner; Am child, youngster.

pi·que m. pique, resentment; chigger (insect); flea; Am. small chili pepper; Am. trail; **a − de** in danger of, on the point of; **echar a −** to sink (a ship); to destroy; **irse a −** to capsize; to sink.

pi·que·te m. prick; bite, sting (of insects); small hole; picket, stake; picket (military); Am. small band of musicians; Am. small corral; Am. cutting edge of scissors.

pi·ra·gua f. Ríopl., Carib., Ven., Col., Andes Indian canoe.

pi·rá·mi·de f. pyramid.

pi·ra·ta m. pirate.

pi·ra·te·ar v. to pirate.

pi·ro·po m. flattery, compliment; a variety of garnet (a semiprecious stone); **echar un −** to "throw a bouquet"; to compliment.

pi·rue·ta f. whirl; somersault; caper; **hacer −s** to cut capers; to turn somersaults; to do stunts.

pi·sa·da f. footstep; footprint; **dar una −** to step on, stamp on; **seguir las -s de** to follow in the footsteps of; to imitate.

pi·sa·pa·pe·les m. paperweight.

pi·sar v. to step on, tread upon; to trample under foot; to pound; to cover (said of a male bird).

pis·ci·na f. swimming pool, swimming tank; fish pond.

pi·so m. Ven. rut; Am. tread (of a wheel). See **rodadura**.

pi·so m. floor; story; pavement, apartment, flat; tread; Ríopl., Mex., Carib., Ven. fee for pasturage rights; Am. table scarf; Am. stool, footstool; Am. small rug.

pi·són m. heavy mallet (for pounding, flattening, crushing).

pi·so·te·ar v. to tramp, tramp on, trample; to tread.

pi·so·tón m. hard step, stamp (of the foot); **dar un −** to step hard, stamp (upon).

pis·ta f. track, trace, trail; clew; race trarck; **− de aterrizaje** landing field.

pis·to·la f. pistol; **pistolera** f. holster.

pis·tón m. piston; Col: cornet.

pi·ta f. Am. agave or century plant; Am. fiber, or thread made from the fiber, of the agave or maguey.

pi·tar v. to toot; to whistle; *Ríopl., Andes* to smoke; *Ven.* to hiss; *Carib., Mex.* to slip away, escape; *Am.* **-se una cosa** to steal something; *Ch., Col., Ven., C.A. (pitado)* **salir pitando** to leave on the run.

pi·ta·zo m. toot, whistle, blast.

pi·ti·llo m. cigarrete; **pitillera** f. cigarette case.

pi·to m. whistle; cigarette; *Am.* tick (*an insect*); **no vale un** – it is not worth a straw; *Am.* **no saber ni – de una cosa** not to know anything about a subject.

pi·za·rra f. slate; blackboard; **pizarrín** m. late pencil; **pizarrón** m. blackboard.

piz·ca f. pinch, small bit; *Mex.* harvest.

pla·ca f. badge, insignia; plaque, tablet; metal plate; photographic plate; license plate; *Ven.* scab or skin blemish.

pla·cen·te·ro[38] adj. pleasant, agreeable.

pla·cer[38] v. irr. to please, content; m. pleasure; sand bank, shoal; *placer* (*place where gold is obtained by washing*); *Am.* pearl fishing.

pla·ce·ro m. **placera** f. market vendor.

plá·ci·do adj. placid, calm.

pla·ga f. plague; calamity.

pla·gar[7] v. to plague, infest; **-se de** to become plagued or infested with.

pla·giar v. to plagiarize, steal and use as one's own (*the writings, ideas, etc. of another*); to kidnap, abduct.

plan m. plan; design; project; drawing; mine floor; *Am.* clearing; *Am.* building grounds of a ranch.

pla·na f. page; plain, flat country; mason's trowel; tally sheet; **enmendar la – a uno** to correct a person's mistakes.

plan·cha f. flatiron; metal plate; gangplank; blunder; *Cuba* railway flatcar; *Ven., Col.* dental plate; **– de blindaje** armor plate; **hacer una** – to make a ridiculous blunder; **tirarse una** – to place oneself in a ridiculous situation.

plan·cha·do m. ironing; clothes ironed or to be ironed; adj. *Am.* smart, clever; *Am.* brave; *Ven.* dolled up, dressed up; *Am.* broke, penniless.

plan·char v. to iron; to smooth out; *Mex.* to leave (*someone*) waiting; *Am.* to strike with the flat of a blade; *Am.* to flatter; *Mex., Ven.* – **el asiento** to be a wallflower at a dance.

pla·nea·dor m. glider airplane.

pla·ne·ar v. to plan; to glide (*said of an airplane or bird*).

pla·neo m. planning; glide, gliding (*of an airplane*).

pla·ne·ta m. planet.

pla·no adj. plane, flat, level; m. plane; plan; map; **de** – flatly, clearly, openly; **dar de** – to hit with the flat of anything.

plan·ta f. (*ser orgánico*) plant; plantation; (*proyecto*) plan; ground plan, ground floor; (*del pie*) sole of the foot; **– baja** ground floor; **buena -** good looks; **echar -s** to brag.

plan·ta·ción f. plantation; planting.

plan·tar v. to plant; to strike (*a blow*); **-se** to stand firm; to balk; *Am.* to doll up, dress up; **dejar a uno plantado** to "stand someone up", keep someone waiting indefinitely.

plan·te·ar v. to plan; to establish; to carry out; to state, present (*a problem*); to try.

plan·tel m. establishment; firm; plant; nursery.

plan·tío m. planting; plantation; recently planted garden; tree nursery.

plas·ma m. plasma.

plás·ti·co adj. plastic.

pla·ta f. silver; silver money; **hablar en** – to speak in plain language; *Carib., C.A., Ven., Col.* money.

pla·ta·for·ma f. platform; **– de lanzamiento** launching pad.

pla·ta·nal, platanar m. grove of banana trees; banana plantation.

plá·ta·no m. banana; banana tree; plane tree.

pla·te·a f. main floor of a theatre; a lower box seat.

pla·te·a·do adj. silver-plated; silvery.

pla·te·ar v. to silver, plate, cover with silver.

pla·tel m. platter; tray.

pla·te·ro m. silversmith; jeweler.

plá·ti·ca f. conversation, talk, chat; informal lecture.

pla·ti·ca·dor m. talker; adj. talkative.

pla·ti·car[6] v. to converse, talk, chat.

pla·ti·llo m. saucer; pan (*of a pair of scales*); cymbal; stew.

pla·ti·no m. platinum.

pla·to m. plate; dish; dinner course; **– de tocadiscos** turntable.

pla·tón m. large plate; platter.

pla·tu·do adj. *Am.* wealthy, rich.

pla·ya f. beach, shore; *Ven.* wide, open space in front of a ranch house; *Riopl., Andes* **– de estacionamiento** parking lot.

pla·za f. (*pública*) plaza, public square; public market; (*empleo*) job; employment; *Riopl., Ch., Cuba., Ven.* park, promenade; **– de armas** parade ground; public square; fortress; **– fuerte** fortress; **– de gallos** cockpit (*for cockfights*); **– de toros** bull ring; **sacar a-** to bring out into the open, make public; **sentar –** to enlist; **plazoleta, plazuela** f. small square, court.

pla·zo m. term, time; **a** – on credit; in installments.

ple·a·mar m. flood tide, high tide.

ple·be f. rabble; masses.

ple·be·yo adj. plebeian.

ple·bis·ci·to m. plebiscite, direct vote.

ple·ga·di·zo adj. folding; pliable, easily bent.

ple·gar[1,7] v. to fold; to pleat; to crease; **-se** to bend, yield, submit.

ple·ga·ria f. supplication, prayer; prayer hour.

plei·to m. litigation, lawsuit; dispute; debate; duel; **– de acreedores** bankruptcy proceedings; **pleitista** m. & f. quarrelsome person.

ple·ni·po·ten·cia·rio m. plenipotentiary (*diplomatic*

agent having full power or authority); *adj.*
plenipotentiary, having full power.

ple·ni·tud *f.* plenitude, fullness, completeness;
abundance.

ple·no *adj.* full, complete; **sesión plena** joint session;
en – día in broad daylight, openly; **en – rostro** (*or*
en plena cara) right on the **face**; *m.* joint sesion (*of
a legislative body*).

plie·go *m.* sheet of paper; sealed letter or document.

plie·gue *m.* fold, crease, pleat.

plo·ma·da *f.* plumb, lead weight, plumb bob.

plo·ma·zo *m. Col., Ven., Mex.* shot, bullet.

plo·me·ría *f.* plumbing; plumber's shop; lead roof.

plo·me·ro *m.* plumber.

plo·mi·zo *m.* leaden, lead-colored.

plo·mo *m.* lead; plumb, lead weight; bullet; boring
person; **a – vertical;** vertically; *adj. Carib., Mex.*
lead-colored.

plu·ma *f.* (*de ave*) feather; plume; (*instrumento*) pen;
quill; **– estilográfica** (*or* **– fuente**) fountain pen;
plumada *f.* dash, stroke of the pen, flourish; **plumaje** *m.* plumage; plume, **plumero** *m.* feather
duster; box for feathers; feather ornament (*on hats,
helmets, etc.*); **plumón** *m.* down; feather mattress;
plumoso *adj.* downy, feathery.

plu·ral *adj.* plural.

plu·vial *adj.* rain (*used as adj.*); **capa – cope** (*long
cope used by priests during certain religious
ceremonies*).

plu·vió·me·tro *m.* rain gauge.

po·bla·ción *f.* (*acto*) populating; settlement; (*número*) population; (*lugar*) town, city.

po·bla·do *m.* inhabited place; village; *p.p.* populated;
covered with growth.

po·bla·dor *m.* settler (*of a colony*).

po·blar² *v. irr.* to populate, people; to colonize, settle;
to stock (*a farm*); to breed; **-se** to become covered
(*with leaves or buds*).

po·bre *adj.* poor; *m.* poor man, beggar; **pobrete** *m.*
poor devil, poor wretch; **pobretón** *m.* poor old
fellow, poor wretch.

po·bre·za *f.* poverty; need; lack, scarcity; barrenness.

po·cil·ga *f.* pigsty, pigpen.

po·ci·llo *m.* cup.

po·co *adj.* little, scanty; small; short (*time*); **-s** few,
some; *m.* a little, a bit; *Adv.* little; **a –** presently, after
a short time; **a – rato** (*or* **al – rato**) after a short
while; **– a –** slowly, little by little; **a los -s meses**
after a few months; **por – me caigo** I almost fell;
tener en – a to hold in low esteem.

po·da·de·ra *f.* pruning hook or knife.

po·dar *v.* to prune, trim, cut off.

po·den·co *m.* hound.

po·der³⁹ *v. irr.* to be able; can; may; **él puede mucho**
(*or* **poco**) he has much (*or* little) power; **puede
que** it is possible that, it may be that, perhaps; **hasta
más no –** to the utmost, to the limit; **no – más** not
to be able to do more; to be exhausted; **no puede
menos de hacerlo** he cannot help doing it; **no –
con la carga** not to be equal to the burden, not to be
able to lift the load; *Col., Ven.* **-le a uno algo** to be
worried or affected by something, *m.* power,
authority.

po·de·río *m.* power, dominion; might; wealth.

po·de·ro·so *adj.* powerful; wealthy.

po·dre *f.* pus; decayed matter; **podredumbre** *f.*
corruption, decay; pus; rotten matter.

po·dri·do *adj.* rotten; *p.p. of* podrir.

po·drir¹⁶ **= pudrir¹⁶**.

po·e·ma *m.* poem.

po·e·sía *f.* poetry; poem.

po·e·ta *m.* poet; **poetastro** *m.* bad poet.

po·é·ti·co *adj.* poetic; **poética** *f.* poetics.

po·e·ti·sa *f.* poetess.

po·la·co *adj.* Polish; *m.* Polish, Polish language; Pole.

po·lai·na *f.* legging.

po·lar *adj.* polar.

po·le·a *f.* pulley.

po·len *m.* pollen.

po·li·cía *f.* police; *m.* policeman.

po·li·cial *m. Col., Ven.* policeman.

po·li·lla *f.* moth; larva of the moth.

po·lí·ti·ca *f.* politics; policy; *Am.* **– de campanario**
politics of a clique.

po·li·ti·cas·tro *m.* bad or incapable politician.

po·lí·ti·co *adj.* political; politic; polite; **madre política** mother-in-law; *m.* politician.

pó·li·za *f.* policy, written contract; draft; customhouse
certificate; **– de seguros** insurance policy.

po·li·zon·te *m.* policeman.

po·lo *m.* pole (*of a magnet or of an axis*); polo (*a
game*); **– acuático** water polo.

pol·trón *adj.* lazy, idle; **silla poltrona** easy chair.

pol·va·re·da *f.* cloud of dust; **armar** (*or* **levantar**)
una – to kick up the dust; to raise a rumpus.

pol·ve·ra *f.* powder box; compact; powder puff.

pol·vo *m.* dust; powder; pinch of snuff or powder; **–
férrico** iron oxide filings (*coating for recording tape*);
-s toilet powder; **-s para dientes** tooth powder; **limpio de – y paja** entirely free; net; *Am.* cleaned out,
without a penny; *Am.* innocent, ignorant, unaware;
Mex., Col., Ven. **tomar el –** to escape, 'beat it'.

pól·vo·ra *f.* gunpowder; fireworks.

pol·vo·re·ar *v.* to powder, sprinkle with powder.

pol·vo·rien·to *adj.* dusty.

pol·vo·rín *m.* powder magazine; priming powder;
powder flask; *Am.* tick (*parasitic insect*); *Riopl.*
spitfire, quicktempered person.

po·lla *f.* pullet (*young hen*); young lass; pool (*in cards*).

po·lla·da *f.* hatch, brood; flock of chicks.

po·lle·ra *f.* woman who raises and sells chikens;
chiken coop; a bell-shaped basket for chikens;

petticoat; *Ríopl.*, *Ch.*, *Col.*, *Andes* skirt.

po·lli·no *m.* young donkey, ass.

po·llo *m.* young chiken; nestling, young bird; Spain young man; **polluelo** *m.* chick.

pom·pa *f.* pomp; pageant, procession; bubble; pump.

pom·po·so *adj.* pompous.

pó·mu·lo *m.* cheek bone.

pon·che *m.* punch (a beverage); **ponchera** *f.* punch bowl.

pon·cho *m. Andes*, *Ch.*, *Ríopl.* poncho; cape.

pon·de·ra·ción *f.* pondering, careful consideration, weighing; exaggeration.

pon·de·rar *v.* (*pensar*) to ponder, consider, weigh; (*exagerar*) to exaggerate; to extol.

pon·de·ra·ti·vo *adj.* exaggerating.

pon·de·ro·so *adj.* ponderous, heavy.

po·ner[40] *v. irr.* to put; to place; to set; to lay; to suppose; **– como nuevo a alguien** to cover someone with insults; **– en claro** to clarify; **– en limpio** to recopy, make a clean copy; **– todo de su parte** to do one´s best; **pongamos que...** let us suppose that...; **-se** to place oneself; to become; **-se** a to begin to; **-se al corriente** to become informed; **-se de pie** to stand up; *Carib.*, *Mex.*, *Ch.*, *Andes* **-se bien con alguien** to ingratiate oneself with someone, get on his good side; *Am.* **ponérsela** to get drunk.

po·nien·te *m.* west; west wind; **el sol –** the setting sun.

pon·tón *m.* pontoon; scow, flat-bottomed boat; long bridge; pontoon bridge.

pon·zo·ña *f.* venom, poison.

pon·zo·ño·so *adj.* venomous, poisonous.

po·pa *f.* poop, stern; **viento en –** speedily; going well.

po·po·te *m. Mex.* straw for brooms; *Mex.* drinking straw or tube.

po·pu·la·cho *m.* populace, rabble.

po·pu·lar *adj.* popular.

po·pu·la·ri·dad *f.* popularity.

po·pu·lo·so *adj.* populous, densely populated.

po·qui·to *adj.* very little; *Cuba*, *Ven.*, *Col.* timid, shy; *m.* a small bit; **a -s** in small quantities.

por *prep.* by; for; for the sake of, on account of, on behalf of; because of; through; along; on exchange for; in the place of; during; about, around; to, with the idea of; **– ciento** percent; **– consiguiente** consequently; **– entre** among, between; **– escrito** in writing; **– poco se muere** he almost died; **está – hacer** it is yet to be done; **él está – hacerlo** he is in favor of doing it; **recibir – esposa** to receive as a wife; **tener –** to consider, think of as; **¿– que?** *interr. Adv.* why? for what reason?.

por·ce·la·na *f.* porcelain, china; enamel.

por·cen·ta·je *m.* percentage.

por·ción *f.* portion; part, share; **una – de gente** a lot of people.

por·che *m.* porch.

por·dio·se·ar *v.* to beg.

por·dio·se·ro *m.* beggar.

por·fí·a *f.* stubbornness, obstinacy; persistence, insistence; **a –** in competition; with great insistence.

por·fia·do *adj.* stubborn, obstinate, persistent.

por·fiar[17] *v.* to persist; to insist; to dispute obstinately; to argue.

por·me·nor *m.* detail.

por·me·no·ri·zar[9] *v.* to detail, tell in detail; to itemize.

po·ro *m.* pore.

po·ro·so *adj.* porous.

po·ro·to *m. Ch.*, *Ríopl.*, *Andes* bean; *Ch.*, *Ríopl.*, *Andes* runt.

por·que *conj.* because; so that.

por·qué *m.* cause, reason, motive.

por·que·ría *f,* filth; filthy act or word; nasty piece of food; trifle, worthless object.

po·rra *f.* club, stick; *Am.* **mandar a uno a la –** to send someone to the devil; **porrazo** *m.* blow; knock; bump; **porrón** *m.* wine vessel with long snout.

por·ta *f.* porthole; cover for a porthole; goal (*in football*).

por·ta·a·vio·nes *m.* airplane carrier.

por·ta·da *f.* façade, front (*of a building*); title page.

por·ta·dor *m.* carrier; bearer; tray.

por·tal *m.* portal; entrance, vestibule; portico, porch; *Am.* Christmas crèche; **-es** arcades, galleries; **portalón** *m.* large portal; gangway (*of a ship*).

por·ta·mo·ne·das *m.* pocketbook, coin purse.

por·ta·pa·pe·les *m.* briefcase.

por·ta·plu·mas *m.* penholder.

por·tar *v. Am.* to carry; **-se** to behave.

por·tá·til *adj.* portable.

por·ta·vio·nes *m.* aircraft carrier; also **portaaviones**.

por·ta·voz *m.* megaphone; mouthpiece; spokesman.

por·taz·go *m.* toll.

por·ta·zo *m.* bang or slam of a door; **dar un -** to bang or slam the door.

por·te *m.* portage, cost of carriage; freight; postage; manner, bearing; size, capacity; *Am.* birthday present; *C.A.* size.

por·tear *v.* to carry on one´s back; *Am.* to get out in a hurry.

por·ten·to *m.* portent; wonder, marvel.

por·ten·to·so *adj.* marvelous, extraordinary, amazing, terrifying.

por·te·ño *adj.* from a port; *Ríopl.* from Buenos Aires.

por·te·rí·a *f.* porter´s quarters; main door of a building.

por·te·ro *m.* doorkeeper, doorman; janitor.

pór·ti·co *m.* portico, porch.

por·ti·lla *f.* porthole; small gate or passageway.

por·tón *m.* gate.

por·tu·gués *adj.* Portuguese; *m.* Portuguese; Portuguese language.

por·ve·nir *m.* future.

pos: en - de after; in pursuit of.

po·sa·da *f.* lodging; inn; boardinghouse; dwelling, home; *Mex.* **las -s** a Christmas festivity lasting nine days; **posadero** *m.* innkeeper.

po·sa·de·ras *f. pl.* posterior, buttocks, rump.

po·sar *v.* to lodge; to rest; to sit down; to pose (*as a model*); to perch (*said of birds*); **-se** to settle (*said of sediment*); to perch (*said of birds*).

pos·da·ta *f.* postscript.

po·se·e·dor *m.* possessor, owner.

po·se·er[14] *v.* to possess, own; to master, know well; **-se** to have control of oneself.

po·se·sión *f.* possession.

po·se·si·vo *adj. & m.* possessive.

po·se·sor *m.* possessor, owner.

po·si·bi·li·dad *f.* possibility.

po·si·ble *adj.* possible; **hacer lo -** to do one's best; **-s** *m. pl.* goods, property, means.

po·si·ción *f.* position; posture; status, rank, standing; placing.

po·si·ti·vo *adj.* positive; effective; true; practical.

pos·po·ner[40] *v. irr.* to postpone, put off; to put after; to subordinate.

pos·pues·to *p.p. of* **posponer**.

pos·ta *f.* (*bala*) small bullet; (*apuesta*) bet, wager; (*relevo*) relay (*of post horses*); post station; **-s** buckshot; **por la -** posthaste; fast, speedily; *m.* postboy, courier, messenger.

pos·tal *adj.* postal; **tarjeta -** postcard.

post·da·ta = posdata.

pos·te *m.* post, pillar.

pos·ter·gar[7] *v.* to delay; to postpone; to disregard someone's right.

pos·te·ri·dad *f.* posterity.

pos·te·rior *adj.* posterior, back, rear; later.

pos·ti·go *m.* wicket, small door or gate; shutter; peep window.

pos·ti·zo *adj.* false, artificial; *m.* switch, false hair.

pos·tra·ción *f.* postration, collapse, exhaustion; dejection, lowness of spirits.

pos·trar *v.* to postrate; to humiliate; to throw down; to weaken, exhaust; **-se** to kneel to the ground; to be weakened, exhausted; to collapse.

pos·tre *m.* dessert; **a la -** at last.

pos·tre·r(o) *adj.* last; hindmost, nearest the rear.

pos·tu·lan·te *m. & f.* petitioner; applicant, candidate.

pós·tu·mo *adj.* posthumous, after one's death.

pos·tu·ra *f.* posture, position; bid; wager; pact, agreement; egg-laying.

po·ta·ble *adj.* drinkable; **agua -** drinking water.

po·ta·je *m.* pottage, thick soup; porridge; mixed drink.

po·te *m.* pot; jar; jug; *Carib., Ven., Mex., Ríopl.* flask; *Am.* buzzard.

po·ten·cia *f.* potency; power; faculty, ability; powerful nation.

po·ten·te *adj.* potent, powerful, strong.

po·tes·tad *f.* power; dominion, authority.

po·tran·ca *f.* filly, young mare.

po·tre·ro *m.* herdsman of colts; fence din pasture land; *Carib., Mex., C.A. Ven., Col., Ch.* cattle ranch, stock farm.

po·tro *m.* colt; rack, torture; *Col., Ven., Mex., Ch., Ríopl.* wild horse.

po·yo *m.* stone or brick bench (*usually built against a wall*).

po·zo *m.* well; hole, pit; mine shaft; hold of a ship; *Am.* pool, puddle; *Ríopl., Ch., Ven., Col., Mex.* spring, fountain.

prác·ti·ca *f.* practice; exercise; custom, habit; method.

prac·ti·can·te *m. & f.* doctor's assistant; hospital intern.

prac·ti·car[6] *v.* to practice; to put into practice.

prác·ti·co *adj.* practical; experienced, skilful; *m.* **- de puerto** harbor pilot.

pra·de·ra *f.* prairie; meadow.

pra·do *m.* meadow, field; lawn.

pre·ám·bu·lo *m.* preamble, introduction, prologue.

pre·ca·rio *adj.* precarious.

pre·cau·ción *f.* precaution.

pre·ca·ver *v.* to guard (*against*), keep (*from*); to warn, caution; **-se** to guard oneself (*against*); to take precautions.

pre·ca·vi·do *adj.* cautious, on guard.

pre·ce·den·cia *f.* precedence; priority.

pre·ce·den·te *adj.* preceding; *m.* precedent.

pre·ce·der *v.* to precede; to have precedence.

pre·cep·to *m.* precept; rule; order.

pre·cep·tor *m.* teacher, tutor.

pre·cia·do *adj.* prized, esteemed; precious, valuable.

pre·ciar *v.* to appraise; to value; **-se de** to boast of, be proud of.

pre·cio *m.* price, value, worth; esteem.

pre·cio·so *adj.* precious, valuable; fine, exquisite; beautiful.

pre·ci·pi·cio *m.* precipice; ruin.

pre·ci·pi·ta·ción *f.* precipitation; rush, haste, hurry.

pre·ci·pi·ta·do *adj.* precipitate, hasty, rash; *m.* precipitate (*chemical term*).

pre·ci·pi·tar *v.* to precipitate; to hasten, rush; to hurl, throw headlong; **-se** to throw oneself headlong; to rush (into).

pre·ci·pi·to·so *adj.* precipitous, steep; rash.

pre·ci·sar *v.* to determine precisely; to force, compel, make necessary; *Ríopl., Col., Ven., Mex., Andes;* to be necessary or urgent; *Am.* to need.

pre·ci·sión *f.* precision, exactness; accuracy; compulsion, force, necessity; *Am.* haste.

pre·ci·so *adj.* necessary; precise, exact; clear; *m. Am.* small travelling bag.

pre·coz *adj.* precocious.

pre·cur·sor *m.* precursor, forerunner.

pre·de·cir[27] *v. irr.* to predict, prophesy, forecast, foretell.

pre·des·ti·nar *v.* to predestine.

pre·di·ca·ción *f.* preaching.

pre·di·ca·do *adj.* & *m.* predicate; *p.p. of* **predicar**.

pre·di·ca·dor *m.* preacher.

pre·di·car[6] *v.* to preach.

pre·dic·ción *f.* prediction.

pre·di·lec·ción *f.* predilection, preference, liking.

pre·di·lec·to *adj.* favorite, preferred.

pre·dis·po·ner[40] *v. irr.* to predispose, bias, prejudice.

pre·dis·pues·to *p.p. of* **predisponer** & *adj.* predisposed, prejudiced, biased.

pre·do·mi·nan·te *adj.* predominant; prevailing, ruling.

pre·do·mi·nar *v.* to predominate, prevail.

pre·do·mi·nio *m.* predominance; sway, influence.

pre·fa·cio *m.* preface.

pre·fec·to *m.* prefect (*military of civil chief; sometimes a mayor, sometimes governor of a province, as in Peru*).

pre·fe·ren·cia *f.* preference; **de –** with preference; preferably.

pre·fe·ren·te *adj.* preferable; preferred; preferential; **acciones -s** preferred shares.

pre·fe·ri·ble *adj.* preferable.

pre·fe·rir[3] *v. irr.* to prefer.

pre·fi·jar *v.* to prefix; to set beforehand (*as a date*).

pre·fi·jo *m.* prefix.

pre·go·nar *v.* to proclaim, cry out; to make known.

pre·gun·ta *f.* question; **hacer una –** to ask a question.

pre·gun·tar *v.* to ask, inquire.

pre·gun·tón *adj.* inquisitive.

pre·jui·cio *m.* prejudice.

pre·la·do *m.* prelate.

pre·li·mi·nar *adj.* & *m.* preliminary.

pre·lu·diar *v.* to be the prelude or beginning of; to initiate, introduce; to try out (*a musical instrument*).

pre·lu·dio *m.* prelude; introduction.

pre·ma·tu·ro *adj.* premature, untimely.

pre·me·di·ta·do *adj.* premeditated, deliberate.

pre·miar *v.* to reward.

pre·mio *m.* prize; reward; recompense; premium; **a -** with interest, at interest.

pre·mi·sa *f.* premise (*either of the first two propositions of a syllogism*).

pre·mu·ra *f.* pressure, urgency, haste.

pren·da *f.* (*fianza*) pawn, pledge, security; token; (*partes del vestido*) article of clothing; anything vauable; loved person; jewel; **-s** good qualities, gifts,

talents; **– de vestir** garment; **juego de -s** game of forfeits; **en – de** as a proof of, as a pledge of.

pren·dar *v.* to pawn, pledge; to charm, please; **-se de** to get attached to; to fall in love with.

pren·de·dor *m.* clasp; stickpin; tie pin; brooch; *Am.* lighter.

pren·der *v.* (*asir*) to seize, catch, grab; to bite (*said of an insect*); to fasten, clasp; to arrest, imprison; (*empezar*) to take root; to begin to burn; catch fire; *Riopl., Carib., C.A., Mex.* to light (*a lamp*); *Am.* to start, begin, undertake; **– el fuego** to start the fire; *Col.* **-las** to take to one's heels; **-se** to dress up.

pren·de·ro *m.* pawnbroker; second-hand dealer.

pren·sa *f.* press; printing press.

pren·sar *v.* to press.

pre·ña·do *adj.* pregnant; full.

pre·ñez *f.* pregnancy.

pre·o·cu·pa·ción *f.* preoccupation; worry; bias, prejudice.

pre·o·cu·par *v.* to preoccupy; to worry; to prejudice; **-se** to be preoccupied; to worry; to be prejudiced.

pre·pa·ra·ción *f.* preparation.

pre·pa·rar *v.* to prepare; **-se** to get ready; to be prepared.

pre·pa·ra·ti·vo *adj.* preparatory; *m.* preparation.

pre·pa·ra·to·rio *adj.* preparatory.

pre·po·si·ción *f.* preposition.

pre·rro·ga·ti·va *f.* prerogative, right, privilege.

pre·sa *f.* prey; dam; fang, tusk; claw; **hacer –** to seize.

pre·sa·giar *v.* to foretell.

pre·sa·gio *m.* presage, omen, sign.

pres·bí·te·ro *m.* priest.

pres·cin·dir *v.* to disregard, set aside, leave aside; to omit; to dispense (*with*).

pres·cri·bir[52] *v.* to prescribe.

pres·cri·to *p.p. of* **prescribir**.

pre·sen·cia *f.* presence; figure, bearing; **– de ánimo** presence of mind, serenity.

pre·sen·ciar *v.* to see, witness; to be present at.

pre·sen·ta·ción *f.* presentation; personal introduction; *Ven.* petition.

pre·sen·tar *v.* to present; to introduce; **-se** to appear, present oneself; to introduce oneself; to offer one's services; *Am.* to have recourse to justice, file suit.

pre·sen·te *adj.* present; *m.* present, gift; **al –** now, at the present time; **por el (la, or lo) –** for the present; **mejorando lo –** present company excepted; **te·ner –** to bear in mind.

pre·sen·ti·mien·to *m.* presentiment, foreboding.

pre·sen·tir[3] *v. irr.* to have a presentiment, foreboding or hunch.

pre·ser·va·ción *f.* preservation.

pre·ser·var *v.* to preserve, guard, protect, keep.

pre·si·den·cia *f.* presidency; office of president; presidential term; chairmanship.

pre·si·den·cial *adj.* presidential.

pre·si·den·te *m.* president; chairman; presiding judge.sss

pre·si·dia·rio *m.* prisoner, convict.

pre·si·dio *m.* garrison; fortress; penitentiary, prison; **diez años de** – ten years at hard labor (*in a prison*).

pre·si·dir *v.* to preside; to direct.

pre·si·lla *f.* loop, fastener; clip.

pre·sión *f.* pressure.

pre·so *m.* prisoner; *p.p. irr. of* **prender** imprisoned.

pres·ta·do *adj. & p.p.* loaned, lent; **dar** – to lend; **pedir** – to borrow.

pres·ta·mis·ta *m. & f.* moneylender.

prés·ta·mo *m.* loan.

pres·tar *v.* to loan, lend; *Col., Ven., C.A., Andes* to borrow; **– ayuda** to give help; **– atención** to pay attention; *Andes* **presta acá** give it here, give it to me; **-se** to lend oneself or itself.

pres·te·za *f.* promptness, speed.

pres·ti·di·gi·ta·ción *f.* juggling, sleight of hand.

pres·ti·di·gi·ta·dor *m.* juggler.

pres·ti·gio *m.* prestige; influence, authority; good reputation.

pres·to *adj.* quick; nimble; prompt; ready; *Adv.* soon, at once; **de** – quickly, promptly.

pre·su·mi·do *adj.* conceited, presumptuous; *p.p. of* **presumir**.

pre·su·mir *v.* to presume; to boast; to show off; *Am.* to court, woo; **– de valiente** to boast of one's valor.

pre·sun·ción *f.* presumption, assumption; conceit, arrogance.

pre·sun·to *adj.* presumed; supposed; prospective; **heredero** – heir apparent.

pre·sun·tuo·so *adj.* presumptuous, conceited.

pre·su·po·ner [40] *v. irr.* to presuppose, take for granted, imply; to estimate.

pre·su·pues·to *p.p. of* **presuponer** presupposed; estimated; *m.* budget, estimate.

pre·su·ro·so *adj.* quick, prompt; hasty.

pre·ten·cio·so *adj.* presumptuous; conceited.

pre·ten·der *v.* to pretend; to solict, seek; to claim; to try; to court.

pre·ten·dien·te *m.* pretender, claimant, suitor; office seeker.

pre·ten·sión *f.* pretension; claim; presumption; pretense.

pre·té·ri·to *adj.* preterite, past; *m.* preterite, the past tense.

pre·tex·to *m.* pretext, pretense, excuse.

pre·til *m.* stone or brick railing; *Am.* ledge; *Mex., Ven.* stone or brick bench (*built against a wall*).

pre·ti·na *f.* belt, girdle; waistband.

pre·va·le·cer [13] *v. irr.* to prevail.

pre·va·le·cien·te *adj.* prevalent, current.

pre·ven·ción *f.* prevention; foresight, preparedness; bias, prejudice; provision, supply; admonition, warning; police station; guardhouse.

pre·ve·ni·do *adj. & p.p.* prepared, ready; forewarned; cautious; supplied.

pre·ve·nir [48] *v. irr.* to prevent, avoid; to prepare beforehand; to foresee; to warn; to predispose; **-se** to get prepared, get ready.

pre·ver [48] *v. irr.* to foresee.

pre·vio *adj.* previous; *m. Am.* preliminary examination.

pre·vi·sión *f.* foresight.

pre·vis·to *p.p. of* **prever**.

prie·to *adj.* dark, black; tight; compact; *Riopl., Ven., Col., Mex., C.A., Andes* dark-complexioned, swarthy.

pri·ma *f.* female cousin, premium; prime (*first of the canonical hours*).

pri·ma·cía *f.* priority, precedence; superiority.

pri·ma·rio *adj.* primary, principal.

pri·ma·ve·ra *f.* spring; primrose; print, flowered silk cloth.

pri·ma·ve·ral *adj.* spring, pertaining to spring.

pri·mer(o) *adj.* first; former; leading, principal; **primera enseñanza** primary education; **primera materia** raw material; **de buenas a primeras** all of a sudden, unexpectedly; **a primera luz** at dawn; *Adv.* first; rather.

pri·mi·cia *f.* first fruit; first profit; **-s** first fruits.

pri·mi·ti·vo *adj.* primitive; primary; original.

pri·mo *m.* cousin; simpleton, sucker, dupe; **– hermano** (*or* **- carnal**) first cousin; *Carib.* **coger a uno de** - to deceive someone easily; *adj.* first; **número** - prime number.

pri·mo·gé·ni·to *adj. & m.* first-born; **primogenitura** *f.* birthright; rights of the first-born.

pri·mor *m.* beauty; excellence; exquisiteness; skill, ability.

pri·mo·ro·so *adj.* excellent, fine, exquisite; skillful.

prí·mu·la *f.* primrose.

prin·ce·sa *f.* princess.

prin·ci·pal *adj.* principal; renowned, famous; **piso** - main floor (*usually, the secon floor*); *m.* principal, capital sum; chief, head.

prín·ci·pe *m* prince; *adj.* princeps, first (*edition*).

prin·ci·pian·te *m.* beginner.

prin·ci·piar *v.* to begin.

prin·ci·pio *m.* principle; beginning; origin, source, entrée (*main dinner course*); **a -s de** towards the beginning of.

prin·gue *m. & f.* grease drippings (*from bacon, ham, etc.*).

prio·ri·dad *f.* priority; precedence.

pri·sa *f.* speed, haste; **de** (*or* **a**) - quickley, speedily; **a todo** - with the greatest speed; **eso corre** - that is urgent; **dar - a** to hurry; **darse** - to hurry; **tener** (*or* **estar de)** - to be in a hurry.

pri·sión *f.* prison; imprisonment; seizure; shackle; **-es** shackles, fetters, chains.

pri·sio·ne·ro *m.* prisoner.

pris·ma *f.* prism.

pris·ti·no *adj.* first, early, former, primitive.

pri·va·ción *f.* privation; want, lack; loss.

pri·va·do *adj.* private; personal; unconscious; *p.p.* deprived; *m.* favorite.

pri·var *v.* (*destituir*) to deprive; to prohibit; (*tener aceptación*) to enjoy the favor of someone; to be in vogue; **-le a uno del sentido** to stun, daze; **ya no privan esas costumbres** those customs are no longer in vogue or in existence; **-se** to lose consciousness; **-se de** to deprive oneself of.

pri·va·ti·vo *adj.* exclusive; particular, distinctive.

pri·vi·le·gia·do *adj.* privileged.

pri·vi·le·giar *v.* to favor; to give a privilege to.

pri·vi·le·gio *m.* privilege; exemption; patent; copyright; **- de invención** patent on an invention.

pro *m. & f.* profit, advantage; **en - de** on behalf of: **en - y en contra** pro and con, for an against; **hombre de -** man of worth.

pro·a *f.* prow.

pro·ba·bi·li·dad *f.* probability.

pro·ba·ble *adj.* probable.

pro·bar[2] *v. irr.* (*examinar*) to test; to taste; to prove; to try; to try on; (*gustar*) to suit, agree with; **no me prueba el clima** the climate does not agree with me.

pro·be·ta *f.* test tube; pressure gauge.

pro·bi·dad *f.* integrity, uprightness, honesty.

pro·ble·ma *m.* problem.

pro·ce·den·te *adj.* proceeding (from), originating; according to law.

pro·ce·der *v.* to proceed; to originate; to behave; to take action (*against*); *m.* behavior, conduct.

pro·ce·di·mien·to *m.* procedure; method; process; conduct.

pró·cer *m.* distinguished person; hero; great statesman.

pro·ce·sa·do *p.p. & adj.* relating to, or included in, a lawsuit; accused, prosecuted; *m.* defendant.

pro·ce·sar *v.* to prosecute; to accuse; to indict; to sue.

pro·ce·sión *f.* procession; parade.

pro·ce·so *m.* process; lawsuit, legal proceedings; lapse of time;- **verbal** minutes, record.

pro·cla·ma *f.* proclamation, ban; marriage banns.

pro·cla·ma·ción *f.* proclamation.

pro·cla·mar *v.* to proclaim.

pro·cu·ra·dor *m.* attorney.

pro·cu·rar *v.* (*pretender*) to try, endeavor; (*obtener*) to procure, obtain, get.

pro·di·gar[7] *v.* to lavish; to bestow upon; to asquander, waste.

pro·di·gio *m.* prodigy, wonder, marvel; miracle.

pro·di·gio·so *adj.* prodigious, marvelous; fine, exquisite.

pró·di·go *adj.* prodigal, wasteful; lavish; generous; *m.* spendthrift.

pro·duc·ción *f.* production; produce.

pro·du·cir[25] *v. irr.* to produce; to bring about; to yield; **-se** to express oneself, explain oneself; *Col., Ven.* to occur, happen.

pro·duc·ti·vo *adj.* productive; fruitful; profitable.

pro·duc·to *m.* product; yield; result.

pro·duc·tor *m.* producer; *adj.* producing, productive.

pro·e·za *f.* prowess; *Col.* boast, exaggeration.

pro·fa·na·ción *f.* profanation.

pro·fa·nar *v.* to profane; to defile.

pro·fa·no *adj.* profane, not sacred, irreverent; lay, uninformed (*about a branch of learning*).

pro·fe·cí·a *f.* prophecy; prediction.

pro·fe·rir[3] *v. irr.* to utter, express, speak.

pro·fe·sar *v.* to profess; to avow, confess.

pro·fe·sión *f.* profession; avowal, declaration.

pro·fe·sio·nal *adj., m. & f.* professional.

pro·fe·sio·nis·ta *m. & f. Am.* professional.

pro·fe·sor *m.* professor, teacher; **profesorado** *m.* faculty; body of teachers; teaching profession; professorship.

pro·fe·ta *m.* prophet.

pro·fé·ti·co *adj.* prophetic.

pro·fe·ti·zar[9] *v.* to prophesy.

pro·fi·cien·te *adj.* proficient, skilled.

pro·fi·la·xis *f.* prophylaxis (*disease prevention*).

pró·fu·go *adj. & m.* fugitive.

pro·fun·di·dad *f.* profundity, depth.

pro·fun·di·zar[9] *v.* to deepen; to go deep into.

pro·fun·do *adj.* profound; deep; low.

pro·fu·so *adj.* profuse; lavish.

pro·gra·ma *m.* program; plan.

pro·gre·sar *v.* to progress.

pro·gre·sis·ta *m. f. & adj.* progressive.

pro·gre·si·vo *adj.* progressive.

pro·gre·so *m.* progress.

pro·hi·bi·ción *f.* prohibition; ban.

pro·hi·bir *v.* to prohibit, forbid.

pró·ji·mo *m.* neighbor, fellow being; *Ríopl., Carib., C.A.* **ese** - that fellow.

pro·le *f.* progeny, offspring.

pro·le·ta·ria·do *m.* proletariat, working class.

pro·le·ta·rio *adj.* proletarian, belonging to the working class; plebeian; *m.* proletarian.

pro·li·jo *adj.* prolix, too long, drawn out, too detailed; boring, tedious.

pro·lo·gar[7] *v.* to preface, write a prefase for.

pró·lo·go *m.* prologue.

pro·lon·ga·ción *f.* prolongation, extension; lengthening.

pro·lon·gar[7] *v.* to prolong, lengthen, extend.

pro·me·diar *v.* to average; to divide or distribute into two equal parts; to mediate; **antes de - el mes** before the middle of the month.

pro·me·dio *m.* middle; average.

pro·me·sa *f.* promise.

pro·me·te·dor *adj.* promising, hopeful.

pro·me·ter *v.* to promise; to show promise; *Ríopl., C.A.*, to affirm, assure; **-se** to become engaged, betrothed.

pro·me·ti·do *adj. & p.p.* betrothed; *m.* fiancé, betrothed; promise.

pro·mi·nen·te *adj.* prominent.

pro·mi·so·rio *adj.* promissory.

pro·mo·ción *f.* promotion, advancement.

pro·mon·to·rio *m.* promontory, headland, cape; anything bulky; bulge.

pro·mo·tor *m.* promoter.

pro·mo·ve·dor *m.* promoter.

pro·mo·ver⁷ *v. irr.* to promote; to advance.

pro·mul·ga·ción *f.* promulgation, publication, proclamation (*of a law*).

pro·mul·gar⁷ *v.* to promulgate, proclaim, announce publicly.

pro·nom·bre *m.* pronoun.

pro·nos·ti·car⁶ *v.* to prophesy, predict.

pro·nós·ti·co *m.* forecast; prediction; omen.

pron·ti·tud *f.* promptness; quickness.

pron·to *adj.* quick, speedy; ready; prompt; *Adv.* soon; quickly; **de** – suddenly; **al** – at first; **por de** (*or* **por lo**) – for the present; *m.* sudden impulse.

pro·nun·cia·ción *f.* pronunciation.

pro·nun·ciar *v.* to pronounce; to utter; **-se** to rise up in rebellion.

pro·pa·ga·ción *f.* propagation, spread, spreading.

pro·pa·gan·da *f.* propaganda.

pro·pa·gar⁷ *v.* to propagate, reproduce; to spread.

pro·pa·lar *v.* to spread (*news*).

pro·pa·sar·se *v.* to overstep one's bounds; to exceed one's authority, go too far.

pro·pen·sión *f.* tendency, inclination; bent, natural tendency or ability.

pro·pen·so *adj.* prone, susceptible, inclined.

pro·pi·cio *adj.* propitious, favorable.

pro·pie·dad *f.* property; ownership; attribute, quality; propriety, appropriateness.

pro·pie·ta·rio *m.* proprietor, owner.

pro·pi·na *f.* tip (*voluntary gift of money for service*).

pro·pi·nar *v.* to give (*something to drink*); to give (*a beating, kick, slap*); *Am.* to tip, give a tip to; – **una paliza** to give a beating.

pro·pio *adj.* proper; suitable; own; same; **amor** – vanity, pride, selfesteem; *m.* messenger.

pro·po·ner⁴⁰ *v. irr.* to propose; to resolve; to present; **-se** to resolve, make a resolution.

pro·por·ción *f.* proportion; dimension; ratio; opportunity; chance.

pro·por·cio·nar *v.* to proportion; to adapt, adjust; to furnish; supply; give.

pro·po·si·ción *f.* proposition; proposal; assertion.

pro·pó·si·to *m.* purpose, aim, design; **a** – apropos, suitable, fitting; by the way; **de** – on purpose; **fuera de** – irrelevant, beside the point.

pro·pues·to *f.* proposal, offer; proposition.

pro·pues·to *p.p. of* **proponer.**

pro·pul·sar *v.* to propel.

pro·pul·sión *f.* propulsion; – **a chorro** (*por reacción*) jet propulsion; – **a cohete** rocket propulsion.

pro·pul·sor *m.* propeller; *adj.* propelling.

pro·rra·te·ar *v.* to prorate, distribute or assess proportionally; to average.

pro·rra·teo *m.* apportionment, proportional distribution.

pró·rro·ga *f.* renewal, extension of time.

pró·rro·gar⁷ *v.* to put off, postpone; to adjourn; to extend (*time limit*).

pro·rrum·pir *v.* to break forth; – **en llanto** to burst into tears; – **en una carcajada** to let out a big laugh.

pro·sa *f.* prose.

pro·sai·co *adj.* prosaic; dull; tedious.

pros·cri·bir⁵² *v.* to proscribe, banish; to outlaw.

pros·crip·ción *f.* banishment.

pros·crip·to, proscrito *p.p. of* **proscribir**; *m.* exile, outlaw.

pro·se·guir⁵,¹² *v. irr.* to continue; to follow.

pros·pe·rar *v.* to prosper.

pros·pe·ri·dad *f.* prosperity; success.

prós·pe·ro *adj.* prosperous; successful.

prós·ta·ta *f.* prostate.

pros·ti·tuir³² *v.* to prostitute, corrupt.

pros·ti·tu·ta *f.* prostitute.

pro·ta·go·nis·ta *m. & f.* protagonist (*main character or actor*).

pro·tec·ción *f.* protection; support.

pro·tec·cio·nis·ta *adj.* protective; **tarifa** – protective tariff; *m. & f.* protectionist (*follower of the economic principles of protection*).

pro·tec·tor *m.* protector, guardian; *adj.* protecting, protective.

pro·tec·to·ra·do *m.* protectorate.

pro·te·ger¹¹ *v.* to protect; to shelter; to defend.

pro·teí·na *f.* protein.

pro·teí·ni·co *adj.* related to the proteins.

pro·tes·ta *f.* protest; protestation.

pro·tes·ta·ción *f.* protestation, solemn declaration; protest.

pro·tes·tan·te *m.* Protestant; one who protest.

pro·tes·tar *v.* (*confesar*) to assert, assure; to avow publicly; (*negar*) to protest; – **una letra** to protest a draft.

pro·tón *m.* proton.

pro·to·plas·ma *m.* protoplasm.

pro·tu·be·ran·cia *f.* protuberance, bulge.

pro·tu·be·ran·te *adj.* protuberant, prominent, bulging.

pro·ve·cho *m.* profit; benefit; utility; advantage; **hombre de** – worthy, useful man.

pro·ve·cho·so *adj.* profitable; useful; beneficial; advantageous.

pro·ve·e·dor *m.* provisioner, provider; supply man.

pro·veer[14,52] *v. irr.* to provide; to supply; to confer, bestow; to decide; **-se de** to supply oneself with.

pro·ve·nir[48] *v. irr.* to originate, arise, como (*from*).

pro·ver·bio *m.* proverb.

pro·vi·den·cia *f.* providence; foresight; Providence, God; legal decision, sentence; provision, measure; **tomar una –** to take a step or measure.

pro·vi·den·cial *adj.* providential.

pro·vin·cia *f.* province.

pro·vin·cial *adj.* provincial.

pro·vin·cia·no *adj. & m.* provincial.

pro·vi·sión *f.* provision; supply, stock.

pro·vi·so·rio *adj.* provisional, temporary.

pro·vis·to *p.p. of* **proveer.**

pro·vo·ca·ción *f.* provocation; dare, defiance.

pro·vo·ca·dor *adj.* provoking; – provoker.

pro·vo·car[6] *v.* to provoke; to excite, rouse; to stimulate.

pro·xi·mi·dad *f.* proximity, nearness.

pró·xi·mo *adj.* next; neighboring; near; **del – pasado** of last month.

pro·yec·ción *f.* projection; jut.

pro·yec·tar *v.* to project; to plan; to throw; to cast, **-se** to be cast (*as a shadow*).

pro·yec·til *m.* projectile.

pro·yec·tis·ta *m. & f.* designer; schemer, planner.

pro·yec·to *m.* project; plan; **– de ley** bill (*in a legislature*).

pru·den·cia *f.* prudence, practical wisdom, discretion.

pru·den·te *adj.* prudent, wise, discreet.

prue·ba *f.* proof; trial; test; fitting; sample; evidence; *Andes, Ríopl., Col., C.A.* acrobatic performance, stunt, trick, sleight of hand; **a – de incendio** fireproof.

pru·ri·to *m.* itch; keen desire.

pú·a *f.* prick; barb; prong; thorn; quill (*of a porcupine, etc.*); sharp, cunning person; *Ríopl.* cock's spur; **alambre de -s** barbed wire.

pu·bli·ca·ción *f.* publication.

pu·bli·car[6] *v.* to publish; to reveal; to announce.

pu·bli·ci·dad *f.* publicity.

pú·bli·co *adj. & m.* public.

pu·che·ro *m.* pot, kettle; meat and vegetable stew; pout; **hacer -s** to pout.

pu·cho *m.* cigar or cigarette butt; *C.A.* something of little value.

pu·dien·te *adj.* powerful; rich, wealthy; *m.* man of means.

pu·dín *m.* pudding.

pu·dor *m.* modesty; shyness.

pu·drir[16] *v.* to rot; to vex, annoy; **-se** to rot.

pue·ble·ro *m. Ríopl.* townsman (*as opposed to countryman*).

pue·blo *m.* town, village; people, race, nation; propulace; common people.

puen·te *m.* bridge; *Carib., Mex., Ríopl.* dental bridge; *Am.* knife and fork rest; **– colgante** suspension bridge; **– levadizo** drawbridge.

puer·ca *f.* sow.

puer·co *m.* pig; hog; **– espín** porcupine; **– jabalí** wild boar; *adj.* filthy, dirty; coarse, ill-bred.

pue·ril *adj.* puerile, childish.

puer·ta *f.* door; gate; entrance; **– accesoria (excusa,** *or* **falsa)** side door; **– de golpe** spring door; trap door; **– franca** open door; free entrance or entry; **– trasera** back door; **a – cerrada** secretly, behind closed doors; *Am.* **en –** in view, in sight, very near.

puer·to *m.* port; harbor; refuge; mountain pass; **– franco** free port.

pues *conj.* since, because, for, inasmuch as; then; *Adv.* then; well; **– bien** well then, well; **– que** since.

pues·ta *f.* set, setting (*of a star or planet*); stake at cards; **– de sol** sunset.

pues·te·ro *m. Carib., Mex., Ríopl.* vendor, seller (*at a stand or stall*); *Ríopl.* man in charge of livestock on Argentine ranches.

pues·to *p.p. of* **poner** placed, put, set; **mal** (*or* **bien**) **–** badly (*or* well) dressed; *m.* place; vendor's booth or stand; post, position, office; military post; *Andes, Ríopl.* station for watching and taking care of cattle on a ranch; **– de socorros** first-aid station; **– que** *conj.* since.

pu·gi·la·to *m.* boxing.

pu·gi·lis·ta *m.* boxer, prize fighter.

pug·na *f.* struggle; conflict; **estar en – con** to be in conflict with; to be opposed to.

pug·nar *v.* to fight; to struggle; to strive; to persist.

pu·jan·za *f.* push, force, power.

pu·jar *v.* to make a strenuous effort; to grope for words; to falter; to outbid (*offer a higher bid than*); *C.A.* to grunt; *Am.* to reject; *Ven.* to dismiss; *Am.* **– para adentro** to forbear, keep silent; *Am.* **andar pujado** to go around crestfallen; to be in disgrace.

pu·ji·do *m. Am.* grunt (*due to strenuous effort*).

pul·cri·tud *f.* neatness, trimness; excellence, perfection.

pul·cro *adj.* neat, trim; beautiful.

pul·ga *f.* flea; *Ríopl.* small and insignificant person; **tener malas -s** to be illtempered; *Col., Andes* **ser de pocas -s** to be touchy, oversensitive; **pulgón** *m.* blight, plant louse.

pul·ga·da *f.* inch.

pul·gar *m.* thumb.

pu·li·do *adj.* polished, refined; polite; neat; exquisite.

pu·li·men·tar *v.* to polish.

pu·li·men·to *m.* polish; gloss.

pu·lir *v.* to polish.

pul·món *m.* lung.

pul·mo·nar adj. pulmonary, pertaining to the lungs.
pul·mo·nía f. pneumonia.
pul·pa f. pulp.
pul·pe·ría f. Riopl., C.A., Ch., Ven., Andes country general store; Am. tavern.
pul·pe·ro m. Riopl., C.A., Ch., Ven., Andes owner of a country store or tavern.
púl·pi·to m. pulpit.
pul·po m. octopus.
pul·que m. Mex. pulque (fermented juice of the maguey).
pul·sa·ción f. pulsation, beat, throb; pulse, beating.
pul·sar v. to pulsate, throb, beat; to feel the pulse of; to sound out; examine; to play (the harp); Mex., C.A. to judge or try the weight of (by lifting).
pul·se·ra f. bracelet, wrist bandage; **reloj de -** wrist watch.
pul·so m. pulse; steadiness; tact; Riopl., Carib., Col. bracelet, wrist watch; **un hombre de -** a prudent, steady man; Cuba, Mex. **beber a -** to drink straight down, gulp down; **levantar a -** to lift with the strength of the wrist or hand; **sacar a - un negocio** to carry out a deal by sheer perseverance.
pu·lu·lar v. to swarm; to multiply rapidly; to sprout, bud.
pul·ve·ri·zar[9] v. to pulverize.
pu·lla f. taunt; mean dig, quip, cutting remark; filthy word or remark.
pu·ma f. puma, mountain lion.
pu·na f. Andes cold, arid tableland of the Andes; Riopl. desert; Andes sickness caused by high altitude.
pun·do·nor m. point of honor.
pun·ta f. point, tip; bull's horn; cigar or cigarette butt; Ven., gang, band, herd, a lot (of things, people, etc.); Am. small leaf of fine tobacco; Am. jeer, cutting remark; **-s** point lace; scallops; **de -** on end; **de -s** (or **de puntillas**) on tiptoe; Am. **a - de** by dint of, by means of; **estar de - con** to be on bad terms with; **sacar - a un lápiz** to sharpen a pencil; **tener sus -s de poeta** to be something of a poet.
pun·ta·da f. stitch; hint; Andes prick, pricking, sting, sharp pain; **no he dado - en este asunto** I have left this matter completely untouched.
pun·tal m. prop; support, basis; bull's horn; Col. snack (between meals).
pun·ta·pié m. kick (with the toe of the shoe).
pun·ta·zo m. Col., Ven., Mex., Cuba stab, jab.
pun·te·ar v. to pluck (the strings of a guitar); to play (a guitar); to make dots; to engrave, draw or paint by means of dots; to stitch; to tack (said of a boat).
pun·te·ría f. aim.
pun·te·ro m. pointer; chisel; blacksmith's punch; C.A., Col., Ch. clock or watch hand; Am. leader of a parade: Cuba, Mex., Ven., Col. leading ox (or other animal); Am. guide.

pun·tia·gu·do adj. sharp, sharp-pointed.
pun·ti·lla f. small point; tip; small dagger, tracing point; point lace; Ven. penknife; Am. toe rubber; Am. ridge (of a hill); **de -s** on tiptoe; **puntillazo** m. stab (with a dagger).
pun·to m. (parada) period; stop; point; dot; (puntada) stitch; mesh; (sitio) place; moment; (mira) gun sight; **- de admiración** exclamation mark; **- de interrogación** question mark; **- y coma** semicolon; **dos -s** colon; **al -** at once, immediately; **a - de** on the point of; **de -** knitted, porous knit, stockinet or jersey weave; **en -** exactly, on the dot; **a - fijo** with certainty; **subir de -** to increase or get worse.
pun·tua·ción f. punctuation.
pun·tual adj. punctual, prompt; exact.
pun·tua·li·dad f. punctuality, promptness; certainty.
pun·tuar[18] v. to punctuate.
pun·za·da f. puncture; prick; sharp pain.
pun·zan·te adj. sharp; pricking; piercing, penetrating.
pun·zar[9] v. to puncture; to sting; to prick; to punch, perforate.
pun·zón m. punch, puncher; pick; awl.
pu·ña·da f. punch, box, blow with the fist.
pu·ña·do m. fisful, hanful; **a -s** abundantly; by handfuls.
pu·ñal m. dagger.
pu·ña·la·da f. stab; sharp pain; **coser a -s** to stab to death.
pu·ñe·ta·zo m. punch, blow with the fist.
pu·ño m. fist; fistful, hanful; cuff; hilt, handle; Ven., Col. blow with the first; **a - cerrado** firmly; **ser como un -** to be stingy; **tener -s** to be strong, courageous.
pu·pi·la f. pupil (of the eye).
pu·pi·lo m. ward; boarding-school pupil; boarder.
pu·pi·tre m. desk, school desk.
pu·ré m. purée, thick soup.
pu·re·za f. purity; chastity.
pur·ga f. purge, laxative, physic.
pur·gan·te adj. purgative, laxative; m. purgative, physic, laxative.
pur·gar[7] v. to purge; to purify; to atone for; **-se** to purge oneself; to take a laxative.
pur·ga·to·rio m. purgatory.
pu·ri·fi·car[6] v. to purify.
pu·ro adj. (limpio) pure; clean; chaste; (sólo) mere, only, sheer; **a pura fuerza** by sheer firce; **a puros gritos** by just shouting; m. cigar.
púr·pu·ra f. purple; purple cloth.
pur·pú·re·o adj. purple.
pus m. pus.
pu·ta f. whore, prostitute.
pu·ta·ti·vo adj. reputed, supposed; **padre -** foster father.
pu·tre·fac·ción f. putrefaction, decay, rotting.

pu•tre•fac•to *adj.* putrid, rotten, decayed.

Q

que *rel. pron.* that; which; who; whom; **el** – who; which; the one who; the one which; *conj.* that; for, because; **más (menos)** – more (less) than; **el mismo** – the same as; – (= *subj.*) let, may you, I hope that; **por mucho** no matter how much; **quieras - no** whether you wish or not.

qué *interr. adj. & pron.* what?; what a!; *interr. adv.* how; **¡– bonito!** how beautiful! **¿a –?** what for?; **¿para – ?** what for?; **¿por – ?** why?; **¿ – tal?** how?; hello; **¡ – más da!** what's the difference! **¡a mí – !** so that! and what's that to me!

que•bra•cho *m.* quebracho, breakax wood.

que•bra•da *f.* ravine; gorge; failure, bankruptcy; *Ríopl., Col., Ven., C.A., Mex.* brook.

que•bra•di•zo *adj.* breakable; brittle; fragile; delicate.

que•bra•do *adj.* broken; weakened; ruptured; bankrupt; rough or rugged (*ground*); *m.* common fraction; *Ven.* navigable waters between reefs.

que•bran•tar *v.* to break; to break open; to pound, crush; to violate (*a law*); to weaken; to vex; *Mex., Col.* to tame, break in (*a colt*); **– el agua** to take the chill off the water.

que•bran•to *m.* breaking, grief, affliction; discouragement; damage, loss.

que•brar [1] *v. irr.* to break; to crush; to interrupt; to wither (*said of the complexion*); to become bankrupt; **-se** to break; to get broken; to be ruptured; **-se uno la cabeza** to rack one's brain.

que•bra•zón *m. Ven., Col.* breakage, breaking.

que•chua *adj. Am.* Quichuan; *m. & f.* Quichua, Quichuan Indian; *m.* Quichuan language.

que•dar *v.* to stay; to remain; to be left over; to be left (*in a state or condition*); **– en** to agree to; *Am.* **– de** to gree to; **– bien** to acquit oneself well; to come out well; *Am.* to suit, become (*said of a dress, hat, etc.*); *Am.* **–bien con alguien** to please someone; **-se** to remain; **-se con una cosa** to keep something; to take something (*buy it*); *Am.* **-se como si tal cosa** to act as if nothing had happened.

que•do *adj.* quiet, still; gentle; *adv.* softly; in a low voice; **quedito** *adj.* nice and quiet; *adv.* very softly.

que•ha•cer *m.* work, occupation; task, duty, chore.

que•ja *f.* complaint; groan, moan; grudge.

que•jar•se *v.* to complaint; to grumble; to moan; to lament.

que•ji•do *m.* moan; groan.

que•jo•so *adj.* complaining whining.

que•jum•bre *f.* whine, moan; murmur, complaint; **-s** *m. Cuba, Ven.* grumbler, whiner; **quejumbroso** *adj.* whining, complaining.

que•ma•da *f.* burned forest; *Am.* burn.

que•ma•do *m.* burned portion of a forest; *Col.* burned field; *Am.* hot alcoholic drink; *adj.* dark, tan; *Am.* peeved, piqued; *Col., Ven.,* Cuba, *Mex.* ruined; *p.p.* of **quemar.**

que•ma•du•ra *f.* burn; scald; smut (*plant disease*).

que•mar *v.* to burn; to scal; to scorch; to sell at a loss; to annoy; *Am.* to deceive, swindle; **-se** to burn; to be hot.

que•ma•zón *f.* (*calor*) burn, burning; great heat; fire, conflagration; (*desazón*) pique, anger; bargain sale; *Am.* mirage on the pampas.

que•re•lla *f.* quarrel; complaint; controversy.

que•re•llar•se *v.* to complain.

que•ren•cia *f.* affection; longing; favorite spot; haunt; stable.

que•rer [1] *v. irr.* to want, wish, desire; to will; to be willing; to love; **– decir** to mean; **sin –** unwillingly; **no quiso hacerlo** he refused to do it; **quiere llover** it is trying to rain, it is about to rain; **como quiera** in any way; **como quiera que** since; no matter how; **cuando quiera** whenever, **donde quiera** wherever; anywhere; **-se** to love each other; *Ríopl., Ven., Col.* to be on the pont of, be about to; **se quiere caer esa pared** that wall is about to fall.

que•ri•do *p.p.* wanted, desired; *adj.* beloved, dear; *m.* lover; **querida** *f.* darling; mistress.

que•se•rí•a *f.* dairy, creamery, cheese factory; **que•sera** *f.* dairy, cheese factory; cheese disch; dairymaid, woman cheese vendor or cheesemaker; **quesero** *adj.* pertaining to cheese; *m.* cheesemaker.

que•so *m.* cheese; *Ven.* **– de higos** fig paste.

qui•cio *m.* hinge of a door; **sacar a uno de –** to exasperate someone.

qui•chua = que•chua.

quie•bra *f.* (*rotura*) break; crack; fissure; fracture; (*pérdida*) loss, damage; bankruptcy.

quien *rel. pron.* who, whom; he who, she who; **quién** *interr. pron.* who? whom?

quien•quie•ra *pron.* whoever, whosoever, whomsoever.

quie•to *adj.* quiet, still; calm.

quie•tud *f.* quiet, stillness, calmness.

qui•ja•da *f.* jaw; jawbone.

qui•la•te *m.* carat (*twenty-fourth part in weight an value of gold*); unit of weight for precious stones and pearls; **-s** qualities; degree of perfection or purity.

qui•lla *f.* keel.

qui•me•ra *f.* absurd idea, wild dancy.

quí•mi•ca *f.* chemistry.

quí•mi•co *adj.* chemical; *m.* chemist.

qui•na, qui•ni•na *f.* quinine.

quin•ca•lla *f.* hardware.

quin•ca•lle•rí•a *f.* hardware; hardware store;

hardware trade.

quin·ce·na *f.* fortnight; semimonthly pay.

quin·ta *f.* (*casa*) villa, country house; (*militar*) draft, military conscription; (*cartas*) sequence of five cards.

quin·ta·e·sen·cia *f.* quintessence, pure essence, purest form.

quios·co *m.* kiosk, small pavilion.

qui·rúr·gi·co *adj.* surgical.

quis·qui·llo·so *adj.* touchy, oversensitive.

quis·to: bien — well-liked, well received, welcome; **mal —** disliked; unwelcome.

qui·ta·man·chas *m.* cleaner, stain remover

qui·tar *v.* to remove; to take away (*off, or from*); to rob of; to deprive of, to subtract, to parry (*in fencing*); **-se** to take off (*clothing*); to remove oneself, withdraw; **-se de una cosa** to give up something; get rid of something; **-se a alguien de encima** to get rid of someone; **¡quita allá!** don't tell me that!; **¡quítese de aquí!** get out of here!

qui·ta·sol *m.* large sunshade, parasol.

qui·te *m.* parry (*in fencing*); dodge, dodging; *Ven., Col., Mex.* **andar a los -s** to be on the defensive; to take offense easily; to be afraid of one's own shadow; **eso no tiene —** that can't be helped.

qui·zá, quizás *adv.* perhaps, maybe.

R

ra·ba·di·lla *f.* end of the spinal column; tail of a fowl; rump.

rá·ba·no *m.* radish; **tomar el — por las hojas** to take one thing for another; to misinterpret something.

ra·bia *f.* rabies, rage; **tener - a alguien** to hate someone; *Riopl., Carib., Mex.* **volarse de —** to get furious, angry.

ra·biar *v.* to have rabies; to rage; to rave; to suffer a severe pain; **— por** to be dying to or for, be very eager to; **quoma que rabia** it burns terribly.

ra·bie·ta *f.* tantrum, fit of temper.

ra·bi·no *m.* rabbi.

ra·bio·so *adj.* rabid (*having rabies*), mad; furious, angry, violent.

ra·bo *m.* tail; **de cabo a —** from beginning to end; **mirar con el — del ojo** to look out of the cornet of one's eye.

ra·ci·mo *m.* bunch; cluster.

ra·cio·ci·nio *m.* reasoning.

ra·ción *f.* ration; allowance; supply.

ra·cio·nal *adj.* rational; reasonable.

ra·cio·na·mien·to *m.* rationing.

ra·cio·nar *v.* to ration.

ra·dar *m.* radar.

ra·da·ros·co·pio *m.* radarscope.

ra·dia·ción *f.* radiation, **- cósmica** cosmic radiation.

ra·diac·ti·vi·dad *f.* radioactivity

ra·diac·ti·vo *adj.* radioactive

ra·dia·dor *m.* radiator

ra·dian·te *adj.* radiant; shining; beaming.

ra·di·ar *v.* to radiate; to radio, to broadcast.

ra·di·cal *adj.* (*básico*) fundamental, basic; radical; (*extremista*) extreme; *m.* radical; root of a word.

ra·di·car *v.* to take root; to be, be found (*in a certain place*); **-se** to take root; to locate, settle.

ra·dio *m.* radius; radium; *m. & f.* radio.

ra·dio·di·fun·dir *v.* to broadcast by radio. *See* **difundir.**

ra·dio·di·fu·sión *f.* broadcasting. *See* **difusión.**

ra·dio·di·fu·so·ra, ra·dio·e·mi·so·ra *f.* broadcasting station.

ra·dio·es·cu·cha *m. & f.* radio listener.

ra·dio·fó·ni·co *adj.* radio (*used as adj.*); **estación radiofónica** radio station.

ra·dio·gra·fía *f.* radiography, X-ray radiography; X-ray picture.

ra·dio·gra·fiar[17] *v.* to take X-ray pictures.

ra·dio·lo·cu·tor *m.* radio announcer. *See* **locutor.**

ra·dio·te·le·fo·nía *f.* radiotelephony, radio wireless.

ra·dio·te·le·gra·fía *f.* radiotelegraphy, radio, wireless telegraphy.

ra·dio·yen·te = radioescucha.

ra·er[24] *v. irr.* to scrape off; to rub off; to scratch off; to fray; to erase.

rá·fa·ga *f.* gust of wind; flasch of light.

ra·í·do *p.p. & adj.* scraped off; rubbed off; frayed; worn, threadbare.

ral·gón *m.* large root; root of a tooth.

ra·íz *f.* root; origin; foundation; **— cuadrada** square root; **a — de** close to, right after; **de -** by the roots, completely; **echar raíces** to take root, become firmly fixed.

ra·ja *f.* slice; splinter; crack; split, crevice; **hacer -s** to slice; to tear into strips; to cut into splinters; **hacerse uno -s** to wear oneself out (*by dancing, jumping or any violent exercise*).

ra·ja·du·ra *f.* crack, crevice.

ra·jar *v.* to split; to crack; to cleave; to slice, to chartter; to brag; *Col., Cuba, Mex., Andes* to defame, insult; *Col.* to flunk, fail (*a student*); **-se** to split open; to crack; *Mex.* to get a fraid, back down.

ra·ja·ta·blas *m. Col.* reprimand, scolding; **a —** in great haste.

ra·le·a *f.* bree, race, stock; species, kind.

ra·le·ar *v.* to thin out, make less dense; to become less dense.

ra·lo *adj.* sparse, thin, thinly scattered.

ra·lla·dor *m.* grater.

ra·llar *v.* to grate; to grate on, annoy; *Am.* to goad, spur.

ra•ma *f.* branch, limb; **en** – crude, raw; **andarse por las -s** to beat about the bush, not to stick to the point.

ra•ma•da *f.* branches, foliage; arbor; *Am.* shed, tent.

ra•ma•je *m.* foliage; branches.

ra•mal *m.* strand (*of a rope, etc.*); branch; branch railway line; halter.

ra•me•ra *f.* harlot, prostitute.

ra•mi•fi•car•se *v.* to branch off, divide into branches.

ra•mi•lle•te *m.* bouquet; flower cluster.

ra•mo *m.* bunch (*of flowers*), bouquet; line, branch (*of art, science, industry, etc.*); branch, bough; **domingo de -s** Palm Sunday.

ra•mo•ne•ar *v.* to cut off twigs or tips of branches; to nibble grass, twigs, or leaves; *Am.* to eat scraps or leftovers.

ram•pa *f.* ramp; apron (*aiport*); **– de cohetes, – de lanzamiento** launching ramp.

ram•plón *adj.* coarse, crude, uncouth; slovenly.

ram•plo•ne•ría *f.* coarse act or remark; crudeness, coarseness; slovenliness.

ra•na *f.* frog.

ran•cio *adj.* rancid, stale; old (*wine*); **linaje** – old, noble lineage.

ran•che•ro *m. Mex.* rancher, farmer; **ranchería** *f.* group of huts; *Col.* inn (*for* **arrieros**).

ran•cho *m.* campo; hamlet; mess (*meal for a group and the group itself*); *Carib., Ven., Col., Andes, Ríopl.* hut; *Carib., Ven., Col., Andes, Ríopl.* country house; *Mex.* ranch, small farm (*usually for cattle raising*).

ran•go *m.* rank, position.

ra•nu•ra *f.* groove; slot.

ra•par *v.* to shave off; to crop (*hair*); to strip bare, rob of everything.

ra•paz *adj.* rapacious, grasping, greedy; *m.* lad; **rapaza** *f.* lass, young girl.

ra•pé *m.* snuff (pulverized tobacco).

ra•pi•dez *f.* rapidity, speed.

rá•pi•do *adj.* rapid, swift; *m.* rapids.

ra•pi•ña *f.* plunder; **ave de** – bird of prey.

ra•pi•ñar *v.* to plunder; to steal.

ra•po•sa *f.* fox.

rap•tar *v.* to kidnap, abduct.

rap•to *m.* (*delito*) abduction, kidnapping; (*sentimiento*) ecstasy, rapture; outburst.

ra•que•ta *f.* racket (*used in games*); tennis.

ra•quí•ti•co *adj.* rickety, feeble, weak, skinny, sickly.

ra•re•za *f.* rarity; oddity; strangeness; freak; curiosity; queer act or remark; peculiarity; **por** - seldom.

ra•ro *adj.* rare; thin, not dense; scarce, strange, odd; ridiculous; **rara vez** (*or* **raras veces**) rarely, seldom.

ras : a – de flush with, even with; **al – con** flush with; **estar - con** - to be flush, perfectly even.

ras•ca•cie•los *m.* skyscraper.

ras•car *v.* to scratch; to scrape; *Andes* to dig up potatoes; *Am.* **– uno para adentro** to seek one's

own advantage, look out for oneself.

ra•se•te *m.* sateen.

ras•ga•do *adj.* torn; open; *Col.* generous; *Am.* outspoken; **ojos -s** large, wideopen eyes.

ras•ga•du•ra *f.* tear, rip. rent.

ras•gar *v.* to tear; to rip.

ras•go *m.* (*propiedad*) trait, characteristic; (*rúbrica*) stroke of the pen, flourish; (*hazaña*) feat; *Am.* irrigation ditch; *Ven.* **un – de terreno** a parcel of land; **-s** features; traits.

ras•gón *m.* large tear, rent, rip.

ras•gu•ñar *v.* to scratch; to claw.

ras•gu•ño *m.* scratch.

ra•so *adj.* (*llano*) plain; flat, smooth; (*despejado*) clear, cludless; *Ríopl., Mex.* even, level (*when measuring wheat, corn, etc.*); *Am.* scarce, scanty; **soldado** – private; **al** – in the open air; *m.* satin.

ras•pa•du•ra *f.* scrape; scarping; erasure; shaving (of wood or metal).

ras•par *v.* to scrape, scrape off; to steal; *Andes* to scold, upbraid; *Col.* to leave.

ras•tra *f.* drag; sled; large rake; harrow; **a -s** dragging; unwillingly.

ras•tre•a•dor *m.* trailer, tracker, tracer.

ras•tre•ar *v.* to trail, track, trace; to rake, harrow; to drag (*a dragnet*); to skim; scrape the ground.

ras•tre•ro *adj.* low, vile.

ras•tri•llar *v.* to rake; to comb (*flax or hemp*); *Ven.* to scrape; *Am.* to shoot; *Am.* to barter, exchange; *Am.* to pilfer, steal (*in stores*).

ras•tri•llo *m.* rake; *Am.* barter, exchange; *Am.* business deal.

ras•tro *m.* track, trail, scent; trace, sign; rake, harrow; slaughterhouse.

ras•tro•jo *m.* stubble.

ra•su•ra *f.* shave, shaving.

ra•su•rar *v.* to shave.

ra•ta *f.* rat; *m.* pickpocket.

ra•te•ar *v.* to pilfer; to pick pockets; to creep, crawl.

ra•te•rí•a *f.* petty larceny; meanness.

ra•te•ro *m.* pickpocket; *adj.* contemptible, mean.

ra•ti•fi•car *v.* to ratify.

ra•to *m.* short time, little while; **buen** – pleasant time; long time; **-s perdidos** leisure hours; **a -s** at intervals, from time to time; **pasar el** – to while away the time, kill time; *Am.* **¡hasta cada** – ! so long!; see you later!

ra•tón *m.* mouse; *Am.* **tener un** – to have a hangover; **ratonera** *f.* mousetrap.

rau•dal *m.* torrent, downpour, flood; *Ríopl., Ch., Col., Ven., Andes* rapids.

rau•do *adj.* rapid, swift.

ra•ya *f.* line; dash; stripe; boundary line; part in the hair; *Mex.* pay, wage; *Mex.* **día de** – payday; **tener a** – to keep within bounds; to hold in check; **pasar de la** – to overstep one's bounds, take undue liberties; *m.*

sting ray (*a species of fish*).

ra·ya·dor *m. Mex.* paymaster; *Am.* umpire in a game.

ra·yar *v.* to line, make lines on: to streak; to scratch, mark; to cross out; *Mex.* to pay or Collect wages; *Am.* to stop a horse all of a suden; *Am.* to spur a horse to run at top speed; **– el alba** to dawn; **– en** to border on; *Am.* **–se uno** to help oneself; to get rich.

ra·yo *m.* ray, beam; lightning, thunderbolt; spoke; **-s X** X-rays; **-s infrarrojos** infrared rays.

ra·za *f.* race; clan; breed, fissure, crevice; **caballo de –** thoroughbred horse.

ra·zón *f. (facultad)* reason; *(justicia)* right, justice; *(cuenta)* ratio; account, information, word, message; **– social** firm, firm name; **a – de** at the rate of; **¡con –!** no wonder!; **dar –** to inform; **dar la – a una persona** to admit that a person is right; **perder la –** to lose one's mind; **poner en –** to pacify; **tener –** to be right.

ra·zo·na·ble *adj.* reasonable.

ra·zo·na·mien·to *m.* reasoning.

ra·zo·nar *v.* to reason; to discourse, talk; to argue.

re·a·bier·to *p.p. of* **reabrir.**

re·a·brir[12] *v.* to reopen.

re·ac·ción *f.* reaction; **– nuclear** nuclear reaction; **– en cadena** chain reaction.

re·ac·cio·nar *v.* to react.

re·ac·cio·na·rio *adj. & m.* reactionary.

re·a·cio *adj.* stubborn, obstinate.

re·ac·tor *m.* reactor; **– atómico** atomic reactor; **- nuclear** nuclear reactor.

re·a·jus·tar *v.* to reajust.

re·a·jus·te *m.* readjustment.

re·al *adj.* real; royal; *m.* army camp; fairground; real *(Spanish coin worth one fourth of a peseta)*; **-es** *Andes* money *(in general)*; **levantar el –** (or **los -es**) to break camp.

re·al·ce *m. (adorno)* embossment, raised work, relief; *(lustre)* prestige; lustre, splendor; **dar –** to enhance; to emphasize.

re·a·le·za *f.* royalty *(royal dignity)*.

re·a·li·dad *f.* reality; truth; fact; **en –** really, truly, in fact.

re·a·lis·mo *m.* realism; royalism.

re·a·lis·ta *adj.* realistic; royalist; *m.* realist; royalist.

re·a·li·za·ción *f.* realization, fulfillment; conversion into money, sale.

re·a·li·zar[9] *v.* to realize, fulfill, make real; to convert into money; to sell out.

re·al·zar[9] *v.* to emboss; to raise; to enhance; to make stand out; to emphasize.

re·a·ni·mar *v.* to revive; to comfort; to cheer; to encourage.

re·a·nu·da·ción *f.* renewal.

re·a·nu·dar *v.* to renew, resume, begin again.

re·a·pa·re·cer[13] *v. irr.* to reappear.

re·a·su·mir *v.* to resume.

re·a·ta *f.* lariat, rope, lasso.

re·a·vi·var *v.* to revive.

re·ba·ja *f.* deduction; reduction; discount.

re·ba·jar *v.* to diminish; to lower, reduce; to tone down *(a painting)*; to humiliate; **-se** to lower or humble oneself.

re·ba·na·da *f.* slice.

re·ba·nar *v.* to slice.

re·ba·ño *m.* flock; herd

re·ba·tir *v.* to be at over and over, to repel, resist; to refute; to rebut *(come back with an argument)*; to argue; to parry *(in fencing)*.

re·ba·to *m.* alarm, call to arms; surprise attack.

re·be·lar·se *v.* to rebel.

re·bel·de *adj.* rebellious; *m.* rebel, defaulter *(one who fails to appear in court)*.

re·bel·día *f.* rebelliousness; defiance; default, failure to appear in court; **en –** in revolt.

re·be·lión *f.* rebellion, revolt.

re·ben·ca·zo *m. Riopl., Ch., Andes* crack of a whip; Am- lash, stroke with a whip.

re·ben·que *m.* rawhide whip.

re·bor·de *m.* edge, border.

re·bo·san·te *adj.* brimming, overflowing.

re·bo·sar *v.* to overflow, brim over; to abound.

re·bo·tar *v.* to reboun, bounce back or again, to make rebound; to repel, reject; to annoy, vex, **-se** to become vexed; upset; *Col., Mex.* to become clouy or muddy *(said of water)*; *Am.* **rebotársele a uno la bilis** to get angry, become upset.

re·bo·te *m.* rebound, bounce; **de –** on the rebound; indirectly.

re·bo·zar[9] *v.* to muffle up; **-se** to muffle oneself up; to wrap oneself up.

re·bo·zo *m.* shawl; **sin –** frankly, openly.

re·bu·llir[20] *v. irr.* to stir, move; to boil up.

re·bus·ca *f.* research; search: searching; gleaning; residue.

re·bus·car[6] *v.* to search thoroughly; to pry into; to glean.

re·buz·nar *v.* to bray.

re·buz·no *m.* bray.

re·ca·bar *v.* to obtain, gain by entreaty.

re·ca·do *m.* message; erran; gift; daily food supply, daily marketing; precaution; equipment; *Riopl, Andes* sadle and trappings; **– de escribir** writing materials; **-s a** regards to.

re·ca·er[24] *v. irr.* to fall (upon); to fall again; to relapse; to have a relapse.

re·ca·í·da *f.* relapse; falling again.

re·ca·lar *v.* to saturate, soak through; to reach port; to come within sight of land; to land, end up, stop at; *Am.* **– con alguien** to "land" on somebody, take it out on somebody.

re·cal·car[6] *v.* to emphasize; to harp on; to press down.

re·cal·ci·tran·te *adj.* obstinate, diso-bedient, stubborn.

re·ca·ien·tar[1] v. irr. to reheat, warm over; to overheat, heat too much.

re·ca·mar v. to embroider (usually with gold or silver).

re·cá·ma·ra f. dressing room; Mex., C.A., Col. bedroom; Riopl., Col. chamber for an explosive charge.

re·ca·pi·tu·lar v. to recapitulate, sum up, tell briefly.

re·car·go m. overload; extra load; extra charge; increase (of fever); new charge, new accusation.

re·ca·ta·do adj. cautious, prudent; modest; p.p. concealed.

re·ca·tar v. to cover, conceal; -se to show timidity; to be cautious; to hide (from), shun.

re·ca·to m. caution, prudence; reserve, restraint; secrecy; modesty.

re·cau·da·ción f. collection, collecting; office of tax collector.

re·cau·da·dor m. tax collector.

re·cau·dar v. to collect (money, taxes, rents, etc.)

re·cau·do m. collection, collecting; precaution; bond, security; Mex. spices, seasonings; Am. daily supply of vegetables; estar a buen — to be safe; poner a buen — to place in safety.

re·ce·lar v. to suspect, fear; -se de to be suspicious or afraid of.

re·ce·lo m. suspicion, fear.

re·ce·lo·so adj. suspicious, disfrustful, feartul.

re·cep·ción f. reception; admission.

re·cep·tá·cu·lo m. receptacle.

re·cep·ti·vo adj. receptive, capable of receiving, quick to receive.

re·cep·tor m. receiver; adj. receiving.

re·ce·ta f. recipe; prescription.

re·ce·tar v. to prescribe (a medicine).

re·ci·bi·dor m. receiver; reception room.

re·ci·bi·mien·to m. reception; welcome; reception room; parlor.

re·ci·bir v. to receive; to admit, accept: to go out to meet; — noticias de to hear from; -se de to receive a title or degree of.

re·ci·bo m. (monetario) receipt; (acción) reception; (sala) reception room; parlor; sala de - reception room; estar de — to be at home for receiving callers; ser de — to be acceptable, be fit for use.

re·cie·dum·bre f. strength, force, vigor.

re·cién adv. recently, lately, newly (used before a past participle); Riopl., Ch., Andes just now; Riopl. Ch., Andes a short time ago; Riopl., Ch., Andes — entonces just then.

re·cien·te adj. recent, new.

re·cin·to m. enclosure; precinct.

re·cio adj. strong, robust; harsh; hard, severe; fast; adv. strongly; harstly rapidly; hard; loud.

re·ci·pien·te m. receptable, container; recipient; receiver (he who receives).

re·cí·pro·co adj. reciprocal, mutual.

re·ci·ta·ción f. recitation, recital.

re·ci·tal m. musical recital.

re·ci·tar v. to recite.

re·cla·ma·ción f. protest, complaint; claim, demand.

re·cla·ma·dor m. claimant; complainer.

re·cla·man·te m. & f. claimant; complainer; adj. complaining; claiming.

re·cla·mar v. (protestar) to complain, protest (against); (exigir) to claim, demand; to lure, call back (a bird).

re·cla·mo m. (protesta) protest; claim; advertisement; (llamada) call; bird call; decoy bird; lure.

re·cli·nar v. to recline, lean; -se to recline, lean back.

re·clu·ir[32] v. irr. to seclude, shut up; -se to isolate oneself.

re·clu·so m. recluse, hermit; adj. shut in, shut up.

re·clu·ta f. recruiting; Am. roundup of cattle; m. recruit.

re·clu·ta·mien·to m. recruiting; levy; draft.

re·clu·tar v. to recruit, enlist; Am. to round up (cattle).

re·co·brar v. to recover, regain; -se to recover; to recuperate.

re·co·bro m. recovery.

re·co·do m. bend, turn; elbow (of a road).

re·co·ger[11] v. (juntar) to gather; to collect; to pick up; (ceñir) to take in, tighten; (abrigar) to shelter; -se to retire, go home; to withdraw; to seclude oneself; to take shelter.

re·co·gi·mien·to m. seclusion; concentration of thought, composure; retreat; collecting, gathering.

re·co·lec·ción f. collecting, gathering; harvest, crop; summary.

re·co·lec·tar v. to harvest; to gather.

re·co·men·da·ble adj. praiseworthy, laudable; advisable.

re·co·men·da·ción f. recommendation; request.

re·co·men·dar[1] v. irr. to recommend; to commend, praise; to enjoin, urge; to advise.

re·com·pen·sa f. recompense; compensation.

re·com·pen·sar v. to recompense, rewar; to compensate.

re·con·cen·trar v. to concentrate, bring together; to hide in the depth of one's heart; -se to concentrate, become absorbed in thought, collect one's thoughts.

re·con·ci·lia·ción f. reconciliation.

re·con·ci·liar v. to reconcile; -se to be come reconciled.

re·cón·di·to adj. hidden, concealed; profound.

re·co·no·cer[13] v. irr. to recognize; to admit, acknowledge; to examine carefully; to reconnoiter, scout, explore.

re·co·no·ci·mien·to m. recognition; acknowledgment; gratitude; examination; scouting, exploring.

re·cons·truir[32] v. irr. to reconstruct, rebuild.

re·con·tar[2] v. irr. to recount; to tell, relate.

re·co·pi·lar *v.* to compile; to digest, make a digest of.

re·cor·da·ción *f.* recollection; remembrance.

re·cor·dar[2] *v. irr.* to remember; to recall; to remind; *Am.* to rouse, awaken; **-se** to remember; to wake up.

re·cor·da·ti·vo *m.* reminder; *adj.* reminding.

re·cor·da·to·rio *m.* reminder.

re·co·rrer *v.* to go over; to travel over; to read over; to look over; to overhaul.

re·co·rri·do *m.* trip, run; mileage, distance traveled.

re·cor·tar *v.* to trim, clip; to shorten; to cut out (*figures*); to pare off; **-se** to project itself (*as a shadow*); to outline itself.

re·cor·te *m.* clipping; cutting; outline, *Mex.* gossip, slander.

re·cos·tar *v.* to recline, lean; **-se** to recline, lean back.

re·co·ve·co *m.* turn, bend; nook; sly or underhanded manner.

re·cre·a·ción *f.* recreation.

re·cre·ar *v.* to entertain, amuse; to gratify, please; **-se** to amuse oneself; to take elight (in).

re·cre·o *m.* recreation, entertainment; place of amusement.

re·cru·de·cer[13] *v.* to recur, break out again, flare up, become worse (*said of an illness or evil*).

rec·tán·gu·lo *m.* rectangle; *adj.* rectangular, right-angled.

rec·ti·fi·car[6] *v.* to rectify, correct, amend; to refine (*liquors*).

rec·ti·tud *f.* rectitude, uprightness, righteousness; straightness; accuracy.

rec·to *adj.* straight; right; just, honest; **ángulo -** right angle; *m.* rectum; *adv. C.A.* straight ahead.

rec·tor *m.* college or university president; principal; rector, curate, priest.

re·cua *f.* drove of pack animals; drove, crowd.

re·cuen·to *m.* recount.

re·cuer·do *m.* remembrance; recollection; souvenir, keepsake; memory; **-s** regards; *adj. Ríopl., Col., Ven.* awake.

re·cu·la·da *f.* recoil.

re·cu·lar *v.* to recoil, spring back, to fall back, go back, retreat; to yield, back down.

re·cu·pe·ra·ción *f.* recovery.

re·cu·pe·rar *v.* to recuperate recover, regain; **-se** to recuperate, recover one's health.

re·cu·rrir *v.* to resort (to); to have recourse (to).

re·cur·so *m.* recourse, resort; petition, appeal; **-s** means, resources; **sin -** without remey; without appeal.

re·cu·sar *v.* to reject, decline.

re·cha·zar[9] *v.* to reject; to repel, drive back; to rebuff.

re·chi·fla *f.* hooting; hissing; ridicule.

re·chi·flar *v.* to hoot; to hiss; to ridicule.

re·chi·na·mien·to *m.* creak; squeak; squeaking; gnashing.

re·chi·nar *v.* to squeak; to creak; *Am.* to be furious, angry; *Am.* to grumble, growl; **– los dientes** to gnash one's teeth.

re·chi·no = rechinamiento.

re·chon·cho *adj.* plump; chubby; squat.

re·chu·par·se *v.* to smack one's lips.

red *f.* net; netting; network; snare; **redecilla** *f.* small net, mesh; hair net.

re·dac·ción *f.* (*acto*) wording; editing; (*lugar*) newspaper offices; editorial department; (*cuerpo*) editorial staff.

re·dac·tar *v.* to word, compose; to edit.

re·dac·tor *m.* editor.

re·dar·güir[12] *v. irr.* to retort, answer back; to contradict, call in question; to reargue.

re·de·dor *m.* surrounding; **al** (*or* **en**) **–** around, about.

re·den·ción *f.* redemption.

re·den·tor *m.* redeemer, savior; **el Redentor** the Savior.

re·dil *m.* sheepfold.

re·di·mir *v.* to redeem; to ransom; to set free.

ré·di·to *m.* interest, revenue, yield.

re·di·tuar[18] *v.* to produce, yield (*interest*).

re·do·blar *v.* to double; to clinch (*a nail*); to reiterate, repeat; to roll (*a drum*).

re·do·ble *m.* roll (*of a rum*).

re·do·ma *f.* flask, vial.

re·do·món *m. Ríopl.* half-tame horse or bull; *adj. Ríopl.* half-civilized, rustic.

re·don·da *f.* surrounding district, neighborhood; whole note (*music*); **a la –** all around, round-about.

re·don·de·ar *v.* to round, make round; to round off; to round out.

re·don·del *m.* arena, bull ring; circle.

re·don·do *adj.* round; whole, entire; clear, evident; *Andes* stupid; *Mex.* honest; **en -** all around.

re·do·pe·lo: a – against the grain.

re·dor *m.* round mat; **en –** around.

re·duc·ción *f.* reduction; cut, discount; decrease.

re·du·ci·do *p.p. & adj.* reduced; compact, small.

re·du·cir[25] *v. irr.* to reduce; to reduce; to diminish; to convert (into); to reset (*a bone*); **-se** to adapt oneself; adjust oneself; to be constraine, forced.

re·e·di·fi·car[6] *v.* to rebuild, reconstruct.

re·e·lec·ción *f.* re-election.

re·e·le·gir[11] *v.* to re-elect.

re·em·bol·sar *v.* to reimburse, refund, repay, pay back.

re·em·bol·so *m.* reimbursement, refund.

re·e·mi·tir *v.* to emit again; to issue again: to rebroadcast; to relay (*a broadcast*).

re·em·pla·za·ble *adj.* replaceable.

re·em·pla·zar[9] *v.* to replace; to substitute.

re·em·pla·zo *m.* replacement; substitute, substitution.

re·fac·ción *f.* (*alimento*) light lunch, refreshment; (*compostura*) repair, reparation; *Mex., Col.* spare part; *Carib.* help, aid, loan.

re·fa·jo *m.* underskirt; short skirt.

re·fe·ren·cia *f.* reference; narration, account.

re·fe·ren·te *adj.* referring.

re·fe·rir[3] *v. irr.* to refer; to narrate; to relate; **–se** to refer (to), relate (to).

re·fi·na·mien·to *m.* refinement.

re·fi·nar *v.* to refine; to purify.

re·fi·ne·rí·a *f.* refinery

re·flec·tor *m.* reflector; floodlight.

re·fle·jar *v.* to reflect, to think over; **–se** to be reflected.

re·fle·jo *m.* reflection, image; reflex; *adj.* reflected; reflex.

re·fle·xión *f.* reflection; meditation, consideration.

re·fle·xio·nar *v.* to reflect, meditate, think over.

re·fle·xi·vo *adj.* reflexive; reflective, thoug-htful.

re·flu·jo *m.* ebb, ebb tide.

re·for·ma *f.* reform; reformation; improvement.

re·for·ma·dor *m.* reformer.

re·for·mar *v.* to reform; to correct, amend; to improve; **–se** to reform.

re·for·mis·ta *m. & f.* reformer.

re·for·zar[2,9] *v.* irr. to reinforce; to strenghten.

re·frac·ción *f.* refraction.

re·frac·ta·rio *adj.* refractory; impervious; rebellious, unruly; stubborn.

re·frán *m.* popular proverb or saying.

re·fre·nar *v.* to restrain, keep in check; to curb; to rein.

re·fren·dar *v.* to legalize by signing; to countersign (*confirm by another signature*); **– un pasaporte** to visé a passport.

re·fres·can·te *adj.* refreshing.

re·fres·car[6] *v.* to refresh, renew; to cool; to get cool (*said of the weather*); **–se** to cool off; to take the fresh air; to take a cooling drink or refreshment; *Cuba, C.A.* to take an afternoon refreshment.

re·fres·co *m.* refreshment.

re·fres·que·ría *f. Mex., C.A., Ven.* refreshment shop, outdoor refreshment stand.

re·frie·ga *f.* strife, fray, scuffle.

re·fri·ge·ra·ción *f.* refrigeration; light meal or refreshment.

re·fri·ge·ra·dor *m. Am.* refrigerator, freezer; *adj.* refrigerating, freezing; refreshing.

re·fri·ge·rio *m.* refreshment; relief, comfort; coolness.

re·fuer·zo *m.* reinforcement.

re·fu·gia·do *m.* refugee; *p.p. of* **refugiar.**

re·fu·giar *v.* to shelter; **–se** to take shelter or refuge.

re·fu·gio *m.* refuge, shelter.

re·ful·gen·te *adj.* refulgent, radiant, shining.

re·fun·dir *v.* to remelt, refound, recast (*metals*); to recast, rewrite reconstruct.

re·fun·fu·ñar *v.* to grumble, mumble, growl, mutter.

re·fun·fu·ño *m.* grumble, growl; **refunfuñón** *adj.* grouchy; grumbly, grumbling.

re·fu·tar *v.* to refute.

re·ga·de·ra *f.* sprinkler; *Mex.* shower, bath.

re·ga·dí·o *adj.* irrigable, that can be irrigated; irrigated; *m.* irrigated land; **tierras de –** irrigable lands.

re·ga·lar *v.* (*dar*) to give, present as a gift; to regale; (*recrear*) to entertain; to delight, please; **–se** to treat oneself well, live a life of ease.

re·ga·lo *m.* present, gift; pleasure, delight; dainty, delicacy; luxury; comfort.

re·ga·ña·dien·tes: a – much against one's wishes; unwillingly.

re·ga·ñar *v.* to growl; to grumble; to quarrel; to scold.

re·ga·ño *m.* scolding, reprimand.

re·ga·ñón *m.* grumbling; scolding; quarrelsome; *m.* growler, grumbler, scolder.

re·gar[1,7] *v. irr.* to irrigate; to water, to sprinkle, scatter; *Col.* to spill, throw off (*said of a horse*); **–se** *Am.* to scatter, disperse (*said of a group, herd, etc.*).

re·ga·te·ar *v.* to haggle, bargain; to dispute; to sell at retail; to race (*in a regatta or boat race*).

re·ga·zo *m.* lap.

re·gen·tar *v.* to direct, conduct, manage, **– una cáte-dra** to teach a course (*at a university*).

re·gen·te *m.* regent; manager; *adj.* ruling.

re·gi·dor *m.* councilman, alderman; *adj.* governing, ruling.

ré·gi·men *m.* regime; government, rule, management; **– lácteo** milk diet.

re·gi·mien·to *m.* regiment; (*administrativo*) administration; municipal council; position of alderman.

re·gio *adj.* regal, royal; splendid, magnificent.

re·gión *f.* region.

re·gir[5,11] *v. irr.* to rule, govern; to direct, manage; to be in force (*said of a law*); to move (*said of the bowels*).

re·gis·tra·dor *m.* registrar, recorder; city clerk, official in charge of records; inspector (*in a customhouse*); searcher; *adj.* registering; **caja re-gistradora** cash register.

re·gis·trar *v.* to examine, inspect, scrutinize; to register, record; **–se** to register, enroll.

re·gis·tro *m.* search, inspection; registra-tion; census; registration office; register; record; registration certificate; watch regulator; bookmark; organ stop; *Ven.* wholesale textile store.

re·gla *f.* (*precepto*) rule; ruler; order; precept, principle; (*medida*) measure, moderation; menstruation; **en –** in order, in due form; **por – general** as a general rule; usually.

re·gla·men·to *m.* regulations, rules; rule, bylaw.

re·go·ci·ja·do *adj.* joyful, merry, gay; *p.p. of* **rego-cijar.**

re·go·ci·jar *v.* to gladden, delight; **–se** to be glad; to rejoice.

re·go·ci·jo *m.* joy; rejoicing.

re·gor·de·te *adj.* plump.

re·gre·sar *v.* to return.

re·gre·so *m.* return; **estar de –** to be back.

re·gue·ro *m.* stream, rivulet; trickle; irrigation ditch.

re·gu·la·ción *f.* regulation; adjustment.

re·gu·la·dor *m.* regulator; controller, governor (*of a machine*); *adj.* regulating.

re·gu·lar *v.* to regulate, to adjust; *adj.* regular; ordinary; moderate; fair, medium; **por lo –** as a rule, usually; *adj.* fairly well.

re·gu·la·ri·dad *f.* regularity.

re·gu·la·ri·zar[9] *v.* to regulate, make regular.

re·ha·cer[31] *v. irr.* to remake, to make over; to repair; **-se** to recover one's strength; to rally.

re·hén *m.* hostage; **en rehenes** as a hostage.

re·huir[32] *v. irr.* to shun, avoid; to shrink (from).

re·hu·sar *v.* to refuse; **-se a** to refuse to.

rei·na *f.* queen.

rei·na·do *m.* reign.

rei·nan·te *adj.* reigning; prevailing.

rei·nar *v.* to reign; to rule; to prevail.

re·in·ci·dir *v.* to relapse, slide back (into).

rei·no *m.* kingdom.

re·in·te·gro *m.* reimbursement, refund.

re·ir[15] *v. irr.* to laugh; **-se de** to laugh at; *Riopl., Andes, Col., Ven., Carib.* **– de dientes para afuera,** to laugh outwardly, laugh hypocritically.

rei·te·rar *v.* to reiterate, repeat.

re·ja *f.* grate, grating; plowshare (*blade of the plow*); plowing; *Carib., C.A.* jail.

re·ji·lla *f.* small grating, lattice; small latticed window; fireplace grate; cane upholstery, *Ch.* wire dishcover.

re·jo·ne·ar *v.* to fight a bull from horseback (*Portuguese style*).

re·ju·ve·ne·cer[13] *v. irr.* to rejuvenate, make young; **-se** to become rejuvenated.

re·la·ción *f.* relation; story, account; long speech in a play; *Riopl.* verse recited alternately by a couple in a folk dance; **-es** personal relations, connections, acquaintances.

re·la·cio·nar *v.* to relate, connect; **-se** to be related, connected; to become acquainted, establish friendly connections.

re·la·ja·ción *f.,* **relajamiento** *m.* relaxation; laxity; slackening; hernia.

re·la·jar *v.* to relax; to slacken, to release from a vow or oath; **-se** to get a hernia or rupture; to become weakened; to become lax (*said of laws, customs, etc.*).

re·la·jo *m. Carib., Mex.* disorderly conduct; lewdness; scandal.

re·la·mer·se *v.* to lick one's lips; to gloat; to boast; to slick oneself up.

re·lám·pa·go *m.* lightning; flash;

re·lam·pa·gue·ar *v.* to lighten; to flash; to sparkle.

re·lam·pa·gue·o *m.* flashing; sheet lightning.

re·la·tar *v.* to relate, narrate.

re·la·ti·vo *adj.* relative; **– a** relative to, regarding.

re·la·to *m.* narration, account, story.

re·lé *m.* relay; **– de televisión** television relay system.

re·le·gar[7] *v.* to relegate, banish; to postpone; to set aside, put away.

re·len·te *m.* night dampness; *Am.* fresh night breeze.

re·le·var *v.* to relieve; to release; to absolve; to replace, substitute; to emboss; to make stand out in relief.

re·le·vo *m.* relief (*from a post or military duty; person who relieves another from the performance of a duty*).

re·li·ca·rio *m.* reliquary (*small box or casket for keeping relics*); *Col., Ven., Cuba, Mex., Andes* locket.

re·lie·ve *m.* relief, embossment, raised work; **-s** scraps, leftovers; **de –** in relief; prominent, outstaning; **poner de –** to make stand out; to emphasize.

re·li·gión *f.* religion.

re·li·gio·si·dad *f.* religiousness, piety; faithfulness.

re·li·gio·so *adj.* religious, faithful; punctual; *m.* friar, monk.

re·lin·char *v.* to neigh.

re·lin·cho *m.* neigh.

re·li·quia *f.* relic; vestige; **-s** relics, remains.

re·loj *m.* clock; watch; **– de pulsera** wristwatch; **– de sol** (*or* **– solar**) sundial; **– despertador** alarm clock.

re·lu·cien·te *adj.* shining; sparkling.

re·lu·cir[13] *v. irr.* to glitter, sparkle; to shine.

re·lum·bran·te *adj.* brilliant, flashing, resplendent.

re·lum·brar *v.* to glare; to glitter.

re·lum·bre *m.* glare, glitter.

re·lle·nar *v.* to refill; to fill up; to pad; to stuff.

re·lle·no *adj.* stuffed; *m.* meat stuffing; filling.

re·ma·char *v.* to clinch; to hammer down; to flatten; to rivet; to fix firmly; **-se** *Am.* to be tight-lipped, stubbornly silent.

re·ma·che *m.* clinching; fastening; securing; riveting; rivet.

ro·ma·nen·te *m.* remainder, balance; remnant; residue.

re·mar *v.* to row; to struggle.

re·ma·ta·do *adj.* & *p.p.* (*acabado*) finished; (*vendido en subasta*) sold at auction; **loco –** completely crazy.

re·ma·tar *v.* (*acabar*) to finish; to end; to give the final or finishing stroke; (*vender*) to auction; (*afinazar*) to fasten (*a stitch*); *Am.* to stop (*a horse*) suddenly; *Am.* to buy or sell at auction; **-se** to be finished, be completely destroyed or ruined.

re·ma·te *m.* (*fin*) finish, end; (*postura*) highes bid at an auction; sale at auction; (*punta*) pinnacle, spire; *Am.* selvage, edge of a fabric; **de –** absolutely, without remey; **loco de –** completely crazy, stark mad.

re·me·dar *v.* to imitate; to mimic.

re·me·diar v. to remedy; to help; to avoid.

re·me·dio m. remedy; help; amendment; recourse, resort; **sin** – without help, unavoidable; **no tiene** – it can't be helped.

re·me·do m. imitation; mockery.

re·mem·bran·za f. remembrance, memory.

re·me·mo·rar v. to remember, call to mind.

re·men·dar[1] v. irr. to mend, patch; to darn; to repair.

re·men·dón m. cobbler, shoe repairman; mender, patcher.

re·me·ro m. rower.

re·me·sa f. shipment; remitance, payment.

re·me·sar v. to remit; to ship.

re·mien·do m. mend; mending; patch; darn; repair; **a -s** piecemeal, piece by piece.

re·mil·ga·do adj. prudish, prim, affected.

re·mil·go m. prudery, primness, affectation.

re·mi·nis·cen·cia f. reminiscence.

re·mi·sión f. (disculpa) remission; forgiveness; (remesa) remittance, remitting; (diminución) abatement, slackening; Mex., Ven. anything shipped or sent.

re·mi·ten·te m. & f. sender; shipper.

re·mi·tir v. (enviar) to remit; to send; (diferir) to defer; to pardon; to refer; to abate, **-se** to defer, yield (to another's judgment).

re·mo m. oar; hard and long work; leg of a horse; **al** – at the oar; at hard labor.

re·mo·jar v. to soack, to steep; Am. to tip, bribe.

re·mo·jo m. soaking; steeping; Am. tip bribe.

re·mo·la·cha f. beet.

re·mol·ca·dor m. towboat, tug, tugboat; **lancha remolcadora** tugboat.

re·mol·car[6] v. to tow, tug; to take (a person) in tow.

re·mo·li·no m. swirl, whirl; whirlwind; whirlpool; commotion; Riopl. pin wheel; Am. ventilating wheel (fan); – **de gente** throng, crowd.

re·mo·lón adj. indolent, lazy.

re·mol·que m. tow; towrope; **llevar a** – to tow; to take in tow.

re·mon·tar v. (alzar) to elevate, raise; (reparar) to repair, patch up; to resole; to revamp; Am. to go up; Riopl., Carib., C.A.: Ven., Col. to go upstream; **-se** to rise; to soar, fly upward; to date (from), go back (to); Riopl. to take to the woods or hills.

ré·mo·ra f. impediment, obstacle, hindrance.

re·mor·di·mien·to m. remorse.

re·mo·to adj. remote, distant; improbable.

re·mo·ver[2] v. irr. to remove; to dismiss; to stir.

rem·pu·jar v. to jostle, push.

rem·pu·jón m. jostle, push.

re·mu·da f. change; substitution; replacement; change of clothes; spare tire; relay of horse; Am. spare horse, spare pack animal.

re·mu·dar v. to change; to replace.

re·mu·ne·ra·ción f. remuneration, compensation; pay, reward.

re·mu·ne·rar v. to remunerate, compensate, pay, reward (for services).

re·na·cer[13] v. irr. to be reborn; to spring up, grow up again.

re·na·ci·mien·to m. renascence, renaissance; revival, rebirth.

ren·co adj. lame.

ren·cor m. rancor, resentment, hatred, grudge.

ren·co·ro·so adj. resentful, spiteful.

ren·di·ción f. surrender; submission; yield, profit.

ren·di·do p.p. & adj. tired out, fatigued; devoted; obsequious, servile.

ren·di·ja f. crack, crevice.

ren·di·mien·to m. yiel, output, profit; surrender; submission; fatigue.

ren·dir[5] v. irr. to subdue; to surrender, hand over; to yield, produce; to fatigue; to render, do (homage); Cuba, Ven. – **la jornada** to en or suspend the day's work; **-se** to surrender, give up; to become fatigued, worn out.

re·ne·ga·do m. renegade, traitor; adj. renegade, disloyal; wicked.

re·ne·gar[1,7] v. irr. to deny insistently; to detest; to blaspheme; curse; – **de** to deny, renounce (one's faith); Am. to hate, protest against.

ren·glón m. line (written or printed); item; Riopl., Col., Ven., Mex., Carib., Andes line of business, specialty.

re·nom·bra·do adj. renowned, famous.

re·nom·bre m. renown, fame.

re·no·va·ción f. renovation, restoration; renewal.

re·no·var[2] v. irr. to renovate; to renew; to replace.

ren·que·ar v. to limp.

ren·ta f. rent, rental; income; revenue.

re·nuen·cia f. reluctance, unwillingness.

re·nuen·te adj. reluctant, unwilling.

re·nue·vo m. (vástago) sprout, shoot; (acto) renovation, restoration.

re·nun·ciar v. to renounce; to resign; to refuse; to renege (fail to follow suit in cards).

re·ñi·dor adj. quarrelsome.

re·ñir[5,19] v. irr. to quarrel; to fight; to scold.

re·o adj. guilty; m. culprit, criminal; defendant.

re·o·jo : **mirar de** – to look out of the corner of one's eye; to look scornfully.

re·pan·ti·gar·se[8] v. to lounge, stretch out (in a chair).

re·pa·ra·ción f. reparation; repair; indem·nity.

re·pa·rar v. (renovar) to repair; to regain; to recover, (corregir) to make amends for, atone for; to remedy; to ward off (a blow); Am. to rear, buck (said of horses); – **en** to observe, notice.

re·pa·ro m. (arreglo) repair; restoration; (observación) notice, observation; (duda) doubt, objection; (abrigo) shelter; parry (fencing); Mex. suden bound or leap of a horse.

re•par•ti•mien•to *m*. distribution, division; assessment.

re•par•tir *v*. to distribute; to allot.

re•par•to *m*. distribution; mail delivery; cast of characters.

re•pa•sar *v*. to review, look over, go over again; to mend (*clothes*); to pass by again.

re•pa•so *m*. review; revision.

re•pe•len•te *adj*. repellent, repulsive, repugnant.

re•pe•ler *v*. to repel; to rejest.

re•pen•te *m*. sudden movement; *Am*. attack, fit; **de -** suddenly.

re•pen•ti•no *adj*. sudden.

re•per•cu•tir *v*. to resound, echo back; to rebound; to reflect back (*as light*).

re•pe•ti•ción *f*. repetition.

re•pe•ti•do *p.p*. repeated; **repetidas veces** repeatedly, often.

re•pe•tir⁵ *v. irr*. to repeat; to belch.

re•pi•car⁶ *v*. (*tañer*) to chime, ring; (*hacer menudo*) to mince, chop fine; *Carib., Ven*. to drum, tap (*with the fingers or heels*); **-se** to boast; to be conceited.

re•pi•que *m*. (*tañido*) chime, ringin, peal; (*acción de picar*) mincing, chopping.

re•pi•que•te•ar *v*. to chime ring; to jingle; *Am*. to tap (*with fingers or heels*).

re•pi•que•te•o *m*. chiming, ringing; jingling; tinkling; *Riopl., Carib., Ven*. clickking sound of heels.

re•pi•sa *f*. shelf, ledge; sill; wall bracket; **— de venta-na** window sill.

re•ple•gar¹·⁷ *v. irr*. to fold, pleat; **-se** to retreat, fall back.

ré•pli•ca *f*. reply, answer, retort; replica, copy; *Am. m*. examiner.

re•pli•car⁶ *v.*to reply, answer back; to retort.

re•plie•gue *m*. fol, crease; retreat (*of troops*).

re•po•llo *m*. cabbage.

re•po•ner⁴⁰ *v. irr*. (*devolver*) to replace, put back; to restore; (*contestar*) to reply, retort; **-se** to recover one's health or fortune; to collect oneself, become calm.

re•por•ta•je *m*. newspaper report; reporting.

re•por•tar *v*. to check, control, restrain; to attain, obtain; to bing; to carry; *Am*. to report; **-se** to control oneself.

re•por•te *m*. report, news.

re•pór•ter, reportero *m*. reporter.

re•po•sa•do *p.p*. & *adj*. reposed; quiet, calm; restful.

re•po•sar *v*. to repose; to rest; to lie buried; **-se** to settle (*said of sediment*).

re•po•si•ción *f*. replacement; recovery (*of one's health*).

re•po•so *m*. repose, rest; calm.

re•pos•ta•da *f*. sharp answer, back talk.

re•pren•der *v*. to reprimand, scold.

re•pren•si•ble *adj*. reprehensible, deserving reproof.

re•pren•sión *f*. reproof, rebuke.

re•pre•sa *f*. dam; damming, stopping; *Col., Ven*. reservoir.

re•pre•sa•lia *f*. reprisal.

re•pre•sar *v*. to bank, dam; to recapture (*a ship*) from the enemy; to repress, check.

re•pre•sen•ta•ción *f*. representation; play, perfor-mance; authority, dignity; petition, plea.

re•pre•sen•tan•te *adj*. representing; *m*. & *f*. representative; actor.

re•pre•sen•tar *v*. (*declarar*) to represent; to declare, state; to express, show; (*actuar*) to act, play, perform; **-se** to imagine, picture to oneself.

re•pre•sen•ta•ti•vo *adj*. representative.

re•pre•sión *f*. repression, control, restraint.

re•pri•men•da *f*. reprimand, rebuke.

re•pri•mir *v*. to repress, check, curb; **-se** to repress oneself; to refrain.

re•pro•bar² *v. irr*. to reprove, blame; to condemn; to flunk, fail.

re•pro•char *v*. to reproach.

re•pro•che *m*. reproach.

re•pro•duc•ción *f*. reproduction.

re•pro•du•cir²⁵ *v. irr*. to reproduce.

rep•til *m* reptile.

re•pú•bli•ca *f*. republic.

re•pu•bli•ca•no *adj*. & *m*. republican.

re•pu•diar *v*. to repudiate; to disown.

re•pues•to *m*. stock, supply, provisions; sideboard; **de -** spare, extra; *p.p*. of **reponer** & *adj*. recovered (*from an illness, loss, fright, etc.*); replaced; restored.

re•pug•nan•cia *f*. repugnance, disgust; aversion; dislike, reluctance.

re•pug•nan•te *adj*. repugnant, disgusting, loathsome.

re•pug•nar *v*. to be repugnant; to disgust; to oppose, contradict.

re•pu•li•do *adj*. polished up, slick; shiny; spruce.

re•pul•sa *f*. repulse; rebuff; rebuke.

re•pul•sar *v*. to repule, repel, reject.

re•pul•si•vo *adj*. repulsive, repugnant.

re•pu•ta•ción *f*. reputation.

re•pu•tar *v*. to repute.

re•que•brar¹ *v. irr*. to compliment, to flatter; to flirt with; to court, woo; to break again.

re•que•ma•do *p.p*. & *adj*. burne; parched; tanned, sunburned.

re•que•mar *v*. to parch, dry up; to burn; to overcook; se to become overheated; to burn inwardly; to get tanned, sunburned.

re•que•ri•mien•to *m*. requisition; require-ment; summons; **-s** amorous advances, insinuations.

re•que•rir³ *v. irr*. (*exigir*) to require; to need; to summon; (*indagar*) to examine, investigate; (*avisar*) to notify; **— de amores** to court, woo.

re•que•són *m*. cottage cheese.

re•quie•bro *m*. flattery; compliment.

re·qui·si·to *m.* requirement, requisite; **– previo** prerequisite.

res *f.* head of cattle; any large animal.

re·sa·bio *m.* disagreeable aftertaste; bad habit.

re·sa·ca *f.* undertow; surge, surf; redraft (*of a bill of exchange*); *Am.* beating, thrashing; *Mex.*, *Ríopl.* mud an slime (*left by a flood*).

re·sal·tar *v.* to stand out; to project, just out; to rebound, bounce or spring back; to be evident, obvious.

re·sar·cir[10] *v.* to indemnify, compensate, repay; to make amends for; **-se de** to make up for.

res·ba·la·de·ro *m.* slide, slippery place.

res·ba·la·di·zo *adj.* slippery.

res·ba·lar *v.* to slide; **-se** to slip; to slide; to skid; **resbalársele a uno una cosa** to let a thing slide off one's back, be impervious to a thing.

res·ba·lón *m.* sudden or violent slip; slide; error; **darse un –** to slip.

res·ba·lo·so *adj.* slippery.

res·ca·tar *v.* to ransom; to redeem; to barter, exchange, trade; *Am.* to resell.

res·ca·te *m.* ransom; redemption; barter, exchange.

res·col·do *m.* embers, hot cinders, hot ashes; doubt, scruple.

re·se·car[6] *v.* to dry up; to parch.

re·se·co *adj.* very dry; dried up, parched, thin, skinny.

re·sen·ti·mien·to *m.* resentment; impair-ment, damage (*to one's health*).

re·sen·tir·se[3] *v. irr.* (*tener pesar*) to show resentment, hurt, or grief; to resent, (*empeorar*) to weaken; to become worse.

re·se·ña *f.* military review; book review; brief account; sign, signal.

re·se·ñar *v.* to review (*a book*); to review (*troops*); to autline briefly, give a short account of.

re·se·ro m. *Ríopl.* cowboy, herdsman; *Am.* dealer in livestock.

re·ser·va *f.* reserve; reservation; exception; caution; **a – de** reserving the right to, intending to; **sin –** without reserve, frankly.

re·ser·va·ción *f.* reservation.

re·ser·var *v.* to reserve; to put aside; to postpone; to exempt; to keep secret; **-se** to conserve one's strength, spare oneself (*for another time*).

res·fria·do *m.* cold (*illness*); *p.p. of* **resfriar**; *adj. Ríopl.* indiscreet.

res·friar[17] *v.* to cool; to chill; **-se** to catch cold; to cool.

res·frí·o *m.* chill; cold.

res·guar·dar *v.* to guard, defend; to shield; **–se de** to guar oneself against; to seek shelter from.

res·guar·do *m.* defense; securituy; guarantee; guard.

re·si·den·cia *f.* residence; office or post of a resident foreing minister; *Am.* luxurious dwelling.

re·si·den·te *adj.* resident, residing; *m. & f.* resident, dweller; resident foreign minister; *Col.*, *C.A.*, *Ríopl.* alien resident.

re·si·dir *v.* to reside; to live, dwell; to be inherent, belong (to).

re·si·duo *m.* residue; remainder.

re·sig·na·ción *f.* resignation.

re·sig·nar *v.* to resign; to hand over; **-se** to resign oneself.

re·si·na *f.* resin.

re·sis·ten·cia *f.* resistace

re·sis·ten·te *adj.* resistant; resisting.

re·sis·tir *v.* to resist; to tolerate, endure; **-se** to resist, struggle.

re·so·lu·ción *f.* (*ánimo*) resolution; courage, determination; (*resultado*) solution; **en –** in brief.

re·sol·ver[2,52] *v. irr.* to resolve, decide, to solve; to dissolve; **-se** to resolve, decide; to be reduced (to), dissolve (into).

re·so·llar[2] *v. irr.* to breathe hard; to pant.

re·so·nar[2] *v. irr.* to resound.

re·so·plar *v.* to puff, breathe hard; to snort.

re·so·pli·do *m.* puff, pant; snort.

re·sor·te *m.* spring; elasticity; means (*to attain an object*); *Col.* elastic, rubber ban; *Ven.* **no es de mi –** it doesn't concern me.

res·pal·dar *v.* to endorse; to guarantee; *Am.* to back, support; **-se** to lean back; *Ch.* to protect one's rear.

res·pal·do *m.* back (*of a chair or sheet of paper*); protecting wall; endorsement; *Am.* protection, security, guarantee.

res·pec·ti·vo *adj.* respective.

res·pec·to *m.* respect, relation, reference; point, matter; **(con) – a** (*or* **– de**) with respect to, with regard to.

res·pe·ta·ble *adj.* respectable.

res·pe·tar *v.* to respect.

res·pe·to *m.* respect; reverence, regard; consideration.

res·pe·tuo·so *adj.* respectful; respectable.

res·pin·gar[7] *v.* to buck; to balk (*said of a horse*); to grumble; to curl up (*said of the edge of a garment*).

res·pin·go *m.* buck, balking; muttering, grumbling.

res·pi·ra·ción *f.* respiration, breathing.

res·pi·rar *v.* to breathe.

res·pi·ro *m.* breathing; breath; respite, pause, moment of rest; extension of time (*for payment*).

res·plan·de·cer[13] *v. irr.* to shine; to glitter.

res·plan·de·cien·te *adj.* resplendent, shining.

res·plan·dor *m.* splendor, brilliance, brightness; *Am.* sun's glare.

res·pon·der *v.* to respond; to answer; to correspond, harmonize; to answer (for), be responsible (for).

res·pon·dón *adj.* saucy, pert, insolent (*in answering*).

res·pon·sa·bi·li·dad *f.* responsibility.

res·pon·sa·ble *adj.* responsible.

res·pues·ta *f.* response, answer, reply.

res·que·bra·du·ra, resquebrajadura *f.* fissure, crevice, crack.

res·que·bra·jar = resquebrar.

res·que·brar[1] *v. irr.* to crack; to split.

res·qui·cio *m.* crack, slit, crevice; opening; *Col., Ven., Mex.* vestige, sign, trace.

res·ta *f.* subtraction (*as an arithmetical operation*); remainder.

res·ta·ble·cer[13] *v. irr.* to re-establish; to restore; **-se** to recover.

res·tan·te *adj.* remaining; *m.* residue, remainder.

res·ta·ñar *v.* to staunch (*a wound*); to check the flow of.

res·tar *v.* to deduct; to subtract; to remain, be left over; to strike back (*a ball*).

res·tau·ra·ción *f.* restoration.

res·tau·ran·te *m.* restaurant.

res·tau·rar *v.* to retore; to recover; to re-establish; to repair.

res·ti·tu·ción *f.* restitution, restoration, return.

res·ti·tuir[32] *v. irr.* to return, give back: to restore.

res·to *m.* rest, remmainder; stakes at cards; return (*of a tennis ball*); player who returns the ball; **-s** remains.

res·tre·gar[1,7] *v. irr.* to rub hard; to scrub.

res·tric·ción *f.* restriction; restraint, curb; limitation.

res·trin·gir[11] *v.* to restrict; to restrain; to limit.

re·su·ci·tar *v.* to resuscitate; bring to life; to come to life; to revive.

re·suel·to *p.p. of* **resolver** resolved, determined; *adj.* resolute, bold; quick.

re·sue·llo *m.* breath; breathing, panting.

re·sul·ta *f.* result; effect, consequence; **de -s** as a result, in consequence.

re·sul·ta·do *m.* result, effect, consequence.

re·sul·tan·te *adj.* resulting; *f.* resultant (*force*).

re·sul·tar *v.* to result; to spring, arise as a consequence; to turn out to be; **resulta que** it turns out that.

re·su·men *m.* résumé, summary; **en -** summing up, in brief.

re·su·mi·de·ro *m. Am.* = **sumidero.**

re·su·mir *v.* to summarize, sum up; **-se** to be reduced or condensed.

re·sur·gir[11] *v.* to arise again; to reappear.

re·ta·blo *m.* altarpiece, religious picture hung as a votive offering; series of pictures that tell a story.

re·ta·guar·dia *f.* rear guard.

re·tal *m.* remnant.

re·tar *v.* to challenge, defy; to reprimand, scold; *Ch., Andes* to insult.

re·tar·dar *v.* to retard, delay.

re·ta·zo *m.* remnant; piece; fragment.

re·te·ner[45] *v. irr.* to retain; to keep; to withhold; to detain.

re·tin·tín *m.* jingle, tinkle; sarcastic tone or ring.

re·ti·ra·da *f.* retreat; withdrawal.

re·ti·ra·do *p.p. & adj.* retired; distant, remote; isolated; pensioned.

re·ti·rar *v.* to withdraw; to take away; **-se** to retire, withraw; to retreat.

re·ti·ro *m.* retreat; retirement; withdrawal; place of refuge; pension of a retired officer.

re·to *m.* challenge; defiance; *Ríopl.* scolding; *Andes* insult.

re·to·ba·do *adj. Col., Ríopl.* saucy; *Andes* stubborn, unruly; *Andes* peevish; *Am.* sly, astute.

re·to·bar *v. Col., Andes* to cover with leather; *Am.* to wrap with leather, oilcloth, or burlap; *Am.* to tan (*leather*); **-se** *Ríopl.* to rebel, talk back; act saucy; *Andes, Col.* to become disagreeable an aloof.

re·to·car[6] *v.* to retouch, touch up; to finish, perfect.

re·to·ñar *v.* to sprout; to bud; to sprout again; to reappear.

re·to·ño *m.* sprout, shoot; bud.

re·to·que *m.* retouching; finishing touch.

re·tor·cer[2,10] *v. irr.* to twist; to retort; to distort; **-se** to wriggle; to squirm.

re·tor·ci·mien·to *m.* twisting; squirming.

re·tó·ri·ca *f.* rhetoric.

re·tor·nar *v.* to return; to give back.

re·tor·no *m.* return; repayment; barter.

re·to·zar[9] *v.* to gambol, frisk about, frolic, romp; to stir within (*said of passions*).

re·to·zo *m.* frolic; **retozón** *adj.* frisky, playful.

re·trac·tar·se *v.* to retract, take back one's word.

re·tra·er[46] *v. irr.* to withdraw, draw back, take back; **-se de** to withdraw from; to keep aloof or away from; to shun.

re·trai·mien·to *m.* retirement; reserve, aloofness, shyness.

re·tran·ca *f. Cuba* brake; **retranquero** *m. Am.* brakeman.

re·tran·car[6] *v. Cuba* to brake, put the brake on; *Cuba* **se ha retrancado el asunto** the affair has come to a standstill.

re·tra·sa·do *p.p. & adj.* behind, behind time; backwar; postponed, delayed.

re·tra·sar *v.* to delay, retard; to set back; to go backward; **-se** to fall behind; to be late, behind time.

re·tra·so *m.* delay.

re·tra·tar *v.* to portray; to photograph; to copy, imitate; **-se** to be portrayed; to be photographed; to be reflected.

re·tra·to *m.* portrait; photograph; copy, imitation, reflection.

re·tre·te *m.* toilet, water closet; place of retreat.

re·tro·ce·der *v.* to turn back; to fall back, draw back; to recede.

re·tro·ce·so *m.* retrogression, backward step; retreat; setback; relapse.

re·trué·ca·no *m.* pun.

re·tum·bar *v.* to resound; to rumble.

re·tum·bo *m.* loud echo or sound; rumble (*of thunder, cannon, etc.*).

reu·ma m. & f., **reumatismo** m. rheumatism.

reu·nión f. reunion; meeting.

reu·nir v. to reunite; to unite; to group; to gather; to assemble; to collect, **-se** to meet, assemble; to reunite.

re·van·cha f. revenge; return game or match.

re·ve·la·ción f. revelation.

re·ve·la·dor adj. revealing; m. developer (in photography).

re·ve·lar v. to reveal; to develop (a film).

re·ven·de·dor m. retailer, reseller; ticket scalper.

re·ven·ta f. resale.

re·ven·tar[1] v. irr. (estallar) to burst, to burst forth; to explode; to smash; (fatigar) to fatigue, exhaust; to bother; **-se** to burst, to blow out, explode.

re·ven·tón m. burst, bursting; blowout; steep hill; hard work, toil; adj. bursting.

re·ver·de·cer[13] v. irr. to grow fresh and green again; to gain new strength and vigor.

re·ve·ren·cia f. reverence; bow.

re·ve·ren·ciar v. to revere, venerate.

re·ve·ren·do adj. reverend; Cuba, Ríopl., Mex., Andes large, big (ironically).

re·ve·ren·te adj. reverent.

re·ver·so m. reverse; back side.

re·ver·tir[3] v. irr. to revert.

re·vés m. reverse; back, wrong side; back stroke or slap; backhanded thrust (in fencing); misfortune; **al –** backwards; wrong side out; in the opposite way; from left to right.

re·ves·tir[5] v. irr. to dress, clothe; to coat, cover with a coating; **-se** to dress, put on an outer garment or vestment, to be invested (with power, authority, etc.); **-se de paciencia** to arm oneself with patience.

re·vi·sar v. to revise; to review; to examine, inspect.

re·vi·sión m. revision; review (of a case), new trial.

re·vi·sor m. corrector; inspector, overseer.

re·vis·ta f. (inspección) review; inspection; (publicación) magazine, journal; (proceso) second trial or hearing; **pasar –** to pass in review; to examine carefully; to review (troops).

re·vis·tar v. to review, inspect (troops).

re·vi·vir v. to revive.

re·vo·ca·ción f. repeal, cancellation.

re·vo·car[6] v. to revoke, repeal.

re·vol·car[6] v. (derribar) to knock down; to turn over and over; to floor, defeat; (suspender) to fail, flunk; **-se** to wallow; to roll over and over; to flounder.

re·vo·lo·te·ar v. to fly about, flutter around; to hover; to circle around.

re·vol·ti·jo, revoltillo m. jumble, mixture, mess; tangle, muddle; **revoltillo de huevos** scrambled eggs.

re·vol·to·so adj. turbulent, unruly, rebellious; mischievous; intricate; m. agitator, troublemaker; rebel.

re·vo·lu·ción f. revolution.

re·vo·lu·cio·na·rio adj. revolutionary; m. revolutionist; revolutionary.

re·vol·ver[2] v. irr. to revolve; to turn over; to stir up; to mix up; to turn around swiftly (a horse); **-se** to move back and forth; to roll over and over; to change (said of the weather).

re·vól·ver m. revolver, pistol.

re·vue·lo m. whirl; stir, commotion; flying around.

re·vuel·ta f. revolt, revolution; second turn, turn, bend; quarrel, fight; Am. sudden turning of a horse.

re·vuel·to p.p. of **revolver** & adj. confused; mixed up; intricate, complicated; choppy (sea); changeable (weather); **huevos -s** scrambled eggs.

rey m. king.

re·yer·ta f. quarrel, dispute.

re·za·ga·do adj. back, behind; m. straggler, slowpoke; latecomer.

re·za·gar[7] v. to leave behind; to separate (the weak cattle) from the herd; Am. to reserve, set aside; **-se** to lag behind.

re·zar[9] v. to pray; to say or recite (a prayer); to mutter, grumble; **así reza el libro** so the book says; **eso no reza conmigo** that has nothing to do with me.

re·zo m. prayer.

re·zon·gar[7] v. to grumble, growl, mutter.

re·zon·gón adj. growling, grumbling; m. grumbler; growler; scolder.

re·zu·mar v. to ooze; to leak; **se rezuma** it oozes, it seeps through.

rí·a f. mouth of a river, estuary.

ria·chue·lo m. rivulet, brook.

ri·ba·zo m. bank, ridge.

ri·be·ra f. shore, bank, beach.

ri·be·re·ño adj. of pertaining to, or living on, a river bank.

ri·be·te m. trimming, border, edge, binding; addition; **tiene sus –s de poeta** he is something of a poet.

ri·be·te·ar v. to bind, put a binding on; to border, trim the edge or border of.

ri·ca·cho adj. quite rich (often said sarcastically); **ricachón** adj. extremely rich, disgustingly rich.

ri·co adj. rich, wealthy; delicious; exquisite; **ricote = ricacho.**

ri·di·cu·li·zar[6] v. to ridicule, deride.

ri·dí·cu·lo adj. ridiculous; queer, strange; m. ridicule; ridiculous situation; **hacer el –** to be ridiculous; to act the fool.

rie·go m. irrigation; watering.

riel m. rail; **-es** track, railroad track.

rien·da f. rein, bridle; moderation, restraint; **a - suelta** with free rein, without restraint; violently, swiftly; **soltar la –** to let loose, act without restraint; **tirar las -s** to draw rein, tighten the reins; to restrain.

rien·te adj. laughing, smiling.

ries·go m. risk.

ri·fa f. raffle; scuffle, quarrel.

ri•far *v.* to raffle; to scuffle, quarrel.

ri•fle *m.* rifle.

ri•gi•dez *f.* rigidity, stiffness; severity, strictness.

ri•gi•do *adj.* rigid, stiff; severe, strict.

ri•gor *m.* rigor; severity; harshness; rigidity, stiffness; **en -** in reality; strictly; **ser de** – to be absolutely indispensable, be required by custom.

ri•go•ro•so, riguroso *adj.* rigorous; harsh; severe; strict.

ri•ma *f.* rhyme; **-s** poems.

ri•mar *v.* to rhyme.

rim•bom•ban•te *adj.* high-sounding; resounding.

ri•me•ro *m.* pile, heap.

rin•cón *m.* corner, nook; *Am.* narrow valley.

rin•co•na•da *f.* corner; nook.

rin•co•ne•ra *f.* corner cupboard, corner table, corner bracket.

rin•gle•ra *f.* tier, row, line.

ri•no•ce•ron•te *m.* rhinoceros.

ri•ña *f.* quarrel, dispute, fight.

ri•ñón *m.* kidney; center, interior.

rí•o *m.* river.

ri•pio *m.* rubble, stone or brick fragments; padding (*in a verse, speech, etc.*), useless word.

ri•que•za *f.* riches; wealth.

ri•sa *f.* laugh; laughter; **rcvontar de** – to burst with laughter; **tomar a** – to take lightly; to laugh off.

ri•sa•da *f.* gale of laughter, loud laugh.

ris•co *m.* rocky cliff, crag; honey fritter.

ri•si•ble *adj.* laughable, ridiculous.

ri•so•ta•da *f.* guffaw, big laugh.

ris•tra *f.* string (*of onions, garlic, etc.*); series, row.

ri•sue•ño *adj.* smiling; pleasant; delightful.

rít•mi•co *adj.* rhythmical.

rit•mo *m.* rhythm.

ri•to *m.* rite, ceremony.

ri•val *m. & f.* rival, competitor; enemy.

ri•va•li•dad *f.* rivalry, competition; enmity.

ri•va•li•zar[9] *v.* to rival, compete.

ri•za•do *p.p.* curled; *adj.* wary, curly; *m.* curling; curls.

ri•zar[9] *v.* to curl; to ripple; to ruffle, gather into ruffles; **-se** to curl one's hair; to curl.

ri•zo *m.* curl; *adj.* curly; **rizoso** *adj.* curly.

ro•a•no *adj.* roan (*red, bay, or chestnutcolored, mixed with white; applied to a horse*).

ro•bar *v.* to rob, steal; to abduct, kidnap.

ro•ble *m.* oak tree; oak wood; **robledal, robledo** *m.* oak grove.

ro•bo *m.* robbery, theft; loot, plunder.

ro•bus•to *adj.* robust, vigorous.

ro•ca *f.* rock, boulder; rocky cliff, crag.

ro•ca•llo•so *adj.* rocky.

ro•ce *m.* graze; friction; contact; **no tener – con** to have no contact with (*a person*).

ro•cia•da *f.* sprinkling; spray; dew; sprinkle, shower; volley of harsh words.

ro•ciar[17] *v.* to sprinkle; to spray; to fall (*said of dew*).

ro•cín *m.* nag, hack; draft horse; coarse, ill-bre man; *Riopl.*, *Mex.*, *Andes* riding horse.

ro•cí•o *m.* dew; sprinkle; shower; spray; *adj. Am.* reddish, roan (*horse*).

ro•co•so *adj.* rocky.

ro•da•da *f.* rut, wheel track; *Riopl.* tumble, fall.

ro•da•do *adj.* dapple (horse); *p.p. of* **rodar**.

ro•deo *f.* rolling; rut; **– del neumático** tire tread.

ro•da•ja *f.* disk; small wheel; round slice.

ro•da•je *m.* works (*of a watch*); **– de película** the filming of a movie.

ro•dar[2] *v. irr.* to roll; to revolve; to roam, wander about; to fall down (*rolling*); *Am.* **– a patadas** to kick down.

ro•de•ar *v.* to go around; to go by a roundabout way; to surround, encircle; *Riopl.*, *Cuba*, *Ven.* to round up (*cattle*).

ro•de•la *f.* round shield; *Mex.* padded ring for carrying loads on the head; *Am.* round slice; *Am.* kettle lid; *Am.* hoop; *Am.* game of rolling a hoop.

ro•de•o *m.* detour, roundabout way; circumlocution, roundabout expression; dodge, evasion; corral, stockyard; rodeo, roundup.

ro•di•lla *f.* knee; **de -s** on one's knees; **hincarse de -s** to kneel down.

ro•di•llo *m.* roller; rolling pin; road roller.

ro•er[51] *v. irr.* to gnaw; to corrode, eat away; to torment, harass.

ro•gar[2,7] *v. irr.* to pray, beg, besseech; **hacerse de –** to let oneself be coaxed.

ro•jez *f.* redness.

ro•ji•zo *adj.* reddish.

ro•jo *adj.* red; red, radical.

ro•ju•ra *f.* redness.

ro•lli•zo *adj.* plump; *m.* log.

ro•llo *m.* roll; bundle; rolling pin; log.

ro•ma•di•zo *m.* nasal catarrh, head cold.

ro•man•ce *adj.* Romance, Romanic (*language*); *m.* Romance language; Spanish language; romance, chivalric novel; ballad; eight-syllable meter with even verses rhyming in assonance; **en buen –** in plain language.

ro•má•ni•co *adj.* Romanesque (*architecture*); Romance (*language*).

ro•ma•no *adj. & m.* Roman.

ro•man•ti•cis•mo *m.* romanticism.

ro•mán•ti•co *adj.* romantic; sentimental; *m.* romantic; sentimentalist.

ro•me•ría *f.* pilgrimage.

ro•me•ro *m.* pilgrim; rosemary (*shrub*).

ro•mo *adj.* blunt; snub-nosed.

rom•pe: de – y rasga resolute, bold; **al –** *Am.* suddenly.

rom•pe•ca•be•zas *m.* puzzle, riddle.

rom•pe•o•las *m.* breakwater, mole.

rom•per[52] *v.* to break; to shatter; to tear; to wear through; *Ven.* to leave suddly or on the run; **– el alba**

to dawn; **– a** to start to; **-se** to break.

rom•pien•te *m.* shoal, sand bank; reef; **-s** breakers, surf.

rom•pi•mien•to *m.* rupture, breadk; crack; breach; quarrel.

ron *m.* rum.

ron•car[6] *v.* to snore; to roar; to brag.

ron•co *adj.* hoarse; harsh-sounding.

ron•cha *f.* hive; welt.

ron•da *f.* patrol; night serenaders; round (*of a game; of drinks, etc.*); *Ríopl., C.A., Andes* ring- aroun-a-rosy (*a children's game*); **hacer la – a** to court; *Am.* to surround, trap (*an animal*).

ron•dar *v.* to go around, hover around; to patrol; to make the rounds; to serenade.

ron•que•ra *f.* hoarseness.

ron•qui•do *m.* snore; snort.

ron•ro•ne•ar *v.* to purr.

ron•ro•ne•o *m.* purr.

ron•zal *m.* halter.

ro•ña *f.* scab, mange; filth; infection; stinginess; trickery; *Ríopl., Col., Ven., Cuba* ill will, grudge; *Am.* **hacer –** to fake an illness.

ro•ño•so *adj.* scabby, mangy; dirty; stingy; *Carib., Mex.* spiteful; *Am.* fainthearted, cowardly.

ro•pa *f.* clothing, clothes; **– blanca** linen; **– vieja** ol clothes; stew made from leftover meat; **a quema –** at close range (*when shooting*); suddenly, without warning.

ro•pa•je *m.* clothes, clothing, apparel; robe.

ro•pe•ro *m.* clothier; wardrobe, clothespress; wardrobe keeper; *Am.* clothes rack.

ro•que•ño *adj.* rocky; hard, like rock.

ro•sa *f.* rose; red spot on the skin; rose color; *Ch., Mex.* rosebush; **– de los vientos** (*or* **– náutica**) mariner's compass.

ro•sa•do *adj.* rosy, rose-colored; frosted (*drink*); *Am.* roan, reddish-brown (*horse*).

ro•sal *m.* rosebush.

ro•sa•rio *m.* rosary; **– de desdichas** chain of misfortunes.

ros•bif *m.* roast beef.

ros•ca *f.* screw an nut; screw thread; spiral, twist; ring-shaped roll; *Mex., Ven., Col.,* ring-shaped cushion (*for carrying loads on the head*); *Am.* circle of card players.

ro•se•ta *f.* rosette; small rose; **-s** popcorn; **rosetón** *m.* large rosette; rose window.

ro•si•llo *adj.* light red; roan (*horse*).

ros•tro *m.* face; **hacer –** to face.

ro•ta *f.* rout, defeat; ship's course; Rota (*ecclesiastical court*); rattan palm tree.

ro•ta•ción *f.* rotation.

ro•ta•rio *m.* member of the Rotary Club.

ro•ta•ti•vo *adj.* rotary; *f.* printing press.

ro•ta•to•rio *adj.* rotary.

ro•to *p.p. irr. of* **romper** & *adj.* broken; shattered; torn; worn out, ragged; *m. Ch.* person of the poorer class.

ro•tu•lar *v.* to label; to letter.

ró•tu•lo *m.* title, inscription; label.

ro•tun•do *adj.* round; sonorous; **una negativa rotunda** a flat denial.

ro•tu•ra *f.* breach, opening; break; tear, rip; rupture; fracture.

ro•tu•rar *v.* to break ground; to plow (*new ground*).

ro•za•du•ra *f.* friction; chafe; chafing.

ro•za•mien•to *m.* friction; rubbing.

ro•zar[9] *v.* to graze; to scrape; to chafe; to clear of underbrush; **-se con alguien** to have connections, contact, or dealings with someone.

ro•zón *m.* graze, sudden or violent scrape; short, broad scythe.

rua•na *f. Col., Ven.* a woolen poncho.

rua•no = roano.

ru•bí *m.* ruby.

ru•bi•cun•do *adj.* reddish; ruddy, healthy red; reddish-blond.

ru•bio *adj.* blond, blonde.

ru•bor *m.* blush; bashfulness, shyness.

ru•bo•ri•zar•se[9] *v.* to blush; to feel ashamed.

rú•bri•ca *f.* scroll, flourish (*added to a signature*); title, heading; **de –** according to ritual, rule, or custom.

ru•cio *adj.* grey (*horse or donkey*); **– rodado** dapple-grey.

ru•de•za *f.* rudeness; coarseness; roughness.

ru•do *adj.* rude; coarse; rough; stupid.

rue•ca *f.* distaff (*used for spinning*).

rue•da *f.* (*maquina*) wheel; circle; spread of a peacock's tail; round object: (*grupo*) circle; group; **en –** in turn; in a circle; **hacer la – a** to court; to flatter.

rue•do *m.* circuit; tour; border, rim; circumference.

rue•go *m.* prayer, supplication, request.

ru•fián *m.* ruffian; bully.

ru•gi•do *m.* roar; rumbling.

ru•gir[11] *v.* to roar; to bellow.

ru•go•so *adj.* wrinkled; furrowed.

rui•bar•bo *m.* rhubarb.

rui•da•zo *m.* big noise.

rui•do *m.* noise; din; dispute; talk, rumor; **hacer** (*or* **meter**) **–** to make a noise; to create a sensation; to cause a disturbance.

rui•do•so *adj.* noisy; loud; sensational.

ruin *adj.* (*vicioso*) vile, base, mean; vicious (*animal*); (*mezquino*) small; petty; puny; stingy.

rui•na *f.* ruin; destruction; downfall.

ruin•dad *f.* baseness; meanness; stinginess; mean or vile act.

rui•no•so *adj.* ruinous; in a state of ruin or decay.

rui•se•ñor *m.* nightingale.

rum•ba *f. Ven., Col., Carib., Mex., Ríopl.* rumba (*dan-*

ce and music); *Carib.*, *Ven.*, *Andes* spree; *Carib.*, *Ven.*, *Andes* **irse de** – togo on a spree.

rum•be•ar v. *Riopl.*, *Andes* to head (towars), take a certain direction; *Am.* to cut a path through a forest; *Am.* to go on a spree.

rum•bo m. (*ruta*) direction, course; route; (*pompa*) pomp; ostentation; *Am.* cut on the hea; *Am.* revel, noisy spree; **hacer – a** to head or sail towards; *Am.* **ir al –** to be going in the right direction, be on the right track.

rum•bo•so adj. pompous, ostentatious; generous.

ru•miar v. to ruminate; to chew the cud, to ponder, meditate.

ru•mor m. rumor, report; murmur; rumble.

run•fla f. series (*of things of the same kind*); sequence (*in cards*).

run•rún m. rumor; murmur.

rup•tu•ra f. rupture; break; fracture

ru•ral adj. rural.

ru•so adj. Russian; m. Russian; Russian language.

rús•tico adj. rustic, rural; crude, coarse; m. peasant; **en** (*or* **a la**) **rústica** unbound, paper-bound.

ru•ta f. route, course, way.

ru•ti•na f. routine.

S

sá•ba•do m. Saturday.

sá•ba•na f. bed sheet; altar cloth.

sa•ba•na f. *Col.* savanna, treeless plain; *Col.* **ponerse en la –** to become suddenly rich.

sa•ban•di•ja f. small reptile; small lizard.

sa•ba•ñón m. chilblain.

sa•be•dor adj. knowing; aware, informed.

sa•ber[42] v. irr. to know; to know how to, to be able to; to learn, find out; *Riopl.*, *Ven.*, *Col.* to be in the habit of; **– a** to taste of, taste like; **sabe bien** it tastes good; **a –** namely; that is; *Am.* **¡a – si venga!** who knows whether he will come!; **un no sé qué** an indefinable something; **¿sabe Vd. a la plaza?** do you know the way to the square?; m. knowledge, learning.

sa•bi•du•rí•a f. wisdom; knowledge.

sa•bien•das : a – consciously, knowingly.

sa•bio adj. wise; judicious; learned; m. savant, scholar; sage, wise man.

sa•ble m. saber; **sablazo** m. blow with a saber, saber wound; **dar un sablazo** to strike for a loan.

sa•bor m. savor, taste, flavor.

sa•bo•re•ar v. to savor, flavor, season, to relish, taste with pleasure; to enjoy; **-se** to eat or drink with relish; to smack one's lips.

sa•bo•ta•je m. sabotage.

sa•bo•te•ar v. to sabotage.

sa•bro•so adj. savory, tasty; delicious; dilightful.

sa•bue•so m. hound.

sa•ca•bo•ca•dos m. punch (*tool*).

sa•ca•cor•chos m. corkscrew.

sa•ca•mue•las m. & f. tooth puller; quack dentist.

sa•car[6] v. to draw, draw out, pull out, get out, or take out; to get, obtain; to infer; to make (*a copy*); to take (*a snapshot or picture*); to stick out (*one's tongue*); to serve (*a ball*); **- a bailar** to ask to dance, lead on to the dance floor; **– a luz** to publish; **– el cuerpo** to dodge; **– en claro** (*or* **– en limpio**) to deduce, conclude; *Am.* **– el sombrero** to take off one's hat; *Am.* **¡sáquese de allí!** get out of there!

sa•ca•ri•na f. saccharine.

sa•cer•do•cio m. priesthood.

sa•cer•do•te m. priest.

sa•ciar v. to satiate, satisfy; **-se** to be satiated, satisfied completely.

sa•co m. sack, bag; sackful, bagful; loose-fitting coat; sack, plundering; *Am.* suit coat; **– de noche** overnight bag, satchel.

sa•cra•men•to m. sacrament.

sa•cri•fi•car[6] v. to sacrifice.

sa•cri•fi•cio m. sacrifice.

sa•cri•le•gio m. sacrilege.

sa•cri•le•go adj. sacrilegious.

sa•cris•tán m. sacristan, sexton; *Am.* busybody, meddler.

sa•cro adj. sacred.

sa•cro•san•to adj. sacrosanct, holy and sacred.

sa•cu•di•da f. shake, jolt, jerk.

sa•cu•di•mien•to m. shaking, shake, jerk; shock, jolt.

sa•cu•dir v. to shake; to jerk; to beat; to beat the dust from; to shake off; **-se** to shake oneself; to brush oneself off; **-se de alguien** to shake someone off, get rid of someone.

sá•di•co adj. sadistic, cruel.

sa•e•ta f. arrow, dart.

sa•ga•ci•dad f. sagacity.

sa•gaz adj. sagacious, shrewd.

sa•gra•do adj. sacred; consecrated; m. asylum, refuge.

sa•hu•mar v. to perfume with incense; to fumigate.

sa•hu•me•rio m. vapor, fume; incense; burning of incense; fumigation.

sai•ne•te m. one-act comedy or farce; delicacy, tasty tidbit; flavor, relish; sauce.

sa•jón adj. & m. Saxon.

sal f. salt; wit, humor; grace; *Mex.*, *Cuba*, *C.A.*, *Col.*, *Andes* misfortune, bad luck.

sa•la f. parlor; hall, large room; **– de justicia** courtroom.

sa•la•do adj. salty; salted; witty; charming; *Am.* costly; *Mex.*, *Cuba*, *C.A.*, *Col.*, *Andes* **estar –** to be unlucky; m. *Am.* salt pit, salt mine.

sa•lar v. to salt; to cure or preserve with salt; *Mex.*, *Cuba*, *C.A.*, *Col.*, *Andes* to bring bad luck (to); *Am.* to dishonor; *Am.* to ruin, spoil; *Am.* to bribe; *Am.* to feed salt to cattle; *m. Am.* salt pit.

sa·la·rio *m.* salary, wages.

sal·chi·cha *f.* sausage; **salchichón** *m.* large sausage.

sal·dar *v.* to balance, settle (*an account*).

sal·do *m.* balance, settlement (*of an account*); bargain sale.

sa·le·di·zo = salidizo.

sa·le·ro *m.* (*vaso*) saltcellar, saltshaker; place for storing salts; salt lick; (*gracia*) wit, grace, charm; *Am.* salt dealer.

sa·li·da *f.* departure; exit; sally; outlet; way out; loophole; outskirts; outcome; jut, projection; outlay, expenditure; witty remark; **– de pie de banco** silly remark, nonsense; **– del sol** sunrise; *Cuba* **– de teatro** evening wrap.

sa·li·di·zo *m.* jut, ledge, projection; *adj.* salient, jutting, projecting.

sa·lien·te *adj.* salient, staning out; projecting; *m.* salient, salient angle; jut, projection.

sa·li·na *f.* salt mine or pit; salt works.

sa·lir [43] *v. irr.* (*partir*) to go out; to leave, depart; to get out (*of*); to come out; to sprout; to come (*from*); (*resultar*) to turn out to be; **– bien** to turn out well; to come out well; **– a su padre** to turn out to be or look like his father; *Am.* **– a mano** to come out even; **-se** to get out, slip out; to leak out; **-se con la suya** to get one's own way.

sa·li·tral *m.* saltpeter bed or mine.

sa·li·tre *m.* saltpeter; **salitrera** *f.* saltpeter mine or bed; **salitroso** *adj.* nitrous, abounding in saltpeter.

sa·li·va *f.* saliva.

sal·mo *m.* psalm.

sal·mo·diar *v.* to chant, to talk in a monotone or singsong.

sal·món *m.* salmon.

sal·mue·ra *f.* brine.

sa·lo·bre *adj.* briny, salty.

sa·lón *m.* salon, hall, large room; salted meat or fish.

sal·pi·ca·du·ra *f.* spatter, splash.

sal·pi·car [6] *v.* to sprinkle, spray, spatter.

sal·pi·cón *m.* hash; hodgepodge; *Ec.* fruit drink.

sal·pi·men·tar [1] *v. irr.* to salt and pepper.

sal·pi·mien·ta *f.* salt and pepper.

sal·pu·lli·do *m.* rash, skin eruption.

sal·sa *f.* sauce; gravy; *Am.* sound whipping or beating; **salsera** *f.* sauce dish.

sal·ta·mon·tes *m.* grasshopper.

sal·tar *v.* (*brincar*) to jump; to jump over; to leap; to bounce; to skip; (*estallar*) to burst, break into pieces; to come off; **– a la vista** to be obvious, evident; **– a tierra** to disembark, land; *Mex.* **– las trancas** to lose one's patience; to lose one's head.

sal·te·a·dor *m.* bandit, highway robber.

sal·te·ar *v.* to assault, attack; to hold up, rob; to take by surprise; to jump or skip around.

sal·to *m.* jump; leap; precipice; gap; **– de agua** waterfall; **a -s** by jumps; **en un** (*or* **de un**) **–** in a jiffy; quickly **dar un –** to jump, leap.

sal·tón *adj.* jumping, shipping, hopping; jumpy; protruding; *Col.* half-cooked; **ojos -es** popeyes, bulging eyes; *m.* grasshopper.

sa·lu·bre *adj.* healthy, healthful.

sa·lu·bri·dad *f.* healthfulness, health; sanitation.

sa·lud *f.* health; welfare; salvation; **¡–!** greetings!; your health!

sa·lu·da·ble *adj.* wholesome, healthful beneficial.

sa·lu·da·dor *m.* greeter; healer, quack.

sa·lu·dar *v.* to salute, greet; to fire a salute.

sa·lu·do *m.* salute, nod, greeting.

sa·lu·ta·ción *f.* salutation; greeting.

sal·va *f.* salvo, salute with guns; greeting, welcome.

sal·va·ción *f.* salvation.

sal·va·do *m.* bran.

sal·va·dor *m.* savior, rescuer; Savior; *adj.* saving.

sal·va·guar·dar *v.* to safeguard, defend, protect.

sal·va·guar·dia *m.* safeguard, protection; guard; *f.* safe-conduct paper, passport; password.

sal·va·ja·da *f.* savage act or remark.

sal·va·je *adj.* savage, wild; *m.* savage.

sal·va·jez *f.* wildness, savagery.

sal·va·jis·mo *m.* savagery; *Am.* savage act or remark. *See* **salvajada.**

sal·va·men·to *m.* salvation, rescue; place of safety; salvaje (*rescue of property*); **bote de –** lifeboat.

sal·var *v.* (*librar*) to save; to except; to exclude; (*vencer*) to clear, jump over, **-se** to be saved; to save oneself, escape.

sal·va·vi·das *m.* life preserver; **lancha –** lifeboat.

¡sal·ve! *interj.* hail!; **Salve** *f.* Salve f. Salve Regina, prayer to the Virgin Mary.

sal·via *f.* sage (*a plant*).

sal·vo *adj.* saved; safe; *prep.* save, except but; **a –** safe, without injury; **en –** in safety; out of danger.

sal·vo·con·duc·to *m.* safe-conduct, pass.

san *adj.* (*contr. of* **santo**) saint.

sá·na·lo·to·do *m.* cure-all.

sa·nar *v.* to heal, cure; to recover, get well.

sa·na·to·rio *m.* sanitarium.

san·ción *f.* sanction.

san·cio·nar *v.* to sanction; to authorize, ratify.

san·da·lia *f.* sandal.

san·dez *f.* stupidity; folly; foolish remark.

san·dí·a *f.* watermelon.

san·dio *adj.* silly, foolish.

sa·ne·a·mien·to *m.* sanitation; drainage of land.

sa·ne·ar *v.* to make sanitary (*land, property, etc.*); to drain, dry up (*land*).

san·grar *v.* to bleed; to drain; to tap (*a tree*); to pilfer; to exploit (*someone*); to indent (*a line*).

san·gre *f.* blood; **– fría** calmness, coolness of mind; **a – fría** in cold blood.

san·grí·a *f.* a refreshing Spanish drink made of red wine, fruit juice, and sugar.

san·grien·to *adj.* bleeding; bloody; bloostained; bloodthirsty, cruel.

san·gui·jue·la *f.* leech.

san·gui·na·rio *adj.* bloody, cruel; bloodthirsty, murderous.

sa·ni·dad *f.* health; soundness; healthfulness; sanitation; – **pública** health department.

sa·ni·ta·rio *adj.* sanitary.

sa·no *adj.* (*de salud*) sound, healthy; healthful; sane, sensible; (*íntegro*) whole; unbroken; undamaged; – **y salvo** safe and sound.

san·se·a·ca·bó that's all; that's the end.

san·tia·mén: en un – in a jiffy.

san·ti·dad *f.* sanctity, holiness, saintliness; **su Santidad** his Holiness.

san·ti·fi·car *v.* to sanctify; to consecrate.

san·ti·guar *v.* to bless; to make the sign of the cross; to beat, hit, punish; -**se** to cross oneself; to show astonishment (*by crossing oneself*).

san·tí·si·mo *adj.* most holy; *m.* the Holy Sacrament.

san·to *adj.* saintly, holy; sacred; **esperar todo el** – **día** to wait the whole blessed day; – **y bueno** well and good; *Riopl., Col., Ven., Mex., Carib., Andes* **¡santa palabra!** that's my final an last word! *m.* saint; saint's day; *Mex., Ven.* **tener el** – **de espaldas** to have a streak of bad luck; **santurrón** *m.* religious hypocrite, affectedly pious person.

san·tua·rio *m.* sanctuary; *Col.* buried treasure; *Am.* Indian idol.

sa·ña *f.* fury, rage.

sa·ñu·do *adj.* furious, enraged.

sa·po *m.* toad; *Col.* despicable little man; *Col.* chubby person; *Am.* sly person; **echar** -**s y culebras** to swear, curse.

sa·que *m.* serve, service (*in tennis*); server.

sa·que·ar *v.* to sack, plunder, pillage, loot.

sa·que·o *m.* sacking, pillaging, plunder; loot, booty.

sa·qui·llo *m.* small bag, handbag, satchel.

sa·ram·pión *m.* measles.

sa·ra·o *m.* soirée, evening party.

sa·ra·pe *m. Mex.* serape, blanket.

sar·cas·mo *m.* sarcasm.

sar·cás·ti·co *adj.* sarcastic.

sar·di·na *f.* sardine.

sar·gen·to *m.* sergeant.

sar·men·to·so *adj.* vinelike; full of vine shoots; gnarled; knotty.

sar·mien·to *m.* shoot or branch of a vine.

sar·na *f.* itch; mange.

sar·no·so *adj.* itchy, scabby, mangy.

sar·pu·lli·do = **salpullido.**

sa·rro *m.* tartar (*on teeth*); crust, sediment (*in utensils*).

sar·ta *f.* string (*of beads*); series.

sar·tén *f.* frying pan.

sas·tre *m.* tailor.

sa·tá·ni·co *adj.* satanic, devilish

sa·té·li·te *m.* satellite; suburban development; – **artificial** artificial satellite.

sa·tén *m.* sateen.

sá·ti·ra *f.* satire.

sa·tí·ri·co *adj.* satirical.

sa·ti·ri·zar[9] *v.* to satirize.

sa·tis·fac·ción *f.* satisfaction; apology, excuse; **tomar** – to vindicate oneself; to take revenge; **dar una** – to offer an apology; to apologize.

sa·tis·fa·cer[31] *v. irr.* to satisfy; to pay (*a debt*); – **una letra** to honor a draft; -**se** to be satisfied; to take satisfaction.

sa·tis·fac·to·rio *adj.* satisfactory.

sa·tis·fe·cho *p.p. of* **satisfacer** satisfied, gratified; *adj.* content, contented.

sa·tu·rar *v.* to saturate; to satiate.

sau·ce *m.* willow.

sa·via *f.* sap.

sa·xó·fo·no *m.* saxophone; also **saxofón.**

sa·zón *f.* (*época*) season, opportune time; (*sabor*) taste, flavor; ripeness; **a la** – then, at that time; **en** – in season, ripe; opportunely; *adj. Riopl., Mex., Cuba*, ripe.

sa·zo·na·do *adj. & p.p.* seasoned; mellow, ripe; expressive (*said of a phrase*).

sa·zo·nar *v.* to season; to flavor; -**se** to become seasoned; to ripen, mature.

se *adj. pron.* (*before* **le, la, lo, las,** *and* **los**) to him, to her; to you (*formal*); to them; *refl. pron.* himself, herself, yourself (*formal*), yourselves (*formal*) themselves; *reciprocal pron.* each other, one another.

se·bo *m.* tallow, fat.

se·ca·dor *m. Am.* dryer (*clothes, hair*).

se·can·te *adj.* drying, blotting; **papel** – blotter, *f.* secant (*math*).

se·car[9] *v.* to dry; to wipe dry; -**se** to dry or wipe oneself; to dry up; to wither; to get thin.

sec·ción *f.* section; division; cutting.

sec·cio·nar *v.* to section.

se·co *adj.* (*sin humedad*) dry; dried, whithered; (*áspero*) harsh; abrupt; plain, unadorned; **en** – on dry land, out of the water; **para en** – to stop short, stop suddenly; **a secas** plain; alone, without anything else; *Mex., Carib., Riopl., Andes* simply, straight to the point; **comer pan a secas** to eat just bread; *Mex., Ven.*, **bailar a secas** to dance without musical accompaniment.

se·cre·ción *f.* secretion.

se·cre·tar *v.* to secrete.

se·cre·ta·rí·a *f.* secretary's office; position of secretary.

se·cre·ta·rio *m.* secretary; confidant; **secretaria** *f.* woman secretary; secretary's wife.

se·cre·te·ar *v.* to whisper; -**se** to whisper to each other.

se·cre·to adj. secret, hidden; secretive; m. secret; secrecy; secret place; **– a voces** open secret; **en –** secretly; **hablar en –** to whisper.

sec·ta f. sect.

se·cuaz m. partisan, follower.

se·cue·la f. sequel, óutocome, consequence.

se·cuen·cia f. sequence.

se·cues·tra·dor m. kidnapper; confiscator.

se·cues·trar v. to seize; to kidnap; to confiscate.

se·cues·tro m. kidnapping; seizure.

se·cu·lar adj. secular; lay, worldly; centennial; m. secular, secular priest.

se·cun·dar v. to second, favor, back up.

se·cun·da·rio adj. secondary.

sed f. thrist; craving, desire; **tener –** to be thirsty.

se·da f. silk; **como una –** soft as silk; sweet-tempered; smoothly, easily.

se·dal m. fishing line.

se·dán m. sedan.

se·da·ti·vo adj. & m. sedative.

se·de f. seat, see; **Santa Sede** Holy See.

se·den·ta·rio adj. sedentary.

se·de·ño adj. silky, silken.

se·de·rí·a f. silk goods; silk shop.

se·de·ro m. silk dealer or waver; adj. silk, pertaining to silk; **industria sedera** silk industry.

se·di·ción f. sedition.

se·di·cio·so adj. seditious, turbulent.

se·dien·to adj. thirsty; dry, parched; anxious, desirous.

se·di·men·to m. sediment; dregs, grounds.

se·do·so adj. silken, silky.

se·duc·ción f. seduction.

se·du·cir[25] v. irr. to seduce; to entice; to charm.

se·duc·ti·vo adj. seductive, alluring; inviting, enticing.

se·duc·tor adj. tempting, fascinating; m. seducer; tempter; charming person.

se·ga·dor m. harvester; reaper; **segadora** f. harvester, mowing machine; woman reaper.

se·gar[1,7] v. irr. to mow, reap; to cut off.

se·glar adj. secular, lay; m. layman.

seg·men·to m. segment.

se·gui·da f. succession; series, continuation; **de –** without interruption, continuously; **en –** at once, immediately.

se·gui·do p.p. followed; continued; adj. continuous; straight, direct; adv. without interruption; Am. often; Col., Ven. **de –** at once, immediately.

se·gui·dor m. follower.

se·gui·mien·to m. pursuit.

se·guir[5,12] v. irr. to follow; to continue; to pursue; **-se** to follow as a consequence.

se·gún prep. according to; conj. as; according to; **– y conforme** (or **– y como**) exactly as, just as; that depends.

se·gun·dar v. to repeat a second time; to second.

se·gun·de·ro m. second hand (of a watch or clock).

se·gun·do adj. & m. second.

se·gu·ri·dad f. security; safety; certainty; **alfiler de –** safety pin.

se·gu·ro adj. secure; sure, certain; safe; Ríopl., Mex., Carib., Andes honest, trustworthy; m. assurance; insurance; safety device; **a buen – (al –,** or **de –)** truly certainly; **en –** in safety; **sobre –** without risk; without taking a chance; Am. **irse uno del -** to lose one's temper; Ch., Mex., Cuba., Andes **a la segura** without risk.

se·lec·ción f. selection choice.

se·lec·cio·nar v. to selećt, choose.

se·lec·to adj. select, choice.

sel·va f. forest; jungle.

se·llar v. (imprimir) to stamp; to seal; (cerrar) to close tightly, seal; (concluir) to conclude.

se·llo m. seal; stamp; Am. official stamped paper.

se·má·fo·ro m. traffic light.

se·ma·na f. week; week's wages; **días de –** week days; **entre –** during the week.

se·ma·nal adj. weekly; **– mente** adv. weekly, every week.

se·ma·na·rio m. weekly publication; adj. weekly.

sem·blan·te m. countenance; facial expression; appearance.

sem·blan·za f. portrait, literary sketch.

sem·bra·do m. sown groun; cultivared field.

sem·brar[1] v. irr. to sow; to scatter.

se·me·jan·te adj. similar, like; such a; m. fellow man; **nuestros -s** our fellow men.

se·me·jan·za f. resemblance, similarity; simile; **a – de** in the manner of.

se·me·jar v. to resemble; **-se** to resemble.

se·men·tal adj. sowing (crops); breeding (animals); used as stud.

se·mi·con·so·nan·te f. semiconsonant.

se·mi·lla f. seed.

se·mi·lle·ro m. seed bed; plant nursery; **– de vicios** hotbed of vice.

se·mi·na·rio m. seminary; plant nursery, seed plot.

se·mi·vo·cal f. semivowel.

sem·pi·ter·no adj. everlasting; evergreen.

se·na·do m. senate.

se·na·dor m. senator

sen·ci·llez f. simplicity; plainness.

sen·ci·llo adj. simple; easy; plain; unadorned; unaffected; m. loose change, small coins.

sen·da f. path; way, course.

sen·de·ro m. path.

sen·dos adj. pl. one for each of two or more persons or things.

se·nec·tud f. senility, old age.

se·nil adj. senile.

se·no m. (pecho) breast, bosom; (hueco) cavity,

hollow; womb; lap; cove, bay; innermost recess; sinus (*cavity in a bone*); sine (*math*); *C.A.* armpit.

sen·sa·ción *f.* sensation.

sen·sa·cio·nal *adj.* sensational.

sen·sa·tez *f.* prudence, common sense.

sen·sa·to *adj.* sensible, wise, prudent.

sen·si·bi·li·dad *f.* sensibility; sensitiveness.

sen·si·ble *adj.* sensitive; perceptible; regrettable.

sen·si·ti·vo *adj.* sensitive.

sen·sual *adj.* senual; sensuous.

sen·sua·li·dad *f.* sensuality; lewdness.

sen·ta·da *f.* sitting; **de una** — at one sitting.

sen·ta·do *adj.* seated; sitting; **dar por** — to take for granted.

sen·tar[1] *v. irr.* to seat; to set; to establish; to become, suit, fit; to agree with one (*as food or climate*); **-se** to sit down; to settle down; *Col.* **-se en la palabra** to do all the talking, monopolize the conversation.

sen·ten·cia *f.* sentence; verdict; judgment, maxim, proverb; statement.

sen·ten·ciar *v.* to sentence; to pass judgment on; to decide.

sen·ti·do *p.p.* felt; experienced; *adj.* heartfelt, filled with feeling; sensitive; touchy; **dar -se por** — to take offense; to have one's feelings hurt; **estar — con alguien** to be offended or peeved at someone; *m.* sense; meaning; judgment; **aguzar el** — to prick up one's ears; **perder el** — to faint.

sen·ti·men·tal *adj.* sentimental.

sen·ti·men·ta·lis·mo *m.* sentimentalism, sentimentality.

sen·ti·mien·to *m.* sentiment; sensation, feeling; grief, regret.

sen·tir[3] *v. irr.* to feel; to sense; to hear; to regret; **-se** to feel (*well, strong, sad, etc.*); to feel oneself, consier oneself; to feel resentment; to feel a pain; **sin-** without being realized or felt; inadvertently; unnoticed; *m.* feeling; judgment, opinion.

se·ña *f. familiar contraction of* **señora**.

se·ña *f.* sign, mark; signal; password; **-s** adress (*name and place of residence*); **por más -s** an additional proof.

se·ñal *f.* (*marca*) sign, mark; signal; trace, vestige; scar; (*indicio*) reminder; indication; token, pledge; *Ríopl., Andes* earmark, brand (*on the ear of livestock*); **en – de** in proof of, in token of.

se·ña·lar *v.* to mark; to point out; to indicate; to determine, fix; to appoint; to signal; to assign; *Am.* to earmark, brand (cattle); **-se** to distinguish oneself.

se·ñor *m.* mister; sir; owner; master, lord; gentleman; **el Señor** the Lord.

se·ño·ra *f.* lady; madam; mistress; Mrs.

se·ño·re·ar *v.* to lord it over, domineer; to dominate; to master, control.

se·ño·rí·a *f.* lordship.

se·ño·ril *adj.* lordly.

se·ño·rí·o *m.* dominion, rule; domain of a lord; lordship; dignity; mastery, control; body of noblemen.

se·ño·ri·ta *f.* miss; young lady.

se·ño·ri·to *m.* master, young, gentleman.

se·ñue·lo *m.* decoy; lure, bait; *Ven.* leading or guiding oxen.

se·pa·ra·ción *f.* separation.

se·pa·ra·do *p.p. & adj.* separate; separated; **por -** separately.

se·pa·rar *v.* to separate; to set aside; to remove (from); to dismiss (from); **-se** to separate; to retire, resign; to withdraw, leave.

se·pa·ra·ta *f.* reprint (*of an article*).

sep·ten·trio·nal *adj.* northern.

sep·tiem·bre *m.* September.

se·pul·cral *adj.* sepulchral (*pertaining to sepulchers or tombs*); **lápida** – tombstone.

se·pul·cro *m.* sepulcher, tomb, grave.

se·pul·tar *v.* to bury; to hide.

se·pul·tu·ra *f.* burial; grave; **dar** – to bury.

se·que·dad *f.* dryness; gruffness.

se·quí·a *f.* drought

sé·qui·to *m.* retinue, following.

ser[44] *v. irr.* to be; to exit; to happen, occur; **– de** (*or* **para**) **ver** to be worth seeing; *m.* being; essence, nature, existence; *Am.* **estar en un** – to be always in the same condition.

se·re·nar *v.* to pacify; to calm down; *Col.* to drizzle, rain gently; **-se** to become serene, calm down; to clear up (*said of the wather*).

se·re·na·ta *f.* serenade.

se·re·ni·dad *f.* serenity, calm.

se·re·no *adj.* serene, calm; clear, cludless; *m.* night humidity, dew; night watchman; **al** – in the night air.

se·rie *f.* series.

se·rie·dad *f.* seriousness; gravity; earnestness; dignity.

se·rio *adj.* serious; grave; earnest; dignified; formal; **en** – seriously.

ser·món *m.* sermon; reproof.

ser·mo·ne·ar *v.* to preach; to admonish, reprimand.

ser·pen·te·ar *v.* to wind, twist, turn, zigzag

ser·pien·te *f.* serpent, snake.

se·rra·do *aj.* toothed, notched (*like a saw*); jagged.

se·rra·na *f.* mountain girl; **serranilla** *f.* lyric poem with a rustic theme.

se·rra·ní·a *f.* mountainous region; chain of mountains.

se·rra·no *m.* mountaineer; *adj.* of, pertaining to, or from the mountains.

se·rrar = aserrar.

se·rrín *m.* sawdust.

se·rru·cho *m.* handsaw.

ser·vi·ble *adj.* serviceable, useful.

ser·vi·cial *adj.* helpful, obliging.

ser·vi·cio *m.* service; table service; tea or coffee set; chamber pot; *Am.* toilet water closet.

ser·vi·dor *m.* servant; waiter; **– de Vd.** at your service; **su seguro** – yours truly.

ser·vi·dum·bre *f.* domestic help, servants; servitude, slavery; service.

ser·vil *adj.* servile; **servilón** *adj.* very servile; *m.* bootlicker, great flatterer.

ser·vi·lis·mo *m.* servility, servile behavior or attitude; servile submission.

ser·vi·lle·ta *f.* napkin.

ser·vir [5] *v. irr.* to serve, to be of use; **– de** to serve as, act as; to be used as; **– para** to be good for; to be used for; **-se** to serve or help oneself; to be pleased to; **-se de** to make use of; **sírvase Ud. hacerlo** please do it.

ses·ga·do *adj.* slanting, oblique, bias.

ses·gar [7] *v.* to slant; to cut on the bias; to follow an oblique line.

ses·go *m.* bias; slant; diagonal cut; turn; **al –** on the bias; diagonally, obliquely.

se·sión *f.* session; meeting, conference.

se·so *m.* brain; wisdom, intelligence; **devanarse los -s** to rack one's brain.

ses·te·ar *v.* to snooze, take a nap.

se·su·do *adj.* sensible, wise, prudent; *Mex., C.A.* stubborn.

se·ta *f.* mushroom.

se·to *m.* fence; hedge.

seu·dó·ni·mo *m.* pseudonym, pen name.

se·ve·ri·dad *f.* severity; strictness; seriousness.

se·ve·ro *adj.* severe; strict; stern.

se·vi·lla·no *adj.* of, from, or pertaining to Seville, Spain.

se·xo *m.* sex.

se·xual *adj.* sexual.

si *conj.* if; whether; **¡– ya te lo dije!** but I already told you!; **– bien** although; **por – acaso** just in case.

sí *adv.* yes; **– que** certainly, really; **un – es no es a** trifle, somewhat; *m.* assent, consent; *refl. pron.* (*used after a prep*) himself, herself, yourself (*formal*), themselves; **de por –** separately, by itself; **estar sobre –** to be on the alert.

si·co·lo·gí·a *f.* pysichology.

si·co·ló·gi·co *adj.* psychological.

si·có·lo·go *m.* psychologist.

si·dra *f.* cider.

sie·ga *f.* reaping, mowing; harvesting; harvest, harvest season.

siem·bra *f.* sowing; seedtime, sowing time; sown field.

siem·pre *adv.* always; *Mex., C.A., Col., Andes* in any case, anyway; **para** (*or* **por**) **–** forever, for always; **por – jamás** forever and ever; **– que** whenever; provided that; *Am.* **– si me voy** I've decided to go anyway.

siem·pre·vi·va *f.* evergreen; everlasting.

sien *f.* temple (*of the forehead*).

sier·pe *f.* serpent, snake.

sie·rra *f.* saw; rocky mountain range.

sier·vo *m.* serf; slave; servant.

sies·ta *f.* siesta, afternoon nap; early afternoon; **dor·mir la –** to take an afternoon nap.

si·fón *m.* siphon; siphon bottle; trap (*in plumbing fixtures*).

si·gi·lo *m.* secret; secrecy.

si·glo *m.* century; period, epoch; the world, worldly matters.

sig·ni·fi·ca·ción *f.* meaning; significance.

sig·ni·fi·ca·do *m.* significance, meaning.

sig·ni·fi·car [6] *v.* to signify; to mean; to make known, show; to matter, have importance.

sig·ni·fi·ca·ti·vo *adj.* significant.

sig·no *m.* sign; marck; symbol.

si·guien·te *adj.* following.

sí·la·ba *f.* syllable.

si·la·ba·rio *m.* speller, spelling book.

sil·bar *v.* to whistle; to hiss.

sil·ba·to *m.* whistle.

sil·bi·do *m.* whistle; hiss.

si·len·cia·dor *m.* silencer; muffer (*or an automobile*).

si·len·cio *m.* silence; pause; *adj. Am.* silent, quiet, motionless.

si·len·cio·so *adj.* silent, quiet.

si·lue·ta *f.* silhouette.

sil·ves·tre *adj.* wild, uncultivated.

sil·vi·cul·tor *m.* forester; **silvicultura** *f.* forestry.

si·lla *f.* chair; saddle; **– de montar** sadle; *Ven.* **– de balanza** rocking chair. *See* **mecedora.**

si·llón *m.* large chair; easy chair; *Am.* **– de hamaca** rocking chair.

si·ma *f.* chasm, abyss.

sim·bó·li·co *adj.* symbolic.

sim·bo·lis·mo *m.* symbolism.

sím·bo·lo *m.* symbol; **– de la fe** (*or* **de los Apósto·les**) the Apostle's creed.

si·me·trí·a *f.* symmetry.

si·mé·tri·co *adj.* symmetrical.

si·mien·te *f.* seed.

sí·mil *m.* simile; similarity; *adj.* similar.

sim·pa·tí·a *f.* sympathy; accord, harmony; liking.

sim·pá·ti·co *adj.* sympathetic, congenial; pleasant, agreeable, nice.

sim·pa·ti·zar [9] *v.* to be attractive to; to get on well with; to be congenial; **no me simpatiza** I don't like him.

sim·ple *adj.* simple; mere, plain; pure, unmixed; naive, innocent; silly, foolish; *m.* simpleton.

sim·ple·za *f.* simplicity; simpleness, stupidity, foolishness.

sim·pli·ci·dad *f.* simplicity; candor.

sim·pli·fi·car [6] *v.* to simplify.

sim·plis·ta *adj.* simplistic; *m. & f.* a person who is inclined to oversimplify.

sim·plón *m.* simpleton.

si•mu•la•cro *m.* mimic battle, sham or mock battle; image, vision.

si•mu•lar *v.* to simulate, feign.

si•mul•tá•ne•o *adj.* simultaneous.

sin *prep.* without; besides, not counting; **– que** *conj.* without; **– embargo** nevertheless, still, yet; **– qué ni para qué** without rhyme or reason.

si•na•pis•mo *m.* mustard plaster; irritating person, nuisance, pest, bore.

sin•ce•rar *v.* to square, justify, excuse; **-se** to square oneself (with), justify oneself (with).

sin•ce•ri•dad *f.* sincerity.

sin•ce•ro *adj.* sincere.

sín•co•pa *f.* syncopation; syncope.

sin•di•car[6] *v.* to syndicate; **-se** to syndicate, form a syndicate.

sin•di•ca•to *m.* syndicate.

sín•di•co *m.* receiver (*person appointed to take charge of property under litigation or to liquidate a bankrupt business*); trustee.

si•ne•cu•ra *f.* sinecure (*easy and well paid position*).

sin•fo•ní•a *f.* symphony.

sin•gu•lar *adj.* singular; unique; striking; odd, strange.

sin•gu•la•ri•zar[6] *v.* to single out, choose; to distinguish; **-se** to distinguish oneself to be singled out.

si•nies•tro *adj.* sinester; left (*side*); *m.* unforessen loss, damage; **siniestra** *f.* left hand; left-hand side.

sin•nú•me•ro *m.* great number, endless number.

si•no *conj.* but; *prep.* except; **no hace – lo que le mandan** he only does what he is told; **– que** *conj.* but; *m.* fate, destiny.

si•nó•ni•mo *m.* synonym; *adj.* synonymous.

sin•ra•zón *f.* injustice, wrong.

sin•sa•bor *m.* displeasure; trouble, grief, distress.

sin•ta•xis *f.* syntax.

sín•te•sis *f.* synthesis; summary.

sin•té•ti•co *adj.* synthetic.

sin•te•ti•zar[6] *v.* to synthesize.

sín•to•ma *m.* symptom; indication, sign.

sin•to•ni•zar[9] *v.* to tune in (on).

si•nuo•so *adj.* sinuous, wining; wavy.

sin•ver•güen•za *m. & f.* shameless, person; scoundrel.

si•quia•tra *m. & f.* psychiatrist, alienist.

si•quia•trí•a *f.* psychiatry.

si•quie•ra *adv.* at least; even; **ni –** not even; *conj.* even though.

si•re•na *f.* siren; whistle, foghorn.

sir•vien•te *m.* servant; waiter; **sirvienta** *f.* housemaid; waitress.

si•sa *f.* petty theft; dart (*made in a garment*).

si•sal *m. Am.* sisal or sisal hemp (*fiber used in ropemaking*).

si•sar *v.* to take in (*a garment*); to pilfer; to cheat out of, defraud.

si•se•ar *v.* to hiss.

si•se•o *m.* hiss, hissing.

sis•te•ma *m.* system.

sis•te•má•ti•co *adj.* systematic.

si•tial *m.* chair of a presiding officer; place of honor.

si•tiar *v.* to besiege; to surround.

si•tio *m.* site, location; place, spot, space; siege; *Am.* cattle ranch; *Mex.* taxicab station; **poner – a** to lay siege to.

si•to *adj.* situated, located.

si•tua•ción *f.* situation; position; location; state, condition; *Mex.*, *Carib.*, *Ven.*, *Col.* **hombre de la –** man of the hour, man of influence.

si•tua•do *p.p.* situated; placed.

si•tuar[18] *v.* to locate; to place; **-se** to station oneself, place oneself; to be located, placed, situated.

so: – capa de under the guise of; **– pena de** under penalty of; **– pretexto de** under the pretext of.

so•ba•co *m.* armpit.

so•bar *v.* (*ablandar*) to rub; to knead; to massage; to touch, handle, to fondle, pet; (*fastidiar*) to bother; to beat, slap; *Col.*, *Ven.*, *Mex.* to set bones; *Col.* to flay, skin; *Am.* to win (*in a fight*); *Am.* to tire out (*a horse*).

so•be•ra•ní•a *f.* sovereignty.

so•be•ra•no *adj. & m.* sovereign.

so•ber•bia *f.* pride, arrogance; ostentation, pomp.

so•ber•bio *adj.* proud, haughty, arrogant; pompous; superb, magnificent; spirited (*horse*).

so•bor•nar *v.* to bribe.

so•bor•no *m.* bribery; bribe; *Andes* overload (*on a pack animal*), extra load.

so•bra *f.* surplus, excess; **-s** leftovers, leavings; **de –** more than enough; superfluous, unnecessary.

so•bra•do *m.* attic; loft; *Am.* pantry shelf; **-s** *Col.*, *Ven.* leftovers, leavings; *adj.* leftover; excessive; superfluous; forward, brazen; **sobradas veces** many times, repeatedly.

so•bran•te *adj.* leftover, surplus, excess, spare; *m.* surplus, excess, remainder.

so•brar *v.* to exceed; to remain, be left over; to be more than enough.

so•bre *prep.* (*encima de*) over; above; on, upon; (*acerca de*) about; approximately; besides; **– ma•nera** excessively; **estar – sí** to be cautious, on the alert; **– que** besides, in adition to the fact that; *m.* envelope; adress (*on an envelope*).

so•bre•ca•ma *f.* bedspread.

so•bre•car•ga *f.* overload; overburden.

so•bre•car•gar[7] *v.* to overload; to overburden.

so•bre•car•go *m.* purser (*on a ship*); *f.* airline hostess.

so•bre•co•ger[11] *v.* to surprise, catch unaware; to startle; **-se** to be startled; **-se de miedo** to be seized with fear.

so•bre•en•ten•der[1] *v. irr.* to assume, understand; **-se** to be assumed, be obvious, be understood.

so•bre•ex•ci•ta•ción *f.* overexcitement; thrill.

so•bre•ex•ci•tar *v.* to overexcite.

so·bre·hu·ma·no *adj.* superhuman.

so·bre·lle·var *v.* to endure, bear; to tolerate; to lighten (*another's burden*).

so·bre·me·sa *f.* table runner; after dinner conversation at the table; **de –** during the after dinner conversation.

so·bre·na·dar *v.* to float.

so·bre·na·tu·ral *adj.* supernatural.

so·bre·nom·bre *m.* surname; nickname.

so·bre·pa·sar *v.* to exceed; to excel; **-se** to overstep, go too far.

so·bre·po·ner[40] *v. irr.* to lay on top; **-se** to dominate oneself; **-se a** to overcome; to dominate.

so·bre·pues·to *p.p.* of **sobreponer**; *m.* appliqué (*trimming laid on a dress*); *C.A.* mend, patch.

so·bre·pu·jar *v.* to exceed, excel, surpass; to outweigh.

so·bre·sa·lien·te *adj.* outstanding; projecting; excellent; *m. & f.* substitute (*a person*); understudy (*substitute actor*).

so·bre·sa·lir[43] *v. irr.* to stand out; to project, jut out; to excel.

so·bre·sal·tar *v.* to startle, frighten; to assail; to stand out clearly; **-se** to be startled, frightened.

so·bre·sal·to *m.* start, scare, fright, shock; **de –** suddenly.

so·bres·cri·to *m.* address (*on an envelope*).

so·bres·tan·te *m.* overseer; boss, foreman.

so·bre·suel·do *m.* overtime pay, extra pay or wages.

so·bre·to·do *m.* overcoat.

so·bre·ve·nir[48] *v. irr.* to happen, occur, come unexpectedly; to follow, happen after.

so·bre·vi·vien·te *m. & f.* survivor; *adj.* surviving.

so·bre·vi·vir *v.* to survive.

so·brie·dad *f.* sobriety, soberness, temperance, moderation.

so·bri·na *f.* niece.

so·bri·no *m.* nephew.

so·brio *adj.* sober, temperate, moderate.

so·ca·rrón *adj.* cunning, sly, crafty.

so·ca·rro·ne·rí·a *f.* craftiness, slyness, cuning.

so·ca·var *v.* to dig under; to undermine.

so·ca·vón *m.* tunnel; cave, cavern; underground passageway.

so·cial *adj.* social; sociable, friendly.

so·cia·lis·ta *adj.* socialist, socialistic; *m. & f.* socialist.

so·cie·dad *f.* society; partnerhip; company, firm, corporation; **– anónima** (*or* **– por acciones**) stock company.

so·cio *m.* associate, partner; member.

so·cio·lo·gí·a *f.* sociology.

so·co·rrer *v.* to help, aid, assist.

so·co·rro *m.* help, aid, assistance, relief; *Am.* partial advance payment on a workman's wages.

so·dio *m.* sodium.

so·ez *adj.* low, vile, vulgar; coarse, illmannered.

so·fá *m.* sofa, davenport.

so·fo·can·te *adj.* suffocating, stiffling.

so·fo·car[6] *v.* to suffocate, choke; to smother; to bother; to embarrass.

so·fo·co *m.* suffocation, choking; upset, annoyance; embarrassment.

so·fre·nar *v.* to check; to control; to reprimand.

so·ga *f.* rope; *Ven., Col., Andes, Ch.* leather lasso or rope.

so·juz·ga·mien·to *m.* subjugation, subjection.

so·juz·gar[7] *v.* to subjugate, subdue, subject.

sol *m.* sun; sunshine; sol (*fifth note of the scale*); *Am.* sol (*monetary unit of Peru*); **de – a –** from sunrise to sunset; **hace –** it is sunny; **tomar el –** to bask in the sun; to enjoy the sunshine.

so·la·na *f.* sunny place; sunroom; sun porch; intense sunlight; **solanera** *f.* sunburn; sunny place.

so·la·pa *f.* lapel.

so·la·pa·do *adj.* sly, crafty, cunning, deceitful, underhanded.

so·lar *m.* lot, plot of ground; ancestral mansion, manor; *Carib., Mex.* tenement house; *Mex., Ven.* back yard; *Col.* town lot, field (*for growing alfalfa, corn, etc.*); *adj.* solar, of the sun.

so·lar[2] *v. irr.* to sole (shoes); to pave, floor.

so·la·rie·go *adj.* manorial, pertaining to a manor; **casa solariega** ancestral manor or mansion.

so·laz *m.* solace, comfort; relaxation, recreation.

so·la·zar[7] *v.* to console, cheer, comfort; **-se** to seek relaxation or pleasure; to enjoy oneself.

sol·da·do *m.* soldier; **– raso** private; **– de línea** regular soldier.

sol·da·du·ra *f.* soldering; welding; solder.

sol·dar[2] *v. irr.* to solder; to weld.

so·le·a·do *adj.* sunny; *p.p.* sunned.

so·le·ar *v.* = **asolear.**

so·le·dad *f.* solitude; loneliness; homesickness; lonely retreat.

so·lem·ne *adj.* solemn; imposing; **– disparate** downright foolishness, huge blunder.

so·lem·ni·dad *f.* solemnity; solemn ceremony.

so·ler[2,51] *v. irr.* to have the custom of, be in the habit of.

sol·fe·ri·no *adj.* reddish-purple.

so·li·ci·tan·te *m. & f.* solicitor; applicant.

so·li·ci·tar *v.* to solicit; to apply for; to beg, ask for; to court, woo.

so·lí·ci·to *adj.* solicitous, careful; anxious, concerned; diligent.

so·li·ci·tud *f.* solicitude; care, concern, anxiety.

so·li·da·ri·dad *f.* solidarity union; bond, community of interests.

so·li·dez *f.* solidity; compactness.

so·li·di·fi·car[6] *v.* to solidify.

só·li·do *adj.* solid; firm; strong; *m.* solid.

so·li·lo·quio *m.* soliloquy, monologue.

so·lis·ta *m. & f.* soloist.

so·li·ta·ria *f.* tapeworm.

so·li·ta·rio *adj.* solitary; lonely; *m.* recluse, hermit; solitaire (*card game*); solitaire (*gem set by itself*).

so·lo *adj.* sole, only; single; alone; lonely **a solas** alone; *m.* solo; **sólo** *adv.* only.

so·lo·mi·llo, so·lo·mo *m.* sirloin; loin; loin of pork.

sol·tar *v. irr.* to loosen, untie, unfasten; to let loose; to set free; to let go; to let out; to utter; **-se** to set oneself free; to come loose; to lose restraint; to loosen up; **-se a** to begin to, start to.

sol·te·ro *adj.* single, unmarried; *m.* bachelor; **solte·ra** *f.* spinster; **solterón** *m.* old bachelor; **solterona** *f.* old maid.

sol·tu·ra *f.* looseness; freedom; facility, ease; agility, nimbleness; release (*of a prisoner*).

so·lu·ción *f.* solution; loosening, untying.

sol·ven·tar *v.* to pay (*a bill*), settle (*an account*); to solve (*a problem or difficulty*).

so·llo·zar *v.* to sob.

so·llo·zo *m.* sob.

som·bra *f.* (*oscuridad*) shadow; shade; darkness; (*abrigo*) shelter, protection; (*imagen*) image, reflection (*in the water*); *Am.* guide lines (under writing paper), *Ven.* awning, sunshade; **hacer —** to shade; to cast a shadow (on).

som·bre·a·do *adj.* shady; shaded.

som·bre·ar *v.* to shade; **-se** Mex., *Ven.*, *Col.*, to seek the shade, stand in the shade.

som·bre·re·ría *f.* hat shop.

som·bre·ro *m.* hat; **— de copa** top hat, high hat; **— hongo** derby; **— de jipijapa** Panama hat; *C.A.*, *Col.*, *Ven.* **— de pelo** top hat.

som·bri·lla *f.* parasol, sunshade.

som·brí·o *adj.* somber, gloomy; shady.

so·me·ro *adj.* superficial, shallow; summary, concise.

so·me·ter *v.* to submit; to subject; **-se** to submit.

so·me·ti·mien·to *m.* submission; subjection.

som·no·len·cia *f.* drowsiness, sleepiness; **con —** sleepily.

son *m.* sound; tune; rumor; **en — de guerra** in a warlike manner; **sin ton ni —** without rhyme or reason.

so·na·ja *f.* jingles, tambourine (*to accompany certain dances*); rattle; **sonajero** *m.* child's rattle.

so·nan·te *adj.* sounding; ringing; sonorous; **en dine·ro — y contante** in hard cash.

so·nar *v. irr.* to sound; to ring; to sound familiar; **— a** to sound like; seem like; **-se** to blow one's nose; **se suena que** it is rumored that.

son·da *f.* plumb, string with lead weight (*for sounding the depth of water*); sounding; surgeon's probe.

son·dar = sondear.

son·de·ar *v.* to sound, fathom; to sound out; to probe; to examine into.

son·de·o *m.* sounding, fathoming.

so·ne·to *m.* sonnet.

so·ni·do *m.* sound.

so·no·ro *adj.* sonorous; **consonante sonora** voiced consonant.

son·re·ír *v. irr.* to smile; **-se** to smile.

son·rien·te *adj.* smiling, beaming, radiant.

son·ri·sa *f.* smile.

son·ro·jar·se *v.* to blush.

son·ro·jo *m.* blush.

son·ro·sa·do *adj.* rosy.

son·sa·car *v.* to lure away; to draw (*someone*) out; to extract (*a secret*); to take on the sly.

so·ña·dor *m.* dreamer

so·ñar *v. irr.* to dream; **— con** (*or* **— en**) to dream of; **— despierto** to daydream.

so·ño·lien·to *adj.* sleepy, drowsy.

so·pa *f.* soup; sop; **estar hecho una —** to be sopping wet; *Am.* **es un —s** he is a fool.

so·pa·po *m.* chuck, tap, pat (*under the chin*); slap.

so·pe·tón *m.* box, slap; **de —** all of a sudden, unexpectedly.

so·plar *v.* (*despedir aire*) to blow; to blow away; to blow up, inflate; (*robar*) to swipe, steal; (*informar*) to prompt; to "squeal" on, inform against; *Col.*, *Ven.*, *Mex.*, *Cuba*, *Andes* **— una bofetada** to strike a blow; **-se** to swell up, puff up; to eat up, gobble up; to gulp down; **se sopló el pastel** he gobbled up the pie; *Am.* **-se a uno** to deceive someone, get the best of someone.

so·ple·te *m.* blow torch; blowpipe.

so·plo *m.* (*de aire*) blowing; puff, gust of wind; breath; (*aviso*) whispered warning or advice; "squealing", informing; **en un —** in a jiffy, in a second.

so·plón *m.* informer, "squealer" (*one who tells on someone*), tattletale.

so·por·tal *m.* arcade.

so·por·tar *v.* to support, hold up, bear; to stand, endure, tolerate.

so·por·te *m.* support.

sor·ber *v.* to sip; to suck; to swallow; to absorb; to snuff up one's nose.

sor·be·te *m.* sherbet; fruit ice; *C.A.*, *Mex.*, *Ven.* cone, ice-cream cone; *Am.* silk top hat.

sor·bo *m.* sip, swallow, gulp; sniff.

sor·de·ra, sor·dez *f.* deafness.

sór·di·do *adj.* sordid.

sor·di·na *f.* mute (*of a musical instrument*).

sor·do *adj.* deaf; silent, noiseless; dull; muffled; **con·sonante sorda** voiceless consonant; *m.* deaf person; **hacerse el —** to pretend not to hear; to turn a deaf ear.

sor·do·mu·do *adj.* deaf and dumb; *m.* deaf-mute.

sor·na *f.* slyness, cunning; sneer.

so·ro·che *m.* *Andes* shortness of breath, sickness caused by high altitude; *Am.* blush, flush.

sor·pren·den·te *adj.* surprising.

sor•pren•der v. to surprise; **-se** to be surprised.

sor•pre•sa f. surprise.

sor•te•ar v. to draw lots; to raffle; to dodge; to shun; to fight (*bulls*) skillfully.

sor•te•o m. drawing or casting of lots; raffle.

sor•ti•ja f. ring; finger ring; ringlet, curl.

so•sa f. soda.

so•se•ga•do adj. calm, quiet, peaceful.

so•se•gar[1,7] v. to calm, quiet; to be quiet; **-se** to quiet down.

so•sie•go m. calm, peace, quiet.

sos•la•yo: **al** — obliquely; slanting; on the bias; **de** — oblique, slanting; at a slant; sideways; **mirada de** — side glance; **pegar de** — to glance, hit at a slant.

so•so adj. flat, tasteless, insipi; dull, silly; awkwar.

sos•pe•cha f. suspicion; mistrust.

sos•pe•char v. to suspect; to mistrust.

sos•pe•cho•so adj. suspicious; m. suspect.

sos•tén m. support; prop; supporter; brassière.

sos•te•ner[45] v. irr. to sustain; to hold; to support, maintain; to defend, uphold; to endure.

sos•te•ni•do p.p. & adj. sustained; supported, held up; m. sharp (*in music*).

so•ta f. jack (*at cards*); m. Am. foreman, boss, overseer.

so•ta•na f. cassock (*black outer robe of a priest*).

só•ta•no m. cellar, basement.

so•to m. grove; thicket.

so•tre•ta m. Andes, Riopl. nag, old horse.

so•viet m. soviet; **soviético** adj. soviet, of, or pertaining to, soviets.

sua•ve adj. soft; smooth; mild; bland; gentle.

sua•vi•dad f. softness; smoothness; mildness; gentlenes.

sua•vi•zar[9] v. to smooth; to soften.

su•bal•ter•no adj. & m. subordinate.

su•bas•ta f. public auction.

su•bas•tar v. to sell at auction.

súb•di•to m. subject.

su•bi•da f. rise; ascent; carrying up; **de** — on the way up; **muchas -s y bajadas** many ups and downs; much going up and down.

su•bir v. to ascend, go up, climb; to raise, lift; to carry up; to mount; **– al tren** to board the train, get on the train.

sú•bi•to adj. sudden; **de** — suddenly.

su•ble•va•ción f. revolt, uprising, insurrection.

su•ble•var v. to excite to rebellion; **-se** to revolt.

su•bli•me adj. sublime.

sub•ma•ri•no m. & adj. submarine; m. **– atómico** atomic submarine.

su•bor•di•na•do adj. & m. subordinate.

su•bor•di•nar v. to subordinate; to subdue.

su•bra•yar v. to underline; to emphasize.

sub•sa•nar v. to mend, remedy, repair (*a damage, error, defect, etc.*); to make up for (*an error, fault, etc.*); to excuse (*a fault or error*).

subs•cri•bir = **suscribir**.

subs•crip•ción = **suscripción**

subs•crip•tor = **suscritor.**

sub•se•cre•ta•rio m. undersecretary,

sub•se•cuen•te adj. subsequent.

sub•si•guien•te adj. subsequent.

sub•sis•ten•cia f. living, livelihood; sustenance; permanence.

sub•sis•tir v. to subsist; to exist; to last.

subs•tan•cia = **sustancia.**

subs•tan•cial = **sustancial.**

subs•tan•cio•so = **sustancioso.**

subs•ti•tu•í•ble = **sustituíble.**

subs•tan•ti•vo = **sustantivo.**

subs•ti•tu•ción = **sustitución**

subs•ti•tu•ir = **sustituir.**

subs•ti•tu•to = **sustituto.**

subs•trac•ción = **sustracción**

subs•tra•er = **sustraer.**

sub•sue•lo m. subsoil.

sub•te•nien•te m. second lieutenant.

sub•te•rrá•ne•o adj. subterranean, underground; m. underground; cave, tunnel, vault.

su•bur•ba•no adj. suburban; m. suburban resident.

su•bur•bio m. suburb.

sub•ven•ción f. subsidy.

sub•ven•cio•nar v. to subsidize.

sub•yu•gar v. to subdue.

suc•ción f. suction.

su•ce•der v. to happen, occur; to succeed, follow.

su•ce•sión f. succession; heirs, offspring.

su•ce•si•vo adj. successive; **en lo** — hereafter, in the future.

su•ce•so m. event; outcome, result.

su•ce•sor m. succesor.

su•cie•dad f. dirt, filth; filthiness; filthy act or remark.

su•cin•to adj. compact, concise, brief.

su•cio adj. dirty; foul, filthy.

su•cu•len•to adj. juicy.

su•cum•bir v. to succumb; to yield.

su•cur•sal f. branch, branch office (*of a post office, bank, etc.*); adj. branch (*used as an adj.*).

su•che adj. Ven. sour, unripe; m. Andes pimple; Ch. office boy, insignificant employee; Andes suche (a tree).

sud m. south; south wind; **sudeste** m. & adj. southeast; **sudoeste** m. & adj. southwest.

su•da•me•ri•ca•no adj. & m. South American.

su•dar v.to sweat, perspire; to ooze; to toil.

su•dor m. sweat, perspiration; toil.

su•do•ro•so adj. sweaty, sweating, perspiring.

sue•co adj. Swedish; m. Swede; Swedish language, **hacerse el** — to pretend not to see or understand.

sue•gra f. mother-in-law.

sue•gro m. father-in-law.

sue•la f. sole of a shoe; shoe leather.

suel•do *m.* salary.

sue•lo *m.* soil, ground; floor; pavement; bottom.

suel•to *adj.* (*no atado*) loose; free, easy; (*ágil*) agile, nimble; blank (*verse*); *m.* small change; short newspaper article, news item.

sue•ño *m.* sleep; dream; sleepiness, drowsiness; **en - s** in one's sleep; **conciliar el -** to get to sleep; **tener -** to be sleepy.

sue•ro *m.* serum.

suer•te *f.* (*fortuna*) fate; fortune; chance; luck; (*clase*) sort, kind; way, manner; (*truco*) trick; **de - que** so that, in such a way that; and so; **echar -s** to cast lots; **tener -** to be lucky; **tocarle a uno la -** to fall to one's lot; to be lucky.

sué•ter *m. Am.* sweater.

su•fi•cien•te *adj.* sufficient; competent, able.

su•fi•jo *m.* suffix; *adj.* suffixed.

su•fra•gar[7] *v.* to defray, pay; to help, aid; *Am.* **- por** to vote for.

su•fra•gio *m.* suffrage; vote; help, aid.

su•fri•do *adj.* suffering, long-suffering, patient; **mal - ** impatient.

su•fri•dor *m.* sufferer; *adj.* suffering.

su•fri•mien•to *m.* suffering; patience, endurance.

su•frir *v.* to suffer; to endure; to allow, permit, to sustain; to undergo; **- un examen** to take an examination.

su•ge•ren•cia *f. Am.* suggestion, hint.

su•ge•rir[3] *v. irr.* to suggest; to hint.

su•ges•tión *f.* suggestion; hint.

su•ges•ti•vo *adj.* suggestive.

sui•ci•da *m. & f.* suicide (*person who commits suicide*).

sui•ci•dar•se *v.* to commit suicide.

sui•ci•do *m.* suicide (*act of suicide*).

sui•zo *adj. & m.* Swiss.

su•je•ción *f.* subjection; control; submission.

su•je•ta•pa•pe•les *m.* paper clip.

su•je•tar *v.* to subject; to control; to subdue; to fasten; to grasp, hold; **-se** to subject oneself; to submit; to adhere (to).

su•je•to *adj.* subject; liable; fastened; under control; *m.* subject matter; subject; fellow, individual.

sul•fa•mi•da *f.* common name for the sulfa drugs.

sul•fa•to *m.* sulphate.

sul•fu•rar•se *v.* to get angry.

sul•fú•ri•co *adj.* sulphuric.

sul•fu•ro *m.* sulphide.

sul•tán *m.* sultan.

su•ma *f.* sum; addition; substance; summary; **en -** in short.

su•ma•dor *adj.* adding; **máquina sumadora** adding machine.

su•mar *v.* to add; to add up (to), amount (to); to sum up; **-se a** to join.

su•ma•rio *m.* summary; indictment; *adj.* summary, brief, concise; swift (*punishment*).

su•mer•gi•ble *adj.* submergible; *m.* submarine.

su•mer•gir[11] *v.* to submerge, plunge, sink; to immerse; **-se** to submerge; to sink.

su•mi•de•ro *m.* sink; sewer, drain.

su•mi•nis•trar *v.* to give, supply with, provide with.

su•mir *v.* to sink; to submerge; to immerse; *Ríopl., Mex., Carib.,* to dent; **-se** to sink; *Andes* to shrink, shrivel; *Andes* to cower, crouch in fear; *Am.* **-se el sombrero hasta las cejas** to pull one's hat over one's eyes.

su•mi•sión *f.* submission; obedience.

su•mi•so *adj.* submissive; obedient; meek.

su•mo *adj.* supreme, highest, high; greatest; **- pontífice** Sovereign Pontiff (*the Pope*); **a lo -** at the most.

sun•tuo•so *adj.* sumptuous, magnificent, luxurious.

su•per•a•bun•dan•cia *f.* superabundance, great abundance, overflow.

su•pe•rar *v.* to surpass; to exceed; to overcome.

su•pe•rá•vit *m.* surplus.

su•per•fi•cial *adj.* superficial; shallow; frivolous; **superficialidad** *f.* superficiality, shallowness, frivolity.

su•per•fi•cie *f.* surface; area.

su•per•fluo *adj.* superfluous.

su•pe•rin•ten•den•te *m.* superintendent; supervisor; overseer.

su•pe•rior *adj.* superior; higher; better; upper; *m.* superior; father superior; **superiora** *f.* superior, mother superior.

su•pe•rio•ri•dad *f.* superiority; excellence.

su•per•la•ti•vo *adj. & m.* superlative.

su•per•só•ni•co *adj.* supersonic

su•pers•ti•ción *f.* superstition.

su•pers•ti•cio•so *adj.* superstitious

su•per•vi•ven•cia *f.* survival.

su•per•vi•vien•te = sobreviviente.

su•plan•tar *v.* to supplant; to forge (*a document or check*).

su•ple•men•tar *v.* supplement.

su•ple•men•ta•rio *adj.* supplementary, extra.

su•ple•men•to *m.* supplement, supply, supplying.

su•plen•te *adj., m. & f.* substitute.

sú•pli•ca *f.* entreaty; request; petition; prayer.

su•pli•can•te *adj.* suppliant, beseeching; m & f. suppliant; petitioner.

su•pli•car[7] *v.* to beg, entreat, implore; to pray humbly; to appeal, petition.

su•pli•cio *m.* torture; torment; anguish; execution; instrument of torture; scaffold, gallows.

su•plir *v.* to supply; to make up for; to subtitute, take the place of (*temporarily*).

su•po•ner[40] *v. irr.* to suppose; to assume; to be important.

su•po•si•ción *f.* supposition; asumption.

su•pre•ma•cí•a *f.* supremacy.

su·pre·mo *adj.* supreme; final, last.

su·pre·sión *f.* suppression; omission; elimination.

su·pri·mir *v.* to suppress; to abolish; to omit.

su·pues·to *p.p.* of **suponer** supposed, assumed; — **que** supposing that; since; **por** — of course, naturally; *m.* supposition; assumption.

su·pu·ra·ción *f.* formation or discharge of pus.

su·pu·rar *v.* to fester, form or discharge pus.

sur *m.* south; south wind; **sureste** *m.* southeast; **su·roeste** *m.* southwest.

su·ra·me·ri·ca·no = **sudamericano.**

sur·car⁶ *v.* to furrow; to plow; to plow through; to cut through.

sur·co *m.* furrow; rut; grove; wrinkle.

su·re·ño *adj.* southern, from the south; *m.* a southerner.

sur·gir¹¹ *v.* to surge, rise; to spurt, spout; to appear.

sur·ti·do *m.* stock, supply, assortment; *adj.* assorted.

sur·ti·dor *m.* supplier; spout, jet.

sur·tir *v.* to provide, supply, stock (*with*); to spout, spurt; — **efecto** to produce the desired result; — **un pedido** to fill an order.

sus·cep·ti·ble *adj.* susceptible; sensitive; touchy.

sus·ci·tar *v.* to raise, stir up, provoke.

sus·cri·bir⁵² *v.* to subcribe; to endorse; to agree (to); **-se** to subscribe.

sus·crip·ción *f.* subcription.

sus·cri·to *p.p.* of **suscribir.**

sus·cri·tor *m.* subscriber.

su·so·di·cho *adj.* aforesaid, above-mentioned

sus·pen·der *v.* (*colgar*) to suspend; to hang; (*detener*) to stop; to efer; (*no aprobar*) to fail, flunk; to dismiss temporarily; to astonish.

sus·pen·sión *f.* suspension; postponement, delay; uncertainty; cessation; a system of supporting devices (*automobile*).

sus·pen·so *adj.* suspended; hanging; pending; perplexed, astonished; **en** — in suspense; *m.* failure (*in an examination*).

sus·pi·caz *adj.* suspicious.

sus·pi·rar *v.* to sigh; to sigh (for), long (for).

sus·pi·ro *m.* sight; brief pause (*in music*).

sus·tan·cia *f.* substance; essence; *Andes* broth.

sus·tan·cial *adj.* substantial; nourishing.

sus·tan·cio·so *adj.* substantial, nourishing.

sus·tan·ti·vo *m.* noun; *adj.* substantive; real; independent.

sus·ten·tar *v.* to sustain; to support; to feed, nourish; to maintain; uphold.

sus·ten·to *m.* sustenance; food; support.

sus·ti·tu·ción *f.* substitution.

sus·ti·tu·í·ble *adj.* replaceable.

sus·ti·tu·ír³² *v. irr.* to substitute.

sus·ti·tu·to *v.* substitute.

sus·to *m.* scare, fright.

sus·trac·ción *f.* subtraction.

sus·tra·er⁴⁶ *v. irr.* to subtract; to remove, withdraw; — **se a** to evade, avoid, slip away from.

su·su·rrar *v.* to whisper; to murmur; to rustle; **-se** to be whispered or rumored about.

su·su·rro *m.* whisper; murmur; rustle.

su·til *adj.* subtle; keen; clever; crafty; thin, fine, delicate.

su·ti·le·za, su·ti·li·dad *f.* subtlety; keenness, cleverness; cunning; thinness, fineness.

su·yo *adj.* his, of his; her, of hers; your, of yours (*formal*); their, of theirs; *pron.* his, hers, yours (*formal*), theirs; **de** — naturally, by nature; **salirse con la suya** to get one's own way; **hacer de las suyas** to be up to one's tricks; **los -s** his (hers, theirs); his (her, their) own people.

T

ta·ba·co *m.* tobacco; *Carib:, Ven., Col.* cigar; snuff; *Col.* blow with the fist; **tabaquería** *f.* tobacco store, cigarstore.

tá·ba·no *m.* horsefly, gadfly.

ta·ber·na *f.* tavern, bar, liquor store.

ta·ber·ná·culo *m.* tabernacle.

ta·bi·que *m.* partition, partition wall.

ta·bla *f.* board, plank; plate of metal; slab; table, list; strip of ground; *Col.* chocolate tablet; **-s** draw, tie (*in games*); stage boards, the stage; **a raja** — cost what it may; *Am.* in great haste; **hacer** — **rasa de algo** to dis regard, omit, or ignore something; *Am.* to clear away all obstacles in the way of something.

ta·bla·do *m.* platform, stage; scaffold; floor boards.

ta·ble·ro *m.* board; panel; timber, piece of lumber; chessboard, checkerboard; store counter; large work table; gambling table; *Col., Ven., Mex.* bkackboard; **poner al** — to risk, endanger; — **de mando** control panel.

ta·ble·ta *f.* tablet; small thin board; memorandum pad.

ta·ble·te·ar *v.* to rattle; to make a continuous rattling or tapping sound.

ta·ble·te·o *m.* rattling sound; tapping.

ta·bli·lla *f.* tablet; slat, small thin board; splint; small bulletin board; **-s** wooden clappers.

ta·blón *m.* plank; large, thick boar.

ta·bu·re·te *m.* stool; footstool.

ta·ca·ñe·ría *f.* stinginess, tightness, miserliness.

ta·ca·ño *adj.* stingy, tight, miserly; sly.

tá·ci·to *adj.* tacit, implied; silent.

ta·ci·tur·no *adj.* taciturn, silent, sullen; sad.

ta·co *m.* wad; roll; plug, stopper; billiard cue; bite, snack; swear word; *Mex., C.A.* Mexican folded tortilla sandwich; *Am.* leather legging; *Ch., Andes* short, fat person; *Mex.* heel of a shoe; *Am.* pile, heap; **echar**

-s to curse, swear; *Mex.* **darse uno –** to strut, put on airs.

ta·cón *m.* heel of a shoe.

ta·co·ne·ar *v.* to click the heels, walk hard on one's heels.

ta·co·ne·o *m.* click, clicking (*of the heels*).

tác·ti·ca *f.* tactics.

tac·to *m.* tact; touch, sense of touch.

ta·cha *f.* flaw, defect, blemish.

ta·char *v.* (*borrar*) to cross out; to scratch out; to blot out; (*culpar*) to blame; to find fault with; to censure.

ta·chón *m.* stud; trimming, braid; blot.

ta·cho·nar *v.* to stud, ornament with studs; to adorn with trimming.

ta·chue·la *f.* tack, small nail; *Am.* metal dipper; *Am.* runt, "shorty".

ta·fe·tán *m.* taffeta; **– inglés** court plaster.

ta·hur *m.* gambler; cardsharp.

tai·ma·do *adj.* sly, crafty; *Am.* sullen, gloomy, gruff.

tai·ta = tatita. *See* **tata**.

ta·ja·da *f.* slice; cut.

ta·ja·lá·piz *m.* pencil sharpener.

ta·jan·te *adj.* cutting, sharp.

ta·jar *v.* to slice; to cut; to sharpen (*a pencil*).

ta·jo *m.* cut; gash; cutting edge; sheer cliff; chopping block.

tal *adj.* such; such a; **– cual** such as; so-so, fair; **– vez** perhaps; **el – Pedro** that fellow Peter; **un – García** a certain García; **– para cual** two of a kind; **un – por cual** a nobody; *adv.* just as, in such a way; **estaba – como le dejé** he was just as I left him; **con – (de) que** provided that; **¿qué –?** how are you?; hello!

ta·la·bar·te *m.* sword belt.

ta·la·drar *v.* to bore, drill; to pierce; to penetrate.

ta·la·dro *m.* auger, drill; bore, drill hole; *Am.* mine tunnel.

tá·la·mo *m.* bridal bed or chamber

ta·lan·te *m.* disposition; mood; appearance, manner.

tal·co *m.* talc (*a soft mineral*); **– en polvo** talcum powder.

ta·le·ga *f.* money bag, sack.

ta·len·to *m.* talent; ability, natural gift.

ta·len·to·so *adj.* talented, gifted.

ta·lis·mán *m.* talisman, charm.

ta·lón *m.* heel; stub, check, coupon.

ta·lo·na·rio *m.* stub book; **litro –** stub book.

ta·lo·ne·ar *v.* to tap with one's heel; to wal briskly.

ta·lo·ne·o *m.* tapping with the heel; loud footsteps.

ta·lla *f.* (*altura*) stature, height; (*labrado*) carving; (*lance entero*) round of a card game; (*rescate*) ransom; *Am.* chat; *Am.* thrashing, beating.

ta·llar *v.* to carve; to cut (*stone*); to appraise; to deal (*cards*); *Am.* to court, make love; *Andes, Col.* to bother, disturb.

ta·lla·rín *m.* noodle.

ta·lle *m.* figure, form; waist; fit (*of a dress*); looks, appearance; *Ven.* bodice.

ta·ller *m.* workshop; laboratory; studio; factory.

ta·llo *m.* stalk; stem, shoot, sprout.

ta·mal *m. Mex., C.A.* tamale; *Am.* vile trick, intrigue; *Am.* clumsy boundle.

ta·ma·ño *m.* size; *adj.* such a; of the size of; **– disparate** such a (big) mistake; **– como un elefante** big as an elephant; **tamañito** *adj.* very small; **tamañito así** about this little; **se quedó tamañito** he was (left) astonished, amazed.

tam·ba·le·ar·se *v.* to totter, stagger, sway, reel.

tam·bién *adv.* also, too; likewise.

tam·bor *m.* drum; drum-like object; drummer; pair of embroidery hoops; *Mex.* bedspring, spring mattress; **– de freno** brake drum; **tambora** *f.* bass drum; **tamboril** *m.* small drum; **tamborilero** *m.* drummer.

tam·bo·ri·le·ar *v.* to drum; to extol.

ta·miz *m.* fine sieve.

ta·mi·zar *v.* to sift; to blend.

tam·po·co *conj.* either (*after a negative*); **no lo hizo – he** did not do it either; **ni yo –** nor I either.

tan *adv.* (*contr. of* **tanto**) so, as; such a

tan·da *f.* turn; round, bout; task; gang, group; shift, relay; *Col., Ven., Mex., Carib:* section of a theatrical performance.

tan·gen·te *adj. & f.* tangent; **salirse por la –** to go off at a tangent; to avoid the issue.

tan·gi·ble *adj.* tangible.

tan·go *m.* tango.

tan·que *m.* tank; reservoir; *Col., Ven.* pond; *Mex.* swimming pool.

tan·tán *m.* clang; knock! knock!; sound of a bell, drum, etc.

tan·te·ar *v.* to probe, test; to sound out, feel out; to estimate, calculate approximately; *Cuba, Ven., Riopl.* to grope, feel one's way; *Am.* to lie in wait; *Mex.* to fool, make a fool of; *Ven., Mex., C.A.* **¡tantee Vd.!** just imagine!.

tan·te·o *m.* trial, test; calculation, estimate; score; **al - by guess;** hit or miss.

tan·to *adj., pron. & adv.* so much, as much; so; **-s** so many, as many; *m.* certain amount; counter, chip (*to keep score*); **cuarenta y –s** forty odd; **el – por ciento** percentage, rate; **un –** (*or* **algún –**) somewhat; **– como** as well as; as much as; **– . . . como** both. . . and; **– en la ciudad como en el campo** both in the city and in the country; **entre** (*or* **mientras**) **–** meanwhile; **por lo –** therefore.

ta·ñer *v.* to play (*an instrument*); to ring.

ta·ñi·do *m.* sound, tune; ring; twang (*of a guitar*).

ta·pa *f.* cover; lid; book cover; heel lift.

ta·pa·cu·bos *m.* hubcap.

ta·pa·de·ra *f.* cover, lid; one who shields another.

ta·par *v.* to cover; to plug, stop up; to veil; to hide; *Am.* to fill (*a tooth*); *Am.* to crush, crumple; *Am.* to cover with insults; **-se** to cover up; to wrap oneself up.

ta·pa·rra·bo *m.* loincloth; trunks.

ta·pe·ra *f. Am.* ruins; *Riopl., Andes* abandoned room or house.

ta·pe·te *m.* rug; table scarf.

ta·pia *f.* adobe wall; wall fence.

ta·piar *v.* to wall up; to block up (*a door or window*).

ta·pi·ce·ría *f.* tapestry; upholstery; tapestry shop; tapestry making.

ta·piz *m.* tapestry.

ta·pón *m.* plug, stopper, cork; bottle cap.

ta·qui·gra·fía *f.* shorthand.

ta·quí·gra·fo *m.* stenographer.

ta·qui·lla *f.* ticket office; box office, file (*for letters, papers, etc.*); *Am.* tavern, liquor store.

ta·ra·re·ar *v.* to hum.

ta·ra·re·o *m.* hum, humming.

ta·ras·ca·da *f.* snap, bite; snappy or harsh answer.

tar·dan·za *f.* delay; slowness.

tar·dar *v.* to delay; to be late; to be long (in); to take long (in); **-se** to delay oneself; to be delayed, **a más** – at the very latest.

tar·de *f.* afternoon; *adv.* late, **de – en –** from time to time, now and then.

tar·dí·o *adj.* late, slow.

tar·do *adj.* slow, lazy; tardy; late; stupid, dull; **tardón** *adj.* very slow; *m.* slowpoke, slow person.

ta·re·a *f.* task, job; anxiety, care.

ta·ri·fa *f.* tariff; list of duties, taxes, or prices; fare.

ta·ri·ma *f.* wooden plantform; low bench.

tar·je·ta *f.* card; **– postal** postcard.

ta·rro *m.* earthen jar; *Mex.* horn (*of an animal*); *Ch., Cuba, Andes* can; *Andes* top hat.

tar·ta *f.* tart.

tar·ta·mu·de·ar *v.* to stutter, stammer.

tar·ta·mu·de·o *m.* stammer, stammering.

tar·ta·mu·do *m.* stutterer, stammerer; *adj.* stuttering, stammering.

tar·te·ra *f.* griddle; baking pan.

ta·ru·go·m wooden block; wooden peg; blockhead, dunce; *adj. Andes* mischievous, devilish.

ta·sa *f.* measure; standard; rate, appraisal; valuation.

ta·sa·ción *f.* assessment, valuation, appraisal.

ta·sa·jo *m.* piece of jerked beef.

ta·sar *m.* to measure; to appraise; to rate.

ta·ta *f.* daddy, dad; *Mex., Andes* chief (*said by Indians to a superior*); **tatita** *m.* daddy; *Mex., Andes* dear chief or daddy (*said by Indians*).

ta·ta·ra·nie·to *m.* great-great-grandson.

tau·ro·ma·quia *f.* bullfighting.

ta·xe·ar *v.* to taxi (*said of a plane*).

ta·xi, ta·xí·me·tro *m.* taxi, taxicab.

ta·xis·ta *m. & f.* taxi driver.

ta·za *f.* cup; bowl; basin of a fountain.

ta·zón *m.* large cup; bowl; basin of a fountain.

té *m.* tea; *f.* T-square, T-shaped ruler.

te *obj. pron.* you (*fam. sing.*); to you; for you; yourself.

te·a·tral *adj.* theatrical.

te·a·tro *m.* theater; stage, scene, setting; **hacer -** to put on airs, show off.

te·cla *f.* key (*of a piano, typewriter, etc.*); **dar uno en la -** to hit the nail on the head, find the right way to do something.

te·cla·do *m.* keyboard.

te·cle·ar *v.* to finger the keys; to play the piano; to type.

te·cle·o *m.* fingering; movement of the keys (*typewriter, piano*).

téc·ni·ca *f.* technique.

téc·ni·co *adj.* technical; *m.* technical expert, technician.

te·co·lo·te *m. Am.* owl.

te·cha·do *m.* roof; shed; *p.p.* of **techar**.

te·char *v.* to roof.

te·cho *m.* roof; ceiling.

te·chum·bre *f.* roof; ceiling.

te·dio *m.* tediousness; boredom; bother.

te·dio·so *adj.* tedious, boring, tiresome.

te·ja *f.* tile; linden tree; *Am.* rear part of a saddle; **de -s abajo** here below, in this world.

te·ja·do *m.* roof; shed.

te·ja·ma·nil *m.* shingle, small thin board.

te·jar *m.* tile factory; *v.* to cover with tiles.

te·je·dor *m.* weaver.

te·jer *v.* to weave; to interlace; to braid; to knit.

te·ji·do *m.* textile, fabric; texture, weave; weaving, tissue.

te·jo *m.* disk; quoit; wight.

te·jón *m.* badger; bar of gold.

te·la *f.* cloth; membrane; web; film (*on the surface of liquids*); **– adhesiva** adhesive tape; **– de cebolla** onion skin; flimsy fabric; *Am.* **– emplástica** court plaster; **– metálica** wire screen; **poner en – de juicio** to call in question.

te·lar *m.* loom.

te·la·ra·ña *f.* cobweb, spider's web.

te·le·fé·ri·co *m.* telpher; car suspended on aerial cables.

te·le·fo·ne·ar *v.* to telephone.

te·le·fó·ni·co *adj.* telephonic, telephone (*used as adj.*); **receptor** – telephone receiver.

te·lé·fo·no *m.* telephone; **telefonista** *m. & f.* telephone operator.

te·le·gra·fí·a *f.* telegraphy.

te·le·gra·fiar[17] *v.* to telegraph.

te·le·grá·fi·co *adj.* telegraphic.

te·lé·gra·fo *m.* telegraph; **– sin hilos** (*or* – **inalámbrico**) wireless telegraph; **telegrafista** *m. & f.* telegraph operator.

te·le·gra·ma *m.* telegram.

te·les·co·pio *m.* telescope.

te·les·quí *m.* ski lift.

te·le·ti·po *m.* teletype.

te·le·vi·sión f. television.

te·lón m. theater curtain; **– de boca** drop curtain; **– de foro** drop scene.

te·ma m. theme; subject; f. fixed idea, mania.

tem·blar[1] v. irr. to tremble; to shake; to quiver.

tem·blón adj. tremulous, trembling, shaking, quivering.

tem·blor m. tremor, trembling; shiver; quake; **– de tierra** earthquake.

tem·blo·ro·so adj. trembling, shaking.

te·mer v. to fear; to dread, to suspect.

te·me·ra·rio adj. rash, reckless.

te·me·ri·dad f. temerity, recklessness; folly.

te·me·ro·so adj. fearful; suspicious; timid.

te·mi·ble adj. terrible, dreadful.

te·mor m. fear; dread, suspicion.

tém·pa·no m. thick slice or chunk (of anything); kettledrum; drumhead (parchment stretched over the end of a drum); **– de hielo** block of ice; iceberg.

tem·pe·ra·men·to m. temperament; climate.

tem·pe·ra·tu·ra f. temperature.

tem·pes·tad f. tempest, storm.

tem·pes·tuo·so adj. tempestuous, stormy.

tem·pla·do p.p. & adj. (moderado) tempered; tuned; moderate; temperate; lukewarm; (valiente) brave; Andes in love; Am. half-drunk; Am. hard, severe; **estar mal –** to be in a bad humor.

tem·plan·za f. temperance; moderation; mildness.

tem·plar v. to temper; to moderate; to calm; to soften; to tune; **-se** to be tempered, moderate, to control oneself; Andes to fall in love; Col. to take to one's heels; Am. to stuff oneself.

tem·ple m. temper; temperament, valor, courage, harmony (of musical instruments); Am. sweetheart, **de mal –** in a bad humor.

tem·plo m. temple; church.

tem·po·ra·da f. period of time, season; **- de ópera** opera season.

tem·po·ral adj. temporal; secular, worldly; temporary; m. weather; storm; spell of rainy weather.

tem·pra·ne·ro adj. habitually early or ahead of time; **ser –** to be an early riser.

tem·pra·no adj. early; premature; adv. early.

te·na·ci·dad f. tenacity, tenaciousness; perseverance.

te·na·ci·llas f. pl. small tongs; pincers, tweezers; sugar tongs; curling iron.

te·naz adj. tenacious; firm, strong, resistant, stubborn.

te·na·zas f. pl. pincers; pliers; tongs; forceps (for pulling teeth); **tenazuelas** f. pl. tweezers, small pincers.

ten·de·de·ro m. place tohang or spread clothes; clothesline.

ten·den·cia f. tendency, inclination.

ten·der[1] v. irr. (extender) to spread out; to hang to dry; to stretch out; to lay out; (propender) to tend, have a tendency, move (toward); Carib:, Mex., C.A., Riopl.

Andes to make (a bed); **-se** to stretch oneself out; to lay all one's cards on the table; to run at full gallop.

tén·der m. tender (of a train).

ten·de·ro m. storekeeper; tentmaker.

ten·dón m. tendon, sinew.

ten·du·cho m. wretched little shop.

te·ne·bro·so adj. dark, shadowy; gloomy.

te·ne·dor m. table fork; holder, possessor, keeper; **– de libros** bookkeeper.

te·ne·du·ría f. office and position of bookkeeper; **– de libros** bookkeeping.

te·ner[45] v. irr. to have; to possess; to hold; **– en mucho** to esteem highly; **– por** to consider, judge; **– que** (+ inf.) to have to; **– gana** (or **– ganas**) **de** to desire, feel like; **– miedo** (**sueño, frío, hambre,** etc.) to be afraid (sleepy, cold, hungry, etc.); **– . . . años** to be . . . years old; **-se** tostand firm: to hold on.

te·ne·ría f. tannery.

te·nien·te m. first lieutenant; substitute, deputy.

te·nis m. tennis.

te·nor m. tenor; text, literal meaning; kind, sort, nature.

ten·sión f. tension; strain.

ten·so adj. tense; tight, taut.

ten·ta·ción f. temptation.

ten·tá·cu·lo m. tentacle, feeler.

ten·ta·dor adj. tempting; m. tempter; the devil.

ten·ta·le·ar v. to grope, feel around; to finger, touch; to fumble (for something).

ten·tar[1] v. irr. to tempt; to touch, feel with the fingers; to grope; to attempt, try; to test; to probe, examine with a probe.

ten·ta·ti·va f. attempt, trial.

ten·ta·ti·vo adj. tentative.

te·nue adj. delicate, thin; flimsy; worthless.

te·ñir[5,19] v. irr. to dye; to tinge; to darken (the color of a painting).

te·o·lo·gal, te·o·ló·gi·co adj. theological.

te·o·lo·gía f. theology.

te·o·ría f. theory.

te·ó·ri·co adj. theoretical.

te·qui·la m. Mex. tequila (liquor made from the maguey plant).

ter·ce·ro adj. third; m. third person; mediator, go-between; tertiary (member of the third order St. Francis).

ter·ciar v. (atravesar) to sling across one's shoulders; (dividir) to divide into three parts; (intervenir) to intervene, mediate; to meddle, join (in); (equilibrar) to balance the load on a pack animal; Mex., Col. to load or carry on the back; Am. to adulterate, add water to; Am. to mix.

ter·cio adj. third; m. one third; half of a mule load; military regiment or division; Col., Carib:, Mex. bale, bundle; **hacer uno mal –** to hinder, interfere, **– de varas** the banderilla part of the bullfight.

ter·cio·pe·lo m. velvet.

ter•co *adj.* obstinate, stubborn; hard; *Am.* harsh, severe.

ter•gi•ver•sar *v.* to distort, twist.

ter•mi•na•ción *f.* termination, end; ending.

ter•minal *adj.* terminal, final.

ter•mi•nan•te *adj.* closing, endign; decisive, final.

ter•mi•nar *v.* to terminate, end; to finish; -se to end.

tér•mi•no *m.* end; completion; goal, object, boundary, limit; terminal; term; word, phrase; **en otros -s** in other words; **por – medio** on an average; as a rule; **primer –** foreground.

ter•mo *m.* thermos bottle.

ter•mó•me•tro *m.* thermometer.

ter•mo•nu•clear *adj.* thermonuclear.

Ter•mos *f.* Thermos bottle (*trademark*).

ter•mós•ta•to *m.* thermostat.

ter•ne•ra *f.* calf; veal.

ter•ne•za *f.* tenderness; softness; affection; affectionate word; caress.

ter•no *m.* group or combination of three; suit of clothes; *Carib:*, *Mex.* set of jewels (*earrings, necklace, and brooch*); *Am.* cup and saucer; **echar** (*or* **soltar**) **un –** to utter a bad word; to curse, swear.

ter•nu•ra *f.* tenderness.

ter•que•dad *f.* obstinacy, stubbornness.

te•rra•do *m.* terrace; flat roof.

te•rra•mi•ci•na *f.* Terramycin.

te•rra•plén *m.* railroad embankment.

te•rra•te•nien•te *m.* & *f.* landholder.

te•rra•za *f.* terrace, veranda; flat roof.

te•rre•mo•to *m.* earthquake.

te•rre•nal *adj.* earthly, worldly.

te•rre•no *m.* land; ground; field; *adj.* earthly, worldly.

te•rres•tre *adj.* terrestrial; earthly.

te•rri•ble *adj.* terrible.

te•rrí•fi•co *adj.* terrific.

te•rri•to•rio *m.* territory.

te•rrón *m.* clod; lump (*of sugar*).

te•rror *m.* terror.

ter•so *adj.* polished, smooth.

ter•tu•lia *f.* evening party; social gathering; club; conversation; *Riopl.*, *Cuba*, *Ven.* theater gallery.

ter•tu•lia•no, **ter•tu•lio** *m.* member of a **tertulia.**

te•sis *f.* thesis.

te•són *m.* grit, endurance, pluck, persistence.

te•so•n•ero *adj. Mex.*, *Cuba*, *Andes* tenacious, stubborn, persevering, pesistent.

teso•re•ría *f.* treasury; **tesorero** *m.* treasurer.

te•so•ro *m.* treasure, trasury.

tes•ta *f.* head; crown of the head, front.

tes•ta•men•to *m.* testament; will.

tes•ta•ru•dez *f.* stubbornness, obstinacy.

tes•ta•ru•do *adj.* stubborn.

tes•ti•go *m.* & *f.* witness; *m.* testimony, proof, evidence; **– de cargo** witness for the prosecution; **– de vista** eyewitness.

tes•ti•mo•niar *v.* to give testimony of; to serve as a witness.

tes•ti•mo•nio *m.* testimony; proof, evidence; **levantar falso –** to bear false witness.

tes•tuz *m.* nape; crown of the head (*of certain animals*).

te•ta *f.* teat, nipple; breast, udder.

te•te•ra *f.* teapot; teakettle; *Mex.*, *Cuba*, *Col.* **tetero** nursing bottle.

té•tri•co *adj.* sad, melancholy, gloomy.

tex•til *adj.* textile.

tex•to *m.* text; quotation; textbook.

tez *f.* complexion, skin.

ti *pers. pron.* (*used after prep.*) you; yourself (*fam. sing.*).

tí•a *f.* aunt; older woman; *Ven.* **– rica** pawnshop; **no hay tu –** there is no use or hope; there is no way out of it; **quedarse una para –** to remain an old maid.

ti•bio *adj.* tepid, lukewarm, indifferent; *Am.* annoyed, angry.

ti•bu•rón *m.* shark.

ti•co *adj.* & *m. Am.* Costa Rican (*humorous nickname*).

tiem•po *m.* time; weather; tense, **a –** in time, on time; **a su –** in due time, at the proper time; **a un –** at one and the same time; **andando el –** in time, as time goes on.

tien•da *f.* store; tent, **– de campaña** camping tent, army tent.

tien•ta *f.* probe (*surgical instrument*); **a -s** gropingly, feeling one's way; **andar a -s** to grope, feel one's way.

tien•to *m.* touch; tact; blind man's stick; steady hand; blow; tentacle, feeler (*of an insect*); *Andes, Riopl.* saddle strap, leather strap, thong; *Am.* snack; *Am.* swallow of liquor; **dar un –** to make a trial or attempt; **hacer algo con mucho –** to do something with great care or caution; **perder el –** to lose one's skill; *Andes* **tener a uno a los -s** to keep someone within sight; *Ven.* **tener la vida en un –** to be in great danger.

tier•no *adj.* tender, soft; young; recent, new; sensitive, affectionate; *Am.* green, unripe.

tie•rra *f.* earth; land; ground; soil; native land; **– adentro** inland; **– firme** mainland; solid ground; **dar en – con alguien** to overthrow someone; **echar por –** to knock down; to demolish; **tomar –** to land.

tie•so *adj.* stiff, rigid; stuck-up; firm: stubborn.

ties•to *m.* flowerpot; broken piece of earthenware; *Am.* pot.

tie•su•ra *f.* stiffness.

ti•fo *m.* typhus; **tifoidea** *f.* typhoid fever.

ti•fón *m.* typhoon; waterspout.

tifus m. typhus.

ti•gre *m.* tiger.

ti•je•ra *f.* (*usually* **tijeras**) scissors; saw horse, **silla de - folding** chair; **tener buena –** (*or* **tener buenas - s**) to have a sharp tongue; to be a gossip.

ti•je•re•ta•da f., **tijeretazo** m. snip, cut, clip (*with the scissors*).

ti•je•re•te•ar v. to snip, cut, clip (with scissors); to criticize others, gossip.

til•dar v. to accent (*a word*); to put a tilde over the **n**; to stigmatize.

til•de f. tilde (*mark over an* **n**); blemish; jot, bit, speck; *Col.* accent mark.

tim•brar v. to stamp, mark with a seal.

tim•bre m. revenue stamp; seal; crest (*on a coat of arms*), call bell; tiembre (*quality of tone, tone color*); merit, fame; glorious deed, *Am.* postage stamp.

tl•mi•dez f. timidity; shyness.

tí•mi•do adj. timid; shy.

ti•món m. helm; rudder; beam of a plow.

ti•mo•ne•ar v. to steer (*a ship*).

ti•mo•ra•to adj. timorous, timid.

tím•pa•no m. eardrum; kettledrum.

ti•na f. large earthen jar; vat, tank, rub; bathtub.

ti•na•co m. tank, vat, tub.

ti•na•ja f. large earthen jar.

ti•nie•blas f. pl. darkness; obscurity; ignorance, confusion; Tenebrae (*Holy Week religious service*).

ti•no m. acumen, keen insight, good judgment; tact; accurate aim; good sense of touch; tank, vat.

tin•ta f. ink; dye; tint, hue; **-s** paints; **– simpática** invisible ink; **saber de buena** – to know on good authority.

tin•te m. tint, hue; tinge; color; dye; dyeing.

tin•te•ri•llo m. shyster. See **picapleitos**.

tin•te•ro m. inkwell, inkstand; ink roller (*printing*); *Am.* writing materials, desk set.

tin•ti•ne•ar v. to tinkle.

tin•ti•ne•o m. tinkle, tinkling.

tin•to adj. tinged; red (*wine*); *Am.* darkred, *p.p. irr.* of **teñir**.

tin•to•re•ría f. cleaner's and dyer's shop.

tin•to•re•ro m. dyer.

tin•tu•ra f. tincture; tint, color; dye.

tin•tu•rar v. to tincture; to tinge; to dye.

ti•ño•so adj. scabby, mangy; stingy

tí•o m. uncle; old man; good old man, fellow, guy; *Riopl., Mex., Ven., Andes* **el cuento del** – deceitful story (*told to extract money*).

tío•vi•vo m. merry-go-round.

tí•pi•co adj. typical; *Am.* corrected (*edition*).

ti•ple m. & f. high soprano singer; m. treble; soprano voice; treble guitar.

tipo m. type; class; model, standard; fellow, guy; *Am.* rate of interest, *Am.* **– de cambio** rate of exchange; **buen** – good-looking fellow.

ti•po•gra•fía f. typography, printing; press, printing shop.

ti•ra f. strip; stripe; *Mex.* **estar hecho -s** to be in rags, *Ven.* **sacar a uno las -s** to tan one's hide, beat one to pieces.

ti•ra•bu•zón m. corkscrew.

ti•ra•da f. throw; issue, edition, printing; *Am.* tirade, long speech; *Am.* sly trick; *Am.* dash (*on horseback*); **de una** - all at once, at one fell swoop.

ti•ra•dor m. shooter; thrower; slingshot; bell cord; handle; printer; *Am.* leather belt with pockets; **– de goma** slingshot.

ti•ra•nía f. tyranny.

ti•rá•ni•co adj. tyrannical.

ti•ra•no adj. tyrannical; m. tyrant.

ti•ran•te adj. pulling; stretched, taut; strained; m. trace (*of a harness*); brace; **-s** suspenders; supporters (*for stockings*).

ti•ran•toz f. tension, tightness; strain; pull.

ti•rar v. (*lanzar*) to throw; to throw away; to shoot, fire; (*imprimir*) to draw; to print; (*atraer*) to pull; to attract; *Am.* to cart; **– a** to tend toward; to resemble; to aim at; **– de** to pull, tug; **– bien a la espada** to handle a sword well; **ir tirando** to get along; **a todo** (*or* **a más**) – at the most; *Am.* **al** – haphazardly; **-se** to throw oneself; to lie down; *Mex., C.A., Col., Ven., Riopl., Andes* **tirársela de** to boast of.

ti•ri•tar v. to shiver.

ti•ro m. (*disparo*) throw; shot; (*pieza*) piece of artillery; (*alcance*) range of a gun; shooting range; (*carga*) charge of a gun; team (*of horses*); chimney draft; mine shaft; *Am.* issue, printing; *Am.* cartage, transport; **-s** *Am.* suspenders; **– al blanco** target practice; *Ch., Andes* **al** – at once; *Ven.* **de a** (*or* **de al**) – at once; completely; **caballo de** – draft horse; **ni a -s** absolutely not (*not even if you shoot me*).

ti•rón m. jerk, sudden pull; **de un** – all at once, with one big pull.

ti•ro•ne•ar v. *C.A., Mex., Riopl.* to pull, jerk; *Col.* to attract.

ti•ro•te•ar v. to shoot around, to shoot at random; **-se** to exchange shots.

ti•ro•te•o m. shooting; exchange of shots; skirmish.

ti•rria f. aversion, grudge; **tenerle – a una persona** to have a strong dislike for someone; to hold a grudge against someone.

tí•si•co adj. tubercular, consumptive.

ti•sis f. tuberculosis, consumption.

tí•te•re m. puppet; ridiculous little fellow; **-s** puppet show.

ti•ti•la•ción f. flicker; twinkle; **titileo** m. flickering; twinkling; glimmer.

ti•ti•lar v. to flicker; to twinkle.

ti•tu•be•ar v. to hesitate; to totter, stagger; to grope; to stutter, stammer.

ti•tu•be•o m. hesitation, wavering.

ti•tu•lar v. to entitle; to name; **-se** to be called or named; to call oneself; to receive a title; adj. titular, in name only.

tí•tu•lo m. (*letrero*) title; heading; sign; inscription; (*derecho*) claim, legal right; (*grado*) degree, diplo-

ma; credential; titled person; merit; bond, certificate; **a – de** under the pretext of; in the capacity of.

ti·za f. chalk.

tiz·na·do adj. sooty, covered with soot; smutty; dirty; Ven. drunk; p.p. of **tiznar**.

tiz·nar v. to smudge, smut; to smear with soot.

tiz·ne m. soot; smut; **tiznón** m. smudge.

ti·zón m. firebrand (piece of burning wood); rust, blight (on plants); stain (on one's honor).

to·a·lla f. towel.

to·bi·llo m. ankle.

to·ca·dis·cos m. record player; phonograph.

to·ca·do m. headdress; hairdo, coiffure; adj. "touched", half-cruzy; p.p. of **tocar**.

to·ca·dor m. dressing table; boudoir, dressing room; dressing case; player (of a musical instrument).

to·car v. to touch; to play (an instrument); to toll, ring; to knock, rap; **– en** to stop over in; **-le a uno** to fall to one's lot; to be one's share; to be one's turn; to concern one; **-se** to fix one's hair, to become "touched", go slightly crazy.

to·ca·yo m. namesake.

to·ci·no m. bacon; salt pork; lard.

to·cón m. stub, stump (of a tree, arm or leg).

to·da·vía adv. still; yet; even.

to·do adj. all, whole; every, each; **– hombre** every man; **-s los días** every day; **a – correr** at full or top speed; m. whole; all; everything; **-s** everybody; **ante – first** of all; **así y –** in spite of that, **con –** in spite of that; **del –** wholly.

to·do·po·de·ro·so adj. almighty.

to·ga f. gown, robe (worn by a judge, professor, etc.); Roman toga.

tol·de·ría f. Riopl. Indian camp, Indian village.

tol·do m. awning; pomp, vanity; Riopl. Indian hut.

to·le·ran·cia f. tolerance, toleration; **tolerante** adj. tolerant.

to·le·rar v. to tolerate; to allow; to overlook, let pass.

to·le·te m. Col., Mex., Cuba stick, club, cudgel; Am. raft.

to·ma f. taking; seizure, capture, dose; tap (of a water main); Am., irrigation ditch; **– de corriente** plug, electric outlet.

to·mar v. (ASIR) to take; to grasp, catch; to capture, (beber) to drink; **– a pechos** to take to heart, take seriously; **-lo a mal** to take it amiss; **– el pelo a** to make fun of, make a fool of; **– por la derecha** to turn to the right; **-se con** to quarrel with.

to·ma·te m. tomato.

to·mi·llo m. thyme.

to·mo m. tome, volume; Am. heavy person; Am. dull, silent person; Am. **buen – a** heavy drinker; **de – y lomo** bulky; important.

ton: sin – ni son without rhyme or reason.

to·na·da f. tune, song; Andes singsong; Andes, Mex., Carib:, Riopl. local accent; **tonadilla** f. little tune;

short popular song.

to·nel m. keg, cask, barrel.

to·ne·la·da f. ton.

to·ne·la·je m. tonnage.

tó·ni·co adj. & m. tonic.

to·no m. tone; tune, key, pitch; accent; manner; vigor, strength; **de buen –** of good taste, stylish; **subirse de –** to put on airs.

ton·te·ra = tontería.

ton·te·rí·a f. foolishness; stupidity.

ton·to adj. foolish; stupid; **a tontas y a locas** recklessly, without thought; m. fool; dunce; Col., Ch. a game of cards.

to·par v. to collide with, run into, bump into; to encounter; to find; to run across; to butt; Am. to gamble; Col. to light with the fists; Carib., Mex., Riopl., Andes, Col. to meet, greet.

to·pe m. butt, bump, collision; encounter; bumper; **hasta el –** up to the top; **estar hasta los -s** to be filled up.

to·pe·ta·da f., **topetazo** m. butt; bump, blow on the head; **topetón** m. hard bump, collision; butt.

to·pe·tear v. to butt; to bump.

tó·pi·co m. topic, subject.

to·po m. mole (small animal); dunce; awkward person.

to·que m. touch; ringing; beat (of a drum); tap, sound (of a trumpet, clarinet, etc.); assay; **piedra de –** touchstone; **¡allí está el –!** there is the difficulty!; there is the real test!.

to·qui·lla f. triangular handkerchief; ribbon; hatband.

tor·be·li·no m. whirlwind; rush, bustle, confusión.

tor·ce·du·ra f. twist; sprain, strain.

tor·cer[2.10] v. irr. to twist; to turn; to bend; to sprain, to distort; **-se** to become twisted, bent, or sprained; to get crooked; to go astray; to turn sour (said of wine); Am. to get offended, angry.

tor·ci·do p.p. & adj. twisted, turned, bent; crooked; angry, resentful; Am. unfortunate, unlucky; **estar – con** to be on unfriedly terms with; m. twisted roll of candied fruit; coarse silk twist; Mex., Carib: gesture or look of disdain; Andes lasso made of twisted leather.

tor·di·llo adj. greyish, dapple-grey.

tor·do adj. dapple-grey; m. thrush; dappe-grey horse.

to·re·ar v. to perform in a bullfight; to incite, provoke (a bull); to tease.

to·re·ro m. bullfigter; adj. relating to bullfighting.

tor·men·ta f. storm, tempest; misfortune.

tor·men·to m. torment; torture; rack (instrument of torture), anguish; pain.

tor·nar v. to return; to turn; to change, alter; **– a hacer-lo** to do it again.

tor·na·so·la·do adj. iridescent, rainbowcolored; changeable (silk).

tor·ne·ar v. to turn in a lathe; to do lathe work; to fight in a tournament.

tor·ne·o *m.* tournament.

tor·ni·llo *m.* screw; clamp, vise; **faltarle a uno un —** to have little sense, "have a screw loose".

tor·no *m.* turn; lathe; turnstile; revolving server, winch or windlass (*machine for lifting or pulling, turned by a crank*); **— de hilar** spinning wheel; **en —** around.

to·ro *m.* bull; *Mex.*, *Col.* difficult question; **-s** bullfight; *Am.* **estar en las astas del —** to be in a predicament.

to·ron·ja *f.* grapefruit.

tor·pe *adj.* stupid, dull; clumsy; slow; lewd.

tor·pe·de·ar *v.* to torpedo.

tor·pe·do *m.* torpedo; **torpedero** *m.* torpedo boat.

tor·pe·za *f.* stupidity, dullness, clumsiness; slowness; moral turpitude, lewdness.

to·rre *f.* tower; turret, castle (*in chess*).

to·rren·te *m.* torrent; flood; **— de voz** powerful voice.

to·rre·ón *m.* large tower (*of a fortress, castle, etc.*).

tó·rri·do *adj.* torrid.

tor·sión *f.* twist; sprain.

tor·ta *f.* torte, round cake; round loaf.

tor·ti·lla *f.* omelet; *Mex.*, *C.A.* tortilla (*flat, thin cornmeal cake*).

tór·to·la *f.* turtledove.

tor·tu·ga *f.* tortoise; turtle.

tor·tuo·so *adj.* tortuous, twisting, winding; sly.

tor·tu·ra *f.* torture; grief, affliction.

tor·tu·rar *v.* to torture.

tor·vo *adj.* grim, stern, severe.

tos *f.* cough; **— ferina** whooping cough.

tos·co *adj.* coarse, harsh, rough.

to·ser *v.* to cough; *Am.* to brag, boast.

tos·que·dad *f.* coarseness, crudeness, roughness; rudeness.

tos·ta·da *f.* toast, toasted bread; *Am.* boring visit or conversation; *Ven.* toasted **tortilla; dar** (*or* **pegar**) **una — a uno** to play a mean trick on someone; *Am.* to make someone very angry.

tos·ta·do *p.p.* & *adj.* toasted; roasted; tanned; *Am.* worn out, tired out; *m.* toasting; *Am.* roasted corn.

tos·ta·dor *m.* toaster.

tos·tar² *v. irr.* to toast; to tan; to overheat; to roast (*coffee*).

tos·tón *m.* toast dipped in oil; small roasted pig; *Mex.*, *C.A.* coin worth half a Mexican peso.

to·tal *adj.* & *m.* total.

to·ta·li·dad *f.* entirety, whole.

to·ta·li·ta·rio *adj.* totalitarian.

tó·xi·co *adj.* toxic.

to·xi·na *f.* toxin (*poison produced within animals and plants*).

to·za *f.* wooden block; stump; log; piece of bark.

tra·ba *f.* bond, tie; binding or locking device; fastener, fetter, shackle; hindrance, obstacle.

tra·ba·do *adj.* *Col.*, *Riopl.*, *Mex.* tonguetied; *p.p.* of **trabar**.

tra·ba·ja·dor *adj.* industrious; *m.* worker, laborer.

tra·ba·jar *v.* to work; to labor; to strive.

tra·ba·jo *m.* work; labor; difficulty, obstacle, trouble; hardship.

tra·ba·jo·so *adj.* laborious, difficult; troublesome; *Am.* unobliging; *Am.* demanding.

tra·ba·len·guas *m.* tongue twister.

tra·bar *v.* to join, fasten; to clasp; to shackle; to brace, to impede; **— amistad con alguien** to become friends with someone; **— batalla** to join in battle; **— conversación** to be engaged in conversation; to engage in conversation; **-se** *Riopl.*, *Mex.*, *Ven.* to stammer; **-se de palabras** to get into an argument.

trac·ción *f.* traction.

trac·tor *m.* tractor.

tra·di·ción *f.* tradition.

tra·di·cio·nal *adj.* traditional.

tra·duc·ción *f.* translation.

tra·du·cir²⁵ *v. irr.* to translate; to interpret.

tra·duc·tor *m.* translator.

tra·er⁴⁶ *v. irr.* to bring; to carry; to lead, conduct; to have; to bring about; to wear; **— a uno inquieto** to keep one disturbed; **— a uno a mal —** to mistreat someone; to bother someone; **-se bien** to dress well; to carry oneself well.

tra·fa·gar⁷ *v.* to traffic, trade; to roam about; to bustle, hustle; to toil.

trá·fa·go *m.* trade, commerce; bustle, hustle; toil.

tra·fi·can·te *m.* trader; dealer; tradesman.

tra·fi·car⁶ *v.* to traffic; trade; *Ven.* to pass or move back and forth (*as traffic*). See **transitar.**

trá·fi·co *m.* traffic; trade, commerce.

tra·ga·luz *f.* skylight.

tra·gar⁷ *v.* to swallow; to gulp; to engulf, swallow up.

tra·ge·dia *f.* tragedy.

trá·gi·co *adj.* tragic.

tra·go *m.* swallow, gulp; misfortune; *Am.* brandy, hard liquor; **a -s** slowly, by degrees; **echar un —** to take a drink; **tragón** *m.* glutton; *adj.* gluttonous.

trai·ción *f.* treason; treachery; **a —** treacherously, deceitfully.

trai·cio·nar *v.* to betray.

trai·cio·ne·ro *adj.* treacherous; deceitful; *m.* traitor.

traí·do *adj.* used, old, worn out; **muy - y llevado** very worn out; *p.p.* of **traer.**

trai·dor *adj.* treacherous; *m.* traitor; betrayer.

tra·je *m.* dress; suit; gown; **— de etiqueta** (**— de ceremonia,** *or* **— de parada**) formal gown; formal suit; dress uniform; **— de luces** bullfighter's costume; *Col.*, *C.A.*, *Mex.*, *Riopl.* **— sastre** woman's tailor-made suit.

tra·je·a·do *p.p.* & *adj.* dressed, clothed.

tra·jín *m.* traffic, going and coming; hustle, bustle, commotion.

tra·ji·nar *v.* to carry, cart back and forth; to go back and forth; to bustle, hustle.

tra•ma f. plot; sheme; conspiracy; woof (*horizontal threads of a fabric*).

tra•mar v. to weave; to plot; to scheme.

tra•mi•tar v. to transact; to take legal steps; to negotiate.

trá•mi•te m. transaction, procedure, step, formality.

tra•mo m. stretch, lap, span; short distance; regular interval; flight of stairs.

tram•pa f. trap; snare, hatch, trap door; hinged section of a counter; spring door; fraud; trick.

tram•pe•ar v. to trick, cheat, swindle.

tram•pis•ta m. & f. cheat, crook, swindler.

tram•po•lín m. springboard.

tram•po•so adj. deceitful, tricky; m. swindler, cheat.

tran•ca f. crossbar, bolt; pole, prop; club, stick; *Ven.*, *Riopl.* rustic gate, *Riopl.* fence with gates; *Mex.*, *Ven.* **saltar las -s** to jump over the fence; to lose one's patience, rebel, get angry; *Ch.*, *Riopl.*, *Andes*, *Mex.* **tener una** - to be drunk.

tran•ce m. critical moment; dangerous situation; **el último** – the last moment of life; **a todo** – at any cost, cost what it may.

tran•co m. stride, long step; threshold; **a -s** hurriedly; **en dos -s** in a jiffy; *Riopl.* **al** – striding, with long steps.

tran•que•ar v. to stride along.

tran•que•ra f. stockade, wooden fence; *Riopl.*, *Cuba*, *Ven.*, large gate (*made with* **trancas**).

tran•qui•li•dad f. tranquillity, peacefulness.

tran•qui•li•zar v. to quiet, calm down; to pacify; **-se** to become tranquil, calm down.

tran•qui•lo adj. tranquil, peaceful.

tran•sac•ción f. transaction, negotiation; compromise.

tran•sar v. *Am.* to compromise, yield, give in.

trans•a•tlán•ti•co adj. transatlantic; m. transatlantic steamer.

trans•bor•dar = **trasbordar.**

trans•bor•do = **trasbordo.**

trans•cen•den•cia f. consequence, importance; penetration.

trans•cen•den•tal adj. consequential, important, far-reaching.

trans•cu•rrir v. to pass, elapse.

trans•cur•so m. passing, lapse (*of time*).

tran•seún•te m. passer-by; pedestrian; transient; adj. transient.

trans•fe•ren•cia f. transference, transfer.

trans•fe•rir v. irr. to transfer.

trans•for•ma•ción f. transformation.

trans•for•ma•dor m. transformer.

trans•for•mar v. to transform.

trans•gre•dir v. to transgress.

trans•gre•sión f. transgression.

trans•gre•sor m. transgressor, offender.

tran•si•ción f. transition.

tran•si•gen•te adj. compromising, yielding, pliable.

tran•si•gir v. to compromise, yield, make consessionns; to settle by compromise.

tran•sis•tor m. transistor.

tran•si•ta•ble adj. passable (*road*).

tran•si•tar v. to pass or move back and forth (*as traffic*).

trán•si•to m. transit; traffic; passing; passage; transition; **de** – on the way, in transit, passing through.

tran•si•to•rio adj. transitory.

trans•mi•sión f. transmission; – **automática** automatic transmission.

trans•mi•sor m. transmitter; adj. transmitting.

trans•mi•tir v. to transmit.

trans•pa•ren•cia f. transparency.

trans•pa•ren•te adj. transparent; lucid, clear; m. window shade; stained-glass window.

trans•po•ner v. irr. to transpose; to transfer; to transplant; to go beyond, go over to the other side; **-se** to hide from view, go behind; to set, go below the horizon.

trans•por•ta•ción f. transportation, transport.

trans•por•tar v. to transport, to transpose (*music*); **-se** to be transported, carried away by strong feeling; to be in ecstasy.

trans•por•te m. transport, transportation; transport vessel; ecstasy; **- de locura** fit of madness.

trans•pues•to p.p. of **transponer**.

trans•ver•sal adj. transversal, transverse; **sección -** cross section.

trans•ver•so adj. transverse, cross.

tran•vía m. streetcar; streetcar track.

tra•pa•ce•ar v. to swindle, cheat; to racketeer.

tra•pa•ce•ría f. racket, fraud, swindle.

tra•pa•ce•ro m. racketeer; cheat, swindler; adj. cheating, deceiving

tra•pa•cis•ta m. & f. racketeer; swindler, cheat.

tra•pe•a•dor m. *Am.* mopper; *Andes*, *Ven.*, *Col.*, *C.A.*, *Mex.*, *Cuba* mop.

tra•pe•ar v. *Am.* to mop; *Am.*, to beat up, give (*someone*) a licking.

tra•pi•che m. sugar mill; press (*for extracting juices*); *Andes* grinding machine (*for pulverizing minerals*).

tra•pi•son•da f. escapade, prank; brawl; noisy spree.

tra•po m. rag; *C.A.*, *Ven.*, *Ur.* cloth; -s clothes; **a todo - at** full sail; speedly; **poner a uno como un -** to make one feel like a rag; **sacarle a uno los -s al sol** to exhibit somebody's dirty linen; **soltar el -** to burst out laughing or crying.

tra•po•so adj. *Am.* ragged, tattered, in rags.

trá•que•a f. trachea, windpipe.

tra•que•te•ar v. to rattle; to shake; to jolt; to crack, crackle.

tra•que•te•o m. rattling; shaking; jolting; cracking, crackling; *Riopl.*, *Col.*, *Ven.*, *C.A.*, *Mex.*, *Carib.*, *Andes* uproar, din; *Am.* noisy, disorderly traffic.

tras *prep.* after; in search of; behind, in back of; **- de** behind, after; besides, in addition to; *interj.* ¡ **- !** bang!

tras•bor•dar *v.* to transfer.

tras•bor•do *m.* transfer.

tras•cen•den•cia = transcendencia.

tras•cen•den•tal = transcendental.

tra•se•gar[1.7] *v. irr.* to upset, overturn; to change from one place to another; to pour from one container to another.

tra•se•ro *adj.* rear, hind, back; *m.* rump.

tras•la•dar *v.* to move, remove; to transfer, to postpone; to translate; to transcribe, copy.

tras•la•do *m.* transfer; transcript, written copy.

tras•lu•cir•se[13] *v. irr.* to be translucent; to be transparent, clear, evident.

tras•no•char *v.* to sit up all night; to stay awake all night; to spend the night out.

tras•pa•lar *v.* to shovel.

tras•pa•pe•lar *v.* to mislay, misplace (*a paper, letter, document, etc.*); **-se** to become mislaid among other papers.

tras•pa•sar *v.* to pass over, cross over, to go beyond; to pass through; to pierce; to transfer (*property*); to trespass.

tras•pa•so *m.* transfer, transgression, trespass.

tres•pie *m.* stumble, slip; **dar un -** to stumble or trip

tras•plan•tar *v.* to transplant.

tras•po•ner[40] = transponer.

tras•qui•la, tras•qui•la•du•ra *f.* shearing, clip, clipping; bad haircut.

tras•qui•lar *v.* to shear, to clip; to crop; to cut badly (*hair*).

tras•ta•zo *m.* thump, blow.

tras•te *m.* fret, stop (*of a guitar*); *Am.* utensil, implement; **dar al - con** to destroy, ruin.

tras•to *m.* household utensil; piece of junk; rubbish, trash; **-s** utensils; implements; **-s de pescar** fishing tackle.

tras•tor•nar *v.* to overturn; to upset; to disturb.

tras•tor•no *m.* upset; disorder; disturbance.

tras•tro•car[2.6] *v. irr.* to invert, change; to upset.

tra•su•dar *v.* to perspire, sweat slightly.

tra•su•dor *m.* slight perspiration or sweat.

tra•ta•ble *adj.* friendly, sociable; manageable.

tra•ta•do *m.* treaty; treatise.

tra•ta•mien•to *m.* treatment; title of courtesy; form of address.

tra•tan•te *m. & f.* dealer, tradesman, trader.

tra•tar *v.* to treat; to handle; to discuss; to have social relations with; **- con** to have dealings with; **- de** to try to; to treat of, deal with; **-le a uno de** to address someone as; to treat someone as; **- en** to deal in; **-se bien** to treat oneself well; to behave well; **-se de** to be a question of; **no se trata de eso** that isn't the question, that isn't the point.

tra•to *m.* (*acuerdo*) treatment; deal, pact; trade,

(*manera*) manner, behavior; social relations; dealings; *Am.* **- pampa** unfair deal; ¡ **- hecho!** it's a deal!; **tener buen -** to be affable, sociable.

tra•vés *m.* crossbeam; reverse, misfortune; **a** (*or* **al**) **- de** trough, across; **de -** across; **dar al - con** to ruin, destroy; to squander; **mirar de -** to squint in a sinister manner.

tra•ve•sa•ño *m.* crosspiece, crossbar, bolster, long bedpillow; *Ven., Andes* railway tie.

tra•ve•se•ar *v.* to romp, frisk, frolic; to fool around; to misbehave.

tra•ve•sí•a *f.* crossing; sea voyage; wind blowing towards a coast; *Am.* wasteland, desert land; *Am.* partition wall or fence.

tra•ve•su•ra *f.* mischief; prank; lively wit.

tra•vie•sa *f.* railway tie; rafter, crossbeam; *Col.* midyear crop.

tra•vie•so *adv.* mischievous; lively; restless; **a cam•po -** (*or* **a campo traviesa**) cross-country.

tra•yec•to *m.* run, stretch, lap, distance (*traveled over*).

tra•yec•to•ria *f.* path (*of a bullet, missile, etc.*).

tra•za *f.* (*plan*) plan; design; plot; invention; (*apariencia*) appearance; semblance; aspect; indication, sign; **darse -s** to use one's wits or ingenuity; **tener -s de** to have the appearance or signs of; **tiene** (*or* **lleva**) **-s de no acabar nunca** it looks as if he would never end.

tra•za•do *m.* draft, plan, sketch, outline; drawing; *p.p. & adj.* traced, sketched, outlined.

tra•zar[9] *v.* to trace, sketch; to draw, mark out; to plan.

tré•bol *m.* clover.

tre•cho *m.* space, distance; lap (*in a race*); **a -s** by or at intervals; **de – en -** at certain points or intervals; from time to time.

tre•gua *f.* truce; rest, respite.

tre•me•dal *m.* quagmire, bog.

tre•men•do *adj.* tremendous, huge; terrible.

tre•men•ti•na *f.* turpentine.

tre•mo•lar *v.* to flutter, wave (*as a flag*).

tré•mo•lo *m.* tremolo (*of the voice*), quaver.

tré•mu•lo *adj.* tremulous, trembling, quivering; flickering.

tren *m.* train; *Am.* traffic; **– correo** mail train, **– de aterrizaje** landing gear; *Ven., Carib.:* **– de lavado** laundry; *Cuba, Ven.* **– de mudadas** moving company; **– de recreo** excursion train; **– mixto** freight and passenger train.

tren•za *f.* tress; braid; *Mex., Cuba, Ven.* string (*of garlic, onions, etc.*); **trencilla** *f.* braid.

tren•zar[9] *v.* to braid; **-se** to braid one's hair; *Riopl., Andes, Col.,* to fight hand to hand.

tre•par *v.* to climb; to clamber; **-se** to climb; to clamber; to perch.

tre•pi•da•ción *f.* jar, vibration; trembling, shaking.

tre•pi•dar *v.* to shape, vibrate, tremble, jar.

tre•ta *f.* trick, wile; **malas -s** bad tricks, bad habits.

tri•án•gu•lo *m.* triangle.

tri•bu *f.* tribe.

tri•bu•la•ción *f.* tribulation, trouble.

tri•bu•na *f.* rostrum (*speaker's platform*).

tri•bu•nal *m.* tribunal; court of justice; body of judges.

tri•bu•tar *v.* to pay tribute, pay homage.

tri•bu•ta•rio *adj. & m.* tributary.

tri•buto *m.* tribute; contribution, tax.

tri•ful•ca *f.* fight, quarrel, wrangle, row.

tri•go *m.* wheat.

tri•gue•ño *adj.* swarthy; brunet; dark.

tri•lla•do *p.p.* beaten; *adj.* trite, hackneyed, commonplace; **camino -** beaten path.

tri•lla•do•ra *f.* threshing machine.

tri•llar *v.* to thresh; to beat, mistreat; *Cuba* to cut a path.

tri•mes•tre *m.* quarter, period of three months; quarterly payment, income, or salary; **trimestral** *adj.* quarterly.

tri•nar *v.* to trill (*in singing*); to warble; to quaver (*said of the voice*); to get furious.

trin•chan•te *m.* carving fork; carving knife; carver.

trin•char *v.* to carve (*meat*).

trin•che *m.* *Col., Ven., C.A., Mex.* fork; *Am.* carving table; *Am.* **plato –** carving platter.

trin•che•ra *f.* trench; ditch; *C.A., Ven., Andes* stockade, fence; *Am.* curved knife.

trin•che•ro *m.* carving table; plato – carving platter.

tri•ne•o *m.* sleigh; sled.

tri•no *m.* trill (*in singing*).

tri•pa *f.* intestine, bowel; paunch, belly; **-s** entrails, insides.

tri•ple *adj. & m.* triple.

tri•pli•car *v.* to triplicate, triple, treble.

tri•pu•la•ción *f.* crew, ship's company.

tri•pu•lar *v.* to man (*a ship*).

tri•quem. crack, snap; *Mex.* utensil, trinket; *Col.* clever trick in a game; *Am.* drink made from barley; **-s** *Mex.* poor household utensils, goods, etc.

tris•car *v.* to romp, frisk, frolic; **to stamp or shuffle the feet,** *Am.* to tease, make fun of.

tris•te *adj.* sad; sorrowful; *Mex.* bashful, backward; *m. Riopl.* melancholy love song.

tris•te•za *f.* sadness; sorrow; *Am.* tick fever.

tris•tón *f.* wistful, quite sad, melancholy.

triun•fal *adj.* triumphal.

triun•fan•te *adj.* triumphant.

triun•far *v.* to triumph; to trump (*at cards*).

triun•fo *m.* triumph; trump card; trophy.

tri•vial *adj.* trivial, commonplace, trite.

tri•za *f.* shred, fragment, small piece; cord, rope (*for sails*); **hacer -s** to tear into shreds; to tear to pieces.

tro•car *v. irr.* to change; to barter, exchange; to do one thing instead of another; **-se** to change; to be transformed; to exchange.

tro•cha *f.* path, trail; *Riopl.* gauge (*of a railway*); *Col.*

trot; *Am.* slice or serving of meat.

tro•fe•o *m.* trophy; booty, spoils.

troj, tro•je *m.* barn, granary.

tro•le *m.* trolley.

trom•ba *f.* waterspout.

trom•bón *m.* trombone.

trom•pa *f.* trumpet; trunk of an elephant; large spinning top; *Am.* snout; *Col.* cowcatcher (*of a locomotive*).

trom•pa•da *f.* blow with the first; bump.

trom•pe•ta *f.* trumpet; *m.* trumpeter; useless individual; *Andes* drunk, drunkard; *Andes* bold, shameless fellow.

trom•pe•te•ar *v.* to trumpet, blow the trumpet.

trom•po *m.* spinning top; stupid fellow, dunce.

tro•na•da *f.* thunderstorm.

tro•nar *v. irr.* to thunder; to explode; burst; *Mex., C.A.* to execute by shooting; **– los dedos** to snap one's fingers; **por lo que pueda -** just in case.

tron•co *m.* tree trunk; log; stem; trunk (*of the human body*); team (*of horses*).

tron•char *v.* to bend or break (*a stalk or trunk*); to chop off; to break off; **-se** to break off or get bent (said of a stalk or trunk); *Col.* to get twisted or bent.

tro•ne•ra *f.* opening; porthole (*through which to shoot*); small, narrow window; pocket of a billiard table; *m.* madcap, reckless fellow.

tro•ni•do *m.* thunder; detonation; sharp, sudden sound.

tro•no *m.* throne.

tro•pa *f.* troop; crowd; *Riopl.* herd of cattle, drove of horses (*often* **tropilla**).

tro•pel *m.* throng; bustle, rush; jumble, confusion.

tro•pe•zar *v. irr.* to stumble; to blunder; **– con** to meet, come across, encounter.

tro•pe•zón *m.* stumbling; stumble; slip; **a –es** falteringly, stumbling slong clumsily; **darse un –** to stumble, trip.

tro•pi•cal *adj.* tropical.

tró•pi•co *m.* tropic.

tro•pie•zo *m.* stumble; stumbling block; slip, fault; dispute.

tro•pi•lla *f.* small troop; *Am.* drove of horses guided by the **madrina**; *Mex.* pack of dogs; *Am.* group of spare saddle horses.

tro•pi•lle•ro *m.* *Am.* horse wrangler, herdsman.

tro•tar *v.* to trot; to hurry.

tro•te *m.* trot; **al –** quickly.

tro•va•dor *m.* troubadour, minstrel.

tro•za *f.* log.

tro•zar *v.* to cut off, break off (*a piece*); to break or cut into pieces.

tro•zo *m.* piece, bit, fragment; passage, selection.

tru•co *m.* clever trick; pocketing of a ball (*in the game of pool*); *Am.* blow with the fist; *Andes, Riopl.* a card game; **-s** game of pool (*game similar to billiards*).

tru•cu•len•cia *f.* cruelty, ferocity, ruthlessness.

tru•cu•len•to *adj.* cruel, fierce, ruthless.

tru•cha *f.* trout; *Am.* vendor's portable stand.

true•no *m.* thunder; explosion, report of a gun; wild youth, troublemaker; *Am.* firecracker, rocket.

true•que, true•co *m.* exchange; barter; *Col., Ven., Andes* change, small money; **a** (*or* **en**) – **de** in exchange for.

tru•hán *m.* scoundrel; swindler; cheat; buffoon, jester.

tu *adj.* thy; your (*fam. sing.*).

tú *pers. pron.* thou; you (*fam. sing.*).

tua•let = **lavado**.

tu•ber•cu•lo•sis *f.* tuberculosis; **tubercu-loso** *adj.* tuberculous, tubercular.

tu•be•rí•a *f.* tubing, piping; pipe line.

tu•bo *m.* tube; pipe; lamp chimney; – **de ensayo** test tube; – **de escape** tail pipe.

tuer•ca *f.* nut (of a screw); **llave de -s** wrench.

tuer•to *adj.* one-eyed; blind in one eye; *m.* wrong, injustice; **a – o a derecho** (*or* **a tuertas o a derechas**) rightly or wrongly; thoughtlessly.

tué•ta•no *m.* marrow; pith; innermost part; **mojado hasta los -s** soaked through and through.

tu•fo *m.* vapor, fume; disagreeable odor; airs, conceit; **tufillo** *m.* whiff, pungent odor.

tul *m.* tulle (*a thin, fine net for veils*); tul, tulc *m. Mex* a kind of reed or bulrush (*used in the manufacture of seats and backs of chairs.*).

tu•li•pán *m.* tulip.

tu•lli•do *p.p.* crippled; paralyzed; numb.

tu•llir•se[20] *v. irr.* to become crippled; to become nimb or paralyzed.

tum•ba *f.* tomb; grave; *Col., Cuba, Mex.* felling of timber; *Ven.* forest clearing.

tum•bar *v.* to knock down; *Col., Mex., Cuba* to fell timber; **-se** to lie down.

tum•bo *m.* tumble; somersault; **dar -s** to jump, bump along.

tu•mor *m.* tumor; **tumorcillo** *m.* boil; small tumor.

tu•mul•to *m.* tumult, uproar; mob, throng.

tu•mul•tuo•so *adj.* tumultuous.

tu•na *f.* prickly pear.

tu•nan•te *m. & f.* rascal, rogue, scamp; loafer; *Andes, Ch., C.A.* libertine, licentious or lewd person.

tun•da *f.* whipping, thrashing; shearing (*the nap of cloth*).

tun•dir *v.* to lash, beat, whip; to shear (*the nap of cloth*).

tú•nel *m.* tunnel.

tú•ni•ca *f.* tunic; gown, robe.

tu•pi•do *adj.* dense; compact, thick; blocked, obstructed.

tu•pir *v.* to press, pack, squeeze together; to stop up, clog; **-se** to get stopped up; to stuff oneself; to become dense (*as a forest*); *Am.* to get astonished or confused.

tur•ba *f.* mob, throng.

tur•ba•ción *f.* disturbance, confusion; embarrassment.

tur•ba•mul•ta *f.* throng, mob, crowd.

tur•bar *v.* to perturb, to disturb; to trouble; **–se** to get disturbed, confused, embarrassed.

tur•bio *adj.* muddy; muddled, confused.

tur•bión *m.* thunderstorm; heavy shower.

tur•bo•rre•ac•tor *m.* turbojet.

tur•bu•len•to *adj.* turbulent; restless; disorderly.

tur•co *adj.* Turkish; *m.* Turk; Turkish, Turkish language; *Am.* peddler.

tu•ris•mo *m.* tourist travel; touring, sightseeing; **oficina de** – travel bureau; **turista** *m. & f.* tourist; **turístico** *adj.* tourist; related to tourism.

tur•nar *v.* to alternate; **-se** to alternate; to take turns.

tur•no *m.* turn, alternate order.

tu•rrón *m.* nougat, nut confection; almond cake; *Mex.* **romper el** – to decide to use the **tú** form of address (*as a mark of close friendship*).

tu•sa *f. Am.* corn, corncob; *Cuba, Mex.* corn husk; *Am.* corn silk, tassel of an ear of corn.

tu•sar *v. Cuba, Mex., Riopl., Andes* to shear; *Riopl.* to cropo, cut badly (*hair*).

tu•te•ar *v.* to address familiarly (*using the* **tú** *form*).

tu•te•la *f.* guardianship; guidance, pro-tection.

tu•te•lar *v.* to guide, coach, direct; *adj.* guiding, guardian (*used as adj.*).

tu•tor *m.* tutor; guardian.

tu•yo *poss. adj.* your, of yours (*fam. sing.*); *poss. pron.* yours.

U

u *conj.* (*before works beginning with* **o** *or* **ho**) or.

u•bi•car[6] *v. Am.* to locate; -se to be situated or located.

u•bre *f.* udder.

u•fa•nar•se *v.* to glory (in); to be proud (of).

u•fa•no *adj.* proud; gay; self-satisfied.

u•jier *m.* usher, doorman.

úl•ce•ra *f.* ulcer; sore.

ul•te•rior *adj.* ulterior; further; later.

ul•ti•mar *v.* to put an end to; *Am.* to give the finishing blow; kill.

úl•ti•mo *adj.* last, final; ultimate; latest; **estar en las últimas** to be on one's last legs; to be at the end of one's rope, be at the end of one's resources.

ul•tra•jar *v.* to outrage, insult; to scorn.

ul•tra•je *m.* outrage, insult.

ul•tra•mar *m.* country or place across the sea; **de -s** overseas, from across the sea; **en** (*or* **a**) – overseas.

ul•tra•vio•le•ta *adj.* ultraviolet.

u•lu•lar *v.* to howl, shriek, hoot.

u•m•bral *m.* threshold.

um•brío *adj.* shady.

un(o) *indef. art.* a, an; **-s** some, a few; **-s cuantos** a few; **uno** *pron. & num.* one.

u·ná·ni·me *adj.* unanimous.

u·na·ni·mi·dad *f.* unanimity, complete accord.

un·ción *f.* unction (*anointing with oil*); religious fervor; spiritual grace; **Extremaunción** Extreme Unction (*the Last Sacrament of the Church*).

un·cir[10] *v.* to yoke.

un·gir[11] *v.* to anoint; to consecrate.

un·güen·to *m.* ointment; salve.

ú·ni·co *adj.* only, sole; unique, singular, rare.

u·ni·dad *f.* unity; unit.

u·ni·fi·car[6] *v.* to unify; to unite.

u·ni·for·mar *v.* to standardize; to make uniform; to furnish with uniforms.

u·ni·for·me *adj. & m.* uniform.

u·ni·for·mi·dad *f.* uniformity.

u·ni·la·te·ral *adj.* unilateral, one-sided.

u·nión *f.* union.

u·nir *v.* to unite; to join; to bring together; **-se** to unite, join together; to wed.

u·ni·ver·sal *adj.* universal.

u·ni·ver·si·dad *f.* university.

u·ni·ver·so *m.* universe.

un·tar *v.* to anoint, to smear; to oil, grease; to bribe, to corrupt; **-se** to smear oneself; to get smeared.

un·to *m.* grease, fat; ointment.

un·tuo·si·dad *f.* greasiness; **untuoso** *adj.* unctuous; oily, greasy.

uña *f.* fingernail; toenail; claw, hoof; hook (*on a tool*); **a - de caballo** at full gallop, at full speed; **largo de -s** prone to stealing; *Mex., C.A., Ven., Col., Andes* **largas -s** thief; **vivir de sus -s** to live stealing; *Mex., C.A., Ven., Col., Andes* **echar la -** to steal, **ser - y carne** to be inseparable friends.

u·ra·nio *m.* uranium.

ur·ba·ni·dad *f.* courtesy, politeness; refinement.

ur·ba·no *adj.* urban; courteous, polite.

ur·be *f.* metropolis, large city.

ur·dim·bre *f.* warp (*of a fabric*); scheme.

ur·dir *v.* to warp (*in weaving*); to plot, scheme; to invent (*a lie, story, etc.*).

u·re·mia *f.* uremia.

ur·gen·cia *f.* urgency, pressing need.

ur·gen·te *adj.* urgent, pressing.

ur·gir[11] *v.* to urge; to be urgent.

ur·na *f.* urn; **- electoral** ballot box.

u·rra·ca *f.* magpie.

u·sa·do *p.p. & adj.* used; accustomed; worn; threadbare.

u·san·za *f.* usage, custom, habit.

u·sar *v.* to use; to wear; to wear out; to be accustomed; **-se** to be in use, be in vogue.

u·so *m.* (*empleo*) use; usage; wear; (*costumbre*) usage; practice; habit; custom; **al – de la época** according to the custom or usage of the period; **estar en buen –** to be in good condition (*said of a thing*).

us·ted *pers. pron.* (abbreviated as **Ud., V.,** or **Ud.**) you.

u·sual *adj.* usual; ordinary, customary.

u·su·fruc·to *m.* use, enjoyment; profit.

u·su·fruc·tu·ar[18] *v.* to enjoy the use of; to make use of.

u·su·ra *f.* usury.

u·su·re·ro *m.* usurer, loan shark.

u·sur·par *v.* to usurp.

u·ten·si·lio *m.* utensil; implement, tool.

ú·te·ro *m.* uterus, womb.

ú·til *adj.* useful; profitable; **-se** *m. pl.* tools, instruments.

u·ti·li·dad *f.* utility; profit; usefulness.

u·ti·li·zar[9] *v.* to utilize; to use.

u·va *f.* grape; **– espina** gooseberry; **– pasa** raisin; **estar hecho una –** to be tipsy, drunk.

V

va·ca *f.* cow; **carne de –** beef; **cuero de –** cowhide; *Am.* **hacer –** to play hooky, play truant, cut class; to join in a quick business deal.

va·ca·ción *f.* vacation (*usually* **vacaciones**).

va·ca·da *f.* herd of cows.

va·can·cia *f.* vacancy.

va·can·te *adj.* vacant, unfilled, unoccupied; *f.* vacancy.

va·ciar[17] *v.* (*dejar vacío*) to empty; to drain; to flow; (*amoldar*) to cast into a mold; (*ahuecar*) to hollow out; **-se** to spill; to empty; to become empty; to flow (into).

va·cie·dad *f.* emptiness; nonsense, silliness.

va·ci·la·ción *f.* hesitation; wavering; doubt.

va·ci·lan·te *adj.* vacillating, hesitating, wavering; unsteady.

va·ci·lar *v.* to vacillate, waver, hesitate; to sway.

va·cí·o *adj.* empty; vacant; unoccupied; hollow; *m.* void; hollow; vacuum; vacancy; gap, blank.

va·cu·na *f.* vaccine; vaccination; cowpox (*eruptive disease of the cow*); **vacunación** *f.* vaccination; **– antipoliomelítica** antipolio inoculation.

va·cu·nar *v.* to vaccinate.

va·de·ar *v.* to ford; to wade; to avoid (*a difficulty*).

va·do *m.* ford; **no hallar -** to find no way out.

va·ga·bun·de·ar *v.* to tramp around, wander, rove; to loiter.

va·ga·bun·do *adj.* vagabond, wandering; *m.* vagabond, tramp; vagrant; wanderer.

va·gar[7] *v.* to wander, roam; to loiter, to loaf; *m.* leisure; loitering.

va·go *adj.* vague; roaming; idle; vagrant; *m.* vagrant, tramp.

va·gón *m.* railway car or coach; **vagoneta** *f.* small railway car or tram (*used in mines*); **vagonada** *f.* carload.

va·gue·ar = vagar.

va·hi·do *m.* dizziness, dizzy spell.

va·ho *m.* vapor, steam, fume, mist; odor.

vai·na *f.* sheath, scabbard; case; pod. husk; *Ven., Col., C.A., Mex.* bother, nuisance; *Ven., Col.* luck.

vai·ni·lla *f.* vanilla.

vai·vén *m.* sway; fluctuation, wavering; traffic, coming and going; **-es** comings and goings; ups and downs; inconstancy.

va·ji·lla *f.* tableware; set of dishes; **– de plata** silverware; **– de porcelana** chinaware.

va·le *m.* bond, promissory note; voucher; adieu, farewell; *m. & f. Col., Ven., Mex.* comrade, pal, chum.

va·le·de·ro *adj.* valid, binding, effective.

va·le·dor *m.* defender, protector; *Am.* pal, comrade.

va·len·cia·no *adj.* Valencian, of or from Valencia, Spain; *m.* Valencian.

va·len·tí·a *f.* courage, valor; exploit; boast.

va·len·tón *adj.* blustering, boastful; *m.* bully, braggart.

va·ler [17] *v. irr.* to favor, protect; to cost; to be worth; to be worthy; to be equivalent to; to be valid; to prevail; to be useful; **– la pena** to be worth while; **– por** to be worth; **-se de** to avail oneself of, make use of; **más vale** it is better, **¡válgame Dios!** heaven help me! good heavens!

va·le·ro·so *adj.* valiant, brave; valuable.

va·lí·a *f.* worth, value; influence.

va·li·dez *f.* validity; stability, soundness.

vá·li·do *adj.* valid.

va·lien·te *adj.* valiant, brave; powerful; *m.* brave man; bully.

va·li·ja *f.* valise, satchel; mailbag.

va·li·mien·to *m.* favor, protection; **gozar de –** to enjoy protection or favor.

va·lio·so *adj.* valuable; worthy, wealthy.

va·lor *m.* value; worth; price; significance; valor, courage; boldness; efficacy; power; **-es** stocks, bonds.

va·lo·ra·ción *f.* valuation, appraisal.

va·lo·rar *v.* to evaluate, value, appraise.

va·lo·ri·zar [9] *v. Cuba, Ven., Riopl., Andes* to value, appraise; *Am.* to realize, convert into money.

vals *m.* waltz.

val·sar *v.* to waltz.

va·lua·ción *f.* valuation, appraisal.

va·luar [18] *v.* to value, price, appraise; to rate.

vál·vu·la *f.* valve.

va·lla *f.* stockade, fence; barrier; obstacle; *Cuba, Col.* cockpit (*for cockfights*).

va·lla·do *m.* stockade, fenced-in place; fence.

va·lle *m.* valley; vale.

va·na·glo·ria *f.* vainglory, boastful vanity.

va·na·glo·riar·se [17] *v.* to glory, take great pride (in), boast (of).

va·na·glo·rio·so *adj.* vain, boastful, conceited.

van·guar·dia *f.* vanguard.

va·ni·dad *f.* vanity; conceit; emptiness.

va·ni·do·so *adj.* vain, conceited.

va·no *adj.* vain; empty; hollow; *m.* opening in a wall (*for a door or window*).

va·por *m.* vapor, steam, mist; steamer, steamship.

va·po·ro·so *adj.* vaporous, steamy, misty; vaporlike.

va·pu·le·ar *v.* to beat, whip, thrash.

va·pu·le·o *m.* beating, whipping, thrashing.

va·que·rí·a *f.* herd of cows; stable for cows; dairy.

va·que·ri·zo *m.* herdsman; *adj.* pertaining to cows; **vaqueriza** *f.* stable for cows.

va·que·ro *m.* cowherd, herdsman; cowboy; *Cuba* milkman; *adj.* relating to cowherds, cowboys, or cattle.

va·que·ta *f.* sole leather; cowhide; *Mex.* **zurrar a uno la –** to tan someone's hide, beat someone up.

va·ra *f.* twig; stick; rod; wand; staff; yard, yardstick; thrust with a picador's lance.

va·ra·de·ro *m.* shipyard.

va·rar *v.* to beach (*a boat*); to run aground; to stop, come to a standstill (*said of business*).

va·re·ar *v.* to beat, to whip; to sell by the yard; to measure with a **vara** *Am.* to exercise (*a horse before a race*).

va·ria·ble *adj.* variable, unstable, changeable; *f.* variable.

va·ria·ción *f.* variation.

va·ria·do *p.p. & adj.* varied; variegated.

va·riar [17] *v.* to vary; to change, to shift. to differ.

va·rie·dad *f.* variety; variation, change.

va·ri·lla *f.* small rod; wand; long, flexible twig; rib (*of an umbrella or fan*); corset stay; *Mex.* peddler's wares.

va·ri·lle·ro *m. Mex.* peddler.

va·rio *adj.* various; different; changeable; varied; **-s** various, several.

va·rón *m.* male, man; *Am.* long beam, timber.

va·ro·nil *adj.* manly; strong; brave.

va·sa·llo *adj. & m.* vassal; subject.

vas·co, vas·con·ga·do *adj. & m.* Basque.

va·si·ja *f.* vessel, container, receptacle.

va·so *m.* drinking glass; glassful; vase; vessel; hull of a ship; horse's hoof; **– de elección** person chosen by God.

vás·ta·go *m.* (*de planta*) shoot, sprout; stem; (*persona*) scion, offspring; *Mex., Col., Ven.* stem, trunk of a banana tree.

vas·to *adj.* vast, extensive, large.

va·te *m.* bard, poet.

va·ti·ci·nar *v.* to prophesy, predict, foretell.

va·ti·ci·nio *m.* prophecy, prediction.

ve·cin·dad *f.* vicinity; neighborhood; neighborliness; **casa de –** tenement.

ve·cin·da·rio *m.* neighborhood, neighbors; vicinity.

ve·ci·no *m.* neighbor; resident; citizen; *adj.* neighboring; next, near.

ve·dar *v.* to prohibit, to impede.

ve·ga *f.* fertile lowland or plain; *Cuba, Ven.* tobacco plantation.

ve·ge·ta·ción *f.* vegetation.

ve·ge·tal *adj.* vegetable; *m.* vegetable, plant.

ve·ge·tar *v.* to vegetate.

ve·he·men·te *adj.* vehement, passionate, impetuous; violent.

ve·hí·cu·lo *m.* vehicle.

vein·te·na *f.* score, twenty.

ve·jes·to·rio *m.* wrinkled old person.

ve·je·te *m.* little old man.

ve·jez *f.* old age.

ve·ji·ga *f.* bladder; blister; smallpox sore; **– de la bilis** (*or* **– de la hiel**) gall bladder.

ve·la *f.* vigil, watch; night watch; candle; sail; **a toda** **–** under full sail; at full speed; **en –** on watch, without sleep; **hacerse a la –** to set sail.

ve·la·da *f.* watch, vigil; evening party; evening function or meeting.

ve·la·dor *m.* night watchman; keeper, guard; lamp table; bedside table; candlestick; *Riopl., Mex., Cuba, Col.* lamp shade.

ve·lar *v.* to keep vigil; to stay up at night; to be vigilant, to watch over, to veil; to cover, hide.

ve·la·to·rio *m.* wake (*vigil over a corpse*). *See* **velorio**.

ve·lei·do·so *adj.* inconstant, fickle, changeable.

ve·le·ro *m.* sailboat; sailmaker; candlemaker; *adj.* swift-sailing; **buque –** sailboat.

ve·le·ta *f.* weathervane, wathercock; *m. & f.* fickle person.

ve·lís *m. Mex.* valise.

ve·lo *m.* veil; curtain, covering; **– del paladar** velum, soft palate.

ve·lo·ci·dad *f.* velocity.

ve·lo·cí·me·tro *m.* speedometer.

ve·lo·rio *m. Am.* wake (*vigil over a corpse*); *Mex., C.A., Ven., Col., Ch., Andes* dull party.

ve·loz *adj.* swift, quick, fast.

ve·llo *m.* hair (*on the body*); down, fuzz; nap (*of cloth*).

ve·llón *m.* fleece, tuft of wool; sheepskin with fleece, silver and copper alloy; an ancient copper coin.

ve·llo·so *adj.* hairy; downy, fuzzy.

ve·llu·do *adj.* hairy; downy; fuzzy; *m.* plush; velvet.

ve·na *f.* vein; lode, vein of metal ore; mood, disposition; **estar en –** to be in the mood; to be inspired.

ve·na·do *m.* deer; venison, deer meat; *Mex.* **pintar –** to play hooky.

ven·ce·dor *adj.* conquering, winning, victorious; *m.* conqueror, winner, victor.

ven·cer[10] *v.* to conquer, vanquish; to defeat; to overcome; to surpass; to win; **-se** to control oneself; to mature, fall due; **se venció el plazo** the time limit expired.

ven·ci·do *p.p. & adj.* conquered; defeated; due, fallen due.

ven·ci·mien·to *m.* conquering, defeat; maturity (*of a debt*), falling due; expiration (*of a period of time*).

ven·da *f.* bandage.

ven·da·je *m.* bandage.

ven·dar *v.* to bandage; to blindfold.

ven·da·val *m.* strong wind, gale.

ven·de·dor *m.* vendor, seller, peddler.

ven·der *v.* to sell; to betray; **-se** to be sold; to sell oneself, accept a bribe.

ven·di·mia *f.* vintage; profit.

ven·du·ta *f. Col.* auction; *Cuba* small fruit and vegetable store.

ve·ne·no *m.* venom, poison.

ve·ne·no·so *adj.* poisonous.

ve·ne·ra·ble *adj.* venerable.

ve·ne·ra·ción *f.* veneration, reverence.

ve·ne·ran·do *adj.* venerable, worthy of respect.

ve·ne·rar *v.* to venerate, revere; to worship.

ve·ne·ro *m.* water spring; source, origin; lode, layer, seam (*of mineral*).

ve·ne·zo·la·no *adj.* Venezuelan; *m.* Venezuelan; *Ven.* Venezuelan silver coin.

ven·ga·dor *adj.* avenging, revenging; *m.* avenger.

ven·gan·za *f.* vengeance, revenge.

ven·gar[7] to avenge, revenge; **-se de** to take revenge on.

ven·ga·ti·vo *adj.* vindictive, revengeful.

ve·nia *f.* pardon; permission, leave; bow, nod; *C.A., Ven., Riopl.* military salute.

ve·ni·da *f.* arrival, return; river flood, onrush of water; attack (*in fencing*).

ve·ni·de·ro *adj.* coming, future; **en lo –** in the future; **-s** *m. pl.* successors.

ve·nir[48] *v. irr.* to come; to arrive; to fit; **-le a uno bien** (*or* **mal**) to be becoming (*or unbecoming*); **– a menos** to decline, decay; **– a pelo** to come just at the right moment; to suit perfectly; to be pat, opportune, to the point; **– en** to agree to; **– sobre** to fall upon; **¿a qué viene eso?** what is the point of that?; **-se abajo** to fall down; to collapse; to fail.

ve·no·so *adj.* veined, venous (*of or pertaining to the veins; with veins*).

ven·ta *f.* sale; roadside inn; *Ur.* store, vendor's stand; **– pública** auction.

ven·ta·ja *f.* advantage; gain, profit; bonus; odds.

ven·ta·jo·so *adj.* advantageous, beneficial, profitable; *Mex.* self-seeking, profiteering.

ven·ta·na *f.* window; window shutter; *Col.* clearing (*in a forest*); **– (or ventanilla) de la nariz** nostril.

ven·ta·rrón *m.* gale, strong wind.

ven·te·ar *v.* (*oler*) to scent, sniff; (*soplar*) to blow, be windy; (*poner al aire*) to air; (*indagar*) to nose around; *Ven.* to toss in the wind; *Am.* to flee; *Am.* to outrun; **-se** to expel air, break wind; *Col.* to stay outdoors.

ven·te·ro *m.* innkeeper.

ven·ti·la·ción *f.* ventilation.

ven·ti·la·dor *m.* ventilator, fan (*for ventilation*).

ven·ti·lar *v.* to ventilate; to air.

ven·tis·ca *f.* blizzard, snowstorm; snowdrift.

ven·tis·car[6] *v.* to snow hard and blow (*as in a blizzard*); to drift (*as snow in a blizzard*).

ven·tis·que·ro *m.* blizzard, snowstorm; glacier; snowdrift; snow-capped mountain peak.

ven·to·le·ra *f.* gust of wind; pride, vanity; whim; pin wheel; **darle a uno la – de** to take the notion to.

ven·to·so *adj.* windy.

ven·tu·ra *f.* happiness; fortune, chance; risk, danger; **a la –** at random; **buena –** fortune; **por –** perchance.

ven·tu·ro·so *adj.* fortunate, lucky; happy.

ver[49] *v. irr.* to see; to look, to look at, to look into, examine; **– de** to try to, see to it that; **a más** (*or* **hasta más**) – good-bye; **no - la hora de** to be anxious to; **no tener nada que – con** not to have anything to do with; **-se** to be seen, to be; **-se obligado a** to be obliged to, be forced, to; **a mi modo de –** in my opinion; **de buen –** good-looking, **ser de –** to be worth seeing.

ve·ra *f.* edge; **a la – del camino** at the edge of the road.

ve·ra·ci·dad *f.* truthfulness.

ve·ra·ne·an·te *m. & f.* summer resorter, vacationist, or tourist.

ve·ra·ne·ar *v.* to spend the summer.

ve·ra·ne·o *m.* summering, summer vacation.

ve·ra·nie·go *adj.* summer, of summer.

ve·ra·no *m.* summer.

ve·ras *f. pl.* reality, truth, **de –** in truth; truly; in earnest.

ve·raz *adj.* truthful.

ver·bal *adj.* verbal; oral.

ver·be·na *f.* verbena (*a plant*); festival or carnival (*on eve of a religious holiday*).

ver·bi·gra·cia *adv.* for instance, for example.

ver·bo *m.* verb; **el Verbo** the Word (*second person of the Trinity*).

ver·bo·so *adj.* verbose, wordy.

ver·dad *f.* truth; ¿–? really?; is that so?; isn't that so?; **– de Perogrullo** truism, evident truth; **de –** (*or* **a la–**) in truth, in earnest; **en –** really, truly.

ver·da·de·ro *adj.* real; true; truthful; sincere.

ver·de *adj.* green; unripe; young; off-color, indecent; *m.* green; verdure; *Ur., Ven.* country, countryside.

ver·de·ar *v.* to grow green; to look green.

ver·di·ne·gro *adj.* dark-green.

ver·dor *m.* verdure, greenness.

ver·do·so *adj.* greenish.

ver·du·go *m.* executioner; cruel person; torment; rapier (*light sword*); lash, whip; welt; shoot of a tree; **verdugón** *m.* large welt.

ver·du·le·ra *f.* woman vendor of green vegetables, **verdulería** *f.* green vegetable store or stand.

ver·du·ra *f.* verdure; greenness; green vegetables.

ve·re·da *f.* path; *Ch., Riopl., Andes* sidewalk; *Col.* small village, *C.R.* bank of a stream.

ve·re·dic·to *m.* verdict.

ver·gon·zo·so *adj.* shameful, disgraceful; shy, bashful; *m.* species of armadillo.

ver·güen·za *f.* shame; disgrace, shyness, bashfulness; **tener –** to have shame; to be ashamed.

ve·ri·cue·to *m.* rugged, wild place (*often rocky*).

ve·rí·di·co *adj.* truthful; true.

ve·ri·fi·car[6] *v.* to verify; to confirm; to test, check; to carry out, fulfill; **-se** to be verified; to take place.

ve·ri·jas *f. pl. Riopl., Mex.* groin (*hollow between lower part of abdomen and thigh*); *Am.* flanks of a horse.

ver·ja *f.* grate, grating.

ve·rru·ga *f.* wart; nuisance.

ver·sa·do *adj.* versed, skilled, expert.

ver·sar *v.* to deal (with), treat (of); **-se en** to become versed in.

ver·sión *f.* version; translation.

ver·so *m.* verse; meter; **– suelto** (*or* **– libre**) free or blank verse.

ver·ter[1] *v. irr.* to pour; to empty; to spill; to translate; to flow down.

ver·ti·cal *adj.* vertical.

vér·ti·ce *m.* top, apex, summit.

ver·tien·te *f.* slope; watershed; *adj.* flowing.

ver·ti·gi·no·so *adj.* whirling, dizzy, giddy.

vér·ti·go *m.* dizziness, giddiness; fit of madness.

ves·tí·bu·lo *m.* vestibule, lobby.

ves·ti·do *m.* clothing, apparel; dress; garment; suit.

ves·ti·du·ra *f.* vestment; attire, apparel; raiment.

ves·ti·gio *m.* vestige, sign, trace.

ves·tir[5] *v. irr.* (*cubrir*) to dress; to clothe; to put on; to adorn; to cover; (*llevar*) to wear; **-se** to dress, get dressed; to be clothed; to be covered.

ves·tua·rio *m.* wardrobe, apparel; theatrical costumes; cloakroom; dressing room; vestry (*room for church vestments*).

ve·ta *f.* vein, seam (*of mineral*); streak, grain (*in wood*); stripe; *Am.* rope.

ve·te·a·do *adj.* veined; striped; streaked.

ve·te·ra·no *adj. & m.* veteran.

ve·te·ri·na·rio *m.* veterinary.

ve·to *m.* veto.

ve·tus·to *adj.* old, ancient.

vez *f.* time, occasion; turn; **a la –** at the same time; **cada – más** more and more; **cada – que** whenever; **de – en cuando** from time to time; **de una –** all at once; **en – de** instead of; **otra –** again; **una que otra –** rarely, once in a while; **tal –** perhaps; **a veces** sometimes; **raras veces** seldom; **hacer las veces de** to take the place of.

ví·a *f.* way; road; track; railroad track; conduit; **Vía Crucis** the Way of the Cross; **Vía Láctea** the Milky Way.

via·duc·to *m.* viaduct.

via·jan·te *m.* traveler; **– de comercio** traveling salesman.

via·jar *v.* to travel.

via·je *m.* voyage; trip; travel; **– de ida y vuelta** (*or* **– redondo**) round trip.

via·je·ro *m.* traveler; *adj.* traveling.

vian·da *f.* viands, food; meal.

vian·dan·te *m. &* adj. wayfarer, walker, pedestrian; passer-by; vagabond.

viá·ti·co *m.* provisions for a journey; viaticum (*communion given to dying persons*).

ví·bo·ra *f.* viper.

vi·bra·ción *f.* vibration.

vi·bran·te *adj.* vibrant, vibrating.

vi·brar *v.* to vibrate.

vi·ce·pre·si·den·te *m.* vice-president.

vi·ce·ver·sa *adv.* vice versa, conversely.

vi·cia·do *adj.* contaminated, foul; corrupt; *p.p. of* **vi·ciar.**

vi·ciar *v.* to vitiate, corrupt; to adulterate; to falsify, **-se** to become corrupt.

vi·cio *m.* vice; bad habit; fault; craving; **de –** as a habit; **hablar de –** to talk too much; **-s** *Am.* articles and ingredients used for serving **mate.**

vi·cio·so *adj.* vicious, evil, wicked; having bad habits; licentious; faulty, incorrect (*grammatical construction, reasoning, etc.*).

vi·ci·si·tud *f.* vicissitude; **-es** vicissitudes, ups and downs, changes of fortune or condition.

víc·ti·ma *f.* victim.

vic·to·ria *f.* victory, triumph; victoria (*carriage*).

vic·to·rio·so *adj.* victorious.

vi·cu·ña *f.* vicuña (*an Andean animal allied to the alpaca and llama*); vicuña wool; vicuña cloth.

vid *f.* vine, grapevine.

vi·da *f.* life; living; livelihood; **– mía** dearest; **hacer –** to live together; **pasar a mejor -** to die; **tener la – en un hilo** to be in great danger.

vi·da·li·ta *f. Am.* melancholy song of Argentina and Chile.

vi·den·te *m.* seer, prophet; *adj.* seeing.

vi·dria·do *m.* glaze; glazed earthenware; *p.p. & adj.* glazed.

vi·driar[17] *v.* to glaze (*earthenware*).

vi·drie·ra *f.* glass window; glass door; *Am.* show case, show window; **– de colores** stained-glass window.

vi·drie·ro *m.* glazier (*one who installs windowpanes*); glass blower; glass maker; glass dealer.

vi·drio *m.* glass; any glass article.

vi·drio·so *adj.* glassy; brittle; slippery, icy; touchy, irritable.

vie·jo *adj.* old; ancient; worn-out; *m.* old man; **– verde** old man who boast of his youth and vigor; *Am.* **los - s** the old folks (applied to one's parents); **viejoto** *f.* old hag.

vien·to *m.* wind; scent; **hace –** it is windy; **a los cua-**
tro **-s** in all directions; **vientecito** *m.* gentle breeze.

vien·tre *m.* abdomen; belly; bowels; entrails; womb.

vier·nes *m.* Friday.

vi·ga *f.* beam; rafter.

vi·gen·cia *f.* operation (*of a law*); **entrar en –** to take effect (*said of a law*); **estar en -** to be in force (*said of a law*).

vi·gen·te *adj.* effective, in force (*as a law*).

vi·gía *f.* lookout, watchtower watch (*act of watching*); reef; *m.* lookout, watchman

vi·gi·lan·cia *f.* vigilance.

vi·gi·lan·te *adj.* vigilant, watchful; *m.* watchman.

vi·gi·lar *v.* to keep guard; to watch over.

vi·gi·lia *f.* vigil, watch; wakefulness, sleeplessness; night hours (*spent in study*); eve before certain church festivals; vesper service; **día de –** day of abstinence; **comer de -** to abstain from meat.

vi·gor *m.* vigor; **en –** in force (*said of a law*); **entrar en –** to become effective (*as a law, statute, etc.*).

vi·go·ri·zar[6] *v.* to invigorate, tone up, give vigor to, strengthen.

vi·go·ro·so *adj.* vigorous.

vi·hue·la *f.* guitar.

vil *adj.* vile, base, low, mean.

vi·le·za *f.* villainy; baseness; vile act.

vi·li·pen·diar *v.* to revile.

vi·lo: en – in the air; suspended; undecided; in suspense; **llevar en –** to waft.

vi·lla *f.* villate; villa, country house.

vi·llan·ci·co *n.* carol; Christmas carol.

vi·lla·ní·a *f.* villainy; lowliness.

vi·lla·no *adj.* rustic, uncouth; villainous, mean, base; *m.* villain; rustic, peasant.

vi·llo·rrio *m.* small village, hamlet.

vi·na·gre *m.* vinegar; **vinagrera** *f.* vinegar cruet.

vin·cu·lar *v.* to tie, bond, unite; to entail (*limit the inheritance of property*); to found, base (on).

vín·cu·lo *m.* bond, tie, chain; entailed inheritance.

vin·di·car[6] *v.* to vindicate; to avenge; to defend, assert (*one's rights*); **-se** to avenge oneself; to defend oneself.

vi·no *m.* wine; **- amontillado** good grade of pale sherry (*originally* from *Montilla*); **– tinto** dark-red wine; **vinería** *f. Riopl., Andes* wineshop; **vinero** *adj. Am.* pertaining to wine; **vinoso** *adj.* winy.

vi·ña *f.* vineyard.

vi·ñe·do *m.* vineyard.

vio·la·ción *f.* violation.

vio·la·do *adj.* violet, *m.* violet, violet color; *p.p.* violated.

vio·lar *v.* to violate; to rape.

vio·len·cia *f.* violence.

vio·len·tar *v.* to force to break into (*a house*); **-se** to force oneself; to get angry.

vio·len·to *adj.* violent; impetuous; forced; strained; unnatural.

vio·le·ta *f.* violet.

vio•lín *m.* violin; *m. & f.* violinist; *Ven.* **estar hecho un** - to be very thin.

vio•li•nis•ta *m. & f.* violinist.

vi•ra•da *f.* tack, change of direction, turn.

vi•ra•je *m.* change of direction; turn.

vi•rar *v.* to turn, turn around, change direction; to tack (*said of a ship*).

vir•gen *adj. & f.* virgin.

vir•gi•nal *adj.* virginal, virgin, pure.

vi•ril *adj.* virile, manly.

vi•ri•li•dad *f.* virility, manhood, manly strength, vigor.

vi•rrei•na•to *m.* viceroyalty (*office or jurisdiction of a viceroy*).

vi•rrey *m.* viceroy.

vir•tud *f.* virtue.

vir•tuo•so *adj.* virtuous; *m.* virtuoso (*person skilled in an art*).

vi•rue•la *f.* smallpox; pock (*mark left by smallpox*); **-s locas** (*or* **-s bastardas**) chicken pox.

vi•ru•ta *f.* wood shaving.

vi•sa *f.* visa, visé; **visado** *p p.* of **visar**; *m.* visa, visé.

vi•sa•je *m.* grimace; wry face, **hacer -s** to make faces.

vi•sar *v.* to visé; to approve; to O.K.

vis•co•so *adj.* slimy, sticky.

vi•se•ra *f.* visor; eye shade; *Cuba, Mex.* blinder (*on a horse's bridle*).

vi•si•ble *adj.* visible; evident; conspicuous, notable.

vi•si•llo *m.* window curtain.

vi•sión *f.* vision; sight; fantasy; apparition; sight (*ridiculous-looking person or thing*).

vi•sio•na•rio *adj. & m.* visionary.

vi•si•ta *f.* visit, call; visitor; callers, company; **– de cumplimiento** (*or* **– de cumplido**) formal courtesy call, **– domiciliaria** police inspection of a house; home call (*of a social worker, doctor, etc.*).

vi•si•ta•ción *f.* visitation, visit.

vi•si•ta•dor *m.* visitor, caller; inspector.

vi•si•tan•te *m. & f.* caller, visitor; *adj.* visiting.

vi•si•tar *v.* to visit; to inspect.

vis•lum•brar *v.* to catch a glimpse of; to guess, surmise; **-se** to be faintly visible.

vis•lum•bre *f.* glimmer; glimpse; vague idea; faint appearance.

vi•so *m.* appearance, semblance; pretense, pretext; luster, brilliance, glitter; glass curtain; **a dos -s** with a double view; with a double purpose.

vis•pe•ra *f.* eve, evening or day before; time just before; **-s** vespers; **en -s de** on the eve of; about to.

vis•ta *f.* (*panorama*) view; landscape; sight; (*sentido*) sight; vision; (*acción*) look, glance; **a – de** in the presence of; in from of, within view of; **pagadero a la –** payable at sight or upon presentation; **¡hasta la –** ! good-bye!; **bajar la –** to lower one's eyes; **conocer de –** to know by sight; **hacer la – gorda** to pretend not to see; **pasar la – por** to glance over;

perder de – to lose sight of; **tener a la –** to have before one; to have received (*a letter*).

vis•ta•zo *m.* glance; **dar un – a** to glance over.

vis•to *p.p.* of **ver** seen; *adj.* evident, clear **bien –** well thought of, proper; **mal –** looked down upon, improper; **– bueno** (V°.B°.) approved, (O.K) **dar el – bueno** to approve, O.K.; **– que** whereas considering that.

vis•to•so *adj.* showy; colorful.

vi•tal *adj.* vital; important, necessary.

vi•ta•li•cio *adj.* for life; *m.* life-insurance policy, lifetime pension.

vi•ta•li•dad *f.* vitality.

vi•ta•mi•na *f.* vitamin.

ví•tor *m.* cheer, applause; **¡–!** hurrah!

vi•to•re•ar *v.* to cheer, applaud.

vi•tri•na *f.* glass case; show cas; show window.

vi•tua•llas *f. pl.* victuals, food, provisions.

vi•tu•pe•rar *v.* to revile, insult, call bad names.

vi•tu•pe•rio *m.* affront, insult; reproach; censure.

viu•da *f.* widow.

viu•dez *f.* widowhood.

viu•do *m.* widower.

vi•vac, vi•va•que *m.* bivouac, military encampment; *Am.* police headquarters.

vi•va•ci•dad *f.* vivacity; brightness; liveliness.

vi•va•ra•cho *adj.* lively; vivacious, gay.

vi•vaz *adj.* vivacious, lively; bright, keen, witty.

ví•ve•res *m. pl.* food supplies, provisions.

vi•ve•ro *m.* fish pond, fish hatchery, tree nursery.

vi•ve•za *f.* vivacity; animation, liveliness, quickness; brilliance, cleverness.

ví•vi•do *adj.* vivid; colorful.

vi•vien•da *f.* dwelling; apartament.

vi•vien•te *adj.* living.

vi•vir *v.* to live; to endure, last; **¡viva!** hurrah! long live; **¿quién vive?** who goes there?; *m.* existence, living.

vi•vo *adj.* (*no muerto*) alive; living; (*ágil*) lively; quick; (*vistoso*) vivid; bright; (*listo*) clever, wide-awake; **tío –** merry-go-round; **al –** vividly; **de viva voz** by word of mouth; **tocar en lo –** to hurt to the quick, touch the most sensitive spot.

viz•ca•cha *f. Andes, Riopl.* viscacha (*South American rodent about the size of a hare*).

viz•ca•che•ra *f. Andes, Riopl.* viscacha burrow or hole; *Am.* room filled with junk; **vizcacheral** *m. Andes, Riopl.* ground full of viscacha burrows.

vis•caí•no *adj.* Biscayan, of or from Biscay, Spain.

vo•ca•blo *m.* word, term.

vo•ca•bu•la•rio *m.* vocabulary.

vo•ca•ción *f.* vocation; aptness, talent.

vo•cal *adj.* vocal; oral; vowel; *f.* vowel: *m.* voter (*in an assembly or council*).

vo•ce•ar *v.* to shout; to cry out; to hail.

vo•ce•ci•ta *f.* sweet little voice.

vo•ce•ría *f.* clamor, shouting.

vo•ce•río *m. Am.* clamor, shouting

vo•ce•ro *m.* spokesman.

vo•ci•fe•rar *v.* to shout, clamor; to yell; to boast loudly of.

vo•de•vil *m.* vaudeville.

vo•lan•te *adj.* flying; floatin; **papel** (*or* **hoja**) − handbill, circular; *m.* ruffle, frill; steering wheel; balance wheel; flywheel.

vo•lar² *v. irr.* to fly; to fly away; to explode; to irritate, pique; to rouse (*bird game*); **-se** *Carib:, Col.* to fly off the handle, lose one's temper.

vo•lá•til *adj.* volatile; fickle, changeable; flying.

vol•cán *m.* volcano; *Col.* precipice; *Am.* swift torrent, *C.A.* **un − de** many; lots of; a pile of.

vol•cá•ni•co *adj.* volcanic.

vol•car²,⁶ *v. irr.* to overturn; to capsize; to upset; to make dizzy; **-se** to upset, get upset.

vo•le•ar *v.* to volley, hit (*a ball*) in the air.

vo•li•ción *f.* volition.

vol•ta•je *m.* voltage.

vol•te•ar *v.* to turn, turn around; to revolve; to turn inside out; to overturn; to tumble or roll over; to turn a somersault; *Am.* to go prying around; *Col., Ven., C.A., Mex., Andes* − **la espalda** to turn one's back; **-se** to turn over; to change sides.

vol•te•re•ta *f.* somersault, tumble.

vol•tio, volt *m.* volt.

vo•lu•ble *adj.* fickle, moody; changeable; twining (*as a climbing wine*).

vo•lu•men *m.* volume.

vo•lu•mi•no•so *adj.* voluminous, bulky, very large.

vo•lun•tad *f.* will; desire; determination; benevolence, good will; consent; **última** − last will, testament; **de** (*or* **de buena**) − willingly, with pleasure.

vo•lun•ta•rio *adj.* voluntary, willful; *m.* volunteer.

vo•lun•ta•rio•so *adj.* willful.

vo•lup•tuo•so *adj.* voluptuous; sensual.

vo•lu•ta *f.* scroll, spiral-like ornament; **-s de humo** spirals of smoke.

vo•lver²,⁵² *v. irr.* (*regresar*) to return; (*dar vuelta*) to turn; to turn up, over, or inside out; to restore; − **loco** to drive crazy; − **a** (+ *inf.*) to do again; − **en sí** to come to, recover one's senses; − **por** to return for; to defend; **-se** to become; to turn; to turn around; to change one's ideas; **-se atrás** to go back; to back out, go back to one's word; **-se loco** to go crazy.

vo•mi•tar *v.* to vomit.

vó•mi•to *m.* vomit, vomiting.

vo•ra•ci•dad *f.* voraciousness, greediness.

vo•rá•gi•ne *f.* vortex, whirlpool.

vo•raz *adj.* voracious, ravenous, greedy.

vór•ti•ce *m.* vortex, whirlpool; whirlwind, tornado; center of a cyclone.

vo•ta•ción *f.* voting; vote, total number of votes.

vo•tan•te *m. & f.* voter.

vo•tar *v.* to vote; to vow; to curse; ¡**voto a tal**! by Jove!.

vo•to *m.* vote; vow; prayer; votive offering; oath; wish; − **de confianza** vote of confidence.

voz *f.* (*capacidad*) voice; (*sonido*) shout, outcry; (*palabra*) word; rumor; − **común** common rumor or gossip; **a − en cuello** (*or* **a − en grito**) shouting; at the top of one's lungs; **en − alta** aloud; **a voces** shouting; with shouts; **secreto a voces** open secret; **dar voces** to shout, yell.

vo•za•rrón *m.* loud, strong voice.

vuel•co *m.* upset; overturning; capsizing; tumble.

vue•lo *m.* flight; width, fullness (*of a dress or cloak*); frill, ruffle; jut, projection (*of a building*); **al** (*or* **a**) − on the fly; quickly; **levantar** (*or* **alzar**) **el** − to fly away, to soar.

vuel•ta *f.* (*giro*) turn; return; repetition; (*parte opuesta*) reverse side; cuff, facing of a sleeve; cloak linig; (*cambio*) change (*money returned*); **a la** − around the corner; on returning; **a la − de los años** within a few years; *Am.* **otra** − again; **dar -s** to turn over and over, to wander about; **dar una** − to take a walk; **estar de** − to be back; **no tiene − de hoja** there are no two ways about it.

vuel•to *p.p.* of **volver**; *m. Am.* change (*money returned*).

vues•tro *poss. adj.* your, of yours (*fam. pl.*); *poss. pron.* yours.

vul•gar *adj.* common, ordinary; in common use; low, vile, base.

vul•ga•ri•dad *f.* vulgarity, coarseness, commonness.

vul•ga•ris•mo *m.* slang, slang expression, vulgar or ungrammatical expression.

vul•go *m.* populace, the common people; *adv.* commonly, popularly.

Y

y *conj.* and.

ya *adv.* already; now; finally; soon, presently; in time; ¡−! now I see!; I understand; enough!; − **lo creo**! I should say so!; yes, of course!; − **no** no longer; − **que** since; although; − **se ve** of course; it is clear; − **voy** I am coming.

ya•cer⁵⁰ *v. irr.* to lie (*in the grave*); to be lying down; to lie, be situated.

ya•ci•mien•to *m.* bed, layer (*of ore*); − **de petróleo** oil field.

yan•qui *m. & f.* North American, native of the united States; Yankee.

yan•tar *v.* to eat; *m.* food, meal.

ya·ra·rá f. Riopl. Argentine poisonous snake.

yar·da f. yard (unit of measure).

ya·te m. yacht.

ye·dra = **hiedra.**

ye·gua f. mare; Am. cigar butt; adj. Am. big, large; **yeguada** f. herd of mares.

yel·mo m. helmet.

ye·ma f. egg yolk; bud, shoot; candied egg yolk; - **del dedo** finger tip.

yer·ba = **hierba.**

yer·ba·bue·na f. mint; peppermint.

yer·be·ro m. Méx., Cuba, Ven., Col., Andes herb vendor.

yer·mo m. desert, wilderness; adj. desert uninhabited; uncultivated; sterile.

yer·no m. son-in-law.

ye·rro m. error, fault, mistake.

yer·to adj. stiff, motionless, rigid.

yes·ca f. tinder; anything highly inflam-mable; incentive (to passion); Riopl., Mex. **estar hecho una** – to be in great anger.

ye·so m. gypsum, chalk; plaster; chalk (for blackboard); – **blanco** whitewash; – **mate** plaster of Paris; **yesoso** adj. chalky.

yo pers. pron. I.

yo·do m. iodine.

yu·go m. yoke; marriage tie; burden.

yun·que f. anvil.

yun·ta f. yoke of oxen; pair of draft animals.

yu·yo m. Cuba, Mex., Riopl. Andes wild grass, weeds; Am. an herb sauce; Am. garden stuff; Andes **estar** – to be lifeless, insipid; Col. **volverse uno** – to faint.

Z

za·ca·te m. Mex., C.A. grass, forage; hay.

za·fa·do adj. impudent, brazen, shameless; Ven. smart, wide-awake, keen; Col., Mex., Andes "touched", halfcrazy, p.p. of **zafar.**

za·far v. to release, set free; to dislodge; Am. to exclude; -**se** to slip away, to dodge; to get rid (of); to get loose; Col., Ven., Andes to get dislocated (said of a bone); Col., Mex., Andes to go crazy; Col. to use foul language.

za·fio adj. coarse, uncouth, rude.

za·fir, za·fi·ro m. sapphire.

za·fra f. sugar-making season; sugar making; sugar crop.

za·ga f. rear; **a la** – (a or en –) behind.

za·gal m. young shepherd; lad; **zagala** f. young shepherdess; lass, maiden; **zagalejo** m. young shepherd; short skirt; petticoat.

za·guán m. vestibule.

za·he·rir[3] v. irr. to hurt (feelings); to censure, reprove; to reproach.

zai·no adj. treacherous; vicious; chestnut-colored (horse).

za·la·me·ro m. fawner, flatterer, servile person; **zalamería** f. flattery, scraping and bowing.

za·le·a f. pelt, undressed sheepskin.

zam·bo adj. knock-kneed; m. Riopl., Ven., Andes Indian and negro halfbreed; Col., a species of South American monkey.

zam·bu·lli·da f. dive, dip, plunge.

zam·bu·llir[20] v. to plunge, dip, duck; -**se** to dive; to plunge.

zam·bu·llón m. quick, sudden dip or dive.

za·na·ho·ria f. carrot.

zan·ca f. long leg of any fowl; long leg; long prop; **zancada** f. stride, long step.

zan·co m. stilt; **andar en -s** to walk on stilts.

zan·cón adj. lanky, long-legged; Col., Guat., Mex. too short (skirt or dress).

zan·cu·do adj. long-legged; m. Mex., C.A., Ven., Col., Andes mosquito.

zán·ga·no m. drone; loafer, sponger; Am. rogue, rascal.

zan·go·lo·te·ar v. to shake, jiggle; -**se** to shake; to waddle; to sway from side to side.

zan·go·lo·te·o m. jiggle, jiggling; shaking; waddling.

zan·guan·ga f. feigned illness; **hacer la** – to pretend to be ill; **zanguango** adj. lazy; silly; m. fool.

zan·ja f. ditch; trench; Am. irrigation ditch.

zan·jar v. to excavate; to dig ditches in; to settle (disputes).

za·pa·llo m. Pan., Col., Ven., Andes pumpkin; squash.

za·pa·pi·co m. pickaxe.

za·pa·ta f. half-boot; – **de freno** brake shoe.

za·pa·te·a·do m. a Spanish tap dance.

za·pa·te·ar v. to tap with the feet; to tapdance.

za·pa·te·o m. tapping with the feet; Am a popular tap dance.

za·pa·te·ría f. shoe store; shoemaker's shop.

za·pa·te·ro m. shoemaker; shoe dealer.

za·pa·ti·lla f. slipper, pump.

za·pa·to m. shoe.

za·ran·da·jas f. pl. trifles, trinkets, worthless things.

za·ran·de·ar v. to winnow (separate the chaff from grain); to sift out; to move (something) quickly; wiggle, jiggle; C.A., Riopl. to whip, lash, mistreat, abuse; -**se** to wiggle, jiggle; to bump along; to waddle; to strut, swagger.

za·ran·de·o m. jiggle, jiggling; sifting; waddling; strutting.

zar·ci·llo m. earring; tendril (coil of a climbing vine); Andes, Mex. earmark (on the ear of an animal).

zar·pa f. paw, claw; weighing anchor; **echar la** – to grasp, seize; **zarpada** f. pounce; blow with a paw; **zarpazo** m. blow with the paw; big blow, thud; hard fall.

zar·par *v.* to weigh anchor; to set sail.

zar·za *f.* bramble; blackberry bush.

zar·za·mo·ra *f.* blackberry.

zar·zue·la *f.* Spanish musical comedy.

zig·zag *m.* zigzag.

zig·za·gue·ar *v.* to zigzag.

zinc = cinc.

zó·ca·lo *m.*base (*of a pedestal*); *Mex.* public square.

zo·día·co *m.* zodiac.

zo·na *f.* zone; band, girdle; shingles (*a disease*).

zon·zo *adj.* dull, stupid, silly, foolish.

zo·o·lo·gia *f.* zoology.

zo·o·ló·gi·co *adj.* zoological; **jardin** – zoo.

zo·pen·co *adj.* stupid, dull, thick-headed *m.* blockhead, dunce.

zo·pi·lo·te *m. Mex. C.A.* buzzard.

zo·que·te *m.* (*cosa*) block, chunk of wood; hunk of bread; (*persona*) blokhead, dunce, fool; ugly fat person; *Am.* grease, dirt, filth; *Am.* slap.

zo·rra *f.* fox; foxy person; drunkenness; prostitute; **pillar una** – to get drunk.

zo·rro *m.* fox; foxy person; **-s** fox skins; duster made of cloth or leather strips. **estar hecho un** – to be drowsy; **hacerse uno el** – to pretend to be stupid or not to hear; *adj.* foxy; **zorrillo, zorrino** *m. Riopl.* skunk; **zo-rruno** *adj.* foxy.

zor·zal *f.* thrush; crafty fellow; *Am.* fool, scapegoat, dupe.

zo·zo·bra *f.* foundering; sinking; anxiety, worry.

zo·zo·brar *v.* to founder; to capsize; to sink; to be in great danger; to fret, worry.

zum·bar *v.*to buzz; to hum; to ring (*said of the ears*); to scoff at ; to strike, hit; *Ven., Col.* to throw out or away; *Andes* to punish; **– una bofetada** to give a slap; **-se** *Am.* to slip away, disappear.

zum·bi·do *m.* buzzing, humming; ringing (*in one's ears*); hit, blow, whack.

zum·bón *adj.* funny, playful; sarcastic; *m.* jester.

zu·mo *f.* juice; profit; **zumoso** *adj.* juicy.

zur·ci·do *m.* darn; darning; *p.p. of* **zurcir**.

zur·cir[10] *v.* to darn; to invent, make up (*lies*).

zur·do *adj.* left-handed; left; **a zurdas** with the left hand; clumsily.

zu·ro *m.* cob, corncob.

zu·rra *f.* beating, flogging; tanning (*of leather*).

zu·rrar *v.* to flog, thrash; to tan (*leather*).

zu·rrón *m.* pouch; bag; leather bag; *Ven., Col.* big coward.

zu·ta·no *m.* so-and-so; a certain person. (*Used often with* **Fulano** *and* **Mengano**).

Hojas de Práctica

Preposiciones de lugar

The meat is
on the table.

The truck is **in front of** the car.

The car is
behind the truck.

The cat is **under** the table.

Sam is **between** Kim and Tom.

The bird is **in /
inside** the cage

The temperature
is **below** zero

Kim is **next to / beside** Sam.

The girl
is leaning
against the wall.

Tom is **opposite /
across from** Kim

The house is **among** the tress.

Preposiciones de movimiento

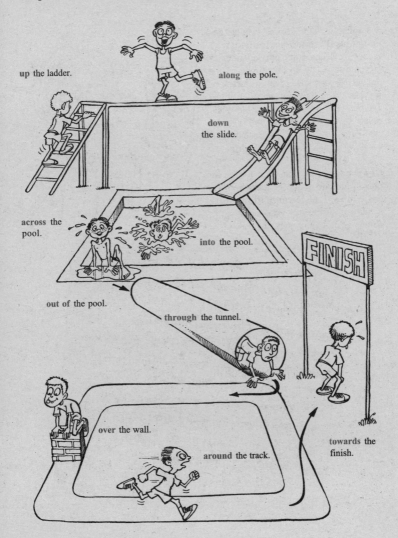

up the ladder.

along the pole.

down
the slide.

across the
pool.

into the pool.

out of the pool.

through the tunnel.

FINISH

over the wall.

around the track.

towards the
finish.

Cómo corregir sus propios textos

Si comete muchos errores y faltas de
ortografía al escribir una carta, una
redacción o cualquier otro documento, a
la gente le puede costar trabajo
entenderlo. Además, estos errores
pueden bajarle la calificación en un
examen. Por eso, es importante que
revise su trabajo y corrija todos los
errores que encuentre, paa lo cual puede
ser de gran ayuda este diccionario.

Observe ahora un texto que fue escrito
por un alumno y que contiene numerosos errores. Intente corregirlos con la
ayuda del diccionario y las pistas que
damos en la página siguiente.

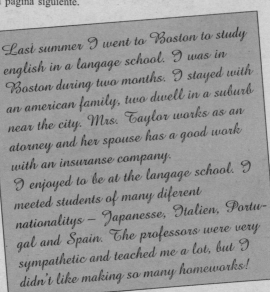

Last summer I went to Boston to study
english in a langage school. I was in
Boston during two months. I stayed with
an american family, two dwell in a suburb
near the city. Mrs. Taylor works as an
atorney and her spouse has a good work
with an insuranse company.
I enjoyed to be at the langage school. I
meeted students of many diferent
nationalitys – Japanesse, Italien, Portu-
gal and Spain. The professors were very
sympathetic and teached me a lot, but I
didn't like making so many homeworks!

Pistas para la corrección de textos

☐ **1. ¿He utilizado la palabra correcta?**

En este diccionario incluimos notas sobre palabras que la gente tiende a confundir. Busque entradas como *sympathetic, work* o cualquier otra que lo haga dudar.

☐ **2. ¿He escogido el estilo más adecuado?**

Puede que algunas de las palabras que ha utilizado sean demasiado formales o informales para el texto que escribió. Compruébelo en las entradas correspondientes de nuestro diccionario.

☐ **3. ¿He combinado correctamente las palabras?**

¿Se dice to *make your homework* o to *do your homework?* Si no está seguro, consulte las entradas de los verbos correspondientes, donde encontrará un ejemplo que se lo aclare.

☐ **4. ¿Qué proposición debo utilizar?**

¿Se dice *close to* o *close from?* Las preposiciones en inglés pueden llegar a ser una pesadilla... ¡¡parece como si cada sustantivo, adjetivo y verbo llevara una preposición diferente!! Este diccionario le ayudará a la hora de hacer la elección.

☐ **5. ¿He acertado con la estructura sintáctica?**

¿Enjoy to do sth o *enjoy doing sth?* La entrada *enjoy* le ayudará a solucionar esta duda. Asegúrese de comprobar este tipo de estructuras en el texto.

☐ **6. ¿He cometido faltas de ortografía?**

Tenga cuidado con aquellas palabras que se parecen a las de su propia lengua, ya que a menudo se escriben de distinta manera. Fíjese también en los nombres de países y nacionalidades (encontrará una lista en el apéndice 2). Compruebe las terminaciones del plural, las formas en *-ing,* las dobles consonantes, etc.

☐ **7. ¿Es el texto gramaticalmente correcto?**

¿Se ha fijado en si los sustantivos son contables o incontables? ¿Ha utilizado el pasado y el participio correctos en los verbos? Consulte la lista de verbos irregulares del apéndice 5 para asegurarse.

Ahora ya puede darle la vuelta a la página y comprobar las respuestas.

Respuestas

Last summer I went to Boston to study **English** in a language school. I was in Boston **for** two months. I stayed with an American family, who **live** in a suburb near the city. Mrs. Taylor works as an attorney, and her **husband** has a good **job** with an insurance company. I **enjoyed being** at the language school. I **met** students of many different nationalities — Japanese, italian, **Portuguese** and **Spanish**. The teachers were very nice and **taught** me a lot, but I didn't like **doing** so **much homework!**

Cómo archivar el vocabulario nuevo

A la hora de aprender vocabulario, es importante ordenar y archivar todas aquellas palabras nuevas que se quieran recordar. He aquí algunas sugerencias sobre cómo hacerlo.

Cuadernos de vocabulario

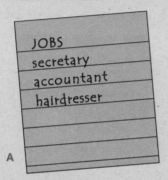

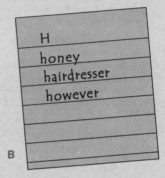

A muchos estudiantes les gusta tener un cuaderno especial para anotar el vocabulario. Hay dos maneras de organizar dicho cuaderno: por temas (como en el dibujo A) o por orden alfabético (dibujo B). Escriba unas cuantas palabras al principio, y añada después otras a medida que las vaya aprendiendo.

Fichas de vocabulario

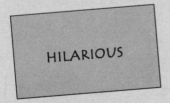

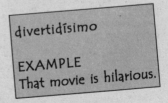

parte anterior de la ficha   *parte posterior de la ficha*

Otra manera de organizar el vocabulario es escribir cada palabra nueva en una ficha y guardar todas las fichas en un fichero. Escriba la palabra en una cara de la ficha y la traducción, acompañada de algún ejemplo, en la otra cara. Esto le será muy útil cuando quiera repasar lo que ha aprendido: mire la palabra e intente recordar cómo se traduce al español; o, si prefiere, mire la traducción y trate de adivinar de qué palabra se trata.

Cómo anotar información adicional sobre una palabra

Puede que le interese recordar ciertos detalles sobre una palabra. Búsquelos en el diccionario y decida cuáles quiere anotar en su cuaderno o en sus fichas de vocabulario. Trate de dar siempre un ejemplo, pues le ayudará a recordar cómo se usa la palabra en inglés.

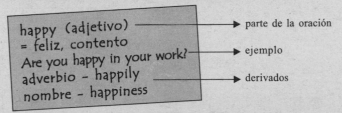

happy (adjetivo) ──────▶ parte de la oración
= feliz, contento
Are you happy in your work? ──────▶ ejemplo
adverbio - happily ──────▶ derivados
nombre - happiness

Ejercicio 1
Establezca, con la ayuda del diccionario, cuáles son los detalles más importantes de las siguientes palabras, y a continuación anótelos.

bleed   deaf   on the ball   fluent   swap

Cuadros sinópticos y diagramas

A veces puede ser interesante agrupar las palabras por familias. Observe los dos métodos que mostramos a continuación:

a) Cuadros sinópticos

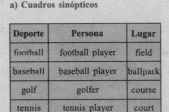

Deporte	Persona	Lugar
football	football player	field
baseball	baseball player	ballpark
golf	golfer	course
tennis	tennis player	court

b) Diagramas

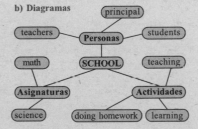

Ejercicio 2
a. *Haga un cuadro sinóptico utilizando palabras que se refieran a trabajos, lugares de trabajo y cosas que la gente utiliza en el trabajo.*
b. *Haga un diagrama que muestre vocabulario relacionado con las vacaciones. Puede agrupar las palabras según se refieran a lugares donde alojarse, métodos de transporte o actividades.*

Cómo redactar una carta
Cartas formales

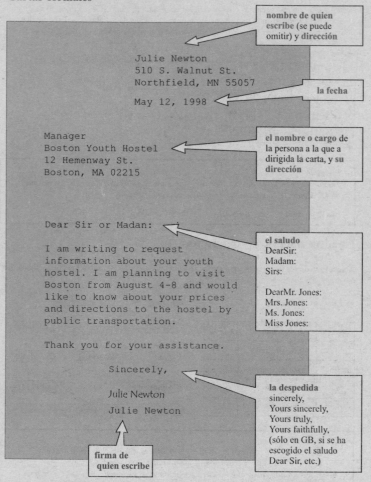

nombre de quien escribe (se puede omitir) y dirección

```
                    Julie Newton
                    510 S. Walnut St.
                    Northfield, MN 55057

                    May 12, 1998
```

la fecha

```
Manager
Boston Youth Hostel
12 Hemenway St.
Boston, MA 02215
```

el nombre o cargo de la persona a la que a dirigida la carta, y su dirección

```
Dear Sir or Madan:

I am writing to request
information about your youth
hostel. I am planning to visit
Boston from August 4-8 and would
like to know about your prices
and directions to the hostel by
public transportation.

Thank you for your assistance.

        Sincerely,

        Julie Newton
        Julie Newton
```

el saludo
DearSir:
Madam:
Sirs:

DearMr. Jones:
Mrs. Jones:
Ms. Jones:
Miss Jones:

la despedida
sincerely,
Yours sincerely,
Yours truly,
Yours faithfully,
(sólo en GB, si se ha escogido el saludo Dear Sir, etc.)

firma de quien escribe

Es importante recordar que este tipo de cartas debe redactarse en estilo formal y por lo tanto se debe evitar utilizar contracciones como *I'm, I'd,* etc.

Cartas informales

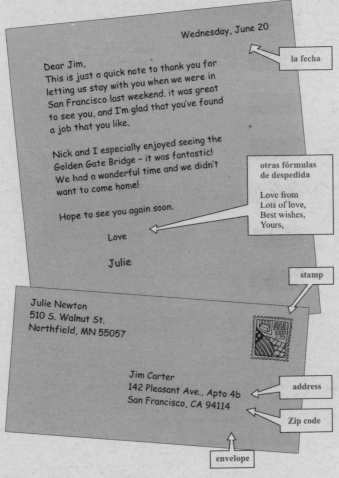

Wednesday, June 20

la fecha

Dear Jim,
This is just a quick note to thank you for letting us stay with you when we were in San Francisco last weekend. it was great to see you, and I'm glad that you've found a job that you like.

Nick and I especially enjoyed seeing the Golden Gate Bridge – it was fantastic! We had a wonderful time and we didn't want to come home!

Hope to see you again soon.

Love

Julie

otras fórmulas de despedida

Love from
Lots of love,
Best wishes,
Yours,

stamp

Julie Newton
510 S. Walnut St.
Northfield, MN 55057

Jim Carter
142 Pleasant Ave., Apto 4b
San Francisco, CA 94114

address

Zip code

envelope

Es importante recordar que este tipo de cartas se redacta en un estilo más informal, y que en ellas se pueden utilizar contracciones como *I'm, you're, didn't,* etc.

La hora

10:00	ten o'clock
5:15	a quarter after five five fifteen
6:30	six thirty half past six
3:45	a quarter to four three forty-five
11:10	ten past eleven eleven ten
11:40	twenty to twelve eleven forty
14:07	seven minutes past two two o seven*

What time is it?

What's the time?

It's ten o'clock?

*El "reloj de veinticuatro horas" no se utiliza en el lenguaje hablado, salvo para leer horarios de aviones y buses.

Si se quiere especificar que son las 06:00 y no las 18:00, se puede decir *six o'clock in the morning*. 15:30 se diría *half past three in the afternoon* y 22:00 sería *ten o'clock in the evening*.

En lenguaje más formal se utiliza a.m./p.m. para distinguir entre las horas de la mañana y las de la tarde.

60 seconds	=	1 minute
60 minutes	=	1 hour
24 hours	=	1 day

Ejemplos
The train leaves at 6:56 a.m.
Something woke me at two o'clock in the morning.
Office hours are 9 a.m. to 4:30 p.m.

Vamos a llamar por teléfono

¿Cómo se expresan los números de teléfono?

(617) 731-0293 area code six one seven, seven three one, o two nine three

637-2335 six three seven, two three three five

Para hacer una *llamada telefónica* (a **telephone call**), *levantamos* el *auricular* (**pick up the receiver**) y *marcamos* un número de teléfono (**dial a telephone number**). Cuando el teléfono *suena* (the telephone **rings**), la persona a la que llamamos lo *contesta* (**answers it**). Si esa persona está hablando por teléfono en ese momento, el teléfono estará *ocupado* (**busy**).

La puntuación inglesa

. El *punto seguido* o **period (.)** pone fin a la frase, siempre que ésta no sea una pregunta o una exclamación:

We're leaving now
That's all.
Thank you

También se utiliza en abreviaturas:
Acacia Ave
Walton St.

? El *signo de interrogación* o **question mark (?)** se pone al final de una frase interrogativa directa:
"Who's that man?" Jenny asked.
Pero nunca al final de una interrogativa indirecta:
Jenny asked who the man was.

! El *signo de admiración* o **exclamation point (!)** se pone al final de una frase que expresa sorpresa, entusiasmo, miedo, etc.
What an amazing story!
How well you look!
Oh no! The cat's been run over!

También se utiliza con interjecciones y palabras onomatopéyicas:
Bye!
Ow!
Crash!

, La coma o **comma (,)** indica una breve pausa dentro de una frase:
I ran all the way to the station, but I still missed the train.
However, he may be wrong.

También utilizamos la coma para citar a una persona o para introducir una frase en estilo directo:
Fiona said, "I'll help you".
"I'll help you", said Fiona, "but you'll have to wait till Monday".

La coma puede separar los elementos de una enumeración o de una lista (no es obligatoria delante de *"and"*).
It was a cold, rainy day.
This store sells records, tapes, and compact discs.

: Los *dos puntos* o **colon (:)** se utilizan para introducir citas largas o listas de objetos:
There is a choice of main course: roast beef, turkey or omelette.

; El *punto y coma* o **semicolon (;)** se utiliza para separar dos partes bien diferenciadas dentro de una oración:
John wanted to go; I did not.

También puede separar elementos de una lista cuando ya hemos utilizado la coma:

The school uniform consists of navy skirt or pants; gray, white or pale blue shirt; navy sweater or cardigan.

? *El apóstrofo* o **apostrophe** (') puede indicar dos cosas:

a) que se ha omitido una letra, como en el
caso de las contracciones
hasn't, don't, I'm y *he's*

b) el genitivo sajón:
Peter's scarf
Jane's mother
my friend's car

Cuando un sustantivo acaba en s, no siempre
es necesario añadir una segunda. s. p. ej. en
Jesus' family

Observemos que la posición del apóstrofo es
distinta cuando acompaña a sustantivos que
están en singular y en plural:

the girl's keys
(= las llaves de una niña)
the girls' keys
(= las llaves de varias niñas)

" " Las *comillas* o **quotation marks (" ")**, se
utilizan para introducir las palabras o los
pensamientos de una persona:

"Come and see", said Martin.
Angela shouted, "Over here!"
"Will they get here on time?"she wondered.

Cuando queremos destacar una palabra, o bien
la utilizamos con un sentido poco común o
irónico, dicha palabra suele aparecer entre co
millas:

The word "conversation" is often spelled
incorrectly.
La palabra "conversación" a menudo se escribe incorrectamente.

The "experts" were unable to answer a sim-
ple question.

Los "expertos" fueron incapaces de contestar
una pregunta tan sencilla.

- El *guión* o *hyphen (-)* se usa para unir dos
o más palabras que forman una unidad:

mother-in-law
a ten-ton truck

También se usa para unir un prefijo a una palabra:
non-violent
anti-American
y en números compuestos:
thirty-four
seventy-nine

Cuando tenemos que partir una palabra al final
de una línea, lo hacemos por medio de un guión.

— La *raya* o **dash (–)** se utiliza para separar
una frase o explicación dentro de una oración más amplia. También la podemos encontrar al final de la oración, para resumir
su contenido:

A few people – not more than ten – had already
arrived.
The burglars had taken the furniture, the TV
and stereo, the paintings – absolutely
everything.

( ) El *paréntesis* o **parentheses ( )** sirve para
resaltar información adicional dentro de
una oración:

Two of the runners (Johns and Smith) finished
the race in under an hour.

Los números y letras que indican distintos
apartados se marcan también mediante paréntesis:

The camera has three main advantages:
1. *its compact size*
2. *its low price and*
3. *the quality of the photographs.*
What would you do if you won a lot of money?
a. *save it*
b. *travel around the world*
c. *buy a new house*

El sistema de educación en los Estados Unidos

Escuelas

La mayoría de los niños norteamericanos van a escuelas oficiales, que son gratuitas. En los Estados Unidos éstas se llaman **public schools**. (No deben confundirse con las **public schools** británicas). También existen los colegios particulares (**private schools**) que a veces son respaldados por organizaciones religiosas.

Evaluaciones

No existe un sistema nacional de exámenes, aunque algunas escuelas y algunos estados hacen sus propios exámenes al final de cada semestre. En general, se evalúa a los alumnos por el proceso de **continuous assessment**, lo que significa que los maestros evalúan a los alumnos durante todo el año con base en sus calificaciones en pruebas, discusiones, y trabajo escrito y oral. Si los estudiantes quieren continuar su educación, algunas universidades y colegios les exigen presentar un examen, el **SAT (Scholastic Aptitude Test)**.

Grado

Los alumnos pueden graduarse en **high school** si han reunido suficientes **units** (aproximadamente 120 horas de clase en una materia). Casi todos los alumnos reúnen **units** en materias básicas (y obligatorias) llamadas **requirements** en sus primeros años de **high school**. En los dos últimos años pasan a materias electivas y más especializadas llamadas **electives.**

Estudios superiores

La mayoría de los programas universitarios tienen una duración de cuatro años. Muchas universidades son privadas, pero los estudiantes también tienen que pagar para asistir a las universidades públicas. No hay exámenes finales; los estudiantes reciben un **degree** si han reunido suficientes **credits** en la materia elegida.

Esta tabla muestra como se organiza generalmente la educación en los Estados Unidos, aunque existen sistemas diferentes en algunos estados.

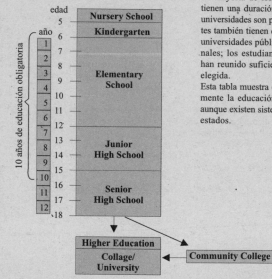

El gobierno en los Estados Unidos

El sistema federal

La constitución de los Estados Unidos divide el poder entre el gobierno federal (**the federal government**) y los gobiernos de los estados individuales (**state governments**). Cada estado tiene sus propias leyes y su propio sistema de gobierno. El gobierno federal se ocupa de asuntos nacionales como la economía y la política exterior.

El gobierno federal está compuesto por tres ramas: la ejecutiva, bajo el mando del presidente (**President**); la legislativa (el congreso o **Congress**, compuesto por el senado o **Senate** y la Cámara de Representantes o **House of Representatives**); y la judicial (la Corte Suprema o **Supreme Court** y las cortes federales). El congreso hace las leyes pero el presidente tiene el poder de vetarlas o **veto**; la Corte Suprema puede declarar que una ley va en contra de la constitución.

Las elecciones

Cada estado elige dos senadores (**senators**) y varios representantes (**representatives**) a la Cámara (el número depende de la población de cada estado).

La elección de los representantes se lleva a cabo cada dos años. Los senadores se eligen por un período de seis años; cada dos años la tercera parte de éstos se somete a nuevas elecciones. El presidente no es elegido directamente por los ciudadanos, sino por el colegio electoral (**electoral college**), que está compuesto por delegados (**delegates**) de los cincuenta estados. Las elecciones presidenciales se llevan a cabo cada cuatro años.

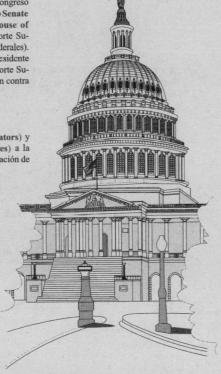

Apéndices

En esta sección se encuentran los apéndices a los que hacemos referencia a lo largo del diccionario:

Apéndice 1
Expresiones numéricas
Números

Cardinales		Ordinales	
1	one	1st	first
2	two	2nd	second
3	three	3rd	third
4	four	4th	fourth
5	five	5th	fifth
6	six	6th	sixth
7	seven	7th	seventh
8	eight	8th	eighth
9	nine	9th	ninth
10	ten	10th	tenth
11	eleven	11th	eleventh
12	twelve	12th	twelfth
13	thirteen	13th	thirteenth
14	fourteen	14th	fourteenth
15	fifteen	15th	fifteenth
16	sixteen	16th	sixteenth
17	seventeen	17th	seventeenth
18	eighteen	18th	eighteenth
19	nineteen	19th	nineteenth
20	twenty	20th	twentieth
21	twenty-one	21st	twenty-first
22	twenty-two	22nd	twenty-second
30	thirty	30th	thirtieth
40	forty	40th	fortieth
50	fifty	50th	fiftieth
60	sixty	60th	sixtieth
70	seventy	70th	seventieth
80	eighty	80th	eightieth
90	ninety	90th	ninetieth
100	a/one hundred	100th	hundredth
101	a/one hundred and one	101st	hundred and first
200	two hundred	200th	two hundredth
1,000	a/one thousand	1,000th	thousandth
10,000	ten thousand	10,000th	ten thousandth
100,000	a/one hundred thousand	100,000th	hundred thousandth
1,000,000	a/one million	1,000,000th	millionth

Ejemplos

528	*five hundred and twenty-eight*
2,976	*two thousand, nine hundred and seventy-six*
50,439	*fifty thousand, four hundred and thirty-nine*
2,250,321	*two million, two hundred and fifty thousand, three hundred and twenty-one*

En inglés se utiliza una coma (y NO un punto) para marcar el millar, por ejemplo *25,000*.

En cuanto a números como 100, 1.000, 1.000.000, etc. se pueden decir de dos maneras, *one hundred* o *a hundred*, *one thousand* o *a thousand*.

0 (cero) se pronuncia *zero, nothing*, o/Ø /, *nought* (*GB*) dependiendo de las expresiones.

Quebrados

1/2	a half
1/3	a/one third
1/4	a quarter
2/5	two fifths
1/8	an/one eighth
1/10	a/one tenth
1/16	a/one sixteenth
1 1/2	one and a half
2 3/8	two and three eighths

Hay dos maneras de expresar los quebrados en inglés: lo normal es decir one eighth of the cake, two thirds of the population, etc.; pero su profesor de matemáticas puede pedirle que resuelva el siguiente ejercicio:

Multiply two over five by three over eight (2/5 x 3/8).

Expresiones matemáticas

+	plus
−	minus
x	times *o* multiplied by
÷	divided by
=	equals
%	per cent
3^2	three squared
5^3	five cubed
6^{10}	six to the tenth power

Ejemplos

$6 + 9 = 15$	*Six **plus** nine equals/is fifteen*
$5 \times 6 = 30$	*Five **times** six equals thirty/ Five **multiplied by** six is thirty.*
75%	*Seventy-five **per cent** of the class passed the test.*

Decimales

0.1	(zero) point one
0.25	(zero) point two five
1.75	one point seven five

En inglés se utiliza una coma (y NO un punto) para marcar los decimales.

Peso

	Sistema en los Estados Unidos			Sistema Métrico Decimal	
	1 ounce	(oz.)	=	31.103 grams	(g)
16 ounces	= 1 pound	(lb.)	=	0.373 kilogram	(kg)
2.000 pounds	= 1 ton	(t.)	=	0.907 metric ton	(m.t.)

Ejemplos
The baby weighed 7 lb 4 oz (seven pounds four ounces).
For this recipe you need 500g (five hundred grams) of flour.

Longitud

	Sistema en los Estados Unidos			Sistema Métrico Decimal	
	1 inch	(in.)	=	25.4 millimeters	(mm)
12 inches	= 1 foot	(ft.)	=	30.48 centimeters	(cm)
3 feet	= 1 yard	(yd.)	=	0.914 meter	(m)
1 760 yards	= 1 mile		=	1.609 kilometers	(km)

Ejemplos
Height: 5 ft 9 in (five foot nine/five feet nine)
The hotel is 30 yds (thirty yards) from the beach
The car was doing 50 mph (fifty miles per hour)
The room is 11' x 9'6" (eleven foot by nine foot six/ekeveb feet bt bube feet six).

Superficie

Sistema en los Estados Unidos			Sistema Métrico Decimal
	1 square inch	(sq in.)	= 6.452 square centimeters
144 square inches =	1 square foot	(sq ft.)	= 929.03 square centimeters
9 square feet =	1 square yard	(sq yd.)	= 0.836 square meter
4,840 square yards =	1 acre		= 0.405 hectare
640 acres =	1 square mile		= 2.59 square kilometers/259 hectares

Ejemplos
They have a 200-acre farm.
The fire destroyed 40 square miles of woodland.

Capacidad (líquidos)

Sistema en los Estados Unidos			Sistema Métrico Decimal
	1 cup		= 0.2371 liter (l)
2 cups =	1 pint	(pt.)	= 0.4731 liter (l)
2 pints =	1 quart	(qt.)	= 0.9461 liter (l)
8 pints =	1 gallon	(gal.)	= 3.7851 liters

Ejemplos
I bought a quart of milk at the store
The gas tank holds 12 gallons.

En las recetas de cocina, una taza (a cup) de ingredientes como la harina o el azúcar equivale a 0.275 litros

Moneda

EEUU	Valor de la moneda/billete	Nombre de la moneda/billete
1¢	a cent	a penny
5¢	five cents	a nickel
10¢	ten cents	a dime
25¢	twenty-five cents	a quarter
$ 1	a dollar	a dollar bill
$ 5	five dollars (five bucks*)	a five-dollar bill
$10	ten dollars (ten bucks*)	a ten-dollar bill
$20	twenty dollars (twenty bucks*)	a twenty-dollar bill
$50	fifty dollars (fifty bucks*)	a fifty-dollar bill
$100	a hundred dollars (a hundred bucks*)	a hundred-dollar bill

Ejemplos
$5.75: five seventy-five
$0.79: seventy-nine cents
The apples are $1.29 (a dollar twenty-nine/one twenty-nine) a pound.
We pay $400 a month for rent

* Las expresiones que aparecen entre paréntesis son más coloquiales.

Fechas

Cómo escribirlas:

4/15/98 (GB 15/4/98)
4-15-98 (GB 15.4.98)
April 15, 1998
15 April 1998 (GB)

Cómo decirlas:

April fifteenth, nineteen ninety-eight
The fifteenth of April/April the fifteenth, nineteen ninety-eight (GB)

Ejemplos

Her birtdhay is on April 9/9th (April ninth)
The restaurant will be closed May 3-June 1 (from May third through June first).

Apéndice 2
División territorial de los Estados Unidos

Los Estados que configuran EEUU

Alabama	(AL)	/ˌælə'bæmə/
Alaska	(AK)	/ə'læskə/
Arizona	(AZ)	/ˌæri'zoʊ nə/
Arkansas	(AR)	/'ɑːrkənsɔː/
California	(CA)	/ˌkælɪ'fɔːrnjə/
Colorado	(CO)	/ˌkɑlə'rædoʊ/
Connecticut	(CT)	/kə'netɪkət/
Delaware	(DE)	/'deləweər/
Florida	(FL)	/'flɔːridə/
Georgia	(GA)	/'dʒɔːrdʒə/
Hawaii	(HI)	/hə'waɪi/
idaho	(ID)	/'aɪdəhoʊ/
Illinois	(IL)	/ˌɪlɪ'nɔɪ/
Indiana	(IN)	/ˌɪndi'ænə/
Iowa	(IA)	/'aɪəwə/
Kansas	(KS)	/'kænzəs/
Kentucky	(KY)	/kən'tʃki/ *
Louisiana	(LA)	/luːˌzi'ænə/
Maine	(ME)	/meɪn/
Maryland	(MD)	/'merɪlənd/
Massachusetts	(MA)	/ˌmæsə'tʃuːsɪts/
Michigan	(MI)	/'mɪʃɪgən/
Minnesota	(MN)	/ˌmɪnɪ'soʊ tə/
Mississippi	(MS)	/ˌmɪsɪ'sɪpi/
Missouri	(MO)	/mɪ'zʊri/
Montana	(MT)	/mɑn'tænə/
Nebraska	(NE)	/nə'bræskə/
Nevada	(NV)	/nə'vɑdə, nə'vædə/
New Hampshire	(NH)	/nuː 'hæmpʃər/
New Jersey	(NJ)	/ˌnuː 'dʒɜːrzi/
New Mexico	(NM)	/ˌnuː 'meksɪkoʊ/
New York	(NY)	/ˌnuː 'jɔːrk/
North Carolina	(NC)	/ˌnɔrθ kærə'laɪnə/
North Dakota	(ND)	/ˌnɔkoʊ tə/
Ohio	(OH)	/oʊ 'haɪoʊ/
Oklahoma	(OK)	/ˌoʊ klə'hoʊ mə/
Oregon	(OR)	/'ɔːrɪgən/
Pennsylvania	(PA)	/ˌpensəl'veɪnjə/
Rhode island	(RI)	/roʊ d 'aɪlənd/
South Carolina	(SC)	/ˌsaʊ θ kærə'laɪnə/
South Dakota	(SD)	/ˌsaʊ θ də'koʊ tə/
Tennessee	(TN)	/ˌtenə'siː/
Texas	(TX)	/'teksəs/
Utah	(UT)	/'juːtɑ/
Vermont	(VT)	/vər'mɑnt/
Virginia	(VA)	/vər'dʒɪnjə/
Washington	(WA)	/'wɑʃɪtən, 'wɔː-/
West Virginia	(WV)	/ˌwest vər'dʒɪnjə/
Wisconsin	(WI)	/wɪs'kɑnsɪn/
Wyoming	(WY)	/waɪ'oʊ mɪ/

Ciudades principales

Atlanta	/ət'læntə/
Anchorage	/'æŋkərɪdʒ/
Baltimore	/'bɔːltɪmɔːr/
Boston	/'bɔːstən, 'bɑs-/
Chicago	/ʃɪ'kɑgoʊ/
Cincinnati	/ˌsɪnsɪ'næti/
Cleveland	/'kliːvlənd/
Dallas	/'dæləs/
Denver	/'denvər/
Detroit	/dɪ'trɔɪt/
Honolulu	/ˌhɑnə'luːluː/
Houston	/'hjuːstən/
Indianapolis	/ˌɪndiə'næpəlɪs/
Kansas City	/ˌkænzəs'sɪti/
Los Angeles	/lɔːs 'ændʒələs, lɑs-/
Miami	/maɪ'æmi/
Milwaukee	/mɪl'wɔːki/
Minneapolis	/ˌmɪni'æpəlɪs/
New Orleans	/nuː'ɔːrliːənz, ɔːr'liːnz/
New York	/ˌnuː'jɔːrk/
Philadelphia	/fɪlə'delfiə/
Pittsburgh	/'pɪtsbɜːrg/
San Diego	/sæn di'eɪgoʊ/
San Francisco	/ˌsæn frən'sɪskoʊ/
Seattle	/si'ætl/
St. Louis	/seɪnt 'luːɪs/
Washington D.C.	/'wɑʃɪtən ˌdiː 'siː, 'wɔː-/

Apéndice 3
Las Islas Británicas

Great Britain (GB) o **Britain** está formada por inglaterra - **England** /iˑɡlənd/, Escocia - **Scotland** /ˈskɑtlənd/ y Gales - **Wales** /weɪlz/.

El estado político es oficialmente conocido como **the United Kingdom (of Great Britain and Northern Ireland) (UK)** e incluye Irlanda del Norte además de Gran Bretaña. Sin embargo muchas veces se usa el término **Great Britain** como sinónimo de **United Kingdóm**. Cuando hablamos de **the British Isles** nos referimos a la isla de Gran Bretaña y la isla de Irlanda /ˈaiərlənd/.

Ciudades principales de las Islas Británicas

Aberdeen /ˈæbərdiːn/
Bath /bæθ; GB bɑːθ/
Belfast /ˈbelfæst/
Berwick-upon-Tweed /ˌberik əpɑn twiːd/
Birmingham /ˈbɜːrmiˑəm/
Blackpool /ˈblækpuːl/
Bournemouth /ˈbɔːrnməθ/
Bradford /ˈbrædfərd/
Brighton /ˈbraɪtn/
Bristol /ˈbrɪstl/
Caernarfon /kərˈnɑrvn/
Cambridge /ˈkeimbridʒ/
Canterbury /ˈkæntərberi; GB -bəri/
Cardiff /ˈkɑrdɪf/
Carlisle /ˈkɑrlaɪl/
Chester /ˈtʃestər/
Colchester /ˈkoʊˑltʃestər/
Cork /kɔːrk/
Coventry /ˈkʃ vəntri; GB ˈkɒv-/
Derby /ˈdɑrbi/
Douglas /ˈdʃ ɡləs/
Dover /ˈdoʊ vər/
Dublin /ˈdʃ blɪn/
Dundee /dʃ nˈdiː/
Durham /ˈdɜːrəm; GB ˈdʃ r-/
Eastbourne /ˈiːstbɔːrn/
Edinburgh /ˈednbɜːrə/
Ely /ˈiːli/
Exeter /ˈeksɪtər/
Galway /ˈɡɔːlweɪ/
Glasgow /ˈɡlæsɡoʊ; GB ˈɡlɑːz-/
Gloucester /ˈɡlɔːstər/
Hastings /ˈheɪstɪŋz/
Hereford /ˈherɪfərd/
Holyhead /ˈhɑlihed/
Inverness /ˌɪnvərˈnes/

Ipswich /ˈipswitʃ/
Keswick /ˈkezɪk/
Kingston upon Hull /ˌkiˑstən əpɑn ˈhʃl/
Leeds /liːdz/
Leicester /ˈlestər/
Limerick /ˈlimərik/
Lincoln /ˈliˑkən/
Liverpool /ˈlɪvərpuːl/
London /ˈlʃ ndən/
Londonderry /ʃ ndənderi/
Luton /ˈluːtn/
Manchester /ˈmæntʃestər/
Middlesbrough /ˈmɪdlzbrə/
Newcastle upon Tyne /ˌnuːkæsl əpɑn
ˈtam; GB ˈnjuːkɑːsl -/
Norwich /ˈnɔːritʃ; GB ˈnpridʒ/
Nottingham /ˈnɑtiˑəm/
Oxford /ˈɑksfərd/
Plymouth /ˈplɪməθ/
Poole /puːl/
Portsmouth /ˈpɔːrtsməθ/
Ramsgate /ˈræmzɡeɪt/
Reading /ˈredɪŋ/
Salisbury /ˈsɔːlzberi/
Sheffield /ˈʃefiːld/
Shrewsbury /ˈʃuːzberi; GB ˈʃroʊ zbəri/
Southampton /saʊ θˈhæmptən/
St. Andrews /seɪnt ˈændruːz; GB snt/
Stirling /ˈstɜːrlɪŋ/
Stoke-on-Trent /ˌstoʊ k ɑn ˈtrent/
Stratford-upon-Avon /ˌstrætfərd əpɑn ˈeɪvn/
Swansea /ˈswɑnzi, US tb -si/
Taunton /ˈtɔːntn; GB -tən/
Warwick /ˈwɔːrɪk/
Worcester /ˈwʃ stər/
York /jɔːrk/

Apéndice 4
Verbos irregulares

Infinitivo	Pasado	Participio	Infinitivo	Pasado	Participio
arise	arose	arisen	feed	fed	fed
awake	awoke	awoken	feel	felt	felt
be	was/were	been	fight	fought	fought
bear[2]	bore	borne	find	found	found
beat	beat	beaten	flee	fled	fled
become	became	become	fling	flung	flung
begin	began	begun	fly	flew	flown
bend	bent	bent	forbid	forbade	forbidden
bet	bet, betted	bet, betted	forecast	forecasted,	forecasted,
bid	bid	bid		forecast	forecast
bind	bound	bound	forget	forgot	forgotten
bite	bit	bitten	forgive	forgave	forgiven
bleed	bled	bled	freeze	froze	frozen
bless	blessed	blessed	get	got	gotten;
blow	blew	blown			(GB) got
break[1]	broke	broken	give	gave	given
breed	bred	bred	go[1]	went	gone
bring	brought	brought	grind	ground	ground
broadcast	broadcast	broadcast	grow	grew	grown
build	built	built	hang	hung,	hung,
burn	burned,	burned,		hanged	hanged
	burnt	burnt	have	had	had
burst	burst	burst	hear	heard	heard
bust[2]	busted,	busted,	hide[1]	hid	hidden
	bust	bust	hit	hit	hit
buy	bought	bougt	hold	held	held
cast	cast	cast	hurt	hurt	hurt
catch	caught	caught	keep	kept	kept
choose	chose	chosen	kneel	kneeled, knelt	kneeled,
cling	clung	clung	knit	knitted	knitted
come	came	come	know	knew	known
cost	cost,	cost,	lay[1]	laid	laid
	costed	costed	lead[2]	led	led
creep	crept	crept	lean[2]	leaned, leant	leaned, leant
cut	cut	cut	leap	leaped,	leaped,
deal[3]	dealt	dealt		leapt	leapt
dig	dug	dug	learn	learned,	learned,
dive	dove;	dived		learnt	learnt
	(GB) dived		leave	left	left
do[2]	did	done	lend	lent	lent
draw[2]	drew	drawn	let	let	let
dream	dreamed,	dreamed,	lie[2]	lay	lain
	dreamt	dreamt	light	lighted, lit	
drink	drank	drunk	lose	lost	lost
drive	drove	driven	make[1]	made	made
eat	ate	eaten	mean[1]	meant	meant
fall	fell	fallen	meet[1]	met	met

Infinitivo	Pasado	Participio	Infinitivo	Pasado	Participio
mistake	mistook	mistaken	speed	sped,	sped,
misunder	misunder	misunder		speeded	speeded
-stand	-stood	-stood	spell	spelled,	spelled,
mow	mowed	mown,		spelt	spelt
		mowed	spend	spent	spent
overcome	overcame	overcome	spill	spilled,	spilled,
pay	paid	paid		spilt	spilt
plead	pled; *(GB)*	pled;	spin	spun	spun
	pleaded	*(GB)* pleaded	spit	spat; *(esp*	spat; *(esp*
prove	proved	proven;		USA)* spit	USA)* spit
	(GB) proved		split	split	split
put	put	put	spoil	spoiled,	spoiled,
quit	quit,	quit,		spoilt	spoilt
	quitted	quitted	spread	spread	spread
read	read	read	spring	sprang	sprung
ride	rode	ridden	stand	stood	stood
ring²	rang	rung	steal	stole	stolen
rise²	rose	risen	stick²	stuck	stuck
run¹	ran	run	sting	stung	stung
saw²	sawed	sawed;	stink	stank,	stunk
	(GB) sawn			stunk	
say	said	said	stride	strode	strode
see	saw	seen	strike	struck	struck
seek	sought	sought	string	strung	strung
sell	sold	sold	strive	strove	striven
send	sent	sent	swear	swore	sworn
set²	set	set	sweep	swept	swept
sew	sewed	sewn, sewed	swell	swelled	swollen,
shake	shook	shaken			swelled
shed²	shed	shed	swim	swam	swum
shine	shone	shone	swing	swung	swung
shoe	shod	shod	take	took	taken
shoot	shot	shot	teach	taught	taught
show	showed	shown,	tear²	tore	torn
		showed	tell	told	told
shrink	shrank,	shrunk	think	thought	thought
	shrunk		throw¹	threw	thrown
shut	shut	shut	thrust	thrust	thrust
sing	sang	sung	tread	trod	trodden,
sink	sank	sunk			trod
sit	sat	sat	wake	woke	woken
sleep	slept	slept	wear	wore	worn
slide	slid	slid	weave	wove,	woven,
sling²	slung	slung		weaved	weaved
slit	slit	slit	weep	wept	wept
smell	smelled,	smelled,	win	won	won
	smelt	smetl	wind²	wound	wound
sow²	sowed	sown, sowed	wring	wrung	wrung
speak	spoke	spoken	write	wrote	written

Apéndice 5
La pronunciación

Hay palabras que tienen más de una
pronunciación posible. En el *New Chicago*
se encuentran las más comunes, ordenadas
por su frecuencia de uso.

     either /ˈiːðər, ˈaiðər/

Si la pronunciación de la palabra cambia
mucho en inglés británico, se indica
mediante la abreviatura *GB*.

     salon /səˈlɑn; *GB* ˈsælpn/

/ˈ/   indica el acento principal de la palabra.
     money /ˈmʌni/ lleva el acento en la
     primera sílaba
     lagoon /ləˈguːn/ se acentúa en la
     segunda sílaba

/ˌ/   muestra el acento secundario de la
   palabra.
     pronunciation /prəˌnʌnsiˈeiʃn/ lleva el
     acento secundario en la sílaba /ˌnʌn/ y
     el acento principal en la sílaba /ˌeiʃn/

r   En inglés americano hablado siempre se
     pronuncia la **r** final.
     Sin embargo, en inglés británico no se
     pronuncia la **r** final, salvo que la
     palabra siguiente empiece por vocal.
     La **r** no se pronuncia en la frase *His car*
     broke down, pero sí en *His car is*
     brand new.
     Por esta razón, en la versión británica
     aclaramos esta dificultad añadiendo una
     r entre paréntesis en la transcripción
     fonética.
     chauffeur /ʃoʊˈfɜːr; *GB* ˈʃəʊ fə(r)/

ɑː/ɑ Además, hay dos símbolos fonéticos
     que sólo aparecen en la versión
     británica:

ɑː   **bath** (bæθ; *GB* bɑːθ/

ɑ   **off** /ɔːf; *GB* ɑf/

Formas tónicas y átonas

Algunas palabras de uso frecuente (**an, as,
from, that, of,** etc) tienen dos pronunciacio-
nes posibles, una tónica y otra átona. De las
dos, la forma átona es la más frecuente.
Tomemos por ejemplo el caso de la
preposición **from** /frəm, frɑm/, que
normalmente se pronuncia /frəm/, como en la
frase

   He comes from Spain.

Ahora bien, si aparece al final de la oración,
o le queremos dar un énfasis especial,
utilizamos la pronunciación tónica /frɑm/,
como en el caso de

   The present's not ˈfrom John, it's ˈfor him.

Palabras derivadas

En muchas ocasiones, la pronunciación de
una palabra derivada es la suma de la
pronunciación de sus elementos. En estos
casos no damos la transcripción fonética, ya
que es predecible.

slowly	=	**slow**	+	**ly**
/ˈsloʊ li/		/sloʊ/	+	li/
astonishingly	=	**astonish**	+ **ing**	+ **ly**
/əˈstɑnɪʃɪŋli/		/əˈstɑnɪʃ/	+ iŋ +	li/

Pero a veces el acento de la palabra cambia al
añadirle las desinencias, y en estos casos sí
mostramos la pronunciación.

photograph	/ˈfoʊ təgræf/
photographer	/fəˈtɑgrəfər/
photographic	/ˌfoʊ təˈgræfik/
photography	/fəˈtɑgrəfi/

En el caso de las derivadas terminadas en
-tion, la norma de que el acento recaiga sobre
la penúltima sílaba se cumple con
regularidad, y por lo tanto no indicamos la
pronunciación.

alter	/ˈɔːlter/
alteration	/ˌɔːltəˈreiʃn/
confirm	/kənˈfɜːrm/
confirmation	/ˌkɑnfərˈmeiʃn/

Apéndice 6
Adjectives of Nationality / Gentilicios

Argeria	argelino
Argentina	argentino
Asunción	asunceño
Basutolandia	basutolandés
Bechuanalandia	bechuanalandés
Bélgica	belga
Birmania	birmano
Bogotá	bogotano
Bolivia	boliviano
Brasil	brasileño
Bruselas	bruselense
Buenos Aires	bonaerense or porteño
Bulgaria	búlgaro
Burundi	burundi
Camboya	camboyano
Camerún	camerunés
Canadá	canadiense
Caracas	caraqueño
Ceilán	ceilanés
Colombia	colombiano
Congo (both)	congoleño
Costa de Marfil	marfileño
Costa Rica	costarricense
Cuba	cubano
Chad	chadiano
Checoslovaquia	checoslovaco
Chile	chileno
China	chino
Chipre	chipriota
Dahomey	dahomeyano
Dinamarca	dinamarqués or danés
Ecuador	ecuatoriano
El Salvador	salvadoreño
España	español
Estados Unidos de América	estadounidense
Etiopía	etíope
Filipinas	filipino
Finlandia	finlandés or finés
Francia	francés
Gabón	gabonés
Gambia	gambio
Ghana	ghanés
Ginebra	ginebrino
Grecia	griego
Guatemala	guatemalteco
Guayaquil	guayaquileño
Guinea	guineo

Haití	haitiano
Honduras	hondureño
Hungría	húngaro
Ifni	ifneño
India	indio
Indonesia	indonesio
irak	iraqués
Irán	iranio
Irlanda	irlandés
Islandia	islandés
Israel	israelí
Italia	italiano
Jamaica	jamaicano
Japón	japonés
Jordania	jordanio
Jerusalém	jerosolomitano
Kenia	kenio
Kuwait	kuwaiteño
Laos	laosiano
La Paz	paceño
Líbano	libanés
Liberia	liberiano
Libia	libio
Lima	limeño
Lisboa	lisboeta or lisbonense
Londres	londinense
Luxemburgo	luxemburgués
Madagascar	malache
Madrid	madrileño
Malasia	malayo
Malavi	malavio
Malí	maliense
Managua	managüense
Marruecos	marroquí
Mauritania	mauritano
México (Méjico)	mexicano (mejicano)
Mongolia	mongol
Montevideo	montevideño or montevideano
Nepal	nepalés
Nicaragua	nicaragüense
Níger	nigerino
Nigeria	nigeriano
Noruega	noruego
Nueva York	neoyorquino
Nueva Zelandia	neozelandés
Países Bajos	holandés
Pakistán	pakistano
Panamá	panameño
Paraguay	paraguayo

París	parisiense
Perú	peruano
Polonia	polaco
Portugal	portugués
Puerto Rico	puertorriqueño or portorriqueño
Reino Unido de Gran Bretaña e irlanda del Norte	británico
República Arabe Unida	egipcio
República Centroafricana	centroafricano
República Dominicana	dominicano
República Socialista Soviética de Bielorrusia	bieloruso
República Socialista Soviética de Ucrania	ucranio
Río de Janeiro	carioca
Río Muni	riomuniense
Rodesia	rodesio
Rumania	rumano
Rwanda	rwandés
San José	josefino
São Paulo	paulistano
Santa Cruz	cruceño
Santiago	santiagueño or santiaguino
Senegal	senegalés
Sierra Leona	leonense
Siria	sirio
Somalia	somalí
Suazilandia	suazilandés
Sudáfrica	sudafricano
Sudán	sudanés
Suecia	sueco
Tailandia	tailandés
Tanganyica	tanganyikano
Tanzania	tanzanio
Tegucigalpa	tegucigalpense
Tenerife	tinerfeño
Tetuán	tetuaní
Togo	togolés
Trinidad y Tobago	trinitario
Túnez	tunecí
Turquía	turco
Uganda	ugandés
Unión de Repúblicas Socialistas Soviéticas	ruso
Uruguay	uruguayo
Venecia	veneciano or véneto
Venezuela	venezolano
Viena	vienés
Yemen	yemenita
Yugoslavia	yugoslavo
Washington	washingtoniano
Zambia	zambio
Zanzíbar	zanzibareño

Phonetic Manifestations of the Consonant Phonemes of Spanish

Voice	Bilabial		Labiodental		Interdental		Dental		Alveolar		Palatal		Velar		Glottal	
	vs	vd	vs	vd	vs	vd	vs	vd	vs	vd	vs	vd	vs	vd	vs	vd
Occlusive	p	b											k	g		
Fricative	ø	ƀ	f		θ	ð						y	x	ǥ	h	
Sibilant							s	z	S	Z	Š	Ž				
Affricate											č	ŷ				
Nasal										n		ñ		ŋ		
Lateral										l		ļ				
Vibrant										r rr						
Semiconsonant		w										j				

Parte Segunda Inglés-Español

Al Lector

El auge que desde el principio de la Segunda Guerra Mundial viene cobrando en la América Española el aprendizaje del inglés, nos ha movido a recopilar en este breve Diccionario las voces y locuciones más indispensables de esta lengua tal como se habla y escribe en los Estados Unidos de América.

Al igual que en la Sección española-inglesa hemos antepuesto la abreviatura *Am.* y otras de señalados países o regiones a aquellos vocablos o modismos que son de uso exclusivo en alguna región de la América española, o bien de uso frecuéntísimo en ésta, aunque ya hayan caído en desuso en la Península. Todo lo cual no excluye la posibilidad de que alguna acepción así designada se oiga en labios de un español o sea de uso esporádico en España.

Lo que sí hemos procurado con gran ahínco y anhelamos lograr, presentando al estudioso este caudal indispensable de palabras, es el acercamiento lingüístico de las Américas, como base para nuestra mutua comprensión y como instrumento poderosísimo para nuestra solidaridad.

LOS EDITORES

Lista de Abreviaturas

adj.	adjetivo	*irr.*	irregular
adv.	adverbio	*p.p.*	participio pasado o pasivo
art.	artículo	*pers.*	personal
art. indef.	artículo indefinido	*pl.*	plural
aux.	auxiliar	*pos.*	posesivo
comp.	comparativo	*prep.*	preposición
conj.	conjunción	*pron.*	pronombre
contr.	contracción	*pron. pers.*	pronombre personal
defect.	defectivo	*pron. pos.*	pronombre posesivo
etc.	etcétera	*s.*	sustantivo
ger.	gerundio	*sing.*	singular
gram.	gramatical, gramática	*subj.*	subjuntivo
imperf.	imperfecto	*v.*	verbo
indic.	indicativo	*v. defect.*	verbo defectivo
interj.	interjección	*v. irr.*	verbo irregular.
interr.	interrogativo		

Abreviaturas especiales de Indicación Regional

Am.[1]	Americanismo
Andalucía	
Andes	(Ecuador, Perú, Bolivia)
Arg.	Argentina
Bol.	Bolivia
Carib.	(Cuba, Puerto Rico, República Dominicana)
C.A.	Centroamérica (Guatemala, El Salvador, Honduras, Nicaragua, Costa Rica)
Ch.	Chile

---

1. Esta abreviatura se emplea para indicar uso general hispanoamericano; se implica a la vez carácter arcaizante en cuanto a España. Se usa también para señalar los vocablos ya poco usados que puedan encontrarse en obras literarias del siglo pasado.

Col.	Colombia		
C.R.	Costa Rica		
Cuba			
Ec.	El Ecuador		
Esp.	España		
Guat.	Guatemala		
Hond.	Honduras		
Méx.	México		
N. Esp.	Norte de España		
Nic.	Nicaragua		
Pan.	Panamá		
Par.	Paraguay		
Perú			
P.R.	Puerto Rico		
Ríopl.	Río de la Plata (La Argentina Oriental, el Uruguay)		
S.A.	Sudamérica		
Sal.	El Salvador		
Ur.	El Uruguay		
Ven.	Venezuela		

Pronunciación Inglesa

I. Vocales

Símbolo Fonético	Ortografía inglesa	Ortografía fonética	Explicación de los sonidos
i	see pea	si pi	Equivalentes a la *i* in *hilo*.
	bit	bɪt	El sonido más aproximado es la *i* en *virtud*, pero la [I] inglesa es una *i* más abierta tirando a *e* cerrada.
e	late they	let ðe	Equivale aproximadamente a *ei*; la *i* de este diptongo es muy relajada y más abierta que en español.
ɛ	bet	bɛt	El sonido más aproximado en español es la *e* abierta de *perro*.
æ	sat	sæt	Es una vocal intermedia entre la *a* y la *e*.
ɑ	car	kɑr	Equivale aproximadamente a la *a* en *cargo*.
ɔ	forge	fɔrdʒ	Equivale aproximadamente a la *o* en *corto, corre*.
o	mode	mod	Equivale aproximadamente a *ou*; la *u* de este diptóngo es muy relajada y más abierta que en español.
U	pull	pUl	El sonido más aproximado en español es la *u* en *turrón*, pero la [U] inglesa es todavía más abierta.
u	June Moon	dʒun mun	Equivale aproximadamente a la *u* en *uno*.
ə	cudgel apply	kʌdʒəl əplaɪ	Es una *e* muy relajada. No tiene equivalente en español.
ɚ	teacher	títʃɚ	Es una *e* muy relajada articulada simultáneamente con la *r*. No tiene equivalente en español.

Símbolo fonético	Ortografía inglesa	Ortografía fonética	Explicación de los sonidos
ɝ	earth	ɝθ	Es un sonido intermedio entre la *e* y la *o* articulando simultáneamente con la *r*. Se acerca más a la *e* que a la *o*. No tiene equivalente en español.
ʃ	duck	dʃk	Es una vocal intermedia entre la *e* muy abierta y la *o*. Se acerca más a la *o* que a la *e*. No tiene equivalete en español.

II. Diptongos

aI	aisle	aIl	Equivale aproximadamente a *ai* en *aire*.
	nice	naIs	
aU	now	naU	Equivale aproximadamente a *au* en *causa*.
ɔI	coy	kɔI	Equivale aproximadamente a *oy* en *hoy*. El segundo elemento del diptongo es más abierto y débil, tirando a *e*.
ju	used	juzd	Equivale aproximadamente a *iu* en *ciudad*.
jU	cure	kjUr	Equivale aproximadamente al diptongo *iu*, pero la *u* es más abierta.

III. Consonantes

p	paper	pépɚ	Equivale aproximadamente a la *p* española, pero es aspirada.
b	bat	bæt	La *b* inglesa es semejante a la *b* inicial española, pero se pronuncia más explosivamente.
t	tea	ti	Es bastante diferente a la *t* española. Se articula colocando flojamente la lengua arriba de los dientes incisivos superiores y es aspirada.
d	day	de	Equivale a la *d* inicial española pronunciada con mayor énfasis y se articula arriba de los dientes.
k	cat	kæt	Equivale aproximadamente a la *c* española delante de *a, o, u* pronunciada con aspiración.
	kill	kIl	
g	go	go	Equivale aproximadamente, a la *g* inicial delante de *a, o, u: goma, guerra, gana;* sólo que la *g* inglesa se pronuncia con mayor explosión.
	gum	gʃm	
	ago	əgó	
f	fun	fʃn	Equivale aproximadamente a la *f* española.
	affair	aʃáér	
v	very	vérI	De vez en cuando se oye en español como ultracorrección. Es una labiodental que se articula con el labio inferior y los dientes incisivos superiores.
θ	thin	θIn	Equivale aproximadamente a la *z* en el castellano *cazar*.
ð	then	ðɛn	Equivale aproximadamente a la *d* española en *nada*.
	other	ʌ ðɚ	
s	send	sɛnd	Equivale aproximadamente a la *s* inicial española de Hispanoamérica; *santo*.
	case	kes	
	cent	sɛnt	
z	rose	roz	Equivale aproximadamente a la *s* sonora en *mismo*, pero se pronuncia con más sonoridad en inglés.
	these	ðiz	
	zero	zíro	
ʃ	sheet	ʃit	Es una *s* palatal que no tiene equivalente en español. Suena como la *ch* francesa; *chapeau*.
	machine	maʃín	
	nation	néʃən	
ʒ	vision	viʒən	Es una palatal fricativa sonora, semejante a la *y* argentina y uruguaya o la *j* de *jouer* en fráncés.

tʃ	chase	tʃes	Equivale aproximadamente a la *ch* en *charla*.
dʒ	judge	dʒ ʃdʒ	No tiene equivalente exacto en español. Se parece a la *y* de *inyectar* en la pronunciación de muchos hispanoamericanos.
m	much	mʃtʃ	Equivale aproximadamente a la *m* española.
n	none	nʃn	Equivale aproximadamente a la *n* española en *nada*.
	any	énI	
ŋ̩	eaten	itŋ̩	No tiene equivalente en español. Representa la *n* sin la articulación
	button	bÁtŋ̩	de la vocal anterior.
	lesson	lésŋ̩	
ŋ	ankle	æ̃ŋkl	Equivale a la *n* española en *mango, banco*.
	angle	æ̃ŋg l̩	
	ring	rIŋ	
l	late	let	La *l* inicial equivale aproximadamente a la *l* española en *lado*. La
	altar	ɔ́ltɚ	*l* final de sílaba es más débil que la inicial y semejante a la portuguesa
	fall	fɔl	o a la catalana.
	folly	fálI	
l̩	able	éb l̩	No tiene equivalente en español. Se pronuncia como la *l* final de
	ankle	ankl	sílaba, omitiendo la vocal precedente.
w	weed	wid	Equivale a la *u* de los diptongos; *ui, ue, ua, ou*.
	well	wɛl	
	wall	wɔl	
h	hat	hæt	No tiene equivalente exacto en español. Equivale aproximadamente
	whole	hol	a una *j* suave que se reduce a una simple aspiración.
hw	where	hwɛr	Equivale a una *j* suave seguida de una *w* arriba explicada, y se usa en la mayoría de los dialectos norteamericanos.
j	year	jIr	Equivale a la *i* española en los diptongos *ie, ia, io, iu: hiena*.
	yawn	jɔn	
	yet	jɛt	
r	rose	roz	No tiene equivalente en español. La punta de la lengua se arrolla hacia atrás sin tocar el paladar. A veces se pierde al grado de vocalizarse.

Pronunciación de la *S* del Plural[3]

I. La **-s** del plural es sorda cuando la palabra termina en las consonantes sordas representadas por los símbolos fonéticos [p], [t], [k], [f], [Θ]. Pronúnciase como la *s* de *santo*: **caps** [kæps], **gates** [gets], **cats** [kæts], **books** [bUks], **cliffs** [klIfs], **lengths** [leŋkΘs].
Las excepciones más comunes son: **oath** [oΘ], **oaths** [oðz]; **leaf** [lif], **leaves** [livz]; **wife** [walf], **wives** [walvz]; **knife** [nalf], **knives** [nalvz]; **calf** [kæf], **calves** [kævz]; **half** [hæf], **halves** [hævz].

II. La **-s** del plural es sonora cuando la palabra termina en vocal (incluyendo la **-y** que se cambia en **-ies**), o en las consonantes sonoras representadas por los símbolos fonéticos [b], [d], [g], [v], [ð], [m], [n], [ŋ], [l]: **cries** [kralz], **robes** [robz], **beds** [bɛdz], **logs** [lɔgz], **stoves** [stovz], **lathes** [leðz], **farms** [farmz], **bins** [blnz], **kings** [klŋz], **falls** [fɔz], **furs** [fɝz], **papers** [pépɚz], **plows** [plaUz].

III. Cuando la palabra termina en las consonantes representadas por los símbolos [s], [ʃ], [tʃ], [z], [ʒ], [dʒ], se añade **-es** [Iz], o s [Iz], si la palabra termina en **-ce, -se, -dge, -ge**: **face** [fes], **faces** [fésiZ]; **kiss** [kls], **kisses** [kísIz]; **ash** [æʃ], **ashes** [æʃIz]; **lunch** [l&ntʃ], **lunches** [l&ntʃIz]; **rose** [roz], **roses** [rózIz]; **judge** [dʒ ʃdʒ], **judges** [dʒ ʃdʒIz].

---

3. Las mismas reglas se aplican a la pronunciación del genitivo y de la tercera persona del presente de indicativo, singular: **keeps** [kips]; **Kate's** [kets]; **saves** [sevz]; **John's** [dʒanz]; **judges** [dʒ ʃdʒíz]; **Alice's** [ælIstz].

El Sustantivo

I. Género

En la gramática inglesa el género tiene papel mínimo y resulta ser fenómeno léxico. Son masculinos los nombres de varón o animal macho, y son femeninos los nombres de mujer o animal hembra. Los demás son neutros. El artículo definido the se aplica a todos los sustantivos, singular y plural: **the man** el hombre; **the men** los hombres; **the book** el libro; **the books** los libros; **the woman** la mujer; **the women** las mujeres. En ciertos sustantivos se distingue el género femenino por medio del sufijo **-ess: actor** actor; **actress** actriz. A veces es indispensable indicar el género por medio de las palabras **male** o **female**, **boy** o **girl**, **man** o **woman**, **she** o **he**; **baby boy** niño; **baby girl** niña; **woman writer** escritora; **she-bear** osa. En otros casos hay una palabra distinta para cada género; **uncle** tío; **aunt** tía.

II. Plural de los Sustantivos[4]

1. Generalmente se forma el plural añadiendo **-s** al singular: **paper, papers** papel, papeles; **book, books** libro, libros; **chief, chiefs**, jefe, jefes.
2. Los sustantivos que terminan en **-ch** (pronunciada como la ch española), **-ss, –x, -sh, -z,** y **-o** añaden **-es** para formar el plural: **arch, arches**, arco, arcos; **kiss, kisses**, beso, besos; **box, boxes**, caja, cajas; **dish, dishes** plato, platos; **buzz, buzzes**, zumbido, zumbidos; **hero, heroes**, héroe, héroes. Nótese que los sustantivos terminados en **-ch** (pronunciada [k]) forman el plural añadiendo **-s: monarch, monarchs**, monarca, monarcas.
3. Los sustantivos que terminan en **-fe**, y ciertos sustantivos que terminan en **-f**, también cambian estas letras en v y añaden **-es: leaf, leaves**, hoja, hojas; **life, lives**, vida, vidas; **wife, wives** esposa, esposas; **knife, knives**, cuchillo, cuchillos.
4. Para formar el plural de los sustantivos terminados en **-y** precedida de consonante cámbiese la **-y** en **-ies: fly, flies** mosca, moscas; **cry, cries** grito, gritos; **family, families**,familia, familias; **quantity, quantities** cantidad, cantidades. Nótese que los sustantivos terminados en **-y** precedida de vocal forman el plural añadiendo **-s** al singular: **day, days** día, días.
5. Ciertos sustantivos forman el plural de una manera irregular: **man, men** hombre, hombres; **woman, women** mujer, mujeres; **mouse, mice** ratón, ratones; **louse, lice** piojo, piojos; **goose, geese** ganso, gansos; **tooth, teeth** diente, dientes; **foot, feet** pie, pies; **ox, oxen** buey, bueyes.
6. Ciertos sustantivos que terminan en **-is** forman el plural cambiando la **i** de la terminación en **e: axis, axes** eje, ejes; **the crisis, the crises** la crisis, las crisis.

El Adjetivo

El adjetivo inglés es invariable en cuanto a género y número. Normalmente se coloca delante del sustantivo: **an interesting book** un libro interesante; **a large table**, una mesa grande; **beautiful women** mujeres hermosas.

Los comparativos y superlativos. Aunque no hay una regla general, por lo común los adjetivos monosílabos, los adjetivos acentuados en la última sílaba y algunos bisílabos fácilmente pronunciados forman *el comparativo de aumento y el superlativo* añadiendo **-er** y **-est**. Los demás adjetivos van precedidos de **more** y **most**. Nótese que (1) sólo se añaden **-r** y **-st** a los que terminan en **-e** muda; (2) los adjetivos terminados en **-y** cambian esta letra en **i**; (3) los adjetivos terminados en consonante precedida de vocal doblan la consonante:

Positivo	*Comparativo*	*Superlativo*
tall alto	**taller** más alto	**the tallest** el más alto
wise sabio	**wiser** más sabio	**the wisest** el más sabio

4. Véase las reglas para la pronunciación del plural.

polite cortés	**politer** más cortés	**the politest** el más cortés
happy feliz	**happier** más feliz	**the happiest** el más feliz
fat gordo	**fatter** más gordo	**the fattest** el más gordo
careful cuidadoso	**more careful** más cuidadoso	**the most careful** el más cuidadoso

El superlativo absoluto se forma anteponiendo **very** y a veces **most: very intelligent** muy inteligente; **she is a most beautiful woman** es una mujer hermosísima.

El comparativo y el superlativo de inferioridad se forma con los adverbios **less** y **least: less important** menos importante; **the least important** el menos importante.

El comparativo de igualdad se forma con el adverbio **as: poor as** tan pobre como; **as much as** tanto como; **as much money as** tanto dinero como.

Los adjetivos siguientes forman el comparativo y el superlativo de una manera irregular:

good, well	**better**	**best**
bad, ill	**worse**	**worst**
little	**less, lesser**	**least**
far	**father, further**	**farthest, furthest**
much, many	**more**	**most**
old	**older, elder**	**oldest, eldest**

El Adverbio

Fórmanse muchos adverbios, añadiendo **-ly** al adjetivo: **courteous** cortés, **courteously** cortésmente; **bold** atrevido, **boldly** atrevidamente. Existen las irregularidades siguientes en la formación de los adverbios que terminan en **-ly**: (1) los adjetivos terminados en **-ble** cambian la **-e** en **-y: posible, possibly**; (2) los terminados en **ic** añaden **-ally: poetic, poetically**; (3) los terminados en **-ll** añaden sólo la **-y: full, fully**; (4) los terminados en **-ue** pierden la **-e** final: **true, truly**; (5) los terminados en **-y** cambian la **-y** en **i: happy, happily**.

Como los adjetivos, la mayor parte de los adverbios forman *el comparativo y el superlativo* con los adverbios **more** (más), **most** (más), y **very** (muy). Asimismo los adverbios monosílabos lo añaden **-er** y **-est**:

Positivo	*Comparativo*	*Superlativo*	*Superlativo Absoluto*
boldly	more boldly	most boldly	very boldly
generously	more generously	most generously	very generously
soon	sooner	soonest	very soon
early	earlier	earliest	very early
late	later	latest	very late
near	nearer	nearest	very near
fast	faster	fastest	very fast

Los adverbios siguientes forman el comparativo y el superlativo de una manera irregular:

well	better	best	very well
badly, ill	worse	worst	very badly
little	less	least	very little
much	more	most	very much
far	father, further	farthest, furthest	very far

Sufijos Comunes en Inglés

-dom	denota dominio, jurisdicción, estado, condición etc. ; **kingdom** reino; **martyrdom** martirio; **boredom** aburrimiento; **freedom** libertad.
-ed, -d	es la terminación del pretérito y del participio pasivo o pasado de los verbos irregulares: **I**

	called llamé, **called** llamado.
-ee	indica la persona que recibe la acción: **addressee** destinatario; **employee** empleado.
-eer	denota oficio u ocupación: **engineer** ingeniero; **auctioneer** subastador.
-en	a) terminación del participio de muchos verbos irregulares: **fallen, broken, shaken**;
	b) sufijo que significa hecho de: **golden** dorado, de oro; **wooden** de madera; **leaden** de plomo;
	c)terminación verbal equivalente a hacer: **whiten** hacer blanco, emblanquecer; **darken** hacer obscuro, obscurecer.
-er	a) indica la persona que hace o el agente de la acción del verbo: **player** jugador; **speaker** orador;
	b) indica el residente de un lugar: **New Yorker habitante** o residente de Nueva York; **islander** isleño;
	c) denota ocupación: **carpenter** carpintero; **baker** panadero.
	d) es la terminación del comparativo de adjetivos y adverbios; **taller** más alto; **faster** más aprisa.
-ees	únase para formar el género femenino de ciertos sustantivos: **actress** actriz; **princess** princesa; **countess** condesa.
-est	terminación del superlativo: **tallest** el más alto.
-fold	sufijo que significa veces: **twofold** dos veces; **hundredfold** cien veces.
-ful	a) equivalente a lleno, y tratándose de adjetivos es igual a **-oso**: **hopeful** lleno de esperanzas; **careful** cuidadoso; **willful** voluntarioso; **merciful** misericordioso; **glassful** un vaso (lleno);
	b) indica a veces hábito o inclinación: **forgetful** olvidadizo;
	c) es a veces equivalente a los sufijos españoles **-ado, -ada: handful** puñado; **spoonful** cucharada.
-hood	indica estado, condición, carácter, grupo; a menudo equivale a **-dad: motherhood** maternidad; **brotherhood** fraternidad; **childhood** niñez; **likelihood** probabilidad.
-ician	denota especialidad en cierto ramo: **musician** músico; **technician** técnico; **electrician** electricista.
-ie	sufijo diminutivo: **birdie** pajarito; **Annie** Anita.
-ing	a) sufijo del gerundio: **speaking** hablando;
	b) sufijo de participio activo: **threatening** amenazante; **surprising** sorprendente;
	c) úsase a menudo para formar adjetivos: **running water** agua corriente; **drinking water** agua potable; **waiting room** sala de espera; **washing machine** máquina lavadora;
	d) únase para formar sustantivos: **understanding** entendimiento; **supplying** abastecimiento; **clothing** ropa; **covering** cobertura; equivale al infinitivo castellano: **swimming is good excercise** el nadar es un buen ejercicio.
-ish	a) úsase para formar ciertos adjetivos de nacionalidad: **Spanish** español; **English** inglés; **Turkish** turco;
	b) indica semejanza: **boyish** como niño, aniñado; **womanish** como mujer, mujeril, afeminado; **whitish** blancuzco, medio blanco, que tira a blanco.
-less	equivale a sin, falto de: **childless** sin hijos; **penniless** sin dinero, en ciertos casos el sufijo inglés se traduce por medio de un prefijo: **countless** innumerable, sin número; **endless** interminable, sin fin.
-like	significa semejanza, y equivale a como, a manera de: **lifelike** que parece vivo; **childlike** como niño, infantil; **tigerlike** como tigre.
-ly	a) sufijo adverbial: **slowly** lentamente; **happily** felizmente; **possibly** posiblemente;
	b) añadido a ciertos sustantivos equivale a como a la manera de: **motherly** como madre, materno; **gentlemanly** como caballero, caballeroso; **friendly** amigable; **manly** varonil;
	c) equivale a cada en estos ejemplos: **daily** cada día, diario; **weekly** cada semana, semanal; **monthly** cada mes, mensual; **yearly** cada año, anual.
-ness	úsase para formar sustantivos abstractos: **goodness** bondad; **darkness** obscuridad; **foolishness** tontería; **shamelessness** desvergüenza.
-ship	a) úsase para formar sustantivos abstractos: **friendship** amistad; **relationship** relación, parentesco;
	b) denota arte o destreza: **horsemanship** equitación;

	c) expresa dignidad, oficio, cargo, o título: **professorship** profesorado o cátedra; **chairmanship** presidencia (de un comité, asamblea, etc.); **lordship** señoría;
	d) a veces expresa un solo estado y su duración: **courtship** galanteo, cortejo, noviazgo.
-some	expresa en alto grado la cualidad representada por el vocablo al cual se añade: **tiresome** que cansa, cansado; **quarrelsome** dado a riñas, pendenciero; **loathsome** que repugna, asqueroso; **burdensome** gravoso.
-th	úsase para formar números ordinales; **fifth** quinto; **tenth** décimo.
-ty	a) terminación de los múltiplos de diez: **twenty** veinte; **thirty** treinta; **forty** cuarenta;
	b) terminación de muchos sustantivos abstractos; equivale frecuentemente al sufijo español **-tad** o **-dad**: **beauty** beldad; **partenity** paternidad; **falsity** falsedad.
-ward, -wards	denota hacia: **homeward** hacia casa; **downward** hacia abajo.
-ways,-wise	expresan manera, dirección, posición, etc.: **edgewise** de lado; **sideways** de lado; **lengthwise** a lo largo.
-y	a) terminación equivalente a los sufijos españoles **-ia**, **-ía**: **victory** victoria, **glory**, gloria **courtesy** cortesía; **biology** biología; **astronomy** astronomía;
	b) sufijo diminutivo: **doggy** perrito; **Johnny** Juanito;
	c) Denota abundancia, y es a menudo equivalente a **-udo**, **-oso**, **-ado**; **rocky** lleno de rocas, rocoso, pedregoso; **rainy** lluvioso; **hairy** lleno de pelo, peludo; **bulky** abultado; **wavy** ondulado; **angry** enojado;
	d) Expresa semejanza: **rosy** rosado, como una rosa, color de rosa.

Verbos Irregulares de la Lengua Inglesa

Se denominan verbos irregulares los que no forman el pretérito o el participio pasivo con la adición de **-d** o **-ed** al presente. Obsérvese que en ciertos verbos coexiste la forma regular al lado de la irregular. En otros coexisten dos formas irregulares juntamente con la regular.

Presente	Pretérito	Participio pasivo o pasado
abide	abode	abode
am, is, are	was, were	been
arise	arose	arisen
awake	awoke, awaked	awaked, awoke
bear	bore	born, borne
beat	beat	beat, beaten
become	became	become
befall	befell	befallen
beget	begat	begotten
begin	began	begun
behold	beheld	beheld
bend	bent	bent
bereave	bereft, bereaved	bereft, bereaved
beseech	besought, beseeched	besought, beseeched
beset	beset	beset
bet	bet	bet
bid	bid, bade	bidden, bid
bind	bound	bound
bite	bit	bitten, bit
bleed	bled	bled
blow	blew	blown
break	broke	broken
breed	bred	bred
bring	brought	brought

build	built	built
Presente	*Pretérito*	*Participio pasivo o pasado*
burn	burnt, burned	burnt, burned
burst	burst	burst
buy	bought	bought
can (verbo defectivo)	could	–
cast	cast	cast
catch	caught	caught
chide	chided, chid	chided, chidden
choose	chose	chosen
cleave	cleft, clove, cleaved	cleft, cloven, cleaved
cling	clung	clung
clothe	clad, clothed	clad, clothed
come	came	come
cost	cost	cost
creep	crept	crept
crow	crew, crowed	crowed
cut	cut	cut
deal	dealt	dealt
dig	dug, digged	dug, digged
dive	dived, dove	dived, dove
do	did	done
draw	drew	drawn
dream	dreamt, dreamed	dreamt, dreamed
drink	drank	drunk
drive	drove	driven
dwell	dwelt, dwelled	dwelt, dwelled
eat	ate	eaten
fall	fell	fallen
feed	fed	fed
feel	felt	felt
fight	fought	fought
find	found	found
flee	fled	fled
fling	flung	flung
fly	flew	flow
forbear	forbore	forborne
forbid	forbade	forbidden
foresee	foresaw	foreseen
foretell	foretold	foretold
forget	forgot	forgotten, forgot
forgive	forgave	forgiven
forsake	forsook	forsaken
freeze	froze	frozen
get	got	got, gotten
gild	gilt, girded	gilt, gilded
gird	girt, girded	girt, girded
give	gave	given
go	went	gone
grind	ground	ground
grow	grew	grown

5. Es regular cuando significa «ahorcar.»

hang[5]	hung	hung
Presente	*Pretérito*	*Participio pasivo o pasado*
have, has	had	had
hear	heard	heard
heave	hove, heaved	hove, heaved
hew	hewed	hewn, hewed
hide	hid	hidden, hid
hit	hit	hit
hold	held	held
hurt	hurt	hurt
inlay	inlaid	inlaid
keep	kept	kept
kneel	knelt	knelt
knit	knit, knitted	knit, knitted
know	knew	known
lay	laid	laid
lead	led	led
lean	leaned, leant	leaned, leant
leap	leapt, leaped	leapt, leaped
learn	learned, learnt	learned, learnt
leave	left	left
lend	lent	lent
let	let	let
lie[6]	lay	lain
light	lit, lighted	lit, lighted
load	loaded	loaded, laden
lose	lost	lost
make	made	made
may (verbo defectivo)	might	—
mean	meant	meant
meet	met	met
melt	melted	melted, molten
mistake	mistook	mistaken
mow	mowed	mown, mowed
must (verbo defectivo)	——	——
ought (verbo defectivo)	ought	—
pay	paid	paid
put	put	put
quit	quit, quitted	quit, quitted
read [rid]	read [rçd]	read [rçd]
rend	rent	rent
rid	rid, ridded	rid, ridded
ride	rode	ridden
ring	rang, rung	rung
rise	rose	risen
run	ran	run
saw	sawed	sawn, sawed
say	said	said
see	saw	seen
seek	sought	sought
sell	sold	sold

6. Es regular cuando significa «mentir.»

send	sent	sent
Presente	Pretérito	Participio pasivo o pasado
set	set	set
sew	sewed	sewn, sewed
shake	shook	shaken
shall	should	—
shave	shaved	shaved, shaven
shear	sheared	shorn, sheared
shed	shed	shed
shine[7]	shone	shone
shoe	shod	shod
shoot	shot	shot
show	showed	shown, showed
shred	shred, shredded	shred, shredded
shrink	shrank, shrunk	shrunk, shrunken
shut	shut	shut
sing	sand, sung	sung
sink	sank	sunk
sit	sat	sat
slay	slew	slain
sleep	slept	slept
slide	slid	slid, slidden
sling	slung	slung
slink	slunk	slunk
slit	slit	slit
smell	smelt, smelled	smelt, smelled
smite	smote	smitten
sow	sowed	sown, sowed
speak	spoke	spoken
speed	sped, speeded	sped, speeded
spell	spelled, spelt	spelled, spelt
spend	spent	spent
spill	spilled, spilt	spilled, spilt
spin	spun	spun
spit	spit, spat	spit, spat
split	split	split
spread	spread	spread
spring	sprang, sprung	sprung
stand	stood	stood
stave	staved, stove	staved, stove
steal	stole	stolen
stick	stuck	stuck
sting	stung	stung
stink	stunk	stunk
strew	strewed	strewn, strewed
stride	strode	stridden
strike	struck	struck, striken
string	strung	strung
strive	strove, strived	striven, strived
swear	swore	sworn
sweep	swept	swept

Presente — *Pretérito* — *Participio pasivo o pasado*

7. Es por lo común regular cuando significa «pulir, dar brillo.»

swell	swelled	swollen, swelled
Presente	*Pretérito*	*Participio pasivo o pasado*
swim	swam	swum
swing	swung	swung
take	took	taken
teach	taught	taught
tear	tore	torn
tell	told	told
think	thought	thought
thrive	throve, thrived	thriven, thrived
throw	threw	thrown
thrust	thrust	thrust
tread	trod	trod, trodden
understand	understood	understood
undertake	undertook	undertaken
undo	undid	undone
uphold	upheld	upheld
upset	upset	upset
wake	woke, waked	waked
wear	wore	worn
weave	wove	woven
wed	wedded	wedded, wed
weep	wept	wept
wet	wet, wetted	wet, wetted
will (verbo auxiliar)	would	——
win	won	won
wind	wound	wound
withdraw	withdrew	withdrawn
withhold	withheld	withheld
withstand	withstood	withstood
work	worked, wrought	worked, wrought
wring	wrung	wrung
write	wrote	written

Inglés/Español

A

a [ə, e] *art. indef.* un, una; **what –** ...! ¡qué...!; **such** **–** tal; tan.

a·ban·don [əbǽndən] *v.* abandonar; dejar; *s.* abandono, desahogo, desenvoltura; entrega.

a·ban·doned [əbǽndənd] *adj.* abandonado, dejado; perverso; inmoral.

a·ban·don·ment [əbǽndənmənt] *s.* abandono, abandonamiento; desamparo; desenvoltura, desembarazo.

a·bashed [əbǽʃt] *adj.* humillado, avergonzado.

a·bate [əbét] *v.* bajar; rebajar; disminuir acabar con; mitigar (se); calmarse.

a·bate·ment [əbétmənt] *s.* disminución, merma, rebaja, descuento; mitigación.

ab·bess [ǽbəs] *s.* abadesa.

ab·bey [ǽbɪ]s. abadía, monasterio.

ab·bot [ǽbət] *s.* abad.

ab·bre·vi·ate [əbrívɪet] *v.* abreviar, acortar, reducir.

ab·bre·vi·a·tion [əbrívɪéʃən] *s.* abreviación, abreviatura.

ab·di·cate [ǽbdəket] *v.* abdicar, renunciar.

ab·do·men [ǽbdəmən] *s.* abdomen; vientre.

ab·duct [æbd ʌkt] *v.* secuestrar, raptar, *Am.* plagiar (*a alguien*).

ab·duc·tion [æbd ʌkʃən] *s.* rapto, robo, secuestro (*de una persona*).

ab·er·ra·tion [æbəréʃən] *s.* aberración, extravío (*de la mente*).

a·bet [əbét] *v.* incitar; fomentar.

a·bey·an·ce [əbéəns] *s.* suspensión; **in-** pendiente.

ab·hor [əbhɔ́r] *v.* aborrecer, odiar, abominar.

ab·hor·rence [əbhɔ́rəns] *s.* aborrecimiento, aversión.

a·bi·de [əbáɪd] *v.* quedar, permanecer; morar, habitar; aguardar; soportar, tolerar; **to – by** conformarse a ; atenerse a.

a·bil·i·ty [əbíləɪ] *s.* habilidad, capacidad.

ab·ject [æbdʒékt] *adj.* abatido; vil.

ab·ju·re [æbdʒúr] *v.* abjurar.

a·ble [éb l] *adj.* hábil, capaz; competente; **able –** **bodied** de cuerpo sano; **to be – to** poder; saber.

a·bly [éblɪ]*adv.* hábilmente.

ab·nor·mal [æbnɔ́rm l] *adj.* anormal.

a·board [əbórd] *adv.* a bordo; en el tren; **to go –** embarcarse; **all – !** ¡viajeros al tren!; *Méx., C.A.* ¡vámonos!

a·bo·de [əbód] *s.* morada, domicilio, casa; *pret. &* *p.p. de* **to abide**.

a·bol·ish [əbálɪʃ] *v.* abolir, anular.

ab·o·li·tion [æbəlíʃən] *s.* abolición.

a·bom·i·nable [əbómnəb l] *adj.* abominable, aborrecible.

a·bort [əbɔ́rt] *v.* abortar.

a·bor·tion [əbɔ́ʃən] *s.* aborto.

a·bound [əbáUnd] *v.* abundar; **to – with** abundar en.

a·bout [əbáUt] *prep.* (*concerning*) acerca de, tocante a, respecto de; (*near, surrounding*) alrededor de, por;*adv.* (*almost*) casi, poco más o menos; **at –** **ten o'clock** a eso de las diez; **to be – one's business** atender a su negocio; **to be – to** estar para, estar a punto de; **to face –** dar media vuelta; **to** **have no money – one's person** no llegar dinero consigo.

a·bove [əbr ʌv] *prep.* por encima de; sobre; *adv.* arriba; **– all** sobre todo; **above-mentioned** susodicho, ya mencionado; **from –** de arriba; del cielo, de Dios.

a·bra·si·ve [əbrésɪv] *adj.* abrasivo; tosco.

a·breast [əbrést] *adj. adv.* al lado; **to keep abreast** ponerse al corriente.

a·bridge [əbrídʒ] *v.* abreviar; compendiar, condensar; privar (*a uno de sus derechos*).

a·broad [əbrɔ́d] *adv.* en el extranjero; fuera de casa; **to go –** ir al extranjero; **to spread –** divulgar o publicar por todas partes.

a·brupt [əbr ʌpt] *adj.* repentino; precipitado; áspero, brusco; escarpado; **-ly** *adv.* de repente; bruscamente.

ab·scess [ǽbsɛs] *s.* absceso.

ab·sence [ǽbe ŋ s] *s.* ausencia; falta; **– of mind** abstracción; **leave of –** licencia (*para ausentarse*).

ab·sent [ǽbe ŋ s] *adj.* ausente; abstraído, distraído; **absent-minded** absorto, abstraído; [æbsént] *v.* **to** **– oneself** ausentarse.

ab·so·lute [ǽbsəlut] *adj.* absoluto; **the –** lo absoluto; **-ly** *adv.* absolutamente; en absoluto.

ab·so·lut·ion [æbsəlúʃən] *s.* absolución.

ab·solve [əbsálv] *v.* absolver, remitir; perdonar, alzar la pena o el castigo.

ab·sorb [əbsɔ́rb] *v.* absorber.

ab·sorb·ent [əbsɔ́rbənt] *adj. & s.* absorbente.

ab·sorp·tion [əbsɔ́rpʃən] *s.* absorción; abstracción; embebecimiento.

ab·s·tain [əbstén] *v.* abstenerse, privarse.

ab·stinence [ǽbstənəns] *s.* abstinencia.

ab·stract [ǽbstrækt] *adj.* abstracto; *s.* sumario; extracto; **in the** – en abstracto; [æbstrǽkt] *v.* abstraer; considerar aisladamente; separar, retirar; resumir, compendiar.

ab·strac·tion [æbstrǽkʃən] *s.* abstracción; idea abstracta.

ab·surd [əbsə́rd] *adj.* absurdo; insensato ridículo; disparatado.

ab·surd·i·ty [əbsə́dətɪ] *s.* absurdo, disparate.

a·bun·dance [əbʌ́ndəns] *s.* abundancia, copia.

a·bun·dant [əbʌ́ndənt] *adj.* abundante, copioso.

a·buse [əbjús] *s.* abuso; maltrato; ultraje; [əbjúz] *v.* abusar de; maltratar; injuriar; ultrajar.

a·bu·sive [əbjúsɪv] *adj.* abusivo; insultante, injurioso.

a·byss [əbís] *s.* abismo; sima.

ac·a·dem·ic [əkædémɪk] *adj.* académico; escolar.

a·cad·e·my [əkǽdəmɪ] *s.* academia; colegio, instituto; escuela preparatoria.

ac·cede [æksíd] *v.* acceder, consentir.

ac·cel·er·ate [ækséləret] *v.* acelerar (se).

ac·cel·er·a·tion [ækseləréʃən] *s.* aceleración.

ac·cel·er·a·tor [ækséləretə] *s.* acelerador.

ac·cent [ǽksɛnt] *s.* acento; [æksɛ́nt] *v.* acentuar; recalcar.

ac·cen·tuate [æksɛ́ntʃUet] *v.* acentuar; recalcar; realzar.

ac·cept [əksɛ́pt] *v.* aceptar; admitir; acoger; aprobar.

ac·cept·a·ble [əksɛ́ptəb‖] *adj.* aceptable; grato; acepto.

ac·cep·tance [əksɛ́ptəns] *s.* aceptación; aprobación; buena acogida, recibimiento.

ac·cess [ǽksɛs] *s.* acceso; ataque (*de una enfermedad*); arrebato (*de furia*).

ac·ces·si·ble [æksésəb‖] *adj.* accesible; asequible; obtenible.

ac·ces·so·ry [ǽksésərɪ] *adj.* accesorio; adjunto; *s.* accesorio; cómplice; **accessories** cosas accesorias, adornos, adminículos.

ac·ci·dent [ǽksədənt] *s.* accidente; percance, contratiempo; **by** – por casualidad.

ac·ci·den·tal [æksədɛ́nt‖] *adj.* accidental; casual; -**ly** *adv.* accidentalmente; por casualidad.

ac·claim [əklém] *v.* acalmar, aplaudir; *s.* aclamación, aplauso. ▲

ac·cla·ma·tion [ækləméʃən] *s.* aclamación, aplauso.

ac·cli·mate [əkláɪmət] , [ǽkləmet] *v.* aclimatar (se); acostumbrar (se).

ac·cli·ma·tize [əkláɪmətaɪz] *v.* aclimatar (se).

ac·com·mo·date [əkɑmədét] *v.* (*adjust*) acomodar, ajustar, ayudar, hacer un favor; (*lodge*) hospedar, alojar, tener cabida para; **to** – **oneself** confortarse, adaptarse.

ac·com·mo·da·tion [əkɑmədéʃən] *s.* favor, ayuda; conveniencia; alojamiento (*en un hotel, casa, etc.*); cabida; adaptación; ajuste.

ac·com·pa·ni·ment [əkʌ́mpənɪmənt] *s.* acompañamiento.

ac·com·pa·nist [əkʌ́mpənɪst] *s.* acompañador, acompañante.

ac·com·pa·ny [əkʌ́mpənɪ] *v.* acompañar.

ac·com·plice [əkɑ́mplɪs] *s.* cómplice.

ac·com·plish [əkɑ́mplɪʃ] *v.* cumplir; completar; lograr, conseguir; realizar, efectuar.

ac·com·plished [əkɑ́mplɪʃt] *adj.* cumplido; realizado; consumado; establecido; diestro; perfecto.

ac·com·plish·ment [əkɑ́mplɪʃmənt] *s.* cumplimiento; logro, realización; habilidad; perfección; mérito, proeza.

ac·cord [əkɔ́rd] *s.* acuerdo, convenio, armonía, concierto; **of one's own** – voluntariamente; espontáneamente; **in**- **with** de acuerdo con; **with one** – unánimemente; *v.* otorgar, conceder, dar; concordar.

ac·cor·dance [əkɔ́rdn̩s] *s.* conformidad, acuerdo; **in** – **with** de acuerdo con, de conformidad con.

ac·cord·ing [əkɔ́rdɪŋ] – **to** según; conforme a; de acuerdo con; – **as** según (que), a medida que.

ac·cord·ing·ly [əkɔ́rdɪŋlɪ] *adv.* en conformidad,; así; como tal; por lo tanto; por consiguiente.

ac·cor·di·on [əkɔ́rdɪən] *s.* acordeón.

ac·cost [əkɔ́st] *v.* abordar (*a alguien*) en la calle, acosar molestar, perseguir.

ac·count [əkáUnt] *s.* (*bill*) cuenta, computación; (*story*) relato; **on** – **of** a causa de; con motivo de; por; **on my** – por mi; **on my own** – por mi propia cuenta; **on no** – de ninguna manera; **of no** – de ningún valor o importancia; **to turn to** – aprovechar, hacer útil y provechoso; *v.* dar cuenta (a); considerar, tener por; **to** – **for** dar cuenta o razón de; explicar; **how do you** – **for that?** ¿cómo se explica eso?

ac·count·a·ble [əkáUntəb‖] *adj.* responsable; explicable.

ac·count·ant [əkáUntənt] *s.* contador, tenedor de

libros.

ac•count•ing [əkáUntɪŋ] s. contabilidad, contaduría.

ac•cred•it [əkrédɪt] v. acreditar.

ac•crue [əkrú] v. acumular (se).

ac•cul•tur•ate [ək Áltʃðet] v. aculturar (se).

ac•cu•mu•late [əkjúmjəlet] v. acumular (se), juntar (se), amontonar (se).

ac•cu•mu•la•tion [əkjumjəléʃən] s. acumulación, amontonamiento.

ac•cu•ra•cy [ǽkjərəsɪ] s. precisión, exactitud, esmero.

ac•cu•rate [ǽkjərɪt] adj. preciso, exacto; correcto; esmerado; cierto, certero; acertado; **-ly** adv. con exactitud; correctamente; con esmero.

ac•curs•ed [ək ŕ́st] adj. maldito; infame.

ac•cu•sa•tion [ǽkjəzéʃən] s. acusación.

ac•cuse [əkjúz] v. acusar; denunciar.

ac•cus•er [əkjúzə•] s. acusador, delator, denunciador.

ac•cus•tom [ək Ástəm] v. acostumbrar; **to – oneself** acostumbrarse **to be -ed to** tener la costumbre de, acostumbrar, soler; estar acostumbrado a, estar hecho a.

ace [es] s. as; as, el mejor de su clase (como un aviador excelente); **within an – of** a punto de; muy cerca de.

ac•e•tate [ǽsatet] s. acetato.

a•cet•y•lene [əsétəlin] s. acetileno.

ache [ek] s. dolor; **tooth –** dolor de muelas; v. doler.

a•chieve [ətʃív] v. acabar, llevar a cabo; realizar; conseguir, lograr; alcanzar.

a•chieve•ment [ətʃívmənt] s. logro, realización; proeza hazaña.

ac•id [ǽsɪd] adj. ácido; agrio; s. ácido.

a•cid•i•ty [əsídətɪ] s. acidez

ac•knowl•edge [əknálɪdʒ] v. reconocer, admitir; confesar; **to – receipt** acusar recibo.

ac•knowl•edg•ment [əknálɪdʒmənt] s: reconocimiento, expresión de gratitud; confesión, admisión; **– of receipt** acuse de recibo.

a•corn [ékɔrn] s. bellota.

a•cous•tics [əkústɪks] s. acústica.

ac•quaint [əkwént] v. enterar informar; dar a conocer; familiarizar; **to – oneself with** ponerse al corriente de; enterarse de to be **-ed with** conocer a (una persona); estar esterado de (algo); conocer (una ciudad, un país, etc.).

ac•quain•tance [əkwéntəns] s. conocimiento; conocido; **-s** amistades.

ac•qui•esce [ǽkwɪés] v. asentir; consentir, quedar conforme.

ac•qui•es•cence [ǽkwɪés n̩ s] s. asentimiento, consentimiento; conformidad.

ac•quire [əkwáɪr] v. adquirir; obtener, conseguir; contraer (costumbres, vicios).

ac•qui•si•tion [ǽkwəzíʃən] s. adquisición.

ac•quit [əkwít] v. absorver, exonerar; pagar, redimir, librar de (una obligación); **to – oneself** web quedar bien; portarse bien.

ac•quit•tal [əkwít⌡] s. absolución.

a•cre [ékə•] s. acre (medida de superficie).

ac•ro•bat [ǽkrəbæt] s. acróbata.

ac•ro•nym [ǽkrənɪm] s. acrónimo.

a•cross [əkrɔ́s] prep. a través de; al otro lado de; por; por en medio de; adv. a través, de través; **to go – atravesar**; **to come –, run –** encontrarse con; tropezar con.

a•cryl•ic [əkrílɪk] adj. acrílico.

act [ækt] s. acto; acción, hecho; v. hacer, desempeñar (un papel); representar (en el teatro); obrar; actuar; portarse; funcionar; **to – as** servir de, estar de.

act•ing [ǽktɪŋ] s. representación, desempeño (de un papel dramático); acción, actuación; adj. interino, suplente.

ac•tion [ǽkʃən] s. acción; acto; actuación; funcionamiento.

ac•ti•vate [ǽktɪvet] v. activar.

ac•tive [ǽktɪv] adj. activo.

ac•tiv•ism [ǽktəvɪzm] s. activismo.

ac•tiv•ist [ǽktəvɪst] s. activista.

ac•tiv•i•ty [æktívətɪ] s. actividad.

ac•tor [ǽktrə•] s. actor.

ac•tress [ǽktrɪs] s. actriz.

ac•tu•al [ǽktuʃUəl] adj. (legitimate) verdadero, real; (current) actual, existente; **-ly** adv. realmente, en realidad; de hecho, efectivamente.

a•cu•men [əkjúmɪn] s. caletre, tino, perspicacia.

a•cute [əkjút] adj. agudo; perspicaz; penetrante.

ad•a•mant [ǽdəmænt] adj. duro; firme, inflexible.

a•dapt [ədǽpt] v. adaptar; **to – oneself** adaptarse, acomodarse.

ad•ap•ta•tion [ædəptéʃən] s. adaptación.

add [æd] v. sumar; añadir, agregar.

ad•dict [ǽdɪkt] s. adicto (persona adicta al uso de narcóticos); **drug –** morfinómano.

ad•dic•ted [ədíktɪd] adj. adicto, dado, entregado, habituado.

ad•di•tion [ədíʃən] s. adición; suma; añadidura, aditamiento; **in – to** además de.

ad•di•tion•al [ədíʃən⌡] adj. adicional.

ad•di•tive [ǽdətɪv] s. & adj. aditivo.

ad•dress [ədrés] s. (street) dirección, domicilio, señas; sobrescrito; (speech) discurso, arenga, conferencia; **form of –** tratamiento; v. dirigir, poner la dirección, señas o sobrescrito a; hablar, dirigir la palabra a; dirigirse a; **to – oneself to a task** aplicarse a una tarea.

ad·dress·ee [ədrɛsí] *s.* destinatario.

ad·duce [ədús] *v.* aducir.

ad·e·quate [ǽdəkwɪt] *adj.* adecuado; proporcionado; suficiente.

ad·here [ədhír] *v.* adherirse; pegarse.

ad·her·ence [ədhírəns] *s.* adherencia.

ad·he·sion [ədhíʒən] *s.* adhesión.

ad·he·sive [ədhísɪv] *adj.* adhesivo; pegajoso; **– tape** tela adhesiva, esparadrapo.

ad·ja·cent [ədʒésŋt] *s.* adyacente, contiguo.

ad·jec·tive [ǽdʒɪktɪv] *s.* adjetivo.

ad·join [ədʒɔ́ɪn] *v.* estar contiguo o adyacente a, lindar con.

ad·journ [ədʒŕn] *v.* aplazar, diferir; **to – the meeting** suspender o levantar la sesión; **meeting -ed** se levanta la sesión.

ad·journ·ment [ədʒŕnmənt] *s.* aplazamiento, levantamiento (*de una sesión*).

ad·junct [ǽdʒʌŋkt] *s.* adjunto, aditamento, añadidura; asociado, acompañante; *adj.* adjunto, unido, subordinado.

ad·just [ədʒʌ́st] *v.* ajustar, acomoda; arreglar; graduar; **to – oneself** ajustarse, adaptarse, conformarse.

ad·just·ment [ədʒʌ́stmənt] *s.* ajuste, ajustamiento; arreglo; regulación.

ad·lib [ædlíb] *v.* improvisar; expresarse espontáneamente.

ad·min·is·ter [ədmínəstə] *v.* administrar; dirigir, regir, gobernar; aplicar (*remedio, castigo, etc.*); **to – an oath** tomar juramento.

ad·min·is·tra·tion [ədmɪnəstréʃən] *s.* administración; dirección, gobierno; gerencia; manejo.

ad·min·is·tra·tive [ədmínəstreɪtɪv] *adj.* administrativo; ejecutivo; gubernativo.

ad·min·is·tra·tor [ədmínəstretə] *s.* administrador.

ad·mi·ra·ble [ǽdmərəb]] *adj.* admirable; **admirably** *adv.* admirablemente.

ad·mi·ral [ǽdmərəl] *s.* almirante.

ad·mi·ra·tion [ædməréʃən] *s.* admiración.

ad·mire [ədmáɪr] *v.* admirar; estimar.

ad·mir·er [ədmáɪrə] *s.* admirador; pretendiente.

ad·mis·si·ble [ædmísab]] *adj.* admisible.

ad·mis·sion [ədmíʃən] *s.* (*entrance*) entrada, precio de entrada o de ingreso; (*confession*) confesión, admisión.

ad·mit [ədmít] *v.* admitir, aceptar; confesar, reconocer; conceder; dar entrada.

ad·mit·tance [ədmítŋs] *s.* entrada; derecho de entrar; admisión.

ad·mon·ish [ədmánɪʃ] *v.* amonestar.

ad·mo·ni·tion [ædməníʃən] *s.* amo-nestación consejo.

a·do [ədú] *s.* actividad; bulla; disturbio.

ad·o·be [ədóbɪ]*s.* adobe; casa de adobe.

ad·o·les·cence [ædɛ́sŋs] *s.* adolescencia.

ad·o·les·cent [ædɛ́sŋt] *adj. & s.* adolescente.

a·dopt [ədápt] *v.* adoptar.

a·dop·tion [ədápʃən] *s.* adopción.

a·dor·a·ble [ədórəb]] *adj.* adorable; encantador.

a·d·o·ra·tion [ædəréʃən] *s.* adoración.

a·do·re [ədór] *v.* adorar.

a·dorn [ədɔ́rn] *v.* adornar; ornar; embellecer.

a·dorn·ment [ədɔ́rnmənt] *s.* adorno.

a·re·nal [ədrín]] *adj.* suprarrenal.

a·dren·a·lin [ædrénəlɪn] *s.* adrenalina.

a·drift [ədríft] *adj. & adv.* a la deriva, flotando, flotante.

a·droit [ədrɔ́ɪt] *adj.* hábil, diestro.

a·dult [ədʌ́lt] *adj. & s.* adulto.

a·dul·ter·ate [ədʌ́ltəret] *v.* adulterar.

a·dul·ter·er [ədʌ́ltərə] *s.* adúltero.

a·dul·ter·y [ədʌ́ltərɪ] *s.* adulterio.

ad·vance [ədvǽns] *v.* (*progress*) avanzar, adelantar; progresar; acelerar; (*promote*) promover, proponer; (*pay beforehand*) pagar por adelantado (*anticipado*); *s.* avance; progreso; adelanto, anticipo; alza, aumento de precio; **-s** requerimientos, pretensiones, insinuaciones; **in –** por adelantado, con anticipación.

ad·vanced [ədvǽnst] *adj.* avanzado; adelantado; **in years** entrado en años; viejo, anciano.

ad·vance·ment [ədvǽnsmənt] *s.* adelantamiento, mejora, progreso; promoción.

ad·van·tage [ədvǽntɪdʒ] *s.* ventaja; beneficio, provecho; **to have the – over** llevar ventaja a; **to take – of** aprovecharse de; **to take – of a person** abusar de la confianza o paciencia de alguien

ad·van·ta·geous [ædvəntédʒəs] *adj.* ventajoso; provechoso.

ad·vent [ǽdvɛnt] *s.* advenimiento; venida.

ad·ven·ture [ədvɛ́ntʃə-] *s.* aventura; riesgo.

ad·ven·tur·er [ədvɛ́ntʃərə] *s.* aventurero.

ad·ven·tur·ous [ədvɛ́ntʃərəs] *adj.* aventurero; atrevido; aventurado, arriesgado.

ad·verb [ǽdvɝb] *m.* adverbio

ad·ver·sar·y [ǽdvə-sərɪ] *s.* adversario, antagonista, contrario.

ad·verse [ədvɝ́s] *adj.* adverso; opuesto, contrario; hostil; desfavorable.

ad•ver•si•ty [ədvɔ́ˑsətɪ] s. adversidad; infortunio.

ad•ver•tise [ǽˑdvɚˑtaɪz] s. anunciar; avisar, dar viso.

ad•ver•tise•ment [ædvəˑtáɪzmənt] s. anuncio, aviso.

ad•ver•tis•er [ǽˑdvɚˑtaɪzɚˑ] s. anunciador, anunciante.

ad•ver•tis•ing [ǽˑdvəˑtaɪzɪŋ] s. anuncios; arte o negocio de anunciar.

ad•vice [ədváɪs] s. aviso, advertencia; consejo; noticia.

ad•vis•a•ble [ədváɪzəb‖] adj. conveniente; prudente; recomendable.

ad•vise [ədváɪz] v. (counsel) aconsejar; (inform) avisar, informar, advertir; **to – with** consultar con; aconsejarse con.

ad•vis•er, ad•vis•or [ədváɪzɚˑ] s. consejero, aconsejador.

ad•vo•cate [ǽˑdvəkɪt] s. abogado; defensor, intercesor; partidario; [ǽˑdvəket] v. abogar por; defender.

aer•i•al [ɛ́rɪəl] adj. aéreo; s. antena.

aer•o•dy•nam•ic [ɛrodɑɪnǽˑmɪk] adj. aerodinámico; aerodynamics s. aerodinámica.

aer•o•plane [ɛ́rəplen] = **airplane.**

aer•o•sol [ɛ́rosol] s. aerosol.

aes•thet•ic [ɛsθɛ́tɪk] adj. estético; **-s** s. estética.

a•far [əfɑ́r] adv. lejos; **from –** desde lejos.

af•fa•ble [ǽˑfəb‖] adj. affable, amable.

af•fair [əfɛ́r] s. (social) función, tertulia, fiesta, convite; (venture) asunto; negocio; lance; cosa; **love –** amorío.

af•fect [əfɛ́kt] v. afectar; conmover; fingir; hacer ostentación de.

af•fec•ta•tion [æfɪktéʃ(ə)n] s. afectación.

af•fect•ed [əfɛ́ktɪd] adj. (emotion) afectado, conmovido, enternecido; (feigned) fingido, artificioso.

af•fec•tion [əfɛ́kʃən] s. afecto, cariño; inclinación; afección, dolencia.

af•fec•tion•ate [əfɛ́kʃ(ə)nɪt] adj. afectuoso, cariñoso.

af•fi•da•vit [æfədévɪt] adj. declaración jurada.

af•fil•i•ate [əfílɪet] v. afiliar; afiliarse, unirse, asociarse.

af•fin•i•ty [əfínətɪ] s. afinidad.

af•firm [əfɔ́ˑm] v. afirmar, asegurar, aseverar.

af•fir•ma•tive [əfɔ́ˑmətɪv] adj. afirmativo; s. afirmativa.

af•fix [əfíks] v. fijar, pegar; **to – one's signature** poner su firma, firmar.

af•flict [əflíkt] v. afligir; **to be -ed with** padecer de, sufrir de, adolecer de.

af•flic•tion [əflíkʃən] s. aflicción; pena, dolor; achaque; angustia; infortunio.

af•flu•ent [ǽˑflʊənt] adj. acaudalado; abundante.

af•ford [əfɔ́rd] v. proveer, proporcionar; **I cannot – that expense** no puedo hacer ese gasto; **he cannot – to waste time** no le conviene perder el tiempo; no tiene tiempo que perder; **I cannot – that risk** no puedo (o no quiero) exponerme a ese riesgo.

af•fric•ate [ǽˑfrɪkət] adj. & s. africado.

af•front [əfr ʌnt] s. afrenta, agravio, ultraje; v. afrentar, agraviar, ultrajar.

a•fire [əfáɪr] adj. ardiendo, quemándose.

a•float [əflót] adj. & adv. flotante; flotando; a flote; a flor de agua; a bordo; inundado; a la deriva, sin rumbo; **the rumor is –** corre la voz.

a•foot [əfÚt] adv. a pie; en marcha, en movimiento

a•fore•said [əfórsɛd] adj. susodicho, ya dicho.

a•fraid [əfréd] adj. miedoso, medroso; atemorizado, amedrentado; **to be –** temer, tener miedo.

a•fresh [əfréʃ] adv. de nuevo, desde el principio.

A•fri•can [ǽfrɪkən] adj. & s. africano; negro.

af•ter [ǽˑftɚˑ] prep. (temporal) después de, tras, tras de; (position) detras de; (following) en busca de; adv. después; detrás; conj. después (de) que; adj. subsiguiente; siguiente; **– all** después de todo; de todos modos; **day – tomorrow** pasado mañana; **afterdinner** de sobremesa **–effect** consecuencia, resultado; **–math** consecuencias, resultados (usualmente desastrosos); **–thought** idea tardía.

af•ter•noon [ǽftəˑnún] s. tarde.

af•ter•taste [ǽˑftəˑtest] s. dejo, dejillo (sabor que quema en la boca)

af•ter•wards [ǽˑftəˑwɚˑdz] adv. después.

a•gain [əgén] adv. otra vez, de nuevo; además por; otra parte; **– and –** repetidas veces, **never –** nunca jamás; **to come –** olver; **to do it –** volver ha hacerlo.

a•gainst [əgénst] prep. contra; frente a; en contraste con; **– in the grain** a contrapelo, a redopelo; **– a rainy day** para cuando llueva.

age [edʒ] s. edad; época; siglo; generación; **of –** mayor de edad; **old –** vejez, ancianidad; **to become of –** llegar a mayor de edad; **under –** menor edad; v. envejecer (se).

ag•ed [édʒɪd, édʒd] adj. viejo, anciano, añejo; envejecido; **– forty years** de cuarenta años; **– in wood** añejado en toneles o barriles (dícese del vino).

a•gen•cy [édʒənsɪ] s. agencia; medio, intermedio.

a•gen•da [ədʒɛ́ndə] s. temario; asuntos que han de tratarse en una reunión.

a•gent [édʒənt] s. agente; intermediario, representante; apoderado.

ag•gran•dize [ǽˑgrəndaɪz] v. engrandecer; agrandar.

ag•gra•vate [ǽˑgrəvet] v. agravar. empeorar, irritar. exasperar.

ag•gre•gate [ǽˑgrɪgɪt] s. agregado, conjunto, colección; *adj.* agregado, unido; **in the** – en conjunto.

ag·gres·sion [əgréʃən] *s.* agresión

ag·gres·sive [əgrésɪv] *adj.* agresivo; emprendedor.

ag·gres·sor [əgrésə] *s.* agresor.

a·ghast [əgǽst] *adj.* espantado, pasmado.

ag·ile [ǽdʒəl] *adj.* ágil

ag·il·i·ty [ədʒílɪəɪ] *s.* agilidad.

ag·i·tate [ǽdʒətet] *v.* agitar; turbar, perturbar; alborotar; discutir acaloradamente; maquinar, tramar.

ag·i·ta·tion [ædʒətéʃən] *s.* agitación; alboroto.

ag·i·ta·tor [ǽdʒətetə] *s.* agitador; alborotador, revoltoso.

a·go [əgó] *adj. & adv.* pasado; en el pasado; **many years** – hace muchos años; muchos años ha, mucho tiempo ha; **long** – hace mucho tiempo; ha mucho.

ag·o·nize [ǽgənaɪz] *v.* agonizar; sufrir angustiosamente; retorcerse de dolor; luchar.

ag·o·ny [ǽgənɪ] *s.* agonía; angustia; tormento; dolor; lucha.

a·gree [əgrí] *v.* (*accede*) acordar, concordar, consentir, estar de acuerdo, ponerse de acuerdo; (*suit*) sentarle bien a uno (*dícese del clima, del alimento, etc.*).

a·gree·a·ble [əgríəb⎮⎮] *adj.* agradable, afable; complaciente; conveniente; satisfactorio.

a·gree·ment [əgrímənt] *s.* (*concord*) acuerdo, convenio, conformidad; (*gramatical*) concordancia; **to be in** – estar de acuerdo; **to come to** – ponerse de acuerdo.

ag·ri·cul·tur·al [ægrɪk⋀ltʃərəl] *adj.* agrícola.

ag·ri·cul·ture [ǽgrɪk⋀ltʃə] *s.* agricultura.

ag·ri·cul·tur·ist [ægrɪk⋀ltʃərɪst] *s.* agricultor.

a·ground [əgráUnd] *adj. & adv.* encallado.

a·head [əhéd] *adv.* delante, al frente; adelante; **– of time** adelantado; antes de tiempo; **to go** – ir adelante; **to get** – adelantar(se).

aid [ed] *s.* ayuda, auxilio, socorro; ayudante, auxiliar; *v.* ayudar, auxiliar, socorrer.

ail [el] *s.* adolecer, padecer; **what -s you?** ¿qué tienes?, ¿qué te aflige?

ail·e·ron [élərən] *s.* alerón.

ail·ment [élmənt] *s.* achaque, dolencia.

aim [em] *s.* (*pointing*) puntería; tino; (*objective*) fin, objeto; proposición; *v.* apuntar (*un arma*); dirigir, asestar, dirigir la puntería, aspirar (a); **to** – **to please** proponerse (o tratar de) agradar.

aim·less [émlɪs] *adj.* sin propósito, sin objeto.

air [ɛr] *s.* (*atmosphere*) aire, brisa; (*music*) tonada; **in the** – en el aire; indeciso, incierto; **in the open** – al raso, al aire libre; **to be on the** – emitir, radiodifundir; **to put on -s** darse tono; *adj.* de aire; aéreo; – **brake** freno neumático; –**line** línea aérea; ruta aé-

rea, **by** –**mail** por correo aéreo; por vía aérea; por avión; **air – conditioned** de aire acondicionado; *v.* airear; orear; ventilar; publicar; ostentar.

air·borne [érborn] *aéreo*; aerotransportado.

air·craft [érkræft] *s.* avión aeroplano; aeronave; aviones.

air·line [érlaɪn] *s.* aerovía; línea aérea; compañía de transporte aéreo.

air·plane [érplen] *s.s.* aeroplano; avión; – **carrier** portaaviones.

air·port [érport] *s.* aeropuerto, aeródromo.

air·ship [érʃɪp] *s.* aeronave.

air·tight [értáɪt] *adj.* hermético.

air·y [érɪ] *adj.* airoso; aireado, ventilado; ligero; tenue.

aisle [aɪl] *s.* pasillo, pasadizo; nave (*de una iglesia*).

a·jar [ədʒár] *adj.* entreabierto, entornado.

a·larm [əlórm] *s.* alarma; rebato; inquietud; – **clock** despertador; *v.* alarmar; inquietar.

al·bum [ǽlbəm] *álbum.*

al·co·hol [ǽlkəhol] *s.* alcohol.

al·co·hol·ic [ælkəhɔ́lɪk] *adj.* alcohólico.

al·cove [ǽlkov] *s.* alcoba.

al·der·man [ɔ́ldə·mən] *s.* concejal, regidor.

ale [el] *s.* cerveza de tipo espeso y amargo.

a·lert [əlɜ́t] *adj.* alerto; vigilante; despierto; vivo; listo; alarma, rebato; **to be on the** – estar alerta.

al·fal·fa [ælfǽlfə] *s.* alfalfa.

al·ge·bra [ǽldʒəbrə] *s.* álgebra.

al·i·bi [ǽləbaɪ] *s.* coartada; excusa.

a·li·en [éljən] *s.* extranjero; residente extranjero; *adj.* extraño, ajeno.

al·ien·ate [éljənet] *v.* enajenar; apartar, alejar (*a una persona de otra*).

al·ien·ist [éljənɪst] *s.*alienista; psiquiatra.

a·light [əláɪt] *v.* apearse, desmontarse, bajar (de); posarse (*dícese de los pájaros, mariposas, etc.*).

a·lign [əláɪn] *v.* alinear (se).

a·like [əláɪk] *adj.* semejante; parecido; **to be** – parecerse; asemejarse; ser iguales; *adv.* del mismo modo.

al·i·mo·ny [ǽləmonɪ] *s.* asistencia de divorcio; alimentos.

a·live [əláɪv] *adj.* vivo; con vida; viviente; activo; – **with** lleno de.

all [ɔl] *adj.* todo (el); todos (los); *s.* todo; todo el mundo, todos; *adv.* enteramente; – **at once** de una vez; de un tirón; de repente; – **right** bueno, bien; – **the worse** tanto peor; – **not at** – de ninguna manera; no hay de qué; **nothing at** – nada en absoluto; – **told** (*o* **in** –) en conjunto; **once (and) for** – por última vez; una vez por todas; **to be** – **in** estar agotado, estar rendido de fatiga; **it is** – **over** se acabó, ha terminado todo.

al·lay [əlé] v. aliviar; calmar.

al·le·ga·tion [æləgéʃən] s. alegación, alegato; aseveración.

al·lege [əlédʒ] v. alegrar; declarar; sostener, asegurar.

al·le·giance [əlídʒəns] s. lealtad, fidelidad; homenaje.

al·le·go·ry [ǽləgorɪ] s. alegoría.

al·ler·gy [ǽlə·dʒɪ] s. alergia (*sensibilidad anormal a ciertos alimentos o sustancias*).

al·le·vi·ate [əlívɪet] v. aliviar.

al·ley [ǽlɪ] s. callejón; callejuela; **blind –** callejón sin salida; **bowling –** boliche, *Am.* bolera.

al·li·ance [əláɪəns] s. alianza.

al·lied [əláɪd] adj. aliado; relacionado.

al·li·ga·tor [ǽləgetə·] s. lagarto; caimán; – **pear** aguacate.

al·lot [əlót] v. asignar; repartir.

al·low [əláU] v. permitir, dejar; conceder; admitir; asignar; abonar; **to – for certain errors** tener en cuenta ciertos errores.

al·low·a·ble [əláUəb]] adj. permisible, admisible, lícito.

al·low·ance [əláUəns] s. asignación; abono, pensión; ración, rebaja, descuento; permiso; concesión; **monthly –** mesada, mensualidad; **to make – for** tener en cuenta.

al·loy [ǽlɔɪ] s. aleación, ligar, mezcla (*de dos o más metales*); [əlɔ́ɪ] v. alear, ligar, mezclar (*metales*).

al·lude [əlúd] v. aludir.

al·lure [əlúr] v. seducir, cautivar; atraer, halagar.

al·lure·ment [əlúrmənt] s. seducción, tentación; atractivo, halago.

al·lur·ing [əlúrɪŋ] adj. seductivo, halagüeño, encantador.

al·lu·sion [əlúʒən] s. alusión; indirecta, insinuación.

al·ly [əláɪ] v. unir; aliarse; **to – oneself (itself) with** aliarse con, unirse con; [ǽlaɪ] s. aliado.

al·ma·nac [ɔ́lmənæk] s. almanaque, calendario.

al·might·y [ɔlmáɪtɪ] adj. todopoderoso, omnipotente.

al·mond [ámənd] s. almendra; **– tree** almendro.

al·most [ɔ́lmost] adv. casi; **I – fell down** por poco me caigo.

alms [omz] s. limosna; **– box** cepo o cepillo, alcancía (*para limosnas*).

a·loft [əlɔ́ft] adv. en alto; arriba.

a·lone [əlón] adj. solo; solitario; único; adv. sólo, solamente; **all – a solas**; completamente solo; solito; **to let – no tocar**; no molestar; dejar en paz; no hacer caso de.

a·long [əlɔ́ŋ] prep. a lo largo de; por; al lado de; **– with** junto con; en compañía de; **all –** todo el tiempo;

de un extremo a otro; **all – the coast** por toda la costa; **to carry – with one** llevar consigo; **to go – with** acompañar; **to get –** ir bien; **to get – with** llevarse bien con; **get –!** ¡vete! ¡váyase! ¡largo de aquí!

a·long·side [əl ɔ́ ŋsáɪd] prep. & adv. al lado (de); al costado (de); lado a lado.

a·loof [əlúf] adj. aislado, apartado, retirado; huraño; reservado; adv. aparte; lejos.

a·loof·ness [əlúfnɪs] s. alejamiento, desapego, aislamiento.

a·lound [əláUd] adv. alto, recio, fuerte, en voz alta.

al·pha·bet [ǽlfəbet] s. alfabeto.

al·read·y [ɔlrédɪ] adv. ya.

al·so [ɔ́lso] adj. también, además, igualmente.

al·tar [ɔ́ltə·] s. altar; **high – altar mayor**; **– piece** retablo.

al·ter [ɔ́ltə·] v. alterar; cambiar; variar.

al·ter·a·tion [ɔltəréʃən] s. alteración, cambio; mudanza; modificación.

al·ter·nate [ɔ́ltə·nɪt] adj. alternativo; alterno; alternado; s. suplente; **-ly** alternativamente, por turno; [ɔ́ltə·net] v. alternar; variar; turnar.

al·ter·na·tive [ɔlt ɚ́nɑtɪv] adj alternativo; s. alternativa.

al·ter·na·tor [ɔlt ɚnétə·] s. alternador.

al·though [ɔlðó] conj. aunque, si bien, bien que.

al·tim·e·ter [ǽltímətə·] s. altímetro.

al·ti·tude [ǽltətjud] s. altitud, altura, elevación.

al·to [ǽlto] s. & adj. contralto.

al·to·geth·er [ɔltəg ɚ́ðə·] adv. del todo, completamente; en conjunto.

a·lu·mi·num [əlúmɪnəm] s. aluminio.

a·lum·nus [əl ʌ́mnəs] s. graduado, ex-alumno.

al·ways [ɔ́lwɪz] adv. siempre.

am [æm] *1ª persona del presente de indic. del verbo* **to be:** soy, estoy.

a·mal·ga·mate [əmǽlgəmet] v. amalgamar; combinar; unir.

a·mass [əmǽs] v. amontonar, acumular, apilar, *Am.* amasar.

am·a·teur [ǽmətʃUr] s. aficionado; novicio, principiante.

a·maze [əméz] v. pasmar, maravillar, asombrar.

a·maze·ment [əmézmənt] s. pasmo, admiración, asombro.

a·maz·ing [əmézɪŋ] adj. pasmoso, asombroso, maravilloso.

am·bas·sa·dor [æmbǽsədə·] s. embajador.

am·ber [ǽmbə·] s. ámbar; color de ámbar; adj. ambarino; de ámbar.

am·bi·gu·i·ty [æmbɪgjúetɪ] s. ambigüedad.

am·big·u·ous [æmbígjʊəs] adj. ambiguo.

am·bi·tion [æmbíʃən] s. ambición, aspiración.

am·bi·tious [æmbíʃəs] adj. ambicioso.

am·biv·a·lent [æmbívələnt] adj. ambi-valente.

am·ble [ǽmbḷ] v. andar, vagar.

am·bu·lance [ǽmbjələns] s. ambulancia.

am·bush [ǽmbʊʃ] s. emboscada; celada; acecho; **to lie in —** estar emboscado, estar al acecho; v. emboscar; poner celada a.

a·me·na·ble [əmínabḷ] adj. dócil; tratable.

a·mend [əménd] v. enmendar; rectificar; **-s** s. pl. satisfacción, compensación; **to make — for** resarcir, dar satisfacción por, compensar por.

a·mend·ment [əméndmənt] s. enmienda.

A·mer·i·can [əmérəkən] adj. & s. (continental) americano: (U.S.A) norteamericano.

am·e·thyst [ǽməθɪst] s. amatista.

a·mi·a·ble [émɪəbḷ] adj. amable, afable, amistoso.

am·i·ca·ble [ǽmɪkəbḷ] adj. amigable, amistoso.

a·mid [əmíd] prep. en medio de; entre; **amidst** [əmídst] = **amid.**

a·miss [əmís] adj. errado, equivocado; impropio; adv. mal; fuera de lugar, impropiamente; **to take —** llevar a mal.

am·mo·nia [əmónjə] s. amoníaco.

am·mu·ni·tion [æmjənfʃən] s. munición.

am·ne·sia [æmníʒə] s. amnesia.

am·nes·ty [ǽmnɛstɪ] s. amnestía.

a·mong [əm ʌ ŋ] prep. entre, en medio de; **amongst** [əm ʌ ŋst] = **among.**

am·o·rous [ǽmərəs] adj. amoroso.

a·mor·phous [əmɔ́rfəs] adj. amorfo.

am·or·tize [ǽmɜ̆taɪz] v. amortizar.

a·mount [əmáUnt] s. suma; cantidad; total; importe; valor; v. montar, subir, importar ascender (a); valer; **that -s to stealing** eso equivale a robar.

am·pere [ǽmpɪr] s. amperio.

am·phi·the·a·ter [ǽmfəθíəɪə] s. anfiteatro.

am·ple [ǽmp ḷ] adj. amplio; abundante; bastante; suficiente.

am·pli·fy [ǽmpləfaɪ] v. ampliar; amplificar.

am·pu·tate [ǽmpjətet] v. amputar.

a·muse [əmjúz] v. divertir, entretener, distraer; **to-oneself** divertirse.

a·muse·ment [əmjúzmənt] s. diversión, entretenimiento, pasatiempo, recreo, distracción.

a·mus·ing [əmjúzɪŋ] adj. divertido, entretenido; gracioso chistoso.

an [ən, æn] art. indef. un, una.

a·nach·ro·nism [ənǽkrənɪzm] s. anacronismo.

a·nal·o·gous [ənǽləgəs] s. análogo.

a·nal·o·gy [ənǽlədʒɪ] s. analogía, semejanza.

a·nal·y·sis [ənǽləsɪs] s. análisis.

an·a·lyze [ǽnḷaɪz] v. analizar.

an·ar·chist [ǽnəkɪst] s. anarquista.

an·ar·chy [ǽnəkɪ] s. anarquía.

a·nat·o·my [ənǽtəmɪ] s. anatomía.

an·ces·tor [ǽnsɛstə] s. antepasado; **-s** abuelos, antepasados.

an·ces·tral [ænsɛ́strəl] s. solariego, de los antepasados; hereditario.

an·ces·try [ǽnsɛstrɪ] s. linaje, abolengo, ascendencia.

an·chor [ǽŋkə] s. ancha; **to drop —** anclar, echar anclas, dar fondo, fondear; **to weigh -** llevar el ancla; v. anclar; echar anclas; fijar, asegurar.

an·cho·vy [ǽntʃovɪ] s. anchoa; anchova.

an·cient [énʃənt] adj. antiguo; vetusto; **the -s** los antiguos; la antigüedad.

and [ənd, ænd] conj. y; e (delante de i o hi); **— so forth** etcétera; y así sucesivamente; **let us try – do it** tratemos de hacerlo; **let us go – see him** vamos a verle.

An·da·lusian [ændəlúʒən] adj. andaluz.

an·ec·dote [ǽnɪkdot] s. anécdota..

a·ne·mi·a [ənImɪə] s. anemia.

an·es·thet·ic [ænəsθɛ́tɪk] adj. & s. anestésico.

a·new [ənjú]adv. otra vez, de nuevo; nuevamente.

an·gel [éndʒəl] s. ángel.

an·gel·ic [ændʒɛ́lɪk] adj. angélico.

an·ger [ǽŋgə] s. enojo, enfado, ira, cólera; v. enojar, enfadar, encolerizar.

an·gi·na [ændʒáɪnə] s. angina; **— pectoris** angina de pecho.

an·gle [ǽŋgḷ] s. ángulo; (interior) rincón; (exterior) esquina; punto de vista, aspecto; v. pescar.

An·glo-Sax·on [ǽŋglosǽksṇ] adj. & s. anglosajón.

an·gry [ǽŋgrɪ] adj. enojado; colérico.

an·guish [ǽŋgwɪʃ] s. angustia, ansia, pena, dolor.

an·gu·lar [ǽŋgjələ] adj. angular; anguloso.

an·i·mal [ǽnəm ḷ] s. & adj. animal.

an·i·mate [ǽnəmɪt] adj. animado, viviente; **animated cartoon** dibujo animado; [ǽnəmet] s. animar, alentar.

an·i·ma·tion [ænəmáʃən] s. animación; viveza.

an·i·mos·i·ty [ænəmósətɪ] s. animosidad, ojeriza, inquina, rencor.

an·ise [ǽnɪs] s. anís.

an•kle [ǽŋkḷ] s. tobillo.

an•nals [ǽn|z] s. pl. anales.

an•nex [ǽnɛks] s. (building) pabellón, ala; (dependent addition) anexo; añadidura; [ənéks] v. anexar.

an•nex•a•tion [ænɛkséʃən] s. anexión.

an•ni•hi•late [ənáɪəlet] v. aniquilar; anonadar.

an•ni•ver•sa•ry [ænəv ə́ sərɪ] s. & adj. aniversario.

an•no•tate [ǽnotet] v. anotar.

an•no•ta•tion [ænotéʃən] s. anotación, acotación, nota.

an•nounce [ənáUns] v. anunciar; proclamar.

an•nounce•ment [ənáUnsmənt] s. anuncio; aviso; noticia.

an•nounc•er [ənáUnsə] s. anunciador; radio – locutor.

an•noy [ənɔ́ɪ] v. molestar; fastidiar; incomodar; enfadar.

an•noy•ance [ənɔ́ɪəns] s. molestia; fastidio; enfado.

an•nu•al [ǽnjUəl] adj. anual; s. anuario; planta anual; ly adv. anualmente, cada año, todos los años.

an•nu•i•ty [ənúətɪ] s. anualidad; renta anual.

an•nul [ən ʌ́l] v. anular; abolir.

an•nul•ment [ən ʌ́lmənt] s. revocación; anulación.

a•noint [ənɔ́ɪnt] v. ungir; untar; administrar la Extremaunción.

a•non [ənɑ́n] adv. pronto, luego; otra vez.

a•non•y•mous [ənɑ́nəməs] adj. anónimo.

an•oth•er [ən ʌ́ðə] adj. & pron. otro; one – uno a otro, unos a otros.

an•swer [ǽnsə] s. respuesta, contestación; réplica; solución; v. responder; contestar; replicar; to – for ser responsable de (o por); responder de; ser (salir) fiador de; to – the purpose ser adecuado; servir para el objeto.

ant [ænt] s. hormiga; – eater oso hormiguero; – hill hormiguero.

ant•ac•id [ænt ǽ sɪd] v. & adj. antiácido.

an•tag•o•nism [ænt ǽ gənɪzəm] s. antagonismo, oposición, antipatía.

an•tag•o•nist [ænt ǽ gənɪst] s. antagonista, adversario.

an•tag•o•nize [ænt ǽ gənaɪz] v. contrariar, oponerse a, hostilizar.

an•te•ce•dent [æntəsid ŋ t] adj. & s. antecedente.

an•te•lope [ǽnt ǀ op] s. antílope.

an•ten•na [ænténə] (pl. antennae [ænténi]) s. antena.

an•te•ri•or [æntírɪə] adj. anterior; delantero.

an•te•room [ǽntɪrum] s. antecámara; sala de espera.

an•them [ǽnθəm] adj. himno.

an•thol•o•gy [ænθɑ́lədʒɪ] s. antología.

an•thra•cite [ǽθrəsaɪt] s. antracita.

an•thro•pol•o•gy [ænθrəpɑ́lədʒɪ] s. antropología.

an•ti•air•craft [æntɪɛ́rkræft] adj. antiaéreo.

an•ti•bi•ot•ic [æntɪbaɪɑ́tɪk] s. & adj. antibiótico.

an•ti•bod•y [ǽntɪbɑdɪ] s. anticuerpo.

an•tic•i•pate [æntɪ́səpet] v. anticipar (se); prever; esperar.

an•tic•i•pa•tion [æntɪsəpéʃən] s. anticipación; expectación; previsión.

an•tics [ǽntɪks] s. pl. travesuras, cabriolas.

an•ti•dote [ǽntɪdot] s. antídoto.

an•ti•freeze [ǽntɪfriz] s. anticongelante.

an•tip•a•thy [æntɪ́pəθɪ] s. antipatía, repugnancia.

an•ti•quat•ed [ǽntəkwetɪd] adj. anticuado.

an•tique [æntík] adj. antiguo; anticuado; s. antigualla.

an•tiq•ui•ty [æntɪ́kwətɪ] adj. antigüedad; vejez, ancianidad.

an•ti•sep•tic [æntəséptɪk] adj. & s. antiséptico.

an•ti•so•cial [æntɪsófəl] adj. antisocial; s. Am. criminal.

an•tith•e•sis [æntɪ́θəsɪ] antítesis.

ant•ler [ǽntlə] s. asta, cuerno (del venado, ciervo, etc.).

an•vil [ǽnvɪl] s. yunque.

anx•i•e•ty [æŋzáɪətɪ] s. ansiedad; zozobra; ansia; anhelo, afán.

anx•ious [ǽŋkʃəs] adj. ansioso; inquieto, preocupado; anheloso, deseoso; -ly adv. con ansiedad, con ansia, ansiosamente.

an•y [ɛ́nɪ] adj. & pron. cualquier(a), cualesquier (a); alguno, algunos, in – case de todos modos, en todo caso; I have not – bread no tengo pan; he does not sing – more ya no canta; she does not want to work – more no quiere trabajar más.

an•y•bod•y [ɛ́nɪbɑdɪ] pron. alguien, alguno; cualquiera; not ... – no... nadie, no... ninguno; he does not know – no conoce a nadie.

an•y•how [ɛ́nɪhaU] adv. de todos modos; de cualquier modo.

an•y•one [ɛ́nɪwʃn] pron. = anybody.

an•y•thing [ɛ́nɪθɪŋ] pron. alguna cosa; cualquier cosa; algo; not ... – no ... nada; not ... to know – no saber nada; you wish todo lo que viera Vd.

an•y•way [ɛ́nɪwe] adv. de todos modos; en cualquier caso.

an•y•where [ɛ́nɪhwɛr] adv. dondequiera; en cualquier parte o lugar; en todas partes; not ... – no... en (o a) ninguna parte; not to go – no ir a ninguna parte.

a•part [əpárt] *adj.* aparte; separadamente; a un lado, *adj.* aislado, separado; **to take –** desarmar desmontar **to tear –** despedazar, hacer pedazos.

a•part•ment [əpártmənt] *s.* departamento, piso, apartamento; vivienda, habitación.

ap•a•thy [ǽpəθɪ] *s.* apatía, indiferencia, indolencia.

ape [ep] *s.* mono; *v.* remendar, imitar.

ap•er•ture [ǽpə•ʃə•] *s.* abertura.

a•pex [épɛks] *s.* ápice, cumbre.

a•pha•sia [əfézɪə] *s.* afasia.

a•piece [əpis] *adv.* cada uno, a cada uno, por persona.

a•poc•ope [əpákəpɪ] *s.* apócope.

ap•o•gee [ǽpədʒɪ] *s.* apogeo.

a•pol•o•get•ic [əpaledʒétɪk] *adj.* que se excusa o disculpa.

a•pol•o•gize [əpálədʒaɪz] *v.* disculparse, excusarse.

a•pol•o•gy [əpálədʒɪ] *s.* apología; excusa, disculpa, justificación, satisfacción.

ap•o•ple•xy [ǽpəplɛksɪ] *s.* apoplejía.

a•pos•tle [əpós̩] *s.* apóstol.

ap•os•tol•ic [æpəstálɪk] *s.* apostólico.

a•pos•tro•phe [əpóstrəfɪ] *s.* apóstrofe; *(punctuation)* apóstrofo.

ap•pall [əpɔ́l] *v.* aterrorizar, aterrar; asombrar, espantar.

ap•pall•ing [əpɔ́lɪŋ] *adj.* aterrador, espantoso; asombroso.

ap•pa•ra•tus [æpərétəs] *s.* aparato; aparatejo.

ap•par•el [əpǽrəl] *s.* ropa; ropaje; vestidos; indumentaria.

ap•par•ent [əpǽənt] *adj.* aparente; visible; claro, evidente; patente; **heir –** heredero presunto; **-ly** *adv.* aparentemente, al parecer, por lo visto.

ap•pa•rit•ion [æpəríʃən] *s.* aparición; aparecido, espectro, fantasma.

ap•peal [əpíl] *s.* *(legal)* apelación, recurso; *(request)* súplica; *(attraction)* atracción, atractivo, llamamiento; *v.* apelar; recurrir, acudir; atraer, despertar interés o simpatía; llamar la atención.

ap•pear [əpɪ́r] *v.* aparecer (se); parecer; comparecer.

ap•pear•ance [əpírəns] *s.* apariencia, semblante; porte, facha; aparición.

ap•pease [əpíz] *v.* apaciguar, aplacar; pacificar; conciliar; sosegar.

ap•pease•ment [əpízmənt] *s.* apaciguamiento; conciliación.

ap•pen•dix [əpéndɪks] *s.* apéndice.

ap•per•tain [æpə•tén] *v.* pertenecer.

ap•pe•tite [ǽpətaɪt] *s.* apetito; gana, deseo.

ap•pe•tiz•er [ǽpətaɪzə•] *s.* aperitivo.

ap•pe•tiz•ing [ǽpətaɪzɪŋ] *adj.* apetecible; apetitoso.

ap•plaud [əplɔ́d] *v.* aplaudir.

ap•plause [əplɔ́z] *s.* aplauso.

ap•ple [ǽp] *s.* manzana; **– tree** manzano **Adam's - nuez** *(de la garganta);* *Ven., C.A. Col.* manzana; **of my eye** niña de mis ojos.

ap•ple•sauce [ǽp̩sɔs] *s.* compota de manzana.

ap•pli•ance [əpláɪəns] *s.* utensilio, instrumento; herramienta.

ap•pli•cable [ǽpləkəb̩] *adj.* aplicable.

ap•pli•cant [ǽpləkənt] *s.* solicitante, aspirante, candidato.

ap•pli•ca•tion [æpləkéʃən] *s.* *(dedication)* aplicación; *(petition)* solicitud, petición; *Méx., Carib., Ven.* aplicación.

ap•plied [əpláɪd] *adj. & p.p.* aplicado; **– for** pedido, solicitado.

ap•ply [əpláɪ] *v.* aplicar(se); **to – to** dirigirse a, acudir a, recurrir a; **to –** for solicitar, pedir; **to – oneself** aplicarse, dedicarse; **to – on account** acreditar en cuenta.

ap•point [əpɔ́ɪnt] *v.* *(designate)* nombrar, designar, señalar; *(furnish)* amueblar, equipar; **a well -ed house** una casa bien amueblada.

ap•point•ee [əpɔɪntí] *s.* electo.

ap•point•ment [əpɔ́ɪntmənt] *s.* *(desig-nation)* nombramiento, designación; *(engagement)* cita, compromiso; **-s** mobiliario, mueblaje; accesorios.

ap•por•tion [əpórʃən] *v.* repartir proporcionadamente; prorratear.

ap•por•tion•ment [əpórʃənmənt] *s.* prorrateo, distribución, repartimiento.

ap•prais•al [əpréz̩] *s.* tasa, valuación.

ap•praise [əpréz] *v.* avaluar, valuar, tasar.

ap•pre•ci•able [əpríʃrəb̩] *adj.* *(prized)* apreciable; *(perceived)* perceptible; *(quantity)* bastante.

ap•pre•ci•ate [əpríʃɪet] *v.* apreciar; estimar; agradecer; **to – in value** subir de valor.

ap•pre•ci•a•tion [əprɪʃéʃən] *s.* apreciación; aprecio; valuación; agradecimiento; aumento, alzar, subida *(de precio).*

ap•pre•hend [æprɪhénd] *v.* aprehender, asir, prender; comprender; percibir.

ap•pre•hen•sion [æprɪhénʃən] *s.* aprehensión, aprensión, recelo, desconfianza, presentimiento; captura.

ap•pre•hen•sive [æprɪhénsɪv] *adj.* aprensivo.

ap•pren•tice [əpréntɪs] *s.* aprendiz; novicio, principiante; *v.* poner de aprendiz.

ap•pren•tice•ship [əpréntɪsʃɪp] *s.* aprendizaje.

ap·prise [əpráɪz] v. enterar, informar; apreciar.

ap·proach [əprótʃ] s. acercamiento; aproximación; acceso, entrada; **method of -** técnica o modo de plantear (*un problema*); v. acercarse, aproximarse; abordar. (*a alguien*).

ap·pro·ba·tion [æprəbéʃən] s. aprobación.

ap·pro·pri·ate [əpróprɪɪt] adj. apropiado, propio, apto, conveniente, a propósito; [əpróprɪet] v. apropiarse, apoderarse de; asignar (*una suma de dinero*).

ap·pro·pri·a·tion [əproprɪéʃən] s. apropiación, asignación, suma asignada.

ap·prov·al [əprúvl] s. aprobación, asentimiento.

ap·prove [əprúv] v. aprobar; asentir a.

ap·prox·i·mate [əpróksəmɪt] adj. aproximado; aproximativo; **-ly** adv. aproximadamente, casi, poco más o menos; [əpróksəmet] v. aproximar; aproximarse, acercarse.

a·pri·cot [éprɪkat] s. albaricoque; *Am.* chabacano.

A·pril [éprəl] s. abril.

a·pron [éprən] s. delantal.

ap·ro·pos [æprəpó] adv. a propósito; adj. oportuno; pertinente; **- of** a propósito de.

apt [æpt] adj. apto, capaz; pertinente, a propósito; **- to** propenso a.

ap·ti·tude [ǽptɪtjud] s. aptitud, capacidad; habilidad.

a·quar·i·um [əkwérɪəm] s. acuario; pecera.

a·quat·ic [əkwǽtɪk] adj. acuático.

aq·ue·duct [ǽkwɪdʌkt] s. acueducto.

A·rab [ǽrəb] adj. & s. árabe.

A·ra·go·nese [ærəgəníz] adj. & s. aragonés.

ar·bi·ter [ásbɪtə] s. árbitro, arbitrador, juez árbitro.

ar·bi·trar·y [árbətrɛrɪ] adj. arbitrario; despótico.

ar·bi·tra·te [árbətret] v. arbitrar; decidir; someter al arbitraje.

ar·bi·tra·tion [arbətréʃən] s. arbitraje, arbitración.

ar·bi·tra·tor [árbətretə] s. arbitrador, árbitro; mediador.

ar·bor [árbə] s. emparrado, enramada, glorieta.

arc [ark] s. arco; **- lamp** lámpara de arco.

ar·cade [arkéd] s. arcada; galería; soportal.

arch [artʃ] s. arco; bóveda; **semicircular —** arco de medio punto; **— enemy** enemigo acérrimo; v. arquear (se); enarcar (se).

ar·chae·o·lo·gy [arkɑ́ɪədʒɪ] s. arqueología.

ar·cha·ic [arkéɪk] adj. arcaico, desusado, anticuado.

arch·bish·op [ártʃbíʃəp] s. arzobispo.

arch·er·y [ártʃərɪ] s. tiro de flechas.

ar·chi·pel·a·go [arkəpéləgo] s. archipiélago.

ar·chi·tect [árkɪtekt] s. arquitecto.

ar·chi·tec·tur·al [arkɪtéktʃərəl] adj. arquitectónico.

ar·chi·tec·ture [árkətɛktʃə] s. arquitectura.

ar·chives [árkaɪvz] s. archivo.

arch·way [ártʃwe] s. pasadizo (*bajo un arco*); arcada, galería abovedada.

arc·tic [árktɪk] adj. ártico.

ar·dent [árdṇt] adj. ardiente; apasionado.

ar·dor [árdə] s. ardor; enardecimiento; fervor.

ar·du·ous [árdʒUəs] adj. arduo, trabajoso.

are [ar] 2ª *persona y pl. del presente de indic. del verbo* **to be** eres, estás; somos, estamos; sois, estáis; son, están.

ar·e·a [ɛ́rɪə] s. area, superficie; espacio; región.

a·re·na [əríná] s. arena, redondel, plaza.

Ar·gen·tine [árdʒəntin] adj. & s. argentino.

ar·gue [árgjU] v. argüir; debatir; altercar; **to - into** persuadir a.

ar·gu·ment [árgjəmənt] s. argumento; razonamiento; sumario, resumen.

ar·id [ǽrɪd] adj. árido.

a·rise [əráɪz] v. levantarse; elevarse; surgir; provenir.

a·ris·en [ərízṇ] p.p. de **to arise**.

ar·is·toc·ra·cy [ærəstákrəsɪ] s. aristocracia.

aris·to·crat [ərístəkræt] s. aristócrata.

aris·to·crat·ic [ərɪstəkrǽtɪk] adj. aristocrático.

arith·met·ic [əríθmətɪk] s. aritmética.

ark [ark] s. arca; **- of the covenant** arca del testamento; **Noah's —** arca de Noé.

arm [arm] s. (*anatomy*) brazo; (*weapon*) arma; **- in -** de bracete, de bracero; *Am.* de brazo, de brazos; **at -'s length** a una brazada; **with open -s** con los brazos abiertos; v. armar (se).

ar·ma·da [armádə] s. armada, flota.

ar·ma·ment [árməmənt] s. armamento.

ar·ma·ture [ármətʃə] s. armadura.

arm·chair [ármtʃɛr] s. silla de brazos, sillón, butaca.

armed forces [ármd fórsəz] s. fuerzas armadas.

arm·ful [ármfUl] s. brazada.

ar·mi·stice [árməstɪs] s. armisticio.

ar·mor [ármə] s. armadura; blindaje, coraza; arnés; v. blindar, acorazar.

ar·mored [árməd] p.p. blindado, acorazado.

ar·mor·y [ármərɪ] s. armería, arsenal.

arm·pit [ármpɪt] s. sobaco.

ar·my [ármɪ] s. ejército; muchedumbre; **- doctor** médico militar; **regular -** tropa de línea.

a·ro·ma [ərómə] s. aroma; fragancia.

ar·o·mat·ic [ærəmǽtɪk] adj. aromático.

a·rose [əróz] pret. de **to arise**.

a·round [əráUnd] adv. alrededor; en derredor; a la redonda; en torno; en derredor; cerca; **all -** por todos lados; prep. alrededor de; cerca de; **- here** por aquí; **to go - in circles** dar vueltas; **to go - the world** dar la vuelta al mundo.

a·rouse [əráUz] v. despertar, *Riopl., C.A., Ven.* recordar (*al dormido*); excitar; promover.

ar·raign [ərén] v. acusar; procesar (*a un criminal*).

ar•range [ərénʒ] v. arreglar; disponer, colocar; acomodar; hacer arreglos (para), hacer planes (para).

ar•range•ment [ərénʒmənt] s. arreglo; disposición; colocación, orden; convenio.

ar•ray [əré] s. arreglo, formación, orden; orden (de batalla); pompa; gala, atavío; v. formar (trapas); poner en orden; ataviar, adornar.

ar•rears [ərírz] s. pl. atrasos, pagos o rentas vencidos y no cobrados; in — atrasado (en el pago de una cuenta).

ar•rest [ərést] s. arresto, captura, aprensión, detención; v. aprehender o prender, arrestar; detener; llamar, atraer (la atención).

ar•ri•val [əráɪv] s. llegada; arribo; venida; the new -s los recién llegados.

ar•rive [əráɪv] v. llegar; arribar; to at a result lograr (o conseguir) un resultado.

ar•ro•gance [ǽrəgəns] s. arrogancia.

ar•ro•gant [ǽrəgənt] adj. arrogante.

ar•row [ǽro] s. saeta, fleta.

ar•se•nal [árs ŋ əl] s. arsenal. ·

ar•se•nic [árs ŋ ɪK] s. arsénico.

ar•son [ársən] s. delito de incendio.

art [art] s. arte; destreza; astucia; fine -s bellas artes; master of -s licenciado en letras, maestro en artes.

ar•ter•y [ártərɪ] s. arteria.

art•ful [ártfəl] adj. artero, mañero, ladino.

ar•ti•choke [ártɪʃok] s. alcachofa.

ar•ti•cle [ástɪk] s. artículo; — of clothing prenda de vestir, — of merchandise mercancía, mercadería.

ar•tic•u•late [ɑrtɪ́kjəlɪt] adj. articulado; claro, inteligible; capaz de hablar; [ɑrtɪ́kjəlet] v. articular; enunciar; enlazar.

ar•tic•u•la•tion [ɑrtɪkjəléʃən] s. articulación; coyuntura.

ar•ti•fact [ártəfækt] s. artefacto.

ar•ti•fice [ártəfɪs] s. artificio; ardid.

ar•ti•fi•cial [ɑrtəfɪ́ʃəl] adj. artificial; postizo; afectado, artificioso.

ar•til•le•ry [ɑrtɪ́lərɪ] s. artillería; — man artillero.

ar•ti•san [ástəz ŋ] s. artesano; artífice.

art•ist [ártɪst] s. artista.

ar•tis•tic [ɑrtɪ́stɪk] adj. artístico; -ally adv. artísticamente.

as [əz] adv., conj., prep. como; mientras; a medida que, según; en el momento en que; — hasta donde; — for (— to) en cuanto a ; — if como si; it were por decirlo así; — large — tan grande como; — much — tanto como; — well tan bien; también; — yet hasta ahora, todavía; — long — you wish todo el tiempo que Vd. quiera; strong — he is aunque es tan fuerte; the same — lo mismo que.

as•bes•tos [æsbéstəs] s. asbesto.

as•cend [əsént] v. ascender; subir, elevarse.

as•cen•sion [əsénʃən] s. ascensión; subida.

as•cent [əsént] s. ascenso; subida; ascensión.

as•cer•tain [æsətén] v. averiguar, indagar.

as•cet•ic [əsétɪk] adj. ascético; s. asceta.

as•cribe [əskráɪb] v. atribuir, imputar, achacar.

ash [æʃ] s. ceniza; — tray cenicero; — tree fresno; Ash Wesnesday miércoles de ceniza; ash-colored adj ceniciento, cenizo.

a•shamed [əʃémd] adj. avergonzado, corrido; to be — tener vergüenza; avergonzarse.

a•shore [əʃór] adv. a tierra: en tierra; to go — desembarcar.

A•siat•ic [əʒɪ ǽ tɪk] adj. & s. asiático.

a•side [əsɛ́ɪd] adv. aparte; a un lado; al lado; s. aparte (en un drama).

ask [æsk] v. (request) pedir, rogar, solicitar; (inquire) preguntar; (invite) invitar; to — for pedir; to — for (about, after) preguntar por; to — a question hacer una pregunta.

a•skance [əskǽns] adv. de soslayo; con recelo, recelosamente; to look — mirar con recelo; no aprobar.

a•sleep [əslíp] adj. dormido; to fall — dormirse; my arm is — se me ha dormido (entumecido o entumido) el brazo.

as•par•a•gus [əspǽrəgəs] s. espárrago.

as•pect [ǽspɛt] s. aspecto.

as•phalt [ǽsfɔlt] s. asfalto.

as•pi•ra•tion [æspəréʃən] s. aspiración; anhelo.

as•pire [əspáɪr] v. aspirar; anhelar, ambicionar.

as•pi•rin [ǽ sp•ɪn] s. aspirina.

ass [æs] s. asno, burro; pollino.

as•sail [əsél] v. asaltar, acometer, agredir.

as•sail•ant [əsélənt] s. asaltador, agresor.

as•sas•sin [əsǽsɪn] s. asesino.

as•sas•si•nate [əs æ s ŋ et] s. asesinar.

as•sas•si•na•tion [æs ŋ éʃən] s. asesinato.

as•sault [əs ó lt] s. asalto, acometida, ataque; v. asaltar, acometer, atacar; violar.

as•say [əsé] v. ensayar (metales); analizar, examinar; contrastar (pesas, monedas); s. ensaye (de metales); contraste (de pesas, moneda).

as•sem•ble [əsémb] v. reunir(se), congregar(se), juntar(se); convocar; armar, montar (maquinaria).

as•sem•bly [əsémblɪ] s. asamblea; reunión; montaje (de maquinaria); — hall salón de sesiones; paraninfo.

as•sent [əsént] s. asentimiento; consentimiento; v. asentir; consentir.

as•sert [əs ś t] v. aseverar, asegurar, afirmar; to — oneself hacerse valer; obrar con firmeza; vindicarse.

as•ser•tion [əs ə́ʃən] *s.* aserción, aserto, afirmación.

as•sess [əsés] *v.* avaluar; tasar; asignar, imponer (*impuestos, multas, contribuciones, etc.*).

as•sess•ment [əsésmənt] *s.* avaluación, tasación; imposición (*de contribuciones, multas, etc.*); contribución, impuesto.

as•set [ǽ sɛt] *s.* cualidad, ventaja; **-s** capital, fondos, caudal; haber, activo; **personal —s** bienes muebles.

as•sid•u•ous [əsídʒUəs] *adj.* asiduo, diligente.

as•sign [əsáɪn] *v.* asignar; señalar, designar; traspasar, ceder a favor de.

as•sign•ment [əsáɪnmənt] *s.* asignación; designación; cesión (*de bienes*); tarea (*asignada*); lección (*señalada*).

as•sim•i•late [əsím ɪ et] *v.* asimilar (se), absorber (se).

as•sist [əsɪ́st] *v.* asistir, ayudar.

as•sis•tance [əsɪ́stəns] *s.* asistencia, ayuda.

as•sis•tant [əsɪ́stənt] *s.* asistente; ayudante, auxiliar; *adj.* subordinado, auxiliar.

as•so•ci•ate [əsóʃɪɪt] *adj.* asociado; *s.* asociado; socio; compañero; colega; [əsóʃɪɛt] *v.* asociar (se); relacionar.

as•so•ci•a•tion [əsosɪéʃən] *s.* asociación; sociedad; conexión, relación.

as•sort [əsɔ́ rt] *v.* ordenar, clasificar.

as•sort•ed [əsɔ́ rtɪd] *adj.* surtido, mezclado, variado, de todas clases.

as•sort•ment [əsɔ́ rtmənt] *s.* variedad; clasificación; surtido; colección, grupo.

as•sume [əsúm] *v.* asumir; tomar; dar por sentado, dar por supuesto; arrogarse, apropiarse.

as•sump•tion [əs ʌ́mpʃən] *d.* suposición; toma, apropiación; presunción; asunción (*de la Virgen*).

as•sur•ance [əʃÚrəns] *s.* seguridad, certeza; convicción; confianza; **life —** seguro de vida *Véase* **insurance**.

as•sure [əʃÚr] *v.* asegurar; afirmar, infundir confianza,

as•sured•ly [əʃÚrɪdlɪ] *adv.* seguramente; sin duda, con seguridad.

as•ter•isk [ǽ stərɪsk] *s.* asterisco.

as•tig•ma•tism [əstɪ́gmətɪzem] *s.* astigmatismo.

a•ston•ish [əstáni] *v.* asombrar, pasmar, espantar.

a•ston•ish•ing [əstániʃɪŋ] *adj.* asombroso, pasmoso, maravilloso.

a•ston•ish•ment [əstániʃmənt] *s.* asombro, pasmo, sorpresa.

a•stound [əstáUnd] *v.* pasmar, aterrar, aturdir.

a•stray [əstré] *adv.* fuera de camino; *adj.* desviado; extraviado, descaminado; **to go —** perderse; errar el camino; extraviarse; **to lead —** desviar, extraviar;

llevar por mal camino, seducir.

a•stride [əstré] *adv.* a horcajados.

as•tro•dome [ǽ strədom] *s.* astródomo.

as•trol•o•gy [əstrálədʒɪ] *s.* astrología.

as•tro•naut [ǽ strenɔt] *s.* astronauta.

as•tron•o•mer [əstránəmə·] *s.* astrónomo.

as•tron•o•my [əstránəmɪ] *s.* astronomía

as•tro•phys•ics [æstroffsɪks] *s.* astrofísica.

As•tu•rian [æstjúrɪən] *adj.* & *s.* asturiano.

as•tute [əstjú] *adj.* astuto, sagaz.

a•sun•der [əs ʌ́ndə·] *adj.* separado; **to cut —** separar, apartar; dividir en dos.

a•sy•lum [əsáɪləm] *s.* asilo; hospicio; **orphan —** orfanato, casa de huérfanos, *Méx., C.A., Andes* orfanatorio.

at [æt] *prep.* a; en; en (la) casa de; **— last** or fin, al fin; **— once** al punto; **to be — work** estar trabajando; **to enter — that door** entrar por aquella puerta.

ate [et] *pret. de* **to eat.**

a•the•ist [éθɪɪst] *s.* ateo.

ath•lete [ǽ θlit] *s.* atleta.

ath•let•ic [æθlétɪk] *adj.* atlético.

ath•let•ics [æθlétɪks] *s.* gimnasia; atletismo; deportes.

At•lan•tic [ətlǽ tɪk] *adj.* atlántico; *s.* el Atlántico.

at•las [ǽ tləs] *s.* atlas.

at•mos•phere [ǽ tmosɪr] *s.* atmósfera; ambiente.

at•mos•pher•ic [ætməsférɪk] *adj.* atmosférico.

at•om [ǽ təm] *s.* átomo; **— bomb** bomba atómica.

a•tom•ic [ətómɪk] *adj.* atómico; **— age** edad atómica; **— energy** fuerza atómica; **— pile** pila atómica **— weight** peso atómico.

a•tone [ətón] *v.* expiar, purgar; reparar.

a•tone•ment [ətónmənt] *s.* expiación; reparación.

a•tro•cious [ətróʃəs] *adj.* atroz.

a•troc•i•ty [ətrásətɪ] *s.* atrocidad; maldad.

at•tach [ət ǽ ʃ] *v.* unir, juntar; sujetar, pegar, adherir; poner (*sello o firma*); embargar (*bienes*); asignar; atribuir.

at•tach•ment [ət ǽ ʃmənt] *s.* adhesión; apego; afición, cariño; embargo (*de bienes*); accesorio.

at•tack [ət ǽ k] *s.* ataque, asalto, acceso; *v.* atacar; acometer, embestir.

at•tain [ətén] *v.* lograr, conseguir, alcanzar; llegar a.

at•tain•ment [əténmənt] *s.* logro, consecución; adquisición; dote habilidad.

at•tempt [ətémpt] *s.* tentativa; prueba, ensayo; esfuerzo; atentado; *v.* tentar, intentar; procurar, tratar (de), probar; **to — the life of** atentar contra la vida de.

at•tend [əténd] *v.* atender, cuidar, mirar por; asistir a; acompañar.

at•ten•dance [əténdəns] *s.* asistencia; presencia;

concurrencia.

at•ten•dant [əténdənt] *s.* acompañante; sirviente; servidor; asistente; *adj.* acompañante.

at•ten•tion [əténʃən] *s.* (*care*) cuidado; (*courtesy*) fineza, urbanidad, atención; **to pay** – hacer caso; prestar atención.

at•ten•tive [əténtɪv] *adj.* atento; cortés.

at•test [ətést] *v.* atestiguar, atestar; certificar; dar fe.

at•tic [ǽtɪk] *s.* desván.

at•tire [ətáɪr] *s.* atavío; vestidura; vestido, traje; *v.* ataviar, adornar.

at•ti•tude [ǽtətjud] *s.* actitud; postura.

at•tor•ney [ətǝ́ʳnɪ] *s.* abogado; procurador; apoderado; **– general** fiscal (*de una nación o estado*); **district** – fiscal de distrito; **power of** – procuración, poder.

at•tract [ətrǽkt] *v.* atraer; cautivar; **to – attention** llamar la atención.

at•trac•tion [ətrǽkʃən] *s.* atracción; atractivo; **-s** diversiones; lugares o sitios de interés.

at•trac•tive [ətrǽktɪv] *adj.* atractivo; seductor; simpático.

at•trac•tive•ness [ətrǽktɪvnɪs] *s.* atracción; atractivo.

at•trib•ute [ǽtrəbjut] *s.* atributo; propiedad; [ətríbjut] *v.* atribuir, achacar.

at•tri•tion [ətríʃən] *s.* agotamiento; atrición.

auc•tion [ɔ́kʃən] *s.* subasta, almoneda, remate, *Am.* venduta; *v.* subastar; rematar.

au•da•cious [ɔdéʃəs] *adj.* audaz, atrevido, osado.

au•dac•i•ty [ɔdǽsətɪ] *s.* audacia, osadía; descaro.

au•di•ble [ɔ́dəbḷ] *adj.* audible.

au•di•ence [ɔ́dɪəns] *s.* auditorio, concurrencia, público; audiencia.

au•di•o freq•uen•cy [ɔdɪofríkwɛnsɪ] *s.* audiofrecuencia.

au•di•o-vis•u•al [ɔdɪovíʒuəl] *adj.* audio-visual.

au•dit [ɔ́dɪt] *v.* intervenir (*cuentas*); asistir a (*una clase*) de oyente; *s.* intervención, comprobación de cuentas.

au•di•tion [ɔdíʃən] *s.* audición.

au•di•tor [ɔ́dɪtǝ] *s.* interventor (*de cuentas*); oyente.

au•di•to•ri•um [ɔdətórɪəm] *s.* salón de conferencias o conciertos; paraninfo.

au•di•to•ry [ɔ́dətɪrɪ] *adj.* auditivo.

au•ger [ɔ́gǝ] *s.* taladro, barrena.

aught [ɔt] *s.* algo.

aug•ment [ɔgmɛ́nt] *v.* aumentar.

au•gur [ɔ́gǝ] *s.* agorero; *v.* augurar, pronosticar; **to – well** (*o* **ill**) ser de buen (*o* mal) agüero.

Au•gust [ɔ́gǝst] *s.* agosto.

aunt [ænt] *s.* tía.

aus•pices [ɔ́spɪsɪz] *s. pl.* auspicios; protección.

aus•pi•cious [ɔspíʃǝs] *adj.* propicio; favorable.

aus•tere [ɔstíʳ] *adj.* austero, adusto, severo.

aus•ter•i•ty [ɔstérǝtɪ] *s.* austeridad, severidad.

Aus•trian [ɔ́strɪən] *adj. & s.* austríaco.

au•then•tic [ɔθénɪtk] *adj.* auténtico.

au•thor [ɔ́θǝ-] *s.* autor; escritor.

au•thor•i•ta•tive [əθ ɔ́rətetɪv] *adj.* autorizado, que se tiene autoridad; autoritario.

au•thor•i•ty [əθ ɔ́rǝtɪ] *s.* autoridad; facultad; **to have on good** – saber de buena tinta.

au•thor•ize [ɔ́θǝraɪz] *v.* autorizar.

au•to [ɔ́to] *s.* auto, automóvil.

au•to•crat [ɔ́tǝkræt] *s.* autócrata.

au•to•graph [ɔ́tǝgræf] *s.* autógrafo.

au•to•mat•ic [ɔtǝmǽtɪk] *adj.* automático; **-ally** *adv.* automáticamente.

au•to•mo•bile [ɔ́tǝmǝbil] *s.* automóvil.

au•ton•o•my [ɔtánǝmɪ] *s.* autonomía.

au•top•sy [ɔ́topsɪ] *s.* autopsia.

au•tumn [ɔ́tǝm] *s.* otoño.

au•tum•nal [ɔt ʌ́n] *adj.* otoñal.

aux•il•ia•ry [ɔgzíljǝrt] *adj. & s.* auxiliar.

a•vail [əvél] *v.* aprovechar; beneficiar; **to – oneself of** aprovecharse de; *s.* aprovecho; ventaja; **of on** – de ninguna utilidad o ventaja.

a•vail•a•ble [əvéləbḷ] *adj.* disponible; aprovechable; obtenible.

av•a•lanche [ǽvǝ|æntʃ] *s.* alud; torrente.

av•a•rice [ǽvǝrɪs] *s.* avaricia.

av•a•ri•cious [ævǝríʃǝs] *adj.* avaro, avariento.

a•venge [əvéndʒ] *v.* vengar; vindicar.

a•veng•er [əvéndʒǝ] *s.* vengador.

a•ve•nue [ǽvǝnu] *s.* avenida.

a•ver [əvǝ́·] *v.* afirmar asegurar.

av•er•age [ǽvrɪdʒ] *s.* promedio, término medio; **on an** – por término medio, *adj.* medio, mediano; ordinario; *v.* promediar, calcular o sacar el promedio; **to – a loss** prorratear una pérdida; **he -s 20 miles an hour** avanza o recorrer un promedio de 20 millas por hora.

a•verse [əvǝ́·s] *adj.* adverso, renuente.

a•ver•sion [əvǝ́·ʒən] *s.* aversión; malquerencia; inquina.

a•vert [əvǝ́·t] *v.* apartar, desviar; evitar; impedir.

a•vi•a•tion [evɪéʃən] *s.* aviación.

a•vi•a•tor [évɪetǝ] *s.* aviador.

av•o•ca•do [ɔvəkádo] s. aguacate.

av•o•ca•tion [ævəkéʃən] s. distracción; ocupación de distracción o diversión.

a•void [əvɔ́ɪd] v. evitar, eludir.

a•vow [əváU] v. confesar, reconocer, admitir.

a•vow•al [əváUəl] s. confesión, admisión.

a•wait [əwét] v. esperar, aguardar.

a•wake [əwék] adj. despierto; alerto; **wide – awake** muy despierto; avispado; v. despertar (se).

a•wak•en [əwékən] v. despertar (se).

a•ward [əwéɔ́rd] s. premio; decisión, sentencia; v. asignar; otorgar; conferir; adjudicar (un premio, medalla, etc.).

a•ware [əwér] adj. consciente; enterado, sabedor, cauto; sobre aviso.

a•way [əwé] adv. lejos; fuera; adj. ausente; **rigth –** ahora mismo; ahorita; **two miles –** a diez millas de aquí; **to give –** regalar; **to go –** irse; **to take –** quitar.

awe [ɔ] s. pavor; pasmo; **to stand in –** quedarse, o estar pasmado; pasmarse; v. aterrorizar; infundir pavor; maravillar.

aw•ful [ɔ́fUl] adj. terrible; horroroso; tremendo; impresionante; **-ly** adv. terriblemente; horrorosamente, muy.

a•while [əhwáɪl] adv. (por) un rato; (por) algún tiempo.

awk•ward [ɔ́kwə·d] adj. torpe, desmañado; molesto, embarazoso; incómodo; inconveniente.

awl [ɔl] s. lezna, punzón.

awn•ing [ɔ́nɪŋ] s. toldo.

a•woke [əwók] pret. & p.p. de **to awake.**

ax, axe [æks] s. hacha.

ax•is [ǽksɪs] pl. **axes** [ǽksɪz] s. eje.

ax•le [ǽks] s. eje (de una rueda); **front –** eje delantero, **rear –** eje trasero.

aye [e] adv. sí; s. voto afirmativo.

Az•tec [ǽztɛk] adj. & s. azteca.

az•ure [ǽʒə·] adj. azul; s. azur, azul celeste.

B

bab•ble [bǽb|] s. balbuceo; parloteo, charla; v. balbucear; parlotear, charlar.

babe [beb] s. = **baby.**

ba•boon [bæbún] s. mandril (especie de mono).

ba•by [bébɪ] s. nene, bebé, criatura; Andes, Ch. guagua; C.A. tierno; adj. infantil; de niño – **girl** nena; – **sitter** [bébɪsftə·] s. cuidaniños, niñera por horas; v. mimar.

bach•e•lor [bǽtʃələ·] s. bachiller; soltero.

ba•cil•lus [bəsíləs] s. bacilo.

back [bæk] s. (anatomy) espalda; lomo (de animal); (opposite side) revés; respaldo (de silla), espaldar; **behind one's –** a espaldas de uno, a espaldas vueltas; **in – of** detrás de, tras, **to fall on one's –** caer de espaldas, caer boca arriba; **to turn one's –** volver las espaldas; adj. posterior; trasero; retrasado, atrasado, rezagado; **– pay** sueldo atrasado; **– yard** patio interior; corral; adv. atrás, detrás; **– and forth** de aquí para allá; **to come –** volver, regresar; **to give -** volver; v. respaldar, endosar; sostener, apoyar, retroceder; hacer retroceder; **to – down** hacerse (para) atrás; retractarse.

back•bone [bǽkbón] s. espinazo, esquina dorsal; firmeza; apoyo, sostén.

back•er [bǽkə·] s. fiador; sostenedor, defensor.

back•ground [bǽkgraUnd] s. fondo; educación; experiencia; **to keep in the –** dejar en último término; quedarse en último término; mantenerse retirado.

back•hand [bǽkhænd] s. revés; escritura inclinada a la izquierda; **-ed stroke** revés; **a -ed remark** una ironía; una indirecta.

back•ing [bǽkɪŋ] s. apoyo, garantía; endose, endoso; respaldo.

back•lash [bǽklæ] s. contragolpe; culateo.

back•log [bǽklɔg] s. reserva pendiente.

back•stage [bækstédʒ] adv. detrás del telón.

back•ward [bǽkwəd] adj. atrasado; retrasado, retrógrado; lerdo, tardo; huraño, tímido, esquivo; adv. = **backwards.**

back•ward•ness [bǽkwə·dnɪs] s. torpeza; atraso; timidez.

back•wards [bǽwə·dz] adv. hacia (o para) atrás; de espaldas; **to go –** retroceder, andar hacia (o para) atrás.

ba•con [békən] s. tocino.

bac•te•ri•a [bæktírɪə] s. pl. bacterias.

bac•te•rio•log•y [bæktɪrɪóledʒɪ] s. bacteriología.

bad [bæd] adj. malo; perverso; dañoso; podrido; **to go from – to worse** ir de mal en peor; **to look –** tener mal cariz, tener mala cara o mal aspecto; **ly** adv. mal, malamente.

bade [bæd] pret. de **to bid.**

badge [bædʒ] s. insignia, divisa; distintivo.

badg•er [bǽdʒə·] s. tejón; v. atormentar, acosar, molestar.

bad•ness [bǽdnɪs] s. maldad.

baf•fle [bǽf|] v. desconcertar, confundir; frustrar, impedir.

bag [bæg] s. (sack) saco, bolsa, talega; costal; (baggage) maleta; zurrón, morral; v. ensacar; cazar; agarrar; adueñarse de; inflarse; abolsarse.

bag•gage [bǽgɪdʒ] s. equipaje; bagaje; **– car** furgón, vagón de equipajes; **– check** talón, contraseña de equipajes; **– tag** marbete, etiqueta.

bag•pipe [bǽgpaɪp] s. gaita.

bail [bel] s. fianza, caución; **to let out on –** poner en libertad bajo fianza; v. dar fianza; salir fiador; achicar (agua), vaciar; **to – out of a plane** tirarse (con paracaídas) de un aeroplano.

bait [bet] s. cebo; atractivo, aliciente; v. tentar, atraer; cebar; acosar, perseguir.

bake [bek] v. hornear, cocer al horno; calcinar.

bak•er [békə] s. panadero, pastelero, hornero.

bak•er•y [békərɪ] s. panadería, pastelería, tahona.

bak•ing [békɪŋ] s. hornada; cocimiento; **– powder** levadura.

bal•ance [bǽləns] s. (instrument) balanza; (equilibrium) contrapeso, equilibrio. balance; (debit, credit) saldo; **– of payments** balanza de pagos; **– wheel** volante del reloj; **– of trade** balanza comercial; **– of power** equilibrio político; **to lose one's –** perder el equilibrio; v. contrapesar; pesar; balancear(se); equilibrar; saldar (una cuenta).

bal•co•ny [bǽlkənɪ] s. balcón; galería (de teatro).

bald [bold] adj. calvo; pelado, sin vegetación; escueto; sin adornos; **– spot** calva.

bale [bel] s. bala, fardo (de mercancías); v. embalar, enfardar, empacar.

balk [bok] v. oponerse, rebelarse, resistirse; pararse de repente; negarse a seguir; encabritarse; **to some one's plans** frustrar los planes de alguien.

ball [bol] s. (plaything) pelota, bola; (string, thread) ovillo; (weapon) bala; (dance) baile; **– game** juego de pelota; béisbol; v. ovillar; **to – up** enredar, confundir.

bal•lad [bǽləd] s. romance; copla, canción; balada.

bal•last [bǽləst] s. lastre; grava (usada en terraplenes, caminos, etc.); v. lastrar, poner el lastre a (una embarcación).

bal•let [bæléé] s. ballet.

bal•loon [bələún] s. globo (aerostático).

bal•lot [bǽlət] s. balota, Am. boleta, cédula para votar; votar; voto; **– box** urna electoral; v. balotar, votar.

ball point [bɔ́ pɔɪnt] s. bolígrafo.

balm [bam] s. bálsamo.

balm•y [bámɪ] adj. balsámico; fragante; refrescante suave; algo loco, chiflado.

bal•sam [bɔ́səm] s. bálsamo; especie de abeto.

bam•boo [bæmbú] s. bambú.

ban [bæn] s. bando, proclama; excomunión; prohibición; **marriage -s** (o **banns**) amonestaciones; v. proscribir, prohibir; condenar.

ba•nan•a [bənǽnə] s. banana; plátano; **- tree** banano; plátano.

band [bænd] s. (group) banda, partida, pandilla, cuadrilla; (musicians) banda; (strip) faja, lista, cinta, tira; partida, pandilla, cuadrilla; **rubber –** liga de goma; v. unir, juntar; atar. ligar; **to – together** confederarse, juntarse.

band•age [bǽndɪdʒ] v. venda, vendaje; v. vendar.

ban•dit [bǽndɪt] s. bandido, bandolero.

bang [bæŋ] s. golpe, golpazo; estallido; fleco (de pelo) ; **with a –** de golpe, de golpazo; de repente; con estrépito; **–!** ¡pum!; v. golpear; hacer estrépito; cortar (el pelo) en fleco; **to – the door** dar un portazo.

ban•ish [bǽnɪ] v. proscribir, desterrar; **to – fear** desechar el temor.

ban•ish•ment [bǽnɪʃmənt] s. proscripción; destierro.

ban•is•ter [bǽnɪstə] s. balaustre; barandilla, barandal, pasamano.

ban•jo [bǽndʒo] s. banjo.

bank [bæŋk] s. (institution) banco; (in card game) banca; (of a river) orilla, ribera, banda; escarpa; (pile) montón; **saving –** caja de ahorros; adj. bancario; de banco; v. depositar en un banco; amontonar (tierra o arena); cubrir con cenizas, tapar (el fuego); ladear (un aeroplano); **to – upon** (o **on**) contar con.

bank•book [bǽŋkbUk] s. libreta de banco.

bank•er [bǽŋkə] s. banquero.

bank•ing [bǽŋkɪŋ] s. transacciones bancarias, banca; adj. bancario, de banca; **– house** banca, casa de banca.

bank•note [bǽŋknot] s. billete de banco.

bank•rupt [bǽŋkyʃpt] adj. en quiebra, arruinado, insolvente; v. quebrar; arruinar.

bank•rupt•cy [bǽŋkrʃptsɪ] s. bancarrota, quiebra; **to go into –** declararse insolvente; quebrar, hacer bancarrota.

ban•ner [bǽnə] s. bandera, estandarte, perdón; adj. primero, principal, sobresaliente.

ban•quet [bǽŋkwɪt] s. banquete; v. banquetear.

bap•tism [bǽptɪzəm] s. bautismo; bautizo.

Bap•tist [bǽptɪst] s. bautista.

bap•tize [bæptáɪz] v. bautizar.

bar [bɑr] s. (of iron) barra; barrote; tranca; (obstacle) barrera, obstáculo; (of justice) tribunal; foro; (saloon) cantina, taberna;   (counter) mostrador; (piece) barra (de jabón); pastilla (de chocolate); **sand –** banco de arena; **-s** reja; **to be admitted to the –** recibirse de abogado; v. atrancar (la puerta); estorbar; prohibir; excluir.

barb [bɑrb] s. púa.

bar•bar•i•an [bɑrbɛ́rɪən] s. & adj. bárbaro; salvaje.

bar•bar•ous [bɑ́rbərəs] adj. bárbaro; salvaje; inculto.

bar•be•cue [bárbɪkju] *s. Méx., C.A., Col.* barbacoa; *Riopl.* churrasco; *v.* hacer barbacoa; *Riopl.* churrasquear.

barbed [bɑrbd] *adj.* con púas; **— wire** alambre de púas.

bar•ber [bárbə] *s.* barbero; peluquero.

bar•ber•shop [bárbəʃɑp] *s.* barbería; peluquería.

bard [bɑrd] *s.* bardo, vate, poeta.

bare [bɛr] *adj.* (*naked*) desnudo; descubierto; pelado; (*evident*) manifiesto, patente; (*unfurnished*) desamueblado, vacío; **— majority** mayoría escasa; **to lay —** poner en manifiesto, hacer patente, revelar; **to ride — back** montar en pelo.

bare•foot [bérfʊt] *adj.* descalzo, con los pies desnudos; **-ed** [bérfʊtɪd] **= barefoot.**

bare•head•ed [bérhédɪd] *adj.* descubierto, sin sombrero.

bare•legg•ed [bérlégɪd] *adj.* con las piernas desnudas; sin medias.

bare•ly [bérlɪ] *adv.* apenas; escasamente; **— three pounds** tres libras escasas.

bare•ness [bérnɪs] *s.* desnudez.

bar•gain [bárgɪn] *s.* (*agreement*) convenio, pacto; negocio, trato; (*cheap*) ganga; **— sale** ganga *Méx., C.A., Ven., Andes* barata; **intro the —** por añadidura; de ganancia; **to make a —** cerrar un convenio; *v.* regatear; negociar; **to — for** regatear; contar con, esperar.

barge [bɑrdʒ] *s.* lanchón; barca.

bar•i•tone [bǽrəton] *s. & adj.* barítono.

bar•i•um [bǽrɪəm] *s.* bario.

bark [bɑrk] *s.* ladrido; corteza (*de árbol*); barco velero, *v.* ladrar; descortezar, quitar la corteza.

bar•ley [bárlɪ] *s.* cebada.

barn [bɑrn] *s.* establo, cuadra; granero, troje; pajar; **streetcar —** cobertizo para tranvías.

bar•na•cle [bárnəkəl] *s.* cirrópodo.

barn•yard [bárnjord] *s.* corral; **— fowl** aves de corral.

ba•rom•e•ter [bərómətə] *s.* barómetro.

bar•on [bǽrən] *s.* barón.

ba•roque [bərók] *adj. & s.* barroco.

bar•rage [bəráʒ] *s.* fuego de barrera, presa.

bar•rel [bǽrəl] *s.* barril, barrica, tonel, cuba; cañón (*de fusil, pistola, etc.*); *v.* embarrilar (*meter en barril*).

bar•ren [bǽrəe] *adj.* árido; estéril.

bar•ren•ness [bǽrənnɪs] *s.* aridez; esterilidad.

bar•rette [bərét] *s.* broche, prendedor (*para sujetar el pelo*).

bar•ri•cade [bærəkéd] *s.* barricada, barrera; *v.* poner barricadas; obstruir el paso con barricadas.

bar•ri•er [bǽrɪə] *s.* barrera, valla; obstáculo.

bar•ter [bártə] *v.* permutar, trocar, cambiar; *s.* permuta, trueque, cambio.

base [bes] *s.* base; basa; fundamento; *adj.* bajo, vil, ruin; inferior; *v.* basar, fundar; establecer.

base•ball [bésbɔl] *s.* baseball o béisbol.

base•ment [bésmənt] *s.* sótano.

base•ness [bénɪs] *s.* bajeza, ruindad, vileza.

bash•ful [bǽʃfəl] *adj.* tímido, encogido, vergonzoso.

bash•ful•ness [bǽʃfəlnɪs] *s.* timidez, vergüenza; cortedad, apocamiento.

ba•sic [bésɪk] *adj.* básico, fundamental.

ba•sin [bésɳ] *s.* palangana, jofaina; lebrillo; tazón (*de fuente*); estanque, depósito de agua; **river —** cuenca de río.

ba•sis [bésɪs] (*pl.* **bases** [bésɪz]) *s.* base, fundamento.

bask [bæsk] *v.* calentarse (*al sol*); asolearse, tomar el sol.

bas•ket [bǽskɪt] *s.* cesta, cesto, canasta.

bas•ket•ball [bǽskɪtbɔl] *s.* básquetbol.

bas•que [bæsk] *adj. & s.* (*person*) vasco; (*language*) vascuence, vasco; (*territory*) vascongado, vasco.

bass [bes] *s.* bajo (*en música*); *adj.* bajo, grave; **— drum** tambora, bombo; **— horn** tuba.

bas•tard [bǽstəd] *s. & adj.* bastardo.

baste [best] *v.* hilvanar; pringar (*empapar la carne con grasa*); apalear.

bat [bæt] *s.* palo, *Méx., Carib., Ven., C.A.* bate (*de béisbol*); garrote; golpe, garrotazo; murciélago; *v.* apalear; dar palos; *Méx., Carib., Ven., C.A.* batear; **not to — an eye** no pestañear.

batch [bætʃ] *s.* hornada; colección, grupo, conjunto.

bath [bæθ] *s.* baño.

bathe [beð] *v.* bañar (se)

bath•er [béðə] *s.* bañista.

bath•house [bǽθhaʊs] *s.* casa de baños; bañadero.

bath•robe [bǽθrob] *s.* bata de baño.

bath•room [bǽθrum] *s.* baño, cuarto de baño.

bath•tub [bǽθtʃb] *s.* bañera, tina.

ba•thy•sphere [bǽθɪsfɪr] *s.* batisfera.

bat•tal•ion [bətǽljən] *s.* batallón.

bat•ter [bǽtə] *s.* batido, masa; *Am.* bateador (*de béisbol*); *v.* golpear; **to — down** demoler.

bat•ter•y [bǽtərɪ] *s.* batería; acumulador; asalto.

bat•tle [bǽtḷ] *s.* batalla, lucha, combate; *v.* batallar, luchar, combatir.

bat•tle•field [bǽtḷfild] *s.* campo de batalla.

bat•tle•ship [bǽtḷʃɪp] *s.* buque de guerra, acorazado.

bawl [bɔl] *s.* aullido; grito; *v.* aullar; gritar; pregonar; **to — out** regañar, reprender.

bay [be] *s.* bahía; ladrillo, balido, aullido; **– rum** ron de laurel; **– tree** laurel **– window** ventana saliente, mirador; **to hold at –** tener a raya; *adj.* bayo; *v.* dar aullidos, ladridos o balidos.

bay·o·net [béənɪt] *s.* bayoneta; *v.* traspasar; herir con bayoneta.

ba·zaar [bəzár] *s.* bazar, feria.

ba·zoo·ka [bəzúka] *s.* bazuca.

be [bi] *v.* (*innately*) ser; (*state or condition*) estar, verse, hallarse, encontrarse; **to – cold (warm, hungry, right,** etc.): tener frío (calor, hambre, razón, *etc.*); **to – in a hurry** tener prisa; **he is to –** ha de ser; va a ser; **it is cold (hot, windy,** etc.**)** hace frío, (calor, viento, *etc.*).

beach [bitʃ] *s.* playa, ribera; *v.* varar, poner en seco (*una embarcación*), encallar.

beach·head [bítʃhed] *s.* cabeza de playa.

bea·con [bíkən] *s.* faro, fanal; boya luminosa; señal; **aviation –** radiofaro.

bead [bid] *s.* cuenta (*de rosario, collar, etc.*) abalorio; glóbulo; gota (*de sudor*); **-s** rosario; collar de cuentas; *v.* adornar con abalorios o cuentecitas.

beak [bik] *s.* pico (*de ave*); espolón (*de nave*).

beam [bim] *s.* rayo (*de luz o de calor*); sonrisa; viga; vigueta, brazo (*de balanza*); **radio –** línea de radiación, radiofaro; *v.* emitir (*luz, rayos*); brillar; sonreír, estar radiante de alegría; radiar, transmitir por radio.

beam·ing [bímɪŋ] *adj.* radiante, resplandeciente; sonriente.

bean [bin] *s.* judía, habichuela; *Méx., C.A., Ven., Col., Ch., Riopl.,* fríjol; *Ch., Riopl.,* poroto; **coffee –** grano de café; **Lima –** haba; **string –** judía o habichuela verde; *Méx., C.A.* ejote; *Ch., Ríopl.,* poroto.

bear [bɛr] *s.* oso, osa; bajista (*el que hace bajar los valores en la Bolsa*); *v.* (*stand*) soportar; llevar; sobrellevar; tolerar, aguantar, (*give birth*) parir, dar a luz; producir; **to – down** deprimir; apretar; **to – a grudge** guardar rencor; **to – in mind** tener en cuenta, **to – on a subject** tener relación con un asunto; **to – oneself with dignity** portarse con dignidad; **to – out** confirmar; **to – testimony** dar testimonio.

beard [bɪrd] *s.* barba, barbas; aristas (*de trigo o maíz*); **-ed** *adj.* barbado, barbudo.

bear·er [bérə-] *s.* portador; mensajero. **bearing** [bérɪŋ] *s.* (*posture*) porte, presencia; (*relation*) relación, conexión, (*direction*) rumbo, orientación; (*mechanical*) cojinete; **ball –** cojinete de bolas; **beyond –** inaguantable, insufrible; **to lose one's -s** perder el rumbo, desorientarse; **fruit –bearing** *adj.* fructífero.

beast [bist] *s.* bestia, animal.

beat [bit] *s.* golpe; toque (*de tambor*); latido, palpitación; compás; ronda (*que hace el policía*); *v.* batir; golpear; azotar; vencer; ganar; marcar (*el compás*);

pulsar, latir; sonar (*tambores*); **to – around the bush** andarse por las ramas; valerse de rodeos; *pret. & p.p. de* **to beat.**

beat·en [bít ŋ] *p.p. de* **to beat** & *adj.* batido; vencido; fatigado; **– path** camino trillado.

beat·er [bítə-] *s.* batidor; molinillo golpeador **egg –** batidor de huevos.

be·a·tif·ic [biətífɪk] *adj.* beatífico.

beat·ing [bpitɪŋ] *s.* paliza, tunda, zurra; latido, pulsación.

be·at·i·tude [bɪ ǽ tətjud] *s.* beatitud, bienaventuranza; **the Beatitudes** las bienaventuranzas.

beau [bo] *s.* galán, pretendiente.

beau·te·ous [bjútɪəs] *adj.* bello, hermoso.

beau·ti·ful [bjútəfəl] *adj.* bello, hermoso.

beau·ti·fy [bjútəfaɪ] *v.* hermosear, embellecer.

beau·ty [bjútɪ] *s.* belleza, hermosura; beldad; **- parlor** salón de belleza.

bea·ver [bívə-] *s.* castor; **– board** cartón para tabiques.

be·came [bɪkém] *pret. de* **to become.**

be·cause [bɪk ɔ z] *conj.* porque; **– of** *prep.* por, a causa de.

beck·on [békən] *s.* seña, llamada; *v.* llamar a señas.

be·come [bɪk ʌ m] *v.* (*suit*) sentar bien a, quedar bien a; convenir a; (*turn out to be*) hacerse; ponerse, llegar a ser; convertirse en; **to – crazy** volverse loco; enloquecer; **to – angry** enojarse; **to – frightened** asustarse; **to – old** envejecer (se); **what has – of him?** ¿que ha sido de él?; ¿qué se ha hecho él?; *p.p. de* **to become.**

be·com·ing [bɪk ʌ mɪŋ] *adj.* propio, conveniente; decente, decoroso; **that dress is – to you** le sienta bien ese traje.

bed [bɛd] *s.* cama, lecho; cauce (*de un río*); fondo (*de lago o mar*); cuadro (*de jardín*); yacimiento (*mineral*); **to go to –** acostarse; **to put to –** acostar.

bed·bug [bédbʃg] *s.* chinche.

bed·clothes [bédkloz] *s. pl.* ropa de cama.

bed·ding [bédɪŋ] *s.* = **bedclothes.**

bed·pan [bédpæn] *adj.* en cama; comodín.

bed·rid·den [bédrɪdən] *adj.* en cama; postrado.

bed·rock [bédrák] *s.* roca sólida; lecho de roca.

bed·room [bédrum] *s.* cuarto de dormir, alcoba, *Méx., C.A.* recámara.

bed·side [bédsaɪd] *s.* **at the –** al lado de la cama; **- table** velador, mesilla de noche.

bed·spread [bédspréd] *s.* colcha, sobrecama.

bed·time [bédtaɪm] *s.* hora de acostarse, hora de dormir.

bee [bi] *s.* abeja; reunión (*para trabajar o competir*); **to have a – in one's bonnet** tener una idea metida en la cabeza.

beech [bitʃ] *s.* haya; **– nut** nuez de haya, hayuco.

beef [bif] *s.* carne de vaca o toro; vaca, toro

(*engordados para matar*); **roast** – rosbif.

beef•steak [bífstek] *s.* bistec, biftec o bisté.

bee•hive [bíhaɪv] *s.* colmena; abejera.

been [bɪn, bɛn] *p.p. de* **to be.**

beer [bɪr] *s.* cerveza; – **tavern** cervecería.

beet [bit] *s.* remolacha, *Am.* betabel.

bee•tle [bútl] *s.* escarabajo.

be•fall [bɪfɔl] *v.* sobrevenir, acaecer, suceder.

be•fall•en [bɪfɔlən] *p.p. de* **to befall.**

be•fell [bɪfél] *pret. de* **to befall.**

be•fit [bɪfít] *v.* convenir.

be•fore [bɪfór] *adv.* (*temporal*) antes; (*spatial*) delante; al frente; *prep.* antes de; delante de; enfrente de; ante; *conj.* antes (de) que.

be•fore•hand [bɪfórhænd] *adv.* de antemano, por adelantado, con antelación, con anticipación.

be•friend [bɪfrénd] *v.* ofrecer o brindar amistad a; favorecer, amparar.

beg [bɛg] *v.* rogar, suplicar, pedir; mendigar, pordiosear; **to – the question** dar por sentado lo mismo que se arguye.)

be•gan [bɪɡǽn] *pret. de* **to begin.**

be•get [bɪɡét] *v.* engendrar; causar, producir.

beg•gar [béɡɚ] *s.* mendigo, pordiosero; pobre; infeliz, miserable.

be•gin [bɪɡín] *s.* comenzar, empezar, principiar.

be•gin•ner [bɪɡínɚ] *s.* principiante; novicio.

be•gin•ning [bɪɡínɪŋ] *s.* principio; comienzo; empiezo; origen; – **with** comenzando con (*o* por); a partir de; **at the** – al principio.

be•got [bɪɡát] *pret. & p.p. de* **to beget.**

be•got•ten [bɪɡátŋ] *p.p. de* **to beget.**

be•guile [bɪɡáɪl] *v.* engañar; defraudar; seducir.

be•gun [bɪɡʌn] *p.p. de* **to begin**

be•half [bɪhǽf]: **in (on) – of** por; en nombre de; a favor de; en defensa de; **in my -** en mi nombre; a mi favor; por mí.

be•have [bɪhév] *v.* portarse, conducirse, obrar, proceder (*bien o mal*); – **your-self!** ¡pórtate bien¡

be•hav•ior [bɪhévjɚ] *s.* comportamiento, proceder, conducta; funcionamiento; reacción.

be•head [bɪhéd] *v.* decapitar, degollar, descabezar.

be•held [bɪhéld] *pret. & p.p. de* **to behold.**

be•hind [bɪháɪnd] *adv.* detrás; atrás; a la zaga, en zaga; *prep.* detrás de, tras; – **one's back** a espaldas de uno; – **time** atrasado, retrasado; **from** – por detrás; **to arrive ten minutes – time** llegar con diez minutos de retraso; **to fall** – atrasarse; retrasarse.

be•hold [bɪhóld] *v.* contemplar, mirar; – ! ¡he aquí¡

be•hoove [bɪhúv] *v.* serle necesario a uno; corresponderle a uno; atañerle a uno.

be•ing [bíɪŋ] *s.* ser; ente; esencia; existencia; *ger. de* **to be** siendo; **for the time –** por ahora; por el momento.

be•lat•ed [bɪlétɪd] *adj.* tardío; atrasado.

belch [bɛltʃ] *v.* eructar; **to – forth** echar, arrojar, vomitar; *s.* eructo.

bel•fry [bélfrɪ] *s.* campanario.

Bel•gian [béldʒɪən] *adj. & s.* belga.

be•lief [bəlíf] *s.* creencia; fe; convicción; opinión.

be•liev•a•ble [bəlívəbl] *adj.* creíble.

be•lieve [bəlív] *v.* creer; pensar; **to – in** creer en; tener en; confiar en.

be•liev•er [bəlívɚ] *s.* creyente, fiel.

be•lit•tle [bɪlítl] *v.* menospreciar, apocar, empequeñecer; dar poca importancia a.

bell [bɛl] *s.* campana; campanilla; **cow –** cencerro, esquila; **call –** timbre; **jingle –** cascabel – **flower** campanilla, campánula.

bell•boy [bélbɔɪ] *s.* mozo de hotel, botones.

belle [bɛl] *s.* beldad, mujer bella.

bel•lig•er•ent [bəlídʒɚənt] *adj. & s.* beligerante.

bel•low [bélo] *s.* bramido, rugido; *v.* rugir, bramar, berrea; gritar.

bel•lows [béloz] *s.* (*sing. & pl.*) fuelle.

bel•ly [bélɪ] *s.* barriga; panza; vientre; estómago.

bel•ly•ache [béliek] *s.* dolor de barriga (*estómago*).

be•long [bəlɔŋ] *v.* pertenecer, corresponder; **it does not – here** está fuera de su sitio; está mal colocado.

be•long•ings [bəlɔŋɪŋz] *s. pl.* posesiones, bienes, efectos, cosas.

be•lov•ed [bɪlʌvɪd] *adj.* querido, amado.

be•low [bɪló] *adv.* abajo; bajo; debajo; **here –** aquí abajo, en este mundo, de tejas abajo; *prep.* bajo, debajo de.

belt [bɛlt] *s.* cinturón, cinto; correa; zona; **sword –** talabarte; *v.* ceñir, fajar.

be•moan [bɪmón] *v.* lamentarse de, quejarse de.

bench [bɛnt] *s.* banco, banca; tribunal.

bend [bɛnd] *s.* curva; vuelta, recodo; *v.* encorvar (se); doblar (se), *Am.* enchuecar (se)inclinar (se); someter (se), ceder; **to – one's efforts** esforzarse (por), dirigir sus esfuerzos.

be•neath [bɪníθ] *prep.* debajo de, bajo; indigno de; inferior a.

ben•e•dic•tion [bɛnədíkʃən] *s.* bendición.

ben•e•factor [bénəfæktɚ] *s.* benefactor, bienhechor; patrón.

ben•ef•i•cent [bənéfəsŋt] *adj.* benéfico.

ben•e•fi•cial [bɛnəfíʃəl] *adj.* beneficio; ventajoso, provechoso.

ben•e•fit [bénəfɪt] *s.* beneficio; provecho, ventaja; – **performance** función de beneficio; *v.* beneficiar; hacer bien; **to – by the advice** aprovecharse del concejo; **he -ed by the medicine** le hizo bien la medicina.

be•nev•o•lence [bənévələns] *s.* benevolencia.

be·nev·o·lent [bənévələnt] *adj.* benévolo.

be·nign [bɪnáɪn] *adj.* benigno; afable.

bent [bɛnt] *s.* inclinación; tendencia; propensión; *pret. & p.p. de* **to bend**; *adj.* encorvado; inclinado, doblado; corvo; gacho; **to be – on** estar resuelto a.

ben·zene [bénzin] *s.* benceno.

be·queath [bɪkwíð] *v.* heredar, legar, dejar en testamento.

be·quest [bɪkwést] *s.* legado, donación.

be·rate [bɪrét] *v.* regañar, reñir, reprender.

be·ret [bəré] *s.* boina.

ber·ry [bérɪ] *s.* baya (*como mora, fresa, etc.*); grano (*de café*).

berth [bɝθ] *s.* litera (*de un camarote*); **to give a wide – to** sacarle el cuerpo a, hacer a un lado para dejar pasar.

be·seech [bɪsíʧ] *s.* suplicar, rogar.

be·set [bɪsét] *v.* atacar; rodear; acosar; *pret. & p.p. de* **to beset.**

be·side [bɪsáɪd] *prep.* (*spatial*) al lado de; cerca de; (*in adition*) además de; fuera de; **to be – oneself** estar fuera de sí, estar loco; **that is – the question** eso no hace el caso; no se trata de eso; *adv.* además.

be·sides [bɪsáɪdz] *adv.* además; *prep.* además de.

be·siege [bɪsíʤ] *v.* sitiar, cercar; acosar, importunar.

be·sought [bɪsɔ́t] *pret. & p.p. de* **to beseech.**

best [bɛst] *adj.* mejor; *adv.* mejor; más; **the –** el mejor; lo mejor; **– girl** novia; querida; **– man** padrino de boda; **– seller** éxito de venta; de mayor venta; **at –** a lo más; cuando más; **to get the – of a person** vencer o ganarle a una persona; **to make the – of** sacar el mejor partido de.

be·stow [bɪstó] *v.* otorgar, conferir; **to – gifts upon** hacer regalos (*o* dádivas) a; **time well –ed** tiempo bien empleado.

bet [bɛt] *s.* apuesta; *v.* apostar; *pret. & p.p. de* **to bet.**

be·ta·ke [bɪték] *v.* **to – oneself** encaminarse, dirigirse.

be·ta·ken [bɪtékən] *p.p. de* **to betake.**

be·took [bɪtÚk] *pret. de* **to betake.**

be·tray [bɪtré] *v.* traicionar, vender, hacer traición; revelar, no guardar (*un secreto*); **to – one's ignorance** hacer patente su ignorancia.

be·tray·er [bɪtréə] *s.* traidor, traicionera.

be·troth·al [bɪtrɔ́θəl] *s.* esponsales, compromiso, mutua promesa de matrimonio.

be·t·roth·ed [bɪtrɔ́θt] *s.* prometido, desposado; novio, novia.

bet·ter [bétə] *adj.* mejor; *adv.* mejor; más; **– half** cara mitad; **so much the –** tanto mejor; **to be – off** estar mejor así; estar en mejores condiciones; **to change for the –** mejorar (se); **to get –** mejorar (se), restablecerse, aliviarse; *v.* mejorar; **to – oneself** mejorarse, mejorar de situación.

bet·ter·ment [bétəmənt] *s.* mejoramiento, mejora, mejoría.

be·tween [bətwín] *prep.* entre, en medio de; *adv.* en medio de.

bev·el [bévəl] *adj.* biselado; *v.* biselar.

bev·er·age [bévrɪʤ] *s.* bebida.

be·wail [bɪwél] *v.* lamentar; quejarse de.

be·ware [bɪwér] *v.* guardarse (de), cuidarse (de); **– !** ¡cuidado! ¡guárdese!.

be·wil·der [bɪwíldə] *v.* confundir, turbar, perturbar, dejar perplejo; **to be -ed** estar turbado o perplejo; estar desorientado.

be·wil·der·ment [bɪwíldəmənt] *s.* perplejidad, aturdimiento.

be·witch [bɪwíʧ] *v.* hechizar; aojar; encantar, cautivar.

be·yond [bɪjónd] *adv.* más allá, más lejos; *prep.* allende; más allá de; fuera de: **– my reach** fuera de mi alcance.

bi·as [báɪəs] *s.* (*tendency*) prejuicio; inclinación, tendencia; (*diagonal*) sesgo, oblicuidad; **on the –** sesgado, al sesgo, de lado; *adj.* sesgado, oblicuo; *v.* predisponer, inclinar, influír en.

bib [bɪb] *s.* babero; pechera (*de delantal*).

Bi·ble [báwbəl] *s.* Biblia.

bib·li·cal [bíblɪk] *adj.* bíblico.

bib·li·og·ra·pher [bíblɪógrəfə] *s.* bibliógrafo.

bib·li·og·ra·phy [bɪblɪógrəfɪ] *s.* bibliografía.

bick·er [bíkd] *v.* disputar, reñir.

bi·cy·cle [báɪsɪk] *s.* bicicleta; *v.* andar en bicicleta.

bid [bɪd] *s.* postura, oferta; envite (*en naipes*); turno (*para envidiar*); invitación; oferta (*precio*); mandar invitar, convidar, rogar; envidar (*en naipes*); **to – fair** parecer muy probable; **to – good-bye** decir adiós; despedirse; **to – up** alzar, pujar (*la oferta es una subasta*); *pret. & p.p. de* **to bid.**

bid·den [bídŋ] *p.p. de* **to bid & to bide.**

bide [baɪd] *v.* guardar; **to – one's time** esperar una buena oportunidad.

bi·en·ni·um [baɪénɪəm] *s.* bienio.

bier [bɪr] *s.* féretro.

big [bɪɡ] *adj.* grande; importante; imponente; **– Dipper** Osa Mayor; **– game** caza mayor; **– sister** hermana mayor; **– with child** encinta; **to talk –** darse bombo, *Am.* darse corte; **big-bellied** panzudo, panzón, barrigón; **big-hearted** magnánimo.

big·a·my [bíɡəmɪv] *s.* bigamia.

big·ot [bíɡət] *s.* fanático.

big·ot·ry [bíɡətrɪ] *s.* fanatismo; intolerancia.

bi·ki·ni [bɪkíɪ] *s.* traje bikini.

bile [baɪl] *s.* bilis, hiel; cólera, mal humor.

bi·lin·gual [baɪlíŋɡwəl] *adj. & s.* bilingüe.

bill [bɪl] *s.* (*statement*) cuenta; factura; (*poster*) cartel, anuncio; (*bank note*) billete de banco; programa de teatro; (*bird*) pico; (*legislative*) proyecto de ley;

– of exchange libranza, letra de cambio; **– of fare** lista de platos; **– of lading** conocimiento de embarque; **– of rights** declaración de derechos; **– of sale** escritura o acta de venta; *v.* cargar en cuenta; enviar una cuenta a; **to – and coo** acariciarse y arrullas (*como las palomas*).

bill•board [bílbord] *s.* cartelera.

bill•fold [bílfld] *s.* cartera.

bil•liards [bílja·dz] *s.* billar.

bil•lion [bíljən] *s.* billón, millón de millones; mil millones (*en los Estados Unidos y en Francia*).

bil•low [bílo] *s.* oleada; ola grande; *v.* alzarse en olas.

bin [bɪn] *s.* arcón, depósito; **coal** – carbonera; **grain** – granero.

bind [baɪnd] *v.* (*unite*) unir, juntar; (*tie*) ligar; amarrar; vendar; ceñir; (*compel*) restringir; obligar, compeler; (*enclose*) encuadernar, empastar; rivetear.

bind•ing [báɪndɪŋ] *s.* encuadernación; ribete, cinta; **cloth** – encuadernación en tela; **paper** – encuadernación en rústica; *adj.* obligatorio.

bi•og•ra•phy [baɪógrəfɪ] *s.* biografía.

bi•ol•o•gy [baɪólədʒɪ] *s.* biología.

bi•par•ti•san [baɪpórtəzən] *adj.* de dos partidos; bipartito.

birch [bɜ·tʃ] *s.* abedul.

bird [bɜ·d] *s.* ave; pájaro; persona extraña o mal vista; **of** – **prey** ave de rapiña; **– seed** alpiste; **– shot** perdigones.

birth [bɜ·θ] *s.* nacimiento; parto; linaje; origen, principio; **– certificate** certificado (*o* fe) de nacimiento; **– control** control de la natalidad; limitación de partos; **– rate** natalidad; **to give** – dar a luz, parir.

birth•day [bɜ́·θde] *s.* cumpleaños; natalicio.

birth•place [bɜ́·θples] *s.* lugar de nacimiento, suelo natal.

birth•right [bɜ́·θraɪt] *s.* derechos naturales o nacimiento; naturalidad; primogenitura.

bis•cuit [bískɪt] *s.* bizcocho; galleta; panecillo.

bish•op [bíʃəp] *s.* obispo; alfil (*en ajedrez*).

bi•son [báɪsŋ] *s.* bisonte, búfalo.

bit [bɪt] *s.* pedacito; trocito; pízca, migaja, poquito; bocado (*del freno*); taladro, **I don't care a –** no me importa un ardite; *pret.* & *p.p. de* **to bite.**

bitch [bɪtʃ] *s.* perra; ramera, prostituta.

bite [baɪt] *s.* mordedura, mordisco; becado, bocadito; picadura (*de insecto*); *v.* morder; mordiscar; picar.

bit•ten [bɪtŋ] *p.p. de* **to bite.**

bit•ter [bítə·] *adj.* amargo; agrio, acre; áspero; mordaz; **to fight to the – end** luchar hasta morir; **–s** *s. pl.* amargo; **-ly** *adv.* amargamente; con amargura.

bit•ter•ness [bítə·nɪs] *s.* amargura, amargor; rencor; aspereza.

black [blæk] *adj.* negro; oscuro; sombrío; **black-and-blue** amoratado, lleno de moretones; **– mark**

mancha, estigma, marca de deshonra; *s.* negro; luto; **– out** obscurecimiento: **to put down in – and white** poner por escrito; *v.* teñir de negro; embetunar, dar bola o betún a (*los zapatos*).

black•ber•ry [blǽkbɛrɪ] *s.* zarzamora, mora.

black•bird [blǽkbɜ·d] *s.* mirlo.

black•board [blǽkbord] *s.* encerado; pizarrón; pizarra.

black•en [blǽkən] *v.* ennegrecer; obscurecer; teñir de negro; denigrar.

black•head [blǽkhɛd] *s.* espinilla.

black•ish [blǽkɪʃ] *adj.* negruzco.

black•jack [blǽkdʒæk] *s.* (*weapon*) cachiporra flexible; (*card game*) veintiuna.

black•mail [blǽkmel] *s.* chantaje, extorsión; *v.* ejercer el chantaje, extorsionar.

black•ness [blǽknɪs] *s.* negrura; obscuridad.

black•smith [blǽksmɪθ] *s.* herrero; **-'s shop** herrería.

blad•der [blǽdə·] *s.* vejiga.

blade [bled] *s.* hoja (*de navaja, cuchillo, etc.*); hoja (*de hierba*); espada; pala (*de remo*); aspa (*de hélice*); **shoulder** – espaldilla o paletilla.

blame [blem] *s.* culpa; *v.* culpar; echar la culpa a; **to be to** – tener la culpa.

blame•less [blémlɪs] *adj.* inculpable.

blanch [blæntʃ] *v.* blanquear; palidecer; escaldar (*almendras*).

bland [blænd] *adj.* blando; suave.

blank [blæŋk] *adj.* (*no writing*) en blanco; (*void*) vacío; (*confused*) aturdido; **– cartridge** cartucho vacío; **– face** cara sin expresión; **– form** blanco, forma en blanco, *Mex. C.A., Ven.*, esqueleto; **– verse** verso suelto o libre; *s.* blanco; vacío; hueco, intermedio; papel en blanco; forma en blanco; **application** – forma (*o* blanco) para memorial o solicitud.

blan•ket [blǽŋkɪt] *s.* manta; frazada; cobertor; *Ríopl. C.A. Méx., Ven., Col.* cobija; *Méx.* sarape, poncho; *adj.* general, inclusivo, que abarca un grupo o clase.

blare [blɛr] *s.* fragor; son de trompetas; clarinada; *v.* trompetear, proclamar; sonar (*las trompetas*); hacer estruendo.

blas•pheme [blæsfím] *v.* blasfemar.

blas•phe•my [blǽsfɪmɪ] *s.* blasfemia.

blast [blæst] *s.* (*wind*) ráfaga de viento, golpe de viento; soplo repentino; (*trumpet*) trompetazo; (*whistle*) silbido; (*explosion*) explosión; estallido; carga de dinamita; **– furnace** alto horno; *v.* volar (*con dinamita, etc.*); destruir.

blaze [blez] *s.* llama, llamada; incendio; resplandor; **– of anger** arranque de ira; *v.* arder; resplandecer; **to – a trail** abrir (*o* marcar) una senda.

bleach [blitʃ] *s.* blanqueador; blanqueo; *v.* blanquea (se); desteñir (se).

bleach•ers [blítʃɚz] *s. pl.* graderías, *Am.* glorietas.

bleak [blik] *adj.* yermo, desierto; helado.

blear [blɪr] *v.* nublar (*los ojos*).

blear•y [blírɪ] *adj.* nublado, inflamado, lagrimoso, lagañoso.

bleat [blit] *s.* balido; *v.* balar.

bled [blɛd] *pret. & p.p. de* **to bleed.**

bleed [blid] *v.* sangrar; desangrar; extorsionar.

blem•ish [blɛmɪʃ] *s.* marcha, tacha, defecto; *v.* manchar; empañar.

blend [blɛnd] *s.* mezcla, entremezcla; gradación (*de colores, sonidos, etc.*); mezclar, entremezclar; graduar (*colores o sonidos*); entremezclarse, fundirse; armonizar.

bless [blɛs] *v.* bendecir; **God – you!** ¡que Dios te bendiga!

bless•ed [blɛsɪd] *adj.* bendito; santo; beato; bienaventurado; **the whole – day** todo el santo día; [blɛst] *pret. & p.p. de* **to bless.**

bless•ing [blɛsɪŋ] *s.* bendición; gracia; don, beneficio.

blest [blɛs] *adj.* = **blessed.**

blew [blu] *pret. de* **to blow.**

blight [blaɪt] *s.* pulgón (*parásito*); tizón (*honguillo parásito*); quemadura (*enfermedad de las plantas*); roña (*de las plantas*); malogro; ruina; *v.* destruir, arruinar; frustrar (*esperanzas*).

blimp [blɪmp] *s.* dirigible pequeño.

blind [blaɪnd] *adj.* ciego; tapado, oculto; hecho a ciegas; **– alley** callejón sin salida; **– choice** selección hecha a ciegas; **– flying** vuelo ciego, vuelo a ciegas; **– man** ciego; **– man's buff** juego de la gallina ciega; **– date** [blaɪnddet] *s.* cita a ciegas; persiana, cortinilla; biombo; venda (*para los ojos*); anteojera (*para resguardar los ojos de caballo*); **to be a – for someone** ser tapadera de alguien; *v.* cegar; ofuscar; encubrir; tapar.

blind•er [blaɪndɚ] *s.* anteojera, *Am.* visera (*para caballos de tiro*).

blind•fold [blaɪndfold] *v.* vendar (*los ojos*); *adj.* vendado (*de los ojos*); *s.* venda (*para los ojos*).

blind•ly [blaɪndlɪ] *adv.* ciegamente; a ciegas.

blind•ness [blaɪndnɪs] *s.* ceguera, ceguedad.

blink [blɪŋk] *v.* pestañeo; parpadeo; guiño; guiñada; *v.* pestañear; parpadear; guiñar.

blip [blɪp] *s.* bache de radar.

bliss [blɪs] *s.* beatitud, bienaventuranza, gloria; felicidad.

blist•er [blɪstɚ] *s.* ampolla, vejiga (*en piel o en cualquier superficie*); *v.* ampollar, levantar ampollas; ampollarse.

blitz [blɪts] *s.* ataque relámpago.

bliz•zard [blɪzɚd] *s.* ventisca; *v.* ventiscar.

bloat [blot] *v.* inflar (se); abotagarse.

blob [blɑb] *s.* burbuja.

block [blɑk] *s.* (*piece*) bloque, trozo de piedra; zoquete; (*city section*) manzana (*de casas*); *Am.* cuadra; (*obstacle*) estorbo, obstáculo; (*group*) grupo, sección; (*hat*) horma; **– pulley** polea; **chopping –** tajo; *v.* estorbar; tapar; bloquear; planchar (*sobre horma*); parar (*una pelota, una jugada*); **to – out** esbozar, bosquejar; **to – the door** impedir el paso; **to – up a door** tapiar una puerta.

block•ade [blɑkéd] *s.* bloqueo; obstrucción; *v.* bloquear.

block•head [blɑkhɛd] *s.* zoquete, tonto, zopenco.

blond(e) [blɑnd] *adj. & s.* rubio, blondo; *Méx.*, huero, güero; *Guat.* canche; *Sal., Hond.,* chele; *C.R.* macho; *Col.* mono; *Ven.* catire.

blood [blʌd] *s.* sangre; **– count** análisis cuantitativo de la sangre; **– pudding** (*o* **– sausage**) morcilla; **– relative** pariente consanguíneo; **– vessel** vena, arteria; **in cold –** en sangre fría; **– bank** banco de sangre; **– poisoning** septicemia.

blood•shed [blʌdʃɛd] *s.* matanza; derrame, derramamiento o efusión de sangre.

blood•shot [blʌdʃɑt] *adj.* inyectado de sangre.

blood•thirst•y [blʌdθɝstɪ] *adj.* sanguinario.

blood•y [blʌdɪ] *adj.* sangriento; ensangrentado; sanguinario, feroz.

bloom [blum] *s.* flor; florecimiento, floración; lozanía; color rosado (*en las mejillas*) *v.* florecer, *Am.* florear.

bloom•ing [blúmɪŋ] *adj.* floreciente; fresco, lozano, vigoroso.

blos•som [blásəm] *s.* flor; floración, florecimiento; *v.* florecer.

blot [blɑt] *s.* marcha, borrón; tacha; *v.* manchar; borrar; secar (*con papel secante*); emborronar, echar manchas o borrones; **to –out** borrar, tachar; destruir; **this pen -s** esta pluma echa borrones; **blotting paper** papel secante.

blotch [blɑtʃ] *v.* emborronar o borronear, manchar, cubrir con manchas; *s.* mancha, borrón.

blot•ter [blátɚ] *s.* papel secante; libro borrador.

blouse [blaUs] *s.* blusa.

blow [blo] *s.* (*stroke*) golpe; porrazo; (*shock*) choque, sorpresa, desastre; (*wind*) sopo, soplido; **to come to -s** venir a las manos; *v.* soplar; ventear; resoplar; sonar (*una trompeta*); fanfarronear; **to – a fuse** quemar un fusible; **to – one's nose** sonarse; **to – one's brains out** levantarse la tapa de los sesos; **to – open** abrirse; **to – out** apagar (se); estallar, reventar (se) (*un neumático*); **to – over** pasar; disiparse; **to – up** inflar, hinchar; volar (*con dinamita*); estallar; reventar.

blo•wer [blóɚ] *s.* soplar; fuelle; ventilador, aventador.

blown [blon] *p.p. de* **to blow** & *adj.* soplado; inflado; **full-blown rose** rosa abierta.

blow•out [blóaUt] s. reventón (de neumático); escape violento de gas, aire, etc.

blow•pi•pe [blópaɪp] s. soplete.

blow•torch [blótɔrtʃ] s. soplete.

blue [blu] adj. azul; triste, melancólico; s. azul; the -s melancolía, morriña, murria; v. azular, teñir de azul.

blue•bell [blúbɛl] s. campanilla azul (flor).

blue•bird [blúbɝd] s. pájaro azul, Am. azulejo.

blue•jay [blúdʒe] s. gayo, especie de azulejo (pájaro).

bluff [blʌf] s. acantilado, escarpa; risco; fanfarronada; fanfarrón, farsante; v. fanfarronear; alardear, hacer alarde; echar bravatas; embaucar.

bluff•er [bl ʌ́fɚ] s. farsante, fanfarrón.

blu•ing [blúɪŋ] s. añil (para ropa blanca).

blu•ish [blúɪʃ] adj. azulado, azulejo.

blun•der [bl ʌ́ndɚ] s. disparate, desatino; despropósito; v. disparatar; desatinar; equivocarse.

blunt [blʌnt] adj. despuntado, embotado; brusco, grosero, Méx., claridoso; v. despuntar, embotar.

blur [blɝ] s. mancha; tacha; nube, cosa obscura o confusa; v. empañar; borronear, manchar, nublar, ofuscar; empañarse, nublarse.

blush [blʌʃ] s. sonrojo; rubir; v. sonrojarse, ruborizarse, ponerse colorado.

blus•ter [bl ʌ́stɚ] v. ventear o soplar recio (el viento) ; fanfarronear; s. ventolera, ventarrón, fuerte golpe de viento; jactancia, fanfarronada.

blus•ter•ing [bl ʌ́stɚɪŋ] adj. fanfarrón, jactancioso; – wind ventarrón.

boar [bor] s. jabalí.

board [bord] s. (wood) tabla, tablero; mesa; (meals) comidas; (directors) junta, consejo; (pasteboard) en pasta; cartón; the -s las tablas, el teatro; room and – cuarto y comida, pensión completa; asistencia; – of directors junta directiva; bulletin – tablilla para anuncios; free on (f.o.b.) franco a bordo; on – a bordo; en el tren; to go by the – caer en el mar; perderse; ser descartado; v. ir a bordo; subir (al tren); entablar, cubrir con tablas; tomar a pupilaje, dar asistencia, pensión o pupilaje; residir o comer (en casa de huéspedes).

board•er [bórdɚ] s. huésped, pupilo, pensionista.

board•ing•house [bórdɪŋhaUs] s. casa de huéspedes, pensión.

boast [bost] s. jactancia; alarde; bravata; gloria, orgullo; v. jactarse, alardear; hacer alarde de; ostentar.

boast•ful [bóstfəl] adj. jactancioso.

boast•ful•ness [bóstfəlnɪs] s. jactancia; ostentación.

boat [bot] s. bote; barco; buque; lancha, chalupa

boat•house [bóthaUs] s. casilla o cobertizo para botes.

boat•ing [bótɪŋ] s. paseo en lancha o bote to go –

pasear en bote.

boat•man [bótmən] (pl. boatmen [bótmɛn]) s. barquero.

bob [bab] s. meneo, sacudida; pesa (de metal); to wear a – llevar el pelo corto (o en melena); v. menearse; to – one's hair cortarse el pelo en melena; to – up aparecer de repente; to – up and down saltar, brincar; cabecear (dícese de una embarcación).

bob•bin [babɪn] s. carrete; bobina.

bob•white [babhwáɪt] s. cordorniz.

bode [bod] pret. & p.p. de to bide.

bod•ice [badɪs] s. corpiño, jubón.

bod•i•ly [bad ǀ ɪ] adj. corpóreo; corporal; adv. todos juntos, colectivamente; they rose – se levantaron todos a una, se levantaron todos juntos.

bod•y [bádɪ] s. cuerpo; agregado, conjunto, gremio; carrocería (de automóvil); fuselaje (de aeroplano); – of water extensión de agua; – politic grupo político; estado.

bod•y•guard [bádɪgord] s. guardaespaldas.

bog [bag] s. pantano; tremendal; v. hundir (se); atascarse.

Bo•he•mian [bohímɪən] adj. & s. bohemio.

boil [bɔɪl] s. hervor; tumorcillo; to come to a– soltar el hervor, hervir; v. hervir; cocer; bullir; to – down hervir hasta evaporar; abreviar.

boil•er [bɔ́ɪlɚ] s. caldera, marmita; caldera de vapor; calorífero central.

boil•ing point [bɔ́ɪlɪŋpɔɪnt] s. punto de ebullición.

bois•ter•ous [bɔ́ɪstərəs] adj. bullicioso; estrepitoso; ruidoso; tumultuoso.

bold [bold] adj. atrevido, osado; arriesgado; audaz, insolente; claro, bien, delineado; – cliff risco, escarpado; bold-faced descarado; bold-faced type negritas.

bold•ness [bóldnɪs] s. atrevimiento; osadía; audacia; descaro, insolencia.

bo•lo•gna [bəlóní] s. especie de embutido.

Bol•she•vik [bólʃəvɪk] adj. & s. bolchevique.

bol•ster [bólstɚ] s. travesaño, almohada larga (para la cabecera de la cama); refuerzo, sostén, soporte; v. sostener, apoyar; apuntalar; to – someone's courage infundirle ánimo a alguien.

bolt [bolt] s. (door lock) pestillo, cerrojo; (pin) perno, tornillo grande; (movement) salida de repente; (cloth) rollo; thunder – rayo; v. cerrar con cerrojo; tragar, engullir; romper con (un partido político); echarse a correr, lanzarse de repente; caer como rayo; to – out salir de golpe.

bomb [bam] s. bomba; v. bombardear; – shelter [bámʃɛltɚ] s. refugio antiaéreo.

bom•bard [bambárd] v. bombardear, cañonear.

bom•bar•dier [bambɚdír] s. bombardero.

bom•bard•ment [bambárdmənt] s. bombardeo,

cañoneo.

bom·bast·ic [bɑmbǽstɪk] *adj.* ampuloso, altisonante.

bomb·er [bámɚ] *s.* bombardero, avión de bombardeo.

bon·bon [bánbɑn] *s.* bombón, confite.

bond [bɑnd] *s.* lazo, vínculo; ligadura; fianza, vale; obligación, bono.

bond·age [bándɪdʒ] *s.* servidumbre, esclavitud.

bonds·man [bándzmən] *s.* fiador.

bone [bon] *s.* hueso; espina (*de pez*) **-s** restos; osamenta; **– of contention** materia de discordia; **to make no -s about it** no pararse en pelillos; obrar francamente; *v.* deshuesar, quitar los huesos o espinas.

bon·fire [bánfaɪr] *s.* hoguera, fogata.

bon·net [bánɪt] *s.* gorra; sombrero (*de mujer*).

bo·nus [bónəs] *s.* prima, premio, gratificación.

bon·y [bónɪ] *adj.* huesudo.

boo [bu] *v.* mofarse, burlarse (*a gritos*); **– !** *interj.* ¡bu!; **-s** *pl.* rechifla, gritos de mofa.

boo·by [bubɪ] *s.* bobo, bobalicón.

book [buk] *s.* libro; **The book** la Biblia; **cash** – libro de caja; **memorandum** – libreta; **on the -s** cargado en cuenta; **to keep -s** llevar los libros o la contabilidad; *v.* inscribir, asentar (*en un libro*); **to – passage** reservar pasaje.

book·case [búkkes] *s.* estante, estantería, armario para libros.

book·end [búkɛnd] *s.* apoyalibros, sujetalibros.

book·keep·er [búkkipɚ] *s.* tenedor de libros, contador.

book·keep·ing [búkkipɪŋ] *s.* teneduría de libros, contabilidad, **double entry** – partida doble.

book·let [búklɛt] *s.* librillo, librito, cuaderno, folleto.

book·sell·er [búksɛlɚ] *s.* librero.

book·shelf [búkʃɛlf] *s.* estante, repisa para libros.

book·shop [búkʃɑp] *s.* librería.

book·store [búkstor] *s.* librería.

boom [bum] *s.* (*noise*) estampido; (*increase*) alza, auge (*en el mercado o bolsa*); bonanza, prosperidad momentánea, *v.* rugir, resonar, hacer estampido, prosperar, medrar, florecer, estar en bonanza, fomentar.

boon [bun] *s.* don, bendición, gracia, favor; *adj.* jovial, congenial.

boor [bur] *s.* patán, hombre zafio o grosero.

boor·ish [búrɪʃ] *adj.* grosero, zafio.

boost [bust] *s.* empuje, empujón (*de abajo arriba*); **– in prices** alza o auge de precios; *v.* empujar, alzar, levantar; hacer subir.

boost·er [bústɚ] *s.* aumentador; (*rocket*) cohete de lanzamiento; (*electronics*) amplificador.

boot [but] *s.* bota, calzado; **to –** por añadidura de ganancia, *Méx.,* depilón, *Ven.,* de ñapa; *Ríopl., Andes* de yapa (*llapa*); *v.* dar un puntapié; **to – out**

echar a puntapiés, hechar a patadas.

boot·black [bútblæk] *s.* limpiabotas.

booth [buθ] *s.* casilla, puesto.

boot·leg·ger [bútlɛgɚ] *s.* contrabandista (*de licores*).

boot·lick·er [bútlɪkɚ] *s.* servilón, zalamero.

boo·ty [bútɪ] *s.* botín, saqueo.

bo·rax [bóræks] *s.* bórax.

bor·der [bɔ́rdɚ] *s.* borde, margen, orilla; orla, franja; ribete; frontera; *v.* ribetear, guarnecer, (*el borde*) orlar; **to on** (*o* **upon**) lindar con; confinar con; rayar en; **it -s on madness** raya en locura.

bore [bor] *s.* taladro, barreno; agujero (*hecho con taladro*); calibre (*de un cañón, cilindro, etc.*); persona o cosa aburrida; *v.* taladrar, horadar, barrenar; aburrir; fastidiar; *pret. de* **to bear.**

bored [bord] *adj.* cansado, aburrido; *p.p. de* **to bore.**

bore·dom [bórdəm] *s.* aburrimiento, tedio, hastío, fastidio.

bo·ric ac·id [bórɪk ǽsəd] *s.* ácido bórico.

bor·ing [bórɪŋ] *adj.* aburrido fastidioso, tedioso.

born [bɔrn] *p.p. de* **to bear** & *adj.* nacido, innato; **to _be —** nacer.

borne [born] *p.p.* **to bear.**

bor·ough [bɝ́o] *s.* villa; distrito de municipio.

bor·row [bɔ́ro] *v.* pedir prestado; tomar prestado; tomar fiado.

bor·row·er [bɔ́rəwɚ] *s.* el que pide prestado.

bos·om [búzəm] *s.* seno; pecho, corazón; pechera (*de camisa*); **in the – of the family** en el seno de la familia; *adj.* querido; **– friend** amigo íntimo.

boss [bɔs] *s.* jefe; patrón; mayoral, capataz; **political –** cacique político; *v.* mandar, dominar dirigir.

boss·y [bɔ́sɪ] *adj.* mandón, autoritario.

bot·a·ny [bátṇ ɪ] *s.* botánica.

botch [bɑtʃ] *s.* chapucería.

both [boθ] *adj.* & *pron.* ambos, entrambos, los dos; **– this and that** tanto esto como aquello; **– of them** ambos, ellos dos, los dos; **– (of) his friends** sus dos amigos, ambos amigos.

both·er [bɑðɚ] *s.* molestia, fastidio; incomodidad; enfado; *v.* molestar(se); fastidiar, enfadar, incomodar, estorbar.

both·er·some [bɑðɚsəm] *adj.* molesto.

bot·tle [bɑt]] *s.* botella; *v.* embotellar.

bot·tle·neck [bɑt]nɛk] *s.* embotellamiento, gollete.

bot·tom [bɑtəm] *s.* fondo; base; fundamento; asiento (*de silla*) **to be at the – of the class** ser el último de la clase; **what is at the – of all this?** ¿qué hay en el fondo de todo esto?.

bou·doir [budwár] *s.* tocador.

bough [baU] *s.* rama.

bought [bɔt] *pret.* & *p.p. de* **to buy.**

bouil·lon [búljɑn] *s.* caldo.

boul·der [bólda] *s.* peña, roca, guijarro grande, pedrusco.

boul·e·vard [búlavard] *s.* bulevar.

bounce [baUns] *s.* bote, rebote (*de una pelota*); salto, brinco; *v.* hacer saltar; saltar, brincar; brotar; echar, arrojar (*a alguien*); echar, despedir de un empleo.

bounc·er [baUnsa] *s.* apagabroncas.

bound [baUnd] *s.* (*jump*) salto, brinco; (*bounce*) bote, rebote; (*limit*) límite, confín; *adj.* ligado; confinado; obligado; ceñido; encuadernado; **to be – for** ir para, ir con rumbo a; **to be – up in one's work** estar absorto en su trabajo; **it is – to happen** es seguro que sucederá; **I am- to do it** estoy resuelto a hacerlo; *v.* botar, resaltar; saltar, brincar; limitar; ceñir, cercar; *pret .& p.p. de* **to bind.**

bound·a·ry [báUndarɪ] *s.* límite, linde; confín; frontera.

bound·less [báUndlɪs] *adj.* ilimitado; sin límites, sin término.

boun·ti·ful [báUntafal] *adj.* generoso, liberal; abundante.

boun·ty [báUntɪ] *s.* largueza, generosidad; don, favor, gracia, premio, recompensa.

bou·quet [buké] *s.* ramillete, ramo de flores; aroma, fragancia.

bour·geois [bUrʒwá] *adj. & s.* burgués.

bout [baUt] *s.* combate, lucha, contienda, asalto; **a – of pneumonia** un ataque de pulmonía.

bow [baU] *s.* (*inclination*) reverencia; inclinación, saludo; (*of a ship*) proa; *v.* hacer una reverencia, inclinarse (*para saludar*); someterse; **to – one's head** inclinar la cabeza **-ed down** agobiado.

bow [bo] *s.* arco (*para tirar flechas*); arco (*de violín*); curva; lazo, moño (*de cintas*); **bow-legged** *adj.* patizambo, patituerto; *v.* arquear; tocar (*un instrumento*) con arco.

bow·els [báUalz] *s. pl.* intestinos; entrañas; tripas.

how·er [báUa] *s.* enramada, ramada, glorieta.

bowl [bol] *s.* cuenco; tazón; jícara; boliche, bola; **wash – palangana**, lavamanos, **-s** juego de bolos; *v* bolear, jugar a los bolos, jugar al boliche

box [baks] *s.* caja; estuche; palco de teatro; casilla; compartimento; **– car** furgón; **– office** taquilla; **– seat** asiento de palco; *v.* encajonar; meter en una caja; abofetear; boxear.

box·er [báksa] *s.* boxeador, pugilista.

box·ing [báksɪŋ] *s.* boxeo, pugilato.

boy [bɔɪ] *s.* niño; muchacho; mozo.

boy·cott [bɔ́kat] *v.* boycotear, *s.* boycoteo.

boy·hood [bɔ́ɪhUd] *s.* niñez; mocedad, juventud.

boy·ish [bɔ́ɪʃ] *adj.* pueril; juvenil; aniñado.

brace [bres] *s.* traba; tirante; apoyo, refuerzo; corchete ({ }); **carpenter's – berbiquí;** *v.* trabar; apoyar, reforzar; asegurar; estimular, fortalecer; **to – up** animarse, cobrar ánimo.

brace·let [bréslɪt] *s.* brazalete, pulsera.

brack·et [brǽkɪt] *s.* ménsula, soporte, sostén; repisa; **-s** paréntesis cuadrados; *v.* colocar entre paréntesis; unir; agrupar.

brag [bræg] *s.* jactancia; *v.* jactarse (de); hacer alarde de.

brag·gart [brǽgat] *adj. & s.* jactancioso, fanfarrón.

braid [bred] *s.* trenza; galón, trencilla; *v.* trenzar; galonear, guarnecer con galones.

brain [bren] *s.* cerebro; seso; **to rack one's -s** devanarse los sesos, romperse la cabeza; *v.* saltar la tapa de los sesos; **– trust** [bréntrʌst] *s.* grupo de consejeros; **– washing** [brénwoʃɪŋ] *s.* lavado cerebral.

brake [brek] *s.* freno; *Ven., Col.,* retranca; *Méx., Ríopl., C.A., Carib.,* garrote; **– lining** forro de freno; **– shoe** zapata de freno; **– drum** tambor de freno; **– fluid** fluído de freno **to apply the -s** frenar; *v.* frenar, enfrenar; *Ven., Col.,* retrancar; *Méx., Ríopl., C.A. Carib.* dar garrote.

brake·man [brékman] *s.* guardafrenos, *Ven., Col.,* retranquero, *Méx., Ríopl., C.A., Carib.,* garrotero.

bram·ble [brǽmb l] *s.* zarza, breña.

bran [brænd] *s.* salvado.

branch [bræntʃ] *s.* rama (*de árbol*); ramo (*de la ciencia*); sucursal; bifurcación; sección; tributario (*de un río*); ramificación; **– railway** ramal; *v.* ramificarse; bifurcarse

brand [brænd] *s.* (*make*) marca; marca de fábrica; hechura; (*cattle mark*) hierro; *Ríopl., Méx.,* fierro (*de marcar*) estigma; **brand-new** nuevecito, flamante, acabado de hacer o comprar; *v.* marcar, herrar, marcar (*con hierro candente*); difamar; **to – as** motejar de.

bran·dish [brǽndɪʃ] *v.* blandir; *s.* floreo, moliente.

bran·dy [brǽndɪ] *s.* aguardiente; coñac.

brash [bræʃ] *adj.* insolente; impetuoso; temerario.

brass [bræs] *s.* latón, bronce; desfachatez, descaro; **-s** utensilios de latón, instrumentos musicales de metal; **band** banda, murga.

bras·sière [brazír] *s.* corpiño, sostén (*para ceñir los pechos*)

brat [bræt] *s.* mocoso.

bra·va·do [bravádo] *s.* bravata; jactancia.

brave [brev] *adj.* bravo, valiente, valeroso; *v.* arrostrar; desafiar, hacer frente a.

brav·er·y [brévarɪ] *s.* valor, valentía.

brawl [brɔl] *v.* reyerta, pendencia, riña; alboroto; *v.* armar una pendencia, alborotar, reñir.

bray [bre] *s.* rebuzno; *v.* rebuznar.

bra·zen [brézṇ] *adj.* bronceado; de bronce; de latón; descarado, desvergonzado.

bra·zier [brezja] *s.* brasero.

breach [britʃ] *s.* (*opening*) brecha, abertura;

(*infraction*) infracción; rompimiento; **– of faith** abuso de confianza; **– of promise** violación de un compromiso; *v.* abrir brecha.

bread [brɛd] *s.* pan; **– box** caja para pan; *v. Méx.*, *C.A.*, empanizar; *Ríopl.*, *Ch.*, empanar.

breadth [brɛdθ] *s.* anchura, ancho; extensión; amplitud.

break [brek] *s.* rompimiento; rotura; interrupción, pausa; bajón (*en la bolsa o mercado*); **to have a bad (good)** – tener mala (buena) suerte; **to make a bad** – cometer un disparate; *v.* romper (se), quebrantar (se); quebrar (se); amansar, domar; arruinar; **to – away** fugarse, escaparse; **to – into** forzar la entrada en, allanar (*una morada*); **to – loose** escaparate, desprenderse, soltarse; **to-out** estallar (*una guerra*); **to – out of prison** escaparse de la cárcel, **to – a promise** faltar a la palabra; **to – up** desmenuzar, despedazar; disolver; perturbar.

break•a•ble [brékəb] *adj.* quebradizo.

break•down [brédaʊn]*s.* parada imprevista; (*automovile*) avería, pane.

break•er [brékə-] *s.* rompiente (*ola*); **law** – infractor.

break•fast [brɛkfəst] *s.* desayuno; **to eat** – tomar el desayuno; *v.* desayunarse.

break•through [brékθru] *s.* adelanto repentino; brecha.

break•wa•ter [brékwɔtə-] *s.* rompeolas, malecón.

breast [brɛst] *s.* pecho; seno; teta; pechuga (*de ave*); **to make a clean-of it** confesarlo todo.

breath [brɛθ] *s.* aliento; resuello; respiro; soplo, hálito; **in the same** – al mismo instante, con el mismo aliento; **out of** – sin aliento, jadeante, **under one's** – en voz baja, entre dientes.

breathe [brið] *v.* respirar; resollar; tomar aliento; exhalar; **to – into** infundir; **he -ed his last** exhaló el último suspiro; **he did not –a work** no dijo palabra.

breath•less [brɛθlɪs] *adj.* jadeante; sin aliento.

breath•tak•ing [brɛθtekɪŋ] *adj.* conmovedor; emocionante.

bred [brɛd] *pret. & p.p. de* **to breed.**

breech•es [brítʃɪz] *s. pl.* bragas, calzones; **riding** – pantalones de montar.

breed [brid] *s.* casta, raza; relea, especie; *v.* criar; procrear, engendrar; educar; producirse; multiplicarse.

breed•er [brídə-] *s.* criador; animal de cría.

breed•ing [brídɪŋ] *s.* cría, crianza; educación; modales.

breeze [briz] *s.* brisa, vientecillo.

breez•y [bríz1] *adj.* airoso, ventilado; refrescado (*por la brisa*); animado, vivaz; **it is** – hace brisa.

breth•ren [brɛðrɪn] *s. pl.* hermanos (*los fieles de una iglesia o los miembros de una sociedad*).

brev•i•ty [brɛ́vəti] *s.* brevedad.

brew [bru] *s.* cerveza; mezcla; *v.* fermentar, hacer (*licores*); preparar (*té*) fomentar, tramar; fabricar cerveza, amenazar (*una tormenta, calamidad, etc.*).

brew•er•y [brúəri] *s.* cervecería, fábrica de cerveza.

bri•ar, bri•er [bráiə-] *s.* zarza; rosal silvestre.

bribe [braɪb] *s.* soborno, cohecho; *v.* sobornar, cohechar.

brib•er•y [bráɪbəri] *s.* soborno, cohecho.

brick [brɪk] *s.* ladrillo; ladrillos; *v.* enladrillar.

brick•bat [bríkbæt] *s.* pedazo de ladrillo; insulto.

bri•dal [bráɪd] *adj.* nupcial; de bodas; de novia; **– dress** vestido de novia.

bride [braɪd] *s.* novia, desposada.

bride•groom [bráɪdgrum] *s.* novio, desposado.

brides•maid [bráɪdzmed] *s.* madrina de boda.

bridge [brɪdʒ] *a.* puente; caballete de la nariz; **draw** – puente levadizo; **suspension** – puente colgante; *v.* tender un puente; **to a gap** llenar un vacío.

bri•dle [bráɪd] *s.* brida, freno de caballo; freno, restricción; **– path** camino de herradura; *v.* embridar, enfrenar; reprimir, subyugar; erguirse, erguir la cabeza.

brief [brif] *adj.* breve, corto, conciso; *s.* sumario, resumen; informe, memorial; breve apostólico; **to hold a – for** abogar por; **-ly** *adv.* brevemente; en resumen, en breve.

brief•case [brífkes] *s.* portapapeles, cartera grande.

brief•ing [brifɪŋ] *s.* reunión preparatoria.

bri•gade [brɪgéd] *s.* brigada.

bright [braɪt] *adj.* (*light*) brillante, claro, luciente; radiante; (*smart*) inteligente; (*cheerful*) alegre; listo, vivo; **– color** color subido.

bright•en [bráɪt ŋ] *v.* abrillantar, pulir, dar lustre; avivar (se); alegrarse (se); animar (se); aclararse, despejarse (*el cielo*).

bright•ness [bráɪtnɪs] *s.* brillo, lustre, esplendor; claridad; viveza, agudeza, inteligencia.

bril•liance [bríljəns] *s.* brillantez, brillo; lustre; resplandor.

bril•liant [bríljənt] *adj.* brillante; resplandeciente; espléndido; talentoso; *s.* brillante; diamante.

brim [brɪm] *s.* borde, margen, orilla; ala (*de sombrero*); **to fill to the** – llenar o arrasar hasta el borde; **to be filled to the** – estar hasta los topes; estar de bote en bote; *v.* – **over** rebosar.

brine [braɪn] *s.* salmuera.

bring [brɪŋ] *v.* traer; llevar; ocasionar, causar; **to – about** producir, efectuar, ocasionar; **to – down** bajar; **to – forth** dar a luz; producir; **to – to** resucitar; **to – up** criar, educar; **to – up a subject** traer a discusión un asunto.

brink [brɪŋk] *s.* borde, orilla, margen; **on the – of** al borde de.

brisk [brɪsk] *adj.* vivo, animado; fuerte; rápido; **-ly** *adv.* aprisa; fuerte.

bris•tle [brɪs❙] s. cerda; v. erizar (se); **to – with** estar erizado (o lleno) de.

brist•ly [brɪs❙ɪ] adj. serdoso; erizado.

Bri•tish [brɪtɪʃ] adj. británico; **the –** los ingleses.

brit•tle [brɪt❙] adj. quebradizo; frágil.

broach [brotʃ] v. traer a colación, comenzar a hablar de (un asunto).

broad [brɔd] adj ancho; amplio, vasto extenso; tolerante; **– hint** insinuación clara; **in – daylight** en pleno día; **broad-minded** tolerante; de amplias miras.

broad•cast [brɔ́dkæst] s. radiodifusión, difusión, emisión; transmisión; v. difundir; radiodifundir, radiar, emitir.

broad•cloth [brɔ́dklɔθ] s. paño fino de algodón o de lana.

broad•side [brɔ́dsaɪd] s. (guns) andanada; (announcement) hoja suelta de propaganda.

bro•cade [brokéd] s. brocado.

broil [brɔɪl] v. asar (se).

broke [brok] pret. de **to break**; adj. quebrado, arruinado; pelado, sin dinero; **to go –** quebrar, arruinarse.

bro•ken [brókən] p.p. de **to break** & adj. roto; rompido; quebrado; quebrantado, arruinado; abatido; **– English** inglés champurrado o champurreado; inglés mal pronunciado.

bro•ker [brókɚ] s. corredor, agente; bolsista; **money – cambista**, corredor de cambio.

bron•chi•tis [brɑnkáɪtɪs] s. bronquitis.

bron•co, bron•cho [bráŋko] s. potro o caballo bronco, Ríopl. redomón; **– buster** domador.

bronze [brɑnz] s. bronce; color de bronce; v. broncear.

brooch [brutʃ] s. broche (alfiler de pecho).

brood [brud] s. pollada; nidada; cría; casta; v. empollar; **to – over** cavilar.

brook [brUk] s. arroyuelo, riachuelo, C.A., Col., Ven., quebrada; Méx., Ríopl. arroyo, cañada; v. tolerar, aguantar.

broom [brum] s. escoba; retama (arbusto); **– stick** palo o mango de escoba.

broth [brɔθ] s. caldo.

broth•er [brʌðɚ] s. hermano; cofrade.

broth•er•hood [brʌðɚhUd] s. hermandad; fraternidad; cofradía.

broth•er-in-law [brʌðɚɪnlɔ] s. cuñado.

broth•er•ly [brʌðɚlɪ] adj. fraternal.

brought [brɔt] pret.& p.p. de **to bring.**

brow [braU] s. ceja; frente.

brown [braUn] adj. moreno; café; castaño; pardo oscuro; tostado; v. tostar (se).

browse [braUz] v. hojear; ramonear, pacer, pastar (el ganado).

bruise [bruz] s. magulladura, cardenal, contusión; v. magullar (se); estropear (se).

bru•net, bru•net•te [brunét] adj. moreno, trigueño.

brunt [brʌnt] s. fuerza (de un golpe o ataque); **the – of the battle** lo reñido del combate.

brush [brʌʃ] s. (tooth, clothes) cepillo; (pain, shaving) broca; (artist's) pincel; (vegetation) matorral; (contact) roce; encuentro; v. cepillar, acepillar; rozar; **to – aside** desechar, echar a un lado; **to – up** cepillarse; repasar (una materia, una técnica, etc.).

brush•wood [brʌʃwUd] s. broza; maleta, matorral, zarzal.

brusque [brʌsk] adj. brusco.

bru•tal [brút❙] adj. brutal, bruto.

bru•tal•i•ty [brutǽlətɪ] s. brutalidad.

brute [brut] s. bruto, bestia; adj. bruto, brutal; bestia.

bub•ble [bʌb❙] s. burbuja; borbollón; ampolla; v. borbotar; hacer espuma; bullir; **to over with joy** rebosar de gozo.

bub•ble gum [bʌb❙ gʌm] s. chicle; hinchable; chicle de globo.

buck [bʌk] s. macho cabrío, cabrón; gamo; macho (del ciervo, antílope, etc.); corveta, respingo (de un caballo); embestida; **– private** soldado raso; **to pass the –** Ríopl., Andes, pasar el fardo; v. cabriolear, respingar; embestir; encabritarse; bregar con (el viento); **to up** cobrar ánimo; **the horse –ed the rider** el caballo tiró al jinete.

buck•et [bʌkɪt] s. cubo, cubeta, balde.

buck•le [bʌk❙] s. hebilla; v. abrochar con hebilla; doblarse; abollarse; **to – down to** aplicarse con empeño a; **to – with** luchar con.

buck•shot [bʌkʃɑt] s. posta, perdigón.

buck•skin [bʌkskɪn] s. badana; ante.

buck•wheat [bʌkhwɪt] s. trigo sarraceno.

bud [bʌd] s. botón, yema; capullo, pimpollo; retoño; v. echar botones o retoños; florecer.

bud•dy [bʌdɪ] s. camarada; compañero.

budge [bʌdʒ] v. mover (se), menear (se), bullir.

budg•et [bʌdʒɪt] s. presupuesto.

buff [bʌf] s. piel de ante o búfalo; color de ante; pulidor; **blindman's –** juego de la gallina ciega; v. pulir, pulimentar.

buf•fa•lo [bʌf❙o] s. búfalo.

buf•fet [bʌfé] s. aparador; repostería; mostrador para refrescos; fonda de estación.

buf•fet•ing [bʌfətɪŋ] s. golpeteo, bataneo.

buf•foon [bʌfún]s. bufón; payaso.

bug [bʌ g] s. insecto; bicho; microbio.

bug•gy [bʌgɪ] s. cochecillo.

bu•gle [bjpug❙] s. clarín; corneta; trompeta.

build [bɪld] *s.* estructura; taller, forma, hechura; *v.* edificar, construir; fabricar; **to – up one's health** reconstituir su salud.

build·er [bíldə·] *s.* constructor.

build·ing [bíldɪŋ] *s.* edificio; construcción.

build-up [bíldʃp] *s.* refuerzo paulatino.

built [bɪlt] *prep.& p.p. de* **to build.**

bulb [bʃlb] *s.* bulbo (*de la cebolla y otras plantas*); planta bulbosa; **electric light –** bombilla, bujía eléctrica, ampolla, *Méx.*, *C.A.*, *Andes.*, foco; *Ríopl.*, bombita.

bulge [bʌldʒ] *s.* bulto; protuberancia; panza; *v.* abultar; combate.

bulg·y [bʌldʒɪ] *adj.* abultado.

bulk [bʌlk] *s.* bulto, volumen; masa; **the – of the army** el grueso del ejército.

bulk·y [bʌlkɪ] *adj.* abultado, voluminoso, grueso.

bull [bʊl] *s.* toro; alcista (*el que hace subir los valores de la bolsa*); disparate, error; **Papal –** bula; **– fight** corrida de toros; **– fighter** torero, **bull's-eye** centro del blanco; tiro perfecto.

bull·dog [bʊldɔg] *s.* perro dogo, perro de presa.

bull·doz·er [bʊldozə·] *s.* topadora; buldózer.

bul·let [bʊlɪt] *s.* bala.

bul·le·tin [bʊlət ŋ] *s.* boletín; **– board** tablilla para fijar anuncios o avisos.

bull·frog [bʊlfrɔg] *s.* rana grande.

bul·lion [bʊljən] *s.* oro (*o plata*) en barras; metálico; lingotes de oro o plata.

bul·ly [bʊlɪ] *s.* pendenciero, valerón, fanfarrón, matón; *adj.* excelente, magnífico;.*v.* intimidar; echar bravatas.

bul·wark [bʊlwə·k] *s.* baluarte; defensa.

bum [bʌm] *s.* holgazán, vagabundo; gorrón; borracho; **to go on a –** irse de juerga; *adj.* malo, mal hecho, de ínfima calidad; inútil, inservible; **to feel –** estar indispuesto; *v.* holgazanear; vivir de gorra.

bum·ble-bee [bʌmb|bi] *s.* abejorro, abejón.

bump [bʌmp] *s.* (*blow*) tope, choque; golpe; (*lump*) chichón; abolladura; hinchazón; joroba, protuberancia; *v.* topar, topetear; chocar, abollar; **to – along** zarandearse, ir zarandeándose; **to – off** derribar; matar.

bump·er [bʌmpə·] *s.* parachoques, defensa; tope; *adj.* grande; excelente; **– crop** cosecha abundante.

bun [bʌn] *s.* bollo (*de pan*).

bunch [bʌntʃ] *s.* manojo, puñado; racimo (*de uvas, plátanos, etc.*); grupo; **– of flowers** ramillete de flores; *v.* juntar (se), agrupar (se).

bun·dle [bʌnd|] *s.* lío, bulto, fardo, hato; haz; paquete; *v.* liar, atar; envolver; **to up** abrigarse; taparse bien.

bun·ga·low [bʌŋgəlo] *s.* casita de un piso.

bun·gle [bʌŋg|] *v.* chapucear; estropear; echar a perder.

bun·ion [bʌnjən] *s.* juanete.

bunk [bʌŋk] *s.* litera, camilla (*fija en la pared*); embuste, tontería, paparrucha, papa.

bun·ny [bʌnɪ] *s.* conejito.

buoy [bɔɪ] *s.* boya; *v.* boyar. mantener a flote; **to – up** sostener, apoyar.

buoy·ant [bɔɪənt] *adj.* boyante, flotante; vivaz, animado, alegre.

bur·den [bɝdŋ] *s.* carga, peso; cuidado; gravemente; *v.* cargar; agobiar.

bur·den·some [bɝdŋsəm] *adj.* gravoso; pesado.

bu·reau [bjʊro] *s.* oficina; despacho; división, ramo; cómoda, **travel –** oficina de turismo; **weather –** oficina de meteorología, observatorio metereológico.

bur·glar [bɝglə·] *s.* ladrón (*que se mete en casa ajena*).

bur·gla·ry [bɝglərɪ] *s.* robo.

bur·ial [bɛrɪəl] *s.* entierro; **– place** cementerio.

bur·lap [bɝlæp] *s.* arpillera, tela burda de cáñamo.

bur·ly [bɝlɪ] *adj.* corpulento, voluminoso, grandote.

burn [bɝn] *s.* quemadura; *v.* quemar (se); incendiar; arder; abrasar (se).

burn·er [bɝnə·] *s.* quemador; mechero; hornilla.

bur·nish [bɝnɪʃ] *v.* bruñir; pulir; *s.* bruñido, pulimento.

burnt [bɝnt] *pret. & p.p. de* **to burn.**

bur·row [bɝo] *s.* madriguera, conejera; *v.* hacer madrigueras en; escarbar; socavar, minar; esconderse.

burst [bɝst] *s.* reventón, explosión; estallido; **– of laughter** caracajada; *v.* reventar (se); abrirse; estallar; **to – into** entrar de repente; **to – into tears** prorrumpir en lágrimas; **to – with laughter** estallar o reventar de risa; *pret. & p.p. de* **to burst.**

bur·y [bɛrɪ] *v.* enterrar; sepultar; **to be buried in thought** estar absorto, meditabundo o pensativo.

bus [bʌs] *s.* autobús, omnibús, *Méx.*, camión; *C.A.* camioneta; *Ríopl.* colectivo; *Ch.*, micro; *Carib.*, guagua.

bus·boy [bʌsbɔɪ] *s.* ayudante de camarero.

bush [bʊʃ] *s.* arbusto; mata; matorral, breñal; **rose –** rosal; **to beat around the –** andarse por las ramas.

bush·el [bʊʃəl] *s.* fanega (*medida de áridos*).

bush·ing [bʊʃɪŋ] *s.* buje.

bush·y [bʊʃɪ] *adj.* matoso, espeso; lleno de arbustos.

bus·i·ly [bízɪlɪ] *adv.* diligentemente.

busi·ness [bíznɪs] *s.* negocio; ocupación; comercio; asunto; **– house** casa de comercio, establecimiento mercantil; – **transaction** negocio, transacción comercial; **to do – with** negociar con, comerciar con; **he has no – doing it** no tiene derecho a hacerlo; **not to be one's –** no concernirle a uno, no importarle a uno; **to make a – deal** hacer un trato.

busi·ness·like [bíznɪslaɪk] *adj.* eficaz, eficiente, práctico; formal.

busi·ness·man [bíznɪmæn] *s.* hombre de negocios, comerciante.

bust [bʌst] *s.* busto; pecho (*de mujer*); **to go out on a –** salir o ir de parranda; *v.* reventar; quebrar; domar (*un potro*).

bus·tle [bʌs l] *s.* bulla, bullicio, trajín, alboroto; polisón (para abultar las caderas); *v.* bullir (se); menearse; trajinar.

bus·y [bízɪ] *adj.* ocupado; activo; **– body** entrometido; **– street** calle de mucho tráfico; *v.* **to – oneself** ocuparse.

but [bʌt] *conj., prep. & adv.* pero, mas; sino; menos, excepto; sólo, no ... más que; **– for you** a no ser por Vd., **not only... – also** no sólo... sino (que) también; **I cannot help –** no puedo menos de; **she is – a child** no es más que una niña.

butch·er [bútʃɚ] *s.* carnicero; **-'s shop** carnicería; *v.* matar (*reses*); hacer una matanza o carnicería; destrozar.

butch·er·y [bútʃɚɪ] *s.* carnicería, matanza.

but·ler [bʌtlɚ] *s.* despensero, mayordomo; **–s' pantry** despensa.

butt [bʌt] *s.* culata (*de rifle*); colilla (*de cigarro*); tope; topetazo; cabezada; **the – of ridicule** el blanco de las burlas; *v.* topetear, embestir; **to – in** entremeterse; **to – into a conversation** meter baza, *Am.* meter su cuchara.

but·ter [bʌtɚ] *s.* manteca, mantequilla; *v.* enmantecar, untar con manteca o mantequilla.

but·ter·cup [bʌtɚkʃp] *s.* botón de oro (*flor*).

but·ter·fly [bʌtɚflaɪ] *s.* mariposa.

but·ter·milk [bʌtɚmɪlk] *s.* suero de mantequilla.

but·ter·scotch [bʌtɚskótʃ] *s.* confite o jarabe de azúcar y mantequilla.

but·tocks [bʌtɚks] *s. pl.* nalgas, asentaderas.

but·ton [bʌt ŋ] *s.* botón; **– hook** abotonador; *v.* abotonar (se).

but·ton·hole [bʌtŋ hol] *s.* ojal; *v.* hacer ojales; **to – someone** detener, demorar a uno (*charlando*).

but·tress [bʌtrɪs] *s.* contrafuerte; refuerzo, sostén; *v.* sostener, reforzar, poner contrafuerte.

buy [baɪ] *v.* comprar; **to – off** sobornar; **to – up** acaparar.

buy·er [báɪɚ] *s.* comprador.

buzz [bʌz] *s.* zumbido; murmullo; *v.* zumbar; murmurar; **to – the bell** tocar el timbre.

buz·zard [bʌzɚd] *s.* buitre, *Am.* aura, *Méx., C.A.* zopilote, *Ríopl.*, carancho; *Col., Andes* gallinazo.

by [baɪ] *prep.* por; cerca de; sal lado de; junto a; según; **– and –** luego, pronto; **– drint of** a fuerza de; **– far** con mucho; **– night** de noche; **– the way** de paso; a propósito; entre paréntesis; **– this time** ya; a la hora de ésta; **- two o'clock** para las dos; **days gone –** días pasados.

by·gone [báɪgon] *adj.* pasado; **let -s be -s** lo pasado pasado; lo pasado pisado.

by·law [báɪlo] *s.* estatuto; reglamento.

by·pass [báɪpæs] *s.* desviación.

by·path [báɪpæθ] *s.* atajo, vereda.

by·prod·uct [báɪprodʌkt] *s.* producto secundario o accesorio.

by·stand·ers [báɪstændɚz] *s.* circunstantes, presentes; mirones.

C

cab [kæb] *s.* coche de alquiler; taxímetro, taxi; casilla (*de una locomotora*); **– driver** cochero; chófer.

cab·bage [kǽbɪdʒ] *s.* col, repollo, berza.

cab·in [kǽbɪn] *s.* cabaña, choza, bohío, barca, camarote (*de buque*); **airplane –** cabina de aeroplano.

cab·i·net [kǽbənɪt] *s.* gabinete; armario; escaparate, vitrina.

ca·ble [kéb l] *s.* cable, amarra; cablegrama; **– address** dirección cablegráfica; *v.* cablegrafiar.

ca·ble·gram [kéb græm] *s.* cablegrama.

cab·man [kǽbmən] *s.* cochero; chófer.

cack·le [kǽk l] *s.* cacareo; charla; risotada, *v.* cacarear; parlotear, charlar.

cac·tus [kǽktəs] (*pl.* **cacti** [kǽktaɪ]) *s.* cacto.

cad [kæd] *s.* canalla (*m.*); malcriado.

ca·dence [kéd n s] *s.* cadencia.

ca·det [kədét] *s.* cadete.

ca·fé [kəfé] *s.* café, restaurante.

caf·e·te·ri·a [kæfətíriə] *s.* restaurante (*en donde se sirve uno mismo*).

caf·fein [kǽfiɪn] *s.* cafeína.

cage [kedʒ] *s.* jaula; *v.* enjaular.

cake [kek] *s.* pastel; bizcocho; bollo; torta; *Ven., Col.*, panqué; pastilla (*de jabón*); **– of ice** témpano de hielo; *v.* apelmazarse, formar masa compacta.

ca·lam·i·ty [kəlǽmətɪ] *s.* calamidad.

cal·ci·um [kǽlsɪəm] *s.* calcio.

cal·cu·late [kǽlkjəlet] *v.* calcular; **to – on** contar con.

cal·cu·la·tion [kælkjəléʃən] *s.* cálculo; cómputo, cuenta.

cal·cu·lus [kǽlkjələs] *s.* cálculo.

cal·en·dar [kǽləndə-] *s.* calendario, almanaque; – **year** año corriente.

calf [kæf] (*pl.* **calves** [kævz]); *s.* ternero, ternera, becerro, becerra, pantorrilla (*de la pierna*); – **skin** piel de becerro o becerrito.

cal·i·ber [kǽləbə-] *s.* calibre.

cal·i·co [kǽləko] *s.* calicó (*tela de algodón*).

call [kɔl] *s.* (*summons*) llamada; llamamiento; (*visit*) visita; (*demand*) demanda, pedido; **within** – al alcance de la voz; *v.* llamar; gritar; hacer una visita; pasar (*lista*); **to** – **at a port** hacer escala en un puerto; **to** – **for** ir por; demandar, pedir; **to** – **on** visitar a; acudir a (*en busca de auxilio*); **to** – **to order a meeting** abrir la sesión; **to** – **together** convocar; **to** – **up on the phone** llamar por teléfono.

call·er [kɔ́lə-] *s.* visita, visitante; llamador (*el que llama*).

cal·lous [kǽləs] *adj.* calloso; duro.

cal·lus [kǽləs] *s.* callo.

calm [kɑm] *s.* calma; sosiego; *adj.* calmo, tranquilo, quieto, sosegado; *v.* calmar, sosegar, tranquilizar; **to** – **down** calmarse; **-ly** *adv.* tranquilamente, con calma.

calm·ness [kómnɪs] *s.* calma, sosiego, tranquilidad.

cal·o·rie [kǽlərɪ] *s.* caloría.

ca·lum·ny [kǽləmɪ] *s.* calumnia.

came [kem] *pret. de* **to come.**

cam·el [kǽm l] *s.* camello.

cam·e·o [kǽmɪo] *s.* camafeo.

cam·er·a [kǽmərə] *s.* cámara fotográfica.

cam·ou·flage [kǽməflɑʒ] *s.* camuflaje; disfrazar; *v.* encubrir, disfrazar.

camp [kæmp] *s.* campo; campamento; – **chair** silla de tijera; **political** – partido político; *v.* acampar.

cam·paign [kæmpén] *s.* campaña; *v.* hacer campaña; hacer propaganda.

cam·phor [kǽmfə-] *s.* alcanfor.

cam·pus [kǽmpəs] *s.* campo (*de una universidad*).

can [kæn] *s.* lata, bote, envase; – **opener** abrelatas; *v.* envasar, enlatar; *v. defect. y aux.* (*usado sólo en las formas* **can** *y* **could**) poder, saber.

Ca·na·dian [kənédɪən] *adj. & s.* canadiense.

ca·nal [kənǽl] *s.* canal; **irrigation** – acequia.

ca·nar·y [kənɛ́rɪ] *s.* canario.

can·cel [kǽns l] *s.* cancelar; anular; tachar; revocar.

can·cel·la·tion [kæns éʃən] *s.* cancelación; anulación; revocación.

can·cer [kǽnsə-] *s.* cáncer.

can·did [kǽndɪd] *s.* cándido, franco, sincero.

can·di·da·cy [kǽndədəsɪ] . candidatura.

can·di·da·te [kǽndədet] *s.* candidato; aspirante.

can·dle [kǽnd l] *s.* candela, vela; bujía; cirio; **-power** potencia lumínica (*en bujías*).

can·dle·stick [kǽnd l stɪk] *s.* candelero; palmatoria.

can·dor [kǽndə-] *s.* candor, sinceridad.

can·dy [kǽndɪ] *s.* dulce, confite, bombón; **-shop** confitería, dulcería; *v.* confitar, azucarar; almibarar, garapiñar; cristalizarse (*el almíbar*); **candied almonds** almendras garapiñadas.

cane [ken] *s.* caña; – **plantation** (*o –field*) cañaveral; *C.A.* cañal; – **chair** silla de bejuco; **sugar** – caña de azúcar; **walking** – bastón; **to beat with a** – bastonear, apalear.

ca·nine [kénaɪn] *adj.* canino, perruno.

canned [kænd] *adj.* enlatado, envasado, conservado, (*en lata o en vidrio*); – **goods** conservas alimenticias.

can·ner·y [kǽnərɪ] *s.* fábrica de conservas alimenticias.

can·ni·bal [kǽnəb l] *s.* caníbal.

can·non [kǽnən] *s.* cañón.

can·non·ade [kænənéd] *s.* cañoneo; *v.* cañonear.

can·not [kǽnot] = **can not** no puedo, no puede, no podemos, *etc.*

can·ny [kǽnɪ] *adj.* sagaz; astuto.

ca·noe [kənú] *s.* canoa, *Ríopl.* piragua, *Méx.* chalupa.

can·on [kǽnən] *s.* canón; ley; regla; criterio; norma; canónigo.

can·o·py [kǽnəpɪ] *s.* dosel, pabellón; (*airplane*) capota, cúpula.

can·ta·loup·e [kǽnt op] *s.* melón.

can·teen [kæntín] *s.* cantina; cantimplora.

can·ton [kǽntən] *s.* cantón, región, distrito.

can·vas [kǽnvəs] *s.* lona; lienzo; toldo; cañamazo.

can·vass [kǽnvəs] *s.* inspección; escrutinio; indagación, encuesta, pesquisa; solicitación (*de votos*); *v.* examinar, escudriñar; recorrer (*un distrito solicitando algo*); hacer una encuesta, solicitar votos o pedidos comerciales.

can·yon [kǽnjən] *s.* cañón; garganta.

cap [kæp] *s.* (*head covering*) gorro, gorra, boina; (*bottle, wheel*) tapa, tapón; (*mountain*) cima, cumbre; **percussion** – cápsula fulminante; *v.* tapar, poner tapón a; **that –s the climax** eso es el colmo.

ca·pa·bil·i·ty [kepəbílətɪ] *s.* capacidad, aptitud.

ca·pa·ble [képəb l] *adj.* capaz, hábil, competente.

ca·pa·cious [kəpéʃəs] *adj.* capaz, amplio, espacioso.

ca·pac·i·ty [kəpǽsətɪ] *s.* capacidad; cabida; habilidad; aptitud; **in the – of a teacher** en calidad de maestro.

cape [kep] *s.* capa; capote; cabo, promontorio.

ca·per [képə-] *s.* cabriola; voltereta; brinco; **to cut - s** cabriolar, retozar, hacer travesuras; *v.* cabriolar, retozar, juguetear, brincar.

cap·il·lar·y [kǽpɪlɛrɪ] *s.* & *adj.* capilar.

cap·i·tal [kǽpət] *s.* capital (*f.*), ciudad principal; (*m.*), caudal; chapitel (*de una columna*); letra mayúscula; **to make – of** sacar partido de, aprovecharse de; *adj.* capital; principal; excelente; **– punishment** pena capital, pena de muerte.

cap·i·tal·ism [kǽpət ɪzəm] *s.* capitalismo.

cap·i·tal·ist [kǽpət ɪst] *s.* capitalista; **-ic** *adj.* capitalista.

cap·i·tal·i·za·tion [kæpət əzéʃən] *s.* capitalización.

cap·i·tal·ize [kǽpət aɪz] *v.* capitalizar; sacar provecho (de); escribir con mayúscula.

cap·i·tol [kǽpət] *s.* capitolio.

ca·pit·u·late [kəpítʃəlet] *v.* capitular.

ca·price [kəprís] *s.* capricho.

ca·pri·cious [kəpríʃəs] *adj.* caprichoso.

cap·size [kǽpsáɪz] *v.* zozobrar, volcar (se).

cap·sule [kǽps] *s.* cápsula.

cap·tain [kǽptɪn] *s.* capitán; *v.* capitanear, mandar; servir de capitán.

cap·ti·vate [kǽptəvet] *v.* cautivar.

cap·tive [kǽptɪv] *s.* & *adj.* cautivo, prisionero.

cap·tiv·i·ty [kæptívətɪ] *s.* cautiverio, prisión.

cap·tor [kǽptə-] *s.* aprehensor o aprensor.

cap·ture [kǽptʃə-] *s.* captura; aprensión; presa; toma; *v.* capturar; aprender; tomar (*una ciudad*).

car [kor] *s.* coche, automóvil, auto, *Am.* carro; vagón (*de ferrocarril*); camarín (*de ascensor*), ascensor, *Am.* elevador; **dining –** coche comedor; **freight –** furgón, vagón de carga.

car·a·mel [kǽrəm] *s.* caramelo.

car·at [kǽrət] *s.* quilate.

car·a·van [kǽrəvæn] *s.* caravana.

car·bol·ic [karbálɪk] *adj.* carbólico.

car·bon [kárbən] *s.* carbono; **– copy** copia en papel carbón; **– paper** papel carbón; **– monóxide** monóxido de carbón; **– dioxide** dióxido de carbono.

car·bu·re·tor [kárbəretə-] *s.* carburador.

car·cass [kárkəs] *s.* esqueleto; cuerpo descarnado; despojo; res (*muerta*); casco (*de un buque*).

card [kord] *s.* (*missive*) tarjeta; (*playing*) naipe, carta; carda (*para cardar lana*); **– index** índice de fichas; fichero; **– sharp** fullero; **file –** ficha, papeleta; **post – tarjeta postal; pack of -s** baraja, naipes; **to play -s** jugar a la baraja, jugar a los naipes; *v.* cardar (*lana*).

card·board [kordbord] *s.* cartón; **fine –** cartulina.

car·di·ac [kárdɪæk] *adj.* cardiaco, cardíaco.

car·di·nal [kord əl] *adj.* cardinal; principal, fundamental; rojo, bermellón; **– number** número cardinal; *s.* cardenal (*dignatario eclesiástico*); **– bird** cardenal.

care [kɛr] *s.* (*worry*) cuidado; aflección; ansiedad; (*caution*) cuidado, cautela, esmero; (*responsibility*) cargo, custodia; **to take – of** cuidad de; *v.* tener interés (por); **to – about** tener interés en (*o* por); preocuparse de; importarle a uno; **to – for** cuidar de; estimar, tenerle cariño a; gustarle a uno; simpatizarle a uno (*una persona*); **to – to** querer, desear, tener ganas de; **what does he – ?** ¿a él qué le importa?

ca·reer [kərír] *s.* carrera, profesión.

care·free [kɛrfri] *adj.* libre de cuidado, sin cuidado, despreocupado.

care·ful [kɛrfəl] *adj.* cuidadoso; esmerado; cauteloso; **to be –** tener cuidado; **-ly** *adv.* cuidadosamente, con cuidado; con esmero.

care·ful·ness [kɛrfəlnɪs] *s.* cuidado; esmero; cautela.

care·less [kɛrlɪs] *adj.* descuidado; negligente; indiferente; **-ly** *adv.* sin cuidado, sin esmero; descuidadamente.

care·less·ness [kɛrlɪsnɪs] *s.* descuido; falta de esmero; desaliño; negligencia.

ca·ress [kərés] *s.* caricia; *v.* acariciar.

care·tak·er [kɛrtekə-] *s.* cuidador, guardián, vigilante, celador.

car·fare [kárfɛr] *s.* pasaje de tranvía.

car·go [kárgo] *s.* carga, cargamento; flete.

car·i·ca·ture [kǽrɪkətʃə-] *s.* caricatura; *v.* caricaturar o caricaturizar.

car·load [kárlod] *s.* furgonada; vagonada, carga de un furgón o vagón.

car·nal [kárn] *adj.* carnal.

car·na·tion [karnéʃən] *s.* clavel; color encarnado o rosado.

car·ni·val [kárnəv] *s.* carnaval; fiesta, holgorio; feria, verbena.

car·niv·o·rous [karnívərəs] *adj.* carnívoro, carnicero.

car·ol [kǽr əl] *s.* villancico; **Christmas –** villancico de Navidad; *v.* cantar villancicos; celebrar con villancicos.

car·om [kǽrəm] *s.* carambola; rebote.

ca•rouse [kəráUz] *v.* andar de parranda, *Ríopl., Ch.* andar de farra; embriagarse.

car•pen•ter [kárpəntə] *s.* carpintero.

car•pen•try [kárpəntrɪ] *s.* carpintería.

car•pet [kórpɪt] *s.* alfombra; **small** – tapete.

car•riage [kǽrɪdʒ] *s.* carruaje, coche; acarreo, transporte; porte; – **paid** porte pagado; **good**- buen porte, garbo, manera airosa.

car•ri•er [kǽrɪə-] *s.* portador; mensajero; carretero; trajinante; transportador; *Am.* cargador; **airplane** – portaaviones; **disease** – transmisor de gérmenes contagiosos; **mail** – cartero.

car•rot [kǽrət] *s.* zanahoria.

car•ry [kǽrɪ] *v.* llevar; acarrear, transportar; *Am.* cargar; sostener (*una carga*); traer consigo; ganar, lograr (*una elección, un premio, etc.*); **to – away** llevarse; cargar con; entusiasmar, encantar; **to – on** continuar; no parar; **to – oneself well** andar derecho, airoso, garboso; **to – out** llevar a cabo, realizar; sacar.

cart [kɑrt] *s.* carro, carreta, vagoncillo; *v.* acarrear.

cart•age [kártɪdʒ] *s.* carretaje, acarreo.

cart•er [kártə-] *s.* carretero; acarreador.

car•ton [kárt ɳ] *s.* caja de cartón.

car•toon [kɑrtún] *s.* caricatura.

car•toon•ist [kɑrtúnɪst] *s.* caricaturista.

car•tridge [kártrɪdʒ] *s.* cartucho; – **belt** cartuchera, canana; – **box** cartuchera – **shell** cápsula.

carve [kɑrv] *v.* tallar; labrar; cincelar; esculpir; trinchar, tajar (*carne*).

carver [kárvə-] *s.* trinchador; trinchante (*cuchillo*); entallador, escultor.

carv•ing [kárvɪŋ] *s.* talla, obra de escultura, entalladura; – **knife** trinchante.

cas•cade [kæskéd] *s.* cascada, salto de agua.

case [kes] *s.* (*instance*) caso; (*box*) caja; (*pillow*) funda, cubierta; (*scabbard*) vaina; **window** – marco de ventana; **in – that** caso que, en caso de que, dado que; **in any** – en todo caso; **just in** – por si acaso; – **work** trabajo con casos.

case•ment [késmənt] *s.* puertaventana.

cash [kæʃ] *s.* dinero contante; – **box** cofre; – **payment** pago al contado; – **on delivery (c.o.d.)** contra reembolso, cóbrese al entregar; – **register** caja registradora (*de dinero*); **to pay** – pagar al contado; *v.* cambiar, cobrar (*un cheque*).

cash•ew [kǽʃju] *s.* anacardo.

cash•ier [kæʃír] *s.* cajero.

cask [kæsk] *s.* tonel, barril, cuba.

cas•ket [kǽ skɪt] *s.* ataúd; **jewel** – joyero, cofrecillo.

cas•se•role [kǽsərol] *s.* cacerola.

cas•sock [kǽ sək] *s.* sotana.

cast [kæst] *s.* tirada (*al pescar*), molde; matiz; apariencia; defecto (*del ojo*); reparto (*de papeles dramáticos*); actores; – **iron** hierro fundido o colado; *v.* echar; tirar; arrojar; lanzar; moldear; repartir (*papeles dramáticos*); escoger (*para un papel dramático*); **to – a ballot** votar; **to – a statue in bronze** vaciar una estatua en bronce; **to – about** buscar; hacer planes; **to – aside** desechar, **to – lots** echar suertes; **to be – down** estar abatido; *pret. & p.p. de* **to cast.**

cas•ta•nets [kæ stənɛts] *s. pl.* castañuelas.

caste [kæst] *s.* casta; **to lose** – perder el prestigio social.

Cas•til•ian [kæstíljən] *s. & adj.* castellano.

cas•tle [kǽs ⌡] *s.* castillo; alcázar; fortaleza; torre, roque (*en ajedrez*).

cas•tor oil [kǽ stə- oil] *s.* aceite de ricino.

cas•trate [kǽstret] *v.* capar, castrar.

ca•su•al [kǽʒUəl] *adj.* casual; accidental.

ca•su•al•ty [kǽʒUəltɪ] *s.* baja o pérdida (*en el ejército*); accidente.

cat [kæt] *s.* gato; gata.

cat•a•log•ue [kǽt ɔg] *s.* catálogo, *v.* catalogar.

cat•a•ract [kǽtərækt] *s.* catarata.

ca•tarrh [kətár] *s.* catarro.

ca•tas•tro•phe [kətǽstrəfɪ] *s.* catástrofe.

catch [kætʃ] *s.* presa; botín; pesca; pestillo (*de la puerta*); trampa; cogida (*de la pelota*); – **phrase** frase llamativa; – **question** pregunta tramposa; **he is a good** – es un buen partido; **to play** – jugar a la pelota; *v.* coger; prender, asir; alcanzar; enganchar; comprender; ser contagioso, pegarse; **to – a glimpse of** vislumbrar; **to – cold** coger un resfriado, resfriarse; **to – on** comprender, caer en la cuenta; **to – one's eye** llamarle a uno la atención; **to – sight of** avistar; **to – unaware** sorprender, coger desprevenido; **to – up with** alcanzar a, emparejarse con.

catch•er [kǽtʃə-] *s.* cogedor, agarrador; parador; cácher o receptor (*en béisbol*).

catch•ing [kǽtʃɪŋ] *adj.* pegajoso, contagioso; atractivo.

cat•e•chism [kǽtəkɪzəm] *s.* catecismo.

cat•e•go•ry [kǽtəgorɪ] *s.* categoría.

ca•ter [kétə-] *v.* surtir, *v.* abastecer, proveer los alimentos (*para banquetes, fiestas, etc.*); **to – to** proveer a las necesidades o al gusto de; **to – to the taste of** halagar el gusto de.

cat•er•pil•lar [kǽ təpɪlə-] *s.* oruga, – **tractor** tractor.

ca•the•dral [kəθídrəl] *s.* catedral.

cath•ode [kǽθod] *s.* cátodo; – **rays** rayos catódicos.

Cath•o•lic [kǽθəlɪk] *s. & adj.* católico.

Cath•o•lic•ism [kəθálɪsɪzəm] *s.* catolicismo.

cat•sup [kǽtsəp] *s.* salsa de tomate.

cat·tle [kǽtl] s. ganado, ganado vacuno; **– raiser** ganadero, *Ríopl.*, estanciero; **raising** ganadería; **– ranch** hacienda de ganado, *Méx.*, *C.A.* rancho, *Ríopl.*, estancia; *Ven.*, *Col.*, hato.

caught [kɔt] *prep. & p.p. de* **to catch.**

cau·li·flow·er [kɔ́ləflauɚ] s. coliflor.

cause [kɔz] s. causa; *v.* causar; originar; **to –** to hacer; inducir a.

cau·tion [kɔ́ʃən] s. precaución, cautela; aviso, advertencia; **– !** ¡cuidado! ¡atención!; *v.* prevenir, avisar, advertir.

cau·tious [kɔ́ʃəs] *adj.* cauto, cauteloso, cuidadoso; precavido.

cav·a·lier [kævəlír] s. caballero; galán; *adj.* orgulloso, altivo, desdeñoso.

cav·al·ry [kǽvlrɪ] s. caballería.

cave [kev] s. cueva; caverna; *v.* **to – in** hundirse; desplomarse.

cav·ern [kǽvɚn] s. caverna.

cav·i·ty [kǽvətɪ] s. cavidad, hueco; (*tooth*) carie.

caw [kɔ] s. graznido; *v.* graznar.

cease [sis] *v.* cesar; parar, desistir; dejar de

cease·less [síslɪs] *adj.* incesante.

ce·dar [sídɚ] s. cedro.

cede [sid] *v.* ceder.

ceil·ing [sílɪŋ] s. techo (*interior*); cielo máximo (*en aviación*); altura máxima (*en aviación*); **– price** precio máximo.

cel·e·brate [sɛ́ləbret] *v.* celebrar.

cel·e·brat·ed [sɛ́ləbrétɪd] *adj.* célebre, renombrado.

cel·e·bra·tion [sɛləbréʃən] s. celebración; fiesta.

ce·leb·ri·ty [səlɛ́brɪtɪ] s. celebridad; renombre.

cel·er·y [sɛ́lɚ ɪ] s. apio.

ce·les·tial [səlɛ́stʃəl] *adj.* celestial; celeste.

cell [sɛl] s. celda; célula; pila eléctrica.

cel·lar [sɛ́lɚ] s. bodega, sótano.

cel·lu·loid [sɛ́ljəlɔɪd] s. celuloide.

ce·ment [səmɛ́nt] s. cemento; **reinforced –** cemento armado; *v.* unir, cementar, pegar con cemento; cubrir con cemento.

cem·e·ter·y [sɛ́mɛtɛrɪ] s. cementerio.

cen·sor [sɛ́nsɚ] s. censor; censurador, crítico; *v.* censurar (*cartas, periódicos, etc.*).

cen·sor·ship [sɛ́nsɚʃɪp] s. censura.

cen·su·re [sɛ́nʃɚ] s. censura, crítica, reprobación; *v.* censurar, criticar, reprobar.

cen·sus [sɛ́nsəs] s. censo.

cent [sɛnt] s. centavo (*de peso o dólar*); **per –** por ciento.

cen·ten·ni·al [sɛntɛ́nɪəl] *adj. & s.* centenario.

cen·ter [sɛ́ntɚ] s. centro; *v.* centrar; colocar en centro; concentrar (se).

cen·ti·grade [sɛ́ntəgred] *adj.* centígrado.

cen·ti·pede [sɛ́ntəpɪd] s. ciempiés, cientopiés.

cen·tral [sɛ́ntrəl] *adj.* central; céntrico; *s.* (la) central de teléfonos.

cen·tral·ize [sɛ́ntrəlaɪz] *v.* centralizar.

cen·trif·u·gal [sɛntrífjUgl] *adj.* centrífugo.

cen·trip·e·tal [sɛntrípɛtl] *adj.* centrípeto.

cen·tu·ry [sɛ́ntʃɚɪ] s. siglo.

ce·ram·ic [sɚǽmɪk] *adj.* cerámico; **ceramics** s. cerámica.

ce·re·al [sírɪəl] *adj.* cereal; *s.* grano.

cer·e·mo·ni·al [sɛrəmónɪəl] *adj.* ceremonial; *s.* ceremonial; rito.

cer·e·mo·ni·ous [sɛrəmónɪəs] *adj.* ceremonioso.

cer·e·mo·ny [sɛ́rəmonɪ] s. ceremonia; ceremonial.

cer·tain [sɝ́tn̩] *adj.* cierto, seguro; **-ly** *adv.* ciertamente; por cierto; de cierto; seguramente; de seguro.

cer·tain·ty [sɝ́tn̩tɪ] s. certeza; certidumbre; seguridad.

cer·tif·i·cate [sɚtífəkɪt] s. certificado; documento; testimonio; **– of stock** bono, obligación; **birth –** partida de nacimiento; **death –** partida (*o* certificado) de defunción.

cer·tif·i·ca·tion [sɚtɪfɪkéʃən] s. certificación.

cer·ti·fy [sɝ́təfaɪ] *v.* certificar; dar fe, atestiguar.

ces·sa·tion [sɛséʃən] s. suspensión, paro.

cess·pool [sɛ́spul] s. cloaca, rezumadero.

chafe [tʃef] s. rozadura; irritación, molestia; *v.* rozar (se); frotar; irritar (se).

chaff [tʃæf] s. hollejo, cáscara; *v.* embromar, bromear.

cha·grin [ʃəgrín] s. mortificación, desazón, pesar; **-ed** *p.p.* mortificado, afligido.

chain [tʃen] s. cadena; **– of mountains** cordillera; **– store** tienda sucursal (*un entre muchas de una misma empresa*); **– reaction** reacción de cadena; reacción eslabonada; *v.* encadenar.

chair [tʃer] s. silla; cátedra; presidencia; **arm –** sillón (de brazos); **easy –** butaca, poltrona; **folding –** silla de tijera; **rocking –** mecedora.

chair·man [tʃérmən] s. presidente (*de una junta*).

chair·man·ship [tʃérmənʃɪp] s. presidencia (*de una junta*).

chal·ice [tʃǽlɪs] s. cáliz (*vaso sagrado*).

chalk [tʃɔk] s. tiza, yeso; greda; *v.* enyesar; marcar con una tiza o yeso; **to – down** apuntar con tiza o yeso (*en el pizarrón*); **to – out** bosquejar, esbozar con tiza.

chalk·y [tʃɔ́kɪ] *adj.* yesoso; blanco.

chal·lenge [tʃǽlɪndʒ] s. desafío; reto; demanda; *v.* desafiar, retar; disputar; poner a prueba; dar el quienvive.

cham·ber [tʃémbɚ] s. cámara; aposento; **– of commerce** cámara de comercio.

cham·ber·maid [tʃémbə·med] *s.* camarera, sirvienta.

cham·ois [ʃǽmɪ] *s.* gamuza.

cham·pi·on [tʃǽmpɪən] *s.* campeón; defensor, *v.* defender.

cham·pi·on·ship [tʃǽmpɪənʃɪp] *s.* campeonato.

chance [tʃæns] *s.* (*opportunity*) oportunidad, ocasión; (*possibility*) posibilidad, probabilidad; (*fortune*) suerte, fortuna; casualidad, azar; (*risk*) riesgo; billete de rifa o lotería; **by** – por casualidad; **game of** – juego de azar; **to run a** – correr riesgo; *adj.* casual, accidental, *v.* arriesgar; **to** – **to** acertar a, hacer (*algo*) por casualidad.

chan·cel·lor [tʃǽnsələ·] *s.* canciller; primer ministro; magistrado, rector de universidad.

chan·de·lier [ʃænd | ír] *s.* araña de luces, *Am.* candil.

change [tʃendʒ] *s.* (*money*) cambio; vuelta, *Am.* vuelto; suelto; *Méx.*, feria; (*fresh clothes*) muda de ropa; (*switch*) mudanza; **the** – **of life** la menopausia; *v.* cambiar; mudar; alterar; **to** – **clothes** mudar de ropa; **to** – **trains** transbordar(se), cambiar de tren.

change·a·ble [tʃédʒəb |] *adj.* mudable, variable; inconstante; – **silk** seda tornasolada.

chan·nel [tʃǽn |] *s.* canal; cauce.

chant [tʃænt] *s.* canto llano o gregoriano; sonsonete; *v.* cantar (*psalmos, himnos, etc.*).

cha·os [kéɑs] *s.* caos; desorden.

cha·ot·ic [keɑ́tɪk] *adj.* caótico.

chap [tʃæp] *s.* grieta, raja, rajadura (*en la piel*); chico; **what a fine – he is!** !qué buen tipo (*o* sujeto) es!; *v.* agrietarse, rajarse (*la piel*).

chap·el [tʃǽp |] *s.* capilla.

chap·er·on (e) [ʃǽpərɑn] *s.* acompañante, persona de respeto; **to go along as a** – *Am.* ir de moscón; *v.* acompañar, servir de acompañante.

chap·lain [tʃǽplɪn] *s.* capellán; **army** - capellán castrense.

chap·ter [tʃǽptə·] *s.* capítulo; cabildo (*de una catedral*).

char [tʃɑr] *v.* requemar, carbonizar.

char·ac·ter [kǽrɪktə·] *s.* carácter; personaje.

char·ac·ter·is·tic [kærɪktərístɪk] *adj.* característico; típico; *s.* característica, rasgo característico; distintivo; peculiaridad.

char·ac·ter·ize [kǽrɪktəraɪz] *v.* caracterizar.

char·coal [tʃɑ́rkol] *s.* carbón; carboncillo (*para dibujar*); – **drawing** dibujo al carbón.

charge [tʃɑrdʒ] *s.* (*custody*) cargo; custodia; cuidado; (*order*) mandato, encargo; (*accusation*) cargo, acusación; (*load*) carga; peso; (*cost*) precio, coste; (*attack*) embestida, asalto, ataque; – **account** cuenta abierta; – **prepaid** porte pagado; **under my** – a mi cargo; **to be in** – **of** estar encargado de; *v.* cargar; cargar en cuenta; cobrar (*precio*); mandar; exhortar; atacar, embestir, asaltar; **to** – **with murder** acusar de homicidio.

charg·er [tʃɑ́rdʒ] *s.* cargador (*de batería*); caballo de guerra; corcel.

char·i·ot [tʃǽrɪət] *s.* carroza; carruaje.

char·i·ta·ble [tʃǽrətəb |] *s.* caritativo.

char·i·ty [tʃǽrətɪ] *s.* caridad; limosna; beneficencia.

char·la·tan [ʃóelət ŋ] *s.* charlatán; farsante.

charm [tʃɑrm] *s.* encanto; atractivo; hechizo; talismán; **watch** – dije; *v.* encantar; cautivar; hechizar.

charm·ing [tʃɑ́mɪŋ] *adj.* encantador, atractivo.

chart [tʃɑrt] *s.* carta (*hidrográfica o de navegar*); mapa; gráfica, representación gráfica; *v.* cartografiar, delinear mapas o cartas; **to** – **a course** trazar o planear una ruta o derrotero.

char·ter [tʃɑ́rtə·] *s.* carta constitucional, constitución, código; título; carta de privilegio; – **member** socio fundador; *v.* fletar (*un barco*); alquilar (*un ómnibus*).

chase [tʃes] *s.* caza; persecución; *v.* cazar; perseguir; **to** – **away** ahuyentar.

chasm [kǽzəm] *s.* abismo; vacío.

chaste [tʃest] *adj.* casto; honesto; puro.

chas·tise [tʃæstáɪz] *v.* castigar.

chas·tise·ment [tʃǽstaɪzmənt] *s.* castigo, escarmiento.

chas·ti·ty [tʃǽstətɪ] *s.* castidad; honestidad; pureza.

chat [tʃæt] *s.* charla. plática; *v.* charlar; platicar.

chat·tels [tʃǽt | z] *s. pl.* enseres, bienes muebles.

chat·ter [tʃǽtə·] *s.* charla, parloteo; castañeo (*de los dientes*); chirrido (*de aves*); *v.* charlar, parlotear, cotorrear; castañear (*los dientes*).

chauf·feur [ʃófə·] *s.* chofer, cochero de automóvil.

cheap [tʃip] *adj.* barato; cursi, de mal gusto; **to feel** – sentir vergüenza; **-ly** *adv.* barato, a poco precio.

cheap·en [tʃípən] *v.* abaratar.

cheap·ness [tʃípnɪs] *s.* baratura; cursilería.

cheat [tʃit] *s.* fraude, engaño; trampa; trampista, tramposo; estafador; embaucador; *v.* engañar; trampear; embaucar; estafar.

check [tʃek] *s.* cheque (*de banco*); talón, marbete, contraseña (*de equipaje, etc.*); marca; señal; cuenta (*de restaurante*); restricción, represión; cuadro (*de un tejido o tela*); comprobación; jaque (*en ajedrez*); – **room** vestuario; – **point** punto de inspección; depósito de equipajes, *C.A.*, *Ven.*, consigna; *v.* refrenar, reprimir, restringir; facturar, depositar (*equipajes*); inspeccionar; confrontar, comprobar; marcar (*con una señal*); dar jaque (*en ajedrez*); **to** – **out of a hotel** desocupar el cuarto o alojamiento de un hotel.

check·book [tʃékbʊk] s. libreta de cheques; libro talonario.

check·er [tʃékə·] s. cuadro; casilla (de un tablero de ajedrez, etc.); pieza (del juego de damas); comprobador; inspector; **-s** juego de damas; **– board** tablero; v. cuadricular, marcar con cuadritos; **-ed career** vida azarosa, vida llena de variedad; **-ed cloth** paño o tela de cuadros.

cheek [tʃik] s. mejilla; carrillo; cachete; descaro, desfachatez; **fat –** mejilla gorda, moflete; **– bone** pómulo.

cheer [tʃɪr] s. alegría; bien ánimo, jovialidad; consuelo; **-s** aplausos, vivas; v. alegrar, alentar, animar; aplaudir, vitorear; **to – up** alentar, dar ánimo; cobrar ánimo, animarse.

cheer·ful [tʃírfəl] adj. animado, alegre, jovial; **-ly** adv. alegremente, con alegría, con júbilo; de buena gana, de buen grado.

cheer·fu·lness [tʃírfənɪs] s. jovialidad, alegría; buen humor.

cheer·i·ly [tʃírəlɪ] = **cheerfully**.

cheer·less [tʃírlɪs] adj. abatido, desalentado, desanimado; triste, sombrío.

cheer·y [tʃírɪ] = **cheerful**.

cheese [tʃiz] s. queso; **cottage –** requesón.

chem·i·cal [kémɪk] adj. químico; s. producto químico.

chem·ist [kémɪst] s. químico.

chem·is·try [kémɪstrɪ] s. química.

cher·ish [tʃérɪʃ] v. acariciar, abrigar (una esperanza, un ideal, etc.); apreciar.

cher·ry [tʃérɪ] s. cereza; **– tree** cerezo.

chess [tʃɛs] s. ajedrez; **– board** tablero de ajedrez.

chest [tʃɛst] s. cofre, arca; caja; pecho; **– of drawers** cómoda.

chest·nut [tʃésnət] s. castaña; **– tree** castaño; adj. castaño; **– horse** caballo zaino.

chew [tʃu] s. mascada, mordisco, bocado; v. mascar, masticar.

chew·ing gum [tʃúɪŋ gʃm] s. goma de mascar; Am. chicle.

chick [tʃɪk] s. polluelo, pollito; pajarito; **chick-pea** garbanzo.

chick·en [tʃíkɪn] s. pollo; polluelo; **– pox** viruelas locas; **chicken-hearted** cobarde, gallina.

chic·o·ry [tʃíkərɪ] s. achicoria.

chide [tʃaɪd] v. regañar, reprender, reprobar.

chief [tʃif] s. jefe, caudillo; cacique (de una tribu); **commander in –** comandante en jefe, adj. principal; **– clerk** oficial mayor; **– justice** presidente de la corte suprema; **-ly** adv. principalmente, mayormente; sobre todo.

chif·fon [ʃɪfán] s. gasa.

chil·blain [tʃílble] s. sabañón.

child [tʃaɪld] s. niño, niña; hijo, hija; **-'s play** cosa de niños; **to be with –** estar encinta.

child·birth [tʃáɪldbɝθ] s. parto, alumbramiento.

child·hood [tʃáɪldhʊd] s. niñez, infancia.

child·ish [tʃáɪldɪʃ] adj. pueril; infantil; **– action** niñería, niñada.

child·less [tʃáɪldlɪs] adj. sin hijos.

child·like [tʃáɪldlaɪk] adj. como niño, aniñado, pueril.

chil·dren [tʃíldrən] pl. de **child**.

Chi·lean [tʃílɪən] adj. & s. chileno.

chil·i [tʃɪlɪ] s. Méx., C.A. chile, Carib., S.A. ají.

chill [tʃɪl] s. frío, resfrío; enfriamiento; escalofrío; calofrío; **-s and fever** escalofríos; adj. frío; v. resfriar(se); enfriar (se); **to come -ed** resfriarse, escalofriarse.

chill·y [tʃɪlɪ] adj. frío; friolento.

chime [tʃaɪm] s. repique, campaneo; **-s** órgano de campanas; juego de campanas; v. repicar, campanear, tocar, sonar, tañer (las campanas); **to – with** estar en armonía con.

chim·ney [tʃímnɪ] s. chimenea, **lamp –** tubo de lámpara, Am. bombilla.

chin [tʃɪn] s. barba.

chi·na [tʃáɪnə] s. loza de china, porcelana, loza fina; vajilla de porcelana; **– closet** chinero.

chi·na·ware [tʃáɪnəwɛr] = **china**.

Chi·nese [tʃaɪníz] adj. chino; s. chino; idioma chino.

chink [tʃɪŋk] s. grieta, hendidura.

chip [tʃɪp] s. astilla; brizna; fragmento; desconchadura; desportilladura; ficha (de pócar); v. astillar, desconchar (se); descascarar (se); desportillar (se); picar, tajar (con cincel o hacha); **to – in** contribuir con su cuota.

chip·munk [tʃípmʌŋk] s. especie de ardilla.

chirp [tʃɝp] s. chirrido; pío; gorjeo; v. chirriar; piar; pipiar; gorjear.

chis·el [tʃíz] s. cincel; v. cincelar; sisar, estafar.

chiv·al·rous [ʃv rəs] adj. caballeresco, caballeroso, galante, cortés.

chiv·al·ry [ʃív rɪ] s. caballería; caballerosidad.

chlo·rine [klóríin] s. cloro.

chlo·ro·form [klórəfɔrm] s. cloroformo.

choc·o·late [tʃ ɔ klɪt] s. chocolate; **– pot** chocolatera.

choice [tʃɔɪs] s. selección; preferencia; escogimiento; cosa elegida; favorito, preferido; alternativa; **to have no other –** no tener otra alternativa; adj. selecto; bien escogido; excelente.

choir [kwaɪr] s. coro.

choke [tʃok] s. sofoco, ahogo; tos ahogada; estrangulación; estrangulador, obturador (de automóvil); v. sofocar (se), ahogar (se); estrangular (se); obstruir, tapar; regularizar (el motor).

chol·er·a [kólərə] s. cólera (m.).

cho·les·ter·ol [kəléstə·ol] s. colesterol.

choose [tʃuz] v. escoger; elegir, seleccionar; **to – to** optar por; preferir; **I do not – to do it** no se me antoja (*o* no es mi gusto) hacerlo.

chop [tʃɑp] s. chuleta, costilla, tajada (*de carne*); **-s** quijadas (*usualmente de animal*); v. tajar, cortar; picar, desmenuzar (*carne*).

chop·py [tʃɑpɪ] adj. picado, agitado.

cho·ral [kórəl] adj. coral.

chord [kɔrd] s. cuerda; acorde.

chore [tʃor] s. tarea; quehacer.

cho·re·og·ra·phy [korɪɑgrəfɪ] s. coreografía.

cho·rus [kórəs] s. coro; v. cantar o hablar en coro; contestar a una voz.

chose [tʃoz] prep. de **to choose.**

cho·sen [tʃózņ] p.p. de **to choose.**

chris·ten [krɪ́sņ] v. bautizar.

chris·ten·ing [krɪ́sənɪŋ] s. bautizo, bautismo.

Chris·tian [krɪ́stʃən] s. & adj. cristiano; **– name** nombre de pila o bautismo.

Chris·ti·an·i·ty [k   rɪ́stʃɪǽnətɪ] s. cristiandad, cristianismo.

Christ·mas [krɪ́sməs] s. Navidad, Pascua de Navidad; **– Eve** Nochebuena; **– gift** regalo de Navidad; aguinaldo; **Merry – !** ¡Felices Navidades! ¡Felices Pascuas!

chrome [krom] s. cromo; adj. cromado.

chro·mi·um [krómɪəm] s. cromo.

chro·mo·some [króməsom] s. cromosoma.

chron·ic [krɑ́tk] adj. crónico.

chron·i·cle [krɑ́nɪk] s. crónica; v. relatar; escribir la crónica de.

chron·i·cler [krɑ́nɪklə] s. cronista.

chron·o·log·i·cal [krɑnəlɑ́dʒɪk] adj. cronológico.

chro·nom·e·ter [krənɑ́mətə] s. cronómetro.

chry·san·the·mum   [krɪsǽnθəməm] s. crisantema, crisantemo.

chub·by [tʃʌ́kɪ] adj. rechoncho; gordiflón.

chuck [tʃʌk] s. mamola, golpecito, caricia (*debajo de la barba*); v. echar, tirar (*lo que no sirve*); **to – under the chin** hacer la mamola.

chuck·le [tʃʌ́kɪ] s. risita; v. reír entre dientes.

chum [tʃʌm] s. compañero, camarada, compinche.

chunk [tʃʌŋk] s. trozo; zoquete.

church [tʃɜ́tɪ] s. iglesia.

church·man [tʃɜ́tʃmən] s. clérigo, eclesiástico, sacerdote.

church·yard [tʃɜ́tʃjɑrd] s. patio de iglesia, camposanto, cementerio.

churn [tʃɜ́n] s. mantequera (*para hacer manteca*); v. batir (*en una mantequera*); agitar, revolver.

ci·der [sáɪdə] s. sidra.

ci·gar [sɪgár] s. cigarro, puro; **– store** tabaquería, estanquillo

cig·a·ret·te [sɪgərét] s. cigarrillo, pitillo, *Méx., C.A., Ven., Col.,* cigarro; **– case** cigarrera, pitillera; **– holder** boquilla **– lighter** encendedor.

cinch [sɪntʃ] s. cincha; ganga, cosa fácil; v. cinchar; apretar.

cin·der [síndə] s. ceniza; carbón, brasa, ascua; cisco; **-s** cenizas; rescoldo.

cin·na·mon [sínəmən] s. canela; **– tree** canelo.

ci·pher [sáɪfə] s. cifra; número; cero.

cir·cle [sɝk] s. círculo; cerco, rueda; v. cercar, circundar; circular, dar vueltas.

cir·cuit [sɝkɪt] s. circuito, rodeo, vuelta.

cir·cu·lar [sɝkjələ] adj. circular; redondo; s. circular; hoja volante.

cir·cu·late [sɝkjəlet] v. circular; poner en circulación.

cir·cu·la·tion [sɝkjəléʃən] s. circulación.

cir·cum·fer·ence [sɚk ʌ́mfərəns] s. circunferencia.

cir·cum·flex [səkəmfleks] adj. circunflejo.

cir·cum·lo·cu·tion [sɝkəmlokjúʃən] s. circunlocución, rodeo.

cir·cum·scribe [sɝkəmskráɪb] v. circunscribir, limitar.

cir·cum·spect [sɝkəmspɛkt] adj. circunspecto; prudente.

cir·cum·spec·tion [sɝkəmspékʃən] s. circunspección, miramiento, prudencia.

cir·cum·stance [sɝkəmstæns] s. circunstancia; incidente; ceremonia, pompa.

cir·cus [sɝkəs] s. circo.

cir·rho·sis [sɪrósɪs] s. cirrosis.

cis·tern [sístən] s. cisterna.

cit·a·del [sítəd] s. ciudadela.

ci·ta·tion [sattéʃən] s. citación; cita; mención.

cite [saɪt] v. citar; citar a juicio; mencionar.

cit·i·zen [sítəzņ] s. ciudadano, paisano.

cit·i·zen·ship [sítəz ŋ ʃɪp] s. ciudadanía.

cit·ron [sítrən] s. acitrón.

cit·rus [sítrəs] s. cidro.

cit·y [sítɪ] s. ciudad, población; municipio; adj. municipal; urbano; **– council** ayuntamiento; **– hall** ayuntamiento, casa municipal.

civ·ic [sívɪk] adj. cívico.

civ·ics [sívɪks] s. derecho político.

civ·il [sív] adj. civil; cortés; **– engineer** ingeniero civil; **– rights** derechos civiles; **– disobedience** desobediencia civil.

ci·vil·ian [səvíljən] s. paisano (*persona no militar*).

ci·vil·i·ty [səvílətɪ] s. civilidad; cortesía, urbanidad.

ci•vi•li•za•tion [sɪv ḷəzéʃən] *s.* civilización.

ci•vil•ize [sív ḷaɪz] *s.* civilizar.

ci•vilized [sív ḷaɪzd] *adj.* civilizado.

clad [klæd] *pret. & p.p. de* **to clothe.**

claim [klem] *s.* demanda; reclamación, reclamo; derecho, título; pretensión; **miner's –** denuncia; *v.* reclamar; demandar; pedir, exigir; afirmar, sostener; **to – a mine** denunciar una mina; **to – to be** pretender ser.

claim•ant [klémənt] *s.* reclamante o reclamador; pretendiente (*a un trono*).

clair•voy•ant [klɛrv ɔ́ɪənt] *adj.* clarividente.

clam [klæm] *s.* almeja.

clam•ber [klǽmbə-] *v.* trepar, encaramarse, subir a gatas, subir gateando.

clam•my [klǽmɪ] *adj.* frío y húmedo.

clam•or [klǽmə-] *s.* clamor; clamoreo; gritería, vocería; *v.* clamar; vociferar, gritar.

clam•or•ous [klǽmərəs] *adj.* clamoroso.

clamp [klæmp] *s.* grapa; tornillo de banco; *v.* afianzar, sujetar; pisar recio.

clan [klæn] *s.* clan; tribu.

clan•des•tine [klændéstɪn] *adj.* clandestino.

clang [klæŋ] *s.* tantán, retintín; campanada, campanillazo; –¡–! ¡tan! ¡tan!; *v.* sonar, repicar (*una campana o timbre*); hacer sonar; tocar fuerte.

clap [klæp] *s.* palmada; golpe seco; **– of thunder** trueno; *v.* palmear, palmotear, aplaudir, dar palmadas; cerrar de golpe (*un libro*); dar una palmada *Am.* palmear (*sobre la espalda*); **to – in jail** meter (*o* encajar) en la cárcel.

clap•per [klǽpə-] *s.* dabajo.

clar•i•fy [klǽrəfaɪ] *v.* aclarar.

clar•i•net [klærɛ́t] *s.* clarinete.

clar•i•ty [klǽrətɪ] *s.* claridad, luz.

clash [klæʃ] *s.* choque, encontrón, colisión; riña, conflicto; estruendo; *v.* chocar; darse un encontrón; hacer crujir; oponerse, estar en conflicto.

clasp [klæsp] *s.* (*fastener*) broche; hebilla; cierre; traba; (*grip*) apretón, apretón de manos; *v.* abrochar; asir, agarrar; sujetar; abrazar; apretar (*la mano*).

class [klæs] *s.* clase; *v.* clasificar.

clas•sic [klǽsɪk] *adj. & s.* clásico; **– scholar** humanista, erudito clásico.

clas•si•cal [klǽsɪk ḷ] *adj.* clásico.

clas•si•cism [klǽsɪsɪzm] *s.* clasicismo.

clas•si•fi•ca•tion [klæsəfəkéʃən] *s.* clasificación.

clas•si•fy [klǽsəfaɪ] *v.* clasificar.

class•mate [klǽsmet] *s.* compañero de clase, condiscípulo.

class•room [klǽsrum] *s.* clase, aula.

clat•ter [klǽtə-] *s.* estrépito, boruca; traqueteo; bullicio; alboroto; *v.* hacer estrépito o boruca; traquetear; meter bulla o alboroto.

clause [klɔz] *s.* cláusula.

claw [klɔ] *s.* garra; zarpa; uña; pinza (*de langosta, cangrejo, etc.*); orejas (*de un martillo*); arañazo; *v.* desgarrar; arañar; raspar.

clay [kle] *s.* barro; arcilla, greda.

clean [klin] *adj.* limpio; puro; *adv.* limpiamente; **clean-cut** bien tallado, de buen talle, de buen parecer; *v.* limpiar; asear; **to – up** limpiar(se), asear (se).

clean•er [klínə-] *s.* limpiador; quitamanchas.

clean•li•ness [klénlɪnɪs] *s.* limpieza; aseo.

cleanly [klénlɪ] *adj.* limpio; aseado; [klɪ́nlɪ] *adv.* limpiamente.

clean•ness [klɪ́nnɪs] *adj.* limpieza; aseo.

cleanse [klɛnz] *v.* limpiar; asear; purificar; depurar.

cleans•er [klɛ́nzə-] *s.* limpiador.

clear [klɪr] *adj.* (*evident*) claro; patente, manifiesto; (*clean*) límpido; despejado; libre (*de culpa, estorbos, deudas, etc.*). **– profit** ganancia neta; **clear-cut** *adj.* bien delineado; clarividente; **to pass – through** atravesar; trasdpasar de lado a lado; **to be in the –** estar sin deudas; estar libre de culpa; *v.* aclarar (se); despejar (se); clarificar; quitar (*estorbos*); desmontar (*un terreno*); salvar; saltar por encima de; librar (*de culpa, deudas, etc.*); sacar (*una ganancia neta*); pasar (*un cheque*) por un banco de liquidación; liquidar (*una cuenta*); **to – the table** levantar la mesa; **to – up** aclarar (se).

clear•ance [klírəns] *s.* espacio (*libre entre dos objetos*); despacho de aduanas; **– sale** saldo, venta (*de liquidación*), *Am.* barata.

clear•ing [klɪ́rɪŋ] *s.* aclaramiento; claro, terreno desmontado o desarbolado; liquidación de balances; **– house** banco de liquidación.

clear•ness [klírnɪs] *s.* claridad.

cleav•age [klɪ́v ṿ] *s.* hendidura.

cleave [kliv] *v.* hender (se); tajar; rajar, partir.

cleav•er [klív-ə-] *s.* cuchilla o hacha (*de carnicero*).

clef [klɛt] *s.* clave (*en música*).

cleft [klɛft] *s.* grieta, hendedura; *adj.* hendido, partido, rajado; *pret. & p.p. de* **to cleave.**

clem•en•cy [klɛ́mənsɪ] *s.* clemencia.

clem•ent [klɛ́mənt] *adj.* clemente.

clench [klɛntʃ] *s.* agarro, agarrada, agarrón; apretón; *s.* agarrar, asir; apretar (*los dientes, el puño*).

cler•gy [klɚ́ dʒɪ] *s.* clero.

cler•gy•man [klɚ́ dʒɪmən] *s.* clérigo, eclesiástico, pastor, sacerdote.

cler•i•cal [klérɪk ḷ] *adj.* clerical, eclesiástico; oficinesco, de oficina; de dependientes.

clerk [klɚk] *s.* dependiente; empleado (*de oficina*); escribiente archivero (*de municipio*); **law –** escribano; *v.* estar de dependiente.

clev•er [klévə-] *adj.* diestro, hábil; listo; talentoso; mañoso; **-ly** *adv.* hábilmente; con destreza; con maña.

clev•er•ness [klévə•nɪs] *s.* destreza, habilidad, maña; talento.

clew [klu] *s.* indicio (*que indica un camino para resolver un misterio o problema*).

cli•ché [kliʃé] *s.* (*plate*) clisé; *Am.* cliché; (*phrase*) cliché.

click [klɪk] *s.* golpecito; chasquido (*de la lengua*); gatillazo (*sonido del gatillo de una pistola*); taconeo (*sonido de tacones*); *v.* sonar (*un pestillo, un broche, un gatillo, etc.*); chasquear (*la lengua*); **to – the heels** cuadrarse (*militarmente*); taconear.

cli•ent [klárənt] *s.* cliente.

cli•en•tele [klarəntél] *s.* clientela.

cliff [klɪk] *s.* risco, precipicio, peñasco, escarpa.

cli•mate [kláɪmɪt] *s.* clima.

cli•max [klámæks] *s.* clímax, culminación; *v.* culminar; llegar al clímax.

climb [klaɪm] *s.* subida, ascenso; *v.* subir; trepar; encaramarse; **to – down** bajar a gatas; desprenderse (*de un árbol*).

climb•er [kláɪmbə-] *s.* trepador; enredadera, planta trepadora.

clime [klaɪm] *s.* clima.

clinch [klɪntʃ] *v.* remachar, redoblar (*un clavo*); afianzar, sujetar, asegurar bien; cerrar (*un trato*); abrazarse fuertemente; *s.* remache; abrazo; agarrón; **to be in a –** estar agarrados o abrazados.

cling [klɪŋ] *v.* pegarse, adherirse.

clin•ic [klínɪk] *s.* clínica.

clink [klɪŋk] *s.* tintín.

clip [klɪp] *s.* (*fastener*) broche, presilla; (*cutting*) tijeretada (*corte con tijeras*); trasquila, trasquiladura; **paper –** sujetapapeles; **to go at a good –** ir a paso rápido; andar de prisa; *v.* recortas, cortar; trasquilar (*el pelo o lana de los animales*); **to – together** sujetar.

clip•per [klípə-] *s.* clíper (*velero o avión de gran velocidad*); trasquilador; recortador; **-s** tijeras; maquinilla (*para recortar el pelo*).

clip•ping [klípɪŋ] *s.* recorte.

cloak [klok] *s.* capa; manto; *v.* tapar, embozar, encubrir.

cloak•room [klókrum] *s.* guardarropa, vestuario.

clock [klɑk] *s.* reloj; **alarm –** despertador; *v.* marcar; cronometrar.

clock•wise [klókwaɪz] *adv.* en el sentido de las manecillas del reloj.

clock•work [klókwɜ·k] *s.* maquinaria de reloj; **like –** con precisión, puntualmente; sin dificultad.

clod [klɑd] *s.* terrón; tonto, necio.

clog [klog] *s.* estorbo, obstáculo; zueco (*zapato de suela gruesa o de madera*); **dance** zapateado; *v.* estorbar, embarazar; obstruir, atorar, tapar; obstruirse, atascarse, azolvarse (*Am.* enzolvarse); atorarse

(*un caño, acequia, etc.*).

clois•ter [klɔ́ɪstə-] *s.* claustro; monasterio; convenio; *v.* enclaustrar.

close [kloz] *s.* fin, terminación, conclusión; *v.* cerrar (se); concluir; **to – an account** saldar una cuenta; **to – in upon** cercar, rodear; **to – out** liquidar, vender en liquidación.

close [klos] *adj.* (*near*) cercano, próximo; aproximado; íntimo; (*tight*) estrecho, ajustado; (*stingy*) cerrado; tacaño, mezquino; (*suffocating*) opresivo; sofocante; **– questioning** interrogatorio detallado o minucioso; **– translation** traducción fiel; **at – rage** de cerca; *adv.* cerca; **-ly** *adv.* aproximadamente; estrechamente; apretadamente; con sumo cuidado a atención.

closed cir•cuit [klozd sɜ́·kət] *s. & adj.* circuito cerrado.

close•ness [klósnɪs] *s.* cercanía, proximidad; aproximación; estrechez; intimidad; tacañería, avaricia; mala ventilación, falta de aire; fidelidad (*de una traducción*).

clos•et [klózɪt] *s.* ropero; alacena, armario; gabinete, retrete, excusado; *v.* encerrar en un cuarto (*para una entrevista secreta*); **to – oneself (themselves)** encerrarse.

clot [klɑt] *v.* coagular (se), cuajar (se); *s.* coágulo, cuajarón.

cloth [klɔθ] *s.* tela, paño, género, trapo; *adj.* de paño; **– binding** encuadernación en tela.

clothe [kloð] *v.* vestir; cubrir; revestir; investir.

clothes [kloz] *s. pl.* ropa; ropaje, vestidos; **suit of –** terno, traje, *Carib., Ven.*, flux; **– line** tendedero; **– pin** pinza, gancho (*para tender la ropa*).

cloth•ier [klóðə-] *s.* comerciante en ropa o paño; ropero, pañero.

cloth•ing [klóðɪŋ] *s.* ropa; ropaje, vestidos.

cloud [klaʊd] *s.* nube; **storm –** nubarrón; *v.* nublar (se), anublar (se); obscurecer; manchar.

cloud•burst [kládbə·st] *s.* chaparrón, aguacero.

cloud•less [kláʊdlɪs] *adj.* claro, despejado; sin nubes.

cloud•y [kláʊdɪ] *adj.* nublado; nubloso; sombrío.

clove [klov] *s.* clavo (*especia*); **– of garlic** diente de ajo.

clo•ven [klóvən] *adj.* hendido; *s. & adj.* **– hoof** patihendido, pie hendido.

clo•ver [klóvə-] *s.* trébol; **to be in –** estar o vivir en la abundancia; sentirse próspero.

clo•ver•leaf [klóvə-lif] *s.* (*highway*) cruce en trébol.

clown [klaʊn] *s.* payaso, bufón; *v.* payasear, bufonear, hacer el payaso.

cloy [klɔɪ] *v.* empalagar; hastiar.

club [klʌb] *s.* club, círculo; casino; garrote, porra; palo; basto (*de la baraja*); *v.* golpear, aporrear, apalear; **to – together** formar club; escotar, pagar la cuota que le toca a cada uno; *Am.* cotizar.

club•house [kl ʌ́ bhaUs] club, casino.

cluck [klʌk] *s.* cloqueo; *v.* cloquear.

clue = **clew.**

clump [klʌmp] *s.* terrón; pisada fuerte; **– of bushes** matorral; **– of trees** grupo de árboles, arboleda; *v.* apiñar, amontonar; **to – along** andar pesadamente.

clum•sy [kl ʌ́ mzı] *adj.* torpe, desmañado; incómodo; difícil de manejar; malhecho.

clung [klʌŋ] *pret. & p.p. de* **to cling.**

clus•ter [kl ʌ́ stə-] *s.* racimo; grupo; *v.* agrupar (se); arracimarse *(formar racimo).*

clutch [klʌtʃ] *s.* apretón fuerte; agarro, agarrón; embrague *(de automóvil);* **-es** garras; uñas; **– pedal** palanca del embrague; **to step on the –** pisar el embrague; desembragar; soltar el embrague; **to throw in the –** embragar; *v.* agarrar; asir; apretar.

clut•ter [kl ʌ́ tə-] *v.* obstruir; atestar *(de cosas);* poner en desorden; *s.* desorden, confusión.

coach [kotʃ] *s.* coche; entrenador *(en deportes);* maestro particular; *v.* aleccionar; guiar, adiestrar, *Am.* entrenar; **to – with** ser instruido o entrenado por.

coach•man [kótʃmən] *s.* cochero.

co•ag•u•late [koǽ gjəlet] *v.* coagular (se), cuajar (se).

coal [kol] *s.* carbón; ascua, brasa; **hard –** carbón de piedra, antracita; **soft –** hulla; **– bin** carbonera; **– dealer** carbonero, *–* **oil** kerosina; **– tar** alquitrán de carbón; *v.* cargar de carbón, echar carbón; proveer (se) de carbón

co•a•li•tion [koəlíʃən] *s.* coalición.

coarse [kors] *adj.* *(crude)* burdo, basto; tosco; áspero; *(rude)* rudo; grosero; vulgar; tosco; **– sand** arena gruesa.

coarse•ness [kórsnıs] *s.* tosquedad; vulgaridad, grosería, rudeza.

coast [kost] *s.* costa; litoral; **– guard** guardacostas, guarda de costas; *v.* costear, navegar por la costa; deslizar (se), resbalar (se) cuesta abajo.

coast•al [kóst]] *adj.* costero, costanero, de la costa.

coast•line [kóstlaın] *s.* costa, litoral.

coat [kot] *s.* chaqueta, americana; *Am.* saco; lana, pelo *(de un animal);* **lady's –** abrigo de señora; **– hanger** colgador; **– of arms** escudo de armas; **– of paint** capa de pintura; *v.* cubrir; revestir; dar una mano *(de pintura);* **to – with sugar** azucarar, bañar en azúcar.

coat•ing [kótıŋ] *s.* capa.

coat•tail [kóttel] *s.* faldón.

coax [koks] *v.* rogar o persuadir con halagos;, halagar, tentar.

cob [kab] *s.* carozo, zuro *(de la mazorca de maíz),*

Ven., Col., Carib., tusa, *Méx., C.A.* olote.

co•balt [kóbɔlt] *s.* cobalto.

cob•bler [káblə-] *s.* remendón *(zapatero);* pudín de bizcocho y frutas.

cob•ble•stone [káb] ston] *s.* guijarro; *adj.* empedrado.

cob•web [kábwɛb] *s.* telaraña.

co•caine [kokén] *s.* cocaína.

cock [kak] *s.* gallo; macho de ave; espita, grifo; martillo *(de armas de fuego);* **– sure** muy seguro de sí mismo; *v.* amartillar *(un arma de fuego);* ladear *(la cabeza),* ladearse *(el sombrero).*

cock•fight [kókfaıt] *s.* pelea de gallos, riña de gallos.

cock•pit [kókpıt] *s.* gallera; *(airplane)* cabina.

cock•roach [kákrotʃ] *s.* cucaracha.

cock•tail [káktel] *s.* cóctel; aperitivo *(de ostras, almejas, frutas, etc.).*

cock•y [kákı] *adj.* arrogante, *Am.* retobado.

co•coa [kóko] *s.* cacao; bebida de cacao, chocolate.

co•co•nut [kókənət] *s.* coco *(fruta).*

co•coon [kəkún] *s.* capullo *(del gusano de seda, etc.).*

cod [kád] *s. N.Esp.* abadejo; *Andalucía, Am.* bacalao.
    cod-line oil aceite de hígado de bacalao.

cod•dle [kád]] *v.* mimar, consentir.

code [kod] *s.* código; clave; **– message** comunicación en clave; **signal –** código de señales.

cod•fish [kádfıʃ] = **cod.**

co•erce [ko ɜ́ s] *v.* forzar, obligar.

co•er•cion [ko ɜ́ ʃən] *s.* coacción.

co•ex•is•tence [koɛgzístəns] *s.* coexistencia.

cof•fee [k ɔ́ fı] *s.* café; **– shop** café; **– tree** cafeto; **black –** café solo.

cof•fee•pot [k ɔ́ fıpat] *s.* cafetera.

cof•fer [k ɔ́ fə-] *s.* cofre, arca.

cof•fin [k ɔ́ fın] *s.* ataúd, féretro.

cog [kag] *s.* diente; **– wheel** rueda dentada.

cog•nate [kágnet] *s.* cognato.

co•her•ent [kohírənt] *adj.* coherente; conexo.

co•he•sion [kohíʒən] *s.* cohesión.

coif•fure [kwafʃUr] *s.* tocado, peinado.

coil [koıl] *s.* rollo; rosca; espiral de alambre; **electric –** bobina; *v.* arrollar (se), enrollar (se); enroscar (se).

coin [koın] *s.* moneda; *v.* acuñar; inventar; forjar *(una frase o palabra).*

co•in•age [k ɔ́ ınıdʒ] *s.* acuñación; sistema monetario; moneda, monedas; inversión *(de una palabra o frase).*

co•in•cide [koınsáıd] *v.* coincidir.

co•in•ci•dence [koínsədəns] *s.* coincidencia; casualidad.

coke [kok] *s.* cok, coque *(combustible).*

cold [kold] *adj.* frío; **– cream** crema cosmética; **– meat** fiambre; **– wave** ola de frío; **– war** guerra fría;

to be – tener frío; **it is** – **today** hace frío hoy; *s.* frío; catarro, resfriado; **to catch a** – resfriarse, acatarrarse.

cold·ness [kóldnɪs] *s.* frialdad; indiferencia, despego.

col·ic [kálɪk] *s.* cólico.

col·lab·o·rate [kəl ǽbəret] *v* colaborar.

col·lab·o·ra·tion [kəlæbəréʃən] *s.* colaboración.

col·lapse [kəl ǽps] *s.* desplome, derrumbe, derrumbamiento; hundimiento, postración; *v.* doblar (se), plegar (se); contraer (*el volumen*); hundirse, derrumbarse, desplomarse, sufrir una postración.

col·lar [kálə] *s.* collar; cuello (*de vestido, camisa, etc.*); collera (*para mulas y caballos de tiro*); *v.* acollarar, poner collar a; coger o agarrar por el cuello; prender.

col·late [kəlét, kólet] *v.* cortejar; colacionar.

col·lat·er·al [kəl ǽtərəl] *adj.* colateral; auxiliar, subsidiario, accesorio; *s.* garantía (*para un préstamo bancario*).

col·league [kálig] *s.* colega.

col·lect [kəlékt] *v.* recoger; coleccionar; obrar; recaudar (*impuestos*); reunir (se); congregarse; **to** – **oneself** calmarse; sosegarse, reportarse.

col·lec·tion [kəlékʃən] *s.* colección; agrupación (*de gente*); recolección, cobranza, cobro, recaudación, colecta.

col·lec·tive [kəléktɪv] *adj.* colectivo.

col·lec·tiv·ism [kəléktəvɪzm] *s.* colectivismo.

col·lec·tor [kəlétə] *s.* colector; coleccionista (*de sellos, objetos artísticos, etc.*); cobrador (*de billetes, deudas, etc.*); recaudador (*de impuestos*).

col·lege [kálɪdʒ] *s.* universidad; – **of engineering** facultad de ingeniería; – **of medicine** escuela (*facultad*) de medicina.

col·lide [kəláɪd] *v.* chocar; estar en conflicto, oponerse.

col·lie [kálɪ] *s.* perro de pastor.

col·li·sion [kəlíʒən] *s.* hoque, colisión; oposición, pugna (*de intereses, ideas, etc.*).

col·lo·qui·al [kəlókwɪəl] *adj.* familiar; – **expression** locución o frase familiar.

col·lu·sion [kəlúʒɪən] *s.* confabulación.

co·lon [kólən] *s.* colon (*del intestino*); dos puntos (*signo de puntuación*).

colo·nel [kɝn̩] *s.* coronel.

co·lo·ni·al [kəlónɪəl] *adj.* colonial.

col·o·nist [kálənɪst] *s.* colono, colonizador.

col·o·ni·za·tion [kələnəzéʃən] *s.* colonización.

col·o·nize [kálənaɪz] *v.* colonizar; establecer en colonia.

col·o·ny [kálənɪ] *s.* colonia.

col·or [k ʌ lə] *s.* color; colorido; **the -s** la bandera; *v.* colorar; colorear; dar colorido; pintar; teñir; iluminar (*una fotografía, grabado, etc.*); ruborizarse.

col·ored [k ʌ lə·d] *adj.* colorado, teñido, colorido, pintado; de color; coloreado; – **person** persona de color.

col·or·ful [k ʌ lə·fəl] *adj.* lleno de color; colorido; vistoso; vivido; pintoresco.

col·or·ing [k ʌ ləɪŋ] *s.* colorido; coloración; colorante.

col·or·less [k ʌ lə·lɪs] *adj.* incoloro; descolorido.

co·los·sal [kəlás] *adj.* colosal.

colt [kolt] *s.* potro.

Co·lum·bia [kəl ʌ mbɪən] *adj.* colombiano, de Colombia; colombino, referente a Cristobal Colón.

col·umn [káləm] *s.* columna.

comb [kom] *s.* peine; peineta (*de mujer*); cresta (*de gallo*); rastrillo, carda (*para lana*); almohaza (*para caballos*); panal (*de miel*); *v.* peinar; rastrillar, cardar (*lana*); escudriñar; **to** – **one's hair** peinarse.

com·bat [kámbæt] *s.* combate, pelea; *v.* combatir.

com·bat·ant [kámbətənt] *adj. & s.* combatiente.

com·bi·na·tion [kambənéʃən] *s.* combinación.

com·bine [kəmbáɪn] *v.* combinar (se), unir (se).

com·bo [kámbo] *s.* bateria de jazz.

com·bus·ti·ble [kəmb ʌ stəb] *adj. & s.* combustible.

com·bus·tion [kəmb ʌ stʃən] *s.* combustión.

come [k ʌ m] *v.* venir; llegar; provenir; **to** – **about** suceder; **to** – **again** volver, volver a venir; **to** – **back** volver, regresar; **to** – **downstairs** bajar; **to** – **in** entrar; **to** – **out** salir; **to** – **of age** llegar a mayor edad; **to** – **off** soltarse, zafarse; **to** – **to** volver en sí; **to** – **to terms** ponerse de acuerdo, ajustarse; **to** – **up** subir; surgir (*una cuestión*); *p.p. de* **to come.**

co·me·di·an [kəmídɪən] *s.* cómico, comediante.

com·e·dy [kámədɪ] *s.* comedia.

come·ly [k ʌ mlɪ] *adj.* agradable a la vista, gentil, bien parecido.

com·et [kámɪt] *s.* cometa.

com·fort [k ʌ mfə·t] *s.* comodidad; bienestar; alivio, consuelo; *v.* consolar, confortar, aliviar.

com·fort·a·ble [k ʌ mfə·təb] *adj.* cómodo; confortable; – **life** vida holgada; – **income** un buen pasar, renta suficiente; **comfortably** *adv.* cómodamente; con comodidad; holgadamente.

com·fort·er [k ʌ mfə·tə] *s.* consolador; edredón, cobertor acolchado.

com·fort·less [k ʌ mfə·tlɪs] *adj.* incómodo; desconsolado.

com·ic [kámɪk] *adj.* cómico, chistoso, gracioso; **-s** *s. pl.* caricaturas, historietas cómicas.

com·i·cal [kámɪk] *adj.* cómico, gracioso.

com·ing [k ʌ mɪŋ] *adj.* que viene, que llega; próximo; venidero; *s.* venida, llegada; – **of Christ**

advenimiento de Cristo.

com·ma [kɒmə] *s.* coma.

com·mand [kəmǽnd] *s. (order)* mando; mandato, orden; mandamiento; *(post)* comandancia; *(dominance)* dominio; **at your** – a la orden de Ud., a la disposición de Ud.; **he has a good – of english** domina bien el inglés; *v.* mandar; **to – respect** inspirar respeto, imponerse.

com·mand·er [kəmǽndə-] *s.* jefe; comandante; teniente de navío; comendador *(de ciertas órdenes)*; **– in chief** comandante en jefe; general en jefe.

com·mand·ment [kəmǽndmənt] *s.* mandamiento; mandato, orden.

com·man·do [kəmǽndo] *s.* comando.

com·mem·o·rate [kəmɛmˊəret] *v.* conmemorar.

com·mence [kəmɛns] *v.* comenzar.

com·mence·ment [kəmɛnsmənt] *s.* comienzo, principio; acto de distribución de diplomas.

com·mend [kəmɛnd] *v.* alabar, elogiar; encomendar, encargar; recomendar.

com·men·da·tion [kaməndéʃən] *s.* encomio, alabanza.

com·ment [kɑmɛnt] *s.* comentario, observación, nota; *v.* comentar; hacer observaciones; hacer comentarios.

com·men·tar·y [kɑmənterɪ] *s.* comentario.

com·men·ta·tor [kɑmənteta-] *s.* comentador; comentarista; **radio –** comentarista radial.

com·merce [kɑmɚs] *s.* comercio.

com·mer·cial [kəmɚʃəl] *adj.* comercial.

com·mis·er·a·tion [kəmɪzəréʃən] *s.* compasión.

com·mis·sar [kɑmɪsar] *s.* comisario.

com·mis·sar·y [kɑmɚsɛrɑ] *s.* comisario.

com·mis·sion [kəmɪ́ʃən] *s.* comisión; encargo; junta; nombramiento; **to put out of –** inutilizar; descomponer, quebrar; retirar del servicio *(un navío)*; *v.* comisionar; encargar; nombrar; poner en servicio *(un navío)*; **-ed officer** oficial comisionado *(alférez u oficial superior a éste).*

com·mis·sion·er [kəmɪ́ʃənə-] *s.* comisionado; comisario; **police –** comisario de policía.

com·mit [kəmɪ́t] *v. (perpetrate)* cometer; *(entrust)* encargar; **to – to memory** aprender de memoria; **to – to prison** encarcelar; **to – oneself** dar o expresar su opinión, expresarse abiertamente, comprometerse.

com·mit·tee [kəmɪ́tɪ] *s.* comité; comisión, junta; **– of one** comisionado o delegado único.

com·mod·i·ty [kəmádətɪ] *s.* mercancía; género, mercadería, artículo de comercio, producto.

com·mon [kɑmən] *adj.* común; general; corriente; vulgar, ordinario; público; **– law** derecho consuetudinario; **– sense** sentido común; **– soldier** soldado raso; **– market** mercado común; **-s** *pl.* refectorio *(de un colegio o universidad)*; ejido, campo común;

-ly *adv.* comúnmente, por lo común.

com·mon·ness [kɑmənnɪs] *s.* vulgaridad, ordinariez; frecuencia.

com·mon·place [kɑmənples] *adj.* común, trivial; *s.* lugar común.

com·mon·wealth [kɑmənwɛlθ] *s.* estado; república; pueblo, colectividad.

com·mo·tion [kəóʃən] *s.* conmoción; tumulto; bullicio; levantamiento.

com·mune [kəmjún] *v.* comunicarse (con); comulgar.

com·mu·ni·cate [kəmjúnəket] *v.* comunicar (se); transmitir.

com·mu·ni·ca·tion [kəmjunəkéʃən] *s.* comunicación.

com·mu·ni·ca·tive [kəmjúnəketɪv] *adj.* comunicativo.

com·mun·ion [kəmjúnjən] *s.* comunión.

com·mu·nism [kɑmjɪnɪzəm] *s.* comunismo.

com·mu·nist [kɑmjʊnɪst] *s. & adj.* comunista.

com·mu·ni·ty [kəmjúnətɪ] *s.* comunidad; sociedad; vecindario, barrio; **– chest** caja de beneficencia, fondos de beneficencia.

com·mute [kəmjút] *v.* conmutar.

com·pact [kəmpǽkt] *adj.* compacto; denso; apretado; conciso, sucinto; [kɑmpǽkt] *s.* pacto, trato, convenio; polvera.

com·pact·ness [kəmpǽktnɪs] *s.* solidez; densidad; concisión.

com·pan·ion [kəmpǽnjən] *s.* compañero; acompañante.

com·pan·ion·ship [kəmpǽnjənʃɪp] *s.* compañerismo, camaradería; compañía.

com·pa·ny [kʌˊmpənɪ] *s.* compañía; sociedad; visita; **ship's –** tripulación; **to keep – with** acompañar a; cortejar a; tener relaciones con, frecuentar la compañía de.

com·pa·ra·ble [kɑmpərəb|] *adj.* comparable.

com·par·a·tive [kəmpǽrətɪv] *adj.* comparativo.

com·pare [kəmpér] *v.* comparar; cotejar; confrontar; contrastar; **beyond –** incomparable, sin parar, sin igual, sin comparación.

com·par·i·son [kəmpǽrən ŋ] *s.* comparación; símil; **beyond –** incomparable; sin comparación; **in – with** comparado con.

com·part·ment [kəmpártmənt] *s.* compartimento, sección, división; departamento.

com·pass [kʌˊmpəs] *s.* compás *(para dibujar)*; brújula; área, ámbito; alcance.

com·pas·sion [kəmpǽʃən] *s.* compasión, lástima.

com·pas·sion·ate [kəmpǽʃənɪt] *adj.* compasivo, misericordioso.

com·pat·i·ble [kəmpǽtəb|] *adj.* compatible.

com·pa·tri·ot [kəmpétrɪət] *s.* compatriota.

com·pel [kəmpél] *v.* compeler, obligar; exigir.

com·pen·sate [kámpənset] *v.* compensar; recompensar; remunerar.

com·pen·sa·tion [kampənséʃən] *s.* compensación; recompensa; remuneración.

com·pete [kəmpít] *v.* competir.

com·pe·tence [kámpətəns] *s.* competencia; aptitud, capacidad.

com·pe·tent [kámpətənt] *adj.* competente; calificado; capaz.

com·pe·ti·tion [kampətíʃən] *s.* competencia; concurso, certamen; contienda.

com·pet·i·tive [kəmpétətɪv] *adj.* en competencia; **– examination** oposición, concurso.

com·pet·i·tor [kəmpétətə·] *s.* competidor; rival; opositor.

com·pile [kəmpáɪl] *v.* compilar, recopilar.

com·placen·cy [kəmplés ŋ sɪ] *s.* complacencia, contentamiento.

com·pla·cent [kəmplés ŋ t] *adj.* complaciente, satisfecho.

com·plain [kəmplén] *v.* quejarse; querellarse.

com·plaint [kəmplént] *s.* queja; quejido, lamento; dolencia, enfermedad; **to lodge a –** hacer una reclamación.

com·ple·ment [kámpləmənt] *s.* complemento; [kámpləmɛnt] *v.* complementar, completar.

com·plete [kəmplít] *adj.* completo; *v.* completar; terminar; **-ly** *adv.* completamente, por completo.

com·plete·ness [kəmplítnɪs] *s.* perfección; minuciosidad; lo completo; lo cabal; lo acabado.

com·ple·tion [kəmplíʃən] *s.* comple-tamiento; terminación, conclusión; cumplimiento.

com·plex [kámplɛks] *s.* complejo; [kəmplɛks] *adj.* complejo; compuesto; complicado.

com·plex·ion [kəmplɛkʃən] *s.* cutis, tez; aspecto.

com·plex·i·ty [kəmplɛksətɪ] *s.* complejidad.

com·pli·ance [kəmpláɪəns] *s.* complacencia; condescendencia; conformidad; cumplimiento; **in – with** en conformidad con; de acuerdo con, conforme a.

com·pli·cate [kámpləket] *v.* complicar.

com·pli·cat·ed [kámpləketɪd] *adj.* complicado.

com·pli·ca·tion [kampləkéʃən] *s.* complicación.

com·plic·i·ty [kəmplísətɪ] *s.* complicidad.

com·pli·ment [kámpləmənt] *s.* cumplido, cumplimiento; requiebro, lisonja, galería; **to send one's -s** enviar saludos; [kámpləmɛnt] *v.* cumplimentar; requebrar; lisonjear; alabar.

com·ply [kəmpláɪ] *v.* consentir, conformarse (con); obrar de acuerdo (con); cumplir (con).

com·po·nent [kəmpónənt] *adj. & s.* componente.

com·pose [kəmpóz] *v.* componer; **to – oneself** sosegarse, serenarse, calmarse.

com·posed [kəmpózd] *adj.* compuesto; tranquilo, sereno, sosegado; **to be – of** estar compuesto de, componerse de, constar de.

com·pos·er [kəmpózə·] *s.* compositor; autor.

com·posite [kəmpózɪt] *adj.* compuesto; *s.* compuesto; mezcla.

com·po·si·tion [kampəzíʃən] *s.* composición; arreglo; compuesto.

com·po·sure [kəmpóʒə·] *s.* compostura, calma, serenidad.

com·pound [kámpaʊnd] *adj. & s.* compuesto; [kampáʊnd] *v.* componer; mezclar, combinar; **to – interest** calcular el interés compuesto.

com·pre·hend [kamprɪhénd] *v.* comprender; abarcar, abrazar, incluir.

com·pre·hen·si·ble [kamprɪhénsəb l] *adj.* comprensible, inteligible.

com·pre·hen·sion [kamprɪhénʃən] *s.* comprensión.

com·pre·hen·sive [kamprɪhénʃɪv] *adj.* comprensivo; inclusivo.

com·press [kámprɛs] *s.* compresa; [kəmprɛs] *v.* comprimir, apretar, condensar.

com·pres·sion [kəmpréʃən] *s.* compresión.

com·prise [kəmpráɪz] *v.* comprender, abarcar, incluir, abrazar; constar de.

com·pro·mise [kámprəmaɪz] *s.* compromiso; arreglo; avenencia; término medio; *v.* comprometer; avenirse, transigir, *Am.* transar.

comp·trol·ler [kəntrólə·] *s.* interventor, *Am.* contralor.

com·pul·sion [kəmp ʌ lʃən] *s.* compulsión, coacción.

com·pul·so·ry [kəmp ʌ lsərɪ] *adj.* obligatorio.

com·pu·ta·tion [kampjətéʃən] *s.* cómputo, cálculo.

com·pute [kəmpjút] *v.* computar.

com·put·er [kəmpjútə·] *s. Esp.* calculadora electrónica; *Arg.* computadora; programadora.

com·put·er·ize [kəmpjútə·aɪz] *v.* someter datos a la calculadora electrónica; suplir con sistema computadora.

com·rade [kómræd] *s.* camarada, compañero.

con·cave [kankév] *adj.* cóncavo.

con·ceal [kənsíl] *v.* encubrir, ocultar, esconder.

con·ceal·ment [kənsílmənt] *s.* encubrimiento.

con·cede [kənsíd] *v.* conceder; otorgar; admitir, reconocer.

con·ceit [kənsít] *s.* presunción, amor propio, vanagloria; concepto, agudeza.

con·ceit·ed [kənsítɪd] *adj.* presuntuoso, presumido, vanidoso, engreído.

con·ceiv·a·ble [kənsívəb l] *adj.* concebible, imaginable, comprensible.

con·ceive [kənsív] *v.* concebir; imaginar.

con·cen·trate [káns ŋ tret] *v.* concentrar(se),

reconcentrar(se).

con•cen•tra•tion [kɔns ŋ tréʃən] s. concentración; reconcentración.

con•cept [kánsɛpt] s. concepto, idea; opinión.

con•cep•tion [kənsépʃən] s. concepción; concepto, idea.

con•cern [kəns ɝ n] s. (*business*) compañía, negociación; negocio; establecimiento mercantil; (*interest*) cuidado; interés; preocupación; **to be of no –** no ser de consecuencia; *v.* concernir, importar, interesar; preocupar; **in all that -s him** en cuanto le atañe, en cuanto le concierne.

con•cerned [kəns ɝ nd] adj. interesado; preocupado, intranquilo, inquieto, ansioso; **to be – about** interesarse por, preocuparse por; **as far as I am –** por lo que me concierne, por lo que me toca, en cuanto a mí me atañe.

con•cern•ing [kəns ɝ nɪŋ] prep. tocante a, respecto a acerca de.

con•cert [kánsɝt] s. concierto; [kəns ɝ t] v. concertar, arreglar (*un plan*).

con•ces•sion [kənséʃən] s. concesión.

con•cil•i•ate [kənsíliet] v. conciliar, poner en armonía; ganar la voluntad de.

con•cise [kənsáɪs] adj. conciso, sucinto.

con•cise•ness [kənsáɪsnɪs] s. concision, brevedad.

con•clude [kənklúd] v. concluir; acabar, terminar; deducir; decidir.

con•clu•sion [kənkləuʒən] s. conclusión.

con•clu•sive [kənklúsɪv] adj. conclusivo, concluyente.

con•coct [kankákt] v. confeccionar; preparar (*combinando diversos ingredientes*); inventar, urdir.

con•coc•tion [kankókʃən] s. conocimiento, menjurje; mezcla.

con•cord [kánkɔrd] s. concordia, conformidad, acuerdo; convenio, pacto.

con•crete [hankrít] adj. concreto; de hormigón, de cemento, s. hormigón, cemento, Am. concreto.

con•cu•bine [kánkjubaɪn] s. concubina.

con•cur [kənk ɝ] v. estar de acuerdo, ser del mismo parecer; unirse.

con•cus•sion [kənk ʌ ʃən] s. concusión.

con•demn [kəndɛ́m] v. condenar; **to – a building** condenar un edificio.

con•dem•na•tion [kandɛmnéʃən] s, condenación.

con•den•sa•tion [kandɛnséʃən] s. condensación; resumen, compendio.

con•dense [kəndɛ́ns] v. condensar(se).

con•de•scend [kandɪsɛ́nd] v. condescender.

con•de•scen•sion [kandɪsɛ́nʃən] s. condescendencia.

con•di•ment [kándəmənt] s. condimento.

con•di•tion [kəndíʃən] s. condición; estado; nota o calificación provisional; **on – that** a condición de que, con tal que; *v.* acondicionar; poner en buena condición; estipular; reprobar provisionalmente (*a un estudiante*).

con•di•tion•al [kəndíʃən l] adj. condicional.

con•do•le [kəndól] v. condolerse; **to – with** dar el pésame a; consolar a.

con•do•lence [kəndóləns] s. pésame.

con•done [kəndón] v. dispensar; perdonar; condonar.

con•duce [kəndjús] v. conducir.

con•du•cive [kəndjúsɪv] adj. conducente.

con•duct [kándʌkt] s. (*behavior*) conducta; comportamiento, proceder, (*handling*) dirección, manejo; [kənd ʌ kt] v. conducir; dirigir, manejar; **to – oneself well** portarse bien.

con•duc•tor [kənd ʌ ktɚ] s. conductor; guía; **orchestra –** director de orquesta; **train –** revisor; cobrador, Am. conductor.

con•duit [kándɪt] s. conducto; caño; cañería, tubería.

cone [kon] s. cono; **paper –** cucurucho; **pine –** piña.

con•fec•tion [kənfékʃən] s. confección; confitura; confite, dulce.

con•fec•tion•er•y [kənféʃənɛrɪ] s. confitería; dulcería; confites, dulces.

con•fed•er•a•cy [ənfédərəsɪ] s. confederación.

con•fed•er•ate [kənfédərɪt] adj. & s. confederado; [kənfédəret] v. confederar(se).

con•fed•er•a•tion [kənfɛdərəeʃən] s. confederación.

con•fer [kənf ɝ] v. conferir, conceder; conferenciar, consultar.

con•fer•ence [kánfərəns] s. conferencia; consulta, junta, sesión

con•fess [kənfɛ́s] v. confesar(se); reconocer, admitir.

con•fes•sion [kənféʃən] s. confesión.

con•fes•sion•al [kənkéʃən l] s. confesionario.

con•fes•sor [kənfésɚ] s. confesor.

con•fi•dant [kanfədǽnl] s. confidente.

con•fide [kənfáɪd] v. confiar; fiar.

con•fi•dence [kánfədəns] s. confianza; confidencia; **– game** estafa; **– man** estafador.

con•fi•dent [kánfədənt] adj. confiado; seguro, cierto; **-ly** adv. confiadamente, con toda seguridad.

con•fi•den•tial [kanfədénʃəl] adj. confidencial; íntimo; secreto; **-ly** adv. en confianza.

con•fine [kánfaɪn] s. confín; [kənfáɪn] v. confinar; encerrar; **to – oneself to** limitarse a; **to be -ed in bed** estar encamado, guardar cama.

con•fine•ment [kənfáɪnmənt] s. encerra-miento; encierro; prisión, encarcelación.

con•firm [kənf ɝ m] v. confirmar.

con·fir·ma·tion [kɑnfəméʃən] *s.* confirmación.

con·fis·cate [kɑ́nfɪsket] *v.* confiscar.

con·fla·gra·tion [kɑnfləgréʃən] *s.* conflagración, incendio.

con·flict [kɑ́nflɪkt] *s.* conflicto, oposición, choque; lucha, combate; [kənflɪkt] *v.* chocar, oponere, estar en conflicto.

con·form [kənfɔ́rm] *v.* conformar (se)

con·for·mi·ty [kənfɔ́rmɪtɪ] *v.* conformidad.

con·found [kɑnfáUnd] *v.* confundir, perturbar, desconcertar, aturdir; **– it!** ¡caramba!

con·front [kənfrʌ́nt] confrontar; carear, poner cara a cara (*a dos reos*); encararse con, afrontar, hacer frente a, arrostrar.

con·fuse [kənfjúz] *v.* confundir; trastornar; embrollar; desconcertar.

con·fused [kənfjúzd] *adj.* confuso; revuelto; .desconcertado, perplejo; **to become –** confundirse; desconcertarse.

con·fus·ing [kənfjúzɪŋ] *adj.* confuso, revuelto; desconcertante.

con·fu·sion [kənfjúʒən] *s.* confusión; desorden; tumulto; perplejidad.

con·geal [kəndʒíl] *v.* congelar(se), helar(se), cuajar(se).

con·gen·ial [kəndʒínjəl] *adj.* congenial; simpático; **to be – with** congeniar con, simpatizar con.

con·ges·tion [kəndʒéstʃən] *s.* congestión; algomeración.

con·glom·er·a·tion [kənglɑməréʃən] *s.* aglomeración.

con·grat·u·late [kəngrǽtʃəlet] *v.* congratular, felicitar, dar el parabién.

con·grat·u·la·tion [kəngrætʃəléʃən] *s.* congratulación, felicitación, barabién, enhorabuena.

con·gre·gate [kɑ́ŋgrɪget] *v.* congregar(se) juntar(se), reunir(se)

con·gre·ga·tion [kɑŋgrɪgéʃən] *s.* congregación; asamblea, reunión; colección, agregado; fieles, feligreses (*de una iglesia*).

con·gress [kɑ́ŋgrəs] *s.* congreso; asamblea.

con·gres·sion·al [kəngréʃən‖] *adj.* perteneciente al congreso.

con·gress·man [kɑ́ŋgrəsmən] *s.* congresista, diputado, representante.

con·jec·ture [kəndʒétʃə·] *s.* conjetura, suposición; *v.* conjeturar, suponer.

con·ju·gate [kɑ́ndʒəget] *v.* conjugar.

con·ju·ga·tion [kɑ́ndʒəgéʃən] *s.* conjugación.

con·junc·tion [kəndʒʌ́ŋʃən] *s.* conjunción.

con·jure [kɑ́ndʒə·] *v.* conjurar; **to – up** evocar; [kəndʒÚr] rogar, implorar.

con·nect [kənékt] *v.* conectar; unir(se), juntar(se); enlazar(se); relacionar(se); acoplar.

con·nec·tion [kənékʃən] *s.* conexión; enlace; vínculo; unión; relación; **-s** parientes; amigos, amistades.

con·nip·tion [kənípʃən] *s.* pataleta; **to have a –** darle a uno una pataleta.

con·nive [kənáɪv] *v.* conspirar; disimular; hacerse cómplice.

con·nois·seur [kɑnəsɝ́] *s.* conocedor, perito.

con·quer [kɑ́ŋkə·] *v.* conquistar; vencer.

con·quer·or [kɑ́ŋkərə·] *s.* conquistador; vencedor.

con·quest [kɑ́ŋkwɛst] *s.* conquista.

con·science [kɑ́nʃəns] *s.* conciencia.

con·sci·en·tious [kɑnʃɪénʃəs] *adj.* concienzudo.

con·scious [kɑ́nʃəs] *adj.* consciente; sabedor; **-ly** *adv.* conscientemente; a sabiendas.

con·scious·ness [kɑ́nʃəsnɪs] *s.* consciencia, estado consciente; **to lose –** perder el sentido o conocimiento.

con·script [kənskrípt] *v.* reclutar; [kɑ́nskrɪpt] *s.* recluta.

con·se·crate [kɑ́nsɪkret] *v.* consagrar; dedicar.

con·se·cra·tion [kɑnsɪkréʃən] *s.* consagración; dedicación.

con·sec·u·tive [kənsékjətɪv] *adj.* consecutivo.

con·sen·sus [kənsɛ́nsəs] *s.* consenso.

con·sent [kənsɛ́nt] *s.* consentimiento; permiso, asentimiento; *v.* consentir; permitir, asentir.

con·se·quence [kɑ́nsəkwɛns] *s.* consecuencia.

con·se·quent [kɑ́nsəkwɛnt] *adj.* consecuente; consiguiente; *s.* consecuente, consiguiente, consecuencia; **-ly** *adv.* por consiguiente, por consecuencia.

con·se·quen·tial [kɑnsəkwɛntʃ‖] *adj.* de consecuencia.

con·ser·va·tion [kɑnsə·véʃən] *s.* conservación; preservación.

con·ser·va·tive [kənsɝ́vətɪv] *adj.* conservador; conservativo; *s.* conservador.

con·ser·va·to·ry [kənsɝ́vətorɪ] *s.* conservatorio; invernadero.

con·serve [kənsɝ́v] *s.* conserva, dulce; *v.* conservr; preservar.

con·sid·er [kənsídə·] *v.* considerar.

con·sid·er·a·ble [kənsídərəb‖] *adj.* considerable; cuantioso; **considerably** *adv.* considerablemente; **considerably older** bastante más viejo.

con·sid·er·ate [kənsídərɪt] *adj.* considerado.

con·sid·er·a·tion [kənsɪdəréʃən] *s.* (*respect*) respeto; consideración; importancia; (*pay*) remuneración; **in – of** en atención a, teniendo en cuenta, en razón de, en vista de.

con·sid·er·ing [kənsíŋ] *prep.* en razón de, en vsita de; en atención a, en consideración de.

con·sign [kənsáɪn] *v.* consignar; enviar, entregar.

con·sign·ee [kənsaɪnəɪ] *s.* consignatario.

con·sign·ment [kənsáɪnmənt] s. consignación.

con·sist [kənsíst] v. consistir (en); constar (de).

con·sis·ten·cy [kənsístənsɪ] s. consecuencia; consistencia, firmeza, solidez.

con·sis·tent [kənsístənt] adj. consecuente, lógico; compatible; consistente, coherente.

con·so·la·tion [kɑnsəléʃən] s. consolación; consuelo.

con·sole [kənsól] v. consolar.

con·sol·i·date [kənsálədet] v. consolidar(se); unir(se), combinar(se).

con·so·nant [kánsənənt] adj. consonante; conforme; s. consonante.

con·sort [kánsɔrt] s. consorte, [kənsɪrt] v. **to – with** asociarse con.

con·spic·u·ous [kənspíkjʊəs] adj. conspicuo, notorio; manifiesto, sobresaliente.

con·spir·a·cy [kənspírəsɪ] s. conspiración, conjuración.

con·spir·a·tor [kənspíretə] s. conspirador, conjurado.

con·spire [kənspáɪr] v. conspirar; tramar, maquinar.

con·sta·ble [kánstəbl] s. alguacil, policía; condestable (título).

con·stan·cy [kánstənsɪ] s. constancia.

con·stant [kánstənt] adj. constante; s. constante, cantidad constante; **-ly** adv. constantemente, continuamente, siempre; a menudo.

con·stel·la·tion [kɑnstəléʃən] s. constelación.

con·ster·na·tion [kɑnstə·néʃən] s. consternación.

con·sti·pate [kánstəpet] v. estreñir.

con·sti·pa·tion [kɑnstəpéʃən] s. estreñimiento.

con·stit·u·ent [kənstítʃʊənt] adj. constituyente; constitutivo; componente; s. componente, elemento; elector, votante.

con·sti·tute [kánstətjut] v. constituir; componer; establecer.

con·sti·tu·tion [kɑnstətjúʃən] s. constitución.

con·sti·tu·tion·al [kɑnstətjúʃən] adj. constitucional, s. paseo a pie, caminata (para hacer ejercicio).

con·strain [kənstrén] v. constreñir; obligar, forzar; apretar, comprimir.

con·struct [kənstrʌ́kt] v. construir, fabricar.

con·struc·tion [kənstrʌ́kʃən] s. construcción; estructura; interpretación.

con·struc·tive [kənstrʌ́ktɪv] adj. constructivo; de utilidad positiva; provechoso.

con·strue [kənstrú] v. interpretar, explicar.

con·sul [kánsl] s. cónsul.

con·su·late [kánslɪt] s. consulado.

con·sult [kənsʌ́lt] v. consultar.

con·sult·ant [kənsʌ́ltənt] s. consultante.

con·sul·ta·tion [kɑnsltéʃən] s. consulta.

con·sume [kənsúm] v. consumir; gastar; perder (el tiempo).

con·sum·er [kənsúmə] s. consumidor.

con·sum·mate [kánsəmet] v. consumar, completar; [kəns ʌ mɪt] adj. consumado, perfecto, completo.

con·sump·tion [kəns ʌ mpʃən] s. consumo, gasto; consunción; tisis, tuberculosis.

con·sump·tive [kəns ʌ mptɪv] adj. tísico.

con·tact [kántækt] s. contacto; v. tocar; poner(se) en contacto con; estar en contacto con.

con·ta·gion [kəntédʒən] s. contagio.

con·ta·gious [kəntédʒəs] adj. contagioso.

con·tain [kəntén] v. contener; encerrar; tener cabida para ; reprimir, refrenar; **to – oneself** contenerse, refrenarse.

con·tain·er [kənténə] s. envase, caja, recipiente.

con·tam·i·nate [kənt ǽ mənet] v. contaminar, viciar, inficionar.

con·tem·plate [kántəmplet] v. contemplar; meditar; tener la intención de; proyectar.

con·tem·pla·tion [kɑntəmpléʃən] s. contemplación; meditación; intención, propósito.

con·tem·po·rar·y [kəntémpərərɪ] adj. contemporáneo; coetáneo.

con·tempt [kəntémpt] s. desdén, menosprecio; desprecio; **– of court** contumacia.

con·tempt·i·ble [kəntémptəbl] adj. despreciable, vil.

con·temp·tu·ous [kəntémptʃʊəs] adj. desdeñoso.

con·tend [kənténd] v. contender; competir; argüir; altercar; sostener, afirmar.

con·tent [kántɛnt] s. contenido; sustancia; capacidad, volumen; **-s** contenido; **table of -s** tabla de materias, índice general.

con·tent [kəntént] adj. contento; satisfecho; s. contento; satisfacción; **to one's heart's –** a pedir de boca, hasta saciarse; a su entera satisfacción; v. contentar; satisfacer.

con·tent·ed [kənténtɪd] adj. contento, satisfecho.

con·ten·tion [kənténʃən] s. contención, contienda, disputa, controversia; tema, argumento; aseveración.

con·tent·ment [kənténtmənt] s. contentamiento, contento.

con·test [kántɛst] s. concurso, certamen; debate; contienda; torneo; [kəntést] v. contender; disputar; luchar por; **to – with** competir con.

con·text [kántɛkst] s. contexto.

con·tig·u·ous [kəntígjʊəs] adj. contiguo; adyacente.

con·ti·nent [kántənənt] s. continente; adj. continente, casto, moderado.

con•ti•nen•tal [kɑntənɛ́nt]] *adj. & s.* continental.

con•tin•gen•cy [gəntɪ́ndʒənsI] *s.* contingencia, eventualidad.

con•tin•gent [kəntɪ́ndʒənt] *adj. & s.* contingente.

con•tin•u•al [kəntɪ́njUəl] *adj.* continuo; frecuente. **-ly** *adv.* de continuo, continuamente, frecuentemente.

con•tin•u•an•ce [kəntɪ́njUəns] *s.* continuación; aplazamiento.

con•tin•u•a•tion [kəntɪnjUéʃən] *s.* continuación.

con•tin•ue [kəntɪ́nju] *v.* continuar.

con•ti•nu•i•ty [kɑntənúətI] *s.* continuidad.

con•tin•u•ous [kəntɪ́njUəs] *adj.* continuo, sin parar, sin cesar.

con•tor•tion [kənt ɔ́ rʃən] *s.* contorsión.

con•tour [kɑntUr] *s.* contorno; perímetro.

con•tra•band [kɑntrəbænd] *s.* contrabando.

con•tract [kɑntrækt] *s.* contrato, pacto, convenio; contrata; **marriage** – esponsales; [kəntr ǽ kt] *v.* contratar; contraer(se), encoger(se); **to – an illness** contraer una enfermedad; **to – the brows** fruncir las cejas.

con•trac•tion [kəntr ǽkʃən] *s.* contracción.

con•trac•tor [kəntr æ ktɚ] *s.* contratista.

con•tra•dict [kɑntrədɪ́kt] *v.* contradecir; contrariar.

con•tra•dic•tion [kɑntrədɪ́kʃən] *s.* contradicción; contrariedad.

con•tra•dic•tor•y [kɑntrədɪ́ktərI] *adj.* contradictorio; opuesto, contrario.

con•trar•y [kɑntrɛrI] *adj.* contrario; opuesto; testarudo, obstinado; *s.* contrario; **on the** – al contrario.

con•trast [kɑntræst] *s.* contraste; [kəntr ǽ st] *v.* contrastar.

con•tra•vene [kɑntrəvín] *v.* contravenir a; oponerse a.

con•trib•ute [kəntrɪ́bjUt] *v.* contribuir.

con•tri•bu•tion [kɑntrəbjúʃən] *s.* contribución; aportación; cuota; dádiva.

con•trib•u•tor [kəntrɪ́bjətɚ] *s.* contri-buidor; colaborador.

con•trite [kɑntraIt] *adj.* contrito.

con•tri•vance [kəntráIvəns] *s.* traza, maquinación; artificio, invención; designio; artefacto, aparato, máquina.

con•trive [kəntráIv] *v.* tramar, maquinar; inventar, idear; proyectar; **to – to** buscar el medio de, tratar de, procurar.

con•trol [kəntról] *s.* (*authority*) mando, manejo: dirección; (*instrument*) freno, regulador; restricción; *Am.* control, **-s** mandos, controles; – **stick** palanca (*de un aeroplano*); – **tower** torre de mando; **to lose – of** one's temper perder la paciencia; *v.* gobernar, manejar, *Am.* controlar; regular, regularizar; restringir; contener, reprimir; tener a raya; **to – oneself** contenerse, dominarse.

con•trol•ler [kəntrólɚ] *s.* interventor, registrador, *Ríopl., C.A., Andes, Ven., Col.* contralor, *Ch., Méx.* controlador; regulador; aparato de manejo y control.

con•tro•ver•sy [kɑntrəvɚ́sI] *s.* controversia, debate, disputa.

co•nun•drum [kən ʌ́ndrəm] *s.* adivinanza, acertijo.

con•va•lesce [kɑnvəlɛ́s] *v.* convalescer

con•vene [kənvín] *v.* juntar, convocar; reunirse.

con•ven•ience [kənvínjəns] *s.* conveniencia, comodidad; **at one's –** cuando le convenga a uno, cuando tenga oportunidad, cuando buenamente pueda.

con•ven•ient [kənvínjənt] *adj.* conveniente; oportuno; cómodo; a propósito; **-ly** *adv.* convenientemente, cómodamente.

con•vent [kɑnvɛnt] *s.* convento.

con•ven•tion [kənvɛ́nʃən] *s.* convención; congreso, asamblea; convenio; costumbre, regla.

con•ven•tion•al [kənvɛ́nʃən]] *adj.* convencional; tradicional.

con•verge [kənvɚ́ dʒ] *v.* converger o convergir.

con•ver•sant [kɑnvɚ•s ŋ t] *adj.* **– with** versado en.

con•ver•sa•tion [kɑnvɚséʃən] *s.* conversación.

con•verse [kənvɚ́ s] *v.* conversar, hablar, platicar.

con•vers•ion [kənvɚ́ ʒən] *s.* conversión.

con•vert [kɑnvɚt] *s.* converso, persona convertida; catecúmeno (*converso reciente*); [kənvɚ́ t] *v.* convertir(se).

con•vex [kɑnvɛ́ks] *adj.* convexo.

con•vey [kənvé] *v.* llevar; transportar; transferir, traspasar; transmitir; comunicar; **to – thanks** expresar agradecimiento, dar las gracias.

con•vey•ance [kənvéəns] *s.* vehículo; transporte; transmisión; entrega; comunicación; traspaso; escritura de propiedad o traspaso.

con•vict [kɑnvIkt] *s.* presidiario; reo; [kənvIkt] *v.* convencer (*de un delito*), declarar culpable; probar la culpabilidad de.

con•vic•tion [kənvɪ́kʃən] *s.* convicción; convencimiento; prueba de culpabilidad.

con•vince [kənvɪ́ns] *v.* convencer.

con•vinc•ing [kənvɪ́nsIŋ] *adj.* convincente.

con•vo•ca•tion [kɑnvəkéʃən] *s.* convocación; asamblea.

con•voke [kənvók] *v.* convocar.

con•voy [kɑnvɔI] *s.* convoy, escolta, guardia; [kənvoI] *v.* convoyar.

con•vulse [kənv ʌ́Is] *v.* crispar; agitar; convulsionar.

con•vul•sion [kənv ʌ́Iʃən] *s.* convulsión, agitación.

coo [ku] *s.* arrullo; *v.* arrullar.

cook [kUk] *s.* cocinero, cocinera; *v.* cocinar, guisar; cocer; **to – up a plan** urdir un plan.

cook·er·y [kÚkərI] *s.* cocina, arte de cocinar.

cook·ie, cook·y [kÚkI] *s.* bizcochito, bollito.

cook·ing [kÚkIŋ] *s.* cocina, arte culinaria: **–stove** cocina de gas, cocina eléctrica, estufa; **– utensils** batería de cocina, trastos de cocina.

cool [kul] *adj.* fresco; frío, indiferente; calmo, sereno; *s.* fresco, frescura; *v.* refrescar; enfriar; templar, calmar; **to – off** enfriarse; calmarse.

cool·ant [kúlənt] *s.* líquido refrigerador.

cool·ness [kúlnIs] *s.* fresco, frescura; frialdad, indiferencia.

coon [kun] *s.* coatí (*cuadrúpedo carnívoro*); negro; **a -'s age** una eternidad, mucho tiempo.

coop [kup] *s.* jaula; **chicken –** gallinero; *v.* enjaular; **to – up** encerrar.

co·op·er·ate [koápəret] *v.* cooperar.

co·op·er·a·tion [koapəréʃən] *s.* cooperación.

co·op·er·a·tive [koápəretIv] *adj.* cooperativo; *s.* cooperativa, sociedad cooperativa.

co·ör·di·nate [koɔ́rdŋ et] *v.* coordinar; [ko1rd/It] *adj.* coordinado.

co·ör·di·na·tion [koordŋ éʃən] *s.* coordinación.

cop [kɑp] *s.* polizonte, policía.

cope [kop] *v.* **to – with** tener suficiente fuerza para; **I cannot – with this** no puedo con esto, no puedo dar abasto a esto.

co·pi·ous [kópIəs] *adj.* copioso, abundante.

cop·per [kápə-] *s.* cobre; polizonte, policía; **– coin** moneda de cobre, centavo; **– kettle** marmita o caldera de cobre; *adj.* cobrizo.

cop·y [kápI] *s.* copia; ejemplar (*de un libro*); manuscrito (*para el impresor*); *v.* copiar; imitar; remedar.

cop·y·right [kápIraIt] *s.* derecho de propiedad literaria; *v.* registrar, obtener patente de propiedad literaria.

co·quette [kokét] *s.* coqueta.

cor·al [kɔ́rəl] *s.* coral; *adj.* coralino, de coral.

cord [kɔrd] *s.* cuerda; cordón, cordel; cuerda (*medida de leña*), tendón; **–s** pantalones de pana; **spinal –** espinazo, espina dorsal.

cor·dial [kɔ́rdʒəl] *adj. & s.* cordial.

cor·du·roy [kɔrdərɔ́I] *s.* pana; **-s** pantalones de pana; **– road** camino de troncos o maderos.

core [kor] *s.* corazón, centro; núcleo; esencia; *v.* cortar el centro o corazón de; despepitar (*una manzana*).

cork [kɔrk] *s.* corcho; tapón; **– tree** alcornoque; *v.* tapar con corcho.

cork·screw [kɔ́rkskru] *s.* tirabuzón, sacacorchos; *adj.* espiral, de forma espiral.

corn [kɔrn] *s.* maíz; grano, cereal; callo (*de los pies a manos*); **– bread** pan de maíz; **– meal** harina de maíz; *v.* salar, curar, acecinar.

corned beef [kɔ́rnd bif] *s.* carne de vaca curada (*en salmuera y salitre*).

cor·ner [kɔ́rnə-] *s.* (*interior*) rincón; rinconada; ángulo; (*exterior*) esquina; angulo; (*monopoly*) monopolio; **– stone** piedra angular; **– table** (**–shelf, – bracket**) rinconera; *v.* arrinconar; acorralar; acaparar, monopolizar.

cor·net [kɔrnét] *s.* corneta.

corn·field [kɔ́rnfild] *s.* maizal, *Am.* milpa.

cor·nice [kɔ́rnIs] *s.* cornisa.

cor·ol·lar·y [kɔ́rəlɛrI] *s.* corolario; consecuencia natural.

cor·o·na·tion [korənéʃən] *s.* coronación.

cor·o·net [kɔ́rənIt] *s.* coronilla, guirnalda.

cor·po·ral [kɔ́rpərəl] *adj.* corporal; corpóreo; *s.* cabo (*militar*).

cor·po·ra·tion [kɔrpəréʃən] *s.* corporación; sociedad mercantil.

corps [kor] *s.* cuerpo (*grupo organizado*), **air –** cuerpo de aviación; **army –** cuerpo de ejército.

corpse [kɔrps] *s.* cadáver.

cor·pu·lent [kɔ́rpjələnt] *adj.* corpulento.

cor·pus·cle [kɔ́rpəs]] *s.* corpúsculo.

cor·ral [kərǽl] *s.* corral; *v.* acorralar.

cor·rect [kərékt] *v.* corregir; *adj.* correcto; **it is –** está bien; **-ly** *adv.* correctamente; **-ly done** bien hecho.

cor·rec·tion [kərékʃən] *s.* corrección.

cor·rect·ness [kəréktnIs] *s.* corrección.

cor·rec·tor [kəréktə-] *s.* corregidor, corrector.

cor·re·late [kɔ́rəlet] *v.* correlacionar.

cor·re·spond [korəspánd] *v.* corresponder; corresponderse, cartearse, escribirse.

cor·re·spon·dence [korəspándəns] *s.* correspondencia.

cor·re·spon·dent [korəspándənt] *adj.* correspondiente; *s.* correspondiente; corresponsal.

cor·re·spond·ing [korəspándIŋ] *adj.* correspondiente; conforme.

cor·ri·dor [kɔ́rədə-] *s.* corredor, pasillo, pasadizo.

cor·rob·o·rate [kərábəret] *v.* corroborar.

cor·rode [kərod] *v.* corroer(se).

cor·ru·gat·ed iron [kɔ́rəgetəd aIə-n] *s.* hierro acanalado.

cor·rupt [kər ʌpt] *adj.* corrompido; perverso, depravado; **to become –** corromperse; *v.* corromper; pervertir; sobornar.

cor·rup·tion [kər ʌpʃən] *s.* corrupción; soborno; descomposición.

cor·set [kɔ́rsIt] *s.* corsé.

cos·met·ic [kozmétIk] *adj. & s.* cosmético.

cos·mic [kázmIk] *adj.* cósmico.

cos·mo·naut [kázmənɔt] *s.* cosmonauta.

cos•mo•pol•i•tan [kɑzməpálət ŋ] *adj.* cosmopolita.

cost [kɔst] *s.* coste, costa o costo; **at all -s** a toda costa; **to sell at** – vender al costo; *v.* costar; *pret. & p.p. de* **to cost.**

cost•ly [kɔ́ stlI] *adj.* costoso.

cos•tume [kɔ́stjum] *s.* vestuario, traje, vestido; atavío; indumentaria.

cot [kɑt] *s.* catre; **folding** – catre de tijera.

cot•tage [kɑ́tIdʒ] *s.* casita, caseta; casa de campo; – **cheese** requesón.

cot•ton [kɑ́t ŋ] *s.* algodón; **–seed** semilla de algodón; – **wool** algodón en rama; – **yarn** hilaza.

couch [kaUtʃ] *s.* canapé, diván; *v.* expresar; estar escondido o en acecho; **-ed in difficult language** expresado en lenguaje difícil.

cough [kɔf] *s.* tos; – **drop** pastilla para la tos; **whooping** – tos ferina; *v.* toser; **to – up** expectorar.

could [kUd] *pret. del. v. defect.* **can.**

coun•cil [káUns] *s.* concilio; consejo; **city** – consejo municipal.

coun•cil•man [káUns mən] *s.* concejal.

coun•cil•or [káUns ə] *s.* concejal.

coun•sel [káUns] *s.* (*advice*) consejo; parecer, dictamen; (*lawyer*) abogado consultor; *v.* aconsejar; recomendar.

coun•se•lor [káUns ə] *s.* consejero; abogado consultor.

count [kaUnt] *s.* (*reckoning*) cuenta, cálculo; cómputo; (*charge*) cargo, acusación; (*noble*) count; *v.* contar; valer, tener importancia; **to – on** contar con, contar en.

count•down [káUntdaUn] *s.* recuento descendiente hasta cero.

coun•te•nance [káUntənəns] *s.* semblante, aspecto; **to give –** favorecer, apoyar; aprobar; *v.* aprobar; favorecer, apoyar; tolerar.

coun•ter [káUntə] *s.* contador; mostrador; tablero; ficha; *adj.* contrario, opuesto; *adv.* al contrario; **to run – to** ser contrario a, oponerse a; *v.* oponerse; contradecir; **to – a blow** devolver un golpe.

coun•ter•act [kaUntə ǽkt] *v.* contrarrestar, neutralizar.

coun•ter•bal•ance [kauntə•b ǽ ləns] *v.* contrapesar; equilibrar; [káUntə•bæləns] *v.* contrapeso.

coun•ter•feit [káUntə•fIt] *v.* falsificación; *adj.* falso; falsificado, falseado; contrahecho; **– money** moneda falsa; *v.* contrahacer, falsificar, falsear.

coun•ter•mand [káUntə•mænd] *s.* contraorden, contramando, revocación, cancelación; [kaUntə•m ǽnd] *v.* contramandar, revocar, cancelar.

coun•ter•part [káUntə•part] *s.* contraparte.

coun•ter•poise [káUntə•ɔqIz] *s.* contrapeso; *v.* contrapesar.

coun•ter•sign [káUntə•saIn] *s.* contraseña.

.count•ess [káaUntIs] *s.* condesa.

count•less [káUntlIs] *adj.* incontable, innumerable.

coun•try [k ʌ́ntrI] *s.* país; tierra; patria; campo; *adj.* campestre; rural; rústico; campesino.

coun•try•man [k ʌ́ntrImən] *s.* compatriota, paisano; campesino, *Méx. C.A.* ranchero, *P.R.* jíbaro; *Cuba* guajiro; *Ch.* huaso; *Arg.* gaucho; *Ec., Col.* paisa.

coun•try•side [k ʌ́ntrIsaId] *s.* campiña, campo.

coun•ty [káUntI] *s.* condado (*división de un estado*).

coup d'é•tat [ku detó] *s.* golpe de estado; cuartelazo.

cou•pé [kupé, kup] *s.* cupé.

cou•ple [k ʌ́p] *s.* par; pareja; *v.* parear; unir; acoplar.

cou•plet [k ʌ́plIt] *s.* copla, versos pareados.

cou•plin [k ʌ́plIŋ] *s.* unión, conexión; acoplamiento; enganche.

cou•pon [kúpɑn] *s.* cupón; talón.

cour•age [k ɝ́Idʒ] *s.* coraje, ánimo, valor.

cou•ra•geous [kərédʒəs] *adj.* valeroso, valiente, animoso.

cou•ri•er [kÚrlə] *s.* mensajero.

course [kors] *s.* (*way*) curso; rumbo, trayecto; (*advance*) marcha, progreso; (*mode*) método; (*study*) asignatura; (*dish*) plato (*de una comida*); – **of conduct** conducta, proceder; **golf** – campo o cancha de golf; **race** – hipódromo, pista; **in the – of a year** en el transcurso de un año; **of** – claro, por supuesto; **to follow a straight** – seguir una línea recta.

court [kort] *s.* patio; plazuela, plazoleta; juzgado, tribunal de justicia; corte; **tennis** – cancha para tenis; – **plaster** tela adhesiva, tafetán inglés, esparadrapo; **to pay – to** hacer la corte a, cortejar, galantear; *v.* cortejar; galantear; buscar; **to – danger** exponerse al peligro.

cour•te•ous [k ɝ́tIəs] *adj.* cortés.

cour•te•sy [k ɝ́təsI] *s.* cortesía, fineza, atención; reverencia.

court•i•er [kórtlə] *s.* cortesano, palaciego.

court-mar•tial [kórtmarʃəl] *s.* consejo de guerra; *v.* someter a consejo de guerra.

court•ship [kórtʃIp] *s.* cortejo, galanteo.

court•yard [kórtjard] *s.* patio.

cous•in [k ʌ́z ŋ] *s.* primo; prima; **first** – primo hermano, primo carnal.

cove [kov] *s.* cala, ensenada.

cov•e•nant [k ʌ́vənənt] *s.* convenio, pacto; contrato.

cov•er [k ʌ́və] *s.* (*lid*) cubierta, tapa, tapadera; (*blanket*) cobija; cobertor; (*binding*) encuadernación; envoltura; (*pillow*) funda; (*shelter*) albergue, abrido; **table** – tapete; **to send under separate** – enviar por separado; *v.* cubrir; tapar; encubrir; abrigar, proteger; abarcar; **to – a distance** recorrer una distancia.

cov•er•age [k Á vərIdʒ] *s.* alcance; (*journalism*) reportaje.

cov•er•ing [k Á vrIŋ] *s.* cubierta; cobertura; envoltura; cobija, abrigo.

cov•et [k Á vIt] *v.* codiciar; ambicionar.

cov•et•ous [k Á vItəs] *adj.* codicioso.

cow [kaU] *s.* vaca; hembra (*de elefante y otros cuadrúpedos*); *v.* atemorizar, acobardar.

cow•ard [káU⋅əd] *adj.* & *s.* cobarde.

cow•ard•ice [káUə⋅dIs] *s.* cobardía.

cow•ard•li•ness [káUə⋅dIInIs] *s.* cobardía.

cow•ard•ly [káUə⋅dlI] *adj.* cobarde; *adv.* cobardemente.

cow•boy [láUbɔI] *s.* vaquero, *Am.* gaucho.

cow•er [káUə⋅] *v.* agacharse (*de miedo o vergüenza*), achicarse, encogerse (*de miedo*), acobardarse.

cow•hide [káUhaId] *s.* cuero de vaca, vaqueta.

cowl [kaUl] *s.* capucha.

cox•swain [kákSən] *s.* timonel.

coy [kɔI] *adj.* recatado, esquivo, modesto; tímido; gazmoño.

coy•o•te [káIot, kaIotI] *s.* coyote.

co•zy [kózI] *adj.* cómodo y abrigado; cómodo y agradable.

crab [kræb] *s.* cangrejo; cascarrabias (*persona de mal genio*); **– apple** manzana silvestre.

crack [kræk] *s.* (*space*) raja, grieta, rendija; (*sound*) crujido; estallido; trueno, estampido; (*blow*) golpe; (*joke*) pulla, chanza; **at the – of dawn** al romper el alba; *adj.* excelente; *v.* rajar(se), hender(se), agrietarse; crujir; estallar; **to – a joke** soltar un chiste; **to – nuts** cascar nueces.

crack•down [kræ kdaUn] *s.* represión severa.

cracked [krækt] *adj.* agrietado, rajado; quebrado; chiflado, loco.

crack•er [krækə⋅] *s.* galleta.

crack•le [kræ k] *s.* crujido; crepitación; chasquido; *v.* crujir, crepitar.

cra•dle [kréd] *s.* cuna.

craft [kræft] *s.* maña, destreza; astucia, artificio, cautela; arte, oficio; embarcación; embarcaciones.

crafts•man [kræ ftsmən] *s.* artesano, artífice.

craft•y [kræ ftI] *adj.* mañoso, astuto, cauteloso, taimado.

crag [kræg] *s.* risco, peñasco.

cram [kræm] *v.* rellenar; atestar; atracar(se), hartar(se); engullir.

cramp [kræmp] *s.* calambre; grapa; *v.* comprimir,

apretar, estrechar; afianzar, sujetar (*con grapa*).

cran•ber•ry [kræ nbərI] *s.* arándano.

crane [kren] *s.* grulla (*ave*); grúa (*máquina para levantar pesos*); *v.* **to – one's neck** estirar el cuello.

cra•ni•um [krénIəm] *s.* cráneo.

crank [kræŋk] *s.* cigüeña, manubrio, manija, manivela; **he is a** – es un maniático; *v.* voltear el manubrio o la cigüeña.

crank•case [kræ ŋkes] *s.* cárter del motor.

cransk•shaft [kræ ŋkʃæft] *s.* cigüeñal.

crank•y [kræ ŋI] *adj.* cascarrabias; maniático; enojadizo.

cran•ny [kræ nI] *s.* grieta, rendija.

crape [krep] *s.* crespón; crespón negro.

crash [kræʃ] *s.* (*noise*) estallido, golpazo, estruendo; (*collision*) choque; (*failure*) fracaso; quiebra; bancarrota; **– landing** aterrizaje violento; aterrizaje de barriga; *v.* estrellar(se); estallar; chocar; **to – an airplane** aterrizar de golpe un aeroplano; **to – into** chocar con, estrellarse contra.

crate [kret] *s.* canasto, cesta, jaula (*para el transprote de mercancías, etc.*); *Am.* huacal; *v.* embalar en jaula

ora•ter [krétə⋅] *s.* cráter.

cra•vat [krəvæt] *s.* corbata.

crave [krev] *v.* ansiar, anhelar, apetecer; **to – mercy (pardon)** pedir misericordia (perdón).

crawl [krɔl] *s.* marcha lenta; natación a la marinera; *v.* arrastrarse; gatear, andar a gatas; marchar lentamente; **to be -ing with ants** hormiguear, estar lleno de hormigas.

cray•on [kréən] *s.* lápiz de color, *Am.* creyón; pastel; tiza, yeso.

craze [krez] *s.* manía, locura; moda; antojo; *v.* enloquecer.

cra•zy [krézI] *adj.* loco; trastornado; **to go – volverse** loco, perder el juicio.

creak [krik] *s.* crujido, rechino, rechinamiento; *v.* crujir, rechinar.

cream [krim] *s.* crema; nata; **– of tomato soup** puré de tomate; **cold –** crema cosmética; **ice –** helado; *v.* desnatar; batir, mezclar (*azúcar y mantenquilla*); preparar (*legumbres*) con salsa de crema.

cream•er•y [krímərI] *s.* lechería, quesería; *Am.* mantequillería.

cream•y [krímI] *adj.* natoso; lleno de crema o nata.

crease [kris] *s.* pliegue; arruga; *v.* plegar, hacer pliegues; arrugar.

cre•ate [krIét] *v.* crear.

cre•a•tion [krIéʃən] *s.* creación; obra.

cre•a•tive [krIétIv] *adj.* creativo, creador.

cre•a•tor [krIétə⋅] *s.* creador

crea•ture [krítʃə⋅] *s.* criatura; ser viviente; animalejo.

cre•dence [kríd ŋ s] *s.* creencia, crédito.

cre·den·tials [krIdénʃəlz] s. pl. credenciales.

cred·i·ble [krédəb]] adj. creíble.

cred·it [krédIt] s. crédito; buena fama; **– and debit** haber y deber; activo y pasivo; **– card** tarjeta de crédito; **on – a** crédito, al fiado, a plazo; **to give –** dar crédito, creer, acreditar, abonar; **that does him –** eso le acredita; v. acreditar; abonar en cuenta; creer, dar crédito; atribuir.

cred·it·a·ble [krédItəb]] adj. loable.

cred·i·tor [krédItə·] s. acreedor.

cred·u·lous [krédʒələs] adj. crédulo.

creed [krid] s. credo; creencia.

creek [krik, krIk] s. riachuelo, arroyo.

creep [krip] v. arrastrarse; gatear, andar a gatas; trepar (las plantas); andar lentamente; deslizarse; sentir hormigueo (en el cuerpo); s. pl. hormigueo, aprensión, horror.

creep·er [krípə·] s. enredadera, planta trepadora.

cre·mate [krímet] v. incinerar.

cre·o·sote [kríəsot] s. creosota.

crepe [krep] = **crape.**

crept [krɛpt] pret. & p.p. de **to creep.**

cres·cent [krés ŋ t] adj. creciente; s. luna creciente; media luna (emblema de turcos y mahometanos).

crest [krɛst] s. cresta; penacho; copete; cima, cumbre; timbre (de un escudo de armas).

crest·fall·en [kréstfolən] adj. cabizbajo, alicaído, abatido.

cre·ton·ne [krItán] s. cretona.

crev·ice [krévIs] s. grieta, hendedura.

crew [kru] s. tripulación; cuadrilla (de obreros); pret. de **to crow.**

crib [krIb] s. camita de niño; pesebre; granero, arcón; armazón (usado en la construcción de edificios); traducción o clave fraudulenta (en un examen); v. enjaular; usar traducción o clave fraudulenta (en un examen).

crick·et [kríkIt] s. grillo; vilorta (juego).

crime [krIm] s. crimen.

crim·i·nal [krímən] adj. & s. criminal.

crimp [krImp] v. rizar; s. rizo.

crim·son [krímz ŋ] adj. & s. carmesí.

cringe [krInʒ] v. encogerse; arrastrarse.

crip·ple [kríp] s. cojo, manco; tullido, baldado, inválido; v. estropear; mutilar, derrengar; baldar; incapacitar.

cri·sis [kráIsIs] s. crisis.

crisp [krIsp] adj. (brittle) quebradizo; tieso; bien tostado; (curly) crespo, encrespado; **– answer** contestación aguda; **– wind** brisa refrescante; v. encrespar.

cri·te·ri·on [kraItírIən] s. criterio.

crit·ic [krítIk] s. crítico; criticón.

crit·i·cal [krítIk]] adj. crítico; criticador, criticón.

crit·i·cism [krítəsIzəm] s. crítica; criticismo.

crit·i·cize [krítəsaIz] v. criticar; censurar.

croak [krok] v. croar; graznar; s. canto de ranas; graznido.

cro·chet [kroʃé] s. labor de gancho; **– hook** aguja de gancho; v. hacer labor de gancho.

crock [krok] s. vasija de loza, jarra.

crock·er·y [krákər] s. loza.

croc·o·dile [krákədaIl] s. cocodrilo. Am. caimán.

cro·ny [krónI] s. compadre, compinche, camarada, compañero.

crook [krUk] s. (thief) falsario; estafador, malente, pícaro; (curve) curva, vuelt; recodo; gancho; **shepherd's –** cayado; v. torcer(se); **to – one's arm** doblar el brazo o codo.

crook·ed [krÚkId] adj. torcido; curvo, encorvado; Am. chueco; Ríopl. chingado; falso, fraudulento.

croon [krun] v. cantar "tristes" (con exagerado patetismo).

crop [krop] s. cosecha; buche (de ave); látigo, Am. cuarta; **– of hair** cabellera; v. segar; recortar; rapar; **to – out** aparecer, asomar; **to – up** brotar, manifestarse inesperadamente.

cross [kros] s. cruz; cruce; cruzamiento (de razas); mezcla; v. cruzar(se); atravesar(se); santiguar(se); encontrarse; contrariar; adj. en cruz, cruzado, transversal; malhumorado; **cross-country** a campo traviesa; **cross-examine** v. interrogar, repreguntar; **cross-eyed** bizco; **– word puzzle** crucigrama.

cross·bar [krɔ́byr] s. travesaño.

cross·ing [krɔ́sIŋ] s. cruce; cruzamiento; encrucijada, crucero; travesía; **railroad –** cruce; **river –** vado.

cross·road [krɔ́srod] s. vía transversal, encrucijada, crucero.

cross sec·tion [krés sékʃən] s. corte transversal; sección transversal.

crouch [krautʃ] v. agacharse, agazaparse.

crow [kro] s. cuervo; canto del gallo; **crow's-foot** pata de gallo (arrugas en el rabo del ojo); v. cantar (el gallo); cacarear; jactarse, hacer alarde.

crow·bar [króbor] s. barra, palanca de hierro.

crowd [kraud] s. muchedumbre; gentío, gente; cuadrilla, pandilla; grupo; v. agolparse, apiñar(se); estrujar, empujar.

crowd·ed [krÚdId] adj. atestado, lleno, apiñado.

crown [kraUn] s. corona; copa (de sombrero); cima; v. coronar.

cru·ci·ble [krúsəb]] s. crisol.

cru·ci·fix [krúsəfIks] s. crucifijo.

cru·ci·fy [krúsəfaI] v. crucificar.

crude [krud] adj. basto, tosco, rudo; inculto; **– oil** petróleo crudo; **– sugar** azúcar bruto, azúcar crudo.

cru·el [krúəl] adj. cruel.

cru·el·ty [krÚəltI] s. crueldad.

cruet [krúIt] *s.* ampolla (*pequeña vasija de cristal*); vinajera (*para servir vino en la misa*); **oil** – aceitera; **vinegar** – vinagrera.

cruise [kruź] *s.* travesía, viaje por mar; excursión; *v.* navegar.

cruis•er [krúzə-] *s.* crucero (*buque*).

crumb [krʌm] *s.* migaja; miga; mendrugo; *v.* desmenuzar, desmigajar.

crum•ble [kr ʌ mb ǀ] *v.* desmenuzar(se); desmoronarse.

crum•ple [kr ʌ mp ǀ] *v.* arrugar(se); ajar, apabullar.

crunch [krʌntʃ] *v.* crujir; mascullar.

cru•sade [kruséd] *s.* cruzada; *v.* hacer una campaña; hacer una cruzada.

cru•sad•er [krusédə-] *s.* cruzado.

crush [krʌʃ] *s.* compresión, presión; estrujamiento, apiñamiento de gente; *v.* estrujar; aplastar; majar; subyugar; **to – stone** moler piedra.

crust [krʌst] *s.* corteza (*de pan, queso, etc.*); costra; mendrugo; *v.* encostrarse, cubrir(se) de costra.

crust•y [kr ʌ stI] *adj.* costroso.

crutch [krʌtʃ] *s.* muleta.

cry [kraI] *s.* grito; lloro, lamento; **a far – from** muy distante de, muy lejos de; *v.* gritar; llorar; clamar; exclamar; vocear; **to – for help** pedir socorro.

crys•tal [krÍst ǀ] *s.* cristal; **– clear** cristalino.

crys•tal•line [krÍst ǀ In] *adj.* cristalino.

crys•tal•lize [krÍst ǀ aIz] *v.* cristalizar(se).

cub [kʌb] *s.* cachorro (*de oso, tigre, lobo, león*); **– reporter** reportero novato.

Cuban [kjúbən] *adj.* & *s.* Cubano.

cube [kjub] *s.* cubo; **– root** raíz cúbica.

cu•bic [kjúbIk] *adj.* cúbico.

cub•ism [kjúbIzm] *s.* cubismo.

cuck•oo [kÚku] *s.* cuco, cuclillo; *adj.* tocado, chiflado, medio loco.

cu•cum•ber [kjúkʌmbə-] *s.* pepino.

cud [kʌd] *s.* rumia; **to chew the –** rumiar.

cud•dle [k ʌ d ǀ] *v.* abrazar, tener en brazos; estar abrazados.

cudg•el [k ʌ dʒəl] *s.* garrote; porra; *v.* aporrar, apalear.

cue [kju] *s.* señal, indicación; pie (*últimas palabras de un parlamento que sirven de señal en el teatro*); **billiard** – taco de billar.

cuff [kʌf] *s.* puño (*de camisa o de vestido*); doblez (*del pantalón*); bofetada; *v.* abofetear, dar de bofetadas.

cull [kʌl] *v.* entresacar; extraer.

cul•mi•nate [k ʌ lmənet] *v.* culminar.

cul•prit [k ʌ lprIt] *s.* reo, delincuente; culpable.

cult [kʌlt] *s.* culto; secta religiosa.

cul•ti•vate [k ʌ ltəvet] *v.* cultivar; labrar, barbechar.

cul•ti•vat•ed [k ʌ ltəvetId] *adj.* cultivado; culto.

cul•ti•va•tion [kʌltəvéʃən] *s.* cultivación, cultivo; cultura.

cul•ti•va•tor [k ʌ ltəvetə-] *s.* cultivador; máquina cultivadora.

cul•ture [k ʌ ltʃə-] *s.* cultura; cultivo.

cul•tured [k ʌ ltʃə-d] *adj.* culto; cultivado.

cum•ber•some [k ʌ mbə-səm] *adj.* engorroso, embarazoso, incómodo.

cun•ning [k ʌ nIŋ] *adj.* astuto, socarrón, sagaz, taimado; diestro; cuco, mono, gracioso, *s.* astucia, maña, sagacidad.

cup [kʌp] *s.* taza, pocillo; copa (*trofeo*).

cup•board [k ʌ bə-d] *s.* armario, aparador; alacena.

cur [kɜ-] *s.* perro mestizo, *Am.* perro chusco; villano, vil, cobarde.

cu•rate [kjÚrIt] *s.* cura.

cu•ra•tor [kjúretə-] *s.* conservador.

curb [kɜ-b] *s.* reborde, encintado (*de la acera*); *Ríopl.* cordón dela acera; freno, restricción; barbada (*del freno de un caballo*); brocal de pozo; *v.* refrenar, reprimir.

curd [kɜ-d] *s.* cuajada; *v.* cuajar(se), coagular(se).

cur•dle [k ɜ- d ǀ] *v.* cuajar(se), coagular(se).

cure [kjUr] *s.* cura, curación; remedio; *v.* curar(se); sanar.

cur•few [kɜ-fju] *s.* queda.

cu•ri•o [kjÚrIo] *s.* curiosidad, objeto raro y curioso.

cu•ri•os•i•ty [kjUrIásətI] *s.* curiosidad; rareza.

cu•ri•ous [kjÚrIəs] *adj.* curioso; extraño, raro.

curl [kɜ-l] *s.* rizo, bucle; espiral (*de humo*); *v.* rizar(se); ensortijar(se); enroscar(se); retorcerse, alzarse en espirales (*el humo*).

curl•y [k ɜ̃ lI] *adj.* rizo, rizoso, rizado, crespo, *Am.* chino.

cur•rant [k ɜ̃ ənt] *s.* grosella; **– bush** grosellero.

cur•ren•cy [k ɜ̃ ensI] *s.* moneda corriente; circulación, **papor** – papel moneda.

cur•rent [k ɜ̃ ənt] *adj.* corriente; común, prevaleciente, en boga; *s.* corriente.

cur•ric•u•lum [kərÍkjələm] *s.* programa de estudios.

curse [kɜ-s] *s.* maldición; calamidad; *v.* maldecir.

curs•ed [k ɜ̃ st] *adj.* maldito.

cur•sive [kɜ-sIv] *adj.* cursivo.

curt [kɜ-t] *adj.* corto; brusco.

cur•tail [kɜ-tél] *v.* cercenar; acortar; restrigir, reducir.

cur•tain [k ɜ̃ t ŋ] *s.* cortina; telón (*de teatro*); *v.* poner cortinas.

cur•va•ture [k ɜ̃ vətʃə-] *s.* curvatura.

curve [kɜ˞v] *s.* curva; *v.* encorvar(se); torcer(se): doblar(se).

curved [kɜ˞vd] *adj.* encorvado; torcido; curvo, corvo, *Méx.*, *C.A.* chueco.

cush·ion [húʃən] *s.* cojín; almohadilla; almohadón; amortiguador (*para amortiguar un sonido o golpe*); *v.* acojinar; amortiguar (un choque).

cus·tard [kÁstə˞d] *s.* flan; natillas.

cus·to·dy [kÁstədɪ] *s.* custodia, cargo, cuidado; **to hold in** – custodiar.

cus·tom [kÁstəm] *s.* costumbre, hábito, uso, usanza; **-s** derechos de aduana; **– made** hecho a la medida; **– tailor** maestro sastre; **– built** construido según pedido.

cus·tom·ar·y [kÁstəmɛrɪ] *adj.* acostumbrado, habitual, usual, de costumbre.

cus·tom·er [kÁstəmə˞] *s.* parroquiano, cliente, marchante.

cus·tom·house [hÁstəmhaUs] *s.* aduana; **– official** aduanero; **– mark** marchamo.

cut [kʌt] *s.* corte (*m*); cortadura; *Am.* cortada; rebanada, tajada; rebaja, reducción (*de precios, sueldos*); hechura (*de un traje*); ausencia (*de la clase*); grabado; **short –** atajo, camino corto; *v.* cortar; tajar; labrar, tallar; segar; rebajar, reducir (*precios, sueldos*); negar el saludo a; alzar (*los naipes*); **to – across** cruzar, atravesar; **to – capers** hacer cabriolas, cabriolar; **to – class** faltar a la clase; **to – out** recortar; excluir; **to be – out for** estar hecho para, tener vocación para; *pret.* & *p.p.* de **to cut.**

cute [kjut] *adj.* mono, cuco, astuto.

cu·ti·cle [kjútɪk l̩] *s.* cutícula.

cut·ler·y [kÁtlərɪ] *s.* cuchillería, cuchillos.

cut·let [kÁtlɪt] *s.* chuleta.

cut·ter [kÁtə˞] *s.* cortador; máquina para cortar; trineo; **wood –** leñador; **coast guard –** barco guardacostas.

cut·ting [kÁtɪŋ] *adj.* cortante; penetrante; mordaz, sarcástico.

cy·ber·net·ics [saɪbə˞nétɪks] *s.* cibernética.

cy·cle [sáɪk l̩] *s.* ciclo.

cy·clone [sáɪklon] *s.* ciclón; huracán.

cyl·in·der [sÍlɪndə˞] *s.* cilindro.

cy·lin·dri·cal [sɪlÍndrɪk l̩] *adj.* cilíndrico.

cym·bal [sÍmb l̩] *s.* címbalo, platillo; **to play the -s** tocar los platillos.

cyn·ic [sÍnɪk] *s.* cínico.

cyn·i·cal [sÍnɪk l̩] *adj.* cínico.

cyn·i·cism [sÍnəsɪzəm] *s.* cinismo.

cy·press [sáɪprəs] *s.* ciprés.

cyst [sɪst] *s.* quiste.

D

dad [dæd] *s.* papá, tata; **daddy** *s.* papaíto o papacito, tata, tatita, *Am.* taita.

daf·fo·dil [dǽfədɪl] *s.* narciso.

dag·ger [dǽgə˞] *s.* daga; puñal; **to look -s at** traspasar con la mirada.

dai·ly [délɪ] *adj.* diario; *adv.* diariamente; *s.* diario, periódico.

dain·ty [déntɪ] *adj.* delicado, fino, primoroso, exquisito; *s.* golosina, manjar exquisito.

dair·y [dérɪ] *s.* lechería, vaquería; quesería, quesera.

dai·sy [dézɪ] *s.* margarita, maya.

dale [del] *s.* cañada.

dal·ly [dǽlɪ] *v.* juguetear; holgazanear; entretenerse, tardar; malgastar el tiempo.

dam [dæm] *s.* presa, represa; *v.* represar, estancar.

dam·age [dǽmɪdʒ] *s.* daño; perjuicio; avería; **to pay for -s** indemnizar, pagar los daños y perjuicios; *v.* dañar(se); averiar(se).

dame [dem] *s.* dama, señora; **old –** vieja.

damn [dæm] *v.* maldecir; condenar; blasfemar; **– it** ¡maldito sea!

dam·na·tion [dæmnéʃən] *s.* condenación, perdición.

damp [dæmp] *adj.* húmedo; mojado; *s.* humedad; *v.* humedecer, mojar.

damp·en [dǽmpən] *v.* mojar, humedecer; desalentar; amortiguar.

damp·ness [dǽmpnɪs] *s.* humedad.

dam·sel [dǽmz l̩] *s.* damisela.

dance [dæns] *s.* baile; danza; **– music** música de baile; *v.* bailar; danzar.

danc·er [dǽnsə˞] *s.* bailador; bailarín, bailarina; danzante.

dan·de·li·on [dǽnd l̩ aɪən] *s.* diente de león.

dan·druff [dǽndrəf] *s.* caspa.

dan·dy [dǽndɪ] *s.* currutaco, majo, afectado; chulo; *adj.* elegante, excelente.

dan·ger [déndʒə˞] *s.* peligro, riesgo.

dan·ger·ous [déndʒərəs] *adj.* peligroso; arriesgado; **-ly** *adv.* peligrosamente; **-ly ill** gravemente enfermo.

dan·gle [dǽŋg l̩] *v.* pender, colgar, bambolear(se) (*en el aire*).

dap·ple(d) [dǽp l̩ (d)] *adj.* rodado, con manchas (*dícese de los caballos*); **dapple-grey** rucio rodado, tordo, tordillo.

dare [dɛr] *s.* desafío, reto, provocación; **–devil** atrevido, osado; *v.* atreverse, osar; desafiar.

dar•ing [dérɪŋ] *s.* atrevimiento, osadía; *adj.* osado, atrevido, arrojado.

dark [dɑrk] *adj.* obscuro; sombrío; **– horse** caballo desconocido *(que gana inesperadamente la carrera);* candidato nombrado inesperadamente; **– secret** secreto profundo; enigma; **darkskinned** moreno, trigueño; *s.* obscuridad; sombra.

dark•en [dárkən] *v.* obscurecer(se); nublarse.

dark•ness [dárkɪɪs] *s.* obscuridad; tinieblas; sombra.

dark•y [dárkɪ] *s.* negro *(persona).*

dar•ling [dárlɪŋ] *adj. & s.* amado, querido; **my –** vida mía *(o* mi vida), amor mío.

darn [dɑrn] *s.* zurcido; **it is not worth a –** no vale un comino, no vale un pito; *v.* zurcir;–! ¡caramba! ¡canastos!; **-ing needle** aguja de zurcir.

dart [dɑrt] *s.* dardo, flecha; sisa *(en un vestido);* movimiento rápido; *v.* lanzar(se); flechar; **to – out** salir como una flecha; **to – in and out** entrar y salir precipitadamente.

dash [dæʃ] *s. (line)* raya; *(run)* carrera corta; *(vigor)* ímpetu; *(grace)* garbo; pizca *(de sal, azúcar, etc.);* rociada *(de agua);* **–board** tablero de instrumentos; **with a – of the pen** de una plumada; *v.* lanzar(se); echar(se); estrellar(se); salpicar; frustrar *(esperanzas);* **to – by** pasar corriendo; **to – out** salir a la carrera; **to – off a letter** escribir de prisa una carta.

da•ta [détə] *s. pl.* datos.

date [det] *s. (time)* fecha; *(statement)* data; *(appointment)* cita, compromiso; *(fruit)* dátil; **out of –** anticuado, desusado; fuera de moda; **up to –** al día, moderno; **up to this –** hasta ahora, hasta la fecha; *v.* fechar; **to – from** datar de; remontarse a.

daub [dɔb] *v.* embarrar, untar; pintarrajear.

daugh•ter [dɔ́tə·] *s.* hija; **daughter-inlaw** nuera.

daunt [dɔnt] *v.* intimidar, asustar, espantar; desanimar.

daunt•less [dʌ́ntlɪs] *adj.* denodado, intrépido.

dav•en•port [dǽvənport] *s.* sofá.

dawn [dɔn] *s.* alba; amanecer, madrugada; *v.* amanecer; alborear, rayar *(el día);* **it just -ed upon me** acabo de dar cuenta.

day [de] *s.* día; **– after tomorrow** pasado mañana; **– before yesterday** anteayer o antier; **– laborer** jornalero; **by –** de día; **by the –** por día; **eight-hour –** jornada de ocho horas; **to win the –** ganar la jornada, triunfar.

day•break [débrek] *s.* amanecer, alba; **at –** al amanecer, al romper el día, al rayar el día.

day•light [délaɪt] *s.* luz del día.

day•time [détaɪm] *s.* día *(tiempo de luz natural);* **in the –** durante el día; de día.

daze [dez] *s.* aturdimiento; deslumbramiento; **to be in a –** estar aturdido; *v.* aturdir; ofuscar; deslumbrar.

daz•zle [dǽz]] *s.* brillantez; *v.* deslumbrar; ofuscar.

dea•con [díkən] *s.* diácono.

dead [dɛd] *adj.* muerto; **– air** aire viciado o estancado; **– letter** carta no reclamada; **– loss** pérdida absoluta; *adv.* completamente, absolutamente; sumamente, muy; **– sure** completamente seguro; **– tired** muerto de cansancio; *s.* **the –** los muertos; **in the – of the night** en el sigilo de la noche; **in the – of winter** en lo más crudo del invierno.

dead•en [dɛ́d ŋ] *v.* amortiguar.

dead•head [dɛ́dhɛd] *s.* persona que no paga la entrada; colado.

dead•ly [ɛ́dlɪ] *adj.* mortal; fatal; como la muerte, cadavérico; *adv.* mortalmente; **– dull** sumamente aburrido.

deaf [dɛf] *adj.* sordo; **deaf-mute** *s. & adj.* sordomudo.

deaf•en [dɛ́fən] *v.* ensordecer; amortiguar, apagar *(un sonido).*

deaf•en•ing [dɛ́fənɪŋ] *adj.* ensordecedor, estruendoso.

deaf•ness [dɛ́fnɪs] *s.* sordera.

deal [dil] *s.* trato, negocio; mano *(en el juego de naipes);* distribución, reparto *(de los naipes);* **a great – of** una gran cantidad de, mucho; **to give a square –** tratar con equidad; *v.* tallar *(en juegos de naipes);* distribuir, repartir; dar *(un golpe);* **to – in** comerciar en; **to – with** tratar de *(un asunto);* tratar con; negociar con.

deal•er [dílə·] *s.* negociante, comerciante, tratante; tallador *(en el juego de naipe).*

deal•ings [dílɪŋz] *s. pl.* relaciones *(comerciales o amistosas);* comercio, tratos; negocios.

dealt [dɛlt] *pret. & p.p. de* **to deal.**

dean [din] *s.* deán *(dignidad eclesiástica);* decano *(de universidad).*

dear [dɪr] *adj. (beloved)* querido, amado; *(expensive)* caro; costoso; *adv.* caro; **– me!** ¡Dios mío!; **oh –!** ¡ay!; **my –** querido mío; **Dear Sir** Muy señor mío; **-ly** *adv.* cariñosamente; a precio alto; **my -ly beloved** muy amado mío; muy amados míos.

dearth [dɜθ] *s.* escasez, carestía, insuficiencia.

death [dɛθ] *s.* muerte; mortandad; **– rate** mortalidad.

death•bed [dɛ́θbɛb] *s.* lecho de muerte.

de•base [dɪbés] *v.* rebajar el valor de; degradar, humillar, envilecer.

de•bat•a•ble [dɪbétəb]] *adj* discutible, disputable.

de•bate [dɪbǝet] *s.* debate, discusión; *v.* debatir, discutir; considerar; deliberar.

de•bil•i•tate [dǝbílǝtet] *v.* debilitar.

deb•it [dɛ́bɪt] *s.* débito, adeudo, cargo; debe *(de una cuenta);* pasivo *(en contabilidad);* *v.* adeudar, cargar en cuenta.

de•brief•ing [dibrífɪŋ] *s.* informe de vuelo bajo interrogación; informe.

de•bris [dəbríː] *s.* escombros; ruinas.

debt [dɛt] *s.* deuda; adeudo; débito; **bad** — cuenta incobrable; **to run into** — adeudarse, entramparse, cargarse de deudas.

deb•tor [détə] *s.* deudor.

de•bunk [dib ʌ ŋk] *v.* desbaratar; desenmascarar.

de•but [dɪbjú] *s.* estreno; **to make a** – debutar, estrenarse.

dec•ade [dékéd] *s.* década, decenio.

de•ca•dence [dɪkéd ŋ s] *s.* decadencia.

de•cant•er [dɪk ǽ ntə] *s.* garrafa; **large** – garrafón.

de•cay [dɪké] *s.* decaimiento; decadencia, ruina; podredumbre; caries (*de la dentadura*); *v.* decaer; venir a menos; pudrir(se) o podrir(se).

de•cease [dɪsíːs] *s.* muerte, fallecimiento; *v.* morir, fallecer.

de•ceased [dɪdíst] *adj. & s.* muerto, difunto.

de•ceit [dɪsít] *s.* engaño; fraude; trampa.

de•ceit•ful [dɪsítfəl] *adj.* engañador; tramposo; engañoso.

de•ceive [dɪsíːv] *v.* engañar.

De•cem•ber [dɪsémbə] *s.* diciembre.

de•cen•cy [dis ŋ t] *s.* decencia.

de•cent [dís ŋ t] *adj.* decente; decoroso.

de•cide [dɪsáɪd] *v.* decidir, resolver, determinar; **to** – **to** resolverse a, decidirse a.

de•cid•ed [dɪsáɪdɪd] *adj.* decidido, resuelto.

dec•i•mal [désəm]] *adj.* decimal; *s.* decimal, fracción decimal.

de•ci•pher [dɪsáɪfə] *v.* descifrar.

de•ci•sion [dɪsíʒən] *s.* decisión, resolución.

de•ci•sive [dɪsáɪsɪV] *adj.* decisivo; terminante.

deck [dɛk] *s.* cubierta (*de un buque*); baraja; *v.* cubrir; ataviar; **to** – **oneself out** emperifollarse.

dec•la•ra•tion [dɛkləréʃən] *s.* declaración.

de•clare [dɪkl ǽ r] *v.* declarar; afirmar.

de•cline [dɪkláɪn] *s.* declinación; decadencia; mengua; baja (*de precios*); *v.* declinar; decaer; rehusar; **to** – **to do something** negarse a hacer algo.

de•cliv•i•ty [dɪklívəti] *s.* declive.

dé•col•leté [dekɔlté] *adj.* escotado.

de•com•pose [dikəmpóz] *v.* descomponer(se); **corromper**(se), pudrir(se).

dec•o•rate [dékəret] *v.* decorar, adornar; condecorar.

dec•o•ra•tion [dɛkəréʃən] *s.* decoración; adorno; insignia, condecoración.

dec•o•ra•tive [dékəretɪV] *adj.* decorativo; ornamental.

de•co•rum [dɪkórəm] *s.* decoro; circunspección.

de•coy [dɪk ɔ ɪ] *s.* reclamo, señuelo, figura de ave (*que sirve para atraer aves*); cebo (*artificio para atraer con engaño*); trampa, lazo; *v.* atraer con señuelo o engaño.

de•cre•ase [díkris] *s.* disminución o diminución; merma; menga; [dɪkrís] *v.* disminuir(se); mermar; menguar.

de•cree [dɪkríː] *s.* decreto; *v.* decretar; mandar.

de•crep•it [dɪkrépɪt] *adj.* decrépito.

ded•i•cate [dédəket] *v.* dedicar.

ded•i•ca•tion [dɛdəkéʃən] *s.* dedication; dedicatoria.

de•duce [dɪdjús] *v.* deducir, inferir.

de•duct [dɪd ʌ kt] *v.* deducir, descontar, rebajar.

de•duc•tion [dɪd ʌ kʃən] *s.* deducción; rebaja, descuento.

deed [did] *s.* hecho, acción, acto; hazaña; escritura (*de venta o compra*).

deem [dim] *v.* juzgar, creer, considerar.

deep [dip] *adj.* (*down*) hondo; profundo; (*obscure*) oscuro; (*tone*) grave, bajo; – **in debt** cargado de deudas; – **in thought** absorto; – **mourning** luto riguroso; **to go off the** – **end** echarse a pique; caer en el abismo; – **into the night** en las tinieblas de la noche; *s.* **the** – el mar;**-ly** *adv.* profundamente, hondamente; intensamente.

deep•en [dípen] *v.* ahondar, profundizar.

deer [dɪr] *s.* ciervo, venado; **–skin** piel o cuero de venado.

de•face [dɪfés] *v.* desfigurar, estropear, mutilar.

de•fame [dɪfém] *v.* difamar, calumniar, denigrar.

de•fault [dɪf ɔ́ lt] *s.* falla, falta, negligencia (*en un deber, pago, obligación*); deficiencia; *v.* fallar, faltar (*en el cumplimiento de un deber, pago, obligación*); no comparecer a la cita de un tribunal.

de•feat [dɪfít] *s.* derrota, vencimiento; frustración (*de un plan*); *v.* vencer, derrotar; frustrar.

de•fect [dɪfɛ́kt] *s.* defecto.

de•fec•tive [dɪfɛ́ktiv] *adj.* defectuoso; incompleto; subnormal, falto de inteligencia; – **verb** verbo defectivo.

de•fend [dɪfɛ́nd] *v.* defender.

de•fen•dant [dɪfɛ́ndənt] *s.* acusado, demandado, procesado.

de•fend•er [dɪfɛ́ndə] *s.* defensor; abogado defensor.

de•fense [dɪfɛ́ns] *s.* defensa.

de•fense•less [dɪfɛ́nslɪs] *adj.* indefenso, inerme.

de•fen•sive [dɪfɛ́nsɪv] *adj.* defensivo; *s.* defensiva.

de•fer [dɪf ɝ́] *v.* diferir, posponer, aplazar; **to** – **to another's opinion** remitirse o ceder al dictamen de otro.

de•fi•ance [dɪfárəns] *s.* reto, desafío, provocación; oposición; **in** – **of** en abierta oposición con, a despecho de.

de•fi•cienc•y [dɪfíʃənsɪ] *s.* deficiencia; defecto; déficit.

de·fi·cient [dɪfíʃənt] *adj.* deficiente; defectuoso.
def·i·cit [défəsɪt] *s.* déficit.
de·file [dɪfáɪl] *v.* viciar, corromper; profanar; manchar, ensuciar.
de·fine [dɪfáɪn] *v.* definir.
def·i·nite [défənɪt] *adj.* definido; claro, preciso; fijo; **–article** artículo determinado o definido;**-ly** *adv.* definidamente; claramente;**-ly not** terminantemente no.
def·i·ni·tion [dɛfəníʃən] *s.* definición.
de·fin·i·tive [dɪdínətɪv] *adj.* definitivo.
de·flect [dɪflékt] *v.* desviar(se)
de·form [dɪfɔ́rm] *v.* deformar; desfigurar, afear.
de·formed [dɪfɔ́rmd] *adj.* deforme, disforme; deformado; desfigurado.
de·for·mi·ty [dɪfɔ́rmətɪ] *s.* deformidad; deformación.
de·fraud [dɪfrɔ́d] *v.* defraudar.
de·fray [dɪfré] *v.* sufragar, costear, pagar (*gastos*).
deft [dɛft] *adj.* diestro, ágil.
de·functt [dɪf ʌ̀ŋkt] *adj.* diestuo, ágil.
de·fy [dɪfáɪ] *v.* desafiar; retar; oponerse a, resistirse a.
de·gen·er·ate [dɪdʒénərɪt] *adj. & s.* degenerado; [dɪdʒénəret] *v.* degenerar.
de·grad·a·tion [dɛgrədéʃən] *s.* degradación; envilecimiento.
de·grade [dɪgréd] *v.* degradar; envilecer, rebajar.
de·gree [dɪgrí] *s.* grado; rango; **by -s** gradualmente; **to get a –** graduarse.
de·hy·drate [dɪháɪdret] *v.* deshidratar(se).
deign [den] *v.* dignarse, condescender.
de·i·ty [déətɪ] *s.* deidad.
de·ject·ed [dɪdʒéktɪd] *adj.* abatido.
de·jec·tion [dɪdʒékʃən] *s.* abatimiento, melancolía, depresión.
de·lay [dɪlé] *s.* demora, tardanza, dilación, retraso; *v.* demorar; retardar, dilatar; diferir; tardarse.
de·lay·ed ac·tion [dɪléd ǽkʃən] *adj.* atrasado; retardado.
del·e·gate [déləget] *s.* delegado, representante; *v.* delegar, diputar.
del·e·ga·tion [dɛləgéʃən] *s.* delegación, diputación.
de·le·tion [dɪlíʃən] *s.* suspensión.
de·lib·er·ate [dɪlíbərɪt] *adj.* deliberado, premeditado; cauto, prudente; lento;**-ly** *adv.* deliberadamente; con premeditación; [dɪlíbəret] *v.* deliberar.
de·lib·er·a·tion [dɪlɪbəréʃən] *s.* deliberación.
del·i·ca·cy [déləkəsɪ] *s.* delicadeza; sensibilidad; finura; golosina.
del·i·cate [déləkət] *adj.* delicado; frágil; exquisito.
del·i·ca·tes·sen [dɛləkətésn̩] *s.* tienda de fiambres, queso, ensaladas, etc.

de·li·cious [dɪlíʃəs] *adj.* delicioso.
de·light [dɪléaɪt] *s.* deleite; delicia; *v.* deleitar(se); encantar; agradar; **to – in** gozarse en, deleitarse en.
de·light·ed [dɪláɪtɪd] *adj.* encantado; **to be – to** alegrarse de, tener mucho gusto en (*o* de).
de·light·ful [dɪláɪfəl] *adj.* deleitoso; delicioso; ameno, agradable.
de·lin·e·ate [dɪlíɪnɪet] *v.* delinear, trazar.
de·lin·quent [dɪlíŋkwənt] *adj. & s.* delincuente.
de·lir·i·ous [dɪlɪərɪəs] *adj.* delirante; **to be –** delirar, desvariar.
de·lir·i·um [dɪlɪ́rɪəm] *s.* delirio, desvario.
de·liv·er [dɪlívə-] *v.* entregar; librar, libertar; pronunciar (*un discurso*); dar (*un golpe*).
de·liv·er·ance [dɪlívərəns] *s.* liberación, rescate.
de·liv·er·er [dɪlívərə-] *s.* libertador; portador, mensajero.
de·liv·er·y [dɪlívərɪ] *s.* (*giving*) entrega; (*sawing*) liberación; (*birth*) parto; (*speaking*) elocuencia, manera de hacer una conferencia; **– service** servicio de entrega; **– truck** camión (*o* camioneta) de reparto; **mail –** reparto de correo.
dell [dɛl] *s.* cañada, hondonada.
delta wing [déltə wɪŋ] *s.* ala en delta.
de·lude [dɪlúd] *v.* engañar.
de·luge [déljudʒ] *s.* diluvio; *v.* inundar; abrumar.
de·lu·sion [dɪlúʒən] *s.* ilusión; engaño, error.
de·mand [dɪmǽnd] *s.* demanda; exigencia; solicitud; **on –** a solicitud; *v.* demandar, reclamar; exigir.
de·mand·ing [dɪmǽndɪŋ] *adj.* exigente.
de·mean·or [dɪmínə-] *s.* conducta, comportamiento, proceder.
de·ment·ed [dɪméntɪd] *adj.* demente.
de·mise [dɪmáɪz] *s.* fallecimiento.
de·mo·bil·ize [dimób]aɪz] *v.* demovilizar.
de·moc·ra·cy [dəmákrəsɪ] *s.* democracia.
dem·o·crat [déməkræt] *s.* demócrata.
dem·o·crat·ic [dɛməkrǽtɪk] *adj.* democrático.
de·mol·ish [dɪmálɪʃ] *v.* demoler.
de·mon [dímən] *s.* demonio.
dem·on·strate [démənstret] *v.* demostrar.
dem·on·stra·tion [dɛmənstréʃən] *s.* demostración; prueba; (*protest*) manifestación.
de·mon·stra·tive [dɪmánstrətɪv] *adj.* demostrativo; efusivo.
den [dɛn] *s.* guarida; escondrijo; cueva, lugar de retiro.
de·ni·al [dɪnáɪəl] *s.* negación; negativa; **self-denial** abnegación.
den·i·grate [dénɪgret] *v.* calumniar; ennegrecer.
de·nom·i·na·tion [dɪnɑmənéʃən] *s.* (*name*) denominación; nombre; título, designación; (*sect*) secta religiosa.
de·note [dɪnót] *v.* denotar.
de·nounce [dɪnáʊns] *v.* denunciar; delatar, acusar.

dense [dɛns] *adj.* denso; espeso, apretado; estúpido.

den·si·ty [dénsətɪ] *s.* densidad; estupidez.

dent [dɛnt] *s.* abolladura; mella; *v.* abollar; mellar.

den·tal [dént l] *adj.* dental; *s.* dental, consonante dental.

den·ti·frice [déntɪfrɪs] *s.* pasta dentífrica; dentífrico.

den·tist [déntɪst] *s.* dentista.

de·nun·ci·a·tion [dɪnʌnsɪéʃən] *s.* denuncia, acusación.

de·ny [dɪnáɪ] *v.* negar; rehusar; **to – oneself** sacrificarse, abnegarse; **to – oneself to callers** negarse a recibir visitas.

de·part [dɪpárt] *v.* partir, salir, irse; desviarse, apartarse.

de·part·ed [dɪpártid] *adj.* ido; ausente; difunto.

de·part·ment [dɪpártmənt] *s.* departamento; distrito; ramo, división; **– store** almacén.

de·par·ture [dɪpártʃə-] *s.* salida, partida; desviación.

de·pend [dɪpɛnd] *v.* depender; **to – on** depender de; contar con, confiar en.

de·pend·a·ble [dɪpɛndəb l] *adj.* seguro, fidedigno, digno de confianza.

de·pend·ence [dɪpɛndəns] *s.* dependencia; confianza.

de·pend·ency [dɪpɛndənsɪ] *s.* dependencia; sucursal.

de·pend·ent [dɪpɛndənt] *adj.* dependiente; subordinado; *s.* dependiente, familiar.

de·pict [dɪpíkt] *v.* pintar, describir; representar.

de·pil·a·to·ry [dɪpíletorɪ] *s.* depilatorio.

de·plete [dɪplít] *v.* agotar; vaciar.

de·plor·a·ble [dɪplórəb l] *adj.* deplorable, lamentable.

de·plore [dɪplór] *v.* deplorar.

de·port [dɪpórt] *v.* deportar; **to – oneself well** portarse bien.

de·port·ment [dɪpórtmənt] *s.* comportamiento, conducta.

de·pose [dɪpóz] *v.* deponer; declarar, atestiguar.

de·pos·it [dɪpázɪt] *s.* depósito; *v.* depositar.

dep·o·si·tion [dɛpəzíʃən] *s.* deposición; declaración.

de·pos·i·tor [dɪpázɪə-] *s.* depositador.

de·pot [dípo] *s.* depósito; almacén; estación de ferrocarril.

dep·re·cate [déprɪket] *v.* desaprobar.

de·pre·ci·ate [dɪpríʃɪet] *v.* depreciar; bajar de precio; abaratar(se); menospreciar.

de·press [dɪprɛs] *v.* deprimir; abatir; deanimar; depreciar, rebajar el valor de.

de·pressed [dɪprɛst] *adj.* abatido, decaído.

de·press·ing [dɪprɛsɪŋ] *adj.* deprimente.

de·pres·sion [dɪprɛʃən] *s.* depresión; decaimiento, abatimiento; rebaja (*de precios*).

de·prive [dɪpráɪv] *v.* privar.

depth [dɛpθ] *s.* profundidad; honduras; fondo; longitud (*de un solar*); gravedad (*de los sonidos*); viveza (*de los colores*); **in the – of the night** en las tinieblas de la noche; **in the – of winter** en lo más crudo del invierno.

de·pu·ta·tion [dɛpjətéʃən] *s.* diputación, delegación; comisión.

dep·u·te [dɪpjút] *v.* diputar, delegar.

dep·u·ty [dépjətɪ] *s.* diputado; agente; delegado.

de·range [dɪréndʒ] *v.* trastornar, desordenar.

der·by [dǽbɪ] *s.* sombrero hongo, *Méx.*, *Ven.*, *Col.* sombrero de bola.

der·e·lict [dérɪlɪkt] *adj.* abandonado; negligente.

de·ride [dɪráɪd] *v.* escarnecer, ridiculizar, mofarse de, burlarse de.

de·ri·sion [dɪríʒən] *s.* mofa, escarnio.

de·rive [dɪráɪv] *v.* derivar(se); provenir; sacar (*provecho*); recibir (*placer*).

der·ma·tol·o·gy [də-mətólədʒɪ] *s.* dermatología.

der·rick [dérɪk] *s.* grúa; armazón (*para la explotación del petróleo*).

de·scend [dɪsɛnd] *v.* descender; bajar; **to – upon** caer sobre, acometer.

de·scen·dant [dɪsɛndənt] *adj.* & *s.* descendiente.

de·scent [dɪsɛnt] *s.* descenso; bajada; descendencia, linaje; descendimiento; declive.

de·scribe [dɪskráɪb] *v.* describir; trazar.

de·scrip·tion [dɪskrípʃən] *s.* descripción; **of all -s** de todas clases.

de·scrip·tive [dɪskríptɪv] *adj.* descriptivo; **– linguistics** lingüística descriptiva.

des·ert [dézə-t] *adj.* desierto, despoblado; estéril; *s.* desierto, yermo; páramo; [dɪzə́t] *v.* abandonar, desamparar; desertar.

de·sert·er [dɪzə́tə-] *s.* desertor.

de·ser·tion [dɪzə́ʃən] *s.* deserción, abandono, desamparo.

de·serve [dɪzə́v] *v.* merecer.

de·serv·ing [dɪzə́vɪŋ] *adj.* meritorio; merecedor.

de·sign [dɪzáɪn] *s.* (*sketch*) dibujo, diseño; (*plan*) designio, propósito, intención; plan, proyecto; *v.* diseñar, trazar; proyectar; idear.

des·ig·nate [dézɪgnet] *v.* designar; señalar, indicar, nombrar.

de·sign·er [dɪzáɪnə-] *s.* diseñador; dibujante; proyectista; intrigante.

de·sir·a·bi·li·ty [dɪzaɪrəbílətɪ] *s.* conveniencia, utilidad.

de·sir·a·ble [dɪzáɪrəb l] *adj.* deseable; agradable; conveniente.

de·sire [dɪzáɪr] *s.* deseo; anhelo, ansia; *v.* desear; anhelar, ansiar.

de·sir·ous [dɪzáɪrəs] *adj.* deseoso.

de·sist [dizíst] v. desistir.

desk [dɛsk] s. escritorio, bufete, pupitre, mesa de escribir.

des·o·late [dés] ɪt] adj. desolado; despoblado, desierto; solitario; [dés] et] v. desolar; asolar, arrasar; despoblar.

des·o·la·tion [dɛs] éʃən] s. desolación; soledad.

de·spair [dɪspér] s. desesperación; desesperanza; v. desesperarse, perder la esperanza.

de·spair·ing [dɪspérɪŋ] adj. desesperado, sin esperanza.

des·patch [dɪspǽtʃ] = **dispatch**.

des·per·ate [désprɪt] adj. desesperado; arriesgado, temerario; — **illness** enfermedad gravísima;**-ly** adv. deseperadamente;**-ly ill** gravísimamente enfermo.

des·per·a·tion [despəréʃn] s. desesperación; temeridad.

des·pi·ca·ble [déspɪkəb]] adj. despreciable; desdeñable.

de·spise [dɪspáɪz] v. despreciar; desdeñar; menospreciar.

de·spite [dɪspáɪt] s. despecho; prep. a despecho de, a pesar de.

de·spoil [dɪspóɪl] v. despojar.

de·spon·dency [dɪspándənsɪ] s. abatimiento desaliento, descaecimiento o decaimiento del ánimo.

de·spon·dent [dɪspándənt] adj. abatido, descaecido o decaído de ánimo, desalentado, desesperanzado.

des·pot [déspət] s. déspota.

des·pot·ic [dɪspátɪk] adj. despótico.

des·pot·ism [déspətɪzəm] s. despotismo.

des·sert [dɪzɝt] s. postre.

des·ti·na·tion [dɛstənéʃən] s. destinación, destino; paradero.

des·tine [déstɪn] v. destinar; **-ed for** con rumbo a, con destinación a; destinado a.

des·ti·ny [déstənɪ] s. destino, sino, hado.

des·ti·tute [déstətjut] adj. destituido, necesitado; falto, desprovisto.

de·stroy [dɪstrɔ́ɪ] v. destruir.

de·stroy·er [dɪstrɔ́ɪə-] s. destruidor; destructor, cazatorpedero, destroyer.

de·struc·tion [dɪstrʌkʃən] s. destrucción; ruina.

de·struc·tive [dɪstrʌktɪv] adj. destructivo.

de·tach [dɪtǽʃ] v. separar, despegar, desprender; destacar (una porción de tropa).

de·tach·ment [dɪtǽtʃmənt] s. separación; desprendimiento; desapego; despego, alejamiento; destacamento (militar).

de·tail [dítel] s. detalle; pormenor; destacamento (militar); **to go into —** detallar, pormenorizar; [dɪtél]

v. detallar, pormenorizar; destacar, asignar.

de·tain [dɪtén] v. detener; entretener, demorar, retardar.

de·tect [dɪtέkt] v. descubrir.

de·tec·tive [dɪtέktɪv] s. detective, detectivo, policía secreto.

de·ten·tion [dɪténʃən] s. detención.

de·ter·gent [dɪtɝdʒənt] s. detergente.

de·te·ri·o·rate [dɪtírɪəret] v. deteriorar(se).

de·te·ri·o·ra·tion [dɪtɪrɪəréʃən] s. deterioro.

de·ter·mi·na·tion [dɪtɝmənéʃən] s. determinación; decisión; resolución, firmeza.

de·ter·mine [dɪtɝmɪn] v. determinar; decidir; **to — to** determinarse a, decidirse a, resolverse a.

de·ter·mined [dɪtɝmɪnd] adj. determinado, decidido, resuelto.

de·test [dɪtést] v. detestar, aborrecer.

de·tour [dítʊr] s. rodeo, desvío, desviación, vuelta; v. dar o hacer un rodeo.

dev·as·tate [dévəstet] v. devastar, arruinar, asolar.

de·vel·op [dɪvéləp] v. desarrollar(se); desenvolver(se); revelar (una película o placa fotográfica); explotar (una mina).

de·vel·op·ment [dɪvéləpmənt] s. (evolution) desarrollo; desenvolvimiento; evolución; crecimiento; (generation) fomento; explotación; (photo) revelado.

de·vi·ate [dívɪet] v. desviar(se).

de·vi·a·tion [dívɪéʃən] s. desviación; desvío, extravío.

de·vice [dɪváɪs] s. artificio; mecanismo, aparato; ardid, recurso; divisa; **left to one's own -s** abandonado a sus propios recursos.

dev·il [dév]] s. diablo; demonio.

dev·il·ish [dévlɪʃ] adj. diabólico; endiablado; travieso.

dev·il·try [dév] trɪ] s. diablura.

de·vi·ous [dívɪəs] adj. desviado; tortuoso; indirecto.

de·vise [dɪváɪz] v. idear, trazar, urdir.

de·void [dɪvóɪd] adj. exento, libre, falto, privado, desprovisto.

de·vote [dɪvót] v. dedicar; consagrar; **to — oneself to** dedicarse a, consagrarse a, aplicarse a.

de·vot·ed [dɪvótɪd] adj. dedicado, consagrado; apegado; **— friend** amigo fiel o leal.

de·vo·tion [dɪvóʃən] s. devoción; piedad; afecto; lealtad.

de·vour [dɪváʊr] v. devorar.

de·vout [dɪváʊt] adj. devoto, piadoso; sincero.

dew [dju] s. rocío, sereno; v. rociar; caer (el rocío).

dew·drop [djúdrop] s. gota de rocío.

dew·y [djúɪ] adj. rociado, húmedo de rocío.

dex·ter·i·ty [dɛkstérətɪ] s. destreza.

dex·ter·ous [dékstrəs] *adj.* diestro.

dex·trose [dékstros] *s.* dextrosa.

di·a·dem [dáɪədɛm] *s.* diadema.

di·ag·nose [daɪəgnós] *v.* diagnosticar.

di·ag·o·nal [daɪǽgən l] *adj.* diagonal, oblicuo; *s.* diagonal.

di·a·gram [dáɪəgræm] *s.* diagrama.

di·al [dáɪəl] *s.* esfera; muestra (*del reloj*), *Méx., C.A.* carátula; – **telephone** teléfono automático; *v.* sintonizar o captar (*una estación radiotelefónica*).

di·a·lect [dáɪəlɛkt] *s.* dialecto.

di·a·logue [dáɪəlog] *s.* diálogo; *v.* dialogar.

di·am·e·ter [daɪǽmətə] *s.* diámetro.

di·a·mond [dáɪmənd] *s.* diamante; rombo (*figura geométrica*).

di·a·per [dáɪəpə] *s.* pañal.

di·ar·rhe·a [daɪəríə] *s.* diarrea.

di·a·ry [dáɪərɪ] *s.* diario.

dice [daɪs] *s. pl. de* **die** dados; *v.* cuadricular, cortar en cuarterones o cubos.

di·chot·o·my [daɪkótəmɪ] *s.* dicotomía.

dic·tate [díktet] *s.* dictado, precepto; *v.* dictar.

dic·ta·tion [dɪktəeʃən] *s.* dictado; mando absoluto; **to take** – escribir al dictado.

dic·ta·tor [díktetə] *s.* dictador.

dic·ta·tor·ship [dɪktétəʃɪp] *s.* dictadura.

dic·tion [díkʃən] *s.* dicción.

dic·tion·ar·y [díkʃənɛrɪ] *s.* diccionario.

did [dɪd] *pret. de* **to do.**

die [daɪ] *s.* (*pl.* **dice**) dado (*para jugar*); (*pl.* **dies**) matriz, molde; cuño (*sello para acuñar moneda*).

die [daɪ] *v.* morir(se); marchitarse, secarse (*las flores, plantas, etc.*); **to** – **out** morirse, extinguirse, apagarse.

die·re·sis [daɪérəsɪs] *s.* diéresis.

di·et [dáɪət] *s.* dieta; régimen; **to be on a** – estar a dieta; **to put on a** – adietar, poner a dieta; *v.* ponerse a dieta; estar a dieta.

dif·fer [dífə] *v.* diferir, diferenciarse, distinguirse; disentir; **to** – **with** no convenir con, no estar de acuerdo con.

dif·fer·ence [dífrəns] *s.* diferencia; distinción; discordia, controversia; **it makes no** – no importa, es igual, da lo mismo.

dif·fer·ent [dífrənt] *adj.* diferente; distinto.

dif·fer·en·ti·ate [dɪfərénʃɪet] *v.* diferenciar(se); distinguir(se).

dif·fi·cult [dífəkʌlt] *adj.* difícil; dificultoso, trabajoso, penoso.

dif·fi·cul·ty [dífəkʌltɪ] *s.* dificultad; apuro, aprieto.

dif·fi·dence [dífədəns] *s.* timidez; desconfianza de sí propio.

dif·fi·dent [dífədənt] *adj.* huraño; tímido.

dif·fuse [dɪfjús] *adj.* difuso; prolijo; [dɪfjúz] *v.* difundir.

dif·fu·sion [dɪfjúʒən] *s.* difusión; diseminación.

dig [dɪg] *v.* cavar; excavar, ahondar; escarbar; trabajar duro; **to** – **under** socavar; **to** – **up** desenterrar; *s.* piquete; pulla, sarcasmo.

di·gest [dáɪdʒɛst] *s.* sumario, compendio; recopilación; código, [dədʒɛst] *v.* digerir; recopilar.

di·gest·i·ble [dədʒéstəb l] *adj.* digestible, digerible.

di·ges·tion [dədʒéstʃən] *s.* digestión

di·ges·tive [dədʒéstɪV] *adj.* digestivo.

dig·ni·fied [dígnəfaɪd] *adj.* digno, mesurado; serio, grave.

dig·ni·tar·y [dígnətɛrɪ] *s.* dignatario.

dig·ni·ty [dígnətɪ] *s.* dignidad.

di·graph [dáɪgræf] *s.* dígrafo.

di·gress [dəgrés] *v.* divagar.

di·gres·sion [dəgréʃən] *s.* digresión, divagación.

dike [daɪk] *s.* dique, represa, zanja.

di·late [daɪlét] *v.* dilatar(se), extender(se), ensanchar(se).

dil·i·gence [dílədʒəns] *s.* diligencia; aplicación, esmero.

dil·i·gent [dílədʒənt] *adj.* diligente, activo, aplicado.

di·lute [dɪlút] *v.* diluir, desleír; aguar; *adj.* diluido.

dim [dɪm] *adj.* penumbroso, obscuro; nublado; confuso; indistinto; deslustrado, sin brillo; *v.* obscurecer; anublar, ofuscar; atenuar.

dime [daɪm] *s.* moneda de diez centavos.

di·men·sion [dəménɪʃ] *s.* dimensión.

di·min·ish [dəmínɪʃ] *v.* disminuir; rebajar.

dim·i·nu·tion [dɪmənjúʃən] *s.* diminución, mengua.

di·min·u·tive [dəmínjetɪv] *adj.* diminutivo; diminuto; *s.* diminutivo.

dim·ness [dímnɪs] *s.* semi-obscuridad, penumbra, ofuscamiento.

dim·ple [dímp l] *s.* hoyuelo.

din [dɪn] *s.* estruendo, fragor, estrépito.

dine [daɪn] *v.* comer, festejar u obsequiar con una comida.

din·er [dáɪnə] *s.* coche-comedor, comensal (*persona que come a la mesa*).

din·gy [dínʒɪ] *adj.* negruzco; manchado, sucio.

dining [dáɪnɪŋ] *ger. de* **to dine**; – **car** coche-comedor; – **room** comedor.

din·ner [dínə] *s.* comida; – **coat** smoking o esmoquin.

dint [ɪnt] *s.*: **by** – **of** a fuerza de.

di·or·ama [daɪərǽmə] *s.* diorama.

dip [dɪp] *s.* zambullida; inmersión; bajada; declive, depresión, *v.* meter(se); zambullirse, mojar (*la pluma en el tintero*); teñir; agachar (*la cabeza*); saludar (*con la bandera*); inclinarse (*un camino*); dar un bajón (*un avión*); hundirse (*el sol en el horizonte*);

to – out vaciar (**con cucharón o cazo**).

diph•the•ri•a [dɪfθírɪə] s. difteria.

diph•thong [dɪfθɔŋ] s. diptongo.

di•plo•ma [dɪplómə] s. diploma.

di•plo•ma•cy [dɪplómәsɪ] s. diplomacia.

dip•lo•mat [dɪpləmæt] s. diplomático.

dip•lo•mat•ic [dɪpləmǽtɪk] adj. diplomático.

dip•per [dɪpə•] s. cucharón, cazo; **the Big Dipper** la Osa Mayor.

dire [daɪr] adj. extremo; horrendo; fatal, de mal agüero.

di•rect [dərɛkt] adj. (*straight*) directo; derecho, en línea recta; *C.A.* recto; (*immediate*) inmediato; **– current** corriente continua; **– object** acusativo; adv. directamente; **-ly** adv. directamente; inmediatamente; en seguida; v. dirigir; guiar; encaminar; dar direcciones u órdenes.

di•rec•tion [dərɛkʃən] s. dirección; administración; gerencia; rumbo.

di•rec•tion•al an•ten•na [dərɛkʃən] ænténə] s. antena direccional.

di•rec•tion•al sig•nal [dərɛkʃən] sígn]] s. señal direccional.

di•rec•tive [dərɛktɪv] adj. directivo; s. orden, mandato.

di•rect•ness [dərɛktnɪs] s. derechura; franqueza; lo directo; **with –** sin rodeos.

di•rec•tor [dərɛktə•] s. director; gerente.

di•rec•to•ry [dərɛktərɪ] s. directorio; junta directiva; **telephone –** guía telefónica.

dir•ig•i•ble [dírədʒəb]] adj. & s. dirigible.

dirt [dɜrt] s. suciedad; mugre; tierra, polvo, lodo.

dirt•y [dɜ́rtɪ] adj. sucio; mugriento, cochino; enlodado; manchado; v. ensuciar; manchar; enlodar.

dis•a•ble [dɪséb]] v. incapacitar.

dis•ad•van•tage [dɪsədvǽntɪdʒ] s. desventaja, **to be at a –** estar en una situación desventajosa.

dis•a•gree [dɪsəgrí] v. (*dissent*) diferir, disentir, no convenir, no estar de acuerdo, (*bad effect*) no sentarle bien a uno (*el clima, la comida, etc.*).

dis•a•gree•a•ble [dɪsəgríəb]] adj. desagradable; áspero, de mal genio.

dis•a•gree•ment [dɪsəgrímənt] s. desavenencia, desacuerdo; disensión; discordia; discordancia.

dis•al•low [dɪsəlaʊ] v. desaprobar; rechazar.

dis•ap•pear [dɪsəpír] v. desaparecer.

dis•ap•pear•ance [dɪsəpírəns] s. desaparición.

dis•ap•point [dɪsəpɔ́ɪnt] v. chasquear; contrariar; decepcionar; faltar a lo prometido; desilusionar; **to be -ed** estar desilusionado o decepcionado; estar desengañado; quedar contrariado.

dis•ap•point•ing [dɪsəpɔ́ɪntɪŋ] adj. desilusionante,

desengañador, decepcionante.

dis•ap•point•ment [dɪsəpɔ́ɪntmənt] s. desilusión, desengaño, decepción; chasco; contrariedad.

dis•ap•prov•al [dɪsəprúv]] s. desaprobación.

dis•ap•prove [dɪsəprúv] v. desaprobar.

dis•arm [dɪsárm] v. desarmar(se).

dis•ar•ma•ment [dɪsárməmənt] s. desarme.

dis•ar•ray [dɪsəré] s. desarreglo, confusión, desorden, v. desarreglar, desordenar.

dis•as•ter [dɪzǽstə•] s. desastre.

dis•as•trous [dɪzǽstrəs] adj. desastroso.

dis•band [dɪsbǽnd] v. dispersar; licenciar (*las tropas*); desbandarse.

dis•be•lieve [dɪsbəlív] v. descreer, no creer.

dis•burse [dɪsbɜ́s] v. desembolsar.

dis•burse•ment [dɪsbɜ́smənt] s. desembolso; gasto.

disc [dɪsk] = **disk.**

dis•card [dískərd] s. descarte; desecho, cosa desechada; [dískárd] v. descartar; desechar.

dis•cern [dɪsɜ́n] v. discernir, distinguir, percibir.

dis•cern•ment [dɪsɜ́nmənt] s. discernimiento.

dis•charge [dɪstʃárdʒ] s. descarga (*de artillería*); descargo (*de una obligación*); desempeño (*de un deber*); exoneración; despedida; licencia (*militar*); pago (*de una deuda*); derrame, desagüe; supuración; v. descargar; exonerar; poner en libertad; despedir; echar, deponer, dar de baja (*a un soldado*); pagar (*una deuda*); arrojar, supurar; desaguar.

dis•ci•ple [dɪsáɪp]] s. discípulo.

dis•ci•pli•ne [dísəplɪn] s. disciplina, v. disciplinar.

dis•close [dɪsklóz] v. descubrir, revelar.

dis•col•or [dɪsk ʌ́lə•] v. descolorar(se), desteñir(se).

dis•com•fort [dɪsk ʌ́lə•] s. incomodidad; malestar.

dis•con•cert [dɪskәnsɜ́t] v. desconcertar.

dis•con•nect [dɪskənɛ́kt] v. desconectar; desunir, separar.

dis•con•nect•ed [dɪskәnɛ́ktɪd] p.p. & adj. desconectado; desunido; inconexo, incoherente.

dis•con•so•late [dɪskáəs] ɪt] adj. desconsolado.

dis•con•tent [dɪskәntɛ́nt] s. descontento; v. descontestar.

dis•con•tent•ed [dɪskәntɛ́ntɪd] adj. descontento; descontentadizo.

dis•con•tin•ue [dɪskәntínju] v. descontinuar; para; suspender, interrumpir; abandonar.

dis•cord [dískərd] s. discordia; disonancia, discordancia; desavenencia.

dis•count [dískaʊnt] s. descuento, rebaja; **– rate** tipo de descuento; v. descontar, rebajar.

dis•cour•age [dɪskɜ́rɪdʒ[v. desanimar, desalentar,

abatir, **to – from** disuadir de.

dis·cour·age·ment [dɪskə́rɪdʒmənt] s. desaliento, abatimiento.

dis·course [dískors] s. discurso; conversación [dískórs] v. disertar, discurrir hablar.

dis·cour·te·ous [dísk ə́tɪəs] adj. descortés, desatento.

dis·cour·te·sy [dɪsk ə́təsɪ] s. descortesía, desatención.

dis·cov·er [dɪsk ʌ́ və] v. descubrir.

dis·cov·er·er [dɪsk ʌ́vərə] s. descubridor.

dis·cov·er·y [dɪsk ʌ́vrɪ] s. descubrimiento.

dis·cred·it [dɪskrédɪt] s. descrédito; deshonra; v. desacreditar, deshonrar; no creer.

dis·creet [dɪskrít] adj. discreto, prudente.

dis·crep·an·cy [dɪskrépənsɪ] s. discrepancia, diferencia; variación.

dis·cre·tion [dɪskréʃən] s. discreción; prudencia; **at one's own –** a discreción.

dis·crim·i·nate [dɪskrɪ́mənet] v. discernir; distinguir; hacer distinciones, hacer favoritismos; dar trato de inferioridad con motivos de prejuicio; **to – against** hacer favoritismos en perjuicio de.

dis·cuss [dɪsk ʌ́s] v. discutir.

dis·cus·sion [disk ʌ́ʃən] s. discusión.

dis·dain [dɪsdén] s. desdén, menosprecio; v. desdeñar, menospreciar; desdeñarse de.

dis·dain·ful [dɪsdénfəl] adj. desdeñoso.

dis·ease [dɪzíz] s. enfermedad.

dis·eased [dɪzízd] adj. enfermo.

dis·em·bark [dɪsɪmbórk] v. desembarcar.

dis·en·tan·gle [dɪsɪnt ǽ ŋg]] v. desenredar, desenmarañar, deshacer (una maraña o enredo).

dis·fig·ure [disfɪ́gjə] v. desfigurar; afear.

dis·fran·chise [dɪsfr ǽ ntʃaɪz] v. privar de derechos de voto o de ciudadanía.

dis·grace [dɪsgrés] s. ignominia, deshonra; vergüenza; **to be in –** estar desacreditado, haber perdido la gracia o el favor; v. deshonrar; degradar; desacreditar; avergonzar.

dis·grace·ful [disgrésfəl] adj. vergonzoso.

dis·guise [dɪsgáɪz] s. disfraz; v. disfrazar.

dis·gust [dɪsg ʌ́ st] s. asco; repugnancia; **disgusto**; v. disgustar, dar asco, repugnar.

dis·gust·ed [dɪsg ʌ́ stɪd] adj. disgustado, descontento; asqueado.

dis·gust·ing [disg ʌ́ stɪŋ] adj. asqueroso repugnante.

dish [dɪʃ] s. plato; manjar, vianda; **-es** vajilla; v. servir.

dis·heart·en [dɪshórt ŋ] v. desalentar, desanimar, descorazonar.

di·shev·el·ed [dɪʃév ɪ d] adj. desgreñado; desaliñado, desaseado.

dis·hon·est [dɪsánɪst] adj. engañoso, falso, tramposo, falto de honradez, fraudulento.

dis·hon·es·ty [dɪsánɪstɪ] s. fraude, falta de honradez.

dis·hon·or [dɪsánə] s. deshonra; afrenta, v. deshonrar; recusar (un giro o cheque).

dis·hon·or·a·ble [dɪsánərəb]] adj. deshonroso; infame.

dish·wash·er [dɪ́ʃwoʃə] s. (person) lavaplatos; (machine) máquina de lavar platos.

dis·il·lu·sion [dɪsɪlúʒən] s. desilusión, decepción, desengaño; v. desilusionar, decepcionar, desengañar.

dis·in·fect [dɪsɪnfékt] v. desinfectar.

dis·in·fect·ant [dɪsɪnféktənt] s. desinfectante.

dis·in·ter·ested [dɪsíntərəstɪd] adj. desinteresado.

disk [dɪsk] s. disco; **– brake** freno de disco.

dis·like [dɪsláɪk] s. antipatía, aversión; v. sentir o tener aversión por; **I – it** me repugna, no me gusta, me desagrada.

dis·lo·cate [dísloket] v. dislocar, descoyuntar.

dis·lodge [dɪslódʒ] v. desalojar.

dis·loy·al [dɪsl ɔ́ ɪəl] adj. desleal.

dis·mal [dízm]] adj. lúgubre, sombrío, tétrico.

dis·man·tle [dɪsm ǽ nt]] v. desmantelar; desmontar, desarmar.

dis·may [dɪsmé] s. desmayo, desaliento, pavor, v. desalentar, desanimar; atemorizar.

dis·miss [dɪsmɪ́s] v. (discharge) despedir, expulsar, destituir; (dispel) desechar; (allow to leave) licenciar, dar de baja; (close) dar por terminado (un pleito o caso jurídico); **to – the meeting** disolver la junta, levantar la sesión.

dis·miss·al [dɪsmɪ́s]] s. despedida, expulsión, destitución (de un cargo).

dis·mount [dɪsmáUnt] v. desmontar; apear(se); desarmar (un cañón, una máquina); desengastar (joyas).

dis·o·be·di·ence [dɪsəbídɪəns] s. desobediencia.

dis·o·be·di·ent [dɪsəbídɪ́ənt] adj. desobediente.

dis·o·bey [dɪsəbé] v. desobedecer.

dis·or·der [dɪs ɔ́ rdə] s. (confusion) desorden; trastorno; confusión; (illness) enfermedad; v. desordenar; trastornar; desarreglar.

dis·or·der·ly [dɪs ɔ́ rdə·lɪ] adj. desordenado; desarreglado, revoltoso; escandaloso; adv. desordenadamente.

dis·own [dɪsón] v. repudiar, desconocer, negar.

dis·par·age [dɪsp ǽ rɪdʒ] v. desacreditar; desdorar.

dis·pas·sion·ate [dɪsp ǽ ʃənɪ] adj. desapasionado.

dis•patch [dɪspǽtʃ] s. despacho; envío; parte (m.), comunicación, mensaje; prontitud, expedición; v. despachar; enviar, expedir; matar.

dis•pel [dɪspél] v. disipar; dispersar.

dis•pen•sa•ry [dɪspénsərɪ] s. dispensario.

dis•pen•sa•tion [dɪspənséʃən] s. dispensa, exención; dispensación; distribución.

dis•pense [dɪspéns] v. (give) dispensar, dar; repartir, distribuir; administrar (la justicia); despachar (recetas, medicamentos); **to – from** eximir de, dispensar de; **to – with** omitir; pasarse sin, prescindir de.

dis•per•sal [dɪspɝ́s l] s. dispersión; desbandada.

dis•perse [dɪspɝ́s] v. dispersar(se), disipar(se), esparcir(se).

dis•place [dɪsplés] v. desalojar; desplazar; poner fuera de su lugar; suplantar.

dis•play [dɪsplé] s. manifestación, exhibición; ostentación; v. exhibir; mostrar, manifestar; desplegar.

dis•please [dɪsplíz] v. desagradar; disgustar, fastidiar.

dis•pleas•ure [dɪsplézɚ] s. desagrado, disgusto, descontento.

dis•pos•al [dɪspóz l] s. disposición; arreglo; venta (de bienes).

dis•pose [dɪspóz] v. disponer; arreglar; influir; **to – of** deshacerse de.

dis•po•si•tion [dɪspəzíʃən] s. disposición; arreglo; aptitud, inclinación; venta; **good (bad)** – buen (mal) genio.

dis•prove [dɪsprúv] v. refutar.

dis•pute [dɪspjút] s. disputa; v. disputar.

dis•qual•i•fy [dɪskwóləfaɪ] v. inhabilitar, incapacitar, descalificar.

dis•re•gard [dɪsrɪgárd] s. desatención, falta de atención, negligencia, descuido; falta de respeto o consideración; v. desatender, no hacer caso de, desentenderse de.

dis•re•spect [dɪsrɪspékt] s. desacato, falta de respeto.

dis•re•spect•ful [dɪsrɪspéctfəl] adj. irrespetuoso.

dis•sat•is•fied [dɪssǽtɪsfaɪd] adj. descontento, malcontento, mal satisfecho.

dis•sat•is•fy [dɪssǽtɪsfaɪ] v. descontentar, no satisfacer.

dis•sect [dɪsékt] v. disecar, hacer una disección; analizar.

dis•sem•ble [dɪsémb l] v. disimular, fingir.

dis•sen•sion [dɪsénʃən] s. disensión, discordia.

dis•sent [dɪsént] v. disentir; s. desacuerdo; disensión, desavenencia.

dis•sim•u•la•tion [dɪsɪmjəléʃən] s. disimulo.

dis•si•pate [dísəpət] v. disipar(se).

dis•si•pa•tion [dɪsəpéʃən] s. disipación.

dis•so•lute [dɪsəlut] adj. disoluto.

dis•so•lu•tion [dɪsəlúʃən] s. disolución.

dis•solve [dɪzálv] v. disolver(se); anular.

dis•suade [dɪswéd] v. disuadir.

dis•taff [dístæf] s. rueca.

dis•tance [dístəns] s. distancia; lejanía; alejamiento; **in the –** a lo lejos, en lontananza.

dis•tant [dístənt] adj. (far) distante; apartado, lejano, remoto; (aloof) esquivo; **to be – from** distar de; **-ly** adv. de lejos; remotamente; a distancia; en lontananza.

dis•taste [dɪstést] s. disgusto, aversión, repugnancia.

dis•taste•ful [dɪstéstfəl] adj. desagradable, repugnante.

dis•tem•per [dɪstémpɚ] s. moquillo; pepita (de las gallinas).

dis•tend [dɪsténd] v. dilatar, ensanchar.

dis•til [dɪstíl] v. destilar.

dis•til•la•tion [dɪstɪléʃən] s. destilación.

dis•till•er•y [dɪstíləri] s. destilería.

dis•tinct [dɪstíŋkt] adj. distinto, claro; diferente; **-ly** adv. distintamente, claramente, con claridad.

dis•tinc•tion [dɪstíŋkʃən] s. distinción.

dis•tinc•tive [dɪstíŋktɪv] adj. distintivo.

dis•tin•guish [dɪstíŋgwɪʃ] v. distinguir; discernir.

dis•tin•guished [dɪstíŋgwɪʃt] adj. distinguido.

dis•tin•guish•ing [dɪstíŋgwɪʃɪŋ] adj. distintivo, característico.

dis•tort [dɪstɔ́rt] v. desfigurar, deformar, torcer, falsear; tergiversar.

dis•tract [dɪstrǽkt] v. distraer; perturbar.

dis•trac•tion [dɪstrǽkʃən] s. distracción, diversión; perturbación; **to drive to –** volverse loco.

dis•tress [dɪstrés] s. angustia, aflicción, congoja; dolor; **to be in –** tener una aflicción; estar apurado; estar en zozobra (un navío); v. angustiar, acongojar, afligir; **to be -ed** estar afligido o apurado.

dis•trib•ute [dɪstríbjUt] v. distribuir, repartir.

dis•tri•bu•tion [dɪstrəbjúʃən] s. distribución; repartimiento.

dis•trib•u•tor [dɪstríbjətɚ] s. distribuidor.

dis•trict [dístrɪkt] s. distrito; **– attorney** fiscal de distrito.

dis•trust [dɪstrʎst] s. desconfianza; recelo; v. desconfiar; recelar.

dis•trust•ful [dɪstrʎstfəl] adj. desconfiado, sospechoso, receloso.

dis•turb [dɪstɝ́b] v. turbar, perturbar, inquietar; desarreglar; incomodar, molestar; **don't – yourself!** ¡no se moleste Vd.!

dis•tur•bance [dɪstɝ́bəns] s. disturbio; perturbación; desorden; alboroto; molestia.

dis•use [dɪsjús] *s.* desuso; **to fall into** – caer en desuso; caducar.

ditch [dɪtʃ] *s.* zanja; foso; **irrigation** – acequia; *v.* zanjar, abrir zanjas; meter en la zanja; **to – someone** deshacerse de alguien.

dit•to [dɪ́to] *s.* ídem, lo mismo.

di•u•re•tic [daɪjʊRétɪk] *adj.* & *s.* diurético.

di•van *s.* diván.

dive [dáɪv] *v.* zambullida (*echándose de cabeza*), buceada, chapuz; picada (*descenso rápido de un avión*); *Méx.* clavado; garito, leonera; *v.* echarse de cabeza; zambullirse (*de cabeza*); bucear; sumergirse (*un submarino*); **to – into someone** abalanzarse sobre alguien.

div•er [dáɪvǝ-] *s.* buzo; zambullidor.

di•verge [dǝvɚdʒ] *v.* divergir, irse apartando, separarse; diferir.

di•vergen•ce [dǝvɚdʒǝns] *s.* divergencia; diferencia (*de opiniones*).

di•vers [dáɪvǝ-z] *adj.* diversos, varios.

di•verse [dǝvɚs] *adj.* diverso; diferente.

di•ver•sion [dǝvɚʒǝn] *s.* diversión, recreo; desviación.

di•ver•si•ty [dǝvɚsǝtɪ] *s.* diversidad, diferencia, variedad.

di•vert [dǝvɚt] *v.* divertir, entretener; distraer; desviar, apartar.

di•vide [dǝváɪd] *v.* dividir(se); partir.

div•i•dend [dívǝdɛnd] *s.* dividendo.

di•vine [dǝváɪn] *adj.* divino; *v.* adivinar.

di•vin•i•ty [dǝvínǝtɪ] *s.* divinidad; deidad, teología.

di•vi•sion [dǝvíʒǝn] *s.* división.

di•vorce [dǝvórs] *s.* divorcio; *v.* divorciar(se).

di•vulge [dǝvʌ́ldʒ] *v.* divulgar.

diz•zi•ness [dízɪnɪs] *s.* vahído o vaguido, desvanecimiento, mareo, vértigo.

diz•zy [dízɪ] *adj.* desvanecido, mareado; confuso; aturdido; – **speed** velocidad vertiginosa.

do [du] *v.* hacer; **to – away with** deshacerse de; prescindir de; **to – a lesson** estudiar una lección; **to – one's hair** peinarse, arreglarse el pelo; **to – the dishes** lavar los platos; **to – up** envolver; limpiar, arreglar; lavar o planchar; **to – well in business** prosperar en los negocios; **to – without** pasarse sin; **to have nothing to – with** no tener nada que ver con; **that will** – basta, bastará; **that won't** – eso no sirve; eso no resultará bien; **this will have to** – habrá que conformarse con esto; **how – you–?** ¿cómo está Vd.?; **–you hear me?** ¿me oye Vd.? **yes, I** – sí, le oigo; **I – say it** sí lo digo.

doc•ile [dás•] *adj.* dócil.

dock [dɑk] *s.* muelle, desembarcadero; dársena; **dry** – carenero, dique de carena; *v.* entrar en el muelle; atracar, meter (*una embarcación*) en el muelle o dique; **to – the wages** rebajar la paga.

doc•tor [dáktǝ-] *s.* doctor; médico, facultativo; *v.* medicinar, curar; **to – oneself** medicinarse, tomar medicinas.

doc•trine [dáktrɪn] *s.* doctrina.

doc•u•ment [dákjǝmǝnt] *s.* documento; [dákjǝmɛnt] *v.* documentar.

dod•der [dɑdǝ-] *v.* tambalear; temblar.

dodge [dɑdʒ] *s.* evasión, evasiva; *v.* evadir(se); escabullirse; hurtar el cuerpo; **to – around a corner** dar un esquinazo.

doe [do] *s.* cierva; hembra (*del antílope, del gamo, de la liebre*).

dog [dɔg] *s.* perro, perra; can; **hot** – salchicha caliente, *Ch., C.A.* perro caliente; *Ríopl.* pancho; **to put on a lot of** – emperifollarse; darse mucho tono; *Ríopl.* darse mucho corte; *v.* seguir la pista de, perseguir, acosar; *adv.* sumamente, completamente; **dog-tired** cansadísimo.

dog•ma [dɔ́gmǝ] *s.* dogma.

dog•mat•ic [dɔgmǽtɪk] *adj.* dogmático.

doi•ly [dɔ́ɪlɪ] *s.* mantelito (*para platos, vasos, lámparas, etc.*).

do•ings [dúɪŋz] *s. pl.* hechos, acciones, acontecimientos; **great** – mucha actividad, fiesta, función.

do-it-your•self [duɪtjʊrsɛ́lf] *adj.* proyectado para que uno pueda hacer sus propios trabajos manuales en casa.

dole [dol] *s.* reparto gratuito (*de dinero o alimento*); ración, limosna; *v.* repartir gratuitamente.

dole•ful [dólfǝl] *adj.* lúgubre, triste, lastimoso.

doll [dɑl] *s.* muñeca, muñeco; *v.* **to – up** emperifollarse, ataviarse; **dolly** *s.* muñequita.

dol•lar [dálǝ-] *s.* dólar.

dol•phin [dɔ́lfɪn] *s.* delfín.

do•main [domén] *s.* dominio; heredad.

dome [dom] *s.* cúpula: media naranja (*de iglesia*).

do•mes•tic [dǝmɛ́stɪk] *adj.* doméstico; hogareño; nacional, del país, *Am.* criollo; *s.* criado, sirviente.

dom•i•cile [dámǝsaɪl] *s.* domicilio.

dom•i•nant [dámǝnǝnt] *adj.* dominante.

dom•i•nate [dámǝnet] *v.* dominar.

dom•i•na•tion [damǝnéʃǝn] *s.* dominación, dominio.

dom•i•neer [damǝnír] *v.* dominar, señorear.

dom•i•neer•ing [damǝnírɪŋ] *adj.* dominador, mandón, imperioso, tiránico.

do•min•ion [dǝmínjǝn] *s.* dominio.

dom•i•no [dámǝno] *s.* dominó, traje de máscara; disfraz; ficha (*de dominó*); **dominoes** dominó (*juego*).

don [dɑn] *s.* don (*título*); caballero; *v.* ponerse, vestirse.

do•nate [dónet] *v.* donar, regalar, hacer donación.

do•na•tion [donéʃən] s. donación; regalo, dádiva.

done [dʌn] p.p. de **to do** hecho; terminado, acabado; **to be – in** estar rendido de cansancio; **the meat is well –** está bien asada la carne.

don•key [dóŋkɪ] s. burro, asno.

doo•dad [dúdæd] s. chuchería, chisme.

doom [dum] s. hado, sino, destino; mala suerte, perdición, ruina; **the day of –** el día del juicio final; v. condenar, sentenciar; predestinar; **to be -ed to failure** estar predestinado al fracaso.

door [dor] s. puerta; entrada.

door•bell [dórbɛl] s. campanilla o timbre (de llamada).

door•knob [dórnɑb] s. tirador de puerta, perilla, manija.

door•man [dórmæn] s. portero.

door•step [dórstɛp] s. escalón de la puerta; umbral.

door•way [dórwe] s. puerta, entrada; vano (de la puerta).

dope [dop] s. (narcotic) narcótico; opio; droga; menjurje, medicamento; (information) información; **– fiend** morfinómano, **he is a –** es un zoquete, v. narcotizar; **to – out** adivinar, conjeturar; **to – oneself up** medicinarse demasiado.

dor•mi•to•ry [dɔ́rmetorɪ] s. dormitorio.

dose [dos] s. dosis; v. medicinar; **to – oneself** medicinarse.

dot [dɑt] s. punto; **on the –** en punto; v. marcar con puntos; poner el punto (sobre la i).

dot•age [dótɪdʒ] s. chochez; **to be in one's –** chochear.

dote [dot] v. chochear; **to – on** estar loco por.

dou•ble [dʌ́bḷ] adj. doble; doblado; **– boiler** baño de María; **– deal** trato doble; **– entry** partida doble; **– standard** norma de conducta sexual más restringida para la mujer; s. doble: **-s** juego de dobles (en tenis); adv. doblemente; **double-breasted** cruzado; **double-faced** de dos caras; v. doblar(se); duplicar(se); **to–up** doblarse; **doubly** adv. doblemente; por duplicado.

doubt [daʊt] s. duda; v. dudar.

doubt•ful [dáʊtfəl] adj. dudoso; dudable.

doubt•less [dáʊtlɪs] adj. indudable, cierto, seguro; adv. sin duda; indudablemente; probablemente.

douche [duʃ] s. ducha; jeringa.

dough [do] s. pasta, masa; dinero.

dough•nut [dónət] s. bollito o buñuelo en rosca.

dove [dʌv] s. paloma.

dove [dov] pret. de **to dive.**

down [daʊn] adv. abajo, hacia abajo; **– to** hasta; **– East** en el este; **– the street** calle abajo; **to cut – prices** reducir o rebajar precios; **to get – to work** aplicarse, **to go** (o **come**) **–** bajar; **to pay –** pagar al contado, **to put –** poner; anotar; apuntar, poner por escrito; adj. abatido, descorazonado; **– grade**

declive, pendiente; **prices are –** han bajado los precios; **to be – on someone** tenerle ojeriza a alguien; s. plumón; vello; pelusa; v. echar por tierra, derribar; rebajar (precios).

down•cast [dáʊnkæst] adj. cabizbajo, abatido; **with – eyes** con los ojos bajos.

down•fall [dáʊnfɔl] s. caída; ruina.

down•pour [dáʊnpor] s. aguacero, chaparrón.

down•right [dáʊnraɪt] adj. claro, positivo, categórico, absoluto; **– foolishness** solemne disparate; adv. enteramente; absolutamente.

down•stairs [dáʊnstɛrz] adv. abajo; en el piso bajo; adj. del piso bajo; s. piso bajo, piso inferior.

down•stream [dáʊnstrím] adv. río abajo, aguas abajo; con la corriente.

down•town [dáʊntáʊn] adv. al centro, en el centro (de una población); adj. del centro; s. centro.

down•ward [dáʊnwəd] adj. descendente; inclinado; adv. (= **downwards**) hacia abajo.

down•y [dáʊnɪ] adj. suave, blando; velloso; plumoso.

dow•ry [dáʊrɪ] s. dote.

doze [doz] s. siestecita, sueño ligero; v. dormitar.

doz•en [dʌ́zṇ] s. docena.

drab [dræb] adj. pardo, pardusco; monótono.

draft [dræft] s. corriente de aire; trago; libranza, letra de cambio; giro bancario; trazado; plan; leva (militar), conscripción; tiro (de estufa, hogar, etc.); calado (de un barco); **– beer** cerveza de barril; **– horse** caballo de tiro; **rough –** croquis, borrador; v. trazar, dibujar, delinear, reclutar, echar leva; redactar (un documento).

drafts•man [drǽftsmən] s. dibujante.

drag [dræg] s. rastra, traba, obstáculo; **to have a – with someone** tener buenas aldabas con alguien; v. arrastrar(se); rastrear; moverse despacio; **to – on and on** prolongarse demasiado, prolongarse hasta el fastidio.

drag•on [drǽgən] s. dragón.

drain [dren] s. (channel) desagüe; desaguadero, conducto; (exhaust) agotamiento; consumo; v. desaguar(se); apurar (un vaso); agotar, consumir; escurrir(se), secar(se), secar(se); desecar (un terreno); Am. drenar.

drain•age [drénɪdʒ] s. desagüe, Am. drenaje; desaguadero; sistema de desaguaderos; desecamiento, desecación (de un terreno, laguna, etc.).

drake [drek] s. pato.

dra•ma [drómə] s. drama.

dra•mat•ic [drəmǽtɪk] adj. dramático.

dram•a•tist [drómətɪst] s. dramaturgo, dramático.

dram•a•tize [drǽmətaɪz] v. dramatizar.

drank [dræŋk] pret. de **to drink.**

drape [drep] s. colgadura, cortina, tapiz; v. colgar, entapizar, adornar con tapices; cubrir, revestir.

drap•er•y [drépərɪ] *s.* tapicería, colgaduras, cortinas; pañerías, paños, géneros.

dras•tic [dráĕstɪk] *adj.* extremo, fuerte, violento; **to take — steps** tomar medidas enérgicas.

draught [dræft] *véase* **draft**.

draw [drɔ] *v. (pull)* tirar; jalar *(halar); (attract)* atraer; sacar; *(design)* debujar, trazar; *(withdraw)* girar, librar *(una libranza)*; hacer *(una comparación)*; correr *(la cortina)*; **to — aside** apartar(se) **to — a breath** aspirar, tomar aliento; **to — lots** echar suertes, sortear; **to — near** acercarse; **to — out** sacar; sonsacar *(a una persona)*; alargar, prolongar; **to — up** acercar(se); redactar *(un documento)*; *s.* empate *(en deportes o juegos)*; número sacado *(en una rifa)*; atracción; **—bridge** puente levadizo.

draw•back [drɔ́bæk] *s.* desventaja; obstáculo, inconveniente.

draw•er [drɔr] *s.* cajón, gaveta; **-s** calzoncillos.

draw•er [drɔ́ə•] *s.* librador, girador; dibujante.

draw•ing [drɔ́ɪŋ] *s. (design)* dibujo; delineación, trazado; *(raffle)* sorteo; **— paper** papel de dibujo; **— room** sala de recibo, recibidor, recibimiento.

drawn [drɔn] *p.p. de* **to draw**.

dread [drɛd] *s.* pavor, temor, aprensión; *adj.* terrible; temido; *v.* temer; *v.* temer; sentir aprensión de.

dread•ful [drɛ́dfəl] *adj.* horrendo; espantoso.

dream [drim] *s.* sueño; ensueño; **to — of** soñar con, soñar en.

dream•er [drimə•] *s.* soñador.

dream•land [drímlænd] *s.* tierra del ensueño; región de los sueños.

dreamt [drɛmpt] **= dreamed.**

dream•y [drímɪ] *adj.* soñoliento; soñador; melancólico; como un sueño; **a — recollection** un vago recuerdo.

drea•ry [drírɪ] *adj.* sombrío; melancólico.

dredge [drɛdʒ] *s.* draga; *v.* dragar.

dregs [drɛgz] *s. pl.* heces, sedimento.

drench [drɛntʃ] *s.* mojada, mojadura, empapada; *v.* empapar; mojar; remojar.

dress [drɛs] *s.* vestido, traje; vestidura, ropaje, atavío; **— rehearsal** ensayo general y último *(antes de una función)*; **— suit** traje de etiqueta; *v.* vestir(se); arreglarse, componerse; aderezar; adobar *(carne o pieles)*; curar *(heridas)*; alinear, formar *(las tropas)*; **to — down** reprender, regañar; **to — up** emperifollarse, acicalarse, ataviarse.

dress•er [drésə•] *s.* tocador, cómoda *(con espejo)*; **she is a good —** viste con elegancia o buen gusto.

dress•ing [drésɪŋ] *s.* aderezo; salsa *(para ensaladas)*; relleno *(para carne, pollo, etc.)*; medicamento, vendajes *(para heridas)*; **a — down** regaño; **— gown** bata; **— room** tocador; **— table** tocador.

dress•mak•er [drésmekə•] *s.* modista.

drew [dru] *pret. de* **to draw**.

drib•ble [dríb |] *v.* gotear; dejar caer en gotas; babear; *s.* goteo; chorrito.

drib•blet [dríblɪt] *s.* gota, gotita; **in -s** gota a gota; en pequeñas cantidades.

dried [draɪd] *pret. & p.p. de* **to dry**; *adj.* seco; paso; **— fig** higo paso.

drift [drɪft] *s. (direction)* rumbo, dirección, tendencia, deriva; *(pile)* montón, amontonamiento *(de arena, nieve, etc.)*; *(off course)* desvío *(de un barco o avión)*; **to get the — of a conversation** enterarse a medias de una conversación; *v.* flotar; ir(se) a la deriva; dejarse llevar por la corriente; amontonarse *(la nieve, la arena)*; esparcirse *(la arena, la nieve, las nubes)*.

drift•wood [dríftwʊd] *s.* madera o leña flotante; madera de playa.

drill [drɪl] *s. (tool)* taladro; barrena; *(training)* ejercicio; adiestramiento; *Am.* entrenamiento; dril *(tela)*; *v.* taladrar, barrenar, perforar; hacer ejercicio; aleccionar; disciplinar *(un ejército)*; adiestrar(se), *Am.* entrenar(se).

drily [dráɪlɪ] *adv.* secamente.

drink [drɪŋk] *s.* bebida; trago; *v.* beber; **to — a toast to** beber a la salud de, brindar por; **— it down!** ¡bébaselo! ¡tráguéselo!

drink•able [dríŋkəb |] *adj.* potable.

drip [drɪp] *s.* goteo; *v.* gotear, caer gota a gota; dejar caer gota a gota.

drive [draɪv] *s. (ride)* paseo en coche; *(road)* calzada, carretera, paseo; *(campaing)* campaña; *(impulse)* empujar; tiro, tirada *(de una pelota)*; *v.* impulsar, impeler, empujar; arrear *(animales)*; conducir, guar o manejar *(un auto)*; forzar; encajar, clavar *(una estaca, cuña, clavo)*; tirar, lanzar *(una pelota)*; dar un paseo en auto; llevar *(a alguien)* en auto; cavar *(un pozo, túnel, etc.)* **to — away** ahuyentar; **to — a good bargain** hacer un buen trato; **to — mad** volver loco; **what are you driving at?** ¿qué quieres decir con eso?

driv•el [drív |] *s.* baba; ñoñería, tontería; *v.* babear; chochear, decir ñoñerías.

driv•el•ing [drɪv | ɪŋ] *adj.* baboso.

driv•en [drívən] *p.p. de* **to drive**.

driv•er [dráɪvə•] *s.* cochero, chófer, mecánico, conductor *(de automóvil)*; arriero *(de animales)*; uno de los palos de golf; **pile —** martinete *(para clavar pilotes)*; **slave —** mandón, tirano; **truck —** carretero, camionero.

drive•way [dráɪvwe] *s.* calzada de entrada, carretera de entrada.

driz•zle [dríz |] *v.* lloviznar; *s.* llovizna.

drone [dron] *s.* zángano; holgazán; zumbido; *v.* zumbar; hablar con monotonía; holgazanear, perder el tiempo.

droop [drup] *v.* doblarse, andar o estar alicaído, estar abatido; languidecer; marchitarse; bajar (*los hombres, los párpados*); **his shoulders**– tiene los hombros caídos; **-ing eyelids** párpados caídos.

drop [drɔp] *s.* (*liquid*) gota; (*descent*) baja; caída; (*incline*) declive; **cough** – pastilla para la tos; **letter** – buzón; – **curtain** telón (*de teatro*); – **hammer** martinete; – **out** dimitente; *v.* dejar caer, soltar; gotear; caer; dejar (*un asunto, una amistad*); **to – a line** poner unos renglones; **to – asleep** quedarse dormido, dormirse; **to – behind** dejar atrás; quedarse atrás; **to – in** hacer una visita inesperada, *Am.* descolgarse; **to – in a mailbox** echar al buzón; **to – out** retirarse; desaparecer; **to – the curtain** bajar el telón.

drought [draUt] *s.* sequía.

drove [drov] *s.* manada, recua, rebaño; tropel; *pret. de* **to drive**.

drown [draUn] *v.* ahogar(se), anegar(se); apagar, ahogar (*un sonido*).

drowse [draUz] *v.* dormitar; estar amodorrado.

drow•si•ness [dráUzInIs] *s.* modorra, somnolencia.

drows•y [dráUzI] *adj.* soñoliento; adormilado, amodorrado; **to become** – amorrarse.

drudge [drʌʒ] *v.* afanarse, atarearse; *s.* trabajador, esclavo del trabajo.

drug [drʌg] *s.* droga; narcótico; **to be a – on the market** ser invendible (*una mercancía*); *v.* jaropar (*administrar drogas en demasía*); narcotizar.

drug•gist [drʌ ́gIst] *s.* boticario, droguista, droguero, farmacéutico.

drug•store [drʌ ́gstor] *s.* botica, droguería, farmacia.

drum [drʌm] *s.* tambor; tímpano (*del oído*); barril, tonel; **bass** – tambora, bombo; –**stick** bolillo de tambor; – **major** tambor mayor; *v.* tocar el tambor; tamborilear; **to – a lesson into someone** meterle a uno la lección en la cabeza, **to – up trade** solicitar o fomentar ventas.

drum•mer [drʌ ́mɚ] *s.* tambor, tamborilero, viajante de comercio, agente.

drunk [drʌŋk] *p.p. de* **to drink**; *adj.* borracho, ebrio, emborrachado, bebido; *Ríopl.* mamado; *C.A.* bolo; *Ch.* cufifo; **to get** – emborracharse, embriagarse.

drunk•ard [drʌ ́ŋkɚd] *s.* borracho, borrachón, beodo, bebedor.

drunk•en [drʌ ́ŋkən] *adj.* borracho, ebrio.

drunk•en•ness [drʌ ́ŋkənnIs] *s.* borrachera, embriaguez.

dry [draI] *adj.* seco; árido; **a – book** un libro aburrido; – **cleaner** quitamanchas; tintorero; – **cleaning** lavado o limpieza al seco; – **goods** lencería, géneros, tejidos, telas; – **measure** medida para áridos; *v.*

secar(se); enjugar; **to – up** secarse, resecarse.

dry•ness [dráInIs] *s.* sequedad; aridez.

dub [dʌb] *v.* doblar (*una película*).

du•bi•ous [djúbIəs] *adj.* dudoso.

duch•ess [d ʌ ́tʃIs] *s.* duquesa.

duck [dʌk] *s.* pato, pata; ánade; dril (*género*); zambullida, chapuz; agachada rápida (*para evitar un golpe*); *v.* zambullir(se), chapuzar(se); agachar(se); agachar (*la cabeza*).

duck•ling [d ʌ ́klIŋ] *s.* patito, anadeja.

dud [dʌd] *s.* bomba que no estalla.

dude [dud] *s.* caballerete, novato.

due [dju] *adj.* debido; vencido, pagadero; **in – time** a su debido tiempo; **the bill is-** se ha vencido la cuenta; **the train is – at two o'clock** el tren debe llegar a las dos; *adv.* directamente; – **east** hacia el este, rumbo al oriente; *s.* derecho, privilegio; **-s** cuota.

du•el [djúəl] *s.* duelo, desafío, combate; *v.* batirse en duelo.

du•et [djúέt] *s.* dúo, dueto.

dug [dʌg] *pret. & p.p. de* **to dig.**

duke [djuk] *s.* duque.

duke•e•dom [djúkdəm] *s.* ducado.

dull [dʌl] *adj.* (*dim*) opaco, empañado; mate; sin brillo; (*boring*) aburrido; (*blunt*) embotado, sin punta, sin filo; (*stupid*) torpe; tardo; – **pain** dolor sordo; – **sound** sonido sordo o apagado; *v.* embotar(se); empañar(se); ofuscar; amortiguar (*un dolor o sonido*).

dull•ness [d ʌ ́lnIs] *s.* (*dimness*) falta de brillo; (*sluggishness*) estupidez, torpeza; (*bluntness*) falta de punta o filo; (*monotony*) aburrimiento; (*heaviness*) pesadez.

du•ly [djúlI] *adv.* debidamente.

dumb [dʌm] *adj.* (*silent*) mudo; silencioso, callado; (*dull*) estúpido, torpe; – **creature** animal.

dumb•ness [d ʌ ́mnIs]*s.* mudez, mutismo; estupidez.

dum•my [d ʌ ́mI] *s.* (*figure*) maniquí, figurón, muñeco; (*fool*) zoquete, tonto; *adj.* falso, fingido.

dump [dʌmp] *s.* montón (*de tierra, carbón, etc.*); terreno, vaciadero, escorial; **garbage**- muladar; basurero; **to be in the -s** estar abatido; *v.* echar, vaciar descargar, echar a la basura.

dunce [dʌns] *s.* zopenco, zoquete, tonto.

dune [djun] *s.* duna o médano.

duna [dʌn] *s.* boñiga, estiércol.

dun•geon [d ʌ ́ndʒən] *s.* mazmorra, calabozo.

dung•hill [d ʌ ́nhIl] *s.* muladar, estercolero.

dupe [djup] *s.* inocentón, incauto, víctima (*de un engaño*); *v.* embaucar.

du•pli•cate [djúpləkɪt] *adj. & s.* doble, duplicado; [djúpləkɪt] *v.* duplicar, copiar.

du·plic·i·ty [djuplísətɪ] *s.* duplicidad, doblez.

du·ra·ble [djÚrəbɫ] *adj.* durable, duradero.

du·ra·tion [djUréʃən] *s.* duración.

dur·ing [dÚrɪŋ] *prep.* durante.

dusk [dʌsk] *s. adj.* crepúsculo, (*vespertino*), anoche-cida; caída de la tarde; sombra, oscuridad; **at —** al atardecer.

dusk·y [dʌskɪ] *adj.* obscuro, negruzco; sombrío.

dust [dʌst] *s.* polvo; tierra; **cloud of —** polvareda; *v.* sacudir el polvo, desempolvar, quitar el polvo; em-polvar, llenar de polvo espolvorear.

dust·er [dʌstɚ] *s.* limpiador; quita polvo; **feather —** plumero.

dust·y [dʌstɪ] *adj.* polvoriento; empolvado, lleno de polvo.

Dutch [dʌtʃ] *adj. & s.* holandés **— treat** convite a escote.

Dutch·man [dʌtʃmən] *s.* holandés.

du·ty [djútɪ] *s.* deber, obligación; derechos aduanales; impuestos;**— free** libre de derechos aduanales.

dwarf [dwɔrf] *s. & adj.* enano; *v.* achicar, empeque-ñecer; impedir el desarrollo o crecimiento de.

dwell [dwɛl] *v.* residir, morar, habitar, vivir; **to- on a subject** espaciarse o dilatarse en un asunto.

dwell·er [dwɛlɚ] *s.* habitante, morador.

dwell·ing [dwɛlɪŋ] *s.* morada, habitación, domicilio.

dwelt [dwɛlt] *s. pret. & p.p. de* **to dewell**.

dwindle [dwíndɫ] *v.* menguar, mermar; disminuir(se); gastarse.

dye [daɪ] *s.* tinte, tintura; *v.* teñir, tinturar.

dy·er [dáɪɚ] *s.* tintorero; **-'s shop** tintorería.

dy·ing [dáɪɪŋ] *adj.* moribundo; agonizante.

dy·nam·ic [daɪnǽmɪk] *adj.* dinámico; enérgico; **- s** *s.* dinámica.

dy·na·mite [dáɪnəmaɪt] *s.* dinamita; *v.* dinamitar, volar con dinamita.

dy·na·mo [dáɪnəmo] *s.* dínamo.

dy·nas·ty [dáɪnəstɪ] *s.* dinastía.

dys·en·ter·y [dísṇtɛrɪ] *s.* disentería.

E

each [ɪtʃ] *adj.* cada; *pron.* cada uno; **— other** el uno al otro, uno(s), a otro(s).

ea·ger [ígɚ] *adj.* anhelante, ansioso, deseoso; **-ly** *adv.* con anhelo; con ahínco; ansiosamente.

ea·ger·ness [ígɚnɪs] *s.* anhelo, ansia, deseo vehe-mente; ahínco; ardor.

ea·gle [ígɫ] *s.* águila.

ear [ɪr] *s.* oreja; oído; **— drum** tímpano **— muff** ore-jera; **— of corn** mazorca; **— of wheat** espiga; **by —** de

oído; **within —shot** al alcance del oído.

earl [ɝl] *s.* conde.

ea·rly [ɝlɪ] *adv.* temprano; *adj.* temprano; primitive, remoto; **— riser** madrugador, tempranero, maña-nero; **at an — date** en fecha a próxima.

earn [ɝn] *s.* ganar, merecer.

ea·rnest [ɝnɪst] *adj.* serio, formal; ardiente; **in —** en serio, con toda formalidad; de buena fe; **ly** *adv.* se-riamente; con ahinco; encarecidamente, ansiosa-mente.

ear·nest·ness [ɝnɪstnɪs] *s.* seriedad; celo; solici-tud; sinceridad; **in all —** con todo ahinco; con toda formalidad; con toda sinceridad.

earn·ings [ɝnɪŋz] *s.* ganancias; sueldo, salario, paga.

ear·ring [írrɪŋ] *s.* arete, zarcillo, pendiente, arraca-da; *C.A.* arito; *P.R.* pantalla.

earth [ɝθ] *s.* tierra; suelo.

earth·en [ɝθən] *adj.* de tierra; de barro.

earth·en·ware [ɝθənwɛr] *s.* loza de barro; trastos, cacharros.

earth·ly [ɝθlɪ] *adj.* terrenal, terrestre, mundano; terreno; **to be of no — use** no servir para nada.

earth·quake [ɝθkwek] *s.* terremoto, temblor de tierra.

earth·worm [ɝθwɝm] *s.* lombriz.

ease [iz] *s.* (*facility*) facilidad; naturalidad; soltura; (*comfort*) comodidad, tranquilidad; **at —** tranquilo; cómodo; *v.* facilitar; aliviar; mitigar; tranquilizar; aligerar (*el peso*); aflojar.

ea·sel [ízɫ] *s.* caballete (*de pintor*).

eas·i·ly [ízəlɪ] *adv.* fácilmente, sin dificultad; cómo-damente.

east [ist] *s.* este; oriente; levante; *adj.* del este, orien-tal; *adv.* al este, hacia el este; en el este.

Eas·ter [ístɚ] *s.* Pascuas, Pascua Florida; **- Sunday** Domingo de Resurrección o de Pascuas.

east·ern [ístɚn] *adj.* oriental del este.

east·ward [ístʃtwəd] *adv. & adj.* hacia el este u orien-te.

eas·y [ízɪ] *adj.* (*simple*) fácil; (*comfortable*) cómodo; tranquilo; **— chair** silla cómoda, poltrona butaca; **easy — going man** hombre cachazudo o calmo; **at an — pace** a paso moderado; **winhin — reach** al alcance; a la mano.

eat [it] *v.* comer; **to — away** corroer, destruir; **to — breakfat** desayunarse, tomar el dasayuno; **to — dinner**, tomar la comida comer; **to — supper** tomar la cena, cenar; **to — one's hear out** sufrir en silencio; **to — one's words** retractarse.

eat·en [ítṇ] *p.p.de* **to eat**.

eaves [ivz] *s. pl.* alero (*de un tejado*).

ebb [ɛb] *s.* reflujo; decadencia; **– tide** marea menguante; **to be at a low** – estar decaído; *v.* menguar, decaer.

eb•on•y [ɛ́bənɪ] *s.* ébano.

ec•cen•tric [ɪkséntrɪk] *adj.* & *s.* excéntrico.

ec•cle•si•as•tic [ɪklizɪǽstɪk] *adj.* & *s.* eclesiástico.

ech•e•lon [ɛ́ʃələn] *s.* escalón.

ech•o [ɛ́ko] *s.* eco; *v.* hacer eco; repetir; resonar, repercutir.

e•clec•tic [ɪklɛ́ktɪt] *adj.* ecléctico.

e•clipse [ɪklɪ́ps] *s.* eclipse; *v.* eclipsar.

ec•o•nom•ic [ɪkənɔ́mɪk] *adj.* económico.

ec•o•no•mic•al [ɪkənɔ́mɪk‖] *adj.* económico.

eco•no•mics [ɪkənɔ́mɪks] *s.* economía, política.

econ•omist [ɪkɔ́nəmɪst] *s.* economista.

econ•omize [ɪkɔ́nəmaɪz] *s.* economizar

econ•o•my [ɪkɔ́nəmɪ] *s.* economía; parsimonia.

ec•sta•sy [ɛ́kstəsɪ] *s.* éxtasis.

ec•u•men•i•cal [ɛkjuménɛk‖] *adj.* ecuménico.

ed•dy [ɛ́dɪ] remolino; *v.* arremolinarse.

Eden [ɪd ŋ] *s.* Edén; paraíso.

edge [ɛdʒ] orilla, borde; filo; **to be on** – estar nervioso.

edge•wise [ɛ́dʒwaɪz] *adv.* de lado; de filo.

ed•i•ble [ɛ́dəb‖] *adj.* & *s.* comestible.

ed•i•fice [ɛ́dəfɪs] *s.* edificio.

ed•i•fy [ɛ́dəfaɪ] *v.* edificar (*moral espiritualmente*).

ed•it [ɛ́dɪt] *v.* redactar, preparar o corregir (*un manuscrito*) para la imprenta; cuidar (*una adición*).

e•di•tion [ɪdɪ́ʃən] *s.* edición.

ed•i•tor [ɛ́dɪtə-] *s.* redactar: director de un periódico; revisor (*de manuscritos*).

ed•i•to•ri•al [ɛdətórɪəl] *adj.* editorial; *s.* editorial (*m.*), artículo de fondo.

ed•i•to•ri•al•ize [ɛdɪtórɪəlaɪz] *v.* expresar opiniones como en artículo de fondo; editorializar.

ed•u•cate [ɛ́dʒəket] *v.* educar; instruir.

ed•u•ca•tion [ɛdʒəkéʃən] *s.* educación; crianza; instrucción, enseñanza; pedagogía.

ed•u•ca•tion•al [ɛdʒəkéʃən‖] *adj.* educativo, docente pedagógico.

ed•u•ca•tor [ɛ́dʒəketə-] *s.* educador.

eel [il] *s.* anguila.

ef•fect [əfɛ́kt] *s.* efecto; **-s** bienes, efectos; **to go into-** hacerse vigente, ponerse en operación (*una ley*); *v.* efectuar; ejecutar; realizar.

ef•fec•tive [əfɛ́ktɪv] *adj.* efectivo; eficaz, vigente (*una ley*); **-ly** *adv.* eficazmente.

ef•fec•tu•al [əfɛ́ktʃUəl] *adj.* eficaz

ef•fem•i•nate [əfɛ́mənɪt] *adj.* afeminado.

ef•fete [ɪfít] *adj.* gastado; estéril; decadente.

ef•fi•ca•cy [ɛ́fɪkəsɪ] *s.* eficacia.

ef•fi•cien•cy [ə-fíʃə-nsɪ] *s.* eficiencia; eficacia.

ef•fi•cient [əfíʃənt] *adj.* eficiente; eficaz

ef•fi•gy [ɛ́fɪdʒɪ] *s.* efigie; **to burn in** – quemar en efigie.

ef•fort [ɛ́fə-t] *s.* esfuerzo; empeño.

ef•fron•ter•y [əfr Ántərɪ] *s.* descaro, desvergüenza, desfachatez.

ef•fu•sive [ɛfúsɪv] *adj.* efusivo, demostrativo, expansivo.

egg [ɛg] *s.* huevo; **fried** – huevo frito o estrellado; **hard-boiled** – huevo cocido, huevo duro; **acrombled -s** huevos revueltos; **soft-boiled** – huevo pasado por agua; *v.* **to – on** incitar.

egg•plant [ɛ́gplænt] *s.* berenjena.

e•go•cen•tric [igosɛntrɪk] *adj.* egocéntrico.

e•got•ism [ɪ́gətɪzəm] *s.* egotismo; egoísmo.

Egyp•tian [ɪdʒɪ́pʃən] *adj.* & *s.* egipcio.

ei•ther [íðə-] *adj.* & *pron.* uno u otro; **– of the two** cualquiera de los dos; **in – case** en ambos casos; *adv.* tampoco; **nor I** – ni yo tampoco; *conj.* o.

e•ject [ɪdʒɛ́kt] *v.* echar, arrojar, expulsar.

e•jec•tion [ɪdʒɛ́kʃən] *s.* expulsión; **– seat** asiento lanzable.

e•lab•o•rate [ɪlǽbərɪt] *adj.* elaborado, primoroso; esmerado; [ɪlǽbəret] *v.* elaborar.

e•lapse [ɪlǽps] *v.* transcurrir, pasar.

e•las•tic [ɪlǽstɪk] *adj.* elástico; *s.* elástico; goma elástica; cordón elástico; liga elástica.

e•las•tic•i•ty [ɪlæstɪsətɪ] *s.* elasticidad.

e•lat•ed [ɪlɛ́tɪd] *adj.* exaltado, gozoso, alborozado.

el•bow [ɛ́lbo] *s.* codo; recodo, ángulo; **to be within – reach** estar a la mano; *v.* codear, dar codazos; **to – one's way thorugh** abrirse paso a codazos.

eld•er [ɛ́ldə-] *adj.* mayor, más grande, más viejo, de más edad; *s.* mayor; anciano; dignatario (*en ciertas iglesias*); **our -s** nuestros mayores; nuestros antepasados.

eld•er•ly [ɛ́ldə-lɪ] *adj.* viejo, anciano.

eld•est [ɛ́ldɪst] *adj.* mayor.

e•lect [ɪlɛ́kt] *adj.* & *s.* electo; elegido; *v.* elegir.

e•lec•tion [ɪlɛ́kʃən] *s.* elección

e•lec•tor [ɪlɛ́ktə-] *s.* elector.

e•lec•tor•al [ɪlɛ́ktərəl] *adj.* electoral.

e•lec•tric [ɪlɛ́ktrɪk] *adj.* eléctrico; **– meter** electrómetro, contador eléctrico; **– storm** tronada, tempestad; **– eye** ojo eléctrico; *s.* tranvía o ferrocarril eléctrico

e•lec•tric•al [ɪlɛ́ktrɪk‖] *adj.* eléctrico; **– engineerring** electrotecnia, ingeniería eléctrica; **– engineer** ingeniero electricista; electrotécnico.

e•lec•tri•cian [ɪlɛktrɪʃən] *s.* electricista.

e•lec•tric•i•ty [ɪlɛktrɪsətɪ] *s.* electricidad.

e•lec•tri•fy [ɪlɛ́ktrəfaɪ] *v.* electrizar; electrificar.

e•lec•tro•car•di•o•graph [ilɛktrokárdɪəgræf] *s.* electrocardiógrafo.

e•lec•tro•cute [ɪlɛ́ktrəkjut] *v.* electrocutar.

e·lec·tron [ɪléktrɑn] *s.* electrón.

e·lec·tron·ics [ɪléktrɑ́nɪks] *s.* electrónica.

el·e·gance [éləgəns] *s.* elegancia.

el·e·gant [éləgənt] *adj.* elegante.

el·e·ment [éləmənt] *s.* elemento.

el·e·men·tal [ɛləmɛ́nt⌡] *adj.* elemental.

el·e·men·ta·ry [ɛləmɛ́ntəɪ] *adj.* elemental.

el·e·phant [éləfənt] *s.* elefante.

el·e·vate [éləvet] *v.* elevar, alzar, levantar.

el·e·va·tion [ɛləvéʃən] *s.* elevación; altura; exaltación.

el·e·va·dor [éləvetə] *s.* ascensor, *Am.* elevador; **grain** — almacén de granos.

e·lic·it [ɪlɪ́sɪt] *v.* extraer, sonsacar; **to – admiration** despertar admiración; **to – applause** suscitar el aplauso o los aplausos.

el·i·gi·ble [élɪdʒəb⌡] *adj.* elegible.

e·lim·i·nate [ɪlɪ́mənət] *v.* eliminar.

e·lim·i·na·tion [ɪlɪ́mənéʃən] *s.* eliminación.

e·lite [ɛlít] *s.* lo selecto; los selectos; los escogidos.

elk [ɛlk] *s.* ante.

el·lip·tic [ɪlɪ́ptɪk] *adj.* elíptico.

elm [ɛlm] *s.* olmo.

e·lope [ɪlóp]*v.* fugarse (*con su novio*).

el·o·quence [éləkwəns] *s.* elocuencia.

el·o·quent [éləkwənt] *adj.* elocuente.

else [ɛls] *adj. & adv.* otro (*úsase solo en ciertas combinaciones*); más, además; **or** – de otro modo; si no; **nobody** – ningún otro; **nothing** – nada más; **somebody** – algún otro, otra persona; **what – ?** qué más?

else·where [élshwɛr] *adv.* en otra parte; a otra parte.

e·lu·ci·date [ɪlúsədet] *v.* elucidar; esclarecer, aclarar, clarificar.

e·lu·ci·da·tion [ɪlusədéʃən] *s.* elucidación; esclarecimiento, explicación.

e·lude [ɪlúd] *v.* eludir, evadir.

e·lu·sive [ɪlúsɪv] *adj.* evasivo; que elude.

e·ma·ci·at·ed [ɪméʃietɪnd] *adj.* demacrado, escuálido, macilento.

em·a·nate [émənet] *v.* emanar, brotar en.

em·a·na·tion [ɛmənéʃən] *s.* emanación; efluvio.

e·man·ci·pate [ɪmǽnsəpet] *v.* emancipar.

e·man·ci·pa·tion [ɪmǽnsəpéʃn] *s.* emancipación.

em·balm [ɪmbám] *v.* embalsamar.

em·bank·ment [ɪmbǽŋkmənt] *s.* terraplén; dique.

em·bar·go [ɪmbárgo] *s.* embargo; prohibición; **to put an – on** embargar.

em·bark [ɪmbárk] *v.* embarcar(se).

em·bar·rass [ɪmbǽrəs] *v.* turbar, desconcertar; apenar; avergonzar; embarazar; **to be financially –ed** encontrarse escaso de fondos.

em·bar·rass·ing [ɪmbǽrəsɪŋ] *adj.* embarazoso,

penoso; desconcertante; angustioso.

em·bar·rass·ment [ɪmbǽrəsmənt] *s.* turbación, vergüenza, desconcierto; aprieto, apuro, dificultad; estorbo, embarazo.

em·bas·sy [émbəsɪ] *s.* embajada.

em·bel·lish [ɪmbélɪʃ] *v.* embellecer, hermosear.

em·ber [émbə] *s.* ascua; **-s** ascuas, rescoldo.

em·bez·zle [ɪmbéz⌡] *v.* desfalcar.

em·bez·zle·ment [ɪmbéz⌡mənt] *s.* desfalco, peculado.

em·bit·ter [ɪmbítə] *v.* amargar.

em·blem [émbləm] *s.* emblema.

em·bod·y [ɪmbádɪ] *v.* encarnar, dar cuerpo a; incorporar, abarcar.

em·boss [ɪmbɔs] *v.* realzar, grabar en relieve.

em·brace [ɪmbrés] *s.* abrazo; *v.* abrazar(se); abarcar.

em·broi·der [ɪmbrɔ́ɪdə] *v.* bordar; recamar; ornar; embellecer.

em·broi·der·y [ɪmbrɔ́dəɪ] *s.* bordado; bordadura; recamo.

em·bry·o [émbrɪo] *s.* embrión.

em·er·ald [émərəld] *s.* esmeralda.

e·merge [ɪmɝ́dʒ] *v.* emerger, surtir.

e·mer·gen·cy [ɪmɝ́ʒənsɪ] *s.* caso fortuito; aprieto; urgencia; emergencia.

em·i·grant [éməgrənt] *adj. & s.* emigrante.

em·i·grate [éməgret] *v.* emigrar.

em·i·gra·tion [ɛməgréʃən] *s.* emigración.

em·i·nence [émənəns] *s.* eminencia.

em·i·nent [émənənt] *adj.* eminente.

e·mit [ɪmít] *v.* emitir; exhalar, arrojar; despedir (*olor, humo, etc.*)

e·mo·tion [ɪmóʃən] *s.* emoción.

e·mo·tion·al [ɪmóʃən⌡] *adj.* emocional; emotivo; sentimental; sensible.

em·pa·thy [émpəθɪ] *s.* empatía.

em·per·or [émpərə] *s.* emperador.

em·pha·sis [émfəsɪs] *s.* énfasis.

em·pha·size [émfəsaɪz] *v.* dar énfasis; hacer hincapié en, subrayar, recalcar; acentuar.

em·phat·ic [ɪmfǽtɪk] *adj.* enfático; recalcado; **-ally** *adv.* enfáticamente.

em·phy·se·ma [ɛmfəsímə] *s.* enfisema.

em·pire [émpaɪr] *s.* imperio.

em·pir·i·cal [ɛmpírək⌡] *adj.* empírico.

em·ploy [ɪmplɔ́ɪ] *v.* emplear; dar empleo a ; ocupar; **to be in his –** ser su empleado; trabajar a sus órdenes.

em·ploy·ee [ɪmplɪ́] *s.* empleado.

em·ploy·er [ɪmplɔ́ɪə] *s.* patrón, amo, principal.

em·ploy·ment [ɪmplɔ́ɪmənt] *s.* empleo; ocupación.

em•pow•er [ɪmpáUə·] v. autorizar, apoderar (*dar poder a sus abogados*).

em•press [émprɪs] s. emperatriz.

emp•ti•ness [émptɪnɪs] s. vaciedad; futilidad, vanidad.

emp•ty [émptɪ] *adj.* vacío; vacante, desocupado; vano v. vaciar, desaguar, desembocar.

em•u•late [émjUlet] v. emular.

en•a•ble [ɪnéb|] v. capacitar, hacer capaz; habilitar; dar poder; facilitar; hacer posible.

en•act [ɪnǽkt] v. decretar, promulgar; hacer el papel de.

e•nam•el [ɪnǽm|] s. esmalte; v. esmaltar.

e•nam•or [inǽmə·] v. enamorar, mover a amar; encantar; **to be –ed of** estar enamorado de.

en•camp [ɪnkǽmp] v. acampar.

en•chant [ɪntʃǽnt] v, encantar; embelesar; hechizar.

en•chant•er [ɪntʃǽntə·] s. encantador: hechicero, mago, brujo.

en•chant•ment [ɪntʃǽntmənt] s. encanto; encantamiento; hechicería.

en•chant•ress [ɪntʃǽntrɪs] s. encantadora; hechicera, bruja.

en•cir•cle [ɪnsɝk|] v. cercar; rodear, ceñir.

en•close [ɪnklóz] v. encerrar; cercar, rodear, circundar; incluir.

en•clo•sure [ɪnklóʒə·] s. recinto, cercado, vallado; remesa, lo remitido (*dentro de una carta*), lo adjunto; encerramiento.

en•com•pass [ɪnkʌ́mpəs] v. abarcar; encuadrar; rodear, ceñir, circundar.

en•coun•ter [ɪnkáUntə·] s. encuentro; combate; v. encontrar(se); encontrarse con; tropezar con.

en•cour•age [ɪnkɝ́ɪdʒ] v. alentar, animar; fomentar.

en•cour•age•ment [ɪnkɝ́ɪdʒmənt] s. aliento, ánimo; estímulo; fomento.

en•croach [ɪnkrótʃ] v. **to – upon** usurpar, invadir, meterse en; quitar (*el tiempo*).

en•cum•ber [ɛnkʌ́mbə·] v. impedir; estorbar.

en•cy•clo•pe•di•a [ɪnsaɪkləpídɪə] s. enciclopedia.

end [ɛnd] s. (*temporal*) fin; cabo; término; (*spatial*) término; extremo; **no – of things** un sin fin de cosas; **odds and –s** retazos; **on-** de punta; **to put an – to** acabar con, poner fin a; v. acabar; terminar; concluir, dar fin.

en•dan•ger [ɪndéndʒə·] v. poner en peligro, arriesgar.

en•dear [ɪndír] v. hacer amar, hacer querer; **to – oneself** hacerse querer.

en•deav•or [ɪndévə·] s. esfuerzo; empeño; tentativa; tarea; v. procurar, tratar de, intentar; esforzarse por o en.

en•dem•ic [ɛndémɪk] *adj.* endémico.

end•ing [éndɪŋ] s. final; terminación; conclusión.

end•less [éndlɪs] *adj.* sin fin, interminable, inacabable; eterno.

en•dorse [ɛndɔ́rs] v. endosar; respaldar; apoyar, garantizar.

en•dorse•ment [ɛndɔ́rsmənt] s. (*signatura*) endose, endoso; (*backing*) respaldo; garantía, apoyo.

en•dors•er [ɛndɔ́rsə·] s. endosante.

en•dow [ɪndáU] v. dotar.

en•dow•ment [ɪndáUmənt] s. dotación; dote, don.

en•dur•ance [ɪndjÚrəns] s. resistencia; aguante; paciencia; duración.

en•dure [ɪndjÚr] v. aguantar, soportar, sufrir; durar, perdurar.

en•e•ma [énəmə] s. lavativa.

en•e•my [énəmɪ] s. enemigo.

en•er•get•ic [enədʒéɪk] *adj.* enérgico.

en•er•gy [énədʒɪ] s. energía.

en•er•vate [énə·vet] v. enervar, debilitar.

en•fold = **infold**.

en•force [ɪnfórs] v. dar fuerza a; hacer cumplir (*una ley*); **to – obediencia** hacer obedecer, imponer obediencia.

en•force•ment [ɪnfórsmənt] s. coacción, cumplimiento forzoso (*de una ley*).

en•gage [ɪngédʒ] v. (*employ*), ocupar; emplear, contratar; (*reserve*) alquilar; (*attract*) atraer; (*mesh*) engranar, acoplar; **to – in battle** trabar batalla; **to – (oneself) to do it** comprometerse a hacerlo; **to be -ed in something** estar ocupado en algo; **to be -ed to be married** estar comprometido para casarse.

en•gage•ment [ɪngédʒmənt] s. compromiso; cita; noviazgo; convenio, contrato; pelea; traba, engrane, acoplamiento (*de maquinaria*).

en•gen•der [ɪndʒéndə·] v. engendrar, producir.

en•gi•ne [éndʒən] s. máquina; motor; locomotora.

en•gi•neer [ɛndʒənír] s. ingeniero; maquinista (*de locomotora*); v. dirigir, planear.

en•gi•neer•ing [ɛndʒənírɪŋ] s. ingeniería; manejo, planeo.

eng•lish [íŋglɪʃ] *adj.* inglés, s. ingles, idioma ingles; **the -** los ingleses.

Eng•lish•man [íŋglɪʃmən] s. inglés.

en•grave [ɪngrév] v. grabar, esculpir.

en•grav•ing [ɪngrévɪŋ] s. grabado; estampa, lámina; **wood -** grabado en madera.

en•gross [ɛngrós] v. absorber; redactar en limpio.

en•gros•sed [ɛngróst] *adj.* absorto, ensimismado.

en•gulf [ɪngʌ́lf] v. engolfar, absorber, tragar.

en•hance [ɪnhǽns] v. realzar, engrandecer.

e•nig•ma [ɪnɪ́gmə] s. enigma.

en•join [ɪndʒɔ́ɪn] v. mandar, ordenar; **to – from** prohibir, vedar.

en•joy [ɪndʒɔ́ɪ] v. gozar de; disfrutar de; **to – oneself** divertirse, gozar, deleitarse; **to – the use of** usufructuar.

en•joy•able [ɪndʒɔ́ɪəb]] adj. agradable, deleitable.

en•joy•ment [ɪndʒɔ́ɪmənt] s. placer, goce; disfrute; usufructo.

en•large [ɪnlɑ́rdʒ] v. agrandar(se); ensanchar; ampliar; **to – upon** explayarse en ; extenderse en ; comentar.

en•large•ment [ɪnlɑ́rdʒmənt] s. (photo) ampliación; ensanchamiento.

en•light•en [ɪnlɑ́ɪt n] v. alumbrar; iluminar; ilustrar, instruir.

en•list [ɪnlɪ́st] v. alistar(se); sentar plaza (de soldado); reclutar.

en•list•ment [ɪnlɪ́srmənt] s. reclutamiento; alistamiento.

en•liv•en [ɪnlɑ́ɪvən] v. avivar, animar, alegrar.

en•mi•ty [ɪnməɪ] s. enemistad.

en•no•ble [ɪnóbḷ] v. ennoblecer.

e•nor•mous [ɪnɔ́rməs] adj. enorme.

e•nough [ən ʌ́f] adj. & adv. bastante; s. lo bastante, lo suficiente; **that is -** eso basta, con eso basta; - !¡basta¡.

en•quire = **inquire**.

en•rage [ɪnrédʒ] v. enrabiar, hacer rabiar; enfurecer.

en•rap•ture [ɪnrǽptʃə·] v. extasiar, embelesar, enajenar.

en•rich [ɪrɪ́ʃ] v. enriquecer.

en•roll [ɪnról] v. alistar(se); matricular(se); inscribir(se); hacerse miembro.

en•roll•ment [ɪnrólmənt] s. alistamiento; registro, matrícula.

en•sem•ble [ɑnsámbḷ] s. (music) conjunto musical; (dress) traje armonioso.

en•sing [ɛ́nsn] s, alférez (de la marina); [ɛ́nsaɪn] bandera; insignia.

en•slave [ɪnslév] v. esclavizar.

en•snare [ɛnsnɛ́r] v. enredar, entrampar, embaucar.

en•sue [ɛnsú] v. sobrevenir, seguir(se), resultar.

en•tail [ɪntél] v. envolver, ocasionar; vincular (una herencia).

en•tan•gle [ɪntǽŋgḷ] v. enredar, enmarañar, embrollar.

en•ter [ɛ́ntə·] v. entrar en ; ingresar en ; asentar (una partida, cantidad, etc.); registrar; salir (al escenario).

en•ter•prise [ɛ́ntə·praɪz] s. empresa.

en•ter•pris•ing [ɛ́ntə·praɪzɪŋ] adj. emprendedor.

en•ter•tain [ɛntə·tén] v. divertir; agasajar; obsequiar; banquetear; acariciar (una idea); abrigar (una esperanza, un rencor); **she –s a great deal** es muy fiestera u obsequiosa.

en•ter•tain•ing [ɛntə·ténɪŋ] adj. entretenido, divertido, chistoso.

en•ter•tain•ment [ɛntə·ténmə·nt] s. entretenimiento; pasatiempo; diversión; fiesta, convite.

en•thu•si•asm [ɪnθjúzɪæzəm] s. entusiasmo.

en•thu•si•ast [ɪnθjúzɪæst] s. entusiasta.

en•thu•si•as•tic [ɪnθjuzɪǽstɪk] adj. entusiasta, entusiástico; **to be –** estar entusiasmado.

en•tice [ɪntɑ́ɪs] v. atraer, tentar, seducir, halagar.

en•tire [ɪntɑ́ɪr] adj. entero; cabal; **the – world** todo el mundo; **-ly** adj. enteramente, por entero.

en•tire•ty [ɪntɑ́ɪrɪ] s. totalidad, entereza; conjunto; todo.

en•ti•tle [ɪntɑ́ɪt]] v. titular, intitular; autorizar, dar derecho.

en•ti•ty [ɛ́ntəɪ] s. entidad; ente, ser.

en•trails [ɛ́ntrəls] s. pl. entrañas; tripas.

en•trance [ɛ́ntrəns] s. entrada; ingreso.

en•treat [ɪntrɪ́t] v. suplicar; rogar, instar.

en•treat•y [ɪntrɪ́ɪ] s. súplica, ruego; instancia.

en•trench = **intrench**.

en•trust [ɪntr ʌ́st] v. confiar; depositar, entregar.

en•try [ɛ́ntrɪ] s. entrada; ingreso; partida; registro, anotación; **double –** partida, doble (en teneduría).

e•nu•mer•ate [ɪnjúmərət] v. enumerar.

e•nun•ci•ate [ɪn ʌ́ nsɪet] v. articular; enunciar, declarar.

en•vel•op [ɪnvéləp] v. envolver.

en•ve•lope [ɛ́nvəlop] s. sobre, cubierta (de una carta).

en•vi•a•ble [ɛ́nvɪəb]] adj. envidiable.

en•vi•ous [ɛ́nvɪəs] adj. envidioso.

en•vi•ron•ment [ɪnvɑ́ɪrənmənt] s. ambiente, medio ambiente.

en•vi•rons [ɪnvɑ́ɪrənz] s. pl. cercanías, contornos, alrededores.

en•voy [ɛ́nvɔɪ] s. enviado.

en•vy [ɛ́nvɪ] s. envidia; v. envidiar.

e•phem•er•al [ɪfémə·]] adj. efímero.

ep•ic [ɛ́pɪk] s. epopeya, poema, épico; adj. épico.

ep•i•dem•ic [ɛpədémɪk] s. epidemia; peste; adj. epidémico.

E•piph•a•ny [ɪpɪ́fənɪ] s. Epifanía.

ep•i•sode [ɛ́pəsod] s. episodio.

e•pis•tle [ɪpɪ́s]] s. epístola, carta.

ep•i•thaph [ɛ́pətæf] s. epitafio.

ep•och [ɛ́pək] s. época.

e·qual [Íkəl] *adj.* igual; **to be – to a task** ser competente (*o* tener suficientes fuerzas) para una tarea; *s.* igual; cantidad igual; *v.* igualar; ser igual a; **ly** *adv.* igualmente; por igual.

e·qual·i·ty [Íhwálətı] *s.* igualdad.

e·qual·ize [Íkwəlaɪz] *v.* igualar, emparejar; equilibrar; nivelar.

e·qua·tion [ɪkwéʒən] *s.* ecuación.

e·qua·tor [ɪkwétə·] *s.* ecuador.

e·qui·lib·ri·um [ikwəlíbrɪəm] *s.* equilibrio.

e·quip [ɪkwíp] *v.* equipar; proveer; habilitar.

e·quip·ment [ɪkwípmənt] *s.* equipo; aparatos; avíos; habilitación

eq·ui·ta·ble [ékwɪtəb ǀ] *adj.* equitativo.

eq·ui·ty [ékwətı] *s.* equidad; justicia.

e·quiv·a·lent [ɪkwívələnt] *adj.* & *s.* equivalente.

e·quiv·o·cal [ɪkwívək ǀ] *adj.* equívoco, ambíguo.

e·ra [Írə] *s.* era, época.

e·rad·i·cate [ɪrædɪket] *v.* desarraigar, extirpar.

e·rase [ɪrés] *v.* borrar; tachar.

e·ras·er [ɪrésə·] *s.* goma, *Am.* borrador; **blackboard – cepillo.**

e·ra·sure [ɪréʃə·] *s.* borradura, raspadura.

e·re [ɛr] *prep.* antes de; *conj.* antes (de) que.

e·rect [ɪrékt] *adj.* erguido; derecho; levantado; *Am.* parado; *v.* erigir; levantar, alzar.

er·mine [ǯ·mɪn] *s.* armiño.

e·rode [ɪród] *v.* erosionar.

e·ro·sion [ɪróʒən] *s.* erosión; desgaste.

e·rot·ic [ɪrátɪk] *adj.* erótico.

err [ɝ]*v,* errar; equivocarse; descarriarse.

er·rand [érənd] *s.* mandado, recado, encargo; **– boy** mandadero.

er·rant [érənt] *adj.* errante; **knight – errant** caballero andante.

er·rat·ic [ɛrǽtɪk]*adj.* inconstante, errático; vagabundo.

er·ro·ne·ous [ərónɪəs] *adj.* erróneo, errado.

er·ror [érə·] *s.* error.

er·u·di·tion [ɛrɪdíʃən] *s* erudición.

e·rup·tion [ɪr ʌ pʃən] *s.* erupción.

es·ca·late [éskəlet] *v.* aumentar; intensificar.

es·ca·pade [éskəped] *s.* trapisonda, travesura.

es·cape [əskép] *s.* escape; fuga, huída; escapada; escapatoria; *v.* escapar (se); fugarse; huir (se); eludir, evadir; **it –s me** se me escapa.

es·cort [éskɔrt] *s.* escolta; acompañante; convoy; [ɪskɔ́rt] *v.* escoltar; convoyar; acompañar.

es·cutch·eon [ɪk ʌ tʃən] *s.* escudo de armas, blasón.

es·pe·cial [əspéʃəl] *adj.* especial; **-ly** *adv.* especialmente.

es·pio·nage [éspɪənɪdʒ] *s.* espionaje.

es·say [ése] *s.* ensayo; [ɛsé] *v.* ensayar.

es·sence [és ŋ s] *s.* esencia.

es·sen·tial [əsénʃəl] *adj.* esencial.

es·tab·lish [əstǽblɪʃ] *v.* establecer.

es·tab·lish·ment [əstǽblɪʃmənt] *s.* establecimiento.

es·tate [əstét] *s.* hacienda, heredad; bienes, propiedades; estado, condición; **country –** finca rural.

es·teem [əstím] *s.* estima, estimación, aprecio; *v.* estimar, apreciar; considerar, juzgar.

es·ti·ma·ble [éstəməb ǀ] *adj.* estimable.

es·ti·mate [éstəmɪt] *s.* (*calculation*) tasa, cálculo aproximado; presupuesto; (*judment*) opinión; [éstə·met] *v.* estimar, tasar, calcular aproximadamente; hacer un presupuesto; juzgar, opinar.

es·ti·ma·tion [ɛstəméʃən] *s.* juicio, opinión; estima; estimación.

es·trange [ɛstréndʒ] *v.* enajenar; apartar.

es·tu·ar·y [ɛstʃ Uɛrı] *s.* estuario o estero, desembocadura de un río.

etch [ɛt] *v.* grabar al agua fuerte.

etch·ing [étʃɪŋ] *s.* agua fuerte, grabado al agua fuerte.

e·ter·nal [ɪt ǯ n ǀ] *adj.* eterno.

e·ter·ni·ty [ɪt ǯ nətı] *s.* eternidad.

e·ther [Íθə·] *s.* éter.

e·the·re·al [ɪθÍtəl] *adj.* etéreo.

eth·i·cal [éθɪk ǀ] *adj.* ético, moral.

eth·ics [éθɪks] *s.* ética, moral.

eth·nic [éθɪks] *adj.* étnico.

et·i·quette [étɪkɛt] *s.* etiqueta (*regla de conducta social*).

et·y·mol·o·gy [ɛtəmálədʒɪ] *s.* etimología

eu·ca·lyp·tus [jukəlíptəs] *s.* eucalipto.

eu·phe·mism [júfəmɪzm] *s.* eufemismo.

Eu·ro·pean [jUrəpÍən] *adj.* & *s.* europeo.

e·vac·u·ate [ɪvǽkjUet] *v.* evacuar, desocupar.

e·vade [ɪvéd] *v.* evadir.

e·val·u·ate [ɪv ǽ ljUet] *v.* valorar, avaluar

e·vap·o·rate [ɪv ǽ pərɛt] *v.* evaporar(se).

e·vap·o·ra·tion [ɪvæpəréjən] *s.* evaporación.

e·va·sion [ɪvéʒən] *s.* evasión, evasiva.

e·va·sive [ɪvésɪv] *adj.* evasivo.

eve [iv] *s.* víspera, vigilia; **Christmas Eve** Nochebuena; **New Year's Eve** víspera del Año Nuevo; **on the – of** en vísperas de.

e·ven [Ívən] *adj.* (*level*) liso, plano, llano, a nivel; (*same*) parejo; uniforme; igual; **– dozen** docena cabal; **– number** número par; **– temper** genio apasible; **to be – with someone** estar mano a mano (*o* estar a mano) con alguien; **to get – whith someone** desquitarse de alguien; *adv.* aún, hasta; **– if** (*o* **– thouh**) aun cuando; **– so** aun así; **not –** ni siquiera, ni aun; *v.* allanar; nivelar (se); igualar (se);

emparejar; **-ly** adv. igualmente; de un modo igual; con uniformidad; con suavidad.

eve•ning [Ívnɪŋ] s. tarde; noche (*las primeras horas*); **– gown** vestido de etiqueta; **– star** estrella vespertina, lucero de la tarde.

e•ven•ness [ivənnɪs] s. lisura; igualddad; **– of temper** apacibilidad o suavidad de genio.

e•vent [ɪvɛ́nt] s. suceso, acontecimiento; incidente, evento; resultado, consecuencia; **in any –** en todo caso; **in the – of** en caso de.

e•vent•ful [ɪvɛ́ntfəl] adj. lleno de sucesos, importante, memorable.

e•ven•tu•al [ɪvɛ́ntʃUəl] adj. eventual; último, final, terminal; **-ly** adv. finalmente, por fin, con el tiempo; eventualmente.

ev•er [ɛ́və] adv. siempre, jamás; alguna vez; **– so much** muchísimo; **for – and –** por (o para) siempre jamás; **hardly –** casi nunca, penas; **if –** si alguna vez; **more than –** más que nunca; **the best friend I – had** el mejor amigo que en mi vida he tenido.

ev•er•green [ɛ́və-grin] s. siempre viva, sempiterna; adj. siempre verde.

ev•er•last•ing [ɛvə-lǽstɪŋ] adj. sempiterno, eterno, perpetuo; duradero; s. eternidad, sempiterna (*planta*); siempreviva; perpetua, flor perpetua.

ev•er•more [ɛvə-mór] adv. para siempre; **for –** para siempre jamás.

eve•ry [ɛ́vrɪ] adj. cada; todo; todos los, todas las; **– bit of it** todo, todito; **– day** todos los días; **– once in a while** de vez en cuando; **– one of them** todos ellos; **– other day** cada dos días, un día sí y otro no.

eve•ry•bod•y [ɛ́vrɪbadɪ] pron. todos, todo el mundo.

eve•ry•day [ɛ́vrɪdé] adj. diario, cotidiano, de todos los días; ordinario.

eve•ry•one [ɛ́vrɪwʌn] pron. todos; todo el mundo; cada uno.

eve•ry•thing [ɛ́vrɪθɪŋ] pron. todo.

eve•ry•where [ɛ́vrɪhwɛr] adv. por (o en) todas partes; a todas partes.

e•vict [ɪvÍkt] v. desalojar; expulsar.

ev•i•dence [ɛ́vədəns] s. evidencia; prueba; demostración, señal; testimonio; **to be in –** mostrarse; v. hacer evidente, evidenciar; patentizar, revelar, mostrar

ev•i•dent [ɛ́vədent] adj. evidente, patente.

e•vil [ív]] adj. malo, malvado, maligno; aciago, de mal agüero; **to cast the – eye** aojar; **the Evil One** el Diablo; s. mal; maldad; adv. mal.

e•vil•do•er [ic]dúə-] s. malhechor

e•voke [ɪvók] v. evocar; **to – laughter** provocar a risa.

ev•o•lu•tion [ɛvəlúʃən] s. evolución.

e•volve [ɪválv] v. desarrollar(se), desenvolver(se); urdir; evolucionar.

ewe [ju] s. oveja.

ex•act [ɪgzǽkt] adj. exacto, v. exigir, **-ly** adv. exactamente; en punto.

ex•act•ing [ɪgzǽjtɪŋ] adj. exigente.

ex•ag•ger•ate [ɪgzǽdʒəret] v. exagerar.

ex•alt [ɪgzɔ́lt] v. exaltar, ensalzar.

ex•al•ta•tion [ɛgzɔltéʃən] s. exaltación

ex•am•i•na•tion [ɪgzæmənəeʃən] s. examen; reconocimiento (*médico*).

ex•am•ine [ɪgzǽmɪn] v. examinar; reconocer (*dícese del médico*).

ex•am•ple [ɪgzǽmp]] s. ejemplo.

ex•as•per•ate [ɪgzǽspəret] v. exasperar, irritar.

ex•ca•vate [ɛ́kskəvet] v. excavar.

ex•ceed [ɪksíd] v. exceder; sobrepasar; propasarse.

ex•ceed•ing•ly [ɪksídɪŋlɪ] adv. sumamente, extremamente; **– well** extremamente bien.

ex•cel [ɪksɛ́l] v. sobresalir (en o entre); sobrepugar (a).

ex•cel•lence [ɛ́ks]əns] s. excelencia.

ex•cel•len•cy [ɛ́ks]ənsɪ] s. excelencia.

ex•cel•lent [ɛ́ks]ənt] adj. excelente.

ex•cept [ɪksɛ́pt] prep. excepto, menos; v. exceptuar.

ex•cept•ing [ɪksɛ́ptɪŋ] prep. excepto, salvo, menos, exceptuando.

ex•cep•tion [ɪksɛ́pən] s. (*exclusion*) excepción; (*opposition*) objeción; **with the – of** a excepción de, con excepción de; **to take –** objetar; ofenderse.

ex•cep•tion•al [ɪksɛ́pən] adj. excepcional.

ex•cess [ɪksɛ́s] s. exceso; sobrante; **– baggage (weight)** exceso de equipaje (*de peso*); **to drink to –** beber en exceso.

ex•ces•sive [ɪksɛ́sɪv] adj. excesivo, **-ly** adv. excesivamente, en exceso, demasiado.

ex•change [ɪkstʃéndʒ] s. (*money*) cambio; (*interchange*) trueque; intercambio, canje (*de publicaciones, prisioneros*); (*stock*) lonja, bolsa; **rate of –** cambio, Am. tipo de cambio; **telephone –** central de teléfonos; v. cambiar; trocar; canjear (*publicaciones, prisioneros*); **to – greetings** saludarse; mandarse felicitaciones.

ex•cite [ɪksáɪt] v. excitar; acalorar; agitar.

ex•cit•ed [ɪksáɪtɪd] adj. excitado, acalorado; animado; **to get –** entusiasmarse; sobreexcitarse; acalorarse; **-ly** adv. acaloradamente, agitadamente.

ex•cite•ment [ɪksáɪtmənt] s. excitación; acaloramiento; agitación; alboroto; animación.

ex•cit•ing [ɪksáɪtɪŋ] adj. excitante, excitador; estimulante.

ex•claim [ɪksklém] v. exclamar.

ex•cla•ma•tion [ɛkskləméʃən] s. exclamación; **– point** punto de admiración.

ex·clude [ɪksklúd] *v.* excluir.

ex·clu·sion [ɪksklúʒən] *s.* exclusión.

ex·clu·sive [ɪksklúsɪv] *adj.* exclusivo; privativo; **– of** sin contar.

ex·com·mu·ni·cate [ɛ́kskəmjúnəket] *v.* excomunicar.

ex·com·mu·ni·ca·tion [ɛkskəmjunəkéʃən] *s.* excomunión.

ex·cre·ment [ɛ́kskrɪmənt] *s.* excremento.

ex·cur·sion [ɪkskɜ́ʒən] *s.* excursión; correría; expedición.

ex·cus·able [ɪkskjúzəb|] *adj.* excusable, disculpable.

ex·cuse [ɪkskjús] *s.* excusa; disculpa; [ɪkskjúz] *v.* excusar; disculpar; perdonar, dispensar; eximir; **– me!** ¡dispense Vd.!; ¡perdone Vd.!

ex·e·cute [ɛ́ksɪkjut] *v.* ejecutar; ajusticiar; llevar a cabo.

ex·e·cu·tion [ɛksɪkjúʃən] *s.* ejecución; desempeño.

ex·e·cu·tion·er [ɛksɪkjúʃənəˑ] *s.* verdugo.

ex·ec·u·tive [ɪgzɛ́kjUtɪv] *adj.* ejecutivo; *s.* ejecutivo, poder ejecutivo; gerente, administrador.

ex·ec·u·tor [ɪgzɛ́kjətəˑ] *s.* albacea, ejecutor testamentario; [ɛ́ksɪkjutəˑ] ejecutor.

ex·em·pla·ry [ɪgzɛ́mplərɪ] *adj.* ejemplar.

ex·empt [ɪgzɛ́mpt] *adj.* exento, libre; *v.* eximir, exentar.

ex·emp·tion [ɪgzɛ́mpʃən] *s.* exención.

ex·er·cise [ɛ́ksə·saɪz] *s.* ejercicio; *v.* ejercitar(se); ejercer (*poder o autoridad*); hacer ejercicio, hacer gimnasia; **to be -d about something** estar preocupado o sobreexcitado por algo.

ex·ert [ɪgzɝ́t] *v.* ejercer; **to – oneself** esforzarse, hacer esfuerzos, empeñarse.

ex·er·tion [ɪgzɝ́ʃən] *s.* ejercicio; esfuerzo, empeño.

ex·hale [ɛkshél] *v.* exhalar, emitir; espirar, soplar,

ex·haust [ɪgz1st] *s.* escape (*de gas o vapor*); *v.* agotar; consumir; debilitar, fatigar; **I am -ed** no puedo más; estoy agotado.

ex·haus·tion [ɪgz1sʃən] *s.* agotamiento; fatiga, postración.

ex·haus·tive [ɛgz1stɪv] *s.* comprensivo; detallado.

ex·hib·it [ɪgzíbɪt] *v.* exhibir; mostrar, exponer.

ex·hi·bi·tion [ɛksəbíʃən] *s.* exhibición; exposición, manifestación.

ex·hil·a·rate [ɪgzíləret] *v.* alborozar, excitar, animar, entusiasmar.

ex·hort [ɪgzɔ́rt] *v.* exhortar.

ex·ile [ɛ́gzaɪl] *s.* destierro, exilio; desterrado; *v.* desterrar; expatriar.

ex·ist [ɪgzíst] *v.* existir.

ex·is·tence [ɪgzístəns] *s.* existencia.

ex·is·tent [ɪgzístənt] *adj.* existente.

ex·it [ɛ́gzɪt] *s.* salida; salida (*del foro*); *v.* vase o vanse (*un personaje o personajes al fin de una escena*).

ex·o·dus [ɛ́ksədəs] *s.* éxodo.

ex·on·er·ate [ɪgzánəret] *v.* exonerar.

ex·or·bi·tant [ɪgzɔ́rbətənt] *adj.* exorbitante.

ex·ot·ic [ɪgzátɪk] *adj.* exótico; raro, extraño.

ex·pand [ɪkspǽnd] *v.* ensanchar(se); dilatar(se) extender(se); agrandar(se); desarrollar (*una ecuación*).

ex·panse [ɪkspǽns] *s.* espacio, extensión.

ex·pan·sion [ɪkspǽnʃən] *s.* expansión; ensanche; desarrollo (*de una ecuación*).

ex·pan·sive [ɪkspǽnsɪv] *adj.* expansivo; efusivo.

ex·pect [ɪkspɛ́kt] *v.* esperar, contar con; **I – so** supongo que sí.

ex·pec·ta·tion [ɛkspɛtéʃən] *s.* expectación; expectativa; esperanza.

ex·pec·to·rate [ɪkspɛ́ktəret] *v.* expectorar, desgarrar.

ex·pe·di·ent [ɪkspídɪənt] *adj.* conveniente, oportuno; ventajoso; prudente, *s.* expediente, medio.

ex·pe·dite [ɛ́kspədaɪt] *v.* facilitar; despachar.

ex·pe·di·tion [ɛkspɪdíʃən] *s.* expedición.

ex·pe·di·tion·ar·y [ɛkspɪdíʃənɛrɪ] *adj.* expedicionario.

ex·pel [ɪkspɛ́nd] *v.* expeler; expulsar.

ex·pend [ɪkspɛ́nd] *v.* gastar; consumir.

ex·pen·di·ture [ɪkspɛ́ndɪtʃəˑ] *s.* gasto; desembolso.

ex·pense [ɪkspɛ́ns] *s.* gasto; coste, costa o costo.

ex·pen·sive [ɪkspɛ́nsɪv] *adj.* costoso.

ex·pen·sive·ness [ɪkspɛ́nsɪvnɪs] *s.* precio subido, coste elevado.

ex·pe·ri·ence [ɪkspírɪəns] *s.* experiencia; aventura, lance; *v.* experimentar; pasar (*penas, sufrimientos*); sentir.

ex·pe·ri·enced [ɪkspírənst] *adj.* experimentado; ducho, perito, experto.

ex·per·i·ment [ɪkspérəmənt] *s.* experimento, prueba; *v.* experimentar, hacer un experimento.

ex·per·i·men·tal [ɪkspɛrəmɛ́nt|] *adj.* experimental.

ex·pert [ɛ́kspɝt] *s.* experto, perito; [ɪkspɝ́t] *adj.* experto, perito, experimentado.

ex·pi·ra·tion [ɛkspəréʃən] *s.* terminación; vencimiento (*de un plazo*); espiración (*del aire*).

ex·pire [ɪkspáɪr] *v.* expirar, morir; acabar, vencerse (*un plazo*); expeler (*el aire aspirado*).

ex·plain [ɪksplén] *v.* explicar.

ex·plain·a·ble [ɪksplénəb|] *adj.* explicable.

ex·pla·na·tion [ɛksplənéʃən] *s.* explicación.

ex·plan·a·to·ry [ɪksplǽnətorɪ] *adj.* explicativo.

ex·plic·it [ɛksplísɪt] *adj.* explícito.

ex•plode [ɪksplód] v. estallar, hacer explosión, *Am.* explotar; reventar; volar (*con dinamita*); desacreditar (*una teoría*).

ex•ploit [ɛ́ksplɔɪt] s. hazaña, proeza; [ɪksplɔ́ɪt] v. explotar; sacar partido de, abusar de.

ex•ploit•a•tion [ɛ̀ksplɔɪtéʃən] s. explotación.

ex•plo•ra•tion [ɛ̀ksplǝréʃǝn] s. exploración.

ex•plore [ɪksplór] v. explorar.

ex•plor•er [ɪksplórǝ·] s. explorador.

ex•plo•sion [ɪksplóʒǝn] s. explosión, estallido.

ex•plo•sive [ɪksplósɪV] adj. & s. explosivo.

ex•port [ɛ́ksport] s. exportación; artículo exportado, mercancía exportada; [ɪkspórt] v. exportar.

ex•por•ta•tion [ɛ̀ksportéʃǝn] s. exportación.

ex•pose [ɪkspóz] v. exponer; exhibir, mostrar, poner a la vista; revelar; desenmascarar.

ex•po•si•tion [ɛ̀kspǝzíʃǝn] s. exposición; exhibición.

ex•po•sure [ɪkspóʒǝ·] s. exposición; revelación; **to die of** — morir a efecto de la intemperie.

ex•pound [ɪkspáUnd] v. exponer, explicar.

ex•press [ɪksprés] adj. (*rapid*) expreso, (*explicit*) explícito, claro; — **company** compañía de expreso; expreso, *Am.* exprés; — **train** tren expreso; adv. por expreso, por exprés; s. expreso; tren expreso, *Am.* exprés; v. expresar; enviar por expreso (*o* por exprés).

ex•pres•sion [ɪkspréʃǝn] s. expresión.

ex•pres•sive [ɪksprésɪV] adj. expresivo.

ex•pul•sion [ɪkspʌ́lʃǝn] s. expulsión.

ex•qui•site [ɛ́kskwÍzɪt] adj. exquisito.

ex•qui•site•ness [ɛ́kskwÍzɪtnɪs] s. exquisitez; primor.

ex•tant [ɪkstǽnt] adj. existente.

ex•tem•po•ra•ne•ous [ɛ̀kstɛmpǝrénɪǝs] adj. improvisado.

ex•tend [ɪksténd] v. extender(se); tender; prolongar(se); alargar(se); agrandar; dilatar, prorrogar (*un plazo*); dar (*el pésame, el parabién, ayuda, etc.*).

ex•tend•ed [ɪksténdɪd] adj. extenso; prolongado; extendido.

ex•ten•sion [ɪksténʃǝn] s. extensión; prolongación; prórroga (*de un plazo*); añadidura, anexo.

ex•ten•sive [ɪksténsɪV] adj. extenso, ancho, dilatado; extensivo., **-ly** adv. extensamente, por extenso; extensivamente; **-ly used** de uso general o común.

ex•tent [ɪkstént] s. extensión; grado, **to a great** — en gran parte, generalmente; **to such an** — **that** a tal grado que; **to the** — **of one's ability** en proporción a su habilidad; **up to a certain** — hasta cierto punto.

ex•ten•u•ate [ɪnsténjUet] v. atenuar, mitigar.

ex•te•ri•or [ɪkstÍrɪǝ·] adj. exterior; externo; s. exterioridad; exterior, porte, aspecto.

ex•ter•mi•nate [ɪkstɝ́mǝnet] v. exterminar, destruir por completo, extirpar.

ex•ter•mi•na•tion [ɪkstɝ̀mǝnéʃǝn] s. exterminio.

ex•ter•nal [ɪkstɝ́n]] adj. externo; exterior; s. exterioridad; lo externo.

ex•tinct [ɪkstíŋkt] adj. extinto; extinguido, apagado.

ex•tin•guish [ɪkstíŋgwɪʃ] v. extinguir; apagar.

ex•tol [ɪkstól] v. enaltecer; ensalzar.

ex•tort [ɪkstɔ́rt] v. obtener por fuerza o amenaza, exigir (*dinero, promesa, etc.*). *Am.* extorsionar.

ex•tor•tion [ɪkstɔ́rʃǝn] s. extorsión.

ex•tra [ɛ́kstrǝ] adj. extraordinario; de sobra, de más, adicional; suplementario; — **tire** neumático de repuesto o de recambio, — **workman** obrero supernumerario; adv. extraordinariamente; s. extra; extraordinario (*de un periódico*); suplemento; gasto extraordinario; recargo (*cargo adicional*); actor suplente o supernumerario.

ex•tract [ɛ́kstrækt] s. extracto; cita, trozo (*entresacado de un libro*); resumen; [ɪkstrǽkt] v. extraer; seleccionar; citar.

ex•traor•di•nar•y [ɪkstrɔ́rdnɛrɪ] adj. extraordinario, **extraordinarily** adv. extraordinariamente; de manera extraordinaria.

ex•trav•a•gance [ɪkstrǽvǝgǝns] s. despilfarro, derroche, gasto excesivo, lujo excesivo; extravagancia, capricho.

ex•trav•a•gant [ɪkstrǽvǝgǝnt] adj. gastador, despilfarrado; extravagante, disparatado; — **praise** elogios excesivos; — **prices** precios exorbitantes.

ex•treme [ɪkstrÍm] adj. (*last*) último; extremo; más remoto, (*excessive*) excesivo; riguroso, radical, — **opinions** opiniones extremadas; — s. extremo; cabo; **to go to** -s extremar, exagerar; hacer extremos, tomar las medidas más extremas; **-ly** adv. extremamente, en extremo.

ex•trem•i•ty [ɪkstrémǝtɪ] s. extremidad, extremo; medida extrema; **in** — en gran peligro; en un apuro.

ex•u•ber•ant [ɪgzjúbǝrǝnt] adj. exuberante.

ex•ult [ɪgz ʌ́lt] v. alborozarse, regocijarse.

eye [aɪ] s. ojo; — **shade** visera; **in a twinkling of an** — en un abrir y cerrar de ojos; **hook and** — macho y hembra; **to catch one's** — llamar la atención; **to have good** -s tener buena vista; **to have before one's** -s tener a (*o* tener ante) la vista; **to keep an** — **on** cuidar, vigilar; **to see** — **to** — estar completamente de acuerdo; v. mirar, observar.

eye•ball [áɪbɔl] s. globo del ojo.

eye•brow [áɪbraU] s. ceja.

eye•glass [áɪglæs] s. lente, cristal (*de anteojo*), ocular (*de microscopio o telescopio*); **-es** lentes, anteojos.

eye•lash [áɪlæʃ] s. pestaña.

eye•lid [áɪlɪd] s. párpado.

eye·sight [áɪsaɪt] *s.* vista; **poor –** male vista.

F

fa·ble [féb] *s.* fábula.

fab·ric [fæbrɪk] *s.* género, tela; tejido; textura, estructura.

fab·u·lous [fæbjələs] *adj.* fabuloso.

fa·çade [fəʃád] *s.* fachada.

face [fəs] *s.* (*human*) cara, rostro; (*building*) fachada, frente; (*surface*) haz, superficie; (*watch*) muestra; *Ríopl.* esfera, *Méx., C.A., Ven., Col.* carátula; **– value** valor nominal; **in the – of** en presencia de, ante, frente a; **to lose –** perder prestigio; **to make -s** hacer muecas o gestos; **to save one's –** salvar el amor propio; *v.* encararse con; enfrentarse con; hacer frente a; mirar hacia; forrar; **to – about** volverse, *Méx., C.A., Ven., Col., Andes* voltearse; **to – danger** afrontar o arrostrar el peligro; **to – with marble** revestir de mármol; **it -s the street** da a la calle.

fa·cil·i·tate [fəsílətət] *v.* facilitar.

fa·cil·i·ty [fəsílətɪ] *s.* facilidad.

fact [fækt] *s.* hecho, dato; verdad, realidad; **in –** de hecho; en realidad.

fac·tion [fækʃən] *s.* facción, bando, partido, pandilla.

fac·tor [fæktɚ] *s.* factor; elemento; agente; *v.* descomponer en factores.

fac·to·ry [fæktrɪ] *s.* fábrica.

fac·ul·ty [fæk|tɪ] *s.* facultad; (*college*) profesorado; cuerpo docente.

fad [fæd] *s.* novedad; manía; moda.

fade [fed] *v.* descolorar(se); desteñir(se); marchitar(se); apagarse (*un sonido*); desvanecerse.

fag·ged [fægd] *adj.* agotado, rendido de cansancio.

fail [fel] *v.* (*not effect*) falter; fallar; fracasar; no tener éxito; (*wane*) decaer; debilitarse; (*go broke*) quebrar, hacer bancarrota; **to – in an examination** fallar en un examen, salir mal en un examen; **to – a student** reprobar o suspender a un estudiante; **to – to do it** dejar de hacerlo, no hacerlo; **don't – to come** no deje Vd. de venir; **without –** sin falta.

fail·ure [féljɚ] *s.* fracaso; malogro; falta; descuido, negligencia; quiebra, bancarrota; debilitamiento.

faint [fént] *adj.* (*weak*) débil, languido; (*indistinct*) imperceptible, tenue, vago, indistinto; **to feel –** sentirse desvanecido; **–hearted** tímido, cobarde; *s.* desmayo; *v.* desmayarse; languidecer, **-ly** *adv.* débilmente; lánguidamente; indistintamente,

vagamente, tenuemente; apenas.

faint·ness [féntnɪs] *s.* languidez, debilidad, desfallecimiento; falta de claridad, vaguedad.

fair [fɛr] *adj.* (*just*) justo, recto, honrado; imparcial; equitativo; (*mediocre*) regular, mediano, (*complexion*) rubio, blondo; *Méx.* huero, *Guat.* canche; *C.R.* macho; *Pan.* fulo; *Col.* mono; *Ven.* catire; (*weather*) claro, despejado; **– chance of success** buena probabilidad de éxito; **– complexion** tez blanca; **– hair** pelo rubio; **– name** reputación sin mancilla; **– play** juego limpio; **– sex** sexo bello; **– weather** buen tiempo, tiempo bonancible; **to act –** obrar con imparcialidad (*o* con equidad); **to play –** jugar limpio; *s.* feria; mercado; exposición; **-ly** *adv.* justamente; imparcialmente; medianamente; **-ly difficult** medianamente difícil; **-ly well** regular, bastante bien.

fair·ness [férnɪs] *s.* justicia, equidad, imparcialidad; blancura (*de la tez*); belleza.

fair·y [férɪ] *s.* hada; **– godmother** hada madrina; **– tale** cuento de hadas.

fair·y·land [férɪlænd] *s.* tierra de las hadas.

faith [feθ] *s.* fe; fidelidad; **in good –** de buena fe; **to have – in** tener fe o confianza en, **to keep –** cumplir con la palabra.

faith·ful [féθfəl] *adj.* fiel, leal; **-ly** *adv.* fielmente; con fidelidad; puntualmente; **-ly yours** suyo afectísimo; siempre suyo.

faith·ful·ness [féθlɪs] *s.* fidelidad; lealtad; exactitud.

faith·less [féθlɪs] *adj.* infiel; sin fe; desleal; falso.

fake [fek] *s.* fraude, trampa; falsedad; embustero; *adj.* falso, fingido; *v.* falsear; fingir; simular.

fal·con [fɔ́lkən] *s.* halcón.

fall [fɔl] *s.* (*drop*) caída; bajada; (*collapse*) ruina; baja (*de precios*); (*season*) otoño; **-s** cascada, catarata, salto de agua; *v.* caer(se); decaer; bajar; **to – asleep** dormirse, quedarse dormido; **to – back** retroceder, **to – behind** atrasarse, rezagarse, quedarse atrás; **to – in love** enamorarse, **to – out with** reñir con, enemistarse con, **to – to one** tocarle a uno, corresponderle a uno; **his plans fell through** fracasaron (*o* se malograron) sus planes.

fal·la·cy [fæləsɪ] *s.* falsedad; error.

fal·len [fɔ́lən] *p.p. de* fall.

fall·out [fclaʊt] *s.* precipitación radiactiva.

fal·low [fælo] *adj.* baldío; *s.* barbecho; *v.* barbechar.

false [fɔls] *adj.* falso; postizo (*dientes, barba, etc.*); fingido, simulado.

false·hood [fɔ́lsʊd] *s.* falsedad, mentira.

false·ness [fɔ́lsnɪs] *s.* falsedad.

fal·si·fy [fɔ́lsəfaɪ] *v.* falsificar, falsear; mentir.

fal·si·ty [fɔ́lsətɪ] *s.* falsedad; mentira.

fal·ter [fɔ́ltɚ] *v.* vacilar, titubear; tambalearse; bambolearse; **to – an excuse** balbucear una excusa; s. temblor, vacilación.

fame [fem] s. fama.

famed [femd] adj. afamado, famoso, renombrado.

fa·mil·iar [fəmíljə·] adj. familiar, íntimo; confianzudo; **to be – with a subject** conocer bien, estar versado en o ser conocedor de una materia; s. familiar.

fa·mil·iar·i·ty [fəmɪlɪǽrətɪ] s. familiaridad; confianza, franqueza.

fam·i·ly [fǽmlɪ] s. familia; **– name** apellido; **– tree** árbol genealógico; **to be in the – way** estar encinta.

fam·ine [fǽmɪn] s. hambre, escasez, carestía.

fam·ished [fǽmɪʃt] adj. hambriento, muerto de hambre; **to be –** morirse de hambre.

fa·mous [féməs] adj. famoso.

fan [fæn] s. abanico; aventador; ventilador; aficionado (a deportes); admirador; abanicar; ventilar.

fa·nat·ic [fənǽtɪk] adj. & s. fanático.

fa·nat·i·cism [fənǽtəsɪzəm] s. fanatismo.

fan·ci·ful [fǽnsɪfəl] adj. fantástico; caprichoso, imaginario.

fan·cy [fǽnsɪ] s. fantasía, antojo, capricho; imaginación; afición, gusto; **to have a – for** tener afición a; **to strike one's –** antojársele a uno; **to take a – to a person** caerle a uno bien (o simpatizarle a uno) una persona; adj. fantástico, de fantasía; de adorno; elegante; **– ball** baile de fantasía o disfraces; **– free** libre de cuidados; **–work** labor; bordado fino, v. imaginar(se); fantasear, forjar; concebir (una idea); **to – oneself** imaginarse; **just – the idea!** ¡figúrate qué idea! **I don't – the idea of** no me gusta la idea de.

fang [fæn] s. colmillo (de ciertos animales).

fan·tas·tic [fæntǽstɪk] adj. fantástico; extravagante.

fan·ta·sy [fǽntəsɪ] s. fantasía.

far [fɑr] adj. lejos; **–away** muy lejos; **– and wide** por todas partes; **– better** mucho mejor; **– off** muy lejos; a lo lejos; **by –** con mucho; **as – as** hasta; en cuanto a; **as – as I know** según parece, a lo que parece; que yo sepa; **so –** hasta ahora, hasta aquí, hasta entonces; **how –?** ¿hasta dónde?; adj. lejano, distante, remoto; **–journey** largo viaje; **it is a – cry from** dista mucho de.

far·a·way [fárəwé] adj. muy lejano, distante, remoto; abstraído.

farce [fɑrs] s. farsa.

fare [fɛr] s. pasaje, tarifa de pasajes; pasajero; comida, alimento; v. pasarla (bien o mal); irle a uno (bien o mal); **to – forth** salir.

fare·well [fɛrwél] s. despedida, adiós; **to bid – to** despedirse de; **– !** ¡adios!

far·fetched [fárfétʃt] adj. traído de muy lejos; forzado; traído por los cabellos; que no hace al caso; improbable, poco creíble.

far-flung [fárflʌŋ] adj. extenso, de gran alcance.

farm [form] s. hacienda, granja, Ríopl. estancia, Méx. rancho; **– hand** peón **– produce** productos agrícolas; v. cultivar, labrar (la tierra); **to – out** dar en arriendo; repartir.

farm·er [fármə·] s. labrador; granjero, agricultor, Méx. ranchero, Ríopl. estanciero, Am. hacendado.

farm·bouse [fármhaUs] s. alquería, finca.

farm·ing [fármɪŋ] s. labranza, agricultura, cultivo de los campos; adj. agrícola.

farm·yard [fármjɑrd] s. corral (de una alquería).

far-off [fárɔf] adj. distante, remoto.

far-sight·ed [fɑrsáɪtəd] adj. (sight) présbite; (foresighted) precavido.

far·ther [fárðə·] adv. más lejos; más; **– on** más adelante; adj. más remoto, más lejano.

far·thest [fárðɪst] adj. más lejano; más remoto; adv. más lejos.

fas·ci·nate [fǽsŋ et] v. fascinar.

fas·ci·na·tion [fæsŋéʃən] s. fascinación.

fash·ion [fǽʃən] s. (style) moda, boga; estilo; (way) manera, modo: **– plate** figurín; **the latest –** la última moda (o novedad); **after a –** medianamente, no muy bien; **to be in –** estar de moda; estilarse; v. forjar, hacer, formar; idear.

fash·ion·a·ble [fǽʃnəb] adj. de moda; de buen tono, elegante.

fast [fæst] adj. rápido, veloz; adelantado (dícese del reloj); firme; fiel (amigo); fijo; disipado, disoluto; adv. aprisa, de prisa, firmemente, fijamente; **– asleep** profundamente dormido; s. ayuno; v. ayunar.

fas·ten [fǽsŋ] v. fijar(se); sujetar(se), asegurar(se), atar, unir, abrochar(se).

fas·ten·er [fǽsŋ ə·] s. broche, abrochador.

fas·tid·i·ous [fæstídɪəs] adj. melindroso.

fat [fæt] adj. gordo; grasiento; mantecoso; **– profits** ganancias pingües; s. grasa, manteca; gordura; **the – of the land** lo mejor y más rico de la tierra.

fa·tal [fét] adj. fatal.

fa·tal·i·ty [fətǽlɪtɪ] s. fatalidad; muerte.

fate [fet] s. hado, sino, destino; fortuna, suerte.

fa·ther [fóðə·] s. padre.

fa·ther·hood [fóðə·hUd] s. paternidad.

fa·ther-in-law [fóðə·rɪnlɔ] s. suegro.

fa·ther·land [fóðə·lænd] s. patria.

fa·ther·ly [fóðə·lɪ] adv. paternal.

fath·om [fǽðəm] v. sondar, sondear; penetrar; s. braza (medida de profundidad).

fath·om·less [fǽðəmlɪs] adj. insondable.

fa·tigue [fətíg] s. fatiga, cansancio; v. fatigar(se), cansar(se).

fat·ness [fǽtnɪs] s. gordura.

fat·ten [fǽtn̩] v. engordar.

fau·cet [fɔ́sɪt] s. grifo, llave, espita, canilla, *Am.* bitoque.

fault [fɔlt] s. (*defect*) falta; defecto, tacha; (*blame*) culpa; (*geological*) falla; **to a** – excesivamente, **to be at** – scr, culpable; **to find – with** criticar a.

fault·find·er [fɔ́ltfaɪndɚ] s. criticón, criticador.

fault·less [fɔ́tlɪs] adj. intachable, sin tacha, perfecto.

fault·y [fɔ́ltɪ] adj. defectuoso, imperfecto.

fa·vor [févɚ] s. favor; **your – of the . . .** su grata (carta) del . . .; v. favorecer.

fa·vor·a·ble [févrəbl̩] adj. favorable; **favorably** adv. favorablemente.

fa·vor·ite [févrɪt] adj. & s. favorito.

fa·vor·i·tism [févrɪtɪzəm] s. favoritismo.

fawn [fɔn] s. cervato, color de cervato; v. adular; halagar.

fear [fɪr] s. temor, miedo, pavor; v. temer.

fear·ful [fírfəl] adj. terrible, espantoso, temible, temeroso; miedoso.

fear·less [fírlɪs] adj. sin temor, intrépido, atrevido, arrojado.

fear·less·ness [fírlɪsnɪs] s. intrepidez, arrojo, osadía, atrevimiento.

fea·si·ble [fízəbl̩] adj. factible, hacedero, dable.

feast [fist] s. fiesta; festín, banquete; v. festejar, obsequiar; banquetear; **to – one's eyes on** deleitar la vista en.

feat [fit] s. proeza, hazaña; acto de destreza, suerte (*en el circo*).

feath·er [féðɚ] s. pluma; **-s** plumaje; **a – in one's cap** un triunfo para uno; **– weight** de peso mínimo; v. emplumar.

feath·er·y [féðɔrɪ] adj. plumoso; ligero, como una pluma.

fea·ture [fítʃɚ] s. facción, rasgo distintivo; película principal (*en el cine*); **-s** facciones (*de la cara*); **– article** artículo sobresaliente o principal; v. destacar, hacer sobresalir; dar realce a; mostrar, exhibir (*como cosa principal*), hacer resaltar.

Feb·ru·ar·y [fébrʊɛrɪ] s. febrero.

fed [fɛd] pret. & p.p. de **to feed; to be – up** estar harto; estar hasta la coronilla, estar hasta el copete.

fed·er·al [fédərəl] adj. federal.

fed·er·a·tion [fɛdərəʃən] s. federación, confederación, liga.

fee [fi] s. honorario (honorarios), derechos; cuota; **admission –** derechos de entrada; precio de entrada.

fee·ble [fíbl̩] adj. débil, endeble; **feebly** adv. débilmente.

feed [fid] s. forraje, pasto, pienso (*para los caballos*); comida, v. alimentar(se); dar de comer, pacer, pastar; **to – coal** echar carbón.

feed·back [fídbæk] s. regeneración.

feel [fil] v. sentir, tocar, tentar; palpar; **to – better** (sad, happy, *etc.*) sentirse mejor (triste, feliz, *etc.*); **to – one's way** tantear el camino; **to – for someone** compadecer a alguien; **it -s soft** está suave; **it -s hot in here** se siente calor aquí; s. tacto, sentido del tacto; **this cloth has a nice –** esta tela es suave al tacto.

feel·er [fílɚ] s. tentáculo, antena (*de los insectos*); tiempo, propuesta (*para averiguar la inclinación o pensamiento de alguien*).

feel·ing [fílɪŋ] s. (*touch*) tacto; sensación; (*emotion*) sentimiento, emoción; pasión; (*pity*) compasión; ternura; **to hurt someone's -s** ofender la sensibilidad de alguien; adj. sensible, compasivo.

feet [fit] pl. de **foot.**

feign [fen] v. fingir.

fell [fɛl] v. derribar, echar abajo; cortar (*un árbol*); pret. de **to fall.**

fel·low [félo] s. socio, miembro (*de una sociedad, colegio, etc.*); becario (*estudiante que disfruta una beca*); camarada, compañero; individuo, tipo, sujeto, hombre; **– citizen** conciudadano; **– man** prójimo; **– member** consocio; colega; **– student** condiscípulo.

fel·low·ship [félofɪp] s. compañerismo; unión; confraternidad; sociedad; beca; **to get a –** obtener una beca.

fel·o·ny [félənɪ] s. crimen.

felt [fɛlt] s. fieltro; adj. de fieltro; pret. & p.p. de **to feel.**

fe·male [fímel] s. hembra; adj. hembra; femenino, mujeril de la mujer; **– cat (dog,** *etc.***)** gata (perra, *etc.*); **– screw** tuerca, hembra de tornillo.

fem·i·nine [fémənɪn] adj. femenino, femenil.

fem·i·nin·i·ty [fɛmɪnínɪtɪ] s. feminidad.

fence [fɛns] s. cerca, valla, vallado, receptor de cosas robadas; **to be on the –** estar indeciso; v. esgrimir; **to – in** cercar, rodear con cerca.

fenc·ing [fénsɪŋ] s. esgrima, cercado.

fend·er [féndɚ] s. guardabarros, guardafango; *Am.* trompa (*de locomotora*); *Ríopl.* parrilla.

fer·ment [fɝ́mɛnt] s. fermento; fermentación; [fɚmént] v. fermentar; hacer fermentar.

fer·ment·a·tion [fɝmɛntéʃən] s. fermentación.

fern [fɝn] s. helecho.

fe·ro·cious [fəróʃəs] adj. feroz, fiero.

fe·roc·i·ty [fərósətɪ] s. ferocidad, fiereza.

fer·ret [férɪt] v. **to – out** buscar, cazar; escudriñar,

indagar.

fer·ry [férɪ] *s.* barca de pasaje (*a través de un río o bahía*); embarcadero; *v.* transportar de una orilla a otra; atravesar (*un río*) en barca de pasaje.

fer·tile [fɜ́·t|] *adj.* fértil; fecundo.

fer·til·i·ty [fɜ́·tílətɪ] *s.* fertilidad.

fer·til·ize [fɜ́·t|aɪz] *v.* fertilizar; abonar; fecundar.

fer·til·iz·er [fɜ́·t|aɪzə·] *s.* abono (*para la tierra*).

fer·vent [fɜ́·vənt] *adj.* ferviente; fervoroso.

fer·vor [fɜ́·və·] *s.* fervor; ardor.

fes·ter [fésta·] *v.* supurar; enconarse (*una llaga*); *s.* llaga, úlcera.

fes·ti·val [féstv|] *s.* fiesta.

fes·tive [féstɪv] *adj.* festivo; alegre.

fes·tiv·i·ty [fɛstívətɪ] *s.* júbilo, regocijo; festividad.

fetch [fɛtʃ] *v.* ir a buscar; coger, traer.

fete [fet] *s.* fiesta; *v.* festejar; agasajar.

fet·id [fétɪd] *adj.* fétido.

fet·ish [fétɪʃ] *s.* fetiche.

fet·ter [fétə·] *v.* engrillar, meter en grillos encadenar; **-s** *pl.* grillos, cadenas, trabas.

fe·tus [fítəs] *s.* feto.

feud [fjud] *s.* riña, pelea, contienda; **old** – enemistad antigua (*entre dos personas o familias*).

feu·dal [fjúd|] *adj.* feudal.

fe·ver [fívə·] *s.* fiebre, calentura.

fe·ver·ish [fívərɪʃ] *adj.* calenturiento, febril.

fe·ver·ish·ness [fívərɪʃnɪs] *s.* calentura; agitación febril.

few [fju] *adj.* & *pron.* pocos; **a** – unos pocos, unos cuantos.

fi·an·cé [fiɑnsé] *s.* novio; **fiancée** *f.* novia.

fi·as·co [fɪæsko] *s.* fiasco.

fib [fɪb] *s.* bola, mentirilla, paparrucha, papa; *v.* echar papas, decir o contar paparruchas.

fib·ber [fíbə·] *s.* paparruchero, cuentero, mentirosillo.

fi·ber [fáɪbə·] *s.* fibra.

fi·brous [fáɪbrəs] *adj.* fibroso.

fick·le [fík|] *adj.* inconstante, voluble, veleidoso, mudable.

fic·tion [fíkʃən] *s.* ficción.

fic·tion·al [fíkʃən|] *adj.* novelesco; ficticio.

fic·ti·tious [fɪktíʃəs] *adj.* ficticio.

fid·dle [fíd|] *s.* violín; *v.* tocar el violín; **to** – **around** malgastar el tiempo; juguetear.

fi·del·i·ty [faɪdélətɪ] *s.* fidelidad.

fidg·et [fídʒɪt] *v.* estar inquieto; agitarse, menearse nerviosamente.

field [fild] *s.* campo; campo o cancha (*de deportes*); – **artillery** artillería de campaña; – **glasses** anteojos de larga vista; – **work** trabajo de investigación en el campo.

fiend [find] *s.* demonio, diablo; **dope** – morfinómano.

fiend·ish [fíndɪʃ] *adj.* diabólico.

fierce [fɪrs] *adj.* feroz, fiero; furioso, espantoso.

fierce·ness [fíɪrsnɪs] *s.* ferocidad; fiereza, vehemencia.

fier·y [fáɪrɪ] *adj.* fogoso; ardiente; vehemente.

fif [faɪf] *s.* pífano.

fig [fɪg] *s.* higo; – **tree** higuera.

fight [faɪt] *s.* lucha; pelea; riña, pleito; **he has a lot of** – **left** le sobra fuerza para luchar; *v.* luchar (con); pelear; combatir; reñir; batirse; **to** – **it out** decidirlo a golpes o con argumentos; **to** – **one's way through** abrirse camino a la fuerza.

fight·er [fáɪtə·] *s.* luchador; combatiente; guerrero; – **airplane** avión de caza.

fight·ing [fáɪtɪŋ] *s.* lucha, combate, pelea; *adj.* combatiente; luchador.

fig·ure [fígjə·] *s.* (*form*) figura; forma; talle (*de una persona*); (*numerical*) cifra, número; valor; precio; **-s** cuentas, cálculos; – **of speech** figura de dicción; **to be good at** – **s** sabe hacer bien las cuentas; ser listo en aritmética; **to cut a poor** – tener mala facha, hacer el ridículo; *v.* figurar; imaginarse, figurarse; adornar con dibujos; calcular; **to** – **on** contar con, confiar en; tener la intención de, proponerse; tomar en cuenta; **to** – **out** descifrar, resolver.

fil·a·ment [fíləmənt] *s.* filamento.

file [faɪl] *s.* (*records*) fichero; archivo; registro, lista; (*cabinet*) guardapapeles; (*line*) fila; (*tool*) lima; – **card** ficha; papeleta; *v.* archivar; guardar en el fichero; registrar, asentar en el registro; limar; desfilar, marchar en fila.

fil·i·al [fílɪəl] *adj.* filial.

fil·i·gree [fíligri] *s.* filigrana.

fill [fɪl] *v.* llenar(se); ocupar (*un puesto*); empastar (*un diente*); servir, atender, despachar (*un pedido*); inflar (*un neumático*); tapar (*un agujero*); **to** – **out** **a blank** llenar un formulario (forma o esqueleto).

fil·let [fɪlé] *s.* filte; cinta; lista de adorno.

fill·ing [fílɪŋ] *s.* relleno; empaste (*dental*); **gold** – orificación.

fil·ly [fílɪ] *s.* potranca.

film [fɪlm] *s.* película; membrana, tela (*formada sobre la superficie de un líquido*); nube (*en el ojo*); *v.* filmar (*cinematografiar*); **her eyes -ed with tears** se le arrasaron los ojos de lágrimas.

fil·ter [fíltə·] *s.* filtro, *v.* filtrar(se).

filth [fɪlθ] *s.* suciedad; porquería; mugre.

filth·i·ness [fílθɪnɪs] *s.* suciedad, porquería.

filth·y [fílθɪ] *adj.* sucio; puerco, cochino; mugriento.

fin [fɪn] *s.* aleta (*de pez*).

fi·nal [fáɪn|] *adj.* final; terminante; definitivo; **-ly** *adv.* finalmente; en fin, por fin.

fi•nance [fənǽns] s. teoría bancaria; *Am.* finanza; **-s** fondos, recursos monetarios; negocios bancarios, *Am.* finanzas; *v.* hacer operaciones bancarias; fomentar (*un negocio o empresa*), *Am.* financiar.

fi•nan•cial [fənǽnʃəl] *adj.* financiero, monetario.

fin•an•cier [fɪnənsír] s. financiero, *Am.* financista.

fi•nanc•ing [fənǽnsɪŋ] s. *Am.* financiamiento.

find [faɪnd] *v.* hallar; encontrar; declarar; **to − fault with** criticar a, censurar a; **to − guilty** declarar o encontrar culpable; **to − out** descubrir; averiguar; *s.* hallazgo.

find•ing [fáɪndɪŋ] s. descubrimiento; hallazgo; fallo, decisión; **-s** resultados, datos (*de una investigación*).

fine [faɪn] *adj.* fino; perfecto, excelente; superior; primoroso; **− arts** bellas artes; **− sand** arena fina o menuda; **− weather** tiempo claro o despejado; **to feel −** sentirse muy bien de salud; **to have a − time** pasar un rato muy divertido; **fine-looking** bien parecido; guapo; **in −** finalmente, en fin, en resumen; *v.* multar; **-ly** *adv.* finamente; con primor; excelentemente; muy bien; perfectamente.

fine•ness [fáɪnnɪs] s. finura; fineza; primor; excelencia, perfección.

fi•nesse [fɪnɛ́s] s. sutileza; artificio; soltura.

fin•ger [fíŋgɚ] s. dedo (*de la mano*); **−print** impresión digital, **the little −** el dedo meñique; **middle −** dedo del corazón, dedo de en medio; **ring −** dedo anular; *v.* tocar, manosear.

fin•ger•nail [fíŋgɚnel] s. uña.

fin•ick•y [fínɪkɪ] *adj.* melindroso.

fin•ish [fínɪʃ] s. fin término, conclusión; (*varnish*) acabado; pulimiento, **to have a rough −** estar sin pulir, sin pulimento o al natural; *v.* acabar, acabar con, terminar, finalizar; pulir, pulimentar.

fin•ished [fínɪʃt] *adj.* acabado; pulido, pulimentado; excelente.

fir [fɚ] s. abeto.

fire [faɪ] s. (*flame*) fuego; lumbre; (*destructive*) quemazón; incendio; **− alarm** alarma de incendios; **− department** cuerpo o servicio de bomberos; servicio de incendios; **− engine** bomba (*para incendios*); **− escape** escalera de salvamento; **− insurance** seguro contra incendios; **to be on −** estar ardiendo, estar quemándose; **to catch −** incendiarse, quemarse; **to set on −** pegar fuego, incendiar; **to be under enemy −** estar expuesto al fuego del enemigo; *v.* incendiar; pegar fuego; inflamar; disparar; **to − an employee** despedir (*o expulsar*) a un empleado.

fire•arm [fáɪrɑrm] s. arma de fuego.

fire•brand [fáɪrbrænd] s. tizón; pavesa.

fire•crack•er [fáɪrkækɚ] s. triquitraque

fire•fly [fáɪrflaɪ] s. luciérnaga.

fire•man [fáɪrmən] s. bombero; fogonero.

fire•place [fáɪrples] s. chimenea, hogar.

fire•prof [fáɪrpruf] *adj.* incombustible; a prueba de incendio; *v.* hacer incombustible.

fire•side [fáɪrsaɪd] s. hogar.

fire•wood [fáɪrwUd] s. leña.

fire•works [fáɪrwɚks] s. fuegos arficiales.

firm [fɚm] *adj.* firme; estable, s. firma, razón social (*nombre de una casa comercial*); compañía; (*comercial o industrial*); **-ly** *adv.* firmemente, con firmeza.

fir•ma•ment [fɚməmənt] s. firmamento.

firm•ness [fɚmnɪs] s. firmeza; estabilidad.

first [fɚst] *adj.* primero; *adv.* primero, en primer lugar, al principio; **from the −** desde el principio; **first-born** primogénito; **first-class** de primera clase; **first-cousin** primo hermano; **first-rate** de primera clase; muy bien; **−hand** de primera mano.

first aid [fɚst éd] s. primeros auxilios.

fish [fɪʃ] s. pez; pescado; **− market** pescadería; **− story** patraña; cuento extravagante o increíble, **neither − nor fowl** ni chicha ni limonada; *v.* pescar.

fish•er [fíʃɚ] s. pescador.

fish•er•man [fíʃɚmən] s. pescador.

fish•er•y [fíʃɚɪ] s. pesquera; pesquería, pesca.

fish•hook [fíʃhUk] s. anzuelo.

fish•ing [fíʃɪŋ] s. pesca, pesquería; **− rod** caña de pescar; **− tackle** avíos o enseres de pescar; **to go −** ir de pesca.

fis•sure [fíʃɚ] s. grieta, hendedura, *Am.* rajadura.

fist [fɪst] s. puño; **to shake one's − at** amenazar con el puño.

fit [fɪt] *adj.* (*proper*) apto; a propósito, propio, conveniente; (*healthy*) sano, de buena salud, en buen estado; capaz; **− to be tied** frenético; **not to see − to do it** no tener a bien hacerlo; *s.* talle (*de un traje*); ajuste; encaje (*de una pieza en otra*); ataque, convulsión; **− of anger** acceso, arrebato o arranque de cólera, **by -s and starts** espasmódicamente; **that suit is a good −** ese traje le entalla (*o le viene*) bien; *v.* ajustar(se); adaptar; encajar(se), caber (en); acomodar; entallar (*un vestido*); venir bien (*un vestido, zapatos, sombrero, etc.*); ser a propósito para, ser propio para; capacitar, preparar; **to − in with** armonizar con; llevarse bien con; **to − out** equipar; proveer; **it does not − the facts** no está de acuerdo con los hechos; no hace al caso.

fit•ness [fítnɪs] s. aptitud; capacidad; conveniencia, propiedad (*de una idea, de una palabra, etc.*); **physical −** buena salud.

fit•ting [fítɪŋ] *adj.* propio, apropiado, a propósito, conveniente; *s.* ajuste; **dress −** prueba de un traje o vestido; **-s** avíos, guarniciones, accesorios.

fix [fɪks] *v.* (*repair*) remendar; componer; reparar,

ajustar; arreglar; (prearrange) fijar; asegurar; **to –
up** arreglar(se); componer(se); s. apuro, aprieto.

fixed [fɪkst] adj. fijo firme.

fix•ture [fíkstʃə·] s. (thing) accesorio fijo; (person)
persona firmemente establecida (en un sitio o empleo); **electric light -s** instalaciones eléctricas
(como brazos de lámparas, arañas).

flab•by [flǽbɪ] adj. blanducho.

flag [flæg] s. bandera; banderola; **– lily** flor de lis; v.
hacer señas con banderolas; adornar con banderas;
decaer, debilitarse, menguar, flaquear.

fla•grant [fléfrənt] adv. flagrante, notorio, escandaloso.

flag•staff [flǽgstæf] s. asta de bandera.

flag•stone [flǽgston] s. losa.

flair [flɛr] s. instinto, penetración, cacumen; disposición o aptitud natural.

flak [flæk] s. fuego antiaéreo.

flake [flek] s. copo (de nieve); escama; hojuela; **corn
-s** hojuelas de maíz; v. descostrarse, descascarse.

flam•boy•ant [flæbɔ́jənt] adj. rimbombante; flameante.

flame [flem] s. llama; flama; **–thrower** lanzallamas;
v. llamear, flamear, echar llamas; inflamar(se);
enardecer(se).

flam•ing [flémɪŋ] adj. llameante; flameante, encendido, ardiente, apasionado; **– red** rojo encendido.

flank [flæŋk] s. flanco; costado; lado; ijar (de un animal); v. flanquear; rodear.

flan•nel [flǽnḷ] s. franela.

flap [flæp] s. (thing) aleta; cubierta (del bolsillo);
(action) golpeteo; aleteo; v. golpetear; aletear, batir
(las alas); hojear con violencia (las páginas).

flare [flɛr] s. llamarada; llama; arranque (de ira);
vuelo (de una falda); v. llamear, echar llamaradas,
tener vuelo (una falda); **to – up** enfurecerse; en-
cenderse; **the illness -ed up** recrudeció la
enfermedad.

flash [flæʃ] s. rayo; destello, llamarada; fogonazo; **–
of hope** rayo de esperanza; **– of lightning** relámpago; **–of wit** agudeza; **– bulb** bombilla de destello;
bombillo flash; **in a –** en un instante; **news –** última
noticia (enviada por radio o telégrafo); v. relampa-
guear; destellar; brillar; centellear; radiar o
telegrafiar (noticias); **to – by** pasar como un relámpago.

flash•ing [flǽʃɪŋ] s. relampagueo, centello; adj.
relumbrante, flameante.

flash•light [flǽʃlaɪt] s. linterna eléctrica.

flash•y [flǽʃɪ] adj. relumbrante; llamativo, de re-
lumbrón, ostentoso; chillante, chillón (dícese de los
colores).

flask [flæsk] s. frasco.

flat [flæt] adj. (no curves) plano, llano, chato; aplas-

tado; (tasteless) insípido; monótono; (without air)
desinflado; **– denial** negativa terminante; **– note**
nota desentonada; **– rate** precio o número redondo;
D – re bemol (nota musical); **–car** vagón de plataforma; **to be –broke** estar completamente pelado;
estar sin dinero; **to fall –** caer de plano; caer mal (un
discurso, chiste, etc.); **to sing –** desafinarse, cantar
desentonadamente; **to refuse -ly** negarse absolutamente; s. plano; palma (**de la mano**); apartamento;
departamento; piso; bemol (en música).

flat•i•ron [flǽtaɪə·n] s. plancha.

flat•ness [flǽtnɪs] s. llanura; lisura; insipidez;
desafinamiento (en música).

flat•ten [flǽt ŋ] v. aplastar(se); aplanar(se);
allanar(se).

flat•ter [flǽtə·] v. lisonjear; adular.

flat•ter•er [flǽtərə·] s. lisonjero, adulador.

flat•ter•ing [flǽtərɪŋ] adj. lisonjero, halagüeño,
adulador.

flat•ter•y [flǽtərɪ] s. lisonja, halago; adulación.

flat•u•lence [flǽtjʊləns] s. hinchazón, flutulencia.

flaunt [flɔnt] v. ostentar; hacer gala de.

fla•vor [flévə·] s. sabor; gusto; condimento; v. sazonar; dar sabor a; condimentar.

fla•vor•less [flévə·lɪs] adj. insípido, sin sabor.

flaw [flɔ] s. defecto; falta; tacha; imperfección.

flaw•less [flɔlɪs] adj. sin tacha; intachable; irreprochable, perfecto.

flax [flæks] s. lino.

flay [fle] s. desollar.

flea [fli] s. pulga.

fled [flɛd] pret. & p.p. de **to flee**.

flee [fli] v. huir; huir de.

fleece [flis] s. vellón, lana; v. trasquilar, esquilar; despojar, estafar, defraudar.

fleet [flit] s. flota, armada; adj. veloz.

fleet•ing [flítɪŋ] adj. fugaz, transitorio, pasajero, efímero.

Flem•ish [flémɪʃ] adj. flamenco; s. flamenco, idioma flamenco; **the –** los flamencos.

flesh [flɛʃ] s. carne; **– and blood** carne y hueso; **–
color** color encarnado, **in the –** en persona.

flesh•y [fléʃɪ] adj. carnoso, gordo, gordiflón.

flew [flu] pret. de **to fly**.

flex•i•bi•li•ty [flɛksəbíləɪ] s. flexibilidad

flex•i•ble [flésəbḷ] adj. flexible.

flick•er [flíkə·] s. titilación, parpadeo, luz trémula;
temblor momentáneo (de emoción); aleteo; especie de pájaro carpintero; v. titilar; temblar; parpadear;
vacilar; aletear; **to – one's eyelash** pestañear.

fli•er [fláɪə·] s. volador; aviador; tren rápido.

flight [flaɪt] s. vuelo; bandada (de pájaros); escua-
drilla (de aviones); fuga, huída; **– of stairs** tramo de
escalera; **to put to –** poner en fuga.

flim·sy [flÍmzɪ] *adj.* endeble, débil; tenue; quebradizo; frágil; baladí; **a – excuse** una excusa baladí.

fling [flɪŋ] *v.* arrojar(se), lanzar(se); tirar; echar; **to
– open (shut)** abrir (cerrar) de golpe; *s.* tiro; tirada, lanzamiento; tentativa; **to go out on a –** irse a
echar una cana al aire.

flint [flɪnt] *s.* pedernal.

flip [flɪp] *v.* arrojar, lanzar al aire; sacudir; dar un
dedazo.

flip·pancy [flÍpənsɪ] *s.* ligereza, frivolidad; impertinencia; petulancia.

flip·pant [flÍpənt] *adj.* ligero (*en sus acciones y
modales*), ligero de cascos; frívolo; impertinente;
petulante.

flirt [flɜt] *s.* coqueta; coquetón, coquetona; *v.*
conquetear.

flir·ta·tion [flɜtéʃən] *s.* coquetería; **to carry on a –**
coquetear.

flit [flɪt] *v.* pasar velozmente; volar; revolotear.

float [flot] *s.* boya, cosa flotante, flotador; corcho (*de
una caña de pescar*); balsa; carro o carroza (*de pro-
cesiones, fiestas, etc.*); *v.* flotar; sobrenadar; boyar;
poner a flote; lanzar al mercado (*una nueva emisión
de valores, bonos, etc.*).

flock [flok] *s.* bandada (*de pájaros, niños, etc.*); rebaño, grey; manada (*de animales*); grupo; **– of people**
gentío, muchedumbre; *v.* agruparse, congregarse;
to – to acudir juntos (*o en bandadas*) a; **to –
together** andar juntos, volar en bandadas, ir en
grupo.

flog [flog] *v.* azotar.

flood [flʌd] *s.* inundación; diluvio; avenida (*de agua*),
crecida; creciente; torrente; **–gate** compuerta (*de
una presa*); esclusa (*de un canal*); **– light** reflector;
proyector de luz; **– tide** flujo (*o marea ascendente*); *v.* inundar.

floor [flor] *s.* (*surface*) suelo; piso; (*story*) piso; (*bottom*)
fondo; **to have the –** tener la palabra; *v.* solar; entarimar, enladrillar, enlosar; echar al suelo, derribar;
asombrar.

flop *v.* (*flap*) caer o colgar flojamente; aletear, menearse; (*throw*) lanzar; dejar caer; (*fail*) fracasar;
fallar; **to – down** dejarse caer; desplomarse, tum-
barse; **to – over** voltear(se); dar vueltas; *s.* fracaso.

flo·rist [flórɪst] *s.* florero, florera; **–'s shop** florería.

floss [flos] *s.* seda floja; pelusa; fibra se dosa; **dental
–** seda dental.

floun·der [fláUndə] *v.* patalear (*en el lodo, nieve,
etc.*); forcejear (*por salir del lodo, nieve, o cualquier aprieto*); revolcarse; tropezar, cometer
errores; *s.* lenguado (*pez*).

flour [flaUr] *s.* harina.

flour·ish [flɜɪʃ] *s.* (*prosper*) florecer, prosperar,
medrar; (*blandish*) blandir; agitar en el aire; (*with
the signature*) rúbrica; *s.* floreo; adorno o rasgo
caprichoso; ostentación.

flour·y [fláUrɪ] *adj.* harinoso.

flow [flo] *s.* flujo; corriente; **– of words** torrente de
palabras; *v.* fluir; correr; flotar, ondear; **to – into**
desembocar en; **to be -ing with riches** nadar en la
abundancia.

flow·er [fláUə] *s.* flor; **– bed** cuadro de jardín; **–
vase** florero; *v.* florecer, *Am.* florear.

flow·er·pot [fláUrpot] *s.* tiesto, maceta.

flow·er·y [fláUrɪ] *adj.* florido.

flow·ing [flóɪŋ] *adj.* fluído, corriente, fluente; suelto,
ondeante.

flown [flon] *p.p. de* **to fly.**

flu [flu] *s.* influenza, gripe.

fluc·tu·ate [flʌktʃUeɪt] *s.* fluctuar.

fluc·tu·a·tion [flʌktʃUéʃən] *s.* fluctuación

flue [flu] *s.* cañón (*de chimenea*); tubo de escape.

flu·en·cy [flúənsɪ] *s.* fluidez; labia.

flu·ent [flúənt] *adj.* fluente, fluído; **to speak -ly** hablar con facilidad.

fluff [flʌf] *v.* mullir; esponjar.

fluff·y [fl ʌ fɪ] *adj* mullido, suave, blando; cubierto
de vello o plumón; **– hair** pelo esponjado o esponjoso.

flu·id [flúɪd] *adj. & s.* fluido.

flung [flʌŋ] *pret. & p.p. de* **to fling.**

flunk [flʌŋk] *s.* reprobación (*en un examen o asignatura*); *v.* reprobar, suspender (*en un examen*); salir
mal, fracasar o fallar (*en un examen*).

flun·ky [fl ʌ ŋkɪ] *s.* lacayo; ayudante servil; zalamero, persona servil.

flur·ry [flɜɪ] *s.* (*weather*) ráfaga; nevisca; (*action*)
agitación

flush [flʌʃ] *s.* sonrojo, rubor; bochorno; flujo rápido;
flux (*de naipes*); *adj.* lleno; rico; parejo, al mismo
nivel; **– with** a flor de, a ras de; *v.* sonrojar(se),
ruborizar(se), poner(se) colorado; hacer rebosar
(*de agua*); **to – out** vaciar (*un depósito*), enjuagar.

flute [flut] *s.* flauta; estría (*de una columna*); *v.* acanalar; estriar (*una columna*).

flut·ter [fl ʌ tə] *s.* aleteo; agitación; alboroto; vuelco
(*del corazón*); *v.* aletear; revolotear; agitar(se); palpitar; menear(se); tremolar (*una bandera*).

flux [flʌks] *s.* flujo.

fly [flaɪ] *s.* mosca; pliegue (*para cubrir botones*); bra-
gueta (*abertura de los pantalones*); **on the –** al vuelo;
to hit a – pegar una planchita o elevar una palomita
(*en beisbol*); *v.* volar; pasar velozmente; huir; ondear; enarbolar (*una bandera*); **to – at** lanzarse sobre,
to – away volar, irse, escaparse; **to – off the handle**
perder los estribos (*o la paciencia*); **to – open (shut)**
abrirse (cerrarse) de repente; **to – up in anger**
montar en cólera.

fly·er = flier.

fly·leaf [fláɪlif] *s.* guarda (*hoja en blanco al principio
y al fin de un libro*).

foam [fom] *s.* espuma; *v.* espumar, hacer espuma.

fo·cus [fókǝs] *s.* foco; distancia focal; *v.* enfocar(se).

fod·der [fádǝ] *s.* forraje.

foe [fo] *s.* enemigo.

fog [fɑg] *s.* niebla, neblina, bruma; velo, nube (*en una película o fotografía*); **–horn** sirena; *v.* anublar, ofuscar, obscurecer; ponerse brumoso, velar(se) (*una película*).

fog·gy [fógɪ] *adj.* brumoso, nublado; obscuro, confuso.

foil [fɔɪl] *s.* oropel, hojuela, laminita de metal, florete (*de esgrima*); realce, contraste; **tin –** hojuela de estaño, *v.* frustrar.

fold [fold] *s.* (*double over*) pliegue, doblez; (*enclosure*) redil; grey, **three –** tres veces; **hundred–** cien veces; *v.* doblar(se); plegar(se); envolver; **to – one's arms** cruzarse de brazos.

fold·er [fóldǝ] *s.* (*pamphlet*) folleto, circular; (*holder*) papelera; plegadera (*máquina para plegar*).

fold·ing [fóldɪŋ] *adj.* plegadizo, **– chair** silla plegadiza, silla de tijera; **– machine** plegadora, máquina plegadora; **– screen** biombo.

fo·li·age [fólɪɪdʒ] *s.* follaje, fronda.

fo·li·o [fólɪo] *s.* folio; infolio, libro en folio; pliego; **– edition** edición en folio.

folk [fok] *s.* gente, pueblo; **-s** parientes, allegados; familia; personas; amigos (*vocativo familiar*); *adj.* popular, del pueblo; **– dance** danza o baile tradicional; **– lore** folklore, cuentos, leyendas y tradiciones populares; **– song** canción popular, canción típica o tradicional; **– music** música del pueblo; música tradicional.

fol·low [fálo] *v.* seguir; ejercer (*un oficio o profesión*); seguir el hilo de (*un argumento*); seguirse (*como consecuencia*); **to – suit** jugar el mismo palo (*en naipes*); seguir el ejemplo, imitar.

fol·low·er [fálǝwǝ] *s.* seguidor, imitador; partidario.

fol·low·ing [fálǝwɪŋ] *s.* séquito, comitiva, partidarios; *adj.* siguiente; subsiguiente.

fol·ly [fálɪ] *s.* locura; necedad, tontería; desatino.

fo·ment [fomɛ́nt] *v.* fomentar.

fond [fɑnd] *adj.* aficionado (a); amigo (de), amante (de); encariñado (con); cariñoso, afectuoso; tierno; **to be – of** querer a (*una persona*); estar encariñado con, ser aficionado a; gustar de (*algo*); **-ly** *adv.* cariñosamente, afectuosamente.

fon·dle [fándl] *v.* acariciar.

fond·ness [fándnɪs] *s.* cariño, afecto; afición.

font [fɑnt] *s.* pila bautismal; fuente.

food [fud] *s.* alimento, sustento, comida.

food·stuff [fúdstʌf] *s.* alimento; producto alimenticio; comestibles.

fool [ful] *s.* tonto, necio, zonzo; payaso; **to play the – payasear, hacer el payaso; *v.* chasquear,

chancear(se); bromear, embromar; engañar; **to – away the time** malgastar el tiempo.

fool·ish [fúlɪʃ] *adj.* tonto, necio, bobo, zonzo.

fool·ish·ness [fúlɪʃnɪs] *s.* tontería, necedad, bobería.

foot [fʊt] *s.* pie; pata (*de animal*); **on –** a pie; **– soldier** soldado de infantería; **to put one's – in it** meter la pata; *v.* andar a pie, **to – it** andar a pie; **to – the bill** pagar la cuenta; subragar los gastos.

foot·ball [fʊ́tbɔl] *s.* fútbol, football.

foot·hold [fʊ́thold] *s.* arraigo; puesto establecido.

foot·ing [fʊ́tɪŋ] *s.* base, posición firme; **to be on a friendly – with** tener relaciones amistosas con; **to lose one's –** perder pie.

foot·lights [fʊ́tlaɪts] *s. pl.* candilejas (*del teatro*); tablas, teatro.

foot·man [fʊ́tmǝn] *s.* lacayo.

foot·note [fʊ́tnot] *s.* nota al pie de una página.

foot·path [fʊ́tpæθ] *s.* vereda, senda, trocha (*para gente de a pie*).

foot·print [fʊ́tprɪnt] *s.* huella, pisada.

foot·step [fʊ́tstɛp] *s.* (*action*) pisada, paso; (*trace*) huella; **to follow in the -s of** seguir las pisadas o huellas de.

foot·stool [fʊ́tstul] *s.* banquillo, taburete, escabel.

fop [fɑp] *s.* currutaco.

for [fɔr] *prep.* por; para; **– all of her intelligence** a pesar de su inteligencia; **– fear that** por miedo (de) que; **– the present** por el presente, por ahora; **as – him** en cuanto a él; **to know – a fact** saber de cierto, saber de hecho; **to pay him – it** pagárselo; **to thank him – it** agradecérselo; *conj.* porque, pues.

for·age [fɔ́rɪdʒ] *s.* forraje, *v.* forrajear; dar forraje a.

for·ay [fɔ́re] *s.* correría, incursión; saqueo; *v.* pillar, saquear.

for·bade [fǝbǽd] *pret. de* **to forbid**.

for·bear [fɔ́rbɛr] *s.* antepasado; [fɔrbɛ́r] *v.* abstenerse de; tener paciencia.

for·bid [fǝbɪ́d] *v.* prohibir; vedar.

for·bid·den [fǝbɪ́dn̩] *adj.* prohibido; vedado; *p.p. de* **to forbid**.

for·bid·ding [fǝbɪ́dɪŋ] *adj.* austero, reservado, pavoroso, impenetrable.

for·bore [fɔrbór] *pret. de* **to forbear**.

for·borne [fɔrbórn] *p.p. de* **to forbear**.

force [fors] *s.* fuerza; cuerpo (*de policía, de empleados, etc.*); **in –** en vigor, vigente; **armed -s** fuerzas armadas; *v.* forzar, obligar; **to – one's way** abrirse paso por fuerza; **to – out** echar por fuerza, echar a la fuerza.

forced [forst] *adj.* forzado.

force·ful [fórsfǝl] *adj.* vigoroso; enérgico.

for·ceps [fɔ́rsǝps] *s.* gatillo (*tenazas para sacar muelas*); pinzas.

forc·i·ble [fórsəb|] *adj.* (*strong*) fuerte, enérgico; potente; eficaz; (*by force*) violento; hecho a la fuerza; **forcibly** *adv.* fuertemente; con energía; forzosamente; por fuerza.

ford [ford] *s.* vado; *v.* vadear.

fore [for] *adj.* anterior, delantero; de proa; *s.* frente; puesto delantero; *adv.* delante, hacia adelante; *interj.* ¡cuidado! (*dícese en el campo de golf*).

fore·arm [fórɑrm] *s.* antebrazo.

fore·bode [forbód] *v.* presagiar; presentir.

fore·bod·ing [forbódɪŋ] *s.* presentimiento; presagio.

fore·cast [fórkæst] *s.* pronóstico; *v.* pronosticar; predecir; *pret. & p.p. de* **to forecast**.

fore·fa·ther [fórfaðɚ] *s.* antepasado.

fore·fin·ger [fórfɪŋgɚ] *s.* (dedo) índice.

fore·foot [fórfʊt] *s.* pata delantera, mano (*de cuadrúpedo*).

fore·go [forgó] *v.* abstenerse de.

fore·gone [forgɔ́n] *p.p. de* **to forego**; **a — conclusion** una conclusión inevitable.

fore·ground [fórgraʊnd] *s.* frente, primer plano; primer término.

fore·head [fɔ́rɪd] *s.* frente (*f.*).

for·eign [fɔ́rɪn] *adj.* extranjero, foráneo; extraño; **— to his nature** ajeno a su índole; **— office** ministerio de relaciones exteriores; departamento de negocios extranjeros; **— trade** comercio exterior; **foreign-born** extranjero de nacimiento.

for·eign·er [fɔ́rɪnɚ] *s.* extranjero; forastero.

fore·lock [fórlɑk] *s.* guedeja.

fore·man [fórmən] *s.* capataz; presidente (*de una jurado*), *Méx., C.A., Ven., Col.* caporal (*de un rancho o hacienda*); *Riopl.* capataz.

fore·most [fórmost] *adj.* (*first*) primero; delantero; (*most important*) principal, más notable; más distinguido.

fore·noon [fornún] *s.* (la) mañana.

fore·run·ner [forr Ánɚ] *s.* precursor, presagio.

fore·saw [forsɔ́] *pret. de* **to foresee**.

fore·see [forsí] *s.* prever.

fore·seen [forsín] *p.p. de* **to foresee** previsto.

fore·sight [fórsaɪt] *s.* previsión.

fore·st [fɔ́rɪst] *s.* bosque, selva; **— ranger** guardabosques; *v.* arbolar, plantar de árboles

fore·stall [forstɔ́l] *v.* prevenir; madrugar.

for·est·er [fɔ́rɪstɚ] *s.* guardabosques; silvicultor; habitante de un bosque.

for·est·ry [fɔ́rɪstrɪ] *s.* silvicultura.

fore·tell [fortél] *v.* predecir, pronosticar, presagiar.

fore·told [fortóld] *pret. & p.p. de* **to foretell**.

for·ev·er [fɚévɚ] *adv.* por (*o* para) siempre.

for·feit [fɔ́rfɪt] *s.* multa; pena; prenda perdida;

game of -s juego de prendas; *v.* perder, perder el derecho a.

for·gave [fɚgév] *pret. de* **to forgive**.

forge [fordʒ] *s.* fragua; forja; *v.* fraguar; forjar; falsear, falsificar, **to — ahead** abrirse paso; avanzar.

for·ger·y [fɔ́rdʒərɪ] *s.* falsificación.

for·get [fɚgét] *v.* olvidar; olvidarse de; **to — oneself** cometer un desmán impensadamente; perder el tino o la paciencia.

for·get·ful [fɚgétfəl] *adj.* olvidadizo; negligente.

for·get·ful·ness [fɚgétfəlnɪs] *s.* olvido; negligencia.

for·get-me-not [fɚgétmɪnɑt] *s.* nomeolvides.

for·give [fɚgív] *v.* perdonar.

for·given [fɚgívən] *p.p. de* **to forgive**.

for·give·ness [fɚgívnɪs] *s.* perdón.

for·giv·ing [fɚgívɪŋ] *adj.* perdonador, misericordioso, de buen corazón.

for·got [fɚgát] *pret. & p.p. de* **to forget**.

for·got·ten [fɚgát ŋ] *p.p. de* **to forget**.

fork [fork] *s.* tenedor, *Méx., Col., Ven., Andes* trinche; horquilla (*para heno*); horcón; bifurcación; *v.* bifurcarse; levantar y arrojar (*heno*) con horquilla.

for·lorn [fɚlɔ́rn] *adj.* desamparado, desdichado.

form [form] *s.* forma; condición, estado; **blank —** blanco, forma en blanco, *Méx., Ven.* esqueleto, *v.* formar(se).

for·mal [fɔ́rm|] *adj.* formal, perteneciente a la forma; convencional, ceremonioso; **— party** reunión de etiqueta; **-ly** *adv.* formalmente, con ceremonia, solemnemente.

for·mal·i·ty [fɔrmǽlətɪ] *s.* formalidad, ceremonia; formalismo.

for·ma·tion [forméʃən] *s.* formación.

for·ma·tive [fɔ́rmətɪv] *adj.* formativo.

for·mer [fɔ́rmɚ] *adj.* primero, precedente, anterior, antiguo; **in — times** en otro tiempo, en días de antaño, antiguamente, anteriormente; **the —** aquél (aquélla, aquéllos, aquéllas); **-ly** *adv.* anteriormente; antes, en tiempos pasados.

for·mi·da·ble [fɔ́rmɪdəb|] *adj.* formidable.

for·mu·la [fɔ́rmjələ] *s.* fórmula.

for·mu·late [fɔ́rmjələt] *v.* formular.

for·sake [fɚsék] *v.* desamparar; abandonar.

for·saken [fɚsékən] *p.p. de* **to forsake** & *adj.* desamparado, abandonado.

for·sook [forsÚk] *pret. de* **to forsake**.

for·swear [forswér] *v.* abjurar.

fort [fort] *s.* fuerte, fortín, fortaleza.

forth [forθ] *adv.* adelante; hacia adelante; **to go —** salir, **and so —** etcétera, y así succesivamente.

forth·com·ing [fórθk Ámɪŋ] *adj.* venidero, próximo; **funds will not be — until** no habrá fondos disponibles hasta.

forth·with [forθwíθ] *adv.* en seguida, pronto, al punto.

for·ti·fi·ca·tion [fɔrtəfəkéʃən] *s.* fortificación.

for·ti·fy [fɔ́rtəfaɪ] *v.* fortificar; fortalecer.

for·ti·tude [fɔ́rtətjud] *s.* fortaleza.

fort·night [fɔ́rtnaɪt] *s.* quincena, quince días, dos semanas.

for·tress [fɔ́rtrɪs] *s.* fortaleza, fuerte.

for·tu·i·tous [fɔrtjúətəs] *adj.* fortuito; inopinado, inesperado.

for·tu·nate [fɔ́rtʃənɪt] *adj.* afortunado; **-ly** *adv.* afortunadamente, por fortuna.

for·tune [fɔ́rtʃən] *s.* fortuna; **– teller** agorero, adivino.

fo·rum [fórəm] *s.* foro; tribunal.

for·ward [fɔ́rwəd] *adj.* (*leading*) delantero; (*progressive*) precoz; progresista; (*daring*) atrevido; descarado; *adv.* adelante; hacia adelante; *v.* transmitir; despachar; reenviar; **to – a plan** fomentar un plan.

fos·sil [fɑ́sl̩] *adj.* fósil; anticuado, *s.* fósil.

fos·ter [fɔ́stə] *v.* criar, nutrir; fomentar, promover; *adj.* putativo; adoptivo.

fought [fɔt] *pret. & p.p. de* **to fight**.

foul [faʊl] *adj.* sucio; asqueroso, puerco, cochino; fétido; vil; injusto; **– air** aire viciado, **– ball** pelota foul (*en beisbol*); **– mouthed** mal hablado, obsceno; **– play** juego sucio, fraude; violencia; **– weather** mal tiempo; *s.* mala jugada (*contraria a las reglas del juego*), trampa, *Am.* chapuza, foul; *v.* ensuciar; violar (*las reglas de un juego*); *Am.* pegar un foul (*en beisbol*).

found [faʊnd] *v.* fundar, establecer; *pret. & p.p. de* **to find**.

foun·da·tion [faʊndéʃən] *s.* fundación; base, fundamento; dotación.

foun·der [fáʊndə] *s.* fundador; fundidor (*de metales*); *v.* zozobrar, irse a pique; fracasar; tropezar; hacer zozobrar.

foun·dry [fáʊndrɪ] *s.* fundición.

foun·tain [fáʊntn̩] *s.* fuente; manantial; **– pen** pluma (de) fuente, pluma estilográfica.

four·score [fórskór] *adj.* cuatro veintenas, ochenta.

fourth [forθ] *adj.* cuarto; *s.* cuarto, cuarta parte; **the – of July** el cuatro de julio.

fowl [faʊl] *s.* ave, gallo, gallina; pollo.

fox [fɑks] *s.* zorra; zorro; persona astuta.

fox·y [fáksɪ] *adj.* zorro, zorruno, astuto.

frac·tion [frǽkʃən] *s.* fracción, quebrado.

frac·ture [frǽktʃə] *s.* fractura; quiebra; rotura; *v.* fracturar, quebrar, romper.

frag·ile [frǽdʒəl] *adj.* frágil.

frag·ment [frǽgmənt] *s.* fragmento.

fra·grance [frégrəns] *s.* fragancia.

fra·grant [frégrənt] *adj.* fragante, oloroso.

frail [frel] *adj.* frágil, endeble, débil.

frail·ty [frélti] *s.* debilidad, flaqueza.

frame [frem] *s.* armazón, armadura, esqueleto; estructura; marco (*de un cuadro, ventana, puerta, etc.*); disposición (*de ánimo*); **embroidery** – bastidor para bordar; **– house** casa con armazón de madera; *v.* formar, forjar; fabricar; enmarcar (*poner en marco*); inventar, **to – someone** conspirar contra una persona, **to – up a charge** forjar un cargo o acusación.

frame·work [frémwɜk] *s.* armazón, esqueleto; estructura.

franc [fræŋk] *s.* franco (*moneda francesa*).

fran·chise [frǽntʃaɪz] *s.* (*privilege*) franquicia; derecho o privilegio político; (*vote*) sufragio, voto.

frank [fræŋk] *adj.* franco, sincero; **very –** francote; *s.* sello de franqueo; franquicia de correos, *v.* franquear, despachar, enviar (*carta*) exenta de franqueo.

frank·furt·er [frǽŋkfətə] *s.* salchicha.

frank·ness [frǽŋknɪs] *s.* franqueza, sinceridad.

fran·tic [frǽntɪk] *adj.* frenético; **-ally** *adv.* frenéticamente.

fra·ter·nal [frətɜ́n̩] *adj.* fraternal.

fra·ter·ni·ty [frətɜ́nəti] *s.* fraternidad; confraternidad.

frat·er·nize [frǽtənaɪz] *v.* fraternizar.

fraud [frɔd] *s.* fraude, engaño; trampa, *Am.* chapuza; trampista; tramposo.

fraud·u·lent [frɔ́dʒələnt] *adj.* fraudulento.

fray [fre] *s.* reyerta, riña, pelea, alboroto; raedura; *v.* raer(se); deshilacharse.

fray·ed [fred] *adj.* raído, deshilachado.

freak [frik] *s.* capricho; rareza, hombre o cosa rara; monstruosidad, fenómeno.

freck·le [frék̩l] *s.* peca; *v.* ponerse pecoso.

freck·led [frék̩ld] *adj.* pecoso.

freck·ly [feékli] *adj.* pecoso.

free [fri] *adj.* (*not bound*) libre; suelto; (*gratis*) gratuito; exento; (*generous*) liberal, generoso; **– of charge** gratis; **– on board (f.o.b.)** libre a bordo; **– port** puerto franco; **– postage** – franco de porte; **to give someone a – hand** dar rienda suelta o libertad de acción a una persona; **– hand drawing** dibujo a pulso, dibujo a mano, **– thinker** libre pensador; *adv.* libremente; gratis, de balde; *v.* librar; libertar; soltar; eximir; **-ly** *adv.* libremente; con soltura.

free·dom [frídəm] *s.* libertad; libre uso; exención.

freeze [friz] *v.* helar(se); congelar(se).

freez·ing [frizɪŋ] *adj.* helado, gracial, **– point** punto de congelación.

freight [fret] *s.* flete; carga; **– train** tren de carga, tren de mercancías; **by –** por carga; *v.* fletar, cargar; enviar por carga.

French [frɛntʃ] *adj.* francés; **to take – leave** marcharse a la francesa, irse sin despedirse; *s.* francés, idioma francés; **the –** los franceses.

French•man [frɛntʃmən] *s.* francés.

fren•zy [frɛnzɪ] *s.* frenesí.

fre•quen•cy [frɪkwənsɪ] *s.* frecuencia.

fre•quent [frɪkwənt] *adj.* frecuente; *v.* frecuentar; **-ly** *adv.* frecuentemente, a menudo.

fresh [frɛʃ] *adj.* (*not stale*) fresco, (*new*) reciente; nuevo; (*bold*) impertinente, entremetido; **– water** agua dulce; **-ly** *adv.* frescamente; con frescura; nuevamente, recientemente; **-ly painted** recién pintado, acabado de pintar.

fresh•en [frɛʃən] *v.* refrescar(se).

fresh•man [frɛʃmən] *s.* novato, novicio, estudiante del primer año.

fresh•ness [frɛʃnɪs] *s.* frescura; frescor, fresco; descaro.

fret [frɛt] *v.* irritar(se); apurarse; estar nervioso; agitarse; *s.* agitación, apuro, preocupación; traste (*de guitarra, mandolina, etc.*); **-work** calado.

fret•ful [frɛtfəl] *adj.* descontentadizo, malhumorado, enojadizo; nervioso.

fri•ar [fráɪə-] *s.* fraile.

fric•tion [frɪkʃən] *s.* fricción; rozamiento; frotación; desavenencia.

Fri•day [fráɪdɪ] *s.* viernes.

fried [fraɪd] *adj.* frito; freído; *p.p. de* **to fry**.

friend [frɛnd] *s.* amigo, amiga.

friend•less [frɛndlɪs] *adj.* sin amigos, solo.

friend•li•ness [frɛdlɪnɪs] *s.* afabilidad; amistad.

friend•ly [frɛndlɪ] *adj.* amistoso, afable, amigable; propicio, favorable; *adv.* amistosamente.

friend•ship [frɛnʃɪp] *s.* amistad.

frig•ate [frɪgeət] *s.* fragata.

fright [fraɪt] *s.* espanto, susto; terror; espantajo, **she is a –** es un adefesio.

fright•en [fráɪtn] *v.* espantar, asustar, atemorizar; **to – away** espantar, ahuyentar; **to get -ed** espantarse, asustarse.

fright•en•ed [fráɪtnd] *adj.* espantado, asustado.

fright•ful [fráɪtfəl] *adj.* espantoso, terrible, horroroso.

frig•id [frɪdʒɪd] *adj.* frígido, frío.

fringe [frɪndʒ] *s.* fleco; flequillo; orla; *v.* adornar con fleco; orlar.

frip•per•y [frɪpərɪ] *s.* perifollos, moños, perejiles, cursilería.

frisk [frɪsk] *v.* retozar, cabriolar, saltar, brincar; registrar (*los bolsillos*), *Ven.*, *Méx.* esculcar.

frisk•y [frɪskɪ] *adj.* retozón, juguetón.

frit•ter [frɪtə-] *s.* fritura, fruta de sartén; *v.* **to – away** malgastar, desperdiciar poco a poco.

friv•o•li•ty [frɪválətɪ] *s.* frivolidad.

friv•o•lous [frɪvələs] *adj.* frívolo.

fro [fro] **to and –** de una parte a otra; de aquí para allá.

frock [frak] *s.* vestido (*de mujer*); **– coat** levita.

frog [frɔg] *s.* rana, broche (*de cordoncillos o galones*); **– in the throat** gallo en la garganta.

frol•ic [frálɪk] *s.* retozo, juego; holgorio, diversión; *v.* retozar, travesear, juguetear.

from [fram, frʌm] *prep.* de; desde; **to take something away – a person** quitarle algo a una persona.

front [frʌnt] *s.* frente (*m.*); fachada; frontispicio; **in – of** enfrente de; delante de; **shirt –** pechera; *adj.* delantero; frontal; frontero; *v.* hacer frente a; **to – towards** mirar hacia; dar a, caer a.

fron•tier [frʌntír] *s.* frontera; *adj.* fronterizo.

frost [frost] *s.* escarcha; helada; *v.* escarchar; helar; cubrir de escarcha.

frost•ing [frɔ́stɪŋ] *s.* escarcha, confitura (*para cubrir un pastel*).

frost•y [frɔ́stɪ] *adj.* escarchado, cubierto de escarcha; helado.

froth [frɔθ] *s.* espuma; *v.* espumar, hacer espuma; echar espuma o espumarajos; **to–at the mouth** echar espumarajos por la boca; enfurecerse.

frown [fraʊn] *s.* ceño; entrecejo; *v.* fruncir el ceño o las cejas; **to – at** mirar con ceño; desaprobar (*algo*).

froze [froz] *pret. de* **to freeze**.

fro•zen [frózṇ] *p.p. de* **to freeze**.

fru•gal [frúgḷ] *adj.* frugal.

fruit [frut] *s.* fruto (*en general*); fruta (*comestible*); **to eat –** comer fruta; **– tree** árbol frutal; *v.* fructificar, producir frutas.

fruit•ful [frútfəl] *adj.* fructuoso; productivo; provechoso.

fruit•less [frútlɪs] *adj.* infructuoso, improductivo, estéril.

frus•trate [frʌ́stret] *v.* frustrar.

frus•tra•tion [frʌstréʃən] *s.* frustración.

fry [fraɪ] *v.* freír(se); *adj.* fritada; **small –** pececillos; gente menuda; **French fries** patatas fritas a la francesa; **-ing pan** sartén.

fudge [fʌdʒ] *s.* dulce (*usualmente de chocolate y nueces*).

fu•el [fjúəl] *s.* combustible; incentivo.

fu•gi•tive [fjúdʒətɪv] *adj.* fugitivo; transitorio; *s.* fugitivo, prófugo.

ful•fill [fʊlfíl] *v.* cumplir; cumplir con; realizar; llevar a cabo; llenar (*un requisito*).

ful•fill•ment [fʊlfílmənt] *s.* cumplimiento.

full [fʊl] *adj.* lleno; completo; harto; pleno; **– dress** traje de etiqueta; **– moon** plenilunio, luna llena; **– skirt** falda de vuelo entero; **– of fun** muy divertido, muy chistoso; **at – speed** a toda velocidad; **in –**

completamente; por completo; **to the** – por completo, por entero, totalmente, enteramente; **to know – well** saber perfectamente, saber a cierta cierta; **full-blooded** de raza pura; **full-fledged** hecho y derecho; maduro; completo; **-y** *adv.* completamente, enteramente, por completo.

full•ness [fÚlnIs] *s.* plenitud; llenura.

fum•ble [fΛmb|] *v.* tentalear, buscar a tientas; chapucear, no coger la pelota o soltarla al correr.

fume [fjum] *v.* exhalar vapor o gas; rabiar; **-s** *s. pl.* vapores, emanaciones, gases.

fu•mi•gate [fjÚməget] *v.* fumigar, sahumar, *Ríopl.* humear.

fun [fΛn] *s.* diversión; burla, broma, chanza, *Carib.*, *Méx.*, *C.A.* choteo; **for** – en (o de) broma; de chanza; de chiste; **full of** – muy divertido; **to have** – divertirse; **to make – of** burlarse de, chancearse con; *Carib.*, *Méx.*, *C.A.* chotear, chotearse con; *Ríopl.* jorobar.

func•tion [fΛŋkʃən] *s.* función; *v.* funcionar.

fund [fΛnd] *s.* fondo, caudal; **-s** fondos, recursos; *v.* consolidar (*una deuda*); prorrogar el plazo de (*una deuda*).

fun•da•men•tal [fΛndəmént|] *adj.* fundamental; *s.* fundamento, principio.

fu•ner•al [fjÚnərəl] *adj.* funeral, fúnebre; *s.* funeral, exequias, funerales.

fun•gus [fΛŋgəs] *s.* hongo; fungosidad.

fun•nel [fΛn|] *s.* embudo; humero (*cañón de chimenea*).

fun•ny [fΛnI] *adj.* (*comical*) chistoso, cómico, gracioso, divertido, (*odd*) extraño, raro; **the funnies** la sección cómica (*de un periódico*).

fur [fɜ] *s.* piel (*de animales peludos o lanudos*); sarro (*en la lengua*); **– coat** abrigo de pieles; *v.* forrar, cubrir o adornar con pieles.

fur•bish [fɚbIʃ] *v.* acicalar, pulir.

fu•ri•ous [fjÚrIəs] *adj.* furioso.

furl [fɜl] *v.* arrollar, enrollar; plegar.

fur•lough [fɜlo] *s.* licencia militar; *v.* dar licencia militar.

fur•nace [fɜnIs] *s.* horno.

fur•nish [fɜnIʃ] *v.* (*equip*) equipar; amueblar; (*provide*) proveer, suministrar, surtir; **to – a room** amueblar un cuarto.

fur•ni•ture [fɜnItʃɚ] *s.* muebles, mobiliario, moblaje, mueblaje.

fur•row [fɜo] *s.* surco; arruga; *v.* surcar; arar.

fur•ther [fɜðɚ] *adj.* adicional; más lejano, más remoto; *adv.* además; más; más lejos; *v.* promover, fomentar, adelantar.

fur•ther•more [fɜðɚmór] *adv.* además.

fur•thest [fɜðIst] *adj.* (el) más lejano, (el) más remoto; *adv.* más lejos.

fur•tive [fɜtIv] *adj.* furtivo.

fu•ry [fjÚrI] *s.* furia; frenesí.

fuse [fjuz] *s.* fusible; mecha; *v.* fundir(se).

fu•se•laje [fjÚz|Idʒ] *s.* fuselaje.

fu•sion [fjÚʒən] *s.* fusión; **nuclear** – fusión nuclear.

fuss [fΛs] *s.* melindre, preocupación inútil; bulla innecesaria; **to make a – over someone** darle a alguien demasiada importancia, desvivirse por alguien; *v.* hacer melindres, inquietarse (*por bagatelas*).

fuss•y [fΛsI] *adj.* melindroso; minucioso (*en demasía*); inquieto, nervioso; **– dress** vestido con demasiados adornos.

fu•tile [fjÚt|] *adj.* fútil; vano.

fu•ture [fjÚtʃɚ] *adj.* futuro; *s.* futuro; porvenir.

fuzz [fΛz] *s.* vello; pelusa

fuzz•y [fΛzI] *adj.* velloso; cubierto de plumón fino; cubierto de pelusa.

G

gab [gæb] *v.* charlar, parlotear; *s.* charla; **gift of** – labia, facundia.

gab•ar•dine [gǽbə·din] *s.* gabardina (*paño*).

gab•ble [gǽb|] *s.* charla, cotorreo; *v.* charlar, cotorrear.

ga•ble [géb|] *s.* gablete (*de un tejado*); **– roof** tejado de caballete o de dos aguas; **– window** ventana con gablete.

gad [gæd] *v.* vagar, callejear; andar de aquí para allá.

gadg•et [gǽdʒIt] *s.* adminículo, artefacto, chisme.

gag [gæg] *s.* (*obstacle*) mordaza; (*joke*) broma, burla; morcilla, chiste (*improvisado por un actor*); *v.* amordazar; dar náuseas, hacer vomitar, basquear; interpolar chistes (*en la escena*).

gage *véase* **gauge**.

gai•e•ty [géətI] *s.* alegría, viveza, alborozo.

gai•ly [gélI] *adv.* alegremente; vistosamente.

gain [gen] *s.* ganancia, provecho; *v.* ganar.

gain•ful [génf|] *adj.* ganancioso.

gait [get] *s.* paso, andadura, marcha.

gale [gel] *s.* ventarrón; **– of laughter** risotada, carcajada, risada.

gall [gɔl] *s.* (*bile*) bilis, hiel; (*bitterness*) amargura; odio; descaro; **– bladder** vejiga de la bilis; *v.* irritar.

gal•lant [gǽlənt] *adj.* valiente; noble; vistoso; [gəl°nt] *adj.* galante, atento, cortés; galanteador; *s.* galán.

gal•lant•ry [gǽləntrI] *s.* galantería; gallardía, valor.

gal·ler·y [gǽlərɪ] s. galería; paraíso, gallinero del (*teatro*).

gal·ley [gǽlɪ] s. galera; cocina (*de un buque*); – **proof** galerada; – **slave** galeote.

gal·lon [gǽlən] s. galón (*aproximadamente cuatro litros*).

gal·lop [gǽləp] s. galope; *v.* galopar, galopear; ir a galope.

gal·lows [gǽloz] s. horca.

ga·losh·es [gəlóʃɪz] s. *pl.* chanclos, zapatos fuertes, zapatones.

gam·ble [gǽmbl] s. jugar, apostar, aventurar (*algo*) en el juego; **to – away** perder en el juego; **to – everything** jugar el todo por el todo; arriesgarlo todo; s. jugada (*en juegos de azar*), apuesta; riesgo.

gam·bol [gǽmbəl] *v.* retozar; cabriolar; juguetear; s. retozo, cabriola.

game [gem] s. juego; deporte; caza (*animales de caza y su carne*); **to make – of** mofarse de, burlarse de; adj. valiente, atrevido; resuelto; – **bird** ave de caza.

gam·ut [gǽmət] s. gama.

gan·der [gǽndɚ] s. ánsar, ganso.

gang [gǽŋ] s. cuadrilla; pandilla; juego (*de herramientas o máquinas*); *v.* agrupar(se); **to – up against** conspirar contra.

gang·plank [gǽŋplæŋk] s. plancha, pasamano (*de un buque*), pasarela.

gan·grene [gǽŋgrin] s. gangrena; *v.* gangrenar(se).

gang·ster [gǽŋstɚ] s. bandolero, bandido, maleante, atracador.

gang·way [gǽŋwe] s. paso, pasadizo; plancha, pasamano; portalón (*de un barco*); –! ¡a un lado! ¡abranse!

gantlet = gauntlet.

gap [gæp] s. brecha, abertura; boquete; hueco; intervalo.

gape [gep] s. (*breach*) brecha, abertura; (*open jaws*) bostezo; boqueada; *v.* boquear, abrir la boca; estar boquiabierto (*mirando*); estar embobado; bostezar.

ga·rage [gərɑ́ʒ] s. garaje.

garb [gɑrb] s. vestido; vestidura; aspecto, apariencia; *v.* vestir, ataviar.

gar·bage [gɑ́rbɪdʒ] s. desperdicios, basura.

gar·den [gɑ́rdn] s. jardín; huerta; huerto; *v.* cultivar un jardín.

gar·den·er [gɑ́rdnɚ] s. jardinero, hortelano; horticultor.

gar·gle [gɑ́rgl] s. gargarismo, *Am.* gárgaras; *v.* gargarizar, hacer gárgaras, *Am.* gargarear.

gar·land [gɑ́rlənd] s. guirnalda.

gar·lic [gɑ́rlɪk] s. ajo.

gar·ment [gɑ́rmənt] s. prenda (*de vestir*).

gar·net [gɑ́rnɪt] s. granate.

gar·nish [gɑ́rnɪʃ] s. aderezo; adorno; *v.* aderezar; adornar; guarnecer.

gar·ret [gǽrɪt] s. desván, buhardilla.

gar·ri·son [gǽrəsn] s. guarnición; *v.* guarnecer o guarnicionar (*una fortaleza*).

gar·ter [gɑ́rtɚ] s. liga (*para sujetar las medias*); *v.* sujetar con liga.

gas [gæs] s. (*gaseous*) gas; (*petroleum*) gasolina; – **burner** mechero; – **stove** estufa o cocina de gas; – **tear** – gas lacrimante o lacrimógeno; *v.* asfixiar con gas; envenenar con gas.

gas·e·ous [gǽsɪəs] adj. gaseoso.

gash [gæʃ] s. cuchillada, herida, incisión; *v.* dar una cuchillada, acuchillar.

gas·o·line [gǽsǀɪn] s. gasolina.

gasp [gæsp] s. boqueada; grito sofocado; *v.* boquear; jadear; sofocarse; abrir la boca (*de asombro*).

gas·tric [gǽstrɪk] adj. gástrico.

gas·tro·in·tes·tin·al [gǽstroɪntéstɪnl] adj. gastrointestinal.

gate [get] s. portón, entrada; puerta; *Ven., Col.* tranquera (*puerta de trancas*).

gate·way [gétwe] s. paso, entrada.

gath·er [gǽðɚ] *v.* recoger; coger; reunir(se), juntar(se); deducir, colegir; fruncir (*en pliegues*); cobrar (*fuerzas*); **to – dust** llenarse de polvo, empolvarse; s. pliegue.

gath·er·ing [gǽðrɪŋ] s. asamblea, reunión; muchedumbre; pliegue.

gaud·y [gɔ́dɪ] adj. vistoso, llamativo, chillón, chillante.

gauge [gedʒ] s. calibrador; indicador; instrumento para medir; medida; calibre (*de un cañón, pistola, etc.*); ancho (*del ferrocarril*); *Ven.* trocha; *v.* medir; calibrar; estimar, calcular.

gaunt [gɔnt] adj. macilento, demacrado, flaco.

gaunt·let [gɔ́ntlɪt] s. guantelete; manopla, **to throw down the** – retar, desafiar.

gauze [gɔz] s. gasa; cendal.

gave [gev] *pret. de* **to give.**

gav·el [gǽvǀ] s. mazo del que preside.

gawk [gɔk] *v.* bobear, mirar embobado; s. simplón, bobo.

gawk·y [gɔ́kɪ] adj. torpe, desmañado; bobo.

gay [ge] adj. alegre; vivo; vistoso; festivo.

gay·e·ty *véase* **gaiety.**

gaze [gez] s. mirada (*fija*); *v.* contemplar, mirar con fijeza, clavar la mirada.

ga·zette [gəzét] s. gaceta.

gear [gɪr] s. (*equipment*) aperos; herramientas; aparejo; equipo; (*wheel*) rueda dentada; (*assembly*) engranaje (*de ruedas dentadas*); **foot–** calzado; **low**

– primera velocidad; **steering** – mecanismo de dirección; **to be in** – estar engranado; **to shift** – cambiar de engrane o velocidad, **to throw in** – engranar; **to throw out of** – desengranar; – **shift lever** palanca de engrane, palanca de cambios; v. engranar.

geese [gis] pl. de **goose**.

Gei·ger counter [gáɪgə-káUntə-] s. contador (de) Geiger.

gel·a·tin [dʒɛlət ŋ] s. gelatina, jaletina.

gem [dʒɛm] s. gema, piedra preciosa; joya, alhaja, panecillo, bollo.

gem·in·ate [dʒɛmənet] v. germinar(se)

gen·der [dʒɛ́ndə-] s. género.

gene [dʒin] s. gen.

gen·er·al [dʒɛ́nərəl] adj. & s. general; **in** – en general, por lo común, por lo general.

gen·er·al·i·ty [dʒɛnərǽ ləti] s. generalidad.

gen·er·al·ize [dʒɛ́nərəlaɪz] v. generalizar.

gen·er·ate [dʒɛ́nəret] v. engendrar; producir; originar.

gen·er·a·tion [dʒɛnəréʃən] s. generación; producción.

gen·er·a·tor [dʒɛ́nə-etə-] s. generador.

ge·ner·ic [dʒɛnɛ́rɪk] genérico.

gen·er·os·i·ty [dʒɛnərásəti] s. generosidad.

gen·er·ous [dʒɛ́nərəs] adj. generoso; magnánimo, liberal; amplio; abundante.

ge·netics [dʒɛnɛ́tɪks] s. genética.

gen·ial [dʒínjəl] adj. genial, afable.

gen·i·tive [dʒɛ́nətɪv] adj. & s. genitivo.

gen·ius [dʒínjəs] s. genio; ingenio, talento.

gen·teel [dʒɛntíl] adj. gentil, cortés; elegante; gallardo.

gen·tile [dʒɛ́ntaɪl] adj. & s. gentil.

gen·tle [dʒɛ́nt] adj. suave; afable; apacible; manso; gentil.

gen·tle·man [dʒɛ́nt mən] s. caballero; **gentlemen** pl. caballeros; señores.

gen·tle·man·ly [dʒɛ́nt mənlɪ] adj. caballeroso, caballero, cortés.

gen·tle·ness [dʒɛ́nt nɪs] s. suavidad, dulzura, apacibilidad; mansedumbre.

gent·ly [dʒɛ́ntlɪ] adv. suavemente; despacio; dulcemente; con ternura; mansamente.

gen·u·ine [dʒɛ́njUɪn] adj. genuino; sincero.

ge·o·graph·i·cal [dʒiəgrǽfɪk] adj. geográfico.

ge·og·ra·phy [dʒióɡrəfɪ] s. geografía.

ge·o·log·ic·al [dʒiəládʒɪk] adj. geológico.

ge·ol·o·gy [dʒiálədʒɪ] s. geología.

ge·o·met·ric [dʒiəmɛ́trɪk] adj. geométrico.

ge·om·e·try [dʒiámətrɪ] s. geometría.

ge·o·phys·ics [dʒiofízɪks] s. geofísica.

ge·ra·ni·um [dʒərénɪəm] s. geranio.

germ [dʒɚm] s. germen; microbio.

Ger·man [dʒɚ́mən] adj. & s. alemán.

ger·mane [dʒə-men] adj. pertinente, relacionado.

ger·mi·nate [dʒɚ́mənet] v. germinar.

ger·und [dʒɛ́rənd] s. gerundio.

ges·ta·tion [dʒɛstéʃən] s. gestación.

ges·tic·u·late [dʒɛstɪ́kjəlet] v. gesticular, hacer gestos o ademanes, accionar, manotear.

ges·ture [dʒɛ́stʃə-] s. gesto; ademán; **a mere** – una pura formalidad; v. gesticular, hacer gestos.

get [gɛt] v. (obtain) obtener, adquirir, lograr, conseguir; (earn) recibir, ganar; (reach) llegar (a); traer; (catch) coger, atrapar; preparar (la lección, la comida, etc.); **to** – **along** llevarse bien (con alguien); ir pasándolo (o ir pasándola); **to** – **angry** ponerse enojado, enojarse; **to** – **away** escaparse; irse; **to** – **down** bajar; **to** – **ill** ponerse enfermo, enfermar(se); **to** – **in** entrar; meter(se); llegar; **to** – **married** casarse; **to** – **off the train** bajar del tren; apearse del tren; **to** – **old** envejecer(se); **to** – **on** subir; montar; **to** – **out** salir; irse; sacar; divulgarse (un secreto); **to** – **over** pasar por encima de; recuperarse de (una enfermedad); olvidar (una ofensa); pasársele a uno (el susto); **to** – **ready** preparar(se); alistar(se); **to** – **rich** enriquecerse, hacerse rico; **to** – **rid of** deshacerse de, desprenderse de; **to** – **through** pasar; terminar; **to** – **together** juntar(se), reunir(se); ponerse de acuerdo; **to** – **up** levantarse; **I got him to dot it** le persuadí a que lo hiciese; **I (have) got to do it** tengo que hacerlo; **I don't** – **it** no lo comprendo; **that's what** – **s me** (or – **s my goat**) eso es lo que me irrita.

ghast·ly [gǽstlɪ] adj. horrible; pálido, lívido, cadavérico.

ghost [gost] s. espectro, fantasma; **the Holy Ghost** el Espíritu Santo; **not to have the** – **of a notion of** no tener la más remota idea de; – **writer** colaborador anónimo.

ghost·ly [góstlɪ] adj. como un espectro; de espectros, de aparecidos.

gi·ant [dʒáɪənt] s. gigante; adj. gigantesco; enorme.

gid·dy [gídɪ] adj. ligero de casos, frívolo; voluble, inconstante; desvanecido; – **speed** velocidad vertiginosa.

gift [gɪft] s. regalo; dádiva, don; dote, talento, prenda; donación.

gift·ed [díftɪd] adj. talentoso, de talento.

gi·gan·tic [dʒaɪgǽntɪk] adj. gigantesco.

gig·gle [gíg] s. risita, risilla; risa falsa; v. reírse falsamente; reírse sofocando la voz; reír con una risilla afectada.

gild [gɪld] v. dorar.

gill [gɪl] s. agalla (de pez).

gilt [gɪlt] *adj. & s.* dorado; *pret. & p.p. de* **to gild.**

gim·mick [gímɪk] *s.* adminículo.

gin [dʒɪn] *s.* ginebra (*licor*).

gin·ger [dʒíndʒɚ] *s.* jengibre; **– ale** cerveza de jengibre.

gin·ger·bread [dʒíndʒɚbrɛd] *s.* pan de jengibre; ornato de mal gusto.

ging·ham [gíŋəm] *s.* guinga (*tela de algodón*).

gip·sy *véase* **gypsy.**

gi·raffe [dʒəræf] *s.* jirafa.

gird [gɚd] *v.* ceñir; rodear; **to – oneself for** prepararse para.

gir·dle [gɚd l] *s.* ceñidor; cinto; faja; *v.* ceñir; fajar; cercar.

girl [gɚl] *s.* niña; muchacha; joven; chica, moza; criada.

girl·hood [gɚlhʊd] *s.* niñez; mocedad, juventud.

girl·ish [gɚlɪʃ] *adj.* pueril; de niña, de muchacha, juvenil.

girt [gɚt] *pret. & p.p. de* **to gird;** *v. véase* **gird.**

girth [gɚθ] *s.* circunferencia; cincha (*para caballos*); faja; *v.* cinchar; ceñir.

gist [dʒɪst] *s.* substancia, esencia.

give [gɪv] *v.* dar; regalar; ceder, dar de sí; **to – away** regalar; entregar; revelar (*un secreto*); **to – back** devolver; **to – birth** dar a luz, parir; **to – in** ceder; darse por vencido; **to – off** emitir; **to – out** divulgar; repartir; agotarse; **to – up** abandonar; desistir; renunciar a; perder la esperanza; rendir(se); ceder, darse por vencido; *s.* elasticidad.

giv·en [gívən] *p.p. de* **to give;** *adj.* (*presented*) dado; regalado; (*inclined*) adicto, entregado; dispuesto, inclinado; **– name** nombre de pila, nombre de bautismo; **– time** hora determinada; **– that** dada que, supuesto que.

giv·er [gívɚ] *s.* dador, donador.

gla·cial [gléʃəl] *adj.* glacial.

gla·cier [gléʃɚ] *s.* glaciar, helero.

glad [glæd] *adj.* contento; alegre; **to be –** to alegrarse de, tener mucho gusto en (*o* de); **–ly** *adv.* alegremente; con mucho gusto; de buena gana.

glad·den [glæd n] *v.* regocijar, alegrar.

glade [gled] *s.* claro herboso (*en un bosque*).

glad·ness [glædnɪs] *s.* alegría, gozo.

glam·our [glæmɚ] *s.* encanto, hechizo; fascinación, embrujo; **– girl** niña hechicera.

glam·or·ous [glæmərəs] *adj.* fascinador, hechicero.

glance [glæns] *s.* mirada, vistazo, ojeada; vislumbre; *v.* echar (*o* dar) un vistazo; vislumbrar; pegar de soslayo; **– off** rebotar de soslayo (*o* de lado).

gland [glænd] *s.* glándula.

glare [glɛr] *s.* (*light*) resplandor, relumbre; (*stare*) mirada furiosa; *v.* resplandecer, relumbrar; **to – at**

mirar enfurecido a.

glass [glæs] *s.* (*substance*) vidrio; cristal; (*receptacle*) vaso; copa (*de cristal*); (*eye*) lente; **looking –** espejo; **–es** anteojos, lentes, gafas; *adj.* de vidrio; **– blower** vidriero, soplador de vidrio; **– case** escaparate.

glass·ware [glæswɛr] *s.* vajilla de cristal, cristalería; **– shop** cristalería.

glass·y [glæsɪ] *adj.* vidrioso.

glaze [glez] *s.* vidriado; lustre; superficie lustrosa o glaseada; *v.* vidriar; glasear; lustrar; poner vidrios a.

gla·zier [gléʒɚ] *s.* vidriero.

gleam [glim] *s.* destello, rayo, fulgor, viso; *v.* destellar, fulgurar, centellear.

glean [glin] *v.* recoger; espigar.

glee [gli] *s.* regocijo; júbilo; **– club** orfeón, masa coral.

glib [glɪb] *adj.* locuaz; de mucha labia; **– excuse** excusa fácil.

glide [glaɪd] *s.* deslizamiento; ligadura (*en música*); planeo (*de un aeroplano*); *v.* deslizarse; resbalarse; planear (*un aeroplano*).

glid·er [gláɪdɚ] *s.* deslizador, planeador (*aeroplano*).

glim·mer [glímɚ] *s.* vislumbre; viso; titileo; **– of hope** rayo de esperanza; *v.* titilar, centellear.

glimpse [glɪmps] *s.* vislumbre; vistazo, ojeada; **to catch a – of** vislumbrar; *v.* vislumbrar.

glint [glɪnt] *s.* fulgor, rayo, destello.

glis·ten [glís n] *v.* relucir, brillar.

glit·ter [glítɚ] *s.* lustre, brillo, resplandor; *v.* relumbrar, relucir, brillar.

gloat [glot] *v.* gozarse (en), deleitar (en); relamerse (*de gusto*).

globe [glob] *d.* globo; esfera.

gloom [glum] *s.* lobreguez, sombra; abatimiento, tristeza, melancolía.

gloom·y [glúmɪ] *adj.* lóbrego, sombrío; triste, melancólico; abatido.

glo·ri·fy [glórəfaɪ] *v.* glorificar.

glo·ri·ous [glórɪəs] *adj.* glorioso; espléndido.

glo·ry [glórɪ] *s.* gloria; *v.* gloriarse; vanagloriarse.

gloss [glos] *s.* (*shine*) lustre, brillo, pulimento; (*note*) glosa, comentario; *v.* lustrar, dar brillo a; pulir; glosar, comentar; **to – over** encubrir, dar colorido de bueno (*a algo que no lo es*).

glos·sa·ry [glósərɪ] *s.* glosario.

gloss·y [glɔ́sɪ] *adj.* lustroso; pulido.

glove [glʌv] *s.* guante; *v.* enguantar, poner guantes.

glow [glo] *s.* incandescencia; brillo (*de un ascua*); calor vivo; fosforescencia; *v.* lucir, brillar (*como un ascua*); fosforecer; estar encendido o enardecido.

glow·ing [glóɪŋ] *adj.* encendido, ardiente.

glow·worm [glówɚm] *s.* luciérnaga.

glue [glu] *s.* cola (*para pegar*); *v.* encolar, pegar (*con cola*).

glum [glʌm] *adj.* hosco.

glut•ton [glʌtn̩] *s.* glotón.

glut•ton•ous [glʌtn̩əs] *adj.* glotón; goloso.

glut•ton•y [glʌtn̩ɪ] *s.* gula, glotonería.

glyc•er•in [glísəɪn] *s.* glicerina.

gnarled [norld] *adj.* nudoso, torcido.

gnash [næʃ] *v.* crujir, rechinar (*los dientes*).

gnat [næt] *s.* jején (*insecto*).

gnaw [nɔ] *v.* roer.

go [go] *v.* (*move*) ir(se); andar; (*function*) marchar, funcionar, servir; **to – around** andar alrededor de; dar vueltas; **to – away** irse; **to – black on one's word** faltar a la palabra; **to – by** pasar por; guiarse por (*una regla*); **to – down** bajar; **to – insane** volverse loco; **to – into** entrar en; investigar; caber en; **to – off** hacer explosión; dispararse; irse, salir disparado; **to – on** proseguir, continuar; **to – out** salir; apagarse; **to – over** pasar por encima de; examinar con cuidado; releer; repasar; recorrer; **to – to sleep** dormirse; **to – under** ir o pasar por debajo de; hundirse; **to – up** subir; **to let –** soltar; **there is not enough to – around** no hay (bastante) para todos; *s.* empuje, energía; **it is a –** trato hecho; **to be on the –** estar en continuo movimiento.

goad [god] *s.* aguijón; *v.* aguijonear; aguijar, incitar.

goal [gol] *s.* meta; fin, objetivo.

goat [got] *s.* cabra; **male –** macho cabrío; **to be the –** ser la víctima, pagar el pato.

goat•ee [gotí] *s.* perilla.

gob•ble [gábl̩] *v.* tragar, engullir; **to – up** engullirse.

gob•bler [gáblə] *s.* pavo.

go–be•tween [góbətwin] *s.* medianero.

gob•let [gáblɪt] *s.* copa grande.

gob•lin [góblɪn] *s.* duende.

god [gɑd] *s.* dios; **God** Dios.

god•child [gádtʃaɪld] *s.* ahijado, ahijada.

god•dess [gádɪs] *s.* diosa.

god•fa•ther [gádfoðə] *s.* padrino

god•less [gádlɪs] *adj.* impío, ateo.

god•like [gádlaɪk] *adj.* como Dios; divino.

god•ly [gádlɪ] *adj.* pío, devoto; divino.

god•moth•er [gádmʌðə] *s.* madrina.

gog•gles [gáglz] *s. pl.* antiparras, gafas.

go•ing [góɪŋ] *ger. & adj.* que anda, marcha o funciona bien; **to be –** ir, irse; *s.* ida, partida; **comings and –s** idas y venidas.

goi•ter [gɔ́ɪtə] *s.* papera; bocio; *Ríopl., Méx., C.A.* buche; *C.A.* güecho.

gold [gold] *s.* oro; **– standard** patrón de oro.

gold•en [góldn̩] *adj.* de oro; áureo; dorado.

gold•finch [góldfɪntʃ] *s.* jilguero amarillo.

gold•fish [góldfɪʃ] *s.* carpa dorada.

gold•smith [góldsmɪθ] *s.* orfebre.

golf [gɑlf] *s.* golf.

gon•do•la [gándələ] *s.* góndola; cabina (*de una aeronave*); **– car** vagón de mercancías (*sin techo*), *Am.* jaula.

gone [gɔn] *p.p. de* **to go** & *adj.* ido; perdido; **he is –** se fué; **it is all –** se acabó; ya no hay más.

gong [gɔŋ] *s.* gong, batintín.

good [gUd] *adj.* bueno; válido; valedero; **– afternoon** buenas tardes; **– day** buenos días; adiós; **– evening** buenas noches; **– morning** buenos días; **– night** buenas noches; **Good Friday** Viernes Santo; **for –** para siempre, permanentemente; **to have a – time** pasar un buen rato; divertirse; **to make –** pagar, compensar; cumplir (*una promesa*); salir bien, tener buen éxito; *s.* bien; beneficio, provecho, ventaja; **–s** bienes, efectos; mercancías.

good–bye [gUdbáɪ] *s. & interj.* adiós.

good–look•ing [gUdlÚkɪŋ] *adj.* bien parecido, guapo.

good•ly [gÚdlɪ] *adj.* grande, considerable; de buena apariencia.

good–na•tured [gÚdnétʃəd] *adj.* de buen genio, bonachón, afable.

good•ness [gÚdnɪs] *s.* bondad; **–!** ¡Dios mío! ¡cielos!

good•y [gÚdɪ] *s.* golosina, bonbón, dulce; *interj.* ¡qué gusto!; **goody–goody** beatuco (*el que afecta virtud*), papanatas.

goof [guf] *v.* chapucear.

goose [gus] *s.* ganso, bobo, tonto; **– flesh** carne de gallina.

goose•ber•ry [gúsbɛrɪ] *s.* grosella; grosellero (*arbusto*).

go•pher [gófə] *s.* roedor semejante a la ardilla.

gore [gor] *s.* (*blood*) cuajarón de sangre; sangre; (*cloth*) cuchillo (*Am.* cuchilla), sesga (*tira de lienzo en figura de cuchilla*); *v.* acornear, herir con los cuernos; hacer una sesga en (*un traje*).

gorge [gɔrdʒ] *s.* cañada, barranco, barranca; *v.* engullir(se), atracarse.

gor•geous [gɔ́rdʒəs] *adj.* primoroso, vistoso, hermosísimo.

go•ril•la [gərílə] *s.* gorila.

go•ry [górɪ] *adj.* sangriento, ensangrentado.

gos•pel [gáspl̩] *s.* evangelio; **it is the – truth** es la pura verdad.

gos•sip [gásɪp] *s.* (*rumors*) chisme, chismería; murmuración, hablilla; (*person*) murmurador, chismero, chismoso; *v.* chismear, murmurar.

gos•sip•y [gásəpɪ] *adj.* chismero, chismoso.

got [gɑt] *pret. & p.p. de* **to get**.

Goth•ic [gáθɪk] *adj.* gótico; *s.* gótico (*idioma de los godos*); estilo gótico.

got•ten [gátn̩] *p.p. de* **to get**.

gouge [gaUdʒ] *s.* gubia (*especie de formón o escoplo curvo*); *v.* excavar con gubia, formón o escoplo; **to – someone's eyes out** sacarle los ojos a alguien.

gourd [gord] s. calabaza.

gour•met [gUrmé] s. gastrónomo.

gout [gaUt] s. gota (*enfermedad*).

gov•ern [g Á və·n] v. gobernar; regir.

gov•erness [g Á və·nɪs] s. institutriz.

gov•ern•ment [g Á və·mənt] s. gobierno.

gov•ern•ment•al [gΛvə·mént ǀ ǀ] adj. gubernativo.

gov•er•nor [g Á və·nə·] s. gobernador; regulador (*de una máquina*).

gown [gaUn] s. vestido (*de mujer*); toga (*de un juez, profesor, etc.*); **dressing –** bata.

grab [græb] v. agarrar asir; arrebatar; s. arrebatiña; agarro, agarrón; presa.

grace [gres] s. gracia; favor; donaire, garbo; **to say – bendecir** la mesa, dar gracias; **to be in the good –s of someone** gozar del favor de uno; v. agraciar, adornar.

grace•full [grésfəl] adj. gracioso, agraciado, garboso; **–ly** adv. graciosamente, con gracia, con garbo.

grace•ful•ness [grésfəlnɪs] s. gracia, donaire, gallardía, garbo.

gra•cious [gréʃəs] adj. afable; cortés; **–!** ¡válgame Dios!

gra•da•tion [gredéʃən] s. graduación; gradación; grado.

grade [gred] s. (*degree*) grado; (*mark*) nota, calificación; (*slope*) cuesta, declive, pendiente; *Am.* gradiente; **– crossing** cruce a nivel (*de un ferrocarril con una carretera*); **the –s** la escuela primaria; v. graduar, clasificar; calificar, dar una calificación; nivelar (*un camino*).

grad•u•al [græ d3Uəl] adj. gradual; **–ly** adv. gradualmente, poco a poco.

grad•u•ate [græ d3UIt] adj. graduado, que ha recibido un grado académico; **to do – work** cursar asignaturas superiores (*al bachillerato*); s. estudiante graduado (*que estudia para licenciado o doctor*); [græ d3Uet] v. graduar(se).

grad•u•a•tion [græd3Ué ʃ ən] s. graduación.

graft [græft] s. (*insertion*) injerto; tejido injertado; (*extortion*) sisa, malversación (*de caudales públicos*); ganancia ilegal, Am. mordida; v. injertar; malversar fondos ajenos; sisar, exigir pago ilegal, Am. morder.

graft•er [græftə·] s. malversador (de fondos públicos), estafador. *C.A.* coyote, *Méx.* mordelón.

grain [gren] s. (*cereal*) grano; (*markings*) fibra (*de la madera*), veta (*del mármol o madera*); **against the – a** (*o al*) redopelo, a contrapelo.

gram [gǽm] s. gramo.

gram•mar [grǽmə·] s. gramática; **– school** escuela primaria.

gram•mat•i•cal [grəmǽtɪk ǀ ǀ] adj. gramatical, gramático.

gran•a•ry [grǽnərɪ] s. granero.

grand [grænd] adj. grande; grandioso, admirable; magnífico.

grand•child [grǽntʃaɪld] s. nieto.

grand•chil•dren [grǽnt ʃɪdrən] s. pl. nietos.

grand•daugh•ter [grǽndotə·] s. nieta.

gran•deur [grǽnd3ə·] s. grandeza, grandiosidad; majestad.

grand•fa•ther [grǽnfáðə·] s. abuelo.

gran•di•ose [grǽndɪos] adj. grandioso, magnífico.

grand•ma [grǽ nma] s. abuela, abuelita, Am. mamá grande.

grand•moth•er [grǽnmΛðə·] s. abuela.

grand•ness [grǽndnɪs] s. grandeza; grandiosidad; magnificencia.

grand•pa [grǽnpa] s. abuelo, abuelito, Am. papá grande.

grand•par•ent [grǽnpɛrənt] s. abuelo, abuela; **–s** abuelos.

grand•son [grǽnsΛn] s. nieto.

grand•stand [grǽnstænd] s. andanada, gradería cubierta.

grange [grend3] s. granja; asociación de agricultores.

gran•ite [grǽnɪt] s. granito (*roca*).

gran•ny [grǽnɪ] s. abuelita; viejecita, vieja.

grant [grænt] s. concesión; subvención; donación; transferencia de propiedad (*mediane escritura*); v. conceder; otorgar; ceder, transferir (*derechos, propiedad, etc.*); **to take for –ed** dar por supuesto, dar por sentado.

gran•u•late [grǽnjələt] v. granular(se).

grape [grep] s. uva.

grape•fruit [grépfrut] s. toronja.

grape•vine [grépvaɪn] s. vid; parra.

graph [græf] s. diagrama, gráfica; v. hacer una gráfica o diagrama.

graph•ic [grǽfɪk] adj. gráfico.

graph•ite [grǽfaɪt] s. grafito.

grap•ple [grǽp ǀ] v. luchar, pelear cuerpo a cuerpo; aferrar, agarrar.

grasp [græsp] v. (*seize*) agarrar; asir; apretar; (*understand*) comprender; abarcar; s. agarro, asimiento; apretón de manos; **to be within one's – estar** al alcance de uno; **to have a good – of a subject** estar fuerte en una materia, saber a fondo una materia.

grass [græs] s. hierba; césped; pasto; *Méx.* zacate; *Méx., Ven., Col.* grama.

grass·hop·per [grǽhopɚ] *s.* saltamontes, saltón, *Méx., C.A.* chapulín.

grass·roots [grǽsruts] *adj.* del pueblo; de la gente.

grass·y [grǽsɪ] *adj.* herboso, *Am.* pastoso.

grate [gret] *s.* (*window*) reja, verja, enrejado; (*grill*) parrilla, brasero; *v.* enrejar, poner enrejado; crujir, rechinar (*los dientes*); rallar (*queso*); **to – on** molestar, irritar.

grate·ful [grétfəl] *adj.* agradecido; grato, agradable.

grat·er [grétɚ] *s.* rallador.

grat·i·ty [grǽtəfaɪ] *v.* complacer, dar gusto, agradar; satisfacer.

grat·ing [grétɪŋ] *s.* reja, enrejado, verja; *adj.* rechinante; molesto, áspero.

grat·is [grǽtɪs] *adv.* gratis, de balde.

grat·i·tude [grǽtətjud] *s.* gratitud.

gra·tu·i·tous [grətjúɪtəs] *adj.* gratuito; sin fundamento; **– statement** afirmación arbitraria.

grave [grev] *adj.* grave; serio; *s.* tumba sepulcro, sepultura; acento grave; **–stone** losa o lápida sepulcral.

grav·el [grǽvl] *s.* grava, guijo, cascajo; cálculos (*en los riñones, la vejiga, etc.*); mal de piedra; *v.* cubrir con grava.

grave·yard [grévjɔrd] *s.* cementerio.

grav·i·ta·tion [grævɪté∫ən] *s.* atracción; gravitación.

grav·i·ty [grǽvətɪ] *s.* gravedad; seriedad.

gravy [grévɪ] *s.* salsa; jugo (*de carne*).

gray [gre] *adj.* gris; cano; entrecano (*que empieza a encanecer*); **– horse** rucio, tordo, tordillo; **– matter** seso; **gray–headed** canoso; *s.* gris, color gris; *v.* encanecer; poner(se) gris.

gray·ish [gréɪ∫] *adj.* grisáceo, pardusco; **– hair** pelo entrecano.

gray·ness [grénɪs] *s.* grisura, gris, calidad de gris; encanecimiento.

graze [grez] *v.* (*feed*) pacer; apacentar, *Am.* pastear, pastar; (*brush*) rozar; raspar; *s.* roce, rozón, raspadura.

grease [gris] *s.* grasa; *v.* engrasar; untar; lubricar; **to – the palm** untar la mano, sobornar.

greas·y [grísɪ] *adj.* grasiento, grasoso.

great [gret] *adj.* gran(de); eminente; magnífico, excelente; **a – deal** una gran cantidad; muchos; mucho; **a – many** muchos; **a – while** un largo rato o tiempo; **–ly** *adv.* grandemente; mucho; muy; en gran parte; sobremanera.

great–grand·child [grétgrǽnt∫aɪld] *s.* biznieto.

great–brand·fa·ther [grétgrǽnfoðɚ] *s.* bisabuelo.

great–grand·moth·er [grétgrǽnmʌðɚ] *s.* bisabuela.

great·ness [grétnɪs] *s.* grandeza.

Grecian [grí∫ən] *adj. & s.* griego.

greed [grid] *s.* codicia; avaricia; gula.

greed·i·ly [grídǀɪ] *adv.* vorazmente; con avaricia; con gula.

greed·i·ness [grídɪnɪs] *s.* codicia; avaricia; gula; voracidad.

greed·y [grídɪ] *adj.* codicioso; avaro; goloso; voraz.

Greek [grik] *adj. & s.* griego.

green [grin] *adj.* (*color*) verde; (*novice*) novato, inexperto; **to grow –** verdear; **the fields look –** verdean los campos; *s.* verde, verdor; césped, prado; campo de golf; **–s** verduras, hortalizas.

green·horn [grínhorn] *s.* novato, pipiolo.

green·house [grínhaUs] *s.* invernáculo, invernadero.

green·ish [grínɪ∫] *adj.* verdoso.

green·ness [grínnɪs] *s.* (*color*) verdor, verdura; (*experience*) inmadurez; impericia.

greet [grit] *v.* saludar; **to – each other** saludarse.

greet·ing [grítɪŋ] *s.* saludo; salutación; **–s!** ¡salud! ¡saludos!

gre·nade [grɪnéd] *s.* granada, bomba pequeña.

grew [gru] *pret. de* **to grow**.

grey = gray.

grey·ish = gray.

grey·ness = grayness.

grey·hound [gréhaUnd] *s.* lebrel, galgo.

grid·dle [grídǀ] *s.* tartera; plancha (*para tapar el hornillo*).

grief [grif] *s.* dolor, pesar; **to come to –** sobrevenirle a uno una desgracia; fracasar.

griev·ance [grívəns] *s.* queja; resentimiento; motivo de queja, injusticia, ofensa.

grieve [griv] *v.* afligir(se); lamentar(se); acongojar(se).

griev·ous [grívəs] *adj.* doloroso, penoso; grave, altroz.

grill [grɪl] *s.* parrilla; **men's –** restaurante para hombres; *v.* asar en parrillas; interrogar (*a un sospechoso*).

grim [grɪm] *adj.* austero, áspero; firo; torvo, siniestro.

grim·ace [grɪmés] *s.* mueca, gesto; *v.* hacer muecas o gestos.

grime [graɪm] *s.* mugre; *v.* ensuciar.

grim·y [gráɪmɪ] *adj.* mugriento.

grin [grɪn] *s.* sonrisa abierta; sonrisa maliciosa; sonrisa canina; *v.* sonreír (*mostrando mucho los dientes*).

grind [graɪnd] *v.* (*crush*) moler; machacar; (*sharpen*) afilar, amolar; (*study hard*) afanarse demasiado; estudiar con empeño; **to – a hand organ** tocar el organillo; **to – one's teeth** rechinar los dientes; *s.* molienda; faena, trabajo penoso; estudiante tesonero; **the daily –** la rutina diaria.

grind·er [gráɪndɚ] *s.* moledor; molinillo (*para moler café*); amolador, afilador; muela (*piedra para afilar*); muela (*diente molar*).

grind·stone (gráɪndston) *s.* piedra de amolar.

grip [grɪp] *v.* (*seize*) agarrar; asir; apretar; empuñar; (*impress*) impresionar; conmover; *s.* agarro; asimiento; apretón; asidero, asa; (*suitcase*) valija, maletín; *Méx.*, velís; **to have a – on someone** tener agarrado a alguien.

grippe [grɪp] *s.* gripe, influenza.

grit [grɪt] *s.* (*gravel*) arenilla, arena; piedra arenisca; (*pluck*) firmeza, tesón; **–s** maíz, avena, o trigo a medio moler; *v.* rechinar, crujir.

grit·ty [grítɪ] *adj.* arenoso; valeroso, firme.

griz·zly [grízlɪ] *adj.* grisáceo, pardusco; **– bear** oso pardo.

groan [gron] *s.* gemido, quejido; *v.* gemir; quejarse; crujir (*por exceso de peso*).

gro·cer [grósɚ] *s.* abacero, *Méx.* abarrotero, *Carib.*, *C.A.* bodeguero; *Ríopl.* almacenero.

gro·cer·y [grósɚɪ] *s.* abacería, tienda de comestibles, *Méx.* abarrotería, *Méx.* tienda de abarrotes; *Carib. C.A.* bodega; **groceries** cometibles, *Méx.* abarrotes.

groom [grum] *s.* (*bridegroom*) novio; (*stable groom*) caballerizo, mozo de caballeriza; establero; *v.* almohazar, limpiar con la almohaza (*a los caballos*), cuidar (*a los caballos*); **to – oneself** asearse, peinarse, componerse; **well–groomed** bien vestido, aseado, limpio.

groove [gruv] *s.* estría, ranura, acanaladura; surco (*en un camino*); muesca, encaje; *v.* acanalar, estriar.

grope [grop] *v.* tentalear,tentar, andar a tientas; **to – for** buscar tentando, buscar a tientas.

gross [gros] *adj.* grueso; burdo; tosco; grosero; **– earnings** ganancias totales; **– ignorance** ignorancia crasa; **– weight** peso bruto; *s.* grueso, totalidad; gruesa (*doce docenas*).

gro·tesque [grotésk] *adj.* & *s.* grotesco.

grot·to [gráto] *s.* gruta.

grouch [graʊtʃ] *s.* mal humor; gruñón, refunfuñón, cascarrabias; **to have a – against someone** tenerle ojeriza (*o mala voluntad*) a una persona; guardarle rencor a alguien; *v.* gruñir, refunfuñar; estar de mal humor.

grouch·y [gráʊtʃɪ] *adj.* gruñón, refunfuñón, malhumorado, cascarrabias.

ground [graʊnd] *s.* (*earth*) suelo, tierra; terreno; (*motive*) motivo, rezón; base, fundamento; **– crew** personal de tierra; **–s** heces, desperdicios, sedimento; **– floor** piso bajo, planta baja, **to break –** roturar, arar; cavar; **to give –** retroceder, ceder; **to hold one's –** mantenerse firme; *v.* conectar (*un alambre*) con la tierra; encallar (*una embarcación*), aterrizar (*un aeroplano*); **to be well –ed** poseer las bases o principios fundamentales; *pret.* & *p.p. de* **to grind**.

ground·less [gráʊndlɪs] *adj.* infundado.

group [grup] *s.* grupo; **– insurance** seguros sociales; *v.* agrupar.

grove [grov] *s.* arboleda, bosquecillo.

grow [gro] *v.* crecer; brotar; cultivar; criar; producir; **to – angry** ponerse enojado o enfadado, enfadarse, enojarse; **to – better** ponerse mejor, mejorar; **to – difficult** dificultarse, hacerse difícil; **to – late** hacerse tarde; **to – old** ponerse viejo, envejecer; **to – out of a habit** perder la costumbre; **to – pale** ponerse pálido, palidecer; **to – tired** cansarse.

growl [graʊl] *s.* gruñido; *v.* gruñir.

growl·er [gráʊlɚ] *s.* gruñón; regañón.

grown [gron] *p.p. de* **to grow** & *adj.* crecido; desarrollado; **– man** hombre maduro, hombre hecho; **– with trees** poblado de árboles.

grown–up [grónʌp] *adj.* crecido, adulto; *s.* adulto.

growth [groθ] *s.* (*increase*) crecimiento, acrecentamiento; aumento; (*development*) desarrollo; (*vegetation*) vegetación; (*tissue*) tumor, lobanillo, excrecencia.

grub·by [grʌ́bɪ] *adj.* roñoso; sucio.

grudge [grʌdʒ] *s.* inquina, rencor, resentimiento, mala voluntad; *v.* tener inquina, envidia o mala voluntad; dar de mala gana.

gruff [grʌf] *adj.* áspero, rudo; grosero.

grum·ble [grʌ́mbḷ] *s.* refunfuno, gruñido, queja; *v.* refunfuñar, gruñir, quejarse.

grum·bler [grʌ́mblɚ] *s.* gruñón; regañón.

grump·y [grʌ́mpɪ] *adj.* malhumorado; gruñón.

grunt [grʌnt] *s.* gruñido, *Méx.*, *C.A.*, *Col.*, *Ven.* pujido; *v.* gruñir, *Ríopl.*, *Méx.*, *C.A.*, *Ven. Andes* pujar.

guar·an·tee [gærəntí] *s.* garantía; fianza; fiador; *v.* garantizar; dar fianza; salir fiador de.

guar·an·tor [gærəntər] *s.* fiador.

guar·an·ty [gærəntɪ] *s.* garantía; fianza; fiador; *v. véase* **guarantee**.

guard [gɑrd] *s.* guarda; guardia; resguardo; **to be on –** estar alerta; estar en guardia; **to keep –** vigilar; *v.* guardar; resguardar; vigilar; **to – (oneself) against** guardarse de.

guard·i·an [gárdɪən] *s.* guardián, custodio; tutor; **– angel** ángel custodio, ángel de la guarda.

guard·i·an·ship [gárdɪənʃɪp] *s.* tutela; guarda, custodia.

guard·rail [gárdrel] *s.* baranda.

Gua·te·ma·lan [gwatəmáлən] *adj.* & *s.* guatemalteco.

guess [gɛs] *s.* conjetura, suposición; adivinación; *v.* adivinar; suponer, creer.

guest [gɛst] *s.* convidado; visita; huésped, pensionista, inquilino.

guf·faw [gʌfɔ́] *s.* risotada, carcajada.

guid·ance [gáɪdŋs] *s.* guía, dirección.

guide [gaɪd] *s.* guía.

guide·book [gáidbUk] s. guía del viajero; **railway –** guía de ferrocarriles.

guide·line [gáidlain] s. norma; precepto.

guild [gild] s. gremio; cofradía; asociación.

guile [gail] s. engaño, astucia.

guilt [gilt] s. culpa, delito; culpabilidad.

guilt·less [gíltlis] adj. libre de culpa; inocente.

guilt·y [gílti] adj. culpable; reo, delincuente.

guise [gaiz] s. aspecto, apariencia; modo; **under the – of** so capa de; disfrazado de.

gui·tar [gitór] s. guitarra.

gulf [gʌlf] s. golfo; abismo.

gull [gʌl] s. gaviota.

gul·let [g ʌ́ lit] s. gaznate.

gul·ly [g ʌ́ li] s. barranco, barranca; hondonada.

gulp [gʌlp] s. trago; v. tragar; engullir; **to – it down** tragárselo.

gum [gʌm] s. (product) goma; (of mouth) encía; **chewing –** goma de mascar, Am. chicle; **– tree** árbol gomífero, Col. gomero; v. engomar, pegar con goma.

gun [gʌn] s. (cannon) cañón; (rifle) fusil, rifle; (shotgun) escopeta; pistola, revólver; **a 21 – salute** una salva de 21 cañonazos.

gun·boat [g ʌ́ nbot] s. cañonero, lancha cañonera.

gun·ner [g ʌ́ nə·] s. artillero, cañonero; ametrallador.

gun·pow·der [g ʌ́ npaUdə·] s. pólvora.

gur·gle [g ə́ g l] v. borbotar, hacer borbollones; s. borbollón, borbotón.

gush [gʌʃ] s. chorro; borbollón, borbotón; efusión (de cariño o entusiasmo); v. chorrear, borbotar, borbollar, borbollonear; brotar; ser demasiado efusivo.

gust [gʌst] s. ráfaga, ventolera.

gut [gʌt] s. tripa, intestino; cuerda de tripa; **to have –s** tener agallas (ánimo).

gut·ter [g ʌ́ tə·] s. arroyo (de la calle o de un camino); gotera (del techo); zanja.

guy [gai] s. (person) sujeto, tipo, individuo; (wire) tirante, alambre, cadena (para sostener algo); v. sostener (algo) con tirantes; burlarse de, mofarse de.

gym·na·si·um [dʒimnéziəm] s. gimnasio.

gym·nas·tics [dʒimnǽstiks] s. pl. gimnasia.

gy·rate [dʒáiret] v. girar.

gy·ro·scope [dʒáirəskop] s. giroscopio.

gyp·sy [dʒípsi] s. adj. gitano.

H

hab·it [hǽbit] s. hábito; costumbre; **drinking –** vicio de la bebida; **riding –** traje de montar.

ha·bit·u·al [həbítʃUəl] adj. habitual; acostumbrado.

hack [hæk] s. (cut) tajo; (cough) tos seca; (horse) caballo de alquiler; rocín; (writer) escritor mercenario; v. tajar, picar; toser con tos seca.

hack·neyed [hǽknid] adj. trillado, muy común.

had [hæd] pret. & p.p. de **to have; you – better do it** es bueno que Vd. lo haga; sería bueno que usted lo hiciese; **I – rather go than stay** preferiría irme a quedarme.

hag [hæg] s. hechicera, bruja; viejota.

hag·gard [hǽgə·d] adj. macilento, flaco.

hag·gle [hǽg l] v. regatear.

hail [hel] s. (storm) granizo; (greeting) saludo; llamada, grito; **Hail Mary** Ave María; interj. ¡salud!; ¡salve!; v. granizar; saludar; llamar; aclamar; **to – from** proceder de, ser oriundo de.

hail·storm [hélstorm] s. granizada.

hair [hɛr] s. pelo; caballo; vello; filamento (de las plantas); **– net** red para el cabello.

hair·brush [hérbrʌʃ] s. cepillo para el cabello.

hair·cut [hérkʌt] s. corte de pelo; **to have a –** hacerse cortar el pelo.

hair·do [hérdu] s. peinado.

hair·dress·er [hérdrɛsə·] s. peluquero; peinadora.

hair·less [hérlis] adj. sin pelo, pelado; lampiño.

hair·pin [hérpin] s. horquilla, Am. gancho (para el pelo).

hair·y [héri] adj. peludo, cabelludo; hirsuto, velloso, velludo.

hale [hel] adj. sano, fuerte, robusto; v. llevar (a una persona) por fuerza.

half [hæf] s. mitad; v. **– an apple** media manzana; adj. medio; **– brother** hermanastro; **– cooked** a medio cocer, medio cocido; **half-past one** la una y media; **half–baked** a medio cocer; a medio planear.

half–breed [hǽfbrid] adj. & s. mestizo.

half–hour [hǽfáUr] s. media hora; adj. de media hora.

half–mast [hǽfmǽst] s. media asta; v. poner a media asta (la bandera).

half–o·pen [hǽfópən] adj. entreabierto; medio abierto, entornado.

half·way [hǽfwe] adj. & adv. a medio camino; parcial, incompleto; **– between** equidistante de; **– finished** a medio acabar; **to do something –** hacer algo a medias.

half–wit·ted [hǽfwítid] adj. imbécil, zonzo.

hal·i·but [hǽləbət] s. mero, hipogloso (pez).

hall [hɔl] s. salón (para asambleas, funciones, etc.); edificio (de un colegio o universidad); vestíbulo; corredor, pasillo, **town –** ayuntamiento.

hall·mark [hɔ́lmark] s. distintivo.

hallo = hello.

hal•low [hǽlo] *v.* santificar; consagrar.

Hal•lo•ween [hǽloín] *s.* víspera de Todos los Santos.

hall•way [hɔ́lwe] *s.* corredor, pasillo; zaguán.

ha•lo [hélo] *s.* halo; aureola.

halt [hɔlt] *s.* alto, parada; *v.* parar(se), detener(se); hacer alto; vacilar.

halt•er [hɔ́ltəɾ] *s.* ronzal, cabestro.

halt•ing [hɔ́ltɪŋ] *adj.* vacilante; **-ly** *adv.* con vacilación.

halve [hæv] *v.* partir por la mitad; partir en dos.

halves [hævz] *pl. de* **half; to go** – ir a medias.

ham [hæm]. *s.* jamón.

ham•burg•er [hǽmbɜ‐gə‐] *s.* carne picada de vaca; bocadillo o emparedado de carne picada, *Am.* hamburguesa.

ham•let [hǽmlɪt] *s.* caserío, aldehuela.

ham•mer [hǽmə‐] *s.* martillo; martinete (*de piano*); **sledge** – macho; *v.* martillar; machacar; clavar.

ham•mock [hǽmək] *s.* hamaca, *Ven., Col.* chinchorro; *Ríopl.* mangangá; coy.

ham•per [hǽmpə‐] *s.* canasto, cesto grande, cuévano; *v.* estorbar, impedir, embarazar.

hand [hænd] *s.* mano; manecilla; aguja (*de reloj*); obrero; letra (*modo de escribir*); **– and glove** uña y carne; **– in** – (cogidos) de la mano; **at** – a la mano, cerca; **made by** – hecho a mano; **on** – disponible; en existencia; listo; a la mano, presente; **on the other** – en cambio, por otra parte; **to have one's –s full** estar ocupadísimo; *v.* entregar, dar; **to – down** bajar (*una cosa para dársela a alguien*); transmitir (*de una a otra generación*); pronunciar (*un fallo*); **to – in** entregar; **to – over** entregar.

hand•bag [hǽndbæg] *s.* bolsa o bolso; saco de noche, maletín.

hand•ball [hǽndbɔl] *s.* pelota; juego de pelota.

hand•bill [hǽndbɪl] *s.* hoja volante (*anuncio*).

hand•cuff [hǽndkʌf] *v.* maniatar; **-s** *pl.* esposas, manillas de hierro.

hand•ful [hǽndfəl] *s.* manojo, puñado.

hand•i•cap [hǽndɪkæp] *s.* desventaja, estorbo, impedimento, obstáculo; ventaja o desventaja (*impuesta en ciertas contiendas*); **– race** carrera de handicap; *v.* estorbar, poner trabas a.

hand•i•work [hǽndɪwɜ‐k] *s.* labor, trabajo hecho a mano; artefacto.

hand•ker•chief [hǽŋkə‐tʃɪf] *s.* pañuelo.

han•dle [hǽndl] *s.* mango, asa; tirador (*de puerta o cajón*); puño (*de espada*); manubrio (*de bicicleta, organillo, etc.*); *v.* manejar; manipular; manosear, tocar; comerciar en; **-s easily** se maneja con facilidad, es muy manuable.

hand•made [hǽndméd] *adj.* hecho a mano.

hand•saw [hǽndsɔ] *s.* serrucho.

hand•shake [hǽndʃek] *s.* apretón de manos.

hand•some [hǽnsəm] *adj.* (*good–looking*) hermoso, guapo, bien parecido; (*generous*) generoso; **a – sum** una suma considerable.

hand•writ•ing [hǽndraɪtɪŋ] *s.* letra (*modo de escribir*), escritura.

hand•y [hǽndɪ] *adj.* a la mano, próximo; hábil, dietro; manuable, fácil de manejar.

hang [hæŋ] *v.* colgar; suspender; ahorcar; inclinar (*la cabeza*); **sentenced to** – condenado a la horca; **to – around** andar holgazaneando por un sitio; rondar; esperar sin hacer nada; **to – on** colgarse de; depender de; estar pendiente de; persistir; **to – paper on a wall** empapelar una pared; **to – with tapestries** entapizar; *s.* modo de caerle la ropa a una persona; modo de manejar (*un mecanismo*); modo de resolver (*un problema*); significado (*de un argumento*); **I don't care a** – no me importa un ardite.

han•gar [hǽŋə‐] *s.* hangar, cobertizo.

hang•er [hǽŋə‐] *s.* colgadero; percha, clavijero; **paper** – empapelador.

hang•ing [hǽŋɪŋ] *s.* muerte en la horca; **-s** colgaduras; *adj.* colgante; colgado.

hang•man [hǽŋmən] *s.* verdugo.

hang•nail [hǽŋnel] *s.* padrastro (*pedacito de pellejo que se levanta junto a las uñas*).

hang–o•ver [hǽŋovə‐] *s.* sobrante, remanente, resto; **to have a** – *Ven., Col., Andes* tener un ratón o estar enratonado (*tras una borrachera*), *Méx.*, estar crudo o tener una cruda; *Ch.* la mona: *C.A.* de goma; *Ríopl.* resaca.

hap•haz•ard [hæphǽzə‐d] *adj.* al azar, al acaso, a la ventura, a la buena de Dios; *adj.* casual; impensado.

hap•haz•ard•ly [hæphǽzə‐dlɪ] *adv.* = **haphazard.**

hap•less [hǽplɪs] *adj.* desventurado, desgraciado.

hap•pen [hǽpən] *v.* suceder, pasar, acontecer, sobrevivir, acaecer; **to – to hear (do, be,** *etc.*) oír (hacer, estar, *etc.*) por casualidad; **to – to pass by** acertar a pasar; **to – on (upon)** encontrarse con, tropezar con.

hap•pen•ing [hǽpənɪŋ] *s.* acontecimiento, suceso.

hap•pi•ly [hǽplɪ] *adv.* felizmente; afortunadamente.

hap•pi•ness [hǽpɪnɪs] *s.* felicidad, dicha, contento.

hap•py [hǽpɪ] *adj.* feliz; dichoso, alegre; afortunado; **to be – to** alegrarse de.

ha·rangue [hərǽŋ] *s.* arenga, perorata; *v.* arengar, perorar.

ha·rass [hǽrəs] *v.* acosar, hostigar, molestar.

har·bor [hárbə] *s.* puerto; asilo, refugio, abrigo; *v.* abrigar; hospedar; albergar.

hard [hard] *adj.* duro; (*stiff*) tieso; (*difficult*) arduo, difícil; — **cash** dinero contante y sonante, metálico; — **coal** antracita; — **liquor** licor espiritoso (*aguardiente, ron etc.*); — **of hearing** medio sordo; — **water** agua cruda; *adv.* fuerte, recio, con fuerza; con empeño, con ahinco; — **by** muy cerca; — **core** núcleo resistente (*de un grupo*); — **hearted** de corazón duro; **hard–working** muy trabajador, industrioso, aplicado.

hard·en [hárdŋ] *v.* endurcer(se).

hard·en·ing [hárdŋɪŋ] *s.* endurecimiento.

hard·ly [hárdlɪ] *adv.* apenas; a duras penas; difícilmente; duramente, con aspereza; probablemente no.

hard·ness [hárdnɪs] *s.* dureza; aspereza; dificultad.

hard·ship [hárdʃɪp] *s.* apuro, aflicción; trabajo, penalidad.

hard·ware [hárdwɛr] *s.* quincalla, quincallería; — **shop** quincallería, ferretería.

hardy [hárdɪ] *adj.* robusto, fuerte, recio, atrevido.

hare [hɛr] *s.* liebre.

hare·brained [hérbrénd] *adj.* atolondrado, ligero de cascos.

hare·lip [hérlɪp] *s.* labio leporino.

har·em [hérəm] *s.* harén.

har·lot [hárlət] *s.* ramera, prostituta.

harm [harm] *s.* daño, mal; perjuicio; *v.* dañar; hacer mal, hacer daño; perjudicar.

harm·ful [hármfəl] *adj.* dañoso; dañino, nocivo, perjudicial.

harm·less [hármlɪs] *adj.* innocuo; inofensivo; no dañoso, inocente.

harm·less·ness [hármlɪsnɪs] *s.* innocuidad; inocencia, falta de malicia.

har·mon·ic [harmánɪk] *adj.* armónico.

har·mo·ni·ous [harmónɪəs] *adj.* armonioso.

har·mo·nize [hármənaɪz] *v.* armonizar; concordar; congeniar.

har·mo·ny [hármənɪ] *s.* armonía.

har·ness [hárnɪs] *s.* guarniciones (*de caballerías*); jaez, aparejo; **to get back in** — volver al servicio activo, volver a trabajar; volver a la rutina; *v.* enjaezar, poner guarniciones a (*un caballo, mula, etc.*).

harp [harp] *s.* arpa; *v.* tocar el arpa; **to — on** repetir constantemente (*una nota, palabra, tema, etc.*); porfiar en.

har·poon [harpún] *s.* arpón; *v.* arponear, pescar con arpón.

har·row [hǽro] *s.* rastro, rastrillo, grada; *v.* rastrear, rastrillar; atormentar; horrorizar.

har·row·ing [hǽrəwɪŋ] *adj.* horrendo, horripilante, que pone los cabellos de punta; espeluznante.

har·ry [hǽrɪ] *v.* acosar, molestar; asolar.

harsh [harʃ] *adj.* tosco, áspero; severo, austero.

harsh·ness [hárʃnɪs] *s.* aspereza; tosquedad; severidad.

har·vest [hárvɪst] *s.* cosecha; siega, agosto; recolección; *v.* cosechar; segar.

hash [hæʃ] *s.* picadillo.

haste [hest] *s.* prisa; apresuramiento; **in** — de prisa; **to make** — darse prisa, apresurarse; *Am.* apurarse.

has·ten [hésŋ] *v.* apresurar(se), precipitar(se); darse prisa.

hast·i·ly [héstɪlɪ] *adv.* aprisa, de prisa, apresuradamente, precipitadamente.

hast·y [héstɪ] *adj.* apresurado; precipitado.

hat [hæt] *s.* sombrero.

hatch [hætʃ] *v.* empollar; criar pollos; idear, maquinar; *s.* cría, nidada, pollada; escotillón, trampa (*puerta en el suelo*); escotilla.

hatch·et [hætʃɪt] *s.* hacha; **to bury the** — echar pelillos a la mar, olvidar rencores o enemistades.

hate [het] *s.* odio; aborrecimiento; *v.* odiar; aborrecer; detestar.

hate·ful [hétfəl] *adj.* odioso, aborrecible.

ha·tred [hétrɪd] *s.* odio, aversión.

haugh·ti·ly [hótɪlɪ] *adv.* con altivez, altaneramente, arrogantemente.

haugh·ti·ness [hótɪnɪs] *s.* altanería, altivez.

haugh·ty [hótɪ] *adj.* altivo, altanero, arrogante.

haul [hol] *v.* (*transport*) acarrear, transprotar; (*pull*) jalar (*halar*); tirar de; (*drag*) arrastrar; **to — down the flag** arriar (*o bajar*) la bandera; *s.* acarreo; transporte; tirón, estirón; buena pesca; ganancia, botín.

haunch [hontʃ] *s.* anca.

haunt [hont] *v.* frecuentar a menudo; andar por, vagar por (*como fantasma o espectro*); **that idea —s me** me persigue esa idea; — **ed house** casa de espantos, fantasmas o aparecidos; *s.* guarida.

have [hæv] *v.* tener; poseer; haber (*v. aux.*); **to — a suit made** mandar hacer un traje; **to — a look at** dar un vistazo a, echar una mirada a; **to — to** tener que; deber; **I'll not — it so** no lo toleraré, no lo permitiré; **what did she — on?** ¿qué vestido llevaba (puesto)?

ha·ven [hévən] *s.* asilo, abrigo, refugio; puerto.

hav·oc [hǽvək] *s.* estrago, estropicio, ruina; **to cause** — hacer estragos.

hawk [hok] *s.* halcón; *v.* pregonar (*mercancías*).

haw·thorn [hóθrn] *s.* espino.

hay [he] *s.* heno, paja, hierba seca; — **fever** catarro asmático.

hay•loft [hélɔft] *s.* henil, pajar.

hay•stack [héstæk] *s.* montón de heno o paja.

haz•ard [hǽzə·d] *s.* azar; riesgo, peligro; estorbo, obstáculo (*en el campo de golf*); *v.* arriesgar, aventurar.

haz•ard•ous [hǽzə·dəs] *adj.* peligroso.

haze [hez] *s.* bruma, neblina, niebla; *v.* atormentar, hostigar (*con bromas estudiantiles*).

ha•zel [hézļ] *s.* avellano; **– nut** avellana; *adj.* de avellano; avellanado, color de avellana.

haz•y [hézı] *adj.* (*weather*) nublado, brumoso; (*mind*) confuso.

he [hi] *pron. pers.* él; **– who** el que, quien; **he–goat** macho cabrío.

head [hɛd] *s.* cabeza; cabecera (*de cama*); jefe; **– of hair** cabellera; **game of –s or tails** juego de cara y cruz, juego de las chapas, *Ven., Col., Andes, Ch.* juego de cara y sello; *Méx.* juego de águila y sol; **to be out of one's –** delirar, estar delirante; **to come to a –** madurar; supurar (*un absceso*); **to keep one's –** conservar la calma, no perder la cabeza; **it goes to his –** se desvanece; se le sube a la cabeza; *adj.* principal, primero; de proa, de frente; **head–on** de frente; *v.* encabezar; ir a la cabeza de; acaudillar, mandar, dirigir; **to – off** atajar; detener, refrenar; **to – towards** dirigirse a, encaminarse a.

head•ache [hédek] *s.* dolor de cabeza.

head•dress [héddrɛs] *s.* tocado, adorno para la cabeza.

head•gear [hédgɪr] *s.* sombrero, gorro, gorra; tocado, toca (*de mujer*); cabezada (*de guarnición para caballo*).

head•ing [hédɪŋ] *s.* encabezamiento, título.

head•land [hédlənd] *s.* cabo, promontorio.

head•light [hédlaɪt] *s.* linterna delantera, faro delantero.

head•line [hédlaɪn] *s.* título, encabezado.

head•long [hédlɔ́ŋ] *adv.* de cabeza; precipitadamente.

head•quar•ters [hédkwɔ́rɾə·z] *s.* cuartel general; jefatura; oficina principal.

head•set [hédsɛt] *s.* receptor de cabeza.

head•strong [hédstrɔŋ] *adj.* testarudo, porfiado, obstinado.

head•way [hédwe] *s.* progreso, avance; **to make –** avanzar, adelantar, progresar.

heal [hil] *v.* curar; sanar; cicatrizar.

health [hélθ] *adj.* salud; sanidad, salubridad.

health•ful [hélθfəl] *adj.* sano; salubre; saludable.

health•ful•ness [hélθfəlnıs] *s.* salubridad; sanidad.

health•y [hélθı] *adj.* sano; saludable.

heap [hip] *s.* montón; pila; *v.* amontonar; apilar.

hear [hɪr] *v.* (*listen*) oír; escuchar; (*get news*) tener noticias; **to – about someone** oír hablar de alguien; **to – from someone** tener noticias de alguien;

to – of saber de, tener noticias de, oír hablar de; **I – d that ...** oí decir que ...

heard [hɝd] *pret. & p.p.* de **to hear**.

hear•er [hírə·] *s.* oyente.

hear•ing [hírɪŋ] *s.* (*sense*) oído; (*trial*) audiencia; examen de testigos; **hard of –** medio sordo, algo sordo; **within –** al alcance del oído; **– aid** aparato auditivo.

hear•say [hírse] *s.* habilla, rumor; **by –** de oídas.

hearse [hɝs] *s.* carroza fúnebre.

heart [hɑrt] *s.* (*organ*) corazón; (*spirit*) ánimo; **at – en realidad, en el fondo; from the bottom of one's –** de corazón, con toda el alma; con toda sinceridad; **to learn by –** aprender de memoria; **to take –** cobrar ánimo; **to take to –** tomar en serio; tomar a pechos; **– attack** ataque cardíaco.

heart•ache [hɑ́rtek] *s.* dolor del corazón; angustia, pesar, congoja.

heart•bro•ken [hɑ́rtbrokən] *adj.* traspasado de dolor, acongojado, angustiado; desengañado.

heart•en [hɑ́rt ŋ] *v.* animar.

heart•felt [hɑ́rtfɛlt] *adj.* sentido, cordial, sincero; **my – sympathy** mi más sentido pésame.

hearth [hɑrθ] *s.* hogar; fogón.

heart•i•ly [hɑ́rtļı] *adv.* de corazón; cordialmente; de buena gana; **to eat –** comer con apetito; comer bien (*o mucho*).

heart•less [hɑ́rtlıs] *adj.* de mal corazón; cruel; insensible.

heart–rend•ing [hɑ́rtrɛndɪŋ] *adj.* angustioso; agudo.

heart•y [hɑ́rtı] *adj.* sincero, cordial; sano, fuerte; **– food** alimento nutritivo; **a – laugh** una buena carcajada; **– meal** comida abundante.

heat [hit] *s.* (*hot*) calor; ardor; (*emotion*) vehemencia; celo (*ardor sexual de la hembra*); calefacción (*para las habitaciones*); corrida, carrera (*de prueba*); *v.* calentar(se); acalorar(se).

heat•er [hítə·] *s.* calentador; calorífero.

hea•then [híðən] *s.* pagano, gentil, idólatra; paganos; *adj.* pagano; irreligioso.

heat•ing [hítıŋ] *s.* calefacción.

heave [hiv] *v.* levantar, alzar (*con esfuerzo*); arrojar, lanzar; exhalar (*un suspiro*); jalar (*un cable*); jadear; basquear; hacer esfuerzos por vomitar.

heav•en [hévən] *s.* cielo.

heav•en•ly [hévənlı] *adj.* celeste; celestial; divino.

heav•i•ly [hévļı] *adv.* pesadamente, lentamente; copiosamente, excesivamente.

heav•i•ness [hévınıs] *s.* pesadez, pesantez; opresión, abatimiento.

heav•y [hévı] *adj.* (*weight*) pesado; (*thick*) grueso; (*coarse*) burdo; (*oppressive*) opresivo; **– rain** aguacero recio o fuerte; **with a – heart** abatido, acongojado.

heav·y·weight [hévɪwet] *s. & adj.* peso pesado (*fuerte*).

hec·tic [héktɪk] *adj.* febril; inquieto.

hedge [hɛdʒ] *s.* seto; vallado, barrera; *v.* cercar; poner valla o seto a; evitar o evadir contestaciones.

hedge·hog [hédʒhɑg] *s.* erizo.

he·don·ism [hídənɪzm] *s.* hedonismo.

hee [hid] *v.* atender; hacer caso; prestar atención; *s.* atención, cuidado; **to pay – to** prestar atención a; hacer caso de

heed·less [hídlɪs] *adj.* descuidado; desatento.

heel [hil] *s.* talón (*del pie o de una media*); tacón (*del zapato*); **head over -s** patas arriba; *v.* poner tacón a; poner talón a.

he·gem·o·ny [hɪdʒməní] *s.* hegemonía.

heif·er [héfɚ] *s.* novilla, vaquilla.

height [haɪt] *s.* altura; elevación; **– of folly** colmo de la locura.

height·en [háɪtn] *v.* avivar; aumentar(se); realzar.

hei·nous [hénəs] *adj.* aborrecible, odioso; malvado.

heir [ɛr] *s.* heredero.

heir·ess [érɪs] *s.* heredera.

held [hɛld] *pret. & p.p. de* **to hold**.

hel·i·cop·ter [hélɛkɑptɚ] *s.* helicóptero.

he·li·um [hílɪəm] *s.* helio.

hell [hɛl] *s.* infierno.

hel·lo [hɛló] *interj.* ¡hola!; ¡halo!

helm [hɛlm] *s.* timón.

hel·met [hɛlmɪt] *s.* yelmo.

help [hɛlp] *s.* (*aid*) ayuda; auxilio; remedio; alivio; (*employee*) criado o criados, empleado o empleados; *v.* ayudar, asistir; auxiliar; remediar; servir (*algo de comer*); **to – down** ayudar a bajar **– yourself** sírvase Vd. (*de comer o beber*); tómelo Vd., está a la disposición de Vd.; **he cannot – it** no puede evitarlo; **he cannot – doing it** no puede menos de hacerlo; **he cannot – but come** no puede menos de venir.

help·er [hɛlpɚ] *s.* ayudante, asistente.

help·ful [hɛlpfəl] *adj.* útil, servicial; provechoso.

help·ing [hɛlpɪŋ] *s.* ayuda; porción (*que se sirve en la mesa*).

help·less [hélplɪs] *adj.* (*defenseless*) desamparado; (*handicapped*) desvalido; imposibilitado; incapaz; (*confused*) perplejo; indeciso (*sin saber qué hacer*); **a – situation** una situación irremediable.

help·less·ness [hélplɪsnɪs] *s.* incapacidad; incompetencia; impotencia, debilidad; abandono, desamparo.

hem [hɛm] *s.* dobladillo, bastilla; *v.* dobladillar, bastillar, hacer dobladillos en (*la ropa*); **to – in** rodear, cercar; **to – and haw** toser y retoser (*fingidamente*); tartamudear, vacilar.

hem·i·sphere [hémɛsfɪr] *s.* hemisferio.

hem·lock [hémlɑk] *s.* cicuta (*hierba venenosa*); abeto

americano.

he·mo·glo·bin [hímoglobɪn] *s.* hemoglobina.

hemp [hɛmp] *s.* cáñamo, *Am.* sisal.

hem·stitch [hémstɪtʃ] *s.* dobladillo de ojo; *v.* hacer (*o echar*) dobladillo de ojo.

hen [hɛn] *s.* gallina; ave hembra.

hence [hɛns] *adv.* de (*o desde*) aquí; desde ahora; por lo tanto, por consiguiente; **a week –** de hoy en ocho días; de aquí a una semana.

hence·forth [hɛnsfórθ] *adv.* de aquí en adelante; de hoy en adelante; desde ahora.

hep·a·ti·tis [hɛpətáɪtɪs] *s.* hepatitis.

her [hɝ] *pron.* la; le, a ella; ella (*con preposición*); *adj.* su (sus), de ella.

her·ald [hérəld] *s.* heraldo; anunciador, proclamador, precursor; *v.* anunciar, proclamar, publicar.

herb [ɝb] *s.* hierba (yerba).

herd [hɝd] *s.* (*animals*) hato; rebaño; manada; tropel; tropilla; (*cattle*) ganado; (*people*) muchedumbre; **the common –** el populacho, la chusma; *v.* reunir, juntar (*el ganado*); ir en manadas, ir juntos.

herds·man [hɝdʒmən] *s.* vaquero, vaquerizo; pastor.

here [hɪr] *adv.* aquí; acá; **– it is** aquí está, helo aquí, aquí lo tiene Vd.; **– is to you!** ¡a la salud de Vd.!; **that is neither – nor there** eso no viene al caso.

here·af·ter [hɪræftɚ] *adv.* de aquí (*o de hoy*) en adelante; desde ahora en adelante; en lo futuro; *s.* **the –** la otra vida.

here·by [hɪrbáɪ] *adv.* por este medio; mediante la presente, por la presente; con estas palabras.

he·red·i·tar·y [hərédətɛrɪ] *adj.* hereditario.

he·red·i·ty [hərédətɪ] *s.* herencia.

here·in [hɪrín] *adv.* aquí dentro; en esto.

her·e·sy [hérəsɪ] *s.* herejía.

her·e·tic [hérətɪk] *s.* hereje.

here·to·fore [hɪrtəfór] *adv.* hasta ahora, hasta el presente.

here·with [hɪrwíθ] *adv.* aquí dentro, con esto, adjunto, incluso.

her·i·tage [hérətɪdʒ] *s.* herencia.

her·met·ic [hɚmétɪk] *adj.* hermético.

her·mit [hɝmɪt] *s.* ermitaño.

her·ni·a [hɝnɪə] *s.* hernia, ruptura, relajamiento.

he·ro [híro] *s.* héroe; protagonista.

he·ro·ic [hɪróɪk] *adj.* heroico.

her·o·in [héroɪn] *s.* heroína.

her·o·ine [héroɪn] *s.* heroína.

her·o·ism [héroɪzəm] *s.* heroísmo.

her·on [hérən] *s.* garza.

her·ring [hérɪŋ] *s.* arenque.

hers [hɝz] *pron. pos.* suyo (suya, suyos, suyas), de

ella; el suyo (la suya, los suyos, las suyas); el (la, los, las) de ella; **a friend of** – un amigo suyo.

her•self [hə•sélf] *pron.* ella misma; se (*como reflexivo*); **by** – sola; por sí (sola); **she – did it** ella misma lo hizo; **she talks to** – ella habla para sí, para consigo misma, habla para sus adentros, habla sola.

hes•i•tant [hézətənt] = **hesitating**.

hes•i•tate [hézətet] *v.* vacilar; titubear; dudar.

hes•i•tat•ing [hésətetɪŋ] *adj.* vacilante; indeciso; irresoluto; **-ly** *adv.* con vacilación.

hes•i•ta•tion [hɛzəté∫ən] *s.* vacilación; titubeo, duda.

hew [hju] *v.* tajar, cortar; picar (*piedra*); labrar (*madera, piedra*).

hewn [hjun] *p.p. de* **to hew**.

hey [he] *interj.* ¡he!; ¡oiga!; ¡oye!

hi•ber•nate [háɪbə•net] *v.* invernar.

hic•cup, hic•cough [híkʌp] *s.* hipo; *v.* hipar, tener hipo.

hick•o•ry [híkərɪ] *s.* nogal americano; – **nut** nuez (*del nogal americano*).

hid [hɪd] *pret. & p.p. de* **to hide**.

hid•den [híd ŋ] *p.p. de* **to hide**; *adj.* oculto, escondido

hide [haɪd] *v.* ocultar(se); esconder(se); **to – from** esconderse de, recatarse de; *s.* cuero, piel; **to play – and seek** jugar al escondite.

hid•e•ous [hídɪəs] *adj.* horrendo, horripilante, feote.

hi•er•ar•chy [háɪərɑrkɪ] *s.* jerarquía.

hi•er•o•glyph•ic [haɪərogléɪfɪk] *adj. & s.* jeroglífico.

high [haɪ] *adj.* alto; – **altar** mayor; – **and dry** enjuto; en seco; solo, abandonado; – **antiquity** antigüedad remota; – **explosive** explosivo de gran potencia; – **tide** pleamar; – **wind** ventarrón, viento fuerte; **in gear** en directa, en tercera velocidad; **two feet** – dos pies de alto; **it is – time that** ya es hora de que; **to be in – spirits** estar muy animado; *adv.* alto; a precio subido; en alto; **to look – and low** buscar por todas partes; **high–grade** de calidad superior; **high–handed** arbitrario, despótico; **high–minded** magnánimo; orgulloso; **high–sounding** altisonante, rimbombante; **high–strung** muy tenso.

high•land [háɪlənd] *s.* tierra montañosa; **the Highlands** las montañas de Escocia.

high•light [háɪlaɪt] *s.* lo más notable.

high•ly [háɪlɪ] *adv.* altamente; sumamente; muy; – **paid** muy bien pagado.

high•ness [háɪnɪs] *s.* altura; elevación; Alteza (*título*).

high•way [háɪwe] *s.* camino real; carretera, calzada.

high•way•man [háɪwemən] *s.* forajido, salteador de caminos, bandido.

hike [haɪk] *s.* caminata, paseo largo; *Am.* andada; *v.*

dar (*o* echar) una caminata.

hill [hɪl] *s.* colina, collado, cerro; montoncillo de tierra; *Andes, Am.* loma; **ant** – hormiguero; **down** – cuesta abajo; **up** – cuesta arriba.

hil•lock [hílək] *s.* collado, otero, montecillo.

hill•side [hílsaɪd] *s.* ladera.

hill•top [híltop] *s.* cumbre, cima (*de una colina*).

hill•y [hílɪ] *adj.* montuoso; accidentado.

hilt [hɪlt] *s.* empuñadura, puño (*de una espada o daga*).

him [hɪm] *pron.* le; lo; él (*con preposición*).

him•self [hɪmsélf] *pron.* él mismo; se (*como reflexivo*); a sí mismo; *véase* **herself**.

hind [haɪnd] *adj.* trasero; posterior; *s.* cierva; – **most** *adj.* último, postrero.

hin•der [híndə•] *v.* estorbar, impedir, obstruir.

hin•drance [híndrəns] *s.* estorbo, obstáculo, impedimento.

hinge [hɪndʒ] *s.* gozne; bisagra; *v.* engoznar, poner goznes; **to – on** girar sobre; depender de.

hint [hɪnt] *s.* indirecta, insinuación; sugestión; **not to take the** – no darse por entendido; *v.* insinuar, intimar, sugerir indirectamente.

hip [hɪp] *s.* cadera.

hip•po•pot•a•mus [hɪpəpátəməs] *s.* hipopótamo.

hire [haɪr] *s.* (*rent*) alquiler; (*pay*) paga, sueldo; *v.* alquilar; emplear, dar empleo, *C.A., Ven., Col.* enganchar, *Am.* conchabar: **to – out** alquilarse, ponerse a servir a otro.

his [hɪz] *pron. pos.* suyo (suya, suyos, suyas), de él; el suyo (la suya, los suyos, las suyas); el (la, los, las) de él; **a friend of** – un amigo suyo; *adj.* su (sus), de él.

hiss [hɪs] *s.* silbido, chiflido; siseo; *v.* sisear, silbar, chiflar.

his•to•ri•an [hɪstórɪən] *s.* historiador.

his•to•ric [hɪstórɪk] *adj.* histórico.

his•to•ri•cal [hɪstórɪkļ] *adj.* histórico.

his•to•ry [hístrɪ] *s.* historia.

his•tri•on•ics [hɪstrɪónɪks] *s.* histrionismo.

hit [hɪt] *v.* pegar, golpear; dar (*un golpe*); dar en (*o* con); chocar; **they – it off well** se llevan bien, congenian; **to – the mark** acertar, atinar, dar en el blanco; **to – upon** dar con; encontrarse con, encontrar por casualidad; *pret. & p.p. de* **to hit**; *s.* golpe; choque; golpe de fortuna; pulla, dicharacho; **to be a great** – ser un gran éxito; **to make a – with someone** caerle en gracia a una persona; **hit–and–run** *adj.* que abandona a su víctima atropellada.

hitch [hɪt∫] *v.* atar, amarrar; enganchar; uncir (*bueyes*); dar un tirón; **to – one's chair nearer to** acercar su silla a; *s.* tiron; obstáculo, impedimento, tropiezo; enganche, enganchamiento.

hitch•hike [hít∫haɪk] *v.* viajar de gorra (*en automóvil*) *Méx.* irse o viajar de mosca; *Ch., Ríopl.* hacer dedo, ir a dedo.

hith·er [híðəˑ] *adv.* acá; **– and thither** acá y allá.

hith·er·to [híðəˑtú] *adv.* hasta aquí, hasta ahora, hasta hoy.

hive [haɪv] *s.* colmena; ejambre; **-s** ronchas (*de la piel*).

hoard [hord] *s.* tesoro escondido; acumulamiento secreto de provisiones; *v.* atesorar, guardar (*con avaricia*); acumular secretamente.

hoarse [hors] *adj.* bronco, áspero, ronco.

hoarse·ness [hórsnɪs] *s.* ronquera; carraspera.

hoar·y [hórɪ] *adj.* cano, encanecido, canoso.

hob·ble [hábḷ] *v.* (*limp*) cojear, renquear; (*tie*) maniatar o manear (*un animal*); (*impede*) impedir, estorbar; *s.* cojera; traba, maniota o manea (*cuerda con que se atan las manos de una bestia*).

hob·by [hábɪ] *s.* afición; trabajo hecho por afición (*no por obligación*).

ho·bo [hóbo] *s.* vagabundo.

hodge·podge [hádʒpadʒ] *s.* mezcolanza, baturrillo.

hoe [ho] *s.* azada, azadón; *v.* cavar, escardar, limpiar con azadón.

hog [hɑg] *s.* puerco, cerdo, cochino; *v.* apropiárselo todo.

hoist [hɔɪst] *v.* alzar, levantar; izar (*la bandera, las velas*); *s.* elevador, *Am.* malacate.

hold [hold] *v.* tener(se); retener; detener; tener cabida para; sostener; mantener(se); opinar; celebrar (*una reunión, etc.*); ocupar (*un puesto*); ser válido (*un argumento o regla*); **to – back someone** detener (*o refrenar*) a alguien; **to – forth** perorar, hablar largamente; **to – in place** sujetar, **to – off** mantener(se) a distancia; mantenerse alejado; **to – on** agarrar(se); asir(se); persistir; **– on!** ¡agárrese bien! ¡deténgase! ¡pare!; **to – someone responsible** hacerle a uno responsable; **to – someone to his word** obligar a uno a cumplir su palabra; **to – oneself erect** tenerse o andar derecho; **to – one's own** mantenerse firme; **to – one's tongue** callarse; **to – out** continuar, durar; mantenerse firme; **to – over** aplazar; durar; continuar en un cargo; **to – still** estarse quieto o callado; **to – tight** apretar; **to – to one's promise** cumplir con la promesa; **to – up** levantar, alzar; detener; asaltar, atracar (*para robar*); **how much does it –?** ¿cuánto le cabe? *s.* agarro; dominio; influencia; autoridad; bodega (*de un barco*); cabina de carga (*de un aeroplano*); **to get – of** asir, agarrar; atrapar; **to take – of** coger, agarrar, asir.

hold·er [hóldəˑ] *s.* (*person*) tenedor, posesor; (*device*) receptáculo; cojinillo (*para coger un trasto caliente*); **cigarrette –** boquilla, **pen–** portaplumas.

hold·up [hóldʌp] *s.* asalto, atraco.

hole [hol] *s.* agujero; abertura; hoyo, hueco, cavidad; bache (*de un camino*); **swimming –** charco,

remanso; **to be in a –** hallarse en un apuro o aprieto.

hol·i·day [háləde] *s.* día de fiesta, día festivo, festividad; **-s** días de fiesta; vacaciones.

holi·ness [hólɪnɪs] *s.* santidad.

hol·low [hálo] *adj.* (*empty*) hueco; vacío; (*concave*) cóncavo; hundido; (*insincere*) falso; *s.* hueco; hoyo; cavidad; concavidad; depresión; cañada, hondonada; *v.* ahuecar; excavar; ahondar.

hol·ly [hálɪ] *s.* agrifolio, acebo.

hol·ster [hólstəˑ] *s.* pistolera, funda (*de pistola*).

ho·ly [hólɪ] *adj.* santo; sagrado, sacro; **– water** agua bendita.

hom·age [hámɪdʒ] *s.* homenaje; reverencia, acatamiento; **to do –** acatar, rendir homenaje, honrar.

home [hom] *s.* casa, hogar; habitación; domicilio; **at – en** casa; *adj.* doméstico; casero; **– office** oficina matriz o central; **– rule** autonomía; **– run** *Méx., C.A., Ven., Col.* jonrón (*en beisbol*); **– stretch** último trecho (*de una carrera*); *adv.* a casa; en casa; **to strike –** herir en lo vivo; dar en el clavo o en el blanco.

home·land [hómlænd] *s.* tierra natal, suelo patrio.

home·less [hómlɪs] *adj.* sin casa; destituido.

home·like [hómlaɪk] *adj.* hogareño, cómodo.

home·ly [hómlɪ] *adj.* feo; llano; sencillo; casero, doméstico.

home·made [hómméd] *adj.* hecho en casa; doméstico, nacional, del país.

home·sick [hómsɪk] *adj.* nostálgico.

home·sick·ness [hómsɪknɪs] *s.* nostalgia.

home·stead [hómstɛd] *s.* heredad; casa y terrenos adyacentes.

home·ward [hómwəˑd] *adv.* a casa; hacia la patria; **– voyage** retorno, viaje de vuelta.

home·work [hómwɝk] *s.* trabajo de casa; trabajo hecho en casa.

hom·i·cide [háməsaɪd] *s.* homicidio; homicida, asesino.

ho·mo·ge·ne·ous [homədʒíniəs] *adj.* homogéneo.

ho·mog·e·nize [hamádʒənaɪz] *v.* homogenizar.

ho·mo·sex·u·al [homəsékʃjUḷ] *adj. & s.* homosexual.

hone [hon] *v.* amolar, asentar, afilar; *s.* piedra de afilar.

hon·est [ánɪst] *adj.* honrado, recto; genuino; **– goods** mercancías genuinas; **-ly** *adv.* honradamente; de veras.

hon·es·ty [ánɪstɪ] *s.* honradez, rectitud.

hon·ey [hʌnɪ] *s.* miel; dulzura; querido, querida.

hon·ey·comb [hʌnɪkom] *s.* panal.

hon·eyed [hʌnɪd] *adj.* meloso; dulce; melifluo.

hon·ey·moon [hʌnɪmun] *s.* luna de miel; viaje de novios, viaje de bodas; *v.* pasar la luna de miel.

hon·ey·suck·le [h ʌ nɪsʌk]] s. madreselva.

honk [hoŋk] s. pitazo (de automóvil); graznido (voz del ganso); v. donar la bocina; graznar.

hon·or [ánə] s. honor; honra; señoría (título); **upon my** – sobre mi palabra; v. honrar; dar honra.

hon·or·a·ble [ánərəb]] adj. honorable; honroso; honrado.

hon·or·a·ry [ánərɛrɪ] adj. honorario, honorífico.

hood [hUd] s. capucha, caperuza; capirote, cubierta (del motor); v. encapuchar, encapirotar.

hood·lum [hUdləm] s. malenate; antisocial.

hoof [hUf] s. casco, pezuña; pata (de caballo, toro, etc.).

hook [hUk] s. gancho, garfio; anzuelo (para pescar); **– and eye** corchete; macho y hembra, **by – or crook** por la buena o por la mala, por angas o por mangas; **on his own** – por su propia cuenta; v. enganchar(se); abrochar(se); pescar, coger con anzuelo; robar, hurtar.

hook·y [hUkɪ]: **to play** – hacer novillos, Carib. capear la escuela, Méx. pintar venado, C.A., Ven., Col. jubilarse; Ríopl. hacerse la rata (la rabona).

hoop [hup] s. aro; argolla; v. poner aro a; ceñir, cercar.

hoot [hut] v. ulular (dícese del buho, lechuza, etc.); rechiflar, ridiculizar; s. alarido, chillido.

hoot·ing [hUtɪŋ] s. grita, rechifla.

hop [hɑp] s. salto, brinco; baile; v. saltar; brincar.

hope [hop] s. esperanza; v. esperar; **to – for** esperar; **to – against – illness** enfermedad incurable; **it is –** no tiene remedio; **-ly** adv. sin esperanza, sin remedio.

hope·ful [hópfəl] adj. esperanzado, lleno de esperanza; **a young –** un joven prometedor; **–ly** adv. con esperanza; con ansia; lleno de esperanza.

hope·less [hóplɪs] adj. sin esperanza, falto de esperanza, desesperanzado; desesperado; irremediable; **– cause** causa pérdida; **– illness** enfermedad incurable; **it is –** no tiene remedio; **-ly** adv. sin esperanza, sin remedio.

hope·less·ness [hóplɪsnɪs] s. falta de esperanza, falta de remedio; desesperanza, desaliento.

horde [hord] s. horda; muchedumbre, gentío; enjambre.

ho·ri·zon [həráɪz n̩] s. horizonte.

hor·i·zon·tal [hərəzóntl]] adj. horizontal.

horn [hɔrn] s. (animal) cuerno; asta; (automobile) bocina, klaxon, trompa; (musical) corneta; trompeta; **– of plenty** cuerno de la abundancia; v. acornear, dar cornadas; **to – in** entremeterse.

hor·net [hɔrnɪt] s. avispón; **-'s nest** avispero.

hor·o·scope [hɔrəskop] s. horóscopo.

hor·ri·ble [hɔrəb]] adj. horrible; **horribly** adv. horriblemente.

hor·rid [hɔrɪd] adj. horrendo, horrible.

hor·ri·fy [hɔrəfaɪ] v. horrorizar, aterrorizar, espantar.

hor·ror [hɔrə] s. horror.

hors d'oeuvre [ɔrdɜ́ vrə] s. entremés; bocadillos.

horse [hors] s. caballo; caballete (de madera), borriquete (de carpinteros); **saddle** – caballo de silla; **– dealer** chalán; **– race** carrera de caballos; **– sense** sentido común.

horse·back [hɔrsbæk] s. lomo de caballo; **to ride –** montar a caballo, cabalgar, jinetear.

horse·fly [hɔrsflaɪ] s. tábano, mosca de caballo.

horse·laugh [hɔrslæf] s. carcajada, risotada.

horse·man [hɔrsmən] s. jinete.

horse·man·ship [hɔrsmən] s. equitación.

horse·pow·er [hɔrspaUə] s. caballo de fuerza.

horse·rad·ish [hɔrsrædɪʃ] s. rábano picante.

horse·shoe [hɔrsʃu] s. herradura.

hose [hoz] s. medias; manga o manguera (para regar); **men's** – calcetines.

ho·sier·y [hóʒrɪ] s. medias; calcetines; calcetería (negocio), **– shop** calcetería.

hos·pi·ta·ble [hɑspɪtəb]] adj. hospitalario.

hos·pi·tal [hɑspɪt]] s. hospital.

hos·pi·tal·i·ty [hɑspɪtǽlətɪ] s. hospitalidad.

host [host] s. huésped (el que hospeda), anfitrión (el que convida); hospedero, mesonero; hueste; ejército, multitud; hostia; **sacred** – hostia consagrada.

host·age [hóstɪdʒ] s. rehén (persona que queda como prenda en poder del enemigo).

host·ess [hóstɪs] s. huéspeda (la que hospeda o convida).

hos·tile [hóst]] adj. hostil.

hos·til·i·ty [hɑstílətɪ] s. hostilidad.

hot [hɑt] adj. caliente; caluroso; cálido; picante (como el pimentón, chile, ají, etc.); furioso; fresco, reciente; **– bed** semillero; **hot–headed** enojadizo, impetuoso; exaltado; **– house** invernáculo, invernadero; **it is – today** hace calor hoy.

ho·tel [hotél] s. hotel.

ho·tel–keep·er [hotélkípə] s. hotelero.

hot·ly [hárlɪ] adv. calurosamente, con vehemencia.

hound [haUnd] s. perro de busca, lebrel, galgo, sabueso, podenco; v. acosar, perseguir; azuzar, incitar.

hour [aUr] s. hora; **– hand** mano horario.

hour·ly [áUrlɪ] adv. por horas; a cada hora; a menudo; adj. frecuente; por horas.

house [haUs] s. (residence) casa; domicilio; (legislature) cámara, asamblea legislativa; **country –** casa de campo; **a full –** un lleno completo (en el teatro); [haUz] v. alojar; hospedar.

house·hold [háUshold] *s.* casa, familia; *adj.* casero; doméstico.

house·keep·er [háUskipə] *s.* casera; ama de llaves; **to be a good** – ser una mujer hacendosa.

house·keep·ing [háUskipɪŋ] *s.* gobierno de casa; quehaceres domésticos.

house·top [háUstɑp] *s.* techumbre, tejado.

house·wife [háUswaɪf] *s.* mujer de su casa; madre de familia.

house·work [háUswɚk] *s.* trabajo de casa; quehaceres domésticos.

hous·ing [háUzɪŋ] *s.* viviendas; programa de construcción de viviendas.

hove [hov] *pret. & p.p. de* **to heave**.

hov·el [h ʌ v]] *s.* choza, cabaña, *Carib., Ven.* bohío, *Méx.* jacal; cobertizo; *Ríopl.* tapera.

hov·er [h ʌ və] *v.* cernese (*como un pájaro*); vacilar; **to – around** revolotear; rondar.

how [haU] *adv.* cómo; **– beautiful!** ¡qué hermoso!; **– early (late, soon)?** ¿cuándo? ¿a qué hora?; **– far is it?** ¿a qué distancia está? ¿cuánto dista de aquí?; **– long?** ¿cuánto tiempo?; **– many?** ¿cuántos? **– much is it?** ¿cuánto es? ¿a cómo se vende? ¿cuál es el precio?; **– old are you?** ¿cuántos años tiene ud.?; **no matter – much** por mucho que; **he knows – difficult it is** él sabe lo difícil que es; él sabe cuán difícil es.

how·e·ver [haUévə] *adv. & conj.* sin embargo, no obstante, con todo, empero; **– difficult it may be** por muy difícil que sea; **– much** por mucho que.

howl [haUl] *s.* aullido, alarido, chillido, grito; *v.* aullar; chillar, dar alaridos; gritar.

hub [hʌb] *s.* cubo (*de una rueda*), eje, centro de actividad.

hub·bub [h ʌ bʌb] *s.* ajetreo; barullo.

huck·ster [h ʌ kstə] *s.* vendedor ambulante.

hud·dle [h ʌ d]] *s.* montón, confusión; tropel; **to be in a** – estar agrupados (*en fútbol para planear una jugada*); **to get in a** – agruparse (*para aconsejarse o planear algo*); *v.* amontonar(se); acurrucarse.

hue [hju] *s.* tinte, matiz.

huff [hʌf] *s.* enojo, rabieta; **to get into a** – enojarse.

hug [hʌg] *v.* abrazar, estrechar; **to – the coast** costear; *s.* abrazo fuerte.

huge [hjudʒ] *adj.* enorme; descomunal.

hull [hʌl] *s.* casco (*de una nave*); armazón (*de una aeronave*); vaina, hollejo (*de ciertas legumbres*); *v.* mondar, pelar desvainar, deshollejar.

hum [hʌm] *v.* canturrear (*o* canturriar), tatarear; zumbar (*dícese de insectos, maquinaria, etc.*); **to – to sleep** arrullar; *s.* canturreo, tarareo; zumbido; *interj.* ¡hum!; ¡ejém!

hu·man [hjúmən] *adj.* humano; *s.* ser humano.

hu·mane [hjumén] *adj.* humano; humanitario.

hu·man·ism [hjəumənɪzm] *s.* humanismo.

hu·man·i·tar·i·am [hjumænətériən] *adj.* humanitario; *s.* filántropo.

hu·man·i·ty [hjum æ nətɪ] *s.* humanidad; **– ies** humanidades.

hum·ble [h ʌ mb]] *adj.* humilde; *v.* humillar; **humbly** *adv.* humildemente, con humildad.

hum·ble·ness [h ʌ mb] nɪs] *s.* humildad.

hu·mid [hjúmɪd] *adj.* húmedo.

hu·mid·i·fy [hjumídəfaɪ] *v.* humedecer.

hu·mid·i·ty [hjumídətɪ] *d.* humedad.

hu·mil·i·ate [hjumílɪet] *v.* humillar.

hu·mil·i·a·tion [hjumɪlɪéʃən] *s.* humillación.

hu·mil·i·ty [hjumílətɪ] *s.* humildad.

hum·ming·bird [h ʌ mɪŋbɚd] *s.* colibrí, pájaro mosca, *Méx.* chuparrosa, *Am.* chupaflor, *Am.* guainumbi; *Ríopl., Ch.* picaflor.

hu·mor [hjÚmə] *s.* humor, humorismo, gracia; capricho; **out of** – de mal humor, malhumorado, disgustado; *v.* seguir el humor (*a una persona*), complacer; mimar.

hu·mor·ous [hjÚmərəs] *adj.* humorístico, gracioso, cómico, chistoso.

hump [hʌmp] *s.* joroba, corcova, giba; *v.* encorvarse.

hump·back [h ʌ mpbæk] = **hunchback**.

hunch [hʌntʃ] *s.* joroba, corcova, giba; presentimiento, corazonada; *v.* encorvar (*la espalda*).

hunch·back [h ʌ ntʃbæk] *s.* joroba; jorobado.

hun·dred [h ʌ ndrəd] *adj.* cien(to); *s.* ciento; **-s** centenares, cientos.

hun·dredth [h ʌ ndrədθ] *adj.* centésimo.

hung [hʌŋ] *pret. & p.p. de* **to hang**.

hun·ger [h ʌ ngə] *s.* hambre; *v.* tener hambre, estar hambriento; **to – for** ansiar, anhelar.

hun·gri·ly [h ʌ ŋgrɪlɪ] *adv.* con hambre, hambrientamente.

hun·gry [h ʌ ŋgrɪ] *adj.* hambriento; **to be** – tener hambre.

hunk [hʌŋk] *s.* pedazo grande; mendrugo (*de pan*).

hunt [hʌnt] *v.* cazar; perseguir; buscar; escudriñar; **to – down** dar caza a; seguir la pista de; **to – for** buscar; *s.* caza, cacería, busca, búsqueda; persecución.

hunt·er [h ʌ ntə] *s.* cazador; buscador; perro de caza, perro de busca.

hunst·sman [h ʌ ntsmən] *s.* cazador.

hurl [hɚl] *v.* arrojar, lanzar.

hur·rah [hərɔ́] *interj.* ¡hurra! ¡viva! *v.* vitorear.

hur·ri·cane [h ɚ́ ɪken] *s.* huracán.

hur·ried [hɚɪd] *adj.* apresurado; **-ly** *adv.* de prisa, apresuradamente; a escape.

hur•ry [hɜ̃ɪ] *v.* apresurar(se); precipitar(se); dar(se) prisa; apurarse; correr; **to – in (out)** entrar (salir) de prisa; **to – up** apresurar(se); dar(se) prisa; *s.* prisa; precipitación; **to be in a –** tener prisa, ir de prisa, estar de prisa.

hurt [hɜ̃t] *v.* hacer daño; dañar; perjudicar; herir; lastimar; doler; **to – one's feelings** darle a uno que sentir; lastimar a uno; **my tooth –s** me duele la muela; *pret. & p.p. de* **to hurt**; *s.* daño; herida; lesión; dolor.

hus•band [hʌ́zbənd] *s.* marido, esposo.

hush [hʌʃ] *v.* acallar, aquietar; callar(se); **–!** ¡chitón! ¡silencio! ¡cállese! ¡quieto!; **to – up a scandal** encubrir un escándalo; *s.* silencio, quietud.

husk [hʌsk] *s.* cáscara, hollejo, vaina; *v.* mondar, pelar, deshollejar.

huskɜ**y** [hʌ́ski] *adj.* ronco; forzudo, fuerte; cascarudo.

hus•tle [hʌ́sl] *v.* apresurar(se); apurarse; menear(se); atropellar; *s.* prisa, apresuramiento, meneo; actividad; **– and bustle** vaivén.

hut [hʌt] *s.* choza, cabaña, *Am.* bohío.

hy•a•cinth [hátəsɪnθ] *s.* jacinto.

hy•brid [háɪbrɪd] *adj.* híbrido.

hy•drau•lic [haɪdrɔ́lɪk] *adj.* hidráulico.

hy•dro•e•lec•tric [haɪdroiléktrɪk] *adj.* hidroeléctrico.

hy•dro•gen [háɪdrədʒən] *s.* hidrógeno.

hy•dro•pho•bi•a [haɪdrofóbɪə] *s.* hidrofobia.

hy•dro•plane [háɪdrəplen] *s.* hidroplano, hidroavión.

hy•giene [háɪdʒin] *s.* higiene.

hymn [hɪm] *s.* himno.

hy•phen [háɪfən] *s.* guión.

hyp•no•sis [hɪpnósɪs] *s.* hipnosis.

hy•poc•ri•sy [hɪpókrəsɪ] *s.* hipocresía.

hyp•o•crite [hípəkrɪt] *s.* hipócrita.

hyp•o•crit•i•cal [hɪpəkrítɪk] *adj.* hipócrita.

hy•poth•e•sis [haɪpáθəsɪs] *s.* hipótesis.

hys•ter•i•cal [hɪstérɪk] *adj.* histérico.

I

I [aɪ] *pron. pers.* yo.

I•beri•an [aɪbírɪən] *adj.* ibérico, ibero.

ice [aɪs] *s.* (*solid*) hielo; (*food*) helado; sorbete; **– cream** helado; **icecream parlor** *Am.* heladería; **– skates** patines de cuchilla; **– water** agua helada; *v.* helar; escarchar, alfeñicar, cubrir con escarcha (*un pastel*).

ice•berg [áɪsbɜ̃g] *s.* montaña de hielo, témpano.

ice•box [áɪsbɑks] *s.* nevera, *Am.* refrigerador.

ice•man [áɪsmæn] *s.* vendedor de hielo.

i•ci•cle [áɪsɪk] *s.* carámbano.

i•con•o•clasm [aɪkɑ́nəklæzəm] *s.* iconoclasmo.

ic•y [áɪsɪ] *adj.* helado, frío; congelado; cubierto de hielo.

i•de•a [aɪdíə] *s.* idea.

i•de•al [aɪdíəl] *adj. & s.* ideal.

i•de•al•ism [aɪdíəlɪzəm] *s.* idealismo.

i•de•al•ist [aɪdíəlɪst] *s.* idealista.

i•de•al•is•tic [aɪdiəlístɪk] *adj.* idealista.

i•den•ti•cal [aɪdéntɪk] *adj.* idéntico.

i•den•ti•fy [aɪdéntəfaɪ] *v.* identificar.

i•den•ti•ty [aɪdéntətɪ] *s.* identidad.

i•de•ol•o•gy [aɪdɪlɑ́dʒɪ] *s.* ideología.

id•i•om [ídɪəm] *s.* modismo, idiotismo.

id•i•o•syn•cra•sy [ɪdɪosínkrəsɪ] *s.* idiosincrasia.

id•i•ot [ídɪət] *s.* idiota.

id•i•ot•ic [ɪdɪótɪk] *adj.* idiota.

i•dle [árd] *adj.* ocioso; perezoso, holgazán; vano; desocupado; *v.* holgazanear; perder el tiempo; funcionar (*el motor solo, sin engranar*); **idly** *adv.* ociosamente; inútilmente; perezosamente.

i•dle•ness [áɪdnɪs] *s.* ociosidad; ocio, desocupación; pereza, holgazanería.

id•ler [áɪdlə] *s.* holgazán, haragán.

i•dol [áɪd] *s.* ídolo.

i•dol•a•try [aɪdólətrɪ] *s.* idolatría.

i•dol•ize [áɪdlaɪz] *v.* idolatrar.

i•dyl [áɪd] *s.* idilio.

if [ɪf] *conj.* si.

ig•nite [ɪgnáɪt] *v.* encender(se), inflamar(se); prender, pegar fuego a.

ig•ni•tion [ɪgníʃən] *s.* ignición, encendido (*de un motor*); **– switch** interruptor de encendido, *Méx., C.A., Ven., Carib.* switch de ignición.

ig•no•ble [ɪgnób] *adj.* innoble; bajo, vil.

ig•no•rance [ígnərəns] *s.* ignorancia.

ig•no•rant [ígnərənt] *adj.* ignorante.

ig•nore [ɪgnór] *v.* no hacer caso de, desatender; desairar.

ill [ɪl] *adj.* enfermo; malo; **– nature** mal genio, mala índole; **– will** mala voluntad, ojeriza, inquina; *s.* mal; enfermedad; calamidad, infortunio; *adv.* mal, malamente; **– at ease** inquieto, intranquilo; **ill-bred** mal criado; **ill–clad** mal vestido; **ill-humored** malhumorado; **ill-mannered** descortés, grosero; **ill-natured** de mala índole, *Ven., Col., Méx.* mal genioso; **ill-advised** mal aconsejado.

il•le•gal [ɪlíg] *adj.* ilegal; ilícito.

il•legit•i•ɜ•mate [ɪlɪdʒítəmɪt] *adj.* ilegítimo; bastardo.

il•lic•it [ɪlísɪt] *adj.* ilícito.

il•lit•er•a•cy [ɪlítərəsɪ] *s.* analfabetismo

il•lit•er•ate [ɪlítərɪt] *adj. & s.* analfabeto.

ill•ness [Ílnɪs] s. mal, enfermedad.

il•lu•mi•nate [ɪlúmənet] v. iluminar; alumbrar; esclarecer.

il•lu•mi•na•tion [ɪlumənéʃən] s. iluminación; alumbrado.

il•lu•sion [ɪlúʒən] s. ilusión.

il•lu•sive [ɪlúsɪv] adj. ilusorio, ilusivo, falaz.

il•lu•so•ry [ɪlúsərɪ] adj. ilusorio, ilusivo, engañoso.

il•lus•trate [ɪləstrét] v. ilustrar; esclarecer.

il•lus•tra•tion [ɪləstréʃən] s. ilustración; grabado, estampa; aclaración, esclarecimiento.

il•lus•tra•tor [íləstretə] s. ilustrador.

il•lus•tri•ous [ɪl Ʌ strɪəs] adj. ilustre.

im•age [Ímɪdʒ] s. imagen.

im•age•ry [Ímɪdʒrɪ] s. conjunto de imágenes, figuras; fantasía.

i•mag•i•nar•y [ɪmédʒənɛrɪ] adj. imaginario.

i•mag•i•na•tion [ɪmædʒənéʃən] s. imaginación; imaginativa.

i•mag•i•na•tive [ɪmédʒənetɪv] adj. imaginativo.

i•mag•ine [ɪmédʒɪn] v. imaginar(se); figurarse.

im•be•cile [Ímbəsɪl] adj. & s. imbécil.

im•bibe [ɪmbátb] v. embeber, absorber; beber.

im•bue [ɪmbjú] v. imbuir, infundir; impregnar, empapar.

im•i•tate [Ímətet] v. imitar; remedar.

im•i•ta•tion [ɪmətéʃən] s. imitación; remedo; adj. imitado, de imitación.

im•i•ta•tor [Ímətetə] s. imitador; remedador.

im•mac•u•late [ɪmékjəlɪt] adj. inmaculado, sin mancha.

im•ma•te•ri•al [ɪmətírɪəl] adj. inmaterial, espiritual; **it is – to me** me es indiferente.

im•me•di•ate [ɪmídɪɪt] adj. inmediato; próximo; **-ly** adv. inmediatamente; en seguida; al punto, en el acto, al instante.

im•mense [ɪméns] adj. inmenso.

im•men•si•ty [ɪménsətɪ] s. inmensidad.

im•merse [ɪmɝs] v. sumergir, sumir.

im•mi•grant [Íməgrənt] adj. & s. inmigrante.

im•mi•grate [Íməgret] v. inmigrar.

im•mi•gra•tion [ɪməgréʃən] s. inmigración.

im•mi•nent [Ímənənt] adj. inminente.

im•mo•bile [ɪmóbɪl] adj. inmóbil.

im•mod•est [ɪmódɪst] adj. deshonesto, impúdico, indecente.

im•mor•al [ɪmɔrəl] adj. inmoral; licencioso.

im•mor•al•i•ty [ɪmərélətɪ] s. inmoralidad.

im•mor•tal [ɪmɔrtḷ] adj. & s. inmortal.

im•mor•tal•i•ty [ɪmɔrtélətɪ] s. inmortalidad.

im•mov•a•ble [ɪmúvəbḷ] adj. inmovible (o inamovible); inmóvil; inmutable.

im•mune [ɪmjún] adj. inmune.

im•mu•ni•ty [ɪmjúnətɪ] s. inmunidad.

im•mu•ta•ble [ɪmjútəbḷ] adj. inmutable.

imp [ɪmp] s. diablillo.

im•pair [ɪmpér] v. dañar, perjudicar, menoscabar, desvirtuar, debilitar.

im•pair•ment [ɪmpérənt] s. menoscabo; perjuicio; deterioro.

im•part [ɪmpórt] v. impartir, dar, comunicar.

im•par•tial [ɪmpórʃəl] adj. imparcial.

im•par•ti•al•i•ty [ɪmpórʃælətɪ] s. imparcialidad.

im•pass•i•ble [ɪmpæscb̹] adj. impasible.

im•pas•sioned [ɪmpæʃənd] adj. apasionado, vehemente, ardiente.

im•pas•sive [ɪmpésɪv] adj. impasible.

im•pa•tience [ɪmpéʃəns] s. impaciencia.

im•pa•tient [ɪmpéʃənt] adj. impaciente.

im•peach [ɪmpítʃ] v. demandar o acusar formalmente (a un alto funcionario de gobierno), **to – a person's honor** poner en tela de juicio el honor de uno.

im•pede [ɪmpíd] v. impedir, estorbar, obstruir.

im•ped•i•ment [ɪmpédəmənt] s. impedimento, obstáculo, estorbo; traba.

im•pel [ɪmpél] v. impeler, impulsar.

im•pend•ing [ɪmpéndɪŋ] adj. inminente, amenazador.

im•per•a•tive [ɪmpérətɪv] adj. imperativo; imperioso, urgente; s. imperativo.

im•per•cep•ti•ble [ɪmpə•séptəb̹] adj. imperceptible.

im•per•fect [ɪmpɝfɪkt] adj. imperfecto; defectuoso; s. imperfecto (tiempo del verbo).

im•pe•ri•al [ɪmpírɪəl] adj. imperial.

im•pe•ri•al•ism [ɪmpírɪəlɪzm] s. imperialismo.

im•per•il [ɪmpérəl] v. poner en peligro, arriesgar.

im•pe•ri•ous [ɪmpírɪəs] adj. imperioso; urgente.

im•per•son•al [ɪmpɝsn̹l] adj. impersonal.

im•per•son•ate [ɪmpɝsn̹et] v. representar (un personaje); remedar, imitar; fingirse otro, pretender ser otro.

im•per•ti•nence [ɪmpɝtṇəns] s. impertinencia; insolencia, descaro.

im•per•ti•nent [ɪmpɝtṇənt] adj. impertinente; insolente, descarado.

im•per•vi•ous [ɪmpɝvɪəs] adj. impermeable; impenetrable; – **to reason** refractario, testarudo.

im•pet•u•ous [ɪmpétʃUəs] adj. impetuoso.

im•pe•tus [Ímpetəs] s. ímpetu.

im•pi•ous [Ímpɪəs] adj. impío.

im•plac•a•ble [ɪmplékəb̹] adj. implacable.

im•plant [ɪmplǽnt] v. implantar, plantar; inculcar, infundir.

im·ple·ment [Ímpləmənt] *s.* herramienta, instrumento; **-s** utensilios, aperos, enseres.

im·pli·cate [Ímplɪket] *v.* implicar, envolver, enredar.

im·plic·it [ImplísIt] *adj.* implícito.

im·plore [Implór] *v.* implorar, rogar; suplicar.

im·ply [Implái] *v.* implicar; querer decir; insinuar.

im·po·lite [Impəláɪt] *adj.* descortés.

im·port [Ímport] *s.* significado, significación, sentido; importancia; importación; **-s** artículos importados; [Impórt] *v.* importar; significar, querer decir.

im·por·tance [Impórtṇs] *s.* importancia.

im·por·tant [Impórtṇt] *adj.* importante.

im·pose [Impóz] *v.* imponer; **to – upon** abusar de (*la amistad, hospitalidad, confianza de alguien*); engañar.

im·pos·ing [Impósɪŋ] *adj.* imponente; impresionante.

im·po·si·tion [Impəzíʃən] *s.* imposición; carga, impuesto; abuso (*de confianza*).

im·pos·si·bil·i·ty [Impasəbíləti] *s.* imposibilidad.

im·pos·si·ble [Impásəb] *adj.* imposible.

im·pos·tor [Impástɚ] *s.* impostor, embaucador.

im·pos·ture [Impástʃɚ] *s.* impostura, fraude, engaño.

im·po·tence [Ímpətəns] *s.* impotencia.

im·po·tent [Ímpətənt] *adj.* impotente.

im·pov·er·ish [Impávərɪʃ] *v.* empobrecer.

im·preg·nate [Imprégnet] *v.* impregnar; empapar; empreñar.

im·press [Ímprɛs] *s.* impresión, marca, señal, huella; [Imprés] *v.* imprimir, estampar, marcar, grabar; impresionar.

im·pres·sion [Impréʃən] *s.* impresión; marca.

im·pres·sive [Imprésɪv] *adj.* impresionante; imponente.

im·print [Ímprɪnt] *s.* impresión; pie de imprenta; [Imprínt] *v.* imprimir; estampar.

im·pris·on [Imprísṇ] *v.* aprisionar, encarcelar.

im·pris·on·ment [Imprízṇmənt] *s.* prisión, encarcelación o encarcelamiento.

im·prob·a·ble [Imprábəb] *adj.* improbable.

im·promp·tu [Imprámptu] *adv.* de improviso.

im·prop·er [Imprápɚ] *adj.* impropio.

im·prove [Imprúv] *v.* mejorar(se); **to – upon** mejorar; **to – one's time** aprovechar el tiempo.

im·prove·ment [Imprúvmənt] *s.* mejoramiento; mejora; progreso, adelanto; mejoría (*de una enfermedad*).

im·pro·vise [Ímprəvaɪz] *v.* improvisar.

im·pru·dent [Imprúdṇt] *adj.* imprudente.

im·pu·dence [Ímpjədəns] *s.* impudencia, descaro, insolencia.

im·pu·dent [Ímpjədənt] *adj.* impudente, descarado, insolente.

im·pulse [Ímpʌls] *s.* impulso; ímpetu; inclinación; **to act on** – obrar impulsivamente.

im·pul·sive [Imp ʌlsʌɪv] *adj.* impulsivo.

im·pu·ni·ty [Impjúnəɪ] *s.* impunidad, falta o exención de castigo.

im·pure [Impjúr] *adj.* impuro; sucio; adulterado.

im·pu·ri·ty [Impjúrəɪ] *s.* impureza.

im·pute [Impjút] *v.* imputar, achacar, atribuir.

in [In] *prep.* en; dentro de; de (*después de un superlativo*); **– haste** de prisa; **– the morning** por (*o* en) la mañana; **– writing** por escrito; **at two – the morning** a las dos de la mañana; **dressed – white** vestido de blanco; **the tallest – his class** el más alto de su clase; **to come – a week** venir de hoy en ocho días, venir dentro de ocho días; *adv.* dentro; adentro; en casa; **to be – and out** estar entrando y saliendo; **to be all –** no poder más, estar rendido de cansancio; **to be – with someone** estar asociado con alguien; disfrutar del aprecio de una persona; **to come – entrar**; **to have it – for someone** tenerle ojeriza a una persona; **to put –** meter; **is the train –?** ¿ha llegado el tren?

in·a·bil·i·ty [Inəbíləɪ] *s.* inhabilidad, incapacidad.

in·ac·ces·si·ble [Inəksésəb] *adj.* inaccesible; inasequible.

in·ac·cu·rate [Inækjərɪt] *adj.* inexacto, impreciso, incorrecto.

in·ac·tive [Inæktɪv] *adj.* inactivo; inerte.

in·ac·tiv·i·ty [Inæktívəɪ] *s.* inactividad, inacción, inercia.

in·ad·e·quate [Inædəkwɪt] *adj.* inadecuado; insuficiente.

in·ad·ver·tent [Inədvɝtṇt] *adj.* inadvertido; descuidado; **-ly** *adv.* inadvertidamente; descuidadamente.

in·ad·vis·a·ble [Inədváɪzəb] *adj.* imprudente.

in·an·i·mate [Inænəmɪt] *adj.* inanimado.

in·as·much [Inəzmʌtʃ]; **– as** visto que, puesto que; en cuanto.

in·at·ten·tive [Inətɛntɪv] *adj.* desatento.

in·au·gu·rate [Inɔ́gjəret] *v.* inaugurar, iniciar; investir de una dignidad o cargo.

in·au·gu·ra·tion [Inɔgjəréʃən] *s.* inauguración.

in·board [Ínbord] *adj.* interior.

in·born [Inbɔ́rn] *adj.* innato, connatural.

in·can·des·cent [Inkəndésṇt] *adj.* incandescente, candente.

in·ca·pa·ble [Inképəb] *adj.* incapaz.

in·ca·pac·i·tate [Inkəpǽsɪtet] *v.* incapacitar.

in·cen·di·ar·y [InséndIɛrɪ] *adj.* incendiario; **– bomb**

bomba incendiaria.

in·cense [ínsɛns] s. incienso; [insɛns] v. inflamar, exasperar.

in·cen·tive [insɛ́ntɪv] s. incentivo, estímulo.

in·ces·sant [insɛ́s ŋ t] adj. incesante, continuo.

inch [ɪntʃ] s. pulgada (*2.54 centímetros*); **by -es** poco a poco, gradualmente; **every – a man** nada menos que todo un hombre; **to be within an – of** estar a dos pulgadas de, estar muy cerca de; v. avanzar muy despacio (*por pulgadas*).

in·ci·dence [ínsɪdəns] s. incidencia.

in·ci·dent [ínswdəns] s. incidente, suceso, acontecimiento.

in·ci·den·tal [ínsədənt] adj. incidental; accidental; contingente; **-s** s. pl. gastos imprevistos; **-ly** adv. incidentalmente; de paso.

in·cip·i·ent [insípɪənt] adj. incipiente.

in·ci·sion [insíʒən] s. incisión.

in·cite [insáɪt] v. incitar.

in·clem·ent [ínklɛmənt] adj. inclemente.

in·cli·na·tion [ɪnklənéʃən] s. inclinación.

in·cline [ínklaɪn] s. declive, pendiente, cuesta; [ɪnkláɪn] v. inclinar(se).

in·close = enclose.

in·clo·sure = enclosure.

in·clude [ɪnklúd] v. incluir, encerrar; abarcar.

in·clu·sive [ɪnklúsɪv] adj. inclusivo; **from Monday to Friday** – del lunes al viernes inclusive.

in·co·her·ent [ɪnkohɛ́rənt] adj. incoherente, inconexo.

in·come [ínkʌm] s. renta, rédito, ingreso, entrada, – **tax** impuesto sobre rentas.

in·com·pa·ra·ble [ɪnkómpərəb]] adj. incomparable, sin par, sin igual.

in·com·pat·i·ble [ɪnkəmpǽtəb]] adj. incompatible.

in·com·pe·tent [ɪnkómpətənt] adj. incompetente.

in·com·plete [ɪnkəmplít] adj. incompleto.

in·com·pre·hen·si·ble [ɪnkəmprɪhɛ́nsəb] adj. incomprensible.

in·con·ceiv·a·ble [ɪnkənsívəb]] adj. inconcebible.

in·con·sid·er·ate [ɪnkənsídərɪt] adj. inconsiderado, falto de miramiento.

in·con·sis·ten·cy [ɪnkənsístənsɪ] s. inconsecuencia; falta de uniformidad (*en la aplicación de una regla o principio*).

in·con·sis·tent [ɪnkənsístənt] adj. inconsecuente, falto de uniformidad.

in·con·spic·u·ous [ɪnkənspíkjuəs] adj. poco llamativo.

in·cons·tan·cy [ɪnkónstənsɪ] s. inconstancia, mudanza.

in·con·stant [ɪnkónstənt] adj. inconstante, mudable, voluble.

in·con·test·a·ble [ɪnkəntɛ́stəb]] adj. incontestable.

in·con·ven·ience [ɪnkənvínjəns] s. inconveniencia; molestia; v. incomodar; molestar.

in·con·ven·ient [ɪnkənvínjənt] adj. inconveniente; inoportuno.

in·cor·po·rate [ɪnkɔ́rpəret] adj. incorporado; asociado; [ɪnkɔ́rpəret] v. incorporar; incorporarse, asociarse (*para formar un cuerpo*)

in·cor·rect [ɪnkərɛ́kt] adj. incorrecto.

in·cor·ri·gi·ble [ɪnkɔ́rɪdʒəb]] adj. incorregible.

in·crease [ínkrɪs] s. aumento; acrecentamiento; crecimiento; incremento; [ɪnkrís] v. aumentar(se), acrecentar(se), crecer.

in·creas·ing·ly [ɪnkrísɪólɪ] adv. más y más; cada vez más.

in·cred·i·ble [ɪnkrɛ́dəb]] adj. increíble.

in·cre·du·li·ty [ɪnkrədúlətɪ] s. incredulidad.

in·cred·u·lous [ɪnkrɛ́dʒələs] adj. incrédulo, descreído.

in·cre·ment [ínkrəmənt] s. incremento.

in·crim·i·nate [ɪnkrímənət] v. acriminar.

in·cu·ba·tor [ínkjubetɚ] s. incubadora.

in·cul·cate [ɪnk ʌ́ lket] v. inculcar, infundir.

in·cur [ɪnkɝ́] v. incurrir en.

in·cur·a·ble [ɪnkjÚrəb]] adj. incurable, irremediable; s. incurable.

in·debt·ed [ɪndɛ́tɪd] adj. adeudado, endeudado; obligado, agredecido.

in·debt·ed·ness [ɪndɛ́tɪdnɪs] s. deuda; obligación.

in·de·cen·cy [ɪndís ŋ sɪ] s. indecencia.

in·de·cent [ɪndísnt] adj. indecente.

in·de·ci·sion [ɪndəsíʒən] s. indecisión.

in·deed [ɪndíd] adv. en verdad, a la verdad; de veras; realmente.

in·de·fen·si·ble [ɪndɪfɛ́nsəb]] adj. indefendible.

in·def·i·nite [ɪndɛ́fənɪt] adj. indefinido.

in·del·i·ble [ɪndɛ́ləb]] adj. indeleble.

in·del·i·cate [ɪndɛ́ləkət] adj. indelicado, indecoroso.

in·dem·ni·fy [ɪndɛ́mnəfaɪ] v. indemnizar.

in·dem·ni·ty [ɪndɛ́mnətɪ] s. indemnización.

in·dent [ɪndɛ́nt] v. dentar, endentar; sangrar (*comenzar un renglón más adentro que los otros*).

in·de·pend·ence [ɪndɪpɛ́ndəns] s. independencia.

in·de·pend·ent [ɪndɪpɛ́ndənt] adj. independiente.

in·de·scrib·a·ble [ɪndɪskráɪbəb]] adj. indescriptible.

in·dex [índɛks] s. índice; v. alfabetizar, ordenar alfabéticamene; poner en un índice; **– finger** índice.

In·di·an [índɪən] adj. & s. indio; **– Ocean** Océano Índico.

in·di·cate [índəket] v. indicar.

in·di·ca·tion [ɪndəkéʃən] s. indicación.

in·dic·a·tive [ɪndíkətɪv] adj. & s. indicativo.

in·dict [ɪndáɪt] v. procesar, demandar (*ante un juez*); enjuiciar, formar causa a.

in·dict·ment [ɪndáɪtmənt] s. acusación (*hecha por el Gran Jurado*), denuncia, proceso judicial.

in·dif·fer·ence [ɪndífrəns] s. indiferencia; apatía.

in·dif·fer·ent [ɪndífrənt] adj. indiferente; apático.

in·dig·e·nous [ɪndídʒənəs] adj. indígena, autóctono, nativo.

in·di·gent [índədʒənt] adj. & s. indigente.

in·di·ges·tion [ɪndədʒéstʃən] s. indigestión.

in·dig·nant [ɪndígnənt] adj. indignado; **-ly** adv. con indignación.

in·dig·na·tion [ɪndɪgnéʃən] s. indignación.

in·dig·ni·ty [ɪndígnətɪ] s. indignidad, afrenta.

in·di·go [índɪgo] s. índigo, añil; – **blue** azul de añil.

in·di·rect [ɪndərékt] adj. indirecto.

in·dis·creet [ɪndɪskrít] adj. indiscreto.

in·dis·cre·tion [ɪndɪskréʃən] s. indiscreción.

in·dis·pens·a·ble [ɪndɪspénsəb l] adj. indispensable.

in·dis·pose [ɪndɪspóz] v. indisponer.

in·dis·posed [ɪndɪspózd] adj. indispuesto.

in·dis·po·si·tion [ɪndɪspəzíʃən] s. indisposición; malestar.

in·dis·tinct [ɪndɪstíŋkt] adj. indistinto.

in·di·vid·u·al [ɪndəvídʒʊəl] adj. individual; s. individuo, sujeto, persona.

in·di·vid·u·al·i·ty [ɪndəvɪdʒʊǽlətɪ] s. individualidad; individuo, persona.

in·di·vis·i·ble [ɪndəvízəb l] adj. indivisible.

in·doc·tri·nate [ɪndɑtrɪnet] v. adoctrinar.

in·do·lence [índələns] s. indolencia, desidia, apatía.

in·do·lent [índələnt] adj. indolente, desidioso, apático.

in·dom·i·ta·ble [ɪndɑmətəb l] adj. indomable.

in·door [índɔr] adj. interior, de casa.

in·doors [índɔrz] adv. dentro, en casa; adentro; **to go** – entrar; ir adentro.

in·dorse = endorse.

in·dorse·ment = endorsement.

in·dors·er = endorser.

in·duce [ɪndjús] v. inducir.

in·duce·ment [ɪndjúsmənt] s. aliciente, incentivo.

in·duct [ɪndʌkt] v. introducir; iniciar; instalar (*en un cargo*).

in·duc·tion [ɪndʌkʃən] s. inducción; instalación (*en un cargo*).

in·dulge [ɪndʌldʒ] v. gratificar, complacer; seguir el humor a (*una persona*); mimar, consentir (*a un niño*); **to** – **in** darse a, entregarse a (*un placer*); darse el lujo de, permitirse el placer de.

in·dul·gence [ɪndʌldʒəns] s. indulgencia; complacencia (*en el vicio o placer*).

in·dul·gent [ɪndʌldʒənt] adj. indulgente.

in·dus·tri·al [ɪndʌstriəl] adj. industrial.

in·dus·tri·al·ist [ɪndʌstriəlɪst] s. industrial; fabricante.

in·dus·tri·ous [ɪndʌstriəs] adj. industrioso, aplicado, diligente.

in·dus·try [índəstrɪ] s. industria; aplicación, diligencia.

in·ef·fa·ble [ɪnɛ́fəb l] adj. inefable.

in·ef·fec·tive [ɪnəkɛ́ktɪv] adj. inefectivo, ineficaz.

in·ef·fi·cient [ɪnɪfíʃənt] adj. ineficaz.

in·el·i·gi·ble [ɪnɛ́lədʒəb l] adj. inelegible.

in·e·qual·i·ty [ɪnɪkwɑ́lətɪ] s. desigualdad; disparidad.

in·ert [ɪnɝ́t] adj. inerte.

in·er·tia [ɪnɝ́ʃə] s. inercia.

in·es·tim·a·ble [ɪnɛ́stəməb l] adj. inestimable.

in·ev·i·ta·ble [ɪnɛ́vətəb l] adj. inevitable.

in·ex·haust·i·ble [ɪnɪgzɔ́stəb l] adj. inagotable.

in·ex·pe·dient [ɪnɛkspídjənt] adj. inoportuno; imprudente.

in·ex·pen·sive [ɪnɪkspénsɪv] adj. económico, barato.

in·ex·pe·ri·ence [ɪnɪkspírɪəns] s. inexperiencia, falta de experiencia.

in·ex·pe·ri·enced [ɪnɪkspírɪənst] adj. inexperto, falto de experiencia.

in·ex·pli·ca·ble [ɪnɛ́ksplɪkəb l] adj. inexplicable.

in·ex·pres·si·ble [ɪnɪksprésəb l] adj. inexpresable, indecible, inefable.

in·fal·li·ble [ɪnfǽləb l] adj. infalible.

in·fa·mous [ínfəməs] adj. infame, ignominioso.

in·fa·my [ínfəmɪ] s. infamia.

in·fan·cy [ínfənsɪ] s. infancia.

in·fant [ínfənt] s. infante, bebé, criatura, nene.

in·fan·tile [ínfəntaɪl] adj. infantil.

in·fan·try [ínfəntrɪ] s. infantería.

in·fect [ɪnfékt] v. infectar, inficionar; contagiar; contaminar.

in·fec·tion [ɪnfékʃən] s. infección; contagio.

in·fec·tious [ɪnfékʃəs] adj. infeccioso; contagioso.

in·fer [ɪnfɝ́] v. inferir, deducir, colegir.

in·fer·ence [ínfərəns] s. inferencia, deducción.

in·fe·ri·or [ɪnfírɪɚ] adj. & s. inferior.

in·fe·ri·or·i·ty [ɪnfɪríˈərətɪ] s. inferioridad; – **complex** complejo de inferioridad.

in·fer·nal [ɪnfɝ́n l] adj. infernal.

in·fer·no [ɪnfɝ́no] s. infierno.

in·fest [ɪnfést] v. infestar, plagar.

in·fi·del [ɪnfəd] adj. & s. infiel.

in·fil·trate [ɪnfíltret] v. infiltrar(se).

in·fi·nite [ínfənɪt] adj. & v. infinito.

in·fin·i·tive [ɪnfínətɪv] adj. & s. infinitivo.

in·fin·i·ty [ɪnfínətɪ] s. infinidad, infinito.

in·firm [ɪnfɜ́ m] adj. enfermizo, achacoso, débil.

in·fir·ma·ry [ɪnfɜ́ mərɪ] s. enfermería.

in·fir·mi·ty ɪnfɜ́ mətɪ] s. enfermedad, achaque; flaqueza.

in·flame [ɪnflém] v. inflamar(se); enardecer(se).

in·flam·ma·tion [ɪnfləméʃən] s. inflamación.

in·flate [ɪnflét] v. inflar; hinchar.

in·fla·tion [ɪnfléʃən] s. inflación; hinchazón.

in·flec·tion [ɪnflékʃən] s. inflexión.

in·flict [ɪnflíkt] v. infligir, imponer.

in·flu·ence [ínflʊəns] s. influencia, influjo; v. influir en; ejercer influencia o influjo sobre.

in·flu·en·tial [ɪnflʊénʃəl] adj. influyente.

in·flu·en·za [ɪnflʊénzə] s. influenza, gripe.

in·flux [ínflʌks] s. entrada, afluencia (de gente).

in·fold [ɪnfóld] v. involver; abrazar; abarcar.

in·form [ɪnfɔ́ rm] v. informar; enterar; avisar; **to – against** delatar a, denunciar a.

in·for·mal [ɪnfɔ́ rm] adj. informal, sin ceremonia, – **visit** visita de confianza; **-ly** adv. informalmente, sin ceremonia, de confianza.

in·form·ant [ɪnfɔ́ rmənt] s. informante.

in·for·ma·tion [ɪnfəméʃən] s. (service) información; (details) informes; (news) noticias; (knowledge) conocimientos, saber.

in·frac·tion [ɪnfrǽkʃən] s. infracción.

in·fringe [ɪnfríndʒ] v. infringir, violar; **to – upon** violar.

in·fu·ri·ate [ɪnfjʊ́rɪet] v. enfurecer.

in·fuse [ɪnfjúz] v. infundir; inculcar.

in·gen·ious [ɪndʒínjəs] adj. ingenioso.

in·ge·nu·i·ty [ɪndʒənəʊt] s. ingeniosidad.

in·grat·i·tude [ɪngrǽtətjud] s. ingratitud.

in·gre·di·ent [ɪngrídɪənt] s. ingrediente.

in·hab·it [ɪnhǽbɪt] v. habitar, vivir en, residir en.

in·hab·i·tant [ɪnhǽbətənt] s. habitante.

in·hale [ɪnhél] v. inhalar, aspirar, inspirar.

in·her·ent [ɪnhírənt] adj. inherente.

in·her·it [ɪnhérɪt] v. heredar.

in·her·i·tance [ɪnhérətəns] s. herencia.

in·hib·it [ɪnhíbɪt] v. inhibir, cohibir, refrenar, reprimir; impedir.

in·hi·bi·tion [ɪnɪbíʃən] s. inhibición, cohibición; prohibición, restricción.

in·hos·pi·ta·ble [ɪnhóspɪtəb] adj. inhospitalario.

in·hu·man [ɪnhjúmən] adj. inhumano.

in·im·i·ta·ble [ɪnímətəb] adj. inimitable.

in·iq·ui·ty [ɪníkwətɪ] s. iniquidad, maldad.

in·i·tial [ɪníʃəl] adj. & s. inicial; v. marcar o firmar con iniciales.

in·i·ti·ate [ɪníʃɪet] v. iniciar.

in·i·tia·tive [ɪníʃɪetɪv] s. iniciativa.

in·ject [ɪndʒékt] v. inyectar; injerir, introducir.

in·jec·tion [ɪndʒékʃən] s. inyección.

in·junc·tion [ɪndʒʌ́ŋkʃən] s. mandato, orden; entredicho.

in·jure [índʒə] v. dañar; herir, lesionar; lastimar.

in·ju·ri·ous [ɪndʒÚrɪəs] adj. dañoso, dañino, perjudicial.

in·ju·ry [índʒərɪ] s. daño; heida, lesión; perjuicio.

in·jus·tice [ɪndʒʌ́stɪs] s. injusticia.

ink [ɪŋk] s. tinta; v. entintar; teñir o manchar con tinta.

in·kling [íŋklɪŋ] s. indicación, indicio, idea, sospecha, noción vaga.

ink·stand [íŋkstænd] s. tintero.

ink·well [íŋkwel] s. tintero.

in·laid [ɪnléd] adj. incrustado, embutido, – **work** embutido, incrustación; pret. & p.p. de **to inlay**.

in·land [ɪnlənd] s. interior (de un país); adj. interior, del interior de un país; adv. tierra adentro.

in·lay [ínlé] v. incrustar, embutir, s. embutido.

in·mate [ínmet] s. residente, asilado (de un hospicio, asilo, casa de corrección, etc.); presidiario; hospiciano.

in·most [ínmost] adj. más interior, más íntimo, más secreto o recóndito; más profundo.

inn [ɪn] s. posada, mesón, fonda.

in·nate [ɪnét] adj. innato, connatural.

in·ner [ínə] adj. interior; íntimo, recóndito; – **most** = inmost.

in·ning [ínɪŋ] s. entrada, cuadro (en beisbol); turno (del bateador en beisbol y otros juegos).

inn·keep·er [ínkipə] s. venteo, mesonero, posadero.

in·no·cence [ínəs s] s. inocencia.

in·no·cent [ínəs ̥t] adj. & s. inocente.

in·noc·u·ous [ɪnókjʊəs] adj. innocuo, inofensivo.

in·no·va·tion [ɪnəvéʃən] s. innovación.

in·nu·en·do [ɪnjUéndo] s. insinuación, indirecta.

in·nu·mer·a·ble [ɪnjúmərəb] adj. innumerable.

in·oc·u·late [ɪnókjələt] v. inocular; contaminar.

in·of·fen·sive [ɪnəfénsɪv] adj. inofensivo.

in·op·por·tune [ɪnəpətjún] adj. inoportuno.

in·put [ínpʊt] s. potencia consumida; (electric) entrada.

in·quire [ɪnkwáɪr] v. inquirir, indagar; preguntar; **to – about** preguntar por; **to – into** indagar, investigar.

in·quir·y [ɪnkwáɪrɪ] s. indagación, investigación; preguntar; interrogatorio.

in·qui·si·tion [ɪnkwəzíʃən] s. inquisición; indagación.

in·quis·i·tive [ɪnkwízətɪv] *adj.* inquisitivo, investigador, preguntón; curioso.

in·road [ínrod] *s.* incursión, invasión, ataque; **to make -s upon** atacar, mermar.

in·sane [ɪnsén] *adj.* insano, loco; **– asylum** manicomio, casa de locos.

in·san·i·ty [ɪnsǽnɪtɪ] *s.* locura.

in·sa·tia·ble [ɪnséʃɪəbl] *adj.* insaciable.

in·scribe [ɪnskráɪb] *v.* inscribir.

in·scrip·tion [ɪnskríp∫ən] *s.* inscripción; letrero.

in·sect [ínsɛkt] *s.* insecto.

in·se·cure [ɪnsɪkjúr] *adj.* inseguro.

in·sen·si·ble [ɪnsénsəbl] *adj.* insensible.

in·sen·si·tive [ɪnsénsətɪv] *adj.* insensible.

in·sep·a·ra·ble [ɪnsépərəbl] *adj.* inseparable.

in·sert [ɪnsɝ́t] *s.* inserción; intercalación; hoja (*insertada en un libro*); circular, folleto (*insertado en un periódico*); [ɪnsɝ́t] *v.* insertar; intercalar; encajar; meter.

in·ser·tion [ɪnsɝ́∫ən] *s.* inserción; introducción.

in·side [ínsáɪd] *s.* interior; **-s** entrañas; *adj.* interior, interno; secreto; *adv.* dentro; adentro; **to turn – out** volver(se) al revés; *prep.* dentro de.

in·sight [ínsaɪt] *s.* penetración, discernimiento; intuición; perspicacia; comprensión.

in·sig·ni·a [ɪnsígnɪə] *s. pl.* insignias.

in·sig·nif·i·cant [ɪnsɪgnífəkənt] *adj.* insignificante.

in·sin·u·ate [ɪnsínjʊet] *v.* insinuar.

in·sin·u·a·tion [ɪnsɪnjʊéʃən] *s.* insinuación; indirecta.

in·sip·id [ɪnsípɪd] *adj.* insípido.

in·sist [ɪnsíst] *v.* insistir en: empeñarse (en); porfiar, persistir.

in·sis·tence [ɪnsístənt] *s.* insistencia, empeño, porfía.

in·sis·tent [ɪnsístənt] *adj.* insistente, porfiado, persistente.

in·so·lence [ínsoləns] *s.* insolencia

in·so·lent [ínsələnt] *adj.* insolente.

in·sol·u·ble [ɪnsáljəbl] *adj.* insoluble.

in·spect [ɪnspɛ́kt] *v.* inspeccionar; examinar, registrar.

in·spec·tion [ɪnspɛ́k∫ən] *s.* inspección; registro.

in·spec·tor [ɪnspɛ́ktə·] *s.* inspector.

in·spi·ra·tion [ɪnspəréʃən] *s.* inspiración.

in·spire [ɪnspáɪr] *v.* inspirar.

in·stall [ɪnstɔ́l] *v.* instalar.

in·stal·la·tion [ɪnstəléʃən] *s.* instalación.

in·stall·ment [ɪnstɔ́lmənt] *s.* instalación; abono(*pago*); entrega o continuación (*semanal o mensual de una novela*); **to pay in -s** pagar por plazos; pagar en bonos.

in·stance [ínstəns] *s.* ejemplo, caso, vez, ocasión; instancia; **for –** por ejemplo.

in·stant [ínstənt] *s.* instante, *adj.* inmediato; urgente; **the 10th –** el 10 del (mes) corriente, **-ly** *adv.* al instante, inmediatamente.

in·stan·ta·ne·ous [ɪnstəntáníəs] *adj.* instantáneo.

in·stead [ɪnstéd] *adv.* en lugar de ello (eso, él, ella, *etc.*); **– of** en lugar de, en vez de.

in·step [ínstɛp] *s.* empeine (*del pie, del zapato*).

in·sti·gate [ínstəget] *v.* instigar.

in·still [ɪnstíl] *v.* inculcar, infundir.

in·stinct [ínstɪŋkt] *s.* instinto.

in·stinc·tive [ɪnstíŋktɪv] *adj.* instintivo.

in·sti·tute [ínstətjut] *s.* instituto; *v.* instituir.

in·sti·tu·tion [ɪnstətjú∫n] *s.* institucion.

in·struct [ɪnstrʌ́kt] *v.* instruir; dar instrucciones.

in·struc·tion [ɪnstrʌ́k∫ən] *s.* instrucción; enseñanza; **lack of –** falta de saber o conocimiento; **-s** órdenes, instrucciones.

in·struc·tive [ɪnstrʌ́ktɪv] *adj.* instructivo.

in·struc·tor [ɪnstrʌ́ktə·] *s.* instructor.

in·stru·ment [ínstrəmənt] *s.* instrumento.

in·stru·men·tal [ɪnstrəmént̩l] *adj.* instrumental; **to be – in** ayudar a, servir de instrumento para.

in·sub·or·di·nate [ɪnsəbɔ́rdɪnət] *adj.* insubordinado.

in·suf·fer·a·ble [ɪnsʌ́frəbl] *adj.* insufrible, inaguantable.

in·suf·fi·cien·cy [ɪnsəfí∫ənsɪ] *s.* insuficiencia; incompetencia; falta, escasez.

in·suf·fi·cient [ɪnsəfí∫ənt] *adj.* insuficiente; anadecuado.

in·su·late [ínsəlet] *v.* aislar.

in·su·la·tion [ɪnsəléʃən] *s.* aislamiento; aislación.

in·su·la·tor [ínsəletə·] *s.* aislador.

in·sult [ínsʌlt] *s.* insulto; *v.* insultar.

in·sur·ance [ɪnʃúrəns] *s.* aseguramiento; seguro; prima, premio (*de una póliza de seguro*); **– agent** agente de seguros; **– company** compañía de seguros; **– policy** póliza de seguro; **accident –** seguro contra accidentes; **fire –** seguro contra incendios; **life –** seguro sobre la vida.

in·sure [ɪnʃúr] *v.* asegurar; asegurarse de.

in·sur·gent [ɪnsɝ́dʒənt] *adj. & s.* insurgente, insurrecto.

in·sur·mount·a·ble [ɪnsə·máʊntəbl] *adj.* insuperable.

in·sur·rec·tion [ɪnsə·rék∫ən] *s.* insurrección, rebelión, alzamiento.

in·tact [ɪntǽkt] *adj.* intacto.

in·te·gral [íntəgrəl] *adj.* integral; integrante; *s.* integral.

in·te·grate [Íntəgret] v. integrar.

in·teg·ri·ty [Intégrətɪ] s. integridad, enteresa.

in·tel·lect [Ínt|ɛkt] s. intelecto; entendimiento.

in·tel·lec·tu·al [Int|ɛktʃUəl] adj. & s. intelectual.

in·tel·li·gence [Intélədʒəns] s. inteligencia; información, noticias, policía secreta.

in·tel·li·gent [Intélədʒənt] adj. inteligente.

in·tel·li·gi·ble [Intélədʒəb|] adj. inteligible.

in·tem·per·ance [Intémpərəns] s. intemperancia.

in·tend [Inténd] v. intentar, pensar, tener la intención de; proponerse; destinar; to – to do it pensar hacerlo.

in·tense [Inténs] adj. intenso.

in·ten·si·fy [Inténsɪfaɪ] v. intensificar.

in·ten·si·ty [Inténsətɪ] s. intensidad.

in·ten·sive [Inténsɪv] adj. intenso, intensivo.

in·tent [Intént] s. intento, intención, propósito; significado; to all -s and purposes en todo caso, en todos sentidos; en realidad; adj. atento, – on absorto en, reconcentrado en; resuelto a, decidido a.

in·ten·tion [Inténʃən] s. intención.

in·ten·tion·al [Inténʃən|] adj. intencional; -ly adv. intencionalmente, adrede, a propósito.

inter [Intɝ́] v. enterrar, sepultar.

in·ter·cede [Intəsíd] v. interceder.

in·ter·cept [Intəsépt] v. interceptar, atajar.

in·ter·cep·tion [Intəsépʃən] s. interceptación.

in·ter·ces·sion [Intəséʃən] s. intercesión.

in·ter·change [Íntətʃendʒ] s. intercambio; cambio, trueque; [Intətʃéndʒ] v. cambiar, trocar; permutar; alternar.

in·ter·course [Íntəkors] s. comunicación; comercio, trato; intercambio (de ideas, sentimientos, etc.).

in·ter·dental [Intədént|] adj. interdental.

in·ter·est [Íntərɪst] s. interés; rédito; participación (en un negocio); v. interesar.

in·ter·est·ed [Íntərɪstɪd] adj. interesado; to be (o become) – in interesarse en (o por).

in·ter·est·ing [Íntərɪstɪŋ] adj. interesante.

in·ter·fere [Intəfír] v. intervenir; interponerse, entremeterse, estorbar, to – with estorbar, frustrar; dificultar.

in·ter·fer·ence [Intəfírəns] s. intervención; obstáculo; interferencia (en la radio).

in·te·ri·or [IntírIə] adj. interior; interno, s. interior.

in·ter·jec·tion [Intədʒékʃən] s. interjección, exclamación; intercalación.

in·ter·lace [Intəlés] v. entrelazar, enlazar, entretejer.

in·ter·lock [Intəlak] v. entrelazar(se); trabar(se).

in·ter·lude [Íntəlud] s. intervalo.

in·ter·me·di·ate [Intəmídɪɪt] adj. intermedio.

in·ter·mi·na·ble [Intɝ́mɪnəb|] adj. interminable, inacabable.

in·ter·min·gle [Intəmíŋg|] v. entremezclar(se), entreverar(se) v. mezclar(se).

in·ter·mis·sion [Intəmíʃən] s. intermisión; intermedio, entreacto.

in·ter·mit·tent [Intəmítŋt] adj. intermitente.

in·tern [Intɝ́n] v. internar, confinar, encerrar, s. practicante (de medicina en un hospital).

in·ter·nal [Intɝ́n|] adj. interno; interior.

in·ter·na·tion·al [Intənǽʃən|] adj. internacional.

in·ter·oce·a·nic [Intəoʃɪǽnɪk] adj. interoceánico.

in·ter·pose [Intəpóz] v. interponer(se).

in·ter·pret [Intɝ́prɪt] v. interpretar.

in·ter·pre·ta·tion [Intɝ́prɪtéʃən] s. interpretación.

in·ter·pret·er [Intɝ́prɪtə] s. intérprete.

in·ter·ro·gate [Intérəget] v. interrogar.

in·ter·ro·ga·tion [Intɛrəgéʃən] s. interrogación.

in·ter·rog·a·tive [Intərogətɪv] adj. interrogativo; s. pronombre o palabra interrogativa.

in·ter·rupt [Intər ʌ́pt] v. interrumpir.

in·ter·rup·tion [Intər ʌ́pʃən] s. interrupción.

in·ter·sect [Intəsékt] v. cortar(se); cruzar(se).

in·ter·sec·tion [Intəsékʃən] s. intersección; street – bocacalle.

in·ter·sperse [Intəspɝ́s] v. entremezclar, esparcir.

in·ter·twine [Intətwáɪn] v. entrelazar, entretejer, trenzar.

in·ter·val [Íntəv|] s. intervalo.

in·ter·vene [Intəvín] v. intervenir; interponerse; mediar.

in·ter·ven·tion [Intəvénʃən] s. intervención.

in·ter·view [Íntəvju] s. entrevista; v. entrevistar, entrevistarse con.

in·tes·tine [Intéstɪn] s. intestino; adj. intestino, interno.

in·ti·ma·cy [Íntəməsɪ] s. intimidad.

in·ti·mate [Íntəmɪt] adj. íntimo; s. amigo íntimo; v. intimar, insinuar; indicar, dar a entender.

in·ti·ma·tion [Intəméʃən] s. intimación, insinuación.

in·tim·i·date [Intɪ́mədet] v. intimidar, acobardar, infundir miedo.

in·to [IntU, Íntə] prep. en; dentro de; hacia el interior.

in·tol·er·a·ble [Intálərəb|] adj. intolerable, inaguantable.

in·tol·er·ance [Intálərəns] s. intolerancia.

in·tol·er·ant [Intálərənt] adj. intolerante.

in·to·na·tion [Intonéʃən] s. entonación.

in·tox·i·cate [Intáksəket] v. embriagar; emborrachar.

in·tox·i·ca·tion [ɪntɑksəkéʃən] *s.* embriaguez; envenenamiento, intoxicación (*estado tóxico o envenenamiento parcial*).

in·tran·si·gent [ɪntrǽnsədʒənt] *adj.* intransigente.

in·tra·ve·nous [ɪntrəvínəs] *adj.* intravenoso.

in·trench [ɪntrɛntʃ] *v.* atrincherar; **to – oneself** atrincherarse; **to – upon another's rights** infringir los derechos ajenos; **to be-ed** estar atrincherado; estar firmemente establecido.

in·trep·id [ɪntrépɪd] *adj.* intrépido.

in·tri·cate [ɪntrəkɪt] *adj.* intrincado, enredado.

in·trigue [ɪntríg] *s.* intriga; enredo, trama; lío, embrollo; *v.* intrigar; tramar, maquinar.

in·tri·guer [ɪntrígə] *s.* intrigante.

in·tro·duce [ɪntrədjús] *v.* introducir; presentar.

in·tro·duc·tion [ɪntrəd ʌkʃən] *s.* introducción; presentación.

in·tro·spec·tion [ɪntrospékʃən] *s.* introspección.

in·tro·vert [ɪntrovət] *s.* introvertido.

in·trude [ɪntrúd] *v.* entremeterse (*o* entrometerse); introducir, meter.

in·trud·er [ɪntrúdə] *s.* intruso, entremetido.

in·tru·sion [ɪntrúʒən] *s.* intrusión, entremetimiento.

in·tru·sive [ɪntrúsɪv] *adj.* intruso.

in·trust = **entrust.**

in·tu·i·tion [ɪntʊíʃən] *s.* intuición.

in·un·date [ɪnəndɛt] *v.* inundar.

in·ure [ɪnjÚr] *v.* habituar, acostumbrar.

in·vade [ɪnvéd] *v.* invadir.

in·vad·er [ɪnvédə] *s.* invasor.

in·val·id [ɪnvǽlɪd] *adj.* inválido (*que no vale*), nulo, de ningún valor.

in·val·id [ɪnvəlɪd] *adj.* inválido, enfermizo, achacoso; **– diet** dieta para inválidos; *s.* inválido.

in·val·u·a·ble [ɪnvǽljeb l] *adj.* de gran precio o valor, inapreciable, inestimable.

in·var·i·a·ble [ɪnvérɪəb l] *adj.* invariable; **invariably** *adv.* invariablemente; sin falta, sin excepción.

in·va·sion [ɪnvéʒən] *s.* invasión.

in·vent [ɪnvént] *v.* inventar.

in·ven·tion [ɪnvénʃən] *s.* invención; invento; inventiva, facultad para inventar.

in·ven·tive [ɪnvéntɪv] *adj.* inventivo.

in·ven·ti·ve·ness [ɪnvéntɪvnɪs] *s.* inventiva.

in·ven·tor [ɪnvéntə] *s.* inventor.

in·ven·to·ry [ɪnvəntorɪ] *s.* inventario; *v.* inventariar.

in·verse [ɪnvə́s] *adj.* inverso.

in·vert [ɪnvə́t] *v.* invertir; trastrocar; volver al revés.

in·vest [ɪnvést] *v.* invertir, colocar (*fondos*); investir

(*de una dignidad o cargo*); revestir (*de autoridad*); sitiar.

in·ves·ti·gate [ɪnvéstəget] *v.* investigar, indagar.

in·ves·ti·ga·tion [ɪnvɛstəgéʃən] *s.* investigación; indagación

in·ves·ti·ga·tor [ɪnvéstəgetə] *s.* investigador; indagador.

in·vest·ment [ɪnvéstmənt] *s.* inversión (*de fondos*).

in·ves·tor [ɪnvéstə] *s.* el que invierte fondos.

in·vig·o·rate [ɪnvígəret] *v.* vigorizar, fortalecer.

in·vin·ci·ble [ɪnvínsəb l] *adj.* invencible.

in·vis·i·ble [ɪnvízəb l] *adj.* invisible.

in·vi·ta·tion [ɪnvətéʃən] *s.* invitación.

in·vite [ɪnváɪt] *v.* invitar; convidar.

in·vit·ing [ɪnváɪtɪŋ] *adj.* atractivo; seductivo, tentador.

in·vo·ca·tion [ɪnvəkéʃən] *s.* invocación.

in·voice [ínvɔɪs] *s.* factura, envío, mercancías enviadas; *v.* facturar.

in·voke [ɪnvók] *v.* invocar.

in·vol·un·tar·y [ɪnvɑléntɛrɪ] *adj.* involuntario.

in·volve [ɪnvɑlv] *v.* complicar, enredar; envolver; implicar, comprometer; **to get -d in difficulties** embrollarse, meterse en embrollos.

in·ward [ínwəd] *adj.* interior; interno; secreto; *adv.* hacia el interior; hacia dentro, adentro, para dentro; **-s** *adv.* = **inward.**

i·o·dine [áɪədaɪn] *s.* yodo.

ire [aɪr] *s.* ira.

ir·i·des·cent [ɪrədésṇt] *adj.* iridiscente, tornasolado, irisado.

iris [áɪrɪs] *s.* iris; arco iris; flor de lis.

Irish [áɪrɪʃ] *adj.* irlandés; *s.* irlandés, idioma irlandés; **the –** los irlandeses.

irk·some [ə́ksəm] *adj.* fastidioso, engorroso, molesto, tedioso.

i·ron [áɪən] *s.* hierro; plancha (*de planchar ropa*); *adj.* férreo, de hierro; **–work** herraje, trabajo en hierro; **–works** herrería; fábrica de hierro; *v.* planchar; **to – out a difficulty** allanar una dificultad.

i·ron·i·cal [aɪrónɪk] *adj.* irónico.

i·ron·ing [áɪənɪŋ] *s.* planchado.

i·ro·ny [áɪrənɪ] *s.* ironía.

ir·ra·di·ate [ɪrédɪet] *v.* irradiar.

ir·ra·tion·al [ɪrǽʃən] *adj.* irracional

ir·reg·u·lar [ɪréɡjələ] *adj.* irregular.

ir·rel·e·vant [ɪréləvənt] *adj.* fuera de propósito, inaplicable al caso, inoportuno, que no viene (*o no hace*) al caso.

ir·re·lig·ious [ɪrɪlídʒəs] *adj.* irreligioso, impío.

ir·re·me·di·a·ble [ɪrɪmídɪəb l] *adj.* irremediable; incurable.

ir·re·proach·a·ble [ɪrɪprótʃəb l] *adj.* irreprochable, intachable.

ir•re•sist•i•ble [ɪrɪzístəb] *adj.* irresistible.

ir•res•o•lute [ɪrézəlut] *adj.* irresoluto, indeciso.

ir•rev•er•ence [ɪrévərəns] *s.* irreverencia, desacato.

ir•rev•er•ent [ɪrévərənt] *adj.* irreverente.

ir•ri•gate [írəget] *v.* regar; irrigar; bañar.

ir•ri•ga•tion ɪrəgéʃən] *s.* riego; irrigación; – canal acequia, canal de irrigación.

ir•ri•ta•ble [írətəb] *adj.* irritable; colérico.

ir•ri•tate [írətet] *v.* irritar.

ir•ri•tat•ing [írətetɪŋ] *adj.* irritante.

ir•ri•ta•tion [ɪrətéʃən] *s.* irritación.

ir•rupt [ɪr ʌ pt] *v.* irrumpir.

is•land [áɪlənd] *s.* isla.

is•lander [áɪləndə·] *s.* isleño.

isle [aɪl] *s.* isla, ínsula.

i•so•late [áɪs et] *v.* aislar.

i•so•la•tion [aɪs éʃən] *s.* aislamiento.

i•so•la•tion•ism [aɪs éʃənɪzəm] *s.* aislamiento.

i•so•metric [aɪsəm_trɪk] *adj.* isométrico.

Is•ra•el [ízríəl] *s.* srael.

is•sue [íʃU] *s.* (*printing*) tirada, impresión; (*stock, bonds*) emisión (*de valores*); (*problem*) problema, tema; (*result*) resultado, consecuencia; **without** – sin prole, sin sucesión; **to take** – **with** disentir o diferir de; *v.* publicar, dar a luz; dar, promulgar (*un decreto*); emitir (*valores, acciones, etc.*); emanar; fluir; salir; brotar; provenir.

isth•mus [ísməs] *s.* istmo.

it [ɪt] *pron. neutro* lo, la (*acusativo*); ello, él, ella (*después de una preposición*); *por lo general no se traduce cuando es sujeto del verbo:* – **is there** está allí; – **is** _ soy yo; – **is raining** llueve, está lloviendo; **what time is** –? ¿qué hora es?; – **is two o'clock** son las dos; **how goes** –? ¿qué tal?

I•tal•ian [ɪtǽljən] *adj. & s.* italiano.

i•tal•ic [ɪrǽlɪk] *adj.* itálico; -**s** *s.* letra bastardilla.

i•tal•i•cize [itǽləsaɪz] *v.* poner en letra bastardilla.

itch [ɪtʃ] *s.* comezón; picazón; sarna (*enfermedad de la piel*); *v.* picar, darle a uno comezón; sentir comezón; t**o be -ing to** tener ansias de.

itch•y [ítʃɪ] *adj.* sarnoso, Méx., *Ven.* sarniento; **to feel** – sentir comezón.

i•tem [áɪtəm] *s.* artículo, detalle, noticia, suelto (*de un periódico*); partida (*de una lista*).

i•tem•ize [áɪtəmaɪz] *v.* pormenorizar detallar; hacer una lista de.

i•tin•er•ant [aɪtínə·ənt] *adj.* ambulante.

i•tin•er•ar•y [aɪtínərɛrɪ] *s.* itinerario; ruta; guía de viajeros.

its [ɪts] *pos. neutro* su (sus), de él, de ella, de ello.

it•self [ɪtsélf] *pron. neutro* mismo, misma; **by** – por sí, de por sí, por sí solo; solo, aislado; **in** – en sí.

i•vo•ry [áɪvrɪ] *s.* marfil; – **tower** torre de marfil.

i•vy [áɪvɪ] *s.* hiedra (yedra).

J

jab [dʒæb] *v.* picar; pinchar; *s.* piquete, pinchazo.

jack [dʒæk] *s.* gato (*para alzar cosas pesadas*); sota (*en naipes*); macho (*del burro y otros animales*); bandera de proa; – **of all trades** aprendiz de todo y oficial de nada; – **pot** premio gordo, premio mayor; – **rabbit** liebre americana; *v.* **to** – **up** solevantar, alzar con gato (*un objeto pesado*).

jack•ass [dʒǽkæs] *s.* asno, burro.

jack•et [dʒǽkɪt] *s.* chaqueta; envoltura; forro (*de un libro*); hollejo (*de la patata*).

jack•knife [dʒǽknaɪf] *s.* navaja.

jag•ged [dʒǽgɪd] *adj.* serrado, dentado.

jail [dʒel] *s.* cárcel; *v.* encarcelar.

jai•ler [dʒélə·] *s.* carcelero.

jam [dʒæm] *v.* estrujar, apachurrar; atorar(se); obstruir(se), atascar(se); apiñar(se), agolpar(se); **to** – **on the brakes** frenar de golpe; to – **one's fingers** machucarse los dedos; **to** – **through** forzar por, meter a la fuerza; *s.* conserva, compota; apretura; atascamiento; **traffic** – aglomeración de transeúntes o automóviles, *Am.* bola; **to be in a** – estar en un aprieto.

jan•i•tor [dʒǽnətə·] *s.* conserje; portero; casero (*encargado de un edificio*).

Jan•u•ar•y [dʒǽnjuɛrɪ] *s.* enero.

Jap•anese [dʒæpəníz] *adj. & s.* japonés.

jar [dʒɑr] *s.* jarra, jarro; tarro; choque; sacudida; trepidación, vibración; **large earthen** – tinaja; *v.* trepidar; hacer vibrar; hacer temblar, menear; **to** – **one's nerves** ponerle a uno los nervios de punta.

jar•gon [dʒɔ́rgən] *s.* jerga, jeringonza.

jas•mine [dʒǽzmɪn] *s.* jazmín.

jas•per [dʒǽspə·] *s.* jaspe.

jaunt [dʒɔnt] *s.* caminata, excursión; *v.* dar un paseíto, hacer una corta caminata.

jaw [dʒɔ] *s.* quijada, mandíbula, *Am.* carretilla, -**s** grapa (*de herramienta*).

jaw•bone [dʒ óbón] *s.* mandíbula, quijada.

jay [dʒe] *s.* grajo; rústico, bobo; **blue** – azulejo; – **walker** el que cruza las bocacalles descuidadamente.

jazz [dʒæz] *s.* jazz (*cierta clase de música sincopada*); *v.* tocar el jazz; bailar el jazz; **to** – **up** sincopar; animar, alegrar.

jea•lous [dʒéləs] *adj.* celoso; envidioso; **to be** – **of someone** tener celos de una persona, tenerle celos a una persona.

jeal•ous•y [dʒéləsɪ] *s.* celos; envidia.

jeer [dʒɪr] *s.* mofa, befa, escarnio, *Carib.* choteo; *v.*

mofar, befar, *Carib.* chotear; **to — at** mofarse de.

jel•ly [dʒélɪ] s. jalea; v. convertir(se) en jalea, hacer(se) gelatinoso.

jeop•ard•y [dʒépə·dɪ] s. riesgo.

jerk [dʒɝk].s. tirón; sacudida, Mex., C.A., *Ven., Col.*, jalón; espasmo muscular; v. sacudir(se); dar un tirón; atasajar (*la carne*); **to — out** sacar de un tirón; **-ed beef** tasajo, *Am.* charqui.

jerk•water [dʒɝkwɔtə·] adj. de mala muerte.

jer•sey [dʒɝzɪ] s. tejido de punto, tejido elástico, *Am.* jersey; chaqueta, blusa, camisa (*de punto*), *Am.* jersey.

jest [dʒɛst] s. broma; chanza; chiste; v. bromear; chancearse.

jes•ter [dʒéstə·] s. chancero, burlón; bufón.

Jes•u•it [dʒéʒʊɪt] s. jesuita.

jet [dʒɛt] s. chorro; surtidor (*de fuente*); **— airplane** avión de reacción; **— engine** motor de reacción; **gas —** mechero de gas; adj. de azabache; **jet-black** negro como el azabache; v. chorrear, salir en chorro.

Jew [dʒʊ] s. judío.

jew•el [dʒúəl] s. joya, alhaja; gema, **— box** estuche, joyero.

jew•el•er [dʒúələ·] s. joyero; **-'s shop** joyería.

jew•el•ry [dʒúəlrɪ] s. joyas, alhajas, pedrería; **— store** joyería.

Jew•ish [dʒúɪʃ] adj. judío.

jif•fy [dʒífɪ] s. instante; **in a —** en un instante, en dos paletas; en un decir Jesús, en un santiamén.

jig [dʒɪg] s. jiga (*música y baile*); **—saw** sierra mecánica (*para recortar figuras*); **—saw puzzle** rompecabezas (*de recortes*); v. tocar una jiga; bailar una jiga; bailotear; menear(se).

jig•gle [dʒígl] v. zangolotear(se), zarandear(se), menear(se); s. zarandeo, meneo, zangoloteo.

jilt [dʒɪlt] v. desairar, dar calabazas, dejar plantado.

jin•gle [dʒŋg l] s. retintín; verso o rima infantil; **— bell** cascabel; v. hacer retintín.

job [dʒɔb] s. tarea, faena; trabajo; empleo, ocupación; **to be out of a —** estar sin trabajo; estar desocupado.

jock•ey [dʒɔkɪ] s. jockey, v. maniobrar (*para sacar ventaja o ganar un puesto*).

join [dʒɔɪn] v. juntar(se); enlazar(se); acoplar; unirse a, asociarse a

joint [dʒɔɪnt] s. (*point*) juntura, coyuntura; (*function*) articulación; conexión; bisagra; (*public place*) garito (*casa de juego*); fonducho, restaurante de mala muerte; **out of —** descoyuntado; desunido; adj. unido, asociado; copartícipe; colectivo; **— account** cuenta en común; **— action** acción colectiva; **— committee** comisión mixta; **— creditor** acreedor copartícipe; **— heir** coheredero; **— sessión** sesión plena; **-ly** adv. juntamente, juntos, unidamente, co-

lectivamente.

joke [dʒok] s. broma; chiste, chanza; v. bromear; chancear(se), *Carib.* chotear; Ríopl. farrear; jorobar.

jok•er [dʒókə·] s. bromista, chancero, guasón, *Carib.* choteador; naipe especial (*que no pertenece a ningún palo*).

jok•ing•ly [dʒókɪŋlɪ] adv. en (*o* de) chanza, en (*o* de) broma; de chiste.

jol•ly [dʒálɪ] adj. jovial; alegre; festivo; v. bromear, chancearse.

jolt [dʒolt] s. sacudida; sacudimiento; choque; v. sacudir.

jos•tle [dʒɔs l] v. rempujar o empujar, dar empellones; codear; s. rempujón, empujón, empellón.

jot [dʒɔt] v. **to — down** apuntar, tomar apuntes; s. jota, pizca.

jour•nal [dʒɝn l] s. diario; periódico; revista; acta (*de una junta o concilio*).

jour•nal•ism [dʒɝn lɪzəm] s. periodismo.

jour•nal•ist [dʒɝn lɪst] s. periodista.

jour•nal•istic [dʒɝn lístɪk] adj. periodístico.

jour•ney [dʒɝnɪ] s. viaje; jornada; v. viajar.

joy [dʒɔɪ] s. júbilo, regocijo; alegría, gusto, deleite; felicidad.

joy•ful [dʒɔ́ɪfəl] adj. regocijado, jubiloso; alegre; -ly adv. con regocijo, regocijadamente, con júbilo, alegremente.

joy•ous [dʒɔ́ɪəs] adj. jubiloso, alegre, gozoso.

ju•bi•lant [dʒúbəl ənt] adj. jubiloso, alegre.

ju•bi•lee [dʒúbl ɪ] s. jubileo; júbilo.

judge [dʒʌdʒ] s. juez; **— advocate** auditor de un consejo militar, v. juzgar.

judg•ment [dʒʌdʒmənt] s. juicio; sentencia, fallo; opinión; discernimiento; **— day** día de juicio final.

ju•di•cial [dʒʊdíʃəs] adj. judicial.

ju•di•cious [dʒʊdíʃəs] adj. juicioso, cuerdo.

jug [dʒʌg] s. cántaro; jarro, jarra; botija, chirona (*cárcel*) *Am.* chirola.

jug•gle [dʒʌg l] v. hacer juegos de manos; hacer suertes; **to — the accounts** barajar (*o* manipular) las cuentas; s. juego de manos, suerte; trampa.

jug•gler [dʒʌglə·] s. prestidigitador, malabarista.

juice [dʒus] s. jugo; zumo.

ju•ic•i•ness [dʒúsɪnɪs] s. jugosidad.

juic•y [dʒúsɪ] adj. jugoso, zumoso; suculento; **a —story** un cuento picante.

juke box [dʒúkbɑks] s. tragamonedas; tragaquintos.

Ju•ly [dʒʊláɪ] s. julio.

jum•ble [dʒʌ́mbl] s. revolver(se), barajar; mezclar(se); s. mezcolanza, revoltijo; confusión.

jump [dʒʌmp] v. saltar; brincar; salvar (*de un salto*);

hacer saltar; comerse una pieza (*en el juego de damas*); **to – at the chance** asir o aprovechar la oportunidad; **to – bail** perder la fianza por evasión; to – **over** saltar por encima de, salvar de un salto; **to – the track** descarrilarse, **to – to conclusions** hacer deducciones precipitadas; *s.* salto; brinco, subida repentina (*del precio*); **to be always on the – andar** siempre de aquí para allá; trajinar, trafagar, ser muy activo.

jump•er [dʒ ʌ mpə] *s.* saltador; chaquetón holgado (*de obrero*); vestido sin mangas (*puesto sobre la blusa de mujer*); **-s** traje de juego (*para niños*).

jump•y [dʒ ʌ mpɪ] *adj.* saltón; asustadizo; nervioso.

junc•tion [dʒ ʌ ŋk∫ən] *s.* unión, juntura; confluencia (*de dos ríos*); empalme (*de ferrocarriles*).

junc•ture [dʒ ʌ ŋkt∫ə] *s.* juntura; coyuntura; **at this – a** esta sazón; en esta coyuntura.

June [dʒun] *s.* junio.

jun•gle [dʒ ʌ ŋg]] *s.* selva; matorral; *Am.* jungla; *Carib.* manigua.

jun•ior [dʒínə] *adj.* menor, más joven; **– college** colegio para los dos primeros años del bachillerato; **John Smith, Junior (Jr.)** John Smith, hijo; *s.* estudiante del tercer año (*en escuela superior, colegio o universidad*).

ju•ni•per [dʒúnɪpə] *s.* junípero; enebro.

junk [dʒʌŋk] *s.* basura; desperdicios; trastos viejos; cosa inservible; **Chinese –** junco chino (*embarcación pequeña*); *v.* desechar, echar a la basura.

ju•ris•dic•tion [dʒʊrɪsdík∫ən] *s.* jurisdicción.

ju•ris•pru•dence [dʒʊrɪsprúd ŋ s] *s.* jurisprudencia, derecho.

ju•ror [dʒúrə] *s.* jurado, miembro de un jurado.

ju•ry [dʒúrɪ] *s.* jurado; **grand –** jurado de acusación.

just [dʒʌst] *adj.* justo; recto; exacto; *adv.* ni más ni menos; exactamente; justamente; precisamente; sólo, no más, nada má; apenas; **– now** ahora mismo; **be – left** acaba de salir, *Am.* salió recién; **she is – a little girl** no es más que una niña; es una niña no más; **to have –** acabar de.

jus•tice [dʒ ʌ stɪs] *s.* justicia, juez; magistrado.

jus•ti•fi•ca•tion [dʒʌstəfəké∫ən] *s.* justificación.

jus•ti•fy [dʒ ʌ stəfaɪ] *v.* justificar.

just•ly [dʒ ʌ stlɪ] *adv.* justamente; con razón.

jut [dʒʌt] *v.* sobresalir, proyectarse, extenderse; *s.* salidizo, proyección.

ju•ve•nile [dʒúvən]] *adj.* juvenil.

K

kan•ga•roo [kæŋgərú] *s.* canguro.

keel [kil] *s.* quilla; *v.* dar de quilla (*voltear un barco*); **to – over** volcar(se); zozobrar; caerse patas arriba, desplomarse.

keen [kin] *adj.* agudo; afilado; perspicaz; ansioso.

keen•ness [kínnɪs] *s.* agudeza; perspicacia; anhelo, ansia.

keep [kip] *v.* guardar; tener guardado; tener; retener; conservar(se); preservar(se); mantener(se); **to – accounts** llevar las cuentas; **to – at it** persistir, seguir dale que dale; **to – away** mantener(se) alejado; **to – back** tener a raya; detener; reprimir, restringir; **to – from** impedir; guardar(se) de; abstenerse de; **to – going** seguir andando, seguir adelante; seguir viviendo; **to – off** no arrimarse, no acercarse; no entrar; mantener(se) a distancia; **to – one's hands off** no tocar; **to – one's temper** contenerse, refrenarse, reprimirse; **to – quiet** estarse quieto o callado; **to – something up** seguir o continuar haciendo algo; **to – to the right** seguir a la derecha; mantenerse a la derecha; **to – track of** llevar la cuenta de; no perder de vista; *s.* manutención, subsistencia; **for -s** para siempre; para guardar, dado, no prestado.

keep•er [kípə] *s.* guardián, custodio; **jail –** carcelero.

keep•ing [kípɪŋ] *s.* custodia; mantenimiento; preservación, conservación; **in – with** en armonía con.

keep•sake [kípsek] *s.* prenda, recuerdo, regalo.

keg [kɛg] *s.* tone, barril.

ken•nel [kén]] *s.* perrera.

kept [kɛpt] *pret. & p.p. de* **to keep**.

ker•chief [kɝ́t∫ɪf] *s.* pañuelo, pañolón.

ker•nel [kɝ́ n] *s.* simiente; grano (*de trigo o maíz*); meollo (*de ciertas frutas como la nuez*); núcleo.

ker•o•sene [kérəsin] *s.* kerosina, petróleo para lámparas.

ket•tle [két] *s.* caldera; **–drum** tímpano; **tea–** marmita, tetera, *Am.* pava (*para el mate*).

key [ki] *s.* (*lock*) llave, clave; (*music*) clave; (*instrument*) tecla; (*land*) cayo; isleta; **– ring** llavero; **to be in –** estar a tono, estar templado; estar en armonía; *v.* poner a tono, afinar, templar (*con llave*); armonizar; **to – up** elevar el tono de; **to be -ed up** estar sobreexcitado; estar en tensión nerviosa.

key•board [kíbord] *s.* teclado.

key•hole [kíhol] *s.* ojo de la cerradura.

key•note [kínot] *s.* nota tónica; idea o principio fundamental.

key•stone [kíston] *s.* clave (*de un arco*); base, fundamento principal.

kha•ki [kókɪ] *s.* kaki, caqui; *adj.* de kaki.

kick [kɪk] *s.* (*foot*) *Esp. coz*; puntapié; *Am.* patada, (*complaint*) queja; protesta; fuerza (*de una bebida*); estímulo; **to have a** – *Am.* patear (*dícese del licor*); *v.* cocear; dar coces o patadas; dar puntapiés; patear; quejarse, protestar; **to – out** echar a patadas; echar, expulsar; **to – the bucket** estirar la pata, morir, *Am.* patear el balde; **to – up a lot of dust** levantar una polvareda.

kid [kɪd] *s.* cabrito; cabritilla (*piel curtida de cabrito*); niño, niña; **– gloves** guantes de cabritilla; *v.* bromear, embromar; chancearse con, *Carib.*, *Méx.* chotear.

kid•nap [kídnæp] *v.* secuestrar, raptar.

kid•nap•per [kídnæpə-] *s.* secuestrador; robachicos, ladrón de niños.

kid•nap•ping [kídnæpɪŋ] *s.* rapto, secuestro.

kid•ney [kídnɪ] *s.* riñón; **– bean** judía, frijol; **– stones** cálculos.

kill [kɪl] *v.* matar; destruir, amortiguar; para (*el motor*); *s.* animal o animales matados (*en la caza*).

kill•er [kílə-] *s.* matador; asesino.

kiln [kɪln] *s.* horno.

ki•lo [kílo], **kilogram** [kílogram *s.* kilo, kilogramo.

kil•o•me•ter [kíləmitə-] *s.* kilómetro.

ki•mo•no [kəmónə] *s.* quimono; bata.

kin [kɪn] *s.* parentela, parientes, familia; **to notify the nearest of** – avisar al pariente o deudo más cercano.

kind [kaɪnd] *adj.* bondadoso; benévolo; amable; **to send one's – regards to** enviar afectuosos saludos a; **kindhearted** de buen corazón; **– of tire** algo cansado; *s.* clase, especie, género; **to pay in** – pagar en especie; pagar en la misma moneda.

kin•der•gar•ten [kíndə-gɑrt ŋ]s. escuela de párvulos.

kin•dle [kɪ́ndl] *v.* encender(se); inflamar(se); incitar; prender (*el fuego*).

kin•dling [kíndlɪŋ] *s.* encendimiento;leña ligera, astilla, *Andes* charamuscas.

kind•ly [káɪndlɪ] *adj.* bondadoso; benigno; benévolo; amable, apacible; *adv.* bondadosamente, amablemente; con benevolencia; por favor; **not to take – to criticism** no aceptar de buen agrado las correcciones.

kind•ness [kíndnɪs] *s.* bondad, amabilidad; gentileza; benevolencia; favor.

kin•dred [kíndrɪd] *adj.* emparentado; allegado; semejante; **– facts** hechos relacionados; **– spirits** espíritus afines.

ki•nes•ics [kaɪnízɪks] *s.* kinésica; quinésica.

king [kɪŋ] *s.* rey; rey (*en ajedrez*); dama (*en el juego de damas*).

king•dom [kíŋdəm] *s.* reino.

king•ly [kíŋlɪ] *adj.* regio; real; majestuoso; *adv.* regiamente; majestuosamente.

kink [kɪŋk] *s.* (*bend*) enroscadura; (*pain*) tortícolis.

kink•y [kíŋkɪ] *adj.* crespo, ensortijado, *Am.* grifo.

kin•ship [kɪ́nʃɪp] *s.* parentesco; afinidad; semejanza.

kins•man [kínzmən] *s.* pariente, deudo.

kiss [kɪs] *s.* beso; *v.* besar.

kit [kɪt] *s.* estuche, caja de herramientas; saco, envoltura (*para guardar instrumentos, herramientas, etc.*); gatito; **medicine** – botiquín; **soldier's** – mochila.

kitch•en [kíʃ ɪn] *s.* cocina; **– ware** trastos de cocina.

kite [kaɪt] *s.* cometa (*f.*), *Méx.*, papalote; *Ch.*, volantín; *Arg.*, barrilete; milano (*pájaro*)

kit•ten [kít ŋ] *s.* gatito.

kit•ty [kítɪ] *s.* gatito, minino.

knack [næk] *s.* destreza, maña, habilidad.

knap•sack [náepsæk] *s.* mochila, morral, alforja.

knave [nev] *s.* bribón, bellaco, pícaro; sota (*de naipes*).

knead [nid] *v.* amasar, sobar.

knee [nil] *v.* rodilla; **knee-deep** hasta la rodilla; metido hasta las rodillas.

kneel [nil] *v.* arrodillarse; hincharse.

knell [nɛl] *s.* doble (*toque de campanas por los difuntos*); *v.* doblar, tocar a muerto.

knelt [nɛlt] *pret. & p.p. de* **to kneel.**

knew [nju] *pret. de* **to know.**

knick•knack [níknæk] *s.* chuchería, baratija, chisme.

knife [naɪf] *s.* cuchillo; cuchilla; **carving** – trinchante; **pocket** – cortaplumas; navaja; *v.* acuchillar.

knight [naɪt] *s.* caballero; campeón; caballo (*en ajedrez*); **– errant** caballero andante; *v.* armar caballero.

knight•hood [náɪthUd] *s.* caballería, orden de la caballería.

knit [nɪt] *v.* tejer (*a punto de aguja*); hacer calcetas o malla; soldarse (*un hueso*); **– one's brow** fruncir las cejas, arrugar la frente; *pret. & p.p. de* **to knit.**

knit•ting [nítɪŋ] *s.* labor de punto; **– needle** aguja de media.

knives [naɪvz] *pl. de* **knife.**

knob [nɑb] *s.* perilla, botón, tirador (*de puerta, cajón, etc.*); protuberancia

knock [nɑk] *v.* (*pound*) golpear, golpetear; llamar o tocar a la puerta; (*criticize*) criticar; censurar o hablar mal de; **to – down** derribar; desmontar (*una máquina o aparato*); **to – off** suspender (*el trabajo*) rebajar (*del precio*); derribar, echar abajo; **to – out** aplastar de un golpe; poner fuera de combate; dejar sin sentido; *s.* golpe; golpeteo; toque, llamada, aldabonazo; crítica, censura; **knock-kneed** zambo, patizambo.

knock•er [nɑ́kə-] *s.* llamador, aldaba, aldabón; citicón; murmurador.

knoll [nol] *s.* colina, loma; eminencia.

knot [nɑt] *s,* nudo; lazo; *v.* anudar (se).

knot•ty [nɑ́tɪ] *adj.* nudoso; dificultoso, enredado.

know [no] *v.* (*to be acquainted with*) conocer; (*to have knowledge of; to know how to*) saber; (*to recognize*)

reconocer; distinguir; **to – how to swim** saber nadar;
to – of saber de; tener conocimiento de; tener noticias de; estar enterado de.

know•ing•ly [nóɪŋlɪ] *adv.* a sabiendas; adrede.

knowl•edge [nólɪdʒ] *s.* conocimiento; saber, sabiduría; pericia; **not to my –** no que yo sepa.

known [non] *p.p. de* **to know.**

knuck•le [n ʌ k]] *s.* nudillo; coyuntura, articulación; artejo; *v.* someterse; **to – down** someterse; aplicarse con empeño al trabajo.

L

la•bel [léb]] *s.* marbete, etiqueta, rótulo; *v.* marcar, rotular; apodar, llamar.

la•bor [lébə‑] *s.* trabajo; labor; obra; mano de obra; la clase obrera; **– union** unión de obreros; **to be in – union** estar de parto; *v.* trabajar; afanarse; estar de parto; elaborar (*un punto*).

lab•o•ra•to•ry [læ̃brətorɪ] *s.* laboratorio.

la•bor•er [lébərə‑] *s.* trabajador, obrero; jornalero, peón.

la•bo•ri•ous [ləbórɪəs] *adj.* laborioso, trabajoso, penoso; industrioso.

lab•y•rinth [læ̃bərɪnθ] *s.* laberinto.

lace [les] *s.* (*cloth*) encaje; (*cord*) cordón, cordoncillo, cinta (*de corsé, etc.*); **gold –** galón de oro (*para guarnecer uniformes*); *v.* atar con cinta o cordón; guarnecer con encajes; enlazar, entrelazar.

lack [læk] *s.* falta, escasez, carencia; deficiencia; *v.* carecer de, faltarle a uno; necesitar; **he -s courage** le falta ánimo.

lack•ey [læ̃kɪ] *s.* lacayo.

lack•ing [læ̃kɪŋ] *adj.* falto. carente.

lac•quer [læ̃kə‑] *s.* laca; *v.* barnizar con laca.

lad [læd] *s.* rapaz, chico.

lad•der [læ̃də‑] *s.* escalera de mano.

lad•en [léd n̩] *adj.* cargado; agobiado, abrumado; *v.* cargar; agobiar.

la•dies [lédɪz] *pl. de* **lady.**

la•dle [léd]] *s.* cucharón; *v.* servir (*sopa*) con cucharón.

la•dy [lédɪ] *s.* señora; dama; **– like** como señora, muy fina, elegante; **– love** amada, querida.

lag [læg] *v.* rezagarse, quedarse atrás, atrasarse; andar lentamente, *s.* retardo o retardación, retraso.

la•goon [ləgún] *s.* laguna.

laid [led] *prep. & p.p. de* **to lay; to be – up** estar incapacitado o estropeado.

lain [len] *p.p. de* **to lie.**

lair [lɛr] *s.* guarida; cueva de fieras.

lake [lek] *s.* lago.

lamb [læm] *s.* cordero; **–kin** corderito.

lame [lem] *adj.* cojo; lisiado; estropeado; **– excuse** disculpa falsa; *v.* hacer cojo; estropear, incapacitar.

la•ment [ləmént] *s.* lamento; *v.* lamentar (se).

lam•ent•a•ble [læ̃məntəb]] *adj.* lamentable; doloroso.

lam•en•ta•tion [læməntéʃən] *s.* lamentación, lamento.

lam•i•nate [læ̃mənet] *v.* laminar.

lamp [læmp] *s.* lámpara; linterna; farol; **–post** poste (de farol); **–shade** pantalla de lámpara.

lance [læns] *s.* lanza; *v.* alancear, lancear, herir con lanza; picar con bisturí.

land [lænd] *s.* tierra; terreno; suelo; *v.* desembarcar, aterrizar (*un avión*); llegar; coger (*un pez*); **to – a job** conseguir una colocación , lograr un empleo.

land-grant [læ̃ndgrænt] *adj.* mediante donación federal de tierras.

land-hold•er [læ̃ndholdə‑] *s.* terrateniente, propietario, hacendado.

land•ing [læ̃ndɪŋ] *s.* (*act*) desembarco, desembarque; aterrizaje (*de un avión*); (*place*) desembarcadero; descanso (*de escaleras*); **– field** campo de aterrizaje; aeropuerto; **– strip** pista de aterrizaje.

land•la•dy [læ̃ndledɪ] *s.* patrona, casera, dueña (*de la casa*).

land•lord [læ̃nslɔrd] *s.* amo, patrón, propietario, dueño; casero.

land•mark [læ̃ndmɔrk] *s.* mojón, señal (*para fijar los confines*); marca; suceso culminante.

land•own•er [læ̃ndonə‑] *s.* terrateniente, propietario, hacendado.

land•scape [læ̃ndskep] *s.* paisaje.

land•slide [læ̃ndslaɪd] *s.* derrumbe, derrumbamiento, desplome; gran mayoría de votos.

lane [len] *s.* seda, vereda; callejuela; ruta, derrotero (*de vapores o aviones*).

lan•guage [læ̃ŋgwɪdʒ] *s.* lengua; idioma; lenguaje.

lan•guid [læ̃ŋgwɪd] *adj.* lánguido.

lan•guish [læ̃ŋgwɪʃ] *v.* languidecer.

lan•guor [læ̃ŋgə‑] *d.* languidez.

lank [læŋk] *adj.* alto y delgado, largucho.

lank•y [læ̃ŋkɪ] *adj.* largucho, zancón, zancudo.

lan•tern [læ̃ntə‑n] *s.* linterna; farol.

lap [læp] *s.* falda, regazo; aleta; etapa, trecho (*de una carrera*); *v.* lamer; **to – over** cruzar (se) sobre, entrecruzar (se).

la•pel [ləpél] *s.* solapa.

lap•i•dar•y [læ̃pɪdɛrɪ] *s. & adj.* lapidario.

lapse [læps] *s.* lapso; transcurso; desliz, error; *v.* deslizarse; pasar, transcurrir; caer en un desliz; decaer (*el entusiasmo, el interés, etc.*); caducar (*un plazo, un contrato, etc.*).

lar•board [lórbə·d] *s.* babor; *adj.* de babor; **– side** banda de babor.

lar•ce•ny [lárs n̩ ɪ] *s.* latrocinio, hurto; ratería.

lard [lord] *s.* lardo, manteca de puerco; *v.* mechar.

large [lordʒ] *adj.* grande; **at –** suelo, libre; sin trabas; en general; **-ly** *adv.* grandemente, en gran parte.

large- scale [lórrdʒskél] *adj.* en grande escala.

lar•i•at [lǽrɪət] *s.* reata.

lark [lork] *s.* (*bird*) alondra; (*fun*) diversión, holgorio, jarana; **to go on a –** ir o andar de jarana.

lar•va [lórvə] *s.* larva.

lar•ynx [lǽrɪŋks] *s.* laringe.

las•civ•i•ous [ləsívɪəs] *adj.* lascivo.

lash [læʃ] *s.* látigo; azote, latigazo; pestaña; *v.* fustigar; azotar; censurar, reprender; amarrar.

lass [læs] *s.* moza, muchacha, doncella.

las•si•tude [lǽsətjud] *s.* dejadez, flojedad, decaimiento de fuerzas.

las•so [lǽso] *s.* lazo, reata, mangana; *v.* lazar, *Am.* enlazar.

last [læst] *adj.* (*in a series*) último; final; (*just passed*) pasado; **– night** anoche; **–year** el año pasado; **at –** por fin, finalmente, al fin; **next to the –** penúltimo; **to arrive –** llegar el último; *s.* fin, término; horma (*de zapato*); *v.* durar; perdurar; **-ly** *adv.* finalmente, en conclusión.

last•ing [lǽstɪŋ] *adj.* duradero; perdurable.

latch [lætʃ] *s.* pestillo, picaporte, aldaba, cerrojo; *v.* cerrar con aldaba.

late [let] *adj.* (*tardy*) tardío; tardo; (*recent*) reciente; último; **– comer** recien llegado; rezagado; **a – hour** una hora avanzada; **the – Mr. X** el finado (*o* difunto) Sr X; **to have a – supper** cenar tarde; *adv.* tarde; **– in the night** a una hora avanzada de la noche; **– into the night** a deshoras de la noche; **– in the week** a fines de la semana; **of –** últimamente, recientemente; hace poco; **to be –** ser tarde; llegar tarde; estar atrasado, venir o llegar con retraso (*el tren*); **the train was ten minutes –** el tren llegó con diez minutos de retraso; **-ly** *adv.* últimamente, recientemente; hace poco, poco ha.

la•tent [lét n̩ t] *adj.* latente.

lat•er [létə·] *adv.* & *adj.* (*comp. de* **late**) más tarde; después, luego; más creciente; posterior.

lat•er•al [lǽtərəl] *adj.* lateral.

lat•est [létɪst] *adv.* & *adj.* (*superl. de* **late**) más tarde; más reciente, más nuevo; último; **the – fashion** la última moda, las últimas novedades, **the – news** las últimas novedades, las noticias más recientes; **at the –** a más tardar.

lathe [leð] *s.* torno (*de carpintero o mecánico*).

lath•er [lǽðə·] *s.* jabonadura, espuma de jabón; *v.* jabonar, enjabonar; espumar, hacer espuma.

La•tin [lǽt n̩] *adj.* latino; *s.* latín.

lat•i•tude [lǽtətjud] *s.* latitud; libertad; amplitud.

lat•ter [lǽtə·] *adj.* último; **towards the – part of the week** a (*o* hacia) fines de la semana; **the –** éste (ésta, esto, etc.).

lat•tice [lǽtɪs] *s.* celosía; enrejado, rejilla.

laud [lɔd] *v.* loar, encomiar, alabar.

laud•a•ble [lɔ́dəb] *adj.* laudable, loable.

laugh [læf] *v.* reir (se); **to – at** reírse de; **to – loudly** reírse a carcajadas; **to – in one's sleeve** reírse para sus adentros; **she -ed in his face** se rió en sus barbas; *s.* risa; **loud –** risotada, carcajada, risada.

laugh•a•ble [lǽfəb] *adj.* risible; ridículo.

laugh•ter [lǽftə·] *s.* risa.

launch [lɔntʃ] *v.* (*put into water*) botar o echar (*un barco*) al agua; (*a rocket*) lanzar; (*begin*) empezar; poner en operación; **to – forth** lanzarse; **to – forth on a journey** emprender un viaje, *s.* lancha.

laun•der [lɔ́ndə·] *v.* lavar y planchar (*la ropa*).

laun•dress [lɔndrɪs] *s.* lavandera.

laun•dry [lɔ́ndrɪ] *s.* lavandería; lavado; ropa (lavada).

lau•rel [lɔ́rəl] *s.* laurel; gloria, honor.

la•va [lóvə] *s.* lava.

lav•a•to•ry [lǽvətɔɪ] *s.* lavabo; lavamanos; lavatorio.

lav•en•der [lǽvəndə·] *s.* espliego, lavándula; *adj.* lila, morado claro.

lav•ish [lǽvɪʃ] *adj.* gastador, pródigo, dadivoso; abundante, copioso; profuso; lujoso; *v.* prodigar; malgastar, despilfarrar; **to – praise upon** colmar de alabanzas a; **-ly** pródigamente; copiosamente; lujosamente.

law [lɔ] *s.* ley; derecho, jurisprudencia; regla; **– student** estudiante de leyes, estudiante de derecho; **law-abiding** observante de la ley.

law-break•er [lɔ́brekə·] *s.* infractor, transgresor.

law•ful [lɔ́fəl] *adj.* legal; lícito; válido; permitido.

law•less [lɔ́lɪs] *adj.* sin ley; ilegal; desenfrenado; revoltoso; licencioso

law-mak•er [lɔ́mekə·.] *s.* legislador

lawn [lɔn] *s.* césped, prado; linón (*tela de hilo o algodón*); **– mower** cortadora de césped.

law-suit [lɔ́sut] *s.* pleito, litigio.

law•yer [lɔ́jə·] *s.* abogado, jurisconsulto.

lax [læks] *adj.* flojo; suelto; relajado.

lax•a•tive [lǽksəɪv] *adj.* & *s.* laxante, purgante.

lax•i•ty [lǽksətɪ] *s.* flojedad, flojera; relajamiento

(de una regla, ley, etc.).

lay [le] *pret de* **to lie.**

lay [le] *v.* colocar; poner; tender, extender; poner *(huevos)*; echar *(la culpa)*; atribuir *(la responsabilidad)*; presentar, exponer; asentar *(el polvo)*; **to – a wager** apostar; **to – aside** poner a un lado; ahorrar; **to – away** *(o* **by)** guardar; **to – bare** revelar; exponer; **to – down** poner, colocar; rendir *(la armas)*; **to – down the law** mandar; dictar **to – hold of** asir, agarrar; **to – off a workman** suspender a un obrero; **to – open** exponer a la vista; **to – out a plan** trazar un plan; **to – up** almacenar; guardar; ahorrar; **to be laid up** estar incapacitado o estropeado; **to – waste** asolar; *s.* lay, balada, canción; situación, orientación *(del terreno)*; *adj.* lego, laico; profano *(no iniciado en una ciencia).*

lay•er [léə‑] *s.* capa; estrato; gallina ponedora.

lay•man [lémən] *s.* lego, seglar, laico.

la•zi•ly [lézɪlɪ] *adv.* perezosamente.

la•zi•ness [lézɪnɪs] *s.* pereza.

la•zy [lézɪ] *adj.* perezoso, holgazán.

lead [lɛd] *s.* plomo; plomada, pesa de plomo.

lead [lid] *v. (guide)* guiar, dirigir; llevar; conducir; mandar *(un ejército)*; *(precede)* ir a la cabeza de; sobresalir entre; ser mano *(en el juego de naipes)*; **to – an orchestra** dirigir una orquesta, llevar la batuta; **to – astray** llevar por mal camino, extraviar, descarriar; **to – the way** ir por delante; mostrar el camino; *s.* delantera, primer lugar; mando, dirección; indicio; papel principal; primer actor.

lead•en [lɛ́dn̩] *adj.* plomizo; aplomado, color de plomo; pesado.

lead•er [lídə‑] *s.* jefe, caudillo *Am.* líder; director; guía; caballo delantero; **-s** puntos suspensivos.

lead•er•ship [lídə‑ʃɪp] *s.* dirección, mando, iniciativa.

lead•ing [lídɪŋ] *adj.* principal; delantero; **– man** primer actor.

lead•off [lídɔf] *adj.* delantero, puntero.

leaf [lif] *s.* hoja; *v.* echar hojas *(un árbol)*, cubrirse de hojas; **to – through a book** hojear un libro.

leaf•less [líflɪs] *adj.* sin hojas, deshojado.

leaf•let [líflɪt] *s.* hojilla; folleto, hoja volante, papel volante, circular.

leaf•y [lífɪ] *adj.* frondoso.

league [lig] *s. (alliance)* liga, confederación; sociedad; *(distance)* legua; *v.* asociar (se); ligarse, coligarse.

leak [lik] *s.* gotera *(en un techo)*; agujero; grieta *(por donde se escapa el agua o el gas)*; escape *(de gas, vapor, electricidad, etc.)*; *v.* gotear (se); rezumar (se); hacer agua *(dícese de un barco)*, salirse, escaparse *(el gas, el vapor, etc.).*

lean [lin] *v. (incline)* inclinar (se); recostar(se); reclinar(se); *(support)* apoyar(se); *adj.* magro; flaco; **year** año estéril; año improductivo.

leant [lɛnt] = **leaned**.

leap [lip] *v.* saltar; brincar; *s.* salto, brinco; **– year** año bisiesto.

leapt [lɛpt] *pret.* & *p.p. de* **to leap.**

learn [lɜ́n] *v.* aprender, saber, averiguar, enterarse de.

learn•ed [lɜ́nɪd] *adj.* erudito; docto.

learn•er [lɜ́nə‑] *s.* aprendedor; estudiante, estudioso.

learn•ing [lɜ́nɪŋ] *s.* erudición, saber; aprendizaje.

learnt [lɜ́nt] *pret.* & *p.p. de* **to learn.**

lease [lis] *v.* arrendar, dar o tomar en arriendo; *s.* arriendo, contrato de arrendamiento.

leash [liʃ] *s.* traílla; cuerda.

least [list] *adj.* (el) mínimo, (el) más pequeño; *adv.* menos; **at –** al menos, a lo menos, por lo menos; **the – lo** (el, la) menos.

leath•er [léðə‑] *s.* cuero, piel; *adj.* de cuero, de piel; **– strap** correa.

leave [liv] *v.* dejar; abandonar; salir (de); partir; irse; **to – out** dejar fuera; omitir; *s.* permiso, licencia; **– of absence** licencia; **to take – of absence** licencia; **to take – of** despedirse de.

leav•en [lévən] *s.* levadura, fermento; *v.* fermentar *(la masa).*

leaves [livz] *pl. de* **leaf.**

leav•ings [lívɪŋz] *s.* sobras, desperdicios.

lec•ture [lɛ́ktʃə‑] *s.* conferencia, discurso; represión; *v.* dar una conferencia; explicar; reprender.

lec•tur•er [lɛ́ktʃərə‑] *s.* conferenciante; lector *(de universidad).*

led [lɛd] *pret.* & *p.p. de* **to lead.**

ledge [lɛdʒ] *s.* borde; salidizo.

ledg•er [lɛdʒə‑] *s.* libro mayor *(en contabilidad).*

leech [litʃ] *s.* sanguijuela.

leer [lɪr] *s.* mirada de soslayo, mirada lujuriosa; *v.* mirar de soslayo, mirar con lujuria.

lee•ward [líwə‑d] *s.* & *adv.* sotavento.

left [lɛft] *pret.* & *p.p. de* **to leave; I have two books – me** quedan dos libros; *adj.* izquierdo; *s.* izquierda; mano izquierda; **at (on, to) the –** a la izquierda.

left-hand•ed [léfthǽndɪd] *adj.* zurdo; a la izquierda; torpe; malicioso, insincero; **– compliment** alabanza irónica.

left•ist [léftɪst] *s.* izquierdista.

left•o•ver [léftovə‑] *adj.* sobrante; **-s** *s. pl.* sobras.

left-wing [léftwɪŋ] *adj.* izquierdista.

leg [lɛg] *s.* pierna; pata *(de animal, mesa, etc.)*; pie o pata *(de banquillo, silla, etc.)*; etapa, trecho *(de una carrera o viaje)*; **to be on one's last -s** estar en las últimas.

leg•a•cy [légəsɪ] *s.* legado, herencia.

le•gal [líg ̩l] *adj.* legal; lícito.

le•gal•ize [légɪt] *v.* legalizar; sancionar, autorizar.

leg•ate [légɪt] s. legado; delegado.

le•ga•tion [lɪgéʃən] s. legación; embajada.

leg•end [lédʒənd] s. leyenda; letrero, inscripción.

leg•end•ar•y [lédʒəndɛrɪ] adj. legendario.

leg•gings [légɪŋz] s. pl. polainas.

leg•i•ble [lédʒəb‿l] adj. legible.

le•gion [lídʒən] s. legión.

leg•is•late [lédʒɪslet] v. legislar.

leg•is•la•tion [lɛdʒɪsléʃən] s. legislación.

leg•is•la•tive [lédʒɪsletɪv] adj. legislativo.

leg•is•la•tor [lédʒɪsletɚ] s. legislador.

leg•is•la•ture [lédʒɪsletʃɚ] s. legislatura, asamblea legislativa.

le•git•i•mate [lɪdʒítəmɪt] adj. legítimo.

lei•sure [líʒɚ] s. ocio; – **hours** horas de ocio; **to be at** – estar ocioso; estar libre o desocupado; **do it at your** – hágalo Vd. cuando pueda o le convenga; hágalo Vd. en sus ratos de ocio.

lei•sure•ly [líʒɚlɪ] adj. lento, deliberado, pausado; adv. sin prisa, despacio, a sus (mis, tus, etc.) anchas.

lem•on [lémən] s. limón; – **tree** limonero; adj. de limón; – **color** cetrino.

lem•on•ade [lɛmənéd] s. limonada.

lend [lɛnd] v. prestar.

lend•er [léndɚ] s. prestador; **money** – prestamista.

lenght [lɛŋkθ] s. largo, largor, largura, longitud; duración; cantidad; (de una sílaba); **at** – largamente, detenidamente; al fin; **to go to any** – hacer cuanto esté de su parte.

length•en [léŋkθən] v. alargar(se); prolongar(se).

length•wise [léŋkθwaɪz] adv. a lo largo; longitudinalmente; adj. longitudinal.

length•y [léŋkθɪ] adj. largo, prolongado.

le•nient [línɪənt] adj. indulgente, clemente, poco severo.

lens [lɛnz] s. lente; cristalino (del ojo).

lent [lɛnt] pret. & p.p. de **to lend**.

Lent [lɛnt] s. cuaresma.

leop•ard [lépɚd] s. leopardo.

less [lɛs] adj. menor; adv. & prep. menos; – **and** – cada vez menos.

less•en [lésɚ] v. aminorar(se), disminuir(se), reducir(se); mermar.

less•er [lésɚ] adj. menor, más pequeño.

les•son [lésn̩] s. lección.

lest [lɛst] conj. no sea que, por miedo de que.

let [lɛt] v. (permit) dejar, permitir; (rent) alquilar, arrendar; – **us** (o **let's**) **do it** vamos a hacerlo, hagámoslo; – **him come** que venga; **to** – **be** no molestar, dejar en paz; no tocar; **to** – **down** bajar; desilusionar; **to** – **go** soltar; **to** – **in** dejar entrar, admitir; **to** – **know** avisar, enterar, hacer saber; **to** – **off** soltar; dejar libre; **to** – **through** dejar pasar; **to** – **up** disminuir; pret. & p.p. de **to let**.

let•down [létdɑʊn] s. aflojamiento; desilusión

le•thal [líθəl] adj. letal.

le•thar•gy [léθədʒɪ] s. letargo; **to fall into a** – aletargarse.

let•ter [létɚ] s. (alphabet) letra; (missive) carta; – **box** buzón; – **carrier** cartero; –**head** membrete; v. rotular, hacer a mano letras de molde.

let•tuce [létɪs] s. lechuga.

lev•el [lév‿l] adj. llano, plano, a nivel; igual; parejo; **level-headed** bien equilibrado, sensato; adv. a nivel; a ras; s. nivel; **to be on the** – obrar rectamente, obrar sin engaño; ser o decir la pura verdad; v. nivelar; igualar; allanar; apuntar, asestar (un arma); **to** – **to the ground** arrasar, echar por tierra.

lev•er [lévɚ] s. palanca; **control** – palanca de mano.

lev•i•ty [lévɪtɪ] s. frivolidad; levedad.

lev•y [lévɪ] s. imposición, recaudación (de tributos, impuestos, etc.); leva, enganche, reclutamiento; embargo (de propiedad); v. imponer, exigir, recaudar (tributos o multas); reclutar; **to** – **on someone's property** embargar la propiedad de alguien

lewd [lud] adj. lujurioso, lascivo, deshonesto.

lewd•ness [lúdnɪs] s. lascivia, lujuria.

lex•i•con [léksɪkən] s. léxico.

li•a•bil•i•ty [laɪəbílɪtɪ] s. responsabilidad; obligación; desventaja; **liabilities** obligaciones, deudas; pasivo.

li•a•ble [láɪəb‿l] adj. responsable, obligado; sujeto, expuesto; propenso; probable.

li•ai•son [liezán] s. enlace; unión.

li•ar [láɪɚ] s. mentiroso, embustero.

li•bel [láɪb‿l] s. libelo; difamación; v. difamar.

lib•er•al [líbərəl] adj. & s. liberal.

lib•er•al•ism [líbərəlɪzm] s. liberalismo.

lib•er•al•i•ty [lɪbər ǽ lətɪ] s. liberalidad; larguezà, generosidad.

lib•er•al•ize [líbə‿əlaɪz] v. liberalizar(se).

lib•er•ate [líbəret] v. libertar, librar; soltar.

lib•er•a•tion [lɪbəréʃən] s. liberación.

lib•er•a•tor [líbəretɚ] s. libertador.

lib•er•tine [líbə‿tin] adj. & s. libertino.

lib•er•ty [líbə‿tɪ] s. libertad; **at** – libre.

li•brar•i•an [laɪbrérɪən] s. bibliotecario.

li•brar•y [láɪbrɛrɪ] s. biblioteca.

lice [laɪs] pl. de **louse**.

li•cense, li•cence [láɪs n̩ s] s. licencia; permiso; título; **driver's** – licencia (pase, certificado o patente) de chófer; título de conductor; licencia para manejar; – **plate** placa (o chapa) de numeración, chapa de circulación, chapa de matrícula; v. licenciar, dar licencia a; permitir, autorizar.

li•cen•tious [laɪsénʃəs] adj. licencioso, disoluto.

lick [lɪk] v. (tongue) lamer; (thrash) dar una tunda o zurra; vencer; **to** – **someone's boots** adular a uno con servilismo; **to** – **the dust** morder el polvo; adu-

lar; *s.* lamedura, *Am.* lamida; lengüetada; *C.A.*
lambida; **salt —** lamedero (*lugar salino donde lame
el ganado*); **not to do a — of work** no hacer absolutamente nada.

lick•ing [líkɪŋ] *s.* zurra, tunda.

lid [lɪd] *s.* tapadera, tapa; **eye—** párpado.

lie [laɪ] *s.* mentira; embuste; **to give the — to** des-
mentir, dar un mentís; *v.* mentir (*pret. & p.p.* **lied**);
tenderse, acostarse; yacer; estar; estar situado;
consistir (en); **to — back** recostarse, echarse hacia
atrás; **to — down** acostarse, echarse, tenderse; **to —
in wait** acechar, espiar.

lieu•ten•ant [luténənt] *s.* teniente; **second —**
subteniente.

life [laɪf] *s.* vida; **from —** del natural; **still —** naturaleza
muerta; **—boat** bote de salvamento, lancha salvavi-
das; **—imprisonment** prisión perpetua; **insurance**
seguro sobre la vida; **— pensión** pensión vitalicia; **—
preserver** salvavidas, cinto o chaqueta de salvamento.

life•less [láɪflɪs] *adj.* sin vida; muerto; examine; inanimado; desanimado.

life•less•ness [láɪflɪsnɪs] *s.* falta de vida; inercia;
falta de animación.

life•like [láɪflaɪk] *adj.* como la vida; natural, que parece vivo.

life•long [láɪflóŋ] *adj.* perpetuo, de toda la vida.

life•time [láɪftaɪm] *s.* vida, transcurso de la vida.

lift [lɪft] *v.* levantar; alzar; elevar; disiparse (*las nubes, la niebla, las tinieblas*) **to — one's hat** quitarse
el sombrero (*para saludar*); *s.* elevación; exaltación
de ánimo; alzamiento, levantamiento; carga; ayuda (*para levantar una carga*); alza (*de un zapato*);
ascensor, *Am.* elevador; **to give someone a — in a
car** llevar a alguien en el auto.

lig•a•ture [lɪ́gətʃur] *s.* ligadura.

light [laɪt] *s.* luz; lumbre; **tail —** *Am.* farito trasero, *Am.*
farol de cola, *Méx.* calavera; *adj.* claro; con luz; de
tez blanca; ligero; leve; frívolo; **— drink** bebida suave; **—headed** frívolo, ligero de cascos; **— hearted**
alegre; **— opera** opereta; **to make —** dar poca
importancia a; *v.* encender(se); iluminar, alumbrar;
to — upon caer sobre; posarse en (*dícese de los
pájaros, mariposas, etc.*).

light•en [láɪt ɳ] *v.* aligerar; iluminar; aclarar; relam-
paguear; alegrar.

light•er [láɪtɚ] *s.* encendedor.

light•house [láɪthaʊs] *s.* faro.

light•ing [láɪtɪŋ] *s.* iluminación; alumbrado.

light•ly [láɪtlɪ] *adv.* ligeramente; levemente;
frivolosamente; sin seriedad.

light•ness [láɪtnɪs] *s.* ligereza; frivolidad; claridad.

light•ning [láɪtnɪŋ] *s.* relampagueo; relámpago; **—
rod** pararrayos.

light•weight [láɪtwet] *s.* peso liviano; peso ligero.

lik•a•ble [láɪkəb]] *adj.* agradable, simpático, placentero.

like [laik] *adv. & prep.* como; del mismo modo que;
semejante a; *adj.* semejante, parecido; **in — manner**
de manera semejante del mismo modo; **to feel —
going** tener ganas de ir; **to look — someone** parecerse a alguien; **it looks — rain** parece que va a
llover, quiere llover; *s.* semejante, igual; **-s** gustos;
preferencias; *v.* gustarle a uno; **he -s books** le gus-
tan los libros; **do whatever you—** haz lo que gustes.

like•ly [láɪklɪ] *adj.* probable, creíble; prometedor; **—
place** lugar a propósito; **it is — to happen** es probable que suceda; *adv.* probablemente.

lik•en [láɪkən] *v.* asemejar, comparar.

like•ness [láɪknɪs] *s.* semejanza; parecido; retrato.

like•wise [láɪkwaɪz] *adv.* igualmente, asimismo, del
mismo modo; también.

lik•ing [láɪkɪŋ] *s.* simpatía; afición; preferencia, gusto.

li•lac [láɪlək] *s.* lila; *adj.* lila, morado claro.

lil•y [lílɪ] *s.* lirio; azucena.

lil•y-white [lɪlihwáɪt] *adj.* blanquísimo; puro;
racialmente segregado.

limb [lɪm] *s.* rama (*de árbol*); miembro (*del cuerpo*);
pierna, brazo.

lim•ber [límbɚ] *adj.* flexible; ágil; *v.* hacer flexible;
to — up agilitar(se), hacer(se) flexible.

lime [laɪm] *s.* cal; lima (*fruta*); liga (*para cazar pájaros*).

lime•light [láɪmlaɪt] *s.* luz de calcio; proscenio; **to
be in the —** estar a la vista del público.

lime•stone [láɪmston] *s.* piedra caliza.

lim•it [lɪ́mɪt] *s.* límite; confín; *v.* limitar.

lim•i•ta•tion [lɪmɪtéʃən] *s.* limitación; restricción.

lim•it•ed [lɪ́mɪtɪd] *adj.* limitado; restringido.

lim•it•less [lɪ́mɪtlɪs] *adj.* ilimitado, sin límites.

limp [lɪmp] *s.* cojera; *v.* cojear; renquear; *adj.* flojo;
flexible.

lim•pid [límpɪd] *adj.* límpido; claro, transparente.

line [laɪn] *s.* (*mark*) línea; renglón; raya; (*cord*) cuerda; (*business*) ramo; giro (*de negocios*); especialidad;
— of goods surtido, línea (*Am.* renglón) de mercancías; **branch railway —** ramal; **pipe —** cañería;
tubería; **to bring into —** alinear; obligar a proceder
de acuerdo con un plan; poner de acuerdo; **to get
in —** meterse en fila, hacer (*o* formar) cola; *v.* linear,
rayar; alinear; forrar; **to — up** alinear(se); formarse, formar fila.

lin•e•age [línɪɪdʒ] *s.* linaje.

lin•e•ar [línɪɚ] *adj.* lineal.

lined [laɪnd] *adj.* rayado; forrado.

lin•en [lính] *s.* lino; ropa blanca.

lin•er [láɪnɚ] *s.* vapor, buque; **air —** avión, transporte
aéreo.

line•up [láɪnəp] *s.* formación.

lin·ger [líŋgɚ] *v.* tardar(se), demorarse, dilatarse; andar ocioso, vagar; perdurar; prolongarse.

lin·ge·rie [læ̃nʒəri] *s.* ropa interior de mujer.

lin·guis·tics [lɪŋgwístɪks] *s.* lengüística.

lin·ing [láɪnɪŋ] *s.* forro.

link [lɪŋk] *s.* eslabón; enlace; **cuff -s** gemelos; *v.* eslabonar(se); enlazar(se).

lin·net [línɪt] *s.* jilguero.

li·no·le·um [lɪnóliəm] *s.* linóleo (*tela impermeable para cubrir el suelo*).

lin·seed [línsid] *s.* linaza; **– oil** aceite de linaza.

lint [lɪnt] *s.* hilas; hilachas.

li·on [láɪən] *s.* león.

li·on·ess [láɪənɪs] *s.* leona.

lip [lɪp] *s.* labio.

lip·stick [lípstɪk] *s.* lápiz para los labios.

liq·uid [líkwɪd] *adj.* líquido; **– assets** valores líquidos (*o realizables*); **– measure** medida para líquidos *s.* líquido.

liq·ui·date [líkwɪdet] *v.* liquidar, saldar (*cuentas*); poner término a.

liq·ui·da·tion [lɪkwɪdéʃən] *s.* liquidación, saldo de cuentas.

liq·uor [líkɚ] *s.* licor; bebida espiritosa (*como aguardiente, ron, etc.*).

lisp [lɪsp] *s.* ceceo; *v.* cecear; balbucir.

list [lɪst] *s.* lista; registro; escora (*inclinación de un barco*); *v.* alistar, registrar poner o apuntar en una lista; hacer una lista de; escorar, inclinarse a la banda.

list·en [lísṇ] *v.* escuchar; atender, dar oídos, prestar atención; **– !** ¡oye! ¡escucha!; ¡oiga! ¡escuche!; **to – in** escuchar por radio; escuchar a hurtadillas (*una conversación*).

lis·ten·er [lísṇɚ] *s.* escuchador, oyente; **radio –** radioescucha, radioyente.

list·less [lístlɪs] *adj.* abstraído; indiferente; indolente; desatento.

list·less·ness [lístlɪsnɪs] *s.* indiferencia, inatención, abstracción.

lit [lɪt] *pret. & p.p. de* **to light**; *adj.* alumbrado; algo borracho.

lit·er·al [lítɚəl] *adj.* literal; **-ly** *adv.* al pie de la letra, literalmente.

lit·er·ar·y [lítɚɛrɪ] *adj.* literario.

lit·er·a·ture [lítɚətʃUr] *s.* literatura; impresos, folletos, circulares.

lit·i·ga·tion [lɪtəgéʃən] *s.* litigio, pleito.

lit·ter [lítɚ] *s.* (*young animals*) camada, cría; (*stretcher*) litera; camilla; cama de paja para animales; (*disorder*) cosas esparcidas; desorden; revoltillo; *v.* desarreglar, revolver, esparcir cosas por.

lit·tle [lítḷ] *adj.* pequeño; poco; **–Bear** Osa Menor; **a – coffee** un poco de café; **a – while** un ratito (*o*

ratico*), un poco; *adv. & s.* poco; **– by –** poco a poco.

live [lɪv] *v.* vivir; **to – down** hacer olvidar, borrar (*el pasado*); **to – up to** vivir en conformidad con, vivir de acuerdo con.

live [laɪv] *adj.* (*not dead*) vivo; (*lively*) enérgico; vivo, activo; **– coal** ascua encendida; **– oak** encina; **– question** cuestión palpitante, cuestión de actualidad; **– wire** alambre cargado; persona muy activa.

live·li·hood [láɪvlɪhUd] *s.* vida, alimento, subsistencia, manutención.

live·li·ness [láɪvlɪnɪs] *s.* viveza, animación; agilidad.

live·long [lívlɔŋ] *adj.* todo; absolutamente todo.

live·ly [láɪvl] *adj.* vivo; vivaz; animado, alegre; airoso; **– horse** caballo brioso; *adv.* vivamente; de prisa.

liv·er [lívɚ] *s.* hígado; vividor.

liv·er·y [lívɚɪ] *s.* librea; caballeriza (*para caballos de alquiler*); **auto –** garage para autos de alquiler.

lives [laɪvz] *pl. de* **life**

live·stock [láɪvstok] *s.* ganado.

live wire [láɪvwáɪr] *s.* persona alerta y vivaz.

liv·id [lívɪd] *adj.* lívido; amoratado.

liv·ing [lívɪŋ] *s.* (*state*) vida; (*means*) manutención, subsistencia; *adj.* vivo; viviente; **– room** sala; **– wage** sueldo suficiente para vivir; **the –** los vivos.

liz·ard [lízɚd] *s.* lagarto; **small –** lagartija.

load [lod] *s.* carga; **ship –** cargamento; **-s of** gran cantidad de; montones de; *v.* cargar; agobiar; colmar.

loaf [lof] *s.* hogaza de pan; **sugar –** azúcar de pilón; *v.* holgazanear, haraganear.

loaf·er [lófɚ] *s.* holgazán haragán, zángano.

loan [lon] *s.* préstamo; empréstito; **– shark** usurero, **– word** préstamo semántico; *v.* prestar (*dinero*).

loath [loθ] *adj.* maldispuesto, renuente; **to be – to** repugnarle a uno.

loathe [loð] *v.* repugnarle a uno; abominar.

loath·some [lóðsəm] *adj.* repugnante, asqueroso; aborrecible.

loaves [lovz] *pl. de* **loaf.**

lob [ləb] *v* volear.

lob·by [lábɪ] *s.* (*placer*) vestíbulo; antecámara, salón de entrada; hall; (*influence*) camarilla (*que busca ventajas ante un cuerpo legislativo*); **hotel –** vestíbulo o patio del hotel; *v.* cabildear (*procurar ventajas a partidarios en una asamblea*).

lobe [lob] *s.* lóbulo.

lob·ster [lábstɚ] *s.* langosta de mar.

lo·cal [lókḷ] *adj.* local; **– train** tren ordinario.

lo·cal·i·ty [lokǽlərɪ] *s.* localidad; comarca.

lo·cal·ize [lókḷaɪz] *v.* localizar.

lo·cate [lóket] *v.* situar, establecer, localizar, averiguar la posición de; avecindarse, radicarse, establecerse.

lo·ca·tion [lokéʃən] *s.* situación; sitio, localidad.

lock [lak] *s.* (*door*) cerradura; (*canal*) esclusa (*de un canal*); llave (*de un arma de fuego*); guedeja (*de pelo*); bucle, rizo; *v.* cerrar con llave; trabar(se), juntar(se); entrelazar(se); **to – in** encerrar; **to – out** cerrar la puerta (*a alguien*), dejar fuera; **to – up** encerrar; encarcelar.

lock·er [lókə·] *s.* alacena; armario.

lock·et [lákɪt] *s.* guardapelo.

lock·out [lókaʊt] *s.* paro (*suspensión del trabajo por parte de los empresarios*); cierre de fábrica.

lock·smith [láksmɪθ] *s.* cerrajero.

lo·co·mo·tive [lokəmótɪv] *s.* locomotora; **– engineer** maquinista.

lo·cust [lókəst] *s.* langosta; saltamontes; cigarra; **– tree** algarrobo; acacia falsa.

lodge [ladʒ] *s.* logia; casita accesoria; casa de campo; *v.* alojar(se); hospedar(se); colocar; **to – a complaint** presentar una queja.

lodg·er [ládʒə·] *s.* huésped, inquilino.

lodg·ing [láʒɪŋ] *s.* alojamiento; hospedaje; vivienda.

loft [lɔft] *s.* desván; galería; balcón interior (*de un templo*); **choir –** coro; **hay–** pajar.

loft·y [lɔ́ftɪ] *adj.* elevado; sublime; altivo.

log [lɔg] *s.* leño; troza; tronco aserrado; corredera, (*aparato para medir las millas que anda la nave*); diario de navegación; **– cabin** cabaña de troncos; *v.* cortar (*árboles*); cortar leños y transportarlos; registrar; (*en el diario de navegación*).

log·ic [ládʒɪk] *s.* lógica.

log·i·cal [ládʒɪkS] *adj.* lógico.

log·roll [lɔ́grol] *v.* lograr aprobación de leyes mediante favores.

loin [lɔɪn] *s.* ijada, ijar, lomo.

loit·er [lɔ́ɪtə·] *v.* holgazanear, vagar, malgastar el tiempo; **to – behind** rezagarse.

loll [lɑl] *s.* arrellanarse o repantigarse, recostarse con toda comodidad.

lone [lon] *adj.* solo, solitario.

lone·li·ness [lónlɪnɪs] *s.* soledad.

lone·ly [lónlɪ] *adj.* solo, solitario; triste; desamparado.

lone·some [lónsəm] *adj.* solo, solitario, triste, nostálgico.

long [lɔŋ] *adj.* largo; **the whole day –** todo el santo día; **three feet –** tres pies de largo; **to be – in coming** tardar en venir; *adv.* mucho, mucho tiempo; **–ago** hace mucho tiempo; **as** (*o* **so**) **– as** en tanto que, mientras que; **how– is it since....?** ¿cuanto tiempo hace que....?; **so –** ¡ hasta luego! ¡adiós!; **long-suffering** sufrido, paciente; **long-winded** prólijo, largo (*en hablar*); **long-distance** de larga distancia; *v.* anhelar; ansiar; **to – for** anhelar, suspirar por.

long·er [lɔ́ŋgə·] *adj.* mas largo; *adv.* más, más tiempo; **no –** ya no; **not....any** ya no; **no...más.**

lon·gev·i·ty [lándʒévɪtɪ] *s.* longevidad.

long·ing [lɔ́ŋɪŋ] *s.* anhelo, añoranza. nostalgia, *adj.* anhelante, anheloso, nostálgico; **-ly** *adv.* con anhelo, anhelosamente con ansia.

lon·gi·tude [lándʒətjud] *s.* longitud.

long·shore·man [lɔ́ŋʃormən] *s.* estibador (*de barco o muelle*), cargador.

long-term [lɔ́ŋtɜ·m] *adj.* a largo plazo.

look [lʊk] *v.* (*see*) mirar; (*seem*) parecer; **it -s well on you** le cae (*o* le sienta) bien; **to- after** atender, cuidar; **to – alike** parecerse; asemejarse; **to – down on a person** mirar con desprecio (*o* menospreciar) a alguien; **to – for** buscar; esperar; **to – forward to** anticipar con placer; **to – into** examinar, investigar; **–out!** ¡cuidado!; ¡tenga cuidado!; **to – out of** asomarse a; **to – over** examinar; dar un vistazo a; **to – up** levantar la vista; buscar; **to – up to** admirar; mirar con respeto; *s.* mirada, vistazo; **-s** apariencia, aspecto; **to have good -s** ser bien parecido.

look·ing glass [lúkɪŋglæs] *s.* espejo.

look·out [lúkaʊt] *s.* vigía; atalaya; mirador; vista perspectiva; **that is your –** ¡eso a usted!; **to be on the –** estar alerta.

loom [lum] *s.* telar; *v.* destacarse, descollar; asomar(se); aparecer.

loop [lup] *s.* (*closed*) lazo, gaza, presilla; (*road*) vuelta, curva; (*electric*) circuito; *v.* hacer una gaza (con *o* en); atar con gaza o presilla; hacer un circuito.

loop·hole [lúphol] *s.* agujero, abertura; salida; escapatoria.

loose [lus] *adj.* (*slack*) suelto; flojo; (*unfettered*) desatado; (*licentious*) desoluto; **– change** suelto, moneda suelta; **– jointed** de articulaciones flojas; **to let –** soltar; *v.* soltar, desatar; aflojar; **-ly** *adv.* sueltamente; flojamente; con poca exactitud, sin fundamento.

loos·en [lús ṇ] *v.* soltar(se), aflojar(se); desatar(se); **to – one's hold** desasirse, soltarse.

loose·ness [lúsnɪs] *s.* (*limberness*) soltura, flojedad; (*laxness*) flojera; holgura; relajación; (*of bowel*) flujo.

loot [lut] *s.* botín, pillaje, saqueo; *v.* saquear, pillar, robar.

lop [lap] *v.* tronchar, desmochar (*Am.* mochar).

lo·qua·cious [lokwéʃəs] *adj.* locuaz, hablador, lenguaraz.

lord [lɔrd] *s.* señor; dueño; amo; lord; **Lord's Prayer** Padre Nuestro; **Our Lord** Nuestro Señor; *v.* señorear, mandar; **to – it over** señorear, dominar.

lord·ly [lɔ́rdlɪ] *adj.* señoril; noble; altivo; despótico; *adv.* altivamente, imperiosamente.

lord·ship [lɔ́rdʃɪp] *s.* señoría (*título*); señorío, dominio.

lose [luz] *v.* perder; **to – sight of** perder de vista.

loss [lɔs] *s.* pérdida; **to be at a** – estar perplejo; no saber qué hacer; **to sell at a** – vender con pérdida.

lost [lɔst] *pret. & p.p.* de **to lose;** *adj.* perdido; extraviado; **– in thought** absorto, abstraído; **to get –** perderse, extraviarse.

lot [lɑt] *s.* (*land*) lote; (*section*) parte, porción; (*luck*) suerte; solar, porción de terreno; **a – of** (*o* **-s of**) una gran cantidad de; mucho; muchos; **to draw -s** echar suertes; **to fall to one's –** tocarle a uno, caerle en suerte; *adv.* mucho; **a – better** mucho mejor.

lo·tion [lóʃən] *s.* loción.

lot·ter·y [lɔ́təri] *s.* lotería.

loud [laUd] *adj.* ruidos; recio, fuerte; chillón, (*dícese también de los colores*); *adv.* ruidosamente, fuerte, recio; alto, en voz alta.

loud-speak·er [láUdspíkə·] *s.* altavoz, altoparlante.

lounge [laUndʒ] *s.* sala de descanso; sofá, diván, canapé; *v.* arrellanarse, repantigarse, recostarse cómodamente, sestear; holgazanear.

louse [laUs] *s.* piojo.

lous·y [láUzɪ] *adj.* piojoso; asqueroso.

lov·a·ble [lΛvəb] *i.* *adj.* amable.

love [lΛv] *s.* (*affection*) amor; cariño; (*fondness*) afición; **– affair** amorío; **to be in –** estar enamorado; **to fall in – with** enamorarse de; **to make – to** enamorar a; *v.* amar, querer; gustar mucho de, gustarle a uno mucho; encantarle a uno algo.

love·li·ness [lΛvlɪnɪs] *s.* belleza, hermosura; amabilidad.

love·ly [lΛvlɪ] *adj.* amable; lindo, bello; exquisito; encantador ameno.

lov·er [lΛvə·] *s.* amante; **music-** aficionado a (*o* amante de)la música.

lov·ing [lΛvɪŋ] *adj.* amante, amoroso, cariñoso, afectuoso; **-ly** *adv.* cariñosamente, afectuosamente.

low [lo] *adj.* (*not high*) bajo; (*base*) vil; (*humble*) humilde; (*downcast*) abatido; débil; (*lacking*) deficiente (*sick*) gravemente enfermo; **– comedy** farsa, sainete; **– gear** primera velocidad; **– Mass** misa rezada; **-key** música de intensidad mínima; **dress with a – neck** vestido escotado(*o* con escote); **to be – on something** estar escaso de algo; **to be in – spirits** estar abatido o desanimado; *adv.* bajo; en voz baja, quedo, quedito; con bajeza, a precio bajo vilmente; *s.* mugido; *v.* mugir.

low·er [lóə·] *adj.* más bajo, inferior; **– case letter** letra minúscula; **– classman** estudiante de los dos primeros años; **– house** cámara de diputados; *v.* bajar; disminuir; rebajar; abatir; humillar.

low·land [lólænd] *s.* tierra baja.

low·li·ness [lólɪnɪs] *s.* bajeza, humildad.

low·ly [lólɪ] *adj.* bajo, humilde; inferior; *adv.* humildemente.

low·ness [lónɪs] *s.* bajeza; humildad; abatimiento;

gravedad (*de tono*): debilidad (*de un sonido*); baratura.

loy·al [lɔ́ɪəl] *adj.* leal, fiel.

loy·al·ty [lɔ́ɪəltɪ] *s.* lealtad, fidelidad.

lu·bri·cant [lúbrɪkənt] *adj. & s.* lubricante.

lu·bri·cate [lúbrɪket] *v.* lubricar.

lu·cid [lúsɪd] *adj.* lúcido; claro; luciente.

luck [lΛk] *s.* suerte; fortuna; **in –** de buena suerte; **in bad –** de mala suerte.

luck·i·ly [lΛkɪlɪ] *adv.* afortunadamente, por fortuna.

luck·y [lΛkɪ] *adj.* afortunado, feliz; **to be –** tener suerte, tocarle a uno la suerte.

lu·cra·tive [lúkrətɪv] *adj.* lucrativo.

lu·di·crous [lúdɪkrəs] *adj.* ridículo.

lug [lΛg] *v.* llevar, traer, *Am.* cargar; **to – away** cargar con, llevarse (*una cosa pesada*).

lug·gage [lΛgɪdʒ] *s.* equipaje.

luke·warm [lúkwɔ́rm] *adj.* tibio, templado; indiferente.

lull [lΛl] *v.* Arrullar; sosegar; calmar(se); *s.* calma, momento de calma.

lull·a·by [lΛləbaɪ] *s.* arrullo, canción de cuna.

lum·ber [lΛmbə·] *s.* madera, maderaje; **– man** maderero, negociante en madera; **-yard** depósito de maderas; **-jack** leñador; *v.* cortar y aserrar madera; explotar los bosques; moverse pesadamente.

lu·mi·nous [lúmənəs] *adj.* luminoso.

lump [lΛmp] *s.* (*mass*) terrón; bulto; (*swelling*) hinchazón, chichón; protuberancia; **– of sugar** terrón de azúcar; *v.* amontonar; consolidar (*gastos*); apelotonarse, aterronarse, formar terrones.

lump·y [lΛmpɪ] *adj.* aterronado.

lu·na·tic [lúnətɪk] *adj. & s.* lunático, loco.

lunch [lΛntʃ] *s.* almuerzo; merienda; **–room** merendero, *Méx., Ven., Carib.* lonchería; *Ríopl.* confitería; *Spain* cafetería; *v.* almorzar; merendar; *Am.* tomar el lonche.

lunch·eon [lΛntʃən] *s.* almuerzo, merienda.

lung [lΛŋ] *s.* pulmón.

lurch [lɜ·tʃ] *s.* sacudida; tambaleo repentino; **to give a –** tambalearse; **to leave someone in the –** dejar a uno plantado, dejar a uno a buenas noches; *v.* tambalearse; dar un tambaleo repentino.

lure [lIUr] *s.* aliciente, atractivo; tentación; cebo o reclamo (*para atraer*); *v.* atraer; seducir; atraer (*con cebo o reclamo*).

lurk [lɜ·k] *v.* estar oculto; estar en acecho; moverse furtivamente.

lus·cious [lΛʃəs] *adj.* exquisito, delicioso, sabroso.

lust [lΛst] *s.* lujuria; deseo vehemente; codicia; *v.* **to – after** codiciar.

lus•ter [l ʌ srə-] s. lustre, brillo.

lus•trous [l ʌ strəs] adj. lustroso.

lust•y [l ʌ stɪ] adj. vigoroso, fornido, robusto.

lute [lut] s. laúd.

lux•u•ri•ant [lʌgʒÚrɪənt] adj. lozano, frondoso, exuberante.

lux•u•ri•ous [lʌgʒÚrɪəs] adj. lujoso; dado al lujo; frondoso.

lux•u•ry [l ʌ kʃərɪ] s. lujo.

lye [laɪ] s. lejía.

ly•ing [láɪŋ] ger. de to lie; adj. mentiroso. **lying-in hospital** casa de maternidad.

lymph [lɪmpf] s. linfa.

lynch [lɪntʃ]v. linchar.

lynx [lɪŋks] s. lince.

lyre [laɪr] s. lira.

lyr•ic [lírɪk] s. poema lírico; adj. lírico.

lyr•i•cal [lírɪk] adj. lírico.

lyr•i•cism [lírəsɪzəm] s. lirismo.

M

mac•a•ro•ni [mækərónɪ] s. macarrón o macarrones.

mac•a•roon [mækərún] s. macarrón, almendrado, bollito de almendra.

ma•chine [məʃín] s. máquina; automóvil; **– gun** ametralladora; **made** hecho a máquina; **political –** camarilla política; **sewing –** máquina para coser.

ma•chin•er•y [məʃínərɪ] s. maquinaria.

ma•chin•ist [məʃínɪst] s. mecánico, maquinista.

mack•er•el [mǽkərəl] s. escombro, caballa (pez).

mad [mæd] adj. loco; rabioso, furioso, enojado; **to drive –** enloquecer, volver loco; **to get –** encolerizarse; **to go –** volverse loco; enloquecerse; **-ly** adv. locamente.

mad•am, mad•ame [mǽdəm] s. madama, señora.

mad•cap [mǽdkæp] s. calavera (m.), adj. temerario; atolondrado.

mad•den [mǽd ŋ] v. enloquecer(se).

made [med] pret. & p.p. de to make; **to be – of** estar hecho de; ser de; **to have something –** mandar hacer algo; **made-up** fingido, falso; artificial, pintado (on afeites).

made-to-or•der [medtu órdɚ] adj. hecho a la medida.

mad•man [mǽdmæn] s. loco.

mad•ness [mǽdnɪs] s. locura; rabia.

mag•a•zine [mægəzín] s. revista; almacén (especialmente para provisiones militares); **powder –** polvorín.

mag•ic [mǽdʒɪk] s. magia; adj. mágico.

mag•i•cian [mədʒíʃən] s. mágico; brujo.

mag•is•trate [mǽdʒɪstret] s. magistrado.

mag•nan•i•mous [mægnǽnəməs] adj. magnánimo.

mag•ne•si•um [mægnízɪəm] s. magnesio.

mag•net [mǽgnɪt] s. imán.

mag•net•ic [mægnétɪk] adj. magnético; **-pole** polo magnético; **– tape** cinta magnética.

mag•net•ize [mǽgnətaɪz] v. magnetizar; cautivar.

mag•nif•i•cence [mægnífəs ŋ s] s. magnificencia.

mag•nif•i•cent [mægnífəs ŋ t] adj. magnífico.

mag•ni•fy [mǽgnəfaɪ] v. agrandar, engrandecer; amplificar; exagerar.

mag•ni•tude [mǽgnətjud] s. magnitud.

mag•pie [mǽgpaɪ] s. urraca; cotorra, hablador, habladora.

ma•hog•a•ny [məhógənɪ] s. caoba.

maid [med] s. criada, sirvienta camarera, Méx. recamarera, Ríopl., Andes mucama; doncella; **– of honor** doncella de honor; **old –** solterona.

maid•en [méd ŋ] s. doncella; virgen; mozuela; soltera: **– lady** mujer soltera; **– voyage** primer viaje (de un vapor).

mail [mel]s. correo; correspondencia; **air –** correo aéreo; **coal of –** malla; **– bag** , valija; **– train** tren correo; v. echar al correo.

mail•box [mélboks] s. buzón.

mail•man [mélmæn] s. cartero.

maim [mem] v. mutilar, estropear.

main [men] adj. principal, mayor, de mayor importancia; s. tubería, cañería principal (de agua o gas); alta mar, océano; **in the –** en su mayor parte; en general, en conjunto; **-ly** adv. principalmente.

main•land [ménlænd] s. continente, tierra firme.

main•spring [ménsprɪŋ] s. muelle real; origen.

main•tain [mentén] v. mantener; sostener, afirmar; guardar.

main•te•nance [méntənəns] s. mantenimiento; sustento; manutención; sostén, sostenimiento.

maize [mez] s. maíz.

ma•jes•tic [mədʒéstɪk] adj. majestuoso.

maj•es•ty [mǽdʒɪstɪ] s. majestad.

ma•jor [médʒɚ] adj. (greater) mayor, más grande; (principal) principal; **– key** tono mayor; s. comandante; mayor, mayor de edad; curso o asignatura de especialización (en la universidad); **– league** liga mayor; v. especializarse (en un curso de estudios).

ma•jor•i•ty [mədʒórətɪ] s. mayoría; mayor edad.

make [mek] v. (do) hacer; (create) fabricar; formar; (deliver) pronunciar (un discurso); **to – a clean breast of** confesar; **to – a train** alcanzar un tren; **to – a turn** dar vuelta; **to – away with** llevarse, robar;

matar; **to – fast** asegurar, afianzar; **to – headway** progresar, adelantar, avanzar; **to – much of** dar mucha importancia a; **to neither head nor tail of** no comprender nada de; **to nothing out of** no comprender nada de, no sacar nada en limpio; **to – out in the distance** distinguir a lo lejos; **to – over** rehacer, alterar (*un traje*); **to – sure** asegurarse; **to – toward** dirigirse a, encaminarse a; **to – up a story** inventar un cuento; **to – up after a quarrel** hacer las paces; **to –up for a loss** compensar pon una pérdida; **to – up one's face** pintarse la cara; **to – up one's mind** resolverse, dedicarse; *s.* hechura, forma; marca (*de fábrica*); manufactura.

mak•er [mékə·] *s.* hacedor; fabricante; artífice.

make•shift [mékʃɪft] *adj.* provisional.

make – up [mékʌp] *s.* (*composition*) compostura, composición, hechura; (*chracter*) naturaleza, carácter; **facial –** aceite, cosmético.

mal•a•dy [mǽlədɪ] *s.* mal, enfermedad.

ma•lar•i•a [məlέrɪə] *s.* malaria, fiebre palúdica, paludismo.

mal•con•tent [mǽlkəntɛnt] *adj. & s.* malcontento.

male [mel] *adj.* macho; varón; masculino; varonil; de hombres, de varones; *s.* macho; varón; hombre.

mal•ice [mǽlɪs] *s.* malicia.

ma•li•cious [məlíʃəs] *adj.* malicioso, perverso, malévolo.

ma•lign [məláɪn] *v.* calumniar, difamar; *adj.* maligno; pernicioso.

ma•lig•nant [məlígnənt] *adj.* maligno; malévolo.

mal•let [mǽlɪt] *s.* mazo, maceta.

mal•nu•tri•tion [mælnutríʃən] *s.* desnutrición.

malt [mɔlt] *s.* malta; **-ed milk** leche malteada.

ma•ma, mam•ma [mómə] *s.* mamá.

mam•mal [mǽml] *s.* mamífero.

mam•moth [mǽməθ] *adj.* gigantesco, enorme.

mam•my [mǽmɪ] *s.* mamita; niñera negra; criada negra.

man [mæn] *s.* hombre; varón; pieza (*de ajedrez*); **– and wife** marido y mujer; **to a –** unánimemente, todos a una; **officers and men** oficiales y soldados; **man-of war** buque de guerra; **– cook** cocinero; *v.* armar, proveer de gente armada; guarecer (*una fortaleza*); tripular (*una embarcación*).

man•age [mǽnɪdʒ] *v.* manejar; gobernar, dirigir; gestionar; **to – to do something** arreglárselas para hacer algo.

man•age•a•ble [mǽnɪdʒəbl̩] *adj.* manejable; domable, dócil.

man•age•ment [mǽnɪdʒmənt] *s.* manejo; dirección; gobierno, administración; gerencia.

man•ag•er [mǽnɪdʒə·] *s.* gerente; director, administrador; empresario.

man•date [mǽndet] *s.* mandato; *v.* asignar por mandato.

mane [men] *s.* melena (*de león*), crin (*del caballo*).

ma•neu•ver [mənúvə·] *s.* maniobra; gestión; *v.* maniobrar; manipular, manejar.

man•ful [mǽnfəl] *adj.* varonil; viril.

man•ga•nese [mǽŋɡənɪs] *s.* manganeso.

mange [mendʒ] *s.* sarna, roña.

man•ger [méndʒə·] *s.* pesebre.

man•gle [mǽŋɡl̩] *v.* magullar, mutilar, destrozar, estropear; planchar en máquina de planchar; *s.* planchadora (*máquina de planchar*).

mang•y [méndʒɪ] *adj.* sarnoso, *Am.* sarniento.

man•hood [mǽnhʊd] *s.* virilidad; edad viril; hombres.

ma•ni•a [ménɪə] *s.* manía.

man•i•cure [mǽnɪkjʊr] *s.* manicura; *v.* manicurar.

man•i•fest [mǽnəfɛst] *adj.* Manifiesto; *s.* manifiesto (*lista de la carga de un buque*); *v.* manifestar; poner de manifiesto; declarar.

man•i•fes•ta•tion [mænəfɛstéʃən] *s.* manifestación.

man•i•fes•to [mænɪfésto] *s.* manifiesto, bando, proclama.

man•i•fold [mǽnəfold] *adj.* múltiple, numeroso, diverso.

man•i•kin [mǽnəkɪn] *s.* maniquí; muñeco; hombrecillo.

ma•nil•a [mənílə] *s.* abacá (*cáñamo de Manila*); **– paper** papel de Manila.

ma•nip•u•late [mənípjəlet] *v.* manipular; manejar.

ma•nip•u•la•tion [mənɪpjəléʃən] *s.* manipulación.

man•kind [mænkáɪnd] *s.* humanidad, género humano; los hombres.

man•ly [mǽnlɪ] *adj.* varonil; viril; *adv.* varonilmente.

man•ner [mǽnə·] *s.* (*way*) manera; modo; género; (*air*) aire, ademán; **-s** maneras, modales; costumbres; **after the – of** a la manera de; **by no – of means** de ningún modo.

man•ner•ism [mǽnə·ɪzm] *s.* costumbre; amaneramiento.

man•nish [mǽnɪʃ] *adj.* hombruno.

ma•noeu•vre = maneuver.

man•or [mǽnə·] *s.* solar, casa solariega.

man•sion [mǽnʃən] *s.* mansión; palacio.

man•slaugh•ter [mǽnslɔtə·] *s.* homicidio impremeditado o casual.

man•tel [mǽnt l̩] *s.* manto (*de una chimenea*); repisa de chimenea.

man•tle [mǽnt l̩] *s.* manto; capa.

man·u·al [mǽnjUəl] *adj.* manual; **– training school** escuela de artes y oficios; *s.* manual; teclado de órgano.

man·u·fac·ture [mænjəfǽktʃə-] *s.* fabricación; manufactura; *v.* fabricar, manufacturar.

man·u·fac·tur·er [mænjəfǽktʃərə-] *s.* fabricate.

man·u·fac·tur·ing [mænjəfǽktʃərɪŋ] *s.* fabricación; *adj.* fabril, manufacturero.

ma·nure [mənÚr] *s.* estiércol, abono; *v.* estercolar, abonar (*la tierra*).

man·u·script [mǽnjəskrɪpt] *adj.* & *s.* manuscrito.

man·y [mɛ́nɪ] *adj.* muchos; **– a time** muchas veces; **a great –** muchísimos; **as – as** tantos como; cuantos; **as – as five** hasta cinco; **how – ?** ¿cuántos?; **three books too –** tres libros más; **too –** demasiados.

map [mæp] *s.* mapa; *v.* trazar un mapa de; **to – out** proyectar, planear.

ma·ple [mépḷ] *s.* arce, *Méx.* meple; *Ríopl.* maple.

mar [mɑr] *v.* desfigurar, estropear.

mar·ble [márbḷ] *s.* mármol; canica (*para jugar*); **to play -s** jugar a las canicas; *adj.* de mármol; marmóreo.

march [mɑrtʃ] *s.* marcha; *v.* marchar, caminar; hacer marchar; **to – in** entrar marchando; **to – out** marcharse; salirse marchando.

March [mɑrtʃ] *s.* marzo.

mare [mɛr] *s.* yegua.

mar·ga·rine [márdʒərɪn] *s.* margarina.

mar·gin [márdʒɪn] *s.* margen; orilla; sobrante; reserva (*fondos*).

mar·gin·al [márdʒɪn] *adj.* marginal; **– note** nota marginal, acotación.

mar·i·gold [mǽrəgold] *s.* caléndula, maravilla.

ma·rine [mərín] *adj.* marino; marítimo; **–corps** cuerpo de marinos; *s.* marino; soldado de marina; **merchant –** marina mercante.

mar·i·ner [mǽrənə] *s.* marinero.

mar·i·time [mǽrətaɪm] *adj.* marítimo.

mark [mɑrk] *s.* marca; señal, seña; nota, calificación; **question –** punto de interrogación; **to come up to the –** alcanzar la norma requerida; **to hit the –** dar en el blanco; **to make one´s –** distinguirse; **to miss one´s –** fallar; errar el tiro; fracasar; *v.* marcar; señalar; notar; observar; calificar, **my words!** ¡advierte lo que te digo!; **to – down** anotar, apuntar; rebajar el precio de.

mark·er [márkə-] *s.* marcador; marca, señal; jalón.

mar·ket [márkɪt] *s.* mercado, plaza; **- place** mercado, plaza; **- price** precio corriente; **meat –** carnicería; **stock –** mercado de valores, bolsa; *v.* vender; vender o comprar en el mercado; **to go – ing** ir de compras.

mar·ma·lade [mórm ̩ed] *s.* mermelada.

ma·roon [mərún] *s.* & *adj.* rojo obscuro.

ma·roon·ed [mərúnd] *adj.* abandonado (*en lugar desierto*) aislado; **to get –** encontrarse aislado, perdido o incomunicado.

mar·quis [márkwɪs] *s.* marqués.

mar·quise [mɔrkÍz] *s.* marquesa.

mar·riage [mǽrɪdʒ] *s.* matrimonio; casamiento, boda; unión, enlace; **– license** licencia para casarse.

mar·riage·a·ble [mǽrɪdʒəbḷ] *adj.* casadero.

mar·ried [mǽrɪd] *adj.* casado; conyugal; **– couple** matrimonio, cónyuges; pareja de casados; **to get – casarse.**

mar·row [mǽro] *s.* meollo, tuétano, medula (*de los huesos*).

mar·ry [mǽrɪ] *v.* casar; casarse; casarse con.

marsh [mɑrʃ] *s.* pantano; ciénaga.

mar·shal [márʃəl] *s.* mariscal; alguacil; jefe de policía (*en ciertas regiones*); maestro de ceremonia; **fire –** jefe de bomberos; *v.* ordenar, arreglar; guiar, conducir con ceremonia.

marsh·mal·low [márʃmælo] *s.* pastilla o bombón de altea.

marsh·y [márʃɪ] *adj.* pantanoso, cenagoso.

mart [mɑrt] *s.* mercado.

mar·tial [márʃəl] *s.* marcial; **– law** estado de guerra.

mar·tin [mártɪn] *s.* avión (*pájaro*).

mar·tyr [mártə-] *s.* mártir; *v.* martirizar, torturar, atormentar.

mar·tyr·dom [mártə-dəm] *s.* martirio.

mar·vel [márv ̩] *s.* maravilla; *v.* maravillarse.

mar·v·el·ous [márv ̩əs] *adj.* maravilloso.

mas·cot [mǽskɑt] *s.* mascota.

mas·cu·line [mǽskjəlɪn] *adj.* masculino; varonil; hombruno.

mash [mæʃ] *v.* majar, amasar; machacar, magullar; **-ed potatoes** puré de papas (*o patatas*); patatas majadas.

mask [mæsk] *s.* máscara; disfraz; careta; *v.* disfrazar, enmascarar; encubrir; **-ed ball** baile de máscaras.

ma·son [mésṇ] *s.* albañil; **Mason** masón, francmasón.

ma·son·ry [mésṇrɪ] *s.* albañilería; mampostería; **Masonry** masonería, francmasonería.

mas·quer·ade [mæskəréd] *s.* mascarada; disfraz, máscara; *v.* enmascararse, disfrazarse; andar disfrazado.

mass [mæs] *s.* masa; montón; mole; mayoría, mayor parte; misa; **– meeting** mitin popular; **– communication** comunicación extensa; **– media** los medios de comunicarse con el público (*radio,* *televisión, periódicos, etc.*); **the -es** las masas, el pueblo; *v.* juntar(se) en masa.

mas•sa•cre [mǽsəkə] *s.* hecatombe, matanza, carnicería, destrozo; *v.* hacer matanza o hecatombe, destrozar.

mas•sage [məsóʒ] *v.* friccionar, dar masaje; *s.* masaje.

mas•sive [mǽsɪv] *adj.* sólido, macizo; voluminoso, imponente.

mast [mæst] *s.* mástil, palo.

mas•ter [mǽstə] *s.* (*head*) amo, dueño, señor; maestro; patrón; (*skilled*) experto, perito; **band –** director de la banda; **– of arts** maestro en artes, licenciado; **-´s degree** licenciatura, grado de licenciado; *adj.* maestro; **- builder** maestro de obras; **- key** llave maestra; *v.* dominar; domar; gobernar; **to – a language** dominar un idioma.

mas•ter•ful [mǽstəfəl] *adj.* magistral; dominante.

mas•ter•ly [mǽstəlɪ] *adj.* magistral; *adv.* magistralmente.

mas•ter•piece [mǽstəpis] *s.* obra maestra.

mas•ter•y [mǽstərɪ] *s.* maestría, arte, destreza; dominio.

mas•tiff [mǽstɪf] *s.* mastín, alano.

mat [mæt] *s.* (*covering*) estera; esterilla, felpudo, tapete; (*gymnasium*) colchoncillo (*de gimnasia*); borde de cartón (*para hacer resaltar una pintura*).

match [mætʃ] *s.* (*pair*) pareja, (*game*) partida, contienda, juego; (*light*) fósforo, cerillo; *Méx.* cerillo; **he has no –** no tiene igual; **he is a good –** es un buen partido; **the hat and coat are a good –** el abrigo y el sombrero hacen juego; *v.* igualar; aparear; hacer juego, armonizar; **to – one´s strength** medir uno sus fuerzas; **these colors do not – well** estos colores no casan bien.

match•less [mǽtʃlɪs] *adj.* sin par, sin igual, incomparable.

mate [met] *s.* compañero, compañera, consorte; macho o hembra (*entre animales o aves*); piloto (*el segundo de un buque mercante*); oficial subalterno (*en la marina*); *v.* aparear(se).

ma•te•ri•al [mətɪrɪəl] *adj.* material; esencial; *s.* material; tejido, género; materia; **raw –** materia prima.

ma•ter•nal [mətɜ́n] *adj.* maternal, materno.

ma•ter•ni•ty [mətɜ́nəti] *s.* maternidad.

math•e•mat•i•cal [mæθəmǽtɪk] *adj.* matemático.

math•e•ma•ti•cian [mæθəmətɪ́ʃən] *s.* matemático.

math•e•mat•ics [mæθəmǽtɪks] *s.* matemáticas.

mat•i•neé [mætŋé] *s.* función de la tarde, *Am.*

matiné.

ma•tri•arch [métrɪɔrk] *s.* matriarca.

ma•tric•u•late [mətrɪ́kjələt] *v.* matricular(se).

ma•tric•u•la•tion [mətrɪkjəléʃən] *s.* matriculación, matrícula.

mat•ri•mo•ny [mǽtrəmonɪ] *s.* matrimonio, casamiento.

ma•trix [métrɪks] *s.* matriz; molde.

ma•tron [métrən] *s.* matrona, madre de familia; ama de llaves; vigilante, cuidadora (*de un asilo, cárcel para mujeres, etc.*).

mat•ter [mǽtə] *s.* (*substance*) material, materia; sustancia; (*affair*) asunto, cuestión; cosa; (*discharge*) pus; **– for complaint** motivo de queja; **– of two minutes** cosa de dos minutos; **as a – of fact** de hecho; en verdad, en realidad; **business -s** negocios; **printed –** impresos; **serious –** cosa seria; **it is of no –** no tiene importancia; **to do something as a – of course** hacer algo por rutina; **what is the –?** ¿qué pasa?; ¿qué tiene Ud.?; **matter-of-fact person** persona de poca imaginación; *v.* importar; supurar; **it does not –** no importa; no le hace.

mat•tress [mǽtrɪs] *s.* colchón; **spring –** colchón de muelles.

ma•ture [mətjÙr] *adj.* maduro; **a – note** un pagaré vencido; *v.* madurar(se); vencerse, hacerse cobrable o pagadero (*un pagaré, una deuda*).

ma•tur•i•ty [mətjÙrətɪ] *s.* madurez; vencimiento (*de una deuda u obligación*).

maul [mol] *v.* magullar; maltratar; manejar rudamente; golpear.

mav•er•ick [mǽvəɪk] *s.* animal sin marca; becerro suelto.

max•im [mǽksɪm] *s.* máxima.

max•i•mum [mǽksəməm] *adj. & s.* máximo.

may [me] *v.* irr. y defect. (*able*) poder; (*permitted*) tener permiso para, serle permitido a uno; (*possible*) ser posible; **– I sit down?** ¿puedo sentarme?; **– you have a good time** que se divierta Ud.; **it – be that** puede ser que, talvez sea que; **it – rain** puede(ser) que llueva, es posible que llueva; **she – be late** puede (ser) que llegue ella tarde.

May [me] *s.* mayo, mes de mayo; **– Day** primero de mayo; **–pole** mayo; **– Queen** maya (*reina de la fiesta del primero de mayo*).

may•be [mébɪ] *adv.* quizás, tal vez, acaso.

may•on•naise [meənéz] *s.* mayonesa.

may•or [méə] *s.* alcalde, alcalde mayor.

maze [mez] *s.* laberinto; confusión; **to be in a –** estar confuso o perplejo.

me [mi] *pron. pers.* me, mi (*después de preposición*); **give it to –** démelo (a mí); **for –** para mí; **with –** conmigo.

mead•ow [médo] *s.* pradera, prado; **– lark** alondra de los prados.

mea•ger [mígə·] adj. escaso, insuficiente; magro, flaco.

meal [mil] s. comida, harina (a medio moler); **corn — harina** de maíz; **-time** hora de comer.

mean [min] adj. (malicious) ruin, bajo, vil; (humble) humilde; (stingy) mezquino, tacaño; (difficult) de mal genio; (sick) malo; indispuesto; (middle) mediano; medio; intermedio; **– distance** distancia media; s. medio; término medio; **-s** medios; recursos; **a man of –s** un hombre pudiente o rico; **by -s of** por medio de; **by all -s** de todos modos; a toda costa; por supuesto; **by no -s** de ningún modo, v. querer decir, significar; pensar, proponerse, tener la intención de; intentar; destinar; **he -s well** tiene buenas intenciones.

me•an•der [miǽndə·] v. serpentear.

mean•ing [mínɪŋ] s. (sense) significado, sentido; significación; (intent) propósito, intención; adj. significativo; **well-meaning** bien intencionado.

mean•ing•less [mínɪŋlɪs] adj. sin sentido, vacío de sentido.

mean•ness [mínnɪs] s. ruindad, vileza, bajeza; mezquindad.

meant [mɛnt] pret. & p.p. de **to mean.**

mean•time [míntaɪm] adv. mientras tanto, entretanto, s. ínterin, entretanto; **in the –** en el ínterin, mientras tanto.

mean•while [mínhwaɪl] = **meantime.**

mea•sles [mízļz] s. sarampión.

meas•ur•a•ble [mɛʒrəbḷ] adj. medible, mensurable; **measurably** adv. marcadamente.

meas•ure [mɛʒə·] s. (dimension) medida; compás (de música); cadencia, ritmo; (law) proyecto de ley; ley; **beyond –** sobremanera; con exceso; **dry –** medida para áridos; **in large –** en gran parte, en gran manera; v. medir.

meas•ured [mɛʒə·d] adj. medido; moderado; acompasado.

meas•ure•ment [mɛʒə·mənt] s. medida; dimensión; tamaño, medición.

meat [mit] s. carne, meollo; sustancia; **– ball** albóndiga; **– market** carnicería; **cold –** fiambre.

meat•y [mítɪ] adj. carnoso; sustancioso.

me•chan•ic [məkǽnɪk] adj. & s. mecánico, **-s** s. mecánica.

me•chan•i•cal [məkǽnɪkḷ] adj. mecánico, maquinal.

mech•a•nism [mɛkənɪzəm] s. mecanismo.

med•al [mɛdḷ] s. medalla.

med•dle [mɛdḷ] v. entrometerse o entremeterse; meterse.

med•dler [mɛdlə·] s. entremetido.

med•dle•some [mɛdḷsəm] adj. entremetido.

me•di•an [mídɪən] adj. mediano, del medio, s. pun-

to, línea o número del medio; mediana.

me•di•ate [mídɪet] v. mediar; intervenir, arbitrar.

me•di•a•tion [midɪéʃən] s. mediación, intervención, intercesión.

me•di•a•tor [mídɪetə·] s. mediador, medianero, árbitro.

med•i•cal [mɛdɪkḷ] adj. médico; **– school** escuela de medicina.

med•i•ca•tion [mɛdɪkéʃən] s. medicación.

med•i•cine [mɛdəsŋ] s. medicina; medicamento; **– ball** pelota grande de cuero; **– cabinet** botiquín; **– man** curandero indio.

me•di•e•val [midɪív] adj. medioeval o medieval.

me•di•o•cre [midɪókə·] adj. mediocre, mediano, ordinario.

me•di•oc•ri•ty [midɪókrəтɪ] s. mediocridad, medianía.

med•i•tate [mɛdətet] v. meditar.

med•i•ta•tion [mɛdətéʃən] s. meditación.

me•di•um [mídɪəm] s. medio; medio ambiente; adj. mediano; intermedio; a medio cocer, a medio asar; **– of exchange** mediador de cambio.

med•ley [mɛdlɪ] s. baturrillo, mezcla, mezcolanza.

meek [mik] adj. manso, dócil, paciente, sufrido.

meek•ness [míknɪs] s. mansedumbre, docilidad.

meet [mit] v. encontrar(se); reunirse; conocer (personalmente), ser presentado a; ir a esperar (un tren, vapor, o a alguien); satisfacer (deseos, requisitos, etc.); pagar (una deuda); sufragar (gastos); responder a (una acusación); **to – in battle** trabar batalla; **to – with** encontrarse con; tropezar con; topar con; reunirse con; s. concurso; contienda (tratándose de deportes); **track –** competencia de atletas.

meet•ing [mítɪŋ] s. reunión; mitin; sesión; asamblea; encuentro.

meg•a•phone [mɛgəfon] s. megáfono, portavoz, bocina.

mel•an•chol•y [mɛlənkɑlɪ] s. melancolía, adj. melancólico.

me•lee [méle] s. reyerta; zafarrancho.

mel•low [mɛlo] adj. maduro, sazonado; dulce, blando, suave; v. madurar(se), sazonar(se); ablandar(se), suavizar(se).

me•lo•di•ous [məlódɪəs] adj. melodioso.

mel•o•dra•ma [mɛlodrɑmə] s. melodrama.

mel•o•dy [mɛlədɪ] s. melodía.

mel•on [mɛlən] s. melón.

melt [mɛlt] v. derretir(se); disolver(se); fundir(se).

mem•ber [mɛmbə·] s. miembro; socio.

mem•ber•ship [mɛmbə·ʃɪp] s. número de miembros o socios; asociación; (los) miembros (de un club o sociedad).

mem•brane [mɛmbren] s. membrana.

me•men•to [mɪmɛnto] s. memento, memoria, recuerdo.

mem·oir [mémwɑr] s. memoria, apuntaciones; **-s** memorias; autobiografía.

mem·o·ra·ble [mémərəb] adj. memorable.

mem·o·ran·dum [mɛmərǽndəm] s. memorándum; memoria, apunte; **– book** memorándum, librito de apuntes, memorial.

me·mo·ri·al [məmóriəl] s. (monument) monumento conmemorativo; (occasion) obra o fiesta conmemorativa; memorial, petición; adj. conmemorativo.

mem·o·rize [méməraɪz] v. aprender de memoria.

mem·o·ry [mémərɪ] s. memoria; recuerdo.

men [mɛn] pl. de **man.**

men·ace [ménɪs] s. amenaza; v. amenazar.

mend [mɛnd] v. remendar; reparar, componer; enmendar; **to – one´s ways** enmendarse, reformarse; s. remiendo; reparación; **to be on the –** ir mejorando.

me·ni·al [mínɪəl] adj. servil, bajo.

men·stru·a·tion [mɛnstrUéʃən] s. menstruo o menstruación.

men·tal [mént] adj. mental.

men·tal·i·ty [mɛntǽlətɪ] s. mentalidad, ingenio.

men·tion [ménʃən] s. mención; alusión, v. mencionar, mentar; **don´t – it** no hay de qué (contestación a "thank you").

men·u [ménju] s. menú, lista de platos.

me·ow [miau] = **mew.**

mer·can·tile [mɝ́kəntɪl] adj. mercantil.

mer·ce·nar·y [mɝ́sṇ ɛrɪ] adj. mercenario.

mer·chan·dise [mɝ́tʃəndaɪz] s. mercancías, mercaderías; **piece of –** mercancía.

mer·chant [mɝ́tʃənt] s. comerciante; negociante; mercader; adj. mercante, mercantil; **– marine** marina mercante.

mer·ci·ful [mɝ́sɪfəl] adj. misericordioso, piadoso.

mer·ci·less [mɝ́sɪlɪs] adj. sin piedad, despiadado, incompasivo.

mer·cu·ry [mɝ́kjərɪ] s. mercurio, azogue.

mer·cy [mɝ́sɪ] s. (favor) merced; favor, gracia; (compassion) misericordia, piedad, compasión; **to be at the – of** estar a merced de.

mere [mɪr] adj. mero; simple, puro; **a – formality** una pura formalidad, no más que una formalidad, una formalidad no más; **a – trifle** una nonada; **-ly** adv. meramente; sólo, solamente; simplemente.

merge [mɝdʒ] v. combinar(se), unir(se); absorber(se); fundirse.

merg·er [mɝ́dʒɚ] s. amalgamación comercial.

me·rid·i·an [mərídɪən] adj. & s. meridiano.

mer·it [mérɪt] s. mérito; v. merecer.

mer·i·to·ri·ous [mɛrətórɪəs] adj. meritorio.

mer·maid [mɝ́med] s. ninfa marina.

mer·ri·ly [mérəlɪ] adv. alegremente, con regocijo.

mer·ri·ment [mérɪmənt] s. alegría, regocijo, júbilo.

mer·ry [mérɪ] adj. alegre; jovial; divertido; festivo; **– Christmas** Felices Navidades, Felices Pascuas; **to make –** divertirse.

mer·ry-go-round [mérɪgəraUnd] s. tío vivo, Méx., C.A. los caballitos; Ríopl. calesita.

mer·ry·mak·er [mérɪmekɚ] s. fiestero; juerguista.

mer·ry·mak·ing [mérɪmenkɪŋ] s. regocijo; jaleo, juerga, jolgorio; adj. regocijado, alegre, festivo, fiestero.

mesh [mɛʃ] s. malla; red; **-es** red, redes; v. enredar, coger con una red, **to – gears** engranar.

mess [mɛs] s. (food) rancho, comida (en el ejército o la marina); (confusion) lío, confusión; (dirt) suciedad; **– of fish** plato o ración de pescado; **to make a – of** revolver, confundir; ensuciar; echar a perder; v. revolver, confundir; ensuciar, echar a perder (generalmente: **to – up**); **to – around** revolver o mezclar las cosas; entrometerse; **messy** [mésɪ] adj. desordenado, desarreglado, sucio.

mes·sage [mésɪdʒ] s. mensaje; parte (m.), comunicación; recado.

mes·sen·ger [mésṇ dʒɚ] s. mensajero; mandadero.

met [mɛt] pret. & p.p. de **to meet.**

me·tab·o·lism [mətǽbəlɪzm] s. metabolismo.

met·al [mɛ́t] s. metal; adj. de metal, metálico.

me·tal·lic [mətǽlɪk] adj. metálico.

met·al·lur·gy [mɛ́t ɝ́dʒɪ] s. metalurgia.

met·a·phor [métəfɚ] s. metáfora.

me·ta·the·sis [mətǽθəsɪs] s. metátesis.

me·te·or [mítɪɚ] s. meteoro; estrella fugaz.

me·te·or·ite [mítɪoraɪt] s. meteorito.

me·te·or·o·log·i·cal [mitɪərəlódʒɪk] adj. meteorológico.

me·te·or·ol·o·gy [mitɪəráledʒɪ] s. meteorología.

me·ter [mítɚ] s. metro; contador (del gas, agua, electricidad, etc.).

meth·od [méθəd] s. método; técnica.

me·thod·i·cal [məθάdɪk] s. metódico.

me·tre = **meter.**

met·ric [métrɪk] adj. métrico; **– system** sistema métrico.

me·trop·o·lis [mətróp ɪs] s. metrópoli.

met·ro·pol·i·tan [mɛtrəpálət ŋ] adj. metropolitano.

met·tle [mɛ́t] s. temple, brío, ánimo, valor.

mew [mju] s. maullido, maúllo, miau; v. maullar.

Mex·i·can [méksɪkən] adj. & s. mejicano o mexicano.

mez·za·nine [mézənin] s. entresuelo.

mice [maɪs] pl. de **mouse.**

mi·crobe [máɪkrob] s. microbio.

mi·cro·film [máɪkrəfɪlm] s. microfilm.

mi·cro·phone [máɪkrəfon] s. micrófono.

mi·cro·scope [máɪkrəskop] s. microscopio.

mi·cro·scop·ic [máɪkrəskópɪk] s. microscópico.

mid [mɪd] adj. medio (úsase por lo general en composición); in – air en el aire; prep. en medio de, entre.

mid·day [mídde] s. mediodía; adj. del mediodía.

mid·dle [mídḷ] adj. medio; intermedio; Middle ages Edad media; – finger dedo de un medio, dedo del corazón; – size tamaño mediano; s. medio, centro, mitad; in the – of en medio de, a la mitad de; towards the – of the month a mediados del mes; –class clase media.

mid·dle-aged [mídḷéʒd] adj. de edad mediana, de edad madura.

mid·dle·man [mídḷmæn] s. revendedor; medianero, corredor, agente.

mid·dle-sized [mídḷsázd] adj. de mediano tamaño, de mediana estatura.

mid·dy [mídɪ] s. guardiamarina (m.); – blouse blusa a la marinera.

midg·et [mídʒɪt] s. enanillo.

mid·night [mídnaɪt] s. medianoche; adj. de (la) medianoche; – blue azul oscuro; – Mass misa de gallo.

mid·riff [mídrɪf] s. diafragma.

mid·ship·man [mídʃɪpmən] s. guardiamarina (m.).

midst [mɪdst] s. medio, centro; in the – of en medio de, entre; in our – entre nosotros.

mid·stream [mídstrim] s. en el medio (o el centro) de la corriente.

mid·sum·mer [mídsʌ́mə] s. pleno verano, solsticio estival, la mitad del verano.

mid·term [mídtə́m]; –examination examen a mitad del curso.

mid·way [mídwé] adj. situado a medio camino; equidistante; adv. a medio camino; en medio del camino.

mid·wife [mídwaɪf] s. partera, comadrona.

mien [min] s. facha, aspecto.

might [maɪt] imperf. de may podía; podría; pudiera, pudiese; s. poder, poderío, fuerza.

might·y [máɪtɪ] adj. poderoso, potente, fuerte; adv. muy, sumamente.

mi·grant [máɪgrənt] adj. migratorio.

mi·grate [máɪgret] v. emigrar.

mi·gra·tion [maɪgréʃən] s. migración.

mike [maɪk] s. = microphone.

mild [maɪld] adj. (gentle) suave; blando; apacible; (moderate) templado, moderado.

mildew [míldu] s. moho; enmohecimiento.

mild·ness [máɪldnɪs] s. suavidad; mansedumbre; apacibilidad; templanza, dulzura.

mile [maɪl] s. milla; – stone mojón.

mile·age [máɪlɪdʒ] s. millaje, número de millas; recorrido (en millas). Compárese kilometraje, número de kilómetros.

mil·i·tant [mílɪtənt] s. militante; belicoso.

mil·i·tar·y [míləterɪ] adj. militar; de guerra; s. the – el ejército; los militares.

mi·li·tia [məlíʃə] s. milicia.

milk [mɪlk] s. leche; – diet régimen lácteo; v. ordeñar.

milk·maid [mílkmed] s. lechera.

milk·man [mílkmən] s. lechero, Am. vaquero.

milk·y [mílkɪ] adj. lácteo; lechoso; Milky way vía láctea.

mill [mɪl] s. (grinder) molino; (factory) fábrica; (money) la milésima parte de un dólar; saw – aserradero; spinning – hilandería; sugar – ingenio de azúcar; textile – fábrica de tejidos; v. moler; aserrar (madera); fabricar; acordonar (el canto de la moneda); to – around arremolinarse (una muchedumbre).

mill·er [mílə] s. molinero; mariposa nocturna.

mil·li·ner [mílənə] s. modista (de sombreros para señoras).

mil·li·ner·y [mílənɛrɪ] s. sombreros de señora; artículos para sombreros de señora; oficio de modista; – shop sombrerería.

mil·lion [míljən] s. millón de; a – dollars un millón de dólares.

mil·lion·aire [mɪljənɛ́r] adj. & s. millonario.

mil·lionth [míljənθ] adj. & s. millonésimo.

mill·stone [mílston] s. muela o piedra de molino; carga pesada.

mim·ic [mímɪk] adj. mímico, imitativo; – battle simulacro; s. imitador, remedador; v. imitar, remedar.

mince [mɪns] v. picar, desmenuzar; not to – words hablar con toda franqueza.

mince·meat [mínsmit] s. picadillo (especialmente el de carne, pasas, manzanas y especias).

mind [maɪnd] s. (brain) mente; (thought) pensamiento; inteligencia; (spirit) ánimo, espíritu; (purpose) propósito, intención; (opinion) parecer, opinión; to be out of one´s – estar loco, haber perdido el juicio; to change one´s – cambiar de parecer; to give someone a piece of one´s – cantarle a alguien la verdad; echarle a alguien un buen regaño; to have a – to estar por; sentir ganas de; to make up one´s – decidirse, resolverse; to my – a mi modo de ver; to speak one´s – freely hablar con toda franqueza; v. cuidar; atender a, hacer caso de; obedecer; I don´t – no tengo inconveniente en ello, never – no importa; no se preocupe; no se moleste; no haga Ud. Caso; to – one´s own business atender a lo suyo, no meterse en lo ajeno.

mind·ful [máɪndfəl] adj. atento (a); cuidadoso (de).

mine [maɪn] pron. pos. mío (mía, míos, mías); el mío

(la mía, los míos, las mías); **a book of –** un libro mío.

mine [maɪn] *s.* mina; **– sweeper** dragaminas; *v.* minar; explotar (*una mina*); extraer (*mineral*).

min·er [máɪnə·] *s.* minero.

min·er·al [mínərəl] *adj.* & *s.* mineral.

min·gle [míŋ]] *v.* mezclar(se); entremezclar(se); confundir(se); juntarse.

min·i·a·ture [mínɪt∫ə·] *s.* miniatura; *adj.* en miniatura; diminuto.

min·i·mal [mínəm]] *adj.* mínimo.

min·i·mize [mínəmaɪz] *v.* empequeñecer.

min·i·mum [mínəməm] *adj.* & *s.* mínimo.

min·ing [máɪnɪŋ] *s.* minería, explotación de minas; *adj.* minero; **– engineer** ingeniero de minas.

min·i·skirt [mínɪskə·t] *s.* minifalda.

min·is·ter [mínɪstə·] *s.* ministro; pastor, clérigo; *v.* ministrar; atender; proveer, socorrer.

min·is·try [mínɪstrɪ] *s.* ministerio; socorro, ayuda.

mink [míŋk] *s.* visón.

min·now [míno] *s.* pececillo de río.

mi·nor [máɪnə·] *adj.* (*young*) menor; de menor edad; (*secondary*) secundario; **– key** tono menor; *s.* menor de edad; premisa menor (*de un silogismo*); tono menor; curso o asignatura menor.

mi·nor·i·ty [mən∫róʊ] *s.* minoría; minoridad, menor edad; menor parte.

min·strel [mínstrəl] *v.* trovador; bardo, vate; actor cómico que remeda al negro norteamericano.

mint [mínt] *s.* (**flavor**) menta, hierbabuena (*yerbabuena*); (*candy*) pastilla o bombón de menta; (*money*) casa de moneda; **a – of money** un montón de dinero, la mar de dinero; *v.* acuñar.

mint·age [míntədʒ] *s.* acuñación; moneda acuñada.

min·u·et [mɪnjʊét] *s.* minué.

mi·nus [máɪnəs] *adj.* negativo; sin, falto de; **seven – four** siete menos cuatro; *s.* menos, signo menos.

min·ute [mínɪt] *s.* minuto; **-s** acta (*de una junta*); **– hand** minutero.

mi·nute [mənjút] *adj.* menudo, diminuto; minucioso, detallado.

mir·a·cle [mírək]] *s.* milagro.

mi·rac·u·lous [mənrǽkjələs] *adj.* milagroso.

mi·rage [mərázʒ] *s.* espejismo.

mire [maɪr] *s.* cieno, fango, lodo; *v.* atascar(se) en el fango; enlodar(se).

mir·ror [mírə·] *s.* espejo; *v.* reflejar.

mirth [m͡з·θ] *s.* júbilo, regocijo, alegría.

mirth·ful [m͡з·θfəl] *adj.* jubiloso, regocijado, gozoso, alegre.

mir·y [máɪrɪ] *adj.* cenagoso, fangoso, lodoso.

mis·ad·ven·ture [mɪsədvéntʃə·] *s.* desgracia; contratiempo.

mis·be·have [mɪsbɪhév] *v.* portarse mal, obrar mal.

mis·car·riage [mɪskǽrɪdʒ] *s.* aborto, malparto; mal éxito; extravío (*de una carta, papel, etc.*).

mis·car·ry [mɪskǽrɪ] *v.* (*fail*) malograrse, frustrarse; extraviarse (*una carta*); (*abort*) abortar.

mis·cel·la·ne·ous [mɪs énɪəs] *adj.* misceláneo, diverso.

mis·chief [míst∫ɪf] *s.* travesura; diablura; mal, daño; diablillo, persona traviesa.

mis·chie·vous [míst∫ɪvəs] *adj.* travieso; malicioso; dañino.

mis·con·cep·tion [mɪskənsép∫ən] *s.* concepto erróneo.

mis·con·duct [mɪskándʌkt] *s.* mala conducta; mala administración; [mɪskənd ʌkt] *v.* maladministrar, manejar mal; **to – oneself** portarse mal, conducirse mal.

mis·deed [mɪsdíd] *s.* fechoría, mala acción.

mis·de·mean·or [mɪsdɪmínə·] *s.* mal comportamiento; fechoría.

mi·ser [máɪzə·] *s.* avaro, avariento.

mis·er·a·ble [mízrəbS] *adj.* miserable; infeliz, desdichado.

mi·ser·ly [máɪzə·lɪ] *adj.* avariento, avaro; tacaño, mezquino.

mis·er·y [mɪ́zrɪ] *s.* miseria, desgracia; estrechez, pobreza; dolor.

mis·for·tune [mɪsf ɪ́t∫ən] *s.* infortunio, desgracia, desastre.

mis·giv·ing [mɪsgívɪŋ] *s.* mal presentimiento, aprensión, recelo, temor.

mis·guid·ed [mɪsgáɪdəd] *adj.* mal aconsejado.

mis·hap [mí͡shæp] *s.* desgracia, contratiempo, accidente.

mis·judge [mɪsdʒ ʌ́dʒ] *v.* juzgar mal.

mis·lay [mɪsléd] *v.* extraviar, perder; poner fuera de su sitio, colocar mal; traspapelar (*una carta, documento, etc.*).

mis·lead [mɪslíd] *v.* guiar por mal camino; extraviar, descarriar; engañar.

mis·led [mɪsléd] pret. & p.p. de **to mislead.**

mis·man·age [mɪsm ǽnɪdʒ] *v.* administrar.

mis·place [mɪsplés] *v.* extraviar, poner fuera de su sitio, colocar mal; traspapelar (*una carta, documento, etc.*).

mis·print [mɪspr ɪ́nt] *s.* errata, error tipográfico, error de imprenta.

mis·pro·nounce [mí͡sprənaʊns] *v.* pronunciar mal.

mis·rep·re·sent [mɪsrɛprɪzént] *v.* falsear, falsificar; tergiversar.

miss [mɪs] *v.* (*not hit*) errar, no acertar; fallar; (*omit*) equivocar; perder; faltar a; (*feel absence of*) echar de menos; Am. extrañar; **he just -ed being killed** por poco lo matan; *s.* error; falla, falta.

miss [mɪs] *s.* señorita; **Miss Smith** la señorita smith.

mis•sile [mís ǀ] s. proyectil; arma arrojadiza; adj. arrojadiza, que se puede arrojar o tirar.

miss•ing [mísɪŋ] adj. ausente; perdido; **one book is** – falta un libro.

mis•sion [míʃən] s. misión.

mis•sion•ar•y [míʃənɛrɪ] adj. & s. misionero.

mis•spell [mɪsspél] v. escribir con mala ortografía, deletrear mal.

mist [mɪst] s. neblina, niebla; llovizna; Ven., Col., Andes. garúa; v. lloviznar; anublar.

mis•take [məsték] s. error, yerro, equivocación; errata (de imprenta); **to make a** – equivocarse; v. equivocar.

mis•tak•en [məstékən] p.p. de **to mistake** & adj. equivocado; errado; erróneo, incorrecto; **to be** – estar equivocado, equivocarse, errar.

mis•ter [mítə·] s. señor.

mis•took [mɪstÚk] pret. de **to mistake.**

mis•treat [mɪstrít] v. maltratar.

mis•tress [místrɪs] s. señora; ama, dueña; querida, amante; **school** – maestra.

mis•tri•al [mɪstráɪl] s. pleito viciado de nulidad.

mis•trust [mɪstr Ást] s. desconfianza; v. desconfiar de.

mis•trust•ful [mɪstr Ástfəl] adj. desconfiado, sospechoso, receloso.

mist•y [místɪ] adj. brumoso; nublado; empañado; vago, indistinto.

mis•un•der•stand [mɪsʌndə·stǽnd] v. comprender mal; entender mal; interpretar mal; no comprender.

mis•un•der•stand•ing [mɪsʌndə·stǽndɪŋ] s. equivocación; mala interpretación, mala inteligencia; desavenencia.

mis•un•der•stood [mɪsʌndə·stÚd] pret. & p.p. de **misunderstand.**

mis•use [mɪsjús] s. abuso; mal uso; malversación (de fondos); [mɪsjúz] v. abusar de; maltratar; usar o emplear mal; malversar (fondos).

mite [maɪt] s. óbolo, friolera, pequeñez; criatura.

mi•ter [máɪtə·] s. mitra; dignidad de obispo.

mit•i•gate [mítəget] v. mitigar.

mit•ten [mít Á] s. mitón (guante de una pieza y sin dedos).

mix [mɪks] v. mezclar(se); unir(se), juntar(se), asociar(se); **to – someone up** confundir a uno; s. mezcla; confusión, lío.

mix•ture [míkstʃə·] s. mezcla; mezcolanza.

mix-up [míksʌp] s. equívoco; enredo.

moan [mon] s. quejido, gemido; v. gemir; quejarse; lamentar(se).

moat [mot] s. foso.

mob [mɑb] s. populacho; muchedumbre, gentío, Am. bola (de gente); v. atropellar; apiñarse o agolparse alrededor de.

mo•bile [mób ǀ] adj. móvil; movible; movedizo.

mo•bi•li•za•tion [mobǀəzéʃən] s. movilización.

mo•bi•lize [móbǀaɪz] v. movilizar.

moc•ca•sin [mákəs Á] s. Am. mocasín (zapato burdo de cuero); Am. mocasín (víbora venenosa).

mock [mɑk] v. (ridicule) mofar, mofarse de; (imitate) remedar, imitar; **to – at** mofarse de; burlarse de; s. mofa, burla, escarnio; mímica; remedo; adj. falso, ficticio, imitado; – **battle** simulacro, batalla fingida.

mock•er•y [mɔ́kərɪ] s. burla, mofa, escarnio; remedo.

mock-up [mɔ́kʌp] s. maqueta; modelo.

mode [mod] s. modo, manera; moda.

mod•el [mɑdǀ] s. (guide) modelo; (pattern) patrón; (figure) figurín, maniquí; adj. ejemplar; modelo; - **school** escuela modelo; v. modelar; moldear, formar; posar, servir de modelo.

mod•er•ate [mádərɪt] adj. moderado; templado; módico; [mádəret] v. moderar(se); templar(se).

mod•er•a•tion [mɑdəréʃən] s. moderación; templanza.

mod•ern [mádə·n] adj. moderno.

mod•ern•ize [mádə·naɪz] v. modernizar.

mod•est [mádɪst] adj. modesto.

mod•es•ty [mádəstɪ] s. modestia.

mod•i•fi•ca•tion [mɑdəfəkéʃən] modificación.

mod•i•fy [mádəfaɪ] v. modificar.

mod•u•late [mádʒələt] v. modular.

mo•hair [móhɛr] s. moer.

Mo•ham•med•an [mohǽmədən] adj. & s. mahometano.

moist [mɔɪst] adj. húmedo; mojado.

mois•ten [mɔ́ɪs Á] v. humedecer, mojar.

mois•ture [mɔ́ɪsʃə·] s. humedad.

mo•lar [mólə·] adj. molar; s. muela.

mo•las•ses [məlǽsɪz] s. melaza, miel de caña.

mold [mold] s. (form) molde, matriz; (substance) moho; tierra vegetal; v. moldear, amoldar; modelar; enmohecer(se), cubrir(se) de moho.

mold•er [móldə·] v. desmoronarse.

mold•ing [móldɪŋ] s. moldura; moldeamiento.

mold•y [móldɪ] adj. mohoso.

mole [mol] s. lunar; topo (animal); dique, malecón, rompeolas.

mol•e•cule [máləkjul] s. molécula.

mo•lest [məlést] v. molestar.

mol•li•fy [máləfaɪ] v. apaciguar.

mol•ten [mólt ŋ] adj. derretido, fundido, en fusión.

mo•ment [mómənt] s. momento; importancia, consecuencia.

mo•men•tar•y [móməntɛrɪ] adj. momentáneo.

mo•men•tous [mómɛntəs] adj. importante.

mo•men•tum [moméntəm] *s.* momento (*de una fuerza*); ímpetu.

mon•arch [mánə·k] *s.* monarca.

mon•ar•chy [mánə·kɪ] *s.* monarquía.

mon•as•ter•y [mánəstɛrɪ] *s.* monasterio.

Mon•day [m ʌ ndɪ] *s.* lunes.

mon•e•tar•y [mánətɛrɪ] *adj.* monetario.

mon•ey [m ʌ nɪ] *s.* dinero; **– changer** cambista; **– order** giro postal; **paper –** papel moneda; **silver –** monedas de plata; **money-making** lucrativo, provechoso, ganancioso.

mon•ger [mángə·] *s.* traficante; defensor.

mon•grel [m ʌ ŋgrəl] *adj. & s.* mestizo, mixto, cruzado, *Am.* chusco (*perro*).

monk [mʌŋk] *s.* monje.

mon•key [m ʌ kɪ] *s.* mono; **-shine** monada, monería; **– wrench** llave inglesa; *v.* juguetear; hacer monerías; payasear; entretenerse; **to – with** juguetear con; meterse con.

mon•o•gram [mánəgræm] *s.* monograma.

mon•o•graph [mánəgræf] *s.* monografía.

mon•o•logue [mán ˌ ɔg] *s.* monólogo, soliloquio.

mo•nop•o•lIze [mənáp ˌ aɪz] *v.* monopolizar, acaparar.

mo•nop•o•ly [mənáp ˌ ɪ] *s.* monopolio.

mon•o•syl•la•ble [mánəsɪləb]] *s.* monosílabo.

mon•o•tone [mánəton] *adj.* monótono.

mo•not•o•nous [mənát ŋ əs] *adj.* monótono.

mo•not•o•ny [mənát ŋ ɪ] *s.* monotonía.

mon•ster [mánstə·] *s.* monstruo; *adj.* enorme.

mon•stros•i•ty [mɑnstrásətɪ] *s.* monstruosidad, monstruo.

mon•strous [mánstrəs] *adj.* monstruoso.

month [mʌnθ] *s.* mes.

month•ly [m ʌ nθlɪ] *adj.* mensual; *s.* publicación mensual; *adv.* mensualmente.

mon•u•ment [mánjəmənt] *s.* monumento.

mon•u•men•tal [mɑnjəmɛnt]] *adj.* monumental; colosal, grandioso.

moo [mu] *s.* mugido; *v.* mugir.

mood [mud] *s.* humor, disposición de ánimo; de modo (*del verbo*); **to be in a good –** estar de buen humor; **to be in the – to** estar dispuesto a, tener gana de.

mood•y [múdɪ] *adj.* (*changing*) caprichoso, voluble, mudable; (*sad*) melancólico, mohíno.

moon [mun] *s.* luna; mes lunar; **once in a blue –** de Pascuas a San Juan.

moon•light [múnlaɪt] *s.* luz de luna; **- dance** baile a la luz de la luna; **- night** noche de luna.

moor [mUr] *v.* amarrar, atracar (*un buque*); anclar; estar anclado; *s.* terreno inculto o baldío.

Moor [mUr] *s.* moro.

Moor•ish [mÚrɪʃ] *adj.* morisco, moro.

mop [mɑp] *s. Am.* trapeador; **dust –** limpiapolvo; **– of hair** greñas, cabellera abundante; *v.* limpiar (*el suelo*), *Am.* trapear; **to – one´s brow** limpiarse (*o secarse*) la frente; **to – up** limpiar; vencer; acabar con.

mope [mop] *v.* andar quejumbroso o abatido.

mor•al [m ɔ rəl] *adj.* moral; **– philosophy** ética, moral, *s.* moraleja; **-s** moral, ética.

mo•rale [mərǽl] *s.* moral, entereza de ánimo.

mor•al•ist [m ɔ rəlɪst] *s.* moralista.

mo•ral•i•ty [mɔrǽləti] *s.* moralidad.

mor•al•ize [m ɔ rəlaɪz] *v.* moralizar.

mor•bid [m ɔ rbɪd] *adj.* mórbido, morboso, malsano.

mor•dant [m ɔ rdənt] *adj.* mordaz.

more [mor] *adj. & adv.* más; **– and –** cada vez más, más y más; **–or less** poco más o menos; **there is no –** no hay más, ya no hay; se acabó.

more•o•ver [moróvə·] *adj.* además.

morn•ing [m ɔ rnɪŋ] *s.* mañana; **good – !** ¡buenos días!; **tomorrow –** mañana por la mañana; *adj.* de la mañana; matutino, matinal; **morning-glory** dondiego de día; **– star** lucero del alba.

mor•phine [m ɔ rfin] *s.* morfina.

mor•row [m ɔ ro]: **on the –** el día de mañana; mañana.

mor•sel [m ɔ rs]] *s.* bocado; manjar sabroso.

mor•tal [m ɔ rt]] *adj. & s.* mortal.

mor•tal•i•ty [mortǽləti] *s.* mortalidad; mortandad.

mor•tar [m ɔ rtə·] *s.* mortero; argamasa; mezcla; **metal –** almirez.

mort•gage [m ɔ rgɪdʒ] *s.* hipoteca, gravamen; *v.* hipotecar.

mor•ti•fy [m ɔ rtəfaɪ] *v.* mortificar; avergonzar.

mo•sa•ic [mozéik] *adj. & s.* mosaico.

Mos•lem [mázləm] *adj. & s.* musulmán.

Mos•qui•to [məskíto] *s.* mosquito; **– net** mosquitero.

moss [mɔs] *s.* musgo; **moss-grown** musgoso, cubierto de musgo; anticuado.

moss•y [m ɔ sɪ] *adj.* musgoso.

most [most] *adv.* más; sumamente, muy; *s.* la mayoría, la mayor parte, el mayor número o cantidad; los más; **– people** la mayoría (*o la mayor parte*) de la gente, **at the –** a lo más, a lo sumo; **for the – part** por la mayor parte; generalmente, mayormente; **the – that I can do** lo más que puedo hacer; **the – votes** el mayor número de votos, los más votos.

most•ly [móstlɪ] *adv.* por la mayor parte; mayormente, principalmente.

moth [mɔθ] *s.* polilla; mariposa nocturna; **-ball** bolita de naftalina; **moth-eaten** apolillado.

moth•er [m ʌ ðə·] *s.* madre; **mother-of-pearl**

madreperla; nácar; *adj.* de madre; materno, maternal; nativo, natal; **– country** madre patria; país natal; **– Superior** superiora; **– tongue** lengua materna; *v.* servir de madre a, cuidar de.

moth·er·hood [m ʌðəhUd] *s.* maternidad.

moth·er-in-law [m ʌðərInlɔ] *s.* suegra.

moth·er·ly [m ʌðə·lɪ] *adj.* maternal, materno.

mo·tif [motíf] *s.* motivo, tema.

mo·tion [mόʃən] *s.* (*movement*) moción; movimiento; (*signal*) ademán; señal, seña; **-sickness** mareo; *v.* hacer una seña o señas; indicar.

mo·tion·less [mόʃənlɪs] *adj.* inmóvil, inmoble.

mo·tion pic·ture [mόʃənpíktʃə·] *s.* cine o cinematógrafo; película; fotografía cinematográfica, **motion-picture** *adj.* cinematográfico.

mo·tive [mόtɪv] *s.* motivo; tema; *adj.* motriz.

mot·ley [mátlɪ] *adj.* abigarrado, multicolor, de diversos colores; variado, mezclado; *s.* mezcla, mezcolanza.

mo·tor [mόtə·] *s.* motor; automóvil; *v.* pasear o ir en automóvil.

mo·tor·bike [mόtə·baɪk] *s.* motocicleta pequeña; moto.

mo·tor·boat [mόtə·bot] *s.* autobote, lancha de gasolina, bote de motor.

mo·tor·car [mόtə·kɑr] *s.* automóvil.

mo·tor·coach [mόtə·kotʃ] *s.* autobús, ómnibus, *Méx.* camión, *Carib.* guagua; *Ríopl.*, CH. micro; C.A. bus.

mo·tor·cy·cle [mόtə·saɪk] *s.* motocicleta.

mo·tor·ist [mόtə·rɪst] *s.* motorista, automovilista.

mo·tor·man [mόtə·mən] *s.* motorista.

mo·tor scoo·ter [mόtə·skutə·] *s.* motoneta.

mot·tled [mát d] *adj.* moteado, jaspeado, manchado.

mot·to [mάto] *s.* mote, divisa, lema.

mould = mold.

moulder = molder.

moulding = molding.

mouldy = moldy.

mound [maUnd] *s.* montecillo, montículo, montón de tierra.

mount [maUnt] *s.* (*elevation*) monte; (*horse*) montura, cabalgadura, caballo; *v.* montar; montar a caballo; subir, ascender; armar (*una máquina*); engastar (*joyas*).

moun·tain [máUnt ŋ] *s.* montaña; *adj.* montañés; de montaña; **– goat** cabra montés; **- lion** puma; **– range** cordillera, cadena de montañas.

moun·tain·eer [maUnt ŋ Ír] *s.* montañés.

moun·tain·ous [máUnt ŋ əs] *adj.* montañoso.

mourn [morn] *v.* lamentar; deplorar; **to – for** llorar a; estar de duelo por.

mourn·ful [mόrnfəl] *adj.* fúnebre; lúgubre; lastimero; triste.

mourn·ing [mόrnɪŋ] *s.* luto; duelo; lamentación; **to be in** – estar de luto, estar de duelo; *adj.* de luto.

mouse [maUs] *s.* ratón; **–trap** ratonera.

mous·tache = mustache.

mouth [maUθ] *s.* boca; abertura; desembocadura, embocadura (*de un río*).

mouth·ful [máUθfəl] *s.* bocado.

mouth·piece [máUθpis] *s.* boquilla (*de un instrumento de viento*); portavoz.

mov·a·ble [múvəb] *adj.* movible, móvil; **-s** *s. pl.* muebles, bienes muebles.

move [muv] *v.* (*motion*) mover(se); (*change*) mudar(se), mudar de casa; (*propose*) proponer, hacer la moción de; (*game*) hacer una jugada (*en ajedrez o damas*); (*emotion*) conmover; inducir; **– away** irse; alejarse; apartarse; **to – foward** avanzar; **to – on** seguir adelante, caminar; **to – out** irse, mudarse, mudar de casa; *s.* movimiento; mudanza (*de una casa a otra*); paso, trámite (*para conseguir algo*); jugada, turno (*en juegos*); **get a – on there!** ¡ande! ¡dése prisa!; *Am.* ¡ándele!.

move·ment [múvmənt] *s.* (*motion*) movimiento; maniobra; meneo; acción; (*mechanism*) mecanismo, movimiento (*de un reloj*); (*bowel*) evacuación.

mov·ie [múvɪ] *s.* cine, película; **-s** cine.

mow [mo] *v.* segar; cortar (*césped*).

mow·er [mόə·] *s.* segador; segadora, cortadora mecánica; máquina segadora.

mown [mon] *adj. & p.p.* segado.

Mr. [místə·] Sr., señor; **Mrs.** [mísɪz] Sra., señora.

much [mʌtʃ] *adj., adv.* & *s.* mucho; **– the same** casi lo mismo; **as – as** tanto como; **how – ?** ¿cuánto?; **not – of a book** un libro de poco valor; **not – of a poet** un poetastro; **so – that** tanto que; **too –** demasiado; **very –** muchísimo; **to make – of** dar mucha importancia a.

muck [mʌk] *s.* (*manure*) estiércol húmedo; (*mire*) cieno; (*filth*) porquería, suciedad.

mu·cous [mjúkəs] *adj.* mucoso; **- membrane** membrana mucosa.

mud [mʌd] *s.* lodo, fango, cieno; **– wall** tapia.

mud·dle [m ʌd] *v.* enturbiar; confundir; embrollar; *s.* confusión, embrollo, lío, desorden.

mud·dy [m ʌ dɪ] *adj.* fangoso, lodoso; turbio; confuso; *v.* enlodar, ensuciar; enturbiar.

muff [mʌf] *s.* manguito (*para las manos*); falla, error (*en ciertos juegos*); *v.* no coger, dejar escapar (la pelota).

muf·fin [m ʌ fɪn] *s.* bollo, panecillo.

muf·fle [m ʌ f] *v.* embozar; tapar; apagar, amortiguar (*un sonido*).

muf·fler [m ʌ flə·] *s.* bufanda; silenciador (*para maquinaria*); mofle.

mug [mʌg] *s.* pichel, vaso con asa.

mu•lat•to [məl ǽ to] s. mulato.

mul•ber•ry [m ʌ́ lbɛrɪ] s. mora; **– tree** moral.

mule [mjul] s. mulo, mula; **muleteer** [julətĺr] s. arriero.

mull [mʌl] v. meditar, ponderar, revolver en la mente; calentar (vino, sidra, etc.) con azúcar y especias.

mul•ti•ple [m ʌ́ ltəp] s. múltiplo; adj. múltiple.

mul•ti•pli•ca•tion [mʌltəpləkéʃən] s. multiplicación; **– table** tabla de multiplicar.

mul•ti•plic•i•ty [mʌltəplísətɪ] s. multiplicidad.

mul•ti•ply [m ʌ́ ltəplaɪ] v. multiplicar(se).

mul•ti•tude [m ʌ́ ltətjud] s. multitud.

mum [mʌm] adj. callado, silencioso; **to keep –** tarse (o quedarse) callado.

mum•ble [m ʌ́ mb] v. murmurar, hablar entre dientes; mascullar; s. murmullo; **to talk in a –** mascullar las palabras, hablar entre dientes.

mum•my [m ʌ́ mɪ] s. momia.

mumps [mʌmps] s. parótidas, paperas.

munch [mʌntʃ] v. mascar ruidosamente, mascullar.

mun•dane [məndén] adj. mundano.

mu•nic•i•pal [mjunísəp] adj. municipal.

mu•nic•i•pal•i•ty [mjunɪsəpǽlətɪ] s. municipio; municipalidad.

mu•ni•tion [mjuníʃen] s. munición; **– plant** fábrica de municiones, arsenal; v. guarnecer, abastecer de municiones.

mu•ral [mjúrəl] adj. & s. mural.

mur•der [m ɝ́ dəˑ] s. asesinato; homicidio; v. asesinar.

mur•der•er [m ɝ́ dərəˑ] s. asesino, homicida.

mur•der•ess [m ɝ́ dərɪs] s. asesina, homicida.

mur•der•ous [m ɝ́ dərəs] adj. asesino, homicida.

mur•mur [m ɝ́ məˑ] s. (noise) murmullo; susurro; (complaint) queja; v. murmurar; susurrar; quejarse.

mus•cle [m ʌ́ s] s. músculo.

mus•cu•lar [m ʌ́ skjələˑ] adj. muscular; musculoso.

muse [mjuz] v. meditar; s. meditación; **Muse** musa.

mu•se•um [mjuzíəm] s. museo.

mush [mʌʃ] s. potaje espeso de maíz; masa de maíz; cualquier masa blanda; sentimentalismo.

mush•room [m ʌ́ ʃrum] s. seta, hongo.

mu•sic [mjúzɪk] s. música; **– stand** atril.

mu•si•cal [mjúzɪk] adj. musical, músico; melodioso; armonioso; aficionado a la música; **– comedy** zarzuela, comedia musical.

mu•si•cian [mjuzíʃən] s. músico.

musk•mel•on [m ʌ́ skmɛlən] s. melón.

musk•rat [m ʌ́ skræt] s. almizclera (roedor semejante a la rata).

mus•lin [m ʌ́ zlɪn] s. muselina.

muss [mʌs] v. desarreglar, desordenar; arrugar.

must [mʌst] v. defect. (por lo general se usa sólo en el presente) deber; deber de; haber de; tener que.

mus•tache [m ʌ́ stæʃ] s. bigote, mostacho.

mus•tard [m ʌ́ stəd] s. mostaza; **– plaster** sinapismo.

mus•ter [m ʌ́ stəˑ] v. pasar lista o revista; juntarse para una formación militar; reunir(se), **to – out** dar de baja; **to – up one's courage** cobrar valor o ánimo; s. revista (de soldados o marinos); **to pass – pasar lista o revista; ser aceptable (en una inspección).

must•y [m ʌ́ stɪ] adj. mohoso, rancio, añejo.

mute [mjut] adj. mudo; s. mudo; letra muda; sordina (de violín).

mu•ti•late [mjút et] v. mutilar.

mu•ti•ny [mjút ɳ ɪ] s. motín; v. amotinarse.

mut•ter [m ʌ́ təˑ] v. murmurar, refunfuñar; hablar entre dientes; s. murmullo, refunfuño.

mut•ton [m ʌ́ tɳ] s. carne de carnero; **– chop** chuleta de carnero.

mu•tu•al [mjút ʃ Uəl] adj. mutuo.

muz•zle [m ʌ́ z] s. hocico; bozal (para el hocico); boca (de arma de fuego); v. abozalar, poner bozal a; amordazar; hacer callar.

my [maɪ] adj. mi (mis).

myr•i•ad [mírɪəd] s. miríada, diez mil; millares, gran cantidad.

myr•tle [m ɝ́ t] s. mirto, arrayán.

my•self [maɪsɛ́lf] pron. yo mismo; me (como reflexivo); a mí mismo; **by –** solo; **I – did it** yo mismo lo hice; **I talk to –** hablo conmigo mismo, hablo para mis adentros.

mys•te•ri•ous [mɪstírɪəs] adj. misterioso.

mys•ter•y [místrɪ] s. misterio.

mys•tic [místɪk] adj. & s. místico.

mys•ti•cal [místɪk] adj. místico.

myth [mɪθ] s. mito, fábula.

my•thol•o•gy [mɪθñlədʒɪ] s. mitología.

N

nab [næb] v. agarrar, coger; arrestar.

nag [næg] s. rocín, caballejo, jaco; v. importunar, irritar (con repetidos regaños).

nail [nel] s. clavo; uña (del dedo), **– file** lima (para las uñas); v. clavar; clavetear; agarrar, atrapar.

na•ive [noív] *adj.* simple, ingenuo, cándido.
naked [nékɪd] *adj.* desnudo.
na•ked•ness [nékɪdnɪs] *s.* desnudez.
name [nem] *s.* (*designation*) nombre; (*fame*) renombre, fama; **– sake** tocayo; **by the – of** nombrado, llamado; apellidado; **family –** apellido; **to call someone -s** motejar o decirle groserías a uno; ponerle apodos a uno; **to make a – for oneself** ganar fama; **what is your – ?** ¿cómo se llama Ud.?; *v.* nombrar; mentar, mencionar; llamar.
name•less [némlɪs] *adj.* sin nombre; anónimo.
name•ly [némlɪ] *adv.* a saber, esto es, es decir.
nap [næp] *s.* siesta; pelo (*de un tejido*); **to take a –** echar un sueño, echar una siesta; *v.* dormitar; echar un sueño; sestear.
nape [nep] *s.* nuca, cogote.
naph•tha [næfθə] *s.* nafta.
nap•kin [næpkɪn] *s.* servilleta.
nar•cis•sus [norsísəs] *s.* narciso.
nar•cot•ic [norkátɪk] *adj.* & *s.* narcótico.
nar•rate [nærét] *v.* narrar.
nar•ra•tion [næréʃən] *s.* narración.
nar•ra•tive [nærətɪv] *adj.* narrativo; *s.* narración; narrativa; relato.
nar•row [næro] *adj.* (*cramped*) estrecho; angosto; limitado; (*intolerant*) intolerante; **– escape** trance difícil, escapada difícil; **– search** búsqueda esmerada; **narrow-minded** fanático, intolerante; **-s** *s. pl.* desfiladero, paso; estrecho o estrechos; *v.* angostar(se), estrechar(se); limitar, restringir, reducir; **-ly** *adv.* estrechamente; **he -ly escaped** por poco no se escapa.
nar•row•ness [nærənɪs] *s.* (*cramped*) estrechez, estrechura, angostura; limitación; (*intolerance*) intolerancia.
na•sal [néz l] *adj.* nasal.
nas•ti•ness [nǽstɪnɪs] *s.* suciedad, porquería; grosería.
nas•tur•tium [næstɜ́rʃəm] *s.* mastuerzo.
nas•ty [nǽstɪ] *adj.* (*foul*) sucio, asqueroso; feo; (*indecent*) grosero; indecente; **a – fall** una caída terrible; **a – disposition** un genio horrible.
na•tal [nétl] *adj.* natal.
na•tion [néʃən] *s.* nación.
na•tion•al [nǽʃənl] *adj.* nacional; *s.* nacional, ciudadano.
na•tion•al•ism [nǽʃənəlɪzm] *s.* nacionalismo.
na•tion•al•i•ty [næʃənǽlətɪ] *s.* nacionalidad.
na•tive [nétɪv] *adj.* nativo; natal; natural; indígena; del país, Am. criollo; **– of** oriundo de, natural de; *s.* nativo, natural, indígena; habitante.
na•tiv•i•ty [nətívətɪ] *s.* nacimiento; natividad (*de la*

Virgen María); **the Nativity** la Navidad.
nat•u•ral [nǽtʃərəl] *adj.* natural; sencillo, sin afectación; *s.* becuadro (*signo musical*); **he is a – for that job** tiene aptitud natural para ese puesto; **-ly** *adv.* naturalmente; con naturalidad.
nat•u•ral•ism [nǽtʃərəlɪzəm] *s.* naturalismo.
nat•u•ral•ist [nǽtʃərəlɪst] *s.* naturalista.
nat•u•ral•iza•tion [nætʃərələzéʃən] *s.* naturalización.
nat•u•ral•ize [nǽtʃərəlaɪz] *v.* naturalizar.
nat•u•ral•ness [nǽtʃərəlnɪs] *s.* naturalidad.
na•ture [nétʃə] *s.* naturaleza; natural, genio, índole; instinto; especie; **to copy from –** copiar del natural.
naught [nɔt] *s.* cero; nada.
naugh•ty [nɔ́tɪ] *adj.* malo, desobediente; travieso, pícaro; malicioso.
nau•sea [nɔ́zɪə] *s.* náusea.
nau•se•ate [nɔ́zɪet] *v.* dar náuseas, dar bascas, asquear, dar asco; sentir náusea; **to be -ed** tener náuseas.
nau•se•at•ing [nɔ́zɪetɪŋ] *adj.* nauseabundo, asqueroso.
nau•ti•cal [nɔ́tɪk l] *adj.* náutico, naval.
na•val [névl] *adj.* naval; **–officer** oficial de la marina.
nave [nev] *s.* nave (*de una iglesia*).
na•vel [névl] *s.* ombligo; **– orange** naranja california (*sin semillas*).
nav•i•ga•ble [nǽvəgəb l] *adj.* navegable.
nav•i•gate [nǽvəgət] *v.* navegar.
nav•i•ga•tion [nævəgéʃən] *s.* navegación; náutica.
nav•i•ga•tor [nǽvəgətə] *s.* navegador, navegante.
na•vy [névɪ] *s.* marina de guerra; armada; **– blue** azul marino; **– yard** astillero, arsenal.
nay [ne] *adv.* no; no sólo ... sino (que) también; *s.* no, voto negativo.
near [nɪr] *adv.* (*space, time*) cerca; (*almost*) casi; **– at hand** cerca, a la mano; **I came – forgetting to do it** por poco se me olvida hacelo; **to come (go, draw) – acercarse; – sighted** miope, *prep.* cerca de; **– the end of the month** hacia fines del mes; *adj.* cercano, próximo; estrecho, íntimo; **– silk** seda imitada; **I had a – accident** por poco me sucede un accidente, *v.* acercarse (a).
near•by [nírbáɪ] *adv.* cerca, a la mano; *adj.* cercano, próximo.
near•ly [nírlɪ] *adv.* casi, cerca de; aproximadamente, próximamente; **I – did it** estuve al punto de

hacerlo, estuve para hacerlo.

near•ness [nínɪs] s. cercanía, proximidad.

neat [nit] adj. pulcro, aseado, limpio; ordenado; esmerado; hábil, diestro; **-ly** adv. aseadamente; esmeradamente; ordenadamente; hábilmente.

neat•ness [nítɪs] s. pulcritud, aseo; limpieza; esmero; claridad.

neb•u•lous [nɛbjuləs] adj. nebuloso.

nec•es•sar•i•ly [nɛsəsɛrəlɪ] adv. necesariamente.

nec•es•sar•y [nɛsəsɛrɪ] adj. necesario; **necessaries** s. pl. necesidades, requisitos.

ne•ces•si•tate [nəsɛsətet] v. necesitar, precisar.

ne•ces•si•ty [nəsɛsətɪ] s. necesidad.

neck [nɛk] s. cuello; pescuezo; garganta; **—of land** istmo; **low —** escote; **— and —** parejos (en una carrera).

neck•lace [nɛklɪs] s. collar; gargantilla.

neck•tie [nɛktaɪ] s. corbata.

ne•crol•o•gy [nɛkrálədʒɪ] s. necrología.

need [nid] s. (lack) necesidad; (poverty) pobreza; **for — of** por falta de; **if — be** si fuere menester, en caso de necesidad; v. necesitar; tener necesidad de; hacerle falta a uno; tener que.

need•ful [nídfəl] adj. necesario; necesitado.

nee•dle [nídl] s. aguja.

nee•dle•point [nídl pɔɪnt] s. encaje de mano.

need•less [nídlɪs] adj. innecesario, inútil.

nee•dle•work [nídl wɜk] s. labor, bordado; costura.

need•y [nídɪ] adj. necesitado, menesteroso.

ne'er [nɛr] adv. contr. de **never, ne'erdo-well** s. persona incompetente; haragán.

ne•ga•tion [nɪgéʃən] s. negación, negativa.

neg•a•tive [nɛgətɪv] adj. negativo; s. negativa; negación, partícula o voz negativa; negativa (de una fotografía).

ne•glect [nɪglɛkt] v. negligencia; descuido; abandono; v. descuidar; desatender; abandonar; **to — to** dejar de, olvidar, olvidarse de.

ne•glect•ful [nɪglɛktfəl] adj. negligente, descuidado.

neg•li•gence [nɛglədʒəns] s. negligencia.

neg•li•gent [nɛglədʒənt] adj. negligente, descuidado.

ne•go•ti•ate [nɪgóʃɪet] v. negociar; agenciar; vencer (un obstáculo o dificultad), dar cima a.

ne•go•ti•a•tion [nɪgoʃIéʃən] s. negociación.

ne•gro [nígro] s. & adj. negro.

Ne•groid [nígrɔɪd] adj. negroide.

neigh [ne] s. relincho; v. relinchar.

neigh•bor [nébɚ] s. vecino; prójimo; adj. vecino; cercano.

neigh•bor•hood [nébɚhUd] s. vecindad; vecindario; inmediación; **in the — of a hundred dollars** cerca de cien dólares.

neigh•bor•ing [nébɚrɪŋ] adj. vecino; cercano; colindante.

nei•ther [níðɚ] pron. ninguno, ni (el) uno ni (el) otro; **— of the two** ninguno de los dos; adj. ninguno; **— of us** ninguno de nosotros; conj. ni; **— ... nor** ni ... ni; **— will I** tampoco yo, ni yo tampoco.

ne•ol•o•gism [niálədʒɪzm] s. neologismo.

ne•o•phyte [níofaɪt] s. neófito.

neph•ew [nɛfju] s. sobrino.

nep•o•tism [nɛpətɪzm] s. nepotismo.

nerve [nɝv] s. (anatomy) nervio; (courage) valor, ánimo; audacia; (effrontery) descaro; **-s** nervios; nerviosidad; **to strain every —** esforzarse hasta más no poder, poner el mayor empeño posible.

nerv•ous [nɝvəs] adj. nervioso.

nerv•ous•ness [nɝvəsnɪs] s. nerviosidad; agitación.

nest [nɛst] s. nido; nidada; **— egg** nidal; ahorros; **— of baskets (boxes, tables)** juego graduado de cestas (cajas, mesitas); **wasp's —** avispero; v. anidar.

nes•tle [nɛsl] v. acurrucar(se); abrigarse; anidar.

net [nɛt] s. red; malla; tejido de mallas; adj. de mallas, de punto de malla; v. redar, enredar, coger con red; cubrir con una red.

net [nɛt] adj. neto; **— price** precio neto; **— profit** ganancia neta o líquida; v. producir una ganancia neta o líquida; obtener una ganancia líquida.

net•tle [nɛt] s. ortiga; v. picar, irritar, enfadar.

net•work [nɛtwɝk] s. red; malla; **radio —** red de estaciones radiofónicas.

neu•rot•ic [njUrátɪk] adj. & s. neurótico.

neu•ter [njútɚ] adj. neutro.

neu•tral [njútrəl] adj. neutral; neutro.

neu•tral•i•ty [njutrǽlətɪ] s. neutralidad.

neu•tral•ize [njútrəlatz] v. neutralizar.

nev•er [nɛvɚ] adv. nunca, jamás; **— mind** no importa; no haga Ud. caso; no se moleste Ud.; **never-ending** perpetuo, eterno; de nunca acabar.

nev•er•the•less [nɛvɚðəlɛs] adv. & conj. sin embargo, no obstante, con todo, empero.

new [nju] adj. (not old) nuevo; moderno; (fresh) fresco; reciente; adv. recién; **— born baby** criatura recién nacida.

new•com•er [njúkʌmɚ] s. recién llegado.

new•ly [njúlɪ] adv. nuevamente, recientemente; **— arrived** recién llegado; **— wed** recién casado.

new•ness [njúnɪs] s. novedad, calidad de nuevo.

news [njuz] s. noticias, nuevas; novedades; **piece of —** noticia, nueva; **— boy** vendedor de periódicos; **— reel** película noticiera; película de noticias mundiales; **— stand** puesto de periódicos.

news•mon•ger [njúzmʌŋgɚ] s. chismoso,

chismero, gacetilla.

news•pa•per [njúzpepɚ] *s.* periódico.

next [nɛkst] *adj.* (*future*) próximo; entrante, que viene; (*following*) siguiente; contiguo; **in the – life** en la otra vida; **to be – in turn** tocarle a uno, ser su turno; *adv.* después, luego; **– best** segundo en cualidad o importancia; *prep.*; **– to** junto a; al lado de; después de.

nib•ble [níb▯] *s.* mordisco; *v.* mordiscar, mordisquear; picar, morder.

nice [naɪs] *adj.* (*attractive*) fino; bueno; amable, simpático; lindo; primoroso; (*refined*) refinado; esmerado; preciso, exacto; **-ly** *adv.* con esmero; con finura o primor; sutilmente, con delicadeza; amablemente; bien; **to get along -ly with** llevarse bien con.

ni•ce•ty [náɪsətɪ] *s.* fineza, finura; delicadeza; exactitud.

niche [nɪtʃ] *s.* nicho.

nick [nɪk] *s.* mella, desportilladura; **in the – of time** en el momento crítico; *v.* mellar, desportillar.

nick•el [níkl̩] *s.* níquel; moneda de cinco centavos; **nickel-plated** niquelado.

nick•name [níknem] *s.* mote, apodo; *v.* apodar, poner apodo a.

niece [nis] *s.* sobrina.

nig•gard•ly [nígɚdlɪ] *adj.* mezquino, ruin, tacaño; *adv.* mezquinamente, ruinmente.

night [naɪt] *s.* niche; **good - !**¡buenas noches!; **tomorrow –** mañana por la noche; *adj.* nocturno; de noche; **– owl** buho; trasnochador; **– watchman** sereno, vigilante nocturno.

night•fall [náɪtfɔl] *s.* anochecer, caída de la tarde, anochecida.

night•gown [náɪtgaʊn] *s.* camisa de dormir, camisa de noche, Am. camisón.

night•in•gale [náɪt ŋ gel] *s.* ruiseñor.

night•ly [náɪtlɪ] *adv.* cada noche, todas las noches; *adj.* nocturno, de noche.

night•mare [náɪtmɛr] *s.* pesadilla.

ni•hil•ism [náɪɪlɪzm] *s.* nihilismo.

nim•ble [nímb▯] *adj.* ágil, ligero; listo.

nip [nɪp] *v.* (*pinch*) pellizcar; (*bite*) mordiscar; (*frostbite*) marchitar, helar (*por la acción del frío*); **to – in the bud** cortar en germen, destruir al nacer; **to – off** despuntar; podar; *s.* pellizco; mordisco; trago.

nip•ple [níp▯] *s.* teta, tetilla, pezón; pezón de goma.

ni•trate [náɪtret] *s.* nitrato.

nitric a•cid [náɪtrɪkǽsɪd] *s.* ácido nítrico.

ni•tro•gen [náɪtrədʒən] *s.* nitrógeno.

no [no] *adv.* no; **– longer** ya no; **there is – more** no hay más; *adj.* ningun(o); **– matter how much** por mucho que; **– one** ninguno, nadie; **– smoking** se prohibe fumar; **I have – friend** no tengo ningún amigo; **of – use** inútil, sin provecho; *s.* no, voto negativo.

no•bil•i•ty [nobílətɪ] *s.* nobleza.

no•ble [nób▯] *s.* & *adj.* noble.

no•ble•man [nób▯mən] *s.* noble.

no•ble•ness [nób▯nɪs] *s.* nobleza.

no•bly [nóblɪ] *adv.* noblemente.

no•bod•y [nóbɑdɪ] *pron.* nadie, ninguno.

noc•tur•nal [nɑktɚn▯] *adj.* nocturno.

nod [nɑd] *v.* inclinar la cabeza (*para hacer una seña, saludar o asentir*); cabecear, dar cabezadas (*dormitando*); *s.* inclinación de la cabeza, saludo; señal de asentimiento (*con la cabeza*).

noise [nɔɪz] *s.* ruido; barullo; sonido; *v.* divulgar; **it is being -d about that** corre el rumor que.

noise•less [nɔ́ɪzlɪs] *adj.* sin ruido, silencioso, quieto; **-ly** *adv.* sin ruido, silenciosamente.

nois•i•ly [nɔ́ɪzɪlɪ] *adv.* ruídosamente.

nois•y [nɔ́ɪzɪ] *adj.* ruidoso.

nom•i•nal [námən▯] *adj.* nominal.

nom•i•nate [námənet] *v.* nombrar, designar.

nom•i•nation [nɑmənéʃən] *s.* nombramiento, nominación.

non•con•form•ist [nɑnkənfɔ́rmɪst] *adj.* & *s.* disidente.

none [nʌn] *pron.* ninguno; ningunos; nada; **I want – of that** no quiero nada eso; **that is – of his business** no le importa a él eso; *adv.* no, de ningún modo; **– the less** no menos; **to be – the happier for that** no estar por eso más contento.

non•en•ti•ty [nɑnɛ́ntətɪ] *s.* nulidad, persona o cosa inútil.

non•in•ter•ven•tion [nɑnɪntɚvɛ́nʃən] *s.* no intervención.

non•par•ti•san [nɑnpártəzən] *adj.* imparcial; independiente.

non•sense [nánsɛns] *s.* tontería, necedad; disparate, desatino.

noo•dle [núd▯] *s.* tallarín, fideo, pasta (para sopa).

nook [nʊk] *s.* rincón; **breakfast –** desayunador.

noon [nun] *s.* mediodía.

noon•day [núnde] *s.* mediodía; *adj.* meridiano, de mediodía; **– meal** comida de mediodía.

noon•tide [núntaɪd] *s.* mediodía.

noon•time [núntaɪm] *s.* mediodía.

noose [nus] *s.* dogal; lazo, nudo corredizo, Am. gaza; *v.* lazar, coger con lazo; hacer un lazo correizo en.

nor [nɔr] *conj.* ni; **neither ... –** ni ... ni.

norm [nɔrm] *s.* norma.

nor•mal [nɔ́rm▯] *adj.* normal; *s.* norma; normal,

línea perpendicular.

north [nɔrθ] s. norte; adj. septentrional; norteño; del norte; **– pole** polo norte, polo ártico; **– wind** cierzo, norte; **North American** norteamericano; adv. al norte, hacia el norte.

north·east [nɔrθíst] adj. & s. nordeste; adv. hacia el nordeste, rumbo al nordeste.

north·east·ern [nɔrθístə·n] adj. del nordeste, nordeste.

north·ern [nɔ́ rðə·n] adj. septentrional; norteño; del norte; hacia el norte; **-lights** aurora boreal.

north·ern·er [nɔ́ rðə·nə·] s. norteño, habitante del norte.

north·ward [nɔ́ rθwə·d] adv. hacia el norte, rumbo al norte.

north·west [nɔrθwést] adj. & s. noroeste; adv. hacia el noroeste.

norht·west·ern [nɔrθwéstə·n] adj. noroeste, del noroeste.

Nor·we·gian [nɔrwídʒən] adj. & s. Noruego.

nose [noz] s. nariz; proa (de un barco); **–dive** picada (de un avión); v. olfatear; **to – around** husmear, curiosear.

nos·tal·gia [nɑstǽldʒɪə] s. nostalgia, añoranza.

nos·trils [nástrəlz] s. pl. narices, ventanas de la nariz.

not [nɑt] adv. no; **– at all** de ningún modo; de nada (contestación a "thank you"); **– at all sure** nada seguro; **– even a word** ni siquiera una palabra.

no·ta·ble [nótəb] adj. notable.

no·ta·ry [nótərɪ] s. notario.

no·ta·tion [notéʃən] s. notación; apunte; anotación.

notch [nɑtʃ] s. muesca, ranura; hendidura; v. ranurar, hacer una ranura en.

note [not] s. nota; apunte, apuntación; **bank –** billete de banco; **promissory –** pagaré, abonaré; v. notar, observar, reparar; **to – down** apuntar.

note·book [nótbʊk] s. libreta, cuaderno, libro de apuntes.

not·ed [nótɪd] adj. notable, célebre, famoso.

note·wor·thy [nótwɝ ðɪ] adj. notable, célebre.

noth·ing [n ʌ́ θɪŋ] s. nada; cero; **for –** por nada; inútilmente; de balde, gratis.

no·tice [nótɪs] s. noticia; aviso, advertencia, anuncio; mención; **to give a short –** avisar a última hora; **to take – of** hacer caso de, prestar atención a; v. notar, observar; prestar atención a; hacer caso a (o de); notificar.

no·tice·a·ble [nótɪsəb] adj. notable; conspicuo; perceptible.

no·ti·fy [nótəfaɪ] v. notificar, avisar.

no·tion [nóʃən] s. noción; idea; capricho; **-s** mercería, artículos menudos (como alfileres, boto-

nes, etc.), chucherías.

no·to·ri·ous [notórɪəs] adj. notorio.

not·with·stand·ing [nɑtwɪθstǽndɪŋ] prep. a pesar de; adv & conj. no obstante, sin embargo; **– that** a pesar (de) que.

nought = naught.

noun [naʊn] s. nombre, sustantivo.

nour·ish [nɝɪʃ] v. nutrir, alimentar.

nour·ish·ing [nɝɪʃɪŋ] adj. nutritivo, alimenticio.

nour·ish·ment [nɝɪʃmənt] s. nutrimento, sustento, alimento; nutrición.

nov·el [náv] s. novela; adj. novel, nuevo; raro, original.

nov·el·ist [náv ɪst] s. novelista.

nov·el·ty [náv tɪ] s. novedad; innovación; **novelties** novedades.

No·vem·ber [novémbə·] s. noviembre.

nov·ice [návɪs] s. novicio; novato, principiante.

now [naʊ] adv. ahora; ya; **– … –** ya … ya, ora … ora; **– and then** de vez en cuando, de cuando en cuando; **– that** ahora que; **he left just –** salió hace poco, Ríopl., Ch., Andes. recién salió.

now·a·days [náʊədez] adv. hoy día.

no·where [nóhwɛr] adv. en ninguna parte, a ninguna parte.

nox·ious [nókʃəs] adj. nocivo.

nu·cle·us [njúklɪəs] s. núcleo.

nude [njud] adj. desnudo.

nudge [nʌdʒ] v. codear, tocar con el codo; s. codazo ligero.

nug·get [n ʌ́ gɪt] s. pepita; pedazo.

nui·sance [njús ŋ s] s. molestia; lata, fastidio; persona o cosa fastidiosa.

null [nʌl] adj. nulo; **– and void** nulo o inválido.

nul·li·fy [n ʌ́ lɪfaɪ] v. invalidar; anular.

numb [nʌm] adj. entumecido o entumido, aterido; **to become –** entumecerse, entumirse, aterirse; v. entumecer.

num·ber [n ʌ́ mbə·] s. número; v. numerar; ascender a (cierto numero); **to – him among one´s friends** contarle entre sus amigos.

num·ber·less [n ʌ́ mbə·lɪs] adj. innumerable, sin número.

nu·mer·al [njúmrəl] s. número, cifra; guarismo; adj. numeral.

nu·mer·i·cal [njumérɪk] adj. numérico.

nu·mer·ous [njúmrəs] adj. numeroso; numerosos, muchos.

nun [nʌn] s. monja.

nup·tial [n ʌ́ p ʃəl] adj. nupcial; **-s** s. pl. nupcias, bodas.

nurse [nɝs] s. (for the sick) enfermera, enfermero;

(*for children*) niñera, aya; *Méx., Ven., Col., Andes* nana, *Am.* manejadora, *Andes* pilmama; *C.A.* china; **wet** – nodriza, ama de cría; *v.* criar, amamantar, dar de mamar, lactar; mamar; cuidar (*a un enfermo*); abrigar (*rencor*).

nurs•er•y [nɔ́srɪ] *s.* cuarto para niños; criadero, semillero (*de plantas*); **day** – sala donde se cuida y divierte a los niños.

nur•ture [nɔ́tʃə] *s.* crianza; nutrimento; *v.* criar; nutrir; cuidar; fomentar.

nut [nʌt] *s.* nuez (*nombre genérico de varias frutas como la almendra, la castaña, la avellana, etc.*); tuerca; loco, tipo raro o extravagante.

nut•crack•er [n ʌ́ t krækə-] *s.* cascanueces.

nut•meg [n ʌ́ t mɛg] *s.* nuez moscada.

nu•tri•ent [nútrɪənt] *s.* nutritivo.

nu•tri•tion [njutrɪ́ʃən] *s.* nutrición; nutrimento, alimento.

nu•tri•tious [njutrɪ́ʃəs] *adj.* nutritivo, alimenticio.

nu•tri•tive [njútrɪtɪv] *adj.* nutritivo.

nut•shell [n ʌ́ t ʃəl] *s.* cáscara de nuez (*o de otro fruto semejante*); **in a** – en suma, en breve, en pocas palabras.

nymph [nɪmf] *s.* ninfa.

O

oak [ok] *s.* roble; encina; **– grove** robledo o robledal; **live** – encina siempreverde.

oar [or] *s.* remo; *v.* remar, bogar.

o•a•sis [oésɪs] *s.* oasis.

oat [ot] *s.* avena (*planta*); **-s** avena, granos de avena.

oath [oθ] *s.* juramento; blasfemia, reniego.

oat•meal [ótmɪl] *s.* harina de avena; gachas de avena.

o•be•di•ence [əbídɪəns] *s.* obediencia.

o•be•di•ent [əbídɪənt] *adj.* obediente.

o•be•si•ty [obísətɪ] *s.* obesidad, gordura.

o•bey [obé] *v.* obedecer.

ob•ject [óbdʒɪkt] *s.* objeto; cosa; complemento (*del verbo*); [əbdʒɛ́kt] *v.* objetar; oponerse; tener inconveniente.

ob•jec•tion [əbdʒɛ́kʃən] *s.* objeción, reparo; inconveniente.

ob•jec•tive [əbdʒɛ́ktɪv] *adj.* objetivo; **– case** caso complementario; *s.* objetivo; fin, propósito.

ob•li•gate [ábləget] *v.* obligar, constreñir; comprometer.

ob•li•ga•tion [ɑbləgéʃən] *s.* (*duty*) obligación; deber (*debt*) deuda; **to be under – to** estar obligado a; estar agradecido a, deber favores a.

o•blig•a•to•ry [əblɪ́gətorɪ] *adj.* obligatorio.

o•blige [əbláɪdʒ] *v.* obligar; complacer; **much –ed!** ¡muchas gracias!; **to be very much –ed to someone** quedar muy agradecido con alguien.

o•blig•ing [əbláɪdʒɪŋ] *adj.* complaciente, obsequioso, comedido, cortés.

o•blique [əblík] *adj.* oblicuo.

o•blit•er•ate [əblɪ́təret] *v.* borrar; arrasar, destruir.

o•bliv•i•on [əblɪ́vɪən] *s.* olvido.

o•bliv•i•ous [əblɪ́vɪəs] *adj.* olvidado, abstraído.

ob•long [áblɔŋ] *adj.* cuadrilongo; oblongo.

ob•nox•ious [əbnákʃəs] *adj.* ofensivo; molesto; odioso.

o•boe [óbo] *s.* oboe.

ob•scene [əbsín] *adj.* obsceno.

ob•scen•i•ty [əbsénətɪ] *s.* obscenidad, indecencia.

ob•scure [əbskjʊ́r] *adj.* obscuro; *v.* obscurecer; ofuscar.

ob•scu•ri•ty [əbskjʊ́rətɪ] *s.* obscuridad.

ob•se•quies [ábsɪkwiz] *s.* exequias, honras, funerales.

ob•se•qui•ous [əbsíkwɪəs] *adj.* obsequioso; servil, zalamero.

ob•serv•a•ble [əbzɝvəb]] *adj.* observable.

ob•ser•vance [əbzɝ́vəns] *s.* observancia; ceremonia, rito.

ob•ser•vant [əbzɝ́vənt] *adj.* observador; observante.

ob•ser•va•tion [ɑbzɝvéʃən] *s.* observación.

ob•ser•va•to•ry [əbzɝ́vətorɪ] *s.* observatorio; mirador.

ob•serve [əbzɝ́v] *v.* observar; guardar (*las fiestas religiosas*); celebrar (*una fiestas*).

ob•serv•er [əbzɝvə-] *s.* observador.

ob•sess [əbsɛ́s] *v.* obsesionar, causar obsesión.

ob•ses•sion [əbsɛ́ʃən] *s.* obsesión; idea fija.

ob•so•lete [ábsəlit] *adj.* anticuado; desusado.

ob•sta•cle [ábstək]] *s.* obstáculo.

ob•sti•na•cy [ábstənəsɪ] *s.* obstinación, terquedad, porfía.

ob•sti•nate [ábstənɪt] *adj.* obstinado, terco, porfiado.

ob•strep•er•ous [əbstrɛ́pə-əs] *adj.* estrepitoso, turbulento.

ob•struct [əbstr ʌ́ kt] *v.* obstruir.

ob•struc•tion [əbstr ʌ́ kʃən] *s.* obstrucción; impedimento, estorbo.

ob•tain [əbtén] *v.* obtener, conseguir, alcanzar, adquirir.

ob•tain•a•ble [əbténəb]] *adj.* obtenible, asequible.

ob•tru•sive [əbtrúsɪv] *adj.* intruso, entremetido.

ob•vi•ate [ábvɪet] *v.* obviar; allanar (*una dificultad*).

ob•vi•ous [ábvɪəs] *adj.* obvio, evidente.

oc•ca•sion [əkéʒən] *s.* (*timely*) ocasión; (*chance*)

oportunidad; (*cause*) motivo, causa; (*event*) acontecimiento; *v.* ocasionar, causar.

oc·ca·sion·al [əkéʒən]] *adj.* ocasional; infrecuente, poco frecuente; **-ly** *adv.* de vez en cuando, a veces.

oc·ci·den·tal [ɑksədént]] *adj. & s.* occidental.

oc·clu·sive [oklúsɪv] *adj. & s.* oclusivo.

oc·cult [ək Ált] *adj.* oculto, misterioso.

oc·cu·pant [ákjəpənt] *s.* ocupante; inquilino.

oc·cu·pa·tion [akjəpéʃən] *s.* ocupación; trabajo, empleo, oficio.

oc·cu·py [ákjəpaɪ] *v.* ocupar.

oc·cur [ək ɜ́r] *v.* ocurrir, suceder; **to — to one** ocurrírsele a uno, venirle a la mente.

oc·cur·rense [ək ɜ́əns] *s.* ocurrencia, suceso, caso, acontecimiento.

o·cean [óʃən] *s.* océano.

o´clock [əklák] *contr.* de **of the clock; it is two** — son las dos.

oc·tave [áktɪv] *s.* octava.

Oc·to·ber [aktóbə-] *s.* octubre.

oc·u·list [ákjəlɪst] *s.* oculista.

odd [ɑd] *adj.* (*rare*) extraño, singular, raro; (*not even*) non, impar; **– change** suelto, cambio sobrante; **– moments** momentos libres, momentos de ocio; **– shoe** zapato suelto (*sin compañero*); **– volume** tomo suelto; **thirty –** treinta y tantos, treinta y pico; **-ly** *adv.* extrañamente, de un modo raro.

odd·i·ty [ádətɪ] *s.* rareza.

odds [ɑdz] *s. pl.* o *sing.* diferencia, disparidad (*en apuestas*); ventaja, puntos de ventaja (*en apuestas*); **– and ends** retazos, trozos sobrantes, pedacitos varios; **the – are against me** la suerte me es contraria, estoy de mala suerte; **to at -s with** estar reñido o enemistado con.

ode [od] *s.* oda.

o·di·ous [ódɪəs] *adj.* odioso.

o·dor [ódə-] *s.* olor; **bad –** mal olor, hedor.

o·dor·ous [ódəɪəs] *adj.* oloroso.

o´er [or] *contr.* de **over.**

of [ɑv, ʌv] *prep.* de; **– course** por supuesto, claro, ya se ve; **– late** últimamente; **a quarter – five** las cinco menos cuarto; **to smell –** oler a; **to taste –** saber a.

off [ɑf] *adv.* (*distant*) lejos, fuera, a distancia; (*not attached*) suelto; apagado (*luz*); (*equivale al reflexivo se en ciertos verbos: marcharse, irse, etc.*); **– and on** de vez en cuando; a intervalos; **ten cents – rebaja de diez centavos; ten miles – a una distancia de diez millas; to take a day – ausentarse por un día; descansar por un día; *adj.* ausente; distante, más remoto; quitado; **the – side** el lado más remoto; **with his hat –** con el sombrero quitado; **the electricity is –** está cortada la electricidad; **to be – in one´s accounts** estar errado en sus cuentas; **to be - to war** haberse ido a la guerra; **to be well –** ser

persona acomodada, estar en buenas circunstancias; *prep.* lejos de; **off-color** de mal color; verde (*indecente*); **– shore** a vista de la costa; **– standard** de calidad inferior; **– the road** desviado, descarriado; a un lado del camino; **to be – duty** no estar de turno; estar libre.

of·fend [əfénd] *v.* ofender.

of·fend·er [əféndə-] *s.* ofensor; transgresor, delicuente.

of·fense [əféns] *s.* ofensa; agravio; delito, culpa; **no – was meant** lo hice (*o lo dije*) sin malicia; **weapon of –** arma ofensiva.

of·fen·sive [əfénsɪv] *adj.* ofensivo; *s.* ofensiva.

of·fer [ɔ́fə-] *v.* ofrecer; **to – to do it** ofrecerse a hacerlo; *s.* oferta; ofrecimiento; promesa; propuesta.

of·fer·ing [ɔ́fərɪŋ] *s.* ofrenda; oferta, ofrecimiento.

off·hand [ɔ́fhænd] *adv.* de improviso, por el momento, sin pensarlo, impensadamente; *adj.* impensado, hecho de improviso; **in an – manner** con indiferencia; descuidadamente; sin plan.

of·fice [ɔ́fɪs] *s.* (*function*) oficio; cargo; función; (*place*) oficina, despacho; **– building** edificio para oficinas; **post –** correo; **box –** taquilla, *Ch., Riopl.* boletería; **through the good –s of** por el intermedio de.

of·fi·cer [ɔ́fəsə-] *s.* (*office holder*) oficial; funcionario; (*police*) policía, gendarme; agente de policía; *v.* comandar, dirigir (*como un oficial*); proveer de oficiales.

of·fi·cial [əfíʃəl] *adj.* oficial; *s.* oficial, funcionario; empleado público.

of·fi·ci·ate [əfíʃɪet] *v.* oficiar.

of·fi·cious [əfíʃəs] *adj.* oficioso, intruso, entremetido.

off·set [ɔfsét] *v.* compensar por; contrapesar.

off·shore [ɔfʃór] *adj. & adv.* (*land*) terral; (*at sea*) lejos de la playa.

off·spring [ɔ́fsprɪŋ] *s.* prole, hijos, descendientes; hijo, vástago; resultado, consecuencia.

off·stage [ɔfstédʒ] *adv. & adj.* entre bastidores.

oft [ɔft] = **often.**

of·ten [ɔ́fən] *adv.* muchas veces, con frecuencia, frecuentemente, a menudo; **how – ?** ¿cuántas veces?; ¿cada cuándo?

o·gre [ógə-] *s.* ogro, gigante, monstruo.

oil [ɔɪl] *s.* aceite; óleo; petróleo; **– can** alcuza; **– painting** pintura al óleo; **– well** pozo de petróleo; **– motor** aceite para motores, *v* aceitar, engrasar, lubricar; untar.

oil·cloth [ɔ́ɪlklɔθ] *s.* hule, tela de hule.

oil·y [ɔ́ɪlɪ] *adj.* aceitoso, oleoso; grasiento.

oint•ment [ɔ́ɪntmənt] s. ungüento.

O.k. [óké] adj. bueno; corriente, convenido; adv. bien; **it´s** – está bien; **to give one´s** – dar el Vº, Bº. (visto bueno); v. dar el Vº, Bº., aprobar.

old [old] adj. viejo; antiguo; añejo; – **maid** solterona; – **man** anciano, viejo; – **wine** vino añejo, **days of** – días antaño; **how** – **are you?** ¿cúantos años tiene Ud.? ¿qué edad tiene Ud.?, **to be** – **enough to …** tener bastante edad para… **to be an** – **hand at** ser ducho en, ser muy perito o experto en.

old•en [óld ŋ] adj. viejo, antiguo, de antaño.

old-fash•ioned [óldfǽ ʃənd] adj. pasado de moda; anticuado; chapado a la antigua.

old-time [óldtáɪm] adj. vetusto, de tiempos antiguos; de antaño.

old-tim•er [óldtáɪmə-] s. antiguo residente.

ol•ive [álɪv] s. oliva, aceituna; – **grove** olivar; – **oil** aceite de oliva; – **tree** olivo; – **branch** ramo de olivo; adj. aceitunado, verde aceituna.

om•e•let [ámɪlɪt] s. tortilla de huevos.

o•men [ómən] s. agüero, presagio.

om•i•nous [ámənəs] adj. siniestro, de mal agüero, amenazador.

o•mis•sion [omíʃən] s. omisión.

o•mit [omít] v. omitir; dejar de.

om•nip•o•tent [amníʃpətənt] adj. omnipotente, todopoderoso.

on [an] prep. en; a; sobre, encima de; – **all sides** por todos lados; – **arriving** al llegar; – **board** a bordo; en el tren; – **condition that** con la condición de que; – **credit** al fiado; – **foot** a pie; – **horseback** a caballo; – **Monday** el lunes; – **purpose** a propósito, adrede; – **sale** de venta; – **time** a tiempo, a plazo; adv. adelante; **farther** – más adelante; **later** – después; – **and** – sin parar, sin cesar, continuamente; adj. puesto; **his hat is** – lleva puesto el sombrero; **the light is** – está encendida la luz.

once [wʌns] adv. una vez, en otro tiempo; – **and for all** una vez por todas, definitivamente, – **in a while** de vez en cuando; – **upon a time** érase que se era; en otro tiempo; **at** – al punto; a un mismo tiempo; **just this** – siquiera esta vez, sólo esta vez; conj. una vez que, cuando; luego que.

– **one** [wʌn] adj. un, uno, – **hundred** cien, ciento; – **thousand** mil; **his** – **chance** su única oportunidad; **the** – **and only** el único; **one-armed** manco; **one-eyed** tuerto; **one-sided** de un solo lado; unilateral; parcial; desigual; **one-way** de un sentido; s. & pron. uno; – **another** uno a otro; – **by** – uno a uno; uno por uno; **the** – **who** el que, la que; **the green** – el verde; **this** – éste, ésta.

one•self [wʌnsέlf] pron. se (reflexivo); **to speak to** – hablar consigo mismo; **by** – solo; por sí, por sí solo.

on•go•ing [ángoɪŋ] adj. que está haciéndose; corriente; que cursa.

on•ion [ʌ́njən] s. cebolla.

on•look•er [álUkə-] s. espectador, mirón.

on•ly [ónlɪ] adj. solo, único; adv. sólo, solamente; conj. sólo que.

On•set [ánsɛt] s. embestida, ataque; impulso inicial, primer ímpetu; arranque.

on•to [ántu] prep. a; sobre.

on•ward [ánwə-d] adv. adelante; hacia adelante.

on•yx [ánɪks] s. onix, ónice.

ooze [uz] v. rezumar(se), escurrir(se).

o•pal [óp]] s. ópalo.

o•paque [opék] adj. opaco; mate.

o•pen [ópən] v. abrir(se); **to** – **into** comunicarse con, tener paso a; **to** – **onto** dar a, caer a, mirar a; adj. abierto; franco, sincero; expuesto (a); – **country** campo raso, campo abierto; – **question** cuestión discutible; – **to temptation** expuesto a caer en la tentación; – **winter** invierno sin nieve; **in the** – **air** al (o en el) aire libre; **open-minded** receptivo; de amplias miras; – **mouthed** boquiabierto, con la boca abierta; **open-end** [ópənɛ́nd] sin límites; sin trabas; s. campo raso, aire libre.

o•pen•ing [ópənɪŋ] s. (hole) abertura; (beginning) apertura, comienzo; (clearing) claro (en el bosque); (vacancy) puesto vacante; oportunidad; adj. primero; – **night of a play** estreno de una comedia; **the** – **number** el primer número (de un programa).

op•er•a [ápərə] s. ópera; – **glasses** gemelos; – **house** ópera, teatro de la ópera; **comic** – ópera cómica, zarzuela.

op•er•ate [ápəret] v. (function) operar; funcionar; obrar; (manage) maniobrar; manejar; **to** – **on a person** operar a una persona.

op•er•a•tion [apəréʃən] s. (function) operación; funcionamiento; (management) manipulación; manejo; maniobra; **to be in** – funcionar, estar funcionando.

op•er•a•tor [ápəretə-] s. operador, cirujano; maquinista, mecánico, operario; especulador (en la Bolsa); **mine** – explotador de minas; **telegraph** – telegrafista; **telephone** – telefonista.

op•er•et•ta [apərétə] s. opereta, zarzuela.

o•pin•ion [əpínjən] s. opinión, parecer.

o•pi•um [ópiəm] s. opio.

op•po•nent [əpónənt] s. contrario, adversario, antagonista.

op•por•tune [apə-tjún] adj. oportuno; a propósito.

op•por•tun•ist [apə-túnɪst] s. oportunista.

op•por•tu•ni•ty [apə-júnətɪ] s. oportunidad; ocasión.

op•pose [əpóz] v. oponer(se); oponerse a.

op•pos•ing [əpózɪŋ] adj. opuesto, contrario.

op•po•site [ápəzɪt] adj. (contrary) opuesto; contrario; (facing) frontero, de enfrente; – **to** frente a; prep. frente a, en frente de; s. contrario; **the** – lo opuesto, lo contrario.

op·po·si·tion [ɑpəzíʃən] *s.* oposición; resistencia.

op·press [əprés] *v.* oprimir; agobiar.

op·pres·sion [əpréʃən] *s.* opresión.

op·pres·sive [əprésɪv] *adj.* (*harsh*) opresivo; (*distressing*) abrumador; gravoso; bochornoso, sofocante.

op·pres·sor [əprésə·] *s.* opresor.

op·tic [ɑ́ptɪk] *adj.* óptico; **-s** *s.* óptica.

op·ti·cal [ɑ́ptɪk] *adj.* óptico.

op·ti·cian [ɑptíʃən] *s.* óptico.

op·ti·mism [ɑ́ptəmɪzəm] *s.* optimismo.

op·ti·mist [ɑ́ptəmɪst] *s.* optimista.

op·ti·mis·tic [ɑptəmístɪk] *adj.* optimista.

op·tion [ɑ́pʃən] *s.* opción, derecho de escoger, alternativa.

op·tion·al [ɑ́pʃən] *adj.* discrecional.

op·u·lence [ɑ́pjələns] *s.* opulencia, riqueza, abundancia.

op·u·lent [ɑ́pjələnt] *adj.* opulento, rico; abundante.

or [ɔr] *conj.* o; u (*delante de o, ho*).

or·a·cle [ɔ́rək] *s.* oráculo.

o·ral [órəl] *adj.* oral; bucal.

or·ange [ɔ́rɪndʒ] *s.* naranja; **– blossom** azahar; **– grove** naranjal; **– tree** naranjo; *adj.* de naranja; anaranjado.

or·ange·ade [ɔrɪndʒéd] *s.* naranjada.

o·ra·tion [oréʃən] *s.* discurso, peroración, arenga.

or·a·tor [ɔ́rətə·] *s.* orador.

or·a·to·ry [ɔ́rətorɪ] *s.* oratoria, elocuencia; oratorio, capilla.

orb [ɔrb] *s.* orbe.

or·bit [ɔ́rbɪt] *s.* órbita; *v.* moverse en órbita.

or·bit·al [ɔ́rbɪt] *adj.* orbital.

or·chard [ɔ́rtʃə·d] *s.* huerto.

or·ches·tra [ɔ́rkɪstrə] *s.* orquesta; **– seat** butaca, luneta, *Am.* platea (*de orquesta*).

or·chid [ɔ́rkɪd] *s.* orquídea.

or·dain [ɔrdén] *v.* ordenar; decretar.

or·deal [ɔrdíl] *s.* prueba penosa.

or·der [ɔ́rdə·] *s.* (*request*) orden (s.); pedido; (*group*) clase; orden; (*arrangement*) orden (m.); **holy -s** órdenes sagradas; **in –** en orden; en buen estado; en regla; **in – to** para, a fin de; **in – that** para que, a fin de que; **made to –** mandado hacer, hecho a la medida; **to be out of –** estar descompuesto; estar desordenado; no estar en regla; *v.* ordenar; mandar; arreglar; pedir (*hacer un pedido*); **to – away** echar, despedir, expulsar.

or·der·ly [ɔ́rdə·lɪ] *adj.* ordenado; en orden, bien arreglado; bien disciplinado; *s.* ordenanza (*solda-*

do); asistente de hospital.

or·di·nal [ɔ́rdɪn] *adj.* ordinal; **– number** número ordinal.

or·di·nance [ɔ́rdnəns] *s.* ordenanza, ley, reglamento.

or·di·nar·i·ly [ord ɛ́rəlɪ] *adv.* ordinariamente, por lo común.

or·di·nar·y [ɔ́rd ɛrɪ] *adj.* ordinario.

ore [or] *s.* mineral.

or·gan [ɔ́rgən] *s.* órgano; **hand –** organillo.

or·gan·ic [orgǽnɪk] *adj.* orgánico; constitutivo, fundamental.

or·gan·ism [ɔ́rgənɪzəm] *s.* organismo.

or·gan·ist [ɔ́rgənɪst] *s.* organista.

or·gan·i·za·tion [orgənəzéʃən] *s.* organización; organismo; entidad; sociedad.

or·gan·ize [ɔ́rgənaɪz] *v.* organizar(se).

or·gan·iz·er [ɔ́rgənaɪzə·] *s.* organizador.

or·gy [ɔ́rdʒɪ] *s.* orgía.

o·ri·ent [ɔ́rɪɛnt] *s.* oriente; *v.* orientar.

o·ri·en·tal [orɪɛ́nt] *adj.* & *s.* oriental.

o·ri·en·tate [ɔ́rɪɛntet] *v.* orientar.

o·ri·en·ta·tion [orɪɛntéʃən] *s.* orientación.

or·i·fice [ɔ́rəfɪs] *s.* orificio.

or·i·gin [ɔ́rədʒɪn] *s.* origen.

o·rig·i·nal [ərídʒən] *adj.* & *s.* original; **-ly** *adv.* originalmente, originariamente; en el principio, al principio.

o·rig·i·nal·i·ty [ərɪdʒənǽlətɪ] *s.* originalidad.

o·rig·i·nate [ərídʒənet] *v.* originar(se).

o·ri·ole [óriol] *s.* oriol (pájaro).

or·na·ment [ɔ́rnəmənt] *s.* ornamento, adorno; [ɔ́rnəmɛnt] *v.* ornamentar, adornar, ornar.

or·na·men·tal [ɔrnəmɛ́nt] *adj.* ornamental, de adorno, decorativo.

or·nate [ɔrnét] *adj.* ornado, adornado en exceso; **– style** estilo florido.

or·phan [ɔ́rfən] *adj.* & *s.* huérfano; **– asylum** hospicio, orfanato, asilo de huérfanos; *v.* dejar huérfano a.

or·tho·dox [ɔ́rθədɑks] *adj.* ortodoxo.

or·thog·ra·phy [orθɑ́grəfɪ] *s.* ortografía.

os·cil·late [ɑ́səlet] *v.* oscilar.

os·ten·ta·tion [ostəntéʃən] *s.* ostentación, boato.

os·ten·ta·tious [ostəntéʃəs] *adj.* ostentoso.

os·trich [ɔ́strɪtʃ] *s.* avestruz.

oth·er [ʌ́ðə·] *adj.* & *s.* otro; **– than** otra cosa que; más que; **every – day** cada dos días, un día sí y otro no; **some – day** otro día.

oth•er•wise [ʌðə-waɪz] *adv.* de otro modo; en otros respetos; *adj.* otro, diferente.

ot•ter [ótə-] *s.* nutria; piel de nutria.

ought [ɔt] *v.* *deffect.* (*por lo general se traduce por el presente y el condicional de* deber) debo, debes, etc.; debería, deberías, etc.; debiera, debieras, etc.

ounce [aUns] *s.* onza.

our [aUr] *adj.* nuestro (nuestra, nuestros, nuestras).

ours [aUrz] *pron. pos.* nuestro (nuestra, nuestros, nuestras); el nuestro (la nuestra, los nuestros, las nuestras); **a friend of –** un amigo nuestro.

our•selves [aUrsélvz] *pron.* nosotros mismos; nos (*reflexivo*); a nosotros mismos; **we –** nosotros mismos; **by –** solos; por nosotros; *véase* **herself.**

oust [aUst] *v.* echar, expulsar.

out [aUt] *adv.* fuera; afuera; hacía fuera; **– of fear** por miedo, de miedo; **– of humor** malhumorado; **– of money** sin dinero; **– of print** agotado; **– of touch with** aislado de, sin contacto con; **– of tune** desentonado; **made –** of hecho de; **to fight it –** decidirlo luchando; **to have it –** with habérselas con; **to speak –** hablar francamente; *adj.* ausente; apagado; **– and – criminal** criminal empedernido; **– and – refusal** una negativa redonda; **– size** tamaño poco común o extraordinario; **before the week is –** antes de que termine la semana; **the book is just –** acaba de publicarse el libro; **the secret is –** se ha divulgado el secreto.

out•break [áUtbrek] *s.* (*eruption*) erupción; (*revolt*) motín, insurrección, tumulto; (*attack*) ataque, arranque (*de ira*); **at the – of the war** al estallar la guerra.

out•burst [áUtbɝst] *s.* explosión; estallido; arranque (*de pasión*); erupción.

out•cast [áUtkæst] *adj.* excluido, desechado; desterrado; *s.* paria (*persona excluida de la sociedad*).

out•come [áUtkʌm] *s.* resultado, consecuencia.

out•cry [áUtkraɪ] *s.* grito; clamor.

out•door [áUtdor] *adj.* externo; fuera de la casa; **– games** juegos al aire libre.

out•doors [aUtdórz] *adv.* puertas afuera, fuera de casa, al aire libre, al raso; *s.* aire libre, campo raso, campiña.

out•er [áUtə-] *adj.* exterior, externo.

out•fit [áUtfɪt] *s.* equipo; pertrechos; *v.* equipar, habilitar, aviar.

out•go•ing [áUtgoɪŋ] *adj.* (*leaving*) saliente; (*extrovert*) extrovertido.

ut•guess [aUtgés] *v.* anticipar; madrugar.

out•ing [áUtɪŋ] *s.* excursión, gira (jira), caminata.

out•law [áUtlɔ] *s.* forajido, bandido; prófugo, fugitivo; *v.* proscribir, declarar ilegal.

out•lay [áUtle] *s.* gasto, desembolso; [áUtlé] *v.* gastar, desembolsar.

out•let [áUtlɛt] *s.* salida; desaguadero, desagüe.

out•line [áUtlaɪn] *s.* (*abstract*) bosquejo, esbozo; (*boundary*) contorno; *v.* bosquejar, esbozar; delinear.

out•live [aUtlív] *v.* sobrevivir.

out•look [áUtlUk] *s.* vista; perspectiva.

out•ly•ing [áUtlaɪŋ] *adj.* circundante, exterior, remoto (*del centro*).

out-of-date [áUtəvdét] *adj.* fuera de moda, anticuado.

out•post [áUtpost] *s.* avanzada.

out•put [áUtpUt] *s.* rendimiento; producción total.

out•rage [áUtredʒ] *s.* ultraje; *v.* ultrajar.

out•ra•geous [aUtrédʒəs] *adj.* afrentoso; atroz.

out•ran [aUtrǽn] *pret. de* **to outrun.**

out•right [aUtráɪt] *adv. & adj.* sin rodeos; cabal; completo.

out•run [aUtrʌn] *v.* aventajar (*en una carrera*); dejar atrás; *p.p. de* **to outrun.**

out•set [áUtsɛt] *s.* comienzo, principio.

out•shine [aUtʃáɪm] *v.* eclipsar, sobrepasar (*en brillo o lucidez*).

out•shone [aUtʃón] *pret. & p.p. de* **to outshine.**

out•side [áUtsáɪd] *adj.* (*external*) exterior; externo; (*foreing*) foráneo, extranjero; *adv.* fuera, afuera; fuera de casa; *prep.* fuera de; *s.* exterior, parte exterior; superficie; lado de afuera; **in a week, at the –** en una semana, a lo sumo; **to close on the –** cerrar por fuera.

out•sid•er [aUtsáɪdə-] *s.* foráneo, persona de fuera; extraño.

out•skirts [áUtskɝts] *s. pl.* alrededores, arrabales, cercanías.

out•spo•ken [áUtspókən] *adj.* franco, francote, *Ven., Méx., C.A., Carib.* claridoso.

out•stand•ing [aUtstǽmdɪŋ] *adj.* sobresaliente; destacado, notable; **- bills** cuenta por cobrar; **- debts** deudas por pagar.

out•stretched [aUtstrétʃt] *adj.* extendido; **with – arms** con los brazos abiertos.

out•ward [áutwə-d] *adj.* (*external*) exterior, externo; (*apparent*) aparente; superficial, *adv.* fuera, hacia fuera; **– bound** que sale, de salida; para fuera, para el extranjero; **-ly** *adv.* exteriormente; por fuera; aparentemente.

out•weigh [aUtwé] *v.* exceder en peso o valor; sobrepujar.

o•val [óvḷ] *adj.* oval, ovalado; *s.* óvalo.

o•va•ry [óvərɪ] *s.* ovario.

o•va•tion [ovéʃən] *s.* ovación.

ov•en [ʌvən] *s.* horno.

o•ver [óvə-] *prep.* sobre; por; por encima de; encima de; a través de; al otro lado de; más de; **– night** por la noche, durante la noche; (*véase* **overnight**); –

to a; **all – the city** por toda la ciudad; *adv.* encima; al otro lado; otra vez, de nuevo; **– again** otra vez, de nuevo; **– against** en contraste con; **– and –** una y otra vez, repetidas veces; **–curious** demasiado curioso; **–generous** demasiado generoso; **– here** acá, aqí; **– there** allá, allí; **two years and –** más de dos años; **to do it –** hacerlo otra vez, volver a hacerlo; *adj.* excesivo; **it is all –** ya se acabó, se ha acabado; ha pasado.

o•ver•alls [óvə-ɔlz] *s. pl. Am.* overol, overoles (*pantalones de trabajo*).

o•ver•ate [ovə-ét] *pret. de* **to overeat.**

o•ver•board [óvə-bord] *adv.* al mar, al agua.

o•ver•came [ovə-kém] *pret. de* **to overcome.**

o•ver•cast [óvə-kæst] *adj.* encapotado, nublado; **to become –** encapotarse, nublarse; [ovə-kǽst] *v.* nublar o anublar; sobrehilar (*dar puntadas sobre el borde de una tela*); *pret. & p.p. de* **to overcast.**

o•ver•charge [ovə-tʃárdʒ] *v.* cargar demasiado; cobrar demasiado.

o•ver•coat [óvə-kot] *s.* sobretodo, abrigo.

o•ver•come [ovə-k ʌ́m] *v.* vencer; rendir; *p.p. & adj.* vencido; rendido; agobiado; **to be – by weariness** estar rendido de fatiga.

o•ver•due [ovə-dú] *adj.* atrasado; vencido sin pago.

o•ver•eat [ovə-ít] *v.* hartarse.

o•ver•eat•en [ovə-ít n] *p.p. de* **to overeat.**

o•ver•ex•cite [óvərıksáít] *v.* sobreexcitar.

o•ver•flow [óvə-flo] *s.* derrame, desbordamiento; inundación; superabundancia; [ovə-fló] *v.* derramarse, desbordarse; rebosar; inundar.

o•ver•grown [óvə-grón] *adj.* denso, frondoso, poblado (*de follaje, herbaje, etc.*); **- boy** muchachón, muchacho demasiado crecido para su edad.

o•ver•hang [ovə-hǽŋ] *v.* colgar por encima de; proyectarse o sobresalir por encima de; adornar con colgaduras; amenazar (*dícese de un desastre o calamidad*).

o•ver•haul [ovə-h ɔ́l] *v.* reparar (*de cabo a rabo*); remendar; alcanzar (*en una carrera*).

o•ver•head [ovə-hɛd] *s.* gastos generales (*renta, seguro, alumbrado, calefacción, etc.*); *adj.* de arriba; elevado; **– expenses** gastos generales; [óvə-hɛ́d] *adv.* encima de la cabeza, arriba; en lo alto.

o•ver•hear [ovə-hír] *v.* oír por casualidad, alcanzar a oír, acertar a oír.

o•ver•heard [ovə-h ɝ́ d] *pret. & p.p de* **to overhear.**

o•ver•heat [óvə-hít] *v.* recalentar(se); calentar(se) demasiado.

o•ver•hung [ovə-h ʌ́ ŋ] *pret. & p.p. de* **to overhang.**

o•ver•land [óvə-lænd] *adv. & adj.* por tierra.

o•ver•lap [ovə-lǽp] *v.* solapar.

o•ver•lay [ovə-lé] *v.* cubrir; incrustar.

o•ver•load [ovə-lód] *v.* sobrecargar; [óvə-lod] *s.* sobrecarga.

o•ver•look [ovə-lÚk] *v.* mirar a (*desde lo alto*); dar a, tener vista a; pasar por alto, omitir; perdonar (*faltas*); descuidar, no notar; inspeccionar, examinar.

o•ver•ly [ovə-lI] *adv.* excesivámente.

o•ver•night [ovə-náIt] *adv.* durante la noche; toda la noche; *adj.* de noche; nocturno; **- bag** saco de noche; **- trip** viaje de una noche.

o•ver•pass [óvə-pǽs] *s.* viaducto.

o•ver•pow•er [ovə-páUə] *v.* subyugar, abrumar, vencer.

o•ver•ran [ovə-rǽn] *pret. de* **to overrun.**

o•ver•ride [ovə-ráId] *v.* anular; invalidar.

o•ver•rule [ovərúl] *v.* anular.

o•ver•run [ovə-r ʌ́n] *v.* desbordarse, mundar; sobrepasar; infestar, invadir; *p.p. de* **to overrun.**

o•ver•seas [óvə-síz] *adv.* en ultramar, allende los mares; *adj.* de ultramar.

o•ver•see [ovə-sí] *v.* dirigir; vigilar.

o•ver•se•er [óvə-síə] *s.* sobrestante, capataz; inspector, superintendente.

o•ver•shoe [óvə-ʃu] *s.* chanclo; zapato de goma, caucho o hule.

o•ver•sight [óvə-saIt] *s.* inadvertencia, negligencia, descuido.

o•ver•step [ovə-stɛ́p] *v.* sobrepasarse, propasarse; traspasar; **to – the bounds** traspasar los límites; propasarse.

o•ver•take [ovə-ték] *v.* alcanzar.

o•ver•tak•en [ovə-tékən] *p.p. de* **to overtake.**

o•ver•threw [ovə-θrú] *pret. de* **to overthrow.**

o•ver•throw [óvə-θro] *s.* (*overturn*) derrocamiento; (*defeat*) derrota, destrucción; caída; [ovə-θró] *v.* derrocar; derribar, echar abajo, volcar; destronar.

o•ver•thrown [ovə-θrón] *p.p. de* **to overthrow.**

o•ver•time [óvə-taIm] *adv. & adj.* en exceso de las horas estipuladas; **– pay** sobresueldo.

o•ver•took [ovə-tÚk] *pret. de* **to overtake.**

o•ver•ture [óvə-tʃ ɚ] *s.* obertura, preludio; propuesta, proposición.

o•ver•turn [ovə-t ɝ́ n] *v.* volcar(se); trastornar; derribar; echar bajo.

o•ver•whelm [ovə-hwɛ́lm] *v.* abrumar, agobiar; oprimir; arrollar.

o•ver•whelm•ing [ovə-hwɛ́lmIŋ] *adj.* abrumador; opresivo; arrollador, irresistible, poderoso.

o•ver•work [óvə-w ɝ́ k] *v.* atarearse, afanarse más de lo debido, trabajar demasiado; *s.* exceso de trabajo.

owe [o] *v.* deber, adeudar.

ow•ing [óIŋ] *adj.* debido; **- to** debido a.

owl [aul] *s.* lechuza, buho, *Méx., C.A.* tecolote.

own [on] *adj.* propio; **a house of his –** una casa suya;

his – people los suyos; **to be on one´s** – no estar a merced ajena; trabajar por su propia cuenta; **to come into one´s** – entrar en posesión de lo suyo; **to hold one´s** – mantenerse firme; *v.* poseer, tener; admitir, reconocer; **to – to** confesar; **to – up** confesar.

own•er [ónə-] *s.* dueño, amo; propietario; poseedor.

own•er•ship [óna-ʃɪp] *s.* posesión, propiedad.

ox [ɑks] (pl. **oxen** [áks ŋ]) *s.* buey.

ox•y•gen [áksədʒən] *s.* oxígeno.

oys•ter [ɔ́ɪstə-] *s.* ostra, ostión.

o•zone [ózon] *s.* ozono.

P

pace [pes] *s.* paso; *v.* pasear, andar; andar al paso; marchar; medir a pasos.

pace•mak•er [pésmekə-] *s.* marcapaso.

pa•cif•ic [pəsífɪk] *adj.* pacífico.

pac•i•fy [pǽsəfaɪ] *v.* pacificar, apaciguar; calmar.

pack [pæk] *s.* fardo, lío, carga; manada (*de lobos*); cuadrilla, pandilla (*de ladrones*); jauría (*de perros*); muchedumbre; baraja (*de naipes*); **– animal** acémila, bestia de carga; *v.* empacar, empaquetar; embalar; enlatar; envasar; apiñar(se); cargar (*una bestia*); hacer (*el baúl, la maleta*); **to – off** despedir de repente; echar a la calle; largarse, irse.

pack•age [pǽkɪdʒ] *s.* paquete; fardo; bulto; cajetilla (*de cigarrillos*).

pack•er [pǽkə-] *s.* empacador; embalador, envasador.

pack•et [pǽkɪt] *s.* paquetillo; cajetilla.

pack•ing [pǽkɪŋ] *s.* (*covering*) embalaje; envase; (*filling*) relleno; **– box** caja para embalar o empacar; **– house** establecimiento frigorífico, fábrica para envasar o enlatar comestibles.

pact [pækt] *s.* pacto, convenio.

pad [pæd] *s.* almohadilla, cojincillo; tableta, bloc de papel; *v.* rellenar; forrar; acolchar.

pad•ding [pǽdɪŋ] *s.* relleno (*de pelo, algodón, paja, etc.*), *Andes* guata; ripio, palabras o frases inútiles.

pad•dle [pǽd l] *s.* pala; remo de canoa; **– wheel** rueda de paleta; *v.* remar con pala; apalear; chapotear (*en el agua*).

pad•dock [pǽdək] *s.* dehesa.

pad•lock [pǽdlɑk] *s.* candado; *v.* cerrar con candado.

pa•gan [pégən] *s. & adj.* pagano.

pa•gan•ism [pégənɪzəm] *s.* paganismo.

page [pedʒ] *s.* página; paje; "botones" (*de hotel*), mensajero; *v.* paginar; vocear, llamar a voces.

pag•eant [pǽdʒənt] *s.* (*parade*) manifestación, desfile, procesión, pompa; (*drama*) representación al aire libre.

paid [ped] *pret. & p.p. de* **to pay.**

pail [pel] *s.* balde, cubo, cubeta.

pain [pen] *s.* dolor; sufrimiento; **-s** esmero; **on (under) – of** so pena de; **to be in** – estar sufriendo, tener dolores; **to take -s** esmerarse, extremarse; *v.* doler; causar dolor; afligir.

pain•ful [pénfəl] *adj.* doloroso; penoso; arduo.

pain•less [pénlɪs] *adj.* sin dolor; libre de dolor.

pains•tak•ing [pénztekɪŋ] *adj.* esmerado, cuidadoso; aplicado.

paint [pent] *s.* (*mixture*) pintura, color; (*rouge*) colorete; *v.* pintar; pintarse (*la cara*); **to – be town red** irse de juerga o de parranda, *Am.* irse de farra.

paint•brush [péntbrʌʃ] *s.* (art) pincel; (*house*) brocha.

paint•er [péntə-] *s.* pintor.

paint•ing [péntɪŋ] *s.* pintura.

pair [pɛr] *s.* par; pareja; **a – of scisors** unas tijeras; *v.* aparear(se); hacer pareja, hacer pares; **to – off** aparear(se).

pa•ja•mas [pədʒǽməz] *s. pl.* pijama.

pal [pæl] *s.* compañero, camarada.

pal•ace [pǽlɪs] *s.* palacio.

pal•ate [pǽlɪt] *s.* paladar.

pa•la•tial [pəléʃ]] *adj.* suntuoso.

pale [pel] *adj.* pálido, descolorido; *v.* palidecer, ponerse pálido o descolorido.

pale•ness [pélnɪs] *s.* palidez.

pal•i•sade [pæləséd] *s.* palizada, estacada; **-s** riscos, acantilados.

pall [pɔl] *v.* empalagar; aburrir; **it -s on me** me empalaga; me aburre; *s.* paño de ataúd; palia (*lienzo que se pone encima del cáliz*).

pal•li•a•tive [pǽljetɪv] *adj. & s.* paliativo.

pal•lid [pǽlɪd] *adj.* pálido.

pal•lor [pǽlə-] *s.* palidez.

palm [pɑm] *s.* palma; palmera; **– Sunday** Domingo de Ramos; **– tree** palma, palmera; *v.* **to – something off on someone** pasar o dar algo indeseable a una persona (*sin que se dé cuenta de ello*).

pal•pa•ble [pǽlpəb]] *adj.* palpable, tangible; evidente.

pal•pi•tate [pǽlpətet] *v.* palpitar, latir.

pal•pi•ta•tion [pælpəté ʃ ən] *s.* palpitación; latido.

pal•try [pɔ́ltrɪ] *adj.* mezquino, miserable, despreciable, insignificante.

pam•per [pǽmpə-] *v.* mimar, consentir (*a un niño*).

pam•phlet [pǽmflɪt] *s.* folleto, *Am.* panfleto.

pan [pæn] *s.* cazuela, cacerola; cazo; platillo (*de ba-*

lanza); **dish** – cazo para lavar platos; **frying** – sartén; *v.* **to – out** (**well**) salir bien, dar buen resultado.

Pan A·mer·i·can [pǽnəmérəkən] *adj.* panamericano.

pan·cake [pǽnkek] *s.* tortita de harina, *Ven., Col.* panqué; *Ríopl.* panqueque.

pan·der [pǽndə·] *s.* alcahuete, encubridor; *v.* alcahuetear, servir de alcahuete.

pane [pen] vidrio, cristal (*de ventana o puerta*); cuadro (*de vidrio*).

pan·el [pǽnḷ] *s.* panel, tablero; cuarterón (*de puerta, ventana, etc.*); tabla (*doble pliegue de una falda o vestido*); **jury** – jurado; *v.* proveer de (*o adornar con*) paneles.

pang [pæŋ] *s.* dolor agudo; angustia, tormento.

pan·han·dle [pǽnhændḷ] *s.* mango de sartén; territorio en forma de mango; *v.* mendigar.

pan·ic [pǽnɪk] *adj. & s.* pánico; **panicstricken** sobrecogido de pánico.

pan·o·ram·a [pænərǽmə] *s.* panorama.

pan·sy [pǽnzɪ] *s.* pensamiento (*flor*).

pant [pænt] *v.* jadear; palpitar; **to – for** anhelar, ansiar.

pan·ther [pǽnθə·] *s.* pantera.

pan·ting [pǽntɪŋ] *s.* jadeo, palpitación; *adj.* jadeante.

pan·to·mime [pǽntəmaɪm] *s.* pantomima.

pan·try [pǽntrɪ] *s.* despensa.

pants [pænts] *s. pl.* pantalones.

pa·pa [pópə] *s.* papá.

pa·pa·cy [pépəsɪ] *s.* papado.

pa·pal [pépḷ] *adj.* papal.

pa·per [pépə·] *s.* (*material*) papel; (*daily*) periódico; (*essay*) tema, ensayos; **-s** papeles, documentos, credenciales; **naturalization -s** carta de naturaleza, certificado de ciudadanía; **– of pins** cartón de alfileres; **on** – escrito; por escrito; *adj.* de papel; para papel; **– doll** muñeca de papel; **– money** papel moneda; **– weight** pisapapeles; *v.* empapelar.

pa·per·back [pépə·bæk] *s. & adj.* libro en rústica.

pa·per·work [pépə·wə·k] *s.* preparación de escritos; papeleo.

pa·pri·ka [pæpríka] *s.* pimentón.

par [pɑr] *s.* (*equality*) paridad, igualdad; (*standard*) valor nominal; **– value** valor a la par; **above** – sobre par, a premio, con prima; **at** – a la par; **below** – bajo par, a descuento; **on a – with** al par de, al nivel de, igual a; **to feel above** – sentirse mejor que de ordinario; **to feel below** – sentirse menos bien que de ordinario.

par·a·ble [pǽrəbḷ] *s.* parábola (*alegoría bíblica*).

par·a·chute [pǽrəʃut] *s.* paracaídas.

par·a·chut·ist [pǽrəʃutɪst] *s.* paracaidista.

pa·rade [pəréd] *s.* (*procession*) desfile, procesión, manifestación; paseo; (*review*) parada; **– ground** campo de maniobras; **to make a – of** ostentar, hacer ostentación de; *v.* desfilar, pasar en desfile; marchar en parada; hacer ostentación de.

par·a·digm [pǽrədɪm], [pǽrədaɪm] *s.* paradigma.

par·a·dise [pǽrədaɪs] *s.* paraíso.

par·a·dox [pǽrədɔks] *s.* paradoja.

par·af·fin [pǽrəfɪn] *s.* parafina.

par·a·graph [pǽrəgræf] *s.* párrafo; *v.* dividir en párrafos.

Par·a·guay·an [pærəgwáɪən] *adj. & s.* paraguayo.

par·al·lel [pǽrəlɛl] *adj. & s.* paralelo; *v.* ser (*o correr*) paralelo a; comparar, cotejar.

pa·ral·y·sis [pərǽləsɪs] *s.* parálisis.

par·a·lyze [pǽrəlaɪz] *v.* paralizar.

par·a·mount [pǽrəmaʊnt] *adj.* importantísimo, superior, supremo, máximo.

par·a·noi·a [pærənɔ́ɪjə] *s.* paranoia.

par·a·pet [pǽrəpɪt] *s.* parapeto.

par·a·phrase [pǽrəfrez] *v.* parafrasear.

par·a·site [pǽrəsaɪt] *s.* parásito.

par·a·sol [pǽrəsɔl] *s.* parasol, sombrilla.

par·a·troops [pǽrətrups] *s.* tropas paracaidistas.

par·cel [pɑ́rsḷ] *s.* paquete; parcela, porción, lote (*de terreno*); **– post** paquete postal; *v.* parcelar, dividir en porciones o parcelas; hacer paquetes; **to – out** repartir.

parch [pɑrtʃ] *v.* resecar(se); tostar(se).

parch·ment [pɑ́rtʃmənt] *s.* pergamino.

par·don [pɑ́rdṇ] *s.* perdón; indulto; **I beg your** – perdone Vd.; dispense Vd.; *v.* perdonar; dispensar; indultar.

pare [pɛr] *v.* mondar, pelar (*manzanas, patatas, etc.*); cortar, recortar; **to – down expenditures** reducir gastos.

par·ent [pérənt] *s.* padre, madre; origen; **-s** padres.

par·ent·age [pérəntɪdʒ] *s.* linaje; padres.

pa·ren·tal [pəréntḷ] *adj.* parental.

pa·ren·the·sis [pərénθəsɪs] (*pl.* **parentheses** [pərénθəsiz]) *s.* paréntesis.

par·ish [pǽrɪʃ] *s.* parroquia.

pa·rish·ion·er [pəríʃənə·] *s.* parroquiano, feligrés; **-s** fieles, feligreses.

park [pɑrk] *s.* parque; *v.* estacionar, dejar (*un automóvil*); estacionarse; **-ing lot** *Ch., Ríopl.* playa de estacionamiento; *Méx., Ven.* estacionamiento; *Col.*

parqueadero; **-ing space** sitio o lugar para estacionarse; **free-ing** estacionamiento gratis; **no - ing** se prohibe estacionarse; no estacionarse.

par·lance [párləns] s. lenguaje.

par·ley [párlɪ] s. parlamento, discusión, conferencia; v. parlamentar, discutir.

par·lia·ment [párləmənt] s. parlamento.

par·lia·men·ta·ry [parləméntərɪ] adj. parlamentario.

par·lor [párlə-] s. sala, salón; sala de recibo; - **car** coche salón; **beauty** – salón de belleza.

pa·ro·chi·al [pərókɪəl] adj. parroquial.

par·o·dy [pǽrədɪ] s. parodia; v. parodiar.

pa·role [pəról] s. palabra de honor; **to put on** – dejar libre (a un prisionero) bajo palabra de honor; v. dejar libre bajo palabra de honor.

par·rot [pǽrət] s. cotorra, loro, perico, papagayo; v. remedar, repetir como loro.

par·ry [pǽrɪ] v. parar, quitar o reparar (un golpe); s. quite, reparo.

pars·ley [párslɪ] s. perejil.

pars·nip [pársnəp] s. chirivía (legumbre).

par·son [párs ŋ] s. pastor, clérigo.

part [part] s. parte (f.); papel (dramático); raya (del cabello); **– and parcel** parte esencial o inherente; **– owner** condueño, dueño en parte; **– time** parte del tiempo; **in foreing -s** en el extranjero, en países extranjeros; **spare -s** piezas accesorias, piezas de repuesto (o de refacción); **do your** – haga Vd. cuanto esté de su parte; v. partir(se); separar(se); **to – company** separarse; **to – from** separarse de, despedirse de, deshacerse de; **to one´s hair** hacerse la raya; **to – with** separarse de, despedirse de, deshacerse de.

par·take [parték] v. tomar parte, tener parte, participar.

par·tak·en [partékən] p.p. de **to partake.**

par·tial [párʃəl] adj. parcial; **-ly** adv. parcialmente, en parte; con parcialidad.

par·ti·al·i·ty [parʃǽlətɪ] s. parcialidad.

par·tic·i·pant [pə-tísəpənt] adj. & s. participante, partícipe, copartícipe.

par·tic·i·pate [pə-tísəpet] v. participar.

par·tic·i·pa·tion [pə-tɪsəpéʃən] s. participación.

par·ti·ci·ple [pártəsɪp]] s. participio; **present -** gerundio.

par·ti·cle [pórtɪk]] s. partícula.

par·tic·u·lar [pə-tíkjələ-] adj. (single) particular; peculiar; (special) esmerado, exacto; escrupuloso; (demanding) quisquilloso; exigente; s. particular, detalle, circunstancia; **in -** en particular, especialmente; **-ly** adv. particularmente; en particular.

part·ing [pártɪŋ] s. (departure) despedida; (division) separación; bifurcación; **the – of the ways** en-

crucijada, bifurcación, cruce de caminos; adj. de despedida, último.

par·ti·san [pártəz ŋ] adj. partidario; parcial; s. partidario, secuaz, seguidor.

par·ti·tion [pə-tíʃən] s. (division) partición, división, separación; (wall) tabique; Am. medianía; v. partir, dividir; repartir.

par·ti·tive [pártətɪv] adj. partitivo.

part·ly [pártlɪ] adv. en parte.

part·ner [pártnə-] s. socio, consocio; compañero; **dancing** – pareja de baile.

part·ner·ship [pártnə-ʃɪp] s. sociedad, compañía.

par·took [partúk] pret. de **to partake**.

par·tridge [pártrɪdʒ] s. perdiz.

par·ty [pártɪ] s. (get-together) tertulia, reunión, fiesta, (group) grupo, partida (de gente); (legal) parte; **hunting** – partida de caza; **political** – partido político.

pass [pæs] s. paso; pase, permiso de entrar; aprobación (en un examen); trance, situación; **- key** llave maestra; **to came to -** suceder; v. pasar; pasar por; pronunciar (sentencia), dar (un juicio o parecer); aprobar (a un estudiante); adoptar (una ley); ser aprobado en (un examen); **to – away** pasar a mejor vida, morir; desaparecer; pasar (el tiempo).

pass·a·ble [pǽsəb]] adj. (penetrable) transitable; (acceptable) pasádero, regular, mediano.

pas·sage [pǽsɪdʒ] s. pasaje; paso, transito; transcurso (del tiempo); pasillo, pasadizo; travesía, viaje por mar; aprobación (de un proyecto de ley); adopción (de una ley).

pas·sage·way [pǽsədʒwe] s. corredor; pasaje.

pass·book [pǽsbʊk] s. libreta de banco.

pas·sen·ger [pǽs ŋ dʒə-] s. pasajero; **the -s** los pasajeros; el pasaje.

pass·er·by [pǽsə-báɪ] s. transeúnte, viandante.

pas·sion [pǽ ʃən] s. pasión; **Passion play** drama de la Pasión; **to fly into a –** montar en cólera, encolerizarse.

pas·sion·ate [pǽ ʃənɪt] adj. apasionado.

pas·sive [pǽsɪv] adj. pasivo; s. voz pasiva.

pass·port [pǽsport] s. pasaporte.

pass·word [pǽsw з ́d] s. consigna, contraseña, santo y seña.

past [pæst] adj. pasado; último; **– master** perito; **the – president** el expresidente, el último presidente; **– tense** tiempo pasado; pretérito; **for some time –** desde hace algún tiempo, de poco tiempo a esta parte; prep. **– bearing** insoportable; **– understanding** incomprensible; **half – two** las dos y media; **woman – forty** cuarentona, mujer de más de cuarenta años; **to go – the house** pasar por (o por enfrente de) la casa; s. pasado; pretérito; pretérito imperfecto; **man with a** – hombre de dudosos antecedentes.

paste [pest] s. pasta; engrudo; v. pegar (con engrudo).

paste•board [péstbord] s. cartón; – **box** caja de cartón.

pas•teur•ize [pǽstəraɪz] v. pasterizar (o pasteurizar).

pas•time [pǽstaɪm] s. pasatiempo.

pas•tor [pǽstə] s. pastor, clérigo, cura.

pas•tor•al [pǽstərəl] adj. pastoril; pastoral; s. pastoral, carta pastoral; écloga; pastorela, idilio.

pas•try [péstrɪ] s. pastelería, pasteles; – **cook** pastelero; – **shop** pastelería.

pas•ture [pǽstʃə] s. pastura, pasto; dehesa; v. pastar, pacer; apacentar(se).

pat [pæt] adj. apto, oportuno; **to have a lesson** – saber al dedillo la lección; **to stand** – mantenerse firme; adv. a propósito; oportunamente; de molde; s. palmadita, caricia, golpecito; – **butter** cuadrito de mantequilla; v. dar palmaditas a; acariciar; pasar la mano (para alisar o acariciar).

patch [pætʃ] s. (repair) remiendo; parche; mancha; (plot) pedazo (de terreno); sembrado; v. remendar; **to** – **up a quarrel** hacer las paces.

pate [pet] s. coronilla (de la cabeza); **bald** – calva.

pat•ent [pǽtn̩t] adj. patente, evidente, manifiesto; de patente; – **leather** charol; – **medicine** medicina de patente; – **right** patente; s. patente; v. patentar.

pa•ter•nal [pətɜ́n̩l] adj. paternal, paterno.

pa•ter•ni•ty [pətɜ́nətɪ] s. paternidad.

path [pæθ] s. senda, sendero; vereda; ruta; trayectoria (de una bala).

pa•thet•ic [pəθétɪk] adj. patético.

pa•thol•o•gy [pæθáládʒɪ]. patología.

pa•thos [péθɑs] s. patetismo, cualidad patética.

path•way [pǽθwe] s. senda, vereda, vía.

pa•tience [péʃəns] s. paciencia.

pa•tient [péʃənt] adj. paciente; pacienzudo; s. paciente, enfermo.

pa•tri•arch [pétrɪork] s. patriarca.

pa•tri•ar•chal [pétrɪórk l̩] adj. patriarcal.

pat•ri•mo•ny [pǽtrɪmonɪ] s. patrimonio.

pa•tri•ot [pétrɪət] s. patriota.

pa•tri•ot•ic [petrɪátɪk] adj. patriótico.

pa•tri•ot•ism [pétrɪətɪzəm] s. patriotismo.

pa•trol [pətról] s. patrulla; ronda; v. patrullar, rondar.

pa•tron [pétrən] s. patrón, patrono; benefactor; cliente, parroquiano; – **saint** santo patrón.

pa•tron•age [pétrənɪdʒ] s. (support) patrocinio, amparo; (clientele) clientela; (manner) condescendencia; **political** – control de nombramientos políticos.

pa•tron•ess [pétrənɪs] s. patrona, protectora.

pa•tron•ize [pétrənaɪz] v. patrocinar, amparar; tratar con condescendencia; favorecer, ser parroquiano de.

pat•ter [pǽtə] v. golpetear ligeramente; talonear; charlar, parlotear; s. golpeteo; golpecitos; taloneo; charla, parloteo.

pat•tern [pǽtən] s. (model) modelo; dechado; muestra; ejemplo; patrón, molde; (desing) diseño, dibujo (en tejidos, telas, etc.); v. **to** – **oneself after** seguir el ejemplo de; **to** – **something alter** (**on**, **upon**) forjar o modelar algo a imitación de.

pau•ci•ty [pɔ́sɪtɪ] s. escasez; falta.

paunch [pontʃ] s. panza, barriga.

pause [poz] s. pausa; s. pausar, hacer pausa; detenerse, parar.

pave [pev] v. pavimentar; **to** – **the way for** preparar o abrir el camino para; **to** – **with bricks** enladrillar; **to** – **with flagstones** enlosar.

pave•ment [pévmənt] s. pavimento; **brick** – enladrillado.

pa•vil•ion [pəvíljən] s. pabellón.

paw [po] s. garra, zarpa; v. echar la zarpa; arañar; manosear; **to** – **the ground** patear la tierra (dícese del caballo).

pawn [pon] s. prenda, empeño; peón (de ajedrez); – **broker** prestamista, prendero; –**shop** empeño, casa de empeños, montepío; **in** – en prenda; v. empeñar, dejar en prenda.

pay [pe] v. (remit) pagar; (pay for) costear; (profit) ser provechoso; (worthwhile) valer la pena; **to** – **attention** prestar atención; **to** – **back** restituir, volver; **to** – **court** hacer la corte; **to** – **down** pagar al contado; **to** – **homage** rendir homenaje; **to** – **one´s respects** presentar sus respetos; **to** – **a visit** hacer una visita; s. pago; recompensa; paga; sueldo; – **day** día de pagos, Am. día de raya; – **master** pagador, Am. rayador; – **roll** nómina.

pay•a•ble [péəb l̩] adj. pagadero

pay•ment [pémənt] s. pago; paga; – **in full** pago total.

pay•off [péof] s. arreglo; pago.

pea [pi] s. guisante, chícharo; **sweet** – guisante de olor.

peace [pis] s. paz.

peace•a•ble [písəb l̩] adj. pacífico, tranquilo.

peace•ful [písfəl] adj. pacífico; tranquilo, quieto, sosegado.

peach [pitʃ] s. melocotón, durazno; persona bella o admirable; – **tree** durazno, duraznero, melocotonero.

pea•cock [píkɑk] s. pavón, pavo real; **to act like a** – pavonearse, hacer ostentación.

peak [pik] s. pico, cumbre, cima; cúspide; punto máximo.

peal [pil] *s.* repique (*de campanas*); **– of laughter** carcajada, risotada; **– of thunder** trueno; *v.* repicar (*las campanas*).

pea•nut [pínət] *s.* cacahuate, *Carib., Ven., Col., Ch., Ríopl., Andes* maní.

pear [pɛr] *s.* pera; **– tree** peral; **alligator –** aguacate, *Ch., Andes., Ríopl.* palta (*variedad sudamericana*).

pearl [pɜˀl] *s.* perla; **– necklace** collar de perlas; **mother-of-pearl** nácar, madreperla.

pearl•y [pɜˀlɪ] *adj.* perlino; nacarado; aperlado.

peas•ant [pézṇt] *adj.* & *s.* campesino, rústico, *P.R.* jíbaro, *Cuba* guajiro; *Col.* paisa; *Ch.* guaso; *Ríopl.* gaucho.

peb•ble [pébḷ] *s.* guija, china, guijarro, piedrecilla.

pe•can [pikón] *s.* pacana.

peck [pɛk] *v.* picar, picotear; *s.* picotazo, picotada; medida de áridos (*aproximadamente 9 litros*); **a – of trouble** la mar de disgustos o molestias.

pe•cu•liar [pɪkjúljə] *adj.* peculiar; raro, singular, extraño.

pe•cu•li•ar•i•ty [pɪkjulɪǽrətɪ] *s.* peculiaridad; peculiaridad; rareza.

ped•a•gogue [pédəgɑg] *s.* pedagogo, dómine.

ped•a•go•gy [pédəgodʒɪ] *s.* pedagogía.

ped•al [pédḷ] *s.* pedal; *v.* pedalear, mover los pedales.

ped•ant [pédṇt] *s.* pedante.

pe•dan•tic [pɪdǽntɪk] *adj.* pedante, pedantesco.

ped•dle [pédḷ] *v.* ir vendiendo de puerta en puerta; **to – gossip** chismear.

ped•dler [pédlɚ] *s.* buhonero; vendedor ambulante.

ped•es•tal [pédɪst] *s.* pedestal.

pe•des•tri•an [pədéstrɪən] *s.* peatón, transeúnte, viandante; *adj.* pedestre.

pe•di•at•rics [pidɪǽtrɪks] *s.* pediatría.

ped•i•gree [pédəgri] *s.* linaje, genealogía.

peek [pik] *v.* atisbar, espiar; *s.* atisbo.

peel [pil] *s.* corteza, cáscara (*de algunas frutas*); pellejo (*de patatas*); *v.* pelar(se), descortezar(se), deshollejar(se); **to keep one's eye -ed** tener los ojos muy abiertos, estar alerta.

peep [pip] *v.* atisbar, espiar; asomar(se); pipiar, piar; *s.* atisbo; ojeada; pío (*de pollo o de ave*).

peer [pir] *s.* (*equal*) par, igual; (*noble*) noble; *v.* mirar con atención, atisbar; asomar; **to – into other people's business** fisgar, curiosear.

peer group [pírgrup] *s.* conjunto de personas de la misma edad y condiciones.

peer•less [pírlɛs] *s.* incomparable; sin par.

peeve [piv] *v.* irritar, poner de mal humor; **to get -d** amoscarse, ponerse de mal humor.

pee•vish [pívɪʃ] *adj.* enojadizo; malhumorado.

peg [pɛg] *s.* espiga, clavo de madera, estaquilla; cla-

vija (*de violín*); **to take a person down –** rebajar o humillar a alguien; *v.* clavar, clavetear; poner estaquillas; **to – along** atarearse, trabajar con tensón.

pe•jo•ra•tive [pədʒórətɪv] *adj.* peyorativo; despectivo.

pel•let [pélɪt] *s.* (*ball*) pelotilla; bola; (*pill*) píldora.

pell-mell [pélmél] *adj.* confuso, tumultuoso; *adv.* a trochemoche, atropelladamente, en tumulto.

pelt [pɛlt] *s.* zalea, cuero (*especialmente de oveja*); piel; *v.* golpear; **to – with stones** apedrear, arrojar piedras a.

pel•vis [pélvɪs] *s.* pelvis.

pen [pɛn] *s.* pluma (*para escribir*); corral; redil; **holder** mango de pluma, portapluma; **- name** nombre de pluma; **fountain –** pluma fuente, pluma estilográfica; **pig –** pocilga, *v.* escribir (*con pluma*); acorralar, encerrar.

pe•nal [pínḷ] *adj.* penal.

pe•nal•ize [pínəlaɪz] *v.* penar; aplicar sanción.

pen•al•ty [pénḷtɪ] *s.* pena, castigo; multa.

pen•ance [pénəns] *s.* penitencia.

pen•cil [pénsḷ] *s.* lápiz; lapicero; **– sharpener** tajalápiz.

pen•dant [péndənt] *s.* pendiente (*adorno que cuelga*); *adj.* pendiente.

pend•ing [péndɪŋ] *adj.* pendiente; colgado; *prep.* durante.

pen•du•lum [péndʒələm] *s.* péndulo.

pen•e•trate [pénətret] *v.* penetrar.

pen•e•trat•ing [pénɪtretɪŋ] *adj.* penetrante.

pen•e•tra•tion [pɛnətréʃən] *s.* penetración.

pen•guin [péŋgwɪn] *s.* pingüino.

pen•i•cil•lin [pɛnəsílɪn] *s.* penicilina.

pen•in•su•la [pənínsələ] *s.* península.

pen•i•tent [pénətənt] *adj.* arrepentido, penitente; *s.* penitente.

pen•i•ten•tia•ry [pɛnəténʃərɪ] *s.* penitenciaría, presidio.

pen•knife [pénnaɪf] *s.* cortaplumas; navaja.

pen•man•ship [pénmənʃɪp] *s.* escritura, caligrafía.

pen•nant [pénənt] *s.* banderola, gallardete.

pen•ni•less [pénɪlɪs] *adj.* pobre, sin dinero.

pen•ny [pénɪ] *s.* centavo (*de dólar*); **to cost a pretty –** costar un ojo de la cara, costar un dineral.

pen•sion [pénʃən] *s.* pensión; retiro (*de un militar*); *v.* pensionar.

pen•sive [pénsɪv] *adj.* pensativo.

pent [pɛnt] *adj.* encerrado; acorralado; **pent-up emotions** sentimientos reprimidos.

pent•house [pénthaʊs] *s.* casa de azotea; colgadizo.

peo•ple [píp]] *s.* gente; pueblo; *v.* poblar.

pep•per [pépɚ] *s.* pimienta; – **plant** pimentero; – **shaker** pimentero; **green -s** pimientos verdes; **red** – pimentón, chile, *Carib., Col., Ven., Andes., Ch., Ríopl.* ají; *v.* sazonar con pimienta; **to – with bullets** acribillar a balazos.

pep•per•mint [pépɚmɪnt] *s.* menta; pastilla o bombón de menta.

per [pɚ] *prep.* por; – **capita** por cabeza; – **cent** por ciento; – **year** al año; **ten cents – dozen** diez centavos por docena (*o* diez centavos la docena).

per•cale [pɚkél] *s.* percal.

per•ceive [pɚsív] *v.* percibir.

per•cent•age [pɚséntɪdʒ] *s.* porcentaje, tanto por ciento.

per•cep•ti•ble [pɚséptəb]] *adj.* perceptible.

per•cep•tion [pɚsépʃən] *s.* percepción.

per•cep•tive [pɚséptɪv] *adj.* perceptivo; sensible.

perch [pɚtʃ] *s.* percha (*para pájaros*); perca (*pez*); *v.* encaramar(se); posarse (*en una percha o rama*).

per•chance [pɚtʃǽns] *adv.* por ventura, acaso, quizás, tal vez.

per•co•late [pɚkəlet] *v.* filtrar(se), colar(se); rezumarse; penetrar.

per•di•tion [pɚdíʃən] *s.* perdición.

per•en•ni•al [pɚénɪəl] *adj.* perenne; continuo; perpetuo.

per•fect [pɚfɪkt] *adj.* perfecto; completo; *s.* tiempo perfecto (*del verbo*); [pɚfékt] *v.* perfeccionar.

per•fec•tion [pɚfékʃən] *s.* perfección.

per•fid•i•ous [pɚfídɪəs] *adj.* pérfido.

per•fi•dy [pɚfədɪ] *s.* perfidia.

per•fo•rate [pɚfəret] *v.* perforar.

per•force [pɚfɔ́rs] *adj.* necesariamente; por fuerza.

per•form [pɚfɔ́rm] *v.* ejecutar; llevar a cabo, cumplir, hacer; funcionar (*una máquina*); desempeñar o representar un papel.

per•form•ance [pɚfɔ́rməns] *s.* ejecución; desempeño, cumplimiento; funcionamiento (*de una máquina o motor*); función, representación; acto, acción.

per•fume [pɚfjum] *s.* perfume; [pɚfjúm] *v.* perfumar.

per•fum•er•y [pɚfjúmərɪ] *s.* perfumería; perfumes.

per•haps [pɚhǽps] *adv.* acaso, tal vez, quizá (*o* quizás), puede ser.

per•i•gee [pérədʒi] *s.* perigeo.

per•il [pérəl] *s.* peligro; riesgo; *v.* poner en peligro.

per•il•ous [pérələs] *adj.* peligroso.

pe•rim•e•ter [pərímətɚ] *s.* perímetro.

pe•ri•od [pírɪəd] *s.* período; punto final; fin, término, no.

pe•ri•od•ic [pɪrɪádɪk] *adj.* periódico.

pe•ri•od•i•cal [pɪrɪádɪk]] *adj.* periódico; *s.* revista, publicación periódica.

pe•riph•er•y [pərífərɪ] *s.* periferia.

per•ish [pérɪʃ] *v.* perecer.

per•ish•a•ble [pérɪʃəb]] *adj.* perecedero; deleznable.

per•jure [pɚdʒɚ] *v.* **to – oneself** perjurar.

per•ju•ry [pɚdʒrɪ] *s.* perjurio, juramento falso.

per•ma•nence [pɚmənəns] *s.* permanencia.

per•ma•nent [pɚmənənt] *adj.* permanente; duradero.

per•me•ate [pɚmɪet] *v.* penetrar, saturar; difundirse por, filtrarse por.

per•mis•si•ble [pɚmísəb]] *adj.* lícito.

per•mis•sion [pɚmíʃən] *s.* permiso, licencia.

per•mis•sive [pɚmísɪv] *adj.* permisivo.

per•mit [pɚmɪt] *s.* permiso, pase; licencia; [pɚmít] *v.* permitir.

per•mu•ta•tion [pɚmjutéʃən] *s.* permutación.

per•ni•cious [pɚníʃəs] *adj.* pernicioso.

per•pen•dic•u•lar [pɚpəndíkjələɚ] *adj. & s.* perpendicular.

per•pe•trate [pɚpétret] *v.* perpetrar, cometer.

per•pet•u•al [pɚpétʃuəl] *adj.* perpetuo.

per•pet•u•ate [pɚpétʃuet] *v.* perpetuar.

per•plex [pɚpléks] *v.* confundir, turbar, aturdir.

per•plexed [pɚplékst] *adj.* perplejo, confuso.

per•plex•i•ty [pɚpléksətɪ] *s.* perplejidad, confusión.

per•se•cute [pɚsɪkjut] *v.* perseguir, acosar.

per•se•cu•tion [pɚsɪkjúʃən] *s.* persecución.

per•se•cu•tor [pɚsɪkjutɚ] *s.* perseguidor.

per•se•ver•ance [pɚsəvírəns] *s.* perseverancia.

per•se•vere [pɚsəvírɚ] *v.* perseverar; persistir.

per•sist [pɚzíst] *v.* persistir; porfiar.

per•sist•ence [pɚzístəns] *s.* persistencia; porfía.

per•sist•ent [pɚzístənt] *adj.* persistente; porfiado.

per•son [pɚs ŋ] *s.* persona.

per•son•a•ble [pɚsənəb]] *adj.* presentable; bien parecido.

per•son•age [pɚs ŋ ɪdʒ] *s.* personaje.

per•son•al [pɚs ŋ]] *adj.* personal; en persona.

per•son•al•i•ty [pɚs ŋ ǽlətɪ] *s.* personalidad; persona, personaje; alusión personal.

per•son•nel [pɚs ŋ él] *s.* personal.

per•spec•tive [pɚspéktɪv] *s.* perspectiva; – **drawing** dibujo en perspectiva.

per•spi•ca•cious [pɚspɪkéʃəs] *adj.* perspicaz.

per•spi•ra•tion [pɚspəréʃən] *s.* sudor.

per·spire [pəˈspáɪr] v. sudar.

per·suade [pəˈswéd] v. persuadir.

per·sua·sion [pəˈswéʒən] s. persuasión; creencia.

per·sua·sive [pəˈswésɪv] adj. persuasivo.

pert [pɜ˞t] adj. insolente, descarado, atrevido, Am. retobado.

per·tain [pəˈtén] v. pertenecer; atañer.

per·ti·nent [pɜ˞tṇ ənt] adj. pertinente, a propósito, al caso.

per·turb [pəˈtɜ˞b] v. perturbar.

pe·rus·al [pəˈrúz |] s. lectura.

pe·ruse [pəˈrúz] v. leer con cuidado.

Pe·ru·vi·an [pəˈrúvɪən] adj. & s. peruano.

per·vade [pəˈvéd] v. llenar, penetrar, difundirse por.

per·verse [pəˈvɜ˞s] adj. perverso; terco, obstinado.

per·vert [pəˈvɜ˞t] v. pervertir; falsear; [pɜ˞vɜ˞t] s. perverso.

pes·si·mism [pɜ˞səmɪzməm] s. pesimismo.

pes·si·mist [pésəmɪst] s. pesimista; -ic adj. pesimista.

pest [pɛst] s. peste, plaga; pestilencia.

pes·ter [péstə˞] v. importunar, molestar.

pes·ti·cide [péstəsaɪd] s. & adj. insecticida.

pes·ti·lence [péstḷəns] s. pestilencia.

pet [pɛt] s. animal mimado, animal casero o doméstico; niño mimado; favorito; adj. favorito; mimado; **- name** nombre de cariño (por lo general diminutivo); v. mimar, acariciar.

pet·al [pét |] s. pétalo.

pet·cock [pétkak] s. llave de desagüe (purga).

pe·ti·tion [pətíʃən] s. petición, súplica; instancia, memorial, solicitud, Am. ocurso; v. solicitar, pedir, dirigir una instancia o memorial a; suplicar, rogar.

pet·ri·fy [pétrɪfaɪ] v. petrificar.

pe·tro·le·um [pətrólɪəm] s. petróleo.

pet·ti·coat [pétɪkot] s. enaguas.

pet·ty [pétɪ] adj. insignificante, pequeño; mezquino; inferior, subordinado; **- cash** fondos para gastos menores; **- larceny** ratería; **- officer** oficial subordinado (en la marina); **- treason** traición menor.

pew [pju] s. banco de iglesia.

pha·lanx [fél æŋks] s. falanje.

phan·tom [fǽntəm] s. fantasma.

phar·ma·cist [fárməsɪst] s. farmacéutico, boticario.

phar·ma·cy [fárməsɪ] s. farmacia, botica.

phar·ynx [fǽrɪŋks] s. faringe.

phase [fez] s. fase.

pheas·ant [fézənt] s. faisán.

phe·nom·e·na [fənómənə] pl. de **phenomenon**.

phe·nom·e·non [fənámənən] s. fenómeno.

phi·lan·thro·py [fɪl ǽn θrəpɪ] s. filantropía.

phil·har·mon·ic [fɪlharmánɪk] adj. filarmónico.

phi·lol·o·gy [fɪláʲlədʒɪ] s. filología.

phi·los·o·pher [fəlásəfə˞] s. filósofo.

phil·o·soph·i·cal [fɪləsáfɪk] adj. filosófico.

phi·los·o·phy [fəlásəfɪ] s. filosofía.

phlegm [flɛm] s. flema.

phone [fon] s. teléfono; v. telefonear.

pho·neme [fónim] s. fonema.

pho·net·ics [fonétɪks] s. fonética.

pho·no·graph [fónəgr æ f] s. fonógrafo.

pho·nol·o·gy [fonáʲlədʒɪ] s. fonología.

phos·phate [fásfet] s. fosfato.

phos·pho·rus [fásfərəs] s. fósforo (elemento químico).

pho·to [fóto] s. fotografía, retrato.

pho·to·graph [fótəgræf] s. fotografía, retrato; v. fotografiar, retratar.

pho·tog·ra·pher [fətágrəfə˞] s. fotógrafo.

pho·tog·ra·phy [fətágrəfɪ] s. fotografía.

phrase [frez] s. frase; expresión, locución; v. frasear; expresar, formular.

phys·ic [fízɪk] s. purga, purgante; v. purgar.

phys·i·cal [fízɪk |] adj. físico.

phy·si·cian [fəzíʃən] s. médico.

phys·i·cist [fízəsɪst] s. físico.

phys·ics [fízɪks] s. física.

phys·i·o·log·ical [fɪzɪəládʒɪk |] adj. fisiológico.

phys·i·ol·o·gy [fɪzɪáʲlədʒɪ] s. fisiología.

phy·sique [fɪzík] s. físico, constitución física, talle, cuerpo.

pi·an·o [pɪ æ no] s. piano; **- bench** banqueta de piano; **- stool** taburete de piano; **grand -** piano de cola; **upright -** piano vertical.

pic·a·resque [pɪkərésk] adj. picaresco.

pick [pɪk] v. (choose) escoger, coger; (break) picar; (clean) mondarse, limpiarse (los dientes); desplumar (un ave); roer (un hueso); falsear (una cerradura); armar (una pendencia); **to - flaws** criticar, censurar; **to - out** escoger; **to - pockets** ratear; **to - up** recoger; **to - up speed** acelerar la marcha; s. pico (herramienta); selección; lo selecto, lo mejor; recolección, cosecha; **ice -** punzón para romper el hielo; **tooth -** mondadientes, palillo para dientes.

pick·axe [píkæks] s. pico, zapapico.

pick·et [píkɪt] s. piquete (estaca o palo clavado en la tierra); piquete (vigilante huelguista); piquete de soldados; v. estacionar piquetes cerca de (una fábrica, campamento, etc.); vigilar (por medio de piquetes); estar de guardia.

pick·le [pík |] s. encurtido; **to be in a -** hallarse en un aprieto; v. encurtir, escabechar; **-ed cucumbers** pepinillos encurtidos; **-ed fish** escabeche, pescado en escabeche.

pick·pock·et [píkpakɪt] s. rata (m.), ratero; Méx.,

pic·nic [píknɪk] *s.* partida de campo, día de campo, comida campestre, *Am.* pícnic; *v.* hacer una comida campestre; ir a un pícnic.

pic·ture [píktʃə·] *s.* (*painting*) cuadro, pintura; (*portrait*) retrato; (*photo*) fotografía; (*engraving*) grabado; (*movie*) película; **– frame** marco; **– gallery** museo o galería de pinturas; *v.* pintar, dibujar; describir; imaginar(se).

pic·tur·esque [pɪktʃərésk] *adj.* pintoresco.

pie [paɪ] *s.* pastel; empanada.

piece [pis] *s.* (*section*) pieza, pedazo, parte; sección; (*passage*) trozo; **– of advice** consejo; **– of land** parcela; **– of money** moneda, **– of news** noticia; **– of nonsense** tontería; **- meal** en pedazos, a pedazos, por partes; *v.* remendar; **– between meals** comer a deshoras; **to – on to** juntar a, pegar a; **to – together** unir, pegar, juntar.

pier [pɪr] *s.* muelle, embarcadero; rompeolas; pilar (*de puente o arco*).

pierce [pɪrs] *v.* atravesar, traspasar; taladrar, agujerear, perforar.

pi·e·ty [páɪətɪ] *s.* piedad, religiosidad.

pig [pɪg] *s.* puerco, cerdo, cochino; *S.A.* chancho; *C.A.* tunco; cuchi; **– iron** hierro en lingotes; **– headed** cabezón, testarudo; **guinea –** conejillo de Indias.

pi·geon [pídʒən] *s.* pichón, paloma.

pi·geon·hole [pídʒənhol] *s.* casilla; *v.* encasillar.

pig·ment [pígmənt] *s.* pigmento, color.

pig·my [pígmɪ] *s.* pigmeo.

pike [paɪk] *s.* pica, lanza; lucio (*pez*).

pile [paɪl] *s.* pila; montón; pelo (*de ciertos tejidos*); pilote; **-s** almorranas (*enfermedad*); **- driver** martinete (*para clavar pilotes*); *v.* apilar(se), amontonar(se); acumular(se).

pil·fer [pílfə·] *v.* pillar, ratear, hurtar, sisar.

pil·grim [pílgrɪm] *s.* peregrino, romero.

pil·grim·age [pílgrəmɪdʒ] *s.* peregrinación, romería.

pill [pɪl] *s.* píldora; persona fastidiosa.

pil·lage [pílɪdʒ] *v.* pillar, saquear; *s.* pillaje, saqueo.

pil·lar [pílə·] *s.* pilar, columna; **to go from – to post** ir de Ceca en Meca.

pil·low [pílo] *s.* almohada; cojín.

pil·low·case [pílokes] *s.* funda de almohada.

pi·lot [páɪlət] *s.* piloto; guía; **- light** (*o* **– burner**) mechero, encendedor (*de una cocina o una estufa de gas*); **harbor –** práctico de puerto; *v.* pilotar o pilotear; dirigir, guiar.

pim·ple [pímp‖] *s.* grano, barro.

pin [pɪn] *s.* alfiler; prendedor; espiga; bolo (*del juego de bolos*); **- money** dinero para alfileres; **- wheel** molinete, *Am.* remolino; **breast –** broche; **safety –** imperdible; *v.* prender (*con alfiler*); asegurar, fijar, clavar; **to – down** fijar, inmovilizar; hacer dar una

contestación definitiva; **to – one´s hope to** poner toda su esperanza en; **to – up** prender con alfileres; colgar (*un dibujo o retrato*), fijar con tachuelas.

pin·cers [pínsə·z] *s. pl.* pinzas; tenazas; **small –** tenacillas.

pinch [pɪntʃ] *v.* (*squeeze*) pellizcar; apretar; (*economize*) economizar; (*arrest*) prender, arrestar; **to – one´s finger in the door** machucarse el dedo en la puerta; *s.* pellizco; pizca, porción pequeña; punzada, dolor agudo; aprieto, apuro; **– hitter** suplente, sustituto.

pinch·ers [pínt∫ə·z] = **pincers.**

pine [paɪn] *s.* pino; **– cone** piña; **– grove** pinar; **– nut** piñón; *v.* languidecer; **to – away** consumirse; **to – for** anhelar, suspirar por.

pine·ap·ple [páɪnæp‖] *s.* piña, ananá o ananás.

pin·ion [pínjən] *s.* piñón.

pink [pɪŋk] *s.* clavel; color de rosa; **in the – of condition** en la mejor condición; *adj.* rosado, color rosa.

pin·na·cle [pínək‖] *s.* pináculo, cumbre.

pint [paɪnt] *s.* pinta (*aproximadamente medio litro*).

pi·o·neer [paɪənír] *s.* explorador, colonizador; fundador, iniciador, precursor; pionero; *v.* explorar, colonizar; fundar, promover.

pi·ous [páɪəs] *adj.* pío, piadoso.

pipe [paɪp] *s.* pipa (*de fumar*); tubo, caño; cañón (*de órgano*); caramillo, flauta; **- line** cañería, tubería; *v.* conducir por cañerías; desaguar por cañería; proveer de tuberías o cañerías; chillar; **to – down** bajar la voz.

pip·er [páɪpə·] *s.* gaitero, flautista.

pip·ing [páɪpɪŋ] *s.* cañería, tubería; cordoncillo (*de adorno para costuras*); chillido, silbido; *adj.* agudo, chillón; **– hot** muy caliente; hirviendo.

pip·pin [pípɪn] *s.* camuesa.

pique [pik] *s.* enojo, resentimiento; *v.* picar, excitar; enojar, irritar; **to – oneself on** picarse de, preciarse de.

pi·rate [páɪrət] *s.* pirata; *v.* piratear; plagiar.

pis·tol [píst‖] *s.* pistola; revólver.

pis·ton [píst ŋ] *s.* pistón, émbolo; **- ring** aro de pistón; **- rod** vástago del émbolo.

pit [pɪt] *s.* hoyo; foso; hueso (*de ciertas frutas*); **– of the stomach** boca del estómago.

pitch [pɪtʃ] *s.* (*throw*) tiro, lanzamiento (*de una pelota*); cabezada (*de un barco*); (*music*) diapasón, tono; (*inclination*) grado, declive, grado de inclinación; pez (*f.*), brea; resina; **– dark** oscurísimo; *v.* tirar, lanzar, arrojar; cabecear (*un barco*); graduar el tono de (*un instrumento o voz*); echarse de cabeza; inclinarse; **to – a tent** armar una tienda de campaña; acampar; **to – into** arremeter contra; reprender, regañar; **– in !** ¡manos a la obra!

pitch·er [pítʃəⱼ] s. cántaro, jarro o jarra; tirador, lanzador (*en béisbol*).

pitch·fork [pítʃfɔrk] s. horca, horquilla (*para hacinar las mieses, levantar la paja, etc.*).

pit·e·ous [pítɪəs] adj. lastimero, lastimoso.

pith [pɪθ] s. meollo, médula; esencia, sustancia.

pit·i·ful [pítɪfəl] adj. lastimoso; lamentable; miserable.

pit·i·less [pítɪlɪs] adj. despiadado, incompasivo, cruel.

pit·y [pítɪ] s. piedad; lástima; compasión; **for — 's sake** por piedad, por Dios; **what a — !** ¡qué lástima!; v. compadecer; tener lástima por; apiadarse de, tener piedad de.

plac·ard [plᴧkard] s. letrero, cartel; v. fijar carteles.

place [ples] s. (*site*) lugar, sitio; localidad; (*position*) puesto; empleo; posición; **— of business** oficina, despacho; **— of worship** templo, iglesia; **market —** plaza, mercado; **in — of** en lugar de, en vez de; **it is no my — to do it** no es mi deber hacerlo, no me toca a mi hacerlo; v. colocar; situar; poner; acomodar, dar empleo a.

plac·id [plǽsɪd] adj. plácido, apacible, sosegado.

pla·gia·rism [plédʒərɪzəm] s. plagio.

plague [pleg] s. plaga; peste, pestilencia; calamidad; v. plagar, infestar; importunar.

plaid [plǽd] s. tartán, tela a cuadros; manta escocesa a cuadros; diseño a cuadros; adj. a cuadros.

plain [plen] adj. (*flat*) llano; (*simple*) sencillo; claro; franco; ordinario; **— fool** tonto de capirote; **— woman** mujer sin atractivo; **in — sight** en plena vista; **plain-clothes man** detective; adv. claramente; **— stupid** completamente estúpido; **plainspoken** franco, francote, sincero; s. llano, llanura.

plain·tiff [pléntɪf] s. demandante.

plain·tive [pléntɪv] adj. lastimero, triste.

plan [plæn] s. plan, proyecto; plano (*dibujo o mapa*); v. planear; proyectar, idear; pensar, proponerse.

plane [plen] s. (*airplane*) avión; aeroplano; (*surface*) plano, superficie plana; cepillo (*de carpintero*); adj. plano, llano; **— tree** plátano falso; v. acepillar, alisar con cepillo (*la madera o los metales*).

plan·et [plǽnɪt] s. planeta.

plank [plæŋk] s. tabla, tablón; principio, base (*del programa de un partido político*); v. entablar, entarimar, cubrir con tablas; asar (*carne*) en una tabla.

plant [plænt] s. (*vegetation*) planta; (*industry*) fábrica; taller; v. plantar; sembrar; implantar; establecer.

plan·ta·tion [plæntéʃən] s. plantación; plantío; sembrado; **coffe —** cafetal; **cotton —** algodonal; **rubber —** cauchal; **sugar —** ingenio de azúcar.

plant·er [plǽntəⱼ] s. plantador, cultivador.

plaque [plæk] s. placa.

plas·ma [plǽzmə] s. plasma.

plas·ter [plǽstəⱼ] s. yeso; emplasto; **— of Paris** yeso, yeso mate; **court —** esparadrapo, tafetán inglés; **mustard —** sinapismo; v. enyesar; emplastar, poner emplastos a; pegar (*carteles, anuncios*); embarrar.

plas·tic [plǽstɪk] adj. plástico.

plat [plæt] s. plano; parcela; v. levantar o trazar un plano.

plate [plet] s. (*eating*) plato; (*metal*) placa; plancha; lámina; **dental —** dentadura postiza; v. platear; dorar; niquelar; blindar, proteger con planchas de metal.

pla·teau [plætó] s. antiplanicie, mesa, meseta.

plat·ed [plétəd] adj. chapeado; blindado.

plate·ful [plétfUl] s. plato, plato lleno.

plat·form [plǽtfɔrm] s. plataforma; tablado; programa de un partido político; **railway —** andén.

plat·i·num [plǽtɪnəm] s. platino.

plat·i·tude [plǽtətjud] s. lugar común, perogrullada.

plat·ter [plǽtəⱼ] s. platel, platón.

play [ple] v. (*game*) jugar; juguetear; (*instrument*) tocar; (*drama*) representar; hacer, desempeñar (*un papel*); manipular (*un instrumento, radio, fonógrafo, etc.*); **to — a joke** hacer una broma, dar un chasco; **to — cards** jugar a los naipes, jugar a la baraja; **to — havoc** hacer estragos, causar daño; **to — tennis** jugar al tenis; **to — the fool** hacerse el tonto, fingirse tonto; **to be all —ed out** no poder más, estar agotado; s. juego; jugada (*acción, mivientо en un juego*); pieza, drama, comedia, representación; recreación, diversión; **— on words** juego de palabras, equívoco; **to give full — to** dar rienda suelta a.

play·er [pléəⱼ] s. (*games*) jugador; (*music*) músico; (*plays*) cómico, actor; artista; **— piano** piano mecánico, pianola; **piano —** pianista; **violin —** violinista.

play·ful [pléfəl] adj. juguetón, retozón; bromista.

play·ground [plégraUnd] s. campo o patio de recreo.

play·mate [plémet] s. compañero de juego.

play·thing [pléθɪŋ] s. juguete.

play·wright [pléraɪt] s. dramático, dramaturgo.

plea [pli] s. súplica; ruego; alegato, defensa; pretexto; **on the — that** con el pretexto de que.

plead [plid] v. abogar; suplicar, argüir; alegar; defender (*una causa*); **to — guilty** declararse o confesarse culpable.

pleas·ant [plézṇt] adj. grato; agradable; simpático.

pleas·ant·ry [plézṇtrɪ] s. chanza, broma, chiste, humorada.

please [pliz] v. agradar, gustar, dar gusto a; complacer; **— do it** haga Ud. el favor de hacerlo, tenga Ud. la bondad de hacerlo; sírvase hacerlo; **as you —** como Ud. quiera, como Ud. guste; **if you —** si me hace Ud. el favor; **to be —ed to** complacerse en, tener gusto en; alegrarse de; **to be —ed with** gustarle a uno, estar satisfecho de (o con).

pleas•ing [plízɪŋ] adj. agradable.

pleas•ure [pléʒɚ] s. placer, gusto; deleite, alegría, gozo; **- trip** viaje de recreo; **what is your - ?** ¿qué deseaba Ud.? ¿en qué puedo servirle?.

pleat [plit] s. pliegue, doblez; v. plegar, hacer pliegues (en)..

ple•be•ian [plɪbíən] adj. & s. plebeyo.

pledge [plɛdʒ] s. promesa; prenda (garantía); fianza; **as a – of** en prenda de; v. prometer; empeñar, dar en prenda); hacer firmar una promesa; **to – one's word** empeñar (o dar) su palabra; **to – to secrecy** exigir promesa de sigilo.

ple•na•ry [plénərɪ] adj. plenario.

plen•i•po•ten•ti•a•ry [plɛnəpəténʃərɪ] adj. & s. plenipotenciario.

plen•ti•ful [pléntɪfəl] adj. abundante, copioso.

plen•ty [pléntɪ] s. abundancia, copia; **– of time** bastante tiempo; **that is –** con eso basta; basta.

pli•a•ble [pláɪəb‖] adj. flexible; manejable, dócil; transigente.

pli•ant [pláɪənt] adj. flexible; dócil; sumiso.

pli•ers [pláɪɚz] s. pl. alicates, tenazas.

plight [plaɪt] s. apuro, aprieto, situación difícil.

plod [plɑd] v. bregar, trafagar, afanarse, trabajar asiduamente.

plo•sive [plósɪv] adj. & s. oclusivo.

plot [plɑt] s. (outline) trama, enredo, argumento; (conspiracy) complot, conspiración; (land) parcela (de tierra), solar; (plan) plano, diagrama; v. tramar, urdir; maquinar, conspirar; hacer el plano o el diagrama de; **to – a curve** hacer una gráfica.

plot•ter [plɑtɚ] s. conspirador; tramador; conjurado.

plough = **plow.**

plow [plaʊ] s. arado; **–share** reja de arado; v. arar; surcar.

pluck [plʌk] v. coger; arrancar; desplumar (un ave); puntear (la cuerdas de una guitarra); **to – at** tirar de; **to – up** arrancar; cobrar ánimo; s. ánimo, valor; tirón.

pluck•y [plʌkɪ] adj. valeroso, animoso.

plug [plʌg] s. (stopper) taco, tapón; (horse) caballejo, penco; (boost) elogio incidental (de un producto comercial o de una persona); **– of tobacco** tableta de tabaco; **electric –** clavija de conexión; **fire –** boca de agua para incendios; **spark –** bujía; v. tapar; **to – along** afanarse, atarearse; **to – in** enchufar, conectar; **to – up** tapar, obstruir.

plum [plʌm] s. (fruit) ciruela; (prize) la cosa menor; la mejor colocación; **– pudding** pudín inglés con pasas; **– tree** ciruelo.

plum•age [plúmɪdʒ] s. plumaje.

plumb [plʌm] s. plomo, pesa de plomo; sonda; **out**

of – no vertical; adj. vertical, a plomo, recto; **– bob** plomo, plomada; adv. a plomo, verticalmente; **– crazy** completamente loco; v. sondear; aplomar (una pared).

plumb•er [plʌmɚ] s. plomero.

plumb•ing [plʌmɪŋ] s. plomería; cañerías (de un edificio); oficio de plomero.

plume [plum] s. pluma; plumaje; penacho; v. adornar con plumas; **to – its wing** alisarse o componerse el plumaje del ala.

plump [plʌmp] adj. rechoncho, regordete, rollizo; adv. de golpe; v. **to – down** dejar(se) caer; desplomarse, sentarse de golpe.

plun•der [plʌndɚ] s. pillaje, saqueo; botín; v. pillar; saquear.

plunge [plʌndʒ] v. zambullir(se), sumergir(se); hundir(se); lanzar(se), arrojar(se), precipitar(se); **to – headlong** echarse de cabeza; s. zambullida; salto (de arriba abajo).

plunk [plʌŋk] v. (instrument) puntear; (place) arrojar.

plu•ral [plúrəl] adj. & s. plural.

plu•ral•i•ty [plúrǽlɪtɪ] s. pluralidad.

plus [plʌs] s. más, signo más; **– quantity** cantidad positiva; **two – three** dos más tres.

plush [plʌʃ] s. felpa; velludo.

Plu•to [plúto] s. Plutón.

plu•ton•ic [plutɑ́nɪk] adj. plutónico.

ply [plaɪ] v. manejar con tesón (un instrumento o herramienta); importunar (con preguntas); hacer con regularidad un recorrido (entre dos puntos); **to – a trade** seguir o ejercer un oficio; **to – oneself with** saturarse de, rellenarse de; s. doblez, pliegue; capa (de tejido, goma, etc.).

pneu•mat•ic [njumǽtɪk] adj. neumático.

pneu•mo•nia [njumónjə] s. pulmonía.

poach [potʃ] v. escalfar (huevos); invadir (un vedado); cazar o pescar en vedado; robar caza o pesca (de un vedado).

pock•et [pɑkɪt] s. bolsillo, faltriquera, C.A. bolsa; tronera (de billar); cavidad; hoyo; v. embolsarse; apropiarse; ocultar (el orgullo o rencor); aguantar (un insulto).

pock•et•book [pɑkɪtbʊk] s. cartera; portamonedas; **woman's –** bolsa.

pock•et•knife [pɑkɪtnaɪf] s. navaja; cortaplumas.

pod [pɑd] s. vaina (de guisante, fríjol, etc.).

po•di•um [pódɪəm] s. podio.

po•em [póɪm] s. poema, poesía.

po•et [póɪt] s. poeta; vate.

po•et•ess [póɪtɪs] s. poetisa.

po•et•ic [poétɪk] adj. poético; **-s** s. arte poética, poética.

po•et•i•cal [poétɪk‖] adj. poético.

po·et·ry [póɪtrɪ] *s.* poesía.

poign·ant [pɔ́ɪnjənt] *adj.* intenso; picante.

point [pɔɪnt] *s.* punto; punta *(de lápiz, espada, tierra, etc.)*; **it is not to the** – no viene al caso; **not to see the** – no caer en la cuenta; no ver el chiste, propósito o intención; **on the – of** a punto de; *v.* apuntar; señalar; indicar; **to – out** señalar, mostrar, indicar.

point-blank [pɔɪntblǽŋk] *adj.* a quema ropa.

point·ed [pɔ́ɪntɪd] *adj.* puntiagudo, agudo; satírico; apto; a propósito, al caso; **– arch** arco apuntado, arco ojival.

point·er [pɔ́ɪntɚ] *s.* *(indicator)* puntero; indicador, señalador; *(dog)* perro de punta y vuelta; *(advice)* indicación, consejo.

poise [pɔɪz] *s.* equilibrio; porte, compostura; *v.* equilibrar(se); balancear(se).

poi·son [pɔ́ɪzŋ] *s.* veneno; ponzoña; *v.* envenenar, emponzoñar.

poi·son·ous [pɔ́ɪzŋəs] *adj.* venenoso, ponzoñoso.

poke [pok] *v.* atizar, remover *(el fuego)*; picar *(con el dedo o cualquier objeto puntiagudo)*; **to – along** andar perezosamente; **to – around** husmear, curiosear; **to – fun at** burlarse de; **to – into** meter en; **to – out** sacar; proyectarse; *s.* pinchazo; piquete; codazo; aguijonada; **slow –** tardón.

po·lar [pólɚ] *adj.* polar; **– bear** oso blanco.

po·lar·i·ty [polǽrɪtɪ] *s.* polaridad.

po·lar·i·za·tion [polɚɪzéʃən] *s.* polarización.

pole [pol] *s.* poste; pértiga, palo largo; asta *(de una bandera)*; garrocha; polo; **Pole** polaco; **north –** polo norte, polo ártico; **south –** polo sur, polo antártico; **– vault** salto con garrocha.

po·lem·ics [polémɪks] *s.* polémica.

po·lice [pəlís] *s.* policía; *v.* vigilar; guardar el orden.

po·lice·man [pəlísmən] *s.* policía *(m.)*, guardia de policía, polizonte, *Ven., Col.* vigilante, *Méx.* gendarme; *Ch.* carabinero.

pol·i·cy [pálɪsɪ] *s.* política; **insurance –** póliza de seguro.

Pol·ish [pólɪʃ] *adj.* polaco; *s.* polaco, idioma polaco.

pol·ish [pálɪʃ] *s.* pulimento; lustre, brillo; urbanidad, cultura; **shoe –** betún, bola; *v.* pulir, pulimentar; dar brillo o lustre a; embolar, dar bola o brillo a *(zapatos)*.

po·lite [pəláɪt] *adj.* cortés, fino, urbano, político.

po·lite·ness [pəláɪtnɪs] *s.* cortesía; fineza, urbanidad.

pol·i·tic [pálətɪk] *adj.* político, prudente; conveniente.

po·lit·i·cal [pəlítɪkḷ] *adj.* político.

pol·i·ti·cian [palətíʃən] *s.* político; politicastro.

pol·i·tics [pálətɪks] *s.* política.

poll [pol] *s.* votación; lista electoral; **-s** comicios; urnas electorales; casilla *(donde se vota)*; **– tax** impuesto *(de tanto de por cabeza)*; *v.* registrar los votos de; votar; recibir *(votos)*.

pol·len [pálən] *s.* polen.

pol·li·nate [pálənet] *v.* polinizar.

po·lo [pólo] *s.* polo.

pol·y·glot [pálɪglat] *s.* polígota.

pome·gran·ate [pʌ́mgrænɪt] *s.* granada; **– tree** granado.

pomp [pamp] *s.* pompa, boato.

pom·pous [pámpəs] *adj.* pomposa, ostentoso.

pond [pand] *s.* charca; estanque; **fish –** vivero.

pon·der [pándɚ] *v.* ponderar, pesar, examinar; **to – over** reflexionar.

pon·der·ous [pándɚəs] *adj.* ponderoso; pesado.

pon·toon [pantún] *s.* pontón, chata, barco chato; flotador *(de hidroavión)*; **– bridge** pontón, puente flotante.

po·ny [pónɪ] *s.* caballito, potrillo; clave o traducción *(usada ilícitamente en un examen)*.

poo·dle [púdḷ] *s.* perro de lanas.

pool [pul] *s.* charco; charca; trucos *(juego parecido al billar)*; polla o puesta *(en ciertos juegos)*; fondos en común, combinación de fondos *(para una empresa o para especular)*; "trust"; **swimming –** piscina; *v.* formar una polla; combinar fondos.

poor [pUr] *adj.* pobre; malo; de mala calidad; **– student** estudiante pobre; mal estudiante; **– little thing** pobrecito; **the –** los pobres; **-ly** *adv.* pobremente; mal.

poor·house [pÚrhaUs] *s.* hospicio, casa de pobres.

pop [pap] *s.* tronido, trueno, estallido; detonación; **– of a cork** taponazo; **soda –** gaseosa; *v.* reventar, estallar; detonar; saltar *(un tapón)*; **to – a question** espetar una pregunta; **to – corn** hacer palomitas de maíz, hacer rosetas de maíz; **to – in and out** entrar y salir de sopetón; **to – one's head out** sacar o asomar de repente la cabeza.

pop·corn [pápkɔrn] *s.* rosetas, palomitas de maíz, *Andes* alborotos; *Ch.* cabritas; *Méx.* esquite.

pope [pop] *s.* Papa.

pop·eyed [pápaɪd] *adj.* de ojos saltones, *Am.* desorbitado.

pop·lar [páplɚ] *s.* álamo; **black –** chopo; **– grove** alameda.

pop·py [pápɪ] *s.* amapola.

pop·u·lace [pápjəlɪs] *s.* pueblo, populacho.

pop·u·lar [pápjələ·] *adj.* popular.

pop·u·lar·i·ty [papjəlǽrətɪ] *adj.* popularidad.

pop·u·late [pápjəlet] *v.* poblar.

pop·u·la·tion [papjəléʃən] *s.* población.

pop·u·lous [pápjələs] *adj.* populoso.

por·ce·lain [pɔ́rslɪn] *s.* porcelana.

porch [prtʃ] *s.* pórtico, porche; galería.

por•cu•pine [prkjəpaɪn] *s.* puerco espín.

pore [por] *s.* poro; *v.* **to – over a book** engolfarse en la lectura.

pork [pɔrk] *s.* puerco, carne de puerco – **chop** chuleta de puerco; **salt** – tocino salado.

por•nog•ra•phy [pornógrəfɪ] *s.* pornografía.

po•rous [prəs] *adj.* poroso.

por•ridge [prɪdʒ] *s.* potaje, gachas.

port [port] *s.* (*harbor*) puerto; (*wine*) oporto; (*left side*) babor (*de un barco*); **– hole** porta, portilla.

por•ta•ble [ptəb]] *adj.* portátil.

por•tal [prt]] *s.* portal.

por•tent [prtɛnt] *s.* portento, presagio, agüero.

por•ten•tous [portɛ́ntəs] *adj.* portentoso; prodigioso; de mal agüero.

por•ter [prtə·] *s.* mozo de cordel, *Méx., C.A.* cargador; *Ríopl.* changador; camarero (en un coche-cama); portero.

port•fo•li•o [portfólɪo] *s.* portafolio, cartera; carpeta; ministerio.

por•tion [pr∫ən] *s.* porción; *v.* repartir.

port•ly [prtlɪ] *adj.* corpulento.

por•trait [prtret] *s.* retrato.

por•tray [portré] *v.* retratar, pintar, dibujar, representar.

por•tray•al [portréəl] *s.* retrato, delineación, delineamiento, representación.

Por•tu•guese [prt∫ɛgiz] *adj. & s.* portugués.

pose [poz] *s.* (*posture*) postura, actitud; (*affected attitude*) afectación; *v.* posar (*como modelo*); colocar(se) en cierta postura; afectar una actitud o postura; proponer, plantear (*una cuestión o problema*); **to – as** fingirse, hacerse pasar por.

po•si•tion [pəzí∫ən] *s.* posición; postura; situación, empleo, puesto.

pos•i•tive [pázətɪv] *adj.* positivo; cierto, seguro; categórico; dogmático.

pos•sess [pəzɛ́s] *v.* poseer.

pos•ses•sion [pəzɛ́∫ən] *s.* posesión.

pos•ses•sive [pəzɛ́sɪv] *adj. & s.* posesivo.

pos•ses•sor [pəzɛ́sə·] *s.* poseedor, posesor, dueño.

pos•si•bil•i•ty [pàsəbílətɪ] *s.* posibilidad.

pos•si•ble [pásəb]] *adj.* posible; **possibly** adv. posiblemente; acaso, tal vez.

post [post] *s.* (*pole*) poste, pilar; (*position*) puesto; empleo; **army –** guarnición militar; **– haste** por la posta, rápidamente; **– office** correo, casa de correos; **post-office box** apartado, casilla postal; **– paid** porte pagado, franco de porte; *v.* fijar (*anuncios, carteles*); anunciar; poner en lista, apostar, situar; echar al correo; **to – an entry** asentar o hacer un asiento (*en teneduría*); **to be well -ed** estar al corriente, estar bien enterado.

post•age [póstdʒ] *s.* porte, franqueo, **– stamp** sello de correo, *Am.* estampilla, *Méx., Ríopl.* timbre.

post•al [póst]] *adj.* postal; **– card** tarjeta postal; **– money order** giro postal.

post•card [póstkɑrd] *s.* tarjeta postal.

post•er [póstə·] *s.* cartel, cartelón; fijador de carteles.

pos•te•ri•or [postírɪə·] *adj.* posterior; trasero.

pos•ter•i•ty [postɛ́rətɪ] *s.* posteridad.

post•hu•mous [póst∫ʊməs] *adj.* póstumo.

post•man [póstmən] *s.* cartero.

post•mas•ter [póstmæstə·] *s.* administrador de correos.

post•pone [postpón] *v.* posponer; aplazar, diferir; postergar.

post•pone•ment [postpónmənt] *s.* aplazamiento.

post•script [pósskrɪpt] *s.* posdata.

pos•ture [póst∫ə·] *s.* postura, actitud; posición; *v.* adoptar una postura.

po•sy [pózɪ] *s.* flor.

pot [pɑt] *s.* pote; olla, puchero, cacharro (*de cocina*); bacín, bacinica (*de cámara o recámara*); **flower –** tiesto, maceta; **– bellied** panzudo, barrigón; **– hole** bache.

po•tas•si•um [pətǽsɪəm] *s.* potasio.

po•ta•to [pətéto] *s.* patata, papa; **sweet –** batata, *Méx., C.A., Ch., Andes* camote, *Carib , Ríopl.* boniato.

po•ten•cy [pót n̩ sɪ] *s.* potencia, poder, fuerza.

po•tent [pót n̩ t] *adj.* potente, poderoso, fuerte.

po•ten•tial [pətɛ́n∫əl] *adj. & s.* potencial.

pot•tage [pátɪdʒ] *s.* potaje.

pot•ter [pátə·] *s.* alfarero, fabricante de vasijas o cacharros de barro; **-'s field** cementerio de pobres y desconocidos.

pot•ter•y [pátərɪ] *s.* cerámica, alfarería; vasijas de barro.

pouch [paʊt∫] *s.* bolsa, saquillo; **mail –** valija; **tobacco –** tabaquera, petaca.

poul•tice [póltɪs] *s.* emplasto.

poul•try [póltrɪ] *s.* aves de corral.

pounce [paʊns] *s.* salto (*para agarrar*); zarpada; *v.* **to – into** entrar de sopetón; **to – upon** abalanzarse sobre, saltar sobre, agarrar.

pound [paʊnd] *s.* libra; golpazo; **– sterling** libra esterlina; *v.* golpear, machacar, martillar.

pour [por] *v.* vaciar, verter; servir (*una taza*); fluir; llover a cántaros, llover recio.

pout [paʊt] *v.* hacer pucheros, lloriquear; poner cara de enfado; *s.* puchero, pucherito.

pov•er•ty [pávə·tɪ] *s.* pobreza.

Pow•der [páʊdə·] *s.* polvo; pólvora (*explosivo*); polvos (*de tocador*); **– compact –** polvera; **– magazine** polvorín; **– puff** polvera, borla, *Ríopl., Ch.* cisne, *Méx., Andes* mota; *v.* empolvar(se); polvorear, espolvear; pulverizar(se); to – one's face empolvarse la cara, ponerse polvos.

pow•er [páUə-] *s.* poder; poderío; potencia; fuerza; **motive** − fuerza motriz; **− of attorney** poder; − **plant** planta de fuerza motriz.

pow•er•ful [páUə-fəl] *adj.* poderoso.

pow•er•less [páUə-lIs] *adj.* impotente.

prac•ti•ca•ble [præ ktIkəb]] *adj.* practicable; factible, hacedero; práctico; − **road** camino transitable.

prac•ti•cal [præ ktIk]] *adj.* práctico; − **joke** chasco, burla pesada; **-ly** *adv.* casi, virtualmente; realmente, en realidad; prácticamente.

prac•tice [præ ktIs] *s.* práctica; ejercicio (*de una profesión*); método; regla, costumbre; clientela; *v.* practicar; ejercer (*una profesión*); ejercitarse.

prac•ticed [præ ktIst] *adj.* práctico, experimentado; experto, perito.

prac•ti•tion•er [præktí ∫ənə-] *s.* profesional; práctico.

prai•rie [prérI] *s.* pradera, llanura.

praise [prez] *s.* alabanza; elogio; encomio; *v.* alabar; elogiar; encomiar.

praise•wor•thy [prézw ʒ ðI] *adj.* laudable.

prance [præns] *v.* cabriolar, hacer cabriolas.

prank [præŋk] *s.* travesura, burla; **to play −s** hacer travesuras.

prate [pret] *v.* parlotear, charlar; *s.* parloteo, charla.

prat•tle [præt]] *v.* parlotear, charlar; *s.* parloteo, charla.

pray [pre] *v.* orar; rezar; rogar, suplicar; − **tell me** dígame por favor, le ruego que me diga.

prayer [prɛr] *s.* oración, rezo; ruego, súplica; −**book** devocionario; **Lord´s** − Padre Nuestro.

preach [prit∫] *v.* predicar; sermonear.

preach•er [prít∫ə-] *s.* predicador.

Preach•ing [prít∫ Iŋ] *s.* predicación, sermón; sermoneo.

pre•am•ble [prIæmb]] *s.* preámbulo.

pre•ar•ranged [priəréndʒd] *adj.* arreglado de antemano.

pre•car•i•ous [prIkérIəs] *adj.* precario; inseguro.

pre•cau•tion [prIk ɔ ∫ən] *s.* precaución.

pre•cede [prisíd] *v.* preceder.

prec•e•dence [prisíd ŋ s] *s.* predecencia; prioridad.

prec•e•dent [présədənt] *s.* precedente.

pre•ced•ing [prisídIŋ] *adj.* precedente, anterior.

pre•cept [prísɛpt] *s.* precepto.

pre•cinct [prísIŋkt] *s.* distrito; recinto; **-s** límites, inmediaciones.

pre•cious [pré ∫əs] *adj.* precioso; querido, amado, caro; − **little** poquísimo, muy poco.

prec•i•pice [présəpIs] *s.* precipicio.

pre•cip•i•tate [prIsípətet] *v.* precipitar(se); *adj.* precipitado, apresurado, atropellado; *s.* precipitado.

pre•cip•i•ta•tion [prIsIpəté ∫ən] *s.* precipitación; lluvia (*o* nieve, rocío, granizo, *etc.*); cantidad de agua pluvial.

pre•cip•i•tous [prIsípətəs] *adj.* precipitoso, escarpado; precipitado.

pre•cise [prIsáIs] *adj.* preciso, exacto.

pre•ci•sion [prIsíʒən] *s.* precisión, exactitud.

pre•clude [prIklúd] *v.* excluir; impedir.

pre•co•cious [prIkó ∫əs] *adj.* precoz.

pre•cur•sor [prikə-sə-] *s.* precursor.

pred•e•ces•sor [prɛdIsésə-] *s.* predecesor.

pre•des•ti•ne [prIdéstIn] *v.* predestinar.

pre•dic•a•ment [prIdíkəmənt] *s.* aprieto, apuro, dificultad.

pred•i•cate [prédIkIt] *adj. & s.* predicado.

pre•dict [prIdíkt] *v.* predecir, vaticinar.

pre•dic•tion [prIdík ∫ən] *s.* predicción, pronóstico, vaticinio.

pred•i•lec•tion [prid] ék ∫ən] *s.* predilección, preferencia.

pre•dis•pose [prIdIspóz] *v.* predisponer.

pre•dom•i•nance [prIdámənəns] *s.* predominio; ascendiente.

pre•dom•i•nant [prIdámənənt] *adj.* predominante.

pre•dom•i•nate [prIdámənet] *v.* predominar.

pref•ace [préfIs] *s.* prefacio; prólogo; *v.* prologar.

pre•fect [prífɛkt] *s.* prefecto.

pre•fer [prIf ʒ] *v.* preferir; **to − a claim** presentar una demanda.

pref•er•a•ble [préfrəb]] *adj.* preferible; preferente; **preferably** *adv.* preferiblemente; preferentemente, de preferencia.

pref•er•ence [préfrəns] *s.* preferencia.

pref•er•red [prIf ʒ d] *p.p. & adj.* preferido; − **shares** acciones preferentes.

pre•fix [prIfIks] *s.* prefijo; [prifíks] *v.* prefijar, anteponer.

preg•nan•cy [prégnənsI] *s.* preñez, embarazo.

preg•nant [prégnənt] *adj.* preñado; lleno, repleto; encinta.

prej•u•dice [prédʒədIs] *s.* (*preconception*) prejuicio, prevención; (*harm*) daño; *v.* predisponer, prevenir; perjudicar.

prel•ate [prélIt] *s.* prelado.

pre•lim•i•nar•y [prIlímənɛrI] *adj. & s.* preliminar.

prel•ude [préljud] *s.* preludio; *v.* preludiar.

pre•ma•ture [primətjÚr] *adj.* prematuro.

pre•med•i•tat•ed [prImédətetId] *adj.* premeditado.

pre•mi•er [prímIə-] *s.* primer ministro; *adj.* primero; principal.

prem•ise [prémIs] *s.* premisa; **-s** terrenos; local.

pre•mi•um [prímIəm] *s.* premio; **at a −** muy escaso, muy caro; **insurance** − prima de seguro.

pre•na•tal [prinét]] *adj.* prenatal.

pre•oc•cu•py [priákjəpaɪ] v. preocupar; ocupar de antemano.

pre•or•bital [pri ɔ́ rbɪt]] adj. preorbital.

pre•paid [pripéd] adj. pagado de antemano; **to send** — enviar porte pagado, enviar franco de porte.

prep•a•ra•tion [prɛpəréʃən] s. preparación; preparativo.

pre•par•a•to•ry [prɪpǽ rətorɪ] adj. preparatorio.

pre•pare [prɪpér] v. preparar(se).

pre•par•ed•ness [prɪpérɪdnɪs] s. preparación, prevención.

pre•pon•der•ant [prɪpándrənt] adj. preponderante.

prep•o•si•tion [prɛpəzíʃən] s. preposición.

pre•pos•sess [pripozés] v. preocupar; predisponer.

pre•pos•ter•ous [prɪpástrəs] adj. absurdo, insensato.

pre•req•ui•site [prirékwəzɪt] s. requisito previo.

pre•rog•a•tive [prɪrágətɪv] s. prerrogativa.

pres•age [prɛ́sɪdʒ] s. presagio; [prɪsédʒ] v. presagiar.

pre•scribe [prɪskráɪb] v. prescribir; recetar.

pre•scrip•tion [prɪskríp ʃən] s. receta; prescripción; precepto, mandato.

pres•ence [prɛ́z ŋ s] s. presencia; — **of mind** aplomo, serenidad.

pres•ent [prɛ́z ŋ t] s. (time) presente; (gift) regalo; **at** — al presente, ahora; **for the** — por ahora; adj. presente; corriente, actual; — **company excepted** mejorando lo presente; — **participle** gerundio; **to be** — asistir, estar presente; [prɪzɛ́nt] v. presentar; regalar, obsequiar.

pres•en•ta•tion [prɛz ŋ téʃən] s. presentación; regalo, obsequio.

pre•sen•ti•ment [prɪzɛ́ntəmənt] s. presentimiento; corazonada.

pres•ent•ly [prɛ́z ŋ tlɪ] adv. luego, pronto, dentro de poco.

pres•er•va•tion [prɛzɚvéʃən] s. preservación; conservación.

pre•serve [prɪz ɝ́ v] v. preservar, guardar; conservar; mantener; s. conserva, compota; **forest** — vedado.

pre•side [prizáɪd] v. presidir; **to** — **at** (— **over) a meeting** presidir una junta.

pres•i•den•cy [prɛ́zədənsɪ] s. presidencia.

pres•i•dent [prɛ́zədənt] s. presidente.

pres•i•den•tial [prɛzədɛ́nʃəl] adj. presidencial.

press [prɛs] v. (bear down) prensar; apretar; comprimir; planchar (ropa); (force) fozar; apremiar; urgir; empujar; **to** — **forward** empujar hacia delante; avanzar, ganar terreno; **to** — **one´s point** pofiar; insistir en su augumento; **to** — **through the crowd** abrirse paso por entre la multitud; **to be hard -ed**

by work estar abrumado de trabajo; **to be hard -ed for money** estar escaso de fondos; s. prensa; imprenta.

press•ing [prɛ́sɪŋ] adj. apremiante, urgente.

pres•sure [prɛ́ʃɚ] s. presión; apremio, urgencia; — **cooker** cocinilla de presión; - **gauge** manómentro.

pres•sur•ize [prɛ́ʃɚaɪz] v. sobrecargar.

pres•tige [prɛstíʒ] s. prestigio.

pre•sum•a•ble [prɪsúməb]] adj. presumible, probable.

pre•sume [prɪzúm] v. presumir; suponer; **to** — **on (upon)** abusar de; **to** — **to** atreverse a.

pre•sump•tion [prɪz ʌ mpʃən] s. presunción; pretención; suposición.

pre•sump•tu•ous [prɪz ʌ mptʃUəs] adj. presuntuoso, pretencioso, presumido.

pre•sup•pose [prisəpóz] v. presuponer.

pre•tend [prɪténd] v. pretender; fingir.

pre•tense [prɪténs] s. pretensión; presunción; ostentación; aparencia; pretexto; **under** — **of** so pretexto de.

pre•ten•sion [prɪtén ʃən] s. pretensión; pretexto.

pre•ten•tious [prɪtén ʃəs] adj. pretencioso.

pre•text [prítɛkst] s. pretexto.

pret•ti•ly [prítɪlɪ] adv. lindamente; agradablemente.

pret•ti•ness [prítɪnɪs] s. lindeza, gracia.

pret•ty [prítɪ] adj. lindo, bonito, bello, Am. chulo; adv. medianamente; bastante; un poco, algo; — **well** regular, así así; bastante bien, medianamente.

pre•vail [prɪvél] v. prevalecer; **to** — **on (upon)** persuadir.

pre•vail•ing [prɪvélɪŋ] adj. predominante; en boga.

prev•a•lent [prɛ́vələnt] adj. prevaleciente; común, corriente.

pre•vent [prɪvɛ́nt] v. prevenir, evitar; impedir; estorbar.

pre•ven•tion [prɪvɛ́n ʃən] s. prevención; precaución.

pre•ven•tive [prɪvɛ́ntɪv] adj. impeditivo.

pre•view [prívju] s. vista previa (anticipada).

pre•vi•ous [prívɪəs] adj. previo; **-ly** adv. previamente; antes; de antemano.

prey [pre] s. presa; víctima; **birds of** — aves de rapiña; v. **to** — **on** cazar; rapiñar, pillar; robar; **it -s upon my mind** me tiene preocupado, me tiene en zozobra.

price [praɪs] s. precio; valor; costo (coste o costa); **at any** — a toda costa, a todo trance; v. apreciar, valuar, fijar el precio de; averiguar el precio de.

price•less [práɪslɪs] adj. sin precio, inapreciable.

prick [prɪk] v. picar; pinchar; punzar; sentir comezón; sentir picazón; **to** — **up one´s ears** aguzar las orejas; s. picadura; punzada; pinchazo; piquete; aguijón; púa.

prick•ly [príklɪ] *adj.* espinoso, lleno de espinas; lleno de púas; **– heat** picazón causada por el calor; **– pear** tuna (*de nopal*).

pride [praɪd] *s.* orgullo; soberbia; *v.* **to – oneself on (upon)** enorgullecerse de, preciarse de.

priest [prist] *s.* sacerdote.

priest•hood [prísthʊd] *s.* sacerdocio.

prim [prɪm] *adj.* remilgado; repulido; peripuesto; estirado.

pri•mar•i•ly [praɪmérəlɪ] *adj.* primariamente, principalmente; en primer lugar.

pri•mar•y [práɪmerɪ] *adj.* (*first*) primario; primero; (*basic*) fundamental; principal; **– colors** colores elementales; **– election** elección primaria; **– school** escuela primaria.

prime [praɪm] *adj.* (*main*) principal; primario, primero; (*select*) selecto, de primera calidad; **– minister** primer ministro; **– number** número primo; *s.* flor (*de la vida o de la edad*); la flor y nata (*lo mejor*); plenitud; número primo; **to be in one's –** estar en la flor de la edad; *v.* preparar, informar, instruir de antemano; cebar (un carburador, bomba o arma de fuego).

prim•er [prɪmə] *s.* abecedario, cartilla de lectura; compendio.

pri•me•val [praɪmívl̩] *adj.* primitivo.

prim•i•tive [prímətɪv] *adj.* primitivo.

prim•ness [prímnɪs] *s.* remilgo, tiesura, demasiada formalidad, dengue, afectación.

primp [prɪmp] *v.* acicalar(se), adornar(se), arreglar(se).

prim•rose [prímroz] *s.* prímula o primavera (*flor*); color amarillo pálido.

prince [prɪns] *s.* príncipe.

prince•ly [prínslɪ] *adj.* noble, regio, magnífico, propio de un príncipe.

prin•cess [prínsɪs] *s.* princesa.

prin•ci•pal [prínsəpl̩] *adj.* principal; *s.* principal, capital; principal, jefe, director.

prin•ci•ple [prínsəpl̩] *s.* principio; regla, ley; fundamento, base.

print [prɪnt] *s.* (*type*) tipo, letra de molde; (*art*) lámina, grabado; estampado (*tejido estampado*); diseño (*estampado*); impresión; **in –** impreso, publicado; **out of –** agotado; *v.* imprimir; estampar; escribir en letra de molde; **-ed fabric** estampado.

print•er [príntə] *s.* impresor.

print•ing [príntɪŋ] *s.* imprenta; impresión; tipografía; **– office** imprenta; **– press** prensa.

pri•or [práɪə] *adj.* previo, anterior, precedente; **– to** anterior a, con antelación a; *s.* prior (*de un monasterio*).

pri•or•i•ty [praɪ ɔ́ rətɪ] *s.* prioridad, precedencia, antelación.

prism [prízəm] *s.* prisma.

pris•on [prízn̩] *s.* prisión, cárcel; *v.* encarcelar.

pris•on•er [prízn̩ə] *s.* prisionero, preso.

pri•va•cy [práɪvəsɪ] *s.* secreto, reserva; retiro; **to have no –** carecer de sitio privado; estar a la vista del público.

pri•vate [práɪvɪt] *adj.* privado; personal; particular; secreto; confidencial; **a – citizen** un particular; **– school** escuela particular; *s.* soldado raso; **in –** en secreto; a solas, privadamente.

pri•va•tion [praɪvéʃən] *s.* privación.

priv•i•lege [prívlɪdʒ] *s.* privilegio.

priv•i•le•ged [prívlɪdʒd] *adj.* privilegiado; **to be – to** tener el privilegio de.

priv•y [prívɪ] *adj.* privado; enterado de; *s.* excusado exterior.

prize [praɪz] *s.* (*reward*) premio, galardón; (*booty*) presa, botín de guerra; **– fight** boxeo público, pugilato; **– fighter** boxeador, pugilista; **- medal** medalla de premio; *v.* apreciar, estimar, tener en gran estima.

prob•a•bil•i•ty [prɑbəbíləɪ] *s.* probabilidad.

prob•a•ble [prɑ́bəb] *adj.* probable; **probably** *adv.* probablemente.

pro•ba•tion [probéʃən] *s.* probación; noviciado; prueba; **to put a prisoner on –** poner a un prisionero en libertad bajo la vigilancia de un juez.

probe [prob] *v.* tentar, reconocer, sondear (*una herida*); escudriñar, examinar a fondo; indagar; *s.* tienta (*instrumento de cirujano*); indagación.

prob•lem [prɑ́bləm] *s.* problema.

pro•ce•dure [prəsídʒə] *s.* procedimiento; proceder.

pro•ceed [prəsíd] *v.* proceder; proseguir; seguir adelante; **to – to** proceder a, comenzar a, ponerse a.

pro•ceed•ing [prəsídɪŋ] *s.* procedimiento; transacción; **-s** transacciones; actas; proceso.

pro•ceeds [prósidz] *s. pl.* producto, ganancia.

proc•ess [prásɛs] *s.* (*series*) proceso; (*method*) procedimiento método; **in – of time** con el transcurso del tiempo, con el tiempo, andando el tiempo; **in the – of being made** en vía de preparación; *v.* preparar mediante un proceso especial, someter a un procedimiento; procesar (*ante un juez*).

pro•ces•sion [prəsɛ́ʃən] *s.* procesión; desfile; **funeral –** cortejo fúnebre.

pro•claim [proklém] *v.* proclamar; promulgar.

proc•la•ma•tion [prɑkləméʃən] *s.* proclamación; proclama.

pro•cliv•i•ty [proklívɪtɪ] *s.* inclinación.

pro•cure [prokjʊ́r] *v.* procurar, conseguir, obtener.

prod [prɑd] *v.* aguijonear; picar.

prod•i•gal [prɑ́dɪg] *adj. & s.* pródigo, gastador.

pro•di•gious [prədídʒəs] *adj.* prodigioso.

prod•i•gy [prádədʒɪ] s. prodigio.
pro•duce [prádjus] s. producto; productos agrícolas; [prədjús] v. producir.
pro•duc•er [prədjúsə] s. productor; **theatrical —** empresario.
prod•uct [prádəkt] s. producto.
pro•duc•tion [prəd ʌ k ʃ ən] s. producción; producto; obra, composición; representación teatral.
pro•duc•tive [prəd ʌ ktɪv] adj. productivo.
profa•na•tion [profənéʃən] s. profanación, desacato.
pro•fane [prəfén] adj. profano; v. profanar.
pro•fess [prəfɛs] v. profesar; pretender.
pro•fes•sion [prəfɛʃən] s. profesión.
pro•fes•sion•al [prəfɛʃən] adj. profesional; s. profesional, Méx. profesionista.
pro•fes•sor [prəfɛsə] s. profesor, catedrático.
prof•fer [prafə] s. oferta, propuesta; v. ofrecer, proponer.
pro•fi•cien•cy [prəfíʃənsɪ] s. pericia, destreza.
pro•fi•cient [prəfíʃənt] adj. proficiente, perito, experto.
pro•file [prófaɪl] s. perfil; contorno.
prof•it [práfɪt] s. (gain) ganancia; lucro; (usefulness) provecho, utilidad, beneficio; **— and loss** pérdidas y ganancias; **net —** ganancia neta o líquida; v. aprovechar; ganar, sacar provecho; **to — by** aprovecharse de, sacar provecho de.
prof•it•a•ble [práfɪtəb] adj. provechoso; lucrativo.
prof•i•teer [profətír] s. extorsionista, carero, explotador, logrero; v. extorsionar, explotar, cobrar más de lo justo.
pro•found [prəfáʊnd] adj. profundo.
pro•fuse [prəfjús] adj. profuso, abundante; pródigo.
prog•e•ny [prádʒenɪ] s. prole.
prog•no•sis [prəgnósɪs] s. pronóstico.
pro•gram [prógræm] s. programa; plan.
prog•ress [prágrɛs] s. progreso; [prəgrɛs] v. progresar.
pro•gres•sive [prəgrɛsɪv] adj. progresivo; progresista; s. progresista.
pro•hib•it [prohíbɪt] v. prohibir; vedar.
pro•hi•bi•tion [proəbíʃən] s. prohibición.
proj•ect [prádʒɛkt] s. proyecto, plan; [prədʒɛk] v. proyectar(se); extender(se), sobresalir.
pro•jec•tile [prədʒɛkt] s. proyectil; adj. arrojadizo; **— weapon** arma arrojadiza.
pro•jec•tion [prədʒɛkʃən] s. proyección; saliente, salidizo.
pro•jec•tor [prədʒɛktə] s. proyector.
pro•le•tar•i•an [proletérɪən] s. proletariado.
pro•lif•ic [prolífɪk] adj. prolífico.
pro•logue [prólɔg] s. prólogo.

pro•long [prəl ɔ ŋ] v. prolongar.
pro•lon•ga•tion [prolʊŋgéʃən] s. prolongación.
prom•e•nade [promənéd] s. paseo; baile (usualmente **prom**); v. pasearse.
prom•i•nent [prámənənt] adj. prominente; notable; saliente; conspicuo.
pro•mis•cu•ous [prəmískjʊəs] adj. promiscuo.
prom•ise [prámɪs] s. promesa; v. prometer; **Promised Land** Tierra de Promisión.
prom•is•ing [prámɪsɪŋ] adj. prometedor.
prom•is•so•ry [práməsorɪ] adj. promisorio; **- note** pagaré.
prom•on•to•ry [práməntorɪ] s. promontorio.
pro•mote [prəmót] v. (favor) promover; fomentar; explotar; adelantar; (raise) ascender; elevar.
pro•mot•er [prəmótə] s. promotor, promovedor.
pro•mo•tion [prəmóʃən] s. promoción; ascenso; adelantamiento.
prompt [prompt] adj. pronto, puntual; listo, presto; v. mover, incitar, inducir; apuntar (servir de apuntador en el teatro); soplar (sugerir al otro lo que debe decir en una clase o teatro).
prompt•ly [prámptlɪ] adv. pronto, prontamente, presto; puntualmente; con prontitud, con presteza.
prompt•ness [prámptnɪs] s. prontitud, presteza; puntualidad.
prom•ul•gate [prəm ʌ lget] v. promulgar.
prone [pron] adj. inclinado; propenso, dispuesto; boca abajo; postrado.
prong [prɔŋ] s. púa, punta.
pro•noun [prónaʊn] s. pronombre.
pro•nounce [prənáʊns] v. pronunciar; declarar.
pro•nounced [prənáʊnst] adj. pronunciado, marcado; **— opinions** opiniones decididas.
pro•nun•ci•a•tion [prənʌnsɪéʃən] s. pronunciación.
proof [pruf] s. prueba; comprobación; adj. impenetrable, resistente; **— against** a prueba de; **—reader** corrector de pruebas de imprenta; **— sheet** prueba, pliego de prueba; **galley —** galerada; **bomb —** a prueba de bomba; **fire —** a prueba de incendios; **water—** impermeable.
prop [prap] s. puntal; sostén, apoyo; v. apuntalar, sostener.
prop•a•gan•da [propəgændə] s. propaganda.
prop•a•gate [prápəget] v. propagar(se).
prop•a•ga•tion [propəgéʃən] s. propagación; diseminación.
pro•pel [prəpél] v. propulsar, impeler.
pro•pel•ler [prəpélə] s. hélice (de un buque o avión); propulsor, impulsor.
prop•er [prápə] adj. propio; conveniente a propósito; justo; correcto; **- noun** nombre propio; **-ly** adv. propiamente; con propiedad, correctamente.
prop•er•ty [prápətɪ] s. propiedad; posesión; pose

siones, bienes.

proph·e·cy [práfəsı] s. profecía.

proph·e·sy [práfəsaı] v. profetizar, predecir, pronosticar, augurar.

proph·et [práfıt] s. profeta.

pro·phet·ic [prəfétık] adj. profético.

pro·pi·tious [prəpíʃəs] adj. propicio, favorable.

pro·por·tion [prəpórʃən] s. proporción; **out of —** desproporcionado; v. proporcionar; **well -ed** bien proporcionado.

pro·pos·al [prəpóz]] s. propuesta; proposición; declaración (de amor).

pro·pose [prəpóz] v. proponer; declararse, hacer propuesta de matrimonio; **to — to do something** proponerse hacer algo.

prop·o·si·tion [prapəzíʃən] s. proposición; propuesta; asunto.

pro·pri·e·tor [prəpráıətə-] s. propietario, dueño.

pro·pri·e·ty [prəpráıətı] s. propiedad, corrección; decoro.

pro·pul·sion [prop ʌlʃən] s. propulsión.

pro·rate [prorét] v. prorratear, repartir proporcionalmente.

pro·sa·ic [prozéık] adj. prosaico.

prose [proz] s. prosa; adj. prosaico.

pros·e·cute [prásıkjut] v. procesar, enjuiciar, demandar ante un juez; llevar adelante (un negocio, empresa, demanda, etc.).

pros·e·cu·tion [prasıkjúʃən] s. prosecución, seguimiento; parte acusadora (en un pleito).

pros·e·cu·tor [prásıkjutə-] s. fiscal; acusador.

pros·pect [práspɛkt] s. (hope) perspectiva, vista; esperanza; expectativa; (candidate) cliente; (chances) probabilidad de éxito; v. explorar, andar en busca de.

pro·spec·tive [prəspéktıv] adj. probable, posible, esperado; presunto.

pros·pec·tor [prəspéktə-] s. explorador, buscador (de minas, petróleo, etc.).

pros·per [práspə-] v. prosperar, medrar.

pros·per·i·ty [prɑspérətı] s. properidad.

pros·per·ous [práspərəs] adj. próspero.

pros·ti·tute [prástətjut] s. ramera, prostituta; v. prostituir.

pros·trate [prástret] adj. postrado; abatido; v. postrar; abatir.

pro·tag·o·nist [protǽɡənıst] s. protagonista.

pro·tect [prətɛ́kt] v. proteger.

pro·tec·tion [prətɛ́kʃən] s. protección; amparo.

pro·tec·tive [prətɛ́ktıv] adj. protector; **— tariff** tarifa proteccionista.

pro·tec·tor [prətɛ́ktə-] s. protector.

pro·tec·tor·ate [prətɛ́ktrıt] s. protectorado.

pro·té·gé [prótəɡe] s. protegido.

pro·tein [prótiın] s. proteína.

pro·test [prótɛst] s. protesta, protestación; [prətést] v. protestar.

prot·es·tant [prátıstənt] adj. & s. protestante.

prot·es·ta·tion [pratəstéʃən] s. protestación, protesta.

pro·to·plasm [prótəplæzəm] s. protoplasma.

pro·to·type [prótotaıp] s. prototipo.

pro·tract [protrǽkt] v. alargar, extender, prolongar.

pro·trude [protrúd] v. sobresalir; resaltar; proyectar(se).

pro·tu·ber·ance [protjúbərəns] s. protuberancia.

proud [praUd] adj. orgulloso; soberbio.

prove [pruv] v. probar; demostrar; comprobar; resultar.

prov·erb [práv ɝ b] s. proverbio; refrán.

pro·vide [prəváıd] v. proveer; abastecer; suplir; estipular; **to — for** hacer provisión para; **to — with** proveer de.

pro·vid·ed [prəváıdıd] conj. con tal (de) que, a condición (de) que; **— that** con tal (de) que.

prov·i·dence [právədəns] s. providencia.

prov·i·den·tial [pravədénʃəl] adj. providencial.

pro·vid·er [prəváıdə-] s. proveedor.

prov·ince [právıns] s. provincia; jurisdicción; **it isn't within my —** no está dentro de mi jurisdicción; no es de mi incumbencia.

pro·vin·cial [prəvínʃəl] adj. provincial; s. provinciano.

pro·vi·sion [prəvíʒən] s. (goods) provisión; abastecimiento; (plan) estipulación; **-s** provisiones; víveres; **to make the necessary -s** tomar las medidas (o precauciones) necesarias.

pro·vi·so [prəváızo] s. condición, estipulación.

prov·o·ca·tion [pravəkéʃən] s. provocación.

pro·voke [prəvók] v. provocar; irritar; enfadar.

prow [praU] s. proa.

prow·ess [práUıs] s. proeza.

prowl [praUl] v. rondar en acecho; fisgonear.

prox·im·i·ty [praksímətı] s. proximidad.

prox·y [práksı] s. apoderado, substituto, delegado; **by —** mediante apoderado.

prude [prud] s. mojigato, persona gazmoña.

pru·dence [prúd ŋ s] s. prudencia.

pru·dent [prúd ŋ t] adj. prudente.

prud·er·y [prúdərı] s. mojigatería, gazmoñería, remilgo.

prud·ish [prúdıʃ] adj. gazmoño, remilgado.

prune [prun] s. ciruela; ciruela pasa; v. podar, recortar.

pry [praı] v. atisbar, espiar; figar, fisgonear; curiosear; **to — a secret out** extraer (o arrancar) un secreto; **to — apart** separar por fuerza; **to — into other people´s affaire** entremeterse en lo ajeno; **to — open** abrir a la fuerza; **to — up** levantar con una palanca.

psalm [sɑm] s. salmo.

pseu·do·nym [sjúd ŋ Im] s. seudónimo.

psy·chi·a·trist [saɪkáɪətrɪst] s. psiquiatra, alienista.

psy·chi·a·try [saɪkáɪətrɪ] s. psiquiatría.

psy·cho·log·i·cal [saɪkəládʒɪk ǀ ǀ] adj. psicológico.

psy·chol·o·gist [saɪkáledʒɪst] s. psicólogo.

psy·chol·o·gy [saɪkóled ʒɪ] s. psicología.

psy·cho·sis [saɪkósɪs] s. sicosis.

pub·lic [p Á blɪk] adj. público; **— prosecutor** fiscal; s. público.

pub·li·ca·tion [pʌblɪkéʃən] s. publicación.

pub·lic·i·ty [pʌblÍsətɪ] s. publicidad, propaganda.

pub·lish [p Á blɪʃ] v. publicar; editar; **-ing house** editorial o editora.

pub·lish·er [p Á blɪʃə∘] s. publicador; editor.

puck·er [p Á kə∘] v. fruncir.

pud·ding [pÚdɪŋ] s. budín, pudín.

pud·dle [p Á d] s. charco.

puff [pʌf] s. resoplido; bocanada (de humo, vapor, etc.); bullón (de vestido); **— of wind** ráfaga, soplo; **— paste** hojaldre; **cream —** bollo de crema; **powder —** polvera, borla, Méx. mota; Ríopl. cisne; v. resoplar, jadear; echar bocanadas; **to — up** inflar(se); ahuecar(se); hinchar(se).

pug [pʌg] s. perro dogo; **— nose** nariz chata, ñata o respingada.

pull [pUl] v. (tug) tirar de; jalar (halar); (extract) sacar; arrancar; (stretch) estirar; **to — apart** desgarrar; despedazar; descomponer; desmontar; **to — down the curtain** bajar la cortinilla; **to — oneself together** componerse, serenarse; **to — over to the right** hacerse a la derecha, desviarse hacia la derecha; **to — up** arrancar; parar (un caballo, un auto); parar, hacer alto; **to — through** salir de un apuro; sacar (a alguien) de un apuro; **the train -ed into the station** el tren llegó a la estación; s. tirón; estirón; ascenso difícil; esfuerzo (para subir); **to have — tener buenas aldabas, tener influencia.

pul·let [pÚlɪt] s. polla.

pul·ley [pÚlɪ] s. polea; garrucha.

pulp [pʌlp] s. pulpa.

pul·pit [pÚlpɪt] s. púlpito.

pul·sate [p Á lset] v. pulsar, latir.

pulse [pʌls] s. pulso; pulsación.

pul·ver·ize [p Á lvəraɪz] v. pulverizar.

pum·ice [p Á mɪs] s. piedra pómez.

pump [pʌmp] s. bomb (para sacar agua); zapatilla; **gasoline —** bomba de gasolina; **hand —** bomba de mano; **tire —** bomba para neumáticos; v. manejar la bomba, Am. bombear; inflar (un neumático); **to — someone** sacarle (o sonsacarle) a una persona la verdad o un secreto.

pump·kin [p Á mpkɪn] s. calabaza.

pun [pʌn] s. equívoco, retruécano, juego de palabras; v. decir retruécanos o equívocos, jugar del vocablo.

punch [pʌntʃ] s. (blow) puñetazo, puñada; (drink) ponche; (drill) punzón, sacabocados; (vitality) fuerza, empuje; vitalidad; **— bowl** ponchera; v. dar un puñetazo, dar una puñada; punzar, horadar, perforar; **to — a hole** hacer un agujero o perforación.

punc·tu·al [p Á ŋktʃUəl] adj. puntual.

punc·tu·al·i·ty [p Á ŋktʃU ǽ lətɪ] s. puntualidad.

punc·tu·ate [p Á ŋktʃUet] v. puntuar.

punc·tu·a·tion [pʌŋktʃUéʃən] s. puntuación.

punc·ture [p Á ŋktʃə∘] v. picar, punzar, pinchar; agujerar, perforar; **-d tire** neumático picado; s. picadura; pinchazo; perforación; **to have a tire —** tener un neumático picado, tener una llanta o goma picada.

pun·ish [p Á nɪʃ] v. castigar.

pun·ish·ment [p Á nɪʃmənt] s. castigo.

punt [pʌnt] s. puntapié, patada.

pu·ny [pjúnɪ] adj. endeble, débil, flaco, enfermizo; insignificante.

pup [pʌp] s. cachorro.

pu·pil [pjúp ǀ] s. discípulo; **— of the eye** pupila, niña del ojo.

pup·pet [p Á pɪt] s. títere, muñeco, monigote; **— show** títeres.

pup·py [p Á pɪ] s. cachorrito.

pur·chase [p ́ tʃəs] v. comprar; mercar; s. compra; merca; **to get a — upon** agarrarse fuerte a.

pur·chas·er [p ́ tʃəsə∘] s. comprador, marchante.

pure [pjUr] adj. puro; **-ly** adv. puramente; meramente.

pu·rée [pjUré] s. puré.

pur·ga·tive [p ́ gətɪv] adj. purgante; s. purga, purgante.

pur·ga·to·ry [p ́ gətorɪ] s. purgatorio.

purge [p ́ dʒ] v. purgar(se); limpiar; purificar(se); s. purga, purgante.

pu·ri·fy [pjÚrəfaɪ] v. purificar(se); depurar.

pur·ist [pjÚrɪst] s. purista.

pu·ri·ty [pjÚrətɪ] s. pureza.

pur·ple [p ́ p] s. púrpura; adj. purpúreo, morado.

pur·port [p ́ port] s. significado; tenor, sustancia; [pə∘pórt] v. pretender, aparentar.

pur·pose [p ́ pəs] s. (intention) propósito, intención; (goal) fin, objeto; **for no —** sin objeto, inútilmente, en vano, para nada; **on —** adrede, de propósito; v. proponerse.

purr [p ́] s. ronroneo (del gato); zumbido (del motor); v. ronronear (el gato).

purse [pés] *s.* bolsillo, portamonedas, bolsa; *v.* **to – one´s lips** fruncir los labios.

pur·su·ant [pə·súənt] *adv.* conforme; de acuerdo con.

pur·sue [pə·sú] *v.* perseguir; seguir; dedicarse a (*una carrera, un estudio*).

pur·su·er [pə·súə·] *s.* perseguidor.

pur·suit [pə·sút] *s.* perseguimiento; busca; ocupación; ejercicio (*de una profesión, cargo, etc.*); **in – of** a caza de, en seguimiento de, en busca de.

pus [pʌs] *s.* pus, podre.

push [pUʃ] *v.* (*shove*) empujar; (promote) fomentar, promover; (*hurry*) apresurar; **to – aside** hacer a un lado, rechazar, apartar; **to – forward** empujar, abrirse paso; avanzar; **to – through** encajar (*encajar por un agujero o rendija*); abrirse paso a empujones; *s.* empuje; empujón, empellón; **– button** botón eléctrico.

push·cart [pUʃkart] *s.* carretilla de manos.

puss·y [pUsɪ] *s.* minino, gatito; **– willow** especie de sauce americano.

put [pUt] *v.* poner; colocar; **to – a question** hacer una pregunta; **to – across an idea** darse a entender bien; hacer aceptar una idea; **to – away** apartar; guardar; **to – before** poner delante, anteponer; proponer ante; **to – by money** ahorrar o guardar dinero; **to – down** apuntar, anotar; sofocar (*una revolución*); rebajar (*los precios*); **to – in words** expresar; **to – in writing** poner por escrito; **to – off** aplazar, posponer; diferir; **to – on** ponerse (*ropa*); **to – on airs** darse tono o ínfulas; **to – on weight** engordar; **to – out** apagar, extinguir; **to – someone out** echar o expulsar a alguien ; molestar o incomodar a alguien; **to – to shame** avergonzar; **to – up** enlatar, envasar (*frutas, legumbres*); apostar (*dinero*); alojar(se); erigir; **to – up for sale** poner de venta; **to – up with** aguantar, tolerar; *pret. & p.p. de* **to put.**

pu·tre·fy [pjútrəfaɪ] *v.* podrir (*o* pudrir), corromper.

pu·trid [pjútrɪd] *adj.* putrefacto, podrido.

put·ter [p ʌ́ tə·] *v.* trabajar sin orden ni sistema; ocuparse en cosas de poca monta; malgastar el tiempo.

put·ty [p ʌ́ tɪ] *s.* masilla; *v.* tapar o rellenar con masilla.

puz·zle [p ʌ́ z]] *s.* rompecabezas, acertijo; enigma; **crossword –** crucigrama; *v.* embrollar, poner perplejo, confundir; **to – out** desenredar, descifrar; **to – over** ponderar; tratar de resolver o descifrar; **to be -d** estar perplejo.

pyr·a·mid [pírəmɪd] *s.* pirámide.

Q

quack [kwæk] *s.* graznido (*del pato*); curandero, matasanos, medicastro; charlatán; *adj.* falso; *v.* graznar.

quag·mire [kw ǽ gmaɪr] *s.* tremendal, cenagal.

quail [kwel] *s.* codorniz.

quaint [kwent] *adj.* raro, extraño; pintoresco.

quake [kwek] *s.* temblor; terremoto; *v.* temblar.

qual·i·fi·ca·tion [kwɑləfəké ʃ ən] *s.* (*condition*) calificación; cualidad, calidad; (*requirement*) requisito; aptitud.

qual·i·fy [kwɑ́ ləfaɪ] *v.* calificar; capacitar; **to – for a position** estar capacitado para una posición; **his studies – him for the job** sus estudios le capacitan para el puesto.

qual·i·ty [kwɑ́ lətɪ] *s.* cualidad; calidad.

qualm [kwɑm] *s.* escrúpulo.

quan·ti·fy [kwɑ́ ntɪfaɪ] *v.* cuantificar.

quan·ti·ty [kwɑ́ ntətɪ] *s.* cantidad.

quar·an·tine [kw ɔ́ rəntin] *s.* cuarentena; *v.* poner en cuarentena, aislar.

quar·rel [kw ɔ́ rəl] *s.* riña, reyerta, pendencia; querella; *v.* reñir; pelear, disputar.

quar·rel·some [kw ɔ́ rəlsəm] *adj.* reñidor, pendenciero.

quar·ry [kw ɔ́ rɪ] *s.* cantera; presa, caza (*animal perseguido*); *v.* explotar (*una cantera*); trabajar en una cantera.

quart [kwɔrt] *s.* cuarto de galón (*0.9463 de un litro*).

quar·ter [kw ɔ́ rtə·] *s.* (*one-fourth*) cuarto, cuarta parte; (*coin*) moneda de 25 centavos; (*district*) barrio, distrito; **-s** morada, vivienda; alojamiento; **from all -s** de todas partes; **to give no – to the enemy** no dar cuartel al enemigo; *adj.* cuarto; *v.* cuartear, dividir en cuartos; descuartizar; acuartelar, acantonar, alojar (*tropas*).

quar·ter·ly [kw ɔ́ rtə·lɪ] *adv.* trimestralmente, por trimestres; *adj.* trimestral; *s.* publicación trimestral.

quar·tet [kwɔrtét] *s.* cuarteto.

quartz [kwɔrts] *s.* cuarzo.

qua·ver [kwévə·] *v.* temblar; *s.* temblor, trémolo (*de la voz*).

quay [ki] *s.* muelle, embarcadero.

queen [kwin] *s.* reina.

queer [kwɪr] *adj.* raro, extraño, singular; excéntrico; **to feel –** sentirse raro, no sentirse bien; *v.* poner en ridículo, comprometer; **to – oneself with** quedar mal con, ponerse mal con.

quell [kwɛl] *v.* reprimir; sofocar (*una revuelta*); calmar.

quench [kwɛntʃ] *v.* apagar (*el fuego, la sed*); reprimir, sofocar, ahogar; templar el ardor de.

que•ry [kwɪ́rɪ] s. (*interrogation*) pregunta; interrogación, signo de interrogación; (*doubt*) duda; v. preguntar, expresar duda; marcar con signo de interrogación.

quest [kwɛst] s. busca; pesquisa.

ques•tion [kwɛ́stʃən] s. (*interrogation*) pregunta; (*issue*) cuestión; problema; duda; proposición; - **mark** signo de interrogación; **beyond —** fuera de duda; **that is out of the —** ¡imposible!; ¡ni pensar en ello!; v. preguntar; interrogar; dudar.

ques•tion•a•ble [kwɛ́stʃənəb]] adj. dudoso; discutible.

ques•tion•er [kwɛ́stʃənɚ] s. interrogador, preguntador.

ques•tion•ing [kwɛ́stʃənɪŋ] s. interrogatorio; adj. interrogador.

ques•tion•naire [kwɛstʃənέr] s. cuestionario, lista de preguntas, interrogatorio.

quib•ble [kwɪ́b]] v. sutilizar, valerse de argucias o sutilezas; andar en dimes y diretes; s. sutileza, argucia.

quick [kwɪk] adj. (*soon*) pronto, presto; (*smart*) listo; (*speedy*) rápido, veloz; agudo; **— temper** genio violento; **— wit** mente aguda; adv. rápidamente, de prisa, con prisa, pronto; s. carne viva; **to cut to the —** herir en lo vivo, herir en el alma.

quick•en [kwɪ́kən] v. acelerar(se); avivar(se); aguzar (*la mente, el entendimiento*).

quick•ly [kwɪ́klɪ] adv. pronto, presto, de prisa, aprisa, rápidamente.

quick•ness [kwɪ́knɪs] s. (*speed*) rapidez; presteza, prontitud; (*alertness*) vivezal; agudeza (*de ingenio*).

quick•sand [kwɪ́ksænd] s. arena movediza.

quick•sil•ver [kwɪ́ksɪlvɚ] s. mercurio, azogue.

qui•et [kwáɪət] adj. quieto; callado; tranquilo; en calma; reposado; s. quietud; sosiego, reposo; calma; silencio; v. aquietar; sosegar; calmar, tranquilizar; **to — down** aquietarse; calmarse; **-ly** adv. quietamente, con quietud; calladamente; tranquilamente.

qui•et•ness [kwáɪətnɪs] s. quietud; sosiego, calma.

quill [kwɪl] s. pluma; cañón (*de pluma de ave*); púa (*de puerco espín*).

quilt [kwɪlt] s. colcha; v. acolchar.

quince [kwɪns] s. membrillo.

qui•nine [kwáɪnaɪn] s. quinina.

quip [kwɪp] s. pulla, dicharacho; agudeza.

quirk [kwɚk] s. chifladura, extravagancia, capricho; peculiaridad mental.

quit [kwɪt] v. (*abandon*) dejar, abandonar; irse; (*cease*) parar, cesar; **to — doing something** dejar de hacer algo; **-s** adj. desquitado; **we are -s** no nos debemos nada, estamos desquitados, Am. estamos a mano; pret. & p.p. de **to quit**.

quite [kwaɪt] adv. bastante; del todo, enteramente; **— a person** una persona admirable; **— so** así es, en efecto; **it´s — the fashion** está muy en boga.

quit•ter [kwɪ́tɚ] s. el que deja fácilmente lo empezado, el que se da fácilmente por vencido; evasor; desertor.

quiv•er [kwɪ́vɚ] v. temblar; estremecerse; s. temblor; estremecimiento.

quiz [kwɪz] s. examen; interrogatorio; cuestionario; v. examinar, interrogar, hacer preguntas.

quiz•zi•cal [kwɪ́zək]] adj. curioso; burlón.

quo•ta [kwótə] s. cuota.

quo•ta•tion [kwotéʃən] s. citación, cita; cotización (*de precios*); **— marks** comillas.

quote [kwot] v. citar; cotizar (*precios*); **to —from** citar a, entresacar una cita de; s. cita, citación; **-s** comillas; **in -s** entre comillas.

quo•tient [kwóʃənt] s. cociente.

R

rab•bi [rǽbaɪ] s. rabí, rabino.

rab•bit [rǽbɪt] s. conejo.

rab•ble [rǽb]] s. populacho, plebe; canalla.

rab•id [rǽbəd] adj. rabioso.

ra•bies [rébiz] s. rabia, hidrofobia.

rac•coon [rækún] s. Méx., C.A., Andes mapache.

race [res] s. (*lineage*) raza; (*competition*) corrida, carrera; contienda; **— track** (o **— course**) pista; **boat — regata**; v. correr; competir en una carrera; ir corriendo; regatear (*competir en una regata*); acelerar (*un motor*).

rac•er [résɚ] s. corredor; caballo de carrera; auto de carrera.

ra•cial [réʃəl] adj. racial.

rac•ism [résɪzm] s. racismo.

rack [ræk] s. (*framework*) percha, colgadero, clavijero; (*torture*) potro de tormento; **baggage —** red; **towel — toallero; to fall Into — and ruin** caer en un estado de ruina total; v. atormentar; **to — one´s brain** devanarse los sesos, quebrarse uno la cabeza.

rack•et [r | kɪt] s. (*instrument*) raqueta (*de tenis*); (*noise*) boruca, estrépito; baraúnda; bullicio; trapacería.

rack•et•eer [rækɪtɪ́r] s. trapacista, trapacero, extorsionista; v. trapacear, extorsionar.

ra•dar [rédor] s. radar.

ra•di•al [rédɪəl] adj. radial.

ra•di•ance [rédɪəns] s. resplandor, brillo.

ra•di•ant [rédɪənt] adj. radiante; resplandeciente, brillante.

ra•di•ate [rédɪet] v. irradiar; radiar.

ra•di•a•tor [rédɪetɚ] s. radiador; calorífero.

rad•i•cal [r | dɪk]] adj. & s. radical.

ra·di·o [rédɪo] s. radio (m. o f.); radiotelefonía; radiotelegrafía; – **commentator** comentarista radial; – **listener** radioescucha, radioyente; – **program** programa radiofónico; **by** – por radio; v. radiar, emitir, transmitir, radiodifundir o difundir.

ra·di·o·ac·tive [redɪoˈæktɪv] adj. radioactivo.

ra·di·ol·o·gy [redɪóɪˈlədʒɪ] s. radiología.

rad·ish [rˈdɪʃ] s. rábano.

ra·di·um [rédɪəm] s. radio (elemento químico).

ra·di·us [rédɪəs] s. radio (de un círculo).

raf·fle [rˈæfl] v. rifa, sorteo; v. rifar, sortear.

raft [ræft] s. balsa; **a – of things** un montón (o la mar) de cosas.

raft·er [rˈæftɚ] s. viga (del techo).

rag [ræg] s. trapo; harapo, andrajo, Am. hilacho; – **doll** muñeca de trapo; **to be in –s** estar hecho andrajos, Am. estar hecho tiras.

rag·a·muf·fin [rˈægəmʌfɪn] s. pelagatos, golfo; granuja, pilluelo.

rage [redʒ] s. rabia, furor; ira; **to be all the** – estar en boga, estar de moda; v. rabiar; enfurecerse; estar enfurecido; bramar; **to – with anger** bramar de ira.

rag·ged [rˈægɪd] adj. andrajoso, harapiento, haraposo, desarrapado, roto; – **edge** borde raído o deshilachado; **to be on the – edge** estar al borde del precipicio; estar muy nervioso.

raid [red] s. incursión, invasión repentina; allanamiento. (de un local); **air** – ataque aéreo, bombardeo aéreo; v. hacer una incursión; invadir de repente; caer sobre; allanar (un local), entrar a la fuerza.

rail [rel] s. (steel bar) riel, carril; (railroad) ferrocarril; (railing) barandal, barandilla; – **fence** empalizada, estacada; **by** – por ferrocarril.

rail·ing [rélɪŋ] s. baranda, barandilla; pasamano (de escalera), balaustrada, barrera; rieles.

rail·road [rélrod] s. ferrocarril; adj. ferroviario; de ferrocarril.

rail·way [rélwe] s. ferrocarril; adj. ferroviario; de ferrocarril; – **crossing** cruce, crucero.

rai·ment [rémənt] s. vestidura, ropaje.

rain [ren] s. lluvia; – **water** agua llovediza; v. llover; – **or shine** que llueva o no; llueva o truene; a todo trance.

rain·bow [rénbo] s. arco iris.

rain·coat [rénkot] s. impermeable; Ch. capa de agua, Méx. manga o capa de hule; Ríopl. piloto.

rain·drop [réndrop] s. gota de agua.

rain·fall [rénfol] s. lluvia, lluvias; cantidad de agua pluvial; aguacero.

rain·y [rénɪ] adj. lluvioso.

raise [rez] v. (lift) levantar, alzar; subir; eregir; (cultivate) criar, cultivar; (collect) reunir; reclutar; **to – a question** hacer una observación o suscitar

una duda; **to – a racket** armar un alboroto; s. aumento de sueldo.

rai·sin [rézn] s. pasa, uva seca.

rake [rek] s. rastro, rastrillo; libertino, perdulario; v. rastrear, rastrillar (la tierra); raspar; barrer (con rastrillo); atizar (el fuego).

ral·ly [rˈælɪ] v. (unite) reunir(se); juntar(se); (improve) recobrar(se); mejorar (de salud); fortalecerse; revivir; tomar nueva vida; **to – to the side of** acudir al lado de; s. junta popular, junta libre; recuperación.

ram [ræm] s. (animal) carnero; (tool) ariete o martillo hidráulico; espolón de buque; **battering** – ariete; apisonar, aplanar a golpes; aplastar de un choque; rellenar, atestar; **to – a boat** chocar con un barco; arremeter contra un barco.

ram·ble [rˈæmbl] v. vagar; divagar; callejear; s. paseo, andanza.

ram·page [rˈæmpedʒ] s. alboroto.

ram·pant [rˈæmpənt] adj. extravagante; desenfrenado.

ram·part [rˈæmpɑrt] s. baluarte, muralla.

ran [ræn] pret. de **to run**.

ranch [ræntʃ] s. hacienda, Méx., C.A. rancho; **cattle** – hacienda de ganado, Méx., C.A. rancho, Ríopl. estancia; Ch. fundo; Ven., Col. hato.

ran·cid [rˈænsɪd] adj. rancio, acedo.

ran·cor [rˈænkɚ] s. rencor, encono.

ran·dom [rˈændəm] adj. impensado; fortuito, al azar; **at** – al azar, a la ventura.

rang [ræŋ] pret. de **to ring**.

range [rendʒ] v. (align) alinear; poner en fila; arreglar; (wander) vagar por; rondar; fluctuar; **to – ten miles** tener un alcance de diez millas (un arma de fuego); s. fila, hilera; alcance; extensión; fluctuación, variación (dentro de ciertos límites); distancia; pastizal, C.A. pastal; estufa; **gas** – cocina de gas; – **of mountains** cordillera, cadena de montañas; – **of vision** campo de visión; **in – with** en línea con; **shooting** – campo de práctica para tirar.

rank [ræŋk] s. (position) rango, categoría; orden; calidad; grado; (line) fila; línea, hilera; **the – and file** el pueblo, la gente ordinaria; la tropa; v. poner en fila; ordenar, arreglar; clasificar; **to – above** sobrepasar a; ser de grado superior a; **to – high** tener un alto rango, categoría o renombre; ser tenido en alta estima; **to – second** tener el segundo lugar; **to – with** estar al nivel de, tener el mismo grado que; **he –s high in athletics** sobresale en los deportes.

ran·sack [rˈænsæk] v. escudriñar; saquear.

ran·som [rˈænsəm] s. rescate; v. rescatar; redimir.

rant [rænt] v. desvariar; disparatar, gritar necedades.

rap [ræp] v. (strike) golpear, dar un golpe; (censure)

criticar, censurar; **to – on the door** llamar o tocar a la puerta; *s.* golpe; **not to care a –** no importarle a uno un ardite.

ra·pa·cious [rəpéʃəs] *adj.* rapaz.

rape [rep] *s.* estupro, violación (*de una mujer*); *v.* forzar, violar (*a una mujer*).

rap·id [rǽpɪd] *adj.* rápido; **-s** *s. pl.* raudal, rápidos (*de un río*).

ra·pid·i·ty [rəpídətɪ] *s.* rapidez, velocidad.

rap·port [rəpɔ́r] *s.* relación de confianza mutua.

rapt [ræpt] *adj.* extasiado; absorto.

rap·ture [rǽptʃə] *s.* éxtasis, rapto.

rare [rɛr] *adj.* (*strange*) extraordinario, extraño; raro; (*precious*) raro; precioso; (*not well-done*) a medio asar, a medio freír, medio crudo; **-ly** adv. rara vez, raras veces; raramente; extraordinariamente.

rar·i·ty [rɛ́rətɪ] *s.* rareza; enrarecimiento (*de la atmósfera*).

ras·cal [rǽsk] *s.* bribón, bellaco, pícaro.

rash [ræʃ] *adj.* temerario, atrevido; precipitado; imprudente; *s.* salpullido, erupción (*de la piel*).

rash·ness [rǽ ʃnɪs] *s.* temeridad.

rasp [ræsp] *v.* chirriar, irritar; *s.* chirrido, sonido áspero; ronquera, carraspera.

rasp·ber·ry [rǽzbɛrɪ] *s.* frambuesa; **– bush** frambueso.

rasp·y [rǽspɪ] *adj.* ronco; áspero.

rat [ræt] *s.* rata; postizo (*para el pelo*).

rate [ret] *s.* proporción; porcentaje, tanto por ciento, *Am.* tipo (de interés); tarifa; precio; **– of exchange** cambio, *Am.* tipo de cambio; **– of increase** incremento proporcional; **at any –** en todo caso, de todos modos; **at that –** a ese paso; en esa proporción; **at the –** of a razón de; **first –** de primera clase o calidad; muy bien; *v.* calificar, clasificar, considerar; tasar, valuar; **he -s as the best** se le considera como el mejor, **he -s high** se le tiene en alta estima.

rath·er [rǽðə] *adv.* algo, un poco, un tanto; más bien; mejor; mejor dicho; **– than** más bien que; **I would – die than** prefiero antes la muerte que; **I would – not go** preferiría no ir.

rat·i·fy [rǽtəfaɪ] *v.* ratificar.

rat·ing [rétɪŋ] *s.* clasificación; rango, grado; clase.

ra·tio [réʃo] *s.* razón, proporción; relación.

ra·tion [réʃən] *s.* ración; *v.* racionar.

ra·tion·al [rǽʃənəl] *adj.* racional.

ra·tion·al·ize [rǽʃənaɪz] *v.* buscar excusas.

ra·tion·ing [réʃənɪŋ] *s.* racionamiento.

rat·tle [rǽt] *v.* traquetear; golpetear; sacudir ruidosamente; confundir, desconcertar; **to – off** decir de corrido (o decir muy aprisa); *s.* traqueteo; golpeteo; **child's –** sonaja, sonajero; **death –** es-

tertor de la muerte.

rat·tle·snake [rǽt snek] *s.* culebra de cascabel, *Ríopl., Ch.* cascabel o cascabela.

rau·cous [rɔ́kəs] *adj.* ronco; estentóreo.

rav·age [rǽvɪdʒ] *s.* estrago, ruina, destrucción; asolamiento; saqueo, pillaje; *v.* asolar, arruinar; pillar, saquear.

rave [rev] *v.* desvariar, delirar, disparatar; bramar; **to – about someone** deshacerse en elogios de alguien.

ra·ven [révən] *s.* cuervo; *adj.* negro lustroso.

rav·en·ous [rǽvənəs] *adj.* voraz; devorador; **to be –** tener un hambre canina.

ra·vine [rəvín] *s.* quebrada, hondonada, barranco (o barranca).

rav·ish [rǽvɪʃ] *v.* encantar; arrebatar; violar (*a una mujer*).

raw [rɔ] *adj.* (*crude*) crudo; áspero; pelado, descarnado; (*untrained*) inexperto, nuevo; **– material** materia prima; **– recruit** recluta nuevo; **– silk** seda en rama, seda cruda; **– sugar** azúcar bruto, azúcar crudo.

raw·hide [rɔ́haɪd] *s.* cuero crudo; **– whip** rebenque.

ray [re] *s.* rayo, raya (*especie de pez*).

ray·on [réan] *s.* rayón, seda artificial.

raze [rez] *v.* arrasar, asolar.

ra·zor [rézə] *s.* navaja de afeitar; **– blade** hoja de afeitar; **safety –** navaja de seguridad.

reach [ritʃ] *v.* (*go as far as*) llegar a; alcanzar; (*touch*) tocar; (*extend*) extenderse; **to – for** tratar de coger; echar mano a; **to – into** meter la mano en; penetrar en; **to – out one's hand** alargar o tender la mano; *s.* alcance; extensión; **beyond his –** fuera de su alcance; **within his –** a su alcance.

re·act [rɪǽkt] *v.* reaccionar.

re·ac·tion [rɪǽkʃən] *s.* reacción.

re·ac·tion·ar·y [rɪǽkʃənɛrɪ] *adj. & s.* reaccionario.

read [rid] *v.* leer; indicar (*dícese de un contador, termómetro, etc.*); **to – law** estudiar derecho; **it –s thus** dice así, reza así; **it –s easily** se lee fácilmente o sin esfuerzo.

read [rɛd] *pret. & p.p.* de **to read**.

read·er [rídə] *s.* lector; libro de lectura.

read·i·ly [rédɪ] *adv.* pronto, con presteza; fácilmente, sin esfuerzo.

read·i·ness [rédɪnɪs] *s.* prontitud, presteza, facilidad; buena disposición; **to be in –** estar preparado, estar listo.

read·ing [rídɪŋ] *s.* lectura; indicación (*de un barómetro, termómetro, etc.*); **– room** sala o salón de lectura.

re·ad·just [riədʒ st] *v.* reajustar, ajustar de nuevo; arreglar de nuevo; readaptar.

re·ad·just·ment [riədʒ ʌ́ stmənt] *s.* reajuste; readaptación; nuevo arreglo.

read·y [rédɪ] *adj.* pronto, listo; preparado; propenso; dispuesto; – **cash** fondos disponibles; dinero a la mano.

read·y-made [rédɪméd] *adj.* hecho, ya hecho.

real [ríəl] *adj.* real, verdadero; **—estate** bienes raíces, bienes inmuebles; **-ly** *adv.* realmente, verdaderamente.

re·al·ism [ríəlɪzəm] *s.* realismo.

re·al·ist [ríəlɪst] *s.* realista; **-ic** *adj.* realista, vivo, natural.

re·al·i·ty [riǽlətɪ] *s.* realidad.

re·al·i·za·tion [rìələzéʃən] *s.* realización; comprensión.

re·al·ize [ríəlaɪz] *v.* (*comprehend*) darse cuenta de, hacerse cargo de; (*achieve*) realizar, efectuar; convertir en dinero.

realm [rɛlm] *s.* reino; dominio, región.

re·al·tor [ríəltə] *s.* corredor de bienes raíces.

reap [rip] *v.* segar; cosechar; recoger; obtener, sacar (*provecho, fruto, etc.*).

reap·er [rípə] *s.* segador, segadora, máquina segadora.

re·ap·pear [riəpír] *v.* reaparecer.

rear [rɪr] *adj.* trasero, posterior; de atrás; – **admiral** contralmirante; – **guard** retaguardia; *s.* espalda, parte de atrás; trasero; fondo (*de una sala, salón, etc.*); cola (*de una fila*); **in the** – detrás, atrás, a la espalda; *v.* criar, educar; encabritarse, empinarse (*el caballo*).

rea·son [ríz ŋ] *s.* razón; causa, motivo; **by** – **of a** causa de; **it stands to** – es razonable; *v.* razonar; **to** – **out** discurrir, razonar.

rea·son·a·ble [ríznəb ḷ] *adj.* razonable, justo; racional; módico, moderado; **reasonably** *adv.* razonablemente; con razón; bastante.

rea·son·ing [ríz ŋ ɪŋ] *s.* razonamiento, raciocinio.

re·as·sure [riəʃúr] *v.* tranquilizar, restaurar la confianza a; asegurar de nuevo.

re·bate [ríbet] *s.* rebaja (*de precios*); *v.* rebajar (*precio*).

reb·el [réb ḷ] *s. & adj.* rebelde; [rɪbél] *v.* rebelarse.

re·bel·lion [rɪbéljən] *s.* rebelión.

re·bel·lious [rɪbéljəs] *adj.* rebelde.

re·birth [rib ɝ́ θ] *s.* renacimiento.

re·bound [rɪbáUnd] *v.* rebotar; repercutir; [ríbaUnd] *s.* rebote; **on the** – de rebote.

re·buff [rɪb ʌ́ f] *s.* desaire; repulsa; *v.* desairar; rechazar.

re·build [ribíld] *v.* reconstruir, reedificar.

re·built [ribílt] *pret. & p.p.* de **to rebuild.**

re·buke [rɪbjúk] *s.* represión, reproche, reprimen-

da, repulsa; *v.* reprender, reprochar.

re·call [ríkɔl] *s.* llamada, aviso (*para hacer volver*); retirada (*de un diplomático*); revocación; [rɪkLI] *v.* recordar; retirar; revocar.

re·ca·pit·u·late [rikəpítʃələt] *v.* recapitular.

re·cede [rɪsíd] *v.* retroceder; retirarse.

re·ceipt [rɪsít] *s.* recibo; fórmula, receta; **-s** entradas, ingresos; **on** – **of** al recibo de; **we are in** – **of your kind letter** … obra en nuestro poder su grata … ; *v.* sellar (*con el recibí*), dar recibo.

re·ceive [rɪsív] *v.* recibir.

re·ceiv·er [rɪsívə] *s.* receptor; recibidor, depositario, síndico; recipiente, receptáculo.

re·cent [rís ŋ t] *adj.* reciente; **-ly** *adv.* recientemente, *Ch., Riopl.* recién (*como en salió recién*); **-ly married** recién casados.

re·cep·ta·cle [rɪséptək ḷ] *s.* receptáculo.

re·cep·tion [rɪsépʃən] *s.* recepción; recibimiento; acogida, acogimiento.

re·cess [rɪsés] *s.* (*niche*) nicho, hueco; (*cessation*) tregua, intermisión; (*period*) hora de recreo o asueto; **in the** —**es of** en la más recóndito de; *v.* suspender el trabajo; levantar (*por corto tiempo*) una sesión; hacer un hueco o nicho en (*la pared*).

re·ces·sion [rɪséʃən] *s.* retroceso; contracción económica.

rec·i·pe [résəpɪ] *s.* receta, fórmula.

re·cip·i·ent [rɪsípɪənt] *s.* recipiente, recibidor; *adj.* receptivo.

re·cip·ro·cal [rɪsíprək ḷ] *adj.* recíproco, mutuo.

re·cip·ro·cate [rɪsíprəkət] *v.* corresponder.

re·cit·al [rɪsáɪt ḷ] *s.* recitación; relación; narración; recital (*músico*).

rec·i·ta·tion [rèsətéʃən] *s.* recitación.

re·cite [rɪsáɪt] *v.* recitar; relatar; decir o dar la lección.

reck·less [réklɪs] *adj.* temerario, atrevido, precipitado; descuidado; – **with one´s money** derrochador.

reck·less·ness [réklɪsnɪs] *s.* temeridad, osadía, descuido.

reck·on [rékən] *v.* contar, computar, calcular; juzgar; suponer; **to** – **on** contar con.

reck·on·ing [rékənɪŋ] *s.* cuenta; ajuste de cuentas; cálculo; **the day of** – el día del juicio.

re·claim [rɪklém] *v.* recobrar, aprovechar (*tierras baldías*); aprovechar o utilizar (*el hule usado*); pedir la devolución de, tratar de recobrar.

re·cline [rɪkláɪn] *v.* reclinar(se), recostar(se).

re·cluse [rɪklús] *adj.* recluso, solitario; *s.* recluso, solitario, ermitaño.

rec·og·ni·tion [rɛkəgníʃən] *s.* reconocimiento.

rec·og·nize [rékəgnaɪz] *v.* reconocer.

re·coil [rɪk ɔ́ɪl] *v.* recular, *Am.* patear (*un arma de fuego*); retroceder, retirarse; *s.* reculada; rebote.

rec·ol·lect [rɛkəlékt] *v.* recordar; [rikəlékt] recobrar, volver a cobrar; recoger, reunir.

rec·ol·lec·tion [rɛkəlɛkʃ ən] s. recuerdo.

rec·om·mend [rɛkəmɛnd] v. recomendar.

rec·om·men·da·tion [rɛkəmɛndéʃ ən] s. recomendación.

rec·om·pense [rékəmpɛns] v. recompensar; s. recompensa.

rec·on·cile [rékənsaɪl] v. reconciliar; ajustar, conciliar; **to – oneself to** resignarse a, conformarse con.

rec·on·cil·i·a·tion [rɛkənsɪlɪéʃ ən] f. reconciliación; ajuste, conciliación; conformidad, resignación.

re·con·noi·ter [rikən ɔ́ɪtə] v. reconocer, explorar; hacer un reconocimiento o exploración.

re·con·sid·er [rikənsíɪdə] v. reconsiderar.

re·con·struct [rikənstr ʌ kt] v. reconstruir, reedificar.

re·con·struc·tion [rikənstr ʌ kʃ ən] s. reconstrucción.

re·cord [rékəd] s. registro; copia oficial de un documento; memoria; historial (de una persona), hoja de servicios; disco (fonográfico); record (en deportes); **to break the speed** – batir el record de velocidad; **an off-the-record remark** una observación que no ha de constar en el acta; observación hecha en confianza; adj. notable, extraordinario; sobresaliente; [rɪk ɔ́ rd] v. registrar; asentar, apuntar; inscribir; grabar en un disco fonográfico.

re·cord·ing [rik ɔ́ rdɪŋ] s. grabación.

re·count [rīkaʊnt] s. recuento, segunda cuenta; [rɪkáʊnt] v. contar, narrar, relatar, referir; [rikáʊnt] recontar, volver a contar.

re·course [rikors] s. recurso, refugio, auxilio; **to have** – **to** recurrir a.

re·cov·er [rɪk ʌ və] v. recobrar(se), recuperar(se); recobrar la salud; reponerse; [rik ʌ və] volver a cubrir.

re·cov·er·y [rɪk ʌ vrɪ] s. recobro, recuperación; cobranza.

rec·re·a·tion [rɛkrɪéʃ ən] s. recreación, recreo.

re·crim·i·nate [rikrímənət] v. recriminar.

re·cruit [rɪkrút] v. reclutar; alistar; s. recluta; novato, nuevo miembro (de una organización).

rec·tan·gle [réktæŋg] s. rectángulo.

rec·ti·fy [réktəfaɪ] v. rectificar.

rec·tor [réktə] s. rector.

rec·tum [réktəm] s. recto.

re·cu·per·ate [rɪkjúpəret] v. recuperar, recobrar; recobrar la salud.

re·cur [rɪkɔ́] v. volver a ocurrir; repetirse; **to – to a matter** volver a un asunto.

red [rɛd] adj. rojo; colorado, encarnado; **red-hot** candente; enfurecido, furioso; muy caliente; **- tape** formalismo, trámites enojosos; **- wine** vino tinto; **to see** – enfurecerse; s. colo rojo; rojo.

red·den [rɛ́d ŋ] v. enrojecer(se); ruborizarse, ponerse rojo; teñir de rojo.

red·dish [rɛ́dɪʃ] adj. rojizo.

re·deem [rɪdím] v. redimir; rescatar; desempeñar (una prenda); cumplir (una promesa).

re·deem·er [rɪdímə·] s. salvador, redentor; **the Redeermer** el Redentor.

re·demp·tion [rɪdɛ́mpʃ ən] s. redención; rescate; **- of a note** pago de una obligación.

red·ness [rɛ́dnɪs] s. rojez o rojura; inflamación.

re·dou·ble [rid ʌ b] v. redoblar; repetir; repercutir.

re·dound [ridáʊnd] v. redundar.

re·dress [rɪdrɛs] v. reparación, enmienda; compensación; desagravio; [rɪdrés] v. enmendar, rectificar, remediar, reparar; desagraviar.

re·duce [rɪdjús] v. reducir; mermar; rebajar; adelgazar(se); subyugar.

re·duc·tion [rɪd ʌ kʃ ən] s. reducción; merma; rebaja.

re·dun·dant [rid ʌ ndənt] adj. redundante.

red·wood [rédwʊd] s. Am. secoya o secuoya (árbol gigantesco de California), madera roja de la secoya.

reed [rid] s. caña; junco, junquillo; lengüeta, boquilla (de ciertos instrumentos de viento); caramillo.

reef [rif] s. arrecife, escollo; banco de arena (en el mar).

reek [rik] v. (fume) exhalar, echar (vaho o vapor); (stink) heder, oler mal; s. hedor, mal olor.

reel [ril] s. (spool) carrete, carretel; (film) cinta cinematográfica; v. aspar, enredar (en carretel); bambolearse, tambalearse; **to – off stories** ensartar cuento tras cuento.

re·e·lect [riəlɛkt] v. reelegir.

re·e·lec·tion [riəlɛkʃən] s. reelección.

re·en·ter [riéntə] v. volver a entrar.

re·es·tab·lish [riəstæblɪʃ] v. restablecer.

re·fer [rɪf ɜ́] v. referir; transmitir, remitir; dejar al juicio o decisión de; referirse, aludir; acudir, recurrir (a un tratado, diccionario, etc.).

ref·e·ree [rɛfərí] s. árbitro; v. arbitrar.

ref·er·ence [réfrəns] s. (mention) referencia; mención, alusión; (sponsor) fiador, el que recomienda a otro; **- book** libro de referencia, libro de consulta; **comercial –s** fiadores, referencias comerciales; **letter of –** carta de recomendación; **with – to** con respecto a, respecto de, en cuanto a.

re·fill [rifíl] v. rellenar.

re·fine [rɪfáɪn] v. refinar, purificar; pulir; perfeccionar.

re·fined [rɪfáɪnd] adj. refinado; pulido, fino, culto.

re·fine·ment [rɪfáɪnmənt] s. refinamiento, finura;

buena crianza; refinación, purificación; perfeccionamiento.

re·fin·er·y [rɪfáɪnərɪ] *s.* refinería.

re·flect [rɪflékt] *v.* reflejar (*luz, calor*); reflexionar; meditar; **to – on one's character** desdecir del carácter de uno.

re·flec·tion [rɪflékʃən] *s.* reflexión; reflejo, imagen; tacha, descrédito; **on –** después de reflexionarlo.

re·flec·tive [rɪfléktɪv] *adj.* reflexivo.

re·flex [rɪfléks] *adj.* reflejo; *s.* reflejo; acción refleja.

re·flex·ive [rɪfléksɪv] *adj.* reflexivo.

re·form [rɪfórm] *v.* reformar(se); *s.* reforma.

ref·or·ma·tion [rɛfəméʃən] *s.* reforma.

re·for·ma·to·ry [rɪfórmətorɪ] *s.* reformatorio.

re·form·er [rɪflmə] *s.* reformador; reformista.

re·frac·tion [rɪfrǽkʃən] *s.* refracción.

re·frac·to·ry [rɪfrǽktərɪ] *adj.* refractario; terço, obstinado, rebelde.

re·frain [rɪfrén] *v.* refrenarse, abstenerse; *s.* estribillo.

re·fresh [rɪfréʃ] *v.* refrescar(se); renovar.

re·fresh·ing [rɪfréʃɪŋ] *adj.* refrescante; renovador, que renueva; placentero.

re·fresh·ment [rɪfréʃmənt] *s.* refresco.

re·frig·er·a·tion [rɪfrɪdʒəréʃən] *s.* refrigeración, enfriamiento.

re·frig·er·a·tor [rɪfrídʒəretə] *s.* nevera, *Am.* refrigerador.

ref·uge [réfjudʒ] *s.* refugio, asilo, amparo.

ref·u·gee [rɛfjUdʒí] *s.* refugiado.

re·fund [rɪfʌnd] *s.* reembolso, reintegro; [rɪfʌnd] *v.* reembolsar, restituir, reintegrar; [rɪfʌnd] consolidar (*una deuda*).

re·fur·bish [rɪfəbɪʃ] *v.* retocar.

re·fus·al [rɪfjúzl] *s.* negativa; desaire; opción (*derecho de recusar un convenio provisional*).

re·fuse [rɪfjúz] *v.* rehusar; negar; desechar; rechazar; **to – to** rehusarse a, negarse a.

ref·use [réfjus] *s.* desechos, basura, sobras, desperdicios.

re·fute [rɪfjút] *v.* refutar.

re·gain [rɪgén] *v.* recobrar; ganar de nuevo.

re·gal [rígl] *adj.* regio, real.

re·gale [rɪgél] *v.* regalar, agasajar; recrear.

re·ga·lia [rɪgélɪə] *s. pl.* galas, decoraciones, insignias.

re·gard [rɪgárd] *v.* (*look*) mirar; (*consider*) considerar; juzgar; estimar; **as –s this** tocante a esto, en cuanto a esto; por lo que toca a esto; *s.* miramiento, consideración; respeto; estima; mirada, **-s** recuerdos, memorias; **in** (o **with**) **– to** con respecto a, tocante a, respecto de.

re·gard·ing [rɪgárdɪŋ] *prep.* tocante a, con respec-

to a, respecto de, relativo a.

re·gard·less [rɪgárdlɪs]: **– of** sin hacer caso de, prescindiendo de.

re·gen·cy [rídʒənsɪ] *s.* regencia.

re·gent [rídʒənt] *s.* regente.

re·gime [rɪʒím] *s.* régimen.

reg·i·ment [rédʒəmənt] *s.* regimiento.

re·gion [rídʒən] *s.* región.

reg·is·ter [rédʒɪstə] *s.* (*recording*) registro; matrícula; (*entry*) archivo; lista; (*machine*) contador; indicador; (*voice*) registro; **cash –** caja registradora; *v.* registrar; matricular(se); inscribir(se); marcar, indicar; mostrar, manifestar; certificar (*una carta*).

reg·is·trar [rédʒɪstror] *s.* registador, archivero.

reg·is·tra·tion [rédʒɪstréʃən] *s.* registro; asiento (*en un libro*); matrícula; inscripción.

Re·gret [rɪgrét] *s.* pesadumbre, dolor; sentimiento, remordimiento; **to send –s** enviar sus excusas (*al rehusar una invitación*); *v.* sentir, lamentar; arrepentirse de.

re·gret·ful [rɪgrétUl] *adj.* deplorable.

re·gret·ta·ble [rɪgrétəbl] *adj.* lamentable.

reg·u·lar [régjələ] *adj.* regular; metódico, ordenado; **a – fool** un verdadero necio, un tonto capirote; **– price** precio corriente; **– soldier** soldado de línea.

reg·u·lar·i·ty [régjəlærətɪ] *s.* regularidad.

reg·u·late [régjəlet] *v.* regular, regularizar.

reg·u·la·tion [rɛgjəléʃən] *s.* regulación; regla, orden; **-s** reglamento; *– uniform* uniforme de regla, uniforme de ordenanza.

reg·u·la·tor [régjələtə] *s.* regulador; registro (*de reloj*).

re·ha·bil·i·tate [rihæbílətət] *v.* rehabilitar.

re·hears·al [rɪhɜ́sl] *s.* ensayo (*de un drama, concierto, etc.*); enumeración, repetición.

re·hearse [rɪhɜ́s] *v.* ensayar; repetir; repasar.

reign [ren] *s.* reino, reinado; *v.* reinar.

re·im·burse [riɪmbɜ́s] *v.* reembolsar.

re·im·burse·ment [riɪmbɜ́smənt] *s.* reembolso, reintegro.

rein [ren] *s.* rienda; *v.* guiar, gobernar; refrenar (*un caballo*).

re·in·car·nate [riɪnkárnet] *v.* reencarnar.

rein·deer [réndɪr] *s.* reno (*especio de ciervo*).

re·in·force [riɪnfórs] *v.* reforzar.

re·in·force·ment [riɪnfórsmənt] *s.* refuerzo.

re·it·er·ate [riítəret] *v.* reiterar, repetir.

re·ject [rɪdʒékt] *v.* rechazar; desechar; descartar; rehusar.

re·joice [rɪdʒɔ́ɪs] *v.* regocijar(se).

re·joic·ing [rɪdʒɔ́ɪsɪŋ] *s.* regocijo, júbilo.

re·join [rɪdʒɔ́ɪn] *v.* reunirse con; volver(se) a unir; [rɪdʒLɪn] replicar.

re·ju·ve·nate [rɪdʒúvənet] v. rejuvenecer.

re·lapse [rɪlǽps] s. recaída; v. recaer, reincidir.

re·late [rɪlét] v. relatar, narrar; relacionar; **it –s to** se relaciona con, se refiere a.

re·lat·ed [rɪlétɪd] adj. relatado, narrado; relacionado; **to become – by marriage** emparentar; **we are –** somos parientes; estamos emparentados.

re·la·tion [rɪléʃən] s. (association) relación; (story) narración; (kinship) parentesco; pariente; **-s** parientes, parentela; **with – to** con relación a, con respecto a, tocante a.

re·la·tion·ship [rɪléʃənʃɪp] s. relación; parentesco.

rel·a·tive [rélətɪv] adj. relativo; s. relativo, pronombre relativo; pariente, deudo; **– to** relativo a; tocante a; referente a.

re·lax [rɪlǽks] v. relajar; aflojar; mitigar(se); esparcirse, recrearse.

re·lax·a·tion [rilækséʃən] s. (loosening) expansión, esparcimiento; aflojamiento o relajamiento; (recreation) solaz, recreo; **– of discipline** relajación de la disciplina; **– of one's mind** esparcimiento del ánimo.

re·lay [ríle] s. relevo, remuda; **– race** carrera de relevo; **electric –** relevador; [rɪlé] v. transmitir, despachar; hacer cundir (una noticia); **to – a broadcast** reemitir (o redifundir) un programa de radio.

re·lease [rɪlís] v. soltar; librar; poner en libertad; relevar, aliviar; **to – a piece of news** hacer pública una nueva; **to – from blame** exonerar; s. liberación; alivio; exoneración; escape.

rel·e·gate [réləget] v. relegar; **to – to a corner** arrinconar, arrumbar.

re·lent [rɪlént] v. mitigar(se); ceder; aplacarse.

re·lent·less [rɪléntlɪs] adj. implacable.

rel·e·vant [réləvənt] adj. pertinente; a propósito.

re·li·a·bil·i·ty [rɪlaɪəbíləti] s. formalidad; puntualidad; integridad.

re·li·a·ble [rɪláɪb‖] adj. formal; puntual; digno de confianza.

re·li·ance [rɪláɪəns] s. confianza; **selfreliance** confianza en sí, confianza en sus propias fuerzas.

rel·ic [rélɪk] s. reliquia.

re·lief [rɪlíf] s. (ease) alivio; descanso, consuelo; (help) ayuda, socorro; (projection) relieve, realce; **low –** bajo relieve; **to be on –** recibir manutención gratuita; **to put in –** realzar, poner en relieve.

re·lieve [rɪlív] v. relevar; librar; ayudar; aliviar; mitigar.

re·li·gion [rɪlídʒən] s. religión.

re·li·gious [rɪlídʒəs] adj. & s. religioso.

re·lin·quish [rɪlíŋkwɪʃ] v. abandonar, dejar.

rel·ish [rélɪʃ] s. (zest) buen sabor; gusto; apetito; goce; (condiment) condimento; entremés; v. saborear, paladear; gustarle a uno, agradarle a uno.

re·luc·tance [rɪlʌ́ktəns] s. repugnancia, renuencia, aversión, desgana.

re·luc·tant [rɪlʌ́ktənt] adj. renuente, refractario, opuesto; **-ly** adv. renuentemente, con renuencia, de mala gana; a redopelo.

re·ly [rɪláɪ] v. **to – on** contar con, confiar en, fiarse de.

re·main [rɪmén] v. quedar(se), permanecer, estarse; restar, faltar.

re·main·der [rɪméndə] s. resto; restante; residuo.

re·mains [rɪménz] s. pl. restos; reliquias; sobras.

re·make [rimék] v. rehacer, hacer de nuevo

re·mark [rɪmɑ́rk] s. observación, nota, reparo; v. notar, observar; **to – on** comentar; aludir a.

re·mark·a·ble [rɪmɑ́rkəb‖] adj. notable; extraordinario; **remarkably** adv. notablemente; extraordinariamente.

rem·e·dy [rémədɪ] s. remedio; cura; v. remediar; curar.

re·mem·ber [rɪmémbə] v. recordar; acordarse; **– me to him** déle Ud. recuerdos (o memorias) de mi parte.

re·mem·brance [rɪmémbrəns] s. recuerdo; recordación; memoria; **-s** recuerdos, saludos.

re·mind [rɪmáɪnd] v. recordar.

re·mind·er [rɪmáɪndə] s. recordatorio, recordativo, memorándum, memoria; advertencia.

re·miss [rɪmís] adj. descuidado, negligente.

re·mis·sion [rɪmíʃən] s. remisión, perdón.

re·mit [rɪmít] v. remitir; remesar, enviar una remesa; perdonar, absolver.

re·mit·tance [rɪmít ŋs] s. remisión, envío, remesa (de fondos).

rem·nant [rémnənt] s. resto; residuo; retazo (de tela, paño, etc.); vestigio.

re·mod·el [rimɑ́d‖] v. rehacer, reconstruir; modelar de nuevo.

re·morse [rɪmɔ́rs] s. remordimiento.

re·mote [rɪmót] adj. remoto; lejano; s. **– control** telecontrol; comando a distancia.

re·mov·al [rɪmúv‖] s. mudanza, traslado; deposición (de un empleo); eliminación; extracción; alejamiento.

re·move [rɪmúv] v. remover; mudar(se), trasladar(se); quitar; eliminar; extirpar; sacar, extraer; deponer (de un empleo); apartar; alejar.

re·moved [rɪmúvd] adj. remoto, distante.

ren·ais·sance [rɛnəsɑ́ns] s. renacimiento.

re·nas·cence [rɪnǽs ŋs] s. renacimiento.

rend [rɛnd] v. desgarrar, rasgar; rajar.

ren·der [réndə] v. dar; entregar; hacer; ejecutar, interpretar (música o un papel dramático); traducir;

to – an account of rendir o dar cuenta de; **to – homage** rendir homenaje; **to – thanks** rendir gracias, dar las gracias; **to – useless** inutilizar, incapacitar.

ren•di•tion [rɛndíʃən] s. (*surrender*) rendición; (*versión*) traducción, ejecución.

re•new [rɪnjú] v. renovar; restaurar; reanudar; prorrogar (*un préstamo*).

re•new•al [rɪnjúəl] s. renovación; reanudación; prórroga.

re•nounce [rɪnáUns] v. renunciar.

ren•o•vate [rɛ́nəvet] v. renovar.

re•nown [rɪnáUn] s. renombre.

re•nowned [rɪnáUnd] adj. renombrado.

rent [rɛnt] s. alquiler; renta, arrendamiento; **it is for** – se alquila, se arrienda; v. alquilar, arrendar.

rent [rɛnt] pret. & p.p. de **to rend;** s. grieta, hendidura; rasgadura, rotura.

rent•al [rɛ́nt]] s. renta, alquiler.

re•o•pen [riópən] v. reabrir(se), volver a abrir(se).

re•pair [rɪpér] v. reparar; remendar; componer; restaurar; **to – to** dirigirse a; s. reparo, reparación; remiendo; compostura; **in** – en buen estado; compuesto.

repa•ra•tion [rɛpəréʃən] s. reparación; desagravio.

rep•ar•tee [rɛpɑrtí] s. respuesta viva; agudeza en el diálogo.

re•pay [rɪpé] v. resarcir; compensar; reembolsar; pagar.

re•pay•ment [rɪpémənt] s. reintegro, pago, devolución, restitución.

re•peal [rɪpíl] v. derogar, abrogar, revocar, abolir (*una ley*); s. abrogación, derogación, revocación, abolición (*de una ley*).

re•peat [rɪpít] v. repetir; s. repetición.

re•peat•ed [rɪpítɪd] adj. repetido; **-ly** adv. repetidamente; repetidas veces, una y otra vez.

re•pel [rɪpél] v. repeler; rechazar; repugnar; **that idea –s me** me repugna (o me es repugnante) esa idea.

re•pel•lent [rɪpélənt] s. repelente; (*water*) impermeable.

re•pent [rɪpént] v. arrepentirse (de).

re•pen•tance [rɪpéntəns] s. arrepentimiento.

re•pen•tant [rɪpéntənt] adj. arrepentido; penitente.

rep•er•toire [rɛ́pətwɑr] s. repertorio.

rep•e•ti•tion [rɛpɪtíʃən] s. repetición.

re•place [rɪplés] v. reponer, volver a colocar; reemplazar; restituir; remudar.

re•placea•ble [rɪpléséb]] adj. reemplazable; sustituible.

re•place•ment [rɪplésmənt] s. reposición; reemplazo; devolución, restitución; substitución.

re•plen•ish [rɪplénɪʃ] v. reabastecer; rellenar, llenar.

re•plete [rɪplít] adj. repleto, atestado.

rep•li•ca [rɛ́plɪkə] s. reproducción, copia exacta.

re•ply [rɪpláɪ] v. replicar, contestar, responder; s. réplica, contestación, respuesta.

re•port [rɪpórt] v. dar cuenta de; avisar; informar; presentar un informe; rendir informe; hacer un reportaje, Am. reportar; denunciar, delatar; presentarse; **to – for duty** presentarse; **it is –ed that** dízque, se dice que, corre la voz que; s. noticia, reporte; informe; memorial; relación; rumor; estallido, disparo; **news** – reportaje.

re•port•er [rɪpóta•] s. reportero, repórter.

re•pose [rɪpóz] v. reposar, descansar; **to – one's confidence in** confiar en; depositar su confianza en; s. reposo.

re•pos•i•to•ry [rɪpázǝtorɪ] s. depósito; almacén.

rep•re•sent [rɛprɪzɛ́t] v. representar.

rep•re•sen•ta•tion [rɛprɪzɛ́ntéʃən] s. representación.

rep•re•sen•ta•tive [rɛprɪzɛ́ntǝtɪv] adj. representativo; representante; típico; s. representante; delegado, diputado.

re•press [rɪprés] v. reprimir; refrenar, restringir; cohibir.

re•pres•sion [rɪpréʃən] s. represión.

re•prieve [rɪprív] v. suspensión temporal de pena; alivio.

rep•ri•mand [rɛ́prəmænd] v. reprender, regañar; s. reprimenda, reprensión; regaño.

re•pri•sal [rɪpráɪz]] s. represalia.

re•proach [rɪprótʃ] v. reprochar; censurar, criticar; echar en cara; s. reproche, reprimenda; censura.

re•pro•duce [riprədjús] v. reproducir.

re•pro•duc•tion [riprəd ʌ́kʃən] s. reproducción.

re•proof [rɪprúf] v. represión, reproche, regaño.

re•prove [rɪprúv] v. reprobar, reprender, censurar.

rep•tile [rɛ́pt]] s. reptil.

re•pub•lic [rɪp ʌ́blɪk] s. república.

re•pub•li•can [rɪp ʌ́blɪkən] adj. & s. republicano.

re•pu•di•ate [rɪpjúdɪet] v. repudiar.

re•pug•nance [rɪp ʌ́gnəns] s. repugnancia; aversión.

re•pug•nant [rɪp ʌ́gnənt] adj. repugnante; antipático.

re•pulse [rɪp ʌ́ls] v. repulsar, repeler; rechazar; repulsa; desaire.

re•pul•sive [rɪp ʌ́lsɪv] adj. repulsivo, repugnante.

rep•u•ta•ble [rɛ́pjətəb]] adj. de buena reputación.

rep•u•ta•tion [rɛpjətéʃən] s. reputación, renombre.

re•pute [rɪpjút] v. reputar; estimar, considerar; s. reputación; renombre, fama; **of ill –** de mala fama.

re•quest [rɪkwést] s. solicitud, petición, demanda;

súplica, ruego; **at the – of** a solicitud de, a instancias de; v. solicitar, pedir, rogar, suplicar.

re·quire [rɪkwáɪr] v. requerir; exigir, demandar.

re·quire·ment [rɪkwáɪrmənt] s. requerimiento, requisito; exigencia; necesidad.

req·ui·site [rέkwəzɪt] s. requisito; adj. requerido, necesario.

req·ui·si·tion [rɛkwəzíʃən] s. requisición, demanda, orden; v. demandar, pedir, ordenar.

re·scind [rɪsínd] v. rescindir.

res·cue [rέskju] v. rescatar; librar; salvar; s. rescate, salvamento, salvación, socorro; **to go to the – of** acudir al socorro de, ir a salvar a.

re·search [rɪsɝ̀tʃ] s. rebusca, búsqueda, investigación; [rɪsɝ̀tʃ] v. rebuscar, investigar.

re·sem·blance [rɪzémbləns] s. semejanza, parecido.

re·sem·ble [rɪzémb l] v. asemejarse a, semejar, parecerse a.

re·sent [rɪzént] v. resentirse de, sentirse de, darse por agraviado de.

re·sent·ful [rɪzéntfəl] adj. resentido; rencoroso.

re·sent·ment [rɪzéntmənt] s. resentimiento.

res·er·va·tion [rɛzɚvéʃən] s. reservación; reserva.

re·serve [rɪzɝ́v] v. reservar; s. reserva.

res·er·voir [rέzɚvwɔr] s. depósito (de agua, aceite, gas, provisiones, etc.); receptáculo; **water –** alberca, aljibe, tanque, estanque.

re·side [rɪzáɪd] v. residir, vivir.

res·i·dence [rέzədəns] s. residencia; domicilio.

res·i·dent [rέzədənt] adj. & s. residente.

res·i·den·tial [rɛzɪdénʃəl] adj. residencial.

res·i·due [rέzədju] s. residuo; resto.

re·sign [rɪzáɪn] v. renunciar; dimitir; **to – oneself to** resignarse a.

res·ig·na·tion [rɛzɪgnéʃən] s. renuncia, dimisión; resignación.

re·sil·ience [rɪzíljəns] s. elasticidad.

res·in [rézŋ] s. resina.

re·sist [rɪzíst] v. resistir; oponerse, resistirse a.

re·sis·tance [rɪzístəns] s. resistencia.

re·sis·tant [rɪzístənt] adj. resistente.

res·o·lute [rézəlut] adj. resuelto.

res·o·lu·tion [rɛzəlúʃən] s. resolución; acuerdo.

re·solve [rɪzálv] v. resolver(se); **to – into** resolverse en, reducirse a, transformarse en; **to – to** acordar; proponerse, resolverse a.

res·o·nance [rézənəns] s. resonancia.

res·o·nant [rézənənt] adj. resonante.

re·sort [rɪzɔ́rt] v. recurrir, acudir; **to – to force** recurrir a la fuerza; s. refugio; morada; **as a last –** como último recurso; **summer –** lugar de veraneo; **vice –** garito; casa de mala fama; **to have – to** recurrir a.

re·sort·er [rɪzɔ́rtɚ] s. **summer –** veraneante.

re·sound [rɪzáʊnd] v. resonar; repercutir; retumbar.

re·source [rɪsórs] s. recurso; **natural -s** recursos o riquezas naturales.

re·spect [rɪspέkt] v. respetar; **as -s** por lo que respecta a, por lo que toca a, tocante a; s. respeto; consideración; **with – to** (con) respecto a, respecto de; por lo que atañe a.

re·spect·a·ble [rɪspέktəb l] adj. respetable.

re·spect·ful [rɪspέktfəl] adj. respetuoso.

re·spect·ing [rɪspέktɪŋ] prep. con respecto a, tocante a.

re·spec·tive [rɪspέktɪv] adj. respectivo.

res·pi·ra·tion [rɛspəréʃən] s. respiración, respiro.

res·pite [rέspɪt] s. tregua, pausa, descanso; intervalo; prórroga.

re·splen·dent [rɪspléndənt] adj. resplandeciente.

re·spond [rɪspánd] v. responder; corresponder; reaccionar.

re·sponse [rɪspáns] s. repuesta, contestación; reacción.

re·spon·si·bil·i·ty [rɪspɑnsəbíləti] s. responsabilidad.

re·spon·si·ble [rɪspánsəb l] adj. responsable; formal, digno de confianza.

rest [rɛst] s. (repose) descanso; reposo; quietud; tregua; pausa; (support) apoya; **at – en** paz; en reposo; tranquilo; **the –** el resto; los demás; v. descansar; reposar; apoyar; **to – on** descansar sobre; apoyar(se) en; basar(se) en; contar con, confiar en, depender de.

res·tau·rant [rέstərənt] s. restaurante. Am. restorán.

rest·ful [rέstfəl] adj. reposado, sosegado, tranquilo.

res·ti·tu·tion [rɛstətjúʃən] s. restitución; devolución.

res·tive [rέstɪv] adj. intranquilo.

rest·less [rέstlɪs] adj. inquieto, intranquilo.

rest·less·ness [rέstlɪsnɪs] s. inquietud, desasosiego, intranquilidad.

res·to·ra·tion [rɛstəréʃən] s. restauración; restitución; renovación.

re·store [rɪstór] v. restaurar; renovar; restituir; restablecer.

re·strain [rɪstrén] v. refrenar, contener, cohibir, reprimir, coartar; restringir.

re·straint [rɪstrént] s. restricción; reserva, circunspección; moderación; cohibición.

re·strict [rɪstríkt] v. restringir, limitar.

re·stric·tion [rɪstríkʃən] s. restricción.

re·sult [rɪzΛlt] v. resultar; **to – from** resultar de; **to – in** parar en; causar; dar por resultado; s. resulta, resultado; **as a –** de resultas, como resultado.

re·sume [rɪzúm] v. resumir, volver a tomar; recomenzar; reanudar, continuar.

rés•u•mé [rɛzumé] *s.* resumen, sumario.
re•sur•gent [risædʒənt] *adj.* resurgente.
res•ur•rec•tion [rɛzərékʃən] *s.* resurrección.

re•sus•ci•tate [rɪs ʌ́sətet] *v.* resucitar; revivir.
re•tail [rítel] *s.* venta al por menor; **at** – al por menor;
— **merchant** detallista, comerciante al por menor;
— **price** precio al por menor; *v.* detallar; vender al
menudeo (o vender al por menor), *Méx., C.A., Ven.,*
Col. menudear.
re•tail•er [rítelə-] *s.* detallista, revendedor, comerciante al por menor.
re•tain [rɪtén] *v.* retener; emplear.
re•tal•i•ate [rɪt ǽ lɪet] *v.* desquitarse, vengarse.
re•tal•i•a•tion [rɪtælɪéʃən] *s.* desquite; desagravio;
represalia, venganza.
re•tard [rɪtárd] *v.* retardar, retrasar, atrasar.
re•ten•tion [rɪténʃən] *s.* retención.
ret•i•cence [rétəsəns] *s.* reserva.
ret•i•nue [rét ŋ ju] *s.* comitiva, séquito, acompañamiento.
re•tire [rɪtáɪr] *v.* retirar(se); jubilar(se); acostarse;
apartarse.
re•tire•ment [rɪtáɪrmənt] *s.* retiro; jubilación.
re•tort [rɪt ɔ́ rt] *v.* replicar; redargüir; *s.* réplica.
re•touch [rit ʌ tʃ] *v.* retocar; *s.* retoque.
re•trace [rɪtrés] *v.* repasar; volver a trazar; **to** – **one's**
steps volver sobre sus pasos, retroceder.
re•tract [rɪt ǽ kt] *v.* retractar, retractarse de; decidirse (de); retraer.
re•treat [rɪtrít] *s.* retiro, refugio, asilo; retirada; re-
treta *(toque de retirada); v.* retirarse; retroceder.
re•trench [rɪtrént ɔ́] *v.* cercenar, reducir, disminuir;
economizar.
re•trieve [rɪtrív] *v.* cobrar *(la caza);* recobrar, recuperar; reparar *(una pérdida).*
ret•ro•ac•tive [retro ǽ ktɪv] *adj.* retroactivo.
ret•ro•flex [rétrofleks] *adj.* retroflejo.
ret•ro•spect [rétrospɛkt] *s.* retrospección; **in** – re-
trospectivamente.
re•turn [rɪt ɔ́ n] *v.* volver, regresar; retornar; devolver; replicar; redituar; producir; restar *(la pelota en*
tenis); **to** – **a favor** corresponder a un favor; **to** – **a**
report rendir un informe; *s.* vuelta, regreso, retorno; recompensa; restitución, devolución; réplica;
resto *(en un juego de pelota);* rédito, ganancia; informe; – **game** desquite, juego de desquite; – **ticket**
boleto de vuelta; **by** – **mail** a vuelta de correo;
election -**s** reportaje de elecciones; **in** – en cambio; **in** – **for** a cambio de, a trueque de; **income tax**
– declaración de rentas; **many happy** -**s** muchas
felicidades (en su día).
re•un•ion [rijúnjən] *s.* reunión; junta.
re•u•nite [rijUnáɪt] *v.* reunir(se), volver a unirse;
reconciliar(se).

re•veal [rɪvíl] *v.* revelar.

rev•el [rév ḷ] *v.* deleitarse, gozarse; parrandear, *Am.*
farrear; andar de parranda, *Ríopl.* andar de farra; *s.*
parranda, juerga, jarana.
rev•e•la•tion [rɛv ḷ éʃən] *s.* revelación;
Revelation(s) Apocalipsis.
rev•el•ry [rév ḷ rɪ] *s.* jaleo, juerga, jarana.
re•venge [rɪvéndʒ] *v.* vengar, vindicar; *s.* venganza;
desquite.
re•venge•ful [rɪvéndʒfəl] *adj.* vengativo.
rev•e•nue [révənju] *s.* renta; rédito; rentas públicas,
ingresos.
re•vere [rɪvír] *v.* venerar.
rev•er•ence [révrəns] *s.* reverencia; veneración; *v.*
reverenciar, venerar.
rev•er•end [révrənd] *adj.* reverendo; venerable.
rev•er•ent [révrənt] *adj.* reverente.
rev•er•ie, rev•er•y [révərɪ] *s.* ensueño; arrobamiento.
re•verse [rɪv ɔ́ s] *adj.* inverso, invertido; contrario,
opuesto; *s.* revés; reverso, dorso; lo contrario; contratiempo; *v.* invertir; voltear; revocar *(una*
sentencia).
re•vert [rɪv ɔ́ t] *v.* revertir, volver atrás, retroceder.
re•view [rɪvjú] *v. (study)* repasar, revisar; revistar;
(inspect) pasar revista a *(las tropas); (criticize)* re-
señar, hacer una reseña de *(un libro); s.* revista;
repaso; reseña, crítica *(de un libro, drama, etc.);*
revisión *(de un caso jurídico, sentencia, etc.).*
re•vile [rɪváɪl] *v.* vilipendiar, vituperar, denigrar.
re•vise [rɪváɪz] *v.* revisar, repasar, releer *(para*
corregir); corregir, enmendar.
re•vi•sion [rɪvíʒən] *s.* revisión; enmienda; edición
enmendada o mejorada.
re•viv•al [rɪvávɪ ḷ] *s. (renewal)* renovación;
revivificación; *(repeating)* renacimiento; nueva presentación *(teatral);* – **meeting** junta para revivir el
fervor religioso; **religious** – despertamiento (o
nuevo fervor) religioso.
re•vive [rɪváɪv] *v.* revivir, resucitar; volver en sí;
renacer; reavivar, reanimar(se); avivar.
re•voke [rɪvók] *v.* revocar, abrogar, anular; renunciar *(en los juegos de naipes).*
re•volt [rɪvólt] *s.* revuelta, rebelión, sublevación; *v.*
rebelarse, sublevarse; **it** -**s me** me da asco, me
repugna.
re•volt•ing [rɪvóltɪŋ] *adj.* repugnante; asqueroso.
rev•o•lu•tion [rɛvəlúʃən] *s.* revolución; vuelta
(que da una rueda).
rev•o•lu•tion•ar•y [rɛvəlúʃənɛrɪ] *adj. & s.* revolucionario.
rev•o•lu•tion•ist [rɛvəlúʃənɪst] *s.* revolucionario.
re•volve [rɪválv] *v.* girar, dar vueltas; rodar; voltear,
dar vueltas a; **to** – **in one's mind** revolver en la

mente, ponderar, reflexionar.

re•volv•er [rɪválvə•] s. revólver.

re•ward [rɪwɔ́rd] v. premiar; recompensar; s. premio, gratificación, recompensa, galardón; albricias (*por haber hallado algún objeto perdido*).

re•write [riráɪt] v. volver a escribir; refundir (*un escrito*).

rhap•so•dy [rǽpsədɪ] s. rapsodia.

rhet•o•ric [rétərɪk] s. retórica.

rheu•ma•tism [rúmətɪzəm] s. reumatismo, reuma.

rhi•noc•er•os [raɪnásərəs] s. rinoceronte.

rhu•barb [rúbarb] s. ruibarbo.

rhyme [raɪm] s. rima; **without— or reason** sin ton ni son; v. rimar.

rhythm [ríðəm] s. ritmo.

rhyth•mi•cal [ríðmɪk] adj. rítmico, acompasado, cadencioso.

rib [rɪb] s. costilla; varilla (*de paraguas*); cordoncillo (*de ciertos tejidos*).

rib•bon [ríbən] s. cinta; listón, banda; tira.

rice [raɪs] s. arroz; **– field** arrozal.

rich [rɪtʃ] adj. rico; costoso, suntuoso; sabroso; **– color** color vivo; **– food** alimento muy mantecoso o dulce.

rich•es [rítʃɪz] s. pl. riqueza, riquezas.

rick•et•y [ríkɪtɪ] adj. desvencijado; raquítico.

rid [rɪd] v. librar, desembarazar; **to get – of** librarse de, deshacerse de, desembarazarse de; pret. & p.p. de **to rid.**

rid•den [ríd ŋ] p.p. de **to ride.**

rid•dle [ríd] acertijo, adivinanza, enigma; v. acribillar, perforar; **to – with bullets** acribillar a balazos.

ride [raɪd] v. (*horse*) cabalgar, montar; (*vehicle*) pasear; ir en (*tranvía, tren*); **to – a bicycle** andar o montar en bicicleta; **to – a horse** montar un caballo; **to – horseback** montar a caballo; **to – over a country** pasar o viajar por un país (*en auto, a caballo o en automóvil*); **to – someone** dominar a alguien; burlarse de alguien; s. paseo (*a caballo o en automóvil*); viaje (*a caballo, en automóvil, por ferrocarril., etc.*).

rid•er [ráɪdə•] s. jinete; pasajero (*de automóvil*); biciclista; motociclista; aditamento, cláusula añadida (*a un proyecto de ley*).

ridge [rɪdʒ] s. espinazo; lomo (*entre dos surcos*); arista, intersección (*de dos planos*); cordillera; cerro; caballete (*de tejado*); cordoncillo (*de ciertos tejidos*).

rid•i•cule [rídɪkjul] v. ridículo; burla, mofa; v. ridiculizar, poner en ridículo.

ri•dic•u•lous [rɪdíkjələs] adj. ridículo.

ri•fle [ráɪf] s. rifle; v. pillar, robar; despojar.

rift [rɪft] s. (*opening*) raja; abertura; (*disagreement*) desacuerdo.

rig [rɪg] v. aparejar; equipar; enjarciar (*un barco de vela*); **to – oneself up** emperifollarse, ataviarse; s.

aparejo, equipo; aparato; atavío, traje.

rig•ging [rígɪŋ] s. jarcia, aparejo.

right [raɪt] adj. (*not left*) derecho; diestro; (*proper*) recto; justo; propio; adecuado; correcto; **– angle** ángulo recto; **– side** lado derecho; derecho (*de un tejido, traje, etc.*); **it is – that** esta bien que, es justo que; **to be –** tener razón; **to be all –** estar bien; estar bien en salud; **to be in one´s – mind** estar en sus cabales; adv. derecho, directamente; rectamente; justamente; bien; correctamente; a la derecha; **– about-face** media vuelta; **– hungry** muy hambriento; **– now** ahora mismo, inmediatamente; **– there** allí mismo, Am. allí mero; **go – home!** ¡vete derechito a casa!; **it is – where you left it** está exactamente (o en el mero lugar) donde lo dejaste; **to hit – in the eye** dar de lleno en el ojo, Am. dar en el mero ojo; s. derecho; autoridad; privilegio; **– of way** derecho de vía; **by – (by –s)** justamente, con justicia; según la ley; **from – to left** de derecha a izquierda; **to the –** a la derecha; **to be in the –** tener razón; v. enderezar; corregir.

right•eous [ráɪtʃəs] adj. recto, justo, virtuoso.

right•eous•ness [ráɪtʃəsnɪs] s. rectitud, virtud.

right•ful [ráɪtfəl] adj. justo; legítimo.

right-hand [ráɪthǽnd] adj. derecho, de la mano derecha; **– man** brazo derecho.

right•ist [ráɪɪst] s. derechista.

right•ly [ráɪtlɪ] adv. con razón; justamente, rectamente; propiamente, aptamente, debidamente.

right-wing [ráɪtwɪŋ] adj. derechista.

rig•id [rídʒɪd] adj. rígido.

ri•gid•i•ty [rɪdʒídətɪ] s. rigidez; tiesura.

rig•or [rígə•] s. rigor; rigidez; severidad.

rig•or•ous [rígə•əs] adj. rigoroso (o riguroso), severo.

rim [rɪm] s. borde, orilla; aro.

rime = **rhyme.**

rind [raɪnd] s. corteza, cáscara.

ring [rɪŋ] s. (*finger*) anillo, sortija, argolla; aro; (*circle*) arena; pista; (*sound*) toque; tañido; repique; (*telephone*) timbrazo; telefonazo; **– leader** cabecilla; **– of defiance** tono de reto; **– of shouts** gritería; **– of a telephone** llamada de teléfono; **ring-shaped** en forma de anillo, anular; **key –** llavero; **– sarcastic** — retintín; v. tocar (*un timbre, una campanilla o campana*); sonar; tañer, repicar; resonar; zumbar (*los oídos*); **to – for something** llamar para pedir algo; **to – the nose of an animal** ponerle una argolla en la nariz a un animal; **to – up on the phone** llamar por teléfono.

ring•let [ríŋlɪt] s. rizo, bucle; pequeña sortija.

rink [rɪŋk] s. patinadero (*cancha para patinar*).

rinse [rɪns] v. enjuagar; lavar; aclarar (*la ropa*); s. enjuague.

ri•ot [ráɪət] s. motín, desorden, alboroto, tumulto; **– of color** riqueza o exceso de colores chillantes; v.

amotinarse, alborotar, armar un tumulto.

rip [rɪp] v. rasgar(se), romper(se); descoser(se); **to – off** rasgar, arrancar, cortar; **to – out a seam** descoser una costura; s. rasgón, rasgadura, rotura; descosido.

ripe [raɪp] adj. maduro, sazonado; en sazón; **- for** maduro para, sazonado para; bien preparado para, listo para.

rip•en [ráɪən] v. madurar(se), sazonar(se).

ripe•ness [ráɪpnɪs] s. madurez, sazón.

rip•ple [rɪ́p |] v. rizar(se), agitar(se), ondear, temblar (la superficie del agua); murmurar (un arroyo); s. onda, temblor, ondulación (en la superficie del agua); murmullo (de un arroyo).

rise [raɪz] v. subir; ascender; alzarse, levantarse; elevarse; surgir; salir (el sol, la luna, un astro); hincharse (la masa del pan); **to – up in rebellion** sublevarse, levantarse, alzarse (en rebelión); s. subida; ascenso; pendiente; elevación; salida (del sol, de la luna, etc.); subida, alza (de precios).

ris•en [rɪ́z ŋ] p.p. de **to rise.**

risk [rɪsk] s. riesgo; v. arriesgar, aventurar, poner en peligro; exponerse a; **to – defeat** correr el riesgo de perder, exponerse a perder.

risk•y [rɪ́skɪ] adj. arriesgado, peligroso, aventurado.

ris•qué [rɪské] adj. escabroso.

rite [raɪt] s. rito, ceremonia.

rit•u•al [rɪ́tʃʊəl] adj. & s. ritual, ceremonial.

ri•val [ráɪv |] s. rival, competidor, émulo; adj. competidor; **the – party** el partido opuesto; v. rivalizar con, competir con.

ri•val•ry [ráɪv | rɪ] s. rivalidad.

riv•er [rɪ́və•] s. río.

riv•et [rɪ́vɪt] s. remache; v. remachar; fijar.

riv•u•let [rɪ́vjəlɪt] s. riachuelo, arroyuelo.

road [rod] s. camino; carretera; vía.

road•side [ródsaɪd] s. borde del camino.

road•way [ródwe] s. camino, carretera.

roam [rom] v. vagar, errar, andar errante.

roar [ror] v. rugir, bramar; **to – with laughter** reír a carcajadas; s. rugido, bramido; **- of laughter** risotada, carcajada.

roast [rost] v. asar(se); tostar (café, maíz, etc.); ridiculizar, criticar; s. asado, carne asada; adj. asado; **- beef** rosbif, rosbí.

rob [rɑb] v. robar, hurtar; **to – someone of something** robarle algo a alguien.

rob•ber [rɑ́bə•] s. ladrón; **highway –** salteador.

rob•ber•y [rɑ́brɪ] s. robo, hurto.

robe [rob] s. manto, traje talar, túnica, toga (de un juez, letrado, etc.); bata; **automobile –** manta de automóvil.

rob•in [rɑ́bɪn] s. petirrojo.

ro•bust [róbʌst] adj. robusto, fuerte.

rock [rɑk] s. roca, peña; peñasco; **- crystal** cristal de roca; **- salt** sal de piedra, sal gema o sal mineral; **to go on the -s** tropezar en un escollo, Am. escollar; v. mecer(se), balancear(se); bambolear(se); estremecer; **to – to sleep** adormecer (meciendo), arrullar.

rock•er [rɑ́kə•] s. mecedora; arco de una mecedero o cuna.

rock•et [rɑ́kɪt] s. cohete.

rock•et•ry [rɑ́kətrɪ] s. cohetería.

rock•ing [rɑ́kɪŋ] s. balanceo; adj. oscilante; **– chair** silla mecedora.

rock•y [rɑ́kɪ] adj. roqueño, rocoso, rocalloso, peñascoso; pedregoso; movedizo; tembloroso; débil, desvanecido.

rod [rɑd] s. vara, varilla; medida de longitud (aproximadamente 5 metros); **fishing –** caña de pescar.

rode [rod] pret. de **to ride.**

ro•dent [ródənt] s. roedor.

rogue [rog] s. pícaro, bribón, tunante, pillo; **s´ gallery** colección policíaca de retratos criminales.

rogu•ish [rógɪʃ] adj. pícaro, pillo, picaresco; travieso.

role [rol] s. papel, parte.

roll [rol] v. (move) rodar; girar; balancearse (un barco); bambolearse; ondular, retumbar (el trueno, un cañón); aplanar, alisar con rodillo; arrollar, enrollar, hacer un rollo o bola; envolver; redoblar (un tambor); pronunciar (la rr doble); **to – over in the snow** revolverse o revolcarse en la nieve; **to – up** arrollar, enrollar, envolver; s. rollo (de un papel, paño, tela, etc.); balanceo (de un barco); retumbo (del trueno, de un cañón); redoble (de un tambor); lista ondulación; oleaje; bollo, rosca, panecillo; **to call the –** pasar lista.

roll•er [rólə•] s. rodillo, cilindro (para aplanar o alisar); rollo (rodillo de pastelero); oleada; **- coaster** montaña rusa; **- skate** patín de ruedas.

Ro•man [rómən] adj. & s. romano; **– nose** nariz aguileña.

ro•mance [rɑmǽns] s. (literatura) romance; novela; cuento; fábula; (affair) aventura romántica; amorío, lance amoroso; v. contar o fingir fábulas; andar en amoríos o aventuras; **Romance** adj. romance, románico, neolatino.

ro•man•tic [rɑmǽntɪk] adj. romántico; novelesco.

ro•man•ti•cism [rɑmǽntəsɪzəm] s. romanticismo.

ro•man•ti•cist [rɑmǽntəsɪst] s. romántico, escritor romántico.

romp [rɑmp] v. triscar, juguetear, retozar, travesear.

roof [ruf] s. techo, techumbre, techado; tejado; **- garden** azotea-jardín; **- of the mouth** paladar; **flat –** azotea; v. techar.

room [rum] s. (in building) cuarto, pieza, sala, habitación; (space) espacio; lugar, sitio; **there is no – for more** no cabe(n) más, no hay lugar o cabida para más; **to make** – hacer lugar; – **mate** compañero de cuarto; *v.* vivir, hospedarse, alojarse.

room•er [rúmɚ] *s.* inquilino.

room•i•ness [rúmɪnɪs] *s.* holgura.

room•y [rúmɪ] *adj.* espacioso, amplio, holgado.

roost [rust] *s.* gallinero; percha de gallinero; *v.* acurrucarse (*las aves en la percha*); pasar la noche.

roost•er [rústɚ] *s.* gallo.

root [rut] *s.* raíz; *v.* arraigar(se); echar raíces; hocicar, hozar (dícese de lo cerdos); **to – for** vitorear, aclamar; **to – out** (o – **up**) desarraigar, arrancar de raíz; **to become -ed** arraigarse.

rope [rop] *s.* (*cord*) soga, cuerda; (lasso) reata, lazo; **to be at the end one´s** – haber agotado el último recurso; estar (o andar) en las últimas; no saber qué hacer; **to know the -s** saber todas las tretas de un asunto o negocio; *v.* amarrar, lazar, enlazar; **to – off** acordelar, poner cuerdas tirantes alrededor de (*un sitio*); **to – someone in** embaucar a alguien.

ro•sa•ry [rózɚɪ] *s.* rosario.

rose [roz] *pret. de* **to rise.**

rose [roz] *s.* rosa; color rosa; – **bush** rosal; – **window** rosetón.

rose•bud [rózbʌd] *s.* capullo o botón de rosa, yema, pimpollo.

ro•sette [rozét] *s.* registro; lista.

ros•trum [róstrəm] *s.* tribuna.

ros•y [rózɪ] *adj.* (*color*) rosado; color de rosa; (*condition*) alegre, risueño; – **future** porvenir risueño.

rot [rot] *v.* pudrir(se); corromperse; *s.* podre, podredumbre, putrefacción.

ro•ta•ry [rótɚɪ] *adj.* rotatorio, giratorio, rotativo.

ro•tate [rótet] *v.* girar, dar vueltas; hacer girar; turnarse; cultivar en rotación.

ro•ta•tion [roté ʃən] *s.* rotación, vuelta; – **of crops** rotación de cultivos.

rote [rot] *s.* rutina, repetición maquinal; **by –** maquinalmente.

rot•ten [rót ŋ] *adj.* podrido, putrefacto; hediondo; corrompido, corrupto.

rouge [ruʒ] *s.* colorete; *v.* pintar(se), poner(se) colorete.

rough [rʌf] *adj.* (*course*) áspero; tosco; fragoso; escabroso; (*rude*) brusco; grosero; (*stormy*) borrascoso, tempestuoso; – **diamond** diamante en bruto; – **draft** borrador; bosquejo; – **estimate** cálculo aproximativo, tanteo; – **ground** terreno escabroso; – **idea** idea aproximada; – **sea** mar picado; - **weather** tiempo borrascoso; *adv.* véase **roughly**; *v.* **to – It** vivir sin lujos ni comodidades, hacer vida campestre.

rough•en [r ʌ fən] *v.* hacer o poner áspero; picar, rascar (*una superficie*); rajarse, agrietarse (*la piel*).

rough•ly [r ʌ flɪ] *adv.* ásperamente; groseramente,

rudamente; aproximadamente; **to estimate** – tantear.

rough•ness [r ʌ fnɪs] *s.* aspereza; escabrosidad; rudeza; tosquedad; **the – of the sea** lo picado del mar; **the – of the weather** lo borrascoso del tiempo.

round [raʊnd] *adj.* redondo; rotundo; circular; **- trip** viaje redondo, viaje de ida y vuelta; **round-trip ticket** boleto (o billete) de ida y vuelta; *s.* vuelta, rotación, revolución; ronda; vuelta (*en el juego de naipes*); tanda, turno (*en ciertos deportes*); escalón, travesaño (*de escalera de mano*); danza en rueda; – **of ammunition** carga de municiones; descarga; **of applause** explosión de aplausos; – **of pleasures** sucesión de placeres; **to make the -s** rondar; *prep. & adv.* véase **around;** – **about** a la redonda; por todos lados; **round-shouldered** cargado de espaldas; **to come – again** volver otra vez; **to go – a corner** doblar una esquina; *v.* redondear; dar vuelta a; **to – a corner** doblar una esquina; **to – out** redondear; completar; **to – up cattle** juntar el ganado, Am. rodear el ganado.

round•a•bout [ráʊndəbaʊt] *adj.* indirecto.

round-up [ráʊnʌp] *s.* rodeo (*de ganado*).

rouse [raʊz] *v.* despertar(se), Ríopl. recordar; excitar; incitar, provocar; levantar (*la caza*).

rout [raʊt] *s.* derrota, fuga desordenada; *v.* derrotar; poner en fuga; **to – out** echar, hacer salir a toda prisa.

route [rut] *s.* ruta, camino, vía; itinerario; *v.* dirigir o enviar por cierta ruta.

rou•tine [rutín] *s.* rutina.

rove [rov] *v.* vagar, errar, andar errante.

rov•er [róvɚ] *s.* vagabundo.

row [raʊ] *s.* riña, pelea, pelotera; *v.* pelearse, reñir, armar una riña o pelotera.

row [ro] *s.* fila, hilera; paseo en lancha; *v.* remar, bogar; llevar en lancha o en bote.

row-boat [róbot] *s.* bote de remos, lancha.

row•er [róɚ] *s.* remero.

roy•al [r ɔ ɪəl] *adj.* real, regio.

roy•al•ist [r ɔ ɪəlɪst] *s.* realista.

roy•al•ty [r ɔ ɪəltɪ] *s.* realeza, soberanía real; persona o personas reales; derechos (*pagados a un autor o inventor*).

rub [rʌb] *v.* (*apply friction*) frotar; restregar; fregar; (*scrape*) raspar; irritar; **to – out** borrar; **to – someone the wrong way** irritar, contrariar, llevarle a uno la contraria; *s.* fricción, friega, frotación; roce; sarcasmo; **there is the –** allí está la dificultad.

rub•ber [r ʌ bɚ] *s.* caucho, goma, *Méx.*, *C.A.* hule; goma elástica; goma de borrar; partida (*en ciertos juegos de naipes*); jugada decisiva (*en ciertos juegos de naipes*); **-s** chanclos, zapatos de goma o de hule; *adj.* de caucho, de goma, *Méx.*, *C.A.* de hule;

– band faja o banda de goma; **– plantation** cauchal; **– tree** *Am.* caucho, *Am.* gomero.

rub·bish [rʌbɪʃ] *s.* basura, desechos, desperdicios; tonterías.

rub·ble [rʌbḷ] *s.* escombros; ripio, cascajo, fragmentos de ladrillos o piedras; piedra en bruto, piedrar sin labrar.

ru·bric [rúbrɪk] *s.* rúbrica.

ru·by [rúbɪ] *s.* rubí.

rud·der [rʌdɚ] *s.* timón.

rud·dy [rʌdɪ] *adj.* rojo; rojizo; rubicundo.

rude [rud] *adj.* rudo; grosero; áspero; brusco; tosco.

rude·ness [rúdnɪs] *s.* rudeza; grosería, descortesía; tosquedad.

rue·ful [rúfəl] *adj.* triste; lastimoso, lamentable.

ruf·fi·an [rʌfɪən] *s.* rufián, hombre brutal.

ruf·fle [rʌfḷ] *v.* rizar, fruncir (*tela*); arrugar; desarreglar; rizar (*la superficie del agua*); perturbar; molestar; *s.* volante (*de un traje*); frunce, pliegue; ondulación (*en el agua*).

rug [rʌg] *s.* alfombra, tapete.

rug·ged [rʌgɪd] *adj.* escabroso, fragoso; áspero; recio, robusto; tosco; borrascoso, tempestuoso.

ru·in [rúɪn] *s.* ruina; **to go to** – arruinarse, caer en ruinas, venir a menos; *v.* arruinar; echar a perder; estropear.

ru·in·ous [rúɪnəs] *adj.* ruinoso; desastroso.

rule [rul] *s.* (*regulation*) regla; reglamento; precepto; (*control*) mando, gobierno; **as a** – por regla general; *v.* regir, gobernar; mandar; dirigir, guiar; dominar; fallar, decidir; rayar (*con regla*); **to** – **out** excluir; **to** – **over** regir, gobernar.

rul·er [rúlɚ] *s.* gobernante; soberano; regla (*para medir o trazar líneas*).

rul·ing [rúlɪŋ] *s.* fallo, decisión; gobierno; *adj.* predominante, prevaleciente; principal.

rum [rʌm] *s.* ron.

rum·ble [rʌmbḷ] *v.* retumbar, hacer estruendo, rugir; *s.* retumbo, estruendo, rumor, ruido sordo; **- seat** asiento trasero (*de cupé*).

ru·mi·nate [rúmənet] *v.* rumiar; reflexionar, meditar.

rum·mage [rʌmɪdʒ] *v.* escudriñar revolviéndolo todo; *s.* búsqueda desordenada; **- sale** venta de prendas usadas (*para beneficencia*).

ru·mor [rúmɚ] *s.* rumor; runrún; *v.* murmurar; **it is –ed that** corre la voz que.

rump [rʌmp] *s.* anca, trasero.

rum·ple [rʌmpḷ] *v.* estrujar, ajar; arrugar; *s.* arruga (*en un traje*).

rum·pus [rʌmpəs] *s.* barullo, alharaca, boruca, batahola.

run [rʌn] *v.* (*on foot*) correr; (*function*) andar; manchar; funcionar; (*flow*) fluir; chorrear; (*go over*) recorrer; (*direct*) dirigir, manejar; (*un negocio, empresa, máquina, casa, etc.*); extenderse (*de un punto a otro*); correrse (*los colores*); ser candidato (*a un puesto político*); **to – a fever** tener calentura; **to – away** huir; fugarse, escaparse; **to – across a person** encontrarse o tropezar con una persona; **to – down** dejar de funcionar (*una máquina, reloj, etc.*); aprehender a (*un criminal*); hablar mal de; atropellar; **to get – down in health** quebrantársele a uno la salud; **to – dry** secarse; **to – into** tropezar con, encontrarse con; chocar con; **– around with** asociarse con; tener amores con; **to – into debt** adeudarse; **to – something into** meter algo en, clavar algo en; **to – out** salirse; **to – out of money** acabársele a uno el dinero; **to – over** derramarse (*un líquido*); atropellar, pasar por encima de; repasar, echar un vistazo a (*la lección, un libro, etc.*); **to – through a book** hojear un libro; **the play ran for three months** se dio la comedia durante tres meses; *s.* carrera, corrida; curso, marcha; recorrido; manejo; **– of good luck** serie de repetidos éxitos; **– of performances** serie de representaciones; **– on a bank** corrida, demanda extraordinaria de fondos bancarios; **in the long** – a la larga; **stocking – carrera**; **the common** – **of mankind** el común de las gentes; **to have the – of** tener el libre uso de; *p.p.* de **to turn.**

run·a·way [rʌnəwe] *adj.* fugitivo; **– horse** caballo desbocado; **– marriage** casamiento de escapatoria; *s.* fugitivo; caballo desbocado; fuga.

rung [rʌŋ] *s.* barrote, travesaño (*de silla, escalera de mano, etc.*); *pret.* & *p.p.* de **to ring.**

run·ner [rʌnɚ] *s.* corredor; tapete (*para un pasillo o mesa*), *Ríopl.* pasillo; carrera (*en una media*); cuchilla (*de patín o de trineo*); contrabandista.

run·ning [rʌnɪŋ] *s.* (*race*) corrida, carrera; (*direction*) manejo, dirección; (*flow*) flujo; **to be out of the** – estar fuera de combate; *adj.* corriente; **– board** estribo; **– expenses** gastos corrientes; **– knot** nudo corredizo; **– water** agua corriente; **in – condition** en buen estado; **for ten days** – por diez días seguidos.

runt [rʌnt] *s.* enano; hombrecillo.

run·way [rʌnwe] *s.* senda; vía; pista (*de aterrizaje*).

rup·ture [rʌptʃɚ] *s.* ruptura; rompimiento, rotura; hernia; *v.* romper(se); reventar.

ru·ral [rúrəl] *adj.* rural, campestre.

rush [rʌʃ] *v.* (*hurry*) apresurar(se); *Am.* apurarse; despachar con prisa; (*attack*) lanzar(se), precipitar(se); abalanzarse; acometer; **to – out** salir a todo correr; **to – past** pasar a toda prisa; *s.* precipitación, acometida; junco; **– chair** silla de junco; **– of business** gran movimiento comercial; **– of people** tropel de gente; **– order** pedido urgente.

Rus•sian [rʌ∫ən] *adj. & s.* Ruso.

rust [rʌst] *s.* moho, orín; tizón (*enfermedad de las plantas*); **– color** color rojizo; *v.* enmohecer(se), oxidar(se).

rus•tic [rʌstɪk] *adj. & s.* rústico, campesino.

rus•tle [rʌsl̩] *v.* susurrar, crujir; menear; **to – cattle** robar ganado; *s.* susurro, crujido.

rust•y [rʌstɪ] *adj.* mohoso, cubierto de orín, oxidado; rojizo; entorpecido, falto de uso; falto de práctica.

rut [rʌt] *s.* rodada; rutina, método rutinario; **to be in a –** hacer una cosa por rutina, ser esclavo de la rutina.

ruth•less [rúθlɪs] *adj.* despiadado, cruel, brutal.

ruth•less•ness [rúθlɪsnɪs] *s.* fiereza, falta de miramiento, truculencia, crueldad.

rye [raI] *s.* centeno.

S

sa•ber [sébɚ] *s.* sable.

sab•o•tage [sǽbətɑʒ] *s.* sabotaje; *v.* sabotear.

sack [sæk] *s.* (*bag*) saco; costal; (*looting*) saqueo, pillaje; *v.* ensacar, meter en un saco; saquear, pillar.

sac•ra•ment [sǽkrəmənt] *s.* sacramento.

sa•cred [sékrɪd] *adj.* sagrado, sacro.

sa•cred•ness [sékrɪdnɪs] *s.* santidad; lo sagrado.

sac•ri•fice [sǽkrəfaɪs] *s.* sacrificio; **to sell at a –** vender con pérdida; *v.* sacrificar.

sac•ri•lege [sǽkrɪlɪdʒ] *s.* sacrilegio.

sac•ri•le•gious [sækrɪlíɪdʒəs] *adj.* sacrílego.

sac•ro•sanct [sǽkrosænkt] *adj.* sacrosanto.

sad [sæd] *adj.* triste.

sad•den [sǽdn̩] *v.* entristecer(se).

sad•dle [sǽdl̩] *s.* silla de montar; silla de bicicleta o motocicleta; **– big** altoza; **– horse** caballo de silla; **– tree** arzón; *v.* ensillar; **to – someone with responsibilities** cargar a alguien de responsabilidades.

sa•dis•tic [sədístɪk] *adj.* sádico, cruel.

sad•ness [sǽdnɪs] *s.* tristeza.

safe [sef] *adj.* (*secure*) seguro; salvo; sin riesgo, sin peligro; (*trustworthy*) digno de confianza; **– and sound** sano y salvo; **safe-conduct** salvoconducto; **to be –** no correr peligro, estar a salvo; *s.* caja fuerte; **-ly** *adv.* seguramente; con seguridad; sin peligro; **to arrive –ly** llegar bien, llegar sin contratiempo alguno.

safe•guard [séfgɑrd] *s.* salvaguardia; resguardo, defensa; *v.* resguardar, proteger, salvaguardar.

safe•ty [séftI] *s.* seguridad; protección; **in –** con seguridad; sin peligro; *adj.* de seguridad; **– device** mecanismo de seguridad; **– pin** imperdible, alfiler de seguridad.

saf•fron [sǽfrən] *s.* azafrán; *adj.* azafranado, color de azafrán.

sag [sæg] *v.* combarse, pandearse; doblegarse; deprimirse, hundirse (*en el centro*); encorvarse; **his shoulders –** tiene las espaldas caídas; *s.* pandeo, flexión, depresión; concavidad.

sa•ga•cious [səgéʃəs] *adj.* sagaz, ladino, astuto.

sa•gac•i•ty [səgǽsətI] *s.* sagacidad; astucia.

sage [sedʒ] *adj.* sabio; cuerdo, prudente; *s.* sabio; salvia (*planta*).

said [sɛd] *pret. & p.p.* de **to say.**

sail [sel] *s.* (*canvas*) vela (*de barco*); (*trip*) viaje o paseo en barco de vela; **under full –** a toda vela; **to set –** hacerse a la vela; *v.* navegar; hacerse a la vela; zarpar, salir (*un buque*); viajar, ir (*en barco, bote, etc.*); pasear en bote de vela; **to – a kite** volar una cometa o papalote; **to – along** deslizarse; navegar; ir bien; **to – along the coast** costear.

sail•boat [sélbot] *s.* bote o barco de vela.

sail•or [sélɚ] *s.* marinero; marino.

saint [sent] *s.* santo; *adj.* santo; san (*delante de nombres masculinos excepto: Santo Tomás, Santo Domingo, Santo Toribio*); *v.* canonizar.

saint•ly [séntlI] *adj.* santo; pío, devoto.

sake [sek] **for the – of** por; por amor a; por consideración a; **for my –** por mí; **for pity´s –** por piedad; ¡caramba¡; **for the – of argument** por vía de argumento.

sa•la•cious [səléʃəs] *adj.* salaz.

sal•ad [sǽləd] *s.* ensalada; **—dressing** aderezo (*para ensalada*).

sal•a•ry [sǽlərI] *s.* salario, sueldo.

sale [sel] *s.* venta; saldo, *Méx., C.A., Andes* barata; *Ríopl., Andes* realización; **– by auction** almoneda, subasta; **-s tax** impuesto sobre ventas; **for (on) –** de venta.

sales•man [sélzmən] *s.* vendedor; dependiente (*de tienda*); **traveling –** agente viajero, viajante de comercio.

sales•wom•an [sélzwUmən] *s.* vendedora; dependiente (*de tienda*).

sa•li•ent [sélIənt] *adj.* saliente, sobresaliente; prominente.

sa•line [sélin] *adj.* salino.

sa•li•va [səláIvə] *s.* saliva.

sal•low [sǽlo] *adj.* amarillento, pálido.

sal•ly [sǽlI] *s.* salida; agudeza, chiste agudo; *v.* salir, hacer una salida; **to – forth** salir.

salm•on [sǽmən] *s.* salmón.

sa•loon [sǝlún] *s.* salón (*de un vapor*); taberna, *Am.* cantina; *Ríopl.* bar; **dining – of a ship** salón-comedor de un vapor.

salt [sɔlt] *s.* (*sodium chloride*) sal; (*wit*) chiste, agudeza; **smelling -s** sales aromáticas; **the – of the earth** la flor y nata de la humanidad; *adj.* salado; salobre; **– cellar** salero; **– mine** salina; **– pork** tocino salado; **– shaker** salero; **– water** agua salada, agua de mar; *v.* salar; **to – one´s money away** guardar o ahorrar su dinero.

salt•pe•ter [sɔltpítǝ] *s.* salitre, nitro; **– mine** salitral, salitrera.

salt•y [sɔ́ltI] *adj.* salado; salobre.

sal•u•tar•y [sǽljUtɛrI] *adj.* saludable.

sal•u•ta•tion [sæljǝtéʃǝn] *s.* salutación, saludo.

sa•lute [sǝlút] *s.* saludo; **gun –** salva; *v.* saludar; cuadrarse (*militarmente*).

sal•vage [sǽlvIdʒ] *s.* salvamento.

sal•va•tion [sælvéʃǝn] *s.* salvación.

salve [sæv] *s.* untura, ungüento; alivio; *v.* aliviar, aquietar, calmar; untar.

sal•vo [sǽlvo] *s.* salva.

same [sem] *adj.* mismo; igual; idéntico; **it is all the – to me** me es igual, me da lo mismo; **the –** lo mismo; el mismo (la misma, los mismos, las mismas).

sam•ple [sǽmpl] *s.* muestra, prueba; **book of –s** muestrario; *v.* probar; calar.

san•a•to•ri•um [sænǝtorIǝm] *s.* sanatorio.

sanc•ti•fy [sǽŋktǝfaI] *v.* santificar.

sanc•tion [sǽŋkʃǝn] *s.* sanción; aprobación; autorización; *v.* sancionar; ratificar; aprobar, autorizar.

sanc•ti•ty [sǽŋktǝtI] *s.* santidad.

sanc•tu•ar•y [sǽŋktʃUɛrI] *s.* santuario; asilo.

sand [sænd] *s.* arena; **– pit** arenal; *v.* enarenar, cubrir de arena; mezclar con arena; refregar con arena.

san•dal [sǽnd |] *s.* sandalia; alpargata; *Méx.* guarache (huarache); *Andes* ojota.

sand•pa•per [sǽndpepǝ] *s.* papel de lija; *v.* lijar, pulir o alisar con papel lija.

sand•stone [sǽndston] *s.* piedra arenisca.

sand•wich [sǽndwItʃ] *s.* bocadillo, emparedado, sándwich; *v.* intercalar, meter (entre).

sand•y [sǽndI] *adj.* arenoso; arenisco; **- hair** pelo rojizo.

sane [sen] *adj.* sano, sensato; cuerdo.

sang [sæŋ] *pret. de* **to sing.**

san•i•tar•i•um [sænǝtérIǝm] *s.* sanatorio.

san•i•tar•y [sǽnǝtɛrI] *adj.* sanitario.

san•i•ta•tion [sænǝtéʃǝn] *s.* saneamiento; salubridad; sanidad.

san•i•ty [sǽnǝtI] *s.* cordura.

sank [sæŋk] *pret. de* **to sink.**

sap [sæp] *s.* savia; tonto, bobo; *v.* agotar, debilitar, minar.

sap•ling [sǽplIŋ] *s.* vástago, renuevo; arbolillo.

sap•phire [sǽfaIr] *s.* zafiro; color de zafiro.

sar•casm [sárkæzǝm] *s.* sarcasmo.

sar•cas•tic [sɑrkǽstIk] *adj.* sarcástico.

sar•dine [sɑrdín] *s.* sardina.

sar•don•ic [sɑrdánIk] *adj.* burlón; sarcástico.

sash [sæʃ] *s.* faja (*cinturón de lana, seda o algodón*); banda, cinta ancha; **window –** bastidor (*o marco*) de ventana.

sat [sæt] *pret. & p.p. de* **to sit.**

satch•el [sǽtʃǝl] *s.* valija, maletín, maleta, saco.

sate [set] *v.* saciar.

sa•teen [sætín] *s.* satén o rasete (*raso de inferior calidad*).

sat•el•lite [sǽt|aIt] *s.* satélite.

sa•ti•ate [séʃIet] *v.* saciar, hartar.

sat•in [sétŋ] *s.* raso.

sat•ire [sǽtaIr] *s.* sátira.

sa•tir•i•cal [sǝtírIk] *adj.* satírico.

sat•i•rize [sǽtǝraIz] *v.* satirizar.

sat•is•fac•tion [sætIsfǽkʃǝn] *s.* satisfacción.

sat•is•fac•tor•i•ly [sætIsfǽktrǝlI] *adv.* satisfatoriamente.

sat•is•fac•to•ry [sætIrfǽktrI] *adj.* satisfactorio.

sat•is•fied [sǽtIsfaId] *adj.* satisfecho, contento.

sat•is•fy [sǽtIsfaI] *v.* satisfacer.

sat•u•rate [sǽtʃǝret] *v.* saturar, empapar.

Sat•ur•day [sǽtǝdI] *s.* sábado.

sauce [sɔs] *s.* salsa; **– dish** salsera; *v.* aderezar con salsa; sazonar, condimentar; insolentarse con.

sauce•pan [sɔ́spæn] *s.* cacerola.

sau•cer [sɔ́sǝ] *s.* platillo.

sau•ci•ness [sɔ́sInIs] *s.* descaro, insolencia.

sauc•y [sɔ́sI] *adj.* descarado, respondón, insolente, *Am.* retobado.

saun•ter [sɔ́ntǝ] *v.* pasearse, vagar.

sau•sage [sɔ́sIdʒ] *s.* salchicha, salchichón; longaniza; chorizo.

sav•age [sǽvIdʒ] *adj.* salvaje; fiero; bárbaro, brutal, feroz; *s.* salvaje.

sav•age•ry [sǽvIdʒrI] *s.* salvajismo; crueldad, fiereza.

sa•vant [sǝvánt] *s.* sabio.

save [sev] *v.* (*rescue*) salvar; (*hoard*) ahorrar; economizar; (*keep*) guardar; resguardar; **to – from** librar de; **to – one´s eyes** cuidarse la vista; *prep.* salvo, menos, excepto.

sav•er [sévə·] s. salvador; libertador; ahorrador; **life — salvavidas.**

sav•ing [sévIŋ] adj. (rescuer) salvador; (economizing) ahorrativo, económico; frugal; s. ahorro, economía; **-s** ahorros; **-s bank** caja o banco de ahorros; prep. salvo, excepto, con excepción de.

sav•ior [sévjə·] s. salvador.

sa•vor [sévə·] s. sabor; dejo; v. saborear; sazonar; **to — of** saber a, tener el sabor de; **it —s of tréason** huele a traición.

sa•vor•y [sévərI] adj. sabroso.

saw [sɔ] s. sierra; **— horse** caballete; v. aserrar, serrar; **it -s easily** es fácil de aserrar; pret. de **to see.**

saw•dust [sɔ́dʌst] s. aserrín, serrín.

saw•mill [sɔ́mIl] s. aserradero.

sawn [sɔn] p.p. de **to saw.**

Sax•on [sǽksŋ] adj. & s. sajón.

sax•o•phone [sǽksəfon] s. saxófono; saxofón.

say [se] v. decir; declarar; — ! ¡diga! ¡oiga usted!; **that is to —** es decir; **to — one´s prayers** rezar, decir o recitar sus oraciones; **to — the least** por lo menos; **it is said that** dizque, se dice que, dicen que; s. afirmación, aserto; **the final —** la autoridad decisiva; **to have a — in a matter** tener voz y voto en un asunto; **to have one´s —** expresarse, dar su opinión.

say•ing [séIŋ] s. dicho, refrán; aserto; **as the — goes** como dice el refrán.

scab [skæb] s. costra (de una herida); roña; esquirol (obrero que sustituye a un huelguista); obrero que acepta un jornal inferior; v. encostrarse (una herida), cubrirse de una costra.

scab•bard [skǽbə·d] s. vaina, funda (de espada, puñal, etc.).

scab•by [skǽbI] adj. costroso; roñoso, sarnoso, tiñoso.

scab•rous [skébrəs] adj. escabroso.

scaf•fold [skǽf]d] s. andamio, tablado; patíbulo, cadalso.

scaf•fold•ing [skǽf]dIŋ] s. andamiada (Am andamiaje), andamios.

scald [skɔld] v. escalar; **to — milk** calentar la leche hasta que suelte el hervor; s. escaldadura, quemadura.

scale [skel] s. escala; platillo de balanza; balanza; escama (de pez o de la piel); costra; **pair of —s** balanza; **platform —** báscula; v. escalar; subir, trepar por; graduar (a escala); medir según escala; pesar; escamar; quitar las escamas a; pelarse, despellejarse; descostrar(se); **to — down prices** rebajar proporcionalmente los precios.

scal•lop [skǿləp] s. onda, pico (adorno); molusco bivalvo; **-s** festón (recortes en forma de ondas o picos); v. festonear, recortar en forma de ondas o

picos; asar con salsa o migas de pan.

scalp [skælp] s. cuero cabelludo; v. desollar el cráneo; revender (boletos, billetes) a precio subido.

scal•y [skélI] adj. escamoso, lleno de escamas; **- with rust** mohoso.

scamp [skæmp] s. pícaro, bribón, bellaco.

scam•per [skǽmpə·] v. correr, escabullirse, escaparse; s. escabullida, carrera, corrida.

scan [skæn] v. escudriñar; examinar, mirar detenidamente; echar un vistazo a (en el habla popular); medir (el verso).

scan•dal [skǽnd]] s. escándalo; maledicencia, murmuración.

scan•dal•ize [skǽnd]aIz] v. escandalizar, dar escándalo.

scan•dal•ous [skǽnd]əs] adj. escandaloso; difamatorio; ver gonzoso.

scant [skænt] adj. escaso, corto; insuficiente; v. escatimar, limitar.

scant•y [skǽntI] adj. escaso; insuficiente.

scar [skɑr] s. (skin blemish) cicatriz; costurón; (mark) raya, marca (en una superficie pulida); v. marcar, rayar; hacer o dejar una cicatriz en.

scarce [skɛrs] adj. escaso; raro; **- ly** adv. escasamente; apenas.

scar•ci•ty [skérsətI] s. escasez; carestía; insuficiencia.

scare [skɛr] v. espantar, asustar; alarmar; sobresaltar; **he —s easily** se asusta fácilmente; **to — away** ahuyentar, espantar; s. susto, sobresalto.

scare•crow [skérkro] s. espantajo; espantapájaros.

scarf [skɑrf] s. bufanda; mantilla; pañuelo (para el cuello o la cabeza); tapete (para una mesa, tocador, etc.).

scar•let [skórlIt] s. escarlata; adj. de color escarlata; **— fever** escarlata, escarlatina.

scar•y [skérI] adj. espantadizo, asustadizo, miedoso.

scat [skæt] interj. ¡zape!

scat•tor [ɔkǽtə·] v esparcir(se); desparramar(se); **- brained** ligero de cascos, aturdido.

scene [sin] s. escena; escenario; decoración; vista; **to make a —** causar un escándalo.

scen•er•y [sínərI] s. paisaje, vista; **stage —** decoraciones.

scent [sɛnt] s. (odor) olor; (substance) perfume; (trace) pista, rastro; **to be on the — of** seguir el rastro de; **to have a keen —** tener buen olfato; v. oler, olfatear, ventear, husmear; perfumar.

scep•ter [séptə·] s. cetro.

scep•tic [sképtIk] adj. & s. escéptico.

scep•ti•cism [sképtəsIzəm] s. escepticismo.

shed•ule [skédʒUl] s. horario; itinerario (de trenes); lista, inventario (adjunto a un documento); v. fijar el día y la hora (para una clase, conferencia, etc.);

scheme I scratch   **450**

establecer el itinerario para (*un tren o trenes*).

scheme [skim] *s.* (*plan*) esquema, plan, proyecto; empresa; (*plot*) ardid, trama, maquinación; **color** – combinación de colores; **metrical** – sistema de versificación; *v.* proyectar, urdir; maquinar, intrigar, tramar.

schem·er [skímə·] *s.* maquinador, intrigante; proyectista.

shem·ing [skímɪŋ] *adj.* maquinador, intrigante; *s.* maquinación.

schism [sízəm] *s.* cisma.

schiz·o·phre·ni·a [skɪzofrínɪə] *s.* esquizofrenia.

schol·ar [skálə·] *s.* escolar, estudiante; becario (*el que disfruta una beca*); erudito, docto.

schol·ar·ly [skálə·lɪ] *adj.* erudito, sabio, docto; *adv.* eruditamente, doctamente.

schol·ar·ship [skálə·ʃɪp] *s.* saber; erudición; beca; **to have a** – disfrutar una beca.

scho·las·tic [skolǽstɪk] *adj.* escolástico; escolar.

school [skul] *s.* escuela; – **of fish** banco de peces; *adj.* de escuela; – **day** día de escuela; - **board** consejo de enseñanza; *v.* enseñar, educar, instruir, aleccionar.

school·boy [skúlbɔɪ] *s.* muchacho de escuela.

school·girl [skúlgɔ̃ˈl] *s.* muchacha de escuela.

school·house [skúlhaʊs] *s.* escuela.

school·ing [skúlɪŋ] *s.* instrucción; enseñanza, educación.

school·mas·ter [skúlmæstə·] *s.* maestro de escuela.

school·mate [skúlmet] *s.* condiscípulo, compañero de escuela.

school·room [skúlrum] *s.* clase, aula.

school·teach·er [skúltitʃə·] *s.* maestro de escuela.

schoo·ner [skúnə·] *s.* goleta; vaso grande para cerveza; **prairie** – galera con toldo.

sci·ence [sáləns] *s.* ciencia.

sci·en·tif·ic [saɪəntífɪk] *adj.* científico; **-ally** *adv.* científicamente.

sci·en·tist [sáləntɪst] *s.* científico, hombre de ciencia.

scin·til·late [síntəlet] *v.* centellear; chispear.

sci·on [sálən] *s.* vástago.

scis·sors [sízə·z] *s. pl.* tijeras.

scle·ro·sis [sklə·ósɪs] *s.* esclerosis.

scoff [skɔf] *s.* mofa, burla, befa, escarnio; *v.* escarnecer; mofarse; **to** – **at** mofarse de, burlarse de, escarnecer a.

scold [skold] *v.* reñir, reprender, regañar; *s.* regañón, persona regañona.

scold·ing [skóldɪŋ] *s.* regaño, represión; *adj.* regañón.

scoop [skup] *s.* (*tool*) cuchara, cucharón; pala; (*quantity*) palada, cucharada; (*winnings*) buen ganancia; **newspaper** – primera publicación de una

noticia; *v.* cavar, excavar; ahuecar; cucharear, sacar con cucharón o pala; achicar (*agua*); **to** – **in a good profit** sacar buena ganancia.

scoot [skut] *v.* escabullirse, correr, irse a toda prisa; **-!** ¡largo de aquí!.

scoot·er [skútə·] *s.* motoneta (*de motor*); monopatín.

scope [skop] *s.* alcance, extensión; esfera, campo.

scorch [skɔrtʃ] *v.* chamuscar; resecar, agostar; *s.* chamusquina, *Am.* chamuscada o chamuscadura.

score [skor] *s.* cuenta; escor (*en el juego*); raya, línea; calificación (*expresada numéricamente*); veintena; **musical** – partitura; **on that** – a ese respeto; **on the** – **of** a causa de, con motivo de; **to keep the** – llevar el escor, llevar la cuenta; **to settle old -s** desquitarse; *v.* marcar el escor, señalar los tantos en un juego; calificar (*numéricamente*); instrumentar (*música*); rayar, marcar con rayas; **to** – **a point** ganar un punto o tanto; **to** – **a success** lograr éxito, obtener un triunfo.

scorn [skɔrn] *s.* desdén, menosprecio; *v.* desdeñar, menospreciar.

scorn·ful [skɔ́rnfəl] *adj.* desdeñoso.

scor·pi·on [skɔ́rpɪən] *s.* escorpión, alacrán.

Scotch [skotʃ] *adj.* escocés; **the** – los escoceses, el pueblo escocés.

scoun·drel [skáʊndrəl] *s.* bellaco, bribón, pícaro.

scour [skaʊr] *v.* fregar, restregar, limpiar; pulir; **to** - **the country** recorrer la comarca (*en busca de algo*).

scourge [skɔ̃ˈdʒ] *s.* azote; *v.* azotar; castigar.

scout [skaʊt] *s.* explorador (*usualmente militar*); **a good** – un buen explorador; una buena persona, un buen compañero; *v.* explorar; reconocer.

scowl [skaʊl] *s.* ceño; *v.* fruncir el ceño, mirar con ceño; poner mala cara.

scram·ble [skrǽmbl̩] *v.* (*move*) gatear; (*eggs*) hacer un revoltillo; (*mix up*) revolver, mezclar; **to** – **for something** forcejear por coger algo; pelearse por coger algo; **to** – **up** trepar o subir a gatas (*una cuesta*); **-d eggs** revoltillo, huevos, revueltos; *s.* revoltillo, confusión; pelea.

scrap [skræp] *s.* (*fragment*) fragmento, pedacito; migaja; (*fight*) riña, reyerta; **-s** sobras; desperdicios; desechos; retales; – **book** álbum de recortes; – **iron** recortes o desechos del hierro; *v.* desechar; tirar a la basura; descartar; reñir.

scrape [skrep] *v.* (*abrasively*) raspar; rasguñar; rascar; (*rub*) raer; rozar; **to** – **along** ir tirando, ir pasándola; **to** – **together** recoger o acumular poco a poco; **to bow and** – ser muy servil; *s.* raspadura; rasguño; aprieto, dificultad; lío.

scrap·er [skrépə·] *s.* (*tool*) raspador; (*scrimping person*) tacaño.

scratch [skrætʃ] *v.* (*mark*) arañar, rasguñar; (*rub*) rascar; raspar; (*line*) rayar; escarbar; (*write badly*) hacer garabatos; **to – out** borrar, tachar; sacar (*los ojos*) con las uñas; *s.* arañazo, araño, rasguño; raya, marca; **to start from –** empezar sin nada; empezar desde el principio; empezar sin ventajas.

scrawl [skrɔl] *s.* garabato; *v.* hacer garabatos, escribir mal.

scraw•ny [skrɔ́ nI] *adj.* huesudo, flaco.

scream [skrim] *s.* chillido, alarido, grito; **he´s a –** es muy cómico o chistoso; *v.* chillar, gritar.

screech [skritʃ] *s.* chillido; **– owl** lechuza; *v.* chillar.

screen [skrin] *s.* (*projection*) pantalla; (*divider*) biombo; mampara; resguardo; (*sifter*) tamiz, cedazo; **– door** antepuerta de tela metálica; **motionpicture – pantalla de cinematógrafo; wire –** pantalla de tela metálica; *v.* tapar; resguardar, proteger con una pantalla o biombo; cerner; proyectar sobre la pantalla, filmar; **to – windows** proteger las ventanas con tela metálica.

screw [skru] *s.* tornillo; **– eye** armella; **– nut** tuerca; **– propeller – thread** rosca; *v.* atornillar; torcer, retorcer; **to – a lid on** atornillar una tapa; **to – up one´s courage** cobrar ánimo.

screw•driv•er [skrúdraIvəˇ] *s.* destornillador.

scrib•ble [skríb]] *v.* garrapatear, hacer garabatos, borronear, escribir mal o de prisa; *s.* garabato.

script [skrIpt] *s.* letra cursiva, escritura; manuscrito (*de un drama, de una película*).

scrip•ture [skríptʃəˇ] *s.* escritura sagrada; **the Scriptures** la Sagrada Escritura, la Biblia.

scroll [skrol] *s.* rollo de pergamino o papel; voluta, adorno en espiral; rúbrica (*de una firma*).

scrub [skrʌb] *v.* fregar; restregar; *s.* friega, fregado; *adj.* achaparrado; bajo, inferior; **– oak** chaparro; **- pine** pino achaparrado; **- team** equipo de jugadores suplentes o menos bien entrenados; **- woman** fregona.

scru•ple [skrúp]] *s.* escrúpulo; *v.* escrupulizar, tener escrúpulos.

scru•pu•lous [skrúpjələs] *adj.* escrupuloso.

scru•ti•nize [skrút ɳ alz] *v.* escudriñar, escrutar.

scru•ti•ny [skrút ɳ I] *s.* escrutinio.

scuff [skʌf] *v.* raspar; arrastrar los pies.

scuf•fle [skʌ́ f]] *s.* refriega, riña, pelea; *v.* forcejear; luchar, pelear; arrastrar los pies.

sculp•tor [skʌ́ lptəˇ] *s.* escultor.

sculp•ture [skʌ́ lptʃəˇ] *s.* escultura; *v.* esculpir, cincelar, tallar.

scum [skʌm] *s.* nata, capa, espuma; escoria; residuo, desechos; canalla, gente baja; *v.* espumar.

scur•ry [skɝ́ I] *v.* escabullirse; echar a correr; apresurarse; *s.* apresuramiento; corrida, carrera.

scut•tle [skʌ́ t]] *v.* echar a correr; barrenar (*un buque*); echar a pique; *s.* escotilla, escotillón; balde

(*para carbón*).

scythe [saIð] *s.* guadaña.

sea [si] *s.* mar; **to be at –** estar en el mar; estar perplejo o confuso; **to put to –** hacerse a la mar; *adj.* marino, marítimo, de mar; **– biscuit** galleta; **– green** verdemar; **– gull** gaviota; **– level** nivel del mar; **– lion** león marino, foca; **– power** potencia naval.

sea•board [síbord] *s.* costa, litoral; *adj.* costanero, litoral.

sea•coast [síkost] *s.* costa, litoral.

seal [sil] *s.* (*stamp*) sello; timbre; (*animal*) foca, león marino; **to set one´s – to** sellar; aprobar; *v.* sellar; estampar; cerrar; tapar; **to – in** encerrar, cerrar herméticamente; **to – with sealing wax** lacrar.

sealing wax [síIɳ wæks] *s.* lacre.

seam [sim] *s.* costura; juntura; cicatriz; filón, veta; *v.* echar una costura, coser.

sea•man [símən] *s.* marino, marinero.

seam•stress [símstrIs] *s.* costurera.

sea•plane [síplen] *s.* hidroavión.

sea•port [síport] *s.* puerto de mar.

sear [sIr] *v.* chamuscar(se), tostar(se); resecar(se); herrar, marcar con hierro candente; *adj.* reseco, marchito.

search [sɝtʃ] *v.* buscar; escudriñar; registrar; examinar; **to – a prisoner** registrar a un prisionero; **to – for something** buscar algo; **to – into** investigar, indagar; *s.* busca, búsqueda; registro, inspección; investigación, pesquisa, indagación; **– warrant** mandato judicial de practicar un registro; **in – of** en busca de.

search•light [sɝtʃlaIt] *s.* reflector.

sea•shore [síʃor] *s.* costa, playa, orilla o ribera del mar.

sea•sick [sísIk] *adj.* mareado; **to get –** marearse.

sea•sick•ness [sísIknIs] *s.* mareo.

sea•side [sísaId] *s.* costa, litoral; playa.

sea•son [síz ɳ] *s.* estación (*del año*); temporada; sazón, ocasión, tiempo; **– ticket** billete de abono; **Christmas –** navidades; **harvest –** siega, tiempo de la cosecha; **opera –** temporada de la ópera; **to arrive in good –** llegar en sazón, llegar a tiempo; *v.* sazonar; condimentar; aclimatar.

sea•son•ing [síz ɳ Iɳ] *s.* condimento; salsa; desecación (*de la madera*).

seat [sit] *s.* (*furniture*) asiento; silla; (*site*) sitio; (*headquarters*) residencia; sede (*episcopal, del gobierno, etc.*); (*body*) nalgas; fondillos, parte trasera (*de los pantalones o calzones*); **– of learning** centro de estudios, centro de erudición; *v.* sentar; asentar; dar asiento a; **to – oneself** sentarse; **it -s a thousand people** tiene cabida para mil personas.

sea•weed [síwid] *s.* alga marina.

se•cede [sisíd] *v.* separarse (*de una federación o unión*).

se•clude [sɪklúd] v. recluir, apartar, aislar; **to – oneself from** recluirse de, apartarse de.

se•clud•ed [sɪklúdId] adj. apartado, aislado; solitario.

se•clu•sion [sɪklúʒən] s. apartamiento, soledad, aislamiento; retiro.

sec•ond [sékənd] adj. segundo; inferior; **– hand** segundero (de reloj); **– lieutenant** subteniente; **second-rate** de segunda clase; mediocre, inferior; **on – thought** después de pensarlo bien; s. segundo; padrino (en un desafío); ayudante; mercancía de segunda calidad; mercancía defectuosa; v. secundar (o segundar), apoyar; apadrinar.

sec•ond•ar•y [sékəndɛrI] adj. secundario; **– education** segunda enseñanza; **- school** escuela secundaria, escuela de segunda enseñanza.

sec•ond-hand [sékəndhǽnd] adj. de segunda mano; usado; de ocasión; indirecto, por intermedio de otro.

sec•ond•ly [sékəndlI] adv. en segundo lugar.

se•cre•cy [síkrəsI] secreto, sigilo, reserva.

se•cret [síkrIt] s. secreto; adj. secreto; escondido, oculto; **- service** policía secreta; **-ly** adv. secretamente, en secreto.

sec•re•tar•i•at [sɛkrətǽriət] s. secretaría.

sec•re•tar•y [sékrətɛrI] s. secretario; escritorio (con estantes para libros).

se•crete [sɪkrít] v. secretar (una secreción); esconder, ocultar.

se•cre•tion [sɪkríʃən] s. secreción.

se•cre•tive [sɪkrítIv] adj. reservado, callado; **- gland** glándula secretoria.

sect [sɛkt] v. secta.

sec•tion [sékʃən] s. sección; trozo; tajada; región; barrio; v. seccionar, dividir en secciones.

sec•u•lar [sékjələ-] adj. & s. secular.

se•cure [sɪkjÚr] adj. seguro; firme; v. asegurar; afianzar; obtener; resguardar; **-ly** adv. seguramente, con seguridad; firmemente.

se•cu•ri•ty [sɪkjÚrətI] s. seguridad; fianza, garantía, prenda; resguardo, protección; **securities** bonos, obligaciones, acciones, valores.

se•dan [sɪdǽn] s. sedán.

se•date [sɪdét] adj. sosegado; tranquilo, sereno; serio.

se•da•tion [sədéʃən] d. sedación.

sed•a•tive [sédətIv] adj. & s. calmante, sedativo.

sed•en•tar•y [séd ŋ tɛrI] adj. sedentario; inactivo.

sed•i•ment [sédəmənt] s. sedimento, heces, residuo.

se•di•tion [sɪdíʃən] s. sedición.

se•di•tious [sɪdíʃəs] adj. sedicioso.

se•duce [sɪdjús] v. seducir.

se•duc•tion [sɪd ʌ kʃən] s. seducción.

see [si] v. ver; **– that you do it** no deje Vd. de hacerlo; tenga Ud. cuidado de hacerlo; **I'll – to it** me

encargaré de ello; **let me –** a ver; **to – a person home** acompañar a una persona a casa; **to – a person off** ir a la estación para despedir a una persona; **to – a person through a difficulty** ayudar a una persona a salir de un apuro; **to – through a person** adivinar lo que piensa una persona, darse cuenta de sus intenciones; **to – to one´s affairs** atender a sus asuntos; **to have seen military service** haber servido en el ejercito; s. sede, silla; **Holy See** Santa Sede.

seed [sid] s. (grains) semilla; (semen) simiente; (fruit) pepita; **to go to –** producir semillas; decaer, declinar; descuidar de su persona, andar desaseado; v. sembrar; despepitar, quitar las pepitas o semillas de; producir semillas.

seed•ling [sídlIŋ] s. planta de semillero; arbolillo (de menos de tres pies de altura).

seed•y [sídI] adj. semilloso, lleno de semillas; raído; desaseado.

seek [sik] v. buscar; pedir, solicitar; **to – after** buscar; **to – to** tratar de, esforzarse por.

seem [sim] v. parecer; **it -s to me** me parece.

seem•ing•ly [símIŋlI] adv. aparentemente, en apariencia, al parecer.

seem•ly [símlI] adj. propio, decente, decoroso.

seen [sin] p.p. de **to see**.

seep [sip] v. escurrirse, rezumarse, colarse, filtrarse.

seer [sIr] s. vidente, adivino, profeta.

seethe [sið] v. bullir, hervir; burbujear.

seg•ment [ségmənt] s. segmento.

seg•re•gate [ségrəget] v. segregar.

seize [siz] v. (grasp) asir, coger, agarrar; apoderarse de; (arrest) prender o aprehender; (take advantage of) aprovecharse de; (capture) embargar, secuestrar; **to – upon** asir; **to become –d with fear** sobrecogerse de miedo.

sei•zure [síʒə-] s. cogida; captura; aprehensión (de un criminal); secuestro, embargo (de bienes); ataque (de una enfermedad).

sel•dom [séldəm] adv. rara vez, raras veces, raramente.

se•lect [səlékt] adj. selecto, escogido; v. elegir, escoger; entresacar.

se•lec•tion [səlékʃən] s. selección, elección.

self [sɛlf]; **by one-** por sí, por sí mismo; **for one- para sí; one´s other –** su otro yo; **his wife and –** su esposa y él (véase **herself, himself, ourselves, themselves,** etc.); **self-centered** egoísta, egocéntrico; **self-conscious** consciente de sí, cohibido, tímido; **self-control** dominio de sí mismo (o de sí propio); **self-defense** defensa propia; **self-denial** abnegación; **self-evident** patente, manifiesto; **self-esteem** respeto de sí mismo; amor propio; **self-government** gobierno autónomo, autonomía; gobierno democrático; **self-interest** propio interés; egoísmo; **self-love** amor propio;

self-possessed sereno, dueño de sí, tranquilo; **self-sacrifice** abnegación; **self-satisfied** pagado de sí, satisfecho de sí.

self•ish [sélfɪʃ] *adj.* egoísta; **-ly** *adv.* con egoísmo, por egoísmo.

self•ish•ness [sélfɪʃnɪs] *s.* egoísmo.

self•same [sélfsém] *adj.* mismo, idéntico, mismísimo.

sell [sɛl] *v.* vender; venderse, estar de venta; **to – at auction** vender en almoneda o subasta, subastar; **to – out** venderlo todo.

sell•er [sélɚ] *s.* vendedor.

selves [sɛlvz] *pl. de* **self.**

sem•blance [sémbləns] *s.* semejanza; apariencia.

sem•i•cir•cle [séməsɚk] *s.* semicírculo.

sem•i•co•lon [sémɘkolɘn] *s.* punto y coma.

sem•i•nar•y [sémɘnɛrɪ] *s.* seminario.

sen•ate [sénɪt] *s.* senado.

sen•a•tor [sénɪtɚ] *s.* senador.

send [sɛnd] *v.* enviar; mandar; despachar; remitir; expedir; lanzar (*una flecha, pelota, etc.*); **to – away** despedir, despachar; **to – forth** despachar, enviar; emitir; echar; **to – someone up for 15 years** condenar a un reo a 15 años de prisión; **to – word** avisar, mandar decir, mandar recado.

send•er [séndɚ] *s.* remitente; transmisor.

se•nile [sínaɪl] *adj.* senil, caduco; chocho.

se•nil•i•ty [sɘníləti] *s.* senectud; chochera o chochez.

sen•ior [sínjɚ] *adj.* (*older*) mayor, de más edad; más antiguo; (*superior*) superior; **– class** clase del cuarto año; *s.* persona o socio más antiguo; estudiante del último año; **to be somebody's – by two years** ser dos años mayor que alguien.

sen•sa•tion [sɛnséʃɘn] *s.* sensación.

sen•sa•tion•al [sɛnséʃɘn] *adj.* sensacional; emocionante.

sense [sɛns] *s.* (*function*) sentido; (*sentiment*) sentimiento; sensación; (*judgment*) juicio, sensatez; (*meaning*) significado; **common –** sentido común; **to make – tener** sentido; **to be out of one's –s** estar fuera de sí, estar loco; *v.* percibir, sentir; darse cuenta de.

sense•less [sénslɪs] *s.* sin sentido; insensato, absurdo; insensible, privado de sentido.

sen•si•bil•i•ty [sɛnsɘbílɘtɪ] *s.* sensibilidad.

sen•si•ble [sénsɘb] *adj.* (*aware*) sensato, razonable, cuerdo; (*appreciable*) sensible, perceptible; **sensibly** *adv.* sensatamente, con sensatez, con sentido común; sensiblemente, perceptiblemente.

sen•si•tive [sénsɘtɪv] *adj.* sensitivo; sensible; quisquilloso, susceptible.

sen•si•tive•ness [sénsɘtɪvnIs] *s.* sensibilidad.

sen•si•tize [sénsɘtaɪz] *v.* sensibilizar.

sen•su•al [sénʃuɘl] *adj.* sensual, carnal, lujurioso.

sen•su•al•i•ty [sɛnʃuǽlɘtɪ] *s.* sensualidad; lujuria.

sent [sɛnt] *pret. & p.p. de* **to send.**

sen•tence [séntɘns] *s.* sentencia, fallo, decisión; oración (*grammatical*); **death –** pena capital; *v.* sentenciar.

sen•ti•ment [séntɘmɘnt] *s.* sentimiento; sentido.

sen•ti•men•tal [sɛntɘmént] *adj.* sentimental.

sen•ti•men•tal•i•ty [sɛntɘmɛntǽlɘtɪ] *s.* sentimentalismo, sentimentalidad.

sen•ti•nel [séntɘn] *s.* centinela.

sen•try [séntrɪ] *s.* centinela.

sep•a•rate [sépɹɪt] *adj.* (*apart*) separado; apartado; solitario; (*different*) distinto, diferente; **-ly** *adv.* separadamente, por separado; aparte; [sépɘret] *v.* separar(se); apartar(se).

sep•a•ra•tion [sɛpɘréʃɘn] *s.* separación.

Sep•tem•ber [sɛptémbɚ] *s.* septiembre.

sep•ul•cher [sépklɚ] *s.* sepulcro, sepultura.

se•quel [síkwɘl] *s.* secuela; continuación, consecuencia; resultado.

se•quence [síkwɘns] *s.* (*continuity*) secuencia, sucesión; serie, continuación; (*result*) consecuencia, resultado; runfla (*serie de tres o más naipes de un mismo palo*).

ser•e•nade [sɛrɘnéd] *s.* serenata; *v.* dar serenata a.

se•rene [sɘrín] *adj.* sereno; tranquilo; claro, despejado.

se•ren•i•ty [sɘrénɘtɪ] *s.* serenidad; calma.

ser•geant [sárdʒɘnt] *s.* sargento; **– at arms** oficial que guarda el orden (*en un cuerpo legislativo*).

se•ri•al [sírɪɘl] *s.* cuento o novela por entregas; *adj.* consecutivo, en serie; **– novel** novela por entregas.

se•ries [síriz] *s.* serie; series.

se•ri•ous [sírɪɘs] *adj.* serio, grave; **-ly** *adv.* seriamente, con seriedad, en serio; gravemente.

se•ri•ous•ness [sírɪɘsnIs] *s.* seriedad; gravedad.

ser•mon [sɝmɘn] *s.* sermón.

ser•pent [sɝpɘnt] *s.* serpiente, sierpe.

se•rum [sírɘm] *s.* suero.

ser•vant [sɝvɘnt] *s.* sirviente; criado; servidor; **-girl** criada, *Ríopl.* mucama; *Andes, Col., Ven.* muchacha de servicio.

serve [sɝv] *v.* (*wait on*) servir; (*supply*) surtir, abastecer; **to – a term in prison** cumplir una condena; **to – a warrant** entregar una citación; **to – as** servir de; **to – for** servir de, servir para; **to – notice on** notificar, avisar, advertir; **to – one's purpose** servir para el caso o propósito; **it –s me right** bien me lo merezco; *s.* saque (*de la pelota en tenis*).

serv•er [sɝvɚ] *s.* servidor; saque (*el que saca la pelota en el juego de tenis*); bandeja; mesa de servicio.

serv·ice [s3'vIs] *s.* servicio; saque (*de la pelota en tenis*); entrega (*de una citación judicial*); **at your** — a la disposición de Vd.; servidor de Vd.; **funeral** — honras fúnebres, funerales, exequias; **mail** — servicio de correos; **table** — servicio de mesa, vajilla; **tea** — juego y servicio de té; — **entrance** entrada para el servicio; - **man** militar; - **station** estación de servicio; *v.* servir; reparar; surtir (*una tienda*).

serv·ice·a·ble [s3'vIsəb |] *adj.* servible; útil; duradero.

ser·vile [s3'v |] *adj.* servil.

ser·vi·tude [s3'vətjud] *s.* servidumbre; esclavitud.

ses·sion [sé|ən] *s.* sesión.

set [sɛt] *v.* (*place*) poner; colocar, asentar; (*fix*) fijar; establecer; ajustar; engastar (*piedras preciosas*); soldificar(se), endurecer(se) (*el cemento, yeso, etc.*); ponerse (*el sol, la luna*); empollar; **to** — **a bone** componer un hueso dislocado; **to** — **a trap** armar una trampa; **to** — **about** ponerse a; **to** — **an example** dar ejemplo; **to** — **aside** poner aun lado, poner aparte; apartar; ahorrar; **to** — **back** retrasar, atrasar; **to** — **forth** exponer, expresar; manifestar; **to** — **forth on a journey** ponerse en camino; **to** — **off** disparar, hacer estallar (*un explosivo*); hacer resaltar; salir; **to** — **on fire** pegar o poner fuego a, incendiar; **to** — **one's jaw** apretar las quijadas; **to** — **one's heart on** tener la esperanza puesta en; **to** — **one's mind on** resolverse a, aplicarse a; **to** — **out for** partir para, salir para; **to** — **out to** empezar a; **to** — **right** colocar bien; enderezar; rectificar; **to** — **sail** hacerse a la vela; **to** — **the brake** frenar, apretar el freno; **to** — **up** erigir, levantar; armar, montar (*una máquina*); parar (*tipo de imprenta*); establecer, poner (*una tienda, un negocio*); **to** — **go** listo para partir; *s.* juego, colección; serie; grupo, clase; partida (*de tenis*); - **of dishes** servicio de mesa, vajilla; - **of teeth** dentadura; **radio** — radio, radiorreceptor; **tea** — servicio para té.

set·back [sétbæk] *s.* atraso, revés, retroceso inesperado.

set·tee [sɛtí] *s.* canapé.

set·ting [sétIŋ] *s.* engaste (*de una joya*); escena, escenario; puesta (*del sol, de un astro*); - **sun** sol poniente.

set·tle [sét |] *v.* (*colonize*) colonizar, poblar; establecer(se); fijar(se); asentar(se); (*solve*) arreglar, poner en orden, ajustar (*cuentas*); zanjar (*una disputa*); pagar, liquidar, saldar; **to** — formalizarse; asentarse; calmarse; poner casa; **to** — **on a date** fijar o señalar una fecha; **to** — **property on (upon)** asignar bienes o propiedad a; **to** — **the**

matter decidir el asunto, concluir con el asunto.

set·tle·ment [sét | mənt] *s.* (*community*) establecimiento; colonia; poblado; población; colonización; (*arrangement*) asignación o traspaso (*de propiedad*); ajuste, arreglo; pago; saldo, finiquito, liquidación; - **house** casa de beneficencia; **marriage** — dote.

set·tler [sétlə-] *s.* colono, poblador, - **of disputes** zanjador de disputas.

set·up [sétəp] *s.* arreglo; organización.

sev·er [sévə-] *v.* desunir(se), partir(se), dividir(se), separar(se); cortar, romper.

sev·er·al [sévrəl] *adj.* varios, diversos; distintos, diferentes.

se·vere [səvír] *adj.* severo; áspero; austero; rígido; riguroso; grave; recio, fuerte.

se·ver·i·ty [səvérətI] *s.* severidad; austeridad; rigidez; gravedad; rigor.

sew [so] *v.* coser.

sew·er [sjÚə] *s.* albañal, cloaca.

sew·ing [sóIŋ] *s.* costura; modo de coser; — **machine** máquina de coser; - **room** cuarto de costura.

sewn [son] *p.p. de* **to sew.**

sex [sɛks] *s.* sexo; — **appeal** atracción sexual.

sex·tant [sékstənt] *s.* sextante.

sex·ton [sékstən] *s.* sacristán.

sex·u·al [sékʃUəl] *adj.* sexual.

shab·by [ʃæbI] *adj.* raído, gastado; andrajoso; mal vestido; vil, injusto; **to treat someone shabbily** tratar a alguien injustamente o con menosprecio.

shack [ʃæk] *s.* cabaña, choza, *Am.* bohío, *Am.* jacal.

shack·le [ʃæk |] *v.* encadenar; trabar, echar trabas a, poner grillos a; estorbar; -**s** *s. pl.* cadenas, trabas, grillos, esposas; estorbo.

shade [ʃed] *s.* (*shadow*) sombra; (*nuance*) tinte, matiz; (*cover*) visillo, cortinilla; pantalla (*de lámpara*); visera (*para los ojos*); **a** — **longer** un poco más largo; - **of meaning** matiz; **in the** — **of** a la sombra de; *v.* sombrear; dar sombra; resguardar de la luz; matizar.

shad·ow [ʃædo] *s.* (*darkness*) sombra; oscuridad; (*phantom*) espectro; **under the** — **of** al abrigo de, a la sombra de; **without a** — **of doubt** sin sombra de duda; *v.* sombrear; obscurecer; **to** — **someone** espiarle a alguien los pasos, seguirle por todas partes.

shad·ow·y [ʃædəwI] *adj.* lleno de sombras; tenebroso; vago, indistinto.

shad·y [ʃédI] *adj.* sombrío, sombreado, umbrío; — **business** negocio sospechoso; - **character** persona de carácter dudoso, persona de mala fama.

shaft [ʃæft] *s.* pozo o tiro (*de mina, o elevador*); cañón de chimenea; columna; eje, árbol (*de maquinaria*); flecha.

shag·gy [ʃægI] *adj.* peludo, velludo; lanudo; desaseado; áspero.

shake [ʃek] v. menear(se); estremecer(se); temblar; sacudir(se); agitar(se); titubear, vacilar; hacer vacilar; dar, estrechar (*la mano*); **to — hands** dar un apretón de manos, darse la mano; **to — one's head** mover o menear la cabeza; cabecear; **to — with cold** tiritar de frío, estremecerse de frío; **to — with fear** temblar de miedo, estremecerse de miedo; s. sacudida; sacudimiento; estremecimiento, temblor; apretón (*de manos*); **hand —** apretón de manos.

shak•en [ʃékən] p.p. de **to shake.**

shake-up [ʃékəp] s. reorganización.

shak•y [ʃékI] adj. tembloroso; vacilante.

shall [ʃæl] v. aux. del futuro del indicativo en las primeras personas (**I, we**); en las demás expresa mayor énfasis, mandato u obligación; **he — not do it** no lo hará, no ha de hacerlo; **thou shalt not steal** no hurtarás.

shal•low [ʃǽlo] adj. bajo, poco profundo; superficial; ligero de cascos.

shal•low•ness [ʃǽlonIs] s. poca hondura, poca profundidad; superficialidad; ligereza de juicio.

sham [ʃæm] s. fingimiento, falsedad, farsa; adj. fingido, simulado; falso; **— battle** simulacro, batalla fingida; v. fingir, simular.

sham•bles [ʃǽmbḷz] s. desorden.

shame [ʃem] s. vergüenza; deshonra; **— on you !** ¡qué vergüenza!; **it is a —** es una vergüenza; es una lástima; **to bring — upon** deshonrar; v. avergonzar; deshonrar.

shame•ful [ʃémfəl] adj. vergonzoso.

shame•less [ʃémlIs] adj. desvergonzado, descarado.

shame•less•ness [ʃémlIsnIs] s. desvergüenza; descaro, desfachatez.

sham•poo [ʃæmpú] s. champú, lavado de la cabeza; v. dar un champú, lavar (*la cabeza*).

sham•rock [ʃǽmrɑk] s. trébol.

shank [ʃæŋk] s. canilla (*parte inferior de la pierna*); zanca.

shan•ty [ʃǽntI] s. choza, cabaña, casucha.

shape [ʃep] s. (*form*) forma; (*figure*) figura; (*condition*) estado, condición; **to be in a bad —** estar mal; **to put into —** arreglar, poner en orden, ordenar; v. formar, dar forma a; tomar forma; **to — one's life** dar forma a, ajustar o disponer su vida; **his plan is shaping well** va desarrollándose bien su plan.

shape•less [ʃéplIs] adj. informe, sin forma.

share [ʃɛr] s. (*portion*) porción, parte; (*participation*) participación; acción (*participación en el capital de una campaña*); v. compartir; repartir; participar; **to — in** participar en, tener parte en; **to — a thing with** compartir una cosa con.

share•hold•er [ʃérholdə] s. accionista.

shark [ʃɑrk] s. (*fish*) tiburón; (*usurer*) estafador; (*expert*) perito, experto; **loan —** usurero; **to be a — at** ser un águila (*o* ser muy listo) para.

sharp [ʃɑrp] adj. (*acute*) agudo, puntiagudo; cortante; punzante; (*biting*) mordaz; picante; (*bright*) astuto; (*clear*) claro, distinto, bien marcado; (*sudden*) repentino; **— curve** curva abrupta, curva pronunciada o muy cerrada; **— ear** oído fino; **— features** facciones bien marcadas; **— struggle** lucha violenta; **— taste** sabor acre; **— temper** genio áspero; **— turn** vuelta repentina; s. sostenido (*en música*); **card —** tahur, fullero; adv. véase **sharply; at ten o'clock —** a las diez en punto.

sharp•en [ʃɑrpən] v. afilar(se); sacar punta a; aguzar(se); amolar.

sharp•ly [ʃɑrplI] adv. agudamente; mordazmente, ásperamente; repentinamente; claramente; **to arrive —** llegar en punto.

sharp•ness [ʃɑrpnIs] s. agudeza; sutileza; mordacidad; rigor; aspereza; acidez.

shat•ter [ʃǽtə] v. estrellar(se), astillar(se), hacer(se) añicos; quebrar(se), romper(se); **to — one's hopes** frustrar sus esperanzas; **his health was —ed** se le quebrantó la salud; **-s** s. pl. pedazos, trozos, añicos, fragmentos; **to break into —** hacer(se) añicos.

shave [ʃev] v. afeitar(se), rasurar(se); rapar(se); acepillar (*madera*); s. rasura, Am. afeitada; **he had a close —** por poco no se escapa; se salvó por milagro.

shav•en [ʃévən] p.p. de **to shave; cleanshaven** bien afeitado.

shav•ing [ʃévIŋ] s. rasura, Am. afeitada; **wood -s** virutas; **— brush** brocha de afeitar; **— soap** jabón de afeitar.

Shawl [ʃɔl] s. mantón, chal.

she [ʃi] pron. pers. ella; **— who** la que; s. hembra; **she-bear** osa; **she-goat** cabra.

sheaf [ʃif] s. haz, gavilla, manojo; lío; v. hacer gavillas.

shear [ʃIr] v. trasquilar, esquilar (*las ovejas*); cortar (*con tijeras grandes*).

shears [ʃIrz] s. pl. tijeras grandes.

sheath [ʃiθ] s. vaina; funda, envoltura.

sheathe [ʃið] v. envainar.

sheaves [ʃivz] pl. de **sheaf.**

shed [ʃɛd] s. cobertizo; tejadillo; Ríopl., Andes galpón (*de una estancia*); v. derramar; difundir; esparcir; mudar (*de piel, plumas, etc.*); ser impermeable (*un paño, abrigo, sombrero, etc*); **to — leaves** deshojarse; pret. & p.p. de **to shed.**

sheen [ʃin] s. lustre, viso.

sheep [ʃip] s. oveja; carnero; ovejas; **— dog** perro de pastor; **— fold** redil; **— skin** zalea; badana; pergamino; diploma (*de pergamino*).

sheep•ish [ʃípIʃ] adj. vergonzoso, encogido, tímido.

sheer [ʃIr] adj. (pure) pure; completo; (thin) fino, delgado, transparente, diáfano; (steep) escarpado; **by – force** a pura fuerza.

sheet [ʃit] s. (bed) sábana; (paper) hoja, pliego (de papel); lámina (de metal); (transfer) traslador, transferir; **to – for oneself** valerse o mirar por sí lo); **– lightning** relampagueo.

shelf [ʃɛlf] s. estante, anaquel; repisa; saliente de roca.

shell [ʃɛl] s. concha; cáscara (de huevo, nuez, etc.); vaina (de guisantes, frijoles, garbanzos, etc.); casco (de una embarcación); armazón (de un edificio); granada, bomba, cápsula (para cartuchos); v. cascar (nueces); desvainar, quitar la vaina a, pelar; desgranar (maíz, trigo, etc.); bombardear.

shel·lac [ʃəlǽk] s. laca; v. barnizar con laca.

shell·fish [ʃɛlfɪʃ] s. marisco; mariscos.

shel·ter [ʃɛ́ltɚ] s. abrigo, refugio, asilo; resguardo, protección; **to take –** refugiarse, abrigarse; v. abrigar, refugiar, guarecer; proteger, amparar.

shelve [ʃɛlv] v. poner o guardar en un estante; poner a un lado, arrinconar, arrumbar.

shelves [ʃɛlvz] s. pl. estantes, anaqueles; estantería.

shep·herd [ʃɛ́pɚd] s. pastor; zagal; **– dog** perro de pastor.

sher·bet [ʃɝbɪt] s. sorbete.

sher·iff [ʃɛ́rɪf] s. alguacil mayor (de un condado en los Estados Unidos).

sher·ry [ʃɛ́rɪ] s. jerez, vino de Jerez.

shield [ʃild] s. escudo, rodela, broquel; resguardo, defensa; v. escudar, resguardar, proteger.

shift [ʃɪft] v. (change) cambiar; mudar(se); alternar(se); variar; desviar(se); (transfer) trasladar, transferir; **to – for oneself** valerse o mirar por sí mismo; **to – gears** cambiar de marcha; **to – the blame** echar a otro su propia culpa; s. cambio; desvío, desviación; tanda, grupo de obreros; turno; **gear – cambio de marcha.

shift·less [ʃftlIs] adj. negligente; holgazán.

shil·ling [ʃɪ́lIŋ] s. chelín.

shim·my [ʃɪ́mI] s. (dance) shimmy; (vibration) abanicuero.

shin [ʃIn] s. espinilla (de la pierna); v. **to – up** trepar.

shine [ʃaɪn] v. (beam) brillar, resplandecer, lucir; (polish) pulir; dar brillo, lustre o bola, embolar (zapatos); s. brillo, lustre, resplandor; **rain or – llueva o truene; **to give a shoe –** dar bola (brillo o lustre) a los zapatos; embolar o embetunar los zapatos; limpiar el calzado.

shin·gle [ʃɪ́ŋgl] s. ripia, tabla delgada, Méx. tejamaní o tejamaní; pelo corto escalonado; letrero de oficina; **-s zona** (erupción de la piel); v. cubrir con tejamaniles; techar con tejamaniles.

shin·ing [ʃáɪnIŋ] adj. brillante; resplandeciente.

shin·y [ʃáɪnI] adj. brillante; lustroso.

ship [ʃIp] s. (naval) buque, barco, navío, nave; (air)

aeronave, avión; **– builder** ingeniero naval, constructor de buques; **– mate** camarada de a bordo; **-yard** astillero; **on –board** a bordo; v. embarcar(se); despachar, enviar; remesar; trasportar; alistarse como marino.

ship·ment [ʃɪpmənt] s. embarque; cargamento; despacho, envío; remesa.

ship·per [ʃɪpɚ] s. embarcador; remitente.

ship·ping [ʃɪpIŋ] s. embarque; despacho, envío; **– charges** gastos de embarque; **– clerk** dependiente de muelle; dependiente encargado de embarques.

ship·wreck [ʃɪprɛk] s. naufragio; v. echar a pique, hacer naufragar; naufragar, irse a pique.

ship·yard [ʃɪpyard] s. astillero.

shirk [ʃɝk] v. evadir, evitar.

shirt [ʃɝt] s. camisa; **– waist** blusa; **in – sleeves** en camisa, en mangas de camisa.

shiv·er [ʃɪ́vɚ] v. tiritar; temblar; estremecerse; s. escalofrío, temblor, estremecimiento.

shoal [ʃol] s. bajío, banco de arena; banco (de peces).

shock [ʃak] s. (blow) choque; sacudida; sacudimiento; golpe; (surprise) sobresalto; **– absorber** amortiguador; **– of grain** hacina o gavilla de mieses; **– of hair** guedeja, greña; **– troops** tropas de asalto; v. chocar, ofender; escandalizar; causar fuerte impresión; horrorizar; sacudir; conmover; hacinar, hacer gavillas de (mieses).

shock·ing [ʃákIŋ] adj. chocante, ofensivo, repugnante; espantoso, escandaloso.

shod [ʃad] pret. & p.p. de **to shoe.**

shoe [ʃu] s. zapato; botín; **brake –** zapata de freno; **horse –** herradura; **– blacking** betún, bola; **– polish** brillo, lustre, bola; **– store** zapatería; v. calzar; herrar (un caballo).

shoe·black [ʃúblæk] s. limpiabotas.

shoe·horn [ʃúhɔrn] s. calzador.

shoe·lace [ʃúles] s. lazo, cinta, cordón de zapato.

shoe·maker [ʃúmekɚ] s. zapatero.

shoe·string [ʃústrIŋ] s. lazo, cinta, cordón de zapato.

shone [ʃon] pret. & p.p. de **to shine.**

shook [ʃʊk] pret. de **to shake.**

shoot [ʃut] v. (firearm) tirar, disparar, descargar; hacer fuego; fusilar; dar un balazo; (throw) lanzar, disparar (una instantánea); fotografiar, filmar (una escena); echar (los dados); brotar (las plantas); **to – by** pasar rápidamente; **to – forth** brotar, salir; germinar; lanzarse; **to – it out with someone** pelearse a balazos; **to – up a place** entrarse a balazos por un lugar; s. vástago, retoño, renuevo; **to – go out for a –** salir a tirar; ir de caza.

shoot·er [ʃútɚ] s. tirador.

shoot·ing [ʃútIŋ] s. tiroteo; **– match** certamen de tiradores (o de tiro al blanco); **– pain** punzada, dolor agudo; **– star** estrella fugaz.

shop [ʃɔp] *s.* tienda; taller; **– window** escaparate, vitrina, aparador, *Riopl.*, *Andes* vidriera; **barber –** barbería; **beauty –** salón de belleza; **to talk –** hablar uno de su oficio o profesión; *v.* ir de tiendas; ir de compras, comprar.

shop•keep•er [ʃópkipə-] *s.* tendero.

shop•per [ʃópə-] *s.* comprador.

shop•ping [ʃópɪŋ] *s.* compra, compras; **to go –** ir de compras, ir de tiendas.

shore [ʃor] *s.* costa, playa, orilla, ribera; puntal; **ten miles off –** a diez millas de la costa; *v.* **to – up** apuntalar, poner puntales.

shorn [ʃorn] *p.p. de* **to shear.**

short [ʃɔrt] *adj.* (*duration*) corto; breve; (*height*) bajo; *Méx.* chaparro; escaso; brusco; **– cut** atajo; **– circuit** cortocircuito; **- wave** onda corta, método corto; **short-legged** de piernas cortas; **– loan** préstamo a corto plazo; **for –** para abreviar; **in –** en resumen, en suma, en conclusión; **in – order** rápidamente, prontamente; **in a – time** en poco tiempo; al poco tiempo; **to be – of** estar falto o escaso de; **to cut –** acortar, abreviar, terminar de repente; **to run – of something** acabársele (írsele acabando) a uno algo; **to stop –** parar de repente, parar en seco.

short•age [ʃórtɪdʒ] *s.* escasez, carestía; déficit; falta.

short•com•ing [ʃórtkʌmɪŋ] *s.* falta, defecto.

short•en [ʃórtṇ] *v.* acortar(se), abreviar(se), disminuir(se).

short•en•ing [ʃórtnɪŋ] *s.* manteca, grasa (*para hacer pasteles*); acortamiento, abreviación.

short•hand [ʃórthænd] *s.* taquigrafía.

short•ly [ʃórtlɪ] *adv.* brevemente; en breve; al instante, pronto, luego; bruscamente, secamente.

short•ness [ʃórtnɪs] *s.* cortedad; brevedad; pequeñez; escasez, deficiencia.

shorts [ʃɔrts] *s. pl.* calzoncillos, calzones cortos.

short•sight•ed [ʃórtsáItɪd] *adj.* miope; corto de vista.

Shot [ʃɑt] *pret. & p.p. de* **to shoot**; *s.* (*discharge*) tiro; disparo; balazo; cañonazo; (*pellet*) bala; balas; (*injection*) inyección; (*throw*) tirada; **– of liquor** trago de aguardiente; **buck –** municiones, postas; **not by a long –** ni con mucho, ni por pienso, nada de eso; **he is a good –** es buen tirador, tiene buen tino; **to take a –** at disparar un tiro a; hacer una tentativa a; **within rifle –** a tiro de rifle.

shot•gun [ʃótgʌn] *s.* escopeta.

should [ʃUd] *v. aux. del condicional en las primeras personas* (**I, we**): **I said that I – go** dije que iría; *equivale al imperfecto del subjuntivo*; **if it – rain** si lloviera; *se usa con la significación de deber*: **you – not do it** no debiera (*o* no debería) hacerlo.

shoul•der [ʃóldə-] *s.* (*person*) hombro; (*animal*) lomo, pernil (*puerco, cordero*); borde, saliente (*de un camino*); **-s** espalda, espaldas; **– blade** espaldilla, paletilla; **straight from the –** con toda franqueza; **to turn a cold – to** volver las espaldas a, tratar fríamente; *v.* cargar al hombro, echarse sobre las espaldas; cargar con, asumir; empujar con el hombro.

shout [ʃaUt] *v.* gritar; vocear; *s.* grito.

shove [ʃʌv] *v.* empujar, dar empellones; **to – aside** echar a un lado, rechazar; **to – off** partir, zarpar (*un buque*); salir, irse; *s.* empujón, empellón; empuje.

shov•el [ʃʌvḷ] *s.* pala; *v.* traspalar.

show [ʃo] *v.* (*exhibit*) mostrar, enseñar; exhibir; (*prove*) probar, demostrar; indicar; (*appear*) verse; asomarse; **- him in** que pase, hágale entrar; **to – off** alardear, hacer ostentación de; lucirse; **to – up** aparecer, presentarse; **to – someone up** hacer subir a alguien; mostrarle el camino (*para subir*); desenmascarar a alguien, poner a alguien en la evidencia; *s.* exhibición; demostración; ostentación; espectáculo; representación, función, apariencia; **– window** escaparate, vitrina, aparador, *Am.* vidriera; **to go to the –** ir al teatro, ir al cine; **to make a – of oneself** exhibirse, hacer ostentación.

show•case [ʃókes] *s.* vitrina, aparador.

show•down [ʃódaUn] *s.* arreglo terminante.

show•er [ʃáUə-] *s.* aguacero, chubasco, chaparrón, lluvia; ducha, baño de ducha; *Méx.* regadera; **bridal –** tertulia para obsequiar a una novia; *v.* llover; caer un aguacero.

shown [ʃon] *p.p. de* **to show.**

show•y [ʃóI] *adj.* ostentoso; vistoso, chillón.

shrank [ʃræŋk] *pret. de* **to shrink.**

shred [ʃɛd] *s.* tira, triza; andrajo; fragmento; pizca; **to be in -s** estar raído; estar andrajoso; estar hecho trizas; **to tear to -s** hacer trizas; *v.* desmenuzar; hacer trizas, hacer tiras; *pret. & p.p. de* **to shred.**

shrew [ʃru] *s.* arpía, mujer brava, mujer de mal genio.

shrewd [ʃrud] *adj.* astuto, sagaz, agudo.

shriek [ʃrik] *v.* chillar, gritar; *s.* chillido, grito.

shrill [ʃrɪl] *adj.* agudo, penetrante, chillón; *v.* chillar.

shrimp [ʃrɪmp] *s.* camarón; hombrecillo insignificante.

shrine [ʃraɪn] *s.* santuario; altar; lugar venerado.

shrink [ʃrɪŋk] *v.* encoger(se); contraer(se); disminuir; **to – back** retroceder; **to – from** retroceder ante, apartarse de; huir de, rehuir.

shrink•age [ʃrínkɪdʒ] *s.* encogimiento; contracción; merma.

shriv•el [ʃrívḷ] *v.* encoger(se); fruncir(se), marchitar(se); disminuir(se).

shroud [ʃraUd] *s.* mortaja; *v.* mortajar; cubrir, ocultar.

shrub [ʃrʌb] *s.* arbusto.

shrub•ber•y [ʃr ʌ bərI] *s.* arbustos.

shrug [ʃrʌg] *v.* encogerse de hombros; *s.* encogimiento de hombros.

shrunk [ʃrʌŋk] *pret.* & *p.p. de* **to shrink.**

shrunk•en [ʃr ʌ ŋkən] *p.p. de* **to shrink.**

shuck [ʃʌk] *s.* hollejo; cáscara.

shud•der [ʃ ʌ də-] *v.* temblar, estremecerse; *s.* temblor, estremecimiento.

shuf•fle [ʃ ʌ f] *v.* barajar; revolver, mezclar; arrastrar (*los pies*); **to – along** ir arrastrando los pies; *s.* mezcla, confusión; evasiva; **- of feet** arrastramiento de pies; **it is your** – a Vd. le toca barajar.

shun [ʃʌn] *v.* esquivar, evadir, rehuir, evitar.

shut [ʃʌt] *v.* cerrar(se); **to – down** parar el trabajo; cerrar (*una fábrica*); **to – in** encerrar; **to – off** cortar (*el gas, la electricidad, el agua, etc.*); **to – off from** incomunicar, aislar de, cortar la comunicación con ; excluir; **to – out** impedir la entrada de; cerrar la puerta a; **to – up** cerrar bien; tapar; encerrar; tapar la boca, hacer callar; callarse; *pret.* & *p.p. de* **to shut;** *adj.* cerrado.

shut•ter [ʃ ʌ tə-] *s.* contraventa; postigo (*de ventana*); cerrador; obturador (*de una cámara fotográfica*).

shut•tle [ʃ ʌ t] *s.* lanzadera; *v.* ir y venir acompasadamente (*como una lanzadera*).

shy [ʃaI] *adj.* tímido, apocado, vergonzoso; asustadizo; esquivo; **to be – on** estar escaso de; **to be – two cents** faltarle a uno dos centavos; *v.* esquivarse, hacerse a un lado; asustarse; **to – at something** retroceder ante algo; respingar (*un caballo*) al ver algo; espantarse con algo; **to – away** esquivarse de repente; respingar (*un caballo*); desviarse, apartarse.

shy•ness [ʃaInIs] *s.* apocamiento, timidez, vergüenza.

shy•ster [ʃáIstə-] *s.* leguleyo, abogadillo tramposo, picapleitos.

sib•i•lant [síbələnt] *s.* sibilante.

sick [sIk] *adj.* enfermo, malo; nauseado; angustiado; **- leave** licencia por enfermedad; **to be – for** languidecer por, suspirar por; **to be – of** estar cansado de; estar harto de; **to be to** (*o* **at**) **one's stomach** tener náuseas; **to make –** enfermar; dar pena, dar lástima; *s.* **the** – los enfermos; *v.* incitar, azuzar (*a un perro*) **– him** ¡síguele!.

sick•en [síkən] *v.* enfermar(se), poner(se) enfermo; dar asco; tener asco; sentir náuseas.

sick•en•ing [síknIŋ] *adj.* nauseabundo repugnante; lastimoso.

sick•le [sík] *s.* hoz.

sick•ly [síklI] *adj.* enfermizo; achacoso, enclenque; malsano.

sick•ness [síknIs] *s.* enfermedad; malestar; náusea.

side [saId] *s.* (*surface*) lado; cara; costado; ladera; falda (*de una colina*); (*faction*) partido, facción; **– by –** lado a lado; **by his –** a su lado; **by the – of** al lado de; **on all -s** por todos lados; **to take -s with** ser partidario de, ponerse al lado de; *adj.* lateral; de lado; oblicuo; incidental; secundario, de menos importancia; **– glance** mirada de soslayo, de través o de reojo; **– issue** cuestión secundaria; **– light** luz lateral; noticia, detalle o ilustración incidental; *v.* **to – with** estar por, ser partidario de, apoyar a, opinar con.

side•board [sáIdbord] *s.* aparador.

side•slip [sáIdslIp] *s.* deslizamiento.

side•track [sáIdtræk] *v.* desviar; echar a un lado.

side•walk [sáIdwɔk] *s.* acera, *Méx.* banqueta, *Ríopl.*, *Ch.*, *Andes* vereda; *C.A.*, *Col.*, andén.

side•ways [sáIdwez] *adv.* de lado, de costado; oblicuamente; hacia un lado; *adj.* lateral, de lado, oblicuo.

siege [sidʒ] *s.* cerco, sitio, asedio; **to lay – to** sitiar, cercar.

sieve [sIv] *s.* tamiz, cedazo; criba; *v. véase* **sift.**

sift [sIft] *v.* cerner, tamizar; cribar.

sigh [saI] *v.* suspirar; *s.* suspiro.

sight [saIt] *s.* (*sense*) vista; (*view*) visión; espectáculo, escena; (*gun*) mira (*de un arma de fuego*); **in – of** a vista de; **payable at –** pagadero a la vista; **he is a –** es un adefesio o mamarracho; **this room is a –** este cuarto es un horror; **to catch – of** vislumbrar, avistar; **to know by –** conocer de vista; **to lose – of** perder de vista; **to see the -s** ver o visitar los puntos de interés; *v.* avistar; ver.

sight•see•ing [sáItsiIŋ] *s.* turismo; **- tour** paseo en auto para ver puntos de interés.

sign [saIn] *s.* (*signal*) signo; seña, señal; (*indication*) muestra; (*placard*) letrero; **- board** cartel; tablero (*para fijar anuncios*); *v.* firmar; contratar, hacer firmar; **to – over property** ceder una propiedad mediante escritura, hacer cesión legal de propiedad; **to – up for a job** firmar el contrato para un empleo; contratar para un empleo.

sig•nal [síɡn] *s.* señal, seña; *v.* señalar, indicar, hacer seña, dar la señal; *adj.* señalado, notable; extraordinario; **– beacon** faro; **– code** código de señales.

sig•na•ture [síɡnətʃə-] *s.* firma.

sign•er [sáInə-] *s.* firmante.

sig•nif•i•cance [sIɡnífəkəns] *s.* significación; significado.

sig•nif•i•cant [sIɡnífəkənt] *adj.* significativo.

sig•ni•fy [síɡnəfaI] *v.* significar.

si•lence [sáIləns] *s.* silencio; *v.* acallar; apagar (*un sonido*); aquietar, sosegar.

si•lent [sáIlənt] *adj.* silencioso; callado; tácito; **– partner** socio comanditario (*que no tiene ni voz ni voto*).

sil•hou•ette [sIlUét] s. silueta; v. perfilar; **to be -d against** perfilarse contra.

silk [sI-k] s. seda; adj. de seda; **– industry** industria sedera; **– ribbon** cinta de seda.

silk•en [sílkən] adj. sedoso; de seda.

silk•worm [sílw ɜ˞ m] s. gusano de seda.

silk•y [sílkI] adj. sedoso, sedeño; de seda.

sill [sIl] s. umbral; **window –** antepecho de ventana.

sil•ly [sílI] adj. necio, tonto, bobo, simple; absurdo, insensato.

silt [sIlt] s. cieno.

sil•ver [sílvə˞] s. (metal) plata; (tableware) cubierto; (dishes) vajilla de plata; (color) color de plata; adj. de plata; plateado; argentino; **– wedding** bodas de plata; v. platear; argentar; **to – a mirror** azogar un espejo.

sil•ver•smith [sílvə-smIθ] s. platero.

sil•ver•ware [sílvə-wɛr] s. vajilla de plata, vajilla plateada; cuchillos, cucharas y tenedores (por lo general de plata o plateados).

sil•ver•y [sílvərI] adj. plateado; argentino.

sim•i•lar [símələ-] adj. semejante; **-ly** adv. semejantemente; de la misma manera.

sim•i•lar•i•ty [sIməlǽrətI] s. semejanza, parecido.

sim•i•le [síməlI] s. símil.

sim•mer [símə-] v. hervir a fuego lento.

sim•ple [símp] adj. simple; sencillo; llano; tonto, mentecato; **simpleminded** ingenuo, simple, simplón; s. simple.

sim•ple•ton [sípl tən] s. simplón, papanatas, papamoscas.

sim•plic•i•ty [sImplísətI] s. sencillez; simplicidad; simpleza; ingenuidad.

sim•pli•fy [símpləfaI] v. simplificar.

sim•ply [símplI] adv. simplemente; sencillamente; solamente.

sim•u•late [símjəlet] v. simular.

si•mul•ta•ne•ous [saImˈtén əs] adj. simultáneo.

sin [sIn] s. pecado, culpa; v. pecar.

since [sIns] conj. desde que; después (de) que; puesto que, como, visto que; dado que; prep. desde, después de; adv. desde entonces; **ever –** desde entonces; **he died long** murió hace mucho tiempo; **we have been here – five** estamos aquí desde las cinco.

sin•cere [sInsír] adj. sincero.

sin•cer•i•ty [sInsérətI] s. sinceridad.

si•ne•cure [sínIkjur] s. sinecura (trabajo fácil y bien pagado).

sin•ew [sínju] s. tendón; fibra, vigor.

sin•ew•y [sIjəwI] adj. nervudo, nervioso o nervoso; fuerte, vigoroso.

sin•ful [sínfəl] adj. pecaminoso; pecador.

sing [sIŋ] v. cantar; **to – out of tune** desentonar(se), desafinar; **to – to sleep** arrullar.

singe [sIndʒ] v. chamuscar; s. chamusquina, Am.

chamuscada, Am. chamuscadura.

sing•er [síŋə-] s. cantor; cantora, cantatriz.

sin•gle [síŋg] adj. (unique) solo; (distinct) individual; particular; (unmarried) soltero; **– entry book-keeping** teneduría por partida simple; **– room** cuarto para uno; **– woman** mujer soltera; **not a – word** ni una sola palabra; s. billete de un dólar; v. **to – out** singularizar, distinguir, escoger; entresacar.

sin•gle•hand•ed [síŋg hǽndId] adj. solo, sin ayuda.

sing•song [síŋsɔŋ] s. sonsonete, cadencia monótona.

sin•gu•lar [síŋgjələ-] adj. singular; raro, extraordinario; s. singular, número singular.

sin•is•ter [sínIstə-] adj. siniestro, aciago, funesto.

sink [sIŋk] v. hundir(se); sumir(se), sumergir(se); echar a pique; irse a pique, naufragar; cavar (un pozo); enterrar, clavar (un puntal o poste); **to – into one´s mind** grabarse en la memoria; **to – one´s teeth into** clavar el diente en; **to – to sleep** caer en el sueño; s. sumidero; fregadero.

sin•ner [sínə-] s. pecador.

sin•u•ous [sínjuəs] adj. sinuoso, tortuoso; con vueltas y rodeos.

si•nus [sáInəs] s. seno, cavidad (en un hueso); **frontal –** seno frontal.

sip [sIp] v. sorber; chupar; s. sorbo.

si•phon [sáIfən] s. sifón; v. sacar (agua) con sifón.

sir [s ɜ˞] s. señor.

si•ren [sáIrən] s. sirena.

sir•loin [s ɜ˞ lɔIn] s. solomillo, solomo.

sir•up [sírəp] s. jarabe.

sis•sy [sísI] adj. & s. afeminado, maricón.

sis•ter [sístə-] s. hermana; **Sister Mary** Sor María.

sis•ter-in-law [sístərInlɔ] s. cuñada, hermana política.

sit [sIt] v. sentar(se); colocar, asentar; posarse (un pájaro); estar sentado; estar situado; empollar (las gallinas); apoyarse, reunirse, celebrar sesión (un cuerpo legislativo, un tribunal); sentar, venir o caer (bien o mal un traje); **to – down** sentarse; **to – out a dance** quedarse sentado durante una pieza de baile; **to – still** estarse quieto; **to – tight** mantenerse firme en su puesto; **to – up** incorporarse; **to – up all night** velar toda la noche; **to – up and take notice** despabilarse.

site [saIt] s. sitio, local, situación.

sit•ting [sítIŋ] s. sesión (de un cuerpo legislativo, tribunal, etc.); sentada; **at one –** de una sentada; adj. sentado; **– hen** gallina ponedora; **– room** sala (de descanso); sala de espera; antesala.

sit•u•at•ed [sítʃUetId] adj. situado, sito, ubicado, colocado.

sit•u•a•tion [sItʃUéʌən] s. (location) situación, colocación, (employment) empleo; posición; (status) situación.

size [salz] s. tamaño, medida; v. clasificar según el tamaño; **to – up** tantear, formarse una idea de, juzgar.

siz•zle [síz ι] v. chirriar (*aplícase al sonido que hace la carne al freírse*); s. chirrido (*de la carne al freírse*).

skate [sket] s. patín; **ice** – patín de hielo, patín de cuchilla; **roller** – patín de ruedas; v. patinar.

skein [sken] s. madeja.

skel•e•ton [skélət ŋ] s. esqueleto; armazón; **- key** llave maestra.

skep•tic = **sceptic.**

sketch [skɛtʃ] s. (*drawing*) boceto; diseño; croquis; (*outline*) esbozo; bosquejo; v. bosquejar; delinear; esbozar, dibujar.

ski [ski] s. esquí; v. esquiar, patinar con esquís.

skid [skɪd] v. patinar, resbalar(se); patinar (*una rueda*); deslizarse.

skill [skɪl] s. destreza, maña, habilidad, pericia.

skilled [skɪld] adj. experto, práctico, experimentado, hábil.

skil•let [skílɪt] s. sartén; cacerola.

skill•ful, skil•ful [skílfəl] adj. experto, diestro, ducho, hábil, perito.

skim [skɪm] v. (*remove layer*) desnatar, quitar la nata a; espumar, quitar la espuma a; (*read*) leer superficialmente; **to – over the surface** rozar la superficie.

skimp [skɪmp] v. escatimar; economizar; ser tacaño; hacer (*las cosas*) con descuido.

skimp•y [skímpɪ] adj. escaso; tacaño.

skin [skɪn] s. piel; cutis; pellejo; cuero; cáscara, hollejo; **to save one´s –** salvar el pellejo; **skin-deep** superficial; v. desollar; pelar; **to – someone (out of his money)** desplumar a una persona, quitarle a uno el dinero.

skin•ny [skínɪ] adj. flaco; descarnado.

skip [skɪp] v. saltar; brincar; saltarse (*unos renglones, un párrafo, etc.*), omitir; saltar por encima de, salvar de un brinco, **to – out** salir a escape, escabullirse, escaparse, s. salto, brinco; omisión.

skip•per [skípə] s. patrón (*de barco*); capitán; saltador, brincador.

skir•mish [skɝ´mɪʃ] s. escaramuza; v. escaramuzar, sostener una escaramuza.

skirt [skɝ´t] s. falda, *Ríopl.* pollera; orilla, borde; **under – enaguas**; v. bordear, orillar, ir por la orilla de; circundar; **to – along a coast** costear.

skit [skɪt] s. parodia, juguete o paso cómico; boceto satírico o burlesco.

skull [skʌl] s. cráneo; calavera.

skunk [skʌŋk] s. *C.A., Méx., Ríopl.* zorrillo o zorrino, *Ven., Col.* mapurite.

sky [skaI] s. cielo; **- blue** azul celeste.

Sky•lark [skáIlork] s. alondra, calandria.

sky•light [skáIlaIt] s. claraboya, tragaluz.

sky•rock•et [skáIrokIt] s. cohete.

sky•scrap•er [skáIskrepə] s. rascacielos.

slab [slæb] s. tabla, plancha, losa; tajada gruesa; **marble –** losa de mármol.

slack [slæk] adj. (*not taut*) flojo; (*sluggish*) tardo, lento; inactivo; **– season** temporada inactiva; s. flojedad, flojera; inactiviadad; **to take up the –** apretar, estirar; **-s** pantalones anchos con pliegues, v. véase **slacken.**

slack•en [slǽkən] v. aflojar(se); flojear; retardar(se); disminuir.

slag [slæg] s. escoria.

slain [slen] p.p. de to **slay.**

slam [slæm] v. cerrar(se) de golpe; dejar caer de golpe; **to – someone** decirle a alguien una claridad o grosería; **to – the door** dar un portazo; s. golpazo; claridad, grosería; **- of a door** portazo; **to make a grand –** ganar todas las bazas (*en el juego de bridge*).

slan•der [slǽndə] s. calumnia, maledicencia; v. calumniar.

slan•der•ous [slǽndərəs] adj. calumnioso.

slang [slæŋ] s. jerga, jerigonza; vulgarismo.

slant [slænt] s. sesgo; inclinación; punto de vista; adj. sesgado; inclinado; oblicuo; v. sesgar; inclinar(se); ladear.

slap [slæp] s. palmada, manazo, manotada; insulto, desaire; v. dar una palmada a, dar un manazo a.

slap•stick [slǽpstɪk] adj. de golpe y porrazo.

slash [slæʃ] v. acuchillar; dar cuchilladas o tajos; cortar; hacer fuerte rebaja de (*precios, sueldos*); s. cuchillada; tajo, raja, cortadura.

slat [slæt] s. tabla, tablilla.

slate [slet] s. pizarra; color de pizarra; lista de candidatos; **– pensil** pizarrín.

slaugh•ter [slɔ´tə] s. carnicería, matanza, *Ríopl.* carneada; **– house** matadero, *Méx., C.A.* rastro; v. matar; *Ríopl.* carnear; hacer una matanza; destrozar.

slave [slev] s. esclavo; **– driver** capataz de esclavos; persona que agobia de trabajo a otra; **- labor** trabajo de esclavos; trabajadores forzados; v. trabajar como esclavo.

slav•er [slǽvə] s. baba; v. babosear, babear.

slav•er•y [slévrɪ] s. esclavitud.

slav•ish [slévɪʃ] adj. servil.

slay [sle] v. matar.

sled [slɛd] s. trineo, rastra.

sleek [slik] adj. liso; pulido, resbaloso; suave; artero, mañoso; v. alisar; pulir.

sleep [slip] v. dormir; **to –it off** dormir la mona; **to – off a headache** curarse con sueño un dolor de cabeza; **to – on it** consultarlo con la almohada; s.

sueño; **to go to** – dormirse, quedarse dormido; **to put to** – adormecer; arrullar (*al nene*).

sleep•er [slípə-] *s.* durmiente; cochecama, coche-dormitorio.

sleep•i•ly [slípIlI] *adv.* con somnolencia.

sleep•i•ness [slípInIs] *s.* sueño, modorra, somnolencia.

sleep•ing [slípIŋ] *adj.* durmiente; dormido; **– car** coche-cama, coche-dormitorio; **– pills** píldoras para dormir; **– sickness** encefalitis letárgica.

sleep•less [slíplIs] *adj.* desvelado, insomne, sin sueño.

sleep•y [slípI] *adj.* soñoliento; amodorrado; **to be –** tener sueño.

sleet [slit] *s.* cellisca; *v.* cellisquear.

sleeve [sliv] *s.* manga.

sleigh [sle] *s.* trineo; **- bell** cascabel; *v.* pasearse en trineo.

sleight [slaIt]: **- of hand** juego de manos; presdigitación, escamoteo.

slen•der [sléndə-] *adj.* delgado; tenue; escaso, insuficiente.

slept [slɛpt] *pret. & p.p. de* **to sleep.**

sleuth [sluθ] *s.* detective (*o* detectivo).

slew [slu] *pret. de* **to slay.**

slice [slaIs] *s.* rebanada, tajada; lonja; *v.* rebanar, tajar; cortar.

slick [slIk] *v.* alisar; pulir; **to – up** alisar bien; pulir bien; pulirse, acicalarse, componerse; *adj.* liso; meloso, suave; aceitoso; astuto, mañoso.

slick•er [slIk] *s.* impermeable de hule (*o* de caucho); embaucador.

slid [slId] *pret. & p.p. de* **to slide.**

slid•den [slíd ŋ] *p.p. de* **to slide.**

slide [slaId] *v.* resbalar(se); deslizar(se); hacer resbalar; patinar; **to – into** meter(se) en; **to – out** (o **– away**) deslizarse, colarse, escabullirse, escaparse; **to let something –** dejar pasar algo; no hacer caso de algo; *s.* resbalón; resbaladero, lugar resbaladizo; ligado (*en música*); véase **landslide; - cover** tapa corrediza; **– rule** regla de cálculo; **microscope –** platina.

slight [slaIt] *s.* desaire, menosprecio, desdén; desatención; *v.* desairar, menospreciar; descuidar, desatender; *adj.* delgado; delicado; leve, ligero; pequeño; insignificante; escaso; **-ly** *adv.* escasamente; ligeramente; un poco, apenas.

slim [slIm] *adj.* delgado; esbelto; escaso.

slime [slaIm] *s.* limo, cieno, fango; baba, secreción viscosa.

slim•y [sláImI] *adj.* viscoso, mucoso, fangoso; baboso.

sling [slIŋ] *s.* honda (*para tirar piedras*); cabestrillo (*para sostener el brazo*); eslinga (*maroma provista de ganchos para levantar pesos*); **– shot** tirador de goma o hule; *v.* tirar, arrojar; **to – a rifle over one´s**

shoulder echarse el rifle al hombro.

slink [slIŋk] *v.* andar furtivamente; **to – away** escurrirse, escabullirse, deslizarse.

slip [slIp] *v.* (*slide*) deslizar(se); resbalar(se); (*err*) cometer un desliz; equivocarse; **to – away** escaparse, escabullirse, escurrirse; **to – in** meter(se); **to – one´s dress on** ponerse de prisa el vestido; **to – out** salirse; sacar a hurtadillas; **to – out of joint** dislocarse, *Am.* zafarse (*un hueso*); **to – something off** quitar(se) algo; **to let an opportunity –** dejar pasar una oportunidad; **it slipped my mind** se me olvidó, se me pasó; **it slipped off** se zafó; *s.* desliz; resbalón; error, equivocación; funda (*de muebles, de almohada*); combinación-enagua; pedazo (*de papel*), papeleta; embarcadero; guía, sarmiento (*para transplantar*); **- knot** nudo corredizo.

slip•per [slIpə-] *s.* zapatilla; babucha; pantufla.

slip•per•y [slIprI] *adj.* resbaloso, resbaladizo; evasivo.

slit [slIt] *v.* cortar, hacer una rendija, abertura o incisión; **to – into strips** cortar en tiras; *pret. & p.p. de* **to slit;** *s.* abertura, hendedura, rendija; cortada; incisión.

slob•ber [slóbə-] *s.* baba; *v.* babosear, babear.

slob•ver•ing [slóbəɾIŋ] *adj.* baboso.

slo•gan [slógən] *s.* lema, mote.

sloop [slup] *s.* chalupa.

slop [slop] *v.* (*soil*) ensuciar; (*splash*) salpicar; (*spill*) derramar(se); *s.* fango suciedad; **-s** lavazas, agua sucia; desperdicios.

slope [slop] *v.* inclinar(se); *s.* inclinación; declive; falda, ladera; cuesta, bajada; vertiente.

slop•py [slópI] *adj.* puerco, sucio, cochino; desaseado; mal hecho.

slot [slot] *s.* (*opening*) abertura, hendedura; (*groove for coins*) ranura (*en que se introduce una moneda*); **- machine** máquina automática que funciona por medio de una moneda, "traganíqueles", "tragamonedas"; *v.* hacer una abertura o hendedura.

sloth [sloθ] *s.* pereza; perezoso (*cuadrúpedo*).

slouch [slaUtʃ] *s.* (*posture*) postura muy relajada o floja; (*person*) persona perezosa o desaseada; **– hat** sombrero gacho; **to walk with a –** andar con los hombros caídos y la cabeza inclinada; *v.* andar agachado; andar caído de hombros; andar alicaído; arrellanarse, repantigarse (*en una silla*).

slov•en•li•ness [slʌvənlInIs] *s.* desaseo, desaliño; suciedad.

slov•en•ly [slʌvənlI] *adj.* desaseado, desaliñado; desarreglado.

slow [slo] *adj.* (*low speed*) lento, despacio; (*late*) tardo; atrasado; (*sluggish*) lerdo; torpe; *adv.* lentamente, despacio; *v.* **to – down** (*o* **– up**) retardar disminuir (*el paso, la marcha, la velocidad*); aflojar el paso; **-**

ly *adv.* despacio, lentamente.

slow•ness [slónIs] *s.* lentitud; torpeza; cachaza.

slug [slʌg] *s.* bala; porrazo, puñetazo; babosa (*molusco sin concha*); haragán; trago (*de aguardiente*); lingote (*de imprenta*); *c.* aporrear, abofetear, dar puñetazos.

slug•gard [slʌgəd] *s.* holgazán, haragán.

slug•gish [slʌgIʃ] *adj.* tardo; inactivo.

sluice [slus] *s.* compuerta; caño, canal; **– gate** compuerta.

slum [slʌm] *s.* barrio bajo; *v.* visitar los barrios bajos.

slum•ber [slʌmbə] *v.* dormitar; dormir; *s.* sueño, sueño ligero.

slump [slʌmp] *v.* hundirse; desplomarse; bajar repentinamente (*los precios o valores*); *s.* desplome, hundimiento, bajón, baja repentina (*de precios, valores, etc.*).

slung [slʌŋ] *pret.* & *p.p. de* **to sling.**

slunk [slʌŋk] *pret.* & *p.p. de* **to slink.**

slush [slʌʃ] *s.* (*snow*) nieve a medio derretir; (*mud*) lodazal, fango; (*refuse*) desperdicios; (*drivel*) sentimentalismo.

sly [slaI] *adj.* astuto, socarrón, zorro, taimado; **on the – a** hurtadillas, a escondidas.

sly•ness [sláInIs] *s.* disimulo, astucia.

smack [smæk] *s.* (*taste*) sabor, dejo; (*kiss*) beso ruidoso; (*crack*) chasquido (*de látigo*); (*slap*) palmada, manotada; **a – of something** una pizca de algo; *v.* dar un beso ruidoso; chasquear (*un látigo*); dar un manazo; **to – of** saber a, tener el sabor de; oler a; **to – one´s lips** chuparse los labios, saborearse, rechuparse, relamerse.

small [smɔl] *adj.* (*size*) pequeño, chico; bajo; (*insignificant*) insignificante; mezquino; **– change** dinero menudo, suelto; **– hours** primeras horas de la mañana; **– letters** letras minúsculas; **– talk** conversación insubstancial, charladuría; **– voice** vocecita; **to feel –** sentirse pequeño o insignificante.

small•ness [smɔlnIs] *s.* pequeñez; bajeza.

small•pox [smɔlpɑcks] *s.* viruelas.

smart [smɑrt] *adj.* (*intelligent*) listo, inteligente; (*astute*) ladino; astuto; agudo; (*stylish*) elegante; **– remark** observación aguda o penetrante; **– set** gente de buen tono; *s.* escozor, *Ríopl.*, *C.A.*, *Méx.* ardor; *v.* picar, escocer, *Ríopl.*, *C.A.*, *Méx.* arder.

smash [smæʃ] *v.* quebrantar, quebrar, romper; destrozar; aplastar; **to – into** chocar con; topar con, darse un tope contra; *s.* quebrazón, quiebra; fracaso; choque o tope violento; derrota completa.

smat•ter•ing [smætərIŋ] *s.* conocimiento superficial y rudimental.

smear [smIr] *v.* embarrar, untar, manchar; **to – with paint** pintorrear, pintarrajear; *s.* mancha.

smell [smɛl] *v.* oler; **to – of** oler a; *s.* olor; olfato; **– of** olor a; **to take a –** oler.

smell•y [smɛlI] *adj.* oloroso; hediondo.

smelt [smɛlt] *v.* fundir (*metales*); *pret.* & *p.p. de* **to smell.**

smile [smaIl] *v.* sonreir(se); *s.* sonrisa.

smil•ing [smáIlIŋ] *adj.* risueño, sonriente; **-ly** *adv.* sonriendo, con cara risueña.

smite [smaIt] *v.* golpear; herir; castigar; afligir; *véase* **smitten.**

smith [smIθ] *s.* forjador; *véase* **blacksmith, goldsmith, silversmith.**

smith•y [smíθI] *s.* herrería, fragua, forja.

smit•ten [smítn̩] *p.p. de* **to smite** & *adj.* afligido; castigado; enamorado; **to be – with a disease** darle a uno una enfermedad.

smock [smɑk] *s.* bata corta, batín.

smoke [smok] *s.* humo; **– screen** cortina de humo; **cloud of –** humareda; **to have a –** dar una fumada, fumar; *v.* fumar, *Am.* chupar (*un cigarro*); humear; ahumar; **to – out** ahuyentar o echar fuera con humo.

smok•er [smókə] *s.* fumador; vagón de fumar; reunión o tertulia de fumadores.

smoke•stack [smókstæk] *s.* chimenea.

smok•ing [smókIŋ] *adj.* humeante; de fumar; para fumadores; **– car** vagón de fumar; **- room** fumadero, cuarto de fumar.

smok•y [smókI] *adj.* humeante; humoso, lleno de humo; ahumado.

smooth [smuð] *adj.* (*even*) liso; terso; igual, parejo; plano, llano; (*serene*) tranquilo; (*pleasant*) suave; (*wise*) sagaz; **– disposition** genio afable; **– manners** maneras o modales afables; **- style** estilo fluído y fácil; **- talker** hablador melifluo y sagaz; *v.* alisar; allanar; pulir; emparejar; **to – over** allanar, alisar, arreglar; **-ly** *adv.* suavemente, blandamente; fácilmente, con facilidad.

smooth•ness [smúðnIs] *s.* (*evenness*) lisura; igualdad, uniformidad; (*pleasantness*) suavidad; afabilidad; tranquilidad; facilidad, fluidez.

smote [smot] *pret. de* **to smite.**

smoth•er [smʌðə] *v.* ahogar(se); sofocar(se); asfixiar(se).

smudge [smʌdʒ] *v.* tiznar, manchar o ensuciar con tizne; ahumar; *s.* tiznón, mancha (*hecha con tizne*); humareda, nube espesa de humo.

smug•gle [smʌgl̩] *v.* contrabandear, hacer contrabando; **to – in** meter de contrabando; **to – out** sacar de contrabando.

smug•gler [smʌglə] *s.* contrabandista.

smut [smʌt] *s.* (*smudge*) tizne; suciedad, mancha; (*obscenity*) obscenidad, dicho obseno o indecente; tizón (*enfermedad de ciertas plantas*); *v.* tiznar; ensuciar, manchar.

smut•ty [sm ʌ tɪ] *adj.* tiznado, manchado de tizne; sucio.

snack [snæk] *s.* bocado, bocadillo, tentempié, bocadito; merienda, comida ligera.

snag [snæg] *s.* (*protuberance*) tocón; raigón; (*obstacle*) tropiezo, obstáculo; **to hit a –** tropezar con un obstáculo; *v.* rasgar; enredar.

snail [senil] *s.* caracol.

snake [snek] *s.* culebra, víbora; *v.* culebrear.

snap [snæp] *v.* (*make sound*) chasquear, dar un chasquido; estallar; (*break*) quebrar(se); (*photograph*) fotografiar instantáneamente; **his eyes –** le chispean los ojos; **to – at** echar una mordida o mordisco a; dar una tarascada a, morder; asir (*una oportunidad*); **to – back at** tirar una mordida a; dar una respuesta grosera a; **to – off** soltarse, saltar; quebrar(se); **to – one´s fingers** tronar los dedos, castañear con los dedos; **to – shut** cerrar(se) de golpe; **to – together** apretar, abrochar; **to – up** agarrar, asir; morder; *s.* chasquido; estallido; mordida, mordisco, dentellada; broche de presión; energía, vigor; galleta; cosa fácil, ganga; **cold –** nortazo; repentino descenso de temperatura; **not to care a –** no importarle a uno un ardite o un comino; *adj.* hecho de prisa, impensado; instantáneo; **– fastener** broche de presión; **– judgment** decisión atolondrada; **– lock** cerradura de golpe.

snap•py [sn ǽ pɪ] *adj.* mordedor, *Ven.*, *C.A.*, *Andes* mordelón; enojadizo, *Méx.* enojón; violento, vivo; elegante; **– cheese** queso acre o picante; **– eyes** ojos chispeantes.

snap•shot [sn ǽ p ʃ ɑt] *s.* instantánea, fotografía instantánea; *v.* sacar una instantánea.

snare [snɛr] *s.* (*trap*) trampa, lazo; (*ambush*) acechanza; red; *v.* enredar; atrapar, coger con trampa; tender lazos a.

snarl [snɑrl] *v.* gruñir; enmarañar(se), enredar(se); *s.* gruñido; maraña, enredo; pelo enmarañado.

snatch [snætʃ] *v.* arrebatar; agarrar; **to – at** tratar de asir o agarrar; *s.* arrebatiña, arrebatamiento; trozo, pedacito; **to make a – at** tratar de arrebatar, tratar de agarrarse a.

sneak [snik] *v.* andar furtivamente; obrar solapadamente; **to – in** meter(se) a escondidas; colarse; **to – out** escurrirse, salirse a hurtadillas; sacar, llevarse (*algo*) a escondidas; *s.* persona solapada.

sneer [snɪr] *v.* (*smile*) sonreír con sorna; (*gesture*) hacer un gesto de desdén; (*ridicule*) mofarse; **to – at** mofarse de; *s.* sorna, mofa, rechifla; gesto desdeñoso.

sneeze [sniz] *v.* estornudar; *s.* estornudo.

sniff [snɪf] *v.* husmear, olfatear; sorber (*por las narices*); resollar para adentro; **to – at** husmear;

menospreciar; *s.* husmeo, olfateo; sorbo (*por las narices*).

snif•fle [snɪf l] *v.* sorber por las narices.

snip [snɪp] *v.* tijeretear; **to – off** cortar de un tijeretazo, recortar; *s.* tijeretada, tijeretazo; pedacito, recorte.

snipe [snaɪp] *v.* tirar, disparar desde un escondite.

snip•er [snáɪpə] *s.* francotirador; tirador emboscado.

snitch [snɪtʃ] *v.* arrebatar; ratear, hurtar.

sniv•el [snɪv l] *v.* moquear; gimotear.

snob [snɑb] *s.* esnob.

snoop [snup] *v.* fisgar, fisgonear, curiosear; *s.* curioso, fisgón.

snooze [snuz] *v.* dormitar, sestear; *s.* siestecita, siestita; **to take a –** echar un sueñecito o siestita; descabezar el sueño.

snore [snor] *v.* roncar; *s.* ronquido.

snor•kel [sn ó rk l] *s.* tubo esnorkel.

snort [snort] *v.* resoplar; bufar; *s.* resoplido, bufido.

snout [snaUt] *s.* hocico, jeta.

snow [sno] *s.* nieve; *v.* nevar; **to be –ed under** estar totalmente cubierto por la nieve.

snow•ball [snóbɔl] *s.* bola de nieve; *v.* tirar bolas de nieve.

snow•drift [snódrɪft] *s.* ventisca, ventisquero, montón de nieve.

snow•fall [snófɔl] *s.* nevada.

snow•flake [snóflek] *s.* copo de nieve.

snow•storm [snóstorm] *s.* fuerte nevada, nevasca.

snow•y [snóɪ] *adj.* nevado; níveo, blanco como la nieve.

snub [snʌb] *v.* desairar, menospreciar; *s.* desaire; **snub-nosed** chato, *Am.* ñato.

snuff [snʌf] *v.* olfatear, husmear, ventear; aspirar (*por la nariz*); despabilar (*una candela*); **to – at** olfatear, ventear; **to – out** apagar, extinguir; **to – up** sorber (*por las narices*); *s.* sorbo (*por la nariz*); rapé, tabaco en polvo; pabilo, mecha quemada (*de una vela*).

snug [snʌg] *adj.* (*squeezed*) apretado; ajustado; compacto; (*comfortable*) abrigado; cómodo.

so [so] *adv.* así; tan, muy; tanto; **so-so** regular; **so-and-so** Fulano (de tal); **– as to** para; **– far** tan lejos; hasta ahora, hasta aquí; **– many** tantos; **– much** tanto; **– much for that** basta por ese lado; **– much the better** tanto mejor; **- that** de modo que; para que; a fin de que; de suerte que; **– then** conque, pues bien, así pues; **and – forth** etcétera; y así sucesivamente; **I believe –** así lo creo; **is that –?** ¿de veras? ¿de verdad?; ¡no diga!; **ten minutes or –** poco más o menos diez minutos, como diez minutos.

soak [sok] *v.* remojar(se); empapar(se); **to – up** absorber, embeber; chupar; **to be –ed through** estar empapado; estar calado hasta los huesos; *s.* remojo, mojada; borrachín; golpe, puñetazo.

soap [sop] *s.* jabón; **– bubble** pompa de jabón, *Ven.,* *Col.* bombita; *Andes, Méx.* burbuja de jabón; **– dish** jabonera; **soft –** jabón blando; lisonja, adulación; *v.* enjabonar.

soap•y [sópI] *adj.* lleno de jabón.

soar [sor] *v.* remontarse; encumbrarse; subir muy alto; remontar el vuelo.

sob [sɑb] *v.* sollozar; *s.* sollozo.

so•ber [sóbæ] *adj.* (*temperate*) sobrio; moderado, templado; (*serious*) serio, grave; (*sane*) cuerdo, sensato; (*calm*) tranquilo, sereno; **to be –** estar en su juicio; no estar borracho; *v.* **to – down** sosegar(se), calmar(se); formalizarse; **to – up** desembriagarse, desemborracharse; bajársele a uno la borrachera.

so•ber•ly [sóbælI] *adv.* sobriamente; cuerdamente, con sensatez; seriamente.

so•ber•ness [sóbænIs] *s.* sobriedad; seriedad.

so•bri•e•ty [səbráIətI] *s.* sobriedad; cordura.

so-called [sók ɔ́ld] *adj.* así llamado, llamado.

so•cia•ble [sóʃəb] *adj.* sociable, social, tratable.

so•cial [sóʃəl] *adj.* social; sociable; tratable, de buen trato; *s.* reunión social; tertulia.

so•cial•ism [sóʃəlIzəm] *s.* socialismo.

so•cial•ist [sóʃIIst] *adj.* & *s.* socialista.

so•cial•ize [sóʃəlaIz] *v.* socializar.

so•ci•e•ty [səsáIətI] *s.* sociedad; compañía.

so•ci•ol•o•gy [sósiálədʒI] *s.* sociología.

sock [sɑk] *s.* (*garment*) calcetín; (*blow*) porrazo, golpe, puñetazo; *v.* pegar, apalear, golpear; *Am.* batear (*una pelota*).

sock•et [sákIt] *s.* cuenca (*del ojo*); portalámparas, enchufe, *Carib.* sóquet.

sod [sɑd] *s.* césped; terrón (*de tierra sembrada de césped*); *v.* cubrir de césped.

so•da [sódə] *s.* soda, sosa; **– fountain** *Am.* fuente de soda; **- water** agua gaseosa; **baking –** bicarbonato de sodio.

so•di•um [sódIəm] *s.* sodio.

so•fa [sófə] *s.* sofá.

soft [sɔft] *adj.* (*bland*) blando; muelle; suave; (*gentle*) tierno; dulce; **soft-boiled eggs** huevos pasados por agua; **– coal** carbón bituminoso; **– drink** bebida no alcohólica; **- metal** metal dulce, metal maleable; **– soap** jabón blando; adulación; **– water** agua dulce; *adv.* véase **softly.**

soft•en [s ɔ́ fən] *v.* ablandar(se); suavizar(se); enternecer(se); templar(se); **to – one´s voice** bajar la voz , hablar quedo (o quedito).

soft-heart•ed [sɔfthártəd] *adj.* de buen corazón.

soft•ly [s ɔ́ ftlI] *adv.* blandamente; suavemente; quedo, quedito.

soft•ness [s ɔ́ ftnIs] *s.* blandura; molicie; suavidad; ternura; dulzura.

sog•gy [ságI] *adj.* remojado; empapado.

soil [sɔIl] *s.* suelo, terreno, tierra; mancha; *v.* ensuciar(se); manchar(se).

so•journ [sódʒɜ́ n] *s.* estada, estancia, permanencia, *Andes, Méx., Ríopl.* estadía; [sodʒDn] *v.* permanecer; estarse, residir por una temporada.

sol•ace [sólIs] *s.* solaz; *v.* solazar.

so•lar [sólæ] *adj.* solar, del sol; **– plexis** plexo solar.

sold [sold] *pret.* & *p.p.* **to sell; to be – on an idea** estar bien convencido de una idea.

sol•der [sádæ] *v.* soldar; *s.* soldadura.

sol•dier [sóldʒæ] *s.* soldado.

sole [sol] *adj.* solo, único; exclusivo; *s.* suela (*del zapato*); planta (*del pie*); lenguado (*pez*); *v.* solar, echar suelas a; **to half-sole** echar o poner medias suelas a.

sole•ly [sóllI] *adv.* sólamente, únicamente.

sol•emn [sáləm] *adj.* solemne.

so•lem•ni•ty [səlémnətI] *s.* solemnidad.

so•lic•it [səlIsIt] *v.* solicitar.

so•lic•i•tor [səlIsətæ] *s.* solicitador, agente.

so•lic•i•tous [səlIsItəs] *adj.* solícito.

so•lic•i•tude [səlIsətjud] *s.* solicitud, cuidado.

sol•id [sálId] *s.* sólido; *adj.* sólido, firme; macizo; sensato; unánime; **– blue** todo azul; **– gold** oro puro; **for one – hour** por una hora entera, por una hora sin parar; **the country is – for** el país está firmemente unido en favor de.

sol•i•dar•i•ty [saləd ɛ́ rətI] *s.* solidaridad.

so•lid•i•fy [səlÍdəfəl] *v.* solidificar(se).

so•lid•i•ty [səlÍdətI] *s.* solidez.

sol•id-state [saledstét] *adj.* física del estado sólido.

so•lil•o•quy [səlÍləkwI] *s.* soliloquio.

sol•i•tar•y [sáletɛrI] *adj.* solitario; solo; *s.* solitario, ermitaño.

sol•i•tude [sáletjud] *s.* soledad.

so•lo [solo] *s.* solo.

so•lo•ist [sóloIst] *s.* solista.

sol•u•ble [sáljəb] *adj.* soluble, que se disuelve fácilmente.

so•lu•tion [səlúʃən] *s.* solución.

solve [sɑlv] *v.* resolver; explicar, aclarar, desenredar.

som•ber [sámbæ] *adj.* sombrío.

some [sʌm] *adj.* algún, alguno; algunos, unos; algo de, un poco de; **– one** alguno, alguno; **– twenty people** unas veinte personas; *pron.* algunos, unos; algo, un poco; una parte.

some•bod•y [s ʌ mbodI] *pron.* alguien; **a –** un personaje de importancia.

some•how [s ʌ mhaU] *adv.* de algún modo, de alguna manera; **– or other** de una manera u otra; por alguna razón.

some•one [s ʌ mwʌn] *pron.* alguno, alguien.

som•er•sault [s ʌ mærsolt] *s.* voltereta; *v.* dar una

voltereta.

some•thing [s ʌ́ mθIŋ] *s.* algo, alguna cosa; un poco; **– else** alguna otra cosa, otra cosa.

some•time [s ʌ́ mtaIm] *adv.* algún día; alguna vez; en algún tiempo; **-s** *adv.* a veces, algunas veces, de vez en cuando.

some•what [s ʌ́ mhwɑt] *s.* algo, alguna cosa, un poco; *adv.* algo, un tanto.

some•where [s ʌ́ mhwɛr] *adv.* en alguna parte; **– else** en alguna otra parte.

son [sʌn] *s.* hijo.

song [sɔŋ] *s.* canción; canto; **the Song of Songs** el Cantar de los Cantares; **– bird** ave canora, pájaro cantor; **to buy something for a** – comprar algo muy barato.

son•ic bar•ri•er [sɑnIkbǽrIɚ] *s.* barrera sónica.

son-in-law [s ʌ́ nInlɔ] *s.* yerno; hijo político.

son•net [sánIt] *s.* soneto.

so•no•rous [sənórəs] *adj.* sonoro.

soon [sun] *adv.* pronto, presto; luego; **– after** poco después (de); al poco tiempo; **as – as** tan pronto como; luego que, así que; **how – ?** ¿cuándo?

soot [sUt] *s.* hollín; tizne.

soothe [suð] *v.* calmar, sosegar; aliviar.

sooth•say•er [súðseɚ] *s.* adivino.

soot•y [sútI] *adj.* tiznado, cubierto de hollín.

sop [sɑp] *v.* empapar; **to – up** absorber; **to be 0sopping wet** estar hecho una sopa, estar mojado hasta los huesos; *s.* sopa (*pan u otra cosa empapada en leche, caldo, etc.*); soborno, regalo (*para acallar, conciliar, o sobornar*).

so•phis•ti•cat•ed [səfIstəketəd] *adj.* mundano; exento de simplicidad.

soph•o•more [sáfəmor] *s.* estudiante de segundo año.

so•pran•o [səprǽno] *s.* soprano; **high –** triple; **– voice** voz de soprano.

sor•cer•er [s ɔ́ rsərɚ] *s.* brujo, hechicero.

sor•did [s ɔ́ rdId] *adj.* sórdido; vil, indecente; mezquino.

sore [sor] *adj.* (*painful*) dolorido; inflamado, enconado; (*grievous*) afligido, apenado; (*injured*) lastimado; picado; (*offended*) ofendido; **– eyes** mal de ojos; **to be – at** estar enojado con; **to have a – throat** tener mal de garganta, dolerle a uno la garganta; *s.* úlcera, llaga; inflamación; lastimadura; pena, aflicción; **-ly** *adv.* dolorosamente, penosamente; **to be -ly in need of** necesitar con urgencia.

sore•ness [sórnIs] *s.* dolor, dolencia; inflamación.

sor•rel [s ɔ́ rəl] *adj.* alazán (*rojo canela*); *s.* color alazán; caballo alazán.

sor•row [sáro] *s.* (*sandness*) dolor, pena, pesar; (*grieving*) pesadumbre; (*repetance*) arrepentimien-

to; *v.* apenarse, afligirse, sentir pena.

sor•row•ful [sárəfəl] *adj.* pesaroso, doloroso, lastimoso, afligido; **-ly** *adv.* tristemente, dolorosamente, con pena, descon-soladamente.

sor•ry [s ɔ́ rI] *adj.* triste, pesaroso, afligido, arrepentido; lastimoso; **I am –** lo siento; me pesa; **I am – for her** la compadezco.

sort [sɔrt] *s.* suerte, clase, especie; **– of tired** algo cansado, un tanto cansado; **all -s of** toda suerte de, toda clase de; **out of -s** de mal humor, malhumorado; indispuesto; *v.* clasificar, ordenar, arreglar; **to – out** separar, clasificar; entresacar; escoger.

sought [sɔt] *pret. & p.p.* de **to seek.**

soul [sol] *s.* alma; bestí a – nadie, ni un alma.

sound [saUnd] *adj.* (*healthy*) sano; cuerdo; sensato; (*firm*) girme, sólido; ileso; **a – beating** una buena zurra o tunda; **– business** buen negocio, negocio bien organizado; **– reasoning** raciocinio sólido; **– sleep** sueño profundo; **– title** título válido o legal; **of – mind** en su juicio cabal; **safe and –** sano y salvo; **to sleep –** dormir profundamente; *v.* son, sonido; tono; brazo de mar; **– wave** onda sonora; *v.* sonar, tocar; sondear; tanear; auscultar (*el pecho, los pulmones*); cantar, entonar (*alabanzas*); **to – out** tantear, sondear.

sound•ness [sáUndnIs] *s.* (*firmness*) solidez; (*healthiness*) cordura, buen juicio; (*validity*) rectitud; validez; **– of body** buena salud corporal.

soup [sup] *s.* sopa.

sour [saUr] *adj.* (*acid-like*) agrio; acre; ácido; desabrido; rancio; (*peevish*) malhumorado; **– milk** leche cortada; *v.* agriar(se); cortarse (*la leche*); fermentar; poner(se) de mal humor.

source [sors] *s.* origen; manantial, fuente.

sour•ness [sáUrnIs] *s.* acidez, agrura, desabrimiento.

souse [saUs] *v.* zambullir; chapuzar.

south [saUθ] *s.* sur, sud; *adj.* meridional; del sur; austral; **South American** sudamericano, suramericano; **– pole** polo sur, polo antártico; *adv.* hacia el sur.

south•east [saUθíst] *s. & adj.* sudeste; *adv.* hacia el sudeste.

south•east•ern [saUθístɚn] *adj.* del sudeste, sudeste.

south•ern [s ʌ́ ðɚn] *adj.* meridional, del sur, austral, sureño; **– Cross** Cruz del Sur.

south•ern•er [s ʌ́ ðɚnɚ] *s.* sureño, meridional, habitante del sur.

south•ward [sáUθwɚd] *adv.* hacia el sur, rumbo al sur.

south•west [saUθwést] *s. & adj.* sudoeste (*o* suroeste); *adv.* hacia el sudoeste.

south•west•ern [sUθwéstɚn] *adj.* sudoeste (*o* soroeste), del sudoeste.

sou•ve•nir [suvənír] *s.* recuerdo, memoria.

sov•er•eing [sóvrln] *s.* & *adj.* soberano.

sov•er•eingn•ty [sóvrlntI] *s.* soberanía.

so•vi•et [sóvIlt] *s.* sóviet; *adj.* soviético.

sow [saU] *s.* puerca.

sow [so] *v.* sembrar.

sown [son] *p.p. de* to sow.

space [spes] *s.* espacio; **– science** ciencia del espacio; ciencia espacial; **– station** estación espacial; **– suit** traje espacial; *v.* espaciar.

space•craft [spéskræft] *s.* nave espacial; astronave.

space•man [spésmæn] *s.* astronauta.

spa•cious [spéʃəs] *adj.* espacioso; dilatado, vasto.

spade [sped] *s.* azada, azadón; espada (*del juego de naipes*); *v.* cavar con la azada.

span [spæn] *s.* palmo; espacio; tramo; arco u ojo (*de puente*); envergadura (*de un aeroplano*); **– of life** longevidad; *v.* medir a palmos; atravesar.

span•gle [spǽŋg‖] *s.* lentejuela; *v.* adornar con lentejuelas; brillar, centellear; **-d with stars** estrellado, sembrado (*o* tachonado) de estrellas.

Span•iard [spǽnjə‣d] *s.* español.

span•iel [spǽnjəl] *s.* perro de aguas.

Span•ish [spǽnIʃ] *adj.* español; *s.* español, idioma español.

spank [spæŋk] *v.* zurrar, dar una tunda, dar nalgadas; *s.* palmada, nalgada.

spank•ing [spǽŋkiŋ] *s.* zurra, tunda, nalgadas.

spar [spɑr] *v.* boxear, pelear.

spare [spɛr] *v.* ahorrar; evitar (*molestias, trabajo, etc.*); perdonar; **I cannot – another dollar** no dispongo de otro dólar, no tengo más dinero disponible; **I cannot – the car today** no puedo pasarme hoy sin el automóvil; **to – no expense** no escatimar gastos; **to – the enemy** usar de clemencia con el enemigo; **to have time to –** tener tiempo de sobra; *adj.* flaco, descarnado; escaso, frugal; mezquino; sobrante; de sobra; de repuesto; **– cash** dinero disponible o de sobra; **– time** tiempo libre, tiempo disponible; **– tire** neumático de repuesto.

spark [spɑrk] *s.* chispa; **– plug** bujía; *v.* chispear, echar chispas, chisporrotear.

spar•kle [spɑ́rk‖] *s.* (*flash*) chispa, centella; brillo, centelleo; (*spirit*) viveza, animación; *v.* centellear; chispear; relucir, brillar.

spar•kling [spɑ́rklIŋ] *adj.* centelleante; reluciente; chispeante; **– wine** vino espumoso.

spar•row [spǽro] *s.* gorrión, pardal.

sparse [spɑrs] *adj.* escaso; esparcido; poco denso, poco poblado; **– hair** pelo ralo.

spasm [spǽzəm] *s.* espasmo.

spas•tic [spǽstlk] *adj.* espástico.

spat [spæt] *pret.* & *p.p. de* to spit; *v.* reñir, disputar;

dar un manazo o sopapo; *s.* sopapo, manotada; riña, desavenencia; **-s** polainas cortas.

spat•ter [spǽtə‣] *v.* salpicar; rociar; manchar; *s.* salpicadura; rociada.

speak [spik] *v.* hablar; decir; recitar; **– to the point!** ¡vamos al grano!; **so to –** por decirlo así; **to – for** hablar por, hablar en nombre o en favor de; pedir, solicitar; apalabrar, reservar; **to – one´s mind** hablar sin rodeos, decir claramente lo que se piensa; **to – out** (*o* **– up**) hablar claro; hablar con toda franqueza; hablar en voz alta.

speak•er [spíkə‣] *s.* orador; conferenciante, conferencista; el que habla; **– of the House** presidente de la cámara de representantes; **loud-speaker** altavoz, altoparlante.

spear [spIr] *s.* lanza; arpón (*para pescar*); brote, retoño, hoja (*de hierba*); *v.* alancear, lancear, herir con lanza.

spear•mint [spÍrmInt] *s.* yerbabuena (*hierbabuena*), menta.

spe•cial [spéʃəl] *adj.* especial; particular; **– delivery** entrega especial de correo; *s.* tren o autobús especial; carta urgente, entrega especial; **-ly** *adv.* especialmente; en especial; sobre todo.

spe•cial•ist [spéʃəlIst] *s.* especialista.

spe•cial•i•za•tion [speʃəllzéʃən] *s.* especialización.

spe•cial•ize [spéʃəlaIz] *v.* especializarse.

spe•cial•ty [spéʃəltI] *s.* especialidad.

spe•cies [spíʃIz] *s.* especie; especies.

spe•cif•ic [spIsÍfIk] *adj.* específico; peculiar, característico; **– gravity** peso específico; *s.* específico; **-ally** *adv.* específicamente; especificadamente; particularmente, en particular.

spec•i•fy [spésəfaI] *v.* especificar; estipular.

spec•i•men [spésəmən] *s.* espécimen, muestra, ejemplar.

speck [spɛk] *s.* mota; manchita; partícula; **not a –** ni pizca; *v.* véase speckle.

speck•le [spék‖] *s.* manchita; mota; *v.* motear, salpicar de motas o manchas; manchar.

speck•led [spék‖d] *adj.* moteado; **– with freckles** pecoso.

spec•ta•cle [spékták‖] *s.* espectáculo; **-s** gafas, anteojos; **to make a – of oneself** ponerse en la evidencia, ponerse en ridículo.

spec•tac•u•lar [spɛktǽkjələ‣] *adj.* espectacular, ostentoso, aparatoso.

spec•ta•tor [spéktetə‣] *s.* espectador.

spec•ter [spéktə‣] *s.* espectro, fantasma, aparecido.

spec•tro•graph [spéktrogræf] *s.* espectrógrafo.

spec•trum [spéktrəm] *s.* espectro.

spec•u•late [spékjəlet] *v.* especular; reflexionar.

spec•u•la•tion [spɛkjəléʃən] *s.* especulación; reflexión.

spec•u•la•tive [spékjəletɪv] *adj.* especulativo; teórico.

spec•u•la•tor [spékjəletə·] *s.* especulador.

sped [spɛd] *pret. & p.p. de* **to speed.**

speech [spitʃ] *s.* hablar; lenguaje, idioma; discurso, arenga; conferencia; parlamento (*de un actor*); **to make a** — pronunciar un discurso, hacer una perorata.

speech•less [spíʃlɪs] *adj.* sin habla; mudo; estupefacto.

speed [spid] *s.* velocidad; rapidez; presteza, prontitud; **- limit** velocidad máxima; **at full** — a toda velocidad; *v.* apresurar(se), acelerar(se), dar(se) prisa; correr; ir con exceso de velocidad; despachar.

speed•i•ly [spídIlI] *adv.* velozmente, rápidamente; a todo correr; de prisa, con prontitud.

speed•om•e•ter [spidámətə·] *s.* velocímetro.

speed•y [spídI] *adj.* veloz, rápido.

spell [spɛl] *s.* (*charm*) hechizo, encanto; (*period*) temporada, corto período; (*sickness*) ataque (*de una enfermedad*); **to put under a** — aojar; hechizar, encantar; *v.* deletrear; significar, indicar; **how is it -ed?** ¿cómo se escribe?

spell•er [spélə·] *s.* silabario; deletreador.

spell•ing [spélIŋ] *s.* ortografía; deletreo; **— book** silabario.

spelt [spɛlt] *pret. & p.p. de* **to spell.**

spend [spɛnd] *v.* gastar; usar, agotar, consumir; **to — a day** pasar un día.

spend•thrift [spénðrɪft] *s.* derrochador, gastador, pródigo.

spent [spɛnt] *pret. & p.p. de* **to spend.**

sphere [sfɪr] *s.* esfera; globo, orbe.

spher•i•cal [sférɪk] *adj.* esférico.

sphynx [sfɪŋks] *s.* esfinge.

spice [spaɪs] *s.* especia; picante; aroma; *v.* condimentar, sazonar con especias.

spic•y [spáɪsI] *adj.* sazonado con especias; picante; aromático.

spi•der [spáɪdə·] *s.* araña; sartén; **— web** telaraña.

spig•ot [spígət] *s.* espita, grifo, canilla.

spike [spaɪk] *s.* espiga; perno; clavo largo; alcayata; pico; *v.* clavar; clavetear.

spill [spɪl] *v.* verter; derramar(se); desparramar(se); hacer caer (*de un caballo*); revelar (*una noticia, un secreto*); *s.* derrame, derramamiento; vuelco; caída (*de un caballo*).

spilt [spɪlt] *pret. & p.p. de* **to spill.**

spin [spɪn] *v.* hilar; girar, dar vueltas, rodar; bailar (*un trompo*); **to – out** prolongar, alargar; **to – yarns** contar cuentos; *s.* giro, vuelta; paseo (*en automóvil, bicicleta, etc.*); barrena (*hablando de aeroplanos*).

spin•ach [spínItʃ] *s.* espinaca.

spi•nal [spáɪn] *adj.* espinal; **— column** columna vertebral, espina dorsal.

spin•dle [spínd] *s.* huso; eje.

spine [spaɪn] *s.* espina; espinazo, espina dorsal, columna vertebral.

spin•ner [spínə·] *s.* hilandero, hilandera; máquina de hilar.

spin•ning [spínIŋ] *s.* hilandería, arte de hilar; **— machine** aparato para hilar, máquina de hilar; **— mill** hilandería; **— top** trompo; **– wheel** torno de hilar.

spin•ster [spínstə·] *s.* soltera; solterona.

spi•ral [spáɪrəl] *adj.* espiral; **— staircase** caracol, escalera espiral; *s.* espiral.

spire [spaɪr] *s.* aguja, chapitel de torre; cúspide, ápice; punto más alto; **— of grass** brizna de hierba.

spir•it [spírɪt] *s.* (*essence*) espíritu; temple; (animation) viveza, animación; ánimo; **low -s** abatimiento; **to be in good -s** estar de buen humor; **to be out of -s** estar triste o abatido; *v.* **to – away** llevarse misteriosamente.

spir•it•ed [spírItId] *adj.* vivo, brioso, fogoso.

spir•i•tu•al [spírItʃUəl] *adj.* espiritual; *s.* espiritual; *s.* espiritual (*tonada religiosa de los negros del sur de los Estados Unidos*).

spit [spɪt] *v.* escupir; expectorar; *pret. & p.p. de* **to spit;** *s.* esputo, saliva; asador.

spite [spaɪt] *s.* despecho, rencor, inquina, ojeriza; **in — of** a despecho de; a pesar de; **out of —** por despecho; *v.* picar, irritar, hacer rabiar.

spite•ful [spáɪtfəl] *adj.* rencoroso.

splash [splæʃ] *v.* salpicar; rociar; enlodar; manchar; chapotear (*en el agua*); *s.* salpicadura; rociada; chapoteo.

spleen [splin] *s.* bazo; mal humor, rencor.

splen•did [spléndId] *adj.* espléndido.

splen•dor [spléndə·] *s.* esplendor; esplendidez.

splice [splaɪs] *v.* empalmar, unir, juntar; *s.* empalme; junta.

splint [splɪnt] *s.* tablilla; astilla; *v.* entablillar.

splint•er [splɪntə·] *s.* astilla; raja; *v.* astillar(se), hacer(se) astillas; romper(se) en astillas.

split [splɪt] *v.* hender(se), rajar(se); resquebrajar(se); partir(se), dividir(se); **to – hairs** pararse en pelillos; **to – one´s sides with laughter** desternillarse de risa, reventar de risa; **to – the difference** partir la diferencia; *pret. & p.p. de* **to split;** *adj.* partido, hendido, rajado; dividido; resquebrajado; *s.* raja, hendedura, grieta; cisma, rompimiento.

splurge [splə·dʒ] *s.* ostentación; fachenda.

spoil [spɔɪl] *v.* (*decay*) dañar(se); echar(se) a perder, podrir(se), corromper(se); (*harm*) estropear(se); arruinar(se); (*overindulge*) consentir, mimar; *s.* botín, presa; **-s of war** botín o despojos de guerra.

spoke [spok] *s.* rayo (*de rueda*); *pret. de* **to speak.**

spo•ken [spókən] *p.p. de* **to speak.**

spokes•man [spóksmən] *s.* portavoz, vocero.

sponge [spʌndʒ] *s. (absorbent)* esponja; *(dependent person)* gorrón, parásito; *v.* lavar o limpiar con esponja; vivir de gorra, vivir en costa ajena; **to – up** chupar, absorber.

sponge•cake [spʌndʒkek] *s.* bizcocho esponjoso.

spong•er [spʌndʒɚ] *s.* esponja, gorrón, pegote, parásito; *Am.* pavo.

spong•y [spʌndʒɪ] *adj.* esponjoso, esponjado.

spon•sor [spánsɚ] *s.* padrino, madrina; patrón *(el que patrocina una empresa)*; defensor; fiador; fomentador, promovedor; *v.* apadrinar; promover, fomentar; patrocinar; ser fiador de.

spon•ta•ne•i•ty [spɑntəníətɪ] *s.* espontaneidad.

spon•ta•ne•ous [spɑnténɪəs] *adj.* espontáneo.

spook [spuk] *s.* espectro, fantasma, aparecido.

spool [spul] *s.* carrete, carretel; *v.* devanar, enredar *(hilo)* en carrete.

spoon [spun] *s.* cuchara; *v.* cucharear, sacar con cuchara.

spoon•ful [spúnfəl] *s.* cucharada.

sport [sport] *s.* deporte; **in – en** broma, de burla; **to make – of** reírse de, burlarse de; **to be a good –** ser buen perdedor *(en el juego)*; ser un buen compañero; *v.* jugar; divertirse; bromear, chancearse; **to – a new dress** lucir un traje nuevo; **-s** *adj.* deportivo; **- clothes** trajes deportivos.

sports car [spórtskar] *s.* coche *(carro)* deportivo.

sports•man [spórtsmən] *s.* deportista; jugador generoso, buen perdedor *(en deportes)*.

spot [spɑt] *s. (blemish)* mancha, mota; *(place)* sitio, lugar; **in –s** aquí y allá; aquí y allá; **on the –** allí mismo; al punto; **to pay – cash** pagar al contado; *v.* manchar, ensuciar; motear; echar de ver, distinguir; avistar; localizar.

spot•less [spátlɪs] *adj.* sin mancha, limpio.

spot•light [spátlaɪt] *s.* faro giratorio.

spot•ted [spátɪd] *adj.* manchado; moteado.

spouse [spauz] *s.* esposo, esposa.

spout [spaUt] *v.* chorrear; brotar; salir en chorro; emitir; declamar, perorar; hablar mucho; *s.* chorro; surtidor; pico *(de teteras, cafetera, jarra, etc.)*; espita.

sprain [spren] *v.* torcer *(una coyuntura o músculo)*; **to – one's ankle** torcerse el tobillo; *s.* torsión, torcedura.

sprang [spræŋ] *pret. de* **to spring.**

sprawl [sprɔl] *v.* despatarrarse; estar despatarrado; tenderse; **to – one's legs** abrir las piernas; *s.* postura floja *(abiertos los brazos y piernas)*.

spray [spre] *s. (liquid)* rocío, rociada; líquido para rociar; *(branch)* ramita; **sea –** espuma del mar; *v.* rociar.

spread [sprɛd] *v.* extender(se); desparramar(se);

esparcir(se); difundir(se), diseminar(se), dispersar(se); propalar(se) *(noticias, rumores, etc.)*, propagar(se); **to – apart** abrir(se), separar(se); **to – butter on** poner mantequilla en; **to – out the tablecloth** tender el mantel; **to – paint on** dar una mano de pintura a; **to – with** cubrir de; untar con; *s.* extensión; amplitud, anchura; envergadura *(de un aeroplano)*; difusión; diseminación; propagación; cubierta, sobrecama; comilitona, festín; mantequilla, queso, etc., que se le unta al pan; *pret. & p.p. de* **to spread.**

spree [spri] *s.* juerga, parranda, holgorio; **to go on a –** andar *(o ir)* de parranda o juerga, *Am.* ir de farra.

sprig [sprɪg] *s.* ramita.

spright•ly [spráItlɪ] *adj.* vivo, animado, brioso; alegre.

spring [sprɪŋ] *v.* saltar; brincar; hacer saltar; **to – a leak** hacer agua *(un barco)*; comenzar a gotearse *(la cañería, el techo, etc.)*; formarse una gotera; **to – a trap** hacer saltar una trampa; **to – at** abalanzarse sobre; **to – from** salir de, nacer de, brotar de; **to – news of a surprise** dar de sopetón una noticia o sorpresa; **to – something open** abrir algo a la fuerza; **to – one's feet** levantarse de un salto; **to – up** brotar; surgir; crecer; levantarse de un salto; *s.* primavera; muelle *(de metal)*; resorte; elasticidad; salto, brinco; manantial, fuente; origen; *adj.* primaveral; **– board** trampolín; **– mattress** colchón de muelles; **– water** agua de manantial.

spring•time [sprɪ́ŋtaɪm] *s.* primavera.

sprin•kle [sprɪ́ŋk] *v. (scatter)* rociar; regar; espolvorear; salpicar; *(rain)* lloviznar; *s.* rociada, rocío; llovizna; **– of salt** pizca de sal.

sprint [sprɪnt] *v.* echar una carrera, *s.* carrera, carrerilla; corrida corta.

sprout [spraUt] *v.* brotar; retoñar, germinar; hacer germinar o brotar; *s.* retoño, renuevo; **Brussels-s** bretones, coles de Bruselas.

spruce [sprus] *s.* abeto; *adj.* pulcro, aseado, pulido; elegante; *v.* **to – up** asearse, componerse, emperifollarse.

sprung [sprʌŋ] *pret. & p.p. de* **to spring.**

spun [spʌn] *pret. & p.p. de* **to spin.**

spur [spɝ] *s.* espuela; acicate; aguijón, estímulo; espolón *(del gallo)*; estribación *(de una montaña)*; **– track** ramal corto *(de ferrocarril)*; **on the – of the moment** impensadamente, sin la reflexión debida; por el momento; *v.* espolear, aguijar, picar, incitar; **to – on** animar, incitar a obrar o a seguir adelante.

spu•ri•ous [spúrIəs] *adj.* espurio.

spurn [spɝn] *v.* rechazar, desdeñar, menospreciar.

spurt [spɝt] *v.* salir a borbotones, chorrear; echar chorros; hacer un repentino esfuerzo *(para ganar una carrera)*; *s.* borbotón, chorrazo, chorro repen-

tino; esfuerzo repentino; **–of anger** arranque de ira;
-s of flame llamaradas.

sput•ter [sp ʌ tə-] v. chisporrotear; refunfuñar; s.
chisporroteo; refunfuño.

spu•tum [spjútəm] s. esputo.

spy [spaI] s. espía; v. espiar; acechar; atisbar; **to – on**
espiar, atisbar.

spy•glass [spálglæs] s. anteojo de larga vista.

squab [skwɒb] s. pichón.

squab•ble [skwɒbl] s. reyerta; v. reñir, disputar.

squad [skwɒd] s. escuadra, patrulla, partida.

squad•ron [skwɑ́drən] s. escuadra; escuadrón.

squal•id [skwɑ́lɪd] adj. escuálido.

squall [skwɔl] s. chubasco; chillido; v. chillar.

squan•der [skwɑ́ndə-] v. despilfarrar, derrochar,
malgastar, disipar.

square [skwɛr] s. (rectangle) cuadro; cuadrado; (central park) plaza; (block) manzana de casas; Am.
cuadra; escuadra (de carpintero); casilla (de tablero de ajedrez, damas, etc.); **he is on the –** de
buena fe; v. cuadrar; ajustar, arreglar, saldar (cuentas); justificar; cuadricular; **to – one's shoulders**
enderezar los hombros; cuadrarse; **to – oneself
with** sincerarse con, justificarse ante; **to – a person
with another** poner bien a una persona con otra;
adj. cuadrado, en cuadro, a escuadra, en ángulo
recto; saldado; justo, recto, equitativo; franco; **–
corner** esquina en ángulo recto; **– meal** comida
completa, comida en regla; **– mile** milla cuadrada;
– root raíz cuadrada; **– dance** danza de figuras;
cuadrilla; **to be – with someone** estar en paz con
alguien, no deberle nada, Am. estar a mano; adv.
véase **squarely.**

square•ly [skwɛrlI] adv. equitativamente, honradamente; firmemente; de buena fe; derecho,
derechamente; **to hit the target – in the middle**
pegar de lleno en el blanco.

squash [skwɑʃ] s. calabaza; v. aplastar, despachurrar o apachurrar.

squat [skwɒt] v. agazaparse, sentarse en cuclillas;
ocupar tierras baldías para ganar título de propietario; adj. agazapado, sentado en cuclillas; rechoncho,
achaparrado, Méx., C.A., Andes chaparro.

squawk [skwɔk] v. (noise) graznar; chillar; (complain)
quejarse; s. graznido; chillido; queja.

squeak [skwik] v. rechinar, chirriar; chillar; s.
rechinamiento; chirrido, chillido.

squeal [skwil] v. chillar; quejarse, protestar; soplar,
delatar; s. chillido.

squea•mish [skwímɪʃ] escrupuloso; delicado; remilgado.

squeeze [skwiz] v. estrujar; despachurrar o apachurrar; exprimir; prensar; apretar; **to – into** meter(se)
a estrujones, encajar(se) en; **to – out the juice**
exprimir el jugo; **to – through a crowd** abrirse

paso a estrujones por entre la muchedumbre; s. es-
trujón; apretón; abrazo fuerte; apretura.

squelch [skwɛltʃ] v. aplastar; acallar, imponer silencio; reprender, **to – a revolt** sofocar o apagar una
revuelta.

squid [skwɪd] s. calamar.

squint [skwɪnt] v. mirar de través; mirar de soslayo;
mirar achicando los ojos, mirar furtivamente, biz-
quear (mirar bizco); s. mirada de soslayo; mirada
bizca; mirada furtiva; **squint-eyed** adj. bisojo o
bizco.

squire [skwaIr] s. escudero; v. acompañar, escoltar.

squirm [skw ɝ m] v. retorcerse; **to – out of a
difficulty** forcejear para salir de un aprieto.

squir•rel [skw ɝ́ əl] s. ardilla.

squirt [skw ɝ t] v. jeringar; echar un chisguete; salir
a chorritos (o a chisguetes); s. jeringazo; chisguete.

stab [stæb] v. apuñalar, dar una puñalada, dar de
puñaladas, acuchillar; pinchar; s. puñalada, cuchillada, estocada; pinchazo.

sta•bil•i•ty [stəbílətI] s. estabilidad.

sta•ble [stéb l] adj. estable; s. establo, cuadra; caballeriza; v. poner (los animales) en la caballeriza.

stack [stæk] s. pila, montón, rimero; hacina (de paja
o heno); chimenea, cañón de chimenea; **library -s**
estanterías o anaqueles de biblioteca; v. amontonar,
apilar.

sta•di•um [stédIəm] s. estadio.

staff [stæf] s. (stick) báculo, cayado, bastón, vara;
(pole) asta (de bandera, de lanza); (group) cuerpo,
consejo administrativo; **– of life** sostén de la vida –
officer oficial de estado mayor; **army –** estado
mayor; **editorial –** redacción; **musical –**
pentagrama; **teaching –** cuerpo docente; v. proveer de funcionarios y empleados (una
organización).

stag [stæg] s. venado, ciervo; macho, hombre; **–
dinner** banquete exclusivo para hombres.

stage [stedʒ] s. (platform) tablado; tablas, escenario;
escena, (theater) teatro; (period) etapa, tramo; período; (stop) parada; **–coach** ómnibus, autobús;
–hand tramoyista; **by easy -s** por grados, gradualmente; v. representar, poner en escena, **to – a
hold-up** hacer un asalto, atracar; **to – a surprise**
dar una sorpresa.

stag•ger [st ǽ gə-] v. (totter) tambalearse, tratabillar,
bambolearse; hacer tambalear; (overwhelm) azo-
rar, asombrar; **to – working hours** escalonar las
horas de trabajo; s. tambaleo; bamboleo.

stag•nant [st ǽ gnənt] adj. estancado; **to become –**
estancarse.

staid [sted] adj. grave, serio.

stain [sten] v. manchar; teñir; colorar; **stained-glass
window** vidriera de colores; s. mancha, mancilla;
tinte, tintura; materia colorante.

stain•less [sténlIs] *adj.* sin mancha, inmaculado, limpio; **– steel** acero inempañable o inoxidable.

stair [stɛr] *s.* peldaño, escalón; **-s** escalera.

stair•case [stérkes] *s.* escalera.

stair•way [stérwe] *s.* escalera.

stake [stek] *s.* estaca; puesta, apuesta; **his future is at** – su porvenir está en peligro o riesgo; **to die at the** – morir en la hoguera; **to have a – in the future of** tener interés en el porvenir de; **to have much at** – irle a uno mucho en una cosa; haber aventurado mucho, *v.* estacar; atar a una estaca; apostar; arriesgar, aventurar; **to – off** señalar con estacas (*un perímetro*).

stale [stel] *adj.* viejo; rancio; gastado, improductivo.

stale•mate [stélmet] *s.* punto muerto; estancación.

stalk [stɔk] *s.* tallo; caña.

stall [stɔl] *s.* casilla, puesto (*de un mercado o feria*); casilla o sección de un establo; *v.* encasillar, meter en casilla; atascarse (*un auto*); pararse (*el motor*); **he is -ing** está haciendo la casilla; **to be -ed in the mud** estar atascado en el lodo.

stal•lion [stǽljen] *s.* caballo de cría, caballo padre, *Ven., Col., Ríopl.* padrillo; *Méx., C.A.* garañón.

stam•mer [stǽmɚ] *v.* tartamudear, balbucear; *s.* tartamudeo, balbuceo.

stam•mer•er [stǽmərɚ] *s.* tartamudo.

stam•mer•ing [stǽmərIŋ] *s.* tartamudeo; *adj.* tartamudo.

stamp [stæmp] *v.* (*affix*) sellar; timbrar; poner un sello a; estampar; (*mark*) marcar, imprimir, señalar; (*with foot*) patear, patalear; **to – one's foot** dar patadas en el suelo, **to – out** extirpar, borrar; *s.* sello; timbre, estampilla; estampa; marca, impresión; patada (*en el suelo*); **postage** – sello, *Am.* estampilla, *Am.* timbre; **revenue** – timbre.

stam•pede [stæmpíd] *s.* estampida; huída en desorden; tropel; éxodo repentino; *v.* arrancar, huir en tropel; ir en tropel; ahuyentar, hacer huir en desorden.

stanch [stontʃ] *v.* restañar, estancar; *adj.* fuerte, firme; leal, constante, fiel.

stand [stænd] *v.* poner derecho, colocar verticalmente; (*rise*) ponerse de pie, levantarse; *Am.* parar(se); (*be erect*) estar de pie; *Am.* estar parado; (*with-stand*) aguantar, sufrir, tolerar; **to – a chance of** tener probabilidad de; **to – an expense** sufragar un gasto; **to – aside** apartarse; mantenerse apartado; **to – back of** colocarse detrás de; salir fiador de, garantizar a, respaldar a; **to – by** mantenerse a corta distancia; apoyar, defender; estar alerta; **to – for** significar, estar por, apoyar; tolerar; **to – in the way** estorbar, **to – on end** poner(se) de punta; erizarse (*el pelo*); **to – one's ground** mantenerse firme; **to – out** resaltar, destacarse; sobre-salir; **to – six feet** tener seis pies de altura; **to – up for** apoyar, defen-

der, **it -s to reason** es razonable; es lógico; *s.* puesto; mesilla; pedestal; posición; actitud; alto, parada (*para resistir*); quiosco, **grand–** andanada, gradería cubierta (*para espectadores*); **music –** atril; **umbrella –** paragüero.

stand•ard [stǽndɚd] *s.* (*norm*) norma; nivel normal; criterio; (*model*) modelo, patrón; *Am.* estándar; (*base*) base, pedestal, (*banner*) estandarte; **gold -** patrón de oro; **to be up to** – satisfacer las normas requeridas; *adj.* normal, que sirve de norma; de uso general; corriente; **standard-bearer** portaestandarte.

stan•dard•iza•tion [stændɚdɪzéʃən] *s.* normalización, uniformación, igualación.

stan•dard•ize [stǽndɚdaɪz] *v.* normalizar, uniformar, *Méx., C.A., Carib.* estandardizar.

stand•by [stǽndbaɪ] *s.* sustituto.

stand•ing [stǽndɪŋ] *s.* (*position*) posición; (*fame*) fama, reputación; **of long** – que ha prevalecido largo tiempo; muy antiguo; *adj.* derecho, en pie; de pie; establecido, permanente, **– water** agua estancada, **there is – room only** no quedan asientos.

stand•point [stǽndpoɪnt] *s.* punto de vista.

stand•still [stǽndstɪl] *s.* alto; pausa; **to come to a** – pararse; hacer alto.

stank [stæŋk] *pret. de* **to stink.**

stan•za [stǽnzə] *s.* estrofa.

sta•ple [stépḷ] *s.* broche de alambre (*para sujetar papeles*); grapa, argolla, armella; artículo principal; **-s** artículos de necesidad prima; *adj.* principal; de uso corriente; indispensable; *v.* asegurar (*papeles*) con broche de alambre; sujetar con armellas.

star [stɑr] *s.* estrella; asterisco; **star-spangled** estrellado; *adj.* sobresaliente, excelente; *v.* estrellar, adornar o señalar con estrellas; marcar con asterisco; presentar como estrella (*a un actor*); lucir(se) en las tablas o el cine, hacer el papel principal.

star•board [stárbord] *s.* estribor; *adj.* de estribor; **– side** banda de estribor; *adv.* a estribor.

starch [stortʃ] *s.* almidón, fécula, *v.* almidonar.

stare [stɛr] *v.* mirar, mirar con fijeza o curiosidad; mirar azorado; clavar la mirada, fijar la vista; *s.* mirada fija, mirada persistente.

star•fish [stárfɪʃ] *s.* estrella de mar.

stark [stork] *adj.* (*utter*) tieso; (*grim*) escueto; **– folly** pura tontería; **– in death** tieso, muerto; **– narrative** narración escueta, sin adornos; *adv.* completamente, totalmente; **– mad** loco de remate; **– naked** enteramente desnudo, en cueros, *Am.* encuerado.

star•light [stárlaɪt] *s.* luz estelar, luz de las estrellas.

star•ry [stárɪ] *adj.* estrellado, sembrado de estrellas; como estrellas, brillante.

start [stort] *v.* comenzar, empezar, principiar;

poner(se) en marcha; partir, salir; dar un salto, sobresaltarse; **the motor -s** el motor arranca; **to – after someone** salir en busca de alguien; **to – off** salir, partir; dar principio a; **to – out on a trip** empezar una jornada, emprender un viaje; **to – the motor** hacer arrancar el motor; *s.* comienzo, empiezo, principio; sobresalto; respingo (*de un caballo*); arranque; ventaja (*en una carrera*).

start•er [stártɚ] *s.* (*automobile*) arranque; (*person*) arrancador; iniciador; (*first*) primero de la serie; **self-starter** arranque automático.

star•tle [stártḷ] *v.* asustar(se), sobresaltar(se), espantar(se).

star•tling [stártlIŋ] *adj.* sobresaltante, pasmoso, asombroso, sorprendente.

star•va•tion [storvéʃən] *s.* inanición, hambre.

starve [storv] *v.* morir(se) de hambre; hambrear; matar de hambre.

state [stet] *s.* estado; condición, situación; **in great –** con gran pompa; *adj.* de estado; del estado; de ceremonia; *v.* declarar, decir; expresar, exponer.

state•ly [stétlI] *adj.* majestuoso, imponente.

state•ment [stétmənt] *s.* (*declaration*) declaración; exposición; (*information*) informe, relato; (*bill*) cuenta, estado de cuentas.

state•room [stétrum] *s.* camarote (*de un buque*).

states•man [stétsmən] *s.* estadista, hombre de estado.

stat•ic [stǽtIk] *adj.* estático; *s.* estática.

sta•tion [stéʃən] *s.* (*operations point*) estación; (*post*) paradero; puesto; (*condition*) estado, posición social; **broadcasting –** transmisora o emisora; *v.* estacionar, colocar, apostar; **– wagon** *Esp.* rubia; *Méx.* camioneta, huayin; *C.A.* camionetilla.

sta•tion•ar•y [stéʃənɛrI] *adj.* estacionario, fijo.

sta•tion•er•y [stéʃənɛrI] *s.* papelería.

sta•tis•tics [stətístIks] *s.* estadística; datos estadísticos.

stat•u•ar•y [stǽtʃUɛrI] *s.* estatuaria, arte de hacer estatuas, colección de estatuas.

stat•ue [stǽtʃU] *s.* estatua.

stat•ure [stǽtʃɚ] *s.* estatura.

sta•tus [stétəs] *s.* estado, condición; posición social o profesional.

stat•ute [stǽtʃUt] *s.* estatuto, ordenanza.

staunch = stanch.

stave [stev] *s.* duela de barril, *v.* poner duelas (*a un barril*); **to – off** mantener a distancia; evitar; rechazar.

stay [ste] *v.* (*remain*) quedarse, permanecer; parar(se); detener(se); (*sojourn*) hospedarse, alojarse; (*check*) resistir; **to – an execution** diferir o aplazar una ejecución, **to – one's hunger** engañar el hambre, **to – up all night** velar toda la noche; *s.*

estada, estancia, permanencia; suspensión; sostén, apoyo; varilla o ballena de corsé, **to grant a –** conceder una prórroga.

stead [stɛd]: **in her (his) –** en su lugar; **to stand one in good –** servirle a uno, ser de provecho para uno.

stead•fast [stɛdfæst] *adj.* fijo, firme; constante.

stead•i•ly [stɛdIlI] *adv.* constantemente; firmemente; sin parar, de continuo; sin vacilar.

stead•i•ness [stɛdInIs] *s.* firmeza; constancia; estabilidad.

stead•y [stɛdI] *adj.* firme, estable, invariable, constante; continuo; *v.* afianzar, mantener firme, asegurar; calmar (*los nervios*).

steak [stek] *s.* biftec o bisté; tajada (*para asar o freír*).

steal [stil] *v.* (*rob*) robar, hurtar; (*move*) andar furtivamente; **to – away** colarse, escabullirse, escaparse, **to – into a room** meterse a hurtadillas en un cuarto; **to – out of a room** salirse a escondidas de un cuarto, colarse, escabullirse; *s.* robo, hurto.

stealth [stɛlθ]: **by –** a hurtadillas, a escondidas, con cautela.

stealth•y [stɛlθI] *adj.* cauteloso, furtivo, secreto.

steam [stim] *s.* vapor; vaho; *adj.* de vapor; por vapor; **– engine** máquina de vapor, **– heat** calefacción por vapor; *v.* cocer al vapor; dar un baño de vapor; saturar de vapor; echar vapor; **to – into port** llegar a puerto (*un vapor*).

steam•boat [stímbot] *s.* buque de vapor.

steam•er [stímɚ] *s.* vapor, buque de vapor.

steam•ship [stímʃIp] *s.* vapor, buque de vapor.

steed [stid] *s.* corcel, caballo de combate; caballo brioso.

steel [stil] *s.* acero; *adj.* acerado, de acero; *v.* acerar, revestir de acero; **to – oneself against** fortalecerse contra.

steep [stip] *adj.* empinado, escarpado, pendiente; muy alto; **– price** precio alto o excesivo; *v.* remojar, empapar; saturar; poner o estar en infusión.

stee•ple [stíp̣ḷ] *s.* aguja, chapitel; cúspide.

steep•ness [stípnIs] *s.* inclinación abrupta; lo empinado, lo escarpado; altura (*de precios*).

steer [stIr] *s.* novillo; buey; *v.* guiar, conducir, manejar, gobernar; timonear; **to – a course** seguir un rumbo: **the car -s easily** se maneja fácilmente el auto, es de fácil manejo.

stel•lar [stélɚ] *adj.* estelar.

stem [stɛm] *s.* tallo; tronco; pedúnculo (*de hoja, flor o fruto*); raíz (*de una palabra*); pie (*de copa*); cañón (*de pipa de fumar*); proa; *v.* estancar, represar; resistir, refrenar; contraponerse a; **to – from** provenir de.

stench [stɛntʃ] *s.* hedor, hediondez.

sten•cil [stɛnṣḷ] *s.* patrón picado; esténcil.

ste•nog•ra•pher [stənógrəfɚ] *s.* estenógrafo, taquígrafo, mecanógrafo.

step [stɛp] s. (*walking*) paso; pisada; (*staircase*) peldaño; escalón, grada; (*degree*) grado; (*effort*) gestión; **– by** – paso a paso; **to be in – with** marchar a compás con; estar de acuerdo con; **to take -s** dar pasos; tomar medidas; gestionar; v. andar, caminar; dar un paso; **to – aside** hacerse a un lado, apartarse; **to – back** dar un paso o pasos atrás; retroceder; **to – down** bajar; **to – off a distance** medir a pasos una distancia; **to – on** pisar, pisotear; **to – on the gas** pisar el acelerador; darse prisa; **to – out** salir; **to – up** subir; acelerar.

step•fa•ther [stépfaðə] s. padrastro.

step•moth•er [stépmʌðə] s. madrastra.

steppe [stɛp] s. estepa.

ster•e•o•type [stírIotaIp] s. estéreotipo.

ster•ile [stérəl] adj. estéril.

ster•il•i•ty [stərílətI] s. esterilidad.

ster•il•ize [stérəlaIz] v. esterilizar.

ster•ling [stə́rlIŋ] s. vajilla de plata esterlina; adj. genuino; de ley; **– silver** plata de ley, plata esterlina; **pound –** libra esterlina.

stern [stə́rn] adj. austero, severo; firme; s. popa.

stern•ness [stə́rnnIs] s. austeridad, severidad; firmeza.

steth•o•scope [stéθəstop] s. estetoscopio.

ste•ve•dore [stívədor] s. estibador, cargador.

stew [stju] v. estofar; preocuparse, apurarse; s. estofado, guisado; **to be in a –** estar preocupado o apurado.

stew•ard [stjúwəd] s. mayordomo; camarero (*de buque o avión*).

stew•ard•ess [stjúwədIs] s. camarera (*de buque o avión*).

stick [stIk] s. palo; vara; garrote; raja de leña; **– of dynamite** barra de dinamita; **control –** palanca (*de aeroplano*); **walking –** bastón; **stick-up** atraco (*para robar*), asalto; v. pegar(se), adherir(se); permanecer; estar pegado, picar, pinchar; herir (*con cuchillo, puñal, etc.*); fijar (*con clavos, alfileres, tachuelas, etc.*); atascarse (*en el fango un carro, auto, etc.*); **to – something in** (o **into**) clavar o meter algo en; encajar en; **to – out** salir, sobresalir; proyectarse; **to – out one's head** asomar la cabeza; **to – out one's tongue** sacar la lengua; **to – to a job** perseverar (o persistir) en una tarea; **to – up** sobresalir, destacarse; estar de punta (*el pelo*); **to – one's hands up** alzar las manos; **to – someone up** asaltar o atracar a alguien (*para robar*); véase **stuck**.

stick•er [stíkə] s. marbete engomado; etiqueta.

stick•y [stíkI] adj. pegajoso.

stiff [stIf] adj. tieso; rígido; entumido; duro; terco; fuerte; **– climb** subida ardua o difícil; **– price** precio alto o subido; **stiff-necked** terco, obstinado; **scared –** yerto, muerto de miedo; s. cadáver.

stiff•en [stífən] v. atiesar(se), poner(se) tieso; entumir(se); endurecer(se); espesar(se); subir de punto, aumentar (*la resistencia*).

stiff•ness [stífnIs] s. tiesura; rigidez; dureza; rigor; terquedad.

sti•fle [stáIfḷ] v. ahogar(se), asfixiar(se), sofocar(se); apagar, extinguir.

stig•ma [stígmə] s. estigma; baldón.

stig•ma•tize [stígmətaIz] v. estigmatizar.

still [stIl] adj. (*quiet*) quieto; callado, silencioso; (*at ease*) tranquilo; inmóvil; **– born** nacido muerto; **– life** naturaleza muerta; v. aquietar; calmar; acallar; adv. todavía, aún; conj. empero, no obstante, sin embargo; s. destiladera, alambique; silencio.

still•ness [stílnIs] s. quietud, calma, silencio.

stilt [stIlt] s. zanco; pilote, puntual, soporte.

stilt•ed [stíltId] adj. tieso, afectado, pomposo.

stim•u•lant [stímjələnt] adj. & s. estimulante.

stim•u•late [stímjəlet] v. estimular.

stim•u•la•tion [stImjəléʃən] s. estimulación, estímulo.

stim•u•lus [stímjələs] s. estímulo.

sting [stIŋ] s. (*pierce*) picar; pinchar, aguijonear; (*irritate*) escocer; Am. arder; (*cheat*) embaucar; estafar; s. picadura; piquete, mordedura, picazón; aguijón; escozor; **– of remorse** remordimiento.

stin•gi•ness [stínd3Inls] s. tacañería, mezquindad.

stin•gy [stínd3I] adj. mezquino, ruin, tacaño; escaso; Ríop., Mex. codo.

stink [stIŋk] v. heder, oler mal; apestar; s. hedor, mal olor; hediondez.

stint [stInt] v. escatimar; ser frugal o económico; **to – oneself** privarse de lo necesario, economizar demasiado; s. tarea, faena, **without –** sin límite; sin escatimar; generosamente.

stip•u•late [stípjəlet] v. estipular.

stip•u•la•tion [stIpjəléʃən] s. estipulación, condición.

stir [stə́r] v. menear(se); mover(se), bullir(se); atizar (*el fuego*); incitar; conmover; perturbar; revolver; **to – up** incitar; conmover; revolver; suscitar (*un argumento, pelea, etc.*); s. meneo, agitación, movimiento; alboroto.

stir•ring [stə́rIŋ] adj. conmovedor.

stir•rup [stírəp] s. estribo.

stitch [stItʃ] v. coser; dar puntadas; s. puntada; punzada; **to be in -es** desternillarse de risa.

stock [stok] s. (*supply*) surtido; existencias, provisión; (*cattle*) ganado; (*lineage*) cepa, linaje, estirpe; (*shares*) acciones, valores; **in –** en existencia; **live-ganado; meat –** caldo de carne; adj. en existencia, existente, disponible; común, trivial; **–answer** contestación corriente, común o trivial; **– company** sociedad anónima; compañía teatral; **– exchange** bolsa; **– farm** hacienda de ganado, Am. rancho, Am.

estancia; – **market** mercado de valores, bolsa; – **room** almacén; – **size** tamaño ordinario (*regularmente en existencia*); –**yard** matadero; *v.* surtir, abastecer; tener en existencia (*para vender*); **to – a farm** surtir o proveer de ganado un rancho; **to – up with** surtirse de, acumular.

stock•ade [stɔkéd] *s.* estacada, empalizada; vallado; *v.* empalizar, rodear de empalizadas.

stock•bro•ker [stɔ́kbrokə] *s.* bolsista, corredor de bolsa.

stock•hold•er [stɔ́kholdə] *s.* accionista.

stock•ing [stɔ́kIŋ] *s.* media.

sto•ic [stɔ́Ik] *adj. & s.* estoico.

stoke [stok] *v.* atizar (*el fuego*); cebar, alimentar (*un horno*).

stole [stol] *pret. de* **to steal.**

sto•len [stólən] *p.p. de* **to steal.**

stol•id [stɔ́lId] *adj.* estólido, insensible.

stom•ach [stΛmək] *s.* estómago; *v.* aguantar, tolerar.

stomp [stɑmp] *v.* pisar violentamente.

stone [ston] *s.* piedra; hueso (*de las frutas*); **within a –'s throw** a tiro de piedra; *adj.* pétreo, de piedra; **Stone Age** Edad de Piedra; **stone-deaf** totalmente sordo, sordo como una tapia; *v.* apedrear; deshuesar (*las frutas*).

ston•y [stónI] *adj.* pedregoso; pétreo, de piedra; duro.

stood [stUd] *pret. & p.p. de* **to stand.**

stool [stul] *s.* (*furniture*) taburete; *C.A.* banquillo; (*toilet*) bacín, bacinica; (*excrement*) excremento; – **pigeon** soplón (*el que delata a otro*).

stoop [stup] *v.* agacharse; doblarse, inclinarse; encorvarse; andar encorvado o caído de hombros; rebajarse, humillarse, abajarse; *s.* encorvamiento, inclinación (*de espaldas*); **to walk with a** – andar encorvado o caído de hombros; **stoop-shouldered** cargado de espaldas, encorvado.

stop [stɑp] *v.* (*pause*) parar(se), hacer alto, detener(se); (*cease*) acabar(se); cesar; parar de, dejar de; (*block*) atajar; reprimir; suspender; obstruir, tapar; **to – at a hotel** hospedarse o alojarse en un hotel; **to – at nothing** no pararse en escrúpulos, **to – from** impedir; **to – over at** hacer escala en; **to – short** parar(se) de sopetón, parar(se) en seco; **to – up** tapar, obstruir; atascar; *s.* parada; alto, pausa; estada, estancia; detención; suspensión; llave (*de instrumento de viento*); traste (*de guitarra*); registro (*de órgano*); – **consonant** consonante explosiva.

stop•o•ver [stɑ́pvə] *s.* parada, escala; **to make a – in** hacer escala en.

stop•page [stɑ́pIdʒ] *s.* detención; obstrucción; **work** – paro.

stop•per [stɑ́pə] *s.* tapón.

stor•age [stɔ́rIdʒ] *s.* almacenaje; – **battery** acumulador; **to keep in** – almacenar.

store [stor] *s.* (*shop*) tienda; almacén; (*supply*) depósito; acopio; **-s** provisiones; bastimentos; víveres; **department** – almacén; **dry-goods** – lencería, *Méx., Ríopl., Andes* mercería, *Am.* cajón de ropa; **fruit** – frutería; **hat** – sombrerería; **grocery** – abacería, tienda de comestibles, *Méx., C.A.* tienda de abarrotes, *Carib.* bodega; **shoe** – zapatería; **to have in** – tener guardado; *v.* almacenar; guardar; abastecer; **to – up** acumular.

store•house [stɔ́rhaUs] *s.* almacén, depósito.

store•keep•er [stɔ́rkipə] *s.* tendero; almacenista; guardalmacén.

store•room [stɔ́rrum] *s.* almacén; bodega; despensa.

stork [stork] *s.* cigüeña.

storm [storm] *s.* (*weather*) tormenta, tempestad, borrasca, temporal; (*disturbance*) tumulto; asalto; – **troops** tropas de asalto; **hail** – granizada; **snow** – nevasca; **wind** – vendaval; *v.* asaltar, atacar; rabiar; **it is -ing** hay tormenta, hay tempestad.

storm•y [stɔ́rmI] *adj.* tempestuoso, borrascoso; turbulento.

sto•ry [stɔ́rI] *s.* (*tale*) cuento, historia, historieta; relato; (*gossip*) chisme; rumor; bola; (*plot*) argumento, trama; (*floor*) piso (*de un edificio*); **newspaper** – artículo de periódico, gacetilla.

stout [staUt] *adj.* corpulento, robusto, fornido; fuerte; firme; leal; valiente.

stove [stov] *s.* estufa; cocina de gas, cocina eléctrica; *pret. & p.p. de* **to stave.**

stow [sto] *v.* meter, guardar; esconder; estibar, acomodar la carga de un barco; rellenar; **to – away on a ship** embarcarse, clandestinamente, esconderse en un barco.

strad•dle [strǽdḷ] *v.* ponerse o estar a horcajadas; ponerse a caballo, cabalgar; favorecer ambos lados (*de un pleito, controversia, etc.*).

strafe [stref] *v.* ametrallar; *Am.* abalear.

strag•gle [strǽgḷ] *v.* vagar, desviarse; extraviarse; andar perdido; dispersarse; **to – behind** rezagarse.

straight [stret] *adj.* (*direction*) recto; derecho; directo; (*proper*) honrado; franco; erguido; correcto; en orden; – **face** cara sería; – **hair** pelo lacio; – **hand of five cards** runfla de cinco naipes del mismo palo; – **rum** ron puro, sin mezcla; **for two hours** – por dos horas seguidas, por dos horas sin parar; **to set a person** – dar consejo a una persona; mostrarle el camino, modo o manera de hacer algo; *adv.* directamente; derecho, en línea recta; francamente; honradamente; –**away** (*o – off*) en seguida, al punto; **to talk – from the shoulder** hablar con toda franqueza o sinceridad.

straight•en [strét ŋ] *v.* enderezar(se); arreglar, poner en orden.

straight•for•ward [stretfɔ́rwəd] *adj.* derecho, recto; honrado; franco, sincero, *adv.* directamente, en línea recta.

straight•ness [strétnɪs] *s.* derechura; rectitud; honradez.

straight•way [strétwe] *adv.* luego, inmediatamente, en seguida.

strain [stren] *v.* (*force*) estirar demasiado, hacer fuerza; poner tirante; violentar, forzar (*los músculos, los nervios, la vista, etc.*); (*sift*) colar, tamizar; **to – one's wrist** torcerse la muñeca; *s.* tensión excesiva; tirantez; torcedura; esfuerzo excesivo; linaje rasgo racial; aire, tonada.

strain•er [strénæ] *s.* coladera; cedazo.

strait [stret] *s.* estrecho; **-s** estrecho; aprieto, apuro; **– jacket** camisa de fuerza.

strait•laced [strétlest] *adj.* estricto.

strand [strænd] *v.* encallar; dejar perdido (*sin medios de salir*), dejar aislado, extraviar; **to be -ed** estar encallado; estar extraviado (*sin medios de salir*) estar aislado, andar perdido; *s.* ribera, playa; ramal (*de cuerda, cable, etc.*); hebra, hilo; **– of hair** guedeja; trenza; **– of pearls** hilera de perlas.

strange [strendʒ] *adj.* extraño; raro, singular; desconocido.

strange•ness [stréndʒnɪs]*s.* extrañeza, rareza.

strang•er [stréndʒæ] *s.* extraño, desconocido; forastero.

stran•gle [strǽŋg|] *v.* estrangular(se).

strap [stræp] *s.* correa; tira de cuero o de tela; correón; tirante; **metal –** banda de metal; *v.* amarrar o atar con correas; azotar (*con correa*); véase **strop.**

strat•a•gem [strǽtədʒəm] *s.* estratagema.

stra•te•gic [stretídʒɪk] *adj.* estratégico.

strat•e•gy [strǽtədʒɪ] *s.* estrategia.

strat•o•sphere [strǽtəsfɪr] *s.* estratosfera.

straw [strɔ] *s.* paja; **I don's care a –** no me importa un comino; *adj.* de paja; pajizo; **straw-colored** pajizo, color de paja; **– hat** sombrero de paja; **– vote** voto no oficial (*para averiguar la opinión pública*).

straw•ber•ry [strɔ́bɛrɪ] *s.* fresa.

stray [stre] *v.* extraviarse, descarriarse, desviarse; perderse, errar el camino; vagar; *adj.* extraviado, perdido; **– remark** observación aislada; *s.* animal perdido o extraviado.

streak [strik] *s.* (*line*) raya, línea, lista; (*vein*) vena; (*trace*) rasgo; (*beam*) rayo (*de luz*); **– of lightning** relámpago, rayo; *v.* rayar, *Am.* listar, hacer rayas o listas en.

stream [strim] *s.* corriente; chorro; río, arroyo, arroyuelo; **– of cars** desfile de autos; **down –** río abajo, agua abajo, con la corriente; **up –** río arriba, agua arriba, contra la corriente; *v.* correr (*el agua*), fluir; brotar, manar; derramarse; flotar (*en el viento*), ondear; **to – out** of salir a torrentes de.

stream•er [strímæ] *s.* banderola; gallardete; listón, cinta (*que flota en el aire*).

stream•lined [strímlaɪnd] *adj.* aerodinámico.

street [strit] *s.* calle.

street•car [strítkɑr] *s.* tranvía.

strength [strɛŋkθ] *s.* fuerza; poder; potencia; fortaleza, **on the – of his promise** fundado en su promesa.

strength•en [strɛ́ŋkθən] *v.* fortalecer(se); reforzar(se).

stren•u•ous [strɛ́njʊəs] *adj.* arduo; enérgico, vigoroso.

strep•to•my•cin [strɛptomáɪsɪn] *s.* estreptomicina.

stress [strɛs] *s.* (*force*) fuerza, esfuerzo; tensión, torsión, compresión; (*importance*) urgencia; énfasis; (*intensity*) acento; *v.* acentuar; recalcar, dar énfasis a, hacer hincapié en.

stretch [strɛtʃ] *v.* estirar(se); alargar(se); tender(se); ensanchar; **to – oneself** estirarse, desperezarse; **to – out one's hand** tender o alargar la mano; *s.* trecho, distancia; extensión; período de tiempo; elasticidad; tensión; esfuerzo (*de la imaginación*); estirón; **home –** último trecho (*de una carrera*).

stretch•er [strɛ́tʃæ] *s.* estirador, ensanchador, dilatador; camilla (*para los heridos*).

strew [stru] *v.* regar, esparcir.

strewn [strun] *p.p. de* **to strew, – with** regado de, cubierto de.

strick•en [stríkən] *p.p. de* **to strike**; *adj.* herido; afligido; agobiado; atacado.

strict [strɪkt] *adj.* estricto, **in – confidence** en absoluta confianza, con toda reserva.

strid•den [strɪ́d ŋ] *p.p. de* **to stride.**

stride [straɪd] *v.* tranquear, caminar a paso largo, dar zancadas, andar a trancos; *s.* zancada, tranco, paso largo.

strife [straɪf] *s.* refriega, contienda, pleito.

strike [straɪk] *v.* (*hit*) dar, golpear, pegar; azotar; herir; atacar; (*collide with*) chocar con; dar con, encontrar (*oro, petróleo, etc.*); ocurrírsele a uno (*una idea*); asumir, afectar (*una postura, una actitud*); dar (*la hora un reloj*); encender (*un fósforo*); acuñar (*moneda*); declararse o estar en huelga; **to – at** amargar; acometer; **to -off** borrar, tachar; cortar; **to – one's attention** atraer o llamar la atención; **to – one's fancy** antojársele a uno; **to – one's . head against** darse un cabezazo contra; **to – out in a certain direction** tomar cierto rumbo, encaminarse o irse en cierta dirección; **to – someone for a loan** darle un sablazo a alguien; **to – up a friendship** trabar amistad; **to – with terror** sobrecoger de terror; **how does she – you?** ¿qué tal le parece? ¿qué piensa Vd. de ella?; *s.* golpe; huelga; descubrimiento repentino (*de petróleo, de una mina, etc.*); **–breaker** esquirol (*obrero que sustituye a un huelguista*).

strik•er [stráIkɚ] s. (*person on strike*) huelguista; (*device*) golpeador.

strik•ing [stráIkIŋ] adj. notable; llamativo; conspicuo, manifiesto; sorprendente; extraordinario; (*on strike*) que está de huelga; que está en huelga.

string [striŋ] s. cuerda; cordel, cinta, cordón; sarta (*de perlas, cuentas, etc.*); fibra (*de habichuelas, porotos, etc.*); fila, hilera; **– bean** habichuela, judía verde, *Méx.* ejote, *Ch., Ríopl.* poroto; **– of lies** sarta de mentiras; v. ensartar; tender (*un cable, un alambre*); desfibrar quitar las fibras a; encordar (*una raqueta, un violín*); encordelar, atar con cordeles, lazos o cuerdas; tomar el pelo, engañar; **to – out** extender(se), prolongar(se); **to – up** colgar.

strip [strIp] v. despojar; robar; desnudar(se); desvestir(se), desmantelar; **to – the gears** estropear el engranaje; **to – the skin from** desollar, pelar; s. tira, lista, listón; **– of land** faja de tierra.

stripe [straIp] s. (*band*) franja, raya, lista, tira; banda, galón; (*kind*) tipo, índole; v. rayar, *Am.* listar, adornar con listas.

striped [stráIpId, straIpt] adj. listado.

strive [straIv] v. esforzarse; luchar, forcejear; hacer lo posible; **to – to** esforzarse por.

striv•en [strívən] p.p. de **to strive**.

strode [strod] pret. de **to stride**.

stroke [strok] s. golpe; ataque, apoplejía; **– of a bell** campanada; **– of a painter's brush** pincelada; **– of lightning** rayo; **– of the hand** caricia; **– of the pen** plumada; **at the – of ten** al dar las diez; v. frotar suavemente, pasar suavemente la mano, acariciar; alisar.

stroll [strol] v. dar un paseo, pasearse; vagar; **to – the streets** callejear; s. paseo, paseíto.

strong [strɔŋ] adj. fuerte; forzudo, fornido, vigoroso; recio; enérgico; firme; bien marcado, acérrimo; **– chance** buena probabilidad; **– coffee** café cargado; **– market** mercado firme; **strong-willed** de voluntad fuerte, decidido; **strong-arm** violento; adv. fuertemente; firmemente.

strong•hold [strɔ́ŋhold] s. fuerte, plaza fuerte.

strop [strɔp] v. asentar (*navajas de afeitar*); s. asentador de navajas.

strove [strov] pret. de **to strive**.

struck [strʌk] pret. & p.p. de **to strike**; **to be – with a disease** darle a uno una enfermedad; **to be – with terror** estar o quedar sobrecogido de terror.

struc•tur•al [strʌ́ktʃərəl] adj. estructural, relativo a la estructura.

struc•ture [strʌ́ktʃɚ] s. estructura; construcción; edificio.

strug•gle [strʌ́gl̩] v. bregar, luchar, purgar; forcejear; esforzarse; s. esfuerzo; contienda; lucha, pugna.

strung [strʌŋ] pret. & p.p. de **to string**.

strut [strʌt] v. pavonearse, contonearse; s. contoneo; tirante, puntal.

stub [stʌb] s. trozo, fragmento, pedazo mochado; tocón (*de árbol*); talón (*de libro talonario, boleto, etc.*); **– book** libro talonario; **– pen** pluma de punta mocha; v. **to – one's foot** dar(se) un tropezón.

stub•ble [stʌ́bl̩] s. rastrojo; cañones (*de la barba*).

stub•born [stʌ́bɚn] adj. terco, testarudo, obstinado, porfiado, cabezón.

stub•born•ness [stʌ́bɚnnis] s. terquedad, testarudez, porfía, obstinación.

stuc•co [stʌ́ko] s. estuco; v. estucar, cubrir de estuco.

stuck [stʌk] pret. & p.p. de **to stick** pegado; atorado; atascado; **– full of holes** agujereado; **stuck-up** tieso, estirado, orgulloso.

stud [stʌd] s. (*knob*) tachón, tachuela de adorno; (*button*) botón postizo para camisa; (*bolt*) perno; **– horse** caballo padre; v. tachonar; clavetear.

stu•dent [stjúdn̩t] s. estudiante.

stud•ied [stʌ́dId] adj. estudiado.

stu•di•o [stjúdIo] s. estudio, taller.

stu•di•ous [stjúdIəs] adj. estudioso; aplicado, estudiado.

stud•y [stʌ́dI] s. estudio; cuidado, solicitud; gabinete de estudio; v. estudiar.

stuff [stʌf] s. (*material*) materia; material; (*cloth*) género, tela; (*thing*) cosa; (*medicine*) menjurje, medicina; (*junk*) cachivaches, baratijas; **of good – de buena estofa**; v. rellenar; henchir; hartar(se), atracar(se), atiborrar(se).

stuff•ing [stʌ́fIŋ] s. relleno; material para rellenar.

stum•ble [stʌ́mbl̩] v. tropezar, dar(se) un tropezón; dar un traspié; hablar o recitar equivocándose a cada paso; **to – upon** tropezar con; s. tropiezo, tropezón, traspié.

stump [stʌmp] s. tocón (*tronco que queda de un árbol*), raigón (*de muela*); muñón (*de brazo o pierna cortada*); **– of a tail** rabo; **to be up a –** hallarse en un apuro, estar perplejo; v. trozar el tronco de (*un árbol*); renquear, cojear; dejar confuso, confundir; **to – the country** recorrer el país pronunciando discursos políticos.

stump•y [stʌ́mpI] adj. rechoncho, *Am.* chaparro; lleno de tacones.

stun [stʌn] v. aturdir, pasmar; atolondrar.

stung [stʌŋ] pret. & p.p. de **to sting**.

stunk [stʌŋk] pret. & p.p. de **to stink**.

stun•ning [stʌ́nIŋ] adj. aplastante; elegante, bellísimo.

stunt [stʌnt] v. achaparrar, impedir el desarrollo de, no dejar crecer; hacer suertes; hacer piruetas; s.

suerte; pirueta, suerte acrobática, maniobra gimnástica; hazaña sensacional.

stu•pe•fy [stjúpəfaI] v. atontar; entorpecer; aturdir, atolondrar, pasmar, dejar estupefacto.

stu•pen•dous [stjupéndəs] adj. estupendo.

stu•pid [stjúpId] adj. estúpido; atontado.

stu•pid•i•ty [stjupídəI] s. estupidez.

stu•por [stjúpə·] s. letargo, modorra; aturdimiento; **in a** – aletargado.

stur•dy [stɜ́·dI] adj. fornido, fuerte, robusto; firme.

stut•ter [st ʌ́ tə·] v. tartamudear; s. tartamudeo; tartamudez.

stut•ter•er [st ʌ́ tərə·] s. tartamudo.

stut•ter•ing [st ʌ́ tərIŋ] adj. tartamudo: s. tartamudeo.

sty [staI] s. pocilga; orzuelo (en el párpado), Méx. perilla; Ríopl. chiquero.

style [staIl] s. estilo; moda; **to be in** – estar de moda, estilarse; v. intitular; nombrar; **to – a dress** cortar un vestido a la moda.

styl•ish [stáIlIʃ] adj. elegante; a la moda.

styl•ize [stáIlaIz] v. estilizar.

sub•di•vi•sión [sʌbdəvÍʒən] s. subdivisión; parcelación de terrenos.

sub•due [səbdjú] v. subyugar, someter, sujetar, dominar; amansar, domar.

sub•dued [səbdjúd] p.p. de **to subdue**; adj. sumiso; sujeto; manso; suave; tenue; **– light** luz tenue.

sub•ject [s ʌ́ bdʒIkt] s. súbdito; sujeto; asunto, tema, materia; adj. sujeto; sometido; inclinado, propenso; expuesto; v. sujetar; someter; subyugar, sojuzgar.

sub•jec•tion [səbdʒékʃən] s. sujeción; dominación; sumisión.

sub•jec•tive [səbdʒéktIv] adj. subjetivo.

sub•ju•gate [s ʌ́ bdʒəget] v. subyugar, sojuzgar.

sub•li•mate [s ʌ́ bləmet] v. sublimar.

sub•lime [səblaÍm] adj. sublime.

sub•ma•rine [səbmərÍn] adj. submarino; s. submarino.

sub•merge [səm ɜ́ dʒ] v. sumergir(se), hundir(se), sumir(se).

sub•mis•sion [səbmÍʃən] s. sumisión, sometimiento.

sub•mis•sive [səbmÍsIv] adj. sumiso.

sub•mit [səbmÍt] v. someter; **to – a report** someter (presentar o rendir) un informe; **to – to punishment** someterse a un castigo.

sub•or•di•nate [səb ɔ́ rd ņ It]adj. s. subordinado; subalterno; dependiente; v. subordinar.

sub•scribe [səbskráIb] v. subscribir(se); firmar; **to – five dollars** prometer una cuota a subscripción de cinco dólares; **to – for** subscribirse a, abonarse a; **to – to a plan** subscribirse a (o aprobar) un plan.

sub•scrib•er [səbskráIbə·] s. suscritor, abonado;

infrascrito (que firma un documento), firmante.

sub•scrip•tion [sənskrÍpʃən] s. subscripción, abono.

sub•se•quent [s ʌ́ bsIkwɛnt] adj. subsiguiente, subsecuente, posterior; **-ly** adv. después, posteriormente, subsiguientemente.

sub•ser•vi•ent [səbs ɜ́ vIənt] adj. servil, servilón.

sub•side [səbsáId] v. menguar, disminuir; bajar (de nivel); calmarse, aquietarse.

sub•si•dize [s ʌ́ bsədaIz] v. subvencionar.

sub•si•dy [s ʌ́ bsədI] s. subvención.

sub•sist [səbsÍst] v. subsistir.

sub•stance [s ʌ́ bstəns] s. substancia (sustancia).

sub•stan•tial [səbstǽnʃəl] adj. substancial, substancioso; sólido; considerable; importante; **to be in – agreement** estar en substancia de acuerdo.

sub•stan•ti•ate [səbstǽnʃIət] v. comprobar; verificar.

sub•stan•tive [s ʌ́ bstəntIv] adj. & s. sustantivo.

sub•sti•tute [s ʌ́ bstətjut] v. sustituir (substituir); reemplazar; s. sustituto, suplente; reemplazo.

sub•sti•tu•tion [s ʌ́ bstətjúʃən] s. sustitución (substitución); reemplazo.

sub•stra•tum [s ʌ́ bstrætəm] s. sustrato.

sub•ter•fuge [s ʌ́ btə·fjudʒ] s. escapatoria; subterfugio.

sub•ter•ra•ne•an [s ʌ́ btərénIən] adj. subterráneo.

sub•tle [s ʌ́ t l̩] adj. sutil.

sub•tle•ty [s ʌ́ t l̩ tI] s. sutileza; agudeza.

sub•tract [səbtrǽkt] v. sustraer (substraer); restar.

sub•trac•tion [səbtrǽkʃən] s. sustracción (substracción), resta.

sub•urb [s ʌ́ b ɜ́ b] s. suberbio, arrabal.

sub•ur•ban [səb ɜ́ bən] adj. & s. suburbano.

sub•ver•sive [səbv ɜ́ sIv] adj. subversivo (en contra de la autoridad constituida); trastornador, destructivo.

sub•way [s ʌ́ bwe] s. subterráneo, túnel; metro, ferrocarril subterráneo.

suc•ceed [səksíd] v. suceder a; medrar, tener buen éxito, salir bien.

suc•cess [səksés] s. éxito, buen éxito; triunfo.

suc•cess•ful [səksésfəl] adj. afortunado; próspero; **to be** – tener buen éxito; **-ly** adv. con buen éxito, prósperamente

suc•ces•sion [səkséʃən] s. sucesión.

suc•ces•sive [səksésIv] adj. sucesivo.

suc•ces•sor [səksésə·] s. sucesor; heredero.

suc•cor [s ʌ́ kə·] s. socorro; v. socorrer.

suc•cumb [sək ʌ m] v. sucumbir.

such [sʌtʃ] adj. tal; semejante; – **a** tal, semejante; – **a good man** un hombre tan bueno; – **as** tal como, tales como; **at – an hour** a tal hora; **at – and – a place** en tal o cual lugar.

suck [sʌk] v. chupar; mamar; **to – up** chupar; sorber; s. chupada; mamada.

suck•er [s ʌ kə-] s. chupador; mamón, mamantón; dulce (que se chupa); primo (persona demasiado crédula).

suck•le [s ʌ k ḷ] v. mamar; amamantar, dar de mamar.

suc•tion [s ʌ kʃən] s. succión; chupada, aspiración.

sud•den [s ʌ d ŋ] adj. súbito, repentino, precipitado; inesperado; **all of a** – de súbito, de repente, de sopetón; -ly adv. de súbito, de repente, de sopetón.

sud•den•ness [s ʌ d ŋ nɪs] s. precipitación; rapidez.

suds [sʌdz] s. espuma, jabonadura.

sue [su] v. demandar; **to – for damages** demandar por daños y perjuicios; **to – for peace** pedir la paz.

su•et [súlt] s. sebo, gordo, grasa.

suf•fer [s ʌ fə-] v. sufrir; padecer.

suf•fer•er [s ʌ fərə-] s. sufridor.

suf•fer•ing [s ʌ fərɪŋ] s. sufrimiento, padecimiento; adj. doliente; sufrido, paciente.

suf•fice [səfáɪs] v. bastar, ser bastante o suficiente.

suf•fi•cient [səfɪʃ ənt] adj. suficiente, bastante; -ly adv. suficientemente, bastante.

suf•fix [s ʌ flks] s. sufijo.

suf•fo•cate [s ʌ fəket] v. sofocar(se), ahogar(se), asfixiar(se).

suf•fo•ca•tion [sʌfəkéʃən] s. asfixia, sofoco.

suf•frage [s ʌ frɪdʒ] s. sufragio; voto.

sug•ar [ʃúgə-] s. azúcar; – **bowl** azucarera; – **cane** caña de azúcar; **lump of** – terrón de azúcar; v. azucarar; cristalizarse (el almíbar), Am. azucararse.

sug•gest [səgdʒést] v. sugerir, indicar.

sug•ges•tion [səgdʒést ʃən] s. sugestión, Am. sugerencia; indicación.

sug•ges•tive [səgdʒéstɪv] adj. sugestivo.

su•i•cide [súəsaɪd] s. suicidio; suicida; **to commit** – suicidarse.

suit [sut] s. traje, terno, Carib., Ven. flux (o flus); palo (de la baraja); demanda, pleito; petición; galanteo; v. adaptar, acomodar; agradar; satisfacer; sentar bien, venir bien; caer bien; convenir; ser a propósito; – **yourself** haz lo que quieras; haga Ud. lo que guste.

suit•a•ble [súteb ḷ] adj. propio, conveniente, debido, a propósito, apropiado, adecuado.

suit•a•bly [sútebḷI] adv. propiamente, adecuadamente, convenientemente.

suit•case [sútkes] s. maleta, valija.

suite [swit] s. serie; comitiva, acompañamiento; – **of rooms** vivienda, apartamento, habitación; **bedroom** – juego de muebles para alcoba.

suit•or [sútə-] s. pretendiente, galán; demandante (en un pleito).

sulk [sʌlk] v. tener murria; estar hosco o malhumorado; s. murria.

sulk•y [s ʌ lkI] adj. malcontento, hosco, malhumorado; **to be** – tener murria.

sul•len [s ʌ lin] adj. hosco, sombrío, tétrico; malhumorado, taciturno.

sul•ly [s ʌ lI] v. manchar, ensuciar, empañar.

sul•phate [s ʌ lfət] s. sulfato.

sul•phide [s ʌ lfaɪd] s. sulfuro.

sul•phur [s ʌ lfə-] s. azufre.

sul•phur•ic [sʌljúrIk] adj. sulfúrico.

sul•tan [s ʌ lt ŋ] s. sultán.

sul•try [s ʌ ltrI] adj. bochornoso, sofocante; **heat** bochorno, calor sofocante.

sum [sʌm] s. suma; cantidad; esencia, substancia; – **total** total; v. suma; **to – up** resumir, recapitular.

sum•ma•rize [s ʌ məraɪz] v. resumir, compendiar.

sum•ma•ry [s ʌ merI] s. sumario, resumen; compendio; adj. sumario; breve.

sum•mer [s ʌ mə-] s. verano; estío; adj. veraniego, estival de verano; – **resort** balneario, lugar de veraneo; v. veranear.

sum•mit [s ʌ mIt] s. cima, cúspide, cumbre.

sum•mon [s ʌ mən] v. citar; convocar, llamar; -s s. notificación; cita judicial, citación, emplazamiento.

sump•tu•ous [s ʌ mptʃUəs] adj. suntuoso.

sun [sʌn] s. sol; – **bath** baño de sol; – **lamp** lámpara de rayos ultravioletas; – **porch** solana; v. asolear; **to – oneself** asolearse, tomar el sol.

sun•beam [s ʌ nbim] s. rayo de sol.

sun•burn [s ʌ nb ɝ n] s. quemadura de sol; v. asolear(se); quemar(se) al sol, tostar(se) al sol.

Sun•day [s ʌ ndI] s. domingo.

sun•di•al [s ʌ ndaɪəl] s. cuadrante solar, reloj de sol.

sun•down [s ʌ ndaUn] s. puesta del sol.

sun•dry [s ʌ ndrI] adj. varios, diversos.

sun•flow•er [s ʌ nflaUə-] s. girasol.

sung [sʌŋ] pret. & p.p. de **to sing**.

sun•glass•es [s ʌ nglæsəz] s. gafas (anteojos) de sol.

sunk [sʌŋk] pret. & p.p. de **to sink**.

sunk•en [s ʌ ŋkən] adj. hundido, sumido.

sun•light [s ʌ nlaIt] s. luz del sol, luz solar.

sun•ny [s Λ nI] *adj.* asoleado o soleado; alegre, risueño, resplandeciente; **– day** día de sol.

sun•rise [s Λ nraIz] *s.* salida del sol, amanecer, amanecida.

sun•set [s Λ nsɛt] *s.* puesta del sol.

sun•shine [s Λ nʃaIn] *s.* luz del sol, solana.

sun•stroke [s Λ nstrok] *s.* insolación.

sup [sΛp] *v.* cenar.

su•perb [sUpDb] *adj.* soberbio.

su•per•fi•cial [supəˈfíʃəl]*adj.* superficial.

su•per•flu•ous [supɜ́ˈflUəs] *adj.* superfluo.

su•per•hu•man [supəˈhjúmən] *adj.* sobrehumano.

su•per•in•tend [suprIntɛ́nd] *v.* dirigir, inspeccionar, vigilar.

su•per•in•ten•dent [suprIntɛ́nd] *s.* superintendente; inspector; capataz.

su•pe•ri•or [səpIrIə-] *adj.* & *s.* superior.

su•pe•ri•or•i•ty [səpIrIɔ́rətI] *s.* superioridad.

su•per•la•tive [səpɜ́ lətIv] *adj.* & *s.* superlativo.

su•per•mar•ket [súpə-mɑrkət] *s.* supermercado.

su•per•nat•u•ral [supə-nǽtʃrəl] *adj.* sobrenatural; **the –** lo sobrenatural.

su•per•sede [supə-síd] *v.* reemplazar.

su•per•sti•tion [supə-stíʃən] *s.* superstición.

su•per•sti•tious [supə-stíʃəs] *adj.* supersticioso.

su•per•vise [supə-váIz] *v.* dirigir, inspeccionar, vigilar.

su•per•vi•sion [supə-víʒən] *s.* inspección, vigilancia.

su•per•vi•sor [supə-rvaIzə-] *s.* superintendente, inspector; interventor.

sup•per [s Λ pə-] *s.* cena.

sup•plant [səplǽnt] *v.* suplantar; reemplazar.

sup•ple [s Λ p ⌐] *adj.* flexible; dócil.

sup•ple•ment [s Λ pləmənt] *s.* suplemento; apéndice; [s Λ pləmɛnt] *v.* suplementar, completar.

sup•pli•ant [s Λ plIənt] *adj.* & *s.* suplicante.

sup•pli•ca•tion [sΛplIkéʃən] *s.* súplica, plegaria; ruego.

sup•ply [səpláI] *v.* proveer; abastecer, surtir; suplir; dar, suministrar; *s.* provisión, abastecimiento; bastimento; abasto; surtido; **supplies** provisiones; materiales; víveres; pertrechos; **– pipe** cañería o caño de abastecimiento, tubería o tubo de suministro.

sup•port [səpórt] *v.* *(keep from falling)* sostener; apoyar; *(provide for)* mantener; sustentar; *(bear)* soportar, aguantar; *s.* apoyo; sostén, soporte, puntal; sustento, manutención; amparo.

sup•port•er [səpórtə-] *s.* defensor; partidario; mantenedor; sostén, apoyo, tirante *(para medias)*.

sup•pose [səpóz] *v.* suponer.

sup•posed [səpózd] *adj.* supuesto; presunto; **-ly** *adv.* supuestamente.

sup•po•si•tion [sΛpəzíʃən] *s.* suposición.

sup•press [səprɛ́s] *v.* suprimir; reprimir, parar, suspender; **to – a revolt** sofocar una revuelta o motín.

sup•pres•sion [səprɛ́ʃən] *s.* supresión; represión.

su•prem•a•cy [səprɛ́məsI] *s.* supremacía.

su•preme [səprím] *adj.* supremo.

sure [ʃUr] *adj.* seguro, cierto; estable; *adv.* véase **surely; be – to do it** hágalo sin falta, no deje Ud. de hacerlo; **-ly** *adv.* seguramente, ciertamente; con toda seguridad; sin falta.

sure•ty [ʃÚrtI] *s.* seguridad; garantía, fianza; fiador.

surf [sɜ́f] *s.* oleaje, rompientes; resaca.

sur•face [sɜ́fIs] *s.* superficie; cara; *v.* alisar, allanar; poner superficie a.

surf•board [sǽfbord] *s.* patín de mar.

sur•feit [sɜ́fIt] *s.* hastío, exceso; *v.* hastiar; empalagar.

surge [sɜ́dʒ] *s.* oleada, oleaje; *v.* agitarse, hinchar(se) *(el mar)*; surgir.

sur•geon [sɜ́dʒən] *s.* cirujano.

sur•ger•y [sɜ́dʒərI] *s.* cirugía.

sur•gi•cal [sɜ́dʒIk ⌐] *adj.* quirúrgico.

sur•ly [sɜ́lI] *adj.* rudo, hosco, malhumorado.

sur•mise [sə-máIz] *v.* conjeturar, suponer, presumir; *s.* conjetura, suposición.

sur•mount [sə-máUnt] *v.* superar, vencer; coronar.

sur•name [sɜ́nem] *s.* sobrenombre, apellido; *v.* apellidar, llamar.

sur•pass [sə-pǽs] *v.* sobrepasar, superar, sobrepujar, exceder, aventajar.

sur•pass•ing [sə-pǽsIŋ] *adj.* sobresaliente, excelente.

sur•plus [sɜ́plΛs] *s.* sobra, sobrante, exceso, excedente, superávit; *adj.* sobrante, excedente, de sobra.

sur•prise [səpráIz] *s.* sorpresa; *v.* sorprender.

sur•pris•ing [səpráIzIŋ] *adj.* sorprendente.

sur•ren•der [sərɛ́ndə-] *v.* rendir(se), entregar(se), darse; ceder; *s.* rendición; entrega; cesión; sumisión.

sur•round [səráUnd] *v.* rodear, cercar, circundar.

sur•round•ing [səráUndIŋ] *adj.* circundante, circunvecino, circunstante.

sur•round•ings [səráUndIŋz] *s. pl.* alrededores, inmediaciones, cercanías; ambiente.

sur•vey [sɜ́ve] *s.* *(inspection)* examen, reconocimiento, enspección, estudio; *(measure)* medición agrimensura *(de un terreno)*; plano *(de un terreno)*; bosquejo o esbozo general *(de historia, literatura,*

etc.); — **course** curso general o comprensivo; [sə·vé]
v. examinar, inspeccionar, reconocer medir (*un terreno*), levantar un plano (el *agrimensor*).

sur•vey•or [sə·véə·] *s.* agrimensor.

sur•viv•al [sə·váIv|] *s.* supervivencia; sobreviviente; resto.

sur•vive [sə·váIv] *c.* sobrevivir; quedar vivo, salvarse.

sur•vi•vor [sə·váIvə·] *s.* sobreviviente.

sus•cep•ti•ble [səsέptəb|] *adj.* susceptible; — **of proof** capaz de probarse; — **to** propenso a.

sus•pect [s ʌspέkt] *s.* sospechoso; [səspέkt] *v.* sospechar.

sus•pend [səspénd] *v.* suspender.

sus•pend•ers [səspéndə·z] *s.* tirantes (*de pantalón*).

sus•pense [səspéns] *s.* (*uncertainty*) suspensión, incertidumbre; (*anxiety*) ansiedad; **to keep in** — tener en suspenso; tener en duda.

sus•pen•sion [səspénʃən] *s.* suspensión; — **bridge** puente colgante.

sus•pi•cion [səspíʃən] *s.* sospecha.

sus•pi•cious [səspíʃəs] *adj.* sospechoso; suspicaz.

sus•tain [səstén] *v.* (*prolong*) sostener; mantener; (*support*) sustentar; (*bear, endure*) aguantar; (*defend*) apoyar, defender; (*undergo*) sufrir (*un daño o pérdida*).

sus•te•nance [s ʌstənəns] *s.* sustento; subsistencia; alimentos; mantenimiento.

swag•ger [swǽgə·] *v.* pavonearse, contonearse; fanfarronear; *s.* pavoneo, contoneo; fanfarronada.

swain [swen] *s.* galán.

swal•low [swálo] *s.* golondrina; trago; *v.* tragar; deglutir.

swam [swæm] *pret. de* **swim**.

swamp [swɑmp] *s.* pantano; ciénaga; — **land** cenegal, terreno pantanoso; *v.* inundar(se); sumergir(se); **to be -ed with work** estar abrumado de trabajo.

swamp•y [swámpI] *adj.* pantanoso, cenagoso, fangoso.

swan [swɑn] *s.* cisne.

swap [swɑp] *v.* cambalachear, cambiar, trocar; *s.* cambalache, cambio, trueque.

swarm [sworm] *s.* enjambre; *v.* pulular; bullir, hervir, hormiguear.

swar•thy [swɔ́rðI] *adj.* trigueño, moreno, *Am.* prieto.

swat [swɑt] *v.* pegar, aporrear; aplastar de un golpe (*una mosca*); *s.* golpe.

sway [swe] *v.* mecer(se); cimbrar(se); balancearse; ladear(se); oscilar; tambalear; influir; *s.* oscilación; vaivén; balanceo; influjo, influencia; mando; predominio.

swear [swεr] *v.* jurar; renegar, blasfemar, echar maldiciones; juramentar, tomar juramento, **to** —

by jurar por; poner toda su confianza en; **to** — **in** juramentar; **to** — **off smoking** jurar no fumar más, renunciar al tabaco.

sweat [swεt] *v.* sudar; trasudar; hacer sudar; *s.* sudor; trasudor.

sweat•er [swέtə·] *s. Am.* suéter; sudador, el que suda.

sweat•y [swέtI] *adj.* sudoroso.

Swede [swid] *s.* sueco.

Swed•ish [swídIʃ] *adj.* sueco; *s.* sueco, idioma sueco.

sweep [slip] *v.* barrer; dragar (*puertos, ríos, etc.*); extenderse; **to** — **down upon** caer sobre; asolar; **to** — **every-thing away** barrer con todo; **she swept into the room** entró garbosamente en la sala; *s.* barrida; extensión; soplo (*del viento*).

sweep•er [swípə·] *s.* barrendero; **carpet** — escoba mecánica.

sweep•ing [swípIŋ] *s.* barrido; **-s** basura; *adj.* abarcador, que lo abarca todo, vasto; asolador; — **victory** victoria completa.

sweet [swit] *adj.* dulce; oloroso; fresco; — **butter** mantequilla sin sal; — **corn** maíz tierno; — **milk** leche fresca; — **pea** guisante de olor; — **potato** batata, *Am.* camote, *Am.* boniato; **to have a** — **tooth** ser goloso, gustarle a uno los dulces; *s.* dulce, golosina; **my** — mi vida, mi alma.

sweet•en [swítṇ] *v.* endulzar(se), dulcificar(se); suavizar.

sweet•heart [swíthUrt] *s.* querida, novia, prometida; amante, querido, galán, novio.

sweet•meat [swítmit] *s.* confite, confitura dulce, golosina.

sweet•ness [swítnIs] *s.* dulzura; melosidad; suavidad.

swell [swεl] *v.* hinchar(se); henchir(se), inflar(se); dilatar(se), abultar(se); acrecentar; *s.* hinchazón; protuberancia; oleaje; *adj.* elegante; muy bueno, excelente, magnífico; **to have a** — **head** creerse gran cosa; ser vanidoso.

swell•ing [swέlIŋ] *s.* hinchazón; chichón, bulto; protuberancia.

swel•ter [swέltə·] *v.* sofocarse de calor.

swept [swεpt] *pret. & p.p. de* **to sweep**.

swerve [swɝv] *v.* desviar(se); torcer; cambiar repentinamente de rumbo; *s.* desvío brusco, cambio repentino de dirección; **to make a** — **to the right** torcer a la derecha.

swift [swIft] *adj.* veloz, rápido.

swift•ness [swíftnIs] *s.* velocidad, rapidez, presteza, prontitud.

swim [swIm] *v.* nadar; flotar; **to** — **across** pasar a nado, atravesar nadando; **my head is swimming** tengo vértigo, se me va la cabeza, estoy desvanecido; *s.* nadada; — **suit** traje de baño o natación.

swim•mer [swímə·] *s.* nadador.

swin•dle [swÍnd ǀ] v. estafar; s. estafa.

swine [swaIn] s. marrano, puerco, cerdo, cochino; marranos, puercos, cerdos.

swing v. columpiar(se), mecer(se), balancear(se); oscilar; hacer oscilar, blandir (*un bastón, espada, etc.*); colgar; girar; hacer girar; **to – a deal** llevar a cabo un negocio; **to – around** dar vuelta, girar; **to – one's arms** girar o menear los brazos; **to – open** abrirse de pronto (*una puerta*); s. columpio; hamaca; balanceo; vaivén; compás, ritmo; golpe, guantada, puñetazo; **– door** puerta giratoria; **– shift** turno de trabajo desde las dieciséis hasta medianoche; **in full** – en su apogeo, en pleno movimiento; **to give someone full** – darle a alguien completa libertad de acción.

swipe [swaIp] v. hurtar, sisar.

swirl [swɝl] v. arremolinarse; girar, dar vueltas; s. remolino, torbellino; vuelta, movimiento giratorio.

Swiss [swIs] [swItʃ] adj. & s. suizo.

switch s. (*change*) mudanza; (*whip*) látigo, (*blow*) azote; *Méx., Andes* chicote, *Ríopl.* rebenque; *Méx., Andes* fuete; latigazo; pelo postizo; cambio; **electric – ** interruptor, conmutador, **railway –** aguja, cambio; **-man** guardagujas, *Andes, Ríopl.* cambiavia; *Méx.* guardavía; v. azotar; desviar(se); cambiar(se); **to – off** cortar (*la comunicación o la corriente eléctrica*); apagar (*la luz eléctrica*); **to – on the light** encender la luz

switch•board [swÍtʃbɔrd] s. cuadro o tablero de distribución; cuadro conmutador.

swiv•el [swÍv ǀ] adj. giratorio.

swol•len [swólən] p.p. de **to swell.**

swoon [swun] v. desvanecerse, desmayarse; s. desmayo.

swoop [swup] v. **to – down upon** caer de súbito sobre; abalanzarse sobre; acometer; **to – off** cortar de un golpe; **to – up** agarrar, arrebatar; s. descenso súbito; arremetida; **at one** – de un golpe.

sword [sord] s. espada; **– belt** talabarte.

swore [swor] pret. de **to swear.**

sworn [sworn] p.p. de **to swear.**

swum [swʌm] p.p. de **to swim.**

swung [swʌŋ] pret. & p.p. de **to swing.**

syl•la•ble [sÍləb ǀ] s. sílaba.

syl•la•bus [sÍləbəs] s. sílabo.

sym•bol [sÍmb ǀ] s. símbolo.

sym•bol•ic [sImbólIk] adj. simbólico.

sym•bol•ism [sÍmb ǀ Izəm] s. simbolismo.

sym•met•ri•cal [sImÉtrIk ǀ] adj. simétrico.

sym•me•try [sÍmItrI] s. simetría.

sym•pa•thet•ic [sImpəθÉtIk] adj. compasivo; favorablemente dispuesto; que compadece; **– towards** favorablemente dispuesto a (o hacia).

sym•pa•thize [sÍmpəθaIz] v. compadecer(se); con-

dolerse.

sym•pa•thy [sÍmpəθI] s. compasión, lástima; armonía **to extend one's** – dar el pésame.

sym•pho•ny [sÍmfənI] s. sinfonía; **– orchestra** orquesta sinfónica.

sym•po•si•um [sImpósIəm] s. coloquio.

symp•tom [sÍmtəm] s. síntoma.

syn•di•cate [síndIkIt] s. sindicato; **newspaper –** sindicato periodístico; [síndIket] v. sindicar, formar un sindicato; sindicarse, combinarse para formar un sindicato; vender (*un cuento, caricatura, serie de artículos, etc.*) a un sindicato.

syn•drome [sÍmdrom] s. síndrome.

syn•o•nym [sÍnənIm] s. sinónimo.

syn•on•y•mous [sInænəməs] adj. sinónimo.

syn•op•sis [sInópsIs] s. sinopsis.

syn•tax [sÍntæks] s. sintaxis.

syn•the•sis [sÍnθəsIs] s. síntesis.

syn•the•size [sÍnθəsaIz] v. sintetizar.

syn•thet•ic [sInθÉtik] adj. sintético.

sy•ringe [sɪrÍndʒ]s. jeringa.

syr•up = **sirup.**

sys•tem [sÍstəm] s. sistema.

sys•tem•at•ic [sIstəmætIk] adj. sistemático.

sys•tem•ic [sIstémIk] adj. sistemático.

T

tab [tæb] s. (*flap*) lengüeta; (*bill*) cuenta.

tab•er•na•cle [tǽbə·næk ǀ] s. tabernáculo.

ta•ble [téb ǀ] s. mesa, tabla (*de materias, de multiplicar, etc.*); **– cover** tapete, cubremesa; **– land** mesa, meseta; v. poner sobre la mesa; formar tabla o índice; **to – a motion** dar carpetazo a una moción, aplazar la discusión de una moción.

ta•ble•cloth [téb ǀ klɔθ] s. mantel.

ta•ble•spoon [téb ǀ spun] s. cuchara grande.

ta•ble•spoon•ful [téb ǀ spunfUl] s. cucharada.

tab•let [tǽblIt] s. tableta; tablilla; pastilla; bloc de papel; lápida, placa.

ta•ble•ware [téb ǀ wɛr] s. vajilla, servicio de mesa.

ta•boo [tæbú] s. tabú.

tab•u•late [tǽbjəlet] v. formar tablas o listas.

tac•it [tǽsIt] adj. tácito.

tac•i•turn [tǽsətɝn] adj. taciturno, silencioso.

tack [tæk] s. tachuela; hilván; virada o cambio de rumbo (*de una embarcación*); amura, jarcia (*para sostener el ángulo de una vela*); **to – change –** cambiar de amura, cambiar de rumbo; v. clavetear con tachuelas; coser, hilvanar; pegar, clavar; juntar, unir;

virar, cambiar de rumbo; zigzaguear (*un barco de vela*).

tack•le [tǽk̬] *s.* aparejo, equipo, enseres, avíos; agarrada (*en fútbol*); atajador (*en fútbol*); **fishing —** avíos de pescar; *v.* agarrar, asir, atajar (*en fútbol*); atacar (*un problema*); acometer (*una empresa*).

tact [tækt] *s.* tacto, tino, tiento.

tact•ful [tǽktfəl] *adj.* cauto, prudente, diplomático.

tac•tics [tǽktıks] *s.* táctica.

tact•less [tǽktlıs] *adj.* falto de tacto o de tino; imprudente, incauto.

taf•fe•ta [tǽfıtə] *s.* tafetán.

tag [tæg] *s.* (*label*) marbete, etiqueta; cartela; (*loose end*) pingajo, rabito, cabo; **to play —** jugar al tócame tú, jugar a la pega; *v.* pegar un marbete a, marcar; **to — after** seguir de cerca a, pisar los talones a; **to — something on to** juntar, añadir o agregar algo a.

tail [tel] *s.* (*animal*) cola, rabo; (*object*) cabo, extremo, extremidad; **— light** farol trasero, farol de cola; **— spin** barrena.

tai•lor [télə] *s.* sastre.

taint [tent] *s.* tacha, mancha; corrupción; *v.* manchar, corromper(se), inficionar(se).

take [tek] *v.* tomar; coger; llevar; conducir; dar (*un paseo, vuelta, paso, salto*); hacer (*un viaje*); asumir; sacar o tomar (*una fotografía*); **to — a chance** aventurarse, correr un riesgo; **to — a fancy to** caerle en gracia a uno; aficionarse a; antojársele a uno; **to — a look at** mirar a, echar una mirada a; **to — a notion to** antojársele a uno; **to — after** salir a, parecerse a; seguir el ejemplo de; **to — amiss** interpretar mal, echar a mala parte; **to — an oath** prestar juramento; **to — apart** desarmar, desmontar; **to — away** llevarse; **to — back one's words** desdecirse, retractarse; **to — back to** devolver (*algo*) a; **to — by surprise** coger desprevenido, coger de sorpresa; **to — care of** cuidar de, atender a; **to — charge of** encargarse de; **to — cold** resfriarse, acatarrarse; **to - down in writing** poner por escrito, apuntar; **to — effect** surtir efecto, dar resultado; entrar en vigencia (*una ley*); **to — excercise** hacer ejercicio; hacer gimnasia; **to — from** quitar a; sustraer de, restar de; **to — in** meter en; recibir; abarcar; embaucar; reducir, achicar (*un vestido*); **to — leave** decir adiós, despedirse; **to — off** quitar; descontar, rebajar; despegar (*un aeroplano*); remedar, parodiar (*a alguien*); **to - offense** ofenderse, darse por ofendido; **to — on a responsibility** asumir una responsabilidad; **to — out** sacar; **to — place** tener lugar, suceder, ocurrir; **to — stock** hacer inventario; **to — stock in** creer, tener confianza en; **to — the floor** tomar la palabra; **to — to heart** tomar a pechos, tomar en serio; **to — to one's heels** poner pies en polvorosa;

to — to task reprender, regañar; **to — up a matter** tratar un asunto; **to — up space** ocupar espacio; **I — it that** supongo que; *s.* toma; **take-off** despegue (*de un aeroplano*); remedo, parodia.

tak•en [tékən] *p.p. de* **to take**; **to be — ill** caer enfermo.

tal•cum [tǽlkəm] *s.* talco; **— powder** talco en polvo.

tale [tel] *s.* (*story*) cuento, relato, fábula; (*gossip*) chisme; **to tell -s** contar cuentos o chismes; chismear, murmurar.

tale•bear•er [télbɛrə] *s.* soplón, chismoso.

tal•ent [tǽlənt] *s.* talento.

tal•ent•ed [tǽləntıd] *adj.* talentoso.

talk [tɔk] *v.* hablar; charlar, platicar, conversar; **to — into** inducir o persuadir a; **to — nonsense** decir tonterías, hablar disparates; **to — out of** disuadir de; **to — over** discutir; **to — up** alabar; hablar claro o recio, hablar en voz alta; *s.* charla, conversación, plática; habla; discurso; conferencia; rumor; **— of the town** comidilla, tema de murmuración.

talk•a•tive [tɔ́k̬ətıv] *adj.* hablador, locuaz, platicador.

talk•er [tɔ́k̬ə] *s.* hablador; conversador; platicador; orador.

tall [tɔl] *adj.* alto; **— tale** cuento exagerado o increíble; **six feet —** seis pies de altura o de alto.

tal•low [tǽlo] *s.* sebo.

tal•ly [tǽlı] *s.* cuenta; **— sheet** plana para llevar la cuenta; *v.* llevar la cuenta; **to — up** contar, sumar; **to — with** corresponder con, concordar con.

tame [tem] *adj.* manso; dócil; **— amusement** diversión poco animada o desabrida; *v.* amansar, domar, domeñar; domesticar.

tam•per [tǽmpə] *v.* **to — with** meterse con, juguetear con; falsificar (*un documento*); **to — with a lock** tratar de forzar una cerradura.

tan [tæn] *v.* (*cure*) curtir, adobar (*pieles*); (*punish*) zurrar, azotar; (*sunburn*) tostar(se) requemar(se); *adj.* tostado, requemado; color de canela; bayo, amarillento; *s.* color moreno, de canela o café con leche.

tang [tæŋ] *s.* sabor u olor picante.

tan•gent [tǽndʒənt] *adj. & s.* tangente; **to go off at a —** salirse por la tangente.

tan•ger•ine [tǽndʒərin] *s.* naranja tangerina o mandarina.

tan•gi•ble [tǽndʒən] *adj.* tangible, palpable; corpóreo.

tan•gle [tǽŋg] *v.* enredar(se), enmarañar(se); confundir(se), embrollar(se); *s.* enredo, maraña, embrollo; confusión.

tank [tæŋk] *s.* tanque; depósito; **swimming —** piscina.

tan•ner [tǽnə] *s.* curtidor.

tan·ner·y [tǽnərɪ] *s.* curtiduría, tenería.

tan·nic a·cid [tǽnɪkǽsəd] *s.* ácido tánico.

tan·ta·lize [tǽnt‖aɪz] *v.* molestar; hacer desesperar; exasperar.

tan·ta·mount [tǽntəməʊnt] *adj.* equivalente.

tan·trum [tǽntrəm] *s.* berrinche.

tap [tæp] *s.* (*blow*) palmadita; golpecito; (*faucet*) espita, grifo, llave; – **dance** zapateado, *Andes, Ríopl.* zapateo; - **room** bar; **beer on** – cerveza del barril, cerveza de sifón; *v.* tocar, golpear ligeramente; dar una palmadita o golpecito; taladrar; extraer; **to** – **a tree** sangrar un árbol.

tape [tep] *s.* cinta, cintilla; – **measure** cinta para medir; – **worm** solitaria; – **recorder** magnetófono; grabadora; **adhesive** – tela adhesiva; esparadrapo; *v.* atar o vendar con cinta; medir con cinta.

ta·per [tépə-] *s.* (*candle*) velita, candela; (*diminished size*) adelgazamiento paulatino; *v.* adelgazar, disminuir gradualmente; **to** – **off** ahusar(se), ir disminuyendo (*hasta rematar en punta*).

tap·es·try [tǽpɪstrɪ] *s.* tapiz, colgadura; tapicería; tela (*para forrar muebles*).

tape·worm [tépwə-m] *s.* tenia, solitaria.

tap·i·o·ca [tæpɪókə] *s.* tapioca.

tar [tɑr] *s.* alquitrán, brea, pez (*f.*); *v.* alquitranar, embrear, poner brea o alquitrán.

tar·dy [tórdɪ] *adj.* tardo, tardío; **to be** – llegar tarde o retrasado.

tar·get [tórgɪt] *s.* blanco; – **practice** tiro al blanco.

tar·iff [tǽrɪf] *s.* tarifa; arancel, impuesto.

tar·nish [tótnɪʃ] *v.* empañar(se); manchar; perder el lustre; *s.* deslustre, falta de lustre, empañamiento; mancha.

tar·ry [tǽrɪ] *v.* demorarse, tardar(se).

tart [tɑrt] *s.* acre, agridulce; agrio; picante; – **reply** respuesta mordaz o agria; *s.* tarta, torta rellena con dulce de frutas.

task [tæsk] *s.* faena, tarea, quehacer; **to take to** – reprender, regañar.

task force [tǽskfɔrs] *s.* agrupación de fuerzas militares para cierta misión.

tas·sel [tǽs‖] *s.* borla.

taste [test] *v.* gustar; probar; saborear, paladear; **to** – **of onion** saber a cebolla; **it** -**s sour** sabe agrio, tiene un sabor o gusto agrio; *s.* gusto; sabor; prueba; afición; **after**– dejo; **in good** – de buen gusto; **to take a** –**of** probar.

taste·less [téstlɪs] *adj.* insípido; desabrido; de mal gusto.

tast·y [téstɪ] *adj.* sabroso, gustoso; de buen gusto.

tat·ter [tǽtə-] *s.* harapo, *Carib.* hilacho.

tat·tered [tǽtə-d] *adj.* roto, harapiento, andrajoso.

tat·tle [tǽt‖] *v.* chismear, murmurar; *s.* habladuría,

murmuración, hablilla; –**tale** chismoso, soplón.

tat·too [tætú] *s.* tatuaje.

taught [tɔt] *pret. & p.p. de* **to teach.**

taunt [tɔnt] *v.* mofarse de, echar pullas; reprochar; *s.* mofa, pulla.

tav·ern [tǽvə-n] *s.* taberna; posada.

tax [tæks] *s.* impuesto, contribución; esfuerzo; *v.* imponer contribuciones a; tasar; abrumar; reprender, reprochar; cobrar (*un precio*); **to** – **one's patience** abusar de la paciencia.

tax·a·tion [tækséʃən] *s.* impuestos, contribuciones; imposición de contribuciones.

tax·i [tǽksɪ] *s.* taxímetro, taxi, automóvil de alquiler; *v.* ir en taxímetro; taxear (*un aeroplano*).

tax·i·cab [tǽksɪkæb] = **taxi.**

tax·i·der·my [tǽksɪdə-mɪ] *s.* taxidermia.

tax·pay·er [tǽkspeə-] *s.* contribuyente.

tea [ti] *s.* té.

teach [titʃ] *v.* enseñar; instruir.

teach·er [títʃə-] *s.* maestro, maestra.

teach·ing [títʃɪŋ] *s.* enseñanza; instrucción; doctrina.

tea·cup [tíkʌp] *s.* taza para té.

tea·ket·tle [tíkɛt‖] *s.* marmita, tetera, *Ríopl.* pava (*para el mate*).

team [tim] *s.* equipo (*de jugadores*); partido, grupo; tronco (*de caballos, mulas, etc.*); yunta (*de bueyes*): – **work** cooperación; *v.* uncir, enganchar; formar pareja; acarrear, transportar; **to** – **up** unirse; formar un equipo.

team·ster [tímstə-] *s.* carretero.

tea·pot [típɑt] *s.* tetera.

tear [tɪr] *s.* lágrima; – **gas** gas lacrimógeno o lacrimante; **to burst into** -**s** romper a llorar; deshacerse en lágrimas.

tear [tɛr] *v.* rasgar(se); desgarrar; romper; **to** – **along** ir a toda velocidad; andar aprisa, correr; **to** – **apart** desarmar, desmontar; separar, apartar; **to** – **away** arrancar; irse; **to** – **down** demoler, derribar (*un edificio*); desarmar, desmontar (*una máquina*); **to** – **off in a hurry** salir corriendo, salir a la carrera; **to** – **one's hair** mesarse los cabellos; *s.* desgarradura, rasgadura; rasgón, rotura; prisa; **wear and** – desgaste.

tear·ful [tʊrfəl] *adj.* lloroso.

tease [tiz] *v.* embromar; molestar; importunar.

tea·spoon [tíspun] *s.* cucharilla, cucharita.

tea·spoon·ful [tíspunfUl] *s.* cucharadita.

teat [tit]s. teta.

tech·ni·cal [tɛknɪk‖] *adj.* técnico.

tech·ni·cian [tɛkníʃən] *s.* técnico.

tech·nique [tɛkník] *s.* técnica.

tech·nol·o·gy [tɛknálədʒɪ] *s.* tecnología.

te·di·ous [tídɪəs] *adj.* tedioso, pesado, aburrido,

fastidioso.

te·di·ous·ness [tídɪəsnɪs] s. tedio.

teem [tim] v. **to – with** abundar en, estar lleno de.

teen-ag·er [tínedʒəˑ] s. joven de la edad de 13 a 19 años; *Col.* cocacolo.

teens [tinz] s. pl. edad de trece a diecinueve años; números de trece a diecinueve; **to be in one's –** tener de trece a diecinueve años.

teeth [tiθ] s. pl. de **tooth; he escaped by the skin of his –** por poco no se escapa, se escapó por milagro.

tel·e·cast [télɛkæst] s. teledifusión.

tel·e·gram [télɛgræm] s. telegrama.

tel·e·graph [télɛgræf] s. telégrafo; v. telegrafiar.

tel·e·graph·ic [tɛlɛgræfɪk] adj. telegráfico.

te·leg·ra·phy [təlégrəfɪ] s. telegrafía.

tel·ep·a·thy [təlépəθɪ] s. telepatía.

tel·e·phone [télɛfon] s. teléfono; **– booth** casilla de teléfono; **– operator** telefonista; **– receiver** receptor telefónico; v. telefonear, llamar por teléfono.

tel·e·scope [télɛstop] s. telescopio; v. enchufar(se), encajar(se) un objeto en otro.

tel·e·vi·sion [télɛvɪʒən] s. televisión.

tell [tɛl] v. (*recount*) decir; contar; expresar; explicar; (*identify*) adivinar; **to – on someone** delatar a alguien, contar chismes de alguien; **to – someone off** decirle a alguien cuatro verdades; **his age is beginning to –** ya comienza a notársele la edad.

tell·er [télɚ] s. narrador, relator; pagador o recibidor (*de un banco*); escrutador de votos.

tel·lu·ri·um [tɛlúrɪəm] s. telurio.

te·mer·i·ty [təmérətɪ] s. temeridad.

tem·per [témpɚ] v. templar; s. temple (*de un metal*); genio, temple, humor; mal genio; **to keep one's –** contenerse, dominarse; **to lose one's –** perder la calma, encolerizarse.

tem·per·a·ment [témprəmənt] s. temperamento; disposición; temple.

tem·per·ance [témprəns] s. templanza, sobriedad.

tem·per·ate [témprɪt] adj templado, moderado, sobrio.

tem·per·a·ture [témprətʃɚ] s. temperatura; **to have a –** tener calentura o fiebre.

tem·pest [témpɪst] s. tempestad.

tem·pes·tu·ous [tɛmpéstʃuəs] adj. tempestuoso, borrascoso.

tem·ple [témpl] s. templo; sien.

tem·po·ral [témpərəl] adj. temporal.

tem·po·rar·i·ly [témpərɛrəlɪ] adv. temporalmente.

tem·po·rar·y [témpərɛrɪ] adj. temporal, transitorio, provisorio; interino.

tempt [tɛmpt] v. tentar; incitar; provocar; atraer.

temp·ta·tion [tɛmptéʃən] s. tentación.

tempt·er [témptɚ] s. tentador.

tempt·ing [témptɪŋ] adj. tentador, atractivo.

ten·a·ble [ténəbl] adj. defendible.

te·na·cious [tɪnéʃəs] adj. tenaz, aferrado.

te·nac·i·ty [tɪnæsətɪ] s. tenacidad; aferramiento; tesón.

ten·ant [ténənt] s. inquilino, arrendatario.

tend [tɛnd] v. cuidar, vigilar, guardar; atender; tender, inclinarse.

ten·den·cy [téndənsɪ] s. tendencia; propensión.

ten·der [téndɚ] adj. tierno; delicado; sensible; **ten·der-hearted** de corazón tierno; s. oferta, ofrecimiento; ténder (*de un tren*); lancha (*de auxilio*), cuidador, vigilante; **legal –** moneda corriente; v. ofrecer.

ten·der·loin [téndɚloɪn] s. filete.

ten·der·ness [téndɚnɪs] s. ternura, terneza; delicadeza.

ten·don [téndən] s. tendón.

ten·dril [téndrɪl] s. zarcillo (*tallito de una planta trepadora*).

ten·e·ment [ténəmənt] s. casa de vecindad.

ten·nis [ténɪs] s. tenis; **– court** cancha de tenis.

ten·or [ténɚ] s. tenor; significado; **– voice** voz de tenor.

tense [tɛns] adj. tenso; tirante; s. tiempo (*del verbo*).

ten·sion [ténʃən] s. tensión; tirantez.

tent [tɛnt] s. tienda de campaña; pabellón; v. acampar.

ten·ta·cle [tétəkl] s. tentáculo.

ten·ta·tive [téntətɪv] adj. tentativo.

ten·u·ous [ténjuəs] adj. tenue.

ten·ure [ténjʊr] s. tenencia.

tep·id [tépɪd] adj. tibio.

term [tɝm] s. término; período; plazo; sesión; **-s** términos, expresiones, palabras; condiciones; **to be on good -s** estar en buenas relaciones; **not to be on speaking -s** no hablarse, no dirigirse la palabra; **to come to -s** ajustarse, ponerse de acuerdo; v. nombrar, llamar, denominar.

ter·mi·na·ble [tɝmɪnəbl] adj. terminable.

ter·mi·nal [tɝmɪnl] adj. terminal, final, último; s. término, fin; estación terminal; **electric -** toma de corriente; borne (*de aparato eléctrico*).

ter·mi·nate [tɝmənet] v. terminar, acabar.

ter·mi·na·tion [tɝmənéʃən] s. terminación, fin; desinencia (*gramatical*).

ter·mite [tɝmaɪt] s. termita.

ter·race [tɛrɪs] s. terraplén; terraza, terrado; v. terraplenar.

ter·res·tri·al [təréstrɪəl] adj. terrestre, terreno, terrenal.

ter·ri·ble [tɛrəb] adj. terrible; **terribly** adv. terriblemente.

ter·ri·er [tɛ́rɪɚ] *s.* perro de busca.

ter·ri·fic [tɚrɪ́fɪk] *adj.* terrífico.

ter·ri·fy [tɛ́rəfaɪ] *v.* aterrar, aterrorizar.

ter·ri·to·ry [tɛ́rətorɪ] *s.* territorio.

ter·ror [tɛ́rɚ] *s.* terror, espanto.

test [tɛst] *s.* prueba, ensayo, experimento; comprobación; examen; **– tube** probeta, tubo de ensayo; **to undergo a** – sufrir una prueba; *v.* probar, ensayar, comprobar, experimentar; poner a prueba; examinar.

tes·ta·ment [tɛ́stəmənt] *s.* testamento.

tes·ti·fy [tɛ́stəfaɪ] *v.* atestiguar, atestar.

tes·ti·mo·ny [tɛ́stəmonɪ] *s.* testimonio.

tet·a·nus [tɛ́tənəs] *s.* tétanos.

text [tɛkst] *s.* texto.

text·book [tɛ́kstbUk] *s.* texto, libro de texto.

tex·tile [tɛ́kst l] *adj.* textil; de tejidos; **– mill** fábrica de tejidos; *s.* tejido, materia textil.

tex·ture [tɛ́kstʃɚ] *s.* textura, contextura; tejido.

than [ðæn] *conj.* que; **more – once** más de una vez; **more – he knows** más de lo que él sabe.

thank [θæŋk] *v.* dar gracias, agradecer; **– heaven!** ¡gracias a Dios!; **– you** gracias; **to have oneself to – for** tener la culpa de; ser responsable de; **-s** *s. pl.* gracias.

thank·ful [θǽŋkfəl] *adj.* agradecido; **-ly** *adv.* agradecidamente, con agradecimiento, con gratitud.

thank·ful·ness [θǽŋkfəlnɪs] *s.* gratitud, agradecimiento.

thank·less [θǽŋklɪs] *adj.* ingrato; **– task** tarea ingrata o infructuosa.

thanks·giv·ing [θæŋksgɪ́vɪŋ] *s.* acción de gracias; **– Day** día de acción de gracias.

that [ðæt] *adj.* ese, esa, aquel, aquella, **– one** ése, ésa, aquél, aquélla; *pron.* ése, ésa, eso, aquél, aquélla, aquello; *pron. rel.* que; **– is** es decir; **– of** el de, la de, lo de; **– which** el que, la que, lo que; *conj.* que; para que, a fin de que; **so** – para que; de modo que, a fin de que, de suerte que, de tal manera que; *adv.* tan; **– far** tan lejos; hasta allá, hasta allí; **– long** así de largo; de este tamaño; tanto tiempo.

thatch [θætʃ] *s.* paja (*para techar*); *v.* techar con paja; **-ed roof** techumbre o techo de paja.

thaw [θɔ] *v.* deshelar(se), derretir(se); volverse más tratable o amistoso; *s.* deshielo, derretimiento.

the [*delante de consonante* ðə; *delante de vocal* ðɪ] *art.* el, la; lo; los, las; *adv.* **– more . . . –less** cuanto más . . . tanto menos; mientras más . . . tanto menos.

the·a·ter [θíətɚ] *s.* teatro.

the·at·ri·cal [θɪǽtrɪk l] *adj.* teatral.

thee [ðì] *pron.* te.

theft [θɛft] *s.* hurto, robo.

their [ðɛr] *adj.* su (sus), de ellos, de ellas.

theirs [ðɛrz] *pron. pos.* suyo (suya, suyos, suyas), de ellos, de ellas; el suyo (la suya, los suyos, las suyas); el (la, los, las) de ellos; **a friend of** – un amigo suyo, un amigo de ellos.

them [ðɛm] *pron.* los, las; les; ellos, ellas (*con preposición*).

the·mat·ic [θɪmǽtɪk] *adj.* temático.

theme [θim] *s.* tema; ensayo; **– song** tema central.

them·selves [ðɛmsɛ́lvz] *pron.* ellos mismos, ellas mismas; se (*como reflexivo*); **to** – a sí mismos; *véase* **herself.**

then [ðɛn] *adv.* entonces; en aquel tiempo; en aquella ocasión; después, luego, en seguida; *conj.* pues, en tal caso; **now** – ahora bien; **now and** – de vez en cuando, de cuando en cuando; **now . . . –** ora . . . ora; ya . . . ya; **well** – conque, pues entonces; ahora bien.

thence [ðɛns] *adv.* desde allí, de allí; desde entonces, desde aquel tiempo; por eso, por esa razón; **–forth** de allí en adelante, desde entonces.

the·o·log·i·cal [θiəládʒɪk l] *adj.* teológico; teologal.

the·ol·o·gy [θiólədʒɪ] *s.* teología.

the·o·ret·i·cal [θiərɛ́tɪk l] *adj.* teórico.

the·o·ry [θíərɪ] *s.* teoría.

ther·a·peu·tic [θɛrəpjútɪk] *adj.* terapéutico.

ther·a·py [θɛ́rəpɪ] *s.* terapia.

there [ðɛr] *adv.* allí, allá, ahí; **– is, – are** hay; **– followed an argument** siguió una disputa.

there·a·bouts [ðɛrəbátUs] *adv.* por allí, por ahí; aproximadamente.

there·af·ter [ðɛrǽftɚ] *adv.* después de eso, de allí en adelante.

there·by [ðɛrəbáɪ] *adv.* en relación con eso; así, de ese modo; por allí cerca.

there·fore [ðɛ́for] *adv.* por eso, por consiguiente, por lo tanto.

there·in [ðɛrɪ́n] *adv.* en eso, en ello; allí dentro.

there·of [ðɛrávʲ] *adv.* de eso, de ello.

there·on [ðɛrán] *adv.* encima; encima de (*o* sobre) él, ella, ello, etc.

there·up·on [ðɛrəpán] *adv.* luego, después, en eso, en esto; por consiguiente, por eso, por lo tanto; encima de (*o* sobre) él, ella, ello, etc.

there·with [ðɛwíθ] *adv.* con eso, con ello, con esto; luego, en seguida.

ther·mal [θɚ·m l] *adj.* termal.

ther·mom·e·ter [θɚ·mámətɚ] *s.* termómetro.

ther·mo·nu·cle·ar [θɚ·monúkljɚ] *adj.* termonuclear.

Ther·mos [θɝ́məs] (*marca de fábrica*): **– bottle** termos.

ther·mo·stat [θɝ́məstæt] *s.* termóstato.

these [ðiz] *adj.* estos, estas; *pron.* éstos, éstas.

the·sis [θísɪs] *s.* tesis.

they [ðe] *pron.* ellos, ellas.

thick [θɪk] *adj.* (*not thin*) espeso; grueso; (*dense*) denso; tupido; (*slow*) torpe, estúpido; **– voice** voz ronca; **one inch –** una pulgada de espesor; *adv. véase* **thickly; thickheaded** cabezudo, testarudo; estúpido; **thick-set** grueso, rechoncho; **thick-skinned** insensible; que no se avergüenza fácilmente; *s.* espesor; densidad, lo más denso; **the – of the crowd** lo más denso de la muchedumbre; **the – of the fight** lo más reñido del combate; **through – and thin** por toda suerte de penalidades.

thick·en [θíkən] *v.* espesar(se); engrosar; **the plot -s** se complica el enredo.

thick·et [θíkɪt] *s.* espesura, maleza, matorral, *Am.* manigua.

thick·ly [θíklɪ] *adv.* espesamente; densamente.

thick·ness [θíknɪs] *s.* espesor; espesura, grueso, grosor; densidad.

thief [θif] *s.* ladrón.

thieve [θiv] *v.* hurtar, robar.

thieves [θivz] *pl. de* **thief.**

thigh [θaɪ] *s.* muslo.

thim·ble [θímbḷ] *s.* dedal.

thin [θɪn] *adj.* (*slim*) delgado; flaco; (*sparse*) ralo; escaso; (*fine*) tenue, fino; transparente; (*weak*) débil; aguado; **– broth** caldo aguado; **– hair** pelo ralo; *v.* adelgazar(se); enflaquecer; aguar (*el caldo*); **to – out** ralear (*el pelo*); ralear o aclarar (*un bosque*).

thine [ðaɪn] *pron. pos.* tuyo (tuya, tuyos, tuyas); el tuyo (la tuya, los tuyos, las tuyas); *adj.* tu, tus.

thing [θɪŋ] *s.* cosa; **no such –** nada de eso; **that is the – to do** eso es lo que debe hacerse; eso es lo debido.

think [θɪŋk] *v.* (*cerebrate*) pensar; (*believe*) creer, juzgar; opinar; **to – it over** pensarlo; **to – of** pensar en; pensar de; **to – up an excuse** urdir una excusa; **to – well of** tener buena opinión de; **– nothing of it** no haga Vd. caso de ello, no le dé Vd. importancia; **what do you – of her?** ¿qué piensa Vd. de ella?; **to my way of-ing** a mi modo de ver.

think·er [θíŋkə·] *s.* pensador.

thin·ly [θínlɪ] *adv.* delgadamente; escasamente.

thin·ness [θínnɪs] *s.* delgadez; flacura; raleza (*del cabello*); enrarecimiento (*del aire*).

third [θɝd] *adj.* tercero; *s.* tercio, tercera parte.

thirst [θɝst] *s.* sed; anhelo, ansia; *v.* tener sed; **to – for** tener sed de; anhelar, ansiar.

thirst·y [θɝstɪ] *adj.* sediento; **to be –** tener sed.

this [ðɪs] *adj.* este, esta; *pron.* éste, ésta, esto.

this·tle [θísḷ] *s.* abrojo; cardo.

thith·er [θíðə·] *adv.* allá, hacia allá, para allá.

tho [ðo] = **though.**

thong [θɔŋ] *s.* correa, tira de cuero, *Am.* guasca.

thorn [θɔrn] *s.* espina, púa; espinoso; abrojo.

thorn·y [θɔ́rnɪ] *adj.* espinoso; arduo, difícil.

thor·ough [θɝ́o] *adj.* (*finished*) completo, entero, cabal, cumplido, acabado; (*careful*) esmerado.

thor·ough·bred [θɝ́obrɛd] *adj.* de casta pura, de raza pura; bien nacido; *s.* animal o persona de casta; caballo de casta.

thor·ough·fare [θɝ́ofɛr] *s.* vía pública, carretera, camino real; pasaje.

thor·ough·ly [θɝ́olɪ] *adv.* completamente, enteramente, cabalmente; a fondo.

those [ðoz] *adj.* esos, esas, aquellos, aquellas; *pron.* ésos, ésas, aquéllos, aquéllas; **– of** los de, las de; **– which** los que, las que; aquellos que; **– who** los que, las que, quienes.

thou [ðaU] *pron.* tú.

though [ðo] *conj.* aunque, si bien, bien qué; aun cuando; sin embargo; **as –** como si.

thought [θɔt] *s.* (*cogitation*) pensamiento; (*idea*) idea, intención; reflexión, meditación; (*concern*) consideración; cuidado; **to be lost in –** estar abstraído; **to give it no –** no pensar en ello, no darle importancia, no hacerle caso; *pret. & p.p. de* **think.**

thought·ful [θɔ́tfəl] *adj.* pensativo; considerado; atento, solícito, cuidadoso; **to be – of others** pensar en los demás, tener consideración o solicitud por los demás; **-ly** *adv.* con reflexión; consideradamente, con consideración; con solicitud.

thought·ful·ness [θ|tfəlnɪs] *s.* consideración, atención, cuidado, solicitud.

thought·less [θ|tlɪs] *adj.* inconsiderado; descuidado; irreflexivo, atolondrado; **-ly** *adv.* inconsideradamente, sin consideración; sin reflexión; sin pensar, descuidadamente, irreflexivamente, atolondradamente.

thought·less·ness [θ|tlɪsnɪs] *s.* irreflexión, inadvertencia, descuido; atolondramiento.

thrash [θræʃ] *v.* trillar, desgranar (*las mieses*); zurrar, azotar; **to – around** revolcarse, agitarse, menearse; **to – out a matter** ventilar un asunto.

thread [θrɛd] *s.* hilo; hebra, fibra; **screw –** rosca de tornillo; *v.* ensartar, enhebrar; **to – a screw** roscar un tornillo; **to – one's way through a crowd** colarse por entre la muchedumbre.

thread·bare [θrɛ́dbɛr] *adj.* raído, gastado.

threat [θrɛt] *s.* amenaza; amago.

threat·en [θrɛ́tɳ] *v.* amenazar; amagar.

threat·en·ing [θrɛ́tnɪŋ] *adj.* amenazante, amenazador.

thresh [θrɛʃ] *véase* **thrash.**

thres·hold [θrɛ́ʃold] *s.* umbral, entrada.

threw [θru] *pret. de* **to throw.**

thrice [θraɪs] *adv.* tres veces.

thrift [θrɪft] *s.* economía, frugalidad.

thrift·y [θríftɪ] *adj.* económico, frugal; próspero.

thrill [θrɪl] *v.* emocionar(se), conmover(se); estremecerse de emoción, sobreexcitarse; *s.* emoción viva, estremecimiento emotivo, sobreexcitación.

thrive [θraɪv] *v.* medrar, prosperar; florecer.

thriv·en [θrɪvən] *p.p. de* **to thrive.**

throat [θrot] *s.* garganta.

throb [θrob] *v.* latir, pulsar, palpitar; *s.* latido, palpitación.

throe [θro] *s.* agonía; congoja.

throne [θron] *s.* trono.

throng [θroŋ] *s.* muchedumbre, multitud, tropel, gentío; *v.* agolparse, apiñarse; atestar.

throt·tle [θrát l] *s.* válvula reguladora, obturador, regulador; **– lever** palanca del obturador o regulador; *v.* ahogar; estrangular; **to – down** disminuir o reducir la velocidad.

through [θru] *prep.* por; a través de; por medio de; por conducto de; por entre; *adv.* de un lado a otro; de parte a parte, a través; de cabo a cabo; desde el principio hasta el fin; completamente, enteramente; **loyal – and –** leal a toda prueba; **to be wet –** estar empapado; estar mojado hasta los tuétanos; **to carry a plan –** llevar a cabo un plan; *adj.* directo, continuo; **– ticket** billete (*Am.* boleto) directo; **– train** tren rápido, tren de servicio directo; **to be – with** haber acabado con; no querer ocuparse más de.

through·out [θruáUt] *prep. (all through)* por todo; por todas partes de; *(during)* desde el principio; hasta el fin de; **– the year** durante todo el año; *adv.* por todas partes; en todas partes; en todo, en todos respetos; desde el principio hasta el fin.

throve [θrov] *pret. de* **to thrive.**

throw [θro] *v.* tirar, arrojar, lanzar; echar; **to – away** tirar, arrojar; malgastar; **to – down** arrojar, echar por tierra, derribar; **to – in gear** engranar; **to – in the clutch** embragar; **to – off a burden** librarse o deshacerse de una carga; **to – aside** echar fuera; expeler; **to – out of gear** desengranar; **to – out of work** privar de trabajo, quitar el empleo a; **to – out the clutch** desembragar; **to – overboard** echar al agua; **to – up** vomitar; *s.* tiro, tirada.

thrown [θron] *p.p. de* **to throw.**

thrush [θrʌʃ] *s.* tordo, zorzal.

thrust [θrʌst] *v.* (*push into*) meter; hincar, clavar; encajar; *(shove)* empujar; **to – a task upon someone** imponer una tarea a una persona, obligar a alguien a desempeñar un quehacer; **to – aside** echar o empujar a un lado; rechazar; **to – in** (*o* **into**) meter en, encajar en, intercalar en; **to – out** sacar; echar fuera; **to – someone through with a sword** atravesar a alguien de parte a parte con la

espada; *pret. & p.p. de* **to thrust**; *s.* estocada, cuchillada, puñalada, lanzada; empuje, empujón o empellón; arremetida, acometida.

thud [θʌd] *s.* porrazo, golpazo, golpe sordo.

thug [θʌg] *s.* ladron, salteador.

thumb [θʌm] *s.* pulgar; **under the – of** bajo el poder o influencia de; *v.* hojear (*con el pulgar*).

thumb·tack [θ ʌ́ mtæk] *s.* chinche.

thump [θʌmp] *s.* golpazo, porrazo, trastazo; golpe sordo; *v.* golpear, golpetear, aporrear, dar un porrazo.

thun·der [θ ʌ́ ndɚ] *s.* trueno; tronido; estruendo; *v.* tronar.

thun·der·bolt [θ ʌ́ ndɚ·bolt] *s.* rayo.

thun·der·ing [θ ʌ́ ndərɪŋ] *adj.* atronador.

thun·der·ous [θ ʌ́ ndərəs] *adj.* atronador, estruendoso.

thun·der·storm [θ ʌ́ ndɚ·storm] *s.* tronada, tormenta o tempestad de truenos.

Thurs·day [θ ɝ́ zdɪ] *s.* jueves.

thus [θʌs] *adv.* así; **– far** hasta aquí, hasta ahora, hasta hoy.

thwart [θwort] *v.* frustrar; estorbar; impedir.

thy [ðaɪ] *adj.* tu, tus.

thyme [taɪm] *s.* tomillo.

thy·roid [θáɪroɪd] *s.* tiroides.

thy·self [ðaɪsélf] *pron.* tú mismo; a tí mismo; te *(como reflexivo)*; *véase* **herself.**

tick [tɪk] *s.* tic tac; funda *(de colchón o almohada)*; garrapata *(insecto parásito)*; *v.* hacer tic tac *(como un reloj)*; latir *(el corazón)*; **to – off** marcar.

tick·et [tíkɪt] *s.* billete, *Am.* boleto; lista de candidatos *(de un partido)*; balota *(para votar)*; **– office** taquilla; despacho de boletos, *Am.* boletería.

tick·le [tík l] *v.* (*touch*) cosquillear, hacer cosquillas; *(feel)* sentir o tener cosquillas; *(please)* halagar, gustarle a uno; **to be -d to death** morirse de gusto, estar muy contento; *s.* cosquilleo, cosquillas.

tick·lish [tíklɪʃ] *adj.* cosquilloso; delicado, arriesgado, difícil.

tid·bit [tídbɪt] *s.* bocado, bocadito, golosina.

tide [taɪd] *s.* marea; corriente; **Christmas –** navidades, temporada de navidad; *v.* **to – someone over a difficulty** ayudar a alguien durante una crisis o dificultad.

tide·wa·ter [táɪdwɔtɚ] *adj.* costanero.

tid·ings [táɪdɪŋz] *s. pl.* noticias, nuevas.

ti·dy [táɪdɪ] *adj.* aseado, limpio, ordenado; **a – sum** una suma considerable; *v.* asear, arreglar, poner en orden; **to – oneself up** asearse.

tie [taɪ] *v.* (*fasten*) atar, liar, ligar; *Am.* amarrar; *(unite)* enlazar, vincular; *(equal)* empatar *(en juegos, etc.)*; **to – tight** amarrar bien, apretar fuerte; **to – up the traffic** obstruir el tráfico; *s.* lazo, ligadura, atadura;

enlace, vínculo; corbata; empate (*en carreras, juegos, etc.*); (*sealed*) travesaño, *Andes, C.A., Méx.* durmiente; *Ríopl., Ch.* travesaño.

tier [ɪr] *s.* fila, hilera, ringlera.

ti•ger [táɪgɚ] *s.* tigre; — **cat** gato montés.

tight [taɪt] *adj.* (*squeezed*) apretado, ajustado, estrecho; (*sealed*) hermético; (*firm*) firme, tieso; (*stingy*) tacaño, mezquino; (*drunk*) borracho; **to be in a — spot** estar en un aprieto; **to close** — apretar, cerrar herméticamente; **to hold on** — agarrarse bien; **it fits** — está muy estrecho o ajustado.

tight•en [táɪtŋ] *v.* apretar; estrechar; estirar, poner tirante.

tight•ness [táɪtnɪs] *s.* estrechez; tirantez, tensión; mezquindad, tacañería.

tight•wad [táɪtwɑd] *s.* tacaño; cicatero.

ti•gress [táɪgrɪs] *s.* tigre hembra.

tile [taɪl] *s.* teja; baldosa, azulejo; — **roof** tejado; *v.* tejar, cubrir con tejas; cubrir con azulejos, embaldosar.

till [tɪl] *prep.* hasta; *conj.* hasta que; *v.* cultivar, labrar, arar; *s.* gaveta o cajón para el dinero.

till•age [tɪ́lədʒ] *s.* labranza, cultivo, labor.

tilt [tɪlt] *s.* ladeo, inclinación; declive; altercación disputa; **at full** — a toda velocidad; *v.* ladear(se), inclinar(se).

tim•ber [tɪ́mbɚ] *s.* madera de construcción; maderaje; madero; viga.

time [taɪm] *s.* tiempo; hora; vez; plazo; **at -s** a veces; **at one and the same** — a la vez; **at this** — ahora, al presente; **behind** — atrasado, retrasado; **from — to** — de vez en cuando; **in** — a tiempo; andando el tiempo; **on** — puntual; con puntualidad; a tiempo; a la hora debida; **several -s** varias veces; **to beat** — marcar el compás; **to by on** — comprar a plazo; **to have a good** — divertirse, pasar un buen rato; **what — is it?** ¿qué hora es?; *v.* cronometrar, medir el tiempo de; regular, poner en punto (*el reloj, el motor*); escoger el momento oportuno para; — **zone** zona horaria; huso horario.

time•less [táɪmlɪs] *adj.* eterno, infinito.

time•ly [táɪmlɪ] *adj.* oportuno.

time•piece [táɪmpis] *s.* reloj; cronómetro.

time•table [táɪmtebl̩] *s.* itinerario, horario.

tim•id [tɪ́mɪd] *adj.* tímido.

ti•mid•i•ty [tɪmadétɪ] *s.* timidez.

tim•ing [táɪmɪŋ] *s.* medida del tiempo; cronometraje; (*pace*) selección del momento oportuno; sincronización.

tim•or•ous [tɪ́mərəs] *adj.* timorato, tímido, miedoso.

tin [tɪn] *s.* estaño; hojalata, lata; cosa de hojalata; — **can** lata; — **foil** hoja de estaño; *v.* estañar, cubrir con estaño; enlatar.

tinc•ture [tɪ́ŋktʃɚ] *s.* tintua; tinte; — **of iodine** tintura

de yodo; *v.* tinturar, teñir.

tin•der [tɪ́ndɚ] *s.* yesca.

tinge [tɪndʒ] *v.* teñir; matizar; *s.* tinte, matiz; dejo, saborcillo.

tin•gle [tɪŋgl̩] *v.* hormiguear, sentir hormigueo; **to — with excitement** estremecerse de entusiasmo; *s.* hormigueo, picazón, comezón.

tin•ker [tɪ́ŋkɚ] *v.* ocuparse vanamente.

tin•kle [tɪ́ŋkl̩] *v.* tintinear; hacer retintín; *s.* tintineo; retintín.

tin•sel [tɪ́ns l̩] *s.* oropel; *adj.* de oropel.

tint [tɪnt] *s.* tinte, matiz; *v.* teñir, matizar.

ti•ny [táɪnɪ] *adj.* diminuto, menudo, chiquitico, chiquitín.

tip [tɪp] *s.* (*point*) punta, extremo, extremidad; (*money*) propina; (*hint*) noticia o aviso secreto; *v.* ladear(se), inclinar(se); dar propina (a); **to — a persona off** dar aviso secreto a; **to — one's hat** tocarse el sombrero; **to — over** volcar(se), voltear(se).

tip•sy [tɪ́psɪ] *adj.* alumbrado, algo borracho, ladeado.

tip•toe [tɪ́pto] *s.* punta del pie; **on** — de puntillas; *v.* andar de puntillas.

ti•rade [táɪred] *s.* invectiva.

tire [taɪr] *s.* llanta, neumático, goma; **flat** — llanta o goma reventada; *v.* cansar(se), fatigar(se).

tired [taɪrd] *adj.* cansado, fatigado; — **out** extenuado de fatiga, rendido.

tire•less [táɪrlɪs] *adj.* incansable, infatigable.

tire•some [táɪrsəm] *adj.* cansado, aburrido, pesado.

tis•sue [tɪ́ʃU] *s.* tejido; — **paper** papel de seda.

ti•tan•ic [taɪntǽnɪk] *adj.* titánico.

ti•tan•ium [taɪténɪəm] *s.* titanio.

tithe [taɪð] *s.* diezmo.

ti•tle [táɪtl̩] *s.* título; — **page** portada.

to [tu] *prep.* a; hasta; hacia; para; — **try** — tratar de; esforzarse por; **a quarter — five** las cinco menos cuarto; **bills — be paid** cuentas por pagar; **frightened — death** muerto de gusto; **from house — house** de casa en casa; **he has — go** tiene que ir; **near** — cerca de; **not — my knowledge** no que yo sepa; *adv.* — **and fro** de acá para allá; **to come** — volver en sí.

toad [tod] *s.* sapo o escuerzo.

toast [tost] *v.* tostar(se); brindar por, beber a la salud de; *s.* tostada; brindis.

toast•er [tóstɚ] *s.* tostador.

to•bac•co [təbǽko] *s.* tabaco.

to•day [tədé] *adv.* hoy; hoy día.

toe [to] *s.* dedo del pie; punta (*de la media, del zapato, etc.*); *v.* **to — in** andar con la punta de los pies para dentro.

toe•nail [tónel] *s.* uña del dedo del pie.

to•geth•er [təgéðɚ] *adv.* juntamente; a un mismo

tiempo, a la vez; juntos; – **with** junto con; **all** – juntos; en junto; **to call** – convocar, juntar; **to come** – juntarse, unirse; ponerse de acuerdo; **to walk** – andar juntos.

toil [tɔɪl] v. afanarse, trafagar, atarearse; s. esfuerzo, trabajo, faena, fatiga.

toi•let [tɔ́ɪlɪt] s. retrete, excusado, común, *Am.* inodoro; – **articles** artículo de tocador; – **case** neceser; – **paper** papel de excusado, papel higiénico.

to•ken [tókən] s. señal, símbolo; prenda; recuerdo; prueba, muestra; ficha (*de metal*); – **payment** pago nominal.

told [told] *pret. & p.p. de* **to tell.**

tol•er•ance [tólərəns] s. tolerancia.

tol•er•ant [tólərənt] *adj.* tolerante.

tol•er•ate [tóləret] v. tolerar.

tol•er•a•tion [toləréʃən] s. tolerancia.

toll [tol] s. doble, tañido (*de las campanas*); peaje; portazgo; – **bridge** puente de peaje; – **gate** barrera de peaje; – **call** llamada por cobrar; **to pay** – pagar peaje o portazgo; v. tañer, doblar (*las campanas*).

to•ma•to [təméto] s. tomate, *Méx.* jitomate.

tomb [tum] s. tumba.

tomb•stone [túmston] s. lápida sepulcral.

tom•cat [tómkæt] s. gato.

tome [tom] s. tomo.

to•mor•row [təmɔ́ro] *adv.* mañana; – **morning** mañana por la mañana; – **noon** mañana al mediodía; **day after** – pasado mañana.

ton [tʌn] s. tonelada.

tone [ton] s. (*pitch*) tono; timbre; (*sound*) sonido; v. dar tono a, modificar el tono de; **to – down** bajar de tono; suavizar; **to – down one's voice** moderar la voz; **to – in well with** armonizar con, entonar bien con; **to – up** subir de tono; tonificar, vigorizar.

tongs [tɔŋz] s. *pl.* tenazas.

tongue [tʌŋ] s. lengua; idioma; **to be tongue-tied** tener trabada la lengua.

ton•ic [tónɪk] s. & *adj.* tónico.

to•night [tənáɪt] *adv.* esta noche, a la noche.

ton•nage [tʌ́nɪdʒ] s. tonelaje.

ton•sil [tónsl] s. amígdala.

ton•sil•li•tis [tonsláɪtɪs] s. amigdalitis.

too [tu] *adv.* también; demasiado; – **many** demasiados; – **much** demasiado; **it is** – **bad!** ¡es una lástima!

took [tUk] *pret. de* **to take.**

tool [tul] s. instrumento; herramienta; – **box** caja de herramientas.

toot [tut] v. tocar o sonar la bocina; pitar; tocar (*un cuerno, trompa o trompeta*); **to** – **one's own horn** alabarse, cantar sus propias alabanzas; s. toque o sonido (*de corneta, trompeta, etc.*); silbido, pitido; pitazo (*de locomotora*).

tooth [tuθ] s. diente; muela; – **mark** dentellada; **to**

fight – and nail luchar a brazo partido; **to have a sweet** – ser amigo de golosinas.

tooth•ache [túθek] s. dolor de muelas.

tooth•brush [túθbrʌʃ] s. cepillo de dientes.

toothed [tuθt] *adj.* dentado.

tooth•less [túθlɪs] *adj.* desdentado.

tooth•paste [túθpest] s. pasta para los dientes, pasta detífrica.

tooth•pick [túθpɪk] s. mondadientes, palillo de dientes.

top [tɑp] s. (*peak*) cumbre, cima; cúspide; tope; pináculo; remate, cabeza; (*surface*) superficie; copa (*de árbol*); (*cover*) tapa, cubierta; (*toy*) trompo; **at the** – **of his class** a la cabeza de su clase; **at the** – **of one's voice** a voz en cuello; **filled up to the** – lleno hasta el tope; **from** – **to bottom** de arriba abajo; **from** – **to toe** de pies a cabeza; **on** – **of** encima de, sobre; *adj.* superior; más alto; –**coat** abrigo, sobretodo; **at** – **speed** a velocidad máxima; v. coronar; exceder; sobresalir, sobrepujar; rematar; **to** – **off** rematar; terminar.

to•paz [tópæz] s. topacio.

top•er [tópæ] s. bebedor, borrachín.

top-heav•y [tɑphévɪ] *adj.* más pesado arriba que abajo.

top•ic [tópɪk] s. tema, asunto, materia, tópico.

top•most [tópmost] *adj.* más alto; superior.

to•pog•ra•phy [təpógrəfɪ] s. topografía.

top•ple [tópḷ] v. echar abajo, derribar; volcar; **to** – **over** venirse abajo; volcarse.

top•sy-tur•vy [tápsɪtɝ́vɪ] *adj. & adv.* patas arriba; en confusión; trastornado; enrevesado, al revés.

torch [tɔrtʃ] s. antorcha; **blow** – soplete.

tore [tor] *pret. de* **to tear.**

tor•ment [tɔ́rmɛnt] s. tormento; [torment] v. atormentar; afligir.

torn [torn] *p.p. de* **to tear** roto, rompido, rasgado.

tor•na•do [tornédo] s. tornado.

tor•pe•do [torpído] s. torpedo; – **boat** torpedero; v. torpedear.

torque [tɔrk] s. fuerza rotatoria.

tor•rent [tɔ́rənt] s. torrente.

tor•rid [tɔ́rɪd] *adj.* tórrido.

tor•sion [tɔ́rʃən] s. torsión.

tor•toise [tɔ́rtəs] s. tortuga.

tor•tu•ous [tɔ́rtʃUəs] *adj.* tortuoso.

tor•ture [tɔ́rtʃɚ] s. tortura, tormento; v. torturar, atormentar.

toss [tɔs] v. tirar, echar, arrojar, lanzar; menear(se); cabecear (*un buque*); **to** – **aside** echar a un lado; desechar; **to** – **up** echar para arriba; aventar; s. tiro, tirada, meneo, sacudida.

tot [tɑt] s. chiquitín, chiquitina, chiquitico, chiquitica, niñito, niñita, nene, nena.

to•tal [tót⎵] *adj.* & *s.* total.

to•tal•i•tar•ian [totælətέrɪən] *adj.* totalitario.

tot•ter [tóta] *v.* tambalear(se), bambolear(se); estar para desplomarse.

touch [tʌtʃ] *v.* tocar; palpar, tentar; conmover, enternecer, compararse con, igualar; **to – at a port** hacer escala en un puerto; **to – off an explosive** prender la mecha de un explosivo; **to – up** retocar; *s.* toque, tacto, sentido del tacto; tiento, **–stone** piedra de toque; **a – of fever** algo de calentura; **to keep in – with** mantener(se) en comunicación con.

touch-and-go [t ʌtʃénegó] *adj.* arriesgado.

touch•ing [t ʌtʃɪŋ] *adj.* conmovedor, enternecedor.

touch•y [t ʌtʃɪ] *adj.* quisquilloso, susceptible, sensible, sensitivo.

tough [tʌf] *adj.* correoso; fuerte; firme; duro; arduo, difícil; terco; empedernido, malvado.

tough•en [t ʌfŋ] *v.* curtir(se); endurecer(se), enpedernir(se); hacer(se) correoso.

tough•ness [t ʌfnɪs] *s.* dureza; correosidad; flexibilidad; tenacidad; resistencia; dificultad.

tou•pee [tupé] *s.* peluca.

tour [tUr] *s.* viaje, excursión; vuelta; jira; *v.* viajar por; recorrer; hacer una jira; hacer un viaje de turismo.

tour•ism [tÚrɪzəm] *s.* turismo.

tour•ist [tÚrɪst] *s.* turista.

tour•na•ment [tɝ́nəmənt] *s.* torneo; certamen, concurso.

tow [to] *v.* remolcar; *s.* remolque; **–boat** remolcador; **–rope** cuerda de remolque; **to take in –** remolcar, llevar a remolque.

to•ward [tord] *prep.* hacia; rumbo a; alrededor de; para, para con; **– four o'clock** a eso de las cuatro.

to•wards [tordz] = **toward.**

tow•el [taUl] *s.* toalla.

tow•er [táUɚ] *s.* torre; torreón; **bell** campanario; *v.* sobresalir, sobrepujar; destacarse, descollar; elevarse.

tow•er•ing [táUrɪŋ] *adj.* encumbrado; elevado, muy alto; sobresaliente.

town [taUn] *s.* (*center*) población, ciudad, pueblo, aldea; (*administration*) municipio; **– hall** ayuntamiento.

town•ship [táUnʃ Ip] *s.* unidad primaria de gobierno local; sección de seis millas cuadradas (*en terrenos públicos*).

tox•in [tóksɪn] *s.* toxina.

toy [tɔɪ] *s.* juguete; *adj.* de juego, de juguete; pequeñito, *v.* jugar, juguetear.

trace [tres] *s.* señal, indicio, vestigio; huella, rastro, tirante (*de una guarnición*); *v.* trazar; calcar; rastrear, seguir la huella de; rebuscar, investigar; **to – the source of** remontarse al origen de, buscar el origen de.

tra•che•a [trékɪə] *s.* tráquea.

tra•cho•ma [trəkomə] *s.* tracoma.

track [træk] *s.* pista, huella, rastro; pisada; vereda, senda; vía; **– sports** deportes de pista; **race –** pista; **railroad –** rieles, vía del tren, vía férrea o ferrovía; **to be off the –** estar extraviado, estar descarrilado; **to be on the – of** rastrear, ir siguiendo la pista de; **to keep – of** llevar la cuenta de; no perder de vista; *v.* rastrear, seguir la huella de; **to – down** coger, atrapar; descubrir; **to – in mud** traer lodo en los pies, entrar con los pies enlodados.

tract [trækt] *s.* área; terreno; folleto; **digestive –** canal digestivo.

trac•tion [trǽkʃən] *s.* tracción.

trac•tor [trǽktɚ] *s.* tractor.

trade [tred] *s.* (*business*) comercio; trato, negocio; (*swap*) trueque, cambio; (*occupation*) oficio; (*customers*) clientela, parroquianos; **– school** escuela de artes y oficios; **– union** gremio obrero o de obreros; *v.* comerciar, negociar, traficar, tratar; trocar, cambiar.

trade•mark [trédmɚk] *s.* marca de fábrica.

trad•er [tréda] *s.* mercader, comerciante, negociante, traficante.

trades•man [trédzmən] *s.* mercader, comerciante, trafidcante; tendero.

tra•di•tion [trədíʃən] *s.* tradición.

tra•di•tion•al [tredíʃən⎵] *adj.* tradicional.

traf•fic [trǽfɪk] *s.* tráfico; tráfago; tránsito; circulación; *v.* traficar, comerciar, negociar.

trag•e•dy [trǽdʒədɪ] *s.* tragedia.

trag•ic [trǽdʒɪk] *adj.* trágico.

trail [trel] *s.* (*trace*) pista, rastro, huella; (*path*) senda, sendero, trocha, vereda; cola (*de vestido*); *v.* arrastrar(se); rastrear, seguir la pista de; andar detrás de; **to – behind** ir rezagado, rezagarse.

train [tren] *s.* (*railroad*) tren; (*dress*) cola (*de vestido*); (*retinue*) séquito, comitiva; *v.* amaestrar(se), ejercitar(se); adiestrar(se) o adestrar(se), *Am.* entrenar(se); educar; disciplinar (*tropas*); apuntar (*un cañón*).

train•er [tréna] *s.* amaestrador; *Méx., C.A., Andes, Ven., Col., Carib.* entrenador.

train•ing [trénɪŋ] *s.* adiestramiento, disciplina, *Méx., C.A., Andes, Ven., Col., Carib.,* entrenamiento; educación; **– camp** campo de entrenamiento o práctica.

trait [tret] *s.* rasgo, característica; cualidad.

trai•tor [tretɚ] *s.* traidor.

tram [træm] *s.* vagoneta (*de una mina de carbón*).

tramp [træmp] *v.* pisotear; andar a pie; vagabundear; *s.* vago, vagabundo; caminata, marcha; pisadas.

tram•ple [trǽmp] v. pisar, hollar, pisotear; **to – on** pisotear, hollar; s. pisadas.

trance [træns] s. rapto, arrobamiento, enajenamiento, éxtasis; **to be in a** – estar arrobado, estar enajenado; estar distraído o ensimismado.

tran•quil [trǽnkwɪl] adj. tranquilo.

tran•quil•iz•er [trǽŋkwəlaɪzɚ-] s. tranquilizador.

tran•quil•li•ty [trǽnkwɪlɪɪ] s. tranquilidad.

trans•act [trænsǽkt] v. tramitar, despachar, llevar a cabo.

trans•ac•tion [trænsǽkʃən] s. transacción, trato, negocio; trámite; negociación; **-s** actas; memorias.

trans•at•lan•tic [trænsətlǽntɪk] adj. transatlántico.

tran•scend [trænsénd] v. trascender, ir más allá de.

trans•con•ti•nen•tal [trænskontənént] adj. transcontinental.

tran•scribe [trænskráɪb] v. transcribir.

tran•script [trǽnskrɪpt] s. transcripción, copia.

trans•fer [trǽnsfɝ] s. transferencia; traslado; traspaso; trasbordo; **– of ownership** cesión o traspado de propiedad; **streetcar** – transferencia, contraseña, cupón de trasbordo; [trænsfɝ̌] v. transferir; trasboradar (un tren a otro), cambiar (de tren, de tranvía); traspasar (propiedad), trasladar.

trans•fig•ure [trænsfɪ́gjɚ] v. transfigurar.

trans•form [trænsfɔ́rm] v. transformar(se).

trans•form•a•tion [trænsfə-méʃən] s. transformación.

trans•gress [trænsgrés] v. transgredir, violar, quebrantar (una ley); pecar; **to – the bounds of** traspasar los límites de.

trans•gres•sion [trænsgréʃən] s. transgresión; violación de una ley; pecado.

trans•gres•sor [trænsgrésɚ] s. transgresor.

tran•sient [trǽnʃənt] s. transeúnte; adj. transeúnte; transitorio, pasajero.

tran•sis•tor [trænzÍstɚ] s. transistor.

tran•sit [trǽnsɪt] s. tránsito; **in** – en tránsito, de paso.

tran•si•tion [trænzÍʃən] s. transición; tránsito, paso.

tran•si•tive [trǽnsətɪv] adj. transitivo.

tran•si•to•ry [trǽnsətɔrɪ] adj. transitorio, pasajero.

trans•late [trænslét] v. traducir, verter; trasladar.

trans•la•tion [trænsléʃən] s. traducción, versión; translación (de un lugar a otro).

trans•la•tor [trænslétɚ] s. traductor.

trans•lu•cent [trænslús ŋt] adj. translúcido; **to be –** traslucirse.

trans•mis•sion [trænsmÍʃən] s. transmisión; caja de velocidades.

trans•mit [trænsmÍt] v. transmitir; emitir.

trans•mit•ter [trænsmÍtə] s. transmisor; emisor.

tran•som [trǽnsəm] s. montante.

trans•par•ent [trænspérənt] adj. transparente.

trans•plant [trænsplǽnt] v. trasplantar.

trans•port [trǽnsport] s. (moving) transporte; acarreo; (rapture) éxtasis; **– plane** aeroplano de transporte; [trænspórt] v. transportar; acarrear; **to be -ed with joy** estar enajenado de placer.

trans•por•ta•tion [trænspə-téʃən] s. transportación, transporte, boleto, pasaje.

trans•pose [trænspóz] v. transponer.

trans•verse [trænsvɝ́s] adj. transverso, transversal, puesto de través.

trap [træp] s. trampa, lazo, red; **– door** trampa; **mouse** – ratonera; v. entrampar, coger con trampa; atrapar.

tra•peze [trəpÍz] s. trapecio.

tra•pezo•id [trǽpəzɔɪd] s. trapezoide; trapecio.

trap•pings [trǽpɪŋz] s. pl. arreos, jaeces, guarniciones.

trash [træʃ] s. basura; hojarasca; cachivaches; gentuza, plebe.

trav•el [trǽv] v. viajar; viajar por; recorrer; s. viajar; tráfico.

trav•el•er [trǽv ɚ] s. viajero; **–'s check** cheque de viajero.

trav•el•ing [trǽv ɪŋ] adj. de viaje, para viaje; **–expenses** gastos de viaje; **– salesman** agente viajero, viajante de comercio.

trav•e•logue [trǽvəlɔg] s. conferencia sobre viajes.

tra•verse [trǽvɚs] v. atravesar, cruzar; recorrer; s. travesaño.

trav•es•ty [trǽvɪstɪ] s. parodia; v. parodiar, falsear.

tray [tre] s. bandeja; batea.

treach•er•ous [trétʃərəs] adj. traicionero, traidor, alevoso.

treach•er•y [trétʃərɪ] s. traición, perfidia, alevosía.

tread [trɛd] v. (tramble) pisar, hollar; pisotear; (walk) andar a pie, caminar; s. paso; pisada, huella; Am. pise (de una rueda); **tire** – rodadura del neumático, Am. banda rodante.

tread•mill [trédmɪl] s. noria; rueda de andar.

trea•son [trÍz ŋ] s. traición.

trea•son•a•ble [trÍznəb] adj. traidor, traicionero.

treas•ure [trέʒə] s. tesoro; v. atesorar.

treas•ur•er [trέʒərɚ] s. tesorero.

treas•ur•y [trέʒərɪ] s. tesorería; tesoro, erario; **Secretary of the Treasury** ministro de hacienda.

treat [trit] v. tratar; curar; convidar, invitar; s. obsequio; agasajo, convite; placer, gusto.

trea•tise [trÍtɪs] s. tratado.

treat•ment [trÍtmənt] s. trato; **medical –** tratamiento médico.

trea•ty [trítɪ] s. tratado, pacto, convenio.

treb•le [trébl] adj. triple; **– voice** voz atiplada; s. tiple; v. triplicar.

tree [tri] s. árbol; **apple-** manzano; **family –** árbol genealógico; **shoe –** horma de zapato; **to be up a –** estar subido a un árbol; estar en un gran aprieto; estar perplejo.

tree•less [trílɪs] adj. pelado, sin árboles, despoblado de árboles.

tree•top [trítɑp] s. copa de árbol.

trel•lis [trélɪs] s. emparrado, enrejado.

trem•ble [trémbl] v. temblar; estremecerse; s. temblor; estremecimiento.

tre•men•dous [trɪméndəs] adj. tremendo.

trem•or [trémə-] s. temblor.

trem•u•lous [trémjələs] adj. trémulo; tembloroso.

trench [trɛntʃ] s. trinchera; zanja, foso.

trend [trɛnd] s. tendencia; rumbo, dirección.

tres•pass [tréspəs] v. invadir, traspasar; violar, infringir; pecar; **to – on property** meterse sin derecho en la propiedad ajena; **no -ing** prohibida la entrada; s. transgresión; pecado.

tress [trɛs] s. trenza; bucle.

tres•tle [trɛsl] s. caballete; puente de caballetes.

tri•al [tráɪəl] s. ensayo, prueba; tentativa; aflicción; juicio, proceso; **– flight** vuelo de prueba.

tri•an•gle [tráɪæŋg] s. triángulo.

tri•an•gu•lar [traɪæŋgjələ-] adj. triangular.

tribe [traɪb] s. tribu.

trib•u•la•tion [trɪbjəléʃən] s. tribulación.

tri•bu•nal [trɪbjún] s. tribunal, juzgado.

trib•u•tar•y [trɪbjətɛrɪ] adj. & s. tributario.

trib•ute [trɪbjut] s. tributo; homenaje.

trick [trɪk] s. treta; suerte; maña, ardid, trampa; travesura; baza (*en el juego de naipes*); **to be up to one's old -s** hacer de las suyas; v. embaucar, trampear, hacer trampa; burlar; **to – oneself up** componerse, emperifollarse.

trick•er•y [trɪkə-rɪ] s. engaños, malas mañas, astucia.

trick•le [trɪkl] v. gotear; escurrir; s. goteo.

trick•y [trɪkɪ] adj. tramposo, Am. mañero; intrincado, complicado.

tried [traɪd] p.p. de **to try** & adj. probado.

tri•fle [tráɪfl] s. fruslería, friolera, nadería, nonada; bagatela; v. chancear(se), bromear; jugar, juguetear.

trig•ger [trɪgə-] s. gatillo (*de pistola, rifle, etc.*).

trill [trɪl] v. trinar; **to – the r** pronunciar la erre doble; s. trino.

tril•o•gy [trɪlədʒɪ] s. trilogía.

trim [trɪm] v. guarnecer, adornar; recortar; podar,

mondar; despabilar (*una vela*); ganarle a uno (*en el juego*); **to – up** adornar, componer; adj. aseado, limpio, pulcro, acicalado; s. adorno, franja, ribete, guarnición; **to be in – for** estar de buena salud para; estar bien entrenado para.

trim•ming [trɪmɪŋ] s. adorno, aderezo, guarnición; orla, ribete, franja; paliza, zurra; **-s** adornos; accesorios; recortes.

trin•i•ty [trɪnətɪ] s. trinidad.

trin•ket [trɪŋkɪt] s. chuchería, baratija.

trip [trɪp] s. viaje, travesía; recorrido, jira; tropezon; v. tropezar; dar un traspié; equivocarse; hacer tropezar, hacer caer; saltar, brincar, corretear.

triph•thong [trɪfθɔŋ] s. triptongo.

tri•ple [trɪpl] adj. & s. triple; v. triplicar.

trip•li•cate [trɪpləkət] adj. triplicado.

tri•pod [tráɪpɑd] s. trípode.

trite [traɪt] adj. trillado, trivial, vulgar.

tri•umph [tráɪəmf] s. triunfo; v. triunfar.

tri•um•phal [traɪ ʌ mf] adj. triunfal.

tri•um•phant [traɪ ʌ mfənt] adj. triunfante; **-ly** adv. triunfantemente, en triunfo.

triv•i•al [trɪvjəl] adj. trivial, insignificante.

trod [trɑd] pret. & p.p. de **to tread.**

trod•den [trɑd ŋ] p.p. de **to tread.**

trol•ley [trɑlɪ] s. trole; tranvía de trole.

trom•bone [trámbon] s. trombón.

troop [trup] s. tropa; cuadrilla.

tro•phy [trófɪ] s. trofeo.

trop•ic [trɑpɪk] s. trópico; **– of Cancer** trópico de Cáncer; **– of Capricorn** trópico de Capricornio; adj. tropical.

trop•i•cal [trɑpɪk] adj. tropical.

trot [trɑt] v. trotar; hacer trotar; s. trote.

trou•ba•dour [trúbədɔr] s. trovador.

trou•ble [tr ʌ bl] v. perturbar, turbar; molestar, incomodar; afligir; preocupar(se); **don't – to come** no se moleste Vd. en venir; s. pena, aflicción; inquietud, perturbación; dificultad; molestia; panne, avería, accidente (*a un mecanismo*); **heart –** enfermedad del corazón; **to be in –** estar en un aprieto o apuro; **it is not worth the –** no vale la pena; **– shooter** investigador de fallas o averías.

trou•ble•mak•er [tr ʌ b] mekə-] s. agitador, alborotador, malcontento.

trou•ble•some [tr ʌ b] səm] adj. molesto, fastidioso, enfadoso, dificultoso; penoso.

trough [trɔf] s. comedero; artesa; batea; **eaves –** canal, gotera del tejado; **drinking –** abrevadero.

trou•sers [tráUzə-z] s. pl. pantalones.

trous•seau [trúso] s. ajuar de novia.

trout [traUt] s. trucha.

trow•el [tráUəl] s. llana, Am. cuchara (*de albañil*).

tru•ant [trúənt] *s.* novillero, holgazán (*que se ausenta de la escuela*); **to play** – hacer novillos, *Am.* capear la escuela, *Am.* pintar venado, *Am.* jubilarse; *adj.* vago, perezoso.

truce [trus] *s.* tregua.

truck [trʌk] *s.* camión; carretón; carreta; basura; baratijas; **garden** – hortalizas, legumbres y verduras; **– garden** hortaliza, huerta de legumbres; *v.* acarrear, transportar en camión o carretón.

trudge [trʌdʒ] *v.* caminar, caminar con esfuerzo; *s.* caminata.

true [tru] *adj.* (*not false*) verdadero; cierto; verídico; fiel; (*exact*) exacto, preciso; legítimo.

tru•ly [trúlɪ] *adv.* (*not falsely*) verdaderamente, en verdad; en realidad; (*exactly*) exactamente, correctamente; fielmente; **very – yours** su seguro servidor.

trump [trʌmp] *s.* triunfo (*en el juego de naipes*); *v.* matar con un triunfo (*en el juego de naipes*); **to – up an excuse** forjar o inventar una excusa.

trum•pet [trʌmpɪt] *s.* trompeta; clarín; **ear** – trompetilla acústica; *v.* trompetear; tocar la trompeta; pregonar, divulgar.

trunk [trʌŋk] *s.* tronco; baúl; trompa (*de elefante*); **– s** calzones cortos (*para deportes*); **– line** línea principal.

trust [trʌst] *s.* (*reliance*) confianza, fe; (*credit*) crédito; (*charge*) cargo; custodia; depósito; (*firms*) trust, sindicato monopolista; *v.* confiar; fiar en, tener confianza en, fiarse de; esperar; dar crédito a.

trus•tee [trʌstí] *s.* fideicomisario, depositario; **university -s** regentes universitarios; **board of -s** patronato; consejo.

trust•ful [trʌstfəl] *adj.* confiado.

trust•ing [trʌstɪŋ] *adj.* confiado.

trust•wor•thy [trʌstwɜ́ðɪ] *adj.* fidedigno, digno de confianza.

trust•y [trʌstɪ] *adj.* fidedigno; honrado, leal; *s.* presidiario fidedigno (*a quien se le conceden ciertos privilegios*).

truth [truθ] *s.* verdad.

truth•ful [trúθfəl] *adj.* verdadero; verídico; veraz.

truth•ful•ness [trúθfəlnɪs] *s.* veracidad.

try [traɪ] *v.* probar, ensayar; hacer la prueba; poner a prueba; intentar, procurar; procesar, enjuiciar, formar causa (*a un acusado*); ver (*una causa*); **to – on a suit** probarse un traje; **to – one´s luck** probar fortuna; **to – someone's patience** poner a prueba la paciencia de alguien; **to – to** tratar de, procurar, intentar; *s.* prueba, tentativa, ensayo.

try•ing [tráɪɪŋ] *adj.* molesto; penoso, irritante.

tub [tʌb] *s.* tina; bañera; baño; batea, cuba; *v.* lavar en tina o cuba.

tu•ba [túbə] *s.* tuba.

tube [tjub] *s.* tubo; **inner** – cámara (*de un neumáti-*

co); **radio** – lámpara o tubo de radio.

tu•ber•cu•lar [tjubɝ́kjələ-] *adj.* tuberculoso, tísico.

tu•ber•cu•lo•sis [tjubɝ́kjəlósɪs] *s.* tuberculosis.

tuck [tʌk] *v.* alforzar, hacer o echar alforzas; **to – in** meter en; **to – in bed** arropar; **to – under one's arm** meter bajo el brazo; **to – up** arremangar, recoger; **to – up one's sleeves** arremangarse; *s.* alforza.

Tues•day [tjúzdɪ] *s.* martes.

tuft [tʌft] *s.* (*cluster*) penacho, copete; borla; (*clump*) macizo (*de plantas*).

tug [tʌg] *v.* remolcar; jalar (*halar*); arrastrar; trabajar con esfuerzo; **to – at** tirar de, jalar; *s.* tirón, estirón, *Am.* jalón; remolcador; **–boat** remolcador; **– of war** lucha a tirones de cuerda.

tu•i•tion [tjuíʃən] *s.* derechos de enseñanza, *Am.* colegiatura.

tu•lip [tjúləp] *s.* tulipán.

tum•ble [tʌmbḷ] *v.* caer(se); voltear; dar volteretas; **to – down** caerse; desplomarse; **to – down** desplomarse; **to – into someone** tropezar con alguien; **to – over** volcar, tumbar, derribar; venirse abajo; *s.* caída, tumbo, vuelco, voltereta, *Am.* rodada; desorden.

tum•bler [tʌmblə-] *s.* vaso (*de mesa*); acróbata.

tu•mor [tjúmə-] *s.* tumor.

tu•mult [tjúmʌlt] *s.* tumulto.

tu•mul•tu•ous [tjumʌ́ltʃuəs] *adj.* tumultuoso.

tu•na [túnə] *s.* atún (*pez*).

tune [tjun] *s.* (*melody*) tonada; (*pitch*) tono; armonía; **to be in** – estar a tono, estar afinado o templado; estar entonado; **to be out of** – estar desentonado o desafinado; desentonar; *v.* afinar, templar; armonizar; **to – in** sintonizar; **to – up the motor** poner al punto el motor.

tu•nic [tjúnɪk] *s.* túnica.

tun•nel [tʌnḷ] *s.* túnel; socavón; *v.* socavar; abrir un túnel.

tur•ban [təbən] *s.* turbante.

tur•bine [təbaɪn] [təbɪn] *s.* turbina.

tur•bu•lent [təbjələnt] *adj.* turbulento; revoltoso.

turf [tɝf] *s.* césped; terrón de tierra (*con césped*); hipódromo, pista (*para carreras*).

Turk [tɝk] *s.* turco.

tur•key [tɝkɪ] *s.* pavo. *Méx.* guajolote (*o guajalote*); *C.A.* jolote, chumpe, chompipe; *Col.* pisco.

Tur•kish [tɝkɪʃ] *adj.* turco; *s.* turco, idioma turco.

tur•moil [tɝmɔɪl] *s.* alboroto; confusión.

turn [tɝn] *s.* (*rotate*) volver(se); voltear(se); girar, dar vueltas, rodar, virar; (*shape*) tornear, labrar al torno; (*become*) ponerse (*pálido, rojo, etc.*); **to – back** volver atrás; volverse, retroceder; devolver;

to – down an offer rechazar una oferta; **to – in** entregar; recogerse, acostarse; **to – inside out** voltear o volver al revés; **to – into** convertir(se) en; **to – off** apagar (*la luz*); cortar (*el agua, el gas, etc.*); **to – off the main road** apartarse de la carretera; **to – on** encender (*la luz*); abrir la llave (*del gas, del agua*); **to – on someone** volverse contra, acometer o caer sobre alguien; **to – out** apagar (*la luz*); echar, expulsar, arrojar; producir, **to – out well** salir o resultar bien; **to – over** volcar(se), voltear(se); doblar; revolver (*en la mente*); **to – over and over** dar repetidas vueltas; **to – sour** agriarse, fermentarse; **to – the corner** doblar la esquina; **to – to** acudir a; volverse a; dirigirse a; convertir(se) en; **to – to the left** doblar o torcer a la izquierda; **to – up** aparecer; **to – up one's nose at** desdeñar; hacer ascos a; **to – up one's sleeves** arremangarse; **to – upside down** trastornar; volcar; **it -s my stomach** me da asco o náusea; *s.* vuelta; revolución; giro; recodo (*del camino*); turno; virada, cambio de rumbo; **– of mind** actitud mental; **at every –** a cada paso; **to be one's –** tocarle a uno; **to do one a good –** hacerle a uno un favor; **to take -s** turnarse.

tur•nip [tɝ́nəp] *s.* nabo.

turn•o•ver [tɝ́nóvɚ] *s.* vuelco (*de un coche*); cambio (*de empleados*); **business –** movimiento de mercancías, número de transacciones; **labor –** movimiento de obreros, cambio frecuente de trabajadores; **apple –** pastel de manzana; **– collar** cuello doblado.

turn•ta•ble [tɝ́ntebl̩] *s.* plato giratorio.

tur•pen•tine [tɝ́pəntaɪn] *s.* trementina; aguarrás.

tur•pi•tude [tɝ́pətjud] *s.* torpeza, vileza.

tur•quoise [tɝ́kwɔɪz] *s.* turquesa.

tur•ret [tɝ́ɪt] *s.* torrecilla; torre blindada; alminar.

tur•tle [tɝ́tl̩] *s.* tortuga; **–dove** tórtola.

tusk [tʌsk] *s.* colmillo.

tu•tor [tútɚ] *s.* tutor, maestro particular; *v.* enseñar, instruir.

tu•xe•do [tʌksído] *s.* esmoquin.

twang [twæŋ] *s.* tañido (*de una cuerda de guitarra*); nasalidad, tonillo gangoso; *v.* puntear, tañer (*una cuerda*); hablar con voz nasal, hablar con tonillo gangoso.

twang•y [twǽŋɪ] *adj.* gangoso, nasal.

tweed [twid] *s.* mezclilla de lana; **– suit** traje de mezclilla.

tweez•ers [twízɚz] *s. pl.* pinzas, tenacillas.

twice [twaɪs] *adv.* dos veces.

twig [twɪg] *s.* ramita; varita.

twi•light [twáɪlaɪt] *s.* crepúsculo; **at –** entre dos luces; *adj.* crepuscular.

twin [twɪn] *adj. & s.* gemelo, mellizo, *Méx.* cuate.

twine [twaɪn] *s.* cuerda, cordel; *v.* enroscar(se), torcer(se), retorcer(se); entrelazar.

twinge [twɪndʒ] *s.* punzada (*dolor agudo*); *v.* punzar.

twin•kle [twɪ́ŋk] *v.* titilar, parpadear, pestañear; chispear; *s.* titilación, parpadeo; pestañeo; guiño, guiñada; **in the – of an eye** en un abrir y cerrar de ojos.

twirl [twɝl] *v.* girar; dar vueltas; *s.* giro, vuelta; molinete, floreo.

twist [twɪst] *v.* (*turn*) torcer(se); (*coil*) enroscar(se); *s.* torsión, torcedura; torzal, cordoncillo (*hecho de varias hebras torcidas*); curva, recodo, vuelta; rosca (*de pan*); **mental –** sesgo de la mente, sesgo mental.

twitch [twɪtʃ] *v.* crisparse, contraerse, torcerse convulsivamente (*un músculo*); temblar (*los párpados*); dar un tirón; *s.* temblor, ligera, colvulsión, contracción nerviosa; tirón.

twit•ter [twɪtɚ] *v.* gorjear (*los pájaros*); temblar; agitarse; *s.* gorjeo; agitación, estremecimiento nervioso.

two-faced [túfest] *adj.* de dos caras.

two-fist•ed [túfɪstəd] *adj.* vigoroso; de dos puños.

two•fold [túfold] *adj.* doble.

two-way [túwe] *adj.* de dos sentidos.

type [taɪp] *s.* tipo; *v.* escribir a máquina.

type•write [táɪpraɪt] *v.* escribir a máquina.

type•writ•er [táɪpraɪtɚ] *s.* máquina de escribir.

type•writ•ing [táɪpraɪtɪŋ] *s.* mecanografía; trabajo de mecanógrafo.

type•writ•ten [táɪprɪtn̩] *adj.* escrito a máquina.

ty•phoid [táɪfɔɪd] *s.* tifoidea, fiebre tifoidea.

ty•phus [táɪfəs] *s.* tifo.

typ•i•cal [típɪk] *adj.* típico.

typ•ist [táɪpɪst] *s.* mecanógrafo; mecanógrafa.

ty•pog•ra•phic•al [taɪpográfɪk] *adj.* tipográfico; **– error** error de máquina.

ty•ran•ni•cal [tɪrǽnɪk] *adj.* tiránico, tirano.

tyr•an•ny [tírɛnɪ] *s.* tiranía.

ty•rant [táɪrənt] *s.* tirano.

U

u•biq•ui•tous [jubíkwɪtəs] *adj.* ubicuo.

ud•der [ʌ́dɚ] *s.* ubre.

ug•li•ness [ʌ́glɪnɪs] *s.* fealdad; fiereza.

ug•ly [ʌ́glɪ] *adj.* feo; fiero; repugnante; de mal genio; desagradable.

ul•cer [ʌ́lsɚ] *s.* úlcera.

ul•te•ri•or [ʌltíɾɪɚ] *adj.* ulterior.

ul•ti•mate [ʌltəmɪt] *adj.* último; final; fundamental; **-ly** *adv.* finalmente, a la larga.

ul•tra•mod•ern [ʌltrəmádɚn] *adj.* ultramoderno.

ul•tra•vi•o•let [ʌltrəvaɪ̃əlɛt] *adj.* ultravioleta.

um•bil•i•cal cord [ʌmbílək│kɔrd] *s.* cordón umbilical.

um•brel•la [ʌmbrɛ́lə] *s.* paraguas; sombrilla.

um•pire [ʌ́mpaɪr] *s.* árbitro, arbitrador; *v.* arbitrar.

un- [ʌn-] *prefijo negativo equivalente a:* sin, no, in-, des-.

un•a•ble [ʌnéb│] *adj.* incapaz, inhábil; **to be – to come** no poder venir.

un•ac•cent•ed [ʌnǽksɛntəd] *adj.* inacentuado.

un•ac•cus•tomed [ʌnək ʌ́stəmd] *adj.* desacostumbrado; insólito, inusitado.

un•af•fect•ed [ʌnəfɛ́ktɪd] *adj.* inafectado, sin afectación, natural, sincero.

un•al•ter•a•ble [ʌn ɔ́ltərəb│] *adj.* inalterable.

u•na•nim•i•ty [junənímətɪ] *s.* unanimidad.

u•nan•i•mous [jʊnǽnəməs] *adj.* unánime.

un•armed [ʌnármd] *adj.* desarmado.

un•at•tached [ʌnətǽtʃt] *adj.* suelto; libre; (*law*) no embargado.

un•a•void•a•ble [ʌnəvɔ́ɪdəb│] *adj.* inevitable, ineludible.

un•a•ware [ʌnəwɛ́r] *adj.* desprevenido; inadvertido, ignorante; incauto; **-s** *adv.* inesperadamente, inopinadamente; impensadamente.

un•bal•anced [ʌnbǽlənst] *adj.* deseouilibrado; **– account** cuenta no saldada.

un•bear•a•ble [ʌnbérəb│] *adj.* inaguantable, insoportable.

un•be•com•ing [ʌnbɪk ʌ́mɪŋ] *adj.* impropio; **an – dress** un vestido que no sienta bien o que cae mal.

un•be•lief [ʌnbəlíf] *s.* incredulidad.

un•be•liev•a•ble [ʌnbəlívəb│] *adj.* increíble.

un•be•liev•er [ʌnbəlívɚ] *s.* descreído, incrédulo.

un•be•liev•ing [ʌnbəlívɪŋ] *adj.* descreído, incrédulo.

un•bend•ing [ʌnbɛ́ndɪŋ] *adj.* inflexible.

un•bi•as•ed [ʌnbáɪəst] *adj.* imparcial, libre de prejuicio.

un•bo•som [ʌnbʊ́zəm] *v.* revelar, confesar, descubrir (*secretos*); **to – oneself** desahogarse con alguien, revelarle sus más íntimos secretos.

un•bound [ʌnbáʊnd] *adj.* desencuadernado, no encuadernado; suelto, desatado.

un•bro•ken [ʌnbrókəm] *adj.* intacto, entero; indómito; ininterrumpido, continuo.

un•but•ton [ʌnb ʌ́t ŋ] *v.* desabotonar, desabrochar.

un•can•ny [ʌnkǽnɪ] *adj.* extraño, raro, misterioso.

un•ceas•ing [ansísɪŋ] *adj.* incesante.

un•cer•tain [ʌnsɝ́t ŋ] *adj.* incierto; dudoso; indeciso.

un•cer•tain•ty [ʌnsɝ́t ŋ ʊ] *s.* incertidumbre; falta de certeza.

un•change•a•ble [ʌntʃéndʒəb│] *adj.* inmutable, inalterable, invariable.

un•changed [ʌntʃéndʒd] *adj.* inalterado, igual.

un•char•i•ta•ble [ʌntʃ ǽrətəb│] *adj.* duro falto de caridad.

un•cle [ʌŋk] *s.* tío.

un•clean [ʌnklín] *adj.* inmundo, sucio; impuro.

un•com•fort•a•ble [ʌnk ʌ́mfətəb│] *adj.* incómodo; molesto.

un•com•mon [ʌnkámən] *adj.* poco común, insólito, raro.

un•com•pro•mis•ing [ʌnkámprəmaɪzɪŋ] *adj.* intransigente; inflexible.

un•con•cern [ʌnkənsɝ́n] *s.* indiferencia.

un•con•di•tion•al [ʌnkəndíʃən│] *adj.* incondicional, absoluto.

un•con•ge•ni•al [ʌnkəndʒínjəl] *adj.* que no congenia, incompatible.

un•con•quer•a•ble [ʌnkáŋkərəb│] *adj.* invencible, inconquistable.

un•con•quer•ed [ʌnkáŋkɚd] *adj.* no conquistado, no vencido.

un•con•scious [ʌnkánʃəs] *adj.* inconsciente; privado.

un•con•scious•ness [ʌnkánʃəsnɪs] *s.* inconsciencia; insensibilidad.

un•con•sti•tu•tion•al [ʌnkánstɪtuʃən│] *adj.* inconstitucional.

un•con•trol•la•ble [ʌnkəntróləb│] *adj.* irrefrenable, ingobernable.

un•con•ven•tion•al [ʌnkənvɛ́nʃən│] *adj.* despreocupado, libre de trabas o reglas.

un•cov•er [ʌnk ʌ́vɚ] *v.* descubrir(se); revelar; destapar(se); desabrigar(se).

unc•tion [ʌ́ŋkʃən] *s.* unción; fervor; **Extreme Unction** Extremaunción.

unc•tu•ous [ʌ́ŋkʃəs] *adj.* untuoso.

un•cul•ti•vat•ed [ʌnk ʌ́ltəvetɪd] *adj.* inculto; baldío.

un•cul•tur•ed [ʌnk ʌ́ltʃɚd] *adj.* inculto; grosero.

un•daunt•ed [ʌnd ɔ́ntəd] *adj.* impávido.

un•de•cid•ed [ʌndɪsáɪdɪd] *adj.* indeciso.

un•de•ni•a•ble [ʌndɪnáɪəb l] *adj.* innegable.

un•der [ʌ́ndə-] *prep.* (*beneath*) bajo; debajo de; (*less*) menos de; **– age** menor de edad; **– cover** a cubierto; **– the cover of** al abrigo de, al amparo de; **– pretense of** so pretexto de; **– twelve** menos de doce; **to be – obligation to** deber favores a; *adv.* debajo; abajo; menos; *adj.* inferior, de abajo (*en ciertas combinaciones*); **– dose** dosis escasa o corta; **– secretary** subsecretario; **– side** lado de abajo, lado inferior; **the – dogs** los de abajo.

un•der•brush [ʌ́ndə-brʌ ʃ] *s.* maleza.

un•der•clothes [ʌ́ndə-kloz] *s. pl.* ropa interior.

un•der•dog [ʌ́ndə-dɔg] *s.* perdidoso, víctima.

un•der•es•ti•mate [ʌ́ndə-réstəmənt] *v.* menospreciar, apreciar en menos de lo justo; salir corto en un cálculo.

un•der•fed [ʌ́ndə-féd] *adj.* malnutrido.

un•der•go [ʌndə-gó] *v.* sufrir, aguantar, padecer.

un•der•gone [ʌndə-g ɔ́ n] *p.p. de* **to undergo**.

un•der•grad•u•ate [ʌndə-grǽdʒUɪt] *s.* estudiante del bachillerato; **– course** cursos o asignaturas para el bachillerato.

un•der•ground [ʌ́ndə-graUnd] *adj.* subterráneo; *s.* subterráneo; *adv.* bajo tierra; en secreto; ocultamente.

un•der•hand•ed [ʌ́ndə-hǽndɪd] *adj.* socarrón, secreto, disimulado, clandestino.

un•der•line [ʌ́ndə-laɪn] *v.* subrayar.

un•der•ly•ing [ʌndə-láɪɪŋ] *adj.* fundamental.

un•der•mine [ʌndə-máɪn] *v.* minar, socavar.

un•der•neath [ʌndə-níθ] *prep.* bajo, debajo de; *adv.* debajo.

un•der•pay [ʌ́ndə-pé] *v.* malpagar; escatimar la paga.

un•der•pin•ning [ʌ́ndə-pɪnɪŋ] *s.* apuntalamiento.

un•der•score [ʌ́ndə-skor] *v.* subrayar.

un•der•sell [ʌndə-sélə] *v.* malbaratar; vender a menos precio que.

un•der•shirt [ʌ́ndə-sh ɜ́ t] *s.* camiseta.

un•der•signed [ʌndə-sáɪnd] *s.* firmante, infrascrito; **the –** el infrascrito, los infrascritos; el que suscribe.

un•der•sized [ʌ́ndə-sáɪzd] *adj.* achaparrado, de tamaño inferior al normal.

un•der•skirt [ʌ́ndə-sk ɜ́ t] *s.* enaguas, refajo.

un•der•staf•fed [ʌndə-st ǽ ft] *adj.* de personal insuficiente.

un•der•stand [ʌndə-st ǽ nd] *v.* entender; comprender; sobrentender.

un•der•stand•a•ble [ʌndə-st ǽ ndəb l] *adj.* comprensible.

un•der•stand•ing [ʌndə-st ǽ ndɪŋ] *s.* comprensión; entendimiento, inteligencia; acuerdo; *adj.* comprensivo.

un•der•stood [ʌndə-stÚd] *pret. & p.p. de* **to understand**; *adj.* entendido; convenido; sobrentendido.

un•der•study [ʌ́ndə-stʌdɪ] *s.* sobresaliente, actor suplente; *v.* servir de sobresaliente o actor suplente.

un•der•take [ʌndə-ték] *v.* emprender; tratar de, intentar; comprometerse a.

un•der•tak•en [ʌndə-tékən] *p.p. de* **to undertake**.

un•der•tak•er [ʌ́ndə-tekə-] *s.* director de funeraria; embalsamador.

un•der•tak•ing [ʌndə-tékɪŋ] *s.* empresa.

un•der•took [ʌndə-tÚk] *pret. de* **to undertake**.

un•der•tow [ʌ́ndə-to] *s.* resaca.

un•der•wa•ter [ʌ́ndə-wɔtə-] *adj.* submarino; subacuático.

un•der•wear [ʌ́ndə-wɛr] *s.* ropa interior.

un•der•went [ʌndə-wént] *pret. de* **undergo**.

un•der•world [ʌ́ndə-w ɜ́ ld] *s.* hampa, bajos fondos de la sociedad, clase criminal.

un•der•write [ʌ́ndə-raɪt] *v.* asegurar; subscribir.

un•de•sir•a•ble [ʌndɪzáɪrəb l] *adj.* indeseable; inconveniente.

un•did [ʌndíd] *pret. de* **to undo**.

un•dis•turbed [ʌndɪst ɜ́ bd] *adj.* impasible; sereno, tranquilo; intacto.

un•do [ʌndú] *v.* deshacer; desatar; desabrochar; desenredar; anular; **to – one's hair** soltarse el cabello.

un•do•ing [ʌndúɪŋ] *s.* destrucción; pérdida.

un•done [ʌnd ʌ́ n] *p.p. de* **to undo**; inacabado, sin hacer; sin terminar; **it is still –** está todavía por hacer, está inacabado; **to come –** desatarse.

un•doubt•ed•ly [ʌndáUtɪdlɪ] *adv.* indudablemente, sin duda.

un•dress [ʌndrés] *v.* desnudar(se), desvestir(se).

un•due [ʌndjú] *adj.* indebido; impropio; excesivo.

un•du•late [ʌ́ndjəlet] *v.* ondular, ondear.

un•du•ly [ʌndjúlɪ] *adv.* indebidamente.

un•dy•ing [ʌndáɪɪŋ] *adj.* imperecedero, eterno.

un•earth [ʌn ɜ́ θ] *v.* desenterrar.

un•eas•i•ly [ʌníz í ɪ] *adv.* intranquilamente, inquietamente, con inquietud; incómodamente.

un•eas•i•ness [ʌnízɪnɪs] *s.* malestar, inquietud, intranquilidad, desasosiego.

un•eas•y [ʌnízɪ] *adj.* ansioso, inquieto, intranquilo; cohibido; incómodo.

un•ed•u•cat•ed [ʌnédʒəketɪd] *adj.* inculto, indocto, falto de instrucción, ignorante.

un•em•ployed [ʌnɪmpl ɔ́ ɪd] *adj.* desocupado, desempleado, cesante; ocioso; **– funds** fondos no invertidos o inactivos.

un•em•ploy•ment [ʌnɪmplɔ́ɪmənt] s. desempleo, cesantía, falta de empleo, desocupación.

un•end•ing [ʌnéndɪŋ] adj. inacabable, interminable.

un•e•qual [ʌnɪ́kwəl] adj. desigual; insuficiente, ineficaz.

un•e•quiv•o•cal [ʌnɪkwívək│] adj. inequívoco.

un•err•ing [ʌnérɪŋ] adj. infalible.

un•es•sen•tial [ʌnɪséʃ│] adj. no esencial.

un•e•ven [ʌnívən] adj. desigual, desparejo; irregular, accidentado; **– numbers** números impares o nones.

un•e•ven•ness [ʌnívənnɪs] s. desigualdad; desnivel; irregularidad, escabrosidad (*del terreno*).

un•e•vent•ful [ʌnɪvéntf│] adj. sin novedad.

un•ex•pect•ed [ʌnɪkspéktɪd] adj. inesperado; **-ly** adv. de improviso, inesperadamente.

un•ex•pres•sive [ʌnɪksprésɪv] adj. sin emoción.

un•fail•ing [ʌnfélɪŋ] adj. que nunca falta, constante, indefectible; infalible.

un•fair [ʌnfér] adj. injusto; tramposo; **to act -ly** obrar de mala fe.

un•faith•ful [ʌnféθfəl] adj. infiel; desleal.

un•fa•mil•iar [ʌnfəmíljə•] adj. poco familiar; desconocido; **to be – with** no tener conocimiento de; no estar al tanto de, ignorar; no conocer bien.

un•fas•ten [ʌnfǽsṇ]v. desabrochar; desatar; aflojar.

un•fa•vor•a•ble [ʌnfévrəb│] adj. desfavorable, contrario, adverso.

un•feel•ing [ʌnfílɪŋ] adj. insensible; incompasivo.

un•fin•ished [ʌnfínɪʃt] adj. inacabado, sin terminar, sin acabar; sin barnizar, sin pulir.

un•fit [ʌnfít] adj. incompetente, inepto, incapaz; inservible; impropio; v. incapacitar.

un•fold [ʌnfóld] v. desenvolver(se), desarrollar(se); desdoblar; revelar.

un•fore•seen [ʌnforsín] adj. imprevisto.

un•for•get•ta•ble [ʌnfə•gétəb│] adj. inolvidable.

un•for•tu•nate [ʌnfɔ́rtʃ'ənɪt] adj. desventurado, infeliz, desgraciado, desdichado; **-ly** adv. desgraciadamente, por desgracia.

un•found•ed [ʌnfáʊndəd] adj. infundado.

un•fre•quent•ed [ʌnfríkwəntəd] adj. poco frecuentado.

un•friend•ly [ʌnfréndlɪ] adj. hostil, enemigo; poco amistoso; adv. hostilmente.

un•fruit•ful [ʌnfrútf│] adj. intructuoso.

un•furl [ʌnfɝ́l] v. desplegar.

un•fur•nished [ʌnfɝ́nɪʃt] adj. desamueblado.

un•gain•ly [ʌngénlɪ] adj. desgarbado, torpe.

un•grate•ful [ʌngrétfəl] adj. ingrato, desagradecido.

un•guard•ed [ʌngárdəd] adj. desprevenido; descuidado.

un•hap•py [ʌnhǽpɪ] adj. infeliz; desgraciado, desventurado, desdichado.

un•harm•ed [ʌnhármd] adj. sin daño, ileso.

un•health•y [ʌnhélθɪ] adj. malsano; insalubre; enfermizo.

un•heard-of [ʌnhɝ́dɑv] adj. inaudito; desconocido.

un•hitch [ʌnhítʃ] v. desenganchar; desatar.

un•ho•ly [ʌnhólɪ] adj. impío, malo.

un•hook [ʌnhúk] v. desenganchar; desabrochar.

un•hurt [ʌnhɝ́t] adj. ileso.

u•ni•form [júnəform] adj. & s. uniforme.

u•ni•for•mi•ty [junəfɔ́tmətɪ] s. uniformidad.

u•ni•fy [júnəfaɪ] v. unificar, unir.

u•ni•lat•er•al [junɪlǽtə•│] adj. unilateral.

un•im•por•tant [ʌnɪmpɔ́rtṇt] adj. insignificante, poco importante.

un•in•hib•it•ed [ʌnɪnhíbətəd] adj. sin inhibición.

un•ion [júnjən] s. unión; **– leader** jefe de un gremio obrero; **trade-union** gremio obrero; **– shop** obreros sindicados o agremiados.

u•nique [juník] adj. único, singular.

u•ni•son [júnəzṇ]: **in –** al unísono (*en el mismo tono*); al compás.

u•nit [júnɪt] s. unidad.

u•nite [jUnáɪt] v. unir(se).

u•ni•ty [júnətɪ] s. unidad; unión.

u•ni•ver•sal [junəvɝ́s│] adj. universal; **– joint** cruceta.

u•ni•verse [júnəvɝ́s] s. universo.

u•ni•ver•si•ty [junəvɝ́sətɪ] s. universidad.

un•just [ʌndʒʌ́st] adj. injusto.

un•jus•ti•fi•a•ble [ʌndʒʌ́stəfaɪəb│] adj. injustificable, injustificado.

un•kempt [ʌnkémpt] adj. desaseado, desaliñado; desgreñado.

un•kind [ʌnkáɪnd] adj. falto de bondad; descortés; cruel.

un•known [ʌnnón] adj. desconocido; no sabido; ignoto; **– quality** incógnita; **it is –** se ignora, no se sabe, se desconoce.

un•law•ful [ʌnlɔ́fəl] adj. ilegal, ilícito.

un•leash [ʌnlíʃ] v. soltar.

un•less [ʌnlés] conj. a menos que, a no ser que.

un•li•censed [ʌnláɪsənzd] adj. sin autorización.

un•like [ʌnláɪk] adj. desemejante, distinto, diferente; prep. a diferencia de.

un•like•ly [ʌnláɪklɪ] *adj.* improbable, inverosímil.

un•lim•it•ed [ʌnlímɪtɪd] *adj.* ilimitado.

un•load [ʌnlód] *v.* descargar; vaciar; deshacerse de (*acciones, mercancías*).

un•lock [ʌnlók] *v.* abrir (*con llave*); soltar, destrabar; revelar, penetrar (*secretos*).

un•loose [ʌnlús] *v.* soltar.

un•luck•y [ʌnlʌ́kɪ] *adj.* (*unfortunate*) desdichado, desventurado, desgraciado, desafortunado; (*of bad omen*) aciago, de mal agüero, funesto; **an — number** un número de mala suerte.

un•man•age•a•ble [ʌnmǽnɪdʒəbl] *adj.* inmanejable, ingobernable, intratable, indomable.

un•manned [ʌnmǽnd] *adj.* desguarnecido; sin tripulación.

un•marked [ʌnmárkt] *adj.* sin identificación.

un•mar•ried [ʌnmǽrɪd] *adj.* soltero.

un•mask [ʌnmǽsk] *v.* desenvascar(se).

un•mer•ci•ful [ʌnmɝ́sɪfəl] *adj.* despiadado, inclemente.

un•mis•tak•a•ble [ʌnməstékəbl] *adj.* inequívoco, claro, inconfundible.

un•moved [ʌnmúvd] *adj.* fijo; inmutable, impasible; indiferente.

un•nat•u•ral [ʌnnǽtʃərəl] *adj.* afectado, artificial; anormal; **an — mother** una madre desnaturalizada.

un•nec•es•sar•y [ʌnnésəsɛrɪ] *adj.* innecesario.

un•no•ticed [ʌnnóʊtɪst] *adj.* inadvertido.

un•o•blig•ing [ʌnəbláɪdʒɪŋ] *adj.* poco complaciente, descortés, descomedido.

un•ob•served [ʌnəbzɝ́vd] *adj.* inadvertido; sin ser visto.

un•ob•tain•a•ble [ʌnəbténəbl] *adj.* inobtenible, inasequible, inaccesible.

un•ob•tru•sive [ʌnəbtrusɪv] *adj.* discreto; sin ser visto.

un•oc•cu•pied [ʌnákjəpaɪd] *adj.* desocupado; vacío; desalquilado.

un•of•fi•cial [ʌnəfíʃl] *adj.* extraoficial.

un•or•gan•ized [ʌnɔ́rgənaɪzd] *adj.* sin organización; inorganizado.

un•o•rig•i•nal [ʌnərídʒən] *adj.* trivial, ordinario.

un•or•tho•dox [ʌnárθədɑks] *adj.* heterodoxo.

un•pack [ʌnpǽk] *v.* desempacar; desembalar.

un•paid [ʌnpéd] *adj.* no pagado; sin pagar; **— bills** cuentas por pagar.

un•pleas•ant [ʌnpléznt] *adj.* desagradable.

un•pleas•ant•ness [ʌnplézntnɪs] *s.* manera desagradable; desazón; desavenencia; **the — of a situación** lo desagradable de una situación; **to have an — with** tener una desavenencia con.

un•prec•e•dent•ed [ʌnprésədɛntɪd] *adj.* sin precedente; inaudito.

un•pre•med•i•tat•ed [ʌnprimédətetəd] *adj.* impremeditado.

un•pre•pared [ʌnprɪpérd] *adj.* desprevenido; no preparado; no listo.

un•pre•ten•tious [ʌnpriténʃəs] *adj.* modesto; sin pretenciones.

un•print•a•ble [ʌnprÍntəb] *adj.* que no puede imprimirse.

un•pro•duc•tive [ʌnprəd ʌ́ ktɪv] *adj.* improductivo.

un•pro•fes•sion•al [ʌnprəféʃən] *adj.* no profesional.

un•prof•it•a•ble [ʌnpráfɪtəb] *adj.* infructuoso.

un•pub•lished [ʌnp ʌ́ blɪʃt] *adj.* inédito, no publicado.

un•qual•i•fied [ʌnkwálɪfaɪd] *adj.* incompetente; inepto.

un•quench•a•ble [ʌnkwéntʃəb] *adj.* inapagable, inextinguible.

un•ques•tion•a•ble [ʌnkwéstʃənəb] *adj.* indisputable, indudable; irreprochable.

un•rav•el [ʌnrǽv] *v.* desenredar; desenmarañar; deshilachar(se); deshilar.

un•re•al [ʌnríel] *adj.* irreal; ilusorio, imaginario.

un•rea•son•a•ble [ʌnrízənəb] *adj.* desrazonable, fuera de razón; irracional.

un•rec•og•niz•a•ble [ʌnrékəgnaɪzəb] *adj.* irreconocible, no conocible, incapaz de reconocerse; desconocido.

un•re•fined [ʌnrɪfáɪnd] *adj.* no refinado; inculto, grosero.

un•re•li•a•ble [ʌnrɪlaɪəb] *adj.* informal; indigno de confianza.

un•rest [ʌnrést] *s.* inquietud, desasosiego.

un•roll [ʌnról] *v.* desenrollar(se), desenvolver(se).

un•ru•ly [ʌnrúlɪ] *adj.* indómito; indócil; desobediente.

un•safe [ʌnséf] *adj.* inseguro, peligroso.

un•sal•a•ble [ʌnséləb] *adj.* invendible.

un•sat•is•fac•to•ry [ʌnsætɪsfǽktrɪ] *adj.* no satisfactorio, inaceptable.

un•scru•pu•lous [ʌnskrúpjʊləs] *adj.* poco escrupuloso.

un•sea•son•a•ble [ʌnsízənəb] *adj.* intempestivo.

un•seat [ʌnsÍt] *v.* destituir.

un•seen [ʌnsÍn] *adj.* no visto, oculto; invisible.

un•sel•fish [ʌnsélfɪʃ] *adj.* desinteresado.

un•sel•fish•ness [ʌnsélfɪʃnɪs] *s.* desinterés, abnegación.

un·set·tled [ʌnsɛ́t‖d] *adj.* (*disturbed*) desordenado, en desorden; turbio; inestable; (*uncertain*) incierto; indeciso; (*unpopulated*) deshabitado; no establecido; **– bills** cuentas no liquidadas, cuentas pendientes; **– weather** tiempo variable; **an – liquid** un líquido revuelto o turbio.

un·shak·en [ʌnʃékən] *adj.* inmóvil, inmovible, firme.

un·sight·ly [ʌnsáItlI] *adj.* feo, desagradable a la vista.

un·skilled [ʌnskÍld] *adj.* inexperto.

un·skill·ful [ʌnskÍlfəl] *adj.* inhábil, desmañado, inexperto.

un·so·cia·ble [ʌnsóʃəb‖] *adj.* insociable, huraño, intratable, arisco.

un·so·phis·ti·cat·ed [ʌnsəfÍstəketəd] *adj.* cándido, sencillo.

un·sound [ʌnsáUnd] *adj.* erróneo, falso.

un·speak·a·ble [ʌnspíkəb‖] *adj.* indecible; inefable; atroz.

un·sta·ble [ʌnstéb‖] *adj.* inestable.

un·stead·y [ʌnstédI] *adj.* inseguro, inestable; movedizo; variable, inconstante.

un·suc·cess·ful [ʌnsəksɛ́sfəl] *adj.* sin éxito; desafortunado; **to be –** no tener éxito.

un·suit·a·ble [ʌnsútəb‖] *adj.* impropio, inapropiado; inepto; inconveniente; incongruente; incompatible.

un·sus·pect·ed [ʌnsəspéktId] *adj.* insospechado.

un·ten·a·ble [ʌnténəb‖] *adj.* insostenible.

un·think·a·ble [ʌnθÍŋkəb‖] *adj.* impensable.

un·ti·dy [ʌntáIdI] *adj.* desaliñado, desaseado, desarreglado, en desorden.

un·tie [ʌntáI] *v.* desatar(se); desamarrar; deshacer (*un nudo o lazo*).

un·til [ʌntÍl] *prep.* hasta; *conj.* hasta que.

un·time·ly [ʌntáImlI] *adj.* inoportuno, prematuro; *adv.* inoportunamente; fuera de sazón; demasiado pronto.

un·tir·ing [ʌntáIrIŋ] *adj.* incansable.

un·told [ʌntóld] *adj.* indecible, innumerable, incalculable, inestimable.

un·touch·ed [ʌnt ʌ ʃt] *adj.* (*unscathed*) intacto, no tocado, íntegro; (*impassive*) impasible, no conmovido; **to leave –** no tocar, dejar intacto; dejar impasible, no conmover.

un·trained [ʌntrénd] *adj.* indisciplinado, falto de disciplina; sin educación; inexperto.

un·tried [ʌntráId] *adj.* no probado, no ensayado, no experimentado; **– law case** causa todavía no vista.

un·troub·led [ʌntr ʌ b‖d] *adj.* sosegado, tranquilo, quieto.

un·true [ʌntrú] *adj.* falso; infiel; desleal; mentiroso.

un·truth [ʌntrúθ] *s.* falsedad; mentira.

un·tu·tored [ʌntútə̇d] *adj.* sin instrucción; ingenuo.

un·used [ʌnjúzd] *adj.* no usado; desacostumbrado; **– to** no hecho a, desacostumbrado a.

un·u·su·al [ʌnjúʒUəl] *adj.* inusitado, insólito; desusado; raro, extraño; extraordinario.

un·var·nished [ʌnvárnIʃt] *adj.* sin barnizar; sin adornos.

un·veil [ʌnvél] *v.* cuitar el velo a; revelar, descubrir.

un·war·rant·ed [ʌnwɔ́rəntəd] *adj.* no justificado.

un·war·y [ʌnwɛ́rI] *adj.* incauto.

un·washed [ʌnwɔ́ʃt] *adj.* no lavado, sin lavar; sucio.

un·wel·come [ʌnwélkəm] *adj.* indeseable, no deseado; mal acogido, mal recibido, mal quisto.

un·whole·some [ʌnhólsəm] *adj.* malsano; insalubre, dañino.

un·wield·y [ʌnwÍldI] *adj.* inmanejable, difícil de manejar, embarazoso, engorroso.

un·will·ing [ʌnwÍlIŋ] *adj.* renuente, maldispuesto, reacio; **to be – to** no querer, no estar dispuesto a; **-ly** *adv.* de mala gana, sin querer.

un·will·ing·ness [ʌnwÍlIŋnIs] *s.* renuencia, falta de voluntad; mala gana.

un·wise [ʌnwáIz] *adj.* imprudente, indiscreto; necio.

un·wont·ed [ʌnw ʌ́ntəd] *adj.* inusitado, inacostumbrado; inédito.

un·wor·thy [ʌnwɔ́ðI] *adj.* indigno.

un·wrap [ʌnrǽp] *v.* desenvolver.

un·writ·ten [ʌnrÍtən] *adj.* no escrito.

up [ʌp] *adv.* (*above*) arriba, hacia arriba; en lo alto; (*standing*) de pie; *adj.* levantado, derecho, erecto; (*finished*) terminado, concluido; **– and down** de arriba abajo; de acá para allá; **-s and downs** altibajos; fluctuaciones, vaivenes; **– the river** río arriba; **– to now** hasta ahora; **his time is –** ha expirado su tiempo; se ha cumplido su plazo; **prices are –** los precios han subido; **that is – to you** queda a la discreción de Vd., eso es cosa suya; **to be – against it** estar perplejo, no saber qué hacer; estar en un aprieto; **to be – on the news** estar al corriente (*o* al tanto) de las noticias); **to be – to one's old tricks** hacer de las suyas; **to eat it –** comérselo; **what's – ?** ¿qué pasa?; *v.* levantar, alzar.

up·braid [ʌpbréd] *v.* reprender, regañar.

up·date [ʌ́pdét] *v.* poner al día.

up·grade [ʌ́pgréd] *v.* adelantar; mejorar.

up·heav·al [ʌphÍv] *s.* trastorno.

up·held [ʌphéld] *pret. & p.p. de* **to uphold.**

up·hill [ʌphÍl] *adv.* cuesta arriba; *adj.* ascendente, trabajoso, arduo.

up·hold [ʌphóld] *v.* sostener, apoyar.

up·hol·ster [ʌphólstə̇-] *v.* entapizar y rellenar (*mue-*

up•hol•ster•y [aphólstrɪ] *s.* tapicería.

up•keep [ʌ́pkip] *s.* manutención.

up•land [ʌ́plənd] *s.* altiplanicie, tierra alta.

up•lift [ʌ́plɪft] *s.* elevación; edificación (*espiritual*); [ʌplɪ́ft] *v.* elevar; edificar (*espiritualmente*).

up•on [əpón] *prep.* en, sobre, encima de; **– arriving** al llegar.

up•per [ʌ́pə·] *adj.* superior; alto; **– berth** litera alta, cama alta (*de un coche dormitorio*); **to have the – hand** ejercer dominio o mando; llevar la ventaja; *s.* litera alta, cama alta; pala (*parte superior del calzado*).

up•right [ʌ́praɪt] *adj.* recto; derecho; vertical; justo, honrado; **– piano** piano vertical; *s.* poste; puntual; piano vertical.

up•right•ness [ʌ́praɪtnɪs] *s.* rectitud.

up•ris•ing [ʌpráɪzɪŋ] *s.* alzamiento, levantamiento; revuelta.

up•roar [ʌ́pror] *s.* tumulto, alboroto, bulla, gritería.

up•roar•i•ous [aprórɪəs] *adj.* estruendoso, bullicioso, tumultuoso.

up•root [ʌprút] *v.* desarraigar, arrancar de raíz.

up•set [ʌpsét] *v.* (*capsize*) volcar, tumbar, (*distress*) trastornar; perturbar, turbar; **to become –** volcarse; turbarse; trastornársele a uno el estómago; *pret. & p.p. de* **to upset**; *adj.* indispuesto, descompuesto; desarreglado, trastornado; [ʌ́psɛt] *s.* vuelco, trastorno; desorden, indisposición.

up•shot [ʌ́pʃot] *s.* resultado, fin.

up•side [ʌ́psáɪd] *s.* lado o parte superior; **– down** al revés; patas arriba; en desorden.

up•stage [ʌpstédʒ] *v.* quitarle la escena a uno.

up•stairs [ʌpstérz] *adv.* arriba, en el piso de arriba; *adj.* de arriba; *s.* piso (*o* pisos) de arriba.

up•start [ʌ́pstart] *s.* advenedizo, principiante presuntuoso.

up-to-date [ʌ́ptʊdét] *adj.* moderno; al corriente, al tanto.

up•turn [ʌ́ptɝn] *s.* alza, subida (*de precios*); mejora.

up•ward [ʌ́pwə·d] *adv.* arriba, para arriba, hacia arriba; más; **– of** más de; *adj.* ascendente, hacia arriba, para arriba.

up•wards [ʌ́pwə·dz] *adv.* = **upward.**

u•ra•ni•um [jʊrénɪəm] *s.* uranio.

ur•ban [ɝ́bən] *adj.* urbano.

ur•chin [ɝ́tʃɪn] *s.* granuja, pilluelo; **sea –** erizo de mar.

urge [ɝdʒ] *v.* urgir, instar; exhortar; recomendar o solicitar con instancia; apremiar, incitar, estimular;

s. impulso; gana, ganas; estímulo.

ur•gen•cy [ɝ́dʒənsɪ] *s.* urgencia; apremio.

ur•gent [ɝ́dʒənt] *adj.* urgente, apremiante.

u•ri•nal [júrɪn‖] *s.* urinario.

u•ri•nate [jÚrənet] *v.* orinar.

u•rine [jÚrɪn] *s.* orina, (los) orines.

urn [ɝn] *s.* urna; **coffee –** cafetera.

us [ʌs] *pron.* nos; nosotros (*con preposición*).

us•age [júsɪdʒ] *s.* usanza; uso; **hard –** uso constante.

use [jus] *s.* (*application*) uso; empleo; (*goal*) utilidad; **it is of no –** es inútil; no sirve; **out of –** desusado, ya no usado; pasado de moda; **to have to further – for** ya no necesitar, ya no tener necesidad de; **what is the – of it?** ¿para qué sirve?; ¿qué ventaja tiene?; ¿qué objeto tiene?; [juz] *v.* usar; emplear; servirse de, hacer uso de; acostumbrar, soler, *Am.* saber; **– your judgment** haz lo que te parezca; **to – up** gastar, agotar; consumir; **to be -d to** estar hecho, acostumbrado o habituado a; **he -d to do it** solía hacerlo, lo hacía.

use•ful [júsfəl] *adj.* útil.

use•ful•ness [júsfəlnɪs] *s.* utilidad.

use•less [júslɪs] *adj.* inútil; inservible.

use•less•ness [júslɪsnɪs] *s.* inutilidad.

ush•er [ʌ́ ʃə·] *s.* acomodador (*en un teatro o iglesia*); ujier; *v.* conducir, llevar, acompañar; introducir.

u•su•al [júʒʊəl] *adj.* usual; corriente, común, general; **-ly** *adv.* usualmente, generalmente, por lo general.

u•su•rer [júʒərə·] *s.* usurero.

u•surp [juzɝ́p] *v.* usurpar.

u•su•ry [júʒərɪ] *s.* usura.

u•ten•sil [juténs‖] *s.* utensilio.

u•ter•us [jútərəs] *s.* útero.

u•til•i•tar•i•an [jUtɪlətérɪən] *adj.* utilitario.

u•til•i•ty [jutílətɪ] *s.* utilidad; servicio.

u•til•ize [jút‖aɪz] *v.* utilizar; aprovechar.

ut•most [ʌ́tmost] *adj.* (*extreme*) sumo, extremo; más distante; más grande, mayor; más alto; (*last*) último; **he did his –** hizo cuanto pudo; **to the –** hasta más no poder.

ut•ter [ʌ́tə·] *v.* proferir; decir, expresar; **to – a cry** dar un grito; *adj.* completo, total; absoluto.

ut•ter•ance [ʌ́tərəns] *s.* declaración; expresión; modo de hablar.

ut•ter•most [ʌ́tə·most] = **utmost.**

u•vu•la [júvjələ] *s.* campanilla, galillo de la garganta.

u•vu•lar [júvjUlə·] *adj.* uvular.

V

va•can•cy [vékənsɪ] s. vacante, empleo vacante; vacío; habitación o apartamento desocupado.

va•cant [vékənt] adj. vacante; vacío; desocupado; libre.

va•cate [vékət] v. desocupar, dejar vacío; dejar vacante.

va•ca•tion [veké∫ən] s. vacación; vacaciones.

vac•ci•nate [væks ŋ et] v. vacunar.

vac•ci•na•tion [væks ŋ é∫ən] s. vacunación.

vac•cine [væksin] s. vacuna.

vac•il•late [væs ɪet] v. vacilar.

vac•u•um [vækjʊəm] s. vacío; − **cleaner** escoba eléctrica.

vag•a•bond [vægəbɑnd] adj. & s. vagabundo.

va•gran•cy [végrənsɪ] s. vagancia.

va•grant [végrənt] adj. vago, vagabundo, errante; s. vago, vagabundo.

vague [veg] adj. vago.

vain [ven] adj. vano; vanidoso; **in** − en vano.

vain•glo•ry [venglórɪ] s. vanagloria.

vale [vel] s. valle; cañada.

val•en•tine [væləntaɪn] s. tarjeta o regalo del día de San Valentín (el día de los enamorados); **to my** − a mi querido, a mí querida.

val•et [vælɪt] s. criado, camarero; planchador de trajes.

val•iant [væljənt] adj. valiente, valeroso.

val•id [vælɪd] adj. válido; valedero.

va•lid•i•ty [vəlídətɪ] s. validez.

va•lise [vəlís] s. valija, maleta, Méx. velís, Méx. petaca.

val•ley [vælɪ] s. valle.

val•or [vælə] s. valor, ánimo, valentía.

val•or•ous [vælərəs] adj. valeroso, valiente.

val•u•a•ble [væljəb] adj. valioso; precioso; preciado; **-s** s. pl. objetos de valor, joyas, alhajas.

val•u•a•tion [væljʊé∫ən] s. valuación, valoración; avalúo; tasa.

val•ue [væljU] s. (price) valor; precio; (merit) mérito; (consideration) estimación, aprecio; v. valorar, avaluar, valuar; apreciar, estimar.

val•ue•less [væljUlɪs] adj. sin valor.

valve [vælv] s. válvula; valva (de los moluscos); **safety** − válvula de seguridad.

vam•pire [væmpaɪr] s. vampiro.

van [væn] s. camión (para transportar muebles); − **guard** vanguardia.

van•dal [vænd] s. vándalo.

vane [ven] s. veleta; aspa (de molino de viento); paleta (de hélice).

van•guard [vængord] s. vanguardia.

va•nil•la [vənílə] s. vainilla.

van•ish [vænɪ∫] v. desvanecerse, desaparecer(se).

van•i•ty [vænətɪ] s. vanidad; − **case** neceser; − **table** tocador.

van•quish [vænkwɪ∫] v. vencer.

van•tage [væntɪdʒ] s. ventaja; **point of** − lugar estratégico.

va•por [vépə] s. vapor; vaho.

va•por•ize [vépə·aɪz] v. vaporizar.

var•i•a•ble [vérɪəb] adj. & s. variable.

var•i•ance [vérɪəns] s. variación, cambio; desavenencia; **to be at** − estar desavenidos; no estar de acuerdo.

var•i•ant [værɪənt] s. variante.

var•i•a•tion [vérɪé∫ən] s. variación; variedad.

var•ied [vétɪd] adj. variado, vario.

var•i•e•gat•ed [vérɪgetɪd] adj. abigarrado.

va•ri•e•ty [vəráɪətɪ] s. variedad.

var•i•ous [vérɪəs] adj. varios; diferentes, distintos.

var•nish [várnɪ∫] s. barniz; v. barnizar.

var•y [vérɪ] v. variar; cambiar.

vase [ves] s. vaso, jarrón.

Vas•e•line [væsəlɪn] s. vaselina.

vas•sal [væs] adj. & s. vasallo.

vast [væst] adj. vasto; inmenso; anchuroso; **-ly** adv. vastamente, sumamente, muy.

vast•ness [væstnɪs] s. inmensidad.

vat [væt] s. tina, tanque.

vaude•ville [vódəvɪl] s. vodevil, función de variedades.

vault [vɔlt] s. bóveda; tumb; **bank** − caja fuerte; depósito; **pole** − salto con garrocha; v. abovedar, edificar una bóveda; dar figura de bóveda; saltar con garrocha; saltar por encima de.

vaunt [vɔnt] v. jactarse; ostentar, alardear; s. jactancia.

veal [vil] s. carne de ternera; − **cutlet** chuleta de ternera.

veer [vɪr] v. virar; s. virada.

veg•e•ta•ble [védʒtəb] s. (plant) vegetal, planta; (food) legumbre; **-s** hortaliza, legumbres; **green -s** verduras; adj. vegetal; de legumbres, de hortaliza; − **garden** hortaliza.

veg•e•tate [védʒətet] v. vegetar.

veg•e•ta•tion [védʒəté∫ən] s. vegetación.

ve•he•mence [víəməns] s. vehemencia.

ve•he•ment [víəmənt] adj. vehemente.

ve•hi•cle [víɪk] s. vehículo.

veil [vel] s. velo; v. velar; tapar, encubrir.

vein [ven] *s.* vena; veta, filón.

veined [vend] *adj.* veteado, jaspeado; venoso.

ve·loc·i·ty [vəlósətı] *s.* velocidad.

vel·vet [vélvɪt] *s.* terciopelo; velludo; *adj.* de terciopelo; aterciopelado.

vel·vet·y [vélvɪtı] *adj.* aterciopelado.

vend·or [véndə-] *s.* vendedor; buhonero, vendedor ambulante.

ve·neer [vənír], *s.* chapa; *v.* chapar o chapear, *Am.* enchapar.

ven·er·a·ble [vénərəb|] *adj.* venerable; venerando.

ven·er·ate [vénəret] *v.* venerar.

ven·er·a·tion [vɛnəréʃən] *s.* veneración.

ve·ne·re·al [vənírɪəl] *adj.* venéreo.

Ve·ne·zue·lan [vɛnəzwílən] *adj. & s.* venezolano.

ven·geance [véndʒəns] *s.* venganza; **with a** – con furia; con violencia.

ven·i·son [vénəzŋ] *s.* venado, carne de venado.

ven·om [vénəm] *s.* veneno, ponzoña.

ven·om·ous [vénəməs] *adj.* venenoso, ponzoñoso.

vent [vɛnt] *s.* (*opening*) abertura; (*escape*) escape; (*utterance*) desahogo; fogón (*de arma de fuego*); **to give – to anger** desahogar la ira, dar desahogo a la cólera; *v.* dar salida o desahogo; desahogar, descargar.

ven·ti·late [vént|et] *v.* ventilar.

ven·ti·la·tion [vɛnt|éʃən] *s.* ventilación.

ven·ti·la·tor [vént|etə-] *s.* ventilador.

ven·ture [véntʃə-] *s.* ventura, riesgo; **business –** especulación; empresa o negocio arriesgado; *v.* aventurar, arriesgar; **to – outside** aventurarse a salir; **to – to** aventurarse a, atreverse a, osar.

ven·tur·ous [véntʃərəs] *adj.* aventurado.

ve·ran·da [vərǽndə] *s.* galería; terraza; balcón corrido.

verb [vɝb] *s.* verbo.

ver·bal [vɝb|] *adj.* verbal; oral.

ver·bal·ize [vɝ·bəlaɪz] *v.* expresar por medio de palabras.

ver·bose [vɝ·bós] *adj.* verboso; palabrero.

ver·dict [vɝ·dɪkt] *s.* veredicto; fallo, decisión, sentencia; **– of "not guilty"** veredicto de inculpabilidad.

ver·dure [vɝ·dʒə-] *s.* verdura, verdor, verde.

verge [vɝdʒ] *s.* borde, margen, orilla; **on the – of** al borde de; a punto de; *v.* **to – on** rayar en, estar al margen de; **to – toward** tender a, inclinarse a.

ver·i·fy [vérəfaɪ] *v.* verificar; comprobar.

ver·i·ly [vérəlı] *adv.* en verdad.

ver·i·ta·ble [vérətəb|] *adj.* verdadero.

ver·mill·ion [və-míljən] *adj.* bermejo.

ver·nac·u·lar [və-nǽkjUlə-] *adj.* vernáculo; *s.* idioma corriente.

ver·sa·tile [və-sət|] *adj.* hábil para muchas cosas; flexible.

verse [vɝs] *s.* verso.

versed [vɝst] *adj.* versado, experto, perito.

ver·sion [vɝ·ʒən] versión.

ver·te·brate [vɝ·təbrɪt] *adj.* vertebrado.

ver·ti·cal [vɝ·tɪk|] *adj.* vertical.

ver·y [vérɪ] *adv.* muy; **– much** muchísimo; **– many** muchísimos; **it is – cold today** hace mucho frío hoy; *adj.* mismo; mismísimo; mero; **the – man** el mismísimo hombre; **the – thought of** la mera idea de.

ves·pers [véspə-z] *s. pl.* vísperas.

ves·sel [vés|] *s.* vasija; vaso; barco, embarcación; **blood –** vaso, vena, arteria.

vest [vɛst] *s.* chaleco; *v.* conferir; **to – with power** revestir de autoridad, conferir poder a.

ves·ti·bule [véstəbjul] *s.* vestíbulo; zaguán.

ves·tige [véstɪdʒ] *s.* vestigio.

vest·ment [véstmənt] *s.* vestidura.

vet·er·an [vétərən] *adj. & s.* veterano.

vet·er·i·nar·y [vétrənɛrɪ] *s.* veterinario o albéitar.

ve·to [víto] *s.* veto; prohibición; *v.* vedar, prohibir; poner el veto a; negarse a aprobar.

vex [vɛks] *v.* molestar, hostigar; incomodar, enfadar; perturbar.

vex·a·tion [vɛkséʃən] *s.* molestia, incomodidad; enojo.

vi·a [váɪə] *prep.* por, por la vía de.

vi·a·ble [váɪəb|] *adj.* viable.

vi·a·duct [váɪədʌkt] *s.* viaducto.

vi·al [váɪəl] *s.* fresco, redoma; **small –** ampolleta.

vi·ands [váɪəndz] *s. pl.* vianda, alimentos, comida.

vi·brate [váɪbret] *v.* vibrar.

vi·bra·tion [vaɪbréʃən] *s.* vibración.

vi·car·i·ous [vaɪkérɪəs] *adj.* vicario.

vice [vaɪs] *s.* vicio; falta, defecto.

vice-pres·i·dent [váɪsprézədənt] *s.* vicepresidente.

vice·roy [váɪsrɔɪ] *s.* virrey.

vice versa [váɪsɪvɝ·sə] viceversa.

vi·cin·i·ty [vəsínətɪ] *s.* vecindad; cercanía; inmediaciones.

vi·cious [víʃəs] *adj.* vicioso; malo; maligno; malicioso; **– dog** perro mordedor, perro bravo.

vi·cis·si·tude [vəsísətjud] *s.* vicisitud, peripecia.

vic·tim [víktɪm] *s.* víctima.

vic·tim·ize [víktɪmaɪz] *v.* inmolar; engañar.

vic·tor [víktə-] *s.* vencedor.

vic·to·ri·ous [vɪktórɪəs] *adj.* victorioso.

vic·to·ry [víktrɪ] *s.* victoria.

vic·tuals [vít|z] *s. pl.* vituallas, víveres.

vie [vaɪ] v. competir.

view [vju] s. (field of vision) vista; paisaje; (opinion) parecer, opinion; (inspection) inspección; (aim) mira, propósito; in – of en vista de; to be within – estar al alcance de la vista; within a – to con el propósito de; con la esperanza o expectación de; con la mira puesta en; v. mirar; examinar.

view•point [vjúpoɪnt] s. punto de vista.

vig•il [vídʒəl] s. vigilia, velada; to keep – velar.

vig•i•lance [vídʒələns] s. vigilancia, desvelo.

vig•i•lant [vídʒələnt] adj. vigilante.

vig•or [vígə] s. vigor.

vig•or•ous [vígərəs] adj. vigoroso.

vile [vaɪl] adj. vil, bajo, ruin; pésimo.

vil•la [vílə] s. quinta, casa de campo.

vil•lage [vílɪdʒ] s. villa, aldea.

vil•lag•er [vílɪdʒə] s. aldeano.

vil•lain [vílən] s. villano, malvado, bellaco.

vil•lain•ous [vílənəs] adj. villano, ruin, vil, bellaco.

vil•lain•y [vílənɪ] s. villanía, vileza.

vim [vɪm] s. vigor, fuerza, energía.

vin•di•cate [víndəket] v. vindicar, vengar.

vin•dic•tive [vɪndíktɪv] adj. vengativo.

vine [vaɪn] s. vid, parra; enredadera.

vin•e•gar [vínɪgə] s. vinagre.

vine•yard [vínjəd] s. viña, viñedo.

vin•tage [víntɪdʒ] s. vendimia; edad, época.

vi•o•late [váɪəlet] v. violar; infringir.

vi•o•la•tion [vaɪəléʃən] s. violación; infracción.

vi•o•lence [váɪələns] s. violencia.

vi•o•lent [váɪələnt] adj. violento.

vi•o•let [váɪəlɪt] s. violeta; violado, color de violeta; adj. violado.

vi•o•lin [vaɪəlín] s. violín.

vi•o•lin•ist [vaɪəlínɪst] s. violinista.

vi•per [váɪpə] s. víbora.

vir•gin [vɝ́dʒɪn] adj. & s. virgen.

vir•gin•al [vɝ́ʒɪn] adj. virginal.

vir•ile [vír] adj. viril.

vir•tu•al [vɝ́tʃUəl] adj. virtual; -ly adv. virtualmente.

vir•tue [vɝ́tʃU] s. virtud.

vir•tu•ous [vɝ́tʃUəs] adj. virtuoso.

vi•sa [vízə] s. visa, visado; v. visar, refrendar.

vis•cer•al [vɪsə] adj. visceral.

visé = visa.

vise [vaɪs] s. tornillo de banco.

vis•i•ble [vízəb] adj. visible.

vi•sion [víʒən] s. visión; vista.

vi•sion•ar•y [víʒənɛrɪ] adj. visionario; imaginario; s. visionario, iluso, soñador.

vis•it [vízɪt] v. visitar; to – punishment upon mandar un castigo a, castigar a; s. visita.

vis•i•ta•tion [vɪzətéʃən] s. visitación, visita; castigo, calamidad.

vis•i•tor [vízɪtə] s. visita; visitador.

vi•sor [vázə] s. visera.

vis•ta [vístə] s. vista, paisaje.

vi•su•al [vízjU] adj. visual, visible.

vi•su•al•ize [vízjUlaɪz] v. representar en la mente.

vi•tal [váɪt] adj. vital.

vi•tal•i•ty [váɪtǽlətɪ] s. vitalidad.

vi•tal•ize [váɪtəlaɪz] v. vitalizar.

vi•ta•min [váɪtəmɪn] s. vitamina.

vi•va•cious [vaɪvéʃəs] adj. vivaz, vivaracho, vivo, alegre, animado.

vi•vac•i•ty [vaɪvǽsətɪ] s. viveza, vivacidad.

viv•id [vívɪd] adj. vívido, vivo; animado.

viv•i•fy [vívəfaɪ] v. vivificar.

vo•cab•u•lar•y [vəkǽbjələrɪ] s. vocabulario.

vo•cal [vók] adj. vocal; oral; – cords cuerdas vocales; to be – hablar, expresarse.

vo•ca•tion [vokéʃən] s. vocación.

vogue [vog] s. boga, moda; in – en boga, de moda.

voice [vɔɪs] s. (vocalization) voz; (speech) habla; (opinion) voto; v. expresar, decir; -d consonant consonante sonora.

voice•less [vɔ́ɪslɪs] adj. mudo; sin voz; – consonant consonante sorda.

void [vɔɪd] adj. vació; nulo, inválido; – of falto de, desprovisto de; s. vacío; v. vaciar, evacuar; anular, invalidar.

vol•a•tile [válət] adj. volátil, inconstante.

vol•can•ic [volkǽnɪk] adj. volcánico.

vol•ca•no [volkéno] s. volcán.

vo•li•tion [volíʃən] s. volición; voluntad.

vol•ley [válɪ] s. descarga, lluvia (de piedras, flechas, balas, etc.); voleo (de la pelota); v. descargar una lluvia de proyectiles; volear una pelota.

volt [volt] s. voltio.

volt•age [vóltɪdʒ] s. voltaje.

vol•u•ble [váljəb] adj. facundo.

vol•ume [váljəm] s. volumen; tomo; bulto; suma, cantidad.

vo•lu•mi•nous [vəlúmənəs] adj. voluminoso.

vol•un•tar•y [váləntɛrɪ] adj. voluntario.

vol•un•teer [valəntír] s. voluntario; adj. voluntario; de voluntarios; v. ofrecer, dar voluntariamente; ofrecerse.

vo•lup•tu•ous [vəl ʌptʃUəs] adj. voluptuoso.

vom•it [vámɪt] s. vómito; v. vomitar, Méx. deponer.

vo•ra•cious [voréʃəs] adj. voraz.

vor•tex [vɔ́rtɛks] s. vórtice; vorágine.

vote [vot] s. voto; votación; v. votar; votar por.

vot•er [vótə] s. votante, elector.

vouch [vatuʃ] v. **to – for** dar fe de; garantizar, responder de; salir fiador de.

vouch•er [vátuʃ ə-] s. comprobante, justificante; recibo; fiador.

vouch•safe [vatuʃséf] v. otorgar, conceder.

vow [vaU] s. voto, juramente; v. votar, jurar, hacer voto de.

vow•el [váUəl] s. & adj. vocal.

voy•age [vɔɪɪdʒ] s. viaje; travesía; v. viajar.

vul•gar [v ʌ lg ə-] adj. soez, ordinario, grosero; vulgar.

vul•ner•a•ble [v ʌ lnə-əb]] adj. vulnerable.

vul•ture [v ʌ ltʃ ə-] s. buitre, Andes, Ríopl. cóndor.

W

wab•ble [wáb]] v. tambalear(se), bambolear(se); vacilar; temblar; s. tamboleo, bamboleo; balanceo.

wad [wɑd] s. taco; bodoque; pelotilla, bolita, rollo; **– of money** rollo de billetes (de banco); dinero; v. atacar (un arma de fuego); rellenar; hacer una pelotilla de.

wad•dle [wád]] v. anadear, contonearse, zarandearse (al andar); s. anadeo; zarandeo, contoneo.

wade [wed] v. vadear, chapotear; andar descalzo por la orilla del agua; **to – through a book** leer con dificultad un libro.

wa•fer [wéf ə-] s. oblea; hostia (consagrada).

waft [wæft] v. llevar en vilo, llevar por el aire; llevar a flote; s. ráfaga de aire; movimiento (de la mano).

wag [wæg] v. menear; sacudir; **to – the tail** colear, menear la cola; s. meneo; bromista, farsante.

wage [wedʒ] v. hacer (guerra); dar (batalla); s. (usualmente **wages**) paga, jornal; **– earner** jornalero, obrero; trabajador; **– scale** escala de salarios (sueldos).

wa•ger [wédʒ ə-] s. apuesta; v. apostar.

wag•gle [wǽg]] s. meneo rápido.

wag•on [wǽgən] s. carro, carretera; carretón.

wail [wel] v. gemir, lamentar; s. gemido, lamento.

waist [west] s. cintura; taller; blusa; **– band** pretina.

waist•coat [wéskot] s. chaleco.

waist•line [wéstlaɪn] s. talle.

wait [wet] v. (stay) esperar, aguardar; (serve) servir; **to – for** esperar, aguardar; **to – on (upon)** servir a; atender a; **to – table** servir la mesa, servir de mozo o camarero (en un restaurante); s. espera; **to lie in – for** estar en acecho de.

wait•er [wét ə-] s. mozo, camarero, sirviente, Méx., C.A. mesero.

wait•ing [wétɪŋ] s. espera; **– room** sala de espera.

wait•ress [wétrɪs] s. camarera, moza, Am. mesera.

waive [wev] v. renunciar a; **to – one's right** renunciar voluntariamente a sus derechos.

waiv•er [wévə-] s. renuncia.

wake [wek] v. despertar(se); **to – up** despertar(se); despabilarse; s. velatorio (acto de velar a un muerto); Am. velorio; estela (huella que deja un barco en el agua); **in the – of** después de, detrás de.

wake•ful [wékfəl] adj. desvelado, despierto; insomne.

wak•en [wékən] v. despertar(se); Ríopl. recordar (a una persona que está dormida).

walk [wɔk] v. andar, caminar, ir a pie, recorrer a pie; pasear; **to – away** irse, marcharse; **to – back home** volverse a casa (a pie); **to – down** bajar; **to – in** entrar; **to – out** salirse, irse; parar el trabajo, declararse en huelga; **to – the streets** callejear; **to – up** subir; s. paseo; senda, vereda, acera; paso (del caballo); manera de andar; **– of life** vocación; **a ten minutes'** – una caminata de diez minutos.

wall [wɔl] s. (interior) pared; (garden) muro; (fort) muralla; **low mud – tapia**; **to drive to the – poner** entre la espada y la pared, poner en un aprieto.

wal•let [wólɪt] s. cartera.

wall•flow•er [w ɔ flaU ə-] s. alelí; **to be a – at a dance** comer pavo, Andes, Méx., planchar el asiento.

wal•lop [wáləp] v. pegar, zurrar, golpear; s. guantada, bofetón, golpazo.

wal•low [wólo] v. revolcarse; chapalear o chapotear (en el lodo).

wall•pa•per [wólpepə-] s. papel (de empapelar).

wal•nut [w ɔ lnɐt] s. nuez de nogal; nogal; **– tree** nogal.

waltz [wolts] s. vals; s. valsar, bailar el vals.

wan [wɑn] adj. pálido, enfermizo, enclenque; lánguido.

wand [wɑnd] s. vara, varita; **magic –** varita de virtud.

wan•der [wándə-] v. vagar, errar; **to – away** extraviarse; **to – away from** apartarse de, desviarse de; **my mind -s easily** me distraigo fácilmente.

wan•der•er [wándərə-] s. vago, vagabundo.

wane [wen] v. menguar; decaer; s. mengua; diminución; **to be on the –** ir menguando; ir desapareciendo.

want [wɑnt] v. (desire) querer, desear; (lack) necesitar; s. falta; necesidad; escasez, carencia, **to be in – estar** necesitado.

want•ing [wántɪŋ] adj. falto; deficiente; necesitado.

wan•ton [wántən] adj. desenfrenado, libre; licencioso; inconsiderado; temerario.

war [w ɔ r] s. guerra; v. guerrear, hacer guerra; **to – on** guerrear con.

war•ble [w ɔ rb]] v. gorjear; trinar; s. gorjeo; trino.

war•bler [w ɔ rblə-] s. cantor; pájaro gorjeador.

ward [word] *s.* pupilo, menor o huérfano (*bajo tutela*); cuadra (*de hospital, prission, etc.*); distrito (*de una ciudad*); *v.* **to – of** resguardarse de; evitar; parar (*un golpe*).

war•den [wɔ́rdṇ] *s.* guardían; alcaide; **prison –** alcaide de una prisión.

ward•robe [wɔ́rdrob] *s.* (*closet*) guardarropa, ropero, armario; (*garments*) vestuario; ropa.

ware•house [wérhaUs] *s.* almacén, depósito.

wares [werz] *s. pl.* artículos, mecancías, mercaderías, efectos.

war•fare [wɔ́rɛr] *s.* guerra.

war•head [wɔ́rhɛd] *s.* punta de combate.

war•like [wɔ́rlaIk] *adj.* guerrero, bélico.

warm [wɔrm] *adj.* (*temperature*) caliente, cálido, caluroso; (*enthusiastic*) acalorado; (*fresh*) reciente; **– hearted** de buen corazón; **– blooded** apasionado; ardiente; **he is –** tiene calor; **it is – today** hacer calor hoy; *v.* calentar(se); **to – over** recalentar; **to – up** calentar(se); acalorarse; entusiasmarse.

warmth [wɔrmθ] *s.* (*heat*) calor; (*friendship*) cordialidad.

warn [wɔrn] *v.* avisar, advertir, amonestar; prevenir; precaver.

warn•ing [wɔ́rnIŋ] *s.* aviso, advertencia, amonestación; escarmiento; **let that be a – to you** que te sirva de escarmiento.

warp [wɔrp] *s.* urdimbre (*de un tejido*); torcedura, deformación; comba; *v.* combar(se), deformar(se), torcer(se); urdir (*los hilos de un telar*).

war•rant [wɔ́rənt] *s.* (*sanction*) autorización; (*right*) garantía, justificación; (*writ*) comprobante; orden, mandato, citación (*ante un juez*); *v.* autorizar; garantizar; justificar.

war•ri•or [wɔ́rɪə] *s.* guerrero.

war•ship [wɔ́rʃIp] *s.* buque de guerra, acorazado.

wart [wɔrt] *s.* verruga.

war•y [wérI] *adj.* cauteloso, cauto, precavido, prevenido; **to be – of** desconfiar de.

was [wɑz] *pret. de* **to be** (*primera y tercera persona del singular*).

wash [wɑʃ] *v.* lavar(se); **to – away** deslavar(se); **to be – ed away by the waves** ser arrastrado por las olas; *s.* lavado; levadura; lavatorio; lavazas, agua sucia; **mouth –** enjuague o enjuagatorio; **–bowl** lavabo, palangana, lavamanos; **–cloth** paño para lavarse; **– dress** vestido lavable; **– room** lavado, lavatorio.

wash•a•ble [wɑ́ʃəb₁] *adj.* lavable.

wash-and-wear [wɔ́ ʃændwɛ́r] *adj.* de lava y pon.

washed-out [wɑ́ʃtáUt] *adj.* desteñido; agotado, sin fuerzas.

washed-up [wɔʃt ʌ́p] *adj.* fracasado.

wash•er [wɔ́ʃə] *s.* lavador; máquina de lavar; arandela (*para una tuerca*); **– woman** lavandera.

wash•ing [wɔ́ʃIŋ] *s.* lavado; ropa sucia o para lavar; ropa lavada; **– machine** lavadora, máquina de lavar.

wash•out [wɔ́ʃaUt] *s.* derrubio; fracaso.

wasp [wɔsp] *s.* avispa.

waste [west] *v.* gastar; desgastar; malgastar, desperdiciar, derrochar; disipar; **to – away** gastarse, consumirse; desgastarse; *s.* desperdicio; gasto inútil; desgaste, desechos, desperdicios; terreno baldío, desierto; *adj.* inútil, desechado; desierto; baldío; **– of time** pérdida de tiempo; **– basket** cesto para papeles; **– land** terreno baldío; **– paper** papeles inútiles, papel de desecho; **to go to –** gastarse, perderse; malgastarse, desperdiciarse; **to lay –** asolar, arruinar.

waste•ful [wéstfəl] *adj.* despilfarrado, gastador; desperdiciado; ineconómico.

watch [wɑtʃ] *v.* (*look*) mirar; observar; (*be alert*) vigilar; velar; cuidar; **– out!** ¡cuidado!; **to – out for** tener cuidado con; cuidar; vigilar; *s.* reloj (de bolsillo); vela, vigilia; guardia; centinela, vigilante; **– chain** cadena de reloj, *Ven.*, *Méx.*, leontina; **– charm** dije; **wrist –** reloj de pulsera; **to be on the –** tener cuidado; estar alerta; **to keep – over** vigilar a.

watch•ful [wɑ́tʃfəl] *adj.* alerto, vigilante, despierto, atento.

watch•man [wɑ́tʃmən] *s.* vigilante, guardia, sereno.

watch•tow•er [wɑ́tʃtaUə] *s.* atalaya, mirador.

watch•word [wɑ́tʃwɜ́d] *s.* contraseña, santo y seña, consigna; lema.

wa•ter [wɔ́tə] *s.* agua; **– color** acuarela; color para acuarela; **– power** fuerza hidráulica; **–shed** vertiente; **– sports** deportes acuáticos; **– supply** abastecimiento de agua; *v.* regar; agua, diluir con agua; abrevar, dar de beber (*al ganado*); beber agua (*el ganado*); tomar agua (*un barco, locomotora, etc.*); **my eyes –** me lloran los ojos; **my mouth -s** se me hace agua la boca.

wa•ter•fall [wɔ́təfɔl] *s.* cascada, catarata, caída de agua.

wa•ter•front [wɔ́təfrʌnt] *s.* terreno ribereño.

wa•ter•mel•on [wɔ́təmɛlən] *s.* sandía.

wa•ter•pow•er [wɔ́təpaUə] *s.* fuerza hidráulica.

wa•ter•proof [wɔ́təpruf] *adj. & s.* impermeable; *v.* hacer impermeable.

wa•ter ski [wɔ́təski] *s.* esquí acuático.

wa•ter•spout [wɔ́təspaUt] *s.* surtidor; tromba; manga de agua.

wa•ter•way [wɔ́təwe] *s.* vía de agua, río navegable, canal..

wa•ter•y [wɔ́tərI] *adj.* aguado; acuoso; mojado,

húmedo.

wave [wev] *v.* ondear; ondular; agitar; blandir (*una espada, bastón, etc.*); **to – aside** apartar, rechazar; **to – good-bye** hacer una seña o ademán de despedida; **to – hair** ondular el pelo; **to – one's hand** hacer una seña o señas con la mano; mover la mano; *s.* onda; ola; ondulación; **– of the hand** ademán, movimiento de la mano; **permanent –** ondulación permanente.

wave•length [wévlɛŋθ] *s.* longitud de onda.

wa•ver [wévɚ] *v.* oscilar; vacilar, titubear; tambalear(se); *s.* vacilación, titubeo.

wav•y [wévɪ] *adj.* rizado, ondulado; ondulante.

wax [wæks] *s.* cera; **– candle** vela de cera; **– paper** papel encerado; *v.* encerar; pulir con cera; hacerse, ponerse; crecer (*la luna*).

way [we] *s.* (*road*) camino; ruta; senda; (*manner*) modo, manera; **– in** entrada; **– out** salida; **– through** paso, pasaje; **a long – off** muy lejos, a una larga distancia; **by – of** por, por vía de; **by – of comparison** a modo de comparación; **by the –** de paso; **in no –** de ningún modo; **on the – to** camino de, rumbo a; **out of the –** fuera del camino; apartado; a un lado; impropio; extraordinario; **to be in a bad –** hallarse en mal estado; **to be well under –** estar (*un trabajo*) ya bastante avanzado; **to give –** ceder; quebrarse; **to have one's –** hacer su capricho, salirse con la suya; **to make – for** abrir paso para.

way•far•er [wéfɛrɚ] *s.* caminante.

way•lay [welé] *v.* estar en acecho de (*alguien*); asaltar; detener (*a una persona*).

way•side [wésaɪd] *s.* borde del camino; **– inn** posada al borde del camino.

way•ward [wéwɚd] *adj.* voluntarioso, desobediente.

we [wi] *pron.* nosotros, nosotras.

weak [wik] *adj.* débil; flaco; endeble; **– market** mercado flojo; **weakminded** de voluntad débil; simple; **– tea** té claro o suave.

weak•en [wíkən] *v.* debilitar(se); desmayar, flaquear, perder ánimo.

weak•ly [wíklɪ] *adv.* débilmente; *adj.* enfermizo, débil, enclenque.

weak•ness [wíknɪs] *s.* debilidad; flaqueza.

wealth [wɛlθ] *s.* riqueza, copia, abundancia.

wealth•y [wélθɪ] *adj.* rico.

wean [win] *v.* destetar; apartar gradualmente (*de un hábito, de una amistad*).

weap•on [wépən] *s.* arma.

wear [wɛr] *v.* (*have on*) llevar, tener o traer puesto; usar; (*waste away*) gastar, desgastar; **to – away** gastar(se), desgastar(se); consumir(se); **to – off** desgastar(se), gastar(se); borrarse; **to – out** gastar(se); desgastar(se), consumir(se); agotar; cansar; **it -s well** es duradero; dura mucho; **as the day wore on** a medida que pasaba el día; *s.* uso,

gasto; durabilidad; **– and tear** desgaste; uso; **men's – ropa** para hombres; **clothes for summer – ropa** de verano.

wea•ri•ly [wírɪlɪ] *adv.* penosamente, con cansancio, con fatiga, fatigadamente.

wea•ri•ness [wírɪnɪs] *s.* cansancio, fatiga.

wear•ing [wérɪŋ] *adj.* cansado, aburrido, fastidioso.

wea•ri•some [wírɪsəm] *adj.* fatigoso, molesto, fastidioso.

wea•ry [wírɪ] *adj.* cansado, fatigado; aburrido; *v.* cansar(se), fatigar(se).

wea•sel [wíẕ] *s.* comadreja.

weath•er [wéðɚ] *s.* tiempo; **weatherbeaten** desgastado o curtido por la intemperie; **– bureau** oficina meteorológica; **– conditions** condiciones atmosféricas; **– vane** veleta; **it is fine –** hace buen tiempo; **to be under the –** estar enfermo; estar indispuesto; *v.* exponer a la intemperie; orear, secar al aire; **to – a storm** aguantar un chubasco; salir ileso de una tormenta.

weave [wiv] *v.* (*cloth*) tejer, entretejer; (*to plan*) urdir; **to – together** entretejer, entrelazar; combinar; *s.* tejido.

weav•er [wívɚ] *s.* tejedor.

web [wɛb] *s.* tela; membrana (*entre los dedos de los pájaros acuáticos*); **spider's –** telaraña.

wed [wɛd] *v.* casarse; casarse con, casar; *p.p. de* **to wed.**

wed•ded [wédɪd] *p.p. & adj.* casado; unido; **– to an idea** aferrado a una idea.

wed•ding [wédɪŋ] *s.* boda, casamiento, nupcias, enlace; **– day** día de bodas; **– trip** viaje de novios; **silver –** bodas de plata.

wedge [wɛdʒ] *s.* cuña; **entering –** cuña, entrada, medio de entrar, modo de penetrar; *v.* acuñar, meter cuñas; **to be -d between** estar encajado entre.

Wednes•day [wɛnzdɪ] *s.* miércoles.

wee [wi] *adj.* diminuto, chiquitico, pequeñito.

weed [wid] *s.* cizaña, mala hierba; *v.* desherbar (*o* desyerbar), quitar o arrancar la mala hierba; **to – a garden** desherbar un huerto; **to – out** escardar; eliminar, arrancar, entresacar.

weed•y [wídɪ] *adj.* herboso, lleno de malas hierbas.

week [wik] *s.* semana; **–day** día de trabajo, día laborable, día hábil; **– end** fin de semana; **a – from today** de hoy en ocho días.

week•ly [wíklɪ] *adj.* semanal, semanario; *adv.* semanalmente, por semana; *s.* semanario, periódico o revista semanal.

weep [wip] *v.* llorar.

weep•ing [wípɪŋ] *adj.* llorón; lloroso; **– willow** sauce llorón; *s.* llanto, lloro, lágrimas.

wee•vil [wív̱] *s.* gorgojo.

weigh [we] *v.* pesar; ponderar, considerar; **to – anchor** zarpar, levar el ancla; **to – down** agobiar;

abrumar; **to – on one's conscience** serle a uno gravoso, pesarle a uno.

weight [wet] *s.* peso; pesa (*de reloj o medida para pesar*); carga; **paper–** pisapapeles; *v.* cargar, sobrecargar; añadir peso a; asignar un peso o valor relativo a.

weight•y [wéti] *adj.* grave, ponderoso; de mucho peso; importante.

weird [wird] *adj.* extraño, raro, misterioso, fantástico.

wel•come [wélkəm] *s.* bienvenida; buena acogida; *adj.* grato, agradable; bien acogido, bien quisto; bienvenido; bien recibido; **– home!** ¡bienvenido!; **– rest** grato reposo o descanso; **you are –** no hay de qué, de nada (*para contestar a* "thank you"); **you are – here** está Vd. en su casa; **you are – to use it** se lo presto con todo gusto; está a su disposición; *v.* dar la bienvenida a; acoger o recibir con gusto.

weld [weld] *v.* soldar(se); *s.* soldadura.

wel•fare [wélfɛr] *s.* bienestar; bien; felicidad; **– work** labor social o de beneficencia.

well [wɛl] *adv.* bien; **he is – over fifty** tiene mucho más de cincuenta años; **– then** pues bien, ahora bien, conque; **well-being** bienestar; **well-bred** bien criado; bien educado; **well-done** bien cocido; **well-fixed** acomodado; **well-groomed** acicalado; **well-meaning** bien intencionado; **well-nigh** casi, muy cerca de; **all is** – a bien; bien de salud, sano; conveniente; **– and good** santo y muy bueno; **well-off** acomodado, adinerado; en buenas condiciones; **well-to-do** próspero, adinerado; **all is –** no hay novedad, todo va bien; **it is – to do it** conviene hacerlo, es conveniente hacerlo.

well [wɛl] *s.* (*shaft*) pozo; (*cistern*) cisterna; (*spring*) manantial; **artesian –** pozo artesiano; *v.* manar; **tears -ed up in her eyes** se le arrasaron los ojos de lágrimas.

welt [wɛlt] *s.* verdugo, verdugón, roncha.

went [wɛnt] *pret. de* **to go.**

wept [wɛpt] *pret. & p.p. de* **to weep.**

were [wɝ] *pret. de* **to be** (*en el plural y en la segunda persona del singular del indicativo; es además el imperfecto del subjuntivo*); **if I –** si yo fuera Vd.; **there –** había, hubo.

west [wɛst] *s.* oeste, occidente, ocaso; *adj.* occidental, del oeste; **West Indies** Antillas; *adv.* hacia el oeste, al oeste; en el oeste.

west•ern [wéstə-n] *adj.* occidental, del oeste.

west•ern•er [wéstə-nə-] *s.* natural del oeste, habitante del oeste, occidental.

west•ward [wéstwə-d] *adv.* hacia el oeste; *adj.* occidental, oeste.

wet [wɛt] *adj.* húmedo; mojado; **– nurse** nodriza, ama de leche; *s.* humedad, antiprohibicionista (*el que favorece la venta de bebidas alcohólicas*); *v.*

mojar; humedecer; *pret. & p.p. de* **to wet.**

wet•back [wétbæk] *s.* panza mojada.

wet•ness [wétnis] *s.* humedad.

whack [hwæk] *v.* golpear, pegar; *s.* golpe; golpazo; tentativa, prueba.

whale [hwel] *s.* ballena; *v.* pescar ballenas.

wharf [hworf] *s.* muelle, embarcadero.

what [hwɑt] *pron. interr.* qué; qué cosa; cuál; *pron. rel.* lo que; **– for?** ¿para qué? *adj.* qué; **– book?** ¿qué libro? **– a man!** ¡qué hombre!; **– happy children!** ¡qué niños más (*o* tan) felices; **take – books you need** tome Vd. los libros que necesite.

what•ev•er [hwɑtɛ́və-] *pron.* cualquiera cosa que, lo que, cuanto, todo lo que; **– do you mean?** ¿qué quiere Vd. decir?; **it – happens** hágalo suceda lo que suceda; *adj.* cualquiera; **any person –** una persona cualquiera; **no money –** nada de dinero.

what•so•ev•er [hwɑtsoɛ́və-] = **whatever.**

wheat [hwit] *s.* trigo; **cream of –** crema de trigo.

whee•dle [hwíd|] *v.* engatusar.

wheel [hwil] *s.* (*disc*) rueda; rodaja; disco; (*bike*) bicicleta; **– chair** silla rodante, silla de ruedas; **steering –** volante (*de automóvil*); rueda del timón; *v.* rodar; hacer rodar; girar; acarrear; andar en bicicletas; **to – around** dar una vuelta; girar sobre los talones; **to – the baby** pasear al bebé en su cochecito.

wheel•bar•row [hwílbæro] *s.* carretilla.

wheeze [hwiz] *s.* resuello ruidoso.

when [hwɛn] *adv. & conj.* cuando; *adv. interr.* ¿cuándo?.

whence [hwɛns] *adv.* de donde; de que.

when•ev•er [hwɛnɛ́və-] *adj. & conj.* cuando, siempre que, cada vez que.

where [hwɛr] *adv.* donde; adonde; en donde; por donde; **–?** ¿dónde?; ¿adónde?

where•a•bouts [hwɛrəbatUs] *s.* paradero; *adv. interr.* ¿dónde?

where•as [hwɛrǽz] *conj.* mientras que; puesto que, visto que, considerando que.

where•by [hwɛrbái] *adv.* por donde, por lo cual; con lo cual.

where•fore [hwɛrfor] *adv.* por qué; por lo cual; por eso, por lo tanto.

where•in [hwɛrín] *adv.* en qué; en donde; en lo cual.

where•of [hwɛráv] *adv.* de que; de donde; de quien, de quienes.

where•up•on [hwɛrəpán] *adv.* después de lo cual; entonces.

wher•ev•er [hwɛrɛ́və-] *adv.* dondequiera que, adondequiera que, por dondequiera que.

where•with•al [hwɛrwɪðəl] *s.* medios, fondos; dinero.

whet [hwɛt] *v.* amolar, afilar; aguzar, estimular.

wheth•er [hwéðə-] *conj.* si; ya sea que, sea que; **– we escape or not** ya sea que escapemos o no; **I doubt**

– dudo (de) que.

which [hwɪtʃ] *pron. interr.* ¿cuál?; ¿cuáles?; *pron. rel.* que; el cual, la cual, los cuales, las cuales; el que, la que, los que, las que; *adj. interr.* ¿qué?; **– boy has it?** ¿cuál de los muchachos lo tiene? ¿qué muchacho lo tiene?; **– way did he go?** ¿por qué camino se fue?; ¿por dónde se fue?; **during – time** tiempo durante el cual.

which·ev·er [hwɪtʃévɚ] *pron. & adj.* cualquiera (que), cualesquiera (que); el que, la que; **– road you take** cualquier camino que Vd. siga.

whiff [hwɪf] *s.* (*waft*) soplo; fumada, bocanada; (*odor*) repentino olor o hedor; *v.* soplar, echar bocanadas.

while [hwaɪl] *s.* rato; tiempo, temporada; **a short –** un ratito; **a short – ago** hace poco, hace poco rato; **to be worth –** valer la pena; *conj.* mientras, mientras que; *v.* **to – away the time** pasar el tiempo.

whilst [hwaɪlst] *conj.* mientras, mientras que.

whim [hwɪm] *s.* capricho, antojo.

whim·per [hwɪmpɚ] *v.* lloriquear, gimotear; quejarse; *s.* lloriqueo, gimoteo; quejido.

whim·si·cal [hwɪmzɪkḷ] *adj.* caprichoso.

whine [hwaɪn] *v.* lloriquear; quejarse; *s.* gemido, quejido.

whin·er [hwaɪnɚ] *s.* llorón, persona quejosa, *Méx.* quejumbres; *Andes* quejumbroso; *Ríopl.* ʃezongón.

whip [hwɪp] *v.* azotar, fustigar; zurrar, dar una paliza a, dar latigazos a; batir (*crema, huevos*); vencer; **to – up** batir; coger o asir de repente; hacer de prisa; *s.* azote, látigo, fuete; batido.

whip·ping [hwɪpɪŋ] *s.* tunda, zurra, paliza; **– cream** crema para batir.

whir [hwɝ] *s.* zumbar; *s.* zumbido.

whirl [hwɝl] *v.* girar, dar vueltas; arremolinarse; **muy head -s** siento vértigo, estoy desvanecido; *s.* giro, vuelta; remolino, espiral (*de humo*); confusión.

whirl·pool [hwɝlpul] *s.* remolino, vorágine, vórtice.

whirl·wind [hwɝlwɪnd] *s.* remolino, torbellino.

whisk [hwɪsk] *v.* barrer; desempolvar (*con escobilla*); batir (*huevos*); **to – away** barrer de prisa; llevarse de prisa, arrebatar; irse de prisa, escaparse; **to – something out of sight** escamotear algo, esconder algo de prisa; *s.* **– broom** escobilla; **with a – of the broom** de un escobillazo.

whisk·er [hwɪskɚ] *s.* pelo de la barba, **-s** barbas; patillas; bigotes (*del gato*).

whis·key [hwɪskɪ] *s.* whisky (*aguardiente de maíz, centeno, etc.*).

whis·per [hwɪspɚ] *v.* cuchichear, hablar en secreto; soplar, decir al oído; susurrar; secretearse; **it is -ed that** corre la voz que; dizque, dicen que; *s.* cuchicheo, secreteo; susurro; murmullo; **to talk in a –** hablar en secreto; susurrar.

whis·tle [hwɪsḷ] *v.* silbar; chiflar; pitar; **to – for someone** llamar a uno con un silbido; *s.* silbido, chiflido; silbato, pito.

whit [hwɪt] *s.* jota, pizca.

white [hwaɪt] *adj.* (*color*) blanco; (*pure*) puro; inocente; (*honorable*) honrado, recto; **-caps** cabrillas o palomas (*olas con crestas blancas*); **– lead** albayalde; **– lie** mentirilla, mentira venial; **white-livered** cobarde; **white-collar** de oficina; **to show the – feather** mostrar cobardía, portarse como cobarde; *s.* banco; clara (*del huevo*).

whit·en [hwaɪtṇ] *v.* blanquear; emblanquecer(se), poner(se) blanco.

white·ness [hwaɪtnɪs] *s.* blancura; palidez; pureza.

white·wash [hwaɪtwaʃ] *v.* (*paint*) blanquear, enjalbegar; (*gloss over*) encubrir, disimular (*faltas, errores*); absolver (*sin justicia*); *s.* lechada.

whith·er [hwíðɚ] *adv.* adonde; **–?** ¿adónde?.

whit·ish [hwáɪtɪʃ] *adj.* blancuzco, blanquecino, blanquizco.

whit·tle [hwɪtḷ] *v.* cortar, mondar; tallar; tajar, sacar punta a (*un lápiz*); **to – down expenses** cercenar o reducir los gastos.

whiz [hwɪz] *v.* zumbar; *s.* zumbido, silbido; **to be a –** ser un águila, ser muy listo.

who [hu] *pron. rel.* quien, quienes, que, el que, la que, los que, las que; **he –** el que, quien; *pron. interr.* ¿quién?; ¿quiénes?; **– is it?** ¿quién es?

who·ev·er [huévɚ] *pron.* quienquiera que, cualquiera que; el que.

whole [hol] *adj.* todo; entero; íntegro; **the – day** todo el día; **-hearted** sincero, cordial; **-heartedly** de todo corazón; con todo ánimo; *s.* todo, total, totalidad; **as a –** en conjunto; **on the –** en general, en conjunto.

whole·sale [hólsel] *s.* venta al por mayor, *Am.* mayoreo; **by –** al por mayor; *adj.* al por mayor, en grandes cantidades; **– dealer** comerciante al por mayor, *Am.* mayorista; **– slaughter** matanza; gran hecatombe; **– trade** comercio al por mayor, *Am.* comercio mayorista; *adv.* al por mayor, por mayor; *v.* vender al por mayor, *Am.* mayorear.

whole·some [hólsəm] *adj.* saludable, sano; salubre; **– man** hombre normalmente bueno o de buena índole.

whol·ly [hólɪ] *adv.* enteramente, completamente, totalmente.

whom [hum] *pron. pers.* a quien, a quienes; que; al que (a la que, a los que, *etc.*); al cual (a la cual, a los cuales, *etc.*); **for –** para quien; **– did you see?** ¿a quién vió Ud.?

whoop [hup] *s.* grito, chillido, alarido; respiro convulsivo (*que acompaña a la tos ferina*); *v.* gritar, vocear, echar gritos; respirar convulsivamente (*al toser*); **to – it up** armar una gritería, gritar; **whooping cough** tos ferina.

whore [hor] *s.* ramera, puta, prostituta.

whose [huz] *pron.* cuyo, cuya, cuyos, cuyas; *pron. interr.* ¿de quién?; ¿de quiénes?; **– book is this?** ¿de quién es este libro?

why [hwaɪ] *adv.* ¿por qué?; **the reason –** la razón por la que (*o* la cual); **–, of course!** ¡sí, por supuesto!; ¡claro que sí!; **–, that is not true!** ¡si eso no es verdad! *s.* porqué, causa, razón, motivo.

wick [wɪk] *s.* mecha, pabilo.

wick•ed [wɪkɪd] *adj.* malvado, malo, inicuo.

wick•ed•ness [wɪkɪdnɪs] *s.* maldad, iniquidad, 0perversidad.

wick•er [wɪkɚ] *s.* mimbre; **– chair** silla de mimbre.

wick•et [wɪkɪt] *s.* postigo; ventanilla.

wide [waɪd] *adj.* ancho; amplio; vasto; extenso; **– apart** muy apartadas; **wide-awake** muy despierto; alerta, vigilante; **– of the mark** muy lejos del blanco; **– open** muy abierto; abierto de par en par; **far and –** por todas partes, extensamente; **to open –** abrir mucho; abrir (*la puerta*) de par en par; **two feet –** dos pies de ancho (*o* de anchura).

wide•ly [waɪdlɪ] *adv.* ampliamente; extensamente; muy; mucho.

wid•en [waɪd n̩] *v.* ensanchar(se), ampliar(se), dilatar(se).

wide•spread [waɪdspréd] *adj.* muy esparcido, muy extensivo; bien difundido; extendido; general, extendido por todas partes.

wid•ow [wɪdo] *s.* viuda.

wid•ow•er [wɪdəwɚ] *s.* viudo.

width [wɪdθ] *s.* ancho, anchura.

wield [wild] *v.* manejar; esgrimir (*la espada a la pluma*); ejercer (*el poder*).

wife [waif] *s.* esposa.

wig [wɪg] *s.* peluca.

wig•gle [wɪg l̩] *v.* menear(se); *s.* meneo.

wig•wam [wɪgwom] *s.* choza de los indios norteños.

wild [waɪld] *adj.* salvaje; (*animal*) feroz, fiero; indómito; montaraz; (*plant*) silvestre; *Ven.*, *Méx.* cimarrón; impetuoso, desenfrenado; bullicioso; violento; loco; enojado; desatinado; ansioso; **to talk –** disparatar, desatinar; *s.* yermo, desierto, monte.

wild•cat [waɪlkæt] *s.* gato montés; **– scheme** empresa arriesgada.

wil•der•ness [wɪldɚnɪs] *s.* yermo, desierto, monte; inmensidad.

wild-eyed [waɪldaɪd] *adj.* de ojos huraños.

wild•ness [waɪldnɪs] *s.* salvajez; ferocidad, fiereza; locura.

wile [waɪl] *s.* ardid, engaño; astucia.

wil•ful, will•ful [wɪlfəl] *adj.* voluntarioso, testarudo, caprichudo; intencional.

will [wɪl] *v.* (*desire*) querer, decidir; (*order*) ordenar, mandar; (*dispose of legally*) legar; *v. defect. y aux.* querer; *rigurosamente debe usarse para formar el* futuro en las segundas y terceras personas; **she – go** ella irá; *en las primeras personas indica voluntad o determinación:* **I – not do it** no lo haré, no quiero hacerlo.

will [wɪl] *s.* (*wish*) voluntad; albedrío; (*legal disposition*) testamento; **free –** libre albedrío; **ill –** mala voluntad, malquerencia.

will•ful [wɪlfʊl] *adj.* voluntario.

will•ing [wɪlɪŋ] *adj.* bien dispuesto, deseoso, complaciente; voluntario; **-ly** *adv.* con gusto, de buena gana, de buena voluntad; voluntariamente.

will•ing•ness [wɪlɪŋnɪs] *s.* buena voluntad, buena gana.

wil•low [wɪlo] *s.* sauce; mimbrera; **weeping –** sauce llorón.

wilt [wɪlt] *v.* marchitar(se); ajar(se); desmayar; languidecer.

wil•y [waɪlɪ] *adj.* astuto, artero.

win [wɪn] *v.* (*achieve*) ganar; lograr, obtener, alcanzar; (*persuade*) persuadir; **to – out** ganar, triunfar; salirse con la suya; **to – over** persuadir; atraer; alcanzar o ganar el favor de.

wince [wɪns] *v.* cejar (*ante una dificultad o peligro*); encogerse (*de dolor, susto, etc.*).

winch [wɪntʃ] *s.* malacate.

wind [wɪnd] *s.* viento, aire; resuello; **– instrument** instrumento de viento; **to get – of** barruntar; tener noticia de.

wind [waɪnd] *v.* enredar; devanar, ovillar; dar cuerda a (*un reloj*); serpentear (*un camino*); dar vueltas; **to – someone around one's finger** manejar fácilmente a alguien, gobernarle; **to – up one's affairs** terminar o concluir uno sus negocios; *s.* vuelta; recodo.

wind•bag [windbæg] *s.* (*instrument*) fuelle; (*person*) parlanchín, hablador.

wind•fall [wɪndfol] *s.* golpe de fortuna, ganancia repentina, herencia inesperada.

wind•ing [waɪndɪŋ] *adj.* sinuoso, tortuoso, que da vueltas; **– staircase** escalera de caracol.

wind•mill [wɪndmɪl] *s.* molino de viento.

win•dow [wɪndo] *s.* ventana; **show –** escaparate, vitrina, aparador, *Am.* vidriera; **– shade** visillo, cortinilla; **– sill** antepecho, repisa de ventana.

win•dow•pane [wɪndopen] *s.* cristal de ventana, vidriera.

wind•pipe [wɪndpaɪp] *s.* tráquea, gaznate.

wind•shield [wɪndʃild] *s.* parabrisa, guardabrisa.

wind tunnel [wɪndtʌn l̩] *s.* túnel aerodinámico.

wind•y [wɪndɪ] *adj.* airoso; ventoso; **it is –** hace aire, ventea, sopla el viento.

wine [waɪn] *s.* vino; **– cellar** bodega.

wing [wɪŋ] *s.* ala; bastidor (*de escenario*); **under the – of** bajo la tutela de; **to take –** levantar el vuelo.

winged [wɪŋd, wɪŋɪd] *adj.* alado.

wing•spread [wɪŋspréd] *s.* envergadura.

wink[wɪŋk] v. guiñar; pestanear, parpadear; s. guiño, guiñada; **I didn't sleep a** – no pegué los ojos en toda la noche.

win•ner[wínə] s. ganador; vencedor; – **of a prize** agraciado, premiado.

win•ning[wíniŋ] adj. (successful) ganancioso; triunfante, victorioso; (charming) atractivo, encantador; **-s** s. pl. ganancias.

win•some[wínsəm] adj. simpatico, atractivo, gracioso.

win•ter[wíntə] s. invierno; – **clothes** ropa de invierno; v. invernar, pasar el invierno.

win•try[wíntrɪ] adj. invernal, de invierno; frío, helado.

wipe[waɪp] v. secar; enjugar; limpiar; **to – away one's tears** limpiarse las lágrimas; **to – off** borrar; limpiar; **to – out a regiment** destruir o aniquilar un regimiento.

wire[fair] s. (strand) alambre; (telegram) telegrama; **by –** por telégrafo; – **entanglement** alambrada; – **fence** alambrado; – **netting** tela metálica, alambrado; **to pull -s** mover los hilos; v. poner alambrado, instalar alambrado eléctrico, atar con alambre; telegrafiar.

wire•less[wáɪrlɪs] adj. inalámbrico, sin hilos; – **telegraphy** radiotelegrafía; s. radiu, radiotelegrafía; telegrafía sin hilos; radiotelefonía; radiograma.

wire tap•ping[wáɪrtæpɪŋ] s. secreta conexión interceptora de teléfono.

wir•y[wáɪrɪ] adj. de alambre; como alambre; nervudo.

wis•dom[wízdəm] s. sabiduría, saber; cordura, prudencia; – **tooth** muela del juicio.

wise[waɪz] adj. (judicious) sabio, cuerdo, sensato; (prudent) discreto, prudente; **the Three Wise Men** los Tres Reyes Magos; **to get –** darse cuenta de; s. modo, manera; **in no –** de ningún modo.

wise•crack[wáɪzkræk] s. bufonada, dicho agudo o chocarrero, dicharacho.

wish[wɪʃ] v. desear, querer; **to – for** desear; anhelar; **I – it were true!** ¡ojalá (que) fuera verdad!; s. deseo.

wish•ful think•ing[wíʃfʊl θíŋkɪŋ] s. optimismo ilusorio.

wist•ful[wístfəl] adj. anhelante, anheloso, ansioso; tristón, melancólico.

wit[wɪt] s. agudeza, sal, chiste; ingenio; hombre agudo o de ingenio; **to be at one's wit's end** haber agotado todo su ingenio; **to be out of one's -s** estar fuera de sí, estar loco; **to lose one's -s** perder el juicio; **to use one's -s** valerse de su industria o ingenio.

witch[wɪtʃ] s. hechicera; bruja.

witch•craft[wítʃkræft] s. hechicería.

with[wɪð, wɪθ] prep. con; para con; en compañía de; **filled –** lleno de; **ill –** enfermo de; **the one – the**

black hat el del (o la del) sombrero negro.

with•draw[wɪðdrɔ́] v. retirar(se); apartar(se); separar(se); **to – a statement** retractarse.

with•draw•al[wɪðdrɔ́əl] s. retirada, retiro.

with•drawn[wɪðdrɔ́n] p.p. de **to withdraw**.

with•drew[wɪðdrú] pret. de **to withdraw**.

with•er[wíðə] v. marchitar(se); ajar(se); secar(se).

with•held[wɪθhéld] pret. & p.p. de **to withhold**.

with•hold[wɪθhóld] v. retener; detener; **to – one's consent** negarse a dar su consentimiento.

with•in[wɪðín] prep. dentro de; – **call** al alcance de la voz; – **five miles** a poco menos de cinco millas; **it is – my power** está en mi mano; adv. dentro, adentro.

with•out[wɪðáʊt] prep. sin; – **my seeing him** sin que yo le viera; adv. fuera, afuera.

with•stand[wɪθstǽnd] v. resistir; aguantar, padecer.

with•stood[wɪθstÚd] pret. & p.p. de **to withstand**.

wit•ness[wítnɪs] s. testigo, testimonio; v. ver, presenciar; ser testigo de; atestiguar, dar fe de.

wit•ti•cism[wítəsɪzəm] s. ocurrencia, agudeza, dicho agudo.

wit•ty[wítɪ] adj. agudo, ocurrente, gracioso, divertido, chistoso; – **remark** dicho agudo, agudeza, ocurrencia.

wives[waɪvz] s. pl. de **wife**.

wiz•ard[wízəd] s. genio, hombre de ingenio; mago; mágico.

wob•ble[wób|] s. bamboleo.

woe[wo] s. miseria, aflicción, infortunio; – **is me!** ¡miserable de mí!

woe•ful[wófUl] adj. miserable; abatido.

woke[wok] pret. de **to wake**.

wolf[wUlf] (pl. **wolves**[wUlvz]) s. lobo.

wom•an[wúmən] (pl. **women**[wímɪn]) s. mujer; – **writer** escritora.

wom•an•hood[wÚmənhUd] s. estado de mujer; la mujer (las mujeres); integridad femenil; feminidad.

wom•an•kind[wÚmənkaɪnd] s. la mujer, las mujeres, el sexo femenino.

wom•an•ly[wúmənlɪ] adj. femenil, mujeril, femenino; adv. femenilmente, como mujer.

womb[wum] s. vientre, entrañar; útero, matriz.

won[wʌn] pret. & p.p. de **to win**.

won•der[wʌ́ndə] s. (marvel) maravilla; prodigio; (emotion) admiración; **in –** maravillado; **no – that** no es mucho que; no es extraño que; v. asombrarse, maravillarse, pasmarse, admirarse; **to – at** admirarse de, maravillarse de; **I – what time it is** ¿qué hora será? **I – when he came** ¿cuándo vendría? **I should not – if** no me extrañaría que.

won•der•ful[wʌ́ndəfəl] adj. maravilloso, admirable; **-ly** *adv.* maravillosamente, admirablemente, a las mil maravillas; **-ly well** sumamente bien.

won·drous [wʌndrəs] *adj.* maravilloso, pasmoso, extraño.

wont [wʌnt] *adj.* acostumbrado; **to be – to** soler, acostumbrar, *C.A.* saber; *s.* costumbre, hábito, uso.

woo [wu] *v.* cortejar, enamorar, galantear.

wood [wUd] *s.* (*material*) madera; (*stick*) palo; (*firewood*) leña, **-s** bosque, selva; **– engraving** grabado en madera; **–shed** leñera, cobertizo par leña; **fire–** leña; **piece of fire–** leño.

wood·cut [wÚdkʌt] *s.* grabado en madera.

wood·cut·ter [wÚdkʌtɚ] *s.* leñador.

wood·ed [wÚdɪd] *adj.* arbolado, poblado de árboles.

wood·en [wÚd ŋ] *adj.* de madera, de palo; tieso.

wood·land [wÚdlænd] *s.* monte, bosque, selva.

wood·man [wÚdmən] *s.* (*vendedor*) leñador; (*dweller*) habitante del bosque.

wood·peck·er [wÚdpɛkɚ] *s.* pájaro carpintero.

wood·work [wÚdwɝk] *s.* maderamen; labrado en madera; obra de carpintería.

woof [wuf] *s.* trama (*de un tejido*); tejido.

wool [wUl] *s.* lana; *adj.* de lana; lanar; **wool-bearing** lanar; **– dress** vestido de lana.

wool·en [wÚlɪn] *adj.* de lana; lanudo; **– mill** fábrica de tejidos de lana; *s.* tejido de lana; género o paño de lana.

wool·ly [wÚlɪ] *adj.* lanudo, de lana.

word [wɝd] *s.* (*vocable*) palabra; vocablo, voz; (*news*) noticia, aviso; (*order*) mandato, orden; **pass–** contraseña; **by – of mouth** de palabra, verbalmente; *v.* expresar; redactar, formular.

word·y [wɝdɪ] *adj.* palabrero, verboso, ampuloso.

wore [wor] *pret. de* **to wear**.

work [wɝk] *s.* (*effort*) trabajo; (*masterpiece*) obra maestra (*task*) tarea; faena; (*em-ployment*) empleo, ocupación; oficio; (*accomplishment*) labor; **-s** taller, fábrica; maquinaria, mecanismo; **at –** trabajando; ocupado; *v.* trabajar; funcionar; obrar; surtir efecto; manejar, manipular; resolver (*un problema*); explotar (*una mina*); hacer trabajar; **to – havoc** hacer estropicios, causar daño; **to – loose** soltarse, aflojarse; **to – one's way through college** sufragar los gastos universitarios con su trabajo; **to – one's way up** subir por sus propios esfuerzos; **to – out a plan** urdir un plan; **to be all -ed up** estar sobreexcitado; **it didn't – out** no dió resultado; **the plan -ed well** tuvo buen éxito el plan.

work·a·ble [wəkəb ǀ] *adj.* practicable; explotable.

work·er [wɝkɚ] *s.* trabajador; obrero; operario.

work·ing [wɝkɪŋ] *s.* funcionamiento, operación; cálculo (*de un problema*); explotación (de una mina); *adj.* obrero, trabajador; **– class** clase obrera o tra-

bajadora; **– hours** horas de trabajo; **a hard-working man** un hombre muy trabajador.

work·ing·man [wɝkɪŋmæn] *s.* trabajador; obrero.

work·man [wɝkmən] *s.* trabajador, obrero, operario.

work·man·ship [wɝkmənʃɪp] *s.* hechura; trabajo; mano de obra.

work·shop [wɝkʃɑp] *s.* taller.

world [wɝld] *s.* mundo; **the World War** la Guerra Mundial; **world-shaking** de gran importancia.

world·ly [wɝldlɪ] *adj.* mundano, mundanal, terreno, terrenal.

worm [wɝm] *s.* gusano; lombriz; **worm-eaten** comido de gusanos; carcomido, apolillado; *v.* **to – a secret out of someone** extraerle o sonsacarle un secreto a una persona; **to – oneself into** insinuarse en, meterse en.

worn [worn] *p.p. de* **to wear**; **worn-out** gastado, roto; rendido de fatiga.

wor·ry [wɝɪ] *s.* inquietud, ansiedad, cuidado, preocupación, apuro, apuración; *v.* inquietar(se), preocupar(se), afligir(se), apurar(se).

worse [wɝs] *adj.* peor; más malo; *adv.* peor; **– and – cada vez peor; **– than ever** peor que nunca; **from bad to –** de mal en peor; **so much the –** tanto peor; **to be – off** estar peor que antes; **to change for the – empeorar(se); **to – get –** empeorar(se).

wor·ship [wɝʃəp] *s.* adoración, culto; veneración; *v.* adorar; reverencia.

wor·ship·er [wɝʃəpɚ] *s.* adorador; **the -s** los fieles.

worst [wɝst] *adj.* peor; *adv.* peor; **the –** el peor; la peor; lo peor; *v.* derrotar.

worth [wɝθ] *s.* valor, valía, mérito; precio; **ten cent's – of** diez centavos de; **to get one's money's – out of** sacar todo el provecho posible del dinero gastado en; *adj.* digno de; **– hearing** digno de oirse; **to be – doing** valer la pena de hacerse; **to be – while** valer la pena.

worth·less [wɝθlɪs] *adj.* sin valor, inútil; despreciable.

wor·thy [wɝðɪ] *adj.* digno; valioso, apreciable; meritorio, merecedor; *s.* benemérito, hombre ilustre.

would [wUd] *imperf. de indic. y de subj. del verbo defect.* **will: she – come every day** solía venir (*o* venía) todos los días; **if you – do it** si lo hiciera Vd.; *expresa a veces deseo*: **– that I knew it!** ¡quién lo supiera!; ¡ojalá que yo lo supiera!; *v. aux. del condicional*: **she said she – go** dijo que iría.

wound [wund] *s.* herida; llaga, lesión; *v.* herir; lastimar; agraviar.

wound [waʊnd] *pret.* & *p.p. de* **to wind.**

wove [wov] *pret. de* **to weave.**

wo•ven [wóvən] *p.p. de* **to weave.**

wow [waʊ] *v.* entusiasmar.

wran•gle [ræ ŋg]] *v.* (*quarrel*) altercar, disputar; reñir; (*herd*) juntar; *Am.* rodear (*el ganado*); *s.* riña, pendencia.

wrap [ræp] *v.* envolver; enrollar; arrollar; **to – up** envolver(se); abrigar(se); tapar(se); **to be wrapped up in** estar envuelto en; estar absorto en; *s.* abrigo, manto.

wrap•per [ræ pə•] *s.* envoltura, cubierta; **woman's –** bata.

wrap•ping [ræpɪŋ] *s.* envoltura; **– paper** papel de envolver.

wrath [ræθ] *s.* ira, cólera, rabia.

wrath•ful [ræθfəl] *adj.* colérico, rabioso, iracundo.

wreath [riθ] *s.* guirnalda, corona; **– of smoke** espiral de humo.

wreathe [rið] *v.* hacer guirnaldas; adornar con guirnaldas; **-d in smiles** sonriente.

wreck [rɛk] *s.* (*destruction*) ruina; destrucción; (*shipwreck*) naufragio; (*accident*) accidente; (*wreckage*) destrozos, despojos (*de un naufragio*); *v.* arruinar; naufragar; echar a pique; destrozar, demoler; **to – a train** descarrilar un tren.

wrench [rɛntʃ] *v.* torcer, retorcer; arrancar, arrebatar; *s.* torcedura, torsión; tirón, arranque, *Andes*, *Méx.*, *C.A.* jalón; llave de tuercas; **monkey –** llave inglesa.

wrest [rɛst] *v.* arrebatar, arrancar; usurpar.

wres•tle [rɛs]] *v.* luchar a brazo partido; luchar; *s.* lucha a brazo partido.

wres•tler [rɛslə•] *s.* luchador (*a brazo partido*).

wretch [rɛtʃ] *s.* miserable, infeliz; villano.

wretch•ed [rɛtʃɪd] *adj.* (*miserable*) miserable; afligido; (*unfortunate*) desdichado, infeliz; (*bad*) bajo, vil; malísimo; **a – piece of work** un trabajo pésimo o malísimo.

wrig•gle [rɪg]] *v.* mener(se); retorcer(se); **to – out of** salirse de, escaparse de; escabullirse de.

wring [rɪŋ] *v.* torcer, retorcer; exprimir, estrujar; **to – money from someone** arrancar dinero a alguien; **to – out** exprimir (*la ropa*).

wrin•kle [rɪŋk]] *s.* arruga; surco; **the latest – in style** la última novedad; *v.* arrugar(se).

wrist [rɪst] *s.* muñeca; **– watch** reloj de pulsera.

writ [rɪt] *s.* auto, orden judicial, mandato jurídico; **the Holy Writ** la Sagrada Escritura.

write [raɪt] *v.* escribir; **to – back** contestar por carta; **to – down** apuntar, poner por escrito; **to – off** cancelar (*una deuda*); **to – out** poner por escrito; escribir

por entero; **to – up** relatar, describir; redactar.

writ•er [ráɪtə•] *s.* escritor; autor.

writhe [raɪð] *v.* retorcerse.

writ•ing [ráɪtɪŋ] *s.* escritura; escrito; composición literaria; forma o estilo literario; **hand–** letra; **– desk** escritorio; **– paper** papel de escribir; **to put in –** poner por escrito.

writ•ten [rít ŋ] *p.p. de* **to write.**

wrong [rɔŋ] *adj.* (*incorrect*) falso, incorrecto; equivocado; (*wicked*) malo; injusto; mal hecho; (*improper*) inoportuno; inconveniente; **the – side of a fabric** el envés o el revés de un tejido; **the – side of the road** el lado izquierdo o contrario del camino; **that is the – book** ése no es el libro; **it is in the – place** no está en su sitio, está mal colocado; *adv.* mal; al revés; **to go –** extraviarse, descaminarse; resultar mal; *s.* mal, daño perjuicio; injusticia; agravio; **to be in the –** no tener razón, estar equivocado; **to do –** hacer mal; *v.* perjudicar; agraviar; hacer mal a.

wrote [rot] *pret. de* **to write.**

wrought [rot] *pret.* & *p.p. irr. de* **to work;** *adj.* labrado; forjado; **– iron** hierro forjado; **– silver** plata labrada; **to be wrought-up** estar sobreexcitado.

wrung [rʌŋ] *pret.* & *p.p. de* **to wring.**

wry [raɪ] *adj.* torcido; **to make a – face** hacer una mueca.

Y

yacht [jɑt] *s.* yate; *v.* navegar en yate.

Yan•kee [jæŋkɪ] *adj.* & *s.* yanqui.

yard [jɑrd] *s.* (*measure*) yarda (*medida*); (*enclosure*) patio; cercado; terreno (*adyacente a una casa*); **back – corral; barn–** corral; **navy –** arsenal; **ship–** astillero.

yard•stick [jɑrdstɪk] *s.* yarda (*de medir*); medida (*metro*, *vara*, *etc.*), patrón, norma.

yarn [jɑrn] *s.* estambre; hilado, hilaza; cuento enredado y poco probable.

yawn [jon] *v.* bostezar; *s.* bostezo.

yea [je] *adv.* sí; *s.* sí, voto afirmativo.

year [jɪr] *s.* año; **–book** anuario; **-'s income** renta anual; **by the –** por año; **leap –** año bisiesto.

year•ling [jɪrlɪŋ] *s.* primal; becerro.

year•ly [jɪrlɪ] *adj.* anual; *adv.* anualmente; una vez al año, cada año.

yearn [j ɝ] *v.* anhelar; **to – for** anhelar; suspirar por.

yearn•ing [j ɝ ɪŋ] *s.* anhelo.

yeast [jist] *s.* levadura, fermento.

yell [jɛl] *v.* gritar, dar gritos, vociferar; *s.* grito, alarido.

yel•low [jélo] *adj.* amarillo; cobarde; – **fever** fiebre amarilla; *s.* amarillo; *v.* poner(se) amarillo.

yel•low•ish [jéloiʃ] *adj.* amarillento.

yelp [jɛlp] *v.* aullar, ladrar; *s.* aullido, ladrido.

yes [jɛs] *adv.* sí.

yes•ter•day [jéstə-dɪ] *adv.* & *s.* ayer; **day before** – anteayer o antier.

yet [jɛt] *adv.* & *conj.* todavía, aún; con todo, sin embargo; no obstante; **as** – todavía, aún; **not** – todavía no.

yield [jild] *v.* (*surrender*) ceder; rendir; someterse; (*produce*) producir; **to** – **five percent** redituar el cinco por ciento; *s.* rendimiento, rendición; rédito.

yo•del [jód|] *s.* canto en que la voz fluctúa entre natural y falsete.

yoke [jok] *s.* yugo; yunta (*de bueyes, mulas, etc.*); *v.* uncir; unir.

yolk [jok] *s.* yema (*de huevo*).

yon•der [jóndə-] *adj.* aquel, aquella, aquellos, aquellas; *adv.* allá, allí, más allá, acullá.

yore [jor]: **in days of** – antaño, en días de antaño.

you [ju] *pron. pers.* tú, usted, vosotros, ustedes; te, le, lo, la, os, las, los; **to** – a tí, a usted, a vosotros, a ustedes; te, le, les; *pron. impers.* se, uno.

young [jʌŋ] *adj.* joven; nuevo; – **leaves** hojas tiernas; – **man** joven; **her** – **ones** sus niños, sus hijitos; **the** – **people** la gente joven, los jóvenes, la juventud; *s.* jóvenes; cría, hijuelos (*de los animales*).

young•ster [j Áŋstə-] *s.* muchacho, niño, jovencito, chiquillo.

your [jUr] *adj.* tu (tus), vuestro (vuestra, vuestros, vuestras), su (sus), de usted, de ustedes.

yours [jUrz] *pron. pos.* tuyo (tuya, tuyos, tuyas); vuestro (vuestra, vuestros, vuestras); suyo (suya, suyos, suyas), de usted, de ustedes; el tuyo (la tuya, los tuyos, las tuyas); el suyo (la suya, los suyos, las suyas); el (la, los, las) de usted; el (la, los, las) de ustedes; **a friend of** – un amigo tuyo, un amigo vuestro; un àmigo suyo, un amigo de usted o ustedes.

your•self [jUrsélf] *pron.* te, se (*como reflexivo*); **to** – a tí mismo; a usted mismo; **you** – tú mismo; usted mimo; *véase* **herself.**

your•selves [jUrsélz] *pron.* os, se (*como reflexivo*); **to** – a vosotros mismos; a ustedes mìsmos; **you** – vosotros mismos; ustedes mismos.

youth [juθ] *s.* joven; juventud; jóvenes.

youth•ful [júθfəl] *adj.* joven, juvenil.

Yule•tide [júltaɪd] *s.* Pascua de Navidad; Navidades.

Z

zeal [zil] *s.* celo, fervor, ardor, entusiasmo.

zeal•ot [zélət] *s.* fanático.

zeal•ous [zéləs] *adj.* celoso, ardiente, fervoroso.

ze•nith [zínɪθ] *s.* cenit, cumbre.

zeph•yr [zéfə-] *s.* céfiro.

ze•ro [zíro] *s.* cero.

zest [zɛst] *s.* entusiasmo; buen sabor.

zig•zag [zigzag] *s.* zigzag; *adj.* & *adv.* en zigzag; *v.* zigzaguear; culebrear, andar en zigzag, serpentear.

zinc [zɪŋk] *s.* cinc (zinc).

zip code [zíp kod] *s.* sistema de cifras norteamericano, establecido para facilitar la entrega de cartas.

zip•per [zípə-] *s.* cierre relámpago, abrochador corredizo o de corredera, *Am.* riqui.

zo•di•ac [zódɪæk] *s.* zodíaco.

zone [zon] *s.* zona; *v.* dividir en zonas.

zoo [zu] *s.* jardín zoológico.

zo•o•log•i•cal [zoθládʒɪk|] *adj.* zoológico.

zo•ol•o•gy [zoálədʒɪ] *s.* zoología.